PELICAN BOOKS

Lord Wedderburn

The Worker
and the Law

THIRD EDITION

Penguin Books

Penguin Books Ltd, Harmondsworth, Middlesex, England
Viking Penguin Inc., 40 West 23rd Street, New York, New York 10010, U.S.A.
Penguin Books Australia Ltd, Ringwood, Victoria, Australia
Penguin Books Canada Limited, 2801 John Street, Markham, Ontario, Canada L3R 1B4
Penguin Books (N.Z.) Ltd, 182–190 Wairau Road, Auckland 10, New Zealand

First published 1965
Reprinted 1968
Second edition 1971
Third edition 1986

Printed and bound in Great Britain by
Cox & Wyman Ltd, Reading
Filmset in Linotron Times by
Rowland Phototypesetting Ltd,
Bury St Edmunds, Suffolk

Contents

Figures

Preface to the Third Edition

This book aims to set out an account of the relationship between British workers and the law. Since it first appeared in 1965 much has happened. Labour law was then little known as a subject; but in the twenty years that have followed, it has been debated, extended and revised again and again. Workers and managers, however, have always known the relevance of the law to their lives, sometimes welcoming, sometimes rejecting its proffered help. It is to them, as well as to lawyers, to the employed and the unemployed, that the following account is directed.

The developments of two decades have put some of the main issues of labour law on everybody's lips. What should a worker's rights be if he or she is dismissed – or about to be dismissed – from a job? What are the rights and liabilities of trade unions in which workers act in association with colleagues? What can the law do about safety at work, or about discrimination on grounds of race or sex or, indeed, for other reasons? What role can law generally play in a rapidly changing labour market? What matters are best left to collective bargaining? It is not possible to understand the content – often the very language – of employment problems and industrial disputes without some understanding of the law that influences attitudes and strategy in them. An introductory book such as this aims to provide a critical sketch of the law as it now is and of how it came to be as it is, together with some perspectives for discussion of the future. For this is an area of law that has changed rapidly; one member of the Royal Commission that investigated it in 1965–8 wrote anxiously:

supposing we made all the right recommendations and supposing the Government gave effect to them all in legislation, how long would it be before the judges turned everything upside down? . . . The ingenuity of lawyers is endless.

Law is not a mystery; it only uses long words. Some understanding of its technical structure is necessary, however, for an understanding of its development and its place in our lives. In this book the reader will find an elementary exposition of law as lawyers argue and practise it, and as judges interpret it. Wherever possible, technical detail is avoided; but we can understand the social significance of the legal doctrines only by resolutely entering the muddy waters of law itself and emerging on the other side, not by skirting round them. Technical law by itself is of limited use, at best an arid game played by keen minds in court rooms and ivory towers. For its significance we need to look at the historical and social setting, to question the values and policies enshrined in the judgments and the legal rules, and to inquire into what is done in other countries about the problems revealed. So the general reader will, it is hoped, find a guide to the impact of law in the employment field, and the student of our social or legal system an introductory account of the whole subject, on which the works and legal sources cited will provide further material. Except for such later references as it was possible to include, the law is stated as on 1 March 1986.

Necessarily, since the last edition was in 1971, my thanks are due to far more people than I can name, especially all the students and colleagues in this period from whom I have learned so much. Let me, however, thank for all their wisdom, friendship, experience, forbearance and assistance: first, Jon Clark (whose help with this edition I especially appreciate); my colleagues in the Comparative Labour Law Group – Ben Aaron, Xavier Blanc-Jouvan, Gino Giugni (now a member of a democratic second chamber), Thilo Ramm and – though, alas, no longer with us – Folke Schmidt, with whom I join Otto Kahn-Freund (both scholars whose remarkable careers left us so greatly in their debt); also Paul Davies, John Griffith, Silvana Sciarra, Bill McCarthy and David Lea; and Mark Freedland, Peter Pain, Bob Simpson, Julian Fulbrook, Bob Hepple, Paul O'Higgins, Colin Turpin, Roy Lewis, Brian Napier, Brian Thompson, Mickey Rubenstein, John Hendy, Johnny Veeder, Jeremy McMullen, Peter Wallington, Carol Harlow, David Richardson, Jim Mortimer, Mark Hall, Roger Bibbings, Breen Creighton, Albert Blyghton, Jack Jones, Spiros Simitis, Reuben Hasson, Guido Balandi, Gérard Lyon-Caen, Wolfgang Däubler, Tiziano Treu, Antoine Lyon-Caen, Jean-Claude Javillier, Alan Boulton, Don Rawson, Charlie Craver; also Lucy Pollard, Miles Litvinoff, Alison Real, Simon Deakin, Ewan McKendrick, Colleen Etheridge, Jonathan Wedderburn, Catherine Pankhurst and Pam Hodges; and most of all my wife Frances, without whose patient help and devoted support at every stage it could never have been accomplished. For the imperfections that remain I am, of course, alone responsible.

Bill Wedderburn
London
13 April 1986

Glossary of Main Abbreviations

A C	Appeal Cases (House of Lords; sometimes Judicial Committee, Privy Council: J C P C)
ACAS	Advisory, Conciliation and Arbitration Service
All E. R.	All England Law Reports
APEX	Association of Professional, Executive and Computer Staff
ASD	Action short of dismissal
ASLEF	Associated Society of Locomotive Engineers and Firemen
ASTMS	Association of Scientific, Technical and Managerial Staffs
AUEW	Amalgamated Union of Engineering Workers (AEU or AUEW(E): Amalgamated Engineering Union)
BIFU	Banking, Insurance and Finance Union
BJIR	British Journal of Industrial Relations
CA	Court of Appeal
CAC	Central Arbitration Committee
CBI	Confederation of British Industry
Ch.	Chancery Division (High Court)
CIR	Commission on Industrial Relations (1970–4)
CLJ	Cambridge Law Journal
CO	Certification Officer
COHSE	Confederation of Health Service Employees
Co. Law.	The Company Lawyer
CPPA	Conspiracy and Protection of Property Act 1875
CPSA	Civil and Public Services Association
CRE	Commission for Racial Equality
Ct S.	Court of Session (Scotland)
DE	Department of Employment
DHSS	Department of Health and Social Security

EA	Employment Act (1980 or 1982)
EAT	Employment Appeal Tribunal
EC	Commission of the European Economic Community
ECHR	European Convention on Human Rights (and Court; Strasbourg)
ECJ	European Court of Justice (EEC; Luxembourg)
EEC	European Economic Community
EETPU	Electrical, Electronic, Telecommunication and Plumbing Union (previously ETU)
EIRR	European Industrial Relations Review
EOC	Equal Opportunities Commission
EPA	Employment Protection Act 1975
EPCA	Employment Protection (Consolidation) Act 1978
Eq. P. A.	Equal Pay Act 1970
FWR	Fair Wages Resolution
GCHQ	Government Communications Headquarters
GMBAT	General, Municipal, Boilermakers' and Allied Trades Union (previously GMW)
GOQ	Genuine occupational qualification
H. and S. Info. Bull.	Health and Safety Information Bulletin
HL	House of Lords (final appeal court; Law Lords as HL 'Judicial Committee')
HSC	Health and Safety Commission
HSE	Health and Safety Executive
HSWA	Health and Safety at Work Act 1974
ICFTD	In contemplation or furtherance of a trade dispute
ICR	Industrial Cases Reports
IDS	Incomes Data Services
ILJ	Industrial Law Journal
ILO	International Labour Organization
Ind. Rel. Jo.	Industrial Relations Journal
Int. Lab. L. R.	International Labour Law Reports
IPCS	Institution of Professional Civil Servants
IRC	Independent Review Committee (TUC)

IRLR	Industrial Relations Law Reports
Ir. R.	Irish Reports
IRRR	Industrial Relations Review and Report (also contains IRLIB: Industrial Relations Legal Information Bulletin)
ISTC	Iron and Steel Trades' Confederation
IT	Industrial tribunal
ITR	Industrial Tribunal Reports
ITWF	International Transport Workers' Federation
J.	'Mr Justice' (High Court judge; e.g. 'Smith J.' – Mr Justice Smith)
JBL	Journal of Business Law
JIC	Joint Industrial Council
JNC	Joint negotiating committee (or council)
KIR	Knight's Industrial Reports
LC	Lord Chancellor (House of Lords; judge and member of the Government)
LCJ	Lord Chief Justice
LIFO	'Last in, first out' (selection in redundancies)
LJ	Lord Justice (Court of Appeal)
LOST	Lay-off or short time (redundancy)
LQR	Law Quarterly Review
LT	Law Times
MLR	Modern Law Review
MR	Master of the Rolls (Court of Appeal)
MSC	Manpower Services Commission
NALGO	National and Local Government Officers' Association
NAS/UWT	National Association of Schoolmasters/Union of Women Teachers
NATSOPA	National Society of Operative Printers (later Graphical and Media Personnel; now merged in SOGAT '82)
NBPI	National Board for Prices and Incomes
NCB	National Coal Board
NCU	National Communications Union (previously Post Office Engineering Union: POEU)
NEC	National Executive Committee (or Council)

NGA	National Graphical Association
NIRC	National Industrial Relations Court (1971–4)
NUJ	National Union of Journalists
NUM	National Union of Mineworkers
NUPE	National Union of Public Employees
NUR	National Union of Railwaymen
NUS	National Union of Seamen
NUT	National Union of Teachers
P.	President (judge of High Court; or NIRC, 1971–4)
QB	Queen's Bench Division (High Court; previously King's Bench Division)
R(FIS), R(I), R(SB), R(U)	Commissioners' and other decisions on social security (family income supplement, injury, supplementary and unemployment benefits)
RRA	Race Relations Act 1976
RSC	Rules of the Supreme Court (Order; Rule)
SC	Session Cases (Scotland)
SCPS	Society of Civil and Public Servants
SDA	Sex Discrimination Act 1975
SLT	Scottish Law Times
SOGAT '82	Society of Graphical and Allied Trades '82
SOSR	Some other substantial reason (unfair dismissal)
SSAT	Social Security Appeal Tribunal
TASS	Technical, Administrative and Supervisory Staffs (until 1976 section of AUEW)
TDA	Trade Disputes Act 1906
TGWU	Transport and General Workers' Union
TLR	Times Law Reports
TSSA	Transport Salaried Staffs' Association
TUA	Trade Union Act (1984 or 1913)
TUC	Trades Union Congress
TULRA	Trade Union and Labour Relations Act 1974 (amended 1976)
TUPE	Transfer of Undertakings (Protection of Employment) Regulations 1981
UCATT	Union of Construction, Allied Trades and Technicians

UCW	Union of Communication Workers (previously UPW)
UKAPE	United Kingdom Association of Professional Engineers
UMA	Union membership agreement or arrangement
USDAW	Union of Shop, Distributive and Allied Workers
VC	Vice Chancellor (High Court judge)
WLR	Weekly Law Reports
YOP	Youth Opportunities Programme
YTS	Youth Training Scheme

[1] Foundations of Labour Law

Most workers want nothing more of the law than that it should leave them alone. A secure job is preferable to a claim to a redundancy payment; a grievance settled in the plant or the office is better than going to a court or to an industrial tribunal. This attitude has long displayed a fundamental feature of British industrial relations. Despite the existence for many decades of statutes, such as the Factories Acts dealing with health and safety in factories, and of many judicial decisions on the law governing employment, observers have often looked in vain for what they might recognize as 'labour law' in Britain. (What follows is based largely on English law but most of it applies equally to the separate Scottish legal system.) We have never had a labour law code, and one expert wrote in 1959: 'When British industrial relations are compared with those of the other democracies they stand out because they are so little regulated by law.'[1]

Since 1960, though, new judgments and a great quantity of new legislation have affected our industrial relationships. If there is still a preference to be left alone, amongst employers as well as workers, there is now a stronger, though not necessarily justified, expectation that the law can be of help in time of trouble at work. Many rights are now stated in the Employment Protection (Consolidation) Act 1978 (EPCA); employers and trade unions are subject to the Employment Protection Act 1975 (EPA), to the Employment Acts 1980 and 1982 (EA 1980, 1982) and to the Trade Union Act 1984 (TUA 1984), all of them amending the Trade Union and Labour Relations Act 1974 (TULRA, as amended in 1976), not to speak of legislation on sex discrimination and equal pay (SDA 1975; Eq. P. A. 1970), race relations (RRA 1976), health and safety at work (HSWA 1974), industrial training and social security.

Moreover, there is extensive legal machinery now special to labour law. The Advisory, Conciliation and Arbitration Service (ACAS) derives its powers and functions from the 1975 statute (the EPA). Many

workers' rights are enforced through industrial tribunals first set up in
1964. They are tripartite, with two lay members from panels nominated
by employers and unions alongside a legal chairman. Since 1975 a
special tripartite Employment Appeal Tribunal (EAT),with a judge as
chairman, has heard appeals from these tribunals (usually only on points
of law, not of fact). Above that there are no special labour courts;
appeals from the EAT go to the normal Court of Appeal and the
(judicial) House of Lords (five Law Lords). So can it still be said that
British industrial relations are 'so little regulated by law'? Is 'voluntarism' still the distinctive mark of the system?

The meaning of, and answers to, those questions are a central part of
our inquiry. In order to confront them and the continuing debate about
'reform' of British labour law and industrial relations – for this is an area
where each of us has a view as to what is 'wrong' with the system
according to our personal policies and prejudices – we need to clear the
ground of a few misconceptions. First, we must ask what is meant by
'regulation by law'. Then we shall examine in outline the curious
evolution of British labour law, putting the most recent changes of the
1970s and 1980s in the legal and social context of the past. For the very
language of modern labour law can lead us astray unless we understand
its origins. In this chapter, then, we describe the emergence of the legal
'immunities' and their relationship to the 'common law', those principles of law created by the judges. This leads to an inquiry into the
diverse legislation of the 1970s and, in turn, to an outline of the new laws
of the 1980s.

Law and labour relations

There are some who hold the view that until recent times there was no
'law' at all in industrial relations in Britain. But of course there was. If an
employer fails to pay wages due to the worker or if the worker walks out
on his or her job, the law (here principles of 'common law') has long
provided remedies for breach of the contract of employment. Statute
law from Parliament governing such matters as conditions of employment, injury at work, or trade union activity has been abundant for
many years – in 1962 enough to furnish one textbook with some seven

hundred pages. The legislation of the last two decades has its roots in the laws of the last two centuries.

The meaning and quality of such laws, however, are strongly affected both by the social forces at work around them and by the different legal sanctions attached to them. For example, there is a radical difference between the Crown prosecuting a group of workers for a crime and their employer suing them in the civil courts for breach of their employment contracts. In the first case, if they have committed a crime, the acts done are regarded as wrongs against society generally, and the sanction is punishment, usually a fine or imprisonment. In the second case there has been a failure to keep a bargain with another person, a civil wrong by breach of contract commonly remedied by the payment of damages to him or her (and in what follows *both* genders are normally included even if only one is stated).

There is a third type of wrongdoing, a civil breach of duty falling, in a way, between the two. This arises where a person commits a 'tort', a civil wrong other than a breach of contract, ranging from a violent assault or a negligent injury to a slander or a 'nuisance' by interfering with the enjoyment of property. The (civil) *tort* must not be confused with a crime. The remedies for a tort are damages and 'injunctions' (orders by the courts to desist – orders that can also be awarded to stop breaches of many types of contract). So, if an employer fails to provide a safe machine for an employee and the latter suffers injury, this may be both a breach of contract by the employer and a tort by him against the worker; and it may also be a crime if the lapse is prohibited by a statute, such as the Factories Act 1961. It is, therefore, never enough to call an act 'unlawful'. We must know what kind of illegality is in issue. Nor, for parallel reasons, should we speak of 'the law' without distinguishing what kind of obligation and sanction is involved.

Law, courts and Parliament

Constitutionally, it is the job of Parliament to make statutes and of judges to interpret them. In reality, things are rather different. Areas not covered by legislation are the domain of the 'common law', principles developed by the judges. They frequently bring to bear the mentality of the common law also to their task of interpreting the Acts that Parliament has passed. We must remember the judges' role when we assess the impact of labour legislation over the last twenty years. Some of it has created criminal offences (a breach of the duty to ensure that an article supplied for use at work is, as far as reasonably practicable, safe is a crime: HSWA 1974 s. 6). A great deal more of it has given statutory rights to employees against their employer sanctioned in civil law by awards of the industrial tribunals (such areas as maternity leave, 'unfair dismissal' or redundancy payments: EPCA Parts III, V and VI). Statutes have recently enlarged the occasions on which judges can grant injunctions based on tort liability against strikers (EA 1980 and 1982), created new rights for trade union members or for non-unionists against employers and unions (EPA 1975; EA 1980 and 1982) and required employers to consult with or disclose information to unions (EPA 1975).

Sometimes, as with injunctions against strikes, the laws are enforced through the ordinary courts. Other claims – especially claims by individual workers under the statutes – come before the industrial tribunals. Some disputes are adjudicated by special bodies; a union complains of an employer's failure to disclose information to a tripartite Central Arbitration Committee (CAC), and *its* awards become terms of each worker's employment contract, enforceable as such through the ordinary courts. Other statutes are different again. Take the Act of 1975 establishing ACAS and describing its functions (EPA). No civil or criminal powers were granted to, or wanted by, ACAS; its pronouncements are not legally binding. But Parliament used the law to set up this machinery with the aim of assisting in, but not regulating, the solution of industrial disputes, both 'individual' (worker against employer) and 'collective' (employers against unions). The law's role in creating machinery to help solve disputes is just as important as the creation of new crimes or torts.

So there has recently been what ACAS called in 1984 'a considerable increase in the quantity of law affecting managers, trade unions and employees'. But 'law' is not all of one type. The 'quantity of law' is not a safe guide to its character, still less to its quality. To judge that we need closer inquiry into the *nature* of the law in question, into its real, as against its purported, social effects (not all 'law' is enforceable or enforced, like speed limits or shop hours on Sundays) and into our own preconceptions about it. Nor is this just a matter of civil and criminal law. The law that sustains ACAS is, we shall see in Chapter 4, part of a long tradition that regards autonomous collective bargaining between employers and trade unions as the normal way to behave in industry. With that has gone a legal tradition whereby the 'primacy' of that voluntary process is recognized by our legal institutions, which have aimed to sustain it but not to regulate it. But that tradition of 'the law' has often escaped the lawyers. Their gaze was concentrated elsewhere. For the English lawyer, the central institution of labour relations has never been (as it is for most employers and workers) the collective bargain between 'workers' and 'employers'. His primary concern in labour law has been with the individual relationship between the employer and each employee, especially the contract of employment, an institution that the leading authority of the post-war era, Sir Otto Kahn-Freund, described as legally 'the corner-stone of the edifice'.[2] The contract of employment is still governed largely by the 'common law' rules of contract law built up by the judges.

Here then is an ancient tension in the system. For the common law assumes it is dealing with a contract made between equals, but in reality, save in exceptional circumstances, the individual worker brings no equality of bargaining power to the labour market and to this transaction central to his life whereby the employer buys his labour power. This *individual* relationship, in its inception,

is an act of submission, in its operation it is a condition of subordination, however much the submission and the subordination may be concealed by that indispensable figment of the legal mind known as the 'contract of employment'.

That contract of employment Kahn-Freund described as 'a command under the guise of an agreement'.[3] One critical question for the operation of the law is how far the courts interpret that contract so as to preserve the employer's power to 'command'. Parliament has in recent years enacted new rights for employees governing their relationships with the employer. But the majority of these rights are not incorporated into the employment contract. For example, the right not to be 'unfairly dismissed' exists under statute, separate from contractual rights – though only for the 'employee', not for a worker who is 'self-employed'. (We shall see in Chapter 2 that, in today's labour market, this is an increasingly difficult distinction to apply.) But this right does not become *part* of the employment contract. We now have, therefore, on the one hand, rights enshrined in the employment contract enforced by civil actions in the ordinary courts and, on the other, a separate, minimum 'floor of rights' for individual workers gradually added over recent years by statutes and enforced largely by civil claims in the industrial tribunals. A claim for 'wrongful' dismissal as a breach of the employment contract (a sacking without notice, for example) will go to the ordinary courts. But a claim for 'unfair' dismissal based on the rights afforded by the employment protection legislation has for many years now gone to an industrial tribunal. Both cases may end up in the same Court of Appeal or even the (judicial) House of Lords, though the second type of case will have come from a tribunal through the EAT. The EAT is an important new institution; the presiding judges have shown a strong inclination to draw upon the industrial experience of the two industrial 'wing-persons' sitting with them. But, as we shall see, it has not revolutionized our labour law system; and in 1984 it disposed of only 686 cases.

Our labour law has, therefore, two systems of protection for individual workers, operating, not always happily, side by side – though as we shall see the common law concepts of the older system tend to dominate (see Chapter 3). A few statutory rights are expressed as compulsory 'terms' of the contract (like the 'equality clause' for equal pay, which we meet in Chapter 6). But most are not. When, therefore, an EEC Directive is imported into our labour law by regulations (as a member State EEC legislation is binding upon us) so as to transfer the contract of employment of a worker from his employer to someone who buys the undertaking, together with all rights 'under or in connection with' that contract (see p. 299), our courts are immediately set a puzzle. Which of the worker's rights are 'connected with' his contract?

The statutory 'floor of rights' now extends into many facets of employment law and even into the law affecting social discrimination (see Chapters 3 and 6); but it does not normally prevent the erection of superior conditions by way of collective bargaining. It was meant to be a floor not a ceiling. Some workers, for instance, derive from collective agreements rights to redundancy payments higher than the sums that employers must pay under redundancy legislation. Legislation of this kind long antedated the recent laws. In the nineteenth century we find Parliament protecting specially vulnerable workers, women and young children, for example. From early in this century legislation has tried to protect exploited workers who are not organized in trade unions by setting minimum conditions to their employment. Such provisions (examined in Chapter 4) recognize and encourage collective organization in trade unions and, like obligations placed on the employer to consult his unions (when, for example, redundancies are proposed), they may be seen as 'props' to, rather than replacements of, the 'voluntary' bargaining process. In this area of labour law, though, public policy has undergone, as we shall see, great changes in recent years.

Collective bargaining and labour law

Such a system assumes the existence of autonomous collective bargaining. Collective bargaining itself, moreover, assumes freedom for workers to organize in independent trade unions, to bargain independently and effectively with the employer. The freedom to combine in autonomous associations is essential to the individual worker to alleviate his subordination. Bargaining cannot be effective if the union is a 'house union' controlled by the employer or if the members have no right to refuse to work on the terms offered by him. Many modern systems of law positively establish rights to do these things. The French or Italian workers has a constitutional *right* to organize, to join a trade union without being penalized for doing so, and to strike. The Swedish employer and (given certain conditions) the United States and the French employer are obliged by law to bargain with their unions. None of these rights exist in Britain. Neither in the statutes nor in the court judgments will we find any positive 'right to organize' for trade unions or for employers' associations (see Chapter 4), nor any legal 'right' to lock out or to strike (Chapters 7 and 8). It must not be assumed that British law is necessarily the worse for that. If industrial relations operate without formal legal rights to the satisfaction of a sufficiently broad social *consensus*, and so long as workers and employers are in practice free to organize, bargain and withdraw labour, the absence of formal legal rights may not be important. Their absence, though, has affected the development of our law, not least about the status of trade unions, their relationships with their members and with employers, and the partial or total withdrawal of labour by workers in disputes with employers. Here in bargaining and conflict we find the clearest expression of Kahn-Freund's observation: 'On the labour side, power is collective power.' As we shall see (p. 96) the 'individual' employer is from the outset an aggregate collection of resources, already a 'collective power' in social terms. The relationship at work is at root a power relationship, and legal intervention can rarely be wholly neutral as between the conflicting interests. The relationship between the employer and his workers and their union is, of course, not the only source of conflict at work. A worker may clash with his union, and the interests of the State or 'the public' (a dangerous term unless it is defined carefully)[4] may be involved.

In any labour law system, the State may try to use 'law' to regulate the terms of that employment relationship or the machinery by which they are bargained. On the other hand, it may intervene only to the extent of holding the ring in order that bargaining should take place between unions and employers to modulate the terms of employment as they see fit. Labour law systems in democracies usually have elements of both approaches. But British labour legislation has largely adopted the stance of 'holding the ring' for over a century. We have no legal minimum wage, no compulsory Works Councils.

So strong did this characteristic become in the century after 1850 that Kahn-Freund and others described it as 'non-intervention' or 'abstention' by the law. What the Webbs had called the 'method of Collective Bargaining' in 1897 spread to become the most important factor in determining wages and terms of employment for the great majority of workers, re-emphasized by the increasing density in the work-force of trade union membership (15 per cent in 1910, growing to a peak of 55 per cent in 1979).[5] The Webbs also predicted that collective bargaining might encounter difficulties so great as to 'lead to its supersession by some form of compulsory arbitration; that is to say, by Legal Enactment'. Yet apart from exceptional periods in wartime, things have not generally gone in this direction. Indeed, as we see in Chapter 4, unlike in most countries with comparable economic systems, not only are bargaining structures in Britain regulated very little by the law as against the efforts of the employers and unions themselves, thereby permitting flexibility more readily than in systems that impose legal structures (as in West Germany, with its mandatory Works Councils and legal rules about where and how certain matters can be negotiated), but the average British collective agreement between a union and employer has itself been rarely enforceable by any legal sanction, though the worker's individual employment contract with his employer is, of course, enforceable in law. Nor do the collective agreements and informal arrangements made at various levels (whether in multi-employer bargaining with unions at industry level, or Joint Industrial Councils or single company agreements or district councils, or shop-floor or plant bargains between managers and shop stewards) normally follow lawyers' lines or distinctions in Britain. They have usually displayed a 'lack of concern for the distinction between conflicts of interest and conflicts of right, which is fundamental in European labour law'.[6] The individual employment contract, though, feeds on the collective bargain however informal the latter may be. We examine the legal relationship between that individual contract and the collective agreement in Chapter 4, not least because it is there that we find the mechanism through which some seven out of ten workers derive their personal rights to the employment terms and conditions negotiated by trade unions.

A Royal Commission set up under Lord Donovan reported in 1968 on industrial relations and labour law (the Donovan Report). It summed up many of the virtues and the vices of the British industrial tradition when it said about its 'reform':

What is needed first of all is a change in the nature of British collective bargaining, and a more orderly method for workers and their representatives to exercise their influence in the factory; and for this to be accomplished, if possible, without destroying the British tradition of keeping industrial relations out of the courts.

Until recently many took this as the yardstick by which to judge the success or failure of our labour laws.

Law, unions and the labour market

The law, then, has never regulated the general patterns of British bargaining. At plant level the shop steward (an employee carrying out representative union functions) grew spontaneously and autonomously to be a predominant influence, elected by workers according to the rules or custom of their union or of their workplace. The shop steward is 'an accepted, reasonable and even moderating influence; more of a lubricant than an irritant', wrote McCarthy for the Donovan Commission; a different figure from that usually portrayed as 'addressing thousands on a football field'[7] – a view later surveys confirmed. Bargaining at plant level between shop stewards and managers became the most informal, yet essential, part of the British system. In recent years, some parts of the bargaining structure have become more formalized. This is illustrated especially in the formulation of clearer written 'procedures' for processing workers' grievances (a CBI survey recorded in 1982 that this had become 'an almost universal practice') and in the relatively greater formality that has accompanied a shift since 1968 from multi-employer to single-employer bargaining for the greater part of industry.[8] Other sectors have changed their patterns less, such as private services or national and local government. In the public sector white-collar unionism grew strong roots many decades ago. By 1980 in the private sector too 'white-collar pay was widely regulated through collective bargaining'.[9] Despite elements of greater formality in procedure, to which legal changes have contributed, it would still be extremely difficult to reduce this patchwork of negotiating, consultative and grievance machinery to clear lines of academic or legal principle.

Like the trade union movement, which is woven into it, the structure cannot be understood apart from its history. The crazy-paving patterns of the trade union movement itself have been much publicized, and we return to the structure of that movement in Chapter 9. But at the outset we must note certain features. There is a high, though decreasing, number of trade unions, of which membership rose to a peak of 13.3 million in 1979; by 1984 it had fallen to 11.1 million. Most important unions are affiliated to the TUC. At its 1985 Congress, the TUC had 91 affiliated organizations comprising 9.9 million members (against 112 in 1979 with 12.1 million). The size and character of unions vary greatly. Whilst the Society of Shuttlemakers hung on with its 49 members, the five largest affiliates maintained 4.8 million members (TGWU, AUEW, GMBAT, NALGO and NUPE). The rise in membership in NALGO and NUPE marks the rising importance of public sector employment. As old manufacturing industries decayed or closed down, the focus of employment moved towards the service and the public sectors. Managerial, technical, banking and similar sectors have more than doubled their membership since 1970, as white-collar employees have come to account for about one-half of the work-force. Indeed, white-collar union density grew from 15 per cent in 1968 to 44 per cent in 1983 in private manufacturing industry, though still languishing at 17 per cent in private services, the only sector with a recent growth in jobs. The figures have importance for legal policy. For we need to ask what 'the law' is trying to do with unions and with the industrial relations system.

It would be a mistake to see British trade unions as very rich or mighty in resources. They own far more property than French or Italian unions; but they do not control banks or similar financial bodies like West German unions, whilst members of the main Swedish unions pay on average more than three times as much as the average British member in union subscriptions. The entire funds and gross assets, including buildings, of all British unions in 1983 amounted to some £980 million (less than £90 per member; the average annual income per member was £36). That total can be matched by many an employer that is a large public company or company group.

Since 1970 our industrial relations system as a whole has been subjected to the ravages of a national and international recession. Over many years before that, we had experienced absolute economic growth but relative international decline, and in particular low levels of capital investment and technical innovation. But the maintenance of 'full' employment had remained a central aim of all governments and had facilitated stronger organizations of work-people, especially at the workplace in decentralized collective bargaining. Rapid economic and social changes have occurred in the last five years. Unemployment (excluding school-leavers) grew from 2.5 per cent of the work-force in 1974 to 5 per cent in 1979, then to over 13 per cent (3.2 million workers) in 1985. Many observers would increase this official figure to 4.0 million, or even more, in reality. Social discrimination at work is particularly serious in that labour market for ethnic minorities and for women (a challenging problem for the law, discussed in Chapter 6).

The latter are particularly affected by the changing patterns of employment. The labour market has fragmented. Some analyse it as being 'segmented' into a 'primary' sector, with higher wages, fringe benefits, good and improving conditions, some stability, and chances of advancement, and a 'secondary' sector with poor conditions, low wages, more arbitrary discipline and greater insecurity, often employment of a casual quality.[10] The two may exist side by side in an industry or even in an enterprise. Recent studies have concentrated upon this division into 'two nations' in employment, where some workers still seem to 'own' a job, while others are tenants made doubly insecure by the recession's effect upon cost-conscious employers. Some companies train and keep their own 'core group' of skilled workers, leaving other functions to those on, or nearer to, a 'periphery', where rings of workers provide a buffer for the core workers through part-time, temporary or casual employment or in various forms of subcontracting or 'outwork'.[11] Beyond them lies the little charted land of the black economy. Whereas a 'precondition for management' of the modern capitalist enterprise once seemed to be 'centralization of employment', now technological change may have facilitated a relatively larger reliance upon an external, 'marginal' work-force to complement the inner ring of workers in the fortress of what they hope is permanent employment.[12] Many of the more marginal jobs are part-time and many of those jobs are held by women. Women now make up more than 40 per cent of the employed work-force. Recent losses of employment, mainly full-time jobs, have been felt in all sectors other than services; and of the 700,000 'new' jobs created in 1984–5 well over half (491,000) were for part-time women workers. The other major area of growth is self-employment, one that introduces great difficulties of definition and of policy into the legal discussion. Other so-called atypical forms of employment, such as temporary work or outwork, have joined casual and part-time work to increase the number of employment relations with which the law has to deal but which lie outside the 'normal' full-time employee–employer nexus. That poses novel problems for the legal concept of 'employment' itself, which we meet in Chapter 2. There is in fact 'a crisis which threatens that very legal concept . . . of the most profound moment for the whole of our labour law'.[13] The same point emerges when we look at young workers coming on to the labour market for the first time, many finding that society offers to them a choice between unemployment and the Youth Training Scheme with an ambiguous work status (discussed in Chapter 6).

These and similar changes in society and the economy determine the lives of workers. Changes in the law have their effects, but for the most part they are accessory, a legal counterpoint to the dominant themes of an economic and industrial score. Whether law – of one type or another – can play a more direct or a more fundamental role, and, if so, to what effect, is one of the issues raised by the events and the policies of modern labour law.

Labour law as a subject

It may be useful at this stage to indicate the main areas that fall within the province of labour law to be dealt with in this book. They are:

(1) The employment relationship between wor½er and employer. We shall examine the concept of 'the employee' (we use the words 'worker' and 'employee' interchangeably, except where the former has a special meaning in areas that we shall indicate); the nature of the individual contract of employment; and the problems of job security connected with its termination.

(2) The area of collective bargaining between trade unions and employers; legal encouragement of, support for, or obstacles to, collective organization and negotiation; and the legal effect of the collective agreement.

(3) Parliamentary provision by statute of a 'floor of rights' for individual employees, and the interpretations of it, from safety at work to rights in respect of job security (especially unfair dismissal and redundancy) and matters such as equal pay, sex and racial discrimination, and protection of wages.

(4) Strikes, lock-outs and industrial action generally; the interplay of Parliament's statutes and the judges' decisions, and the role of the State in industrial conflict.

(5) The status of trade unions, the rights of union members, and the role of the trade union movement.

Other areas of law naturally impinge – for example, social security law, incomes policy and taxation statutes. Some of these are extensive subjects in themselves, but they must be mentioned, however briefly. The main aim in touching upon them as far as space allows is to remind ourselves of the importance they have to the central themes of labour law.

It may be useful to portray a 'skeleton' of the structure in two stages. First, we show the fundamental legal relationships (Figure 1, p. 14). To this we add Parliament's major interventions (Figure 2, p. 15). Legislation adds protection for individual workers, and various measures give support to collective bargaining, often by aid to workers or their unions but sometimes, as we see in Chapter 4, also by strengthening employers' associations against the black-sheep employer.

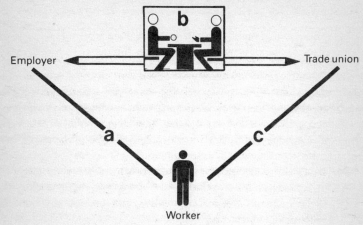

(a) Individual contract of employment

(b) Collective bargaining; collective agreement

(c) Trade union contract of membership (where a member)

Figure 1. The fundamental relationships in labour law

The courts and Europe

We must also note the relationships between our courts and those outside the United Kingdom. Appeals from industrial tribunals, as we saw, go to the EAT, and thence to the ordinary Court of Appeal and House of Lords. Appeals from the County courts and High Court proceed to those same appellate courts. But after the European Communities Act 1972 all of our courts are bound by decisions of the European Court of Justice (ECJ) in Luxembourg. This is now our final court of appeal on matters within its competence under the European Community Treaties. The first area of labour law that has been affected by this new source is equal pay and sex discrimination (Chapter 6); but an increasing number of other matters are being affected by Community law or by proposals of the European Commission (Brussels) for new Regulations or Directives under the Treaties.

We must distinguish European Community law from the decisions of other bodies. The European Court of Human Rights (Strasbourg), for example, is quite separate from the ECJ (Luxembourg). The Stras-

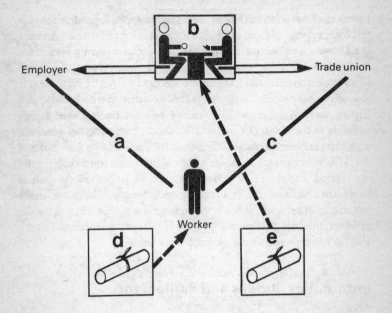

(d) Legislation on individual employment protection and the 'floor of rights'

(e) Legislation providing 'props' to collective bargaining by encouragement or support (but normally not regulation)

Figure 2. Parliament's main interventions in labour law

bourg court, and the Commission on Human Rights with it, were established under the European Convention on Human Rights, which the United Kingdom has ratified; but its decisions do not automatically become part of British law. They are accorded high moral standing, and some of our judges have referred to them and to the Convention for guidance. British governments have even come to regard it as desirable to legislate and change our law in order not to stand in breach of the Convention. But until such legislation is passed, British law does not incorporate any part of the Convention or the judgments under it. A similar relationship exists with the International Labour Organization (ILO), set up after the First World War and now a United Nations agency, with the participation of governments, employers and unions. Britain has ratified many of its Conventions setting labour standards, on

Freedom of Association (No. 87, 1948) for example. Indeed, in the past this country was a pioneer of international labour standards. But neither the Conventions nor the decisions of its various tripartite bodies are 'law' unless established as such by British legislation. If the UK is found to have contravened an ILO Convention, and no Act of Parliament is passed or other similar legal step taken, no action can be brought in a British court by reason of that contravention alone. We shall see an example in the *GCHQ* case (p. 277). Governments do not generally wish to be in breach of these international obligations. We shall find that the UK government, in order to avoid that consequence, recently 'de-ratified' certain ILO Conventions, so as to be able to pursue its policies without the risk of any such breach. There are other international agencies whose work impinges on labour law; but for the moment, the critical point to note is the special position occupied by the ECJ in Luxembourg whose judgments are binding.

Immunities, judges and Parliament

The system emerges: 1871–1906

British labour law today cannot be understood without a grasp of its history. Despite the existence of a large 'quantity' of law, the system that emerged from the nineteenth century was one that expressed 'non-intervention' by the law. The law does not seek to regulate the shape of the employment contract or the outcome of collective industrial negotiation. In that sense the law's policy has been a *laissez-faire* policy. But the emergence of that system did not depend upon some academic choice. To reach it trade unions had to struggle against earlier *interventions* by 'the law'. They needed to persuade Parliament to provide liberation from decisions hostile to their activities, and even to the lawful existence of autonomous unions. As we shall see in Chapter 7, both Parliament and judges had declared unions to be criminal combinations during the first part of the nineteenth century. Parliament relaxed its outright ban in 1824, and statutes of 1859, 1871 and 1875 were fought for and enacted to relieve the expanding workers' movement from the worst consequences of criminal liability. But then the judges turned to the development of civil liability.

As late as 1872, in *R.* v. *Bunn* (p. 519) a judge told the jury trying gas workers accused of organizing a strike that would have plunged the West End of London into darkness, that they were guilty of criminal conspiracy if what they had done was

an unjustifiable annoyance and interference with the masters in the conduct of their business and which in any business would be such annoyance and interference as would be likely to have a deterring effect upon masters of ordinary nerve.

This form of 'conspiracy' had to be excluded by Parliament from industrial disputes ('trade disputes'). That was done in 1875. But the courts replied by creating and extending a civil liability for the *tort* of civil 'conspiracy to injure'. In 1901 they imposed this and other civil liabilities in tort upon trade union funds in the *Taff Vale* decision (p. 525). The unions extracted certain protections against some tort liabilities from the Liberal Government of 1906. But the courts proceeded to declare other activities illegal, including political activity by unions. For this, too, another protective statute was needed in 1913 (it has recently been amended in 1984: Chapter 9). So this period saw the pendulum swing regularly back and forth between judge-made liabilities and cautious parliamentary protection, a process in which the attitude of the judges 'reflected that of the middle class'.[14] Lindley LJ said in 1896: 'You cannot make a strike effective without doing more than is lawful.'

Given the stage of the Industrial Revolution in Britain as compared to equivalent stages of development in other countries, the labour movement had acquired considerable strength and recognition from employers by the turn of the century. Some employers resisted bitterly, like the railway companies; others agreed to bargain relatively quickly. The skilled and semi-skilled 'New Model' unions that were, with the miners and cotton workers, the core of the movement after 1850 were joined as the century closed by unions organizing the unskilled, from dockers to match-girls, the progenitors of the big 'general' unions like the TGWU. Alliances were forged with groups of MPs as the franchise was slowly extended to more (male) voters in 1867 and 1884. But this was still an industrial movement. The Labour Party sprang from a body formed in 1900 and was not formally constituted until 1906; only then did Britain have a party overtly based upon working-class support as the political wing of the labour movement (the earlier Social Democratic Federation never fulfilled that function). By that time the main frame of the labour law system had long been established. Positive legislation with criminal and civil sanctions to secure health and safety standards at work and to protect women and children had been promoted by factory reformers and unions early in the nineteenth century, with a Factory Inspectorate. But the legislation on trade unions, collective bargaining and industrial disputes enacted between 1871 and 1906 was different. It aimed mainly to remove liabilities that the judges continued to impose on unions. Safety and health in factories came to be regarded as appropriate for positive, legislative regulation. The terms and conditions of adult male workers came to be seen as primarily appropriate for collective bargaining.

The 'mix' is not of course immutable. We shall see that in 1974 Parliament used legislation to introduce new rights and duties to consult about safety at work; and various types of 'law' have been used to underpin the protection of minimum conditions for workers. The unions themselves have not been averse to seeking regulation by the 'method of legal enactment' (as with public servants and railwaymen at the turn of the century).[15] It became possible to speak of 'non-intervention' in collective labour relationships because the Acts of 1871, 1875 and 1906 aimed to push back the boundaries of illegalities in the common law that would hamstring the unions. In trade disputes, 'the law' (the common law) which once intervened could not now do so in respect of these excluded liabilities. The critical exclusions were the removal of the doctrine of 'restraint of trade' that made unions unlawful associations (1871: p. 522), the two doctrines of conspiracy to injure in 'trade disputes' (1875, criminal liability: p. 520; 1906, civil liability: p. 581), and the tort of inducing breach of an employment contract in 'trade disputes' (1906: p. 585). Without these exclusions, unions and collective bargaining would encounter immediate illegality, then and now. These and parallel legal provisions came later to be known (perhaps unfortunately) as 'the immunities'. In reality they amounted not so much to 'abstention' by the law as to an exclusion of the judges. The concept of 'non-intervention' of the law was a useful subsequent rationalization.

Judges and the illegality of trade unions

The illegalities in question did not depend, though, upon some whim or prejudice of the judges, nor even upon their 'bias'. Some illegalities had been imposed by statute. The Master and Servant Acts, for example, which traced their ancestry back to the Statute of Labourers 1351, made it a crime for a servant improperly to leave employment until their repeal as late as 1875. But the common law was, and is, part of a social structure with clear ideas about property and contract and 'combinations' inimical to them, and judges gave expression to that. In 1868 Malins VC said of workers who had picketed their employer with placards declaring him 'black':

The jurisdiction of this Court is to protect property . . . to prevent these misguided and misled workmen from committing these acts of intimidation which go to the destruction of property.[16]

Furthermore, the problem of trade union illegality was not unique to Britain. It was common to all comparable industrializing societies. Combination for 'economic purposes' was obnoxious to the *laissez-faire* ideology of the nineteenth century, 'and the spirit of the common law differs only in degree from that of the legal systems of the continent'.[17] In Europe unions and their activities met prohibitions and illegalities parallel in function to ours. The problem arose everywhere, but the solutions everywhere differed. The illegalities

were the natural consequence of systems of law based upon rights of property derived from legal concepts of the seventeenth and eighteenth centuries. . . . The solution offered to that common problem is a central feature of each system of collective labour law.[18]

In these European countries, at different dates but at similar stages of industrial development (Germany 1869, France 1884, Italy 1889, Sweden 1864), the most repressive penal laws were swept away. As we see in Chapter 7, the process began earlier in Britain in 1824, as we would expect with our earlier Industrial Revolution. This stage, however, brought only a bare liberty of association. By itself it was inadequate. Further rights were needed to cope with other illegalities that stopped unions from acting effectively in their members' interests. A trade union is not a passive association; it lives by the struggle to maintain and improve its members' lot. In most of the comparable countries this second phase resulted in one or more of the rights to organize, to bargain and to strike entering the legal system as positive rights. In Britain that was not the case. The industrial liberties permitting bargaining and withdrawal of labour came to rest here almost entirely upon the 'immunities'. It may be possible to argue about the precise frontiers of the immunities, but as the Government White Paper of 1981 put it:

immunities are not simply legal privileges which could be abolished outright. Without some legal protection – however circumscribed – it would be impossible for trade unions or individuals to organise industrial action without risk of civil proceedings and the ultimate safeguard of a collective withdrawal of labour would be effectively nullified.[19]

What the statutory 'immunities' protect are social 'rights'. In substance, behind the form, the statute provides liberties or rights that the common law would deny to workers. The 'immunity' is mere form.

This is one key to an understanding of the structure of British labour law. Many judges, though, have perceived the statutory 'immunity' as something that detracts from the common law rights of other persons and therefore as a 'privilege', which must be construed narrowly. Few have seen 'immunities' as introducing *collective* freedoms before which contract and property must give way. Except for the brief attempt at overall statutory regulation of industrial relations in 1971, the pattern of 'immunities' has since 1906 been the base of our system. In recent times it has rested upon the legislation of 1974 to 1976, which modernized the protections in trade disputes. In 1979 Lord Scarman described this modern structure of the 'immunities' as representing 'what Parliament had intended when it enacted the Act of 1906 – but stronger and clearer than it was then'.[20]

The general approach of judges has been different. In the same 1979 case the Law Lords agreed to reverse an extravagantly narrow meaning put upon the trade dispute 'immunities' by the Court of Appeal (p. 568); but many went out of their way to comment rather differently from Lord Scarman. Lord Diplock said the immunities could even permit claims that would 'bring down the fabric of the present economic system by raising wages to unrealistic levels'. Commentators saw such passages as a 'thinly disguised . . . invitation to the government to propose changes in the law'.[21] This judgment was rendered just two weeks after the publication of Government proposals for radical change in this area brought about in the Employment Act 1980. Similarly, judges usually concentrate on the *form* of the law. Lord Denning MR insisted in 1979 that Parliament had never granted union organizers 'rights' in trade disputes. 'It did not give them a *right* to break the law or to do wrong by inducing people to break contracts. It only gave them immunity if they did.'[22] Doing 'wrong' and breaking 'the law' relate here to the judges' own common law. Some legal writers, therefore, have described trade union liberties as 'immune wrongs'.[23] In the cases of 1979–80 the Law Lords felt obliged to express further opinions about the 'immunities'. They spoke of the 'immunities' as 'unpalatable' and given to 'privileged persons'. Lord Diplock said that they 'tended to stick in judicial gorges', that they are 'intrinsically repugnant to anyone who has spent his life in the practice of the law'. Lord Salmon declared of the law: 'Surely the time has come for it to be altered.' The Bill to alter it had been printed a few days earlier.

This is not to say that all judicial attitudes express a uniformity of attitude. As Griffith has said:

judges like the rest of us are not all of a piece . . . they are liable to be swamped by emotional prejudices . . . their 'inarticulate major premises' are strong and not only inarticulate but sometimes unknown to themselves.

Judges do their honest best, but the great majority 'define the public interest inevitably from the viewpoint of their own class', one that puts priority on maintenance of order, protection of private property and 'containment of the trade union movement'. They may move with the times, but 'it is their function in our society to do so belatedly'.[24] Perhaps we should not be surprised that judges cannot see the social substance behind the legal form. The very semantics of the 'immunities' invite concentration upon the form (though whether a system of 'positive rights' would necessarily fare better in Britain we leave open until Chapter 10). More important is the question: why did Britain *not* acquire a pattern of law that included some at least of the basic industrial *rights* expected in a democratic society? This historical question remains centrally relevant to labour law today.

Why immunities?

For most of this century we have prided ourselves, rightly, upon freedoms that *have* in practice included freedom to organize, to bargain and to withdraw labour in combination. Yet this 'proud edifice' of collective labour law and practice was built without positive legal assistance: 'No Wagner Act, no Weimar Constitution, no Front Populaire legislation'.[25] Why is the buzz-word 'immunity' at the centre of British trade union law? It will not do to explain this by saying that Anglo-Saxon 'common law' countries do things this way (Australia, Canada and the United States do not) or that the lack of written constitutional rights compelled it (though lack of them clearly contributed). The key lies not in legal but in social developments. No doubt this includes the legal machinery along with other parts of the political economy; but in comparable countries, the shape of modern labour law is clearly affected most directly by the character of the labour movement as it emerges with the proletariat of industrial society.

The formative period for Britain was the fifty years before 1914. In a country that had achieved the first Industrial Revolution, permeated with doctrines of *laissez-faire*, a conjunction of three factors combined to produce the idiosyncratic but organic framework of labour law. These were, first, a relatively strong but essentially *industrial* labour movement; second, a gradual, but far from complete, extension of the (male) franchise; and third, the *absence* until late in this period of a distinct political party based upon working-class support with a programme of industrial rights to offer to workers and the unions. The advent of the 'new unions' of the 1880s (organizing unskilled workers) alongside the earlier craft unions had produced a situation 'unique' to Britain. Hobsbawm notes: 'On the continent, unionism developed simultaneously with the mass political labour movement and its parties, and largely under their impulsion.'[26] This was not the case in Britain. Kahn-Freund stressed the importance of the 'craft' tradition for all unions – and for society generally – in Britain; but he placed importance too upon the fact that 'the political movement arose from the trade unions and that in France and in Germany it was the opposite'.[27]

Programmes for 'rights' were not inherently alien notions not understood here. British unions had their radicals and socialists; some of their leaders participated in international associations of 'working men'. But from 1867 onwards, the demands of the movement upon the bourgeois parties at Westminster were directed towards the pragmatic objective of removing common law shackles. The unions were not 'non-political', but they were concerned to 'mitigate the existing system rather than transform it'. Moreover, it is of 'the utmost significance that in Britain the party was the creature of the unions, not their creator'.[28] So too, the absence of universal male franchise is significant when one compares other systems in Europe and in the United States. In some European systems, the influence of the workers' party was so strong that membership of it was a condition of membership of the unions, as for a brief period in Sweden. Naturally, those other countries display great diversity; the unions of Sweden or Germany were, and are, different from the highly 'pluralist' movements in Italy, the Netherlands and France, divided on political or even religious lines; United States 'labour unions', in a movement that never acquired a political wing, are profoundly different from our trade unions. In each system, the character of the labour movement is central to the origins and nature of labour law; in Britain it is crucial.

It may be asked why, even so, history was allowed to construct a system as strange as the British 'immunities'. Why did those who ruled not impose a more rational legal regulation? Why did the advisers and friends of the unions themselves not press them to carry a banner inscribed with 'human rights' rather than 'immunities', a device that might one day be misinterpreted as a demand for 'privilege'? One answer lies in the dominant social ethic of *laissez-faire* in this formative period, expressed not merely as an idea but as a part of the social structure, including the unions. But those who favoured the unions could break from that tradition – the Webbs were one outstanding example – and, what is more, many were not unaware of thinking and practice elsewhere in the world, not only in Europe but also in Australia and New Zealand, which by the turn of the century were in the course of producing a system based upon compulsory arbitration. The labour movement itself, though, appeared to see little of functional value in such structures or in programmes of legal 'rights'. Hobsbawm has noted that workers in labour movements 'spoke the language of *rights* (and still do)', though many theorists of labour movements did not; but the language of human rights 'is unsuited (except rhetorically or agitationally) to the struggle for the achievement of the economic and social changes' that those movements have sought to achieve.[26] Even so, 'rights' might be considered a useful style even if only as the rhetoric of change, secondary though the form may be to the substance of social reality (for workers are not necessarily more 'free' in every country that has a code of labour rights).

From the outset there were people who could have attempted new legal forms. If anyone was the author of the 1871 Act, in which the first 'immunity' lifted the illegality of restraint of trade from the unions in return for making their rules largely unenforceable (Parliament going no further than necessary to recognize them, the unions keeping as far as possible away from the courts), it was Frederick Harrison. In close touch with Positivists, radicals and trade unionists, a lawyer and acquaintance of Marx, he could draft 'rights'. But what he put forward in his Bill of 1869 was not the language of human rights that was soon to be the language of many European labour movements,[29] but rights, objects and liabilities, as he described it, 'for the most part . . . such as courts of law should neither enforce nor modify nor annul'. The challenge of Chartism had been withstood three decades earlier by a State that had come to combine concession with repression; now in the beginnings of 'mid-Victorian liberalism', when it sounded as if 'economics and politics were sundered',[30] the moment seemed ripe both to the unions and to advisers like Harrison to make functional demands in an acceptable form, that of protection from hostile common law doctrines.

Again, take what turned out to be the crucial civil 'immunity', the protection from tort liability in trade disputes for anyone organizing or threatening a strike (in lawyers' terms, the 'immunity' for inducing a breach of the workers' employment contracts). This was piloted into the Trade Disputes Act 1906 as an amendment to s. 3 by Sir Charles Dilke, whose exceptional talent was at the very centre of union activity at Westminster. Only he saw the critical importance of this tort.[31] For many years he chaired an informal committee of unions and advisers; he had managed the 1885 Bill, which confirmed extensions of the franchise; he had supported, Bishop Gore said, 'all the great causes of industrial progress'. Closely associated with Liberals and trade unionists in the land reform association established by John Stuart Mill, he was manifestly capable of putting forward proposals in the form of 'positive rights' for unions and workers. Indeed he drafted the Trade Boards Act 1909 (p. 351) to stop 'sweating'; and he had advised those who were devising the new structures in Australia. When the moment came, though, in 1906 he introduced the critical amendment securing (so it was thought for fifty years) the freedom to organize withdrawals of labour in the form of an 'immunity' in trade disputes. This was what was required and what was politically possible; and there was no political party on hand to press an alternative programme. In a sense it even expressed democratic confidence in Westminster's ability to have its way against the judiciary; and industrially the unions and their members, Phelps Brown put it, resented the employer's authority but 'wanted to limit it by negotiation, not to assume it themselves'.[32] They therefore sought legal protection for a space, immune from ancient wrongs, within which they could negotiate freely and collectively.

Law and social conflict

With the evolution of such a system came the special place of law in industrial relations. The law seemed to protect the area for bargaining between employers and workers. While a community of interest between them undoubtedly exists in certain contexts or times, that bargaining represents the more fundamental conflict of interest between the worker and employer. In real life, conflict exists alongside community of interest. But a common social interest (in avoiding nuclear destruction, for example, or in escaping hyper-inflation) does not abolish divisions between classes or groups while society survives. The fundamental conflict in industrial society is central to the various 'pluralist', radical or Marxist analyses. Rather different is the emphasis of a 'unitary' frame of reference, where the business enterprise, or even society as a whole, is seen as enshrining primarily a common interest, where all can share a common goal because they are all involved in its 'success' (as in one sense they must be).[33]

The structure of the law that emerged after 1918 did not demand adherence to any one of these theories. But judges frequently tend towards 'unitary' analyses. They 'are concerned to preserve and to protect the existing order', as Griffith puts it; so a unitary frame of reference is more natural to them – perhaps to judges in any society – than the more conflictual models of industrial relations. English judges combine with this an instinctive *rapport* with the individual, including the individual worker. They understand his claim to protect himself *against* his union, but much less his need to protect himself *through* his union. In labour law judgments the unitary and the individualistic frames of reference often blend together so that, while the union 'Goliath' is perceived as threatening central interests of society, the protection of the member 'David' assumes the mantle of a shield not just for the member but also for society as a whole. Judges display a dislike for power relationships at the workplace. Even in the E A T it was said in 1983:

Unfortunately a substantial factor in industrial relations negotiations in this country is a display of power by one side in response to which the other side either does or does not yield to the wishes of the person displaying such power.[34]

But social and economic power relationships are at the base of labour law. It is 'sheer utopia', Kahn-Freund said, to see employment as based on anything other than conflicting interests. That is the reason for collective bargaining for which, in our developed system, the law appeared to preserve liberty without formal rights by means of its 'non-intervention', or by – in his better image – 'collective *laissez-faire*'. The collective social forces (employers and unions) were the dominant influence, 'far more than the law and the State', and the unions had not relied in Britain, as they often had elsewhere, upon direct legal sanctions to achieve their strength. By 1959, when the system looked stable, he made his famous declaration, which we now know to have been optimistic: 'What the State has not given, the State cannot take away.'[35] His analysis has been persuasively criticized for giving to 'the principles of the "voluntarist" system a greater stability and permanence in theory than they had in reality', even for advancing the 'myth' that the State promoted an 'equilibrium' by legal abstention.[36] True, it is doubtful whether he foresaw the instability ahead – the stability of a society is usually judged only in the hindsight of history – though he rejected 'equilibrium' as a 'pre-established fact of any economic system'. Many were confident of stability in the Britain of 1960. Few foresaw its condition in 1980. Which of our cherished hopes of today will rank as unreal in 2000?

Such issues are important to what follows. For these analyses invite the lawyer to concentrate upon the social and economic forces so as to see his own material – the immunities and the common law, for instance – in that wider context. Critics of 'pluralism' find that it 'depoliticizes' its material and tends to ignore the existing imbalance in the power relationships. But a unitary frame of reference is more likely to give law a primary role in adjusting social imperfections, holding industrial interests to be coincident, seeing everyone as part of a team or family: one enterprise, one country, one goal. Here, writes Fox, we find emphasis upon authority and loyalty, obedience and trust: 'oppositional behaviour on the part of employees tends . . . to be seen as lacking full legitimacy'. Trade unions may be accepted as 'partners in control' or an 'inescapable social fact'; but their job is as much to regulate members as to represent them. On this quite common view industrial conflict is seen as a social disorder (rather than as an expression of conflicting interests inevitable in industrial or capitalist society) arising at best from misunderstanding, at worst from subversion. Indeed, industrial disorder then comes to be equated with public disorder.

Collective *laissez-faire* and the judges

Judges are often led in this direction. We shall find examples of their unitary thinking, even in the thick of apparently technical areas of employment law such as the judicial interpretation of obligations 'implied' into the employment contract as to co-operation, trust and 'fidelity' (Chapter 3). It is not logically inevitable that workers' interests *must* be subordinated if one adopts a unitary analysis of social problems, but historically this has been the common result. If industrial interests are coincident, it may even seem logical to bring in a judge to stop the bickering and end the battle of power relationships by sorting out the 'merits of disputes'. Sir John Donaldson MR suggested, in 1975 after leaving the Presidency of the National Industrial Relations Court (NIRC), that judges should have the power in a dispute to tell the public which side was 'right'. Invited to advise the Government on labour law in 1983, he felt judges should have the power 'to tackle almost any issues which gave trouble as between employer and workforce'. He saw this as having advantages for both unions and employers. Disputes would no longer be determined 'primarily by the balance of power' but by the yardstick of reasonableness. Ideally strikes should not be permitted at all over grievances 'on which the courts had already ruled'.[37] Such judges believe their perception of what is 'reasonable' can settle industrial conflict.

The integration of social organizations into a 'corporate' system is a common feature in unitary thinking, in many versions integration through the State. Some see this 'corporatist' element in recent British developments, such as the 'bargained corporatism' described by Crouch in the 'Social Contract' of 1974–8 or the proposals on 'industrial democracy' in the same period (when Davies and the present writer preferred to see 'conflictual partnership').[38] There is no simple frame of reference likely to satisfy every complexity of workplace industrial relations,[39] and some such theoretical analyses can obscure problems by their very language; but many can pose useful questions. What is the role, for example, of unions in a democratic State if a government propounds policies compounded of individualism and unitarism? What are the place and meaning in the various political programmes of 'tripartism' (bodies with representatives nominated by employers, unions and the government)?

The latter is a particularly important question. Tripartism is a form widely used and of great importance to labour law in many countries. Italy, commonly considered to be a highly 'conflictual' society, has crept forward by tripartite 'accords' since 1983 in a crisis that expressed itself particularly in the *scala mobile* (indexation of wages). The Australian Government came to power in that very year bearing an 'accord' with the unions that was the basis of its 'prices and incomes' policy and promised 'a total review of federal industrial legislation'. Problems of inflation and 'incomes policy' have frequently seen a resort to such machinery – though, as we shall see (p. 354), the consequential changes in labour law in Britain have not been as great as might have been expected. Questions must arise here how far in such arrangements the State is playing a 'neutral' role, and how far they are directed towards integrating trade unions, and business too, into a strategy of social control.[40] How are the 'social partners' (as they are often called in Europe) to retain independence from the State? Tripartite structures are an international phenomenon, promoted by organizations such as the ILO (see Convention No. 144, 1976, 'Tripartite Consultation'). They do not necessarily lead to integration of unions, as was shown in Italy in 1985 when the trade unions put forward bold plans for restructuring the labour market that involved short-term losses for some redundant workers.

The various theoretical frameworks and the context of social history can illustrate, too, tendencies in judicial, as well as legislative, policy. Judges are not merely the trumpets of the law; they often call the tune. To hear it, the lawyer must look at both the judgments themselves and their interaction with social change. Without the judgments and the statutes the lawyer is not a lawyer. But without an understanding of social change he is a lawyer groping in the dark.

Both world wars were, in this respect, important periods for British labour law. Both in 1915 and in 1940 strikes and lock-outs were made criminal offences, though there were strikes and prosecutions. The story of the prosecution of 1,000 miners in the Kent strike of 1941 (the union 'obligingly' instructing everyone to plead guilty; the accused marching to the court accompanied by colliery bands; everything 'orderly, and even festive', as appendix 6 to the Donovan Report put it, with the Minister and employers eventually negotiating a settlement with union leaders in prison) is a legend of our subject – though after the industrial warfare of the 1984–5 miners' strike it may sound more like a fairy-tale. Yet it was not so much dramatic legal interventions in wartime industrial relations that had lasting effects upon the shape of the law, as the very war itself and the concomitant changes in the place and strength of the unions. Law in courts (or in Parliament) does not always develop in a straight-line relationship with changing social forces. The role of law is too complex for detailed development always to be attributable to some 'aspect of the relations of production which the legal rule is supposed to reflect';[41] and the 'rule of law' is not wholly illusory even if it is highly ambiguous.[42]

Non-intervention and conspiracy

Nevertheless social policies can be detected in the judgments of judges, as well as in the statutes of Parliament. Because labour law is a focal point of conflicting interests within the relations of production, its very sensitivity makes such policies and their relationship to changing social forces of central importance. Let us take as examples the major judgments on civil conspiracy and the adjacent torts. A combination by two or more persons to do an unlawful act (an assault, for example) is in itself a criminal conspiracy if that act is a crime. But in the nineteenth century the judges also held that a combination to 'molest' others was also a crime, even if the acts to be done were not in themselves criminal. We saw that doctrine applied to the gas strikers who were convicted in 1872 of simple criminal conspiracy to annoy their masters. Three years later an Act abolished that liability for simple criminal conspiracy *if* the acts were done in trade disputes (so long, at any rate, as the act to be done by the combination would not itself be a crime). The judges thereupon decided that there existed a *civil* liability for conspiracy, rarely heard of before, actionable by a person injured by the combination. The Act of 1875, they said, had not abolished that. It dealt with crime. They imposed liabilities on trade unionists in *civil* law parallel to the conspiracy liability that the 1875 Act had abolished in criminal law. In 1895 unionists who posted a black list of blackleg workers were made liable for 'conspiracy to injure'; but in 1892 and 1902 the circulation of lists of strikers and trouble-makers by employers' associations was held to be lawful because the employers were defending their legitimate self-interest. In 1892 traders who undercut competitors were held not liable for conspiracy because they, too, were pursuing legitimate objects of their own. At the turn of the century the judges were in fact willing to choose some economic or social objects as less 'legitimate' than others, and workers' interests were coming off worst.

The key decision was *Quinn* v. *Leathem*, 1901, where union officials and members had objected to Leathem's employment of non-union workers in his fleshing business. A lengthy dispute ended in their demanding that he dismiss those workers; nothing else would do; they must go. When Leathem refused, the union approached a butcher, one of his customers, and got him to stop dealing with Leathem under threat of a strike in his shop. Leathem sued for conspiracy, alleging a conspiracy to injure. No unlawful act had been done. The defendant unionists argued that they were pursuing their legitimate interests, like trade competitors. Moreover, they argued that in the decision in *Allen* v. *Flood*[43] four years earlier, a majority of the Law Lords had decided that a union official who had called a strike at Millwall Docks was not civilly liable, even if he was malicious, since in defending his members' interests he had done no act unlawful in itself. The official had not caused the workers there to break their contracts because their employment terms allowed them to leave work without notice. Despite the *Allen* case, the Law Lords in 1901 found for Leathem. The earlier case concerned an 'individual' act promoting a 'trade interest'; this was not the act of one man, it was a combination the purpose of which was 'to injure the plaintiff in his trade'. Moreover, said Lord Lindley, Allen had 'informed' the employers, whereas a threat to call a strike 'is a form of coercion, intimidation, molestation or annoyance, requiring justification'. He added: 'The law is the same for all persons whatever their callings; it applies to masters as well as to men.'[44]

The reasoning of the judgments meant that, since workers act by 'combination', all strike activity after 1901 ran a major risk of encountering tort liability for conspiracy from which employers would obtain damages and injunctions. It looked as though what was lawful for the individual was unlawful for a combination, at any rate one of workers. In 1901 the *Taff Vale* decision[45] allowed these remedies to be pursued against trade unions as such (Chapter 7). From the ensuing uproar emerged the Trade Disputes Act of 1906, replete (or so it was thought) with defences against such liabilities for those who acted in furtherance of trade disputes. Within the golden circle of trade disputes, 'simple' conspiracy to injure (where none of the acts is inherently wrongful) was banned.

But independently of that statute a new wave of judgments began after 1918. A few eminent lawyers had already complained about the 'new world' of civil liabilities, like Lord Chancellor Loreburn who noted that the new 'civil responsibility for conspiracy became very serious'.[46] A few years later, Jenks wrote of the two 1901 decisions: 'The House of Lords had first invented a new civil offence and had then created a new kind of defendant against whom it could be alleged.'[47] Few, if any, judges saw it that way. Indeed, some judgments stressed yet another liability, mentioned in the *Quinn* decision alongside 'conspiracy', namely 'coercion' or wilful 'molestation' done even by one person, wrongful even if no act inherently unlawful was done. Such judgments seemed to fly in the face of *Allen* v. *Flood*. But in 1904 Grantham J. remarked that the Law Lords had 'been getting round [*Allen* v. *Flood*] so there is little left of that case now'. Modern judges, too, have disliked that precedent. Lord Devlin has said it 'dammed a stream of thought [which] would have had a beneficial effect on the law'.[48] We shall see in Chapters 7 and 8 that there are still uncertainties and novelties in this part of our judge-made law, not least because of the invention of new liabilities, such as 'interference with contract' and 'economic duress'.

Immediately after the war, some judges showed a different spirit.[49] In a judgment delivered in July 1920, in *White's* case, the Court of Appeal accepted the objective (whatever *Quinn's* case said) of comprehensive 100 per cent membership for one union at a place of work as legitimate.

Union workers had refused to work with a man who was not a member of their union. Apart from the defence under the Act of 1906 – for this was then a 'trade dispute', though it might not be so today (p. 553) – the court held that the 'compulsion' against the employer and the worker was not a tortious conspiracy. The industrial action was 'bona fide from a trade union point of view'; the workers did not conspire 'to injure' the plaintiff worker, but sought 'to obtain that . . . he should become a member of [their] union'. The inter-union and industrial issues gave 'room for acute difference of opinion', but the court must be 'vigilant' to avoid 'any prepossessions' it might be tempted to feel. In *Reynolds* v. *Shipping Federation*, 1924, an agreement between the seamen's union and the employers' federation blacking men in a breakaway union was held to be legitimate. A seaman belonging to it was barred from employment. His union had gone on strike against a settlement made after employers had demanded a reduction in wages. The collective agreement was 'not against a particular individual', said the court; it showed 'a desire to advance the business interests of employers and employed alike by securing or maintaining those advantages of collective bargaining and control' underpinned by the joint agreement and the National Maritime Board set up in the war. There was no 'capricious' boycott, nor was there a wrongful invasion of the worker's 'right to seek and obtain the employment constituting his livelihood'. There was no liability at all. This was a new judicial approach, one destined not to last, as we shall see.

Even a cursory examination shows that such judgments of the 1920s 'distinguish' the precedent of 1901 on logically slender grounds. Lawyers came to speak of *Quinn's* case as 'depending on its own facts', resting especially on the demand that the non-unionists should 'walk the streets'. That technique is the lawyer's last refuge faced with an unpalatable precedent. The change that had really occurred was manifestly a change – though a temporary change – of social outlook. It was correlated to the events of the time and it affected the judges. The unity of the war did not last long. Even before the boom collapsed, later in 1920, severe strikes hit the railways and the mines; an Emergency Powers Act had been enacted. A year later machine-guns were mounted near pit-heads. Trade unions – consulted, even flattered, in the war by government – now confronted strong attacks by employers and reductions of wages. Government stood aside, though Baldwin's administration of 1922 did significantly avoid the more extreme measures then advocated.[50] But the judges were surely responding in these judgments, 'belatedly' perhaps, to the great surge of patriotism that had engulfed all classes in the war, reflecting upon the spectacle of the slaughter of millions of men who were not before them. In 1920 Scrutton L J, a great but conservative judge, declared thoughtfully in a lecture that judicial impartiality

is rather difficult to attain in any system. I am not speaking of conscious partiality; but the habits you are trained in, the people with whom you mix, lead to your having a certain class of ideas of such a nature that, when you have to deal with other ideas, you do not give as sound and accurate judgments as you would wish. This is one of the great difficulties at present with Labour. Labour says 'Where are your impartial judges? They all move in the same circle as the employers, and they are all educated and nursed in the same ideas as the employers. How can a Labour man or a trade unionist get impartial justice?' It is very difficult sometimes to be sure that you have put yourself into a thoroughly impartial position between two disputants, one of your own class and one not of your class. Even in matters outside trade unionist cases (to some extent in workmen's compensation cases) it is sometimes difficult to be sure, hard as you have tried, that you have put yourself in a perfectly impartial position between the two litigants.[51]

He was making no accusation of bias, merely reflecting upon the facts. Few judges were prepared to engage in parallel humility.

The tort of conspiracy reappeared like a comet in labour law in the *Crofter* case of 1942.[52] In the Outer Hebrides Island of Lewis weavers of tweed cloth made their product from yarn imported through docks on the mainland. In the larger mills on the island cloth was woven from more expensive local yarn. Most mill workers were in a union, the TGWU, as were the dockworkers. The union wanted to secure 100 per cent membership and also a wage increase. The mill owners refused, pointing to the difficulties of local competition from the weavers. Eventually, officials of the TGWU arranged for the dockers to put an embargo on yarn going to the local weavers (without any breach of their employment contracts). The weavers alleged that this arrangement was a tortious 'conspiracy to injure'; but the House of Lords said it was not. All the parties concerned were pursuing their legitimate interests, the mill owners to increase their control of the market and their profits, the union to improve wages and extend membership – all, said Viscount

Simon, 'to create a better basis for collective bargaining'. The combination was not unlawful because its 'object is the legitimate promotion of the interests of the combiners'. This remains true, another Law Lord added, even if each had 'his own axe to grind'.

In such a case a court clearly makes a policy choice. As Evatt J. had said in Australia ten years earlier, such union action may well be seen in two different ways: as a combination 'to injure' the plaintiffs, or as a 'combination to protect or advance the interests of the union'. In 1901 it was natural for judges to take the first view; by 1942 they were prepared to accept the combination's objects as 'legitimate'. Lord Wright in the *Crofter* case advanced the principle that the common law

has for better or worse adopted the test of self-interest or selfishness as being capable of justifying the deliberate doing of lawful acts which inflict harm . . . we live in a competitive or acquisitive society, and the English common law may have felt that it was beyond its power to fix by any but the crudest distinctions the metes and bounds which divide the rightful from the wrongful use of the actor's own freedom.

The background to judicial non-intervention

In a sense this merely restates in principle a central tenet of the individualism of the common law. What had changed, though, since 1901 was a willingness of judges to accept workers' collective organization and interests, something it had taken statute to impose on them in the 'immunities' from 1871 to 1906. In this the judges were thought to be joining in the process of legal 'non-intervention'. Kahn-Freund in 1959 called it 'the abstention of English law in all matters of "union security"'. But it was 'abstention' of a special kind. These developments took place in the shadow of, or during, national wartime struggles. The doctrines of Lord Lindley were hardly to be applied in 1942 at the height of hostilities to the country's largest union, at any rate not if they could be avoided. More important still, none of these cases aimed at 'freedom' for workers as such in industrial conflict. The developments towards a more liberal view of the meaning of 'legitimate objects' arose in decisions where the big battalions of labour and of capital stood together against the dissidents – a small union or a small producer. In *Crofter* that was self-evident. In *White's* case, the individual worker belonged to the radical Workers' Union (later merged in the TGWU), opposed to the

'Curriers' craft union that was currently ensconced in that workplace. In *Reynolds*, the national seamen's union ran a tight pre-entry closed shop with the employers' federation, which they had forced into negotiation during the war. The plaintiff, a 'reliable greaser', had left that union to join a militant splinter union. There can be no doubt that Lord Lindley would have found a remedy for him. Lord Denning MR would have tried to do so forty years later when, as we shall see, he was attempting to create the principle that a civil wrong is done in depriving a person of work by reason of non-membership of a union: 'The reason lies in the man's right to work' (pp. 364 and 791). This was just the formula rejected in 1924 in *Reynolds*.

Such variations in judges' attitudes relate to their feelings or perceptions as much about the social, as about the legal, problems before them. Indeed, the legal principles on 'conspiracy to injure' have become slightly absurd. They make damage done by a combination to injure wrongful, when it is not wrongful if done by one 'person' alone (including one giant company). All the same, this tort of conspiracy to injure is 'too well established to be discarded however anomalous it may seem today'.[53] For our purpose, we may note that no further significant alterations were made in this area of the law of tort between 1930 and 1964. After the defeat of the trade unions in the General Strike of 1926 (discussed on p. 666) a period of industrial peace followed, in great measure based on the weakness of work-people. An Act of 1927, which was not repealed until 1946, made strikes criminal where strikers supported workers outside their own trade or industry that were 'calculated to coerce the Government'. It also rendered certain picketing criminal, banned civil service unions from joining the TUC and prohibited public employees from having a closed shop. The Act was 'probably the least that Baldwin . . . could have introduced'; employers were demanding complete removal of all union 'immunities'; and the Act proved to be 'more irritant than blood-bath'.[54] In the 1930s there was little call for judicial intervention. Trade unions were enfeebled, and 'labour law really rested upon a middle-class acquiescence in the current balance of industrial power'.[55]

Few civil labour law cases were brought before the courts in this period. The 'Mond–Turner' discussions brought unions back into consultations for a kind of 'joint control' of industry, but they were decidedly the weaker party in 'institutionalized co-operation between the trade unions, management and the state'.[56] By contrast, the end of the Second World War ushered in a period of greater strength for organized workers. The wartime prohibitions on strikes were curiously extended for six years after the end of it (though they were not used: p. 344); but the attainment of and commitment to 'full employment' offered unions a base on which greater power could rest. When this was perceived, 'middle-class opinion changed. The social bottom was knocked out of the judges' attitudes of non-intervention.'[55] Whatever its real strength, the trade union movement was now believed to be mighty by those who felt threatened. As has happened before and since, critics contrasted its current depravities and 'disruptive' militancy with the 'responsible' unions of old and the 'heroic sacrifices' of earlier days.[57] Critics of trade unions always swear fidelity to the honourable unions of previous eras.

The courts, though, changed 'belatedly'. There was still a detectable caution in the 1950s. In *Thomson* v. *Deakin*, 1952,[58] another tort, intentionally inducing a breach of contract, was brought back to the Court of Appeal in a labour law context. Union officials had called for a boycott of Thomson's, which had run a non-union shop since 1926. It had a standing contract with Bowater's for delivery of paper. The boycott aimed at non-delivery of supplies by Bowater's lorry drivers, though in the event Bowater's was unwilling to instruct its men to drive the lorries. Thomson's sought an injunction to prevent the continuance of this 'conspiracy' by the officials, which, it alleged, involved the indirect inducement of a breach of their *commercial* contract of supply (Figure 3). The court refused on various grounds, some of which we examine in detail later (p. 589). What matters here is the caution with which the court confined strictly all the possible principles of liability. Conspiracy to injure it brushed aside; these were legitimate union objects. Further, liability for inducing breach of contract attached only to those who had 'actual knowledge' of the particular contract. On the evidence the judges decided that the officials did not have sufficient knowledge about it, though they might (not surprisingly) 'guess or assume' that such a commercial contract of supply existed and would be broken in the boycott. This suspicion was not enough; liability must rest on knowledge.

This approach contrasts markedly with most reported decisions in labour law after 1964. Judges became increasingly prepared to infer knowledge of such business contracts in union defendants. The latter are not now required to know the terms of contracts 'with exactitude' before they are made liable, and they are even 'deemed to know' about such contracts and the likelihood of their interruption. Lord Denning MR has said that if they have 'the means of knowledge – which they deliberately disregarded – that would be enough. Like the man who turns a blind eye.'[59] When we come again to this tort in the context of the Trade Union Act 1984 (Chapter 8) we shall find a judge in 1985 disallowing 'honest doubt' as a defence, which had been recognized in earlier cases; in the earlier cases the doubt arose from lack of knowledge 'as to the facts themselves', but the union before him, he said, had entertained doubts only about 'the legal result of known facts'.[60] In three decades judicial interpretation has significantly expanded liability for this tort. Most leading cases involved trade unions.

These different ways in which judges interpret and weigh the *evidence*, together with the exercise of *discretion* in the procedures and

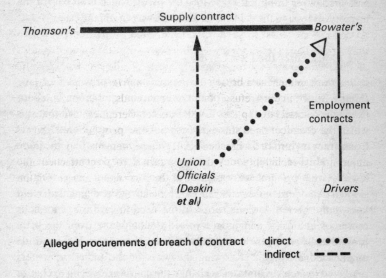

Figure 3. *Thomson* v. *Deakin*, 1952

remedies of the law (an injunction, for example, is a 'discretionary remedy' that the judge can choose to grant or refuse in the last resort), are in practice just as important as their interpretations of the substantive principles of liability. Many practitioners would say more important. In the court room, law is as much about tactics and guile aimed at influencing discretion and presenting the 'merits' of the evidence as it is about logical argument on principle. Many cases, especially on 'labour injunctions' (Chapter 8), are won or lost 'on the facts' according to the judge's attitude to the evidence. In one area of labour law this is of new importance. The industrial tribunals that administer the floor of rights on employment protection have been made the arbiters of the facts, as 'an industrial jury' it has been said. Appellate courts may displace a tribunal's verdict only when it has 'misdirected itself' as to the law or reached 'a conclusion which no reasonable tribunal would have reached' in law on the evidence before it. We shall find, therefore, in Chapters 2 and 3, the EAT and Court of Appeal refusing to upset the tribunal's conclusion, even though the judges have doubts about it, because no error of law can be proved. This distinction between questions of fact and questions of law sometimes mystifies the layman, especially when he sees the lawyer turning the one into the other, which is all part of the mystery. Handling the *evidence* is often the way to win the case.

The 1960s: enter the Law Lords

It was a dramatic intervention in the substantive principles of law, though, which in 1964 broke open the apparent equilibrium in labour law. This decision by the Law Lords was of such importance that it is worthy of examination at this early stage of our inquiry. Some lawyers had by now revived the language of 1901, renewing claims that 'the trade union and its members today occupy a privileged position under the law'.[61] Great prominence was given to the one major union election scandal of modern times in the ETU.[62] New laws were demanded or old laws reinterpreted; lawyers spoke of the need to curb the 'enormous power of unions',[63] and judges voiced doubts about even the basic judicial decisions by the Law Lords on which the legality of some trade union actions rested.[64] Knowing the ways of the judiciary, writers predicted: 'when circumstances change the courts are willing to change their attitude and their policy'.[65] Seeing that collective agreements were binding in other countries which appeared not to suffer our 'plethora' of unofficial strikes (Sweden was the usual example), experts engaged in the simplicities of *post hoc propter hoc* to propose that agreements should be compulsorily enforceable here, with a system of labour courts on the Swedish model.[66] In Whitehall civil servants concerned with the problems of inflation, incomes policy and industrial training looked more expectantly at legal processes. The egalitarian social change of wartime had not survived the brief class armistice of the 1950s as Britain became a less equal, but markedly more prosperous, society. Poverty remained, whether measured in absolute or relative terms.[67] By 1960, however, the trade unions appeared to have the strength to challenge this pattern; and their members showed signs of autonomous strength at the 'grass roots'. Two demands were made about trade unions, a curious dichotomy that has appeared before and since. The unions' 'power' must be controlled to stop their leaders exercising 'tyranny', over both their members and society. The union leaders, however, must be encouraged – or, if need be, compelled – to be more 'responsible' and to 'discipline' their irresponsible members. Both themes, not always mutually concordant, were prominent in the campaign.

It was in this setting that five Law Lords in *Rookes* v. *Barnard*,[68] 1964, drove a 'coach and four', as counsel put it, through the 'immunities' of the Trade Disputes Act 1906. Kahn-Freund described the judgment as a 'frontal attack upon the right to strike'.[69] It went to the roots of labour law, both then and now. An examination of the judges' reasoning is worth undertaking immediately.

Rookes was a draughtsman in a London Airport office of BOAC, where there was an informal 100 per cent union membership agreement. He had once been a militant unionist but, after disagreements, he left the union. Eventually a threat was made in a resolution at a members' meeting to withdraw labour within three days if Rookes were not removed. That was conveyed to BOAC by Barnard and Fistal (two employed draughtsmen who were branch officials) and Silverthorne (a district officer employed by the union). Such a strike would have been a breach of employment contract by each employee. As we shall see, this is the normal consequence of strike action in British law (Chapter 3). But here counsel also conceded that a 'no strikes' clause in a formal collective agreement between BOAC and its unions had been incorporated, in effect written in, to each individual contract of employment.

The notice was clearly a threat to break their contracts. Rookes was eventually given long notice of dismissal by B O A C, which fulfilled all its obligations as the law then stood. He then sued Barnard, Fistal and Silverthorne for conspiracy (Figure 4). It was an unusual case in one respect; the claim was not for an injunction but for damages. But this could not determine the question of liability.

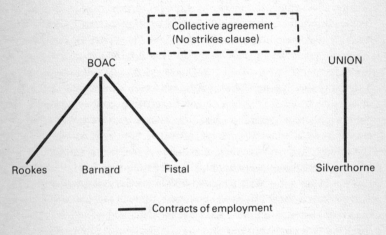

Figure 4. *Rookes* v. *Barnard*, 1964

At the trial in 1961 Sachs J. decided for Rookes, and, after his spirited address, the jury awarded £7,500 damages, including 'exemplary damages' to punish the defendants. The Court of Appeal, however, unanimously decided that Rookes had no cause of action in tort at common law; and even if he had, the defendants would be protected by the Act of 1906. We may recall that this Act had removed liability in a 'trade dispute' for the torts of (1) 'simple conspiracy to injure' and (2) inducing breach of a contract of employment. (We examine the modern law in Chapters 7 and 8.) But the House of Lords restored the finding of liability against all three defendants (by now Silverthorne had died), though it also held that the damages were too high.

What was the legal basis for this liability? There seemed to be none, for three reasons. First, it was not simple conspiracy to injure. Everyone agreed that on the *Crofter* test these defendants had honestly pursued legitimate trade union objectives. (Lord Devlin musingly hinted that he might try to get round *Allen* v. *Flood*, by leaving open the question whether an individual might not be liable, after all, for a malicious, though inherently lawful, act that did damage: '*Quinn* v. *Leathem* without the conspiracy'. But no other Law Lord agreed.) Second, there could not be liability for inducing breach of contract, because Rookes's employment contract had not been broken. Third, even if there had been a tort committed under either of those heads, the 1906 Act protected the defendants for both torts since they had acted in further-ance of a trade dispute.

In answer, the House of Lords created a new liability. Rookes alleged that he was damaged by civil 'intimidation'. The law-books had very little to say about *civil* intimidation. The crime of 'intimidation' was tied down after 1875 to actual or threatened force (p. 541). There were a few old civil cases. They concerned a threat by A to use violence against B unless B withdrew some benefit from C. If C suffered loss in conse-quence, those cases said, he could sue A (if, for example, A said to B, 'I will break your arm if you make that gift to C'). The threat had to be a threat of an *unlawful* act. The last clear example of such a liability had been in 1793. An unduly enthusiastic sea captain (A) had fired cannon near to the canoes of potential customers (B) in order to scare them from trading with a rival ship (C) off the Cameroon coast. There C could sue A. But how was that threat of violence relevant to a peaceful threat to strike? Indeed, lay observers in the court room were understandably puzzled by the very idea of modern industrial rights of workers being determined by precedents about canoes and cannons off the Cameroon coast 170 years earlier.

But Rookes claimed these trade unionists (like A) had made a threat to do an 'unlawful act' against B O A C (B) (namely, strike in breach of contract), which had intentionally damaged him (C). The essential question was: would the courts for the first time classify a breach of employment contract along with violence, within the same category of 'unlawful act'? It had never been done even by the nineteenth-century judges. It is tempting to speculate that no such equation would have been made by the Law Lords in 1942. Nor was it made in *Rookes* by the

Court of Appeal in 1963, which refused to enlarge this 'obscure, unfamiliar and peculiar' tort, and for a good legal reason. The step from violence to breach of contract is in law a giant stride. Whereas the State imposes the legal duties in criminal and in tort law to which every citizen is obliged to conform, in contract 'the obligation is self-assumed', as one authority puts it, and by agreement 'the right self-created'. That is why, in English law, no third party can sue on a contract or derive rights or burdens under it. The Court of Appeal insisted that the employment contract between Barnard and B O A C created rights and duties only for them; B O A C could release Barnard from its obligations; Rookes (a third party) could not derive rights from its breach, still less from the threat to break it. This distinction the House of Lords swept aside. A 'coercive threat' of a breach of contract gave a cause of action just like a coercive threat of violence.

What stands out in the speeches of the Law Lords is their determination to reach this result. 'The injury and suffering caused by strike action', said Lord Hodson, 'is very often widespread as well as devastating, and a threat to strike would be expected to be certainly no less serious than a threat of violence' (the 'expectation' was his). Lord Devlin saw the industrial relations difficulties – on this analysis almost all strike threats would be unlawful – but he refused to 'hobble the common law' (when he was extending it). He found 'nothing to differentiate a threat of a breach of contract from a threat of physical violence'. The law stopped threats of violence, said Lord Reid, and it should not 'turn a blind eye' now that 'subtler means are at least equally effective'. Lord Donovan had said in the Court of Appeal that if this novel liability existed it was 'astonishing' that no one had discovered it before. No one in England had thought of it, ever since 1793.

There were two final problems. First, even if Barnard and Fistal were liable for the new tort of 'intimidation' by threats to break employment contracts, Silverthorne surely could not be. He was not a B O A C employee, so he had no such contract to threaten to break. If he had *induced* a breach of the employees' contracts, he was protected by the 1906 Act. He had done what union officials do every day, represent his members to their employer in a fierce dispute and a strike threat. But conspiracy in a different form was used against him, in the shape of a combination to do *unlawful* acts to cause damage.

The argument went like this: Once the plaintiff proved civil 'intimidation' against any of the defendants, he could sue 'the doer of the act *and the conspirators*, if any, as well' (Lord Devlin). Once one worker threatened to strike, all the other workers and union officials 'conspiring' with him were equally liable. In later judgments Lord Denning found it difficult to see why Silverthorne was not protected. It was because he was treated as a combiner, not an inducer. The semantic change made him a wrongdoer. The combination was one to do 'unlawful' acts, torts of 'intimidation', so the Law Lords could sweep aside the 1906 Act protection for 'simple' conspiracy. Secondly, another part of the 1906 Act protected 'interference with trade, business or employment' in trade disputes (p. 612). Was not this what the defendants – especially Silverthorne – had done? Not so, replied the Law Lords. Here there had been an interference by wrongful 'intimidation' – a tort not mentioned in the 1906 Act. But what was the wrongdoing in respect of which Parliament enacted this 'immunity' for 'interference' if it was not a threat to strike? The Law Lords concluded that the answer was – nothing. This 'immunity' was inserted by Parliament, said Lord Reid, as something 'necessary to achieve their object if the law should go one way but unnecessary if it went the other way'. Historically this was probably true. In 1906 'the law' (that is, the judge-made common law) was 'notoriously uncertain'. But now we knew there was no tort of 'malicious interference' with trade, this provision in the Act was 'unnecessary', it was 'nugatory' (Lord Evershed), 'pointless' (Lord Pearce). The Law Lords deprived these words in the 1906 Act of any legal meaning. But as Lord Donovan had said, it was odd that Parliament allowed one to 'procure the breach of another's contract' in a trade dispute if 'one cannot even threaten to break one's own'. Lord Devlin saw that Parliament in 1906 'did not anticipate that a threat of breach of contract would be regarded as an intimidatory weapon'. No one had dreamed it could be regarded as such a tort until this case. No one expected that 'creative' judges would equate a threat to walk out at work with a threat to punch you on the nose. That is what did the trick.

Legal reasoning. Many aspects of this case illustrate features of the law that non-lawyers find strange. Three judges in the Court of Appeal unanimously had reversed the trial judge and decided the defendants had committed no tort. Five Law Lords in the House of Lords upheld the trial judge. None directed their reasoning primarily to what was 'fair', nor could they do so. The judge's job is to do justice 'according to law', here according to the legal principles of the law of tort and Parliament's statute. The court therefore asks whether the action of the defendant constituted the tort of 'inducing breach of contract' or 'intimidation'. To answer this, the court breaks down the issues into specific questions (Did the defendant know there was a contract? Did he threaten to break a contract?) and then into further questions (Is what he knew 'knowledge' for this purpose? Is a breach of contract an 'illegal act' for the purpose of intimidation?), and so on. By this time there is plenty of room for disagreement. Sometimes this arises at an even earlier point; for example, we shall find judges asking, 'Is what the defendant did reasonable?' This can be judged by many different standards. Naturally, then, judges interpret the law differently; and lawyers often criticize a decision by a court as being out of accord with principle, as *they* see it. But in terms of legal principle what the Law Lords in the House of Lords decide is final (unless they choose to reopen the issue in a later case, which is rarely done). Such a decision binds the 'lower' courts, just as those of the Court of Appeal bind the courts below it. Appeals from the High Court are normally about these legal principles; the facts found by that court are not generally open to appeal. So it is quite possible to have a legal principle settled by a minority of the judges hearing a case, e.g. if the trial judge, all three Court of Appeal judges and two Law Lords decide for the plaintiff, but three Law Lords decide in favour of the defendant. The doctrine of precedent means that the law is as stated by the three Law Lords (in such a case everyone hopes that these three agree in their formulation of the law; if they do not, lawyers have to find the common threads in their reasoning).

Judgments in British cases are, moreover, personalized. We do not normally find an impersonal judgment of 'the court', as with the European Court of Justice. Sometimes a Law Lord or Lord Justice of Appeal will merely agree with a judgment of another member of the court; sometimes one will give a judgment with which all agree. But often one will dissent; the Court of Appeal may 'split' two to one, for example, and then the dissenting judgment can be a fruitful source of arguments for lawyers or judges who in later cases try to 'limit' the principle established by the majority of two. So differences in interpretation are central to the method. The individualism of common law principles is matched by the individual styles of judges. The most famous example in our time is, of course, Lord Denning, whose iconoclastic approach to the doctrine of precedent often delighted those who agreed, and infuriated those who disagreed, with the results that his methods of reasoning produced. He often made it clear that his guiding light is what is 'just' or 'fair'; but, whilst this is attractive because it puts aside much of the legal jargon, it leaves the judge free to apply his own personal concepts of social justice. The Law Lords' judgments in *Rookes* created new principles out of old; but their *methods* were within the traditional reasoning of the common law. This is the way judicial social policy is expressed. Some judges tried in 1968 to mitigate its more unfortunate consequences by excluding threats of breaches of employment contracts that really did no damage to the employer; or, in Lord Denning's case, even by creating a defence of 'justification' against plaintiffs who were 'troublemakers who fomented discord in the docks'.[70] In social terms, though, the *Rookes* decision gave rise to

the impression that the repressive tendencies of the courts, which in the 19th and early 20th centuries had to be repeatedly counteracted by Parliament, are on the point of being revived.[69]

The TUC General Secretary, George Woodcock, said the unions could not 'be responsible to courts, unless those courts are operating the minimum of reasonable sensible laws'. People called for unions to control their hot-heads; how could they do so if their officials were threatened by such laws as these?

By now the relative industrial peace that had continued after the war in what has been called a 'depression mentality' had given rise to the 'shop-floor revolt', which itself unfolded into the 1970s when there were more official union challenges.[71] Some politicians and judges felt there was an 'increasing lawlessness of trade unionists'.[72] Many writs against union officials were issued or threatened, most of them containing (as they contain today) allegations of 'intimidation'. In 1965 the Labour Government passed a short Act granting a limited 'immunity' to preserve the liberty to withdraw labour. It provided that an act done in furtherance of a trade dispute was not to be 'actionable in tort' on the ground only that it consisted in a threat to break a contract of employment or to induce another person to break an employment contract. This was the narrowest possible protection by which Parliament could deal with *Rookes* v. *Barnard*. Like the protections of 1906 it protected threats to cause breaches only of employment contracts. It did not grasp the nettle at the core of the decision, namely the innovation in the law of tort that a breach of contract was an 'illegal act' or 'unlawful means', like violence. But Parliament wished to go no further than restore, as it saw them, the policies of 'non-intervention' in labour law. The pendulum that had been still for decades, after swinging to and fro between judicial intervention and statutory protections, had by these ingenious speeches of the Law Lords been set swinging again.

Parliament and judicial creativity

Some lawyers applauded the Law Lords' decision as remarkably 'creative'. Both in their common law judgments and in their interpretation of statute, judges are sometimes divided into those who 'play safe', sticking rigidly to the rules, and the 'dynamic' judges (like Lord Denning) prepared to modify liabilities, invent new ones or read words into an Act of Parliament. Lord Devlin has placed himself in a middle category, the judicial 'activists' who take account of changes in social consensus but no more. This debate, as Griffith has shown, 'is a somewhat unreal discussion'. No judge is 'creative' on every issue, but some 'get carried away by their personal convictions of where rightness and justice lie', and then 'judicial pronouncements begin to lose their authority and their legitimacy'.[73] Indeed, few of us applaud judges' creativity always. We clap – or groan – at what they have created. Yet it must be understood that judges do and will (to use a neutral word) develop the common law and interpret statutes along lines of their own policies to draw new contours of liability out of old principles. This is an inescapable fact for labour, as for other, law. This process has a legitimacy of its own that is very difficult to question. Most judges have now jettisoned, as Lord Reid put it, the idea that 'in some Aladdin's cave there is hidden the Common Law', which judges need only to find ('we do not believe in fairy tales any more'). But the new principle or the new tort that they create is, upon its creation and its admission into the hallowed corpus of common law, invested with an authority equal to the rules that have been included there for centuries, as if it had been there all along.

This is the case with many startling judicial innovations in labour law. For instance, 'economic duress' can now be committed by a 'threat to break a contract unless money is paid . . . causing the victim's intentional submission arising from the realization that there is no other practical choice open to him'.[74] This creation came on show first, in its modern form, in 1976; if it is applied to industrial relations – and we will see in Chapter 8 that it has been – it has profound effects. Indeed, it puts in question collective bargaining pressure itself. Some Law Lords understood that and in 1982 limited the application of 'economic duress' in industrial relations; but this was at a time when the new legislation of the 1980s had restricted the shape of the statutory immunities almost out of recognition (p. 71). But one could ask why *should* a new doctrine, like 'economic duress', be suddenly imported into union–employer relationships? Are the parties not entitled to more certainty in the law than that?

Our legal and political culture is such that a Bill to change the 'common law' (even when it is new) on industrial relations puts even government on the defensive, despite the 'supremacy' of Parliament. The Labour Government justified its protective statute of 1965 largely on the ground that '*Rookes* v. *Barnard* has thrown trade union law into confusion'. Opponents such as Viscount Dilhorne (a Law Lord in the Lindley tradition) were able to fight strenuously to 'preserve what is the legal position' until a wider inquiry took place – as though the tort of 'intimidation' in its new form had always been as broad as it became in 1964. They were also able to say that the Bill gave 'additional privileges' to unions.[75] The fact that the 'immunity' was the least that could redress an onslaught of *new* common law, to restore the status quo, was an alien thought. Indeed, at this time, such was the pressure to impose new controls on unions that Government was willing to engage in a wider inquiry. A clamour had greeted the increase of unofficial strikes, apparently associated with the growth in workplace organization and bargaining.[76] On the day it produced its 1965 Bill the Government announced the establishment of a Royal Commission chaired by Lord Donovan to consider all aspects of industrial relations, the 'role of trade unions and employers' associations . . . with particular reference to the law'. A significant trigger in the launching of this enterprise was the Law Lords' judgment in *Rookes* v. *Barnard*.

Finding a role for law: 1968–74

In the years 1965 to 1968 all eyes were upon the Donovan Royal Commission. A distinguished member of the Commission, and perhaps the driving force behind its Report, has said:

To many of its critics the Donovan Report seemed to be a defence of voluntarism. The Commission acknowledged many defects in British industrial relations but did not identify the unions as their main cause. They attributed them primarily to the structure of collective bargaining in private industry. . . . The means to reform of collective bargaining was not primarily through the law.[77]

The Report concentrated on private manufacturing industry.[78] There it found a 'formal' system (mainly multi-employer) now confronted by autonomous 'informal' bargaining at shop-steward level, with many issues left to 'custom and practice'. There was little union 'control' of informal bargaining, with its 'wage drift' and fragmentation. Broadly, two schools of thought gave evidence. The first urged that 'the law' should be called in to change the pattern by regulation, compelling collective agreements to be legally enforceable in labour courts, penalizing strikers perhaps by automatic deprivation of rights to social security benefit. This way (one member excepted) the Commission rejected. But it wanted reform, especially to produce 'factory' agreements as an instrument to make bargaining more orderly. The method would be mainly educational, with some legal stimuli that could be accepted by the second school of thought in the tradition of existing legislation that supported but did not regulate the essentially 'voluntary' system. The Report averred that,

properly conducted, collective bargaining is the most effective means of giving workers the right to representation in decisions affecting their working lives, a right which is or should be the prerogative of every worker in a democratic society.

A new 'floor of rights' should be enacted to include a right for workers to challenge unjust dismissal in the industrial tribunals, to join the Act of 1963 on minimum notice rights and the Redundancy Payments Act 1965. Members of unions should enjoy better safeguards under clearer rule-books, and the broad structure of the 'immunities' should remain. On one point here the members split; seven, against five, would allow a clarified protection against liability for the tort of inducing breach of contract (needed because of yet further judicial 'creativeness' after 1964: p. 587) only to official union strikes, not to unofficial strikers.

The argument, though, did not die with the Report. Indeed, the Donovan debate and what followed it have made their mark upon the basic Act of trade union law today, TULRA 1974. A Conservative programme, *Fair Deal at Work*, opted like Donovan for 'reform' but, as its main author Mr (Lord) Carr said, with 'a fundamental difference', seeking 'comprehensive legislation as an instrument of modernization'. Law was to be a primary, rather than a secondary, instrument of change. The Labour Government produced twenty-five proposals in *In Place of Strife* (1969), most of them in line with Donovan recommendations: a new status for the Commission on Industrial Relations (CIR), a law on unjust dismissal, a review tribunal on trade union rules, modernization of the immunities, a union right to information from employers. But some proposals went further, giving legal sanction a more immediate role, as with the proposed right for unions to be recognized by employers for bargaining. Two proposals were different again: to allow the Secretary of State to ban strikes in 'breach of procedure' or without 'adequate joint discussions' for twenty-eight days; and to allow that Minister to order a ballot on an 'official' strike. The orders would be enforced by financial penalties.

Here was the law as a primary intervention. Employers' reactions were mixed. Trade unions vigorously opposed the new legal powers against unions and workers. The other proposals were almost forgotten in the 'battle of Downing Street' that followed,[79] and folklore speaks of *In Place of Strife* as if those proposals never existed. Suddenly the Government announced in – of all things – the Budget speech plans for an 'interim' Bill containing the two 'penal clauses', as the unions called them. The Government was 'ready to discuss alternatives with the TUC'. It did so for two months. After a special conference, the TUC General Council was given further powers to assist in settling unofficial stoppages and, after a 'solemn and binding undertaking' by the TUC, the Government dropped its legislation on 'penal clauses'. Many politicians displayed the characteristic one member of the Commission saw in them: 'Whenever they see anything going wrong, their first instinct is to pass a law to stop it.' Thoughtful managers like Mr Lowry (later to be the second chairman of ACAS in 1980) warned against the amateurish borrowing of foreign legal codes, such as that in the United States. The TUC considerably increased its role, but on a 'voluntary' basis, in the settlement of local disputes (though it could do little – and could the law? – with strikers like the Port Talbot blast-furnacemen, who said in 1969: 'If Jesus Christ . . . asked us to go back we wouldn't go'). The CIR began to provide assistance especially in recognition disputes. For there were, and still are, employers refusing to bargain – especially small firms, those employing mainly women, those with high labour turnover, those in service industries, those in foreign ownership or control, as well as many that would not bargain for white-collar workers, such as banking and insurance companies. A bitter clash over non-recognition lasted ten months and caused riots in Stockport in 1967, after a US-owned firm dismissed unionized workers, ending in closure and withdrawal of its capital. On May Day 1970 the Government promoted a new Bill without the 'penal clauses'. The Minister, Barbara Castle, declared: 'Management these days can no longer function by the arbitrary exercise of traditional prerogative but only by winning the consent of its work people.' Within two months the Conservative Party won the general election.

It would be unreal to suggest that policies to combat inflation, or 'incomes policies', were absent from the Donovan analysis. Arbitration ought, the Report said, to 'take incomes policy into account'; inflation was a consequence of 'full employment' and wage-push. Nevertheless, the Report was primarily concerned with industrial structure, especially at company or 'factory' level. With 'effective control of industrial relations, including pay at the level of the factory and company, by means of properly constructed agreements between companies and trade unions', national incomes policy would 'work'. Variants of anti-inflation policies were pursued by all governments after 1948, and in some periods even by means of statutory prohibitions as in 1966 to 1969 (p. 354). So too, the incoming Conservative Government, although committed to 'economic freedom . . . nevertheless showed a lively interest in voluntary pay restraint'.[80] Indeed, after the successful miners' strike of 1972, it too resorted to 'counter-inflation' legislation. But its reform of labour law in 1971 was not formally linked to anti-inflation objectives, though some believed it to have this function.[81] The objective was said to be 'reform' of industrial relations based upon collective bargaining. There has (as we see in Chapter 4) long been an ambiguous relationship between labour law and incomes policy legislation. In 1971 the Conservative administration aimed to use the law as 'the Government's main instrument' of policy, the method against which Donovan had strongly warned.

The Industrial Relations Act 1971

Although it was an attempt to provide a comprehensive regulatory framework of law for industrial relations, the 1971 Act did not have one unified central theme. One object was certainly to weaken the power of unions and workers at shop-floor level, especially by securing the registration and integration of trade unions on a new central Register. But behind this there were

two different, similar, but not wholly compatible philosophies; as it were two different phantom draftsmen . . . [first] a civil servant concerned mainly to bring order and a tidy structure into collective British industrial relations. The second is quite different, a Conservative lawyer imbued above all else with doctrines of *individual* rights.[82]

Two key institutions were introduced: the NIRC (National Industrial Relations Court) and the Register. (The CIR was also continued, with new functions.) But behind them lay the two interlocking themes. Individual employees were to have a right to complain of 'unfair' dismissal (this was a bipartisan proposal; the Labour proposals of 1970 were broadly similar). But the individual was also given rights to join a registered trade union and *not* to join a union, whether registered or not. Further, the pre-entry closed shop was rendered 'void', and the individual worker given a right to pay to charity in the rare cases where, after complex ballots, a registered union and an employer were allowed to agree upon obligatory union membership in an 'agency shop'. All unions were forbidden to exclude workers in an 'arbitrary' way. Industrial action to disturb individual rights was, along with many other actions, an 'unfair industrial practice' actionable in the NIRC.

But the 'individualist' theme often gave way to another, the demand for order. Registered unions had many rights; they could become 'sole bargaining agents' with remedies for non-recognition enforceable in the NIRC (unregistered unions could not enforce such a status). Other provisions seeking more order included the employers' duties of disclosure to a (registered) union recognized as bargaining agent. Collective agreements in writing were presumed to be legally binding unless otherwise stated (thereby reversing the presumption that emerged from one of the last 'non-interventionist' judgments, the *Ford* case in 1969: p. 319). A union was liable to legal action in the NIRC if it broke an enforceable agreement or if it failed to take 'all such steps as are reasonably practicable' to prevent its members from taking any action that, if taken by the union, would be a breach of it. The same requirement for unions to 'police' their shop-floor members underlay the unfair industrial practices that replaced the 'immunities' in industrial disputes. Here again the NIRC had jurisdiction. The unregistered union was liable across the face of industrial action, not least because it was illegal for it to induce the breach of *any* employment contract or *any* commercial contract. Even registered unions were liable for action against employers 'extraneous' to an 'industrial dispute', a provision that like many others in the Act rendered the detail of the law more, not less, obscure.[83] Further provisions (which Donovan had explicitly rejected) enacted that, where the Government was satisfied that industrial action might be 'gravely injurious to the national economy', it could apply to the NIRC for an order banning it for up to sixty days, during which time a compulsory ballot of the workers was held. These sections had been clumsily imported from the labour law of the United States, where the Taft Hartley Act allowed for 'cooling-off orders' in an 'emergency'. A leading US arbitrator thought 'heating up' might be a better term. So it proved for Britain.[84]

The failure of the 1971 Act is now well documented, but in the 1980s it needs to be reassessed. By 1972 unions affiliated to the TUC had, with few exceptions, refused to register despite the disadvantages (the Registrar had further powers over the rules of registered unions; but only unions on the new Register received customary tax allowances). As Clegg said,

The success of the Act depended on three things: the willingness of unions to register . . . the willingness of employers to institute proceedings against unions and strike leaders; and the capacity of the new court to enforce its decisions.[85]

Not only did unions refuse to stay on the Register; the TUC called for unionists on the industrial tribunals to resign, and 80 per cent of them did so. Massive union demonstrations against the Act were held. Very few large employers even threatened to begin proceedings in the NIRC; experience on the closed shop and collective agreements illustrated their reluctance to ride with the Act. A network of illegalities surrounded even the 'post-entry' closed shop arrangement (where workers must join a union after recruitment). But such wrongs needed a plaintiff to activate them in the NIRC. Surveys have shown that, whilst the spread of the closed shop practice may have slowed down, managements even in nationalized industries did not activate the statute and adopted many subterfuges to 'preserve the status quo'.[86] So too on collective agreements, the Act allowed the parties to insert a clause rebutting the presumption and denying legal force to the bargain as between union and employer (the normal effect for decades before). This they did regularly. Of sixty companies in one survey, fifty-three included such disclaimers in agreements automatically; only two had legally binding agreements (one was about to close; in the other the union had forgotten to ask for it). This experience, it was suggested in 1981, showed that 'without an established basis of consent it is possible that any attempt to impose legally enforceable collective agreements would be hindered by evasion'.[87]

The Government's first attempt to use its 'emergency' provisions was catastrophic. In a pay dispute, the unions on the railways had instituted a work-to-rule and overtime ban, which produced chaos. They argued that the workers were not thereby breaking their employment contracts; they were merely abstaining from zealous co-operation. But in a decision still of importance for labour law generally, the courts rejected this plea (p. 185). This left the way clear for a 'cooling-off' order and a compulsory ballot. By six to one the workers voted for the union demands (and for their union, as they saw it). Soon after, a settlement was agreed on terms favourable to them. The emergency procedure was never used again, not even in the massive miners' strike of 1974.

The NIRC and the rule of law

The NIRC, moreover, could not gain acceptance for its orders, mainly by reason of the law it had to administer, partly because of the bravura style that its President, Sir John Donaldson, chose to adopt in this new, informal jurisdiction. Some unions, like the AUEW, defied the court to the end. The NIRC ordered that it accept a worker, *Mr Goad*, into membership; but it and its members refused throughout many court hearings. A small engineering firm, *Con-Mech*, obtained an order banning industrial action to gain union recognition; the union refused to obey, leading to heavy damages, a fine for contempt and, when this was not paid, sequestration (seizure) of the union's assets. Most managements avoided the NIRC like the plague.[88]

In legal terms the most important case arose from the containerization dispute in the docks. Decasualization had scarcely been achieved when dockworkers, members of the TGWU, saw their work and employment declining with the practice of unloading and loading large containers outside dock areas. They began to 'black' certain haulage firms and their goods in consequence. Immediately the Act took effect in 1972, cases were brought by small and medium-sized haulage firms, such as *Heatons*, in the NIRC to stop this 'unfair industrial practice'. The cases split into two prongs.[89] In the first, the NIRC ordered shop stewards to be imprisoned for contempt because they defied its orders to stop inducing breaches of contracts which clearly arose from the 'blacking'. But the Official Solicitor (an official of the court, not of the Government as most people believed) asked the Court of Appeal to set this aside because of the unsatisfactory evidence on which the NIRC acted. The appeal judges agreed. But some weeks later on another complaint, the NIRC ordered five docks shop stewards to prison for similar contempt. This time there was no reprieve; but there were widespread unofficial strikes in protest. Although the imprisoned dockers explicitly refused to give any promise of obedience (which is the normal way to 'purge' a contempt) the Official Solicitor approached the NIRC for their release. Donaldson P. refused: 'To do so would imperil all law and order. . . . The issue is whether these men are to be allowed to opt out of the rule of law.' The Official Solicitor was told to come back on a given day, in the afternoon.

Meanwhile, in the other prong complaints were pursued against the TGWU itself. The NIRC said the union was liable for its shop stewards, ordered an end to the 'blacking', and when this did not happen fined the union £55,000. The Court of Appeal rejected this judgment and returned the fines. The union was liable only if its dock shop stewards possessed sufficient 'authority' to act as agents of the union as a whole. The Court of Appeal thought they did not. There was no such authority in the union rules. The case was rushed to the House of Lords, which gave judgment with unaccustomed celerity only seven days after argument, on the morning of the very day that the Official Solicitor had been told to return to the NIRC. The unanimous House of Lords judgment held that the TGWU *was* liable for the acts of the shop stewards. At once the NIRC convened and ordered the release of the shop stewards; they had not apologized, or 'purged' their contempt, but the situation, said Donaldson P., was 'entirely changed'. The union was now liable, and 'the cause of the rule of law' would not be advanced by their continued incarceration. The NIRC had, of course, partly stumbled and partly been pushed into a pit where industrial and political battles could no longer be distinguished from legal issues. Industrial disorder was at risk of becoming social disorder. The docks were on strike, and a one-day general strike had been called by the TUC. Immediately afterwards Lord Devlin criticized the 1971 Act and its administration; it went far beyond *consensus* law; judges were beginning to speak not for 'the voice of the community' but for 'the voice of government or the voice of the majority'. But the *Heatons* case turned out to be of more general importance for labour law, for three reasons of great significance for the 1980s.

First, the legal doctrine. The reasoning of the Law Lords' judgment displayed a determination to establish 'implied authority' in the shop stewards necessary to make the union as a whole liable under the Act. No such authority was given to them in the union rules; but one should not expect, they said, 'all the terms' of a union agreement to be 'found in the rule-book alone'. It depends, said the Law Lords, on what 'the members understand' to be those terms. (There were some 1.6 million TGWU members in 1972, and only about one in forty of these were dockers; different trade groups had very different practices about the role of shop stewards.) The courts could look at the shop stewards' handbook, the union journal and all aspects of 'union policy'. From all this the Law Lords deduced that, although the action was said to be 'unofficial', the shop stewards did have an *implied* authority to call for 'blacking' to protect jobs *on behalf of the union as a whole*.

This issue of the vicarious liability of trade unions had scarcely ever arisen before because the 1906 Act had protected unions and their funds from liability in tort. The *legal* problem, whether the union was 'vicariously' responsible for the acts of the stewards, just as a 'master' is for his 'servant' or a principal for his agent, illustrated the difficulty that confronts the transfer of doctrines of commercial and civil law to trade unions. The employer is liable for his employee's acts done in the course of the employment, and the principal for his agent's acts within the scope of his express or implied authority, because the latter becomes part of the former's 'enterprise'. Even so, not everything done that conforms to the principal's 'policy' is within the agent's authority. Nor does a trade union have a command structure analogous to that of a company, whose workers are, Lord Denning once said, 'hands to do the work', while the directors are the directing 'mind and will'. The union is a democratic organization or it is nothing. It might be said that a union must be liable for its *employed* full-time officials on normal principles for they are union employees. But shop stewards work for an employer, not for the union, and are elected by workers in their plant or office. The Law Lords tried to take account of this by insisting that the 'implied authority' came from the 'bottom' (all the members) not from the 'top' (the executive council). The implication of an authority to bind the whole union was unreal, and the fragility of the reasoning was evident when, some years later, the Law Lords held that similar T G W U shop stewards at Heathrow Airport did *not* have any implied authority to bind the union when they called for industrial action there. To this we return in Chapter 7.

But the union was also held to be in contempt of court. The same reasoning underlay this part of the Law Lords' judgment. The T G W U was guilty of contempt of court, said the Law Lords, because its officers had not given the stewards sufficiently clear instructions to *stop* the 'blacking'. This is what the union had to do to obey the order of the NIRC. If necessary the union must withdraw the shop stewards' authority by 'disciplinary action' against them. The Law Lords thus interpreted the Act to put pressure on the union to 'police' its stewards. There is more to be said, both on liability and on 'contempt', as we shall see shortly and in Chapter 8. It is not always easy to answer the question: what must the union do in the face of a particular court order?

Lessons of the 1971 Act: martyrs and law enforcement

Secondly, the imprisonment of the dockers brought home a lesson that it was thought had been learned in Britain and many other countries, that penal sanctions resting upon imprisonment are likely to be counterproductive in labour law. A movement of millions of workers which was so recently illegal is bound to have an ambivalent relationship to law; and workers' leaders who are put in prison tend to become martyrs, just as the Kent miners' leaders imprisoned during the war had done. Anonymous donors have often paid the fines of imprisoned union leaders in order to break the prospect of a potential martyr (it was done for Clarence O'Shea in Australia in 1969 and for Arthur Scargill in Britain in 1984).

The Government gave close consideration to this problem a decade after *Heatons*:

Mass prosecution of strikers can hardly . . . be regarded as a practical proposition. . . . Even in wartime it proved impossible to prevent strikes altogether by making strikers liable to criminal prosecution.

Lord Denning saw it similarly: 'the lesson to be learned from the dockers' cases' was that 'imprisonment should never be used – for contempt of court – in the case of industrial disputes. Some better means must be found.'[90] A further Green Paper of 1983 considered ways of enforcing new legislation against unions. Contempt fines or injunctions were inadequate; perhaps named union officials might be removed from their positions; or the assets of a union be 'frozen'; or the funds be deposited in court (though this had little to offer over sequestration); or union 'privileges', such as the 'immunities' or tax relief, could be stopped. But there was another idea:

it might be thought necessary to make some provision for the taking over by an outside authority of the running of the business of the trade union in the interests of its members.[91]

In other words, put in a manager. Few who read those proposals believed that within two years the judiciary for its part would hit upon the novel, but remarkably similar, remedy of receivership, one that dovetailed neatly into the new Acts of 1980 to 1984 (p. 746). It was to be found that a combination of extended liability for the union, plus a gradation of remedies against it and (above all) its *property*, was a more effective way of enforcing regulatory labour law than remedies that risked the martyr syndrome inherent in the *personal* punishment of individuals. The release of the shop stewards without apology in 1972, because the union was liable, was an important stage in that evolution. We shall see, too, that the issue of 'vicarious liability' was confronted by the legislation of 1982 to avoid the obvious problems of 'implied' authority (p. 530).

Developments were not confined, though, to the 'labour law' legislation. The system evolved as a whole. A little noticed change was made in 1981 in the rules about enforcing the High Court's orders for contempt of court. Previously if a defendant in contempt refused to pay a fine, the ultimate deterrent of imprisonment was close at hand. But the Contempt of Court Act 1981 gave the judges an extra option. They could leave the fine to be enforced, as if it were a debt, by 'Her Majesty's Remembrancer'. (The Queen's Remembrancer is a court official rather less obscure than the Official Solicitor.) Union members might react differently to the sight of bailiffs acquiring their leader's property as against the spectacle of his person in prison. We shall see that this was an important element in the legal dimension of the miners' strike in 1984 (Chapters 8 and 9).

There were, lastly, the industrial relations lessons of the docks dispute of 1972. For the dispute did not end with the judgment by the Law Lords. Dockers saw their places of work, and the 'registered' scheme that had marked the end of the degradations of casualization in 1946 and 1967, gradually dying in the face of a displacement of capital and new technologies, of which containerization was only one example. The TGWU and the dock employers' leaders worked strenuously to reach what became the 'Jones–Aldington' agreements in August 1972. After the lawyers had departed for the summer recess, the dispute was eventually settled, with large increases in redundancy ('severance') payments. The 'Donovan School' was content that its point had been made yet again. Law as a primary instrument could not create such understandings. Its role was 'secondary', auxiliary or promotional. But those who were to draft the legislation of the 1980s had something in mind that was different, a transfer of power back to the common law.

In 1972 a national dock strike had already developed; the Government had sought emergency powers under the Act of 1920, which allowed it to arrange 'essential supplies' (p. 667); but the 1971 Act was useless and unused. The Government had promised to avoid using troops if it could; but it refashioned and streamlined the CCU (Civil Contingencies Unit) in the Cabinet Office, which, though it is given little publicity, 'has remained to this day the central government's principal mechanism for meeting the effects of stoppages in essential industries'.[92]

The industrial lesson was not new. In the words of the great conciliator Askwith: 'It is vain to think that peace can be got by Acts of Parliament.' In the docks in 1972 it was achieved by hard graft at the tables by negotiators who knew the constituencies to which they had to answer.

There is a further point about the 1971 Act. It became common to say – indeed, who did not say? – that its short life had 'proved' that employers in Britain would not, save for a few, go to court to trigger the remedies necessary to 'activate' such laws against workers and trade unions. The dockers' cases appeared to show that unions could not be coerced into controlling stewards and that legal remedies against individuals would not work. Generally,

management seemed anxious to avoid loss of control to outsiders which they felt the use of the new legal institutions implied. In so far as any of them saw a need for change, strategies other than the use or threat of law were generally preferred.[93]

With hindsight, now that willingness to go to the courts in such cases has increased remarkably, we may note three features of the 1971 Act relevant to this issue. First, it was an attempt to break with the traditional organic relationship between law and industrial relations *and* to introduce at a stroke a legally regulated system. 'The law', said Kahn-Freund in 1972, 'has now – to some extent – abandoned its previous policy.' Yet the authors of the Act, although they hoped it would clip the wings of the unions especially on the shop floor, genuinely believed they were making an offer to both sides of industry, a chance for a new 'framework of law'. 'What we are creating', said Secretary of State Carr in introducing the measure, 'are better conditions for positive leadership first from management, and then from the trades unions.' But management either did not understand or did not want the changes required. Its caution sprang from the idea that the new law required it to alter shop-floor practices which it saw no reason to change. And the unions resisted a new law that set out to decrease workers' bargaining power. Secondly, to use this new machinery entailed putting one's fate in the hands of a new, swashbuckling court that was willing, when it could, to take on all the legal and industrial issues at once. After all, its president later affirmed that he would rather have had jurisdiction not for 'curbing industrial action' but to 'investigate the grievances, report to the public and recommend and, if necessary, enforce solutions' to the industrial problems.[94] The same desire shone through in the style of the NIRC. Lastly, the state of the economy did not encourage lawsuits. Unemployment scarcely went above half a million in the early 1970s, the oil crisis and world recession had yet to bite. Workers who took a day off to the cry of 'Kill the Bill' had little doubt their jobs would await them on return. The picture is very different in 1986.

The legislation of the 1980s is also different from the Act of 1971. No 'corporatist' offers of new regulated 'frameworks' are made, nor are there any parallel demands upon management to promote a joint amendment of industrial structures. No tripartite agency oversees industrial relations. No informal, alien court presides, only the High Court judges in their robes. Remedies have been (as we shall see in Chapters 8 and 9) calculated; technical necessities, such as the 'vicarious liability' of unions, ignored by the 1971 statute, carefully considered. It cannot be doubted that what ACAS called the 'significant increase in the volume of legal actions brought before the courts' in 1983–4 was related both to social and economic changes, to changes of attitude, not least among top managers, as well as to the very character of the new laws. Even in the first two years after 1980 commentators had detected 'a mild *frisson*' among managers 'less consensus-minded and welfare-based' in response to the Act of 1980, to a psychological reassurance that the Government was 'on their side' and, within that setting of industrial politics, a greater willingness to make use of legal weapons.[95] There may be another factor. One well known change in British management in the last two decades has been the growth in number and importance of professional personnel managers. But by the mid-1980s that process seems to have been overtaken by an expansion of financial controllers and the rise of managers with an accountancy background. This 'militates against the serious consideration of labour relations matters at top management level', often concealing issues by 'camouflage rhetoric'.[96] It may be that managers at board level who calculate costs in figures rather than in people are more ready to operate the machinery of the courts or to pursue industrial disputes more vigorously. There was evidence of the latter in the NCB's conduct of the prolonged miners' strike that began in 1984, to which we return below.

Law and the Social Contract: 1974–8

We turn to the period 1974–8. Much of the legislation of this period is still on the statute book and, as amended, it therefore belongs in detail to forthcoming chapters. The Labour Government envisaged three phases: first, repeal of the 1971 Act and restoration of the 'immunities'; secondly, modernization of trade union rights in an extended and improved collective bargaining structure, with an extension of the 'floor of rights' for workers; thirdly, further democratization of the political economy with extensions of 'industrial democracy'.

TULRA in context

The early legislation is impossible to understand unless account is taken of the fact that the first Labour Government of 1974 was a minority government; its absolute majority in the House of Commons was acquired only nine months later. The first Act, the Trade Union and Labour Relations Act 1974 (TULRA), for example, into which Opposition clauses had been inserted, was amended to fit its initial purpose only in 1976. The legislative programme as a whole was fashioned as part of the 'Social Contract' with the TUC, itself originally a defensive alliance forged between the TUC and the Labour Party in 1970 to oppose the Industrial Relations Bill; but in retrospect it cannot be said that this legal programme was fully integrated with general social and economic policies. Much of it was based upon an improved model of 'non-intervention' in collective bargaining, because this was thought to be the best method, in the light of the Donovan Report, of extending collective bargaining. The repeal of the 1971 Act in TULRA opened the way to a renewal of the 1906 'immunities' in spring-cleaned form to take account of judicial creativity since then. Changes were needed especially in the protection for trade disputes because of new common law liabilities, such as inducing breach of *commercial* contract. For in their decisions between *Rookes* v. *Barnard* and 1971 the judges had sculpted yet further dimensions of liability on to the tort of inducing breach of contract and some further vague liabilities including 'interference' with contract (all of which have returned into prominence in the 1980s: Chapter 8). For these new torts the old 1906 Act provided no defence (mainly because it dealt only with inducing breach of *employment* contracts). Whilst most judges objected to the new 'immunities', Lord Scarman, we have seen (p. 20) recognized the legislation of 1974–6 as re-enacting the intentions of Parliament in 1906.

The basic purpose of the legislation was to restore and extend the legal base for voluntary collective bargaining together with an improved 'floor of rights' for workers and unions. The T U C and the Government, however, also co-operated in policies to combat inflation and to initiate greater social equality – the Social Contract. By 1975 'national wage guidelines' were introduced, though on a 'voluntary' basis. Despite periods of agreement (such as the imaginative flat-increase-all-round of £6 devised by the T G W U leader Jack Jones in 1975) 'wage restraint' was not, however, an acceptable, perhaps not a viable, policy. Union leaders complained that they could not resist pressure from members when deflationary policies from the Treasury and from the International Monetary Fund slashed subsidies and public expenditure, prevented the investment needed to resist rising unemployment, jettisoned the plan for obligatory 'planning agreements', and failed to take the social measures expected to defend more vulnerable groups in society. The 'wider Social Contract' had, they felt, been betrayed. These divergences grew into a pattern of 'grass-roots' revolt in the industrial discontent of 1978. In the 1970s generally strike patterns began to include more 'large' stoppages, more 'official' union action and more action in the public sector. The immediate 'victims' were often the 'old, the sick, the bereaved, children and the poor' injured by the 'bitterness and frustration' of low-paid workers.[97] The question how to maintain adequate earnings in that sector was unresolved. Unemployment by May 1979 stood at 1.2 million. The Social Contract, which had set out so proudly, disintegrated.[98]

The 1975 Act

The second phase of the legislation, however, had been passed when hopes were higher. The Employment Protection Act 1975 (EPA) aimed to promote, expand and improve collective bargaining on the footing of improved protection for all workers. The Advisory, Conciliation and Arbitration Service (ACAS), run by a tripartite council, was put on a statutory footing but not given powers of compulsion or regulation for its work of settling industrial disputes. It took over the work, and many of the personnel, of industrial relations conciliation, which traced its ancestry back to the Act of 1896. It was, and is, perhaps the supreme 'voluntarist' body of the labour law structure. The EPA gives it power to issue Codes of Practice, which are not law but are to be 'taken into account' by the tribunals and the (tripartite) Central Arbitration Committee (CAC). The aim was to keep such institutions as far away from the High Court and judges' injunctions as possible. But this was the period in which judges began eagerly expanding the jurisdiction of the High Court to subject to 'judicial review' any body with statutory functions. Neither the CAC nor ACAS escaped control by a judiciary that, for the most part, had little understanding of, or sympathy with, the collective rights for workers with which they were meant to deal. One such right gives recognized unions a right to disclosure by the employer of information needed for collective bargaining in accordance with good industrial relations practice (see Chapter 4). Another, enacted following an EEC Directive of 1975, requires the employer to consult with a recognized union upon the proposed redundancies of his employees. A third tackled the vexed question of 'recognition'. For what use were these rights and improved collective bargaining if the whole structure rested upon the employer's choice as to whether he bargained or not? Most industrialized democracies impose on employers some legal duty to bargain. But the last thing that was wanted in Britain was a jurisdiction for the courts to build up tortuous precedents, as in the United States, interpreting 'the duty to bargain in good faith'. This is a real problem and is not solved merely by instituting a 'positive right' for unions to be recognized.

The 1975 solution was a power for ACAS, after satisfying strict procedures of inquiry, to 'recommend' a union for recognition, thereby imposing a duty to bargain reasonably on the employer. But that duty was not enforceable in the ordinary courts; the lessons of the previous years inclined the legislature to avoid court orders, whether against employers or unions. The remedy in this 'auxiliary' legislation was a complaint to the CAC whose sanction for a breach of duty was to be *not* specific enforcement of disclosure, consultation or recognition, but an 'award' of improved conditions thrust into the employment contracts of workers concerned. If the employer did not like CAC awards, next time he could bargain with the union. The weakness of this remedy was one, but only one, of the factors that made the recognition procedure of little value even before it was repealed in 1980 (p. 282). The Act also saw a continuation and enlargement of a special procedure for compulsory arbitration, which had in various forms existed since 1940, for workers whose conditions fell below certain minima.

Legislation such as this was not a breach of the 'voluntary' principle, though an imposed duty to bargain came close to the frontier. These were 'props' to collective bargaining and were meant to improve and extend it both in range and in depth. The 1975 Act also introduced prohibitions against dismissal and discipline of workers on grounds of membership of, or activities for, an independent trade union, together with rights to 'reasonable' time off for trade union activities, which, in the case of recognized union shop stewards, was to be paid leave. In this area and others, it took over themes from the much overlooked Labour Government's 'Industrial Relations Bill' of 1970, which had never been enacted after *In Place of Strife*. Parts had appeared in changed guise in the 1971 Act; but the essential difference now was that the E P A did not repeat the equation of 1971 between the right to be and the right not to be a trade union member. The new 'trade union rights' were couched, though, in terms of rights for individual workers, and their sanction was largely compensation in the industrial tribunals. We shall see that these characteristics, plus the dominant interpretation by the judges on appeal, have been a cause of weakness (p. 309). The Employment Appeal Tribunal (E A T) was also created in 1975, tripartite in structure.

The main jurisdiction of the tribunals and E A T thus came to relate to redundancy and unfair dismissal cases; the latter feature was carried over into T U L R A from the 1970 Bill and 1971 Act. This was at the time a relatively uncontroversial development. But new problems appeared. Unlike the 1971 legislation, there were no provisions in T U L R A or E P A aimed at making the 100 per cent closed shop or *union membership agreement or arrangement* (U M A, as it came to be known) illegal or unworkable. So what was now the legal status of the dismissal of a non-unionist? Would such a worker in a U M A now be entitled to compensation in a tribunal for *unfair* dismissal? The solutions sought along the lines of the Donovan Report to this and allied problems have been a source of debate and publicity ever since. We examine in Chapter 4 the problem of the non-unionist worker in a closed shop. It may be noted here that the unjust hounding of non-unionists is not the everyday sport of either employers or unions who agree on a closed shop; many non-unionists still work in closed shops through mutual toleration; and when in 1982 the Government offered money retrospectively to such workers dismissed between 1974 and 1980 (the period of law that it regarded as morally indefensible for such 'victims'), it was hard put to it to find 400 cases for compensation despite extensive Press advertisements.[99] Statistics do not condone injustice. But we shall see that various measures were taken in 1975, including steps by the TUC, to alleviate problems which were not as widespread as many claimed.

The EPA 1975 also added further individual rights for the worker: in the insolvency of the employer; guarantee payments when on short time; maternity rights to payments and to return to the job after childbirth; rights to written statements on reasons for dismissal. Most of these rights were consolidated in the statute that today contains the great majority of workers' 'individual' legal rights, the Employment Protection (Consolidation) Act 1978 (EPCA), including the modern versions of redundancy and unfair dismissal provisions. Further, in the Sex Discrimination Act 1975 (SDA), which also updated the Equal Pay Act 1970 (Eq. P.A.), and the Race Relations Act 1976 (RRA) laws were passed to protect workers in respect of discrimination affecting them at the workplace (Chapter 6). Here labour law was mobilized to play a role as part of the drive against discrimination in society. The Health and Safety at Work Act 1974 also extended traditional legal sanctions to enforce proper safety and health standards but fused them with new methods, notably the right of recognized unions to appoint 'safety representatives' with rights of consultation (Chapters 4 and 5). The rate of legislation on 'individual' employment since the Redundancy Payments Act 1965 gave the impression that industrial relations were turning to 'the method of Legal Enactment' and away from nonintervention. Although this was a rapid augmentation of employment legislation, such a judgment is too indiscriminate.

First, there has been a lot of employment legislation for many decades. Kahn-Freund's classic analysis in 1959 of 'collective *laissez-faire*' mentioned some thirty-five major enactments concerned with employment and labour relations. The type of law has to be considered, not just the quantity. Secondly, the new legislation extending the 'floor of rights' did not, like the 1971 Act, aim to regulate collective bargaining. It meant to support it, to stimulate voluntary bargaining above the floor, on new subjects, for more workers, at higher levels of entitlement (though whether it was successful in this is another question). Thirdly, whether such legislation provokes greater 'legalism' in the conduct of industrial relations – or (as it has come to be called) greater 'juridification' – depends upon the actual effect it has upon people, whether and to what extent we find

the behaviour of line and personnel managers, shop stewards and full-time officers in dealing with individual and collective issues determined by reference to legal (or what are believed to be legal) norms and procedures, rather than to voluntarily agreed norms and procedures or to 'custom and practice'.[100]

Detecting such consequences, and even more judging the changes of emphasis in the operation of industrial relations, is a difficult matter, as a recent survey of dismissal and the industrial tribunals has concluded.[101]

Industrial democracy

The Labour Government's approach to the third phase, legislation on 'industrial democracy', was cautious. There were many reasons for this. First, it was now 1976 and the Social Contract had begun to crumble as the recession gathered pace. Secondly, what did 'industrial democracy' mean anyway? To most British trade unions, and to employers too, it had always meant collective bargaining. This was the way industry became more 'democratic'. But there were those who put questions provoked by institutions set up by law in countries on the Continent. Diverse types of Works Councils exist by law in other countries. Unions have a minority presence on the 'one-tier' Swedish company board. In West Germany workers occupy half the seats of 'supervisory councils' in coal and steel companies, nearly half in other large companies. British unions had always opposed such structures because they saw them as ensnaring workers' representatives within the enterprise, emasculating them in a 'unitary' structure. Authoritative voices said one had to build either 'in the land of collective bargaining on the pluralistic pattern or in the land of company law on the unitary pattern'.[102]

On the other hand, trade unions had found that, whatever the support given to it, collective bargaining had not overcome certain limitations, in particular the inability to make managements (not least those of the huge transnational enterprises and multinational corporations) negotiate on issues that they chose to exclude from the bargaining table, such as plans for closures, pricing structures and the investment on which jobs depended. In 1974, therefore, the great majority of unions in the TUC determinedly changed tack and produced proposals for trade union participation in new structures of the enterprise, including even representation on company boards. But the representatives of workers must not be in a minority. They saw this as an 'extension of collective bargaining' into the higher reaches of the enterprise. In this they expressed the perspective of a union movement that thought as much in terms of administering agreements and of 'joint regulation' as of the conflict in bargaining.

The Government, which at various times made tentative forays into workers' representation on boards of nationalized corporations, such as British Steel and the Post Office, set up at the end of 1975 a committee headed by Lord Bullock to report within a year on industrial democracy *by way of* 'representation on boards of directors' in the private sector. The Bullock Report[103] included majority recommendations (to which the writer was a signatory) to reform company law along these lines. Boards of directors would have equal representation of shareholders and of workers and a smaller independent element (the '$2x + y$' formula, as it became known). The reaction of company directors and managers to '$2x + y$' was one of explosive opposition. The CBI – even though it had earlier insisted that a company owed a duty, after pursuing profits, to its employees and to the community, to act as 'a good citizen in business' – opposed even the minority report of three industrialists proposing minority employees' representatives on a 'supervisory' board. In view of EEC pressures to 'harmonize' the company law of member States with (minority) workers' representation on boards (the draft Fifth Directive of the EEC, which is still a draft) the Institute of Directors produced, three years later, a document entitled *The Fifth Directive: A Trojan Bullock?*. Nor did all unions or workers support the plan. In the gathering recession of 1978, one shop steward said to the present writer: 'Do you expect me to go on the board to preside over the redundancy of my members?' It was a more difficult question than it had seemed three years earlier. The same year, the Government produced proposals that watered down Bullock; the point had been reached where no one was enthusiastic in the recession for industrial democracy.

Yet this was part of a wider issue that was unlikely to go away. In a related sphere, the Government had produced proposals for parity representation for workers through their unions on the bodies that controlled pension funds (institutions we shall meet again: p. 303). The question was raised whether the pension fund 'belongs' to the employer, and, if not, who should share in its control, still an unanswered puzzle lying beneath the surface of policy on State pensions and welfare law.[104] The general issue was whether workers should have rights to bring influence to bear *inside* the bodies that make the critical decisions affecting their lives, such as boards of directors, nationalized industry boards or pension fund trustees. Extensive experiments have been made elsewhere, in Sweden for example, in industrial and 'economic' democracy to confront this question. Even critics of the Bullock Report saw a possible 'catalyst for reform' in involving British unions in new areas of co-operative, if conflictual, power-sharing. The alternative was to adopt the 'easy answer':

for companies to continue the conflict with the unions, slowly reducing it on the fringes by means of communications and other exercises . . . with little real constructive participation but some 'sham democracy'. Union leaders would of course continue to do their occasional deals in Downing Street. . . . The unions and managements would remain as they have been for years.[105]

But 'industrial democracy' was largely forgotten when the victory of the Conservative Party introduced a new era at the 1979 general election. Deals in Downing Street were no longer to be the way things were done.

Market forces and new legal policies: the 1980s

The administration that took over government in 1979 would have no truck with conventional policies on 'incomes policy' or social contracts. It believed passionately in the economic forces of market competition as the way to contain inflation and achieve prosperity. Its labour law policies were composed accordingly. Introducing one of its first measures, the Order of July 1979 to double the qualifying period of employment required before workers could complain to a tribunal about unfair dismissal, Earl Gowrie said:

In the words of the old song: 'Something's got to give', and in our case it is the ability of our economy to sustain, without the raging inflation which has the same job-destroying effects in the end, the levels of employment to which we have become accustomed.[106]

Inflation rates did fall; but unemployment rose from 5 per cent of the work-force in 1979 to 13 per cent in 1985, when it was still rising. Over 1.3 million workers had then been unemployed for more than one year; more than half a million of the workers unemployed were below twenty-one years of age.

A completely fresh attitude was brought to employment legislation, one that was part of an essential unity in both the economic and the ideological perspectives of the Government. Never before has labour law policy been so fully integrated within a unified, overall policy.[107] This is best illustrated by a brief description of the legal changes between 1979 and 1985. The measures were two Orders of July 1979, the Employment Acts of 1980 and 1982 (E A) and the Trade Union Act 1984 (T U A). Although, in Mr Prior's famous phrase, the measures were introduced 'step by step', or as others had it 'softly, softly', they present a consistent theme under five headings: employment protection; props to bargaining; industrial action; union strength and security; and internal union affairs.

Employment protection

First, important adjustments were made to the 'floor of rights' on employment protection, such as unfair dismissal and maternity rights. Both were restricted, especially for workers in 'small businesses'. A new right to time off for antenatal care was introduced, and a technical improvement in workers' rights in insolvency accepted. The 'July Orders' of 1979 weakened union rights to consultation about redundancies and restricted unfair dismissal claims in 1979 to workers with one year's continuous employment (instead of six months'). The period was increased to two years for workers in small businesses in 1980 and to two years for all newly employed workers in 1985. Introduced because of the alleged 'burdens' of the legislation on business, for which the evidence was rather slender, these gradually increasing qualifying periods excluded millions of workers from the protection not to be unfairly dismissed. Guarantee payments in cases of short-time were reduced, and new limitations were placed upon social security payments, especially by phasing out earnings-related benefit, removing the guarantee of annual indexation with prices, and introducing a deduction from supplementary benefit for the family of a worker on strike, as a sum he is 'deemed' to receive from his union (whether he receives it or not). In 1986 it was proposed to charge workers who applied to tribunals a deposit of £25, refundable only if they won.

The props to bargaining

Secondly, the legal 'props' to the system of collective bargaining, which had set a floor to the minimum conditions for less well organized or low paid workers, were largely dismantled. In 1980 the Schedule of the EPA 1975 was repealed that allowed the CAC to award (via unilateral arbitration) terms of employment for workers employed on terms less favourable than the minimum established by collective bargaining (or, in its absence, the 'general level' of conditions in the industry). The very exceptional 'fair wage' statutes (for lorry drivers, for example) were also repealed or neutralized. Then, freeing itself of obligations to the ILO, the Government in 1982 rescinded the Fair Wages Resolution, which had had similar functions in public contracts, and 'advised' local authorities to remove all such clauses from their contracts. In 1985, again withdrawing from an ILO Convention, it drew up plans for Wages Councils, which have set minimum conditions for nearly 3 million low-paid workers, to restrict their functions (and in particular to exclude young workers from their minimum Wage Orders). In 1980, too, the power of ACAS to impose on an employer an obligation to recognize a union was repealed (this part of the 1975 Act had not, it is true, worked satisfactorily: p. 282).

These measures by themselves amounted to a major withdrawal of legal support from collective bargaining by removing a minimum floor in favour of the pursuit of market forces. Support for the 'union rate' or 'going rate' was replaced by encouragement of the market rate. Young workers especially were the target of an insistence that wage rates were 'too high'. In the week when the Secretary of State reiterated that rising unemployment could be reduced only if the levels of wage increases were reduced, a survey disclosed that in 1984 directors' and managers' pay (apart from fringe benefits) had risen twice as fast as that of manual workers.[108] Economists were divided about the relationship of lower pay and more jobs.[109] Many distinguished names advocated an Employment Institute to promote alternative policies. Certainly the evidence seemed a slender basis on which to destroy so quickly the labour law structures that had since 1891 both contributed to defences against 'sweating' and helped to avoid the economic costs of an unrestricted 'pricing' of labour which might lead to 'maintaining obsolete equipment in existence and discouraging investment through increasing risk'.[110] But the legal changes were a logical part of the drive for lower wages sustained by what the market would bear.

A measure that was advanced as promoting 'participation' of employees was a requirement (EA 1982 s. 1) on companies employing 250 or more people. In the directors' report there must be stated the 'action' taken in the year to provide employees with information, to consult them or their representatives regularly so that their views can be 'taken into account', to encourage employees' 'involvement', e.g. by share schemes, and to achieve a 'common awareness' on financial and economic problems. There is no obligation to take such action, only to report it. Independent trade unions find no place. Moreover, of some 300 directors' reports surveyed in 1985, 17 per cent gave no report, 13 per cent reported on all headings, and only 11 per cent reported consultation specifically with trade unions.[111] On the other hand, the range and character of 'consultation' in private sector companies had been growing for over a decade including consultation with shop stewards. For the most part this still operates as an adjunct to collective bargaining, although 'in a minority of workplaces, joint consultation was being established in the absence of, or perhaps as alternative to, trade union representation and collective bargaining'.[112]

Industrial action

The third area of change concerns workers' industrial action. Here the 'immunities' were chopped back, especially the central immunity in TULRA (s. 13), which, in a trade dispute, protects inducing breach of contract. There are six main areas of restriction.

(1) *Picketing*, however peaceful, that takes place away from a worker's own place of work is deprived of protection, leaving him liable for inducing breach of contract if he, say, persuades a lorry driver not to deliver goods, even if he was in the same union and supporting the trade dispute (EA 1980 s. 16). A union official is in the same position unless he is actually accompanying a member picketing his own workplace and is *his* 'representative'. As we see in Chapter 7, other liabilities can arise in

the course of picketing, and these are accentuated by a new Code of Conduct produced by the Secretary of State, not ACAS, which a court must take into account.

(2) *Secondary action.* No protection is now afforded to workers who take industrial action when their employer is not a party to the trade dispute. This is now called 'secondary action'. It is no defence that their interests are linked with those of the workers whom they support in the 'primary' trade dispute (EA 1980 s. 17). Solidarity or sympathy action, support for the weak by the strong in another employment – a practice as old as trade unionism itself – is banned. The three exceptions in the Act have meant almost nothing, in the light of the judges' interpretations (p. 598).

(3) *Action to extend negotiation or union labour only.* In 1982 the 'immunity' in TULRA s. 13 was also stripped from industrial action to *promote* an extension of recognition or negotiation. The Government made contracts and other business practices unlawful in which one business man either requires another to use union labour for the work *or* requires the other to 'recognize, negotiate or consult with' a trade union. Such practices are common in areas such as the construction industry and local government contracts. They are now illegal (EA 1982 ss. 12, 13). The Act also removes protection from unions or workers who take industrial action of which *one* objective is to secure any of those results or to interrupt the supply of goods and services for any of those reasons (EA 1982 s. 14). This is the provision in the 1980s legislation that most clearly reverses the traditional public policy on promoting collective bargaining. Industrial action to extend consultation with trade unions is banned (p. 606).

(4) *Trade disputes.* The golden formula of the system of 'immunities', on which everything rests, was changed. Industrial action receives 'immunity' only if it constitutes an act done 'in contemplation or furtherance of a trade dispute' ('ICFTD'). But in 1982 the definition (in TULRA s. 29) of a 'trade dispute' was amended. The changes look small; the effect is dramatic. A dispute must now exist between workers and their *own* employer; and it must 'wholly or mainly relate' to the list of employment matters affecting workers of that employer (EA 1982 s. 18). Previously, the employer could be *any* employer; disputes between workers were included; and the dispute needed to be no more than 'connected with' the employment matters listed (p. 553).

Within a year the Court of Appeal showed how great was the change, in *Mercury Communications* v. *Scott-Garner*.[113] As part of its 'privatization' programme the Government passed legislation to sell the shares in British Telecom (BT), after it had been split off from the Post Office by a statute in 1981 and the sector 'liberalized' by admitting private competitors. The major telecommunications union POEU (now NCU) opposed the policy and waged campaigns against it and against the proposed licensing of private firms, such as Mercury, with rights to plug into the BT network. The POEU claimed that the jobs and job opportunities of workers were threatened. It arranged selective strikes. After members had refused management's orders to connect Mercury to BT's network the union declared Mercury and its shareholders 'black'. When Mercury demanded an interim injunction, the judge refused, saying there was a 'trade dispute' (under the traditional definition there certainly would have been). The Court of Appeal (accepting fresh evidence from Mercury on the appeal, an important point: Chapter 8) decided that the dispute was not 'mainly' about fears of redundancy; it was mainly about the Government's privatization programme. The 1982 amendment of the definition, said Donaldson MR, was intended to be 'relatively restrictive'. 'There is massive evidence that the union was waging a campaign against the political decisions to liberalize the industry and to privatize BT.' The union had indeed waged a 'political' campaign. But it claimed that the industrial action was launched against its employer to save jobs – a trade dispute mainly about workers' employment. The 1982 Act, the judges said, required the court to find the 'predominant purpose'; 'we live in a time of high unemployment with fears of redundancy prevalent throughout industry'; but the likely job losses could be absorbed by 'natural wastage or retirement'; nor had the union used the collective agreement procedures to raise the issue with the employer. This was 'in substantial degree a political and ideological campaign'. The union might prove otherwise at the full trial, but it would be 'a close run thing'.

This interpretation puts in question the very concept of 'trade dispute' itself in major strikes. The Green Paper of 1981 said such a definition would 'restrict many types of industrial action which are undoubtedly directed at improving terms and conditions of employment'. Government is today often involved in industrial disputes. Indeed 'so interdependent and interconnected are firms and industries' that there is 'almost no major strike which will not ultimately affect the interests of the economy or community as a whole'.[114] The redefinition of 'trade dispute' questions the general distinction between the 'political' and the 'economic' that is at the root of 'trade dispute'. In a few words Parliament changed disputes that for decades had been 'trade disputes' into 'political disputes'. There was no complaint from the judges.

These innovations in the law of industrial conflict illustrate a dominant characteristic of the new policy. The market is to work as a 'free' market but on the State's terms. Obstacles must be removed. The primary obstacle is trans-enterprise industrial action by workers.

The objective of the policy of restriction is quite specific. It is this: Workers are to be permitted the self-help of lawful industrial action *only within their own employment unit*. That is the rule on which the market is to work. . . . Trans-enterprise solidarity is no longer acceptable to the law.[115]

Capital, however, is rarely limited in similar ways in its trans-enterprise – indeed, transnational – forms, through groups of associated and subsidiary companies. Labour is confined within the employment unit, normally defined by the employer, or by employer and State together.

(5) *Dismissal of strikers*. The power of an employer to dismiss strikers without fear of challenge in the tribunals for 'unfair dismissal' has been extensive since 1974. Briefly, he is at risk of liability here only if he victimizes one or more of those 'taking part' in the industrial action – for example, if he dismisses some strikers but re-engages others. The aim has been to keep the tribunals away from industrial conflict (p. 193). Now, however, he is not liable unless he discriminates amongst workers taking part at the same establishment as the claimant worker and does so at the time of that dismissal (EA 1982 s. 9, amending EPCA s. 62). His position is thus greatly improved. He can treat different plants differently and wait for the strike to erode.

(6) *Strike ballots*. The Act of 1984 introduced a new control (TUA ss. 10, 11). In *any* case where a union authorizes or endorses industrial action, neither the union nor its officials have any 'immunity' (under TULRA s. 13) unless a majority approves in a ballot held strictly in accordance with the Act and with the questions it requires. Unofficial strike action is unaffected. The question the union must ask is whether the worker is 'prepared to take part . . . in a strike involving him in a breach of his contract of employment'. Profound issues both of legal

doctrine and of principle concerning 'ballots' are raised by the 1984 Act, which we must reserve for Chapters 8 and 9. The new legal requirement was said to strengthen the democratic rights of members. A State-imposed strike ballot – as against votes that many unions have long chosen to hold under their own rules – was, however, rejected by the Donovan Report. Union members must use the procedures prescribed by the Act; and there is not (as there is in the law of some other countries that demand workers' ballots) any provision limiting outside inter-ference, e.g. by the employer (p. 625).

The first impact of the new laws

It may be said that doubts about the wisdom of strike ballots – like other issues in the six areas of change – have been overtaken by events. The trade unions greeted all three of the statutes of the 1980s with campaigns of opposition as strong in expression as that which met the Act of 1971. It would have been surprising had that not been so. Indeed, the 1971 Act, hostile though it clearly was to union interests, might be seen as some kind of 'offer' to unions to join in and share in the structures of a new, regulated system. With some show of legitimacy the 1971 Act could, at a pinch, use the language of Donovan. The Acts of 1980 to 1984 are very different. Their central purposes are to change the balance in collective negotiation, to make illegal commercial and industrial pressure for its extension, and to reintroduce the tort liabilities of the common law to regulate industrial relations. For workers, every trade dispute 'immun-ity' restricted is a social right lost. The TUC, therefore, at its special Wembley conference of 1982 agreed upon a campaign of opposition: no participation in ballots under the Acts or acceptance of Government money for them; withdrawal of union wing-persons from tribunals or the EAT in cases involving a UMA; co-ordination of union action by the General Council, if it thought this to be 'justified', and, if necessary, industrial action against the employer concerned, or more widely, in order to support unions 'experiencing legal action by an employer'.

But much has changed since 1971. The 'days of action' against the new laws were better supported than reports had it; but they were nothing like the massive protests of the 1970s. Polls showed that many trade unionists had not voted Labour and that public opinion strongly disliked both the strikes of 1978 and the operation of the closed shop. Not all employers supported further legislation after the first round in 1980; and in 1981 the *Financial Times* warned management that an 'insensitive' use of its new power when employees were 'docile' would be 'certain to breed resentment'.[116] But there was resentment also against the unions. The new Secretary of State, Mr Tebbit, strode into the 1982 Act 'to safeguard the liberty of the individual' and to 'improve the operation of the labour market by providing a balanced framework of industrial relations law'. There had now emerged a 'tougher coordinated business line against . . . [the] softly softly approach'.[117] There were also signs of the new readiness by employers to begin actions in the High Court to enforce 'the law'. This change emerged gradually. In part it may have been related to changes within management itself and in part to the new situation in the labour market. But the new Acts, too, made different demands upon management. The theme protecting individual rights was parallel to that in the 1971 Act, but there was now no promotion by *law* of 'orderly' structures, integrating unions and employers into an industrial framework administered by law in which managers were called upon to initiate change. Instead, in the 1980s the draftsmen called up the ghosts of judge-made common law by stripping unions of 'privileged' statutory protection against it. 'Reform' was replaced in substance and in form by restriction. The law was enforced in the High Court, which no respectable person would call, as the NIRC had been called, a 'class court'. Management was presented with a more docile work-force and a more competitive labour market in which its prerogatives were more powerfully protected; fear of unemployment was widespread for the first time for fifty years. But the legal innovations went further. Any 'second round' of legislation had to take account of the lessons of earlier Acts. In 1972, for example, this had 'put great strain upon the internal [TGWU] solidarity . . . between the road transport section, which worked the rival container depots, and the docks section'.[118] Sectionalism had continued, perhaps increased, in the trade union movement.[119] The tendency of the new laws to divide workers into enterprise groups was facilitated by this. But the 1984 Act made a further contribution; by imposing the requirement of a ballot before official strikes, it was able to claim the banner of 'democracy' as its own.

Union strength and security

Legal remedies often determine the practical impact of legal liabilities. For example the 1981 Green Paper referred to the 'martyrdom' problem. Throughout the world leaders have defied court orders against trade unions: 'individuals may be moved to seek martyrdom by deliberately ignoring an injunction'. This can make laws backfire. Two suggestions were made in 1981. Full liability could be imposed on unions in tort so that court orders could be made against *them*, as well as, or instead of, their officials. Secondly, unions could be required to discipline their officials and even members for unofficial strikes. This, however, might reduce but could not eliminate 'the opportunities to seek martyrdom'. This problem was tackled in the context of union security generally in the 1982 and 1984 Acts. After the *Taff Vale* judgment, 1901 (p. 525), Parliament tried to save unions from the threat of extinction through awards of damages (if a company claims all its losses in even a modest dispute, this may run to millions of pounds) by granting them (though not officials) a blanket immunity from tort liability. That protection was largely re-enacted in 1974 (TULRA s. 14). The 1982 Act (s. 15) removes the protection, though it also recognizes the problem of financial ruin by setting limits to the damages the court can award in any one set of proceedings (p. 531). Those limits do not apply to fines or other sanctions, such as 'sequestration' (seizure) of union property, which the High Court can impose on a body disobeying an order of the court (for 'contempt of court': Chapters 8 and 9). The Government said the new structure aimed 'to bring the trade union movement back within the law of the land'.

In 1984 an incident illustrated the new industrial and legal trends. The union side of the JNC at *Austin Rover*, which bargained for some 25,000 workers, called a strike in a dispute. The company, complaining that there had been no ballot as required by the 1984 Act, at once launched proceedings on a day's notice for interlocutory injunctions against the eight unions represented. Of these, the EETPU disavowed the strike, calling for a ballot. Sections of the AUEW were at risk of liability; but the Court of Appeal held there was no 'need' for any order. True to his ambition to settle industrial and legal issues together, Donaldson MR held hearings in closed session in the Court of Appeal and said it had been indicated to the parties that 'no useful purpose would be served by giving any injunction at this stage' (the injunction is a remedy in the *discretion* of the judge – though normally of the trial judge, not the appellate court). The court thus offered a carrot to unions that agreed to be of good conduct; the AUEW appeared to wish to accept a ballot whilst not breaking TUC policy about boycotting the Act. The strike itself collapsed within two weeks. Orders were made against other unions (though four were ineffective because proper notice of them was not served). TASS proved to the court that its contempt was 'not serious' and was not punished. But the TGWU defied the injunction and was fined £200,000 for contempt – one week *after* the strike collapsed (the money was quietly taken from a bank account some weeks later). Whoever was right or wrong in the dispute, the unions lay like skittles bowled out into the corners of the industrial arena. The willingness of Austin Rover to pursue its actions, especially the contempt proceedings against the country's largest union weeks after the industrial dispute had ended, proclaimed a new employers' attitude and was facilitated by the revived liability of the unions in tort (p. 535).

Another provision in the 1982 Act spelt out precisely for *whom* the union is liable in a code of 'vicarious liability' on industrial torts. When officials authorize or endorse a strike, the union is now liable (1) automatically for the 'top' officials – the President, General Secretary or National Executive Committee; (2) for officials who have express or implied authority under the rules (as in *Heatons*); and (3) for other full-time officers not prevented by the rules from having authority. In the last case, broadly their authorization makes the union liable unless one of the second ('top') group repudiates their action (Chapter 7, p. 532). All of this imposes a tighter doctrine of 'vicarious liability' than under the common law, and is 'an attempt to build a "command" structure into the trade union, since without one the notion of vicarious liability will not work'.[120]

Various functions are fulfilled by bringing the union rather than just its officials into court in tort actions. On the 'carrot' side, the court, having the organization before it, can play a conciliating role if it wishes, gently leading the union back to 'obey the law', leaving it to the top officials to bring recalcitrant members or officials to heel. On the 'stick' side, it can impose unlimited penalties for contempt to the point of sequestration of the entire assets (and now even beyond that: Chapter 9). Just as important to the real world, the strictures of 'the law' can hold up the union to condemnation on the television news before a nation that will know nothing about the legal niceties involved. What will be seen is that the union has acted 'illegally' (as in the miners' strike: Chapter 9). Orders can be made against officials as well; and top officers or trustees may also be made personally liable for breaches of orders against the union.[121] The threat to the funds and to the operation of the union, perhaps long after a dispute is over, is critical to the law's new role. But it also puts the courts in the front line. The policy of 'non-intervention' is not modified; it is reversed.

Closed shops and the law

This strategy interlocks with the new closed-shop legislation, which is rather better known. As we see in Chapter 4, union movements in many democratic countries engage in some kind of 'union security' arrangements, commonly in collaboration with employers. In some countries where unions have from the beginning measured strength by membership rather than by influence or support the tendency towards such arrangements is more pronounced. In Britain it has taken the form of 100 per cent union-membership union–employer arrangements (UMAs) or closed shops (either 'pre-entry', where membership is a condition of engagement, or more usually 'post-entry', where workers join within a given period after hiring unless they fall into an exempted category). By the 1980s Conservative policy had developed a point of principle on this matter. As the Green Paper put it: 'Individual employees should have the right to decide for themselves whether or not to join a trade union.'

By 1982 the Government spoke of the 'conscript army' of unionists. No quarter was given to traditional arguments on the other side, such as that non-unionists should not be 'free-riders' on the engine of collective bargaining from whose machinery they benefited, or that 100 per cent union membership facilitates orderly bargaining. On the contrary, closed shops, it was said, were monopolies that had led workers 'into unemployment'. Not surprisingly, therefore, attempts were made in the 1980s legislation to repair the failure of the 1971 Act and 'outlaw' the UMA. First, as we have seen, commercial and industrial action to induce another employer to maintain a UMA became a tort (EA 1982 ss. 12, 14). This liability lay at the root of the eventual sequestration of the assets of the NGA when it tried to maintain its UMA in the various companies of Mr Shah's group in 1983–4. Each of the companies of his *Messenger Newspapers* group with which it was in dispute was a separate employer. So industrial action by members at one place of work was pressure to induce a *different* employer to adopt a closed shop at another. Secondly, the permitted occasions on which an employer who is party to a UMA can discipline or dismiss a non-unionist were restricted almost to the point of extinction (Chapter 4). If a non-union worker objects by reason of a 'deeply held personal conviction' to joining unions, his dismissal is unfair. Moreover, even if the worker does not fall within one of many such exceptions, the dismissal will now be unfair unless the UMA has been supported in a recent ballot by huge majorities – either 80 per cent of the workers involved, or 85 per cent of those voting (E A 1982 and E A 1980).

What is less well known is that any dismissal by reason of non-unionism is now *always* an unfair dismissal outside a UMA, and one that attracts a 'special award' of money on top of any compensation for loss suffered. This has little to do with the closed shop; but it is of profound importance to the philosophy and practice of the new laws. In 1975 statutory support was provided for workers carrying out trade union activities, with paid time off and special protection against dismissal and discipline. This was justified as part of the social right to organize; such workers are the key people at the workplace to implement the union side of collective bargaining on behalf of all workers, unionists and non-unionists alike. Now that model is changed. The status of trade unionist and of non-unionist at work is equated. The non-unionist, for example, is given the same special procedure of 'interim relief' that is provided for the dismissed unionist (maintaining his employment until the case on unfair dismissal can be fully heard). In addition, though, the non-unionist who is unfairly dismissed or disciplined is able to sue in the tribunal not only the employer but the trade union as well if it has induced his dismissal. This is the procedure of 'joinder' (p. 381). Thus (except for time off) non-unionism receives protection from the law as much as, arguably more than, trade unionism.

Internal union affairs

By 1984 the new policy of restriction moved inside the trade union itself to regulate elections to its executive committee. Since the E T U scandal in 1959 research had not unearthed any major scandals in trade union elections (though allegations of ballot rigging were later made, but not sustained in court, in TGWU elections in 1984). But research has shown that the diverse practices by which national executive committees (NECs) and officials in British unions have been elected for many years do not correlate with particular political or policy characteristics (as we see in Chapter 9).[122] That trade union rules vary greatly is not surprising in a democratic movement. The ILO Convention on Freedom of Association (No. 87, 1948) demands that workers and employers' organizations must have the right to adopt rules and elect representatives 'in full freedom'. The Donovan Report, which concluded: 'It is not practicable to prescribe one set of model election rules', had proposed procedures for dealing with malpractices in union elections; the 1971 Act had gone further, enacting general principles for all unions and more detailed requirements for unions on the Register. But neither went as far as the 1984 Act. In 1983 the ILO Committee of Experts questioned the propriety of detailed government control of election procedures.[123]

Part I of the 1984 Trade Union Act demands that the 'principal executive committee' of each union must be elected at least once every five years by means of a direct vote of the union's members under the Act's procedures, whatever the union rules may say. Many rule-books (of unions as of other bodies) provide for the election of some or all members of the NEC by indirect methods (through directly elected Regional Councils, for example, as in the GMBAT). This is not now permitted. The Act requires that the election must be effected by a direct postal ballot unless the union has 'reasonable grounds' to believe that a workplace ballot will equally satisfy the detailed requirements laid down. No other method, such as voting at branch meetings or in branch ballot boxes, is permitted. Rules are laid down about the permissible constituencies of members and candidatures. Any member may complain to the Certification Officer (CO) and to the High Court (cumulatively) about alleged irregularities (Chapter 9). Such requirements, the Government claimed, were necessary both to 'democratize' unions and 'hand them back to the members', and as the modern price for union 'immunities'.

From 1980 onwards unions have been able to take advantage of State funds to finance certain ballots and have acquired rights to hold secret ballots on an employer's premises so long as they are 'recognized' and the number of employees exceeds twenty (EA 1980 ss. 1, 2). The Certification Officer supervises the application of the detailed regulations governing these funds and may confine payments to the amounts that he considers reasonable. TUC policy has been that affiliated unions should refuse to apply for such grants; but individual unions have been placed in a dilemma when faced with the increasing cost of elections and other ballots forced upon them. Some large unions (notably the EETPU and AUEW) applied for this State money, thereby threatening in 1985 a serious rift in the TUC. The issue of 'ballots' is sometimes discussed as if it involved simple democratic choices. There are more difficult issues, as we see in Chapter 9. Much depends on the type of ballot, its conditions and its purposes, and on the meaning given to 'trade union democracy'.

Political funds

Lastly, Part III of the 1984 Act intervened on the unions' political funds. As we shall see (p. 759), because of a decision by the Law Lords in 1910, trade unions have since an Act of 1913 been permitted to engage in 'political' expenditure only if they maintain a separate 'political fund' approved by the members in a ballot and financed by contributions from which each individual member is exempted if he so wishes (Chapter 9). No similar controls are imposed on the political activities of other associations. Two changes were made in 1984 long after what had been regarded as the authoritative review of this system by Donovan as a constitutional compact. First, the definition of 'political' was widened (TUA 1984 s. 17). An enlarged area of activities may now be included, such as trade union campaigns against 'cuts' in social services. Thus, on the one hand, more and more industrial action is dubbed 'political', whilst, on the other hand, a widened area of social controversy is labelled 'political'. The second change demands that unions' political funds must be legitimated by fresh ballots every ten years. But any union that had not held a ballot within the last nine years was obliged to hold one within one year. The necessary consequence was a series of ballots within most of the fifty trade unions that had political funds in 1985, which most of them had had for decades, to legitimize them afresh. A high proportion of these unions were affiliated to the Labour Party. It was clear, therefore, that this move had constitutional implications. The end of 'political funds' in unions would certainly bankrupt the main opposition party. This issue went beyond industrial law and raised the question of how political parties should be financed in our democracy.

The new policy and collectivism

All these measures increasingly imposed legal restriction upon trade union activities. The Government made it clear that more statutes might follow (in the Prime Minister's words, there might need to be 'a Bill every other year until we have got it right').

In 1985 the Government disclosed that it was considering further legislation, possibly to impose new forms of prohibition upon strike action in 'essential services', or further legal protection for non-unionists and union members (such as a prohibition upon unions' disciplining members who fail to answer a strike call), or the application of compulsory ballot methods to other elections or to committees below the level of the NEC. A further extension of compulsory ballots would reinforce the Government's claim to occupy the ground of 'democracy' and take further advantage of the apparent inability of the TUC to make an effective response, despite its affiliated unions' strong record on internal democracy. Indeed, by 1985 the increasing number of work groups holding ballots on closed shops or on strikes and of unions adjusting the election for their NECs to the 1984 statutory rules, as well as union successes in ballots on political funds, suggested that the TUC would eventually come to treat parts of the 1984 legislation rather differently from that of 1980–2.

The logic of the Acts of 1980–4

The logic of the new policy of government, though, lies in something more profound than ballots of members and removals of legal support for unions or 'props' for collective bargaining (as in the Wages Bill 1986: p. 354), eradication of the 'closed shop', control of union elections, repeal of protective legislation (as in the Sex Discrimination Bill 1986: p. 407; and Shops Bill 1986: p. 412), or even the removal of 'immunities'. The new laws are based upon a modulated rejection of collectivism. This marks them off sharply from the earlier traditions of labour law. They are logically consistent not only with the fiscal and economic policy of the Government but with a broader ideological vision, one entertained by a school of thought largely silent throughout the debates before the Donovan Commission, which were carried on mainly in the language of conservative, pluralist and radical collectivists.

Its leading exponent, Hayek, puts the central point clearly enough: 'There can be no salvation for Britain until the special privileges granted to the trade unions three-quarters of a century ago are revoked.' Wages would be 'higher', he has claimed, and there would be more jobs if wages were 'again determined by the market and if all limitations on the work an individual is allowed to do were removed'. Indeed, 'so long as general opinion makes it politically impossible to deprive the trade unions of their coercive powers, an economic recovery of Great Britain is also impossible'.[124] The 'coercive powers' refer to the legality of industrial action. The Act of 1906 had 'conferred on the labour unions unique privileges', and 'freedom of organisation' is merely a 'battle cry' which must be controlled to defend 'the individual'. Competition must be protected in every respect; the 'big enterprises' should not even be *entitled* to act in 'the public or social interest or to support good causes and generally to act for the public benefit', because that would bring the corporations' power into prominence and inevitably bring about 'public control' by government. In 1984 he reasserted that there is 'no hope for the British economy . . . unless the monopoly of the privileged wielders of force is radically removed'; workers who suffered 'should form a libertarian, anti-labour movement'.[125] A collectivity of individual workers was acceptable but only in order to combat collectivism.

This philosophy is distinct in its simplicity not only from socialist thinking, but from most liberal and conservative analysis of 1940–80. Competition is *the* way to success and freedom, trade unions *the* obstacle.

These convictions stand at the core of the new labour law policies. But the 'market' to which appeal is made for salvation (whether rightly or wrongly in economic terms is, for the present, of no importance) is not exactly a 'free' market. It must not be encumbered with 'monopoly' or 'coercion' caused by workers' collective organizations. It must be free from effective trade unions. It follows that their freedom of combination must be restricted. For the first time in a century, therefore, labour law policy is directed not towards amendment or 'reform' of the collective bargaining system (whether on a pluralist, corporatist or even 'unitary' basis). It points in a different direction. It does not accept the legitimacy of 'collective labour power' in the labour market. Many of the traditional assumptions of recent labour law debates are therefore put in question. Behind pluralist, radical and Marxist analyses stood a very different postulate: the subordination of the individual employee and *his* need and right to find greater dignity and freedom through combination with others, including those employed in other enterprises. The main thrust of the market school has been to emphasize the need to stamp out 'coercion' by the majority against the individual, to see collective organization as *less* free, even less dignified, than individual relations. It has at times played an important role in judges' thinking. But, until recently, it has rarely led policy-makers to reject trans-enterprise collective bargaining itself.

To find a stark expression of this ideology in action we must go back almost one hundred years, beyond even the General Strike (p. 666), when a gas employer, Livesay, 'broke the union in his own works with a combination of "free" (that is, non-union) labour – strongly protected by the police – and a profit-sharing scheme'. Then 'free labour' temporarily broke the emergent dockers' and seamen's unions; and the great engineering lock-out marked the 'employers' counter-offensive' of the 1890s.[126] In 1898 the Free Labour Protection Association demanded for employers 'the right of managing their . . . business without interference from trade unions'. It may be said, rightly, that employers, unions and collective bargaining now are not what they were a century ago. But the new willingness of employers to use actions in the courts shows that this policy cannot be denied merely by arguing, as was so often the fashion after the failure of the 1971 Act, that legal regulation will not 'work' because employers will not use the legal sanctions that are offered.

By 1985 the trickle of legal actions had not yet grown into a flood but its current was strong enough to inhibit such easy answers. Moreover, the tests by which to judge whether labour laws 'work' were not now held in common by the different sides to the debate. Because labour law policy was geared to promotion of 'competitiveness', with the whole of Government policy ostensibly based upon the success in those terms, it could not afford to see the policy fail. Those who opposed the new policies increasingly ran the risk of being seen not as critics with whom to debate and to compromise (the supreme pluralist virtue) but as a domestic enemy within, which must be defeated. The social dangers of such developments were illustrated by the miners' strike of 1984 where a union spoke in unusually challenging tones (as John Lloyd wrote, it 'constituted itself as a revolutionary vanguard'), and government gave no quarter. In such circumstances the old tradition of compromise was squeezed out: 'The mining dispute cannot be *settled*. It can only be *won*.'[127]

1983–5 and the civil courts

This increasing politicization of labour law was graphically illustrated in many of the legal cases brought after 1982 against trade unions. In addition to the *Austin Rover* case (p. 535), the *Messenger* newspaper companies of Mr Shah sought damages and contempt remedies against the NGA, ending in sequestration of the union's assets; various actions were brought against the NUJ, including the *Dimbleby* case, for 'secondary action' (p. 601); the POEU (NCU) lost to *Mercury* under the new definition of 'trade dispute'; partial strikes by teachers, which continued for many months, were challenged in the courts even though ballots were held; many other employers, including British Rail, threatened or issued writs seeking labour injunctions. Unions often compromised or withdrew rather than go into court. One union officer said, 'We are settling three a week.'

The contrast with the 1970s was sharpened in 1985 when the NUR called a strike by its members in the London Underground in face of management's insistence on introducing more trains without guards. The injunction against the union granted at the suit of the employers on a Friday (because no ballot had been held) was followed by a refusal to strike by 70 per cent of the members on the Monday. This was hardly the experience of the railway work-to-rule in 1972. The workers refused to support their own union policy; but union leaders complained that they had been made to feel (wrongly) that it would be 'illegal' for each of them, personally, to withdraw his labour. Whatever the legal substance, the injunction was a central factor in the rhetoric and tactics that led to their defeat. The NUR changed its policy, adopting ballots under the 1984 Act as a requirement for official action. In the subsequent dispute about 'one-man trains' nationally, it held a ballot of the 10,000 guards who were urged to take industrial action. But – to the astonishment of union, management and the pundits – 52 per cent of the guards voted against the proposal. British Rail had already dismissed 200 guards for unofficial action (intimidation and interference, the union claimed, when the ballot had not yet even been held) and in an advertisement campaign threatened to close down the entire railway network. Fear of unemployment patently affected the vote. But the Government was understandably jubilant at this 'proof' that its new laws 'worked'. By 1986 more strike ballots were going the union way; but this was only one of the new hurdles of illegality to be surmounted.

The year-long miners' strike was the centre-piece of the period. Because, like *Rookes* v. *Barnard*, 1964, its legal events are bound to be of importance for many years to come, an outline must be included here (see further Chapters 8 and 9).[128] The strike was a response to an announcement of pit closures by the NCB; an overtime ban on other issues was already in operation in most Area unions (each Area is a separate union in law, in the federal structure of the NUM). The union said huge numbers of jobs would be lost; the NCB disputed the figures but insisted on closing 'uneconomic' pits. The NUM insisted that this was a strike at Area level, approved but not initiated by the National Union. So there was no national ballot, an omission criticized by many. The rule-books of many Areas, however, also required ballots before industrial action. Dissenting members began legal actions against some of the Areas, alleging breach of the contract in the rules and claiming injunctions. In some Areas there was no breach; but in others injunctions were issued, including (as we see in Chapter 9) the Nottinghamshire Area, where the great majority of miners continued to work. In some legal actions the unions did not at first appear in court. The national NUM was often joined as a defendant and was ultimately ordered not to treat the strike as 'official' action. Dissident 'working miners' proceeded to make claims against the individual members of the national and the Area executive committees. One such claim in Derbyshire eventually succeeded to the point of a declaration that some of the Area officials were liable to repay over £1 million.[129] The financing of the strike itself rested far more upon Area than upon National Union funds.

But moneys of the National Union also were alleged to have been put in peril. In October 1984 the High Court found the union and its

President, Mr Scargill, to be in breach of its earlier orders and therefore in contempt. It fined Mr Scargill £1,000 (this was paid by an anonymous donor). The union's fine of £200,000, however, remained unpaid; it remained in contempt of court. The judge ordered sequestration of the union's entire assets. This penalty sprang ultimately from its refusal to accept the order that the strike must not be treated as 'official' because to do so was a breach of the rules. These civil actions did not rest, in juridical terms, upon the Acts of 1980 to 1984. They were based on common law breach of contract, albeit a breach that the unions denied and which in many cases was never fully fought out in the interim proceedings. The base of the liability was the common law, and the avoidance of 'martyrdom' remedies by the judges soon became evident. (If the fine of £1,000 had remained unpaid, the court would have ordered the Queen's Remembrancer to collect it.) It may be said that the NUM and the Areas could have avoided liability by holding the necessary ballots and appearing in court to defend their procedure. What would have happened then we shall never know. The next move by the dissident miners led into uncharted territory. They claimed that the trustees of the NUM had misapplied the funds, or at least put them in jeopardy, in breach of their duties as trustees. The sequestrators had, indeed, been unable to find the national funds because most of them had been transferred at an earlier date to banks abroad, in jurisdictions where the sequestrators were conducting protracted and unsuccessful litigation for their recovery.

The last week of November 1984 was one of unparalleled legal drama. Some 140,000 miners were pursuing their ninth month on strike; the House of Commons was in frequent uproar; soup-kitchens had appeared in mining villages; if the battles between pickets and police had abated, they had not been forgotten. The High Court ordered the union and its trustees to repatriate the funds from abroad to the sequestrators. To do otherwise would only 'postpone the day of reckoning' and increase the costs for those funds. On Thursday 29th, dissident miners applied to have the trustees removed and a receiver appointed to take possession of the assets. The trustees now appeared in court; they asserted the funds were safe; and the claim was adjourned by consent for seven days. The next day the plaintiffs (as the court rules of procedure permit) renewed their claim, vigorously supported by the sequestrators on the urgent need to safeguard the absent funds. The judge asked for assurances that the defendants would obey all the orders of the courts (including the order to desist from treating the strike as 'official'), but they would not give such assurances, offering only a promise that the funds would not be moved. The judge ordered that they be removed as trustees and that a receiver of the national funds be appointed. An appeal was made to the Court of Appeal on the Saturday; but it was rejected. The defendants, already in contempt of the court's orders, must be replaced.[130] A further hearing a week later extended the appointment of a receiver indefinitely. This is yet another example in our labour law of the importance of remedies, which we take up in Chapters 8 and 9.

At the end of 1984, then, two agents of the court had power to take over NUM assets, the sequestrators and the receiver. It was the first time the remedy of receivership had ever been used against a trade union (p. 734). With the strike grinding to an end, the court refused the receiver's request to end sequestration; the union was still in 'open defiance'. In parlous state the miners began to drift back to work, and the strike ended in March 1985. Many months later costs (payable out of the funds) were running at about £1 million. The court allowed the receiver to pay over to each Area union its part of the 'check-off', union subscriptions from miners deducted by the NCB, provided that such payment had the written consent of the sequestrators and that each Area undertook not to feed such sums back to sustain the National Union. As soon as the strike was over the South Wales Area union secured the liberation of *its* funds from sequestration (the fine of £50,000 and costs were deducted); the judge was 'not troubled' by the absence of an apology. But for the national NUM punishment continued (and costs mounted) because of its 'misguided conduct'. It did not end even when the miners who brought the original legal action abandoned it. The grip of the law seemed set to throttle the NUM before it could secure the end of sequestration and appointment of new trustees to replace the receiver (Chapter 9). No public policy intervened like that which released the dockers in 1972. Once taken up, the legal weapons of war are not so easily buried even if industrial hostilities are over.

There had been other civil actions. The deduction from their families' supplementary benefit of amounts 'deemed' to be paid as union strike pay was challenged by miners in the High Court but without success (though the union had no money with which to make such payments).

Injunctions had been granted based on tort against Area unions where the new legislation *did* have relevance. At the outset, the NCB obtained injunctions in respect of miners' picketing at certain pits that were not their own place of work; but as it did not follow up the judgment with proceedings for contempt, the orders merely lay on the record. It was never established whether the reason for this was industrial policy, Government wishes or the reported desire of the Chairman to 'forge contacts' with the working miners who later brought legal actions.[131] Two transport companies obtained injunctions against the South Wales Area union early in the dispute, based upon interference with their trade and unlawful picketing. Defiance of this order led to contempt proceedings and sequestration of the South Wales union's assets. But no big company or nationalized industry brought a serious legal action in the strike. Dissident miners in three Areas sued their union alleging liability by reason of the picketing. In South Wales they obtained an injunction because of 'unreasonable harassment' limiting pickets at certain pits to six, the number in the Secretary of State's code (a decision of some moment: Chapter 7, p. 546).[132]

Nor was civil litigation confined to the miners' unions. A member of the seamen's union obtained an order stopping a levy of members to support the miners. An employer had industrial action by seamen banned (despite a successful ballot, it was still 'secondary action'). Other unions supported the miners financially; but the sequestrators and the Receiver pressed them with questions about their gifts to a union that was in contempt of court many months after the strike had ended. (In 1986 the receiver, still in charge of NUM assets, was actively pursuing legal actions against banks and other third parties involved in the transfer of funds in 1984.) The TUC had hesitated to help the NUM even after the strike with direct finance, in case it was seen as 'aiding or abetting' a contempt (which is itself a contempt – a difficult area of the law that we review in Chapters 8 and 9). Railway workers had engaged in a one-day strike in certain regions – management alleged it was in support of the miners; the union asserted it was in defence of victimized rail workers. British Rail issued a writ but stayed its hand until three months *after* the end of the miners' strike, when it notified two railway unions that it would proceed with the claim for damages unless they admitted within a week their liability to pay £200,000 to compensate it for its losses. By this time many other employers were issuing or threatening writs against unions. It began to be asked whether consumers could sue – commuters stranded by rail strikes, for example (see p. 644). This was a very different world from that of 'legal abstention'.

Criminal law and civil procedures

These civil cases, though, were not what most people thought of when asked about the miners' strike and 'the law'. The more significant impact of 'law' in the perceptions of the public at large lay elsewhere, in the criminal law. For months large numbers of pickets appeared at some pits; and great numbers of police, organized from the 'National Reporting Centre', were transported across the country. Some 10,000 miners were arrested in England and Wales (though 65 per cent were charged with non-violent offences, many were not convicted, and dozens of charges, even of riot, affray and unlawful assembly, the most serious crimes of disorder, were ultimately withdrawn or negatived by acquittals in 1985). Magistrates' courts had appeared to put bail conditions to new uses to exclude miners from picket lines. Serious crimes of violence had been committed on and off picket lines. There was violence by the police, the worst confrontations occurring when they appeared in areas not their own. The Government could not apply for civil injunctions (the new legislation had not revived the 'emergency' procedures of 1971) but it might have encouraged nationalized industries (the Central Electricity Generating Board, or the NCB itself) to seek and enforce such orders.

Critics alleged that the Government favoured a policy of confronting pickets and unions with police rather than with writs, thereby accentuating the image – and ultimately the reality – of the industrial dispute as one of public disorder. Certainly normal social 'order' fragmented in some areas. The life of a 'scab' in Yorkshire or of a striker in Nottinghamshire in 1984 was not pleasant. Passions were intense. But the general public did not, and was not encouraged to, distinguish civil from criminal wrongdoing. When the NUM was portrayed as acting 'illegally' (in breach of contract and of consequent court orders) most people put its wrongdoing into the same category as the crimes of violence that they were shown nightly on television.

This understandable tendency not to distinguish civil from criminal wrongs in industrial disputes – of special importance on picketing

(Chapter 7) – had been noted in surveys earlier in the 1980s.[133] In 1972 the 'special' court, the NIRC, was a body that was felt to be administering not 'the law' but a special law. In 1984 there was something reassuring for the public about the fact that the 'ordinary' law was being applied, by the 'ordinary' courts. But the period illustrated the confusion that can be caused by indiscriminate assertions about breach of 'the law'.

Moreover, the 'interlocutory' procedures of the High Court turned out to be, if anything, more favourable to a plaintiff suing the union than those of the NIRC had been (so long, at any rate, as he had legal aid or other adequate backing for his costs). Evidence in these procedures is given on written affidavit (in very few of them is a witness ever called for cross-examination). The plaintiff can therefore prepare his written documents for weeks and then launch his 'interlocutory' (i.e. interim) action to bring the case into court on, at most, a few days' notice to the defendant. In some cases, he can even do so *ex parte* (that is, without the defendant being present). In theory, the 'full trial' comes months, or years, later; often it is not pursued at all if the plaintiff has already got what he wants. In the NUM case, the contempt was for disobedience of an interim order; but the plaintiffs, understandably, later abandoned their action after the strike without any full 'trial'. In *Stratford* v. *Lindley*[134] (p. 590) the 'interlocutory' injunction, on which an appeal to the House of Lords took place, remained on the record against the union officials for over four years, reappearing in proceedings that went to the Court of Appeal in a wrangle over costs. Most civil cases in the miners' strike involved 'interim' remedies. Whatever the merits of the NUM strike or of the NCB policies – and this book is not concerned with those – the dispute proved that the legal process now has a *potential* for enfeebling combinations of workers or (according to taste) the 'coercive powers' of unions, which it had not enjoyed since the nineteenth century, especially by speedy intervention through remedies available at the discretion of the judges.

By 1986 the inability of unions to take effective lawful industrial action was illustrated in the dispute between the printing unions and the News International group, which dismissed 5,000 striking print workers when it moved production of *The Times* and *Sun* newspapers from Fleet Street to its new plant in Wapping. News International refused to recognize the printing unions in its new plant, and its multi-corporate structure included three different companies for newspaper production and another to organize distribution, thereby dividing its work-force into different employment units. Within two weeks and at the first hearing on 'contempt', SOGAT '82 was fined and lost its £17 million assets in a sequestration for failure to obey a court order to withdraw instructions to members to black distribution of the newspapers. (There had been a ballot of the printing members but not of the distribution workers; and, in any event, their action was arguably 'secondary action'.) The UCW submitted to injunctions prohibiting its Post Office members from blacking the distribution of *Sun* 'bingo' cards. Similar injunctions were enforced against the NGA, which was also fined for disobeying them. The TUC withdrew from taking steps (such as requiring another union, the EETPU, to instruct its members not to cross printers' picket lines in order to work in the Wapping plant) for fear of acting unlawfully. The employer, wrote one commentator, 'does not just have the best cards, he's got the entire pack'.[135]

The judgments in some of these cases will be discussed in detail in Chapters 8 and 9. To most of the public, including many workers outside the disputes concerned, they were taken as evidence that 'the law' could intervene, no matter how powerful the union. To many lawyers they appeared as support for individuals and for small firms who were standing up to mighty unions. It was important that the liabilities rested largely on the common law. Having been taught that unions are 'privileged' institutions and heard the Law Lords declare that union 'immunities' stuck in their 'judicial gorges', many lawyers took the civil judgments to be a reimposition of 'the law of the land'. As Laski noted of English lawyers in 1950: 'There is amongst them a kind of nostalgia for the law as it stood . . . before the Trade Disputes Act 1906.' But a significant body of lawyers also expressed concern for traditional liberties in the face of new interventions by the civil and criminal law, and the new methods employed by what had become a nationally organized police force and by the administration of the criminal law.

The re-entry of the common law

The new labour law in technical terms largely consists, then, in civil cases, in unlocking the common law from the constraints of the 'immunities'. One lawyer defended the policy in this way:

What justification can there be for the unique legal position enjoyed by unions and unionists? The only intellectually respectable answer appears to be Marxism . . . even experienced trade unionists may be able to visualize life after the immunities have disappeared. . . . Life without immunities offers unions an honourable and responsible role as *voluntary* associations active within the limits of the ordinary law of the land to secure the interests of their members.[136]

This soon became a well known statement at the legal heart of the policy. Economists have described the new 'market' policies as measures that cannot work unless the government proceeds to 'break real wage resistance'.[137] The Government itself has proclaimed the need to contain wage increases and to decrease the level of rates, in particular, of young workers. The new legal framework depends, similarly, upon a withdrawal of legislative resistance to the common law. This reintroduces a corpus of rules for social relationships that is by no means 'ordinary', certainly not neutral between contending social classes. The same writer described the ordinary courts as 'well placed to rank conflicting interests and to protect vested rights and legitimate expectations'. But when conflicting interests are judged by the common law, workers find few rights and scant expectations. It is precisely the legitimacy of existing relationships and, in particular, of management's rights that effective trade unionism challenges. The objective of the common law is normally to blunt that challenge.

We have seen that the exceptional 'non-interventionist' decisions of judge-made law have tended to occur when the interests of a union coincide, rather than conflict, with the predominant interests of employers and the State (as in *Reynolds's* case, 1924, or the *Crofter* decision, 1942: p. 32). Recent innovations made in the common law and in its procedures and remedies tend to reinforce the validity of that perception, as we shall see in Chapters 8 and 9. From this point of view, it is only of marginal relevance that many of the miners' cases in 1984–5 did not involve the new legislation. In that litigation it was the common law that continued its long march.

The new statutes of the 1980s have invited the common law to resume its dominion over industrial conflict, union security and the power relationships inherent in employment. They have cleared the ground of laws that had propped up minimum standards as a base for bargaining machinery, much of which is now deplored as an obstacle to lower wages and competitive efficiency. As *The Times* put it in 1984:

A statutory minimum wage, whether established by trade union agreement or official regulation, is a restrictive practice, and one of the worst. It is a major source of economic distortions in Great Britain.[138]

The objection is not to trade union 'coercion', but to trade union 'agreement'. We shall see that, in some respects, the direction of these changes comports with changes in the labour market that do not depend at all upon the law.

At the same time government has insisted – as all Governments habitually do – that its ideology contains the virtues both of the old and of the new regimes. The Secretary of State, Mr Tebbit, introducing the 1982 Bill declared he had no quarrel with the TUC in its demand for three basic rights: the right to combine in order to pursue the collective interest of members; the right to be recognized by employers for collective bargaining; and the right to withhold labour. These were 'the characteristic rights of free trade unions in all democratic countries'. He insisted: 'If those are the rights that trade unions need to function effectively, they have nothing to fear from the Bill.'[139]

It is not difficult to speak in support of these three rights. But there are differing shades of meaning in the apparent common language. In the new application of the formula, the priorities for union organization and collective bargaining are different, for these are to be displaced whenever the needs of 'competitive efficiency' or 'individual rights' demand it. Union strength and security are seen as 'coercion', which the law must prevent. Pressure brought to bear upon employers by combinations of workers *across* the boundaries of enterprises is outlawed. The acceptable face of trade unionism is increasingly restricted to 'enterprise unionism', associations that integrate the interests of individual employees in the common goals of a workplace or a company, rather than organizations based upon a wider solidarity and social role. The new policy feels the need, however, to impose controls on all unions, not only through the common 'law of the land' but through direct legislative regulation over internal elections, strike ballots and the like, in order to enforce uniform, rather than plural, structures of 'democracy', to sustain individualist, rather than collectivist, social ambitions, and to contain the undesirable 'power' felt to be inherent in this form of opposition.[140] Industrial conflict is resisted by mechanisms that include direct application of both civil and criminal remedies. The State replaces collective *laissez-faire* with restrictive *laissez-faire*.

The consequences of this bold change are hard to predict. Nor, as we shall see, are the results necessarily the same at every point of the labour law compass. It cannot be said how far State policy will be driven to intervene by criminal or civil sanction to anticipate or break collective forces judged to be inimical to economic competition in the market, nor what the effects may be upon the social fabric or the democratic machinery of government itself. To address these questions, though, we need to take a more detailed look at the law in the chapters that follow. As with the policies of the past, so-called 'voluntarism' or 'non-intervention', we need to demystify the legal reasoning of current developments. We will examine the legal techniques and the jargon (to which British lawyers are addicted but probably no more than their counterparts in other countries). We need to establish both the principles of the law and their social effects and functions. There is, however, one further preliminary subject, one not irrelevant to an understanding of the legal forms that mask reality in the employment relationship. It concerns the nature of the employer.

Employer and company

In labour law we speak of 'the employer', as we must. But in reality 'he' is rarely an individual. In the public sector (now nearly one-third of the work-force), the employers range from the Crown and nationalized industries to local authorities and the health service. In the private sector he may be a partnership, a co-operative, a building society or a bank. But most workers in this sector are employed by a company registered under the Companies Act (now) 1985. A company, like a nationalized industry or bank, is in law a *separate* person from its shareholders and directors. Sometimes this phenomenon is called the 'corporate veil'. The reason, said Lord Diplock in 1984, why the law here and in other trading countries has permitted the creation of these 'artificial persons' distinct from their controllers 'is to enable business to be undertaken with limited financial liability in the event of the business proving to be a failure'.

Ordinarily, therefore, the individual employee faces an employer fundamentally different from him. First, the employer is in reality a *collective* entity, an aggregation of capital, but endowed with an *indi-*

vidual personality by the law. Secondly, its shareholders enjoy limited liability (i.e. liability limited to their share contributions), the greatest legal 'immunity' of everyday life. Today limited liability is regarded as a normal mechanism for investment; but it was not introduced until 1855 in Britain (as against full liability of partners for their debts), and some writers then called it a 'rogues' charter'. The law sees every company as a separate person, even if it is in a group where subsidiaries are all controlled by a parent company. Where three giant multinational oil companies created subsidiary companies in Nigeria and Britain that failed, causing losses of £75 million to creditors, the giant shareholders could not be made liable for the debts of those other 'persons', their wholly controlled subsidiary companies – a state of the law that has been pronounced 'seriously inadequate'.[141] Each multinational and each subsidiary company is one legal person and one separate employer. Statutes – especially tax statutes – can and do instruct the courts to break with this concept in particular cases; but, so far, British law includes no general principles that permit exceptions. We shall find that this is very important in labour law.

The separate personalities of companies can change the nature and operation of legal principles. Normally, for example, our courts have, as we shall see (p. 142), refused to grant orders to perform personal contracts (orders of 'specific performance') or to grant injunctions that have the same effect. The normal remedy for non-performance of a ·personal contract is damages. The liberal individualism of the developed common law would not allow judges to enforce personal service, though there have been exceptions, as we see in Chapter 2. In 1985 the question arose, though, whether similar reasoning applied to a long-term contract for the management of the Dorchester Hotel.[142] The contract was made between two separate companies; but it plainly required close co-operation between them, and performance of it in reality would be effected by the personal service of human beings. Nevertheless, the Court of Appeal upheld injunctions that had the effect of specifically enforcing the contract (pending arbitration of a dispute). The agreement did not involve the employment of named persons to do the work; and as the parties to it were corporate 'persons', the court said the rule about personal service did not apply.

A person may stand in diverse relationships to a company. In 1961 a man who owned 2,999 shares in a small company (his solicitor owned the other one) had two further capacities – director *and* employee (chief pilot, on terms effectively negotiated with himself). Contrary to the old learning, the courts today are also prepared to treat a director as an employee in his capacity as executive director, provided the tests of a 'contract of service' are met. The ordinary worker sometimes encounters difficulty in knowing which company in a group *is* his employer. In 1980 a carpenter's written particulars said his employer was 'NH Group'; his payslip said 'NH'; but this could refer to at least four companies in the group. After being injured, he sued one of them, 'NHC', but his employer was in law another subsidiary, 'NHS'. The court rightly allowed him to sue 'NHS', even if he was out of time. (The case illustrates the need for accuracy in the particulars: p. 136). Usually, however, judges stick firmly to the 'corporate veil' doctrine. We shall find the House of Lords rejecting the legality of industrial action launched against company A, where it would have been lawful against company B in the same group, even though the two companies had the same shareholding, same parent and same operating base (p. 601).

It is indeed surprising that courts and Parliament have done so little to offset the results of this legal doctrine. Suppose a number of companies operate on a large site, and a worker employed by company A, a subsidiary in the group, transfers to employment in another subsidiary in the group, B, just across the way, doing the same job: is his employment 'continuous'? If he needed to prove that B employs more than twenty persons (as he once did to maintain his statutory rights: p. 235) can he count in the employees at A? The answer obviously should be 'yes'.[143] The employment protection statutes make an exception and allow for this answer *provided* the companies are 'associated employers'; that is, where two companies are under the control of the same 'third person', or where one company has control of the other, 'directly or indirectly' (EPCA s. 153 (4); cf. TULRA s. 30 (1)). On such problems company law uses different concepts (for example, wide definitions of 'connected persons') to probe deeply (though inadequately) into the family and shareholding 'connections' of persons who appear not to have, but do have, control over a company. By comparison the labour law provisions are a neolithic response to the realities of corporate groups.[144] First, to find 'control' *only* where 51 per cent of the shares is owned is an antique doctrine in today's market of fast operators. Next, the courts have interpreted the labour law formula to mean that where X and Y together own 51 per cent in each of two companies, they are 'associated' and count as one for the purposes stated in the Act; but where the shares in Poparm Ltd were held by Z (50 per cent), Mrs Z (30), and a subsidiary of E (20), and shares in E were owned by Z (35) and his brothers (25 and 15), Poparm and E were judged not to be 'associated' (despite the word 'indirectly' in the definition) because Z owned less than 50 per cent of E's shares.[145] Finally, as the definition speaks of *companies*, it has been held to mean literally 'limited companies', excluding any other body such as a nationalized corporation, a partnership or borough council, whatever its relationship to other bodies under the same control or having the same function. One worker was employed for two years by a local authority after ten years' service with others, but his compensation for unfair dismissal (which is in part dependent on length of continuous service) was calculated by reference only to the shorter period. The position of such workers has been improved through collective agreements in parts of the public sector.

It is true that the law saves continuity of employment where there is 'transfer of a business' (not mere sale of assets) and makes similar provision for the 'transfer of (a commercial) undertaking' under regulations of 1981 inspired by the EEC (pp. 207 and 243). The transferor can also protect the position if an offer of re-engagement in a suitable job by him or an associated employer is made before dismissal to a redundant employee, or when a transferee offers such an alternative. The employee's continuity will be preserved; but, broadly, if he unreasonably refuses the job – he has a four-week trial period to test it – his right to a redundancy payment disappears (p. 222). However, not only does this part of the law (of vital interest to so many workers in the 1980s) leave aside transfers of 'assets', it also ignores the commonest method of changing the real ownership of a business, the share take-over where 'the employer', the company, does not change identity in formal terms, though its new controllers – the new 'employers' in reality – may well intend to strip its assets and leave the work-force stranded (as in certain forms of 'hiving off', which the 1981 Regulations only partially confronted: p. 208). Conversely, the same controllers can effect a 'transfer' of assets from one of their companies to another, and then have the second try to argue that 'it' had never been the worker's employer (though the tribunal may well reject such a claim where the transfer is in reality of the whole business).[146]

Because the legal structure is so far removed from reality, increasing difficulty is experienced. When the business of *B. and L. Ltd* (run by B. and L.) closed down its joinery side, an apprentice moved across to a new partnership (situated next door) and was employed as a joiner. The partnership was run by L., the company's managing director; and B. was a partner too. When made redundant, the joiner's right to an award of compensation depended on the employer's 'recognition' of his union (p. 284). The company had recognized it; but the partnership had not; so he lost his money. And in 1984 the EAT refused to 'lift the corporate veil' for a worker made redundant by a subsidiary, after the managing director of the parent had decided upon redundancies in a tightly knit group of companies.[147] If redundancies in all the subsidiaries had been included (and they all operated from the same 'establishment') they would exceed 100 and the worker's position would have been improved (p. 295). The Act had not made similar provision on 'associated employers' for these purposes (EPA s. 99).

In company law the courts have steered an erratic course, departing from the 'corporate veil' doctrine without specific permission from Parliament in a number – an important minority – of cases. Judges have put aside the personality of a company owning the land of a girls' public school to allow it the advantage of development charges; allowed a parent company to claim compensation when the relevant land was owned by a subsidiary (treating it as the parent's 'agent'); assessed rights by regarding the subsidiary as the 'instrument' of the parent; and treated groups of companies as one enterprise for a variety of purposes. Lord Denning MR said in 1976: 'They should not be treated separately so as to be defeated on a technical point.' Reality today is not normally 'the company'; it is the *group* of companies. But if these judicial notions of 'group enterprise' are uncertain, rather 'timid innovations' in company law,[148] the judges' ventures in labour law have been timorousness itself. Against the rare occasions on which judges have suddenly been prepared to treat companies and their controllers together as one 'party' to a trade dispute (p. 555), the reports disclose a steady refusal to 'pierce the veil' of personality. Lord Diplock said in 1984 that the words in an Act 'employer who is party to the dispute' could not be read to include the parent company and all the subsidiaries in the same group run from the same base, so as to permit a union to be in dispute with all of them.[149] The EAT sometimes adverts to an employing company as being 'not independent of outside control (being the subsidiary of a holding company)', as in 1984 where a manager had to obtain the parent's approval for dismissal; but then it was only an irrelevant context to a legal dispute on unfair dismissal. As we shall see, however, the judicial concept of the incorporated employer often carries with it a peculiar metaphysic. In the 1970s judges developed the doctrine of 'economic duress', which can invalidate a transaction if the 'apparent consent' of a party is induced by 'illegitimate' economic pressure, and they have applied it to the 'coercion of the will' of large companies. When this image of the company was suddenly applied in 1982 to industrial relations, it opened up wide vistas of new liability for trade unions (p. 650).

The company and the workers

The characters in the traditional drama of company law have been the shareholders, directors, creditors (including debenture holders), receiver and liquidator – and the corporate puppet itself. The employee was nowhere in the programme. Other company law systems, however, have recognized workers' interests more generally, especially those that, like the West German system, have found a place for Works Councils in their labour law and employee representation on 'supervisory' boards in company law. A decision in 1962 increased dissatisfaction with British company law. The directors of a company sold its main asset (the *New Chronicle* newspaper) and had more than £1 million left after discharging liabilities. They determined to pay this as a gift and compensation to the employees who had to be made redundant (the 1965 Act requiring redundancy payments was not yet passed). A shareholder, who had received no dividends for many years, objected and succeeded in obtaining an injunction to stop these payments.[150] The company appeared to have no capacity to make such gifts, judging by the 'objects' set out in its registered constitution. If so, it was an *ultra vires* act (i.e. one beyond its legal powers), not even ratifiable by the shareholders. In any event, the directors owed to the company a duty to pursue the benefit and interests of the company. 'There are to be no cakes and ale', as a judge said in 1883, 'except such as are required for the benefit of the company.' The 'interests of the company' must be judged by the interests of the *shareholders* on a long-term view, plus (some judges have said) in certain situations those of the creditors. Employees' interests could be considered indirectly only, as they affected the interests of shareholders. The directors here, said the judge in 1962,

were prompted by motives which, however laudable and however enlightened from the point of view of industrial relations, were such as the law does not recognize as sufficient justification.

But the language of reality is different. Directors have for decades said they *do* directly pay heed to the interests of their workers. By 1980 Parliament felt the need to insert a section into the Companies Act *requiring* directors, as part of their duty to the company, 'to have regard', in performing their functions, to the interests of 'the company's employees in general, as well as the interests of its members' (now s. 309, 1985 Act). Many have regarded this as window dressing. The structure of the Act appears to make it clear that shareholders' (and creditors') interests prevail in any crunch situation, not least because the directors are given express permission to act *otherwise* than in the 'best interests of the company' where they make provision for the workers on transfer or cessation of the undertaking (now s. 719).[151] Similarly companies have often adopted for themselves a non-legal 'social responsibility'. As the CBI put it in 1973, 'A company should behave like a good citizen in business.' But this appears to make only a marginal difference to the relative position of shareholders, creditors and workers.[152] Little has changed the legal perception that the interests of shareholders must predominate in directors' considerations because the final yardstick and purpose of the private sector commercial company are the pursuit of profit.

Two further matters are relevant. The company law developments must be sharply distinguished from the debate that has flourished in Europe since the Second World War – and flowered in Britain in the 1970s – about 'industrial democracy'. Whereas the changes in company law have largely brought the law into accord at least with the rhetoric of existing practice, most proposals about industrial democracy have aimed to change the power structure within the enterprise, giving workers more influence over decisions that collective bargaining cannot reach, raising directly the legitimacy of management's role. Some of the proposals, for example the EEC draft Fifth Directive, envisage the participation of employees in the very structure of company government, of which the West German and Swedish models are two very different species. We shall return later to this sensitive area, which can be assessed in Britain only after closer examination of industrial relations and the law, especially as it affects collective bargaining.

The transnational dimension

Calling a company 'the employer' may be mystifying not only because it is already an aggregation of capital with legal personality and may be part of a corporate group, but also because that very group may be transnational in character. A Minister predicted in 1968 'as the international companies develop, National Governments, including our own, will be reduced to the status of a parish council'. By 1982 one in six of the work-force in British manufacturing industry worked in groups owned abroad, whilst 1.3 million abroad worked directly for British-owned groups. Only four national budgets in the Western world exceeded the turnover of General Motors in 1972; and a high proportion of 'exports' are intra-group international transactions (often at special or 'transferred' prices). This is all part of the internationalization of the world economy, in which 'the expansion of multinational activity and interpenetration of national economies during the past several decades has led to a new network of international linkages'.[153]

But if capital moves easily across national frontiers, labour – especially collectively organized labour – cannot. This accounts for the 'relative feebleness of the international responses of [trade union] movements to international accumulations of capital'.[154] Great efforts by trade unions have been made. International trade secretariats have long existed for numerous sectors of industry, scoring a few modest successes (such as the simultaneous union pressure in the USA and Europe on the multinational St Gobain empire in 1968). Cross-frontier shop steward councils exist, though not many get beyond the exchange of information stage; for example, in 1985 shop stewards from Ford plants in Europe, Asia, Africa, Australasia and South America met in face of threatened closures.[155] The problem of co-ordinating bargaining, let alone industrial action, amongst such disparate work-forces with conflicting immediate interests is obvious. Not only do national unions compete; they may belong even within one country to competing international bodies.[156]

In this dimension the EEC Treaty of Rome has little to say. It counterposes 'free movement' of capital to 'free movement' of the *individual* worker (Art. 48 and Reg. 1612/68) and concentrates on the right of nationals of member States to reside and work in other States within the Community (p. 448). This has important consequences for many areas – social security, immigration and family law, as well as labour law. But it is perhaps understandable if local workers faced with a disintegrating domestic labour market do not, in the eyes of some legal writers, 'always play the positive and constructive role that could be expected from them'.[157]But the European Commission long ago proposed a Directive to improve information given to unions and consultation about the world-wide groups of subsidiaries within the EEC (the 'Vredeling' proposals: p. 301). Various other international bodies – the UN Centre on Transnational Corporations, the OECD and the ILO – have elaborated bolder guidelines and Codes of Conduct for multinationals, though these do not have the force of law. Under the OECD Guidelines of 1979 pressure has been put upon enterprises with occasional success in respect of trade union recognition, disclosure of information and consultation.

However, no one yet has found any code of international practice or law to prevent the transnational enterprise 'closing down a subsidiary, even a profitable one' – British unions found that pressure through the OECD could not stop a British Caterpillar plant being closed in 1984 – or to create obligations for the liability of a parent in Detroit or Tokyo for the debts of a subsidiary in Liverpool or Johannesburg, a problem that goes to the heart of the question.[158] A subsidiary of the multinational *Firestone*, accused of breaking the OECD Guidelines and a Swiss collective agreement, actually pleaded the orders of its parent company as a defence in the Swiss court, though without success.[159] As Herman concluded, these corporations have 'helped to create enormous wealth' but they have also 'brought forth new problems whose solutions require protective and control mechanisms – private and governmental, local, national, and international – that do not now exist'.[160]

In truth, the internationalized enterprise adds a new dimension to employment and a critical challenge that labour law has hardly begun to confront. But whether the employer is an international company, a subsidiary company, a small or large company or an individual proprietor, a nationalized industry or a local authority, the worker's relationship with 'him' is the primary relationship on which his living depends. For the English lawyer, too, the individual contract of employment is the initial focus of legal analysis. So the stuff of our inquiry must begin there in the next chapter.

[2] The Employment Relationship

For the English lawyer the fundamental institution to which he is forced to return again and again is the individual contract of employment. This makes inevitable a certain unreality, for the common law sees the employment contract, like other contracts, as 'an agreement by which two or more persons agree to regulate their legal relationships recognized and, generally speaking, enforced by the law'.[1] Few individual contracts of employment are arrived at by the bargaining that is implied in such a description. There is rarely a protracted haggle about terms between employer and employee at the factory gate or the office door. The rights of the parties are often laid down by collective negotiations between employers and workers' trade unions, or they may sometimes be imposed by Parliament in statutes and orders. But the legal starting-point is the individual worker's contract – which he invariably has with the employer, though he may often be unaware that it exists. The lawyer's model of a freely bargained individual agreement is misleading. In reality, without collective or statutory intervention, many terms of the 'agreement' are imposed by the more powerful party, the employer, by what Fox has called 'the brute facts of power'. This is one reason for identifying the real social relationship that the law shrouds, in Kahn-Freund's phrase, under the 'indispensable figment' of contract as one involving the subordination of the individual worker; and it helps us to understand why the courts' interpretation of the parties' 'intention' in such an 'agreement' so frequently results in the consolidation of the superior disciplinary powers of the employer.

The individual employment relationship is today modified not only by collective bargaining but also by a complex network of statutory rights for employees, a 'floor of rights' that regulates the obligations of worker and employer even though they are not (for the most part) inserted in formal terms into the employment contract itself. The best known examples of such statutory rights are the worker's right to complain to a tribunal in respect of his unfair dismissal (EPCA 1978 Part V: the common law normally allowed him to challenge only the adequacy of the notice given, not the fairness) and his right to a statutory payment if dismissed by reason of redundancy (EPCA Part VI: the common law knew of no right to such severance payments). These are both discussed in Chapter 3; other parallel enactments appear in Chapters 5 and 6, such as those on equal pay, discrimination or itemized pay statements. As has already been said, the word 'worker' in this book normally means an employee (though we shall see that sometimes 'worker' has its own legal definition). Parliament has granted most of those statutory rights only to 'employees' in a strict sense, i.e. those who work under a contract of employment, that is 'a contract of service or apprenticeship' (express or implied, oral or in writing). We must therefore at once consider the definition of a 'contract of service' by which the law marks off from the so-called 'independent contractor', or self-employed worker or entrepreneur, the *employee* proper.

The worker enters into his employment on the basis of a voluntary agreement. The right of choice whether or not to work for a particular employer is critical. This is, Lord Atkin said in 1940, 'the main difference between a servant and a serf'. There is a difference between a labour market and forced labour, which is why Parliament has forbidden the courts to 'compel an employee to do any work' by way of an order of 'specific performance' or any equivalent injunction (TULRA s. 16). There are some occasions when the worker's contract is automatically transferred by the law to a new employer (for example, on the transfer of an undertaking under the Transfer of Undertakings (Protection of Employment), or 'TUPE', Regulations of 1981: p. 207); but this is done as part of the employment protection provisions. There are also situations – apparently increasing in range – in which the law allows the worker's choice to be very limited, for example when faced with the employer's demand to replace the existing employment contract with different terms in the interests of business 'efficiency' (Chapter 3).

Legal pressure: social security

But the law knows of, and accepts, rather more direct pressures. Let us look at some of them. Social security law, as regards both (contributory) unemployment benefit and supplementary benefit (for which no qualifying number of contribution payments is required), is based upon the principle that 'the unemployment should be involuntary'.[2] So, even if qualified by payment of the necessary national insurance contributions, the worker without a job will be disqualified from receiving unemployment benefit unless he is 'available' for work on the day in question.[3] He must not place restrictions on his availability that preclude all reasonable prospects of his securing work (such as limits on the rates of pay he will accept) except where this arises from age or sex, or from reasonable conditions that relate to his physical or general circumstances, or unless the absence of such prospects arises from 'adverse industrial conditions' (such as short-time working) in the relevant locality. So too, he must be wholly unemployed; where a worker was suspended from his job after a charge of theft but was paid for the day, he was available for alternative full-time employment but not entitled to unemployment benefit, even though he might be required to repay that remuneration if he was convicted (as he was). A 'non-patrial' citizen whose leave to enter the UK in order to marry does not include permission to work is not available for work (Chapter 6).[4] The worker also fails to qualify if he fails without good cause to apply for or accept a 'suitable' job, or to use reasonable opportunities to secure suitable employment (the social security authorities will notify him of such openings).[5] The definition of 'suitable' work begins by excluding vacancies arising due to a 'trade dispute', goes on to exclude work in his usual occupation and in his district on conditions lower than he might reasonably have expected to obtain, and finally excludes work in his usual occupation in another district on conditions less favourable than those recognized by collective bargaining or 'good employers' in that district. But after a reasonable period of time, employment ceases to be 'unsuitable' merely because it is not in his usual employment or because the conditions are less favourable than those levels. Where a man unemployed for three months refused to take a job in a different trade at the normal rate because he was receiving more by way of social security payments and milk tokens than he would earn as his net weekly income in the job, the Social Security Commissioners disqualified him because this was not 'good cause' for the refusal. And a man who went for his interview for a job in a dirty and unshaven state was held to have neglected to avail himself of a reasonable opportunity of securing suitable employment, which left him similarly disqualified.[6]

Parallel principles apply to supplementary benefit, the means-tested 'safety net' of the social security system (though not to certain payments that can be made for urgent need). Where a claimant under sixty years of age either has been or would be disqualified from unemployment benefit as not 'available' for work, the supplementary benefit will be severely reduced. The reduction is 40 per cent unless a member of the claimant's household 'unit' is pregnant or seriously ill and the claimant does not have capital of more than £100 (in which case the reduction is 20 per cent).[7] The seriousness of these reductions can be gauged from the fact that basic scale rates of supplementary benefit in 1985–6 were £29.50, or £47.85 for a married couple (unemployment benefit was £30.45, or £49.25 for a married couple). The difficulties of interpretation in the regulations had been compounded by two different channels of decision for the two benefits until 1983 when these were merged into one channel of adjudication officers with a Social Security Appeal Tribunal (with appeals to the Commissioners and to the Court of Appeal).[8] The maze of complexity is still growing, however, partly by reason of the impact of EEC law, which attempts to secure equal treatment for workers from one member State residing in another.[9] The Social Security Commissioners have so far interpreted EEC law in a manner that permits disqualification in Britain for voluntary unemployment and for a failure to comply with conditions for residence in Britain through which the claimant becomes unavailable for employment.[10] Since 1982 registration at a Jobcentre is no longer required of a claimant. But he is treated as unavailable for work for purposes of supplementary benefit if he refuses suitable employment without good cause; or if he fails to report for an interview as required after notification; or if he lives in an area where there is a reasonable opportunity of securing short-term work that he has failed to take up; and if he is aged between 18 and 45 and not living with a woman who is over 45 or pregnant, and the social security officer thinks it 'not inappropriate' to withdraw benefit.[11] Further disqualifications are applied to other groups including students.

These regulations represent an attempt to penalize 'work-shy' claimants who fail to take what they see as poorly paid jobs with little future, at least in areas where the MSC takes the view that such work is available. Except in cases of failure to report, the maximum period for withdrawal of benefit is six weeks (to become 13 in 1986). But supplementary benefit can be wholly withheld if a person not receiving unemployment benefit 'appears' to be refusing or neglecting to maintain himself or his family, is directed to attend a course at a Re-establishment Centre and fails or refuses to do so. Beyond that, if a person persistently refuses or neglects to maintain himself or herself, their spouse or children under sixteen, he or she commits a criminal offence.[12]

A further pressure upon young people was introduced in 1985 by regulations that, in addition to reducing supplementary benefit payable to those under 25 in respect of rent and meals, further reduced benefit payable to those between 16 and 25 who were in board and lodgings by insisting upon their moving regularly. There had been complaints that some young people were 'Costa del Dole scroungers'. Penal cuts in benefit were exacted if they failed to move on every few weeks. Once they had left an area, it was forbidden to return to it for at least six weeks. Reports spoke of great hardship and even of one suicide. Some months after their introduction, Mann J. decided that parts of the regulations were *ultra vires* and invalid.[13] Later, the Court of Appeal agreed. The regulations affected some 85,000 people.

In the face of such social security provisions it is hardly possible now to maintain that the only direct pressures on a worker to enter into an employment contract are economic. Alongside State social security provisions stand various others, including the openings for, and pressures upon, the young worker in training schemes (Chapter 6). The worker's choice is still formally free; but the law can require him to exercise it on pain of severe disabilities.

The employee

The contract of employment (or of 'service' as it is still called: EPCA 1978 s. 153) is distinguished from a contract in which the employer has work done by an 'independent', or self-employed, contractor. The distinction is important both for the common law and for many statutes. The 'master', to use the old language, has long been 'vicariously' liable for the tort of his 'servant', in addition to any liability of the servant, if the latter has committed the tort in the course of the employment (e.g. a driver who knocks someone down driving the van on his delivery round). The employer also owes to his employee a duty to provide a reasonably safe system of work. The statutory rights in respect of unfair dismissal and redundancy payments are granted only to 'employees' (EPCA ss. 54, 81: pp. 217, 258), whereas other statutory rights extend to those under both a contract of service and a contract 'personally to execute any work or labour' which includes the self-employed (as in sex discrimination: SDA 1975 ss. 6, 82). The employee has national insurance contributions and income tax under PAYE deducted by the employer from his wage at source. The self-employed worker will not normally suffer such deductions and will obtain more generous allowances for tax purposes. The forms of employment relationship today are not confined to such categories; but this remains the dichotomy fundamental to English law.

How then do we recognize an 'employee'? In 1910 one judge confessed his 'inability to lay down any complete or satisfactory definition of the term "contract of service"', but he recognized the obvious difference between an employed music teacher, e.g. in a school, and 'a skilled music master' giving tuition. This was the image that had come down to the judges from the earlier common law understanding of a 'servant', when the 'agreement' with the master was indeed even more a myth than it is today, but the nature of the *service* required was very real. The master once had property rights in the service – his *servitium* – a concept 'from the days of serfdom and villeinage [which] lingered on', as Lord Goddard once put it, until its extinction by statute as late as 1982. Under various Master and Servant Acts the servant was liable to criminal sanctions, even imprisonment, for leaving work until 1875. It is not the case, as is sometimes suggested, that the common law experienced difficulty with the definition merely because the servant came to have skills that the master did not have. Servants have often been more skilled than their masters. The music teacher was more proficient in his art than the employing school board; skilled crane and train drivers were held a century ago to be servants of incorporated companies, and a ship's captain was treated as a servant in the eighteenth century.[14] The judges carried over the earlier concept of service, built from the fourteenth century upon the status and legal imagery of a pre-industrial society with agricultural and domestic labourers featuring prominently, and they used it to fill 'the empty boxes of the contract clauses', in Fox's phrase, giving to the master powers to demand obedience that derive from the earlier relationships.[15] They could recognize, Davies and Freedland say, the distinction between 'subordinated service and autonomous independent contracting as necessary and stable features of the social structure'.[16]

An unexpected flavour of those earlier eras may be found today in some decisions. In 1981 the question arose whether an architect was an 'employee' for social security purposes. He worked for a housing association alongside architects who were employees; but he did not keep office hours, received no holiday pay and was treated for tax, V A T and insurance contributions as self-employed. Moreover, he was found not to satisfy the 'principal obligation' of an employee, namely 'to serve'. He provided his 'services' without any obligation to present himself, the court noted, for service at the association's premises at any time.[17] There is an echo of the old obligation of the servant to accept employment and present himself for work.[18]

Among the 'tests' that crystallized out for identification of the 'servant' one stood out, namely the right of the master to *control* the servant not only in what he did but also, as it was put in 1880, 'as to the manner in which he shall do his work'. This did not mean that the master could in fact always control it; it meant he had the *right* to say how it should be done. The uncertainty of such a test inevitably begat others. They included the master's power of dismissal, the right of selection of the worker and of tasks to be done, the method of payment and, in modern times, the practice as to tax and social security deductions. In 1924 one judge said the test, 'if there be a final test . . . lies in the nature and degree of detailed control over the [servant]'. But during the last fifty years all the tests have often failed the courts, not – or not only – because the employee cannot be 'controlled' in his art or technology by the 'employer' (as with a surgeon or even a music teacher) – for that was true of skilled workers a century ago. Somervell LJ said in 1951 of a surgeon's negligence that the employer's 'vicarious' liability for the torts of the employee 'is not ousted by the fact that the "servant" has to do work of a more skilful or technical character for which the servant has special qualifications'. Such an employee is hired precisely because of his special skill. The reasons for the new crisis in legal concepts lie elsewhere, namely in the upheavals that social and economic change has brought to the labour market, fragmenting those who sell their labour power into new groupings with which the law is ill-equipped to deal. The judges still have the 'control' test to use, as with the weight-watchers' lecturer in 1984 whose work was closely controlled by the employer's handbook – 'tied hand and foot', he was said to be – and who was held to be an 'employee' despite a clause in his contract saying that he was *not*. An engineer, *Morren*, was also held to be the employee of a council that paid him and could dismiss him, even though the manner of his work on the job was controlled by a consultant.[19] It is to be noticed in all such cases that the junior employee becomes the 'servant' of the employer (of the council, for example), not of the superior 'servants' of that body.

Lord Denning promoted a rather different test in 1952:

[Under] a contract of service a man is employed as part of the business and his work is done as an integral part of the business; whereas under a contract for services his work, although done for the business, is not integrated into it but is only accessory to it.

This 'organization' test can be valuable. It emphasizes the economist's distinction between one who sells his labour power to the enterprise of another and one who operates his own enterprise. Then judges began to ask related but different questions, like was the worker his own boss? These tests are to some extent circular; the worker is not his own boss if he is an employee. But on such grounds a bar steward of a football supporters' club, hired 'on a self-employed basis', was held to be an employee (with the right to complain of unfair dismissal). So too, for social security purposes, an interviewer engaged from time to time by *Market Investigations*, a research company, working when and how she chose, to a pattern set by the company but without sick-pay, holiday entitlement or any prohibitions on working for others, was held to be in 'insurable employment' as an employee, the judge deciding she was not 'in business on her own account' (she provided no tools, risked no capital) but was employed under a series of contracts of service.[20] This type of analysis can be of particular importance to part-time or casual workers.

The use of the 'own-boss' test, however, has produced little greater certainty or rationality than the others. In the *Ready Mixed Concrete* case,[21] L. was engaged to drive a lorry with a rotating drum of concrete for delivery to the company's customers. The company drew up a complicated contract, which declared him to be an 'independent contractor'; but the judge refused to accept this alone as determinative of his status for social security purposes. The company had brought in a scheme of owner-drivers by such contracts with drivers. L. contracted with it to deliver concrete for payment on a mileage basis and, with an associated company, to take the lorry on hire purchase. He wore a uniform and agreed to drive for certain hours according to orders 'as if' he was an employee and to maintain the lorry himself. The court accepted there was a great deal of 'control' – indeed, to the world he must have had the look of subordination – but this was not sufficient if the other provisions of the contract pointed away from 'service'. In a judgment that has been relied upon frequently, the court found that L. was not an employee but a 'small businessman' who 'owned the instrumentalities' of his business (though one might have thought that the 'ownership' was a device arranged by his employing company's group).

The policy element in such judgments was made even clearer in *Young and Woods Ltd* v. *West*.[22] West, a skilled metalworker, chose when hired by the company to be a 'self-employed' worker, not an 'employee', in the factory. He was treated accordingly for the purpose of tax, national insurance, sick-pay and holiday pay. He saved some £500 a year in tax by reason of the arrangement. Four years later he was dismissed. He claimed unfair dismissal as an 'employee'. But the company vigorously replied that everyone knew that if work became short the self-employed were the first to go; and he had chosen that bed to lie upon. The Court of Appeal decided that he was an employee. He was not 'a person in business on his own account'. True, there were 'pointers in both directions'; but in reality his service was the same employment as others who worked the same hours on the same materials at the same hourly rate alongside him. In this area the reasoning evinces a desire by the judges to accept the industrial tribunal's interpretation of the facts (though the nature of the contract is ultimately a question of law). But there is an obvious objection to accepting such a worker as an 'employee': surely it is against public policy to allow him to 'wear two hats' – a self-employed hat for taxation and an employed hat for unfair dismissal. Ackner LJ answered this by remarking that the Inland Revenue might well 'take the appropriate recovery action' for the tax advantages he had improperly gained, making the unfair dismissal case 'a hollow, indeed an expensive, victory'. Whatever the tax consequences, the court clearly disliked the prospect of workers at a factory workbench being self-employed and, for short-term advantage, contracting with their employers out of the employment protection legislation (an unusually forceful application of public policy by judges so often given to preference for 'individual' choice).

The company raised another point. If a contract of employment is consensual, then where the parties expressly categorize it as 'self-employment' this must surely determine the issues, at any rate where there are pointers both ways. In many recent cases, however, judges have refused to accept the 'label' tied to the contract by the parties. In *Ready Mixed Concrete*, the judge said that if the relationship is really 'master and servant, it is irrelevant that the parties have declared it to be something else'. The label is only 'a factor', 'a guide', no more. A previous Court of Appeal decision holding a manager to his self-employed status partly rested on the description in the contract because this was a genuine arrangement for the man to run his own business. But Lord Denning M R had said an arrangement 'to put forward a dishonest description of their relationship so as to deceive the Revenue would clearly be illegal'. In 1970 Fisher J. had also classified workers as self-employed because, if they had been employees, the tax and insurance arrangements would have been illegal. In *West's* case, however, the court preferred to enforce the 'true nature' of the contract, even though it allowed the worker to 'eat his cake and still keep it'. To do otherwise would be

in effect to allow the parties to contract out of the Act and to deprive [a worker] . . . who works as an employee . . . under a contract of service of the benefits which this contract confers.

Even so, where each party knows that the 'label' is accepted by the other and by the Inland Revenue but that it is false, that is 'a deliberate fraud on the Revenue' which neither should be allowed to rely upon. That is an illegal contract.[23] This conclusion, though, apparently depends upon both parties possessing the necessary knowledge and intention. A contract lawful on its face but illegally performed can still be valid and enforced (as where a worker does not know of tax evasion practices or where he innocently sprays illegal chemicals for his employer on a crop). On the other hand, a worker who took a job finding punters for a casino and prostitutes for the punters had no valid contract on which to sue for unfair dismissal (though a contract to find punters would remain lawful if all he did was procure prostitutes on the side). The *West* decision appears to rest upon the intention of the company throughout to deal with this contract in all respects as a 'self-employed' arrangement. Where a lawful contract becomes unlawful for a period (e.g. through a short-term 'fiddle' by lodging allowance) the courts have been strict in deciding that no contract exists during that period so that continuity of employment is broken.[24]

At this point we can see that the semantic tests are less important than the social policy pursued by the court in respect of each issue: qualification for unfair dismissal, category for national insurance purposes, vicarious liability of the employer and so on. So when we find courts accepting as self-employed a chief oboist, or four sessional 'associate' musicians, or a trumpeter and a violinist (who played irregularly with an orchestra), or a music-hall artiste engaged under a weekly contract, we may note that all of these decisions were social security cases; whereas decisions that accepted as 'employees' a television company's researcher and a 'sales representative', even though both bore the label 'self-employed', concerned the employment protection legislation.[25] This distinction, however, is no more than a rough guide to judicial inclination. The legal 'tests' have splintered in the hands of the judges, leaving them to say in the case of a Methodist minister that tax arrangements are no guide (they are 'based on convenience and compromise') that it is 'not practicable to lay down precise tests' or a 'hard and fast list', that there are 'too many variants'; so 'you look at the whole of the picture'.[26] Most courts now appear to use this 'elephant-test' for the employee – an animal too difficult to define but easy to recognize when you see it.

Even within employment protection law, decisions for different purposes are hard to predict. There is a further reason for all this, not of a legal nature. The variety of work patterns in the labour market has recently increased dramatically. This is the social reason for the legal crisis. The number of self-employed workers rose by more than one million in the ten years before 1985, now making up 10 per cent of the entire work-force (2.5 million). Of these, a growing number are women, and many are in small firms employing 200 or less employees, which now account for 25 per cent of the work-force[27] (the legal provisions define 'small firms' differently in several labour law areas: sex discrimination, maternity leave, health and safety, workplace ballots; these might at least be rationalized).[28] Further, the patterns of full-time employment have begun to change (more flexible working hours; earlier retirement) and, more important, to crumble in the face of a cornucopia of alternative relationships: part-time, casual, temporary, freelance, 'off-site labour', outworkers, homeworkers, 'living-in jobs', labour-only contracts, trainees, 'distance employment', telecommuting' and other arrangements. The number of part-time workers has also risen rapidly to 4.5 million, some 85 per cent of them women. The great majority of new jobs created recently are self-employed or part-time. In 1981–4 manufacturing, construction and production industries lost 2.5 million jobs; services gained 0.5 million. Full-time male employment continued to decline in 1984 (by 60,000); women in employment increased by 14,000 full-time but 187,000 part-time. In 1985 'executive leasing' (hiring senior managers for a task or assignment) was on the increase. Overall unemployment crept upwards to 3 million and beyond (the unions claimed 4 million at least in reality on the pre-1982 method of calculation).

The law has been left behind. The legal status of many of the workers in so-called atypical employment is often uncertain.[29] For example, Hakim says of outworkers and homeworkers, 'there is a widespread view among employers in the manufacturing sector that outworkers are customarily self-employed'.[30] As we shall see, the courts show signs of resisting such an automatic conclusion, which would leave unprotected a very vulnerable group of workers. This is a problem too long neglected. In 1973 the ILO noted 'the growing proportion of workers falling outside the scope of labour and social legislation and collective agreements intended to protect all workers', a phenomenon with grave dangers for the exercise of 'trade union rights'.[31] In 1985 Nabisco agreed not to make compulsory redundancies during a three-year agreement, and the union (GMBAT) agreed that the company could take on up to 30 per cent of the work-force as temporary or part-time, with increased use of subcontractors and elimination of traditional work boundaries.[32] Some 40 per cent of employers increased their use of temporary workers in 1980–5. In a weak labour market, full-time workers may perceive such casual or part-time workers as a growing threat. In 1985 a major strike was threatened when the Post Office aimed to recruit up to 20,000 part-time workers, instead of the 8,500 previously agreed with the unions on introducing new technology and more 'flexible' work patterns (the union, though, eventually agreed). In 1986 BP Shipping decided to replace the entire crews of its tankers with labour supplied by agencies.

Skilled part-time workers have been threatened by replacement with lower-paid, unskilled workers, especially in public and private services and in manufacturing.

We saw in Chapter 1 (p. 11) that some observers detect 'segmentation' of the labour market generally and of enterprises in particular, with a full-time core of employees surrounded by rings of part-time, casual and temporary workers reaching out to the periphery (homeworkers, subcontractors and the like). Employers – if they plan the change, and not all have done so – save in costs and 'flexibility of working practices' (which are buzz-words normally masking an increase in management prerogative). The 'high discretion' tasks are now clustered near the core, some of the workers in the inner rings (usually part-time or short-term) being a pool on trial, as it were, on which to draw if more full-time work is available.[33] In 1985 the EEF director-general suggested, for example, a four-level labour force, made up of contracting-out; temporary operatives (when needed); easily acquired staff (on standard terms); and key permanent workers (on superior terms). With those on the periphery the employer will often have a relationship defined not by employment but by commercial contracts, as with subcontracting. The question arises, however, whether some at least of the exterior or temporary workers should not have an entitlement to enter the 'employment' category or at least acquire priority rights to full-time work when it is available, and if they do whether there should be some control of the terms, e.g. to enable them to enter the core on fair terms. This would require an intervention in hiring, as opposed to firing, which our labour law has always been reluctant to make, save for such exceptional cases as racial and sex discrimination. As for collective bargaining, union membership among peripheral workers is usually low; and, in realistic terms, in times of high unemployment we may expect to find that the core workers are represented by a union that does not necessarily see its primary duty to be protection of the marginal groups. Indeed, in 1985 some reports described an invasion of the core jobs by temporary employees hired from agencies which provided one million workers a year.[34]

There remain of course millions of workers in full-time jobs whose legal status as 'employees' is clear. And there are other definitions used for various legal purposes that constitute an experience on which Parliament can draw, a variety of definitions each tailored to the purpose in hand. An Act of 1867 on 'workshops' sought to introduce protection for women and children in 'handicraft' (largely manual labour). As originally enacted this applied to 'home-workers but not out-workers'.[35] Later Factories Acts extended the catchment area; they also required local authority councils to draw up lists of outworkers in certain trades (on which the basic Order of 1911 still remains on the statute book). Some Acts adopt, as that one did, narrow definitions; the term 'workmen' under the Employers and Workmen Act 1875, which was used for other Acts, like the Truck Acts 1831–1940 that regulated payment of wages (Chapter 5), included only those 'engaged in *manual* labour' (other than domestic servants) but it extended also to contracts 'personally to execute any work or labour' (i.e. independent contractors). The definition of 'worker' in TULRA 1974, which is an important category for the law on trade disputes, includes those under a contract of employment or a contract 'to perform personally any work or services' (other than for 'a professional client'), plus government employment (except the armed services) and National Health Service employees; but not the police (s. 30 (1), (2)). Here the self-employed stand equally with employees proper. A similar definition is used for Wages Councils (Wages Councils Act 1979 s. 28; with the addition of 'homeworkers'). The Industrial Training Act 1982 extends to contracts of service and of apprenticeship, to contracts 'for services' and even to *de facto* employment 'otherwise than under a contract' (s. 1 (2)). Few statutes are like the Shop Clubs Act 1902, with no definition at all of workers covered.

The courts have sometimes been quick to place particular relationships outside the range of almost all the known definitions. In 1980, for instance, the Court of Appeal held that a police cadet does not have a contract either of service or of apprenticeship. It held that this contract was one 'to teach and learn', but not to learn a 'trade' like apprentices. They are, said Lord Denning, 'in a class by themselves – police cadets'.[36] So too, a young worker on the Work Experience Programme (Chapter 6) was in 1982 denied a right to sue for unfair dismissal. He was not an 'employee', but engaged 'to train in farming practices and . . . gain working experience'. By 1983, as Government training or work experience programmes sought to offer something to young workers for whom there was no job, the legal position of trainees had become alarming. A young worker on the Youth Opportunities Programme was not

protected even by the Race Relations Act 1976, despite its formula
that covers workers who have contracts of service, or even of *apprenticeship*, or 'personally to execute any work' (RRA s. 78). Yet trainees do
work and they are supposed to be instructed (Parliament should
obviously have given them modified apprentice status). But the court
held there was no contract at all between this trainee and the company
'sponsoring' her learning period (or, if there was, it was analogous to
that of a police cadet), nor was there a contract between her and the
MSC.[37]

The trainee therefore may be in a worse position than a person
helping in a family business (such a worker has been held to have a
'contract personally to execute work'). As we shall see, Parliament
intervened in respect of some of the disadvantages for those on the
Youth Training Scheme; and in 1983 regulations provided some protection against safety and health hazards for YTS trainees (p. 807). When
the conceptual problems seem too heavy to bear, judges tend to take
refuge in denial that there is any contract at all, as they did in the case of
the Methodist minister.[26] Moreover, even if young workers on training
schemes do have contracts with anyone, they are not necessarily contracts of employment, though it is open to the 'employer' to accept a
trainee as his 'employee' *if* he wishes – a point that exposes the social
reality of the arrangement. In the absence of special legislation or
regulations, they lose most of the protections afforded by the law on
employment protection. It has been a struggle even to establish that the
'employer' owes basic statutory duties on safety at work, as when two
boys were left to clean dangerous machinery without proper protective
clothing or instruction in safety procedures (one died of his burns; the
Scottish courts finally made the 'employer' criminally liable).[38] That the
young 'trainee' should have been left with such precarious protection is
remarkable, especially when the 'training' schemes were organized by
public bodies (now the MSC) and when our law provided the apprentice
with more (Chapter 6). Davies and Freedland comment:

The whole development provides a very vivid illustration of the way in which
measures concerned with regulation of labour supply and demand can impinge
upon the more traditional concerns of labour law.[39]

Indeed, some have doubted the very character of the contract of
employment as a suitable basis for labour law.[40]

'Temps', casuals, homework and self-employment

We have seen that in legal terms the 'employee' and the 'self-employee' are two distinct circles intersecting the rings of full-time, part-time, casual, temporary and similar workers who in reality make up the labour market. The 'temporary' worker has long been a problem, especially if provided to the 'user' by an employment agency. It is often, as Hepple and Napier said in 1978,

a matter for speculation whether temporary workers – who in other respects may appear to be 'employees' – are engaged under contracts of employment with either the employment business or the user.[41]

Since then it has become less likely that temporary workers will be the employees of the agency business. In *Wickens's* case they were not, even though the contract described them as having a 'contract of service' and required them to obey 'all reasonable rules' of the agency.[42] The Conduct of Employment Agencies Regulations 1976 (No. 715) were meant to make the worker normally the servant of the agency unless it notified the 'hirer' to the contrary. Moreover, they required the agency to give the worker a written statement with details of the employment, stating whether the contract is one of service (on pain of loss of the agency licence: Employment Agencies Act 1973 s. 2). This had been done in *Wickens*. Despite this, the E A T upheld a tribunal decision that the temporary workers were self-employed. They registered with many agencies if they chose; they had no right to a 'booking' and no duty to accept one. Relying on *Ready Mixed Concrete* the E A T found this contract to be 'inconsistent with the normal features' of, and lacking 'the continuity and care of, the employer for the employee' which is associated with a contract of service. It did not matter that they ran no separate business of their own; otherwise, a casual worker would always be an employee: 'that plainly cannot be the law'. (It might be better law than this precedent.) Leighton suggests that this decision runs counter even to the trends in agency practice, which evince increasing control over the work of the temporary worker.

The agencies appear unlikely to assume many of the burdens of employment protection laws even if the temporaries become their employees. (The workers would often, for example, not acquire the two years' continuous service needed for unfair dismissal rights, or even four weeks for minimum notice rights; and they might not work, or have a contract for, the 16 hours weekly – or 8 hours weekly over five years – normally needed to build the necessary continuity periods for such qualifications: p. 199.)[43] This failure of policy by the courts is made worse by the fact that since 1979 regulations have exempted the employment 'agency' and 'business' (strictly, the latter supplies services of its 'employees'; the former, workers for jobs with the hirer) from the 1973 Act, under which it is a crime not to observe the regulations (these are supplemented by a responsible code produced voluntarily by the agencies' federation). The regulations of 1976, for example, prohibit employment businesses to charge workers fees (with some exceptions such as au pair workers) or to supply replacements in a strike. Public policy once aimed to incorporate the temporary worker into the legal structures by strengthening the bond with the supplying body – the relationship with the user is weak and obscure – requiring in 1975, for example, that the supplier pay social security contributions as for an employee. Recently, though, there has been greater Government support for deregulation, and for self-employment generally, such as relief on job-related accommodation in the Finance Act 1984.

In many industries self-employment is not new. In the 1960s there was already evidence from the Inland Revenue Staff Federation (the tax officers' union) of self-employed barbers who 'rented' their chairs, waiters who 'rented' tables, commercial travellers and office staff with the same status. Then there is the long established practice of 'contract draughtsmen', strongly opposed for decades by the union (TASS). A case in 1967 disclosed the widespread practice of big firms in the electronics industry hiring gangs of 'freelance' skilled labour (though *some* gangs were held by the court to be employees). The army of the self-employed has recently advanced each year with greater rapidity (it increased by 400,000 in 1982–5). One industry that has had long experience is construction, especially in the form of 'labour-only sub-contracting' (or 'the lump') whereby groups of workers either supply themselves, or are supplied through an intermediary supplier, to the 'employer' working the site. They rarely become his employees. They may themselves be a 'partnership'. Sometimes they take on specific tasks as a gang, the gang leader being given a lump sum for distribution. As 'independent contractors', no deductions for PAYE tax or for social security contributions would be made from their pay; on the other hand, the 'employers' avoid statutory obligations owed to employees under many safety laws and much of the employment protection legislation. There have been reports of workers being made bankrupt when the time came to pay their income tax. Others are injured on the job but may not fall within protections provided for employed workers, thereby losing the right to claim damages. Whether they become the 'employees' of the intermediary supplier is a more difficult question. In 1970 the High Court ruled that workmen paid a flat rate by *Labour Force Ltd*, and sent to work for contractors who paid a higher sum to it, the workers being responsible for their own income tax and national insurance contributions, were not the employees of Labour Force. Cooke J. analysed the 'intention' of the parties as his guide; and Fisher J. stressed that the tax arrangements would be illegal if they were employees.[44] The *Wickens* case does not encourage confidence in predicting any different result today.

Labour Force was a case on assessment to a levy for the industry's training board, payable only on 'employees'. The importance of the context of the decision is once again made apparent by *Ferguson* v. *Dawson Ltd*, 1976,[45] where the Court of Appeal held that a building firm was liable under Construction Regulations of 1966 to a scaffolder who fell off a roof where there was no guard-rail, as a worker 'employed' by the firm. The worker (who had 'come along' with four workers, and been taken on) enjoyed the tax advantages of self-employed status. He had given a false name; both sides took the view that he was self-employed. Lawton L J, who dissented, protested that these workers had made themselves self-employed – with the 'advantages which attract many men who work "on the lump"' – and self-employed, not 'employed', they should remain. The majority judges refused to accept 'the label' of the parties, for 'in reality' this was a contract of service. It is noteworthy, though, that it was the employer there who insisted that there were no cards and that they were working purely 'as a lump labour force'.

Ferguson was a decision under statutory safety provisions. Each set of regulations must be interpreted for its proper meaning and scope. At common law, the employer seems to owe a lesser duty to the self-employed than to his own employees in respect of a 'safe system of work'. A timberman in 1967 failed in his action against his 'employer' after being injured by a tree felled by unsupervised methods, because he was self-employed on a daily basis; had he been an employee he might have won. Such cases suggest that the concept of 'employee' might well be abandoned in favour of an enactment to apply the core provisions on safety protecting workers to all those in a position of subordination by provision of their labour power, whether or not they are within the old definition of employee.

Some statutory provisions do, of course, go wider. The legislation against racial and sex discrimination covers those who work under a contract to perform personal work *or* labour (wider than 'employees'; RRA s. 78, SDA s. 82: p. 460). It went further by making it unlawful for an employment agency to discriminate in the terms that it offers, and it included in such agencies a person who provides services 'for the purposes of finding employment for workers or supplying employers with workers' (SDA s. 15, RRA s. 14). Moreover, it banned discrimination by a 'principal' for whom a 'contract worker' did work although employed by another person (SDA s. 9, RRA s. 7). This would seem to be enough to oust discrimination from labour-supply practices. Yet an extraordinary decision of 1980 makes this doubtful.[46] Owner-drivers of taxis paid a firm weekly sums for a telephone link with its office. The firm contacted drivers to notify them of customers. A driver had permission to employ a relief one day; but when the firm discovered she was a woman they refused to operate the system with her. The EAT held there was no unlawful discrimination. There was no contractual link between the firm and the driver obliging him to supply a relief; so s. 9 did not apply, especially as she did the work 'for' him, not for the firm. And the firm did not fall within the 'agency' provisions at all. Yet can it be doubted that Parliament intended that this curious pattern of work relationships should be covered by prohibitions on discrimination?

A committee chaired by Professor Phelps-Brown reported on the construction industry's problems in 1968. It found many deficiencies in the employment structures, in communications, in methods of wage payment, welfare, management training, facilities and the like; but 'self-employment' posed the greatest difficulty. It proposed that 'genuine' self-employment (such as the long tradition for independent roofers) should be accommodated by a statutory register for those 'genuinely' in business on their own account, with a legal presumption that those who paid for construction work by unregistered persons should be deemed to be their employers, and with an extension of liability to workers injured in accidents. Of the 1.9 million workers in the industry, self-employed workers had reached a total of 147,000, with another 200,000 working under 'labour-only' contracts (of whom some were employees of the suppliers) and 100,000 more supplied by intermediary agencies. These numbers were increasing, and the Inland Revenue estimated that up to £3 million was being lost annually in taxes. In 1984 the TUC estimated that self-employment in the industry 'could be as high as 600,000'; and this was in a work-force that with the recession had shrunk to less than one million. The Finance Act 1971 attempted to control evasions of social security contributions and income tax and, as amended by subsequent Finance Acts, the scheme makes payments by contractors to subcontractors subject to deduction of tax unless the subcontractor has a certificate from the Revenue. He can obtain this only if he has a genuine business, with adequate insurance and a good tax record. The purpose of the scheme has become increasingly fiscal as relaxations have been introduced, such as that in the Finance Act 1980 (Sched. 8, on 'contractors'). It would perhaps be illogical for the new policies of 'deregulation' to take a stricter view. The Secretary of State, Mr Tebbit, told an MP in 1982 that he might not 'like the lump, but, properly managed, it is a very effective institution'. Indeed, in 1986 the House of Commons gave a second reading to a Bill to encourage self-employment, its sponsor calling the certification control of the lump 'thoroughly wicked'.

It is instructive to find in a Government survey of small firms in 1985 that the industrial group which complained almost twice as much as any other about the employed and self-employed distinctions in tax treatment was construction. What were once known as the building industry's 'Bedouin workers' have not ceased to wander looking for work where it can be found. But trade unions have not accepted 'the lump'. The continuing struggle against it featured in major judicial decisions on strike law (p. 587) and reached a peak as one of the issues in national action in 1972. But in the building slump of recent years little more than a defensive attitude has been apparent.[47]

Many workers who are, or think they are, self-employed work as casual or 'temporary' workers. A recent survey of twenty-five small firms found that six of them 'mis-labelled' their workers (usually employees were treated as self-employed). Another survey discovered 'massive uncertainty' about status among casual workers who worked at home.[48] The essential characteristic to the parties in these relationships is the temporary or short-term nature. But the law must distinguish the employees from the self-employed. The employees will, of course, be treated as such for tax, social security and employment protection purposes; but they must qualify for many employment benefits with the necessary service (e.g. from June 1985 two years for unfair dismissal for new employees). Moreover, if the worker has been an employee, a change in his status (on a transfer of the business, for example) to one of self-employment is a dismissal, though not necessarily an unfair one.[49] Casual workers are typically provided with work in some sectors by agencies. The possible pattern of their legal status then ranges from a series of indefinite employment contracts, to separate fixed-term employment contracts, or to self-employment contracts for services, or even to no contract at all. Sometimes the worker will find special rules applying to him (for example, the 'seasonal worker', who claims social security benefit in his 'off-season', as in agriculture, tourism or school meals work, must satisfy particular conditions concerning his employment record in that period).[50]

Meanwhile the courts flounder. In 1983 McNeill J. was faced with the question for social security purposes whether two musicians and a comedian were employees of a holiday camp that engaged them for a summer season. They were engaged as a 'drummer/sports organizer', a 'comedian/assistant entertainments/public relations' (he employed his own accountant) and an 'organist/entertainer'. Each was paid weekly and responsible for his own tax and insurance contributions; the band brought its own equipment; it decided the content of performances; but all had full board. The contracts prevented employment elsewhere for the season and gave the camp an option to extend. The judge agreed with the Secretary of State that these were 'employed earners'. He could not find any conclusive factor: neither the 'control' test, nor the label (especially, he thought – significantly – where 'the community has an interest, as here, in the collection of contributions for social security purposes'). Some clauses pointed one way; some the other; 'and some are neutral'. All he could do was look at all the facts 'in the aggregate'. It was the elephant test again.

This judgment introduces a further complication. McNeill J.

addressed the 'facts', but only in order to decide whether the Secretary of State was wrong in law. Similarly, where an appellate court is considering an appeal from an industrial tribunal, as the Court of Appeal did in *O'Kelly* v. *Trusthouse Forte p.l.c.*,[51] it is bound by the facts and can interfere only in case of an error or misdirection as to the law. This permits judges more easily to accept a decision that on its facts could be correct under a variety of legal definitions, without making clear their own view of the law. A hotel kept a list of casual staff for catering, 'regulars' who could be relied upon to offer their services as they were needed and were therefore given preference. O'Kelly and two others, the applicants, had no other jobs; they complained of unfair dismissal when the hotel told them they were unlikely to be needed again. The tribunal (by a majority) said they were not, the EAT said they were, employees. The Court of Appeal restored the tribunal decision. The decision of Ackner LJ is clear: the issue of employee status is one of law; the tribunal had not misdirected itself (though a new point had arisen as to whether a series of individual contracts of service existed that the EAT should have sent back to the tribunal). His approach does not solve the problem of definition; but it does maintain some appellate control in the interests of uniformity of meaning.

By contrast, the judgments of Donaldson MR and Fox LJ open new doors to the winds of uncertainty. They insisted upon 'loyally' accepting the facts found by the tribunal, which it is entitled to assess 'qualitatively'; no question of 'pure' law had arisen; the tribunal's conclusion that the applicants were 'in business on their own account as independent contractors' could not stand with the view that there was a series of individual contracts of service. Above all there was 'no mutuality of obligation', and 'in the industry' they were 'not regarded' as working under an employment contract. This insistence upon the tribunal's superiority masks the fact that it had applied the 'own-boss' test in the face of facts that almost defy its use. The hotel provided uniforms and equipment. There was no multiple employment, no profit sharing. The only 'capital' in the waiters' 'business' appeared to be their persons, their labour power. Would they not have a justified complaint if a lawyer told them over the soup about the *Market Investigations* decision (p. 113)? Even if they are employees, the rules about qualifying periods and normal hours place difficulties in the way of such casual or short-term workers' benefiting from employment protection legislation.[52] The majority's support for the tribunal's findings in *O'Kelly* about 'mutuality of obligation' makes their position worse. As for the practice of 'the industry', that is no safe legal guide; it is merely another 'label' – and where bargaining and union membership, as here, are weak, this practice will be written in the characters of the employer's hand. The severance of the work relationship into separate contracts has been imaginatively used by other judges (e.g. by Pain J.: p. 337), and it is a pity that the majority judges in *O'Kelly* gave so little encouragement to it here.

In all this, British law stands below the standards that would be required by a draft EEC Directive ('Temporary Work and Fixed-Term Contracts').[53] Under that, any short-term worker hired from an employment business or agency would receive protection; the hiring of temporary workers would be generally restricted to cases where there is a temporary reduction in the work-force or a 'temporary or exceptional increase in activity'; protection would extend to social security and working conditions. Member States could set aside the limitations in the Directive for labour supply contracts where the 'social benefits' for temporary workers were equivalent to those for permanent workers. There is also an EEC draft Directive on 'Voluntary Part-Time Work', which bridges the issues of employment status and sex discrimination (in all the member States the greater majority of such workers are women).[54] It aims to extend employment protection rights to such workers, improve their social security rights, include them with employees in schemes for informing or consulting workers (an issue that touches upon the question of trade union membership), and give them some priority over outside candidates for full-time jobs.

One of the many questions that would arise, though, if these Directives became law is how easily the structures of British law would allow for their translation and enforcement. A fundamental problem, for example, would be the definition of 'supply of temporary workers', for the Temporary Work draft Directive defines this by reference to 'a temporary employment contract with workers' made by the business 'in the capacity of employer', placing them temporarily 'at the disposal of a user' (Art. 1). As *Wickens's* case shows, there may be no such employment contract with the supplier in Britain. It is of course not only the British law and labour market that encounters such problems. In member States generally the interaction of the crisis with the legal system produces a varied pattern, so that no 'European' concept of 'employee' is easily discoverable. The European Court of Justice was compelled to leave the scope of 'employees' protected by the Directive (77/187) safeguarding rights on the transfer of an undertaking to the definition of whichever persons were protected in each legal system as workers, pursuant to legislation governing labour law, i.e. in Britain the TUPE Regulations (No. 1794, 1981).[55]

Nor are these the only international indicators that governments should act to protect such workers. An OECD report on part-time employment urged action in 1968; the ILO called for legal regulation of fee-charging agencies in 1949 (Convention No. 96). But the increasing participation of women in the labour market, so often in part-time, short-term or temporary employment, appears to have done little to accelerate legal protection even in the most advanced countries. This may relate to the belief of employers that these types of 'flexible' employment combat rising costs.[56] Recent studies show both that part-time employment is poorly paid and that Britain has led the way in increased part-time employment in face of losses of full-time jobs.[57] Categories of part-time or 'freelance' workers and 'outworkers' generally form part of the secondary labour force with greater vulnerability than equivalent full-time workers in almost every respect. The trade union presence is particularly low.[58] In this situation, Government support for measures such as 'job-splitting' may only increase the tally of those 'employed' by reducing standards for workers on all sides, especially because even those part-time workers who are in law 'employees' are often not accorded fringe benefits, bonuses, shift pay or similar conditions on anything like equal terms to full-time employees. There is also beyond this area the uncharted land of the 'black economy' (or 'clandestine employment'), which thrives on tax evasion. A 1985 research report encouraged government to deal with this by *reducing* legal 'burdens' on the 'legitimate economy' rather than attempting further controls, for fear that the black economy might spread![59] It seems that the ultimate logic of the philosophy of 'deregulation' is to whitewash the black economy.

The 'outworkers' who featured in nineteenth-century legislation have recently attracted renewed attention especially in the form of 'home-workers' (people who work at home). The debate about the effects of the dark Satanic mills on workers in the first half of the nineteenth century has sometimes been characterized as 'domestic [home-] workers v. factory workers'.[60] A century later, their importance and numbers had declined in the post-war economy of full employment; but Townsend's survey of poverty in 1968 discovered many working at home in poor conditions (such as the disabled homeworker making lampshades for £1.50 in a twelve-hour week).[61] In 1985 the TUC puts the number of these 'second-class citizens' at 500,000 (and has urged unions to recruit them), while Government estimated a maximum of 400,000. Huws has shown that pay and conditions are poor not only in the traditional areas (sack-repairing, button packing, the finishing of wearing apparel and similar occupations still listed in the 1911 Order) but also in new areas, from telephone-answering to 'telework' (dear to futurologists, who see work being done in future at home before a VDU). Even these more modern forms of homework frequently attract rates of pay well below that of normal, or even casual, office staff.[62] Hakim reported a sharp increase in workers working 'at or *from*' home (now some 940,000, of whom half work for two or more 'clients'), most of them with a confused employment status.[63] The potential for 'distance employment' as a whole is put by one estimate at 13 million workers.

It was disclosed in a case of 1978 that the Inland Revenue treated homeworkers automatically as self-employed. Yet there has been little debate in Britain, compared with other industrialized countries, about the status and rights of these workers 'external' to the dispersed enterprise or 'para-subordinated' to the employer.[64] The poor conditions and isolation of such workers have been emphasized by both ACAS and the House of Commons Select Committee on Employment. Local authorities have rarely kept proper lists under the old Order. Reform is urgently needed to deal with elementary employment protection, wages and union protection.[65] A 'Homeworkers' Charter' adopted at a national conference in 1985 called for employee status, provisions on safety and for dependants, and minimum wages. But proposals to improve protection through Wages Councils run counter to the current policies on deregulation of the labour market (Chapter 4, p. 350). Nor is it easy to see how, without a fundamental reform of the very concept of 'employment', legal protection could easily prevent evasion of new protective employment rights – for instance by way of 'task' contracts, which can defeat continuity of employment and the very concept of 'dismissal' by providing employment for a particular task, like chopping down a specified tree, which is not a 'fixed-term' contract.[66] Even worse, the EAT accepted in *Brown*, 1986, that employment 'so long as funds are provided by the sponsor' (there the MSC, which supported a lecturer for YTS courses) ends, if the funds are withdrawn, *not* by 'dismissal' but by automatic termination. Homeworkers are highly vulnerable to such manipulation even if they are lucky enough to become employees.

In *Nethermere (St Neots) Ltd* v. *Taverna*[67] the Court of Appeal faced two homeworkers, Mrs T. and Mrs G., who between four and seven hours a day sewed trousers delivered and collected by a driver from N. They made it clear to him when it was worthwhile to call. They had both once worked full-time in N.'s factory; T. had changed to homework after having a baby (a pattern typical of many women workers). The pay was by garment on time sheets. After some four years a dispute about holiday pay led N. to terminate the arrangement. By a majority (the legal chairman being outvoted) the tribunal held they were both employees, not in business on their own account and therefore able to complain of unfair dismissal. N. invited the Court of Appeal to hold that this was wrong in law because there was no 'mutuality of obligation' (cases under a Master and Servant Act of 1823 were cited as precedents, in addition to *O'Kelly*). But the court, by a majority, refused. In earlier decisions of 1978 and 1983 homeworkers had shown that sporadic work on shoes done over seven years and work on a company's books at home qualified them as employees. Even so, the dissenting judge not only refused to see T. and G. as employees; he could find no contract *at all*. The tribunal therefore was wrong in law, he found, because there were none of the mutually binding obligations (either to deliver the trousers or to work on them) necessary to constitute either a series of individual contracts or an 'umbrella' contract. The majority held that there was evidence, albeit 'tenuous', of a contract here, and a contract of service at that. The employee's obligation was 'to serve' subject to the employer's control; an employer's duty was to pay wages (not normally to provide work: p. 178). These incidents existed in an 'umbrella' contract formed by a long course of conduct under which N. agreed to pay the wage rates and T. and G. agreed to sew a 'reasonable' number of garments. Their contract was one of service; so they could claim for unfair dismissal.

Stephenson LJ, delivering the main judgment upholding the tribunal majority, refused 'to say anything about the general position of outworkers'. But it is notable that N. depended on his eleven homeworkers, whose finishing work, done at the *same* rates as internal workers, was 'an essential part of the production' of his factory with seventy internal workers. The arrangement was convenient to both sides. If homeworkers form an integrated part of the productive process in this way, they should surely be counted as part of the work-force, equally protected from arbitrary sacking, and entitled to rates of pay parallel to those paid to internal employees. If T. and G. had been excluded from the range of 'employees', as the tribunal chairman had wished, there would be little hope of protection for any species of homeworkers. But a different tribunal (with a more persuasive chairman perhaps) could in future take that view of similar facts if it concluded that the 'course of dealing' with the homeworker was, in that case, inadequate evidence of 'mutual obligations'. Yet these are workers 'at the bottom of the employment heap'; employment protection laws are 'surely meant to cover all those in a position of economic subservience'.[68] Once again the problem seems to require a different approach, one that protects the worker who is a part of the enterprise, wherever the work is done, without the same definition necessarily applying to legal principles devised for other purposes, such as vicarious liability.

Further, when the Court of Appeal feels unable to propound general guidance, what seems to be needed is an intervention by Parliament that can use flexible machinery (such as Wages Councils or the CAC) to protect those in a subordinate – or 'para-subordinate' – relationship doing certain types of work. Definitions for this purpose need not be the equivalent of those used for tax or social security. Labour law cannot have lost its touch for inventing different types of 'workers' for different purposes; it cannot muddle on in the pretence that the common law 'contract of service' is a formula for all seasons. Such a policy, though, implies more intervention in the labour market, a programme perhaps of more radical regulation. Policies of government in the 1980s so far point in the opposite direction. It might be more profitable, therefore, to enter an immediate plea for definitions that, if they do not increase the area of protection, at least make more certain and rational the types of worker covered by the different legal provisions.

Formation of the employment contract

The *Nethermere* case illustrates the way in which a contract, and here a 'contract of service', may be made informally, by word of mouth or even by the conduct of the parties from which it is inferred. The layman tends to think of a contract as a formal document; but this is not normally required for the contract of employment. The law demands only clear agreement on terms sufficiently certain, which the parties may be taken to intend to be legally binding. The parties may expressly exclude an intention to be legally bound if they wish, though they rarely do. Otherwise, the court will decide whether the agreement appears to be so intended as a whole; the use of words like '*ex gratia* payments' will not be enough to exclude legal obligations if the whole bargain appears to have contractual intent. And even a profit-sharing scheme attached to a contract but stating in its revised form that it did 'not create a legal relationship' was held by the Court of Appeal in 1981 to be part of the contractual agreement.[69] The parties are unlikely to spell out all the terms that will cover every eventuality; but the court will, wherever it can, supply the content of these 'empty boxes of the contract', as Fox has called them, constructing 'implied terms' (which we discuss in Chapter 3).

If the court cannot give a meaning to the mutual obligations, the agreement cannot be a contract. An agreement of 1902 for service at a 'West End salary to be mutually arranged between us' was not a contract, only an agreement to make a contract later. Today however the courts will uphold the contract where a reasonable meaning can be imposed. When mining deputies were bound by contract to work 'such days or part days in each week as may reasonably be required by the management' and refused to work Saturday shifts, the Court of Appeal was able in 1958 to decide that they should work for a reasonable number of days and that their refusal in the circumstances was a breach of contract because it was unreasonable.[70]

Certainty is not enough. Unless the agreement is made in a sealed deed, there must be 'consideration' advanced by each party; that is to say, each must contribute to the bargain a price for the other's promises. This is why the court in *Nethermere* puts such stress upon *mutual* obligations, one promise constituting the price for the other. The promise to work in return for the promise to pay wages is, as Stephenson LJ has suggested, perhaps the 'irreducible minimum'.

Certain parties have at common law only a limited capacity to contract, and others are specially regulated by statute. Merchant seamen, for example, employed on British ships must have a written agreement satisfying the provisions of the Merchant Shipping Act 1970. A contract of apprenticeship to learn a 'trade' may also constitute a contract of 'service' but should be made in writing; it is separately included in the 1978 employment protection provisions (EPCA s. 153 (1)). Two parties with special capacity are minors and the Crown. Minors under 18 years (it was 21 until 1970) are held to their employment contracts by the courts if the contracts are on balance beneficial to them when made, even if particular terms are to their disadvantage. This was at the root of the judges' long-standing control over 'unfair' apprenticeships. A son of Charlie Chaplin, a 'Bohemian' living on social security benefit, tried in 1965 to resile from a contract for a book of neither 'taste nor decency' that was to be ghost-written for him and might expose him to libel actions. The Court of Appeal thought the profits were so great that he must be held to the contract – it enabled him to 'make a start as an author' – even though he had been lured into the project by the money offered.

We have seen that the status of minors who enter arrangements such as the Youth Training Scheme is far from clear. Some may have no contract; others may have contracts but not of employment; some become employees. When we discuss such schemes (Chapter 6), we must remember that a contract not on the whole beneficial will not bind the minor who enters it. It may be thought that engagement for a year (or, from 1986, two years) for 'work experience and training' at (from September 1985) £27.30 a week,[71] is necessarily more beneficial than unemployment (Government policy is to give school-leavers 'the choice of a job, or education or training but not unemployment'). Coke CJ, though, in 1628 bound the apprentice to his deed only where it provided 'good teaching or instruction whereby he may profit himself afterwards'. There is good sense in this rule. In addition, statutory provisions have long restricted the employment of young persons and children (Chapter 5), such as the Act of 1920 that prevents employment of those under 16 in industrial undertakings, and the Children and Young Persons Act 1963, which restricts within narrow limits the employment of a child below school-leaving age (sixteen years).

The position of 'the Crown' – including Ministries and government departments – is still rather uncertain. Since 1947 a citizen can sue the Crown for breach of contract. But does the civil servant or other Crown 'employee' have a contract of service? Two different answers can be found in the cases. Where nothing is said concerning tenure, the Crown can undoubtedly dismiss at pleasure. In the *GCHQ* case in 1985 (p. 277) Lord Diplock declared that the principle that a civil servant's employment can always be terminated at will is a rule 'of which the existence is beyond doubt'; he could therefore have no more than a 'legitimate expectation' to his *future* position, not a contractual right (though an Order in Council of 1982 also gave the Crown power to change 'conditions of service'). Other cases have tended to assume there is a contract of some kind, even of service (but with special incidents such as the right to dismiss) on which the employee of the Crown can at least found his claim for salary.[72] In reality, the civil servant will be protected by his trade union and by the procedures for consultation and grievance built around the Whitley Councils. Collective bargaining honeycombs the civil service; the absence in Britain of a separate system of 'administrative courts' and special laws to govern the public officials, which exist in many other countries, permitted its rapid extension between the two world wars in the public service (we may contrast the obstacles confronting *fonctionnaires* in France or *Beamte* in West Germany; or indeed public servants in the United States, where unions and bargaining were thought to infringe the political 'sovereignty' of federal or state bodies). As Lord Goddard commented in 1957, the established civil servant is 'secure in his employment till he reaches retirement age, apart of course from misconduct or complete inefficiency'.

Modern legislation on employment protection, however, tends to side-step these problems and expressly treat persons in Crown employment (other than the armed services) as in ordinary employment for the purpose of applying statutory provisions. So we find unfair dismissal and other similar rights applied (but not the requirements for written particulars of employment terms, redundancy payments, minimum notice periods: EPCA ss. 111, 121, 138). Civil servants have their own redundancy scheme. Sex and racial discrimination measures apply to them (S D A s. 85; R R A s. 75, but with a number of special provisions). The cloak of the Crown covers government departments and other bodies that act for the Crown, but not commercial corporations in the public sector, such as the National Coal Board or the Gas Council. Even before they are 'privatized', when they are still in fact controlled by the government, they and their employees are governed by the ordinary 'private' law of the contract of employment, subject to any provisions in the Act of Parliament that sets them up.

It must be noted, however, that if a Minister certifies that the action complained of in an employment protection case relating to trade union rights or unfair dismissal was taken for the purpose of 'safeguarding national security', the tribunal must dismiss the case; and Crown employment can be redefined for these purposes as not including any employment group in respect of which a Minister has certified an exception because of national security (EPCA s. 138 (4), Sched. 9., para. 2; EPA s. 121 (4)). In the *GCHQ* case one of the steps taken by the Government to force those working at the Communications Headquarters to discontinue trade union membership was a certificate excluding the civil servants in question from employment protection on grounds of 'national security'.

In 1963 statute made a new requirement about the ordinary contract of employment; the employee must be given by the employer a written statement of the main terms of the contract. Employers often anyway provide their workers with written documents to testify to the terms of the employment. Some are surprisingly wide, like the ICI Works Rule in a case of 1968, which gave the company power to transfer a worker 'to another job with a higher or lower rate of pay, whether day work, night work or shift work', a written provision that would be binding in the contract. Higher up the hierarchy, white-collar and other workers are often provided with a formal written contract. Where the contract itself is set out in writing and accepted by the worker (by signing it, for example) the common law rule is that the parties are bound by it in the absence of misrepresentation or mistake. The Court of Appeal applied this common law rule to a signed contract in the *Gascol* case, 1974 (p. 335).[73]

But the statutory requirements (now in EPCA ss. 1–11) do not require a written *contract*, only a written statement of particulars of the contract. The employer must give this to the employee within thirteen weeks – it has never been fully clear why the employer is given so long – unless the latter falls within an excluded category (such as Crown servants, seamen in large ships, those working ordinarily abroad, and employees who have a written *contract* covering all the requirements and accessible to the worker (s. 5)). The particulars required include: the parties; commencement date; in fixed-term contracts the date of termination; previous employment that will count for continuity (p. 205); remuneration details; hours and holidays, holiday pay and sickness or injury pay; pension arrangements; length of notice required; the 'title of the job' to be done. To this must be added 'a note' specifying (other than in respect to health and safety): disciplinary rules; the person who takes disciplinary decisions; details of grievance procedures; further steps in such procedures; and whether a 'contracting-out' certificate is in force in regard to the State pension scheme (p. 303). Pressures in the 1980s towards 'flexible' working have led to uncertainty about the power of such requirements to protect workers. For example, a 'job title' may be central in a dispute about how and where a worker can be required to work. But today this may not mean much. The agreement, for example, made by Nissan and the AUEW in 1985 confirmed management's wish to have only two grades among manual workers (technicians and manufacturing staff) and two for engineers (senior and other) who must do 'everything an engineer is required to do'. Other car firms often have hundreds of grades and job titles for such workers. Not only does the Nissan agreement use wide job titles to extend 'flexibility' of practices at the discretion of management; it also includes the right to hire, and train, part-time workers. In such circumstances management can maintain a pool of reserve labour that can be brought into the 'core' of the enterprise on full time if required and management will have a vast discretion as to what each worker does.

When terms of employment change, the employer must inform the employee in writing within one month. Without further provision, a flood of paper would have deluged employment, not least because, as we see later (p. 329), most employment contracts incorporate terms of collective agreements. The statute therefore permits the initial statement of written particulars to 'refer the employee to some document' that he can read or that is reasonably accessible to him for details (s. 2). Even more important, the employer may 'indicate' that future changes in the stated terms will be entered up in *this* document. Then, so long as the document remains accessible, he need not inform each employee individually of the changes (s. 4). So, if there is a collective agreement between employers and unions on the minimum weekly wage, and workers are given particulars that refer to their remuneration as that agreed in the agreement 'as varied and in force from time to time', the employer need not notify each worker of a change in the rate, so long as he ensures that the updated agreement is available for the workers to consult. This appears to apply to the 'note' as well as to the statement even when this is not expressly stated, because the 'note' is 'included' in the statement. The 'other document' is not confined to a collective agreement, though this is the most important example; it may be a set of works rules or some other document issued by the employer.

The written statement is not a written contract. It constitutes 'very strong prima facie evidence of what were the terms of the contract between the parties but does not constitute a written contract between the parties'. It is not 'conclusive' but places a 'heavy burden' on the party who alleges the real terms are different. Using this approach, the E A T was able in *System Floors (UK) Ltd* v. *Daniel*[74] to put aside the strict rule of the common law. A worker went to work for employers to which an agency sent him. One of these employers decided to take him on as an employee but failed to notify the agency. After joining the employer he was given a statement of terms, which he signed to acknowledge receipt. When he was dismissed the employers alleged that he had not served for a sufficient period to claim for unfair dismissal. This was correct if the date of commencement of employment in the written statement was correct, and the employers claimed he was bound by that, as in *Gascol's* case. But the E A T held that that was a case where the written document was acknowledged *as* a contract; here it was acknowledged as a receipt so that evidence could be given (and was accepted) that the true date of commencement was earlier – sufficient to establish a qualifying period for the claim. No doubt this was just; but few workers can be expected to catch the fundamental significance of signing a document including contractual terms that is a 'receipt' rather than a 'contract'. There are too many 'ambiguous documents' to make this a sensible industrial distinction.[75] This decision is in fact one of a line of cases in which the E A T has attempted to push the strict common law rules about written contracts aside in order to be fair to individual workers.

Where, as in *Rump's* case, an employer issued a statement of particulars specifying that the worker must transfer to any other workplace in accordance with the Working Rule Agreement and the employer tried to send him to such a place in Scotland, the court allowed the worker to prove a preceding oral agreement in which a manager had said that he would be required to work only in southern England, which it accepted as the true term of the contract.[76] In such cases emphasis is often laid upon the fact that the employer did not do enough to notify the worker of the 'change' in the terms, which he could not vary unilaterally. No such argument will apply where the written statement was produced at the commencement of the employment. The principles of interpretation cannot then easily prevent the unfairness. Mr Jones, employed in tunnelling at a specified pit, was sent to another pit and issued with a new statement of particulars, indicating he was to work at that pit or any other 'place in the UK' the employers specified. Three years later the same power of transfer was asserted in a new statement. He objected to a third move; but the EAT said he was contractually bound to go. Even so, the court insisted that a subsequent statement could change the terms of the contract only if it amounted to an 'agreed variation' and where the employee merely took the document without objection this should be concluded only with 'great caution'.[77] In the result the court implied its own term into the contract (p. 177), one which still obliged him to move his workplace.

Perhaps the most important consequence of the absence of a statement relates to those problems of proof of the terms of the contract, especially where they are relied upon to incorporate terms of a collective agreement. But there had to be a more direct sanction on the employer to make him provide the particulars. The original Act of 1963 provided a criminal sanction. But who was going to prosecute? Nothing illustrated better the absence in Britain of any general 'labour inspectorate' of the French kind. After two years this sanction was displaced, with an embarrassed shuffle, by a civil remedy. This went to the opposite extreme. Instead of providing a remedy that could put a civil penalty on the employer (who for two years had risked a criminal fine), the statute (now EPCA s. 11) enables an employee whose employer fails to give him the written statement to refer the matter to a tribunal 'to determine what particulars ought to have been included or referred to so as to comply' with the law. Although earlier decisions suggested otherwise, the Court of Appeal in *Mears's* case[78] insisted that this gives the tribunal power, on a reference to rectify incomplete statements, to find the specified terms that have been omitted – even 'in the last resort [to] invent them' and determine 'what *should* have been agreed', especially since it is the employer's breach of duty that has made the application to the tribunal necessary.

In a sense this implies a penalty against the employer, though it will be such only if he does not care for the 'invented' terms. More generally, this is part of the judges' inclination in the 1980s to take new powers to mould the shape of the individual contract, as with the 'implied terms' in *Mears's* case (p. 174). Davies and Freedland rightly point out that one difficulty with this approach is that it leaves the employees with 'the weaknesses that they suffer when a model of individual bargaining is employed in matters where collective interests may be at stake',[79] instead posing an 'individuated issue'. They contrast a later case where the judges take account of the 'normal practice' of an industry in order to invent terms. But the practice of an industry may or may not be linked to collective bargaining; if it is not, it may reflect only the strength of managerial prerogative against which the individual workers can offer little. There may be some areas in which the need to write things down has caused an increase in negotiation; but there is less evidence of this than there is of increased formality and 'documentation'. The written statement of particulars has caused many companies to go beyond the limited requirements with wider statements by 'additional written statements'.[80] The statutory provisions on written statements are 'individuated' to their core. The employer 'gives' the statement to the worker, on terms that they have in theory 'agreed'. This 'giving' expresses the power relationship. The only way in which a worker can redress the balance is through collective negotiation with the employer. In the absence of collective bargaining the judges may or may not be a second best; but the statute could make a beginning by giving to the union a right to sue the employer in respect of written statements given to workers who are its members. Arguably it should have the right to challenge the statements given to other workers where these expose terms and conditions that undercut a bargained or decent minimum. The existing enforcement mechanism for providing statements to employees is, in any event, impracticable and should be replaced by an enforcement agency more likely to take action than the individual employee. The latter, however, usually comes across this problem not as one concerning formation of the employment contract, as the lawyer sees it, but one that is raised to prove the contractual terms on termination (in redundancy or unfair dismissal cases) or in a dispute during the contract (Chapter 3). It is in those cases that the worker needs to be given greater room to challenge documents the significance of which he may not have understood at the time of issue. But a better solution would be to require the employer to negotiate their terms.

A personal contract

It is rare today for a breach of an employment contract to give rise to a criminal prosecution. The remedies are civil, an award of damages or an injunction. Yet it must be appreciated how modern is this image. From the Statute of Labourers of 1351 onwards, enactments subjected workers who failed to fulfil their duties to the 'master' to criminal penalties, including imprisonment. Similar penalties did not attach to the masters (who were liable only to damages in civil law) nor, as Houldsworth commented, to any other contract. The Webbs remarked that, in days of 'equality of treatment' before the law, it was difficult 'to understand how the flagrant injustice of the old Master and Servant Acts seemed justifiable even to a middle-class Parliament'.[81] An Act of 1843 dealt particularly severely with outworkers; and benches of magistrates scarcely favoured any of the workers involved. The various statutes were revised in the Master and Servant Act 1867, which nevertheless still retained imprisonment for 'aggravated misconduct'. Prosecutions for leaving or 'neglecting' work were a major mechanism for combating unions and militant workers; and between 1858 and 1875, when they were repealed under the pressure of the labour movement, there were on average 10,000 prosecutions a year under these provisions. As late as 1872 there were 10,400 convictions.[82] It is impossible to over-emphasize these criminal origins of the law attaching to the employment relationship. The New Poor Law and its workhouses pushed labourers unprotected into the market; but it was the criminal law that tied them to their jobs.

Already, though, the civil courts had decided that contracts for personal service or services could not be enforced by specific orders (as against damages for breach). A contract cannot be specifically enforced, said a judge in 1859, between a man and 'his valet or coachman or cook who, however excellent they may be . . . can be replaced'. Judges developed other reasons for this principle: it would be 'impossible to make a man work and therefore the Court never attempts to do it' (1890); or 'a series of orders and a general superintendence' of the performance of such a contract 'could not be conveniently undertaken by any court of justice' (1873). The rule was rationalized on a higher plane in 1890; in the words of Fry LJ, the courts should not 'turn contracts of service into contracts of slavery'. With these concepts attached to employment contracts under civil law, old concepts giving the master a property in his servant (*servitium*) gradually died away, though remnants remained until 1982.

The modern model of the employment contract, as a voluntary consensual relationship sanctioned by the civil law, is suffused with an individualism that ignores the economic reality behind the bargain. Indeed, the entire basis of our law of contract is fragile in a society in which terms of 'agreement' are increasingly dictated by the powerful party. Judges have recognized this, but not to any great extent in employment cases. Recently, for example, judges have expanded the concept of 'economic duress', which permits a person to renounce an agreement and sue the other party for restitution if the latter compelled him to agree by conduct and threats – even, Lord Scarman has said, threats 'of lawful action'. The wrong lies in the 'coercion of the will which vitiates consent'. This has been transferred from commercial law and applied to the consent of a shipowner secured through industrial action.[83]

The question arises whether an employment contract on 'sweated' terms dictated to a destitute worker by a take-it-or-leave-it employer would ever be seen as one induced by 'economic duress'. The orthodox answer would appear to be to the contrary, for the judges have always excluded 'commercial pressure' and mere 'dominant bargaining power'. The likelihood of an English court upsetting an individual contract of employment is low. Where an employee had made a settlement of his unfair dismissal claim through ACAS (binding upon him under EPCA, s. 140), the judge held that on the facts this had not been induced by economic duress; and he added that the doctrine would arise in employment law 'only in the most exceptional cases'.[84] Australian courts have understood English doctrines of equity to permit the setting aside of contracts because they are 'unconscionable'.[85] And in the *Schroeder* case the Law Lords recently clarified the range of contracts that they will declare void in Britain by reason of the doctrine of 'restraint of trade'. They now include standard form contracts that have not been negotiated either by the parties themselves or by organizations representing their interests, but were 'dictated' by the party with superior negotiating power. This was not, said Lord Diplock, based upon 'some 19th century economic theory about the benefit to the general public of freedom of trade'; it rests upon 'the protection of those whose bargaining power is weak against being forced by those whose bargaining power is stronger to enter into bargains that are unconscionable'.[86] The contract in that case bound an unknown songwriter to give exclusive services and all copyright to a company for five years without any obligation on it to provide him with more than trivial payments. The company could terminate the agreement and, in certain events, extend it as it pleased. It was the firm's standard contract; but the Law Lords declared it void.

It may be that this doctrine applies only to contracts that 'sterilize' the exclusive services of the worker without any reasonable benefit being granted by the powerful party; and there are few illustrations, other than in judgments of Lord Denning MR, of contracts being set aside only because of 'inequality of bargaining power'.[87] In contracts for services, the Unfair Contract Terms Act 1977 gives the court a power to set aside on grounds of reasonableness certain types of exemption clause (e.g. on indemnities or certain liabilities for negligence: ss. 2, 4, 8); and certain clauses protecting an employer from liability for negligence, in a contract of employment proper, may be struck down as 'unreasonable', but not if it protects the employee (s. 2, Sched. 1, para 4). But these are statutory rules; the common law does not go so far. Even so, many low-paid workers take jobs with standard conditions from employers who do not engage in collective bargaining. Whilst such a worker might not wish normally to have the contract set aside as 'void', the point could become important in other circumstances. For example, to induce a breach of a 'void' or illegal contract is not a tort, and the same should be true of 'unenforceable' contracts. All three descriptions have been applied to contracts in restraint of trade. The tort of inducing breach of contract is the most common ground of illegality for strikes (Chapter 8). Where a strike by such workers is organized, it should therefore be open to the organizers to plead that they have no need of a trade dispute 'immunity'; they have committed no tort since the workers' unconscionable contracts were forced upon them by those whose bargaining power was stronger or even by economic duress without consultation with the union.

The Court of Appeal and the House of Lords, however, have both clearly taken the view in 1985 that this line of reasoning has gone far enough, if not too far. Lord Scarman spoke for the Law Lords when he said there is no 'general principle of relief against inequality of bargaining power'.[88] Dillon LJ held that in the absence of conduct that is 'unconscionable, coercive or oppressive', and having regard to the fact that 'inequality of bargaining power must anyhow be a relative concept' – it is seldom 'equal' – the courts 'would only interfere in exceptional cases where as a matter of common fairness it was not right that the strong should be allowed to push the weak to the wall'. Dunn LJ added: 'Mere impecuniosity has never been held a ground for equitable relief.'[89] The impecunious worker can expect little from these doctrines, though the reason for this owes more to policy than to logic.

Personal contracts and frustration

Since the contract of employment is personal, the courts lean against 'joint' contracts. In 1984, for example, Mr Monoghan took a job at a club as a steward on a weekly wage, 'inclusive of the services of his wife', an arrangement the judge found 'unusual and contrary to the freedoms cherished in these days'. The club paid her one-third of the wage each week. The question of what was the wage on which compensation for *his* unfair dismissal should be calculated was answered by taking two-thirds of the amount. 'Joint employment' is not impossible, although there must be clear evidence of it. But the unfair dismissal of a husband may create a situation from which a 'substantial reason' for reasonable and *fair* dismissal of a wife working alongside him can be created.[90] A case of this kind may also raise the termination of contract under the doctrine of 'frustration'. The death of one party to the contract will in the ordinary way be an event that automatically terminates it. When Mr and Mrs Berry took a joint contract as 'the steward', the death of Mr Berry ended the contract for him and for his wife too. The doctrine is not confined to death. Where, as in the case of a drummer in a pop group who was schizophrenic, the worker becomes so unfit that there is 'no reasonable likelihood' that he will be able to resume work in the near future or substantially to perform the contract, it is terminated by reason of frustration.[91] Such incapacity is not a breach of contract unless the worker had *guaranteed* the work (e.g. pledged his appearance on a given night) or 'induced' the frustrating event (e.g. by taking harmful drugs that incapacitated him). Where a personal employer dies today, statutory provisions protect the worker's rights in regard to redundancy and unfair dismissal (EPCA, Sched. 12, paras. 8–21).

The courts have restricted the doctrine of frustration in employment protection cases where it might allow the employer too easily to say there was no 'dismissal', only 'automatic termination'. One can find in these cases a good example of the EAT in particular struggling to free itself of rigid common law doctrines in order to produce what it judges to be a just solution between an individual employee and the employer. An employer who appears positively to treat the employment as subsisting, for example, when a worker is away sick for a long time will not be allowed to plead frustration, though in 1977 he was allowed to do so where he had given no such indication. The EAT has been particularly flexible. In *Converfoam Ltd* v. *Bell*, 1981,[92] a works director developed a serious heart condition. He returned to work but was not allowed to occupy his old job; the employers pleaded that the old contract was frustrated by the new risk, with which he could not satisfactorily continue his work. In deciding the contract was not frustrated, the EAT took account of the nature of the employment. With 'a sole wireless operator on a sea-going ship' the risk of recurrent heart attacks might have a very different effect on the contract than in the case of a works manager. Even more uncertainty has arisen in regard to the imprisonment of a worker after a criminal offence. Lord Denning MR in 1974, faced with a foreman sentenced to twelve months' imprisonment for unlawful wounding, insisted that this was a 'frustrating event' ending his employment of twenty-five years' service; and Lawton LJ – relying on 'impossibility' of performance – said, 'as long as he is in prison he cannot do his job'.[93] In 1980 a teacher's contract was terminated by frustration on his conviction for indecent assault even though he launched an appeal (which eventually succeeded). And the Law Lords in 1981 treated the contract of a psychiatrist who was suspended from the medical register as terminated 'by operation of law' in an analogous fashion.

Yet the EAT has tried to avoid the automatic doctrine of frustration, especially in normal contracts, posing instead questions like that of Phillips J. in 1977: 'Has the time arrived when the employer can no longer be expected to keep the absent employee's place open?' *Chakki's* case[94] illustrated the flexibility that it prefers. A lorry driver committed a wounding on his son, was charged but released on bail. The trial occurred during his holiday period; he was sentenced to eleven months' imprisonment but released next day on bail to appeal against sentence. The employers had decided to terminate the employment since they thought he would be unable to return to work in the near future (a view that at this point he shared). The worker (whose appeal succeeded, the new sentence being probation) now complained of an unfair dismissal. The tribunal held the contract had been terminated by frustration not dismissal. Neither party thought he could return to work for 'a considerable length of time'. The EAT decided this was wrong in law; the sentence of imprisonment was 'a potentially frustrating event'; but it was necessary to ask whether a reasonable employer would have considered his probable absence as one necessary to replace the worker with a permanent, rather than temporary, replacement.

The 1985 case of Mr Jerrom, an apprentice, was similar.[95] He signed a 'training service' agreement with the Plumbing Services Joint Board, which included a procedure for terminating contracts. When sentenced to Borstal training for an offence 'which had nothing to do with his work', he was at once dismissed. The EAT found that the tribunal was correct in holding that there was no frustration because such an event was a contingency that brought into play the procedures agreed upon. In such cases as this, with procedures on termination nationally agreed, cases of automatic frustration would be comparatively rare. Such decisions make good sense, though they may put employers in a quandary about whether to employ a replacement. There is a case for legislation making general provision about replacements, as with maternity leave (EPCA s. 61: p. 486). But in 1986 the Court of Appeal in *Notcutt's* case, reverting to an older approach, held a worker was not entitled to notice because his incapacitating coronary attack had frustrated his contract.

A major adjustment of the common law is sometimes necessary to protect workers on the transfer of a business. Since the contract is a personal one, the employer cannot pass to his buyer the workers along with his chattels. Their consent is required to serve a new employer. In 1940 the House of Lords even refused to sanction the transfer of employees' contracts from one company to another under provisions of the Companies Act (now s. 427 of the 1985 Act) that allowed for transfers of all rights and liabilities in the course of an amalgamation. Lord Atkin, in language not unconnected with the causes for which the country was then fighting, declared: 'the right to choose for himself whom he would serve . . . constituted the main difference between a servant and a serf'. It must be observed, however, that had the amalgamation taken a different legal, but the same economic, form the servant could have had no objection. Workers have no legal right to complain where the take-over is accomplished by the second company purchasing shares in the first. Indeed, we shall see that the amendments to this area of law, effected by the Transfer of Undertakings (Protection of Employment) Regulations 1981 (p. 207), which now transfer contracts of employment to a purchaser of 'the undertaking' of a commercial enterprise, are in practice emasculated in Britain because they do not deal with transfers of control of the business to new 'owners' brought about by the purchase of shares with associated practices and mechanisms of company law (such as change of name, or entry into a new corporate group, with all the possibilities of 'asset stripping' this entails). These can be even more important to security of employment than the transfers of the business and its goodwill by one employer to another, which these E E C-inspired regulations address.

Enforcing the personal contract

Let us return to remedies. The primary remedy for breach of contract is generally damages, and this is now true of the employment contract. Specific performance of a personal contract is not available. Statute reconfirms this by prohibiting an order to compel an employee to work (T U L R A s. 16). The judges will not at common law order the *reinstatement* of an employee wrongly dismissed in breach of contract. It was the introduction of the remedy of reinstatement for unfair dismissal that was thought (wrongly: p. 251) to be so important in the new statutory floor of rights on unfair dismissal. We shall see in Chapter 3 that compensation is the normal remedy even for 'unfair dismissal' and that a tiny proportion only of workers unfairly dismissed obtain re-employment either through the awards of tribunals or even in conciliation by ACAS. Even under the wartime Order 1305 the judges would not allow an order for reinstatement. It was, Lord Goddard CJ said,

a remedy which no court of law or equity has ever considered it had power to grant. . . . A court of equity has never granted an injunction compelling an employer to continue a workman in his employment or to oblige a workman to work for an employer.

Statutory exceptions have been enacted; for example, a registered dockworker may be reinstated to his job with a registered employer under the statutory scheme (p. 155). But it is otherwise in the normal case of a contract of service, or indeed a contract for services or even analogous contracts for personal co-operation, such as partnerships. Specific performance by reinstatement is not available. Such contracts are said to involve personal 'trust and confidence', which the law cannot supply. It has been doubted, though, whether the rule is so strict in the modern law because today the work relationship is 'much less personal than the old relationship of master and servant was believed to be', and 'present industrial conditions may in fact force an employer to retain' or to dismiss a worker against his preference.[96] This may accurately describe the judicial state of mind; but it scarcely reflects the reality of the old work relationship between 'master and servant' in a nineteenth-century mill or factory. Moreover what may 'force' the employer today is the strength of the union. It was because of this, as we shall see shortly, that the judiciary began to reconsider the doctrine.

Refusing to grant 'specific performance', the judges also forbade injunctions that would, by prohibiting the defendant from doing certain acts, achieve the same result in a roundabout way. They may, however, grant an injunction to enforce a 'negative stipulation' (the injunction is always a discretionary remedy, given if damages would not be an adequate remedy, whether *mandatory*, ordering the defendant to do something, or *prohibitory*, restraining him from doing something). The negative stipulation could be: 'I agree to work for Jones for two years *and* not for anyone else.' Even then, however, there can be no injunction if its effect would be to enforce the contract of service rather than encourage the defendant towards its performance by cutting off alternatives. An opera singer who had agreed to sing at Lumley's theatre two nights a week and not elsewhere without his consent, but who then agreed to sing at Gye's theatre, was prevented from doing so by an injunction in 1852. Bette Davis was the subject of more difficult litigation. She agreed to act exclusively for a film company for a certain period, and agreed not to engage in any other occupation. The judge granted an injunction, but in narrow terms to stop her acting for other film companies. She could still

employ herself both usefully and remuneratively in other spheres of activity, though not as remuneratively as in her special line. She will not be driven, although she may be tempted, to perform the contract.

But when The Troggs, 'simple persons of no business experience' (pop groups have made a signal contribution to modern employment litigation) made an agreement with a manager for five years, promising to employ no one else in the role, the manager was refused an injunction, since this would in practice amount to an order to employ him.[97]

Such covenants not to work or not to compete may be totally invalid on a different ground (one that some think should have been applied in *Lumley's* case): the doctrine of restraint of trade. The roots of these common law principles governing contracts lie deep in the individualist concepts of *laissez-faire* and doctrines of even earlier vintage to resist 'monopoly'. They are part of a wider public policy that can strike down a contract as involving servitude or slavery, though this is rarely done (a debauched son was in 1919 bound by contract to transfer all his property to his father and avoid his friends, to stop excessive borrowing or drinking, and never to go within eighty miles of Piccadilly Circus; the judge found this was not servitude: it was 'not too wide having regard to the nature and extent of the mischief to be avoided'). We have seen, though, that the Law Lords are now prepared to invalidate a standard form of contract for services if it is rather less than a servile relationship; its 'unconscionable' nature may be enough.

Covenants that 'restrain trade' have long been a central target of judges' hostility, though by the eighteenth century they allowed 'partial restraints'. Until 1900 it was thought they might have criminal consequences. The doctrine was regularly applied to trade unions, which were treated as bodies based upon 'illegal' agreements for this reason. Lord Campbell CJ said in 1855 that to do otherwise would establish a principle upon which the fantastic and mischievous notion of a 'Labour Parliament' might be realised for regulating the wages and the hours of labour in every branch of trade all over the empire.

It is from this source that the doctrine of restraint of trade emerged as an important factor even today (p. 522). By 1894 the courts had constructed the modern doctrine: an agreement in restraint of trade is void and unenforceable when it is 'unreasonable'. Reasonableness is tested now by reference to the interests of the parties to the contract (e.g. taking account of the area and time over which an agreement not to compete is to operate) and to the 'public interest'. If these tests are not met, the contract is unenforceable, unless the judge is willing to 'sever' the illegal part as not being within the main substance of the agreement.

In 1968 the Law Lords clarified which agreements are still subject to the doctrine – the contract of employment is one – and confirmed the right of the courts to strike down such clauses when they are not 'in the public interest'. This latter part of the formula had languished unused for decades. Its revival is an important addition to judicial powers. Lord Reid explained an earlier case in which two neighbouring employers in the same line of business agreed that neither would take on any employee who had been employed by the other within the preceding five years. When one tried to enforce it, the court refused to do so because it was unreasonable. One explanation was that the employers could not be allowed to obtain greater protection by their contract than they could secure by restrictive clauses in contracts with the employees themselves. Lord Reid thought another explanation was that from

their own points of view there was probably very good reason for that; but it could well be held to be against the public interest to interfere in this way with the freedom of their employees.

But, he added, an employee would have no right to complain,[98] even though, if the covenant not to work for the competitor had been inserted in each employment contract, the employee would not have been bound by that. Here the agreement was between the two employers, and in English law a third party cannot derive rights from a contract. But in *Eastham's* case, 1964, footballers who were transferred under the old 'retain and transfer' system operated by agreements between the Football League, the Football Association and the clubs – 'involving the buying and selling of human beings as chattels' – were allowed to challenge the agreements and themselves obtain a 'declaration' from the court that the arrangements were void, even though they were not parties to the contract. A judge granted a parallel declaration in 1978 to a group of cricketers banned from international cricket for joining in the 'World Series', though in this case the ban also procured a breach of contract and was a tort.[99]

What such a plaintiff cannot do in the absence of a tort is sue for damages or, it seems, for an injunction. In 1889 the Law Lords decided that a combination damaging another was not tortious by reason only of restraint of trade. However, the status of a 'declaration' appears to have changed over the years. In origin it was no more than a declaration of rights, without further remedy. But in 1983, when a local council refused to comply with a declaration that the National Front was entitled to use its premises, the judge, though he accepted that this was not a contempt of court (because a declaration is not a 'coercive' order), added that the 'inherent' powers of the court allowed him in these 'exceptional, if not unique' circumstances to punish the council for not accepting the ruling. What is more, the sanction of sequestration of the council's property was preferable to gaoling the councillors, who would 'be happy to don the martyr's crown' (another instance of the modern sensitivity of the judiciary to this factor).[100] This ruling concerned the public duties of a council; but however 'exceptional' it was, the judgment could have very important consequences for labour law generally.

The 'reasonableness' of conditions imposed on an employee's future work or competition with the employer has been the subject of many decisions. The covenant must be reasonable and must relate to the latter's proprietary interests. Even without an express negative covenant the employer is entitled to sue the employee for injury to certain interests, for example where the latter divulges 'trade secrets'. In such a case there is an implied term in the contract of employment restraining the worker, although, as we shall see, it is sometimes difficult to define (Chapter 3, p. 180). It does not, for example, restrict the worker from using his own skill and knowledge. An express negative covenant restraining an employee from competition after the employment is more likely to be reasonable and valid the further up the hierarchy of the firm he is and the more confidential the information he has handled, having regard to the area and duration of the constraint. So a clause stopping a manager of a betting-shop from working in any other such business for three years within twelve miles was held unreasonable; for he rendered no 'personal service' to customers touching the goodwill of the business. But a clause restraining a manager of the branch of a motor parts business from dealings for two years with persons known to him to be customers in his last year of service with the employers was upheld as 'reasonably necessary for the protection of their legitimate trade interests'; and a milk roundsman was held bound by a clause banning him for one year from selling milk or dairy products as a milkman to customers served in his last six months.[101]

The decisions pay varying attention to the maxim:

a servant has often very little choice in the matter. If he wants to get or to keep his employment, he has to sign the document which the employer puts before him . . . if he is not allowed to get work elsewhere, he is very much at the mercy of his employer.[102]

This is in practice merely an approach, not a doctrine. Although the court may strike down a contract because of the restraint put upon a weaker party, it will generally do so only in 'exceptional cases', where there has been 'unconscionable conduct' or use of 'coercive power'. It will not, for instance, reopen contracts to borrow money from a bank (where the customer has 'virtually no bargaining power') or to sell a house in a buyer's market, merely because of the inequality of parties' strength.[103]

The courts have also varied in their approach to the 'public interest'. Clauses in a pension scheme that cancel the worker's right to a pension if, on retirement, he engages in competition with, or activity detrimental to, the employer's interest have been held to be unreasonable in the public interest.[104] But a covenant binding a solicitor (a specialist in industrial property) from acting as a solicitor for five years after retirement from the partnership for anyone who was a client in the previous three years was accepted as reasonable, there being 'a clear public interest in facilitating the assumption by established solicitors' firms of younger men as partners'. This test of 'public interest' has never been applied to monopoly or oligopoly enterprises with real effect. Hence Parliament has often intervened, as in the Restrictive Trade Practices Act 1976 under which certain agreements may be rendered void. Unlike contracts void for restraint of trade, however, agreements void under the Act appear to be combinations to use 'unlawful means' in the law of tort (p. 638). Moreover, it appears that agreements void under the Treaty of Rome Article 85 as distortions or restrictions of competition or acts under Article 86 that are an 'abuse of a dominant position within the common market', give rise to actions in tort. But since this is equated to 'breach of a statutory duty' it seems unlikely that workers, as against rival traders, can bring an action for the breach, as the courts are not likely to hold that the duties under such articles in the Treaty are owed to them.[105]

Procedures, remedies and public law

In *Ridge* v. *Baldwin*, 1964,[106] Lord Reid divided dismissals into three types:

dismissal of a servant by his master, dismissal from an office during pleasure and dismissal from an office where there must be something against a man to warrant his dismissal. The law regarding master and servant is not in doubt. There cannot be specific performance of a contract of service.

The common law did not require the master to give any reasons (as EPCA s. 53 now does), nor to follow any procedure save giving proper contractual notice. Nor would it grant an order or even a declaration against a defendant guilty of a wrongful dismissal. If the injured party accepts the repudiation, the contract ends, and he may sue for damages. If he insists on affirming the contract despite the breach, the contract remains alive; but here 'an unaccepted repudiation', Asquith LJ once said, 'is a thing writ in water'; there is no point in making a declaration. Where the worker accepts the employer's repudiation (or, in some cases, must accept it because there is no alternative) and he claims damages, he may obtain a declaration too as to the *wrongful nature* of the repudiation. Although the latter adds little in law to his position, it is rhetorically valuable, as in *Burdett-Coutts's* case where a local authority purported to give 'notice of changes' in the contract to cut the pay of dinner-ladies (in the face of government cuts so as to 'avoid redundancies'), which neither they nor their union were prepared to accept.[107] In face of the employer's dismissal in breach of contract, the worker may elect whether or not to treat it as at an end. This fundamental rule is still applied – perhaps surprisingly, sometimes to his detriment – even in the modern law of unfair dismissal.[108]

Recent judgments and commentary have however thrown some doubts on these principles, largely by reason of the vitality of different principles of 'public law' governing the duties of public bodies and the rights of those holding an 'office' from which dismissal cannot be effected at pleasure (as it can in the case of the Crown: p. 135) but only for good cause. In the *Ridge* case, for example, a chief constable was granted a declaration that his dismissal was a nullity in breach of the principles of 'natural justice', because he had no chance to answer charges made against him. We at once see the differences from the common law. As to remedy, there is less inhibition upon granting declarations of *nullity* or even injunctions. As to substantive principle, the dismissal is invalid at once, before any election; and there is a duty on the employer to observe fair procedures (the absence of which was one of the reasons for introducing by statute unfair dismissal into the ordinary employment relationship in 1971: p. 233).

The question arises: when do employees enjoy the superior protections of a 'public law' character? It is not surprising that, in an era that has seen such an increase in public employment, dismissal from public 'office' should have demanded growing attention. Even so, it is instructive to examine the cases in which judges have relaxed the common law rules for what they are, in assessing any new policy. We should not make an a priori assumption that this new approach constitutes 'better' law than possible alternatives. In particular, we should ask what public law has to offer the humble worker. The 'offices' in question are of great and uncertain diversity, and the rules applicable to each may affect the whole operation of the employment, not just its termination, either as part of a 'contract' or as a statutory code. For example, an office-holder's failure to perform his duties fully may, because of the statutory scheme, permit him nevertheless to draw full salary (as in the case of the registrar of marriages who would not perform on Saturdays: p. 198). This may put such officers 'in a better position than if they were employees' (though by reason of being such officers, and not 'employees', they may lose the protection of the EPCA).[109]

Statutes may, though, import into such a worker's 'employment' relationship conditions established by collective bargaining. This is done for registered dockers employed by registered port employers under the dockwork scheme administered by Dock Labour Boards (introduced to abolish casual labour by an Act and Order of 1946; now supplemented by an Order and Act of 1967 and 1976). The scheme provides a statutory 'status', including special rules in regard to dismissal (the less protective provisions of unfair dismissal law do not apply: EPCA s. 145); and if these provisions are infringed, e.g. by dismissal without the consent of a local board, the dockworker can obtain a declaration against the Dock Labour Board – 'an entirely different situation from the ordinary master and servant case', said Viscount Kilmuir LC. 'Here the removal of the plaintiff's name from the register being, in law, a nullity he continued to have the right to be treated as a registered dockworker.'[110] The declaration is as to *nullity* of the act, not merely as to the wrongful nature of the act.

Both 'status' and 'office', however, are ambiguous words. The former in this context tends to refer to a comprehensive scheme of rights and duties attached by law to a position that a person takes on voluntarily,[111] whilst the latter frequently echoes property rights that the incidents of medieval common law attached to holders of an 'office' (that is, those who had the right 'to exercise a public or private employment and the fees and emoluments thereunto belonging', the growth of which necessitated the abolition of sinecures, including many court officials, in the nineteenth century).[112] So a Justice of the Peace has no 'contract'; he holds, the EAT has said, an 'office' under the Crown, thereby falling outside the sex discrimination legislation. A company director is sometimes said to enjoy 'a sufficient property interest' to have an office, or analogous status, although now he often has a contract of service with the company.[113] The overlap of contract and 'status' creates special problems. For example, in 1970 *Hannam*, a teacher employed in a school maintained by a local authority, was dismissed by procedures that departed from those of 'natural justice'. He was entitled to a fair hearing under certain statutory provisions; but he failed in his action against the authority for breach of contract because his contract of employment was only with the governors of the school, not with the authority. On the other hand, judges have shown a tendency to incorporate provisions that stem from a statute into the very terms of the employment (e.g. the terms of the Civil Service code went into a coastguard's contract, even though no reference to them was made in the employment terms).[114]

Such employees have often been treated by the judges as having an ordinary contract of employment, but one that is modified by statutory, implied (albeit compulsory) terms. In the case of civil servants, this means attaching the statutory provisions to a contract of employment that the Crown can terminate at will (the rule that the Crown can thereby deprive the civil servant 'in the future of a right under a particular term of his employment' is, said Lord Diplock in the *GCHQ* case, 'beyond doubt').[115]

Other public bodies may be in a different position. Where the terms of employment with a Health Service Board restricted its power of dismissal to narrow grounds (e.g. misconduct or inefficiency), a majority of the Law Lords would not permit dismissal merely by notice in a redundancy. This was a contract for 'a permanent post'. University teachers, though, have been treated on the normal basis of employment 'contracts', even when the university is governed by statute and they are removable only for statutory cause.[116] Moreover, where a college registrar was dismissed for disciplinary offences without observing procedures laid down by the employing council's regulations, the latter were treated by the Court of Appeal as implied terms incorporated into an ordinary 'master and servant' contract. The breach of contract gives the employee a right to damages. This was not a 'public office'; no 'special law' governed the employment by such a 'statutory authority', nor had a 'public employee a greater security of tenure' as such.[117] Further, in 1958 a consultant surgeon employed in the National Health Service was bound only in respect of those terms and conditions issued by the Minister that were 'applicable' to an ordinary 'master and servant contract'; he was entitled to damages, not a declaration. In such cases, an analogy may be drawn with incorporation of 'appropriate' terms of a collective agreement into a contract of employment (Chapter 4). But whereas (contrary to the law in most other European countries) our law makes no *automatic* incorporation of the terms of a collective agreement, leaving the individual contract with the power to incorporate those terms (where they are applicable), the terms introduced by statute or delegated legislation cannot normally be ousted by the individual employment agreement.

There is a different approach, however. The acts of an authority contrary to, or in excess of, its statutory powers are regarded in administrative law as a nullity and void. The docker's case comes at once to mind (p. 155). In *Malloch's* case, a 'certificated' schoolteacher who refused to go on a 'register' was employed by a local authority on terms derived from statutory provisions that gave him the right to a proper hearing before he was dismissed. He was dismissed without a hearing. The Law Lords held that this was a nullity; the 'contract of employment had never been broken' – although to say this was not the same as granting 'reinstatement'. The limits of 'public law' are illustrated here, though. Parliament can always intervene. It did in an Act of 1973, which in just such a case changed the law *retrospectively* to give the teachers' employers the power to dismiss.[118] Indeed, in *Scott* v. *Aberdeen Corpn*[119] the Scottish courts rejected a parallel plea from a teacher who had been similarly dismissed *before* that Act came into force; the Act had by now deprived him of his right to a hearing (in which it was found, in any case, he would have had no defence). But if the employing authority has acted *ultra vires*, in excess of its statutory powers, normally the office-holder can now seek 'judicial review' to bring the public body to heel. Earlier difficulties attaching to the orders of mandamus and *certiorari* (used to enforce public duties or quash certain types of decision of public or administrative bodies), neither of which lay in respect of a contract of employment, were eased when the more flexible procedures of 'judicial review' were introduced in 1977. Now, once 'public law' applies, the judges have asserted their jurisdiction to dispose of a range of orders by which to nullify and quash the offending decision or proceedings. Where a person's rights or 'legitimate expectations' are affected by a decision made, Lord Diplock said in 1984, by someone 'empowered by public law (and not merely, as in arbitration, by agreement between private parties)' judicial review may be obtained where the decision is vitiated by reason of 'illegality' (error of law), 'irrationality' (a decision no person properly applying his mind could have reached) or 'procedural impropriety' (a failure of fairness in procedure) – though there may be 'further grounds', if the judges develop them.[115]

Judges have rapidly widened the scope of judicial review, not least by invalidating actions of local government bodies as 'irrational'. The test is whether the action is 'so unreasonable, that no reasonable authority properly instructed could have reached it'. They struck down in this way concessionary public transport fares for pensioners in 1955 (an Act of Parliament was hastily passed to restore such powers to councils) and in

1983 the renowned low fares scheme of the GLC.[120] By 1985 it was clear that they would advance the frontiers of 'public law' still further. Take the *Liverpool City Corporation* case.[121] The council was in bitter dispute with central government about financial aid and rates. A 'day of action' was called in the city, and the relevant council committee decided that payment would be made only to employees who worked on that day. The applicants were teachers who wished to work but could not because the schools had closed when caretakers went on strike. The judge decided that the committee's decision was 'wholly unreasonable' and quashed it. This meant that the 'public law' remedy indirectly enforced the private, contractual rights of the teachers to their pay (had the employer been a company, they would have been left to the far more laborious remedy of an action to prove breach of their employment contracts). What is more, the judge allowed a parallel application by the local NUT official, thereby opening the avenue of 'public law' remedies to unions to enforce their members' employment rights against public authorities that act in what a court may consider an irrational manner. As we shall see, though, there is no hint that judges are likely to find it irrational to pay inadequate wages.

In the *Liverpool* case, no one argued that the council's teachers were anything other than 'employees' in the ordinary sense. The boundary with 'officers' remains uncertain. Moreover, it is still not clear just when the employer will be exercising a 'public law duty' in regard to employees. In *Benwell's* case, 1985, a prison officer who was accused of disobedience and treated unfairly by the Home Office, in the sense that it adopted unfair procedures contrary to a code of discipline, was granted a declaration as to the invalidity of his dismissal and an order of *certiorari* to quash the Home Office's decision. The judge understood that the earlier decision of *Walsh*, 1984, in which such judicial review had been refused by the Court of Appeal to a senior nursing officer who alleged he had been dismissed unfairly and in breach of the authority's statutory powers, rested upon the fact that the disciplinary procedures there had been 'incorporated into the contract of service', so depriving his case of a 'public law character'.[122] In *Benwell* the Minister's duty to be fair was held to be 'part of the statutory terms' permitting dismissal itself – as they were in *Ridge*, *Vine* and *Malloch*. A nurse and a prison officer might seem at first sight to 'have much in common'; for each there was a disciplinary procedure derived from statutory authority. But nurses enter 'into a contract of employment with health authorities whereas prison officers are appointed by the Home Secretary'.

The Crown employee is 'dismissible at pleasure' with no 'private law remedy' unless afforded one by statute. Without judicial review he has 'nowhere else to go in this country'. The procedures in *Walsh* were deprived of a 'public law character' by reason of being 'incorporated into the contract of service' (no objection being taken, we may note, as to their appropriate nature). The disciplinary dismissal of *Walsh* was not the performance of a public law duty. It was the breach of an employment contract. Donaldson M R had said in that case that the conditions specified by Parliament – 'to underpin the position of public authority employees' – were intended to be inserted in the employee's contract of employment (his 'private law' rights) by the public authority. If this were not done a 'public law' question would arise, and he could apply to the court, which would compel the public authority by mandamus (an order to it to carry out its public duties) to insert them. But in *Benwell* the Home Office had performed the duties imposed on it 'as part of the statutory terms under which it exercises its power' relating to the dismissal.

The introduction of a more rigid distinction than hitherto between 'public law' and 'private law' into our law generally, a development for which the Law Lords led by Lord Diplock in the 1980s are responsible, has brought in train problems many of which are illustrated here. The State employee or 'public servant' has in most Continental countries been treated as quite different from the 'employee', governed by public or 'administrative', rather than by private, law. Indeed, frequently such disputes will be heard by 'administrative' rather than by 'ordinary' courts. As for Britain, the eminent jurist Dicey eighty years ago denied the existence of 'administrative law', and Lord Hewart CJ in 1935 thought it 'Continental jargon'. Their antagonists, both old (like Maitland) and new (such as Jennings, Robson, Griffith or de Smith), have been influential in establishing that we do know of the existence of 'a vast body of administrative law. It comprises the law relating to public administration', even though we have 'no *Conseil d'Etat*, no *Oberverwaltungsgericht*, no separate administrative or constitutional court exercising a broad jurisdiction'.[123] Here, therefore, in the one set of courts, the rejuvenated remedy of judicial review in public law collides with the private law remedies for breach of contract at the new frontier of its territory.

This very uniformity of superior judicial machinery of adjudication makes more problematical the two tendencies of recent years: an extension of 'public law' duties, and the insistence upon their separateness from 'private law'. By 1980 the parallel distinction between an 'employee' and a public 'office-holder' was perceived by writers on administrative law themselves to be 'elusive', 'abstruse', 'bizarre', even 'asinine'; and some came to doubt the wisdom of extending public law remedies into the employment field, when this matter might be better left to clear principles of substance and of remedy in the statutes on 'unfair dismissal'.[124] Since then, however, the courts have not adopted that policy. Decisions such as *Liverpool*, *Walsh* and *Benwell* make the logic of the distinctions fragile. But the very inadequacy of the sanctions against 'unfair dismissal', which we examine in Chapter 3, has refuelled the engines of 'public law', as it edges into the labour law field.

In the 'public law' situation some infringement of statutory powers must be shown. The local authorities that (in breach of contract) reduced the wages of dinner-ladies on the school meals staff, in response to government financial 'cuts', sought to cure their earlier breach of those employment contracts (p. 153) by sending out dismissal notices. The trade union, *NUPE*, applied for 'judicial review'. It alleged that the dismissals, coupled with offers of jobs at lower wages, were a breach of national collective agreements and an industrial procedure that meant that the greatest burden of the 'cuts' fell upon those with the lowest pay. This was, the union alleged, a breach of a public duty by the councils, because they had acted so unreasonably. It could not be a reasonable exercise of statutory powers to penalize the poorest. The Court of Appeal would have none of this. It could find no evidence of 'unreasonableness' in the use of the powers in their administrative law sense.[125] Donaldson MR expressed great 'sympathy for those employees who were adversely affected'; but the rules of administrative law had to be 'applied in a real world in which local authorities and others . . . have to make a choice between different injustices and different hardships'. These were not decisions 'such as no reasonable authority could have reached'. Dillon LJ said it had been illustrated in the unfair dismissal cases on dinner-ladies (p. 245) that different industrial tribunals could come to different decisions on the matter in the field of employment law; but the question of 'reasonableness' in this case, in administrative law, was more 'sophisticated' and more difficult (i.e. could any reasonable authority have taken these decisions?).

This test is said to be different from that used on 'unfair dismissal'. In some situations this is so, but we shall see in Chapter 3 that in the field of 'private' jurisprudence too the test of the 'reasonableness' of an employer's decision to dismiss is often whether the decision falls within the 'band' of decisions that a reasonable or sensible employer could reach, whether or not the tribunal would itself have decided to dismiss. In a leading decision on administrative law in 1948 Lord Greene M R quoted the example of a teacher who is dismissed because she has red hair. In one sense this is 'unreasonable'. In another, it is taking account of 'extraneous matters'; or yet again, a decision 'so absurd that no sensible person could ever dream that it lay within the powers of the authority'. The tests in administrative law and in labour law may not be the same, but they do overlap.

At first sight, public law appears to offer strong protection to certain workers – especially if the decision of a public authority is quashed, thereby possibly protecting a whole class of workers of whom the applicant is only one. Statutory terms, especially on fair procedures for discipline or dismissal, can be enforced where these can be found in a scheme attaching to the employment, giving it an adequate 'public law' character, making the review of the employer's decisions a review of public administration. But these terms, as we saw in the Scottish teachers' cases, can be changed by statute (and often by regulation). And in any event the 'employer' can still argue (except in the case of a Crown servant) that they are really only part of an ordinary 'contract of service'. Breach of the statutory scheme for a public 'office' allows for stronger remedies via judicial review quashing the decision itself.

This still leaves open the definition of an 'office' for that purpose. Some judicial guidance has been given. In *Malloch*, 1971, Lord Reid said:

An elected body is in a very different position from a private employer. Many of its servants in the lower grades are in the same position as servants of a private employer. But many in higher grades or 'offices' are given special statutory status or protection.

In *Walsh*, 1984, Donaldson M R declared:

> Employment by a public authority does not per se inject any element of public law. Nor does the fact that the employee is in a 'higher grade' or is an 'officer'. This only makes it more likely that there will be special statutory restrictions upon dismissal or other underpinning of his employment.

The courts sometimes look for direct protection of the post in the statute or statutory scheme to provide the public law element. No doubt 'a majority of workers in Britain' would prefer to be able to secure such status so as to have the opportunity to ask a court to quash a dismissal (which ordinary 'unfair dismissal' law does not normally provide: p. 250).[126] There is no doubt, too, a case for extending reinstatement remedies to *all* employees. But the Court of Appeal in *Walsh* seemed determined not to allow public law to bring about such a development. Walsh had his conditions, like those of other workers, negotiated by the unions in the Whitley Council. They were then approved by the Minister. These conditions were classified by the judges as inhering in 'private law', expressed as is normal in the contract of employment (by 'incorporation' from the collective agreement: p. 329) rather than as constraints or restrictions put by Parliament upon the employer's powers or freedom of action. In the case of the *NUPE* dinner-ladies,[125] Donaldson M R said it was still 'arguable' that no employee of a local authority was an 'officer' entitled to proceed by way of judicial review unless he holds 'an office which has an existence independent of the person who for the time being fills it'. So too, it was said that if *Walsh's* conditions had been *different* from the common negotiated terms, he might have enjoyed 'an administrative law remedy by way of judicial review'. It could hardly be made clearer that, in respect of the employment terms of public authorities, statutory protections are to apply much more for the exceptional post or 'office'. *Hoi polloi*, those in the 'lower grades', must remain servants save for the few whom statute touches directly (like dockworkers or firemen, where the statutory regulations are a comprehensive scheme controlling all or most of the conditions of service),[127] or where some 'irrational' performance of a public function can be attacked.

The well intentioned applause that has accompanied the promotion of public law remedies, in place of the manifestly inadequate remedies of the common law and, now, of the law of 'unjust dismissal' (p. 258), has sometimes appeared to overlook this significant feature. One could apply a segmentation analysis to this law that is crystallizing on public employment parallel to that applied by some to the labour market. At the core stand the primary group of 'office'-holders, normally protected by statutory provisions and a right to be heard, with a distinct prospect of judicial review (though they may still be accorded *locus standi* also in the industrial tribunals, if they have not been positively excluded by statute as employees). Near or on the periphery one finds workers on lower rates and unstable conditions, poorly unionized or with a union in a weak bargaining position, whose only avenue of complaint for unfair dismissal is the tribunals. In intermediate rings, some workers with a better bargaining position no doubt hope they will one day be 'office'-holders. This was hardly the way we expected 'contract' to give way to 'status'. Public law has come, it seems, to refine the class distinctions of private law.

'Status' as a concept in this jurisprudence contains a marked flavour of social status. We find that this characteristic must be borne in mind, too, in another line of cases where courts have attempted to reinterpret the common law itself in a direction that owes something to the public law approach. When a tape-examiner employed by the BBC was accused of removing tapes, the BBC proposed to dismiss her, subject to her appeal in the internal disciplinary procedures. She applied for judicial review of the decision, contending that it should have been stayed until procedures were completed and the result of a criminal prosecution was known. But Woolf J. held that judicial review was inappropriate here. The procedures were part of her contract of employment, not a part of any public law scheme.[128] Even so, the rules of procedure of the court permitted him to treat the action also as one brought for breach of contract, i.e. a private law action. The contract gave the employee a right to a hearing, a right that today the court would uphold, he thought, by way of declaration and injunction. But the disciplinary tribunal, which she had attended, had now made a decision, even though it was subject to an appeal. There would on the facts be no miscarriage of justice in allowing the decision to dismiss to stand. The bold statements in the judgment of Woolf J. were taken in terms of principle by many to be an indication that the courts might now be more ready to enforce where they could the principles of natural justice, before an ordinary employee's dismissal took effect. It is also true that the liberal spirit of his judgment indicates a willingness to extend such reasoning to all types of employee. There are, however, few other decisions along these lines.

In one rather strange case, the Court of Appeal in 1977 did grant a declaration that the dismissal of *Stevenson*, an employee and full-time officer of a trade union, was 'in breach of the rules, in breach of natural justice, *ultra vires* and null and void'.[129] His contract of employment incorporated a union rule providing that the employment would continue 'so long as he gave satisfaction to the executive committee'. A disciplinary case was brought, but he was given no notice of the charges. The committee purported to dismiss him on three months' notice. If he had complained *qua* member of the union (he was a member, too) earlier decisions made it clear he could utilize the normal right of a member to challenge the validity of an expulsion from the union that had been vitiated by procedures contrary to 'natural justice' and obtain an injunction to stop it (p. 807). But such cases also denied his right to a declaration *qua* employee. The appeal judges held, however, that Stevenson was entitled to a fair hearing as an *employee* because the union was a 'party invested with a power' that it should exercise only after complying with that (contractual) duty. The decision of the committee was, therefore, declared a 'nullity *ab initio*'; but this did 'not declare that the contract of employment is still subsisting'. No injunction was granted.

Just what the declaration did effect remains rather a puzzle; nor is there anything in the judgments to suggest that Stevenson's position was some kind of 'office'. So to decide would, indeed, be to transform trade union officials into 'officers' in a *public* law sense, not only a move wrong in law but an unprecedented incursion of the State into the relationship. To avoid this temptation, it is sometimes suggested that the *Stevenson* declaration was granted because Stevenson was dismissible only for cause, but the *committee* had only a limited power to adjudicate, namely by fair procedures, and the employing union could not adopt the decision reached in breach of that power.[130] But this is not parallel to normal private law principles. If the managing director, or a board, of a company dismisses a worker or a manager in breach of express or implied procedures touching their authority under the company's articles of association, the courts will not by reason only of that grant a declaration of invalidity to the dismissed employee.

Indeed, a few exceptions apart, the company *can* 'adopt' the decision.

If the courts had been generally prepared to invalidate a dismissal at common law because the servant had received no fair hearing by the master, one of the main arguments for statutory protection against unfair dismissal would long ago have disappeared, and the character of dismissal law would have been different. They do so only rarely, and then declare the dismissal only 'wrongful', not invalid or 'void'.[131] The difficulty in *Stevenson* may therefore turn upon the court's choice of the wrong form of declaration, induced by the contingency that the employer was a trade union. The new law of unfair dismissal (Chapter 3) has accepted a worker's right to compensation in some cases when he is deprived of a hearing to appeal against unreasonable dismissal, but only where the employment contract expressly gives him access to this procedure. Even here the judges have differed. For example, *Tipton* was dismissed because of absenteeism. He wished to appeal under the employer's disciplinary procedures, which were part of his employment contract. But the dismissal was effected by the board of directors itself, which was also the final appeal body. No appeal, therefore, was allowed. A tribunal found this to be an unfair dismissal because Tipton had been unreasonably deprived of his contractual right to appeal (whatever the outcome might have been). The Court of Appeal held that this conclusion could not be sustained, because under the legislation the reasonableness of a dismissal is judged by the employer's state of mind and the conduct of the worker at the time of dismissal. The company's refusal to allow an appeal was subsequent to dismissal. Unless there was evidence of a 'closed mind' from the outset (which here was not argued), that decision was irrelevant to whether the company acted reasonably at the time of his sacking. The House of Lords disagreed. Evidence that came to light in the appeal procedures after the initial sacking could go to show the 'strength or weakness' of the employer's claim to have acted reasonably in treating the reason given as sufficient to merit dismissal. The worker should not be deprived of his contractual right to shake the employer's case. Where the facts showed that dismissal was inevitable (as with flagrant dishonesty) the employer might reasonably refuse an appeal, despite the contractual right; but that was not the case here.[132]

When we contrast the few exceptional cases where courts have granted declarations or injunctions against dismissals on a common law basis, we find a mixture of legal, social and industrial policy similar to that appearing to infuse the public law cases. None is more remarkable than the decision in *Hill* v. *Parsons Ltd*, 1972.[133] The judgments were rendered by the Court of Appeal on facts that arose just before the coming into effect of provisions of the Industrial Relations Act 1971. An injunction was granted in interim proceedings to an engineer employed for some thirty-five years by the defendants, so as to block his dismissal. He refused to join the union with which the employers had signed a closed-shop agreement. This had been concluded some six months before the Act would give him new rights not to be dismissed on the ground of non-unionism. The Court of Appeal decided that his proper period of notice was six months and that an injunction would lie to enforce his continued employment. The court's discretion was exercised in his favour because 'damages were not an adequate remedy' and the employer's hand had been forced by the union. Lord Denning M R led Sachs L J on to new paths in order (he delicately put it) 'to step over the trip wires of the previous cases and to bring the law into accord with the needs of today'. In other words, it was a quite unprecedented decision to enforce a personal contract. It maintained Hill's employment until he acquired the new statutory protections under the 1971 Act. In effect, the judges created a right to protection before Parliament's statute ever came into effect as law at all. Like *Stevenson's* case, the *Hill* doctrine has not been given any general application. It is a reserve weapon, rarely used.

Indeed, three years later, *Chappell* claimed an injunction to block his dismissal by employers who had told the union that, unless *all* members individually repudiated a union threat of selective strike action (p. 328), they would all be treated as having 'terminated their own engagements' by reason of it. The judges refused to stop this dismissal even if it might be found later to be unlawful as an 'unfair' dismissal.[134] To do this would be to 'force the employers to continue the contract of service'. *Hill's* case, said the court, was different; the employer had no reason there 'to distrust the employee'. Here, the 'loyalty' of these unionized workers was suspect; mutual confidence had not survived. 'These men', declared Lord Denning M R, 'are seeking equity but are not ready to do it themselves.' It is beating about the bush to see this decision as anything other than a judicial refusal to grant to suspect trade unionists what had previously been granted to a trusty non-unionist. Nor have the courts ever indicated that they will hold up the unfair dismissal of a worker just before he completes his required period of continuous service for a redundancy payment or a claim against unfair dismissal, so as to enable him to qualify for those rights under the statute. After *Hill's* case, one might ask: why not? One answer would clearly be that the court could not enforce this personal contract against the employer whose confidence in the employee had evaporated, merely in order to allow the latter to assert rights that he might acquire under statute a few days or weeks after the moment chosen by the employer to make him unemployed. The remedy, in other words, works only through the collusion of the employer and the court.

There are other, rather different cases in which injunctions have been granted, especially, for example, in favour of teachers. *Jones*, a married teacher, was appointed head of a religious school by the managers (the employers). The employment terms were set out in a letter from the local council (which footed the bill) and included carefully devised procedures for dismissals. The council was obliged to make rules for that matter by statute, and, indeed, dismissals needed its consent. Jones's marriage ended in divorce. The managers and the diocesan bishop appointed a special tribunal to hear the case, and then dismissed him. This procedure did not accord with the council's rules, which required a hearing by, and consent of, that authority. Here the plaintiff avoided the pitfalls in *Hannam's* case (p. 155). First, he picked the right defendant (the school managers). But what was his remedy? The Court of Appeal was prepared to imply into his employment contract a right to the proper procedures referred to in the letter. So the procedure 'adopted for his dismissal', said Roskill L J, 'was not the procedure for which his contract provided'. On this the court based an injunction.[135] There appears to have been little argument about this order being one 'to give effect to a contract of service' (the judge below had said this was an 'exceptional case'); but there was a public law element, albeit a tenuous one. The trouble had arisen partly because the council had failed to promulgate 'rules of management' in breach of its statutory duty. Whilst his cause of action was founded on the contract, the terms of that contract were confined within an area mapped out by the council's public duties.

There was a public law background also to *Irani's* case, 1985.[136] An ophthalmologist worked in a health authority clinic for one afternoon a week, under a part-time contract of employment into which (the parties, it must be noted, agreed) there had been incorporated all the Whitley Council and other NHS conditions of employment. These were set out in a 'blue book' and a 'red book'. He quarrelled with the consultant, faced a panel of inquiry and was dismissed because he and the consultant had 'irreconcilable' differences. His complaint was that the procedures in those conditions had not been properly exhausted. Warner J. granted an interlocutory injunction preventing the authority from implementing its decision to dismiss him until the matter was finally tried. The authority argued that no specific performance of the contract of employment could properly be granted; but the judge (to whom no authorities before 1958 appear to have been cited) disagreed. *Hill's* case rested on three factors: confidence existed between employer and employee; the advent of the 1971 Act's rights was imminent; and damages were not an adequate remedy. Here there was a parallel: the authority still had faith in Irani's 'loyalty'; he was asking for time to gain the protection of the procedures; and damages were inadequate. But the second parallel is fallacious; no *new* rights outside the contract would accrue to the employee. The last point, furthermore, exposed two critical factors. One reason why Irani could not be satisfied with damages on the facts of this case was his desire to continue to work in the National Health Service sector of medicine and to continue to treat his private patients in NHS hospitals. Moreover, in law, the authority was

under a statutory restriction as to the kind of contract which it can make with its servants . . . [and] under a restriction as to the manner in which it can dismiss them.

The court would not allow such a public authority 'to snap its fingers at the rights of its employees under the blue book'. This is surely the point; it is difficult to believe that the *public* nature of this statutory scheme was not a determinative factor in permitting the judge to reach that conclusion. The ophthalmologist, at any rate, fared better than the more peripheral dinner-ladies in terms of the procedures and agreements from whose application they might have a legitimate expectation to receive protection. But their expectations rested only on collective agreements.

The grim contrast with the Court of Appeal in *City and Hackney Health Authority* v. *NUPE*, 1985, is another reminder to those who trust in 'public duties' that they have little to offer as yet to collective bargaining or trade unionists.[137] C. was a hospital porter and NUPE shop steward whose members occupied a hospital that the authority had decided to close. The authority obtained *ex parte* injunctions to stop him and NUPE obstructing entry to it, and also suspended him, refusing to allow him to enter the hospital premises. C. now applied for an injunction ordering them to allow him entry in order 'to carry out his duties as a shop steward and to negotiate' about the closure under a long-standing Whitley Council staff agreement. The judge granted the injunction but he was smartly reversed by the Court of Appeal. By now C. had been dismissed. If he had had any legal right to fulfil his duties as a shop steward in the hospital, this arose from the incorporation into his employment contract of the terms of the Whitley agreement (p. 342). Those terms, it should be noted, did take effect partly by reason of the approval of the Secretary of State and by reason of statutory regulations that said they must be incorporated. In other words, this was not a bare, private law contract of employment, but a contract clothed with the very functions in issue for a shop steward by reason of public regulation controlling the employer in the health service.

Even so, said the court, the 'privileges extended to a shop steward' must come to an end when the employment contract came to an end. They were not like a worker's duties under a (reasonable) covenant restricting competition, which survive the termination of that contract. What is more, said Oliver LJ, the judge's order seemed to be 'specific enforcement' of a personal contract. Here the employers had 'lost all confidence' in this worker. The hospital authorities objected to discussing anything with this 'discredited employee'. The court could not compel an employer to accept the presence of an employee guilty of serious misconduct, especially one in 'constant contact with other members of the staff'. So, despite the undoubted statutory element here, C. did not get his injunction; nor should we think there was much hope that he could. Injunctions, like public law duties, are not there to enforce trade union rights of negotiation against an employer, above all if he has no more 'trust' in a shop steward who has been involved in an occupation of a hospital that must be closed down.

Faced with this plethora of fluctuating authority, few principles of law can be stated with complete confidence. The common law judge must still assume that he will refuse remedies that specifically enforce personal contracts of employment. A worker may become an 'exceptional' case and be granted a declaration (*Stevenson*) or even an injunction (*Hill*). When such unprecedented exceptions in 'private law' will be allowed in cases that are purely contractual remains obscure. The chances of success may increase if his contract of employment incorporates duties or conditions that stem from a statutory code regulating or affecting the employer (*Irani, McClelland*, possibly *Jones*). But mere employment in the 'public sector' does not afford him a right to 'judicial review' to enforce his contract and invalidate the dismissal (*Walsh, Lavelle*). Public bodies normally employ most of their workers on ordinary contracts of employment (*Gunton, Walsh*). Once we enter the field of 'public law', if workers enjoy a statutory 'status', a declaration of nullity and an appropriate order may be made by the court (*Vine, Ridge, Malloch*) or some breach of public duty may be quashed (*Liverpool*). If the exercise of a power of dismissal is challenged, however, on the ground that it was unreasonable, the burden will not be easily discharged of proving that the decision was one 'which no sensible authority acting with due appreciation of its responsibility would have decided to adopt' (*NUPE*) – even though the Law Lords have in other contexts not failed to put local councils and Ministers under this lash in decisions with a controversial content outside the employment field.[138]

There is no indication in any of this that the judges have come near to affording effective protection by injunction to the ordinary worker dismissed in breach of principles of 'fairness' or 'natural justice'. At best, he will be left to damages for inadequate notice at common law (normally a few weeks' wages; p. 210) and such compensation as he may or may not receive from a tribunal for unfair dismissal. Even if he is within the ambit of employment governed by statutory powers, he is unlikely (except in a rare case, such as dockworkers) to enjoy any of the public law remedies. These are more likely to attach to the higher-grade employees. Even on the few occasions in private law when an injunction might on principle be available to him, it will in law be at the discretion of the judge (for the injunction is a discretionary remedy, in the last resort granted only when the judge considers that the 'balance of convenience' lies with the plaintiff: p. 684); but in reality it will also be at the discretion of the employer. For if the employer testifies that he no longer has 'trust' or confidence in the worker or in his 'loyalty', the old common law rule will be applied and *Hill's* case be ousted. The union member in conflict with his employer can therefore expect little from this line of decisions.

The new interventions by judicial review may be seen as a response to the large expansion of public sector employment in recent decades in our society. Yet again, common law courts recognized a rival centre of growing power in their traditional manner. Also, as usual, their response was belated; judicial review markedly extended its grip in the 1980s just when it seemed that the expansion of public employment had been reversed. More important to our study, though, what renewed interest in 'public law' reasoning has also done is valuably to focus attention upon the question of why ordinary workers of no special legal or social status should not enjoy job security to the extent that they are entitled to elementary 'fairness' before they are dismissed. Should they not, moreover, retain the job until any disputed issue on which it would be fair to have a hearing has been determined by a third party, be it a tribunal, arbitrator or other person under an agreed disputes procedure? The right of the employer to dismiss as he pleases is widely believed to have been modified already in the employment protection laws, not least in the restrictions upon unfair dismissal and provisions for redundancy. That belief, though, is not always well founded.

We now turn to these and to other areas of law relating to job security.

[3] Job Security and Dismissal

We must investigate the obligations of employer and employee under the contract of employment in order to understand the ways in which the contract can come to an end and the consequences of its termination. Those obligations may, as in other contracts, be either expressly stated or implied, and any breach gives to the other party a claim for damages as compensation for his loss or, in the case of a very serious breach, a right to end the contract by 'accepting' the breach as a termination. This is what happens in a case of summary dismissal. More usually notice of dismissal will be given by one party to the other to terminate the contract. But legislation has surrounded this common law perception, where termination is either a dismissal with notice or a summary 'wrongful dismissal' in breach of the contract, with a complex web of new and quite separate rules, not least those relating to 'unfair dismissal' and redundancy, on which the industrial tribunals began their work as recently as 1971 and 1965 respectively. Paradoxically, however, experience has shown that the contract of employment now needs even closer inspection. For the employment protection legislation has used its common law concepts, and has therefore both been influenced by them and, in turn, reached back to influence the moulding of their very shape.

Implied obligations in the contract

In any contract the problems of real life are always sufficiently unpredictable to bring to light gaps in what the parties have expressly agreed. The common law will therefore imply a term

of which it can be predicated that 'it goes without saying'; some term not expressed but necessary to give to the transaction such business efficacy as the parties must have intended.[1]

The test is sometimes expressed as one to which, on the suggestion of an 'officious bystander', the parties would respond, 'Oh of course!' But judges began to go further, even before the onset of the employment protection statutes, and held in 1957 that a term could be implied that did not represent the 'intention of the parties' but was a 'necessary condition of the relation of master and man', more akin to 'a question of status'.[2] This extends their power; indeed, by 1982 they were prepared to imply into relationships 'which demand by their nature and subject matter certain obligations' a term that they see as 'necessary' or 're-quired', not satisfying the 'business efficacy or officious bystander tests', even though it 'would not have been at once assented to by both parties' when making the contract and (contrary to normal principle) even taking account of the parties' conduct after they made it.[3]

How will judges decide what is a 'necessary' term of employment *outside* the apparent 'intention' of the parties? It is still the law that no term can be implied in territory that is occupied by an express term; but save where a union is strong or an individual exceptionally qualified and able to dictate conditions, it is the employer who inserts most express terms. No doubt, as one judge declared in 1978, the implied terms 'will reflect the changes in the relationship between employer and employee as social standards change'. More accurately they are determined by the judges' perception of those changes and of what is required by them. The E A T in particular has required higher standards of 'fairness' from the employer; but these have entered the law more as part of the law on unfair dismissal as such (p. 233). Often, though, such cases put in issue the contractual terms. What happens, for example, if the worker is temporarily off sick and nothing has been expressly agreed?

Express terms exclude the court from adding implied terms in the same area. Here the express agreement often takes the form of an occupational sick-pay scheme established at the initiative of the employer, possibly after collective bargaining, the terms entering the employment contract, often by reference in the written particulars (p. 136). An official survey showed that even by 1975 some 80 per cent of employees (although less than 60 per cent of women workers) were covered by such schemes; but only 11.5 per cent received full pay when sick; many schemes operated at the employer's discretion, or for short periods; and most deducted the sickness benefit paid to the worker under the national insurance arrangements. The courts have interpreted such terms by reference to the background bargaining (p. 333), but it might have been thought they would go further and uphold the view that, where an employment contract was silent, the wage was impliedly payable (or the wage less national insurance sickness benefit) while the employment contract continued for the period of sickness. Indeed, this was the approach of older authorities.

In *Mears* v. *Safecar Security Ltd*[3] a very different view was taken. The judges thought the facts pointed to a 'no work, no wages' contract. The 'best indication' as to what term should be implied on sick-pay to the employee, a security guard who was ill for seven months, was 'the fact that he was paid or not paid'. His contract was silent about pay while he was sick. Where he was not paid (as here) the implication should be against any obligation to pay sick-pay even if only the employer, not the worker, would have assented to that idea when the contract was made if the issue had been raised with them. This use of *subsequent* conduct to prove contractual terms that ought to represent the parties' 'intention' is most unusual, and seems here to give legal support to the harder-nosed employer. Indeed, it is a break from the normal rules of law of which the consequences are hard to predict; there is certainly no guarantee that practice in performance of the contract will benefit the employee, not least where the union is weak and the employer's discretion wide.

In an Act of 1982 a volcanic change occurred in national insurance. Sick-pay was now to be paid for the first eight weeks not by the State but by the employer, who recovers the money from insurance funds (the period is extended to twenty-eight weeks in 1986). The employee may himself 'certificate' the first week's sickness; he must suffer 'incapacity for work' in a period of 'entitlement' because of illness on a 'qualifying day' when required to work (regulations of 1985 prohibit the previous practice of employer and worker defining qualifying days by agreement). The rates are related to 'normal (average) weekly earnings' (in 1986, £31.60, where earnings fall between £38 and £55.49; for earnings of £74.50 or above, £46.75). Employees with fixed contracts of less than three months and those at whose workplace there is a 'trade dispute' in which they participated or had a direct interest (p. 677) are disqualified. The latter would cover industrial action by a mass 'sick-out', which workers have in the past used in the USA.

The scheme, introduced by the Government primarily to reduce public expenditure and Civil Service jobs, to tax sickness benefit and to prevent 'overcompensation' by scroungers, shifts administration of welfare on to employers, thereby 'privatizing' sickness benefit without encouraging collective bargaining on occupational schemes. This privatized welfare scheme uses the employer to administer broadly the same concepts as in national insurance and passes disputes not to the industrial, but to the social security tribunals. The scheme is complex (a survey in 1985 estimated that small employers 'got it wrong' in 25 per cent of payments); and it is odd that a Government that justified truncation of the employment protection legislation by reason of the 'burden' on employers (p. 235) should put this administrative weight upon them – though in 1986 an employer became entitled to an additional 8 per cent rebate of the benefit paid, for administrative costs (Regulations No. 318, 1986). The courts, though, have seen the growth of statutory sick-pay as another reason not to saddle the employer with implied terms on the matter.[4] We have yet to see what they will make of the rule that the employer cannot evade sick-pay by dismissing the employee 'solely or mainly for the purpose' of avoiding it – if a worker ever manages to prove that subjective intent.

The *Mears* case[3] raises another issue. Suppose workers accept engagement where the employer operates a practice on which nothing is said to the new employee. One judge in 1918 refused to imply a term into the contract where none of the workers 'when they entered the employment . . . had ever heard of that practice'. On the other hand, in *Sagar* v. *Ridehalgh*,[5] Lawrence LJ held that a Lancashire weaver 'accepted his employment on the same terms as to deduction for bad work as the other weavers at the mill', whether he knew of the practice or not. This dominance of the employer's prerogative might be considered to be out of line with modern thinking. Yet the Court of Appeal held in *Mears* (where again nothing was said):

It was the practice of the company not to pay wages to employees absent sick, and the practice was well known to the company's employees. The company would not have made an exception in the [plaintiff] employee's favour.

The appeal to the knowledge of all the existing workers throws their collective weight into the balance on the employer's side. It is an odd argument; and it does not alter the lack of knowledge in the individual worker. A somewhat stricter view has recently been taken of the principle that a term may be implied into the contract by reason of a 'custom', of the trade or the locality, or as part of the 'custom and practice' that, in British industry, play such 'an important part in shop-floor industrial relations' (though their role may be changing where employment becomes more 'formalized and codified').[6] If a custom is 'reasonable, certain and notorious' the court will enforce it. In 1977 the E A T referred back to a tribunal the issue whether an employer had a right to 'lay off' 'according to the customs of the trade' up and down the country; and in 1978 it tested the lawfulness of an order to a specialist teacher to move to general teaching duties by reference to the duties she was engaged to undertake and to 'the custom and practice of the profession'.

In *Sagar's* case,[5] an additional ground for permitting reasonable deductions from a weaver's wages was the 'general usage . . . prevailing in the weaving trade in Lancashire'. But in 1983 Pain J. rejected an alleged custom of the engineering trade allowing employers to lay off workers without pay where some work was available, partly because the employee 'knew nothing of any such custom' and the custom was not 'notorious at all events so far as the defendants' factory was concerned'.[7] Moreover, the E A T in 1982 thought a unilateral management policy could not become a term as 'established custom and practice' unless it had been drawn to workers' attention or 'followed without exception' for a long period.[8] It is sometimes said that the collective agreement's terms can enter the individual employment contract as terms established by 'custom'; but we shall see in Chapter 4 that this reasoning can be dangerous (p. 332).

The courts therefore have great scope today for 'creativity' in the implication of terms in the contract. They do not usually use it in order to limit managerial prerogative. Moreover, it is here that the dialectic between statute and common law is most pronounced. The common lawyer, Kahn-Freund said, is often 'intellectually helpless in the face of legislation, unable to see statute law and common law as a whole'. With few exceptions (such as equal pay: p. 487) the statutory obligations governing employment do not enter the contract of employment. Indeed, their very enforcement is entrusted to different bodies: guarantee pay (p. 396) to industrial tribunals, recovery of agreed wages to the ordinary courts. But the concepts of common law, above all of contract law, filter back into the language of the statute as applied. Indeed, on many matters – the concept of 'dismissal' for example – Parliament itself naturally uses hallowed concepts of 'the law'.

Two factors have contributed to rather confused tendencies in the case law and have loosened some of the earlier principles of law. First, decisions on implied terms are often called for in litigation where the worker alleges the employer unfairly dismissed him by breaking an obligation which amounted to a 'constructive dismissal' (i.e. a repudiation of the contract, which is treated as a dismissal: p. 222). Here, in employment protection law, the appellate courts will normally regard themselves as bound by the industrial tribunal's findings, unless there is an error of law or a perverse or irrational finding of fact. Secondly, both there and elsewhere the dispute comes to tribunals and judges for whom a search for industrial justice involves managerial authority and promotion of efficiency and profitability in an employment relationship 'analysed as one between individuals, hardly touched by collective bargaining'.[9]

Where, for example, in a 'mobility' case, employers asserted the right to change the place (and kind) of work of Mr Jones, a tunneller, taken on to work at a particular pit (whom they later notified of an obligation to work at any 'place in the UK the employers may decide'), the EAT, though refusing to accept the later notification as an agreed variation of terms, held that the contract was sufficiently ambiguous to permit of an implied term 'which the parties, *if reasonable*, would probably have agreed', to give the contract 'business efficacy'. This would permit the employers to require him to work (at the new kind of work) anywhere within reasonable daily commuting distance from his home.[10] This approach is sometimes said to be liberal. But it is barely contractual.

Manipulating the implied terms

Because of these developments it is no longer easy to set out implied terms under the old headings. The employer is obliged to pay the agreed wages; to take reasonable care to provide a safe system of work (an important duty: see p. 426); to reimburse the servant for expenses in proper performance of his orders; and to avoid orders to do unlawful acts. As to the last, telling employees that they will not be disciplined if they decide to break the law in an emergency may be permissible, the Court of Appeal decided in 1971, at any rate for fire-engine drivers crossing red lights (otherwise the risk of accidents would increase).

The employer is not normally obliged to provide work, so long as he pays the agreed wage. Usually he can, if he wishes, keep the employee idle. He has bought an option on labour power. This is the basis of the employer's right to pay wages due in lieu of notice. Of course, if he unilaterally alters the formula for the wage payment (e.g. from a percentage base to a target, for a salesman) he is in breach. But when we speak of the 'wage–work bargain',[11] the limitations on the employer's obligations need to be remembered. The law has exceptionally departed from this approach where the very nature of the contract means that the employer should offer work because otherwise the employee has no chance to earn anything if there is no work (where, for example, services are rendered at piece-rates, or where he depends on work for his continuing ability to find jobs, as with actors). In such cases there may be today a contractual entitlement to a minimum, such as 'guaranteed week' rates bargained with a union; and statute now provides a rather miserable floor of guarantee payments (p. 396).

Recently the courts have slightly expanded the exceptions. Employers of a chief engineer, for example, may be under a duty to provide him with suitable work;[12] and the employer may be obliged to let a worker earn his living where he is unable or forbidden to take part in other activity.[13] Similar protective decisions have caused judges to suggest a need for the employer to give to a non-unionist 'a fair opportunity' to share in the shift and overtime work so as to earn premiums above the basic wage. But this is very different from an obligation to provide him with job satisfaction or what Lord Denning (quoting Longfellow's 'The Village Blacksmith') called his 'right to work' (a more apt literary embellishment, Hepple rightly noted, might be Blake's dark Satanic mills).[14] The E A T, building on this approach in 1980, confirmed that the employer of a silversmith owed a duty not to exclude him 'arbitrarily or capriciously' from wage increases payable to others working on the same basis.[15] But the judges have pulled back from any general applications of such concepts. A probationary employee was said in 1981 to be owed no duty by the employer 'to support, assist, guide and train her'; and there certainly is no general obligation on the employer to 'treat an employee in a reasonable manner', for such an implied term would be 'too wide and too uncertain'.[16]

This leads us to the modern duties of 'mutual trust', fidelity and confidence.

Employee's implied terms

Before considering that important area, we may note traditional implied obligations for the *employee*: to obey reasonable, lawful orders; to exercise reasonable care and such skill as he should possess; and to act in good faith and fidelity. The duty of reasonable care was turned into a duty to indemnify the master for breach of it in the course of normal employment in *Lister's* case.[17] Lister was a lorry driver. One day in the slaughterhouse he carelessly drove over another employee (who happened to be his father). The company was 'vicariously' liable to the latter when he sued it for damages (p. 427). Before 1948 he might have failed because, in decisions dating from 1837, the courts decided a servant could not sue the master for the carelessness of fellow servants in 'common employment' with him – on the extraordinary ground that each servant 'impliedly agreed' to take the risk of the other's negligence. To decide otherwise would be 'an encouragement to the servant to omit . . . diligence and caution'. This doctrine was finally abolished by statute in 1948. Now 'masters' are insured; and, in *Lister's* case, the insurers who paid the damages used their right to sue Lister in the employer's name (a normal right under such policies). He had broken his duty of care, it was held, and he must pay his employer the amount of the damages paid to his father. But did not modern employers and employees expect that insurers would in reality pay such damages? Should an implied term not allow the driver today to benefit from the insurance policy? Lister argued that this was the modern understanding in employment. By three to two, the Law Lords rejected such a 'novel' term. Viscount Simonds echoed Victorian values in saying:

now to grant the servant immunity from such an action would tend to create a feeling of irresponsibility in a class of person from whom, perhaps more than any other, constant vigilance is owed to the community.

The only reason why no outcry followed the *Lister* case was a gentlemen's agreement among the insurance companies not to bring such actions for indemnity, and a similar agreement limits such actions against doctors in the health service. But this is slender protection for the employee. By 1973 a majority in the Court of Appeal tried to limit its impact by interpreting an indemnity clause falling outside the arrangement so as to disallow such an action against the worker, by way of an implied term needed 'in the realities of the situation'; the parties knew the insurance really paid; and normally, to sue the careless worker 'would not only lead to a strike', said Lord Denning MR: 'It would be positively unjust.'[18] Few sophisticated discussions of insurance and 'fault liability' take such account of the beneficial effects of anticipated strikes upon the law of implied terms. Clauses that exempt the employee from liability are not within the Unfair Contracts Terms Act 1977, but clauses protecting the employer are, and are therefore invalid if unreasonable (s. 2, Sched. 1).

Fidelity, trust and confidence

The decisions about 'constructive dismissal' have had great effect upon the implied duties of loyalty, 'mutual trust' and fidelity. The ancient, rather feudal duties of the employer (to provide medicines, for example) have died out; but in their place has appeared a version that in *Woods* v. *WM Car Services*[19] Lord Denning MR summed up as parallel to 'the cases in the old days' – which he had consulted (after the conclusion of counsel's arguments) 'over the week-end' – in a formula that may be thought unpardonably to beg every question: 'Just as a servant must be good and faithful, so an employer must be good and considerate.' He saw this to be the basis of neither of them doing anything to destroy 'the relationship of confidence between them'.

In this case, the employers had tried to impose additional work on a clerk and unilaterally to demote her from 'chief' secretary. This gave rise to constant friction, especially because they had agreed to continue her employment as it had been under previous owners. But this was not enough to upset an industrial tribunal's decision that the employer had not broken the contract in a fundamental manner. Watkins LJ found her 'obdurate refusal' to accept the new terms unreasonable. He assumed the worker must co-operate in change, whether or not it benefits the employer more than the worker.

Employers must not . . . be put in a position where, through the wrongful refusal of their employee to accept change, they are prevented from introducing improved business methods in furtherance of seeking success for their enterprise.

This approach, subjecting the employment contract to the employer's power to legislate at the workplace in order to improve the methods and the profits of 'the business', is the most important judicial development of the 1980s and underlines, yet again, the subordinate dependence of the employee. For all the special flavour of the old common law, it should not be thought that this phenomenon is confined to England. In other countries of Europe the selfsame tendencies appear; the labour courts of West Germany, for example, have deferred to management prerogative where dismissals are necessitated by 'urgent requirements' of the enterprise.[20]

The employer's own duties, however, have been differently applied by the courts in respect of the various types of employee. Management must not falsely assert or imply dishonesty on a worker's part, as an electrician's case confirmed in 1978. And a breach arose from a failure by Wigan Borough Council to give proper support to a junior manager in an old people's home, who had been sent to Coventry by other workers. For employees of higher, managerial or foreman status – sometimes today termed a position of 'high trust'[21] – the test is rather more strict. So, although 'trenchant criticism' of performance may be justified, when an assistant manager said to an overseer of eighteen years' service, 'You can't do the bloody job anyway' (which was not an expression of his true beliefs), he broke a fundamental obligation not to act 'without reasonable and proper cause' in a way likely seriously to damage the relationship of confidence and trust between the parties. So too, an area manager who suffered a nervous breakdown from persistent criticism, 'undermining his authority in the presence of his subordinates', proved an equivalent breach in 1978.[22] The implied obligation of 'trust and confidence' can be used to the advantage of an employee who has waived an earlier breach by the employer. A company broke the express contract by demoting an employee, with lower salary, but he continued working, thereby waiving the breach. But when the employer later harassed him with complaints and other detriment, the Court of Appeal decided that he could rely upon the whole series of incidents (including those waived) to establish a breach of the implied term, and thereby prove a 'constructive dismissal': p. 222[23] (though whether a dismissal is 'reasonable' or not is, as we shall see, another question: p. 244).

However, such protective phrases are rarely applied to the unskilled, or deskilled, worker. Yet there has been a price exacted of all employees, a slow, creeping extension of the *worker's* duty of fidelity reaching out to a vague duty of positive co-operation. This duty originates in the old law requiring the servant to be faithful, for example not to make use of information or material confidential to the employer such as using trade secrets or canvassing clients for a business he aims to set up later. Collective bargaining has never been accorded priority over this, as employees discovered in 1945 when they disclosed, in breach of contract, information about the business to their union officials that the officials needed to prepare for the bargaining round. So too, an army sergeant in 1951, who had used his uniform and position to make a secret profit of £20,000 by sale of illicit spirits in Egypt, broke his duty. But an employee may take with him on leaving the employment, and subsequently use, his own skill and knowledge including his memory of customers and sales information. This far Mr Fowler, a former sales manager of a concern daily selling chickens in itinerant refrigerated lorries to butchers and restaurants, was allowed to use his knowledge about customers and other sales information in his competing business, even though he dealt a serious blow to his former employer's business, and despite the doctrine that forbids the use of confidential information while the employment subsists.[24]

The Court of Appeal stated that the implied term restricting breach of confidence, whilst it still covered trade secrets, was rather more restricted after the employer leaves the employment than when he is still an employee. This is why employers often impose restrictive covenants (lawful if they are 'reasonable': p. 151). Disclosure of confidential information may be justified if the employee discloses misdeeds 'of a serious nature and importance to the country', or otherwise in the public interest (such as a serious breach of the law or 'breach of the country's security'), as the judge put it in the copyright case arising from the 'Ballsoff Memorandum'.[25]

The good faith requirement at the root of these duties has been extended. An employee innocently obtained invoices relating to her employer's potential customers quite outside her employment duties and showed them to her husband, who found them interesting for his business. Even though she had made no use of opportunities acquired in her work or at work, it was held there was a sufficient case against her for breach of a 'fiduciary duty' (the equitable doctrine that prohibits a person from being in a position where duty and interest conflict) to merit an injunction.[26] Such judgments have borrowed doctrines of company law for use in employment law. Directors, whose position is nearly as high as 'trust' can go, short of the trustee proper, are under strict 'fiduciary duties'; and, now that the old learning which said a director could not be a 'servant' has been swept aside, the director with a contract of service finds that these equitable obligations are sometimes treated as implied terms of it, which survive its termination (though a failure to disclose an intention to act in breach is not itself a breach of duty).[27] Indeed, no employee is obliged gratuitously to disclose personal defects or breaches of duty (as in the 1872 case of a governess who said nothing about being a divorcee or of Mr Bell in 1932 who negotiated with Lever Bros. while a managing director of a subsidiary, knowing all the time he had committed serious breaches). But a supervisory role will usually imply a duty to report on *other* employees' misconduct: 'He may be so placed in the hierarchy as to have a duty to report either the misconduct of his superior . . . or the misconduct of his inferiors.'[28]

Freedland concludes that 'obligations of loyalty and good faith of those in senior managerial or executive positions are particularly strict'.[29] Certainly the expansion of duty has there been widest. But the unusual extension in 1946 of the duty of loyalty and good faith to restrain skilled workers from working in their spare time on valves for deaf-aids for another competing manufacturer (even though they disclosed no trade secrets and did not disable themselves from doing their normal work) must, it seems, be restricted to cases where the moonlighting activity causes serious harm and prejudice to the primary employer (as a case about an 'odd-job' man proves).[30]

The law here is not uninfluenced by the desire to permit directors lawfully to sit on the boards of competing companies, which too wide an implied term against serving competitors might prohibit (as Lord Denning once said the law should). But there is also a need to protect the leisure time of the worker (including his right not to work overtime when his contract does not demand it). He has not sold his whole private life along with his labour power in the wage–work bargain, a point to which we return later (Chapter 6, p. 449). Where, though, the employer spells out an express rule of the employment forbidding 'private trading for gain', the courts can be very tough, as where a Radio Rentals employee in 1982 was dismissed – 'fairly' – for one isolated incident, privately repairing a television set for a lady for £14 (a decision not so far distant from the old approach of the nineteenth century). And an ordinary employee, with no management functions, has more than once been placed under an implied duty to co-operate with the employer.

Duties of co-operation

We have seen that an employee may be obliged to accept considerable changes in his own employment terms to accommodate 'improved business methods' that promote the success of the enterprise. In days of technological change this is of great importance. Is the worker contractually obliged to co-operate in introducing new methods that may lead to the redundancy of himself or his fellows? Can it be an *implied* term of the contract that one party must help in the process that may end the contract to his detriment? When the Inland Revenue planned to introduce a new computerized system to administer PAYE, tax officers objected that this might make many of them redundant. The Revenue refused to guarantee their jobs; the workers, though willing to work, refused to work the new system until an agreement was made with the union on its introduction. Thereupon the Revenue (insisting it was not effecting either discipline or dismissal) refused to pay them any salary.[31] Walton J. held that they were under a duty to adapt themselves 'to new methods and techniques' in the course of the employment, as earlier cases on redundancy had suggested. If they would not, then: 'No work – no pay.' They could not be asked to retrain in 'esoteric skills', but it was not 'nowadays unusual' to ask an employee 'to acquire basic skills as to retrieving information from a computer or feeding such information into a computer'.

The employer must provide the necessary training (a point of some importance in view of the paucity of internal training in British companies; p. 505); but the tax officers must 'come out of the horse and buggy age', even if the changes in working methods and practices were great. The judge scornfully thought it ventured 'on the preposterous' that the workers' union had not appreciated 'the precise terms and conditions of service'. One condition was the duty to co-operate. This judgment was not the end of the story. The 438 tax officers defied the Revenue and remained suspended until it was forced to negotiate a wide-ranging collective agreement, covering all 58,000 staff involved, to bring in the technology with job flexibility but in ways that better avoided redundancies, an agreement, the *Financial Times* judged, 'likely to serve as a model for new technology agreements'. Perhaps it was the method of legal judgment, rather than that of collective bargaining, that represented the horse-and-buggy era as a way of modernizing industry by consent.

In considering non-co-operation by, and suspension of, workers we have now entered the field of industrial action. Suppose workers study the 'works rules' issued by their employer. Often these will be out of date; practice will have gone ahead, management and workers wanting to get on with the job. Indeed, 'rule-breaking' is a well known path to success for both managers and shop stewards.[32] The rules are there to be, at best, renegotiated if difficulties arise. What if the workers decide to observe the rules accurately but meticulously, as a way of exerting pressure? In 1972 the Government alleged a breach of contract by railway workers who had dislocated services when the union instructed them to undertake just such a work-to-rule. If it was a breach of contract the NIRC could order a 'cooling-off' ballot under the 1971 Act (as indeed it did, resulting in a huge majority for the union).[33] Donaldson P. said the employees had broken their duty to behave 'fairly' and 'do a fair day's work'. But the Court of Appeal preferred other ways by which to find a breach of contract. Roskill LJ implied a term that workers, although they could withdraw goodwill, could not interpret the railway rules in a 'wholly unreasonable way which has the effect of disrupting the system'. The term was necessary not to make the workers work, but to make the contract work – the normal test for implied terms. (Yet these were the employer's rules.) Lord Denning MR held that a worker must not 'wilfully obstruct the employer' in his business so as to 'produce chaos'. He thought the rules themselves were not terms of the contracts; but they were instructions on how to do the work and, even if some were outdated (such as the rule about the height of the coal on the engine), they were instructions lawfully given and the workers must construe them reasonably. Buckley LJ went further:

The object . . . was to frustrate the very commercial object for which the contracts of employment were made. . . . [This caused] breaches of an implied term to serve the employer faithfully within the requirements of the contract . . . within the terms of the contract the employee must serve the employer faithfully with a view to promoting those commercial interests for which he is employed.

Clearly, the very question at issue was what *was* 'within the terms (express and implied) of the contract'. A duty of co-operation was judicially imposed that met the employer's (and the Government's) objectives. It has been said that such judgments adopt a 'unitary frame of reference', in so far as they fail to register the parties' conflicting interests; and they do indeed echo the 'duty of collaboration' placed on a West German Works Council, which must never 'imperil the tranquillity' of the enterprise.[34] They provide a legal base for demands like that curtly stated in an NCB direction after the strike of 1984–5 about pit-closure plans, that miners owed duties 'to carry out instructions, to give proper effort and to co-operate to secure efficiency'. But expectations that equivalent duties to 'co-operate' of anything like the same scope will be imposed by courts on the employer seem unduly optimistic. On the other hand, the courts have implied terms to promote 'enlightened pluralism',[35] at the level of what the first President of Industrial Tribunals called 'civilizing' discipline and dismissals. A duty to deal *fairly* with employees has, it is true, been prominent in the EAT, and the duty of mutual trust has been used to prohibit the harassment of employees (e.g. 'persistent and unwanted amorous advances', or abusive language that became intolerable).[36] But judicial manipulation of the duty of fidelity has done (perhaps can do) little to change the substantive subordination of the worker.

In one area Parliament had to intervene. The duty of fidelity was read to mean that a worker's inventions connected with his employment duties (as defined in his contract) belonged to the employer. A statute of 1949 was ineffective to displace this judicial approach. Now the Patents Act 1977 passes property to the employee unless the invention was made in the course of his normal duties or duties assigned to him and the invention could 'reasonably be expected to result' from the work, or unless he had a 'special obligation to further the interests of the employer's undertaking'. The employed inventor however can apply for compensation to the Patents Office or the court where the invention belonging to the employer was of 'outstanding benefit', or where he agreed that the employer should use or develop one belonging to him and agreed payments to him were 'inadequate' in relation to the employer's gains. Compensation is awarded to give him a 'fair share' along guidelines set out in the Act, either as a lump sum or in periodical payments. Agreements excluding the employee's rights are unenforceable, except that a collective agreement can make different provision on compensation. But the employee must be a member of the union that is party to such an agreement (an unusual feature: p. 327).

Obedience, dismissal and strikes

'There is certainly nothing more essential to the contractual relation between master and servant than the duty of obedience,' said Cairns L J in 1974. Refusal to obey orders can be fundamental; and such a breach of the contract 'going to the root' of the contract by either employer or employee allows the other party to treat the contract at an end, *if* he elects to do so. An employer's breach 'going to the root', or 'repudiating' the contract, has come to be called 'constructive dismissal' in relation to redundancy and unfair dismissal law (by reason of its statutory origins: p. 222). Such a breach by the employee gives to the employer the remedy under the common law of summary dismissal without notice, if he elects to use it.

Repudiatory breach and acceptance

Here we find dominant (after a period of uncertainty) the normal principles of the law of contract. Some judges, including Diplock J. in 1959 and Donaldson P. in 1974, thought that (exceptionally) a fundamental breach of an employment contract, and therefore a dismissal, automatically terminated the contract 'without the necessity for an acceptance by the injured party'. They and some other judges have said the employment contract is special. A dismissal must be clear, more than a warning. But there seems to be no special rule about termination of employment contracts. Normally the contract ends when the fundamental breach is accepted by the other party.

On normal principles, the employment contract ends when the innocent party accepts the guilty party's breach. As Megarry V C said in 1978: 'Why should a person who makes a contract of service have the right at any moment to put an end to his contractual obligations?' Later decisions have now moved strongly against any exception for contracts of service from this rule and (although some judges still try to keep elbow-room to apply such doctrines as 'automatic-termination-on-breach' if it suits them)[37] the rather confused case law appears to establish that a repudiatory breach of an employment contract normally causes termination only when accepted by the other party. It may, of course, be easy to infer that an employee has 'accepted' a wrongful dismissal from 'any overt act' (when he takes a permanent job elsewhere, for example) or even by inaction, and therefore quickly to conclude he is under a duty to mitigate his loss. The same is true for the employer. When an employee went abroad without leave for long periods and the employer finally notified him that his employment was at an end, the Court of Appeal held that the finding of an industrial tribunal that the employer should have waited until he returned 'outraged common sense'. This breach could be, and was, accepted by the employer; that was when the contract ended.[38] Repudiatory breach, such as fundamental disobedience by the worker or non-payment of the proper wage by the employer, will terminate the contract if 'accepted' by the other party; but the acceptance must be unequivocal. If the employee resigns because of non-payment of wages, for example, it must be for that reason, not for some other. The application of these normal contractual principles is also the only way to make sense of the statutory provisions about the dismissal of strikers (EPCA s. 62: p. 194; this section is consistent only with this view, because it clearly envisages that the employer 'dismisses' employees who go out on strike).

But when the employment contract is repudiated by the employer the employee must make an unequivocal election to accept the termination of the contract if he is to rely upon it. Faced with some repudiatory failure by the employer, the worker cannot normally go on working at the job and then claim a long time later that it was a 'dismissal'. This notion has been applied narrowly where the employer's default is an 'anticipatory breach' – that is, where he repudiates his obligation *before* the time for performance ('You will get no wages next month'). Where a manager who was a director was told he would be removed from his directorship in a company reorganization, this was an anticipatory breach of his rights under his contract; but his claim to have accepted the renunciation was rejected in 1985 (even though he had said he regarded it as a 'determination of my employment') because he had written about it 'without prejudice', in effect offering to negotiate an 'amicable resolution', which was not the posture of a party who had unequivocally accepted a repudiation.[39] An election to accept a repudiation cannot be provisional. The receipt of salary for a period after the repudiatory breach did not result in a finding that a surgeon had 'waived' the breach (management had improperly insisted that he must take psychiatric tests).[40] Even so, for the ordinary worker, acceptance of the next pay-packet after the employer's breach may be treated as a waiver of it and affirmation of the contract (though staying on for a time under protest or until another job can be found does not always prove affirmation).[41] When the worker leaves because of the employer's breach, the onus is on him if he wishes to rely on 'constructive dismissal', to show 'demonstrably' that he is leaving for that reason.[42]

When the contract requires his attendance at work, Blackburn J. said in 1873, 'it is for the workman to explain why he was absent'. This remains so today. If he has no legally satisfactory explanation, he is in breach of contract. Where he disobeyed an instruction to remain, the old law was very strict. In 1845 a maid who left to visit her dying mother contrary to her employer's express orders was held to be properly dismissed. There could be no defence, proclaimed Baron Alderson, for the pleading 'does not show that the mother was likely to die that night'. By 1959 the courts were ready to adopt a different emphasis and to hold that one act of disobedience could now justify dismissal only if it is of a nature that goes to show (in effect) that the servant is repudiating the contract or 'one of its essential conditions'.

The two cases of the swearing gardeners illustrate the point. In 1969 an employer and his 'perfectionist' wife returned from abroad to find their gardener in rebellious mood, as he had often been before, so much so that he refused to obey their orders, crying: 'I couldn't care less about your bloody greenhouse and your sodding garden.' In the light of his previous bad record, this breach was judged to be enough to justify summary dismissal and, indeed, an award of damages against him (£49 for consequential losses on his tied cottage, such as a new key). Dismissal does not preclude the employer from claiming damages as well, if he can prove consequential loss. An erroneous belief by the employee that the instruction is not within the scope of his contractual duties does not by itself save him.[43] But, although in a domestic situation there is still a 'duty of courtesy and respect towards the employer and his family', the on-the-spot dismissal of a head gardener whose oaths were even more fearsome than the previous horticulturist's profanities was held to be unjustified in 1974. On being criticized for having stopped work early with his electric hedge-cutter (for fear of electrocution in the rain), after being goaded and shouted at aggressively, he retaliated with obscene language (of which by far the most delicate phrase was 'Get stuffed'). There was no background here of inefficiency or insolence (as in the 1969 case). His language was 'grossly improper' but, it was held, his acts did not deliberately flout the contract's essential conditions.[44] (It is not insignificant that in reaching this result the court relied on an insubordination case of 1860, despite its insistence that modern 'mutual respect' had replaced 'Czar–serf' relationships.)

Even if the common law test permits the employer to dismiss, the employment protection legislation may still allow a tribunal to find that the dismissal was 'unfair' (p. 233). And at common law otherwise *wrongful* summary dismissals may be justified on facts discovered by the employer afterwards, but this is not normally allowed in the new law of *unfair* dismissal.[45]

Employment contract and industrial action

The common law of contract makes no special provision for strikes or abstentions from work such as a mass meeting.[46] Its starting-point is quite different from those systems of law that see strikes as

a non-performance of the contract, but it is not a breach of contract, because it is the exercise of a collective right [to strike] . . . to which all individual employment contracts implicitly refer. . . . The principle of suspension in case of a *lawful strike* is today accepted in most countries.[47]

In Britain this has never been accepted. A unilateral suspension of the contract of employment is impossible under the common law unless it arises out of an express or implied term. The employer has no inherent power to lay off without pay; but the nature of the contract (where, for example, work becomes available only with pauses in between) or terms of a collective agreement may give rise to such a right.[48] However, the argument that a trade dispute itself leads to a 'suspension' of the contract has been rejected by the House of Lords, and was equally unacceptable to the Scottish Court of Session in regard to a lock-out.[49]

We may note the British habit of 'pairing off' strikes and lock-outs; many collective agreements, too, apply procedures or limits to the right to strike and the right to lock-out alike; they are treated similarly for redundancy purposes. It is not always so abroad. The constitutional right to strike in Italy and France has no precise counterpart in a right to lock out; indeed, Italian writers liken the latter to an unlawful strike or even unconstitutional acts. The reason is the power of management, which controls the workplace and discipline, the lock-out being only one of many weapons at its disposal. An employer in a British dispute may, it seems, properly demand an undertaking from employees that they will not 'disrupt' the plant on pain of being seen to have 'terminated their own engagements'.[50] Lock-outs are infrequent but they are part of the defensive – sometimes offensive – armoury of management.

It is not only a total withdrawal of labour that constitutes a breach by the worker. A refusal to obey an order to go down a pit with non-unionists was held to be such in 1894. A 'go-slow' usually is a breach (when work is slower than it contractually should be); so too, a work-to-rule may be, as we have seen (p. 185). An overtime ban is a breach if the contract makes overtime obligatory (but not a breach if the overtime is wholly voluntary). A concerted refusal to accept new working terms or technology may be a breach, as in the Inland Revenue case (p. 184), along with unduly prolonged tea-breaks or natural breaks, and the action developed by draughtsmen in 1967, 'working without enthusiasm'. 'The forms of industrial action', said Donaldson P. in 1973, 'are limited only by the ingenuity of mankind.' In Britain it is rare to find they have not occasioned breach of employment contracts.

Does a strike notice cure the breach? There is no belief more widespread, more reasonable, but legally more erroneous than that held by many managers and most workers that a strike notice, equivalent in length to that needed to end the contract, makes industrial action lawful. Of course, sometimes the notice given by strikers *is* a notice to quit. The Merchant Shipping Act 1970 gives a statutory right to strike to seamen in trade disputes, on giving forty-eight hours' notice, after mooring, to 'terminate' their contracts. (There may be other strike notices that activate special arrangements between an employer and the union to suspend contracts.)[51] But most unions and workers do not regard a strike notice as equivalent to asking for the workers' cards. Nor do most employers. It is a notice announcing a withdrawal of labour, – a strike, not a mass resignation. The notice announces a forthcoming breach, and is therefore itself in law an 'anticipatory' breach, which the employer can waive or accept. Thus in *Rookes* v. *Barnard*, 1964, Lord Devlin said the object of the threat to strike was 'to break the contract by withholding labour but keeping the contract alive for as long as the employers would tolerate the breach'. And Lord Denning M R agreed a year later that the normal strike notice is not a notice to terminate: 'that is the last thing any of the men would desire . . . [it is] a notice that the men will not come to work. In short that they will break their contracts'.[52]

However, in *Morgan* v. *Fry*, 1968, Lord Denning made a bold if misconceived effort to invent a doctrine whereby, in the 'modern law as to trade disputes', a term is implied into contracts such that after a strike notice the contract 'is suspended during the strike and revives again when the strike is over'. The employer did not usually want to lose his work-force. There had to be 'something wrong' with his own earlier view; otherwise 'it would do away with the right to strike in this country'.

There a union official for lockmen in London announced that, as from a date two weeks ahead, they would be instructed not to work with non-unionists but would carry out duties otherwise as far as possible. The non-unionists had formed a breakaway union. Russell L J attached the usual status to this notice of impending breach induced by the union (to which we return in Chapters 7 and 8).[53] Lord Denning's sounds an attractive view. But the Donovan Report rejected this very proposal the same year, whilst noting that it would have to be introduced into the law by statute (para. 943). Would the new doctrine apply to all strikes and to other action, e.g. a go-slow? What can the employer do? Dismiss the strikers during suspension for misconduct? Can strikers moonlight in other jobs? When is the strike over, and suppose it is never settled? Lord Denning's well intentioned innovation created more difficulties than it solved because it did not address these questions. Even so, he was right to say there cannot be a *right* to strike without some doctrine suspending the employment contract.

Davies L J in the same case offered an ingenious way out. Were the lockmen really in breach? Suppose an employer says, 'Move that bale', and the worker replies, 'Sorry. It is blacked.' If the employer insists, there is a clear breach; but if he says, 'Oh all right, we'll see about it later; get on with the rest', the employer has either 'waived' the breach or he may have agreed new employment terms. Davies L J thought the notice given was in one sense a termination but also 'an offer to continue on different terms. In the present case this was accepted by the [employers].' When that same argument was used, however, by lightermen who had union instructions not to handle certain barges, claiming that their *daily* contracts of employment must have been similarly varied because the employers knew of their union obligations not to touch the barges that day, the House of Lords refused to countenance the idea. The employer, said Lord Donovan, 'expected his normal reasonable orders to be obeyed'. It is unlikely the judges will accept the analysis offered by Davies LJ except where the employer's sympathies are really with the defendant union and workers (as was the case in *Morgan* v. *Fry*).

All the legal authorities were reviewed in *Simmons* v. *Hoover*, 1977,[54] though in a different context. Employers claimed that they were entitled to terminate the worker's contract of employment, thereby disentitling him to a redundancy payment, because he was participating in a strike (under what is now EPCA s. 82(2)). In a last stand, counsel argued that a strike, preceded by notice, only suspended the contract; this reflected 'daily experience, understanding and practice of those engaged in industrial relations', even though it meant the employer could never terminate the contract. But the EAT concluded that *Morgan* v. *Fry* had not 'revolutionized' the law:

> We accept, of course, that in most cases men are not dismissed when on strike; that they expect not to be dismissed; that the employers do not expect to dismiss them . . . [but] a 'real' strike in our judgment always will be a breach.

Little has been heard of the argument since, though it was raised again in 1986 (p. 634). None of the modern cases doubt that the answer in *Simmons* v. *Hoover* was correct; most take it for granted that employees engaging in any form of industrial action are breaking their contracts.[55] Sometimes this is called 'lack of creativity' in the courts; but it is far more profound. The common law, built on the very pillars of property and contract, cannot accommodate a *right* to strike. That job must be done by statute, which would necessarily be complex.

Strikes and unfair dismissal

Two other associated problems have been much debated and must be mentioned. First, can a striking employee go to a tribunal and claim compensation because he was *unfairly* dismissed? This problem arose only in the 1970s, and especially after 1974 when the new law on unfair dismissal had to live for the first time cheek by jowl with a modest renewal of trade union rights. The basic policy for the industrial tribunals, as the Donovan Report recommended, was that they should not deal with 'collective agreements' or 'industrial disputes' but with individual employment disputes. Otherwise they would have to adjudicate on the merits of strikes – and even among the judges there are few who believe in Sir John Donaldson's creed that

the courts could be given their traditional role of investigating the merits of disputes and helping the party who is right. . . . Ought [the public] not know who is right? Adopting this new approach they *would* know, for the court which investigated the dispute would tell them.[56]

To avoid this fate, the modern legislation included two provisions. First, industrial pressure on the employer is to be ignored in determining the reason for a dismissal (EPCA s. 63; though this provision is now side-stepped: p. 381). Secondly, if a dismissal takes place during a lock-out, a strike or industrial action, the tribunal has no jurisdiction over its fairness so long as the employer has not selectively dismissed (or refused to engage) some only of the relevant employees by way of victimization (EPCA s. 62). But this provision was severely weakened by the 1982 Act in two ways. The 'relevant employees' are now defined, not as *all* the workers taking part in the action, but as those at the establishment of the complainant taking part at the date of his dismissal. Clearly, the employer is now more easily able to wait for the strike to erode, picking off plant by plant those who stay out longest, without fear of the unfair dismissal laws. Also, the provision on re-engagement was changed; the complainant must show that an offer of re-engagement was made to another worker and not to him within three months of his dismissal. The Scottish EAT has even allowed the employer to use this three months period to re-engage workers in batches (1,600 first time, 400 the next) in what it sees as a 'cooling-off' period. The new scheme permits victimization to such a degree that it has been judged 'a blot on the law of unfair dismissal'.[57]

The courts have contributed to this landscape partly by confusing the law. The three main problems are: (1) What is a 'strike or industrial action'? (2) When is an employee 'taking part' in a strike? (3) Just when is discrimination improper so as to revive the jurisdiction of the tribunal to pronounce on 'fairness'?

(1) The Act does not here define *strike or industrial action*.[58] Concerted action to put direct or indirect pressure on the employer is at the core. Breach of contract is not required; so a ban on voluntary overtime, without such breach, used as a bargaining weapon is within the section (though a mere threat of action, it seems, is not).[59]

(2) The test of *taking part* in a strike has become enmeshed with the desire by the EAT (and Court of Appeal) not to disturb findings of fact by the industrial tribunals, to such an extent that it has upheld a finding that a worker was taking part when it might be equally reasonable to find he was not. Attendance at a workers' meeting to discuss a ban on overtime was held not to be enough.[60] It has been held that tribunals must use an objective test; the worker's 'motivation and intention are irrelevant'. Once a worker 'chooses not to go to work during the strike, then . . . the employee', said Kerr LJ, 'should be regarded as taking part in the strike'. Otherwise s. 62 would be 'unworkable', leaving the tribunals to investigate the subjective purpose of workers who may have voted for, or against, a strike, or remained absent through fear of crossing a picket line or for other reasons.[61] If an employee who is absent sick merely talked to the pickets when bringing in medical certificates in such 'cursory acts of comradeship as chatting', the objective test can easily demonstrate that he is not taking part (and a tribunal's contrary reasoned decision was reversed; the judges added that it was dangerous for it to give reasons, since 'a conclusion' standing alone would have been safe and sound).[62] Earlier cases, however, have bequeathed problems (as where different groups of workers engage in parallel action or where lock-outs and strikes overlap). It remains to be seen whether the courts will return to consideration of workers' states of mind. Some sociologists appear to insist that a 'form of behaviour' at work (e.g. absenteeism) must be judged against the 'participants' perceptions' before its place in industrial action is assessed;[63] but to do so would here narrow the range of those 'taking part' and thereby assist the employers.

(3) As to *re-engagement*, the EAT in 1984 decided that where the employer had discriminated and re-engaged selectively, therefore resurrecting the tribunal's jurisdiction, the rule reducing compensation for an employee's 'contributory fault' (p. 256) could not apply. To do so, the court would have to judge 'fault' in the strike that involved a breach of contract, 'precisely the arena from which Parliament in general desired

to exclude it'. In marked contrast to the approach of Sir John Donaldson M R, Browne-Wilkinson J. said in *Moosa's* case:

Industrial disputes are often very complex, having a long history and involving many contributory factors. In no area of English law of which we are aware are courts ever entrusted with the determination and allocation of blame in relation to industrial disputes.[64]

What then is re-engagement in the job? The Court of Appeal permitted an employer to discriminate between actors and stage-hands who were re-engaged, by offering some of the militants in an unofficial strike re-engagement only on a 'second warning' (more vulnerable to be legitimately dismissed for a breach of discipline).[65] The technical reason for the decision was that 'job' in s. 62 did not under the definition in the EPCA require unaltered conditions of employment; it meant 'capacity' or 'job in the colloquial sense', and therefore permitted the employers to pick and choose the precise conditions for the workers. But the policy of the court was clear, Lord Denning M R saying:

It must be remembered that they had been guilty of most serious misconduct. They had been guilty of repudiatory breach of their contract. They had inflicted heavy losses on the National Theatre. They could not fairly claim to be re-engaged on precisely the same terms as the large number of loyal employees who had stayed at work throughout the strike.

No coyness there about judging fault; nor any talk of 'suspension' of contract.

The employer's power to suspend

As the unfair dismissal law edged forward (still carrying the basic contractual burden, as Lord Denning makes clear) the common law contiguous to it lurched towards new controls over workers who withdrew their labour. Although the employer disposes of the power to employ a defensive, offensive or 'sympathetic' lock-out (a weapon Folke Schmidt judged 'far more powerful than the strike'),[66] he naturally prefers to rely upon less costly disciplinary weapons, such as suspension of workers without pay. Only a few years ago Kahn-Freund could write that this was 'a penalty unknown to the common law', needing legitimation in the employment contract.[67] Pain J. has said:

'There is no general right to lay off without pay at common law.' Courts have taken a strict view in their interpretations even where the contract expressly allows for 'lay-off'. Take the case of Mrs Tiffen in 1981, working in the 'rag trade' on modest wages; her employers stipulated for lay-off without pay 'if there is a shortage of work or the firm is unable to operate because of circumstances beyond its control'. She succeeded in establishing 'constructive dismissal' after being laid off for more than a 'reasonable' time. The contract can also be all important in regard to payments, as where teachers in 1971 refused the lawful instruction to supervise school meals but recovered their salary for the days they were 'suspended' because the employer, instead of accepting the repudiation as a termination, suspended them without going through the procedures that the contract laid down as appropriate. But by 1980 procedural reasoning overtook substantive arguments, as often happens in the common law. Workers at a power-station had their pay totally stopped on days they worked to rule. They failed to recover it. The burden of proof, it was held, lay upon them to prove, as persons claiming money under a contract, that they were fully 'ready and willing to perform the contract'.[68] If they were not in a position to assert that, how could the court assist them?

Judicial agility enabled Pain J. to avoid this result in the *Bond and Neads* case,[7] where he regarded supplemental agreements to work special machines as separate temporary contracts collateral to the main employment contracts. The workers had withdrawn from those machines but otherwise worked normally. The employers refused to pay them at all for the relevant days. But they were held liable to pay normal pay; the workers had been ready and willing to perform the normal contract. Moreover, the employers themselves had waived breaches of the special agreements, and any prevention of performance had been theirs.[69] A different, rather less subtle way round the all-or-nothing results of earlier cases was taken in 1984 when a teacher had protested, as his union instructed, against education cuts by refusing to accept five additional pupils into his class of thirty-one. They were sent home, causing the education authority to be in breach of its statutory duty. He was allowed to teach the normal class, but his salary was reduced by six months' pay as 'damage' based on the period of the refusal, a deduction not based on any terms of the contract. This, the court held, was mistaken. The employers had affirmed and accepted his 'imperfect performance' and did not suspend him. So should he not recover in full? Park J. thought not, and remedied the legal gaps. He should recover his full salary if he had properly and fully performed his duties; his refusal to teach the extra children was a breach; so the court would 'make a deduction'. The fraction 5/36 of salary over the period 'while being a far from perfect assessment would probably represent the justice of the case'. Both counsel agreed, no doubt willing to compromise a battle fought in such a legal fog.[70]

The judge followed Nicholls J., who in 1983 had treated similarly *Miles*, a registrar of marriages, who on union instructions had engaged in the modest industrial action of refusing to conduct weddings on Saturday mornings. Of his normal thirty-seven hours, three usually fell on Saturdays; so the local council deducted 3/37 of his pay. The judge approved, because he was entitled to pay only for work done. Once again, no good legal reason was found for this compromise, except that it was a 'fair measure' of his failure to carry out his duties. On appeal, however, his case was removed from the normal employment sphere altogether by a finding that under the Act about registration of marriages he held an 'office' with a 'status', and was not under any contractual relationship with the council. Moreover, the Act, on close analysis of its obscurities, put the council under 'an unqualified obligation to pay while the officer held the office', and without deduction. The Court of Appeal doubted whether deductions would have been proper if he had been an employee, but offered no further guidance.[71] There are very few workers covered by this kind of Act.

The current state of the labour market removes inhibitions from some employers who wish to use the powerful weapon of suspension without pay. It is rather unsatisfactory that case law should offer no better guidance to workers who have committed a partial breach of their contracts (perhaps in a work-to-rule) and wish to recover wages stopped by an employer than that he may be obliged to pay them in full, or nothing, or a fraction, as appears just to the judge whom they happen to be allotted. In earlier decades, collective bargaining might have been invoked to help the limping common law over the hurdles; but today the problem may arise where unions are too weak to make new agreements or to modernize old ones. Critics, however, regard any drift away from a refusal to pay anything at all as inimical to 'productivity', like medieval remuneration, payment 'to upkeep the dignity of office and not for work done', dubbing it a view worthy of the arguments of 'Lord Tite Barnacle of the Circumlocution Office'.[72]

In reality this is yet another demand to turn the screw on employees who dare to withdraw even a fraction of their labour. Where workers break the contract, judges now seem to uphold deductions as sums to be set off against salary. In one month in 1985 teachers in the NUT withdrew 'cover' for absent colleagues (their contractual obligation to cover being in dispute: Chapter 8, p. 631), and local authorities began deducting £2 for each such occasion; the union retaliated by demanding individual hearings within agreed procedures on each deduction. Civil servants were warned that if they took time off to lobby Parliament against the closure of Skillcentres their pay would be 'docked' even if they set off the time from annual leave (see too now the Wages Bill 1986, p. 395). But a dockworker, Mr Gibbons (in a test case involving £500,000), won his claim for arrears of £320 stopped by his employers from the guaranteed pay specified in a collective agreement. The employers had made the mistake of believing that termination of the collective agreement by the union allowed them to stop the payments negotiated in that 'package deal'.[73]

The interpretation by the judges of the degree to which workers are bound to co-operate, and the employer entitled to suspend payment, appears to reflect in great measure the developing right of the employer to discipline the work-force. Moreover, some judges suggest that workers ought to be compliant by negotiating individually with the employer and that employment protection legislation obliges them to do so. In 1986 Kilner Brown J., holding that domestic staff who went on strike against pay cuts of up to 30 per cent by their employer, *Crothall Ltd*, had not been unfairly dismissed, criticized the union for encouraging them to take collective, rather than individual, action. To this pressure towards individuation we shall return.

Notice and continuity

The law did not require the employer to tell the worker why he was dismissing him until 1975 when statute gave the latter a right to a written statement of the reasons within fourteen days of the dismissal, whether summary or with notice (now EPCA s. 53). But the modern section is a poor protection. The employee has to request such a statement, to which he is entitled only if he has six months' continuous employment (in 1986 the Government plans to make it two years); and the employer is liable to pay compensation for his failure to comply only if he 'unreasonably refused' to provide the statement. This puts a premium on indolence, for mere inaction is not normally a refusal. Adequate detail must be given, but reference to other documents is permitted. The EAT made the section even less protective by exculpating an employer who thought the request was not for reasons but for a reference.[74]

Moreover, the employer is not obliged to show to the worker the information he sends to the social security authorities about his dismissal. This may affect his benefit because, even if dismissed unfairly in the eyes of an industrial tribunal, the worker may be guilty of 'misconduct' disentitling him to benefit for a period of up to six weeks in social security law (in 1986 it will become 13 weeks), which has its own tests of what is 'blameworthy, reprehensible and wrong'. The 'main emphasis' of the former is on the employer's conduct whereas in the latter it is upon him.[75] It is uncertain how far the Data Protection Act 1984 will assist a worker, in view of the various exemptions for data held only for 'the collection of any tax or duty', pay-roll data and information held by government departments (ss. 28, 29, 32).

The period of employment today is usually not a fixed time (many 'servants' a century ago were still engaged on the ancient basis of a 'yearly hiring'), and each party can normally end the contract where no ground for summary dismissal arises only by giving notice to terminate it (a very different development from that in the United States where employment after 1877 was presumed to be terminable 'at will').[76] The length of notice may be set out but, if it is not, it will be the period implied (by custom or otherwise) as the reasonable period for ending the contract. In practice, the employer appears also still to have the right to end it on the spot by paying wages in lieu of proper notice,[77] since the sum lost over the period of notice will normally represent the whole of the loss suffered by the worker wrongly sacked. The contract may set out different notice periods for employee and employer. And usually the manual worker still enjoys shorter periods than the managerial or white-collar worker, though few judges would today apply the concept of Lord Goddard CJ in 1945 that the disciplinary 'suspension' of such a worker was no more than 'dismissal with an intimation that . . . the man will be re-employed' (not least because the worker there was on one hour's notice). The House of Lords in a 1957 case even accepted that one employer could not dismiss at all except for cause (e.g. inefficiency); but that case was part of the development of the law about public 'office'.[78]

The court's concept of what is the 'reasonable' notice to be implied has long expressed the preference for longer notice where the employee has higher status, with the period of pay (weekly, monthly, etc.) an important, but not a determinative, consideration. Six months for a cinema controller, one week for a weekly paid foreman, three months for an underwear travelling salesman – such assessments rested on the contracts involved and the tenor of the times when the cases arose.

The notice must be given in accordance with the contract, and this normally means *to* the worker. When an employer tried to rely upon a notice to a union by its employers' association to terminate a collective agreement as notice to its boilermaker employee, Mr Morris, the courts rejected, as in *Gibbons's* case, the idea that this could constitute notice to him (Winn L J taking pleasure in pointing out to him the defects in the union rule-book, which spoke of working men 'ground down . . . by laws made by . . . the Ruling Class').[79] So too, collective bargaining, especially on redundancy, requires the distinction to be held between formal notice to quit and mere informal warning of impending dismissal, during which time off to seek other work may be available (time off after notice of redundancy is provided by E P C A s. 31). Also, a 'trial period' of up to four weeks (or any longer period mutually agreed in writing) to try out a new job is accorded to the worker if he is dismissed by reason of redundancy without losing his right to a redundancy payment if he turns it down, or his employer dismisses him in connection with the change-over (EPCA s. 84).

It was in this area, too, that the courts took up the problem of 'variation'. Where a foreman had continued to work under protest for a few weeks after being demoted to lower wages, the Court of Appeal refused to see it as a 'consensual variation' of the terms. It was in reality a termination; he had never agreed to the 'dictated' terms, and staying at work in those circumstances under protest was not an 'acceptance' of the employer's offer.[80] The courts have similarly leaned against the construction that the parties have terminated the contract 'by agreement'. The two parties may so agree, as where an employee in a firm about to be reorganized asked to be released because it made it easier to find alternative employment – a case of 'Please may I go?', as against 'You have treated me in such a way that I'm going without a by-your-leave.'[81] Where a worker signed a document stating the company would 'assume' he had terminated his contract if he did not return from a visit to his sick father by a given date, the EAT refused to see this as any 'mutual consent' to termination; it was, according to the 'policy' of the employment protection legislation, dismissal[82] – a giant step away from Baron Alderson in 1845. Yet a university lecturer in 1985 who had been invited to take premature retirement was held not to have been dismissed, but to have agreed with his university by mutual consent to terminate the employment contract.

This dismal trend towards the old approach was checked in 1986. Mrs Igbo signed a 'contractual letter' agreeing to return to work the day her holiday to Nigeria ended; if she failed, her contract would 'automatically terminate'. She failed to return because she was ill. The appeal judges refused to accept this termination by 'consent'. The letter limited her right not to be unfairly dismissed, and that is prohibited by the EPCA (s. 140).[83] This reasoning blocked the attempt to draft the employer out of liability for dismissal by a variation to end the contract by 'agreement'. Social security law may not always conclude that a leaving is 'voluntary' where the employer requests early retirement; but, after temporary disqualification from benefit was imposed where workers had left voluntarily 'in the interests of the community' to open up jobs for younger workers, as that was not an adequate 'just cause', Parliament enacted in 1985 that workers dismissed by reason of redundancy after 'volunteering or agreeing' to be dismissed are not to be deemed, for the purposes of unemployment benefit, to have left their employment voluntarily.[84]

Nor has Parliament stood still as regards notice of dismissal. From 1963 onwards statutory minimum notice has ruled the employment contract. Today the employer must give one week's notice to an employee who has one month's, but less than two years', continuous employment, and thereafter one week in addition for each year of service up to a maximum of twelve weeks for twelve years or more; and the employee must give at least one week's notice to quit once he has been employed for four weeks or more (EPCA s. 49). These minima of 'obligatory notice' periods are displaced by any express agreement for longer periods. The employee's notice is often made longer than, or equivalent to, the employer's. One of the swearing gardeners was bound to give the same three months' notice as he was entitled to receive. Although the contract cannot exclude the minima, either party may 'waive' his right to notice or accept 'a payment in lieu of notice' – the former being an undesirable loophole that may allow for pressure on workers unless the worker's 'consent' is carefully considered; and the latter appearing to accept the employer's right to pay wages in lieu.

When the statutory rights to notice arise, minimum sums are laid down that must be paid to the worker during the relevant period, unless he enjoys a right to notice at least one week longer than the minimum (EPCA s. 50). In effect, he is to receive pay even if there is no more work to do (so long as he is ready to work) or if he is incapable through sickness or injury or absent on an agreed holiday. From his normal pay will be deducted payments made by the employer for the period, including sick-pay and holiday pay; but the employer's liability arises only when he 'leaves the service'. If in the period he repudiates the contract and the employer terminates in response, or if he takes part in a strike, the right to payment is lost (EPCA, Sched. 3). We shall see that the nature of the payment for the minimum period of notice creates difficulties (pay in lieu of the notice appears not to be deductible against a compensatory award for unfair dismissal).[85]

The concept of a 'week's pay' is important here and in many other areas (including redundancy, unfair dismissal and statutory 'guarantee payments'). Its meaning varies broadly according to whether there are 'normal working hours', i.e. the pay for the fixed, or minimum, hours under the contract (including overtime hours that are both obligatory for the worker and guaranteed by the employer to provide) excluding benefits in kind. But the worker's pay might still vary with work done. If so, his pay is calculated on the average hourly rate payable over the previous twelve weeks. So too, where there are no 'normal working hours', an average weekly rate over twelve weeks is used. If he does not have twelve weeks' service, a 'fair' amount is to be determined.[86]

If the employer fails to give the minimum notice, he is in breach of contract; and the statutory payments are taken into account in 'assessing his liability for breach of contract' (s. 51). Such a claim would be brought in the ordinary courts. But the tribunals may acquire a jurisdiction that overlaps, as in the case where an employer becomes insolvent, for there the EPCA gives the employee a statutory right to compel the Secretary of State to pay certain amounts to which he was entitled out of the Redundancy Fund; and these include arrears of up to eight weeks' pay, compensation for unfair dismissal and payments for failure to give notice (EPCA s. 122). This, the House of Lords has declared, means that such payments to workers shipwrecked by the insolvency of an employing company blessed with limited liability are subject to the ordinary principles of the law of contract; they impose the normal duty to mitigate loss (by finding other work) and deduction of unemployment benefit received (under *Parson's* case: p. 211).[87] Why if it meant this the Act did not say so (in what Eveleigh LJ has rightly called its 'comprehensive code') was not explained. Lord Bridge did not see the Act as 'a comprehensive code'; he found the scheme of the EPCA as a whole and its background in earlier consolidated statutes 'quite irrelevant'. To this we return below.

There is, as so often, an uneasy fit between social security benefit and common law. If the worker receives a payment 'in lieu' of notice or wages that he would have received for days had his employment not terminated (whether the employer was legally obliged to pay it *or not*), then on each day represented up to a maximum of one year he is disqualified from benefit. Payments made under the *statutory* redundancy provisions are not included (p. 218); they compensate for past service. But what about an agreed 'bounty' or 'severance payment', which may relate both to past *and* future? So long as its dominant feature is a 'gratuity' for the past, the courts have applied a generous interpretation avoiding disqualification, even for an *ex gratia* payment where the worker agrees to improperly short notice or if it represents compensation for loss of consultation with the union over redundancy (p. 294); but if it represents payment consequent on the dismissal for ascertainable days when remuneration would have been paid, Social Security Commissioners still disqualify.[88] It is perhaps odd that much can turn on the description of the payment – certainly a matter on which workers and their unions have to be vigilant in negotiating voluntary redundancies. This area, where common law, statute and social security link up on termination of employment, creates special difficulty. Many problems have been dealt with by regulations, for example the right of the State to recover from an employer the amount of unemployment benefit paid to an employee unfairly dismissed up to the hearing of the tribunal case;[89]

if the compensation paid represents the worker's loss of future wages, he is disqualified from benefit for that period.

An employee employed on a contract for a fixed term of one month or less must be given the minimum notice if continuously employed for three months (EPCA s. 49). That stops an obvious loophole. A provision to protect contracts for a 'specific task' in similar terms is less watertight (s. 49 (4A), added in 1982). Normally minimum notice rights accrue after one month's continuity. This means *continuity of employment*, not necessarily of contract; the employment capacity can vary. The worker can count any period involving work for, or under a contract 'normally' requiring, sixteen hours (EPCA, Sched. 13). A teacher in 1979 was not allowed to count extra hours spent preparing lessons at home, as no implied term to do so would, Lawton LJ said, have been agreed by the employers, and overtime must be obligatory *and* guaranteed to become contractual hours.[90]

If the contract hours are only 8 but the worker has five years' continuity already, the weeks count; or if they are reduced to 8, they count up to a maximum of 26 (or even beyond, where the worker has qualified for his rights and continues actually to work 16 hours). So too, some periods of absence can count. A week, broadly, can count (1) if there is no contract and he is incapable through sickness or injury (even if the contract has ended) up to twenty-six weeks so long as he then returns; or (2) if he is absent on account of a temporary cessation of work (other than strikes), i.e. of work for *him* to do; or (3) where a 'custom or arrangement' provides that he is still employed (EPCA, Sched. 13, para. 9). Weeks of incapability through sickness or absence through pregnancy count up to twenty-six even if there is no contract.

These provisions mark an attempt to break free from contractual tests, a matter of importance since 'continuity' periods are required for most statutory rights (minimum notice, redundancy, unfair dismissal, maternity rights, guarantee payments, etc.). In a liberal interpretation in 1984 the EAT held that 'normal' working hours referred to the original contract of dinner-ladies in Cambridge (on 'variable hours') even where for some time the employees had actually worked less than eight hours. A welder, employed from 1958 to November 1962, re-employed in January 1963 and dismissed in 1967, was held to have nine years' continuity, the break of eight weeks caused by shortage of work in the shipbuilding yard being judged to be a temporary cessation of his work. This test involves hindsight. In *Flack*, 1985, the EAT reaffirmed that a mathematical approach to intermittent gaps in the service of seasonal workers was too restrictive in judging whether they were temporary cessations; the whole history must be considered.

What of the increasing army of part-time workers? *Mrs Ford*, a teacher, was employed for eight years on fixed-term contracts, September to July. In July 1979 she was told by the college that, with a great majority of part-time lecturers, she would not be re-engaged. In an imaginative decision that recognizes the needs of part-time workers, the House of Lords held that her continuity was not necessarily broken by the annual summer holidays; these were temporary, i.e. 'transient', cessations causing her to be 'absent from work'.[91] A bank clerk who worked 'one week on, one week off' was in 1979 allowed to count all the weeks because of an 'arrangement or custom'. If a worker successfully seeks reinstatement after unfair dismissal, continuity is preserved back to dismissal; and the EAT held in 1984 that the same applied to re-engagement by conciliation.

But part-time employees still encounter many problems. They may not work normally for 16 hours or more, or have a contract providing for 16 hours generally (or if they have had one, they may not now be normally in employment for 8 hours) or, if they have employment normally for 8 hours, may not have been employed for five years continuously (or if they have, may not now be working for 8 hours). Women workers, in particular, may find that their weeks' hours suddenly do not fit one of these categories and that continuity is ruptured or never acquired. Where, for example, a worker has worked for many weeks towards, say, the two years' continuity required from 1985 for unfair dismissal rights under a contract for, say, 20 hours maximum normally per week, but then is switched to employment of 30 hours one week and 5 hours the next alternately, her continuity will be broken.[92] In 1986 a part-time lecturer working under three different contracts over fourteen years for Surrey County Council was not permitted to aggregate her normal hours under them to acquire continuity (though the EAT said tribunals would be vigilant to penalize an 'unscrupulous employer' who used a 'mosaic of separate contracts'). Similarly McLeod, a trawlerman, found that he had been employed for years under separate contracts by his employer (each voyage was 'discharged by performance'; and, though it was a trade practice for employers not to poach crews, if they chose to remain loyal they did that 'for their own reasons').[93]

With the growth of temporary and short-term employment, the *Ford* decision has clearly not solved all the problems. And if the rights of part-timers and workers external to the enterprise are ever aligned with those of full-time workers, this jigsaw concept of 'continuity' must be re-examined. A different policy was apparent in the Government proposals in 1986 to increase the basic 16 (8) hours to 20 (12), a new inroad on employment protection. Should not an employer owe to all workers a duty that they should not have their employment terminated *unfairly*?

What if the employer sells his business? Based on Lord Atkin's admirable assertion in 1940 that employees 'are not serfs and cannot be transferred as though they were property', the individualist common law sees this as a rupture that ends continuity, even if workers are oblivious of company A selling its business to company B. The Act seeks to preserve continuity so long as the transfer is of the business, or part of it, not merely of 'the assets' (EPCA, Sched. 13, para. 17). The provision on redundancy requiring 'a change in the ownership of a business' (EPCA s. 94) imports the same test. So, where a medical practice was transferred by four partners to a doctor who had been one of them, the employee's service was continuous, unbroken by the transfer of the undertaking.[94]

The House of Lords has confirmed Lord Denning M R's narrow test: 'you look at the nature of the business of the employer, not at the actual work being done by the men'. So, in *Melon's* case, sale of one of two factories was not a transfer even of part of the business as it was not a 'separate or severable' part, especially as it was in the end used by the buyers for 'a different business' (making different types of garment).[95] And where N. Ltd, intending purchasers, occupied the premises and ran the business as day-to-day licensees, keeping on the owners as consultants and contacting customers, but failed to complete the sale, employees who had moved into the employment of N. Ltd and on dismissal claimed redundancy payments were denied continuity of service as they had been in the employment of N. Ltd only one year.[96] These unsatisfactory decisions suggest that 'continuity' needs a new look, at least to enlarge the notion of 'transfer' in such cases.

The TUPE Regulations 1981, made to implement an EEC Directive, effected a bigger break with the common law. Where there is a transfer of an 'undertaking' or part of it that is a 'commercial venture' (again *as* a business, not merely the assets), the contract of employment of an employee employed immediately before the transfer is not terminated but transferred to the transferee.[97] There is then automatic transfer by law of the employment contract and all rights and duties 'under or in connection with' it (other than pension rights).[98] The TUPE Regulations have sometimes been strangely interpreted, as when the business of managing student-union catering was excluded from 'commercial venture', an unnecessary restriction of the rights of employees of non-profit-making enterprises by the Scottish EAT.[99]

More complex is the practice of 'hiving-down'. Where a liquidator or receiver for the creditors takes over an insolvent company to run it, he often tries to hive off the viable parts of the business to a wholly owned 'paper' subsidiary (retaining the employees). That subsidiary is then sold to a take-over company, which decides which workers it wants. What of the workers who are then dismissed? Are they left stranded with what remains of the old insolvent enterprise? Their limited priority rights in insolvency to unpaid wages and the like (Chapter 5; Companies Act 1985, Sched. 19) are of narrow benefit; they may have redundancy and other rights, which again, the 'employer' being insolvent, would have to be met by the national Redundancy Fund (p. 398). The TUPE Regulations had to make special provision for greater protection. In a hiving-down situation the transfer is, therefore, deemed to occur when the undertaking is finally transferred to the ultimate buyer, or the 'paper' company ceases to be a wholly owned subsidiary, a solution introduced as much to facilitate hiving-down as to protect workers.[100] But uncertainties in the regulations (they are 'a Pandora's box of ambiguities') must, the English EAT has said, be decided in favour of the employees concerned in a transfer having regard to the objectives of the EEC Directive.[101]

A change in partners normally changes the employer, but statute again preserves continuity (EPCA, Sched. 13). What about sales of shares in a company? There is a 'transfer' if one company sells the business to another even if all shares in both are owned by the same people, but not if only the shares in a company are sold. Some attempt is made to assist workers against the legal conundrums of 'corporate personality' (p. 96) by preserving continuity where the transfer of employment is from one to another of 'associated employers' as defined in the Act (s. 153 (4): p. 98). We have seen that this is an unsatisfactory definition. Control is interpreted as requiring active 'majority control' of voting shares (a crude test that is rather different from the company practitioner's understanding of 'control'). Where a hairstylist left a company with shares owned half and half by two brothers to work for another, of the shares of which one brother (who arranged the transfer) owned 85 per cent, he found his continuity had been ruptured ('negative control' was limited to 'stock exchange circles').[102]

Secondly, 'company' is not defined, so it was open to the courts at least to include some other corporate bodies, for as Buckley J. said in 1906 'the word company has no strictly legal meaning'. But the Court of Appeal shattered the continuity of a gardener who had worked for various local authorities (corporate bodies), imposing the narrowest possible meaning of registered 'limited company'. With rare statutory exceptions (such as certain teachers) and a few negotiated schemes that adopt a different definition, all such workers risk loss of continuity. Amongst the exceptions, the Act that abolished the GLC and metropolitan councils in 1985 preserved the continuity of staff who transferred to another authority *without* receiving redundancy payments (Local Government Act 1985 s. 54).

Weeks spent on strike (meaning here a cessation of, or refusal to, work in combination in order to compel an employer, or to compel or aid other employees, in regard to terms and conditions of employment) do not count towards continuity. But neither do those weeks break continuity. If the worker is absent because of a lock-out (closing the place of work, or suspending work, or refusal of further employment, to compel workers to accept terms and conditions), this does not break continuity (EPCA, Sched. 13 paras. 15, 24). In the original Act of 1963, strikes did not break continuity only if they were not in breach of employment contracts; but this provision was eliminated in 1965.

Advocates of legal sanctions against 'unofficial' or 'unconstitutional' action had pressed for automatic loss of redundancy and other rights by 'rupture' in such strikes, but the Donovan Report rejected the idea. A worker deprived of 'seniority' would not be open to the penalty on the next occasion; employers might 'condone' the impropriety of a strike after settlement; for older workers, losing the 'fruits of a lifetime's work' in one strike was intolerable. A comparison with the policy of the 1980s shows less anxiety now about using legal sanctions, but they are increasingly used against the union, rather than wildcat strikers whose breaches of procedure dominated those debates.

What if the employer dismisses the strikers? And can strikers build up continuity for ever by staying out in dispute? There is little danger, we have seen, of unfair dismissal claims, if he has avoided gross victimization. But the courts have taken 'employee' here to include an ex-employee (as the word can by statutory definition) at any rate unless and until the employer 'engages other persons on a permanent basis' to do their work, or he 'permanently discontinues' the employment activity, or unless the strikers take other permanent employment. Applying this test, a carpenter was able to utilize fifteen 'frozen' days on strike (during which he was dismissed) as a link between his re-engagement, a 'temporary cessation of work' and his previous service to make up a continuous period.[103]

Any agreement not to count employment before the strike, or to abolish the link during the frozen strike period, is void (EPCA s. 140). It is perhaps odd that there has as yet been little debate in Britain of the need to restrict the general legal right of the employer to hire replacement workers in a strike, a matter subject to some (if confused) control in the United States and, since 1982, sometimes prohibited in France.[104] The only provisions in Britain relate to replacements of workers absent by reason of pregnancy or 'medical suspension' (EPCA s. 61: p. 486) and of workers who are unfairly dismissed but replaced by a 'permanent' employee (s. 71 (4): p. 250).

Damages and social security

The worker who is 'wrongfully' dismissed today may think about unemployment benefit, redundancy pay or compensation for unfair dismissal, before he considers damages in the costly ordinary courts. Even so, he is entitled to damages under the common law.

Damages

The ordinary rule is that damages for breach of contract meet the loss arising naturally in the ordinary course of things (such as wages for the proper notice period) or such special loss as was in the contemplation of the parties (such as damages for loss of opportunity for an actor to put his name in lights). It has been held that discretionary bonuses are excluded because, Diplock LJ said, 'The law is concerned with legal obligations only . . . not with expectations however reasonable.' But a more liberal attitude allowed a 'reasonable and obliging lad' to recover sums for loss of earnings, instruction and future prospects (including loss of 'status in the labour market') when his employer renounced a four-year apprenticeship contract.[105]

The law imposes a duty 'reasonably to mitigate his loss'. If the worker refuses to take another suitable job he will be penalized to the extent of what he might have earned (or did earn, if he took it). It will not normally be reasonable to expect him to take a cut in wages or an 'important reduction in status'. The duty to mitigate applies to employer and employee, and it is not clear how far the courts would apply to this 'personal contract' the uncertain exception in contract law that allows one party with 'a legitimate interest' to insist on performance in face of breach. Where a sum lost would have been taxed, but damages would not be, the courts assess compensation at that sum (e.g. wages) *less* the amount of tax the worker would pay on it. This means that in order to stop the worker making a profit the courts allow the employer to make a profit. The 'slice' that before would have gone to the Revenue he now keeps. But for some years Parliament has decided that sums paid on such cessation of employment (often 'golden parachutes' for redundant directors) must be taxed in the hands of the recipient except for the first 'slice' (now £25,000). In *Parsons* v. *B N M Laboratories*[106] the court held that if damages were less than that amount the employer must pay damages net of tax; but for amounts beyond it he pays gross. This may not properly represent the loss, however; and in 1984 a judge preferred to calculate the entire loss taking tax into account, so that in order to leave the plaintiff with some £60,000 (his actual loss) the damages awarded had to exceed £83,000 (*Shove's* case).[107]

An even more bizarre situation has arisen in respect of damages and social security benefit. Many of the decisions here arise in personal injury cases for tort (Chapter 5), but compensation for common law wrongs both in tort and in contract is intended to compensate not punish. Since the employer's duty to provide a 'safe system of work' can be based both on tort and on the contract, it would be absurd if the measure of damages differed between the two.

Insurance by plaintiffs has long been regarded by judges as a 'private' matter, too remote to decrease the defendant's duty to pay for the loss he caused (as we saw in *Lister's* case). Thus in 1970 the Law Lords decided that an employer's contributory pension scheme of benefit to the plaintiff must be ignored by reason of its 'intrinsic nature' in assessing his loss. But in *Parsons's* case the worker wrongfully dismissed had received £50 national insurance unemployment benefit. This, said the court, was quite different; in a State insurance scheme, the employer 'should get the benefit of it if he finds it necessary to put one of his employees into unemployment'. Private insurance arose from 'thrift'; here contributions were obligatory (from employer, employee and the State). This Samuel Smiles view of State insurance – a 'subvention for wrongdoers', as Canadian courts have termed it – still seems to be the law despite widespread criticism. Parliament laid down a special code for State industrial injury benefit and for sickness or disablement benefit in personal injuries cases:[108] 50 per cent of benefit paid and likely to be paid to the plaintiff over five years must be deducted from damages. Are other State benefits all to benefit the wrongdoing defendant?

A number of sensible judgments have concluded that no deduction should be made for redundancy payments (due on the dismissal anyway) or discretionary State benefits.[109] If the breach causes personal injuries (p. 438) then, contrary to that view, Parliament decided in 1982 that a deduction should be made against damages for loss of income in respect of benefits accorded by the health service 'at public expense' (not, it seems, fees to private clinics). But the majority court decisions have not only approved the *Parsons* case; they have extended its reach to include supplementary benefit as a deduction from damages (now that it is receivable 'as of right', as was said in the case of the disabled ceiling fixer);[110] and this trend has been confirmed by the House of Lords in *Westwood*, 1984, applying the *Parsons* rule to benefits financed not by ordinary insurance but 'by way of compulsory levies on citizens in different circumstances . . . much more closely analogous to a tax than to a contractual premium payable under an insurance policy'. Indeed, Lord Bridge saw

no analogy at all between the generosity of private subscribers to a fund for the victims of some disaster who also have claims for damages against a tortfeasor and the state providing subventions for the needy out of funds which, in one way or another, have been subscribed compulsorily by various classes of citizens. The concept of public benevolence provided by the state is one I find difficult to comprehend.[111]

This is the mentality of the Poor Laws, a viewpoint ineradicably hostile to the Welfare State. No account is taken of the advantage received in reduced damages by an employer who has broken the most elementary of obligations owed to his employee. The preferential treatment for wrongdoers has become even more strange since 1981, when Parliament made unemployment benefit subject to tax in the hands of a claimant who comes above the tax threshold in a year.

The common law forbids damages for wrongful dismissal to compensate the employee for injured feelings. In 1985 the Court of Appeal reiterated this old principle that 'frustration and mental distress' caused by the breach cannot as such be allowed.[112] So too, a defendant should not be allowed any credit for the basic compensation the worker might receive for unfair dismissal, as in *Shove's* case, for the plaintiff would have such a right even if notice were given, and the 'basic award' in unfair dismissal compensation does not represent loss (p. 253). The practice has grown up of adjourning the tribunal proceedings until the court pronounces on damages so that it can then ensure no further compensation is paid twice over. This means even greater delay. But if the tribunal proceedings come first and the dismissal is found to be 'fair' even though at common law 'wrongful' through inadequate notice, the claimant must return to the ordinary courts for his damages. The Lord Chancellor has power to extend tribunal jurisdiction to 'wrongful dismissal', but this step, which has its own difficulties, has not yet been taken.

Where it is the worker who breaks the contract, what loss arises from the breach for the employer? In 1958 the NCB claimed against *Galley*, a deputy, who had refused to work Saturday shifts, damages for the entire loss of production so caused. The Court of Appeal decided that the measure of damage against each man was not the entire loss caused (as it might have been had the action been for a tortious conspiracy: p. 583) but no more than the net loss suffered through losing *his* output or (where, as here, the worker was not directly related to production) the cost of a replacement deputy on the day in question. This sum (less than £4) was awarded for the breaches on Saturdays up to the date of the writ.[113]

Sometimes the employer can prove greater direct loss and recover it, as where a Scottish council that had arranged to train Miss Neal as a social worker, in return for her covenant to stay two years with it, recovered all the sums stipulated in the contract as refundable (insurance contributions, examination fees, cost of books, etc.) because this was a genuine and proper estimate of sums thrown away on the expectation of her return. Although a trainee, she was treated as an 'employee' (contrast the youth trainees in the YTS: p. 119), and the restrictive covenant was held not to be a restraint of trade provision (p. 150). *Galley's* case was distinguished as different; here the parties must have had in mind, as the likely loss consequent on her breach, not merely the cost of a replacement, but all these larger amounts. But, Miss Neal argued, the council would not suffer all that loss because part of it would be recouped by adjustments in the statutory rate support grant. The Scottish court brushed this aside; it was a 'collateral arrangement', like insurance. It is questionable whether the decision should be accepted in England.[114]

The 1958 decision is still important, however. European legal systems that have allowed actions for breach of contract against individual workers who go on strike have often, as in Sweden, found it necessary to limit the damages recoverable. There is a British precedent in the Merchant Shipping Act 1970 under which liability of a seaman for absence without leave was limited to £100. If the individual worker were made liable for the entire loss of production when he refused to go to work (albeit that he could foresee this because his absence was concerted with others), the law would scarcely provide any liberty to withdraw labour. It is in this connection that the possibilities of tortious conspiracy to do damage by the unlawful means of breach of contract will have to be considered (p. 635), for there the damages in a tort action might not be limited. We shall see (p. 851) that other countries, such as France, have recently encountered similar problems.

Loss of the job and social security

Social security payments, such as unemployment benefit, come to a person in the capacity of citizen, not as worker (though now the employer administers the first slice of sick-pay: p. 174).[115] The insurance principle bases the scheme for unemployment benefit on contributions to the national fund. (In 1985 employers' contribution for lower-paid workers was reduced, to encourage them to create more jobs.) An 'employed earner' with the necessary contributions may claim benefit when unemployed provided he is 'capable' of work and 'available' for employment (p. 108). Benefit is payable for 312 days of unemployment, after which a further thirteen weeks of employment are necessary to resurrect entitlement. Otherwise an unemployed person may apply for supplementary benefit, a means-tested arrangement that has emerged by the Welfare State out of the Poor Laws. This area of complex law is administered by benefit ('adjudication') officers, social security tribunals, appeal tribunals and Commissioners, from whom an appeal is now possible to the Court of Appeal and who have also in the past been made subject to the judges' 'judicial review'.[116] Supplementary benefit is 'not performing its intended role as a small safety net' (some who are eligible do not claim it), though it may be more effective than the safety nets in some other European countries.[117] Plans were drawn up in 1985 by the Government to 'simplify' supplementary benefit. By 1981, 43 per cent of the 2.5 million unemployed were in receipt of only unemployment benefit, 34 per cent in receipt of supplementary benefit only. Many unemployed workers fall into a poverty 'trap' where they become 'progressively worse off as they pay tax and claim benefit at the same time', their fate sometimes made even worse by taking a low-paid job.[118] By 1985–6 unemployment benefit (for a couple under pension age) was £49.25 a week.

The employee can suffer disqualifications from unemployment benefit.[119] There are four main areas; that arising from strikes we deal with in Chapter 8, and the refusal of a 'suitable job' was mentioned in Chapter 2. Otherwise, a worker who voluntarily leaves his job 'without just cause' may be disqualified for up to six weeks (to be increased to 13 in October 1986). 'Voluntary' cessation can include a case where the employer dismisses after the employee has made it 'necessary' to do so (as by refusing to accept an X-ray medical examination); but decisions that volunteering for *dismissal* by reason of redundancy was a 'voluntary' leaving have been reversed by Parliament in 1985.[120] The approach to 'just cause' reveals the fact that until 1980 Commissioners had to be of senior barrister standing (they may now be solicitors). They have held it to be 'just cause' to leave in order not to join a trade union, or to resist a reduction in wages; but not by reason of grievances that the worker should have processed through the usual channels; nor through objections on trade union principle to finding an unskilled non-unionist doing the job.[121]

An equivalent disqualification can be imposed for 'misconduct'. The concept of 'industrial misconduct' imports something 'blameworthy, reprehensible and wrong'. The test often used is whether a reasonable employer would want to dispense with the worker's services. But the test is not confined to activities on the job, as where a park-keeper was convicted of gross indecency in his own time; though a chartered accountant was not disqualified after a conviction for fraud committed before he entered employment. Refusal to join a trade union is not misconduct even in a closed shop; but a fitter whose drunkenness in his own lodgings caused a customer to complain was guilty of 'misconduct'.[122] The private life of the worker, to which we return in Chapter 6, appears sometimes to be invaded by the same social security law that jealously safeguards his objections to trade unionism.

We saw that, where a claimant is, or would be, disqualified from unemployment benefit, his supplementary benefit may be reduced by 40 per cent for six (soon to be 13) weeks (p. 109). This applies to misconduct, leaving work voluntarily or refusing suitable employment without good excuse.[123] Until 1983 the reduction was 20 per cent if the claimant had £100 or less capital (after disregarded items) and if a member of his 'unit' was pregnant, seriously ill, a child under five, or affected by other categories of extreme need. The smaller reduction was restricted from 1984 to cases of pregnancy and serious illness. Assets are strictly assessed; but a claimant owning shares in a company is assessed on their value, not on the assets owned by the company ('a legal person separate and distinct from its members').[124] Some 'single payments' may be made; but a sum for cooking utensils was refused to a claimant because he lived in a hostel (though he was allowed to cook there, with his own utensils) instead of being a home tenant or owner.[125] The institution of appeals to the judges has not liberalized the regime. An award for 'urgent need' for clothes needed by the claimant, in part for a job interview, accepted by the appeal tribunal and Commissioner, was disallowed in 1984 by the Court of Appeal; her clothes needed replacing (for interviews), but this was 'normal wear and tear'. A miner on strike had his 'normal gross income' assessed for benefit not on what he actually brought home but on what his income was when working.[126]

Wherever doubt about unemployment benefit arises, for example when it is not claimed, the worker will be assumed to have left his employment 'voluntarily' for supplementary benefit purposes.[127]

On top of this, the social security authorities have an ultimate power to require a person who is long unemployed and therefore not entitled to unemployment benefit, and who is required to be available for employment, to attend a re-establishment centre if he appears not to be maintaining himself or his wife and children. The sanction is withdrawal of entitlement to benefit. There are nineteen centres, for men only. The aim is to fit those who lack a regular occupation or lack instruction or training to re-enter regular employment. Persistent refusal or neglect to maintain oneself or spouse or children under sixteen is a crime.[128] In 1985 an experimental 'non-coercive' counselling service for the long-term unemployed (1.4 million) was announced.

It would not be right to think of such benefits as the concern only of the unemployed. By the end of 1984, 4.6 million persons were in receipt of supplementary benefit and 7.5 million of housing benefit, and such social security assistance, including child benefit and family income supplement, is of great importance for those in employment but earning low wages. Further, families whose net income did not exceed supplementary benefit but who were not in receipt of it rose on official figures to 1.6 million by 1981 (since when poor families have become relatively poorer). Indeed, some estimates put almost a quarter of the population as living 'in poverty'.[129] Attention may soon focus upon the new poverty as much as on the revival of unemployment. Any solutions that involve a national minimum wage will profoundly affect both social security and labour law.

Redundancy and dismissal

In 1965 Parliament required employers to make 'redundancy payments' to employees who, after two years' continuous employment, were dismissed by reason of 'redundancy' (as defined) and assigned disputes about this to the industrial tribunals. The rationale of this curious Act was somewhat shrouded in mystery. Partly, it arose from the fact that collective bargaining was thought to be slow in responding to problems of unemployment and technological change. Employers and unions, though, were lukewarm; the *Financial Times* thought the Government had given priority to the wrong measure, severance payments instead of improved periodical social security measures. Indeed, what do the lump-sum payments represent? And how did we come to adopt the untranslatable word 'redundancy' – a management term at the outset, since it speaks of 'superfluity' of workers. Why do we not pay for, and write about, 'paucity' (of work)? The Donovan Report explained the Act as intended to promote 'labour-mobility', others as avoiding industrial conflict or relieving 'hardship'. But some, including the first president of tribunals, saw it as compensation for 'loss of a right . . . analogous to a right of property'; and Lord Denning spoke in 1982 of a worker's 'proprietary right in his job' and, earlier, of something 'akin to a right of property'. We can hardly see it that way today.

Redundancy payments

What is compensated is the loss of the particular job.[130] The 'redundant' worker may appear the next day doing the same job for a different employer (other than an associated employer or transferee of the business), as in the case of workers in the health service in 1985 dismissed by contractors. The Act provides for offers of a new contract of employment by the employer. If the worker unreasonably refuses such an offer from his employer or an associated employer (or, by virtue of s. 94, a transferee employer), made before his contract ends, to renew that contract or to make a new contract for suitable alternative employment, taking effect within four weeks of the termination of the old one, he loses his redundancy payment (EPCA s. 82 (3), (5)). If he accepts such an offer he is treated as not 'dismissed' and therefore ineligible (s. 84 (1)).

He may wish to try the new job out. Since 1975 the Act has allowed him a four-week trial period. Where the new terms of employment are different, the four-week period begins on the first day of work in the alternative job. If the worker terminates the new employment in that period, he is treated as being dismissed at the end of the original contract; and the same is true if the employer terminates it for a reason 'connected with or arising out of' the change of employment (s. 84 (3), (6)).[131] In such cases, the reason for dismissal is treated as that of the original dismissal, i.e. redundancy. The trial period can be longer (for example for retraining purposes) so long as it is in writing and made before the new work begins. The addition of the trial period in 1975 was an important innovation. Had it been linked to stronger training and retraining programmes, such a period (extended beyond the inadequate four weeks) could have been a useful part of a flexible restructuring of the labour market by consent. But, as elsewhere, the labour law legislation was not wholly integrated with any such overall policies in the Social Contract period.

The main problems have arisen over whether the worker has unreasonably refused suitable employment, which a large number of tribunal decisions have investigated. The job must be 'suitable' for that employee, but he may refuse 'reasonably'. Whether the worker is 'reasonable' if he refuses, e.g. because of his belief that he cannot do the job properly given his 'pride in his job', is for the tribunal a question of fact; and 'personal factors' such as advanced age must be considered.[132] The job must be 'substantially equivalent'; one that involves a substantial reduction in benefits or fails to offer scope for the worker's skills is likely to be inadequate; but this too is a question of fact.[133]

In the boom of the 1960s it was perhaps understandable to analyse employment rights and workers' own practices, as giving rise to 'property-like rights in the worker'.[134] But before 'rights analogous to property' can be meaningful, either full employment must be secure or payment must be made to compensate, if it can, for loss of a job, possibly for life. For many workers it was true before the insecure 1980s that

The social reality is that contracts of employment are usually, so far as the expectations of the parties are concerned, contracts until retirement age subject to earlier termination as prescribed.[135]

On retirement, social security takes over, with an occupational pension if the worker has one: periodical payments until death. This is one reason why the courts have found it so difficult to assess the 'normal retiring age' (after which a worker's other and separate right not to be *unfairly* dismissed is lost).[136] This analysis must now not be pressed too far. It still applies to those parts of the labour market where stability is the norm. Even before the social policies of the 1980s further depressed their condition it was usual for workers in the 'secondary' market to experience unstable employment, low pay, poor promotion prospects and weak unionization.[137]

It would be reassuring to think that the framework of logic that undoubtedly links workers' statutory redundancy pay, guarantee payments, rights in insolvency, unfair dismissal, social security benefits, and benefits from training and industrial subsidies reflects a consistent threat of labour market policy over the last twenty years, but it would hardly be true.[138] The 'paramount policy' has been said to aim at enabling management, preferably in consultation with unions, to achieve 'needed economies in the use of labour', better productivity and unit costs,[139] a formula refurbished in the 1980s to reduce workers' rights further in many areas. In retrospect, the legal provisions may have provided a floor to encourage collective bargaining and 'industrial and technological change',[140] but in return may have rendered redundancy in its industrial sense more acceptable, surrounded by myths (not least, it has been said, as to the 'joint' character of what is a 'managerial' problem) whilst compensating relatively few workers for what is in law 'redundancy'.[141]

To most Continental observers the lack of control by the public authorities over the dismissal is startling. For the public purse has contributed; but the Act cannot be said to aim at income maintenance; this is left to social security.[142] The scheme (now in EPCA ss. 81–120) requires the employer merely to inform the Secretary of State, shortly before his intention to dismiss, with details (and this approach was maintained when in 1975 employers were required to consult with recognized unions: p. 294) as a condition of obtaining the full rebate from the national Redundancy Fund. This rebate, we shall see, is to be largely abolished. That will increase the importance of the criminal sanction under the 1975 Act on employers who fail to inform the Secretary of State of forthcoming redundancies of ten or more workers (EPA ss. 100, 105).

How is a payment computed, if it is due? With maxima of twenty years' service and (in 1986) £155 a week, there is paid: for each year of service between the ages of 41 and 65 years, one and a half weeks' pay; for each between 21 and 40, one week's pay; and for each between 18 and 20, half a week's pay. A worker made redundant after 64 (59 for women) gradually has these rights tapered off to zero in that year at pensionable age (we may expect it to be 64 for both sexes by 1987: p. 919). The rules on a week's pay and normal working hours have been considered above (p. 203). The employer can claim a rebate from the fund (s. 104), but in 1985 this was reduced from 41 per cent to 35 per cent, and is to be abolished altogether from October 1986, except for firms with fewer than ten employees (Wages Bill 1986 Part III).

Soaring unemployment saw the number of redundancy payments reach nearly 810,000 in 1981, and by 1982 the fund moved into a deficit of £282 million. As the rate of dismissals eased but long-term unemployment grew, the deficit fell in 1984 to £69.7 million; in the same year there were 425,000 payments, 40 per cent up on 1979, the average payment to a worker being some £1,500. Payments in schemes collectively bargained are frequently higher, though some in the private sector were decreasingly generous in the 1980s; some have provided for periodical payments as well as lump sums. In both respects public sector industries have seen higher payments, sometimes supported by special legislation, such as for shipbuilding and coal-mining.

A worker aged 55 with twenty years' service in coal-mining could receive in 1982 (as lump sum plus weekly payments to 65) a total of £34,796, but in shipbuilding it was £7,950.[143] In 1984 B L paid an average of £8,800 to each of 1,700 redundant workers, while from 1985 maximum payments to dockers could reach a total of £25,000 (partly available in weekly payments to encourage voluntary redundancies; the scheme, heavily in debt, was given Government backing for two and a half more years). An estimate by Incomes Data Services put the amount paid in five years since 1979 as £6 billion.[144] With few exceptions, redundancy payments even under 'voluntary' schemes are not princely sums (even if they are not measured against the golden handshakes to directors contemporaneously reaching £100,000 or even £750,000). Young workers even in public sector schemes received small amounts; and average redundancy payments in 1981–2 did not exceed £2,000 in any industries except mining, gas, water and electricity.[145] Such figures hardly explain the regular reports of workers 'in their thirties rushing past shop stewards' to accept offers of redundancy money in areas of high unemployment where the prospect of working again seemed slender.[146]

The statutory scheme has thrown up serious problems on both 'dismissal' and 'redundancy'. The employee who is qualified with two years' service must normally claim his redundancy payment within six months of dismissal, though the tribunal can hear him within the following six months if it is just and equitable to do so (E P C A s. 101).

More important, dismissal must be proved by the employee, but thereafter the statute (s. 91) requires the tribunal to presume that the dismissal was by reason of redundancy. This burden of proof is put on the employer, since it is his 'reason' that is in dispute.

Dismissal

The basic definition of 'dismissal' links the statutory rights for both redundancy and unfair dismissal to the concepts of the common law. 'Dismissal' covers (1) termination of the employment contract by the employer, whether with or without notice; (2) the expiry of a fixed-term contract that is not renewed; and (3) termination by the employee, with or without notice, where he is 'entitled to terminate it without notice by reason of the employer's conduct' (EPCA s. 55, unfair dismissal; s. 83, redundancy, other than a lock-out, s. 92 (4)). But in redundancy cases also, there is no dismissal if the worker's employment is renewed or if he is re-engaged in a new contract offered by the employer or an 'associated employer' before the old one terminates, with no more than a four-week interval (EPCA s. 84). Where, however, any of the conditions of the new contract are different, he is allowed a trial period of four weeks (or longer if agreed in writing), as we have seen. He then still counts as dismissed at the earlier time and for the original reason of redundancy if he leaves for any reason or if the employer dismisses him for a reason connected with the new job during that period. (Similar provisions for a trial period apply to the 'protective award' of compensation that an employer must pay to a worker if he fails to consult with a recognized union over proposed redundancies: EPA 1975 s. 102 (6)–(11): p. 294; and on the transfer of a business, EPCA s. 94: p. 207.) The worker must not wait to leave until after the trial period.

Suppose, however, in a redundancy situation, the employer insists upon a change in a worker's employment conditions so grave that it amounts to a 'constructive dismissal'. The worker has the statutory four weeks in which to make up his mind what to do. But that period seems to run only from the time when, faced with the employer's breach, he should decide what to do about it. In this so-called 'common law period' before he elects whether or not to accept the breach as a termination, the EAT has held that he may continue to work at his old job, in a sense under protest.[147]

It will be seen that termination by consent or by frustration (p. 144) is excluded from the statutory concept of dismissal. The courts have been quick to stamp on any general idea that failure to hire can possibly be a dismissal even if both employer and worker have some reason to feel that it is equivalent (as where ship-repairers were refused a rebate on a payment made to an apprentice when they failed to engage him as a fitter at the end of the apprenticeship contrary to arrangements with the unions, because 'work was not available'). Managerial prerogative to hire, as against fire, is scarcely touched by the employment protection laws. An employee to whom notice is actually given may normally leave before the end of it and still count as 'dismissed' so long as he gives notice to his employer, apparently of any length (EPCA s. 55 (3)); but in a case of redundancy, to preserve his 'dismissal' rights he must give the counter-notice not only during the employer's period of notice required under the contract or by statute but also in writing (s. 85). The employer may after that serve another notice requiring him to stay, in which case the tribunal can award whatever proportion of a payment it finds just. The unwary worker can fall into traps here, like the worker who gave his counter-notice after the employer told the union about closure but before any dismissal notices were issued. But a man declared redundant who later asked permission to switch his date with another worker was held not to have given a counter-notice but to have varied only 'the date of dismissal by mutual consent' with the employer, for which s. 85 was not needed.[148]

The date of dismissal is important in practice especially to the worker for calculating his continuity and getting to the tribunal in time. It is fixed by either expiry of actual notice, date of any other termination, expiry of a fixed term, or expiry of a counter-notice (ss. 55 (4), 90). Termination operates at the time of a summary dismissal, or at the time of departure when the employee leaves with wages in lieu; but the employee is then deprived of his period of notice. The Court of Appeal in 1985 was adamant that a summary dismissal by the employer takes effect there and then, even if there are domestic appeals procedures.[149] That remains so even after the *Tipton* case, 1986.

The expiry of a fixed-term contract, as it should be, is brought within the statutory concept of 'dismissal'. But rights here can be waived where a worker with such a contract for two years or more agrees in writing (not necessarily in the contract: s. 142 (2)). A contract for a fixed term does not lose its character because notice can be given within the term.[150] But a hiring on a 'task' or 'job-by-job' basis is different. This is a contract to do 'a particular task or carry out a particular purpose, then when that task or purpose comes to an end the contract is discharged by performance'.

A lecturer hired at the start of each year in Wiltshire for the academic session was on a fixed-term contract, but the court's reasoning left it unnecessarily open to employers to evade employment protection by hiring employees (especially part-time workers) to do 'particular tasks' rather than for a fixed-term contract or one determinable by notice. In 1986 the EAT made matters worse by accepting that a lecturer hired 'so long as sufficient funds are provided' by the MSC was not dismissed when her job was not renewed because the funds dried up (the specific purpose of her employment had ceased, and her job terminated automatically).[151] It is to be hoped that the Court of Appeal will reverse such an extraordinary interpretation of EPCA s. 83, which speaks of a contract being 'terminated by the employer', whether he is rich or poor. Otherwise we may find companies engaging workers on contracts which are to last 'so long as the shareholders provide sufficient funds'.

Certain additional 'acts' by and 'events' affecting the employer are made 'dismissals' in cases of redundancy (EPCA s. 93). These include the death of a personal employer, where redundancy is presumed; but the right to a redundancy payment is barred if the personal representatives carry on the employment (EPCA, Sched. 12, para. 14). Dissolution of a partnership at common law ends the employment and is within this category. The same is normally true of limited companies that are wound up; but certain types of (voluntary) winding-up appear not to end the employment unless the business is not to be carried on. Short of liquidation, a receiver may be appointed. He can be an agent of either the creditors, or the court (or both), or the company. Where he is not an agent of the company, employment is terminated. But where he is the agent of the company, as where he is also a manager to conduct the business, the employment of workers continues, but, by reason of technicalities of company law, the receiver appears not to be personally liable for breach of the continued contracts.[152] Nor is a claim for redundancy excluded under the Transfer of Undertakings Regulations 1981 (p. 243) where a receiver sells the business and 'economic' reasons demand the dismissal of the worker.[153] The distinctions of company law are quite out of place in labour law and fortunately appear to be largely dropped in the sections giving the employee rights in the employer's 'insolvency' (EPCA ss. 122–127: p. 398). Unhappily, as we shall see in Chapter 9, labour law has in other areas recently been invaded by the remedy of receivership with as yet unforeseeable consequences.

Redundancy

A dismissal is *by reason of redundancy* if it is 'attributable wholly or mainly' to the fact (1)

that his employer has ceased, or intends to cease, to carry on the business for the purposes for which the employee was employed by him, or . . . to carry on that business in the place where the employee was so employed [the 'business' limb; EPCA s. 81 (2) (a)]

or (2)

that the requirements of that business for employees to carry out work of a particular kind, or for employees to carry out work of a particular kind in the place where he was so employed, have ceased or diminished, or are expected to cease or diminish [the 'kind of work' limb; EPCA s. 81 (2) (b)]

– and all the businesses of 'associated employers' are counted as one business. But we must recall that if the worker unreasonably refuses an offer of a suitable job made before dismissal, he is not entitled to a payment by reason of redundancy (s. 82 (6)).

As the present writer suggested in 1966, this area has come to 'provide a lawyers' field day'. Such a definition was bound to leave out many workers who to the ordinary person are dismissed for 'redundancy'. As early as 1967 judges insisted on the primacy of 'the overall requirements of the business', requiring the worker 'to adapt himself to new methods and techniques', so as to reject redundancy where a manager with thirty years' service was dismissed by new employers who introduced new methods of work for which he was unfitted. When owners of the Star and Garter Pub converted it into the Steamboat Inn with a discothèque, they dismissed the barmaid in favour of 'bunny girls' to attract younger customers; but this was not 'redundancy', said the court (whose feel for the subject-matter may have been limited), for the work of the 'bunny' barmaid was not 'work of a different kind' from what the older barmaid had done.[154]

The concept gives wide scope to the courts to control the nature of the employment contract, thereby determining the 'kind of work' a worker is employed to do. Boilermakers dismissed for insisting on existing terms of employment found in 1968 that they were not treated as an obvious instance of redundancy. By 1973 the Court of Appeal was astonished at the idea that men who 'refused to alter restrictive practices' should be so regarded, and held there was no redundancy situation where, as their business declined, employers withdrew free transport (a term of the contract) from a china-clay worker, *Mr Chapman*, and six colleagues in the recession. They could not then get to work. There was no reduction, though, in the work: 'They have employed seven other men in their place to do that work.'[155] The 'property' in the 'job' began to look like what the employer said it was, subject to judicial review. It might have been different, said Lord Denning, if the employer had dismissed them to take on replacements at lower wages. Little has been heard of this as a protection for workers in later cases, nor of the suggestion of Buckley LJ that it might be different if the employer did not pay 'the recognized rate for the job, where one existed, or a fair wage'.

The judges now entered the phase of highly 'creative' manipulation of implied terms leading to the modern, extensive rights for the employer to demand changes in the employment contract to promote 'efficiency'. So, in *Johnson*, clerks whose shifts had been reorganized from a five-day to six-day system failed in 1974 to prove they were redundant when they were dismissed and replaced for objecting, it being 'settled'

that an employer is entitled to reorganize his business so as to improve its efficiency and, in doing so, to propose to his staff a change in the terms and conditions of their employment; and to dispense with their services if they do not agree.

There was no change in the kind of work and no reduction in the work-force. By 1977 *Nolan*, a skilled fitter in a toy factory, dismissed on refusing to change from a long day shift plus overtime and a night shift, to a double day shift, had no chance of success: 'nothing should be done', said Lord Denning MR, 'to impair the ability of employers to reorganize their work force and their terms and conditions of work so as to improve efficiency'.[156] It had been thought that the Act of 1965 provided redundancy payments as compensation for this; but as the recession advanced, the judges responded to changed social conditions – or 'as a result of the general decline in the level of productive activity'[157] – by using it as a reason for *non*-payment. It is not surprising that case law on this aspect seems almost to have died out. We return to it below.

The statute also denies a payment if an employer dismisses (without notice, or by short notice, or on full notice with a statement of reasons), and is entitled to do so summarily, for *misconduct* (s. 82 (2)). Soon after the 1965 Act the courts encountered this provision when an electrician worked in Liverpool but was asked, since work there had diminished, to move to Barrow, a journey not possible within the day. He was dismissed – but not, it was held, for misconduct; his contract included no implied term requiring him to make that journey to his 'place of work'. The implied term of 'obligatory mobility', however, has now received greater geographical, as it has technological, expansion. By 1981 *Jones* the tunneller was, as we saw (p. 139), impliedly required to move his pit and his work.[158]

What, however, does 'attributable' to redundancy mean? Should not the employer who dismisses at the time his business is contracting show some other objective reason to escape, or need the reason rest only on his belief? The Court of Appeal, Lord Denning dissenting, chose the latter in the retrograde decision in *Hindle's* case, 1969. A skilled woodworker on boats with twenty years' service was dismissed, and not replaced, when fibreglass was replacing woodwork. Surely this was a diminution of his kind of work? But management claimed it had dismissed him because he was a thorough but 'slow' and 'unprofitable' worker. This, said the majority judges, was their 'main' ground for dismissal and it was 'genuine'. If the employer convinces a tribunal of this, it matters not that he was mistaken. Redundancy, said Sachs LJ, does not deal with 'ill health or deterioration in the employer's views of the capabilities of the employee'; he was free to 'see if someone could do the job better'. The law must not put a brake on 'the best man for the job'.[159] So much for compensating a man for his job property once the employer decides he has deteriorated and become unprofitable in the midst of technological change.

After 1971 a new factor appeared. Dismissal by reason of redundancy became one of the ways in which an employer could show that dismissal was *fair* (now EPCA s. 57 (2) (c)). This saves the employer if he also acted 'reasonably' and if the selection for redundancy is not improper (see further: p. 244). Sometimes the worker benefits, like the assistant manager who, not being redundant, was *unfairly* dismissed. At first, the advent of unfair dismissal appeared to make some of the judiciary say what they felt about the redundancy payments law. It had been 'clouded by a slipshod acceptance of a bottomless purse', said Kilner Brown J., 'often used to justify bribes to go quietly . . . [its provisions may] have outlived their usefulness . . . real hardship . . . can be dealt with by . . . the unfair dismissal provisions'.[160] It also magnified a more difficult issue. The test of redundancy may turn more either upon an interpretation of the contract (styled by Davies and Freedland the 'job package' approach) or upon an investigation of the actual work done (the 'job function' approach). Both appear in the cases and both have their difficulties.[161] The second leaves the court more free to take its own view of the 'kind of work' (as with the barmaid); the first entangles the test of redundancy with the manipulated express and implied terms. Both can be trimmed to suit the needs of the day by the *Hindle* test, giving the employer's subjective reasoning pride of place. All three give the judges wide scope.

Take the contract of a producer for the B B C that required him to serve the corporation with his best endeavours wherever, however and when it demanded. In fact, he worked on the Caribbean Service, which was closed down, leading to his dismissal. To escape unfair dismissal, the B B C relied on 'redundancy'. But it failed; the court in 1977 used a contractual test, 'very reluctantly', to refuse to tie down the 'work' to that service. He was just a producer; and there was no redundancy for producers generally. But in *Cowen* v. *Haden Ltd*[162] the contract of one of ninety surveyors required him to take on any and all duties reasonably within his capabilities. He was promoted to divisional surveyor. As business fell away the employers abolished that post at divisional level. On being dismissed, he argued that he was unfairly dismissed, *not* redundant; but unsuccessfully. The Court of Appeal concentrated on his contract; it had been 'varied' to make his appointment one at divisional level; so there was no longer a 'need' for his particular kind of work. But for safety's sake the judges also explicitly approved earlier decisions that adopted the 'job function' test, such as *Chapman*. It was inevitable that the two tests should have been mingled in the judgments. The statute talks of the purposes and requirements of the 'business' and the kind of 'work' of the 'employees'. The nature of the work done must clearly be inspected; but it is integrally linked to the contract. Indeed, the very concept of 'employee' also gives a place to the contract test. For if the employer replaces employees with self-employed lump labour, his requirements for *employees* (under a contract of employment) to carry out that work must have diminished, and the dismissals are by reason of redundancy (as with two painters in 1972). In 1985 the E A T committed itself to the view that *Cowen* v. *Haden* had settled the question in favour of the 'contract approach'.[163] Time will tell whether this is the full story. Certainly it would be rash to encourage the worker to rely upon the letter of his contract, for the court may demand that he relinquishes his rights in the face of a proposed reorganization.

A dismissal following workers' refusal to move to day-shift from night-shift working (without obligation under their employment contracts and contrary to a collective agreement) *can* be seen by a tribunal (in a redundancy payments case) as a cessation of a requirement for night-work which has an 'inherent particularity'. This view, taking account of the strain on domestic lives, was swallowed (just) by the E A T.[164] The functional character is here combined with a contract test. Nor does the Court of Appeal keep the two distinct. In *Murphy's* case[165] M. was engaged as second plumber by a school to do plumbing work and to assist with the heating boilers. After alterations the boilers were so troublesome that he wrote claiming extra payments for this work and placing limits on the work he would do outside that was fit for a 'trained plumber'. Eventually the school hired a heating engineer and decided it needed only one plumber. He alleged unfair dismissal. In deciding that M.'s dismissal was by reason of redundancy and fair, the court found that the work of a heating engineer was of a kind 'distinct from general plumbing'. It was for the employers 'as a matter of commercial judgment to decide the size and balance' of the staff. They had now

appointed a different kind of tradesman . . . having different qualifications and skills from those of a plumber to perform functions and assume responsibilities . . . of a more extensive and more responsible kind than the functions [M.] was competent to perform in that respect.

Requirements for 'work of a particular kind' (M.'s combined general plumbing and heating work) had 'ceased' because the maintenance of the modernized plant was 'not plumber's work', and the engineer with wider responsibilities could 'help part-time in the . . . normal plumbing work'. So 'the maintenance of the plant as modernised was not plumber's work'. In this labyrinth of reasoning, M.'s job functions are prominent, but they depend in part upon his contract (and undoubtedly his claim under it) in 'the second plumbing post'.

It was no accident that M. was dismissed just *before* he acquired two years' service to qualify for a redundancy payment. Nor is it accidental that the juggled tests for 'redundancy' now so frequently support the 'fairness' of a dismissal or that they have come to depend so much upon the way management defines the old and the new work. Ironically, a major function of redundancy law has changed; from protecting a particular kind of job right for the innocent worker, it has become in part a package for the legitimation of his dismissal.

Lay-off or short time

Little of this was foreseen in 1965. But an employer clearly might evade payments on dismissal for redundancy by substituting, if it were lawful, by contract weekly 'lay-off' or 'short-time' ('LOST') periods. Where LOST periods (entailing no pay, or less than half normal pay) extend to any 6 weeks within 13, the worker can therefore claim a redundancy payment (EPCA s. 88). But he has to navigate a maze of procedures; and where he does not use that tortuous path, an employer with a contractual right to lay off is not necessarily confined to any reasonable period even when the right stems from a national collective agreement (this is not the courts' idea of a necessary term).[166]

Almost as if in acknowledgement of the 'wrong priority' in 1965, Parliament provided in 1975 for periodical 'guarantee payments' (EPCA ss. 12–18). Briefly, after one month's service an employee has a right to a payment for a day when he would normally work but when no work is provided; any sums payable under the contract reduce the amount. In 1986 this stands at a paltry maximum of £10.70 a day; it is lost if lay-off is caused by a lock-out or strike at the workplace, or if the worker refuses suitable alternative work, or fails to attend when required; and (as amended in 1980) is payable for five days only in a rolling period of three months. There is also a meagre provision for payments where suspension under the contract arises by reason of specified medical grounds (EPCA ss. 19–22). A right to unemployment benefit can arise during a LOST period but it is hedged with rigorous conditions;[167] and even the cautious plans of the 1970s to institute a general legal protection for workers in LOST periods were abandoned in the 1980s.[168]

Judicial creativity will, or can, do little about the subjection of workers if an employer has the contractual right to initiate a LOST period. Without such an agreement – express or implied – the employer has no right as such to lay off without wages; but at common law this will normally be restricted to the notice period. In some types of work, the court may find an obligation to pay even where work is not available; or such a duty may arise from collective bargaining. The courts have been prepared, however, to imply a term suspending the duty to pay workers where natural forces cause a lay-off as when a mine became too unsafe to work, the appeal judges saying the intention of the parties must have been to share the loss of this natural event (would they have said the same if a crop of diamonds had appeared?).[169]

There may now be another problem. An agreement is void if it attempts to exclude or limit a statutory right (EPCA s. 140). Where the employer agreed with a union committee to retain the 'last in, first out' ('LIFO') principle in redundancies, but to permit 'bumping' (the practice whereby a worker is transferred to another job, thereby bumping a second employee into a 'translated redundancy dismissal', which may not be unfair), the arrangement was struck down as depriving the redeployed worker of his right to a redundancy payment, which the Act gives him, if he reasonably refused as unsuitable the alternative employment offered (on new pay and status) in the 'trial period' of four weeks.[170] The decision leaves the section ticking like a time bomb under many current practices for it renders questionable how far a contract of employment can be subjected to alterable terms or to 'variations' that exclude statutory rights, when those very rights interlock with common law concepts based on 'consent'.

Redundancy and bargaining

Since it was one of the objects of the 'floor of rights' legislation to promote collective bargaining above it, certain agreements are excluded from this prohibition against contracting out of the Act and are able to oust the statutory provisions (EPCA s. 140 (2)). They include certain agreed 'dismissal procedures', collective agreements excluding unfair dismissal rights and agreements on redundancy. In such agreements, the employees must be entitled to payments on termination of the employment, and disputes must be referred to an industrial tribunal; the Secretary of State must make an order (s. 96; slightly different conditions are set out for dismissal procedures, where disputes may go to an independent arbitrator or tribunal: s. 65). But no extensive use has been made of such provisions. An Order exists on dismissal whereby the electrical contracting industry has set up its own arbitration system; and continuity provisions for redundancy are varied in a few Orders (e.g. for some teachers; and employees of Electricity Boards – which are not 'associated employers'). But twenty-two Orders have been made exempting agreed schemes for guarantee payments (under EPCA s. 18). Most schemes seem to offer a poor 'improvement' on the depressed, statutory floor of rights.[171] One exempted agreement in a food group requires 'remaining employees to work flexibly' and offers five days' wages for 'LOST' in any calendar quarter. Certain public sector schemes, as in coal, shipbuilding and the docks, operate under their own legislation, or are partly or wholly excluded (e.g. civil servants are not excluded from unfair dismissal but are excluded from minimum notice and redundancy claims, though they have their own machinery on that: EPCA ss. 111, 138).

In fact, bargained schemes for redundancy seem to be more extensive in the public sector than in the private sector. Surveys at the end of the 1970s found that, thirteen years after the introduction of redundancy pay (and some years after legal obligations were imposed to consult with unions on redundancies: p. 294), 52 per cent of firms paid only the statutory minimum, while payments reached one and a half times the minimum in only one-fifth of the rest; but bargaining on redundancy arrangements and payments at workplace level was common (normal in the public sector).[172] Relative workplace bargaining power in the mid-1980s is not what it was in 1979, and commentators suggest that private sector firms have now reduced the margin of supplements for redundancy above the statutory floor.

It is not clear whether the legislation has done much to stimulate collective bargaining on 'redundancy'. Nor has it provided workers with 'property' in jobs. Some argue that it has weakened the strength of industrial action as a countervailing power to management decisions on closures. Although a strike during the statutory notice period does not lose the workers redundancy payments, strikes before that are misconduct, which can give rise to dismissal without notice and no entitlement (EPCA ss. 82, 92); and this seems to include a case where the employer has already notified a union of his proposal to dismiss (p. 193).[173] Workers have undoubtedly received payments under the Act where before 1965 they might have been dismissed without any such money; but the price has been a renewed legitimation of management prerogative over the reorganization of work, which in turn has narrowed the right to redundancy pay itself. Moreover, the legal developments may have stimulated an appetite and practice of negotiation for lump-sum payments when the greater need perhaps was for improved periodical payments for workers and their families in the absence of work. Even radical proposals, such as abolition of the maximum amounts, tend to adhere to the lump-sum concept.[174] But in 1985 the dock employers arranged for an insurance company to turn dockworkers' redundancy payments wholly or partly into weekly paid annuities.

The mistakes of the past, on all sides, might be mitigated by restructuring not only the definition of redundancy but the payments so as to include at least an element of periodical income, as part of a pattern that merges social security and labour market policies. No hint of such an approach appeared in the 1985 'programme for action', *Reform of Social Security* (Cmnd 9691).

Unfair dismissal

If redundancy payments provided a 'lawyers' field day', the advent in 1971 of 'unfair dismissal' legislation saw the real legal battle commence. By this time, most European systems provided some legal protection against 'arbitrary' dismissal. In West Germany workers could claim compensation and (in theory) reinstatement from labour courts. In France dismissals in all but small enterprises needed notification to and approval by the Labour Inspectorate; dismissals must not be unfair; and elected works councillors or union representatives received special protection, a system of rights adjudicated by local *conseils de prud'hommes* (elected employers and employees, normally – to unbelieving Anglo-Saxon eyes – with no legal chairman). The United States had taken a different path and developed squads of private 'grievance arbitrators' to deal with such complaints under US collective contracts. Perhaps some of these perspectives were unduly rosy. Yet the fact remained, in Britain workers had no such rights. When British judges – especially Lord Denning MR – spoke of a 'right to work' they meant the right *not* to be a member of a trade union whilst taking such work as was going. The phrase has been understandably criticized as encouraging 'a false consciousness among workers'.[175] Workers, even shop stewards, whom the Donovan Report accepted with its research surveys as an essential part of industrial relations, were often unfairly sacked without legal redress. The employer's power might be limited by a trade union presence; but what if he did not recognize a union, or if the union was weak?

The ILO Recommendation 119, requiring that dismissal be restricted to good and valid cause, accepted by Britain in 1964, was another stimulus; and it is to be hoped that the new ILO standards of 1982 will one day stimulate further improvements.[176] In 1967 a report of the tripartite National Joint Advisory Committee of the Ministry of Labour proposed remedies through improved collective bargaining; statutory machinery, the committee thought, might import 'a legalistic element' and 'undermine existing voluntary procedures'. But the Donovan Report saw the balance of the argument the other way; both political parties proposed legislation; and the industrial tribunals seemed ready for the work; so the proposals of the 1970 Bill were turned into the less controversial part of the Industrial Relations Act 1971. Apart from legal protection for the individual employee, the new provisions had the aim of reducing strikes about dismissals and the introduction of 'a spur to management practice to create a greater formality to disciplinary arrangements'.[177]

Since then hundreds of thousands of disputes about unfair dismissal have been heard by tribunals and appellate courts. The much amended legislation is now in EPCA ss. 54–80. It is useful to distinguish three stages in such a matter: (1) requirements that the worker be an 'employee' in the strict sense (Chapter 2), who is qualified, was dismissed and has presented his complaint in time; (2) the issue of fairness; (3) remedies.

(1) *Qualified employees and dismissal.* A claim must be presented to a tribunal within three months of the date of dismissal unless this is not reasonably practicable for the worker, in which case the tribunal may

substitute another period (EPCA s. 67). Various categories of employee are excluded, e.g. workers reaching 'normal retiring age' in their employment (s. 64: p. 219) or 'ordinarily' working outside Britain;[178] registered dockworkers; police and armed forces; workers on fixed-term contracts for at least one year who have waived their rights in writing (s. 142 (1)); workers dismissed to safeguard national security (on which a Minister's certificate is final) or whose employment has been specified by certificate as excluded on that ground.[179] The contract of employment must not be illegal (e.g. a fraud on the Revenue); but, as we have seen, if the illegality arises only in performance of the contract, not in its nature or conception, it seems that the worker can enforce statutory rights if not aware that the performance was illegal.[180]

The employee must have the requisite continuity of employment. No period of qualification is required in certain cases, e.g. dismissals related to union membership or activities, or to non-unionism (pp. 312, 369), or arising from sex or racial discrimination (Chapter 6), whilst dismissal on certain medical grounds can be challenged after four weeks (EPCA s. 29). This is one reason for basing a case where possible on such grounds. For the qualifying period in 'ordinary' unfair dismissal cases has recently been extended. In 1971 it was put at two years but was reduced to one year in 1974, then to six months in 1976. The reasons originally given for this requirement were, partly, the fear that tribunals might be overloaded, partly the need for the employer to judge the suitability of the worker.

In 1979, although surveys showed that the legislation had had little – if any – effect on recruitment, the Government increased the period by Order to one year. By the 1980 Act, in a small business (where during the period the employees of the employer and his 'associated employers' never exceeded twenty) the qualification was made two years. So, where an agency had a lot of 'temporaries' but fewer than twenty 'employees', dismissed workers with less than two years' service were excluded from the tribunal.[181] The reason given for extension of the period in 1979 was the heavy burden placed on business by this legislation (though this was 'primarily psychological' and the evidence was 'anecdotal').[182] In 1985 the Government restored the two-year period for employment starting in that year, because 'worry' about these workers' rights could make 'employers reluctant to take workers on'; risk of 'unjustified involvement with tribunals' was said to be a deterrent to recruitment, despite a research finding during the same year that it was not. It seems doubtful that the unemployment figures will fall in response to the anecdotal approach to law reform. In 1983 one in four complainants had less than two years' service; the change is estimated to be likely eventually to affect 3 million workers, in a labour market where short-term engagements increasingly affect continuity.

The meaning of 'dismissal' rests on EPCA s. 55, which we have already mentioned (pp. 222–4). Dismissal arises from (a) a termination by the employer, whether with notice or not; (b) the expiry of a fixed-term contract that is not renewed (but exclusion of rights in writing is here possible in a contract of one year or more: s. 142); or (c) termination by the employee, whether with notice or not, where the employer's conduct is such that it repudiates the contract, and the worker is entitled to terminate it without notice. It is here that the law has felt the strong impact of the doctrine of 'constructive dismissal', where the worker quits in the face of the employer's fundamental breach of contract. We have seen the potent influence of the doctrine upon 'implied terms' and the scope that it gives to the courts (p. 177). Constructive dismissals have arisen from an employer's unilateral change in the formula of wage payment; serious reductions in pay and fringe benefits; demotion (in one case even where a clause in the contract seemed to allow it, because it was so gross that it fell outside the scope); or where the employers failed to support a worker who was harassed by her union colleagues in whose strike she had refused to join the previous year (s. 63: p. 194).

Constructive dismissal, although a breach of contract, is not always 'unfair'. Where Mr Savoia, supervisor in a meringue factory, walked out after being refused his old job on returning from illness, he was constructively dismissed. But the tribunal's decision that in all the circumstances it was a 'fair' dismissal was upheld by the Court of Appeal in 1982. Such cases might be 'rare', said Waite J. in *Cawley* v. *South Wales Electricity Board*, 1985,[183] but they were possible. Mr Cawley was dismissed after he had urinated out of a vehicle. On appeal through the industry's disciplinary procedure, the arbitrator found that dismissal was too severe; instead he should be downgraded, a decision that superseded the earlier dismissal. However, as the alternative job offered was further from home and £1,400 less in salary, he refused it. The tribunal held this to be both a constructive dismissal and also reasonable and fair. The EAT regarded this combination of conclusions in this case as inconsistent. Constructive dismissal rested on the repudiatory breach test; but there was no need for

precedents from ancient cases being cited to the bewilderment of Tribunals and the holding up of business. . . . In ordinary life and in reality you cannot say that a re-engagement offered is reasonable for one purpose and not reasonable for the other.

The constructive dismissal was upheld, but the finding on 'fairness' was set aside, and the case remitted to the tribunal for assessment of compensation. This decision came close to the error, common in decisions before 1978, of testing the employer's breach by a test of reasonableness. The tests of reasonableness and of breach will not always be found to overlap so clearly. The tribunal must apply to constructive dismissal the proper contractual test;[184] and a failure to do so may cause appellate courts to negate the dismissal. So too, an employer's motives are not normally relevant to the issue of breach,[185] whereas they may well be relevant to reasonableness.

The distinction between constructive dismissal and reasonableness appears in *Genower's* case, 1980.[186] A reorganization of a health authority led to his transfer to another post and place of work. This other job, he felt, was far below his special skills; so he resigned. A finding of constructive dismissal by fundamental breach was upheld but so was the finding that it was fair. The right of the employer to reorganize for 'a sound good business reason' was upheld once again as essential; and it was the 'substantial reason' that the Act required before dismissal could be fair. Moreover, the employers had 'behaved in a kindly way' and reasonably towards the employee. *Hollister's* case, 1979, had made it clear that the need to reorganize the business could be a 'substantial reason' even if the changes demanded by the employer involved a breach of the employment contract.

(2) *Fair or unfair.* We have entered the second stage: is the dismissal fair? The answer involves two sub-stages: (a) the employer must show what the *reason* or principal reason for it was, and that this related to either the employee's *capability* (or qualifications) for this kind of work, or his *conduct*, or the fact that he was *redundant* (or unable to do the work without contravening a statute) *or some other substantial reason* ('SOSR') such as to justify dismissing an employee holding his position

(s. 57 (1), (2)). Then, if he surmounts that hurdle: (b) the issue of fairness rests on whether he acted 'reasonably or unreasonably' in dismissing; this is to be decided in accordance with *equity and the substantial merits of the case* (s. 57 (3)). Special questions also arise and are discussed elsewhere concerning pregnancy (p. 450), union membership (p. 312), transfers of undertakings (p. 243) and privacy (p. 451). The Shops Bill 1986 aimed to insert a further category making it automatically unfair to dismiss a 'shop worker' where the reason was a refusal to do shop work on a Sunday unless obliged to do so by virtue of an agreement, but the Bill lapsed after a defeat in Parliament.

(a) The reason. The primary burden of proving the reason is put upon the employer, for he must know what his reason was, the set of facts or beliefs that caused him to dismiss. Civil cases are often won or lost according to who is called upon to shoulder the burden of proving his case on the 'balance of probabilities' (different from the criminal threshold of 'no reasonable doubt'). But, as with redundancy, the 'reason' tends to be what the employer says he had in mind. If employers believe their employee to be guilty of drunkenness, the E A T, using the redundancy test in *Hindle's* case, has said that they need not prove their reason was 'well judged', still less that the worker really was 'a victim of drink'.[187] Nor is the employer held to the reason given to the worker, though he must stick to the reason he gives the tribunal; for he might, Viscount Dilhorne accepted in *Devis* v. *Atkins*, 1977, 'give a reason different from the real reason out of kindness'. But the Law Lords limited the employer there to the facts known to him about the worker's conduct at the time of dismissal (contrary to the common law on wrongful dismissal) though they also reduced the worker's compensation to zero.[188] The precise 'label' does not disqualify a real reason. And when it comes to judging 'reasonableness' (p. 244) the tribunal can have regard to new facts that emerged in the employer's disciplinary procedures for appeals.[189] In *Tipton*, 1986, moreover, the Law Lords enforced the worker's right in his contract of employment to have access to appeal procedures against dismissal and so test the strength or weakness of the reasonableness of the employer's proffered reason for it.

A builder asked his plumber, *McCrory*, about the unusual amount of material drawn for his jobs; when McCrory denied 'stealing', he warned that wages might be 'docked'; then, having held a hearing on the matter, he dismissed him for 'gross misconduct'. He told the tribunal the reason was failure to safeguard goods. The tribunal took it that the real reason *was* 'suspicion of dishonesty' and was held not to have erred in law. But some reasons (such as dishonesty) should be stated at the outset because their addition later deprives the worker of a fair chance of answering them.[190] The limits placed by the judges exclude invented, capricious or subsidiary reasons. We recall, too, that the employer is obliged to give a written statement of the reasons for dismissal to any worker with six months' continuity (EPCA s. 53), a statement by which the employer ought surely to be bound (unless the worker profits from the change). But the reason must exist on the evidence. The Scottish Court of Session has robustly refused to accept a reason that was manifestly 'not established' because it rested on evidence which, on the employer's own showing, should not have been taken into account by him; the decision to dismiss was 'vitiated and inept'. And the EAT has rejected the defence of an employer who, having at various times given conduct, capability and redundancy as the reasons for dismissing an oil-rig worker, could not adequately prove any of them.[191]

The permitted 'reasons' an employer may give are discussed in a great number of decisions, many of them illustrating little more than the variety of factual situations along with the relatively restricted role of appellate courts. *Redundancy* we have considered above (p. 225). *Capability* is widely defined (with reference to skill, aptitude, health or other physical or mental quality), as is 'qualification' (s. 57 (4)). Although theoretically incapacity is distinct from *misconduct*, the employer is in both cases often required to warn the employee or carry out a proper investigation (a requirement that will also relate to his 'reasonableness' in the dismissal).[192] The employee may have an explanation to offer. Whether sick-pay is payable under the contract or not, illness of the worker may, if very prolonged, terminate the contract; but we have seen (p. 144) that the EAT has preferred to restrict this doctrine to long-term contracts and treat the termination by the employer as dismissal in order to judge whether it is 'fair'.

Many cases turn less upon legal principle or the meaning of the terms ('capability', 'conduct', etc.) than upon the refusal of appellate courts to overturn decisions of the tribunals, the 'industrial juries' of the facts, unless there has been an error of law because the tribunal misdirected itself on the law or because 'no reasonable tribunal could have reached that conclusion on the evidence'. In face of a misdirection, the decision will stand 'only if it is plainly and unarguably right', notwithstanding that error. Of course a good advocate may find a question of law in any but the simplest facts; but an appellate court should not seek 'some shadowy point of law on which to hang its hat', as Griffiths LJ has said. It was on this basis that the employee in *Woods's* case (p. 180) ultimately failed to prove constructive dismissal; for, said Lord Denning MR, the appellate court should not interfere merely because it thought it 'might not itself have reached the same conclusion'. 'Conduct' is primarily a matter of fact. It is not limited to breach of contract (though many types of misconduct arise from breaches, such as refusal to obey orders or infringing confidentiality) and the conduct may occur outside working time. But the idiosyncratic Scottish EAT in 1983 refused to include a learner driver's collision with the petrol pump on which she worked as she sped off home, putting the station out of action for months, because it did not affect 'the employer–employee relationship', a decision that sensibly relates 'conduct' to 'capacity'.

The ACAS Code of Practice requires a hearing in many types of misconduct, especially charges of dishonesty; but courts have allowed the employer to dispense with one, not only where guilt is obvious (like the 'red-handed' thief) but also where the case is strong (e.g. where the employee's conduct is such that, whatever the explanation, his continued employment is 'not in the interests of the business').[193] The revised ACAS draft code, 1985, proposes more protective procedures; but, although a complaint that a fair procedure was not used will assist the worker's case, a tribunal can put aside the need for a hearing at which he could have made his case, especially if it decides that on the balance of probabilities he would have been dismissed anyway.[194] This approach, enunciated in the *British Labour Pump* case, which 'forgives' the employer procedural unfairness if he proves he would have dismissed in any event, can make its appearance at the stage of 'conduct' (did the employer properly investigate the alleged misconduct?) or of 'reasonableness' (did the employer act reasonably in his procedures?). But if the tribunal decides the procedure was unreasonable, it is not required always to carry out 'a speculative exercise' as to what might otherwise have happened.

If the employer cannot show capability, conduct, redundancy or statutory prohibition, how does he fare with 'some other substantial reason' (SOSR) of a kind to justify dismissal? Favourably. It means, said Donaldson MR in 1984, 'the category of reasons which could justify the dismissal of *an* employee – not *that* employee, but *an* employee – holding the position which that employee held'. Employees are immediately ranked by diverse tests. The reasons that '*could* justify the dismissal of the office boy' are different from those that '*could* justify the dismissal of the managing director'. Thus SOSR arose from the dismissal of an airport security officer at the behest of a third party, a local authority controlling the workplace.[195] Such an employee has no action against the third party, like those who circulate black-lists of workers (in contrast, we shall see, to the non-unionist, p. 381, who may make certain third parties liable).

'I do not think it is right to lay down a general rule what is and what is not' SOSR, said Eveleigh LJ in 1979. But as early as 1972 tribunals were using the test of 'sound business practice'. Indeed, the employer's 'policy' or 'sound, good business reasons' will normally constitute SOSR. The Act might be thought to evince a narrower intention; for Parliament felt it necessary to state expressly that dismissal of a replacement employee in place of one absent temporarily through pregnancy or 'medical suspension' is (so long as the worker is informed on hiring in writing that this will happen) regarded as dismissal for SOSR (s. 61). The courts have gone very wide; if an employer dismisses in circumstances that he wrongly thinks in law amount to 'redundancy', he can still rely on SOSR – what has been called 'quasi-redundancy'.

It is in the preservation and expansion of the employer's prerogative to manage and to 'reorganize' the business, which we met earlier (p. 226), that SOSR is most influential. To argue, said Lord Denning MR in the notorious *Hollister* case, 1979, that it implied a mandatory duty to consult employees or their union was 'to put a gloss on the statute . . . It does not say anything about "consultation" or "negotiation" in the statute.' Following a 'fair procedure' put the employer's duty too high; he must do what is 'fair and reasonable' in the circumstances, even if business needs meant putting new contracts to the workers.[196] Yet ever since 1972 the Code of Practice has stressed the need for consultation. In redundancy cases it has been called 'one of the fundamentals of fairness'. Even there, however, the courts will not insist upon it, and will find dismissals fair if the employer has some 'cogent reason' for having dispensed with it. The employer, said the EAT in *Howarth Timber*,

1986, who 'ties himself to advance commitments' in consultations prior to redundancies 'may be setting the stage for a drama in which it will be difficult for him to appear in the role of a demonstrably fair employer, should the day of redundancy ever dawn'.[197] One might have thought the question is whether he should engage in consultation with those whose livelihood is threatened in order not to appear but to *be* a 'fair' employer.

Mr Yusuf and his colleagues had their hours (and pay) cut to a four-day week and later refused to work week-end overtime without a customary premium in a further reorganization to a seven-day shift system. They were told their dismissal was 'for redundancy'; but at the tribunal the employers chose to plead the more open-ended SOSR. The majority of the EAT upheld the decision that there was a SOSR because goods 'could most efficiently be produced by way of the seven-day rota shift system', of course 'without the premium payments'. Rarely is the point put so bleakly.[198] What is more, although the EAT had held that it was 'easy' for an employer to prove SOSR *and* reasonableness where it was the worker who broke the terms of a collective agreement, in the case of the Kent dinner-ladies, to which we return (p. 245), the Court of Appeal was shocked at the very idea that a County Council should be prohibited from proving SOSR merely because, like other councils, it had broken the national collective agreements on pay in the face of 'great pressure from the Government to reduce their spending'; a 'quite impossible' argument, said Griffith LJ. (The old law of contract was more protective; in 1966 a court refused to release an employer from his obligation to pay workers just because of pressure from Government about its 'incomes policy'.)

We have seen how managerial prerogative acquired new legal support from the changed role of 'redundancy' (p. 226). In the 1980s the judiciary responded to the crisis by providing, through SOSR, the belt and braces to sustain it in business reorganizations. Faced with SOSR, the employee's last hope is to allege lack of 'reasonableness'. But the judges see this almost as a dilemma. It may be 'perfectly reasonable' both for the worker to refuse to take on extra overtime *and* for the employer to require it (beyond the contract) 'having regard to his business commitments'. So, an employee's refusal to take work in a new area, where he would be worse off, still left the employer with SOSR.[199] The crucial question is whether the employer's offer is within the 'range of offers' an employer might reasonably make. Deterioration in the worker's conditions is just one item in the balance (one was fairly dismissed where he would not accept a loss of 10p an hour, one week's holiday in place of four, reduction in petrol allowance, *and* loss of pension-scheme benefit).[200]

If there is an imposed reorganization that the courts see as 'sound' commercially, and workers engage in a strike or other industrial action, none can claim for unfair dismissal unless the employer victimizes, as we saw (p. 193). If they work on, but protest about the new terms, up to the point of actual or 'constructive' dismissal, the employer can rely on redundancy or SOSR. No doubt SOSR was bound to be a wide category, 'but that it would provide so wide a ragbag of gateways to fair dismissal surely could not have been foreseen . . . managerial prerogative has proved a strong fortress'.[201] We have travelled a long way since 1972, when in the first 1,000 tribunal cases employers' 'attempts to force change of duties' was a prominent reason for unfairness.[202]

Before returning to the test of reasonableness, we must note the startling effect of the Transfer of Undertakings Regulations 1981. If an employee of either transferor or transferee is dismissed 'before or after' the transfer he is treated as unfairly dismissed if the reason is connected with the transfer, unless the reason is 'an economic, technical or organisational reason entailing changes in the workforce'. In this event, the dismissal is regarded as caused by reason of SOSR (Reg. 8). This EEC formula of 'economic, technical or organisational reason' ('ETOR') leaves little to the imagination in terms of employment protection, for, as Collins says, it seems to include 'technical innovation, falling production, rising labour costs, remoulding organizational hierarchies, redefinitions of responsibilities, and that blunt instrument of undisclosed policy – financial exigency', truly a 'most searing attack upon principles of job security'.[203] There must be a 'change in the workforce' as part of ETOR; but if there is, the only argument will then be about 'reasonableness'.[204] Redundancy is not mentioned in the TUPE Regulations, but they have been given a wide interpretation to cover this as SOSR (though the courts have, contrary to their first inclinations, preserved the right to a redundancy payment).[205] The clumsy regulation that transfers all the rights and duties 'under or in connection' with contracts of employment of workers transferred with the undertaking (Reg. 5) operates to transfer the right to claim a redundancy payment, which becomes enforceable against the transferee.[206]

The burden of proving ETOR is upon the employer. Where a dry-dock enterprise went into receivership, workers were thereupon summarily dismissed on the same day that the company bought it from the receiver. A tribunal decided that this was automatically unfair under the TUPE Regulations, that it was unreasonable and could not be for ETOR because no evidence had been given on that point. But the EAT in 1986 thought it 'incontrovertible' that the immediate reason for the summary dismissals was 'redundancy' – the receiver had said so – and, in a case such as this, redundancy was an 'economic' reason, and probably 'organizational' as well (though the dismissals were not 'reasonable').[207] Truly, ETOR has grown to be a mighty son of SOSR.

(b) Reasonableness. What then of the issue of 'reasonableness'? Here again, burden of proof is of some importance. Between 1974 and 1980 the employer carried the burden here, as he does under (a). But two changes were made in 1980. The Government restored what has been called a 'neutral' burden of proof, returning to the 1971 formula whereby, if the employer proves a permitted reason, whether he acted *reasonably or unreasonably in treating it as a sufficient reason* for dismissal is determined *in accordance with equity and the substantial merits of the case* (EPCA s. 57 (3)). It is often said that, in the more informal procedures of a tribunal, this makes little or no difference; if there is a dispute about the real reason the employer must still prove his reason under (a). And he must put in some evidence on the issue of reasonableness. But after 1980 tribunals must decide on the evidence and not continue to give 'the benefit of the doubt' to employees on reasonableness (e.g. from lack of evidence where the employers might fruitfully have tried to find the worker another type of job).[208] In *Howarth Timber*, 1986, the EAT insisted that the new burden of proof *does* make a difference.

Clearly 'reasonableness' and 'sufficiency' are largely questions of fact. But the appellate courts have not encouraged tribunals to review unduly management's standards of fairness. By 1977 the EAT was already saying that they should ask themselves whether the decision was so bad 'that no sensible or reasonable management *could* have arrived at it'. The slightly less brusque version asks whether the dismissal 'fell within the band of reasonable responses which a reasonable employer might have adopted'. Reasonable employers might (a tribunal must not assume they would not) summarily dismiss a foreman on finding that he had not controlled workers' improper practices and that doors and electronic safety systems were unsecured at night.[209] The 'band test' demands that tribunals must look primarily not to standards *they* would set but to standards that similar employers do and might set. The lower the prevailing standards of the worst, the better off the respondent employer can be.

The role of the lay 'wing-persons' is changed by this interpretation: no longer do they offer their own view of reasonable industrial standards; they are there to consider what an employer within a 'band' might have done. The second change in 1980 confirmed this attitude by expressly asserting that tribunals must take account of 'the size and administrative resources' of the undertaking in deciding reasonableness (EPCA s. 57 (3)). More adventurous judges in other fields, though, have tried to nudge management along the road beyond a poor 'general practice', like Mustill J. (p. 429) in his requirement that employers keep up to date regarding health and safety at work in the light of advancing knowledge. In an encouraging parallel, the EAT decided in 1986 that a worker given notice at a time when he was fairly dismissed was nevertheless unfairly dismissed when employers knew that business had recovered before his notice period expired but did not offer alternative work.[210]

The test of 'reasonableness' is one of fact for the tribunal in each case. One must not fall into what Donaldson MR has called the 'elephant trap' of thinking that proof of a good reason, even SOSR or ETOR, necessarily also determines the issue of reasonableness. It does not, even if the tribunal has erred in its approach to SOSR. The Kent dinner-ladies who were dismissed in breach of a national agreement were in the end found to have been dismissed unreasonably, bearing in mind all the circumstances, including the breach of the collective agreements without reference to national level. In two other cases, tribunals had found other councils' dismissals of parallel workers to be reasonable; but the court remarked that it is 'endemic' in a system where no appeal on fact is allowed that 'different Industrial Tribunals will give different answers to broadly similar situations' without risk of legal challenge.[211] If the tribunal goes wrong in law, the appeal courts may send the case back to it or to a different tribunal. Mr Yusuf was held to be reasonably dismissed (p. 242); the case of the airport security officer

p. 241) was sent back to a different tribunal to determine 'reasonableness' on the proper legal tests (which must include the extent of 'injustice' to the worker).

It is not surprising, therefore, that, despite the ever accumulating weight of case law, the EAT has striven to avoid 'a body of judge-made law supplementing' the Act and encouraged tribunals to 'drink at the pure waters' of the Act. In employment law 'a surfeit of case law', said Lawton LJ in 1985, 'can have the same disastrous effect that a surfeit of lampreys had on King John'. Unhappily, with statutes of this complexity, this amounts to giving tribunals an itinerary that begins, 'Do not start from here.' To be more helpful, the EAT has on occasion filled out the code and laid down guidelines – usually guidelines that set a high standard. Thus in disciplinary cases and the like, the employer should give a fair warning and allow the worker a chance to improve, make proper inquiry from which reasonable grounds arise for the reason on which he relies, afford a fair opportunity to the employee to put his case without improper pressure, and act with reasonable consistency. The EAT has stressed the need for 'consultation' with employees in whatever is the 'appropriate' manner, for example when the choice falls upon them for dismissal in a redundancy, and with the individual employee in particular. But recent decisions show that even these guidelines can readily be displaced. They have been displaced where the employee admitted the offence, or was in prison after its commission, or where an 'interview' took place on work deficiencies without a trade union representative to assist a probationer.[212] The Court of Appeal appears to dislike such guidelines. In the end tribunals must 'be their own guide on issues of reasonableness', not search for authority 'in a plethora of precedent', or, as Eveleigh LJ put it in 1983, 'seize upon words in a judgment . . . as though they were laying down some new rule of law'.

The tribunal has long been encouraged by the judges to ask whether, on the *British Labour Pump* principle,[194] the bad employer's decision would have been the same if he had been a good employer; that is, whether if the procedure had not been defective it would have made any difference. If not, the dismissal can still be fair. This principle (a 'gargantuan fish' that can be a 'red herring') is not, the EAT recently said where the dismissal *was* unfair, applicable to every case.[213] But when employers failed to observe a disciplinary procedure that required them to inform a union official of proposed dismissals and could not even show that the result would have been the same had they notified him, this was not enough for them to lose; it was just one 'factor', said the Court of Appeal, not sufficient by itself to invalidate a tribunal's decision that they had acted reasonably.[214]

At this point, the control of management by 'civilized' standards in dismissal has, both in substantive and procedural terms, largely given way to priority for managerial prerogative. The seeds sown in the *James* case, 1973, and *British Labour Pump*, 1979, have grown into triffid doctrines that can blind the tribunals by the reassuring reflection that they have considered all the factors and that things would not have been so different in the end even if the employer had followed all proper procedures. Where an employer of a betting-shop manager was 'virtually certain' a serious theft had occurred but could not say which of two employees had committed it, the dismissal of the manager was upheld as fair even though an internal inquiry acquitted him of 'dishonesty' but not of failure to act 'responsibly'; for these were 'solid and sensible grounds', suspicion here being enough, looked at as 'an ordinary business man would look at it', said the Court of Appeal.[215] Facts that emerge during an internal discipline hearing about a dismissal can be properly considered in judging 'reasonableness'. The EAT has sensibly suggested, therefore, that, where an appeal may be made, the dismissal should be conditional, subject to the outcome of any appeal.[216] There is a case for the law to insist that most dismissals of workers should have that character. In *Tipton*, 1986, the Law Lords perhaps moved in that direction in the case of summary dismissal, which could be effective from its original date if the internal appeal failed, but, if it succeeded, would allow for retrospective reinstatement (p. 165).

So too, the careful and progressive ACAS Code of Practice on disciplinary procedures (which 'shall be taken into account' by tribunals: EPA 1975 s. 6, of which a revised and improved draft was issued in 1985) can be treated as guidance, but can be put aside on similar arguments. Indeed, the paragraph protecting a shop steward from dismissal until discussion with the union (a general European standard) was jettisoned in 1980 on the ground that it aimed to avoid strikes rather than 'secure preferential treatment' for stewards who organized mass meetings, even when a tribunal thought suspension a proper penalty.[217] A statutory provision must be observed, such as the Rehabilitation of Offenders Act 1974, which renders certain convictions 'spent' and therefore not a proper ground of dismissal even if concealed. But acquittal of the worker in a criminal prosecution does not preclude the employer from reopening the same issues in later disciplinary proceedings.

Dismissals for redundancy can also be unfair if unreasonable (s. 57 (3)). The employer needs to explain the history and criteria for selection in the redundancy and the employee's position in it, but not the 'rights and wrongs' of it. In 1982 the EAT put forward five guidelines for reasonable action by the employer, including warning, fair objective criteria, consideration of alternative employment for the worker, and consultation with a recognized union. But a tribunal may put these aside, as in the case where the worker's absenteeism made him an 'inevitable first choice' for redundancy, without warning, without consultation, the rules on fair procedure applying it was said to cases of 'conduct' but not 'redundancy' – once more illustrating the employer's power in the right to pick his reason. The guidelines were not appropriate for small-scale redundancies by a 'small employer' ruined by a customer 'out of the blue'.[218] These cases are a remarkable example of courts changing standards to suit the policy of favouring the small, non-unionized employer.

As the recession moved on, and management's need and desire for control accentuated, the EAT reduced the guidelines to small print – just because procedure is in some way not fair 'it does not follow that the dismissal itself was unfair'.[219] As the numbers, and convenience to management, of part-time, short-term or temporary workers increased, such workers (now increasingly in need of protection) were placed increasingly outside the shield of the statute. A teacher 'filled in' under four successive fixed-term contracts at a school; she was not reappointed when another teacher was taken on permanently to fill the gap; she was not dismissed on grounds of redundancy (she lost only 'the chance', it was said, of applying for the permanent job); but the employers had SOSR and had been reasonable. She knew the 'genuine purpose' for which her short, fixed-term contracts had been made; that gap had now been plugged.[220] Even if the part-time or short-term worker manages to acquire the necessary qualification, then, the employer can dismiss without fear so long as he has made the 'genuine purpose' (filling a gap in the permanent staff) clear to the worker. The decisions in this area of law and their trend taken as a whole testify to the courts making common cause with employers and expressing (give or take the odd frolic of its own by the EAT) instinctive understanding of their needs. Lack of consultation can cause redundancies to be unreasonable; but it is not an easy case to argue.[221]

Parliament was nevertheless determined to go the other way in one type of case. It provided specifically that if an employee is *selected* for dismissal in a redundancy among employees in *similar positions* in the undertaking, in contravention of a relevant *customary arrangement or agreed procedure*, then, unless there are *special reasons* justifying it, the dismissal is automatically unfair (s. 59 (b)). The appellate courts have required the tribunals to make findings on whether a selective dismissal is unfair under either s. 59 (b) or s. 57 (3), though they need not spell out all the facts on which they rely.[222] Great importance is attached to the operation of LIFO arrangements ('last in, first out'), a very common industrial practice for redundancies, relying on seniority as the goddess of rough justice. In this area permission has been extended even to permitting limited discrimination between men and women, so important is the need to have 'agreed criteria' for selection (p. 465), though the employer may also be able to rely upon exceptions.[223] If the employer establishes either 'special reasons' or observance of the agreement under s. 59 (b) it is unlikely that the worker can prove 'unreasonableness' under the broader test. Moreover, it is only the actual 'selection' of the worker that the courts permit to come within this section. This restrictive interpretation does not include 'procedural breaches' through non-consultation with the union so long as the criteria are applied (though one might be forgiven for thinking that consultation must be at the core of such agreements – especially now that Parliament requires consultation with recognized unions about proposed redundancies: p. 294).[224] If s. 59 (b) had required a minimum of consultation for *all* redundancies when first enacted in 1965, its effect might have been greater. Indeed, one now sees how such opportunities were lost when the legislation of 1965 emerged not from a political or a collective bargaining, but from a civil service stable, to which judges relate more easily; for both are part of Weber's 'priesthood – the official guardians of the law'.

On the other hand, the courts have not allowed the plain words of the section to be set aside. They cannot be satisfied here merely by showing that a decision to depart from the agreed procedure was 'within the band of reasonable responses' employers might have made, said the Court of

Appeal in 1985 (though a dissenting judge would have allowed an employer's needs in a commercial catastrophe as a special reason to set even that argument aside).[225] At first the concept of an 'agreement' looks simple. But suppose the labour market is such that the union's strength is enfeebled and the employer imposes a pattern of redundancies, knowing that the union would prefer another, like LIFO. In such a case in 1985 the Court of Appeal found not an express agreement or 'custom', but an 'implied agreement' resting on the shipowners' adoption of criteria for redundancy in 1978 in which the union had acquiesced. The criteria included: age, type of ship, 'management discretion' and choice of seamen for dismissal who happened to be on leave and available. A ship's cook, who alleged he was chosen for dismissal by reason of union activities (p. 312), was held by a tribunal to have been dismissed for redundancy 'fairly and reasonably' (s. 57 (3)). The Court of Appeal could see no breach of s. 59 (b). The criteria made 'commercial good sense' and were 'perfectly fair'.[226] In reality, these practices were imposed on the union by the owners. The implied agreement was a fiction. Such decisions reinforce the general conclusion of the latest authoritative survey: 'employers have no difficulty in showing a reason which may justify dismissal'.[227]

(3) *Remedies*. The primary remedy for unfair dismissal has long been re-employment – either 'reinstatement' (to the same job as if the worker had not been dismissed) or 're-engagement' (by the employer or associated employer to a comparable job). The tribunal must explain to a claimant who wants this remedy the power that it has to order re-employment (EPCA ss. 68–9). Orders can be made only where it is 'practicable' for the employer to comply; and replacement workers are ignored except when the employer shows that it was not practicable for the work to be done otherwise, or not 'reasonable' where the worker has not claimed re-employment for a long period (ss. 69–70). The tribunal must also consider how far the worker 'contributed' to his own dismissal. If the employer fails to comply with an order for re-employment, he does not stand in contempt of court; the ultimate remedy is 'additional compensation' (in cases of racial or sex discrimination between 26 and 52 weeks' pay; in others between 13 and 26: s. 71; except dismissals for non-unionism or trade unionism where special rules apply: p. 369). On a failure to comply, the employer can again argue that the arrangement is 'impracticable', and that it was not practicable for him not to have hired

a replacement (s. 71 (4)). If he purports to comply but does not do so fully, the inadequately re-employed worker may seek compensation for his loss.

But all of this is rather theoretical.[228] Many legal systems purport to secure re-employment for the illegally dismissed worker. Few do. Where workers, whether for trade union reasons or otherwise, refuse to work with the claimant, the employer may well show that re-employment is 'impracticable'.[229] The old common law principles baulking at attempts specifically to enforce 'personal' contracts (and now TULRA s. 16, which forbids such a remedy against a worker) supported that view. Despite the new laws, a variety of reasons has made the remedy very rare in Britain. The courts are especially cautious if re-employment is sought in a small business, where an order for re-employment would in the view of the EAT be 'exceptional'. If the judges have shown little enthusiasm for it, nor have the tribunals nor perhaps even the realistic ACAS conciliators, who enter into the tribunal procedure at an early stage of every case. Employers resist it. But suggestions that claimants are not, when they have adequate knowledge, themselves keen for the remedy have been shown to be questionable. In practice, it has rightly been named 'the lost remedy'.[230] In 1984, of 28,052 complaints dealt with, 7,578 reached the tribunals, of which 28.7 per cent were upheld; but in only 78 cases were orders made for re-employment. Between 1976, when amendments tried to promote re-employment as the primary remedy, and 1984 the percentage of successful cases resulting in re-employment orders averaged 3.7. Other estimates indicate that no more than 4 per cent actually returned to their jobs.[231] There is little improvement if one adds in the re-employment agreed through ACAS conciliation: in 1984, 256 re-employments out of some 13,000 settlements.

The evidence is overwhelming, as the authoritative study has shown, that there is indeed a serious 'gap between the intention that unfairly dismissed workers should get back their jobs and the reality'.[232] Whatever the reason, re-employment is not a primary remedy in the tribunals. It is well known that re-employment in Britain as elsewhere is a normal remedy in 'voluntary', collectively agreed procedures, administered jointly by employer and union; but in the legal procedures, the old common law seems to represent reality: either the law cannot, or the courts will not, enforce the employment relationship.

Comparative considerations, however, suggest that the matter is more complex. United States 'grievance arbitrators' do secure re-employment, supported by the courts. In West Germany labour court reinstatement seems to be 'exceptional'. In Quebec, where the ordinary courts follow the common law, re-employment appears to be effected through arbitrators, penal sanctions and 'labour commissioners', with penalties for contempt of court. Re-employment has not normally been available for workers as a remedy in the French *conseils de prud'hommes* except for the elected works council, union or personnel representatives; but a law of 1985 gave the remedy greater priority, with enhanced compensation as the ultimate sanction, where strikers are dismissed. Most European laws really provide, like ours, 'a much needed transfer payment to cushion displacement and perhaps an opportunity to clear one's name'.[233] Reinstatement has played a larger role in Italy for the local *pretore* (an ordinary judge specializing in labour law), but the order for reinstatement even there seems now to be rather less effective, especially in the smaller enterprises.[234] In Australia, the historic *Broken Hill* award in 1984 by the regulatory Conciliation and Arbitration Commission, creating standard protections for unfair dismissal, redundancy and other workers' (and union) rights, drew back from enforcement by reinstatement – that, the commission decided, would need legislation.[235] Those countries, too, encounter the factor that is a realistic barrier to successful re-employment, namely the high proportion of cases originating in small enterprises and weakly organized or non-union firms.[236] On the other hand, cases in the courts and tribunals are sometimes test actions or cases, which will directly affect many other workers.

The complex interactions between social and legal culture and the machinery chosen for the settlement of such disputes, especially the relationship between resort to law and resort to industrial action, invite us to look more closely at the tribunals in the context of the labour market and of the legal profession. If workers see a dismissal or discipline case as calling for a collective response, the evidence in Britain is that 'the industrial tribunal system operating individual rights will not be preferred to bargaining backed by the threat or taking of industrial action'.[237] There is in many labour law systems a tacit acknowledgement that what the forces of 'voluntary' bargaining or industrial action can, the orders of courts cannot do. Yet this is less pronounced when we deal with workers in the State or public sector of employment, at any rate if we see them as occupying a public 'office' (p. 153). And when the law sets out determinedly to enforce reinstatement generally it is known to use sanctions normally thought to have no place in modern labour law. The millions conscripted to serve in the armed or civil defence forces during the war were assured of a return to their jobs by statutes that saw to it that decisions of 'reinstatement committees', or on appeal of 'umpires', were enforced by awards of compensation *and* by criminal fines against recalcitrant employers. The wartime Act was continued for peacetime conscripts in 1950; and the provisions are with us still, consolidated in the Reserve Forces Act of 1985. It is not immediately obvious that parallel sanctions should not be provided for some at least of the civilian casualties of the recession who are unfairly thrust into unemployment.

Compensation

Given that re-employment is at present largely a 'lost remedy', how do the tribunals and courts dispense the remedy of compensation? The statute lays down the structure (EPCA ss. 72–76A). First, there is the 'basic award' (s. 73). This is calculated like a redundancy payment (one and a half weeks' pay for each year of service over the age of 41, one week between 22 and 41, half a week under 22) with a maximum of 20 years and £155 per week (in 1986): EPCA s. 73. Until 1980 there was a minimum basic two weeks' pay; this now applies only to redundancy cases, and a special basic applies to union and non-union dismissals (p. 369; s. 73 (2), (4A)). The payment is gradually reduced in the year up to retirement age and may also be reduced if the tribunal decides it is just and equitable to do so because of the worker's 'conduct' (whether or not it comes to light only after the sacking). To some extent the basic award might be seen as compensation for loss of an interest in 'the job' were it not for the further provision that the figure must be reduced, too, by the amount of any redundancy payment (either statutory or under a voluntary scheme; s. 73 (9)). Where the employer makes an *ex gratia* payment to the unfairly dismissed worker he can set this off against the basic award, as Chelsea FC did in 1981, if it is seen by the tribunal as compensating the worker for statutory rights.

Secondly there is the 'compensatory' award: 'such amount as the tribunal considers just and equitable . . . having regard to the *loss* sustained' by the worker that is attributable to the employer's action (s. 74). But there is a maximum amount; in 1986 it stands at £8,000. (This amount alone was inexplicably not increased in the annual up-rating of financial limits in 1986.) As early as 1972 the courts asserted that compensation is to be awarded for 'financial loss' only, not for hurt feelings as such or the punishment of the employer. In *Norton Tool Co.* v. *Tewson*[238] the NIRC logically set out four heads: actual loss of wages and benefits; future loss of wages and benefits; loss arising from the manner of the worker's dismissal (such as blackening his name for future job prospects); and loss of protection in respect of unfair dismissal and other statutory rights (e.g. loss of continuity). Each heading has been expanded, though the structure still persists. What may be a fifth category is of great importance, namely pension rights. The difficulties here became so great that the Government Actuary's Department issued an explanatory document to assist the tribunals.[239]

The issue of State 'subsidies' by way of unemployment benefit has also troubled the tribunals. In 1977 'Recoupment' Regulations (No. 674, 1977) provided a solution: the tribunal should not deduct any amount representing unemployment or supplementary benefit received by the worker up to the date of the hearing. Instead they must see to it that the employer will not pay a 'prescribed element' of the compensation to the worker but, on demand, pay that to the Department of Employment. This is at least more rational than the principles of *Parsons's* case (pp. 211 and 438). But tribunals can become exercised on social security matters. Daley, a 'good worker' with eight years' service, was unfairly dismissed. He refused a job at lower pay than unemployment benefit would give him. His compensation included loss for an 'intangible benefit', the loss of his entitlement to minimum notice. That is not compensated as redundancy rights are by the basic award (s. 74 (3)); but the tribunal proceeded to excuse the employer because 'the State', which paid him his benefits, should bear that loss. An appeal was needed to reject this idea, which is contrary to the statutory scheme.[240] Similarly, sums recovered by a claimant should normally not take account of tax.

The calculation even of compensation for lost wages can be difficult. In *Moosa's* case, as we saw (p. 196), a worker was not offered re-engagement after industrial action when other workers were. He took a new job. A tribunal upheld his unfair dismissal claim (under s. 62: p. 194). The new job lasted only eighteen months ending in a dismissal for redundancy. His compensation came to be awarded in 1983 because of various re-hearings and appeals (the periods of time are a good illustration of the delays that can overtake such cases and of the need for interest).[241] The tribunal awarded him wages lost from the dismissal in 1979 to the hearing in 1983, plus twenty-six weeks' future loss of wages as an estimate of that head of loss. It then deducted earnings in the eighteen months' employment, which he had to bring 'into account'. But the amount so calculated exceeded the statutory maximum, so they reduced it to that figure (which was then £5,750). Such a calculation, however, produced a different result from an alternative method. If compensation had been awarded at an earlier hearing, Moosa would have appeared to the tribunal to be in a 'permanent' new job, so loss would then have been awarded for wages lost in the weeks when he was unemployed in 1979, no more. The EAT said that was still the way to compute it in 1983. His 'loss' stopped on entering the new job. The first employer could not be responsible for 'loss' of wages in a period when he was re-employed in an apparently secure post elsewhere. Here the court was guided surely as much by the principle of paying for 'fault' as that demanding compensation to the worker. The first method might seem more 'just and equitable' to someone who had to wait four years for a few thousand pounds.

The employers appealed on two other points, however. First, they argued that compensation must be reduced because Moosa had omitted to 'mitigate' his loss by reasonable steps. This common law principle, based on the duty to act reasonably to reduce the damage, applies here (EPCA s. 74 (4)). But Moosa had not failed to take reasonable steps, any more than workers who failed to take their grievances through the firm's disciplinary procedures, or an employee of fifty-five who after dismissal tried to set up his own business rather than look for another managerial job.[242] The duty reasonably to mitigate one's loss is a matter of fact for the tribunal. Its application, though, can express social values. Indeed, the EAT had to reverse the tribunal in the self-employment case for making a deduction. So too, the court has looked favourably upon self-employment when an employee dismissed by IPC chose to take a self-employed post in a family company; he could still claim compensation for 'future earnings' to the extent that he was worse off and for the loss of the contractual rights he had to redundancy pay higher than the statutory minimum.[243]

A second argument was raised in *Moosa's* case. The compensatory award must be reduced by any amount the tribunal finds 'just and equitable' where the dismissal is to any extent caused or contributed to by any 'action' of the worker (s. 74 (6)). This provides the tribunals with a great discretionary power. Compensation can, as in *Devis* v. *Atkins*, even be 'reduced' by 100 per cent. A reduction for 'contributory fault' has been likened to the assessment for contributory negligence in actions for damages in tort (where someone is injured but was careless about their own safety: p. 435). Sometimes workers are required to show considerable industrial 'care', as when a fork-lift-truck driver failed to be alert to 'safeguard goods', and thefts had occurred. He was unfairly dismissed. He was never found guilty; instead the employer gave him two weeks to find the thief, refusing to contact the police. The EAT declined to upset a tribunal finding of 'contributory fault', reducing his award by 80 per cent even though the employer's own system of care was 'slip-shod'. Once he had been found 'blameworthy', the percentage was for the tribunal to decide, according to what it found 'just and equitable'.[244]

We have seen that reductions can also be made in the *basic* award under provisions that were much amended in 1980 and 1982 to give the employer the benefit of avoiding the principle in *Devis* v. *Atkins* (p. 238) by taking account (if that is 'just and equitable') of the *conduct* of the employee even if it was unknown to the employer at the time of dismissal, albeit that in such a case it could not possibly have contributed in fact to the reason for the latter's unfair sacking (s. 73 (7B); see also s. 73 (7A), reducing a basic award for unreasonable refusal of an alternative post and (7C), which prevents deductions in most redundancy dismissals). The objection to 'rogue' workers profiting too easily by keeping their misdeeds secret prevailed over demands that the employer should pay for what he thought he was doing. Faced with such cases tribunals sometimes adopt a 'split hearing', reserving the issues of 'contributory fault' on the compensatory amount until later, so that evidence of facts unknown to the employer is not heard in determining liability.[245] Contributory fault has a very wide range. Even where the worker is awarded a compulsory amount for unfair dismissal based upon lack of 'capability', the amount may be reduced by a substantial percentage (as with the frozen-food worker who, having a healthy instinct for industrial democracy, threatened to work to rule when he was not granted a share in the profits).[246]

What then of *Moosa*? His ex-employers said lastly that his contributory fault lay in the serious breach of contract inherent in the industrial action, which had caused their selective refusal to re-engage. But the Act makes it clear that no account is to be taken in the *compensatory* award of industrial pressure on the employer (s. 74 (5)) and that the complaint in a selective re-engagement case is still in substance one of 'unfair dismissal'. As we have seen above, EPCA s. 63 excludes that ground, for otherwise the tribunal would have to judge the merits of the industrial action (see also s. 62 on jurisdiction: p. 194). But other, not dissimilar actions of the worker can amount to contributory fault (as in a case of 1979, where one lapsed in payment of union subscriptions after disagreements with colleagues, who then refused to work with him; the reduction was 100 per cent).

Since a 'constructive dismissal' involves a serious breach of contract by the employer, a finding of 'contributory fault' by the worker is possible but rather unlikely – the Scottish EAT has said 'exceptional' – in such a case. The worker in that case failed, however, in his claim for loss of future earnings beyond the date when he *began* a university course, because it was said that he 'effectively took himself out of the labour market'. One wonders whether a similar principle should not apply to the self-employed.[247] Contributory fault can here play a complementary role; being 'lazy, negligent or idle' can contribute to an employer's dismissal that is rendered unfair because of faulty procedures. So too, doing something 'culpable or blameworthy', including according to the Court of Appeal anything unreasonable, foolish or perverse, is included if it has helped to cause the dismissal, even if the worker is correct in thinking that he is standing on his legal rights in a dispute with the employer.[248]

Causation is important. If the employee has no 'control' over the 'action' (say, a case of sheer incompetence or incapability) it may not be a fault that contributes to the dismissal; but a 'defect of character' may be the origin of actions that can be taken into account as contributory fault. A manager who set up the Scottish branch of a 'glorified ship's chandlers' business was dismissed for 'redundancy', but at the trial lack of 'capability' was alleged by the employer. Compensation for unfair dismissal was awarded; he had been given no chance to improve; but a reduction of 40 per cent was upheld for contributory fault arising from his failings as a manager.[249] One might have expected the tribunals and judges in such cases to inquire how diligent senior management had been in discovering any defects in the worker during the qualifying period of employment.

Tribunals that become too generous to workers are called to heel. When casino operators heard that their employee was being prosecuted for possession of cannabis, they sacked him without any further investigation. The casino closed down shortly afterwards. The tribunal awarded compensation because the casino had 'jumped the gun' unfairly. It was hardly a fair procedure. But the EAT, asserting that such employees must, 'like Caesar's wife, be above suspicion' and avoid any 'possible impairment' of their judgment, beat the award into the ground with a 100 per cent reduction. This was fault that could have allowed a common law 'summary dismissal'.[250] The common law is never far away.

Jobs, rights and legal sanctions

The structure of compensation as the main remedy for unfair dismissal is, then, a strange mixture of payments to 'cushion displacement' and adjustments for 'fault'. In 1980 and 1982 further oddities were built into it in a category of abnormal cases. In cases of dismissal on 'trade union' grounds – which in practice normally means dismissal of *non*-unionists (p. 369) – a minimum basic award (in 1986, £2,200) is now supplemented, if the worker *asks* for reinstatement, by a 'special award' of £11,000 minimum up to a maximum £22,000, irrespective of loss. Actual loss (up to the limits of £8,000) can then be the subject of a further compensatory award. If reinstatement is ordered but not reasonably complied with, the special award goes up to a minimum £16,500 and maximum 156 weeks' actual pay. (In all cases there can be reduction for contributory fault.) These penal figures contrast in a bizarre fashion with the normal cases of 'ordinary' unfair dismissal. They can in truth be understood only in the context of the policies promoting non-unionism that underlie the 1980 and, even more, 1982 Act (Chapter 4).

In the normal case the maximum of basic award plus compensatory award for unfair dismissal has been raised annually; for example, from

£9,850 in 1980 (£3,600 plus £6,250) it rose to £12,560 in 1985 (£4,560 plus £8,000). This moved up again to £12,650 in 1986, the basic award being raised in the annual uprating (to £4,650) but not the £8,000 limit on the compensatory award. However, this is nothing like the amount most workers get. In the five years 1980 to 1984 the median awards actually made to workers who won compensation in the tribunals were: £598, £963, £1,201, £1,345 and £1,345. In the first quarter of 1985 it was £1,362. (The unusual jump in 1981 was probably due to the 'shake-out' of established workers in the early 1980s as the redundancy figures suggest: p. 221.)[251] These are not princely sums, though they may not be wholly out of line with amounts awarded in other European jurisdictions (in West Germany the median awards in 1979 ran at about 150 per cent of workers' average net monthly earnings).[252] No more than 550 of the 8,980 compensation awards exceeded £5,000 in Britain in the same five years to 1984. In this period only some 34 per cent of all 156,000 unfair dismissal complaints reached the tribunals at all, and of those the average yearly 'success rate' was 28.3 per cent. Compensation was and is the normal remedy (the first quarter of 1985 ran true to form with only 29 of 667 successful tribunal cases resulting in re-employment awards, the median award in 373 compensation cases being £1,362).

In 1980 a 'pre-hearing assessment' stage was introduced to weed out the weakest cases, in addition to the existing 'sifting' and conciliation procedures; and in the new procedure workers are warned that if they go on with the case they may end up being liable for costs. Over 80 per cent of claimants who receive such a warning regularly settle or drop their case. In 1984 A C A S reported, understandably, that these pre-hearing assessments were unhelpful in its work of conciliation. Successful settlements by way of conciliation do not afford riches. In the same period 1980–4 of cases successfully settled, representing 35 per cent of all cases, re-employment was won in less than 2 per cent, and the median compensation was £305 in 1981 and £709 in 1984. In the first quarter of 1985 nearly one-half of the workers who took compensation to settle their claim that dismissal was unfair received less than £750. These figures show that in tribunal and in conciliation the price of 'job property' is not high, nor is the cushion for displacement so soft.

We should put these figures in a more general context. Apart from the 'special awards' noted above, awards of compensation in all employment protection cases are generally low. Take the discrimination cases to which we come in Chapter 6. Of the seventeen compensation awards in 1984 in all types of sex discrimination in employment, no more than six reached £750; and in eighteen awards based on race discrimination, £750 or more was awarded also only in six. The true place of compensation is further clarified there by noting that of the complaints heard under the S D A some 57 per cent were dismissed by the tribunals in that year, along with an astonishing 82 per cent under the R R A. Remedies for employment protection 'rights' are a major indicator of their worth. Sanctions against unfair dismissal are part of the general weakness.

The survey of 1985 by the Warwick team concluded that the slender use of re-employment and the method of calculating compensation 'serve typically to set a low price on the unfair deprivation of a job and can have little deterrent value for most employers' The qualifying periods confirm the general picture. These periods – one year required in 1979, in place of six months, then two years for employees in small firms in 1980, and now the general two years' requirement imposed in 1985 – have increasingly excluded millions of employees from protection. The qualifying period that began in the 1970s as a protection for the tribunals against submersion in a flood of claims, and as a reasonable period for management's assessment of new recruits, is now used to relieve unfair employers of a 'burden' on business. Before 1985 the tribunals were not overwhelmed; and only incompetent managers need two years to assess a recruit. The evidence in 1978 suggested there was very little sign of employment protection laws 'contributing to the high level of unemployment by discouraging employers from taking on new people'.[253] Research for the Government in 1985 did not point in the opposite direction; small business (unprompted) gave V A T, statistical returns and planning requirements as reasons for 'serious' burdens more often than the employment protection laws. Nothing has shaken the fact that a small employer can expect a successful (or any) tribunal claim very rarely, though much has confirmed the 'misunderstanding or ignorance' that leads managers to blame such legislation for their ills. Employers may think that other employers are deterred from hiring; and saloon-bar lore still believes that 'these days you cannot sack a bad worker'. But this is a poor basis for legal policy.[254]

Among the many different 'functions' of unfair dismissal law, four in particular have been described: compensation to the worker; stimulation of better management policies, especially on manpower planning;

legitimation of existing authority at work; and the provision of a floor of rights on which bargaining may improve.[255] Associated with these has been the aim of reducing strikes. The evidence seems to be that strikes over dismissals have not shown a significant reduction.[256] There are now more formal disciplinary procedures throughout industry, especially in larger firms, a development to which the new laws have clearly contributed (though one cannot tell whether some similar trend might not have appeared without them). Managerial prerogative has not been seriously affected by legal inroads, certainly not for intelligent managements willing to master new procedures and act in an acceptably civilized fashion; indeed, in some respects it is more secure. Compensation to workers who claim successfully is poor and erratic. Meanwhile, in the 1985 labour market it is as well to remember one manager's comment reported by Dickens in 1977: a successful claimant 'may not be regarded as an ideal recruit by employers'.

The role of the industrial tribunals

Tribunals and appellate courts have played a prominent role in legitimating existing authority, especially in cases of reorganization of the business where management needs to enforce its policy, if necessary without consultation with unions, demanding lower terms and conditions from workers. Whilst alleviating the edges of hardship, the new laws have done little to promote job security or job stability; far more to underpin 'efficiency' as management perceives it and the recession demands it, tribunals and courts being 'unwilling to be seen to be imposing their standards of industrial justice', as Collins puts it.

It may not be profitable to attempt a division of 'fault' for this result between the legislation and the tribunals and courts that have administered it. Certainly the latter have been content to be constrained within the range of 'reasonable responses' by management. It has been noted that this leads to unfair dismissal law being 'sterilized': 'far from controlling management discretion and therefore protecting the interest of employees in job security, the law endorses and legitimates a strong conception of managerial authority.'[257] Such a conclusion is made incontrovertible by an examination of the decisions. Yet the tribunals mirror the courts; and could Parliament ask them to do more, at any rate without cutting them off from the Court of Appeal? One can detect in the legislation itself a recognition, albeit sometimes apologetic, both of workers' interests and of the fact that they conflict with those of the employer, a kind of cross-bench pluralism groomed in Whitehall. But, under the guidance especially of the Court of Appeal, the decisions have emphasized the values, standards and rights of management, even more of the 'enterprise' on a unitary footing.[258] The ambivalence among union shop stewards and other officials towards this law (and often the tribunals), as well as the more formalized disciplinary procedures to which it has contributed, is not surprising, though they recognize the marginal leverage that is sometimes offered to protect members and to gain entry to small firms not unionized (though this last has not been assisted by the narrow scope given to 'trade union activity' at work: p. 312).[259]

Instead of contrasting the tribunal law with the common law, the tribunals' function may perhaps be best examined as part of the legal system. No doubt common law concepts ('implied terms', 'dismissal' or 'mitigation of loss') have been allowed undue prominence in the new law, though some of them would have required careful replacement. Lawyers' omnipresence and their delight in precedent may have contributed independently to legalism in tribunals (not too much notice has been taken of Lord Denning's dictum that tribunals must not be 'bent down under the weight of the law books or, what is worse, asleep under them'). But employment protection law, as Munday puts it, 'has an accessible hierarchy of jurisdiction, a growing legal personnel, flourishing series of reports and a fertile fund of highly complex legislative material'.[260] Will not lawyers inevitably use 'legal materials in a lawyer-like manner' in such a setting? Do not charges of 'legalism' simply reflect 'the gulf between what is preached and what has to be done'? Legalism was detected early on in the tribunals. By 1982 over 49 per cent of the employers and 36 per cent of applicants had – sensibly, in view of the system they had entered – legal representation at tribunal hearings in all jurisdictions.[261] Where, after all, is the system of 'tribunals' in Britain that has evaded lawyers and legalism? The old trade union Registrar had an exclusive and 'final' jurisdiction on complaints about political funds from 1913 (and scarcely a murmur of trouble was there in it); but in 1975 the jurisdiction with the Certification Officer was brought into the legal system when an appeal was introduced to the EAT. In 1946 an attempt was made to keep legalism, lawyers and appeals to courts out of the work of the national insurance Commissioners; now the reports of their decisions are not unlike law reports; and, after inroads of 'judicial review' by the court, Parliament established an appeal in 1980 to the Court of Appeal (p. 109). What is more, in 1984 the 'juridifying' step was taken of transferring functions in respect of the Commissioners to the Lord Chancellor. As for unfair dismissal complaints, ACAS noted in 1984 that there had been a marked growth of 'legalism' in its *conciliation* work. Four-fifths of claimants were represented at that stage (ten years before it was just over one-half), and the use of solicitors had particularly increased. Further, citation of 'precedent' is not the exclusive preserve of lawyers; any trade unionist knows that.

This is not to say that there are not good grounds for criticism of the tribunals, their procedure (and Parliament's revision of them, like the encouragement of 'summary form' judgments in 1985), their delays and their cost, in all of which they (and especially some of their legal chairpersons) may fail to measure up to accepted standards. Nor, on the other hand, is it to ignore the heroic efforts of many of those who administer them, the EAT and the conciliation stages (especially some of the legal chairpersons), without whose work the problems would be far worse. Indeed, the authoritative survey of their work has found tribunals to be 'cheap, accessible, free from technicality and expert *in comparison with the ordinary courts*'.[262] This is a credit to them; but it is a very carefully chosen standard. It is a valid standard when it is remembered that the legal chairperson is dominant in the vast majority of cases over the lay members. Labour law in the tribunals is not lay law. To ask whether it could or should be, we need to examine their place in labour law and the legal system; and the legal in the social system.

It may be that the current sense of disappointment with tribunals has its origin elsewhere than in the assessment of their informality, speed or cost. It may lie in the belief that they *could be* generically different. They acquired labour law functions through their gradually increasing jurisdiction over 'individual' employment rights (a category, we must remember, convenient for purposes of analysis, but inadequate to portray reality). This progress had an *ad hoc* appearance: redundancy in 1965; unfair dismissal in 1971; on to maternity rights, discrimination cases and the rest. But the tribunals were not created at the request either of employers or of trade unions. Nor did they spring from the programme of any political party. They were the children of civil servants. The Ministry of Labour established them in 1964 to adjudicate complaints about levies on employers for training. Why the two laymen who sat should include a *union* nominee for *that* work (deciding the meaning of 'trade or industry', or whether a 'business activity' was carried on by the Plas Machunlleth Fox Destruction Society) was obscure. The structure of the tribunals clearly suggested a different role. The full intention of the Ministry was overtly set out in 1965 in evidence to the Donovan Commission:

The nucleus of a system of labour courts exists potentially in these tribunals . . . [for] all disputes between the individual worker and his employer . . . [and] between trade unions and their members.

At the time the proposal for 'labour courts' was revolutionary. It was taken up by the Donovan Report with carefully coined limitations to 'individual' issues between only the employer and his worker, and with a plea for the education of lawyers in industrial relations, something notably lacking at the time. Such courts would provide a 'flexibility' of approach, although (the Ministry perceptively added) relations with the 'ordinary judicial system' would have to be 'defined'.

Once the idea was accepted, it was widely assumed that the tribunals would be extraordinary, *different*, partly because they were tripartite. There was 'little hard-headed debate'; two lay wing-persons were thought to be enough to ensure success.[263] In particular, there was strangely little inquiry about how far they would become 'judges' rather than 'laymen' (indeed, there is little inquiry now on that issue, even in regard to the E A T). Not even when the job was expanded in the 1980s to take in awards of compensation against unions in unfair dismissal cases (p. 381) or unreasonable union exclusion cases (p. 739) was that issue canvassed, though the need to have more women on tribunals and in the chair (in 1982 there were 3 women out of 77 full-time chair-persons) was an understandable and much publicized demand, especially when the tribunals acquired sex discrimination and equal pay cases in 1975 (Chapter 6). The T U C (which in 1981 lost its exclusive right for affiliated unions to nominate when a handful of members of the employees' panel was accepted from non-T U C organizations) criticized the tribunals in a 'review' in 1984. Although alternative procedures were touched upon, the T U C criticism finally concentrated upon 'legalism', 'use of barristers', inadequate compensation, delay and low success rates. The Secretary of State replied that he, too, was concerned about 'legalism' and delays. Managers in 1985 also deplored the 'legalism' of tribunals.

What did this consensus about undue 'legalism' mean? What were the tribunals – as part of the legal system – meant to do about it? What would the Court of Appeal let them do about it? The consensus masked the question: Just what is the job we want the tribunals to do? Is the function easily defined, meaning for the lay members, as one delegate put it to the 1981 TUC (rightly demanding more women members), a job 'which can be done by anyone with a reasonable level of intelligence'? If the job is essentially assessment of compensation for hardship, for displacement from, or discrimination in, a job, perhaps common sense is enough. But the tripartite tribunals are often said to bring to bear the experience of 'experts'; this is why they are 'industrial juries' as to the facts. In this event, it seems wrong not to allow them to impose their own views about standards of conduct in the labour market, though if they set about this seriously one would expect a growing ratio of dissenting judgments; but it must be doubted whether, as at present constructed, they could do so. As Mr Richard Holt MP put it in a 1985 parliamentary debate on the tribunals: 'Why should there be one from either side?' Such a 'balance' showed there was an 'idea of prejudice'. Why not appoint 'virtually anybody', in the same way as the jury system, 'honest people of integrity' rather than 'employers' hacks or trade union nominees'?

The tripartite structure of the tribunals, however, may be seen as a condition of the nature of their task. They are concerned rarely with the safe retention of jobs, mainly with unfairness in their loss, that process by which the individual's subordination is finally tested by his descent into unemployment. It is this individuation of the issues that some see as the vice of the system.[264] But to say this is to say that Parliament (and the Ministry of Labour) should have done something else in 1965 and 1971, or done nothing at all. Is there an alternative now to our tribunal justice on employment protection?

Despite the notorious dangers of comparative labour law (Kahn-Freund, who stressed them, may have been optimistic even in thinking that 'individual' employment law can be 'transplanted' rather more easily than the rest, which cannot),[265] it may be useful to ask briefly about the fate of a neighbouring institution, the French *conseils de prud'hommes*, if only to reflect the tribunals in that comparative glass. For over a century (their origins are still not entirely clear) the *conseils* have dealt with employer–employee disputes (except for public servants). On the basic principle of *paritisme*, the lay employer and employee *conseillers* are equal in number, with no legal chairman (save in exceptional cases of deadlock). Moreover, they are elected, the workers candidates of the unions. They sit as representatives (to English eyes becoming, on occasion, even 'tactical aids in class conflict'; while some French commentary deplores their legalism and their 'integration into the judicial machine').[266] Representation is central. A major issue in the 1979 reforms of the *conseils* was the need to 'represent' another constituency, the *cadres* (that untranslatable category of supervisory and technically qualified employees). Were a magic wand to transplant to Britain the whole of the French substantive law about, say, dismissals, the result here would still be very different from the jurisprudence of the *conseils*; just as the French debate about their reform was very different from what preceded the only occasion when British unions *have* insisted upon the representative character of the employee wing-persons on industrial tribunals, namely the walk-out of 80 per cent of them on the proposal of the TUC in 1972 as a protest against the Industrial Relations Act. (Historians will contrast that vividly with their continuance in office under the Acts of 1980–4 and the 1982 TUC policy that they should not sit on closed-shop cases, which was never enforced.) Otherwise, practice has observed the determined stance of the Lord Chancellor, who said in 1968: 'One sometimes hears the members erroneously referred to as "the employers' representatives" or "the employees' representatives". They are not. They represent no one except the interests of justice.' Three persons were in fact removed from the panel in 1978, but their unions had to be satisfied with an assurance that there were 'strong reasons' for this, though the Government declined to give them. One wonders, did they act as 'representatives'?

In some cases, though, we do favour a 'representative' role. Government has since 1974 encouraged the offices of the industrial tribunals to select one woman member for tribunals considering equal pay and sex discrimination. It has never been clear whether such members 'represent' women. If not, why are they there? For racial discrimination cases, encouragement is given to the selection of a member 'experienced in race relations'. Would the Lord Chancellor allow a requirement that one member should preferably be black? If not, why are women different? The fact is, the 'non-representative' character of our tribunals is a cloak fudging the real problems.

This is not to suggest that either the *conseils* or the tribunals fail to observe the normal principles of fairness, such as treating similar cases in similar fashion. Nor is it to deny the similarities that, in our society, are bound to arise between arbitration and tribunal adjudication. But the distinction between 'collective' and 'individual' issues, useful for limited purposes, is not viable in the last resort here.[267] The crucial differences between *conseils* and tribunals spring from their relationship to the legal system and to the wider society. Industrial tribunals were conceived by British civil servants or the Lord Chancellor's office not as institutions acknowledging conflict, but as bodies that would lend the experience of the two industrial parties disinterestedly to the guiding hand of the legal chairman in a united quest for a reasonable answer that all would recognize. They were not meant to (and they very rarely do) outvote him. The philosophy was not one of compromise-in-conflict but that mixture of decency and humbug which Fox has aptly placed at the heart of the British pragmatic tradition.[268] It is when they depart from this that they are most rapidly called to heel by courts that are confident of their unitary touch in constructing implied terms out of the 'obvious' – really believing that they find themselves, as Donaldson MR averred in 1983, 'on neither side. They have an independent role, akin to that of a referee.'

Disputes before both *conseils* and tribunals are individual in form, but the substance ultimately concerns the collective reality of the social forces. The tripartism of the tribunals, however, deliberately breaks the link with those forces, not least because the 'neutrality' of the wing-persons is made to demand their severance from their constituencies.[269] The *paritisme* of the *conseils* is less likely to foster a belief that the only true substance of the issues before them is individual. A system of informal arbitration might perhaps be in closer contact with collective social relations, possibly along the lines proposed by the Warwick team.[270] True, any such system could today expect invasion by the judiciary, via some offshoot of judicial review or other similar procedure. But, then, one must take one step at a time. Resistance to changing the tribunal system would be fierce, not least even by some who now criticize its 'legalism'. Nor is it true that workers have gained nothing from them. Many households have received something out of dismissals where before they would have had nothing (a factor some theoretical critics of the legislation sometimes overlook); and many tribunal members have laboured valiantly to fulfil that function of direct, if modest, compensation. Nor is there much evidence of so many 'ill-founded' claims to justify building more barriers to stop dismissed workers approaching the tribunals (though the 1986 Government programme for further debilitating the floor of rights proposed, by reason of the 'cost and management effort' required of employers, to charge a deposit of £25 returnable only if the applicant succeeded in, or withdrew, the application to a tribunal).

The tribunals are nevertheless part of the legal system and, for all the unwillingness of some of their members, they are married to the judiciary and to the values of the legal system. Their reform would imply a programme of reform of the legal system, just as re-examination of the 'individual' labour law that they administer will be of little value unless it moderates current fashions for 'individuation' in the labour market and renews the search for links between employment protection legislation and the autonomous collective organization upon which the protection of most workers still depends, and the need for which no system of tribunals or labour courts can replace. It is, therefore, to the relationship between the law and collective bargaining that we now turn.

[4] Collective Bargaining and the Law

Most workers pay less regard to their individual contracts of employment than to the terms of agreements between their union and employer; but the former is crucial to the lawyer whom they or their employer may consult in times of trouble. The relationship between bargaining at collective level and the contract of the individual worker is central to labour law. The levels at which collective agreements are made vary greatly. They may be national or industry-wide, between an employers' association and a group of unions, or 'company' agreements, whether in giants like ICI or in small firms; sometimes they are made with more than one union; they may be 'factory' agreements or 'plant' agreements negotiated between shop stewards and management. There may be separate agreements at different levels touching upon the same matter. Through these bargains workers in combination attempt to secure greater equality than they have individually in the balance of bargaining power. Yet English law has traditionally had little to say about the structures of this bargaining and still less about the obligation to engage in it or the collective agreements that result from it.

This chapter inquires into the relationship of law and collective bargaining and asks how far the law supports, encourages, regulates or inhibits this central institution of British industrial life. After an outline of the context, we consider the encouragement of collective bargaining, recognition of unions and obligations to inform and consult with unions; the right to organize for collective bargaining; collective agreements (their legal effects and relationship to employment contracts); statutory props to the bargaining system (including wages councils); incomes policy; and non-union workers in the collective bargaining system.

The context

According to the Donovan Report (1968):

'Collective bargain' is a term coined by Beatrice Webb to describe an agreement concerning pay and conditions of work settled between trade unions on the one hand and an employer or association of employers on the other.

We are concerned then with all negotiations by employees carried on collectively through their representatives. The resulting agreement between union and employer is at once an industrial peace treaty and a source of rules; it encompasses the terms and conditions of employment, remuneration and other benefits, the distribution of work and the control of jobs. More than that, collective bargaining leads to what Flanders termed 'joint regulation' at the place of work; for it 'is also a rule-making process'.[1] Management and unions may bargain and reach agreement, but all may come to naught without adequate joint administration. If in our society collective bargaining does not intervene to structure work and to control jobs in the enterprise, they normally remain in the hands of management unilaterally. In other countries, such as France, one finds a long tradition of State controls at various levels of the labour market, though whether this necessarily curtails management's power more is another question. Britain has had little equivalent experience, even if one includes the interventions of 'tripartite' bodies, such as ACAS or the Manpower Services Commission. Like most things, this tradition has its merits and its demerits.

Collective bargaining directly affects the terms of employment of some three-quarters of our working population. In no other country has there been such a rich history, with varied and intricate webs of bargaining machinery, and there are few where the process is so flexible and dynamic. Traditional British bargaining has not been hedged around with rigid rules binding the parties to contractual principles or to fixed-term agreements, as in the United States. It has thrived on the parties' ability to raise issues in an agreed procedure as and when they arise. Nor does it normally recognize sharp distinctions between 'disputes of right' (conflicts over interpretation of existing agreements) and 'disputes of interest' (such as a new claim for better conditions or more wages than under existing agreements). Such distinctions are fundamental in most European labour relations systems.[2] They may help to promote greater certainty; but British practice has been dominated by *procedure* and the attainment of an acceptable result. What is more, the 'custom and practice' of each workplace are frequently essential for an understanding of the formal and informal bargaining behaviour.

The system emerged in a context not of rigid guidelines or legal structures but from more than a century of pragmatic, if conflictual, development. Even before 1824, when the first dent was made in the illegality of trade unions, groups of workers (from printers to cabinet-makers) were negotiating 'lists of prices' with employers, artisans who later brought pre-industrial threads into the modern unions. In the wake of the Industrial Revolution came the major growth of trade unions in the nineteenth century and the struggle for union legality, which we discuss elsewhere (p. 513). The modern trade union movement begins with the emergence of the skilled workers in craft unions (what were called the 'New Model' unions) alongside the established unions in cotton and coal-mining, taking with them much of their craft spirit as artisans;[3] later after 1880 the unskilled workers organized in the so-called 'new unions'. Employers' associations, usually regional in the nineteenth century, had the aim in Clegg's words both 'to destroy the unions' and 'to deal with the unions when it suited them'. They, too, began to move, in cotton and shipbuilding for example, towards national bargaining.

By the end of the century a Royal Commission on Labour in 1894 spoke the language not of 'codes of working rules', as in 1869, but of 'collective bargaining'. The victory of the dockers in their strike of 1889 for the dockers' 'tanner', the match-girls' determined strike in 1888, the engineers' lock-out and strike of 1897–8, the harsh stand of the railway companies against union membership – all were part of a struggle through which unions gained what was for that stage of industrial development a remarkably wide area of 'recognition' from employers. It is in this period too that one first sees, in Fox's words, 'the emergence of a "system" of organized industrial relations in Britain, based on autonomous sectional bargaining between representative associations of employers and workers'.

Voluntary collective organization became 'the preferred method' even of government.[4] In 1916 the Cabinet appointed the Whitley Committee, which recommended in favour of 'industrial self-government' in Joint Industrial Councils (JICs). In a development that contrasts with many other countries' practice, and of which the importance must never be underrated, the State came to favour in these formative years trade unionism and collective consultation even in the public service. This process accelerated in the middle of the First World War, just one year after the last report of the 'Commissioners of Industrial Unrest' and the first appearance of shop stewards on the 'red' Clyde. Collective organization, and especially organization by workers, which had before been largely hesitantly acknowledged, was welded into the system amid concern for unrest and the patriotism of the war when trade unions in all countries broke their international links and backed their national governments.

Although the law did not play a direct role in establishing collective bargaining, it was in other ways closely involved in the industrial battles in this crucial half-century before 1918. This was the period in which the roots of the industrial relations system and labour law were planted. The reaction against legal attacks on unions by the nineteenth-century courts is a major reason why modern negotiating structures came to be built upon the autonomous arrangements of the parties (employers and unions) rather than upon legal devices and structures, such as bargaining units regulated by legislation. This experience of hostile judicial intervention caused Winston Churchill to say in 1911: 'It is not good for trade unions that they should be brought in contact with the courts, and it is not good for the courts.'

Exclusion of the courts was the basis of 'voluntarism', as the system was later called. If the law were to demand that the bargainers adopt prescribed patterns, compulsory Works Councils for example, many of the arguments that need to be settled on the shop floor might end up as wrangles in the law courts. More than that, because the legal history of British labour relations consisted to such an extent in efforts to repulse the attacks of the courts upon trade unions, what was 'not good' for the unions came to be regarded as 'not good' for the bargaining system of which they were, and are, an integral part. Bargaining without legal regulation – which is a very different thing from bargaining without 'law' – became the natural thing to do. The law generally might support or prop up the structures here and there, but it was forced to accept for the most part the 'primacy' of voluntary collective negotiation in Britain. It is because our system carries the marks today of this history that it is so sensitive to legal policy inherent in legislation by Parliament or adjudications by the judges.

Union membership doubled, and the practice of bargaining flowered during the First World War. As Phelps-Brown put it:

it came about that the typical British bargaining unit, which in 1914 was still made up of certain occupations in one district of one industry, had become by the end of the war the whole of the wage earners in the whole of an industry.

Beyond this, though, centralization did not go. The TUC, founded in 1868, and the national employers' body formed in 1919 (now the CBI) did not, as happened in Sweden, become centralized, national bargaining parties. But after the war a network of committees, conferences, JICs and the like sprang up. For most of this period trade unions were weak as the economy sagged. Indeed, for the unions, after defeat in the General Strike in 1926, conciliatory negotiation seemed to offer the only realistic route to survival. In the Second World War and after it, trade unionism became stronger. The wartime bipartisan commitment to 'the maintenance of a high and stable level of employment after the war', as it was put by the Government in 1943, became a fundamental point of consensus in British society. Indeed, few believed until relatively recently that 'full employment' was not a fact of life whose continuance could be assumed.

Collective bargaining between 1945 and 1980 must be seen in this setting. The formal arrangements covering bargaining in an industry or other wide sectoral area were more and more supplemented by informal negotiations at plant level, especially through shop stewards, until the latter came to exert, at least in private manufacturing industry, a predominant influence.[5] Plant bargaining came to be associated with the 'drift' of wages above the formally bargained minimum. Industrial relations and labour law here came face to face with the 'anti-wage-push', counter-inflation and incomes policies of various post-war Governments after 1945. As we have seen in Chapter 1, however, the central concern of the Donovan Report about our industrial relations in 1968 concentrated on the fact that 'The formal and informal systems are in conflict.' Industry-wide agreements had been undermined by informal and fragmented factory bargaining. Comprehensive 'factory' agreements should be developed; but the 'conflict between the two systems' could not, said Donovan, be cured by legal compulsion, as many demanded, so as to squeeze the system back into patterns of formal bargaining. 'Reality cannot be forced to comply with pretences.' This was the thesis upon which much of the modern debate about labour law came to revolve. It has profound importance for the law, not least because it prompts the question: how far, if at all, can the law change 'reality'?

We have noted the variety of legislation that followed Donovan (pp. 48–96). In the decade after the Report, 'reform' of labour law was proposed and sometimes attempted. These debates became increasingly clouded by an opaque vocabulary. Commentators and policy-makers often advocate a new 'legal framework', or 'more law', for industrial relations. But these phrases are consistent with diametrically opposed policies and laws; it all depends on the shape of the framework. Also, partly because the bargaining structures in Britain are so varied, so hard to generalize, certainly so remote from the tidy and compartmentalized categories of the lawyer or the civil servant, the replacement of these vague terms by concrete discussion has frequently been difficult to attain. One of the great achievements of the Donovan Report was its offer, to friend and foe alike, of a platform of fact and analysis from which to proceed. Yet public attention was often directed largely to symptoms rather than causes of industrial relations 'problems', especially to strikes.

The phraseology of 'a legal framework' became largely synonymous with the search set by some at the centre of policy for the further containment of 'trade union power'. For many years this school of thought proposed new laws to that end, especially legal enforceability of collective agreements and the outlawing of strikes that were 'unofficial' (without official union support) or 'unconstitutional' (in breach of collectively agreed procedures). As the recession gathered momentum in the 1970s, although conflict was still expressed in short plant-level stoppages, larger-scale 'official' industrial action was growing, especially in the public sector where feelings of social injustice were sharpest. Trade union membership advanced to more than 50 per cent of the work-force (over 40 per cent even of white-collar workers). Official strikes of some duration, often in the public sector, occupied the centre of attention in the period of the 'Social Contract' (1975–9). But for the vast majority of the work-force, who never saw a strike, the decade after 1970 was one in which collective negotiation remained the primary method for determining employment conditions especially at shop steward level and was in many sectors still expanding both in scope and in depth of subject-matter. Trade union 'power', though, brought riches to very few of them.

Despite the vacillations in public policy, since 1968 bargaining structures and practices have undergone changes largely in the direction that Donovan proposed – sometimes moving, it has appeared, almost irrespective of the rapidly changing legislation.[6] By 1980, for example, it was found that there had been a marked reduction, though not an extinction, of 'multi-employer', industry-level bargaining in favour of 'company' negotiation (many employers' associations adopted new advisory and service functions). Also, one could find more job evaluation and more 'professional' personnel managers with more formal disciplinary procedures (a development to which the 'floor of rights' legislation seems to have contributed directly). In the unions, ever more complex organization of shop stewards and 'networks of conveners' developed, all playing a key role in the direct democracy of the workplace, many of them representing workers in plants with a mixed work-force.[7] The regulation of pay by collective bargaining reached more and more white-collar workers as their numbers approached one-half of the work-force.

In the private sector some firms have tried recently to reduce the workplace influence of the union, and in the 'crisis in public sector industrial relations' heavily centralized bargaining structures have been eroded by cash limits, expenditure cuts and the Government's decision in the 1980s not to continue the tradition of being a 'model employer'.[8] A natural part of the drive to reintroduce 'market forces', and thereby to 'price' labour into jobs, is a desire for the increased decentralization of bargaining structures. It is not clear how fast the move in this direction has been, but any such change is of primary significance to the meaning and direction of legal policy. 'Privatization' has been accompanied by decentralization of bargaining (the National Bus Company's decision to do this prior to privatization sparked a TGWU strike ballot in 1985, and shipbuilding unions in 1986 prepared co-ordinated bargaining ahead of the planned privatization of the warship yards). Influential voices advocated rapid decentralization of bargaining whilst calling at the same time for criminal sanctions against strikers in industries deemed by Government to be 'essential'.[9] Few of them had thought through all the consequences for public sector pay structures (p. 360).

Also in the 1980s, profound changes in the labour market beset old and new structures of bargaining. By 1986 a massive total of more than 3 million workers were unemployed at any one time (more than a third of them for over a year). Total union membership fell consequently from its peak of over 13 million in 1979 to 11 million in 1984. In addition, the labour market fragmented, not only dividing geographically but increasingly being segmented into a relatively stable 'primary' sector as against low-paid, often part-time, more harshly disciplined, unstable, 'secondary' groups.[10] Whatever importance the law may or may not have, the meaning and reality of collective bargaining are, for employers and for workers, largely determined by economic and social changes of this kind.

Basic industrial rights

Throughout this kaleidoscopic story, British unions – thought by so many to have such great powers and 'immunities' – have, with tiny exceptions, never enjoyed a legal right to organize or a legal right to bargain with employers, still less a positive legal right to strike. Collective bargaining at any level in industry requires that workers have the liberty to organize in autonomous and effective trade unions and that employers should be willing and able to bargain with them. Some kind of legal backing is needed. Those who think they can do without law of any kind err as greatly as those who think positive legal rights can do everything. The removal of a number of common law obstacles to the legality of their organization (such as restraint of trade: p. 522; or conspiracy – criminal, p. 520; civil, p. 581), left our unions by 1906 with only a limited legal 'freedom' (not a *right*) to organize. Yet successive British Governments have felt able to ratify various ILO Conventions declaring the 'right to organize' and 'freedom of association', such as No. 87 of 1948 (which declares that workers and employers have the right to establish organizations without 'interference' from public authorities). It has long been said that British *practice* secures these liberties, whatever the law says.

It was for breach of that ILO Convention 87, with an interlocking Convention on public employees' rights (No. 151, 1978), that the

Government was condemned by the ILO Freedom of Association Committee. In 1984 it banned trade union membership among staff at the Cheltenham communications 'spy' centre (GCHQ), offering them £1,000 to relinquish employment protection rights along with union membership (200 still refused to do so over a year later). The English courts, in a much criticized decision, found that there had been no breach of the law because the action, taken under the prerogative of the Crown, was 'based on considerations of national security'. This overrode any judicial application of any obligation to deal 'fairly' with staff who had for five decades in the Whitley tradition been encouraged to join unions.[11] (See too p. 136.)

The European Social Charter also supports freedom of organization, as does the Universal Declaration of Human Rights; and the European Convention of Human Rights seeks to establish everyone's right to freedom of association with others 'including the right to form and join trade unions for the protection of his interests' (Art. 11; subject to exceptions: p. 376). This Article has played a prominent role in recent labour law developments. So too, ILO Convention No. 98 of 1949 requires 'appropriate measures' to promote 'voluntary negotiation' of collective agreements and prohibits discrimination against workers for trade union activity. Apart from incidents like the GCHQ saga, how could Britain justify ratification of such ILO texts? They do not enter into British domestic law without legislation, and no such general legislation exists.

The traditional answer given has been our practice. The freedom to form independent unions and the protection of the freedom to organize effectively against interference by employers and the State have for many decades existed in practice. As Donovan put it, 'the trade union movement here is sufficiently strong to make legislation on these matters unnecessary'. Recently, though, the UK Government, perhaps remembering the ILO censure in 1982 for its suspension of the pay agreement that had been the basis of bargaining in the Civil Service since 1925 (a breach of Convention 151, which Britain had ratified), decided that it would not be 'appropriate' for it to ratify a new ILO Convention (No. 154, 1981), which, with Recommendation 163, calls for the 'promotion' of collective bargaining in public and private sectors, with adequate disclosure of information by employers. The Government argued that, whilst wishing to facilitate bargaining, it would not take on an obligation to *promote* it by direct Government 'intervention'. The 1975 objectives of ACAS, however, which are still on the statute book, include promoting the improvement and 'encouraging the extension of collective bargaining' (EPA s. 1). A different reason for the Government's answer to the ILO was no doubt the history of very real difficulty that our law has experienced in accommodating a legal duty placed upon employers to bargain with, or to 'recognize', independent trade unions. Collective bargaining cannot even start if the employer refuses to 'recognize' an independent workers' trade union. How far does our law assist at that level?

Encouraging collective bargaining

Independence and recognition

The great majority of employees work for an employer who recognizes their independent union for bargaining. Many unions have found that, once recognition is granted after a bridgehead of membership, the number of members grows quickly. Growth and recognition are the 'virtuous circle'.[12] Recognition has for decades been customary in the public sector. Public policy after the Whitley Reports (1917–19) has promoted recognition in the private sector too, not least during the two world wars. It has been said that it is in the relatively early recognition by employers of unions in many branches of British industry 'that we can most clearly see the results of the early industrial revolution' in Britain.[13] A wide area of recognition was achieved even before the turn of the century.

Parliament placed on the nationalized corporations that took over coal, steel, electricity and some other services after 1945 a legal obligation to consult and bargain with trade unions; but the formulas in the Acts are general and vague. The duties benefit only such unions as appear to the various corporation boards to be appropriate; they could scarcely ever be enforced by legal action. In default, the Minister might take political action; a complaint might be made to, say, the ILO. Few would expect a writ. Where unions have attempted to construct from such statutes a legal right for their members to have the unions recognized, the member going into court to enforce his right to have his union

accepted for bargaining, judges have consistently refused to interfere
with the public corporations' discretion as to which unions they accept,
so long as it was exercised fairly, especially when inter-union rivalry
might lead to a danger of 'leap-frogging' in pay claims.[14] In a similar
way, the Fair Wages Resolution (p. 347) required a contractor with
government to accord to his workers freedom to join a union; but it did
not prescribe which union he should recognize. 'Recognition' is not an
academic exercise; what matters for workers is the duty to bargain with
the union that is effective about the conditions on which their labour
power is available.

It should not be thought that there are no practical problems about
recognition in Britain. In 1967 a TUC report recorded difficulty for
unions to achieve recognition in small firms, in those with more women
workers, in those in foreign ownership or control or in those with a high
labour turnover, and for white-collar workers. Such obstacles still exist.
In the case of white-collar workers, bargaining, while it is not yet
universal, has undergone a dramatic extension; but this has also been a
field where unions have found the strongest resistance from employers,
even a desire, as one union leader put it in 1983, 'to get rid of them'.
Only in 1985 did the BIFU report a breakthrough in the recruitment of
employees of building societies.

Although a NEDO report of the same year emphasized the importance of involvement of, and consultation with, employees through their
representatives in the introduction and proper use of new technologies,
unions have often found it difficult to recruit and bargain in the
high-technology area. Some giants, such as IBM and others in the
'high-tech belts' (such as Scotland's 'Silicon Glen'), prefer not to have a
unionized work-force. There are those who argue that the new information technologies are conducive to individual bargaining or an 'individuated' market in new employment structures, rather than collective
negotiation (a point to which we return in Chapter 10). Consultation is
not the same as, though it frequently leads to, bargaining. And recognition is sometimes accorded on special terms (as with the one-union,
no-strike deal between the EETPU and a Japanese firm – 'the first
break', it was claimed, 'in the ranks of this non-union cartel'). One such
firm was reported to the OECD for refusing unions recognition in 1985
(it recognized unions in Japan). In 1985 Barclays Bank told unionized
staff transferred to financial services subsidiaries that no union would be

recognized for that growing sector of its affairs (other banks acted similarly); and Bell Canada made its take-over for part of the privatized Cable & Wireless enterprise an occasion for the reconsideration of collective bargaining rights.

Nor is recruitment of union members always easy. Part-time staff and homeworkers, the great majority of them women, along with ethnic-minority groups, have revealed low densities of membership and require major changes in union structure (as a TUC report suggested, 'computers would be a help').[15] Recognition is still a constant problem with some employers, and not just in Britain. At a 1984 conference of the white-collar international trade union body FIET, delegates representing 7.5 million workers in eighty-six countries adopted a new, urgent 'action programme' to achieve wider recognition. In 1984 the Institute of Directors advised firms that they now had far more potential to resist recognition (especially of white-collar unions) than many realized. After the General Strike in 1926, D. C. Thomson, the Scottish printer of *Beano*, locked its doors so tightly against union recognition that we still find the TUC pledging 'a renewed campaign' against the firm at its Congress fifty-six years later in 1982. Even if such managerial policies seem to some 'myopic',[16] they survive, indeed they flourish. Later we must ask how far they may be expected to increase (Chapter 10).

What can the law do? It may sound easy to legislate and compel the employer to recognize an independent trade union to bargain for his workpeople. Some parts of this formula are relatively straightforward. Clearly the union must be *independent*. Our law today designates a union as 'independent' when it is not under the domination or control of one or more employers and is not 'liable to interference' by whatsoever means tending towards such control (TULRA s. 30 (1)). But independence is very different from recognition, for the latter depends on the employer. The mere certificate of the Certification Officer (CO) is conclusive evidence of independence. Indeed, if this issue is raised in court proceedings it must be referred to him for decision (EPA s. 8 (11), (12)). Some unions in the 1970s objected to the CO's certificating white-collar staff associations said to be under the sway of employers. But, as third parties, they have no right of appeal on the matter, whereas a refusal of a certificate to such a body can be appealed by it to the EAT on questions both of fact and of law (EPCA s. 136). Of the 88 associations, with nearly 200,000 members, examined by the CO in

1979, 20 were in banking and finance (with 130,000). In the case of one 'house union' at *Squibb and Sons*, the Court of Appeal upheld the practice of the CO to test the union not by the 'likelihood' of, but by its 'vulnerability' to, interference by the employer.[17] (See too p. 529.)

Most unions have now obtained their certificates of independence, and the flurry of disputes about that status has died down. Few new unions are being formed except out of mergers of existing organizations (which are considered in Chapter 9). Independence *from* the employer is not recognition *by* the employer, however. Unions at Fawley, where the first modern 'productivity' agreements were negotiated, have in recent years found that their bargaining rights have been restricted; they have no legal redress. Can English law enforce a duty to 'recognize' – that is (since it implies more than management passing the time of day with the union), a duty to bargain? Or, as the present writer feared in 1978,[18] is it a 'British paradox' that although a modern democracy ought to compel an employer to bargain collectively with those whose labour power he buys, 'even this small degree of intervention is too strong a burden' for our labour law? Other industrial and legal cultures have absorbed such a duty, sometimes with a labour court to enforce it, as in Scandinavia. Others, like France, have introduced a duty to negotiate recently with new determination.[19] In the United States the 'duty to bargain in good faith' has generated a vast quantity of litigation, the courts rejecting 'surface bargaining' or 'Boulwarism' (named after General Electric's Vice-President, who habitually came up with his final offer first – a phenomenon found by ACAS to be 'common' also in Britain in 1982). The US courts found they had to distinguish 'mandatory' from non-mandatory subjects for bargaining, and both from 'illegal' subjects, when they enforced the duty to bargain.[20]

It may be that British labour relations will continue to reject any attempt to insert a 'duty to bargain'. This does not mean that other rights could not be created. In 1982 French labour law created a new right to be heard (*droit d'expression*) for workers in the plant. Perhaps workers who are members of a union in Britain should be accorded at least the right to call on their union representatives to act on their behalf in disputes with management. This would not be a 'right to bargain' but a right of representation. The bargaining system, as we shall see, already knows of such a right in industrial terms. The common law rejects such concepts because they infringe the employer's property rights to exclude unwanted visitors from the works (see p. 168).

An obligation to recognize?

The Industrial Relations Act 1971 introduced a duty to recognize in Britain as part of its regulatory edifice for legally controlled 'bargaining units' at plant or company level; but the NIRC and other institutions of enforcement were associated with the Union Register, which led to its being much used by breakaway unions.[21] After repeal of that statute, the 1975 Act returned to the question in provisions (ss. 11–16) that, though now repealed, remain of importance. In it 'recognition' means recognition of a union by an employer or associated employers 'to any extent for the purpose of collective bargaining'; and *this* means 'negotiations relating to *or* connected with one or more of the matters' about employment that are within the subject-matter of a valid 'trade dispute' (EPA s. 126: p. 557). This basic definition remains with us today. To this the 1975 Act added an obligation to recognize the union (or 'further recognize' it) when ACAS made a statutory recommendation. ACAS could do this only after exhausting specified procedures of consultation and inquiry about the workers' wishes.

If the employer failed to recognize when obliged to do so, the union could ultimately complain to the CAC, which had the power to make an award improving the *substantive* terms and conditions of the relevant workers' employment contracts. But the CAC interpreted the Act to mean that it could not award 'procedures' such as the right of workers to be represented by shop stewards. It regularly rejected what 'effectively is a request that the Committee order the company to recognize the union'.[22] Nor was it ever very clear what recognition negotiations meant (and certainly not what 'further recognition' meant, where the Act envisaged telling an employer who had bargained to bargain about more). The crunch duty of the employer was to take such steps to carry on such negotiations 'as might reasonably be expected to be taken by an employer ready and willing' to carry out the recommendation (s. 15 (2)) – an ambiguous phrase difficult to interpret.

Many of these depths were never plumbed. Nor were the hopes realized that these provisions could be a 'non-legal' mechanism in the hands of ACAS, although ACAS did manage to settle 80 per cent of its cases by conciliation. First, the approach of the courts (until Lord Scarman's judgments in House of Lords decisions, rendered just as the provisions were being repealed)[23] was out of sympathy with this objective. To do its job ACAS needed a flexible discretion to promote bargaining, far wider than the function of counting up heads for or against recognition. Judges began by regarding the legislation as *depriving* a worker of 'a substantial measure of control over his own working life, compulsorily delegated to an agent' or trade union. Such powers for the 'compulsory acquisition of an individual's right to regulate his working life' must be strictly interpreted, like 'powers of compulsory acquisition of property'.[24] Perhaps the individual barrister fits the conceptual bill (subject to the power of his 'clerk'); but the ordinary worker does not. Normally his individual power to regulate his own working life is very limited. Later, though, even Lord Scarman's more enlightened approach could not solve all the problems of the relationship of the Act with the TUC disputes procedures (p. 824).

Secondly, the wording of the sections allowed the courts to tie ACAS down. In the notorious *Grunwick* affair, a small photographic works in North London with a largely immigrant work-force became the crucible of a massive industrial conflagration, giving rise to complaints to industrial tribunals, a Court of Inquiry report (by Lord Scarman), extensive litigation, and industrial action that included solidarity picketing by coal-miners.[25] More than a third of the work-force was dismissed while on strike demanding recognition for a union they had recently joined. The employer refused – and refused access to ACAS when it tried to carry out its obligation to ascertain the opinions of all the relevant workers including those still at work. ACAS had no powers, and wanted none, to compel the employer to grant access. Nevertheless, because ACAS had 'failed' to consult the workers, the House of Lords declared the recommendation for recognition void. The judges could not read the Act to include the idea that ACAS's duty might end where the employer had effectively made its execution impossible.

There was another dimension, however. 'Tripartite' bodies can work only where there is sufficient consensus. On the ACAS council the three employers and the three union representatives could never agree what the criteria for 'recognition' should be. Employers wanted recognition for groups with defined boundaries set largely by them; but unions want membership and support, so long as it does not infringe inter-union boundaries. The litigation exposed this defect, and by 1979 the chairman (not yet in possession of Lord Scarman's liberal interpretative obituary) told the Government that the procedures could no longer operate satisfactorily. A place was found for repeal of EPA ss. 11–16 in the 1980 Employment Act (s. 19). There was some, but muted, complaint from trade unions. The TUC in 1982 thought the procedures had been 'expensive', 'controversial' and 'marginal', and questioned 'the appropriateness of legislative procedures for promoting recognition'. Only 16,000 workers benefited directly by recommendations (49,000 from the voluntary settlements) from 1,610 claims (though the indirect effects of the ACAS procedures probably secured union recognition for many more). Out of 158 ACAS recommendations, more than 100 employers failed to comply – like the railway companies of the 1890s – 'on principle'. So much for the rule of (this) law.

In 1975 it had been necessary to define 'recognition', and that definition governs a variety of extant legal rights for unions – i.e. disclosure of information (p. 289); consultation over redundancies (p. 294); transfers of undertakings (p. 298); occupational pensions (p. 303) and safety (p. 291); and time off for employees or shop stewards (p. 309). In 1986 no law underpins recognition. Subject to any industrial muscle available to a union, an employer can remove many statutory rights by withdrawing recognition. When, therefore, at the behest of the EEC Directive, the TUPE Regulations 1981 'transfer' the recognition of a union from transferor to transferee employer, if the undertaking maintains its identity (Reg. 9), they generally also transfer the opportunity to terminate it.

ACAS retains and uses its 'voluntary' functions in recognition disputes. In 1983 ACAS dealt with 216 such disputes, 13 per cent of all its conciliation work on 'collective' disputes (under EPA s. 2). This was a considerable decline from the peak of 1,211 in 1977; but ACAS considered that since 1976, although 'economic factors' played a part in the decline, 'voluntary conciliation could be held to have been more successful as a means of securing recognition . . . than statutory procedures'. The 'success rate' was more than 40 per cent for the former against less than 36 per cent for the latter. Recognition, though, is a not uncommon cause of disputes. At 16 per cent of ACAS's work in 1985, it was on the increase. BP, for example, on agreeing to staff status for some industrial workers recently removed recognition in respect of them from their union TGWU, and had the deal ratified by a ballot.

The definition bequeathed by the 1975 Act has given rise to further difficulties in the remaining areas of union rights. The courts accept that recognition may be implied as well as expressed. But they require some 'mutual' assent. The Act requires that this agreement must be 'for the purpose of collective bargaining'. Albury Bros. sacked employees – 'some of them youngsters' – without consulting the union. A few of their workers had shortly before been recruited by an official ('he did not tell the employers anything about it'). The firm was in contact with the union only once but was a member of the employers' association and applied the terms of the agreement between it and the union. The association, said the Court of Appeal, was not an agent of the employers (an important point); so they had never recognized the union.[26] Whether or not plant or 'company' negotiation is preferable in the jewellery trade to industry-wide bargaining, it does seem strange to exclude from 'recognition' in a redundancy case a union whose agreements made at the higher level have been regularly observed by an employer.

Even where the union appears to be recognized, the courts will examine its various functions for different groups. The CAC ruled against *BTP Ltd* when it failed to disclose information concerning junior staff to an independent union that was recognized for bargaining for senior staff, and recognized for junior staff for bargaining on certain specified items and for representations about changes in their conditions or for their grievances. The union wanted the information about junior staff in relation to a new job evaluation scheme. For this it had to be recognized (p. 289). The court quashed the CAC decision as wrong in law. 'Representation' was not 'negotiation'; there was a 'clear linguistic distinction'. The agreement drew this distinction. Even the appeals procedure in the job evaluation scheme did 'not give a negotiating role to the union representative at all'.[27] It is true that 'representation' is a known category industrially, a stepping-stone to 'full bargaining rights'; but the court's decision is very formal. It has been suggested that the *BTP* case should be restricted to the area of disclosure of information, making such limited rights sufficient for other purposes (e.g. consultation on safety or redundancy, discussed below), since the statutory definition speaks of recognition 'to any extent'.[28] But few judges are likely to accept such a view, common sense though it may be. Conduct can certainly supplement the formal agreement. Where one employer stipulated in an agreement that it was *not* 'recognition for negotiation' but only for representation of members, the EAT was willing to contemplate that subsequent conduct at a meeting by the employer in face of a threat to strike over redundancies might have flowered into full recognition under the statute.

But the EAT has also rejected a similar view in a case where the same reasoning was attached to the right of 'recognized unions' to appoint safety representatives. A union of polytechnic teachers did not qualify, it held, merely because it sat on the national salary body (a feature that in France or Italy would have made it a 'representative union' with superior rights). There is no doctrine of 'automatic recognition thrust upon an employer by the action of a third party'. Nor had the union proved any 'inferred recognition' consummated by its dealings with the employers, a process that could be 'as decorous and prolonged as a Victorian courtship', with 'coyness' from the one side and 'persistence' on the other.[29]

The judges, then, have emphasized the subjective wishes of the employer in 'recognition'. The need for workers to be represented plays little part now that the obligation to recognize has gone. It is difficult to believe that this can be the last word from a modern system of labour law on such a central issue.

Restrictions on promotion of recognition

Rights to promote recognition have been restricted severely by a provision in the 1982 Act. The Bill at first made 'void' any clause in a contract for supply of goods or services stipulating that work should be done by union labour (or by non-unionists). This is the forbidden 'union membership' ground. It then proceeded to ban the termination of a commercial contract or (more important) discriminatory business practices including any refusal to enter into one, by making such activity into a 'tort', whenever *one* of the reasons for so acting is the forbidden 'union membership' ground. In that event, any 'person adversely affected' can sue in court (such as excluded contractors, customers or even non-unionist workers alleging injury: EA 1982 s. 12). The object here was said to be to stop Labour-controlled councils from spreading the closed shop. Logically, therefore, the Bill went on also to ban industrial action by workers or unions that puts pressure on a business man for the forbidden reason to induce him to break the statute or to bring about the same result (s. 14). We return to this in Chapter 8 in relation to the 'immunities'. Of course a union – a craft union, for example – that takes industrial action where any one of its (dozen) reasons is maintenance of 100 per cent membership in the trade or district, is bound to infringe these sections; so, although not wholly accurate, it was understandable for a judge to conclude in 1984: 'The closed shop, whether practised by employers or employees, was outlawed by ss. 12 and 14 of the Employment Act 1982.'[30]

When Parliament had nearly finished with the Bill, new provisions were inserted. Local councils, it was claimed, might evade it by requiring contractors not to hire union labour, but to 'recognize' unions. Indeed, it is true that many employers, not just councils, inquire of subcontractors or maintenance firms what their position is in relation to the relevant union. There is no sense in having a pointless dispute with one's own electricians, for example, by hiring a maintenance firm that sends in 'cowboy' non-unionists to do electrical maintenance work below union rates and perhaps badly. From the standpoint of organized workers, the employer in the enterprise next door who refuses to talk to the union of his employees is a standing threat to the minimum conditions bargained by the union in their own firm. It is customary for commentators to condemn workers as selfish, but should they be penalized for attempting to support the interests of their colleagues next door, which overlap with their own? A central feature of trade unionism is that the strong support the weak, rather than leave them to be sucked down by forces of the market.

The logic of the Government in 1982, however, was that such practices must also be banned. A new clause therefore prohibited parallel activities to those already covered by the 'union membership' ground by prohibiting actions on a ground defined as 'union exclusion'. At first this sounds as though unions are to be let in; but this is not the way of statutory linguistics. 'Union exclusion' arises if any *one* ground for a person's action is that 'the person against whom it is taken does not, or is not likely to, recognize, negotiate or consult with a trade union or any union official' (EA 1982 s. 13 (2)). In this provision 'recognition' is undefined and seems not to fall within the strict definition of the EPA. Clauses in a contract with a forbidden requirement are made void (s. 13

(1)). Termination of, or refusal to conclude, a business contract is a tort actionable by 'any person adversely affected' (s. 13 (2)). Industrial action to induce such actions is banned (s. 14 (1)). And industrial action by workers when *one* of the reasons for their action is that the 'supplier' of goods or services (other than the workers' own employer) does not, or is likely not to, recognize, negotiate or consult with a union, is also deprived of immunity where the action can 'reasonably be expected' to interfere with the supply of goods or services (whether or *not* under any commercial contract), unprotected even in trade disputes (s. 14).

Thus a threat of industrial action by the employees of a subcontractor to induce the main contractor in control of a site to engage in early consultation about redundancies or unsafe conditions is unlawful – even if the subcontractor is reluctant to press the powerful contractor on these matters, and even though there is a statutory duty on employers to consult recognized unions on proposed redundancies (EPA s. 99: p. 294) and to consult with union safety representatives (HSWA s. 2: p. 291).[31] The same is true of other demands for consultation, though strictly no liability arises if workers (no doubt taking legal advice) restrain their demands to consultation about 'union rates'. The prohibition is on industrial pressure to recognize or consult with a union. There is no equivalent provision prohibiting either commercial activity or industrial action undertaken for the purpose of inducing an employer to consult with non-unionists or individual employees or, more important, *not* to consult with or recognize a trade union. This is consistent with the philosophy of the legislation (pp. 72–5, 606, 641).

Having abolished the 1975 Act's procedure for obligatory recognition (however unsatisfactory) the legislation of the 1980s here restricts the freedom of workers to withdraw their labour where their interests lie in supporting collective bargaining, or consultation, outside the boundaries of their own employment, even in respect of a company in the same group as their own employer. As we shall see (p. 597), this is one of a number of provisions in the new laws with that purpose.[32] For the present, it is sufficient to register that this part of the 1982 Act reverses the traditional public policy of British labour law. It has been said that the 'liberties' of British trade unionists were 'won by throwing off the shackles of the law', and that the 'price that British trade unions have paid is a lack of legal backing'.[33] In 1982 the price was doubled, but shackles were reimposed. The prohibition of otherwise lawful self-help undertaken to encourage the extension of union recognition is a vote of no confidence in collective bargaining.

Obligatory disclosure of information

In order that collective bargaining relationships should flourish, whether at company, industry or plant level, the employer must give the union adequate information. In some systems, such as that in the USA, this is regarded as part and parcel of the duty to bargain. Other systems, as in Sweden, require disclosure to the union of all relevant information in order to allow, in Folke Schmidt's words, 'all individual employees to get a good picture of the activity of the enterprise'. Although British companies with more than 250 employees have now been required to insert in their directors' reports a description of 'employee involvement' (without mentioning any union), including information systematically distributed (EA 1982 s. 1), there is no obligation to 'involve' them. British law has required information to be disclosed to an independent *recognized* union both for purposes of tripartite industrial planning (in a statute in 1975 now repealed) and on a request by its 'authorized representatives' (i.e. under its rules) 'for the purposes of all the stages' of relevant collective bargaining (EPA s. 17 (1)). This second provision is still effective and important. Where there is no recognition for bargaining, or only preparation for it, or where the CAC – to which disputes are referred – can find only 'representational' rights for the union, disclosure is not obligatory.[34] So too, the statute requires the union to show that disclosure accords with 'good industrial relations practice' and that non-disclosure impedes it 'to a material extent' in bargaining. Furthermore, the information must relate *to matters* and to a description of workers in respect of which the union *is already* recognized. So where the ASTMS wished Kodak to disclose information about early retirement schemes for managers, because this might be relevant to forthcoming staff redundancies, on which Kodak insisted it had no plans, the CAC decided that there could be no material impediment for the bargaining for staff based on the union's 'hypothetical contingency'.[35]

The range of information is not only tied strictly to the existing scope of bargaining, it is also limited by specific exceptions excluding information damaging national security, contravening a statute, relating to an individual (unless he consents) or communicated in confidence or obtained by the employer because of a 'confidence' of another person (s. 18 (1)). These, especially the category of confidential information, have been strictly interpreted (as where firms' tenders to the Ministry of Defence about to privatize their cleaning staff were treated as confidential against a recognized union whose members wished to compete by continuing direct labour).[36] The Act also releases the employer from 'compiling' information where this would involve work or expenditure 'out of reasonable proportion' to its value in the collective bargaining. Even if the CAC does find the employer to be in breach of the Act, moreover, it cannot order disclosure. The remedy, as with the old recognition procedures, this time after *two* obligatory complaints by the union, is an award of improved substantive conditions for the employees concerned (ss. 19–20). The employer who will not tell is allowed to pay for his silence.

The sensible approach of the CAC has been to treat the whole apparatus as an adjunct to the development of consultative and negotiating machinery. Thus, where the union was entitled to formal disclosure from a division of a US multinational enterprise of a range of information, the Committee in 1985 made a declaration as to part of it (registering the union stewards' right to take notes of oral information), but as to the rest recommended that the parties should 'establish joint consultative machinery', in default of which 'further recourse to the Committee' by the union would be available.[37] It is better to nudge multinationals into civilized industrial procedures for disclosure and negotiation than to present them with a series of one-off judgments more likely to frighten them off.

Unions have been understandably disappointed with the Act, especially when the ACAS Code of Practice (No. 2), perhaps taking too generous a view of the statute and its concept of collective bargaining, had suggested in 1977 that the obligation to disclose might reach beyond pay and 'conditions of service' to management policies on manpower, productivity, the order book, costs, profits, transfer prices (in a group) and even investments. Indeed the CAC, which has sensibly tried to find an agreed solution wherever possible, in 1982 expressed its unhappiness about employers who stood on the letter of the Act against its 'spirit' and recommended one union to try 'voluntary agreement' to improve communications. Such agreements often improve on the Act. A

GMBAT 'model' agreement on redundancy in 1982 touched on many items in the ACAS code and more. A union must, of course, have the resources and officials equipped to make use of the information; more information by itself may not contribute much, except perhaps as 'a token of interest and goodwill by the management'.[38] In 1983 the CAC had only sixteen cases on disclosure before it, eleven of which were settled; but it thought these figures might be 'misleading' because of the indirect effectiveness of the Act on its practice. The EPA 1975 is better than nothing but if it was meant to promote significant improvements on disclosure it was, in its scope and its enforcement machinery, woefully inadequate. The obligation to disclose information which stems from EEC law on the transfer of an undertaking we shall consider after describing the obligation on the employer, which also stems from the EEC, to consult unions over proposed redundancies.

Obligatory consultation

Apart from the nationalized industry statutes (p. 278), there are four main areas in which the law has come to demand some consultation by the employer with the representatives of an independent recognized union of his employees. They are: (1) health and safety; (2) proposed redundancies; (3) impending transfer of the undertaking; (4) pension schemes. (A little known Act and regulation of 1936 provided for consultation of women and young workers 'by secret ballot' as the condition for the Minister approving certain shift systems in factories; now Factories Act 1961 s. 97: p. 408). We are concerned not with bargaining, but with 'consultation', which, though it can have rather diverse meanings, leaves the last word with the employer.

(1) *Consultation on safety and health at work.* Conditions on health and safety have been the subject of legislation since the early nineteenth century. Until recently the duties of the employer on such matters have been subject to enforcement by way of criminal prosecution, especially through the Factory Inspectors, and civil actions in tort for damages, typically by injured workers. These well known legal remedies we touch upon below (p. 413). The Health and Safety at Work Act 1974 introduced a new protection, placing on employers the duty to consult the safety representatives appointed by recognized unions with a view to the making and maintenance of arrangements enabling him and his em-

ployees 'to co-operate effectively' on developing and checking safety at work (HSWA s. 2 (4), (7): the limitation to *union* appointments was made by the Labour Government of 1974). If requested, he must set up a safety committee. The Robens Report (1972) had proposed that there should be a statutory requirement 'for participation by employees' with safety representatives 'empowered to carry out inspections'; but, though 'the natural identity of interest of the parties' left much scope for discussion and participation, there was 'no legitimate scope for "bargaining"' on safety and health issues. It proposed 'a general duty to consult', such as that placed on the NCB in 1946. Some questioned whether there is always a necessary conjunction of interests between workers exposed to hazardous processes and an employer whose profits must take the initial expense of their improvement.

Even so, the 1974 legislation built upon this foundation as well as adding to the traditional sanctions. Behind it there now exist various safety regulations, a Code of Practice, and 'notes of guidance', prepared by the Health and Safety Commission and its Executive; and these prescribe more closely the manner in which safety representatives and committees should conduct their work.[39] The representatives, for example, are entitled to have extensive information, to investigate machinery and carry out inspections within certain intervals; and, as in the case of shop stewards today (p. 309), they are entitled to paid time off for training and the execution of their duties (Safety Representatives, etc. Regulations No. 500, 1977, Reg. 4 (2)). Indeed, the safety representative, who must usually have two years' continuity of service, may well be a shop steward (though the regulations are flexible enough to permit representatives not to be even 'employees', e.g. in the case of Actors' Equity and the Musicians' Union, since so many of their members are self-employed). We have seen (p. 119) that adjustments had to be made for 'trainees' as they became a permanent feature of employment structures; this was effected in the Health, etc. (YTS) Regulations No. 1919, 1983. Only in the 'notes of guidance' does much appear about the safety committees, the parties being left to adopt agreed procedures. So too, there are guidance notes on statements of company policy on health and safety, which all firms except those with less than five employees must prepare and circulate (HSWA s. 2 (3)), although a survey of 1985 leaves it doubtful whether many companies publish detailed reports of the kind envisaged by the Robens Committee (the obligation to do so in company reports not having been activated).[40] Guidance rules also exist for the non-unionized firms.

Some concern had been expressed about the possible liability of a safety representative where a worker who is injured alleges that a breach of duty by him contributed to it; but the execution of safety functions does not expose him to civil liability (HSWA ss. 7, 8, 47 (1), and Reg. 4 (1): with one possible exception in another regulation). The HSC has a policy of not prosecuting representatives in the criminal courts; but this must be seen against the background of the Commission's general enforcement policies (p. 420) in which it aims at voluntary agreement with employers wherever possible. It is not unimportant, too, that the employer will – and since 1969 must (p. 415) – be insured. Furthermore, the British safety representative does not have, as his counterpart has in some European countries, the power to stop a machine alleged to be dangerous. The legislation of 1974 is supplemented by sixty-one statutory instruments, sixteen Codes of Practice and innumerable 'notes of guidance' regularly issued by the HSC and HSE.[41]

The new legal regime for health and safety clearly mingles different methods and sanctions in order to improve conditions at work. Indeed, the very line between 'consultation' and 'negotiation' is blurred not only under the Act but by the fact that disputes about the consultative structure with the employer are ordinarily resolved through normal negotiating machinery. Some matters can end up before an industrial tribunal (though few appear to do so) – disputes about time off for safety representatives (p. 312) or an appeal by the employer against an 'improvement notice' issued by an inspector to remedy a breach of the Act or regulations on safety – in which case the tribunal can sit with one or more 'assessors' who have 'special knowledge or experience' (HSWA ss. 21–24; see also p. 267). Nor is that the end of the mixtures. One collective agreement in Yorkshire in 1984 allowed employers (whose business involved very high noise levels, and who feared that some employees might not wear hearing protectors) not to process the matter through the disciplinary procedure (which might lead to a dismissal and possible challenge in the tribunal for unfairness) but to 'refer' a worker guilty of persistent failure to the factory inspector. In the last resort, he could, if the HSC permitted, prosecute the worker for failure to take reasonable care of himself or others, or to co-operate with the employer in not fulfilling his duties (HSWA s. 17).[42] The scope for this particular solution may be small, but it illustrates the flexibility that law and practice has adopted in this area.

Similarly it is not yet clear how effective is the HSC policy of separating sharply the representative's functions from those of a shop steward; as McCarthy said to Donovan, there is a strong 'preference of shop stewards for collective bargaining rather than joint consultation'.[43] In a White Paper on the 'burden on business' the Government in 1985 proposed relaxations in some safety regulations, such as raising the threshold below which a written safety policy is required from 5 to 20 employees, and 'showing' employers how to 'question Inspectors' decisions' on safety.[44]

(2) *Consultation on proposed redundancies*. Proposed redundancies must be the subject of consultation by the employer with the appropriate independent trade union recognized by him. This was the nub of an EEC Directive (75/129) on collective redundancies, which also required notification to 'the competent public authority'.[45] This latter requirement was adopted in 1975 into British law (EPA s. 100) as an obligation to notify the Secretary of State, one that the employer is likely to remember, since failure, apart from being an offence, can result in up to a 10 per cent reduction in his rebate (ss. 104–5: p. 220 and p. 398 on 'redundancy'); the rebate system will apply, however, from 1986 only to employers with less than ten employees (on the enactment of the Wages Bill 1986 Part III). Unlike that of many other countries, however, British law does not require approval by any public authority. Under the same statute of 1975 representatives of the recognized union properly authorized under its own constitution to carry on collective bargaining must be consulted about proposed redundancies at the initiative of the employer (EPA s. 99). The nature of the 'consultation' here is taken up to the brink of a negotiating process, for the employer must set out in writing his reasons, the numbers and descriptions of workers involved and the total employed, the proposed method of selection (which has been touched on in respect of unfair dismissal: p. 249) and proposed method and period of time for carrying out the dismissals. He must then consider the union's answer and reply to it, stating his reasons for rejecting any of its representations (s. 99 (5), (7)). Failure to comply with any one of these requirements means that the employer is in breach of the Act.

Timing. For workers facing the employer in redundancies, as in strikes, much may depend on the timing. The employer is therefore always obliged to begin the consultation 'at the earliest opportunity' (a requirement often forgotten). There then follow two specific time limits: (a) where he proposes to dismiss as redundant at least 100 employees within 90 days or less at one establishment, and (b) where 10 or more are involved within 30 days or less. The statute requires consultation to begin in (a) 'at least 90 days before the first of those dismissals' (s. 99 (1)). The consultation period in (b) was originally 'at least 60 days'; but in 1979 when it excluded many workers from unfair dismissal protection the Government also reduced that period to '30 days', no doubt anticipating the rising tide of redundancies, which by 1981 was to engulf manufacturing industry. But 90 and 30 days from when? Consultation should surely start on the employer's 'proposals' so many days before the first worker in that batch is dismissed – so long as, in any case, the employer began at the *earliest opportunity* (this is overriding even if only one worker is made redundant). The EAT agreed with this approach in a decision concerning notification to the Minister. Clearly if the employer issues redundancy notices on the day 'consultation' begins with the union, this is not 'meaningful consultation' within the section (as the EAT insisted in 1978), and he has not complied (though he may have given adequate 'notice' to the individual workers under their contractual or statutory minimum notice: p. 199). On the other hand, where a group of companies dismisses employees, each company is taken separately (p. 96); so a subsidiary that dismisses 36 out of 157 in the group will fall into the period for (b), not (a).

Both points arose in *Green & Son* v. *ASTMS*[46] along with a more difficult question. What the statute should have demanded was a consultation period that permitted notices to be given only at the end of it. But as it is, an employer can begin consultation, tell the union (say) that ninety dismissals will occur on a particular date, but then dismiss some employees on an earlier date. If the employer engages in only a sham consultative process, he has not fulfilled his obligations, as where he gave the union only half an hour to consider difficult proposals, after which he sent out the first dismissal notices (though significantly the EAT had to correct a tribunal that thought this adequate).[47] The enforcement mechanism of the statute reflects the same dislike felt in 1975 for court orders of which disobedience would be contempt. This gave rise to the indirect sanctions attached to breach of the duty of disclosure and the repealed duty to recognize. (After all, it was only three years since the unions had erupted against court orders that had put shop stewards in gaol for defying orders of the NIRC.)

Remedies. The remedy on redundancy consultation involves two stages. First the *union* must complain to a tribunal (normally within three months of the dismissal) and secure a 'protective award' that will cover the employees dismissed or to be dismissed (EPA s. 101). The union seems not to be liable to members if it fails to do so unless, at any rate, the member can construct a breach of contractual duty out of the rule-book, independently of the section (s. 99 (9)). Secondly, an employee can then claim he is entitled to an amount as a 'protective award', provided the period falls within his notice period (contractual, or minimum statutory notice) and provided he has not 'unreasonably' terminated his own employment (or been *fairly* dismissed for a different reason) during it – *and* provided he has not unreasonably refused an offer of renewal or of re-engagement on 'suitable' alternative terms, or unreasonably refused after accepting a trial period of four weeks or longer agreed in writing (s. 102). If he surmounts all these hurdles, how much does he get? The protective award is calculated on the basis of a 'week's pay' (with the limit of £155 as for redundancy: p. 203). He must set off any payments under his employment contract (e.g. in lieu of notice). There is a statutory maximum: 90 days in category (a); 30 days in category (b); and 28 days in any other case (fewer than ten workers), called the 'protected period' (s. 101 (4), (5)).

There remain two problems. The 'protected period' is to run from 'the date on which the first of the dismissals . . . takes effect' or the date of the award, whichever is earlier (s. 101 (5)). In *Green*, the EAT held that the protected period (say, '90 days' in a category (a) redundancy) is linked to the period of consultation (also 90 days). The protected period is part of a scheme of compensation to ensure consultation. Where, as envisaged there, the employer has paid workers sums in lieu of full wages until the 31st of the month but dismissed them on the 21st, if calculation of the period began with the 21st the workers would have to set off payment for the ten days as paid under their contracts. The section looks forward 'to projected dismissals at a future date' making the employer disclose plans for *those* dismissals, which he anticipates, whether or not actual dismissals occur at different times. The 'protected period' thus runs, it was held, from the proposed date of the first dismissals, whether or not dismissals in fact occurred before it.

Secondly, however, the employer does not always have to pay the maximum. The tribunals must award what is 'just and equitable . . . having regard to the seriousness of the employer's default' (s. 101 (5)). After some uncertainty, the courts determined that, while the object of the protective award is to 'compensate', the compensation is for 'failure to consult', not just the 'loss of actual remuneration'. So awards may, within the maxima, exceed the precise loss. Tribunals must consider the seriousness of the breach, deducting contractual payments, but not earnings from any new job.[48] The employer's fault therefore enters the calculation, a tendency that the statute encourages. For where he encounters 'special circumstances' rendering compliance 'not reasonably practicable', the employer is obliged to take only such steps as are 'reasonably practicable in those circumstances' (EPA s. 99 (8)). Take the onset of insolvency. If this creeps up on the employer the courts will not usually regard it as a special circumstance; but if there is a 'sudden occurrence' – if a prospective take-over bidder withdraws, and the bank refuses credit and appoints a receiver (with 'an element of suddenness'), or when a government loan fails to come through – then the doctrine comes into play. Then the employer must do only what is reasonably practicable.[49] It is true the worker may have rights in the employer's insolvency, but these are not extensive (p. 398).

The way the statutory protection for workers disintegrates into a doctrine of *sauve qui peut* or devil-take-the-hindmost illustrates its weakness. The EAT has insisted that the employer need do nothing 'unless and until a proposal to dismiss one or more [employees] on the ground of redundancy is at least in the mind of the employer'. Or, as the Scottish EAT put it, the employer must *propose*, i.e. 'form some view' about, how many, when and how: 'This goes beyond the mere contemplation of a possible event.' This subjective state of mind of 'the employer' will be fought about months later in the two applications to the tribunal. This weakness may account for the paucity of case law, especially when the judges have drawn back somewhat from their earlier insistence upon consultation in redundancies for the purpose of unfair dismissal (p. 241).

The fact is that most good employers buy out these statutory rights by making payments to employees thrown out of jobs for redundancy. Unions have made agreements that provide for continuous information, sometimes with guaranteed minimum notice or payments in lieu, and provisions on selection, retraining and redeployment.[50] If the Act has had any success it has been in that function which is so difficult to prove: the stimulation of collective bargains, especially at the workplace,[51] above its floor. Even so, the minimum periods of the Act have tended to become ceilings for the 1980s. In 1985 Courtaulds stunned North Wales by announcing closures that involved 1,100 workers, who all received 'ninety days' notice'. Some employers have not announced their redundancies until well after 'proposals' had matured in their minds. The notion of the EAT that the Act was meant to 'result in new ideas being ventilated which avoid the redundancy situation altogether' echoes the gentlemanly days of a decade ago.

Redundancy has been usefully termed by some authors 'controlled labour mobility' in specific situations. Such studies help the lawyer to remember 'the differential resources and power available to those involved'.[52] Control, resources and power are not usually the mark of redundant workers. The law gives consultation rights only to *recognized* unions, and such recognition depends on the employer's choice. In this British practice falls below some international standards. In February 1985 the ILO, interpreting its Principles on multinationals after a complaint against Bankers' Trust in Britain, a branch of a US enterprise, declared that 'notice' of redundancy should be given to workers' 'representatives' even if their union is not recognized. This hardly seems an unreasonable proposition.

(3) *Impending transfers of the undertaking.* 'Transfer' received separate attention from the law by reason of another EEC Directive (77/187), implemented in the Transfer of Undertakings (Protection of Employment), or 'TUPE', Regulations No. 1794, 1981.[53] It is important to remember that when EEC obligations are translated into law by regulations in Britain they cannot be amended in Parliament, as a Bill can. The TUPE Regulations are a monument to the unsatisfactory nature of this process.

The scheme deals with the transfer of all or part of an 'undertaking' in four ways: (a) automatic transfer of the worker's employment contracts, and 'rights connected with it', to the transferee (Reg. 5); (b) automatic transfer of collective agreements and union recognition (Regs. 6, 9); (c) unfairness of a dismissal for a reason connected with the transfer, unless there is an 'economic, technical or organizational reason' that counts as an SOSR (p. 243; Reg. 8; see also p. 208 on Reg. 4 on 'hiving-down'); (d) obligations on the employer to inform and consult with the appropriate independent and recognized union (Regs. 10, 11).

We have noted how 'transfer' does not include sales of shares, nor of assets unless they amount to sale of a going concern or business (p. 207). An 'undertaking' means any trade or business that is a 'commercial venture' (Reg. 2). The 'transfer' of recognition and collective agreements means little in British law since the former is not obligatory and the latter normally not legally enforceable. The courts have appeared to equate the TUPE Regulations as far as possible to the law on transfers of a business in a redundancy, continuity of employment and unfair dismissal.[54] A transfer in which the transferee possesses the undertaking only fleetingly will suffice – and in this event both the contractual rights of employees and their rights to redundancy payments pass to the transferee.[55]

The failure of the regulations to fit the patterns of English law was illustrated by *Angus Jowett Ltd* v. *NUTGW*.[56] An employer failed to consult the union about redundancies; but he transferred the business to another company. Was the right to a 'protective award' for the employees transferred? The EAT agreed that rights to redundancy payments were transferred as they were 'connected with' the contracts of employment, but not the protective award. The draftsman could not have 'intended' this to pass with the transfer because

the employer's duties and liabilities regarding consultation could not be described as duties or liabilities *in connection with* any such contract . . . [they arose from] a failure to consult with the recognised unions.

Workers would think both were rights connected with their redundancy and might ask: Why are not all the employment rights of a worker, for which his employer may incur liability, *connected with* his employment contract?

The truth is that the Directive and Regulations are based upon (no doubt logical) concepts natural to many European systems of law, which see the individual employment *relationship* as one bundle of rights. In Britain a strange dichotomy has emerged. Some rights rest on the contract, others on the statute, with different courts and even different procedures and concepts applicable to them, much as judges try sometimes to stick them together with implied terms. To invent a third category, where the right is contingent upon the *employer*'s action in regard to the union, may catch the transferor company that is trying to escape (though it is likely to be less solvent than the transferee), but it is an analysis based upon the employer's perspective.

Information and consultation. The TUPE Regulations impose duties to inform or consult with the independent recognized union. These may fall on the transferor or transferee or both. The scheme is similar to the duty of consultation in redundancies, yet with important differences. The employer must inform the union of the 'fact' of the impending transfer, the reasons for it, the 'legal, economic and social implications' for, and the measures he will take about, 'affected employees', and (for the transferor) what steps the transferee will take about employees transferred to him (Reg. 10 (2)). Since 'affected employees' means any employees of either transferor or transferee who may be affected *whether or not* employed in the undertaking to be transferred, the ambit is wide, though the duties arise only in respect of workers for whom a union is recognized. Workers affected in a factory in a group where jobs may be reduced by reason of a transfer of an associated undertaking are clearly included. There is no provision here, though, for 'associated employers'; each company 'employer' is a separate entity, a very serious deficiency. The employer must inform the union 'long enough' before the transfer 'to enable consultations to take place'. Since the primary subject-matter is the 'fact' of the impending transfer (quite different from 'proposals' in EPA s. 99), an employer might feel justified in waiting until the 'fact' of the sale is assured. Timing is of critical importance because, if he envisages 'taking measures' in relation to employees represented by the union, he must enter into consultations with the union, consider its representations and reply to them, with his reasons for rejecting any of them (Reg. 10 (5), (6)). But, once again, where there are 'special circumstances' he need do only what is 'reasonably practicable in the circumstances' (Reg. 10 (8)).

By this time the employer's duties scarcely resemble the fine phrases with which we set out. What happens if he breaks them? The remedies require another two-stage assault in the tribunal (Reg. 11). First, the union must complain. The tribunal may declare the complaint 'well founded'. Next the employee must come to the tribunal (normally within three months) to claim the appropriate compensation, i.e. such sum as the tribunal considers 'just and equitable' having regard to the 'seriousness' of the employer's default, but deducting any sum paid to him by the employer as damages or remuneration under his contract or as a protective award during the protected period (just as, vice versa, awards under the TUPE Regulations go to reduce those amounts). Yet the sting is in the tail; appropriate compensation must not exceed *two weeks' pay*. No such limit was in the 1978 draft; nor was it required by the Directive. In 1981 Government spokesmen agreed that there had to be 'some sort of sanction for a breach', but anything more than this would prove 'a very substantial burden on an employer'.

(4) *An EEC draft Directive ('Vredeling')*. In addition to the EEC initiatives that gave rise to the obligations on redundancy consultation in the EPA 1975, and on information and consultations in the TUPE Regulations 1981, a proposal was made in 1980, associated with the name of its originator, Commissioner Vredeling, for more extensive EEC legislation. Like the Directives of 1975 and 1977, if it is ever approved by the Council of Ministers it will be binding on Britain. The objective is to create duties to inform and consult with representatives of employees (in Britain this would mean with independent, recognized trade unions) about the affairs, not just of the company employer in the State concerned, but of the whole group of companies of which it forms a part (or of the entire enterprise where, instead of a number of subsidiary companies, one finds many divisions of the enterprise active in more than one State). The multinational enterprise operating in diverse States would be obliged to disclose details of its affairs in all the countries concerned, no matter where the 'parent' was located (it might be in another EEC State, or it might not). So concerned were some United States multinationals at this prospect that they promoted Bills in Congress to enlist the aid of US law to help them avoid the need to fulfil such obligations.

Yet 'Vredeling' hardly imposes drastic duties. By 1983 the revised text that emerged from the European Parliament and its committees was considerably weakened. It still required the employer within a member State to inform and consult if there were 1,000 or more workers (earlier it was 100) employed within the EEC by all the companies in the *group*, smashing down the 'corporate veil' (p. 97), or where 1,000 were employed in all the different 'establishments' within the EEC States. When the 'decision-making' parent was outside the Community, it would be represented by one subsidiary within an EEC State (Art. 2

(2)). Once a year, each subsidiary should give to the unions information (other than 'secret information') about the group concerning the structure, business development, economic and financial situation, employment, and investment prospects of the group as a whole (Arts. 3, 7: the earlier version had included all plans liable to affect employees' interests). The parent should see that the subsidiary had the necessary information. If this fails, earlier versions had allowed the union to 'bypass' and go straight to the parent; but by 1983 this was weakened and became a right to ask the parent to pass the information on to its subsidiary. Consultation rights arise whenever the parent proposes to take decisions concerning the group or the subsidiary that are likely to have 'serious consequences' for the workers, including closures, transfers, change in 'activities' of the enterprise, working practices, production methods and other measures (Art. 4). Precise information (other than 'secrets') must be provided about these measures, the reasons for them and their 'legal, economic and social consequences' for workers. Decisions must be delayed until the end of the consultation period of thirty days. National laws would include 'appropriate penalties' for breach. These provisions would be a considerable advance on British labour law. Even though they do not furnish a right to negotiate or be recognized, such features as the prohibition of 'decisions' during the consultation period constitute a different mechanism from the consultation about 'proposed redundancies' that we have just discussed.

The 1983 version of 'Vredeling' also came under attack. In France the *patronat* (employers) and the left union confederation CGT were both opposed. The British Government issued a consultative document that began with 'reservations' and ended by expressing 'opposition'.[57] The general hostility of employers had already succeeded in enlarging the exceptions for information covered by 'secrecy', and in inserting an extraordinary option for national legislation to permit consultation to be 'directly with the employees' (Art. 5; i.e. not through unions). The draft was alleged by multinational groups with parents outside the EEC to seek improper 'extra-territorial' effect, and dire threats were heard of the withdrawal of investment and, with it, jobs.

When Ireland acquired the Presidency it made suggestions for a new scheme in 1985.[58] Under this the scope of obligatory disclosures would be narrowed, but the details required expanded. The 'bypass' arrangement would be omitted completely; but the subsidiary would still disclose information on the group as a whole, and the parent would provide it. A new provision proposes to give States an option to permit collective agreements to replace the Directive's requirements by voluntary procedures that are 'as beneficial' as the Directive (analogous to the British concept of a 'floor of rights'). One snag here appears to be the European view, which advisers have given to the Presidency, that collective agreements that are not legally enforceable (p. 323) cannot be regarded as giving adequate effect to a Directive. Moreover, hopes for rapid advance were dashed when, although all member States approved the spirit of the 'new approach', the British Government adhered to its view that no such Directive is needed at all. It does not seem likely that this EEC legislation will come to fruition in the near future; but its structure is of importance when we consider the options for the next two decades.

(5) *Participation in occupational pension schemes.* Occupational pension schemes arranged with employers for employees' retirement grew in importance in the 1960s and, with a steadily ageing population, will continue to do so. More than 11 million workers and some 5 million pensioners are covered by occupational pension schemes (over 5 million of the workers are in the public sector, most with index-linked pensions, although half of them have few other resources in retirement). The employer may set up his own fund, or have it administered by a merchant bank or similar 'adviser', or join in an outside package deal run by a life assurance company; but benefits are often 'relatively meagre', especially in regard to 'inflation proofing'.[59] Partly because of the even greater importance for many older citizens of the State retirement pension (drawn by over 9 million people), this subject has normally been treated as appropriate to social security law, because the citizen is there involved as citizen not worker. But it is true that 'it deserves a central place in any study of labour law'.[60] Indeed, the division of functions in regard to income maintenance between State, employers, unions and employees must raise the question whether and where collective bargaining is to participate in employers' schemes quite apart from specific problems such as the solvency of schemes or the law governing their trustees. As early as 1948 in the USA the NLRB recognized pension plans as *mandatory* subjects of bargaining, despite the protest from the president of General Motors that this development was 'an alien form, imported from East of the Rhine'.[61] Here the TUC

had advanced the claim that workers have a legitimate right to a voice in their pension funds.

In 1975 in Britain the Occupational Pensions Board was given the role of protecting employees in schemes, seeking a sound financial base in respect of the guaranteed minimum pension and promoting disclosure of information to employees. This represented a more bipartisan thread of policy compared with the other proposal in a White Paper of the following year, which sparked controversy because it was seen 'as a specialized example of the debate raised by the Bullock Report' (on Industrial Democracy: p. 835).[62] It proposed that management bodies of pension schemes should draw one-half of their membership from independent trade unions of the workers involved. In truth, this proposal did touch upon a very fundamental issue of power in industry, partly because pension funds control such large resources (in 1982 eleven funds alone had a capital of more than £1 billion) and because they were, and are, prominent among the 'institutional investors' who today own more than 50 per cent of the shares in British public companies. Pension funds, though, do not as such involve any 'democratization' of power merely because the funds are held on trust *for* workers. So too, union trustees of the mineworkers' pension fund were not permitted by the courts in 1984 to consider anything other than the strict financial considerations of the traditional law of trusts (they could not assert the NUM's 'invest in Britain' policy before their duty to maximize return) – a decision that rendered uncertain TUC advice to such union trustees to consider longer-term interests of the economy.[63] The response of the union to this defeat was to have its five trustees resign and not be replaced, thereby paralysing the fund's activities; but in 1985 Megarry V C appointed five retired miners to act, 'deemed to be the nominees of the union' until the union appointed trustees ready to act; but this was by then part of a wider conflict: see Chapter 9.

Concern was expressed by senior accountants in 1985 about Britain importing the United States practice of 'asset-stripping' pension funds, whereby a surplus can be refunded to the parent company (which the Revenue's Superannuation Funds Office could not always block). As Nobles has said, occupational pension schemes are now necessarily part of the employer's business; he 'controls their funding'; and in present conditions independence from him is 'an illusion'. Even so, 'greater independence' could arise for 'trade union appointed trustees' if there were a requirement that the employer negotiate about the fund, in respect of which there is a clear conflict of interest.[64]

In 1975 Parliament required employers who opted to 'contract out' from the State earnings-related pension scheme (SERPS) to give notice of their intention to do so to their independent, recognized unions, and consult with them about it.[65] The scheme of the 1970s aimed ultimately to extend joint administration of pension funds. But this unfinished plan has been left stranded by the tides of policy that have subsequently flowed in a different direction.[66] Further, the Government prefers 'portable pensions', transferable freely between jobs, with a minimum employer contribution. The TUC asserted in 1984 that such a development would 'destabilize' the State scheme, putting 'the pensions of the most vulnerable employees at risk'; and directors of some large companies have described such 'takeaway' pensions as 'disruptive'.

On the other hand, company schemes are open to criticism as impeding job mobility unless proper provision is made for transferability. The Social Security Act 1985 has made a move in that direction requiring schemes regularly to revalue 'deferred' pensions, aiming at a right for those leaving a job to transfer accrued rights in another scheme. Such plans would seek increased 'individual' contracting-out of State earnings-related pensions, a right so far available only to an employer's scheme (the director of the National Association of Pension Funds has called this plan 'a recipe for administrative chaos'). Under the 1985 statute, regulations may impose a duty on the employer to disclose to members of a scheme, their spouses, prospective members *and* independent recognized trade unions information about rights, administration, finances and other matters to be specified. Industrial tribunals will decide disputes about a union's status.

The union, then, reappears with the rights to information, confirmation even in 1986 that this is an important area for labour relations and the law. Such rights are most likely to interest workers in the 'primary' labour market. Whether they insist upon collective negotiation on pensions remains to be seen. By 1985 criticism was also being made both of SERPS and of proposals to abolish it in favour of higher basic pensions, which were being seriously considered by Government. For many, certainly the millions in the poorer, unstable 'secondary' sector of employment, the matter is important since the State pension is likely to remain crucial in their retirement. To them the place of the law in encouraging or compelling employers to institute and discuss supplementary occupational pension schemes, on terms that do not discriminate against weaker groups, is of primary importance. Whereas 64 per cent of male workers are covered by a pension scheme, only 37 per cent of women workers are members. The proposals eventually put forward by the Government, however, in *Reform of Social Security* (Cmnd, 9691, 1985), concentrated upon widening 'the choice', 'simplifying' SERPS and promoting personal pensions, with equal rights to disclosure of information but with free transferability in and out of employers' schemes. It remains to be seen whether any institutions other than the State can cope with the scale of organization required.

Conciliation and arbitration in collective bargaining

The law and voluntary methods

Our law has for a century been utilized in a very different, if less spectacular, manner on industrial problems. Starting with the 'Joint Conciliation Boards' of the 1860s, the practice of arbitration and conciliation was developed with the new 'moderate' unions of the day ('the representatives of the masters met representatives of the Trade Unions on equal terms', as the Webbs rather optimistically put it).[67] Here we can trace again the beginnings of that preference for voluntary rules, for procedures over substantive rules and, above all, for flexibility which was to emerge as distinctive of the system.[68] We must not make the mistake, however, here or elsewhere of thinking that the industrial and legal development was created by some theoretical decision to create 'a voluntary system'. Indeed, one of the streams that flowed into the modern structures was the resistance of many employers to arbitration that went beyond disputes about existing terms of employment; in the 1824 Act, arbitration applied to future rates only 'with the mutual consent of both master and workmen'.[69] After the Royal Commission on Labour of 1894 had declared for a 'rapid extension of voluntary boards', the Conciliation Act 1896 provided machinery on that basis – only 'a skeleton' (powers to compel witnesses were omitted 'at the last moment'), but one that the talented if egotistic conciliator Lord Askwith steered successfully forward through its first test, the Penrhyn quarrymen's fierce battle for recognition in 1897.[70] Lord Penrhyn's natural successor eighty years later was perhaps Mr Ward of Grunwick.

ACAS and the CAC

By now, however, the conciliation service, developed over many years by the Ministry of Labour, has been put on a quasi-independent footing as the Advisory, Conciliation and Arbitration Service (ACAS), run by a tripartite council and with statutory powers under the EPA 1975 (ss. 1–5). As we have seen, ACAS in the *Grunwick* dispute had no power even in a recognition matter in 1977 to compel witnesses. Nor did it want any. ACAS is required to promote the 'improvement of industrial relations', to encourage the 'extension of collective bargaining' and to develop, 'where necessary, reform of collective bargaining machinery'. In actual or imminent industrial disputes, it may offer assistance by conciliation, be requested to assist by the parties and refer them to a third party (always encouraging the primary use of their *own* existing, agreed procedures). In 1985 it achieved 1,104 successful conciliations (82 per cent of all cases), the largest 'source' being joint requests for assistance from both sides. ACAS also has power to provide arbitrators. Of the disputes procedures found in modern industry with provision for settlement by a third party (an increasing trend in the 1970s), 85 per cent name ACAS for the role.[71] The only important matters that stray over the frontiers of 'voluntarism' are its powers to give advice or undertake inquiry 'if it thinks fit'. Such powers are used with care; and the results of such an inquiry, like the misnamed 'Court of Inquiry' that can still be established by the Secretary of State under the Industrial Courts Act 1919, have no binding legal force. As with the inquiry report of Lord Scarman on the *Grunwick* affair, they must rely on persuasion (the company there rejected the recommendations).

Two other aspects of ACAS's work may be noticed. First, in cases alleging lack of consultation on redundancies or breach of the floor of statutory employment protection rights, ACAS has a built-in conciliation function (EPCA s. 133). In particular, large numbers of unfair dismissal cases are settled in this way, avoiding a tribunal hearing. Such a settlement bars further litigation. In 1985 ACAS settled 45 per cent of its 43,000 cases. Secondly, in 1975 it was given the task of issuing Codes of Practice; these do not create offences but give advice to employers and unions and, rather like the Highway Code, are to be considered by tribunals or the CAC (EPA s. 6). The tripartite nature of ACAS and its practice of consultation on drafts give its codes considerable prestige (there are codes on time off, disclosure of information and disciplinary procedures). The Secretary of State now also has power to issue a code, after consultation with ACAS, that is admissible in any *court*, tribunal or the CAC (EA 1980 s. 3); but these codes (on picketing and the closed shop) are much more controversial documents.

We may note in this context the Central Arbitration Committee (CAC; a tripartite, separate body), which stands ready (as its forerunners, the Industrial Arbitration Board and before that the 'Industrial Court', did) to provide arbitration at the parties' request. It also has a few special jurisdictions in which its awards are binding (we have met one in discussing the disclosure of information: p. 289; see too on equal pay p. 492). But generally the CAC aims 'at resolving the problems (not merely applying a rule)', as its 1983 report says. It is a tripartite body, of which the independent chairman and his deputies have shown a resilient determination not to become legalistic, an aim not always shared by High Court judges, who have overturned its decisions (as in the *BTP* case on 'recognition': p. 285; or the *Hy-Mac* decision on equal pay: p. 492).

Here the law does not try to regulate industrial relations by judgments or orders, imprisonment or 'sequestration' of assets. Its primary aim is to provide machinery, its purpose to seek agreement. The ACAS success rate is measured by the disputes that are not litigated but settled wherever possible through the parties' own agreed procedures. ACAS in 1984 noted the difference between legal adjudication and its voluntary arbitration processes. In the former the parties are often strangers or those whose relationship has broken down. In arbitration this is rarely the case: 'an arbitrator has to remember that the parties have to live with and build on his award'.

In 'individual' disputes, such as unfair dismissal, ACAS conciliators play a major role. In the first ten years of its life ACAS received 434,000 complaints of breach of individual employment rights of which 39 per cent were settled in conciliation, 24 per cent withdrawn and 36 per cent referred to the tribunals. In 1985, 48 per cent of cases were settled. In pressing for an agreed settlement ACAS is playing a positive role. But it has been suggested that it should not take a more 'committed' stance than it has for fear of losing the benefits of this 'invisible stage' in the legal process.[72] ACAS continues to express the voluntarist principles of negotiated agreement, if necessary of 'fudged' agreement, as against the sharp swing of the judicial axe. Its lights still burn brightly, while those of many compulsory arbitration courts are dim (such as the French *cour supérieur d'arbitrage*).[73] The habitual use of the law to underpin such work from 1896 to 1975 shows that not all legislation is of the same type in industrial relations. Indeed, it is a pity that ACAS itself puts its report for 1984 in a framework of 'a considerable increase in the quantity of law' in the last decade. The statutory provisions on which it and its functions rest are different in quality from the legislation of the 1980s, and even from the individual floor of employment protection laws that it helps to administer. Law that creates such machinery is modest law, come to facilitate rather than to regulate industrial relations, preferring to pursue its policies with the patience of Job rather than the magisterial hubris of injunction.

Workers' rights to organize

Whatever other encouragement the law gives to collective bargaining, it is a generally accepted part of most labour law systems that there must be some protection for trade union activity at the place of work. There must, for example, be some protection against discrimination or dismissal by an employer who picks on shop stewards or union members. This is fundamental, as ILO Convention 98 makes clear. British law establishes no general 'right to associate'; but in 1975 Parliament tried to give some such protection to individual employees in respect of (1) time off work and (2) trade union membership or activity. This legislation attempted to support the edifice of collective bargaining by edging towards a minimal 'right to associate' constructed 'out of the bricks of certain "individual" employment rights'.[74] Rights were given to individual workers for trade union purposes in order to support and extend its influence. How far this has met with success may be questionable. In any event, these rights are *not* a collective 'right to organize'. They are rights of which the aim is to support trade union activity through the medium of the individual worker's rights. The judges, as we shall see, have therefore interpreted them narrowly, sometimes ignoring the collective purposes behind the individual form.

The question also arises in a British multi-union situation: which union is to be supported? The recognized unions or all unions? The inter-union TUC machinery that helps to solve this problem is considered in Chapter 9. Here we note that whereas rights to time off apply to workers in *recognized* unions only, rights to take part in union activities at work at 'an appropriate time' extend to all those in any independent union.

(1) *Time off work for union activities.* This is afforded in two ways. The employer must permit an employee who is a member of an independent *and* recognized trade union time off that is reasonable in the circumstances without pay to take part in union activity (now EPCA s. 28). This does not include activities that 'consist of industrial action', whether it is lawful or unlawful (s. 28 (2)). The ACAS Code of Practice (1978) on time off states that 'employers and unions should reach agreements . . . appropriate to their own situations'. But the courts have begun to set their own limits upon what is 'reasonable'. Where an employee was given twelve weeks' leave a year for union duties, he was refused ten days' more leave, even if unpaid, to prepare a union magazine, because the tribunal found this to be an unreasonable request.

The second provision deals with shop stewards of such unions. The number of shop stewards in manufacturing industry, along with stewards in services and the public sector, grew by a third to about 300,000 between Donovan and the end of the 1970s. Many of these were 'full-time' stewards or conveners, many in stewards' 'combine' committees, some engaged in 'multi-employer' meetings, whilst still remaining employees.[75] Although their numbers appear to have declined, stewards are important in bargaining, as channels of communication to workers and to other union 'officials' (the legal definition covers both stewards and officials employed by the union: TULRA s. 30), in grievances and discipline disputes, explaining subjects to new recruits, and representing their members.

The ACAS code suggests time off for all these activities. The Act gives the steward a right to time off *with* pay, subject to a reasonable extent and conditions, (a) to carry out his duties as an official concerned with industrial relations between the employer (and an associated employer) and the employees, or (b) to undergo training in industrial relations approved by his union or the TUC, a rare appearance of the TUC in labour legislation (EPCA s. 27). In 1980 the EAT decided that an ASTMS course on job security was 'too wide and general' to be directly related to a senior shop steward's duties (it was 'designed' for officials with wider responsibilities, and dealt with 'import controls' and other policies 'from a union point of view'). Nor was it reasonable for him to expect release when he could not show it would assist him in bargaining with the company about redundancy (though he could have unpaid time off as an employee).[76] Time off to take part in a strike or other industrial action is not included; but where the steward is not engaged in it, though his members are, the code suggests that the 'normal arrangements for time off with pay' should apply. Complaints are taken to a tribunal, which can make an award of compensation, the amount 'just and equitable' in the light of any loss, of non-payment of wages, and of the 'employer's default' (s. 30).

Clearly much is left to the courts' appreciation of reasonableness and of 'industrial relations duties'. Take *Beal*, one of seven stewards who represented union members in one of the 'groups' into which the employer's negotiating machinery was divided. The union set up a national body, to exchange information and plan policy, among stewards in all groups. The employer refused to pay them when they attended a national meeting; the Court of Appeal disagreed. 'Industrial relations' are not limited to collective bargaining, and this was a method of enabling them to perform those duties. Stewards could not, though, 'dress up' an activity to look like such a duty; there must be an industrial relations matter and 'policy' formulation in mind rather than a mere exchange of views. When the case came to the EAT again, it appeared to accept the possibility suggested by the judges earlier that, for such a national meeting, the court might 'apportion' the time (and pay): allocating so much to entitlement under the Act, the rest to unpaid leave (because this portion of a meeting was a mere exchange of views).[77]

But the Court of Appeal treated the issue of reasonableness as separate in the case of eleven stewards in a bakery firm who wished to go to such a meeting. Their attendance could fall within the Act; they could attend the meeting but would not be *paid*, because the tribunal did not regard this as 'reasonable' if all eleven went at the same time. Moreover, when *Ashley*, an AUEW convener, obtained permission to go to similar meetings, and was refused his proper pay as a steward, the EAT upheld a tribunal that had found the meetings not to be 'required' by the union and the 'advisory' function to be too 'remote from actual negotiations' (even though it helped to make union strategy).[78] This brings the tribunals into the thick of union affairs and hardly seems to accord with the spirit of the code. The courts have also expressed an understandable desire to see time off arranged by voluntary agreement; but where there is such a procedure, they have penalized stewards who asked for time off under the statute rather than go through the procedure. In 1986 the Government proposed restricting rights to paid time off to matters within the 'scope of recognition' (fixed by the employer).

If the employee is a union *safety representative* (p. 422) he has further rights to time off (Safety Representatives Regulations No. 500, 1977, and Code of Practice 'Time Off for Training Safety Representatives'). The regulations give the representative a right to take time off with pay as is necessary to perform his functions and to undergo such training as may be necessary having regard to the code. No approval by the union or the TUC is here required for the course of training. One representative's union wanted him to attend a safety training course at a technical college. But the employer's training officer drew up a course and insisted on that. The tribunal was entitled to consider the virtues and vices of the employer's own course; but once it found that the 'trade union aspect' was not fully covered it could not decide it was 'adequate'. The fact that the union would not co-operate in that course was irrelevant; but the college course might be necessary on some aspects.[79] It is obvious that the two critical elements in a training course are what is in the syllabus and who pays.

(2) On *trade union membership and activity* the statute offers protection, first, in regard to dismissal; secondly, against discrimination by the employer at work, 'action short of dismissal'.

Dismissal is automatically unfair if the principal reason was that the employee was, or proposed to become, a member or had taken or proposed to take part (at an appropriate time) in the activities of an independent trade union (EPCA s. 58 (1) (a), (b)). Naturally the union need not here be recognized by the employer. The right is the individual right of a worker to join forces collectively with his colleagues. Nor does his claim for unfair dismissal here require any qualifying period of service (as in ordinary cases of unfair dismissal: p. 235). If a worker is selected for redundancy on any improper trade union ground, his dismissal is naturally unfair (s. 59 (a)). The rights arise at the moment of hiring. Since a claim by a worker with short service, therefore, raises a question of jurisdiction, the judges have placed the onus of proving *this* reason upon the employee (though where some other reason for dismissal is raised concerning unfairness the burden remains on the employer).[80]

The activity must be carried on at an 'appropriate time', which means either outside working hours or with the employer's express or implied consent during these hours (s. 58 (2)). The employer must, it seems, accept trade union activity on the premises when workers would normally be there, using facilities reasonably.[81] It remains true, however, that a 'trade union dismissal' is very difficult to prove. The employer may be able easily to find other valid, or allegedly valid, reasons. Government estimates are that of the 2,257 complaints made of dismissal on trade union grounds in 1979 to 1982 only 106 (less than 5 per cent) were ultimately upheld by a tribunal, far less than the percentage for 'ordinary' unfair dismissal cases. It is true that a worker who manages to prove such a claim is entitled to increased compensation (a minimum basic award in 1986 of £2,200, and a minimum 'special' award of £11,000 if he claims reinstatement, subject to reduction for fault), but these remedies are much more relevant to the non-unionists for whom they were introduced (p. 369).

As so often outside sex or racial discrimination (p. 462), there is no protection against discrimination in the *hiring* of militant trade unionists. One delegate at a union conference in 1985 said he had worked for only two years out of the last twenty because he was blacked. The Economic League has maintained a 'Research (Screening of Labour) Department'. The writer has been present when managers have compared notes about information that can be obtained before hiring from the 'local police Red squad'. This is a serious and much ignored problem (p. 455). *Beyer*, a militant trade unionist, gave a false name for fear of being on such a list and was hired. Shortly afterwards, through management's 'intelligence system', he was discovered and dismissed. He was validly dismissed by reason of the misrepresentation; but the EAT found also that the dismissal could not refer to his taking part in trade union activities in that employment; his 'stormy career' lay in the past.[82] This finding seems to ignore the fact that the Act also protects a worker where the reason is that he 'proposes to take part' in such activities (E P C A s. 58 (1) (b)); but it may be that Beyer was not given time even to do that.

The courts have found it difficult to understand, though, just what these activities are. It is perhaps surprising that no code was issued to help the judiciary in the matter. Early decisions proved that such action as recruiting members, albeit (indeed particularly when) secret from management, is included in such 'activities'; so is a dismissal by reason of complaint to an unrecognized union about the unsafe state of the plant, since the object is 'to discourage employers from penalizing participation in activities of a fairly varied kind'. The words 'trade union' are not 'adjectival; what is being looked for are the activities of a trade union'.[83] But *Mr Chant* was dismissed for acting as spokesman and organizing a petition among his colleagues against machinery that was highly unsafe (he was sacked for 'incapability'), and Mr *Drew* was dismissed for repeatedly complaining about safety and for following what he thought was a union 'go-slow' directive on other matters (he was sacked for 'industrial action'). Neither of them was found to be dismissed for 'trade union activity'.[84] The E A T astonishingly noted that Chant (who had in the normal way recruited for the union at the time) had not sent 'a communication from the union . . . he was not a shop steward'.

Equally unfortunate was the Newmarket trainer's case in 1977. After a return to work from an official strike that lasted twelve weeks, five out of the six employees were dismissed. The trainer said they were redundant – an unfair selection, the workers called it. The E A T, whilst agreeing that an employer could not 'cast into outer darkness' a worker who dared to go on strike, saw no reason to doubt the tribunal's decision that this employer had considered predominantly the 'passions that had been aroused during the strike' and possible abuse, violence or friction between the ex-strikers and other workers; this was a fair basis of selection, because it went to the 'morale and efficiency of the undertaking'.[85] The right to 'propose' to engage in trade union activities hangs on a slender thread when outer darkness is so close for those with a record.

This is a very odd way to interpret a statute designed to protect union activity at work and provide a more secure base for bargaining. In *Carrington* v. *Therm-A-Stor Ltd*[86] the Court of Appeal went one step further. The defendants were a non-union firm until four workers (including one of the four complainants) tried 'to introduce' the TGWU into the factory, recruiting some sixty of the seventy employees. The union asked for recognition. Quick on the draw, management told the chargehands to 'select twenty workers for dismissal'; it was left to them to choose. The firm pleaded 'redundancy'; but the tribunal 'had no difficulty' in concluding that these dismissals were executed, rather like hostages, as a reaction to the union's recognition demand by reason of management's anti-union bias. Yet the Court of Appeal, disagreeing with the E A T, rejected the idea that the dismissals were by reason of union activity or membership. The 'reason' was the chargehands' selection. No 'individual's' membership or activities were impugned. The Court of Appeal was full of 'regret'. The union had a 'justifiable grievance'. So did the workers. Though 'tempted' to give a remedy for this 'indefensible reaction', Donaldson M R could not do so.

In other areas the courts have granted injunctions on more slender grounds than those plaintiffs had presented, as where they see trade union defendants who, they say, are ready to procure a breach, not of a contract, but *if* a contract is made (p. 593). *Carrington's* case was parallel: one where the employer set out to terrorize workers by these dismissals *if* they proposed to indulge in trade union membership and the normal activity of supporting a claim for recognition. But the House of Lords would not grant leave for a final appeal. Such interpretations of employment rights in the hands of individualist common lawyers can remove the keystone from attempts to build out of them a collective 'right to associate'. Of course, the activities of an individual worker may have many facets, as in the case of *Mrs Francis* who publicly criticized her union for not supporting equal pay, which she and her colleagues were demanding. When she was reprimanded, she claimed this was sex discrimination as well as a penalty by reason of her A U E W activities. The E A T accepted that it was not sex discrimination but was by reason of union activity. There had been a meeting of a 'defined group' of workers, not a formal branch meeting; but 'discussion of matters with which an independent trade union is concerned' was enough, 'getting together as union members'.[87] This reasoning is superior to that in *Chant*.

If there is a dismissal for that reason, compensation is 'an inadequate remedy', as Donaldson P. said in 1973. Indeed, why should the dismissal take effect at all, leaving the union members to chase a tribunal?

Parliament partially accepted this logic when it offered such a worker 'interim relief'. If in a union dismissal case the tribunal, at an initial hearing, on a complaint within seven days of the dismissal, decides that the worker is likely to succeed in proving a union dismissal at the full hearing, it may order the continuance of the employment pay and benefits until that hearing (EPCA s. 77, 78). There is a further condition; the worker must produce a 'certificate' signed by an 'authorized' union official affirming reasonable grounds for believing this is so. The tribunals appear to apply this remedy narrowly, especially on proof of the 'likely' final result and even of the official's 'authority' (in 1983 a bank employee failed because he failed to prove the 'actual or implied authority' of the official who had 'averred' his authority and signed the certificate). Interim relief, keeping the worker in his job until a full hearing, is a sensible idea and should be extended. Why should the worker bear the burden until full trial? The remedy was extended in 1982 to one other type of case, where the need for a certificate from a union official is deleted – the dismissal of non-unionists, to which we come later (p. 369).

Action short of dismissal ('ASD') by the employer is also disallowed where it is taken against the worker 'as an individual . . . for the purpose of preventing or deterring him' from being a member or seeking to join an independent union or taking part in its activities (at an appropriate time), or penalizing him for doing so (EPCA s. 23 (1) (a), (b)). We have already met an example in the reprimand administered to Mrs Francis. After complaint to a tribunal (within three months) the remedy is compensation to the worker, not as a 'quasi-fine' on the employer but to recompense him for his loss, including frustration in his wish to be a union member (EPCA ss. 24, 26).

There is a surprising number of ASD cases reported in the tribunals, covering refusal to promote, demotion, transfers to different jobs (in one case with fewer tips) and adverse reports.[88] Normally – and especially after *Carrington* – the individual worker will not be able to build out of the employer's refusal of recognition to his union a case of ASD against him. The employer must show what was the purpose of the ASD; and no account is taken, as in unfair dismissal cases, of industrial pressure contributing to it (s. 25). The prohibition applies to any independent union, not only those recognized. This could have important consequences. For example, in 1979 an employer was held to have infringed the Act where he refused to allow a representative of a worker's union to act for him over a grievance, even though a TUC disputes committee had decided it should expel him so that he could join the appropriate union. When the Post Office reserved scarce car-parking permits for officials of recognized unions and refused one to a member of an unrecognized union, the EAT held it could have 'penalized' him illegally, paying little heed to the argument advanced (and victorious in *Carrington's* case) that it had not taken action 'against an individual'.[89]

The judges have been rather more liberal here in deciding the extent to which an employer must not 'penalize' workers in their use of his premises. A fireman whose union was not recognized by the employers was threatened with disciplinary action if he attended a union meeting in the social club on the premises after working hours; such a meeting was a reasonable use of the premises in the eyes of the tribunal in 1979 (relying on precedents under the 1971 Act); so the threat was unlawful, though no compensation was awarded. ASD, the EAT held where employees had been disciplined for meetings at Heathrow Airport, runs from the time the worker knows it is being taken against him.[90]

The common law and union activity

It is perhaps useful to reflect the common law in the glass of these statutory rights. The latter are imperfect and narrow enough, not sufficient as yet to contribute much to any legal 'right to associate'. But Parliament had to be called in to go even this far. One may legitimately wonder why. Judges have developed 'implied terms' in the employment contract to introduce various rights, rights for the employer in requiring co-operation or for the non-unionist over fair treatment by the employer in distributing overtime work; suggesting 'a fair day's pay for a fair day's work'; Lord Denning even said 'a right to work' (as a non-unionist).[91] Lords Scarman and Denning have said that the common law (like Art. 11 of the European Convention on Human Rights) does 'recognize and protect the right of association', in a case involving a splinter union.[92] What has stopped the same judges extending the modern employer's duty of fidelity – the duty to be 'good and considerate to his servant', as Lord Denning put it – to embrace an obligation to respect his employee's right to organize with his fellows without penalization? Or at least, a right to do so without random victimization, as in *Carrington*? What has stopped them is the pervasive individualism of the common law, its unshakable belief in the reality of apparent market relationships and the accompanying ideology. This is why we find it to be the natural ally of 'free market' policies in the 1980s (Chapters 8 and 10). The common law concepts also underlie the total absence of statutory control over discriminatory refusal to hire for trade union reasons. Curiously, too, this characteristic has played a part in its century-long flirtation with the supreme collective institution, the collective agreement, to which we now come.

Collective agreements

'In this country collective agreements are not legally binding contracts,' said the Donovan Report. This referred to the first of the two possible functions of a collective agreement. The first is the *contractual function*. It may be, and in many countries is, a contract between those who made it (unions and employers). At the same time, it may have a *normative function*, ensuring that the code of conditions or rules agreed in it (the norms) is applied to the 'individual employment relationship'.[93] These two functions must never be confused. Whether the agreement is a 'contract' between union and employer is a separate issue from whether the agreement's terms have been incorporated into the individual employee's contract. Some systems of law make such incorporation automatic; ours does not. The individual employment contract must be the magnet that attracts to itself the metal of the collective agreement.

Legal enforceability of collective agreements

It is astonishing but true that for a century the legal character of the collective agreement was uncertain in Britain. Particular problems prevented some agreements being legally enforceable under the law of contract: the terms might be too vague, for example; or only 'aspirations' (e.g. clauses 'emphasizing the value of consultation'); or sometimes the parties were not easily cognizable by the law. But these problems could be cured by drafting. One curious statute prohibited 'direct enforcement' of contracts between 'one trade union and another'

(TUA 1871 s. 4 (4): see p. 523). This prevented some agreements being enforceable because many employers' associations once fell within the definition of trade union (they no longer do: p. 718). But this section was repealed in 1971, and it never applied to 'company' agreements (between a union and one company). Few lawyers seem ever to have given thought to this issue, however; they were concerned with the individual 'contract of service', and the books on master and servant before 1969 scarcely mentioned collective agreements at all. Even where special difficulties did not arise (as in a clearly drafted company agreement with a union) scarcely any legal actions had been brought to enforce a collective agreement as such.

The *Ford* case and TINALEA

In the 1960s the legal enforcement of collective agreements became a national obsession; but what does 'enforcing' a collective agreement mean? The union is unlikely to sue in the High Court if the employer fails to pay workers the agreed wage. What is invariably at issue is whether the employer can enforce against the union, by legal as well as economic means, the agreed procedures, commonly the 'peace' obligation not to strike, at least until a disputes procedure is exhausted. Such agreements are, as Lord Pearson observed in 1956, 'sacrosanct' but usually by way of 'moral obligation' in British industry. In February 1969, however, the *Ford Motor Co.*[94] did bring a High Court action alleging breach of contract by two unions that had allegedly supported members' strike action in breach of agreed procedures. Ford workers had refused to accept agreements made by a joint negotiating committee. But against them Ford could obtain no injunction (p. 142: TULRA s. 16), and damages would be slender (p. 213). So it sued the unions on the collective agreements. The initial injunctions were granted as *ex parte* 'interlocutory' injunctions (i.e. without hearing the defendants) on a Thursday, ordering the unions to call off the action. The unions could not be heard until Monday to challenge the orders. These interim legal remedies are theoretically given to maintain the status quo until full trial. We return to them in Chapter 8.

The High Court decided that the unions were not liable because the collective agreements were not intended to be legally enforceable contracts. The parties had said nothing on the point; but the court argued that as experienced negotiators ('in the top rank') the union and management representatives must have intended to accept the 'climate of opinion voiced and evidenced by the extra-judicial authorities'. To this Kahn-Freund had signally contributed. As a Continental lawyer, he had at first in the 1940s assumed collective agreements to be 'contracts'; but later research led him to the view that the British agreement was not normally legally binding because the parties did not *intend* it to be. Nothing else fitted the facts. Without an intention to create legal obligations there is no contract, only 'an unenforceable gentleman's agreement'. This is the reason most British collective agreements are not in law 'contracts' enforceable in the courts. In most other countries they are, though it is important to distinguish countries in which the enforceability of agreements has practical importance (as in Sweden and West Germany) from others where it is of much less moment (Italy and France).

The British practice of making collective agreements that are not 'contracts' is all part of collective *laissez-faire*. The Donovan Report agreed with this analysis. Collective agreements are not binding contracts,

not because the law says they are not contracts. . . . It is due to the intention of the parties themselves . . . without both parties intending to be legally bound there can be no contract in the legal sense.

If they chose, the parties could state the opposite, as in the case of boot and shoe industry agreements from 1898 onwards that were made under a trust deed under seal, the strongest evidence of intent to create legal rights and duties. But there was no evidence put to the court from Ford to displace its agreements' presumptive status as 'gentlemen's agreements'. The agreements created social rights, not legal rights, at the level of employer and unions. That characteristic is deeply rooted in the structure of our system of industrial relations. The non-judicial writings (accepted as admissible in evidence over the objection of Ford's counsel) greatly swayed the judge.[95] But they displeased those who wished to use court injunctions against the unions. Indeed, some lawyers were intent upon attacking the thread of logic that held the *Ford* judgment together. The judgment was significantly not taken to appeal, and before further attempts could be made to overturn it in the courts the Industrial Relations Act intervened in 1971.

That Act enacted that written collective agreements were presumed to be intended to be legally binding *unless* the parties declared otherwise. The unions were given a policing role; they were liable, if they failed to take all reasonably practicable steps to prevent all members from contravening such agreements, whether their action had official union support or not. Subsequent research showed that almost every collective agreement made between 1971 and 1974 contained a standard 'TINALEA' clause ('this is not a legally enforceable agreement' – some shop stewards had TINALEA rubber stamps made, ready for use at the end of the negotiation, usually without objection by the management). So this part of the Act became a dead letter.[96] In 1974 TULRA restored the traditional presumption. Now a collective agreement is presumed

not to have been intended by the parties to be a legally enforceable contract unless [it] is in writing and contains a provision which (however expressed) states that the parties intend that [it] shall be a legally enforceable contract [s. 18 (1)].

The 1974 Act was a remarkable event for Kahn-Freund: he had researched the issue in the 1940s, proposed the solution ('no *intention* to make legally enforceable agreements') in the 1950s, propounded it as a member of the Donovan Commission in 1968, helped to convince the High Court in 1969, and argued against the attempt in the 1971 Act to impose the opposite presumption of legal enforceability; on its repeal, he saw Parliament enact that solution as law in 1974. There is 'no contract at all . . . merely an arrangement', to be enforced not through the courts but 'by other means . . . [as is] not unusual in English industrial relations'.[97] To provide otherwise would entail a profound alteration in the character of British collective agreements and collective bargaining. Overseas groups that invest in Britain do sometimes import different 'US-style' agreements, written in more legalistic terms and sometimes negotiated by lawyers; but these are a small minority. Moreover, the advantages are not all one way. In 1985, for example, Oliver LJ said that it followed from the 1974 Act 'that any recognition of the trade union representative or shop steward can be withdrawn' by the employer under the normal collective agreement.

Less is heard today of the demand to make collective agreements legally enforceable. Even the Government Green Paper in 1981 accepted that the imposition of legal enforceability would reverse 'the long-established principle of law' allowing the parties to choose, and could easily be evaded by those determined to do so (by making only oral, informal arrangements, for example). So 'without an established basis of consent' such a change, it thought, would not work.[98] Donovan too had concluded, with two dissentients, that unless bargaining structures were changed it would be 'futile and unjust' to subject workers to legal sanctions for breach of collective agreements. Even in wartime penal measures against workers had failed, such as in the famous prosecution of striking Kent miners in 1942 when the minister settled the dispute by negotiating inside a Kent gaol. The Labour Government proposed a modest exception to Donovan when *In Place of Strife* (1969) suggested powers of government intervention, including 'cooling-off' orders for breach of agreed procedures. In the 1980s very different methods were used to extend legal sanctions over strikes and collective bargaining in the courts (Chapters 7, 8, 9), challenging Donovan's concept of integrated reform, even its concept of 'law and order': 'In industrial relations, "law and order" can be created only by adequate collective bargaining arrangements.'

There have been other rare occasions on which employers have threatened to sue to enforce a procedure, and in 1985 the mining unions were reported to have begun an action to enforce the 'review' procedure ignored by the NCB before closing a pit. But none have resulted in judgments of general moment.

Exceptional cases for collective agreements

There are a few situations where the law plays a more prominent role. We have seen that even an 'implied' collective agreement, inferred from conduct or union acquiescence, can directly affect individual rights, as in the case of the seamen selected for redundancy (p. 249). If there is a dispute about enforceability, the legal definition of 'collective agreement' (any agreement or arrangement between a union and employer relating to an industrial matter that can be the subject of a 'trade dispute' – TULRA s. 30 (1): p. 557) can be decisive for the applicability of the presumption of non-enforceability in s. 18.[99] Where the Minister's agreement is sought for an Order exempting certain agreements from the mandatory floor of rights because the voluntary arrangements are better, conditions are laid down to which the agreements must comply (including power for tribunals to determine disputes: p. 232).[100] Also, as against his employer, the rights of an employee inventor who is a member of a union may be governed by a collective agreement (within the 1974 definition) so long as it exists at the time the invention is made, to the exclusion of the statutory scheme (Patents Act 1977 s. 40 (3), (6).

EEC law. Other adjustments have had to be made to meet EEC law, often fashioned against concepts of very different collective bargaining structures in other member states. The TUPE Regulations 1981, for example, not only 'transfer' to the transferee of an undertaking 'recognition' of a union, which he can withdraw; they enact that a collective agreement passes to the transferee with the undertaking and the employees' contracts, together with any acts done under it and orders made in respect of it (Reg. 6). Once again a normal, non-enforceable collective agreement can be renounced by the transferee; but the regulations have more effect at the level of the individual employee's contract since such renunciation cannot automatically change or terminate that (p. 333).

More difficult have been the issues raised by EEC requirements on equal pay and sex discrimination. From the time of its becoming effective in 1975, the Equal Pay Act 1970 provided a mechanism by which clauses in collective agreements can be scrutinized by the CAC to determine what amendments are needed to remove pay inequality between men and women (p. 492). In this case 'collective agreement' meant any agreement 'as to terms and conditions of employment' between employers and 'organizations of employees' (Eq. PA s. 3 (5)).

The UK Government has been held by the ECJ to stand in violation of the Equal Treatment Directive (76/207), which bans direct or indirect discriminatory treatment in employment and training, requiring that offending provisions in collective agreements, contracts or rules of undertakings or professions 'shall be or may be declared void or may be amended'. The British argument was that making judicial orders to amend non-enforceable collective agreements is like 'beating the air'. Contracts promoting or enshrining unlawful sex discrimination are invalidated by SDA s. 77. The Directive of 1976 goes beyond equal pay to include all discrimination and demands that anyone aggrieved must have a remedy. The ECJ held that British legislation is inadequate (even though it already invalidates all discriminatory employment contracts) by not containing 'corresponding provision regarding . . . non-binding collective agreements' because they do 'have important *de facto* consequences for the employment relationships'. (Workers, said the Advocate General to the court, 'in most cases have no legal training'.) Appropriate means must be found whereby they 'may be rendered inoperative, eliminated or amended'.[101]

Logic did not seem to demand this step in pursuit of the wholly admirable aim of destroying sex discrimination. The nature of British bargaining and agreements suggests that, rather than inventing judicial powers over non-binding agreements, the law should urgently meet the standards of the Directive (and better) by adopting stronger sanctions against employers, unions, workers or others who practise, or plan to practise, discrimination. The search for legal powers to control non-binding collective agreements, prompted by an inadequate understanding of British industrial relations, could be chimerical and might even stimulate unnecessary resistance from unions and employers.

Nevertheless the Government was obliged to obey the ECJ judgment. The Sex Discrimination Bill of 1986 aimed to apply SDA s. 77 to collective agreements as well as to an employer's works rules and to rules of trade unions, employers' associations and professional bodies. Under s. 77, a term requiring or furthering sex discrimination (direct or, it seems, indirect) is 'void' except where the contract is discriminatory against a party to it, in which case the term is 'unenforceable' against that party. In this case such a party and any other 'person interested' in the contract can apply to the court – here the County court – to have the term modified or removed, when all 'persons affected' must be given a chance to appear. This is not likely to occur under collective agreements where the 'parties' are the employer and trade union. (It is indeed to be hoped that the County court procedure would not apply to a collective agreement; for then thousands of workers 'affected' would need to be invited to come and address the court.) But it might be used by a woman worker against the employer's works rules, or by some other person interested to challenge them in her interest. Meanwhile, then, the term in the collective agreement is 'void'. At this point one might have expected the Bill to extend the role of the CAC, an expert tripartite body to which, we shall see (p. 492), the Secretary of State or a party can refer a collective agreement alleged to infringe the equal pay legislation. But the 1986 Bill sought to do the exact opposite, namely to repeal the CAC jurisdiction and amalgamate treatment of equal pay provisions with sex discrimination. This seems to leave no judicial procedure for *pronouncing* the collective agreement 'void', for the County court procedure of s. 77 seems not to apply as the agreement is not discriminatory against a 'party' to it. The Secretary of State, in particular, is left with no role. His role was said under the Equal Pay Act 1970 to be a guarantee against collusive agreements for unequal pay between unions and employers. Was this, it was asked when the Bill was published, the necessary effect on CAC and Minister alike of policies of deregulation?

The Bill was therefore expected in 1986 to require some amendment in Parliament if it was to meet the demands of the ECJ for a law under which collective agreements meting out unequal treatment to men and women employees could be pronounced void. The loss of the CAC procedure was particularly noted as unfortunate. The attempt to tie unequal pay and other discrimination into one bundle, moreover, appeared not to have succeeded. More profoundly, the whole exercise illustrated the paucity of understanding about the relationship between law and industrial culture on the part of the ECJ and the Advocate General in the case, who seemed to consider workers' knowledge about the law a more relevant consideration than the realities of trade union organization. The tone of the ECJ proceedings evinces impatience with this odd system where it is 'not customary' to intend to make collective agreements legally binding, and there is little doubt of the desire in such circles to see Britain fall into line with practice in other countries. The Sex Discrimination Bill illustrated the difficulty and the unreality of fitting British industrial practice to off-the-peg trappings of other systems.

Public law. The breach of collective agreements has received attention in a different context, as we saw in Chapter 2. When a County Council made reductions in services by dismissing catering staff in breach of national collective agreements, their trade union, *NUPE*, sought to challenge their action by way of judicial review.[102] But the Court of Appeal saw no evidence that the council had acted so unreasonably that no reasonable authority could have taken the decisions that it had made. Donaldson MR said there was a 'short answer' to proposals about how it should have reacted to Government expenditure reduction: 'it would involve departing from a very much larger number of nationally agreed collective agreements'. The decision really goes no further than that the council was obliged to take the agreement into account in its deliberations, which it had done. The same circumstances gave rise to complaints of unfair dismissal by the dinner-ladies concerned. The Court of Appeal accepted the tribunal's decision that the dismissals were unreasonable in this case and therefore unfair; but it insisted that dismissals effected to achieve economies in the face of public sector cuts, even if they were in breach of national conditions agreed collectively, could still amount to a 'substantial reason' within EPCA s. 57 (1) (b). The tribunal must balance this as one of the factors in determining whether the dismissals were reasonable within s. 57 (3) (p. 244).

Neither of these decisions affects the legal status of collective agreements, though the status accorded to them in the unfair dismissal cases seems unnecessarily slender. Neither decision would necessarily have been different if the collective agreements had been legally enforceable contracts between the union and the local authorities. On the other hand, judicial review may in the near future have a more immediate impact. If in the *Liverpool* case,[103] the council had founded its claim to cancel the pay of certain teachers on the 'day of action' upon a clause in a collective agreement with the NUT giving it the right to do so, there seems nothing in the judgment to suggest that the result would be different. Whatever the legal status of the agreement, the court would presumably still have quashed the decision, which it saw as one that no reasonable council could make.

Collective agreements and the worker's employment contract

It is sometimes suggested that, although the collective agreement is not normally a contract between the 'collective parties', it may be intended to be an enforceable contract between the employer and each union member represented by the union officials. The member could not enforce a contract made between two other persons. That is the principle of 'privity of contract'. But if one of them is his *agent*, then he can sue as principal on the agreement. This would produce the startling result that the worker could sue for the agreed wage at once on the collective agreement, rather than under his personal contract. Is the union an agent of the worker in the legal sense? This is contrary to the normal understanding. Indeed, the EAT said in 1979: 'Collective arrangements are not by themselves of any legal significance unless and until they are translated into contractual relationships between employer and employee.'

There are many examples of this attitude. When a union consulted with the employer about a reorganization, it was held not to be the worker's 'agent to work out the details of any new contract'; and where an employee died after he had applied for voluntary redundancy and the union had agreed with management the date for such dismissals to take effect, the EAT refused to accept that communication to the union officials was made to them as his agents, because such 'agency' could not stem from the mere fact that he was a member of the union, only from evidence of a 'specific agency'.[104] Such cases turn largely on their facts; but they accord with the older decisions, for example one of 1924 where the Court of Appeal decided that an agreement made by a provincial union with a London union for reciprocal rights of membership was not one that could be enforced by a member when he moved to London since he was a third party to the contract, the union not being his agent. Agency may be proved, as where officials of ACTT were treated by the court in 1962 as agents of three named members on whose behalf they tried to negotiate with an employer the settlement of a debt in a dispute that led to the 'blacking' of the employer. The importance of this approach is that it rejects the inference of agency from union membership as such, requiring it to be proved if alleged.

It would be strange if it were otherwise, for many puzzles would then arise. Collective bargaining involves negotiation, conclusion of agreements and administration of agreements. What would be the position of non-unionists in each of these three? What of union members who reject the collective deal? Is the extent of the 'authority' of union officials to be found in the union rules? How does a member withdraw his authority – must he resign? These questions remind us of the crucial fact that British unions do not normally bargain for their members only. Indeed, the law after 1980 may even make some such agreements illegal as 'action short of dismissal' by the employer (p. 368). A collective agreement usually covers a specific description of, or groups of, workers, union members and non-members alike. Only rarely will even statute treat the union members as the only beneficiaries of a union agreement (one such case is the Patents Act 1977: p. 187). Although some collective agreements speak of the union agreeing 'on behalf of its members', the very manner in which these informally worded agreements are concluded *and* administered proves that it is not 'agency' in the legal sense that is intended. It is different in a system, such as in the United States, where the law provides for 'bargaining units' in which, if it wins an election, a union becomes the 'bargaining agent' of all the workers concerned – a system that has numerous different problems of its own.

It is also important not to mistake an employer's offer negotiated with a union as anything to do with the problem of agency. *Edwards's* case in 1964[105] is sometimes so misdescribed. Officials of BALPA had negotiated new terms by which pilots who agreed to relinquish certain pension rights were entitled to receive payments from the employer. Even though they were described as *ex gratia* payments, a redundant pilot member of BALPA proved his contractual right to a payment, which the court saw as offered by the employer with intent to be bound. But he did not succeed by reason of the union being his agent. The negotiated terms were a 'standing offer' by the employer, which each pilot could accept or not, as he chose, and which before acceptance the employer could withdraw. The device of a 'standing offer' is attractive in some employment situations, as where a conditional notice to strike is given (p. 192); but tribunals sometimes use it in order to find that collectively agreed terms have been accepted by a worker's conduct, when they could properly and easily reach the same conclusion on other grounds.[106]

Lord Denning MR once said that in 'negotiating with employers' a union is in law acting 'on behalf of the men'. The case, *Chappell* v. *Times Newspapers Ltd*,[107] arose from a pay dispute between the NGA and the newspaper proprietors. The union had called out small groups of members so as to disrupt production of newspapers and in a press release said that it would continue to do so. The proprietors stated that, unless instructions to members were withdrawn, they would regard the members employed as having 'accepted instructions to infringe their personal contracts', thereby terminating their employment. This applied to *all* members. Two of them sought an injunction on the ground that they had done or said nothing whatever to break their employment contracts. We have seen that the court refused injunctions because they would not undertake to do nothing in future in breach of contract; they were not sufficiently 'ready and willing' to perform their contracts (p. 166). But in reaching this conclusion Lord Denning pressed his concept of the union acting 'on behalf of' members to the astonishing proposition that in regard to negotiating terms or taking industrial action

the members themselves must be taken to authorize whatever the union or its officials do on their behalf. . . . If the press release was issued by the union on behalf of *all* the men, each one of them must be taken to have authorised it, unless he disavowed it.

Lord Denning based his reasoning upon a decision by the Law Lords on a different problem, namely whether a union was liable under the Act of 1971 for shop stewards who instigated industrial action. That problem (as we saw: p. 54) they confronted by treating the 'authority' of the union (as a non-corporate body) as arising not from delegation 'from the top' (the NEC) but out of authority flowing 'from the bottom'.[108] We return later to the status of a union as a non-corporate body and to its vicarious liability for its 'agents' (pp. 530 and 707). But that analysis did not mean that *each member* was liable for the acts that were unlawful under the 1971 legislation. There was nothing in the decisions of the Law Lords to suggest that a union member who did not intend to follow a union call to take disruptive action could be hauled into court and forced to give an undertaking to that effect as the price of the continuance of the contract by which he earned his daily bread. The Court of Appeal turned the Law Lords' arguments upside down to achieve that result. The reasoning in *Chappell's* case, if generally applied, would disturb the sensible practice of not treating a union as the agent of its members unless evidence of a specific agency is adduced. The reasoning is out of accord with Donovan LJ's insistence in 1963 that the court would require clear proof that a union had the authority necessary to bind its members in law as an agent.[109]

Incorporation of the collective agreement

The customary way to secure the 'normative' function is not agency at all. It is to incorporate the terms of the collective agreement into the personal contract of employment of each worker. This is where most terms are meant to have effect: on hours, wages, sick-pay, holidays, redundancy, pensions. But the contract of employment is not compulsorily subject to those terms. Whereas in some countries the collective agreement has an *automatic* effect upon employment contracts, in

Britain it does not; this is the final reason why the 'agency' analysis must be wrong. Our law preserves the overriding authority of the individual contract of employment, perhaps at once the greatest strength and the greatest weakness of the system.

Express and implied terms

The collective agreement is, however, meant to affect the individual contracts; otherwise the elaborate structure of bargaining would have no legal effect at all. The need is for a mechanism to ensure that each employment contract attracts those terms to itself and embraces them. The best way is for the employment contract to incorporate the collective terms *expressly*. So in *NCB* v. *Galley*, 1958, the mining deputies' contracts stated that their wages were regulated by the 'national agreement for the time being in force' and the agreements subsidiary to it.[110] An express reference to the collective agreement must be clear (a reference to 'the going rate' was once held not to be enough). Sometimes a number of different documents will be incorporated, like the employer's works rules in the *ASLEF* case (p. 185); or 'points of guidance' that were 'incorporated' into a written agreement as 'binding on both parties' concerning the places where an 'outworker' electrician could be sent to work; or in another the rules of the Scottish JNC for the plumbing industry; or where the place to which a worker could be sent was regulated by the rules of the Civil Engineering Construction Conciliation Board.[111] The documents incorporated, like any other, must be properly interpreted. Where the employment terms were stated to be those set out in the national 'memorandum of agreement' between the EEF and CEU it was held to be *implicitly* envisaged in the memorandum (and therefore in the employment contract) that the worker was obliged to travel 'anywhere he was required as a steel erector', to give the contract business efficacy.[112]

Today the most useful vehicle for express incorporation is the written statement of particulars that the employer must give to the employee within thirteen weeks (EPCA s. 1: p. 136). As we have seen, the particulars may refer to any other documents, including collective agreements, and these may be varied from time to time so long as they are accessible to the worker and he is notified that changes may occur (EPCA ss. 2 (3), 4 (3)). Although these particulars are not the contract itself, but evidence of it, employers and workers tend to see them as the contract, and may therefore be surprised when the courts find or imply extensive further terms.[113] Well drafted particulars – with a clause making the employment 'on terms of the collective agreement as varied from time to time' – will allow for such variation, as in the *Galley* case; so, although the contract of employment must be arrived at individually between employer and employee, it may, as the EAT said in 1978, 'as a result of union agreement be varied or altered, perhaps on a national basis'.

Suppose, however, the worker's contract or particulars say nothing about collective agreements. Can the latter operate so as to bring an *implied term* into the contract, something that 'goes without saying' or that the parties to the contract look as though they meant to say even though they did not say so? The normal rules of the law of contract determine that nothing can be implied into a contract to affect any matter covered by a term expressly agreed. For example, a stonemason employed *expressly* at a lower rate than the collectively agreed district JNC rate failed in 1945 to recover the higher rate because he had explicitly agreed to take the lower rate in his contract. A clear personal contract of employment cannot be overridden by a collective arrangement, therefore, even if that is adopted through trade union machinery or by a ballot of workers (as where the majority of unions had agreed in a works committee to the switching of public holidays to different dates, but a personal guarantee had been given to certain workers that no switch would be made unless all the unions agreed).

Nevertheless we have seen courts manipulating implied terms in many areas of the contract of employment (Chapter 3). As early as 1858 we find master printers and compositors implicitly 'taken as bound' by the terms agreed for fifty years in a joint committee. In 1933 a mate's written contract had added to it by the court certain implied rights to shore-leave that were set out in the industry's National Maritime Board's Year Book: 'a perfectly familiar form of engagement which had been applied to him on many occasions before'. This is very close to the implication of 'customary' terms, such as the 'custom and practice in civil engineering' that gave the employer an implied right to send an engineer out of his office to work on site in 1972,[114] or the Lancashire weaver who was taken to accept employment 'on the same terms' as other Lancashire weavers (p. 175).

Kahn-Freund wrote that terms of collective agreements can 'normally' be assumed to be 'customary terms', 'tacitly embodied' in employment contracts as 'crystallized custom'. This can be a little dangerous. It is true that courts and tribunals have come more easily to infer, in the absence of evidence to the contrary, that workers covered by them are working under the terms of the relevant agreement covering the work-force, as in a 1978 case where three employees of the Ford Motor Company, belonging one each to the TGWU, GMWU and AUEW, had incorporated into their terms and conditions of employment the 'Blue Book' (*Agreements and Conditions of Employment of Hourly Paid Employees*, 1976 ed.). But there can be no tacit incorporation if there is obscurity about which terms of collective agreements apply and what they mean; nor if the judge decides that a truly solid custom, acted upon for many years, does not really represent the intention of both parties to create enforceable rights in the employment contract. The repetition of customary but gratuitous tips or bonuses is often given as an example. So too, *Mr Dudfield*, an industrial civil servant, thought he was getting a rise. The national joint council, to which his contractual documents referred, had agreed upon a new rate, and it was a long-standing practice for its collectively agreed wage rates to be paid. But the Government had imposed a 'pay pause', not by a statute, merely as a policy. The court found against Dudfield. Whatever the custom, the council's functions were in law 'purely consultative'. No implied term bound the Ministry to pay.[115]

The concept of 'crystallization' may also lead union workers astray. Craft practices at work tend to be well established and crystallized. Suppose a publisher takes on an experienced printer in his closed shop. He knows the union rules (which are themselves a contract among all union members) and knows the worker has observed them all his working life, like his other printers. Why should the later employment contract displace those rules and customs, or at any rate contain implied terms that cut across those crystallized customs? A subsequent contract made knowingly in breach of an earlier contract is unenforceable. It is true that union rules were not negotiated with the employers; but they may rank as custom in the trade – and in some trades have crystallized hard. Yet the courts have refused to bind the employer to the union's rules; and judges in 1979 rejected such ideas as 'quite untenable'. We recall that acquiescence (by a union) in a practice has been seen as contractual in redundancy cases (p. 250). And when a collective agreement permitted employers to call on safety-men during a strike, its terms were incorporated into the *union's* rules so as to prevent a disciplinary rule being applied to workers called on by the employers.[116] One must consider carefully whose 'custom' it is before adopting the crystallization test. It is not necessarily a safe guide.

Judges sometimes do use the same approach as that of Kahn-Freund without using exactly the same doctrine. In *Howman* v. *Blyth*,[117] for example, an employee who had never received any written particulars fell ill. When he applied for a determination of his rights as to sick-pay, a tribunal declared he was entitled to full pay whilst still employed. The EAT agreed he was entitled to sick-pay, but his contract did not make it clear for how long. The court was here free to imply a term as to duration; this should be a 'reasonable term'; and the best evidence of reasonableness was the 'normal practice' in the industry under its working rule agreement (whereby sick-pay for a limited period made up the difference between pay and State sickness benefit). But this is not quite the implication of 'crystallized custom'; the collective agreement is used as evidence of what is 'reasonable'. It would be open to a particular employer to show that circumstances at his works made 'reasonable' an implied term to pay less.

Five problems on incorporation

We must attend to five other problems in this crucial area. First, the problem of the *pendant* employment contract: what happens if an incorporated collective agreement comes to an end leaving the worker's contract to hang out alone? Suppose the employer, for example, resigns from an employers' federation, and his workers are employed on terms incorporated from an agreement between the federation and their union. It is clear that the employer cannot terminate or unilaterally vary the contracts of employment of his employees merely by giving notice to quit from the federation and the agreement, though such is the confusion about collective agreement and employment contracts that employers have tried to do so.[118] There must be some variation that binds the employees individually. *British Gas* employed workers on terms that stated 'incentive bonus scheme conditions will apply'. Later it issued particulars applying the provisions of the NJC agreement and relating bonuses to the scheme agreed by it. But it then gave notice (as it could do under the agreement) to terminate the collective scheme. The Court of Appeal held the individual terms of the workers' employment had not been affected, the same result as in *Gibbons's* case (p. 199).[119] Kerr LJ agreed that the bonus rates were variable 'collectively by agreement' in the NJC, and those variations would bind the workers individually; but this gave no right to the employer unilaterally to abrogate the bonus scheme for his workers.

The weakness of English law is at once apparent. If the employer drafted the terms of employment so that they stated (absolutely clearly) that the bonuses were payable 'while, and only while, the employer is a party of the NJC agreements', the courts might be compelled to reach a different result. Problems can also arise in the construction of such 'pendant' contracts. In *Burroughs's* case, workers' contracts referred to an EEF national agreement on guaranteed pay, and the employer's right to suspend it during strikes, in a 'federated establishment'. The employers resigned from the EEF; so literally the agreement could no longer apply. The Scottish courts put aside the literal interpretation and applied the clause as continuing in substance to bind both employees and the employer without any change.[120]

Secondly, the problem of bargaining *levels*. 'The level at which bargaining is conducted', ACAS suggested in 1983, 'has a fundamental impact on many aspects of industrial relations.' Suppose there is both plant-level bargaining *and* bargaining at a higher level, either in a company or a multi-employer structure. What is incorporated into the employment contract? In 1964 an ambulance driver, Mr Clift, sued his employers for alleged underpayments on the 'scheduled rates' for stand-by duties. There had been a local agreement in 1955 with his union that modified the rates, and the court decided he was entitled only to the lower rates. The judges' reasoning in such cases is not always clear. In *Loman and Henderson's* case, union officials had made a local agreement that provided for 'a 68-hour guaranteed week'. The national agreement guaranteed a 41-hour week. The employers argued that the contractual week was still 41 hours, and the local agreement was 'a gentleman's agreement for ironing out local difficulties'. The court accepted this argument in order to compute normal working hours, pointing out the difficulties that would arise if 'local legally-binding agreements were made departing from the National Agreement'. This reasoning fed on two errors: the national agreement was, almost certainly, equally a 'gentleman's agreement'; further, British industry, just a year after Donovan, was riddled with local agreements that 'departed from' agreements at a higher level.

The court did little better in the *Gascol* case,[121] where at national level the normal working week was 40 hours, but under a local agreement 54 hours. The court again rejected the local agreement because it was 'binding in honour only'. But there the national agreement did state that it took 'precedence'; and the written particulars prescribed a forty-hour week. Indeed, this problem should melt away in the face of well drafted particulars and agreements. Nothing stops the employment contract incorporating local agreements expressly, as in *Barrett*, or even impliedly, as in *Donelan*, where work-site bonus arrangements between *other* employers and unions were held to have been adopted by a subcontractor and his workers.[122]

Thirdly, however, greater difficulty has been introduced by the problem of confused *sources*. The fact that the collective agreement is not contractually binding does not conclude the issue whether incorporated terms are intended to be binding at the level of the individual contract. The court seems to have overlooked this principle in *Loman and Henderson*. In *Marley*, 1986, the EAT contradicted it.[123] The particulars of the employment contract of a supervisor expressly incorporated a personnel manual that included certain procedures for redundancy ('A25'), which were the terms of a collective agreement between the employer and the union of which Marley was a member. But when he tried to rely upon his 'A25' rights, the EAT held that they were unenforceable because of another clause stating: 'This agreement is binding in honour only and it is not intended to give rise to any legal obligation.' If this decision were correct, it would affect the very fundamentals of our labour law. Employment contracts regularly include binding terms that everyone knows are not binding at collective level. Popplewell J. accepted that the collective agreement 'was part of the engagement' of Marley, part of his employment contract. Moreover, he understood that the TINALEA clause was a hangover from the period of the 1971 Act, now merely confirmatory of the presumption in TULRA s. 18 (p. 321). But he then concluded that the 'A25' terms taken from the collective agreement were not 'intended' to be legally binding in the employment contract *because* they were made not legally binding between the union and the employer. So the clause took 'the whole of A25 out of the sphere of legal enforceability'. He regretted the decision – 'nothing but bad for industrial relations'. It is bad in law, too, and should be reversed by the Court of Appeal. The common intention of the union and the employer is not necessarily – and on this point, not usually – the same as the intention common to the employer and employee.

This type of confusion must be distinguished from the issue of interpretation. If a term of the collective agreement is incorporated into the employment contract with legal effect, it may still profit the worker nothing if, on its proper construction, the employer is entitled unilaterally to deprive him of its benefit. This was the employer's argument that failed in *British Gas*; but in *Cadoux's* case, 1986, it succeeded.[124] The worker claimed rights under a life assurance scheme. His employment contract incorporated national conditions and 'the Authorities' Rules as amended from time to time'. The employers, after consultation with the union, amended the rules unilaterally to introduce a scheme. But later they said they were withdrawing it. The court accepted that these terms were incorporated into the employment contracts, but held that the authorities could always 'alter their Rules at their own hand'. The worker could not therefore now enforce his rights under the scheme. The court relied on the fact that this was an employer's scheme, backed by consultations with the union, not a collective agreement. But, as Napier says, it surely makes no difference that the worker's entitlement 'arose following consultation and not agreement with the trade union'; and the 'legal enforceability of the source material is irrelevant'. Nevertheless, the words in Cadoux's employment could be construed to *mean* that these benefits were not just variable but wholly terminable by the employer at his discretion (an approach to interpretation inferior to that in *Burroughs* and *British Gas*). More generally, decisions such as *Marley* and *Cadoux* show the courts in 1986, both sides of the border, straining even further the basic principles of labour law for the better protection of management prerogative. Until now, as we saw also in *Gibbons*, the courts have been slow to permit the employer to escape from obligations to the employee once he has assumed them merely by exercising his right to withdraw from a scheme negotiated with the union.

Fourthly, some judges have indulged in *separation*, hiving off some obligations as separate contracts. Where firemen did extra part-time duties (under old arrangements made with the union) these were seen as performed under separate contracts, additional to their contracts of employment and terminable on reasonable notice by the employer. This enabled the courts to avoid all the difficulties about 'incorporation of collective agreements in individual contracts'. There were effectively two contracts. The same point was argued in cases arising out of the teachers' strikes in 1985 (p. 631). It is difficult to know when judges will accept this. The EAT has refused to see supplementary pay arrangements 'as creating a collateral or supplementary agreement' for control inspectors, and in 1985 this was upheld on appeal.[125]

In 1983 Pain J., in *Bond* v. *CAV Ltd*,[126] indulged an ingenious spree of separation. Setters did part of their work for a bonus on machines allocated on a 'sign-up procedure' agreed collectively. The terms were 'imported' into their employment contracts. New conditions were 'regularly negotiated' (the case is a good illustration of 'dynamic' British bargaining; 'in a piece-rate situation,' said the manager 'no one really agrees to anything but there is tacit agreement'). There were national, factory, departmental and 'individual' plant agreements. Inefficiencies led to variations of the higher agreements on the shop floor in an '*ad hoc* arrangement', with additional payments to make up piece-rate bonuses. The setters now refused in a dispute to work either 'sign-up' or '*ad hoc*' machines, but otherwise did their normal work. The court held they were entitled to their normal pay, without bonuses. The '*ad hoc*' and 'sign-up' agreements were 'supplemental agreements', which could be terminated on reasonable notice. We have seen that if this approach is followed it could be of profound importance to shop-floor industrial action (p. 197); for the rungs on the ladder of 'industrial action' trodden both by workers and managers are so often, on one side, a withdrawal of co-operation or of extra duties and, on the other, a 'tightening up' of work discipline, both well short of a full strike or lock-out. In such action it may be difficult to know just when a breach of an employment contract has occurred. The law of contract has long been familiar with 'collateral contracts', even about the same subject-matter as the main contract; but it will be interesting to see how far this common-sense solution of separation will be employed by judges in multi-level plant arrangements, slicing them up into separate contracts so that no problem of 'incorporation' arises. Furthermore, now that so much of the law of industrial conflict depends upon such torts as inducing a breach of an employment contract (Chapter 8), attention must be given to the question whether all such supplementary agreements are always contracts 'of employment'. For example, if they are not, breach of their terms does not give rise to 'secondary' strike action (p. 597).

Fifthly, there is the problem of *appropriateness*. Are all the collective terms appropriate for incorporation into the individual contract of employment? Some of them will be only a code agreed between the collective parties, not, as the Privy Council once put it, 'adapted . . . for incorporation with a service agreement'. For example, it is not easy to incorporate into any individual worker's contract such clauses as: 'Each trade union party to this agreement may have shop stewards'; or 'The proportion borne by the aggregate number of boys to the aggregate number of men [in certain boot departments] shall not exceed one boy to every four (or fractional part of four) men.' These are matters between the unions and the employers. Other clauses could be incorporated only with some semantic juggling; whilst many substantive clauses are more readily imported: 'Secretaries of [railway] Line Committees shall be allowed free travel [on their duties].' With minimal ingenuity this could be expressed as a term in the contract of an employee-secretary. Indeed, the designation of terms as 'collective' in character, and unfit to create individual rights, is often, as we see in the cases, a matter more of policy than of semantics.

One difficulty is that judges have not offered any test for what is 'appropriate'. It is not a metaphysical question; to some extent, it turns on the interpretation of the clause to be incorporated. Given that the individual contract incorporates terms of the collective agreement, it may itself point to some clauses rather than others. If it does so, *it* must prevail. The Court of Appeal has, for example, interpreted an arbitration clause in the Burnham agreements on teachers' pay as designed to prevent disputes at collective level, not binding on individuals. But the meaning of the collective clause may also need to be elucidated. In *Camden Exhibition Ltd* v. *Lynott*,[127] shop stewards were said to have induced breaches in workers' contracts by organizing an overtime ban under a clause of the NJC rules stating that overtime to ensure due performance of the employer's contracts 'shall not be subject to restriction but may be worked by mutual agreement and direct arrangement between the employer and the operatives concerned'. Wages, hours and

holiday terms were 'in accordance with' the NJC rules. Russell LJ
thought the rule on overtime was an agreement between the union side
and the employers; there was to be no agreed ceiling on overtime hours;
each man would arrange his own. But Lord Denning thought it went
further, to mean that no 'restriction' would be placed by the union on
overtime, *nor* would the workers 'officially or unofficially impose a
collective embargo'. The second rendering makes the rule much more
appropriate for incorporation. Sometimes general legal policy is involved, as in a case of 1983 where the terms of a conciliation procedure
were 'implied' into the employment contract of a news editor but not so
as to make a disputes procedure prohibit him from bringing a legal
action for defamation in the courts; this was, as counsel said,
'inappropriate for incorporation'.

Incorporation and procedural clauses

We are closer now to another central issue: are 'procedural' clauses
inappropriate for incorporation? There does not seem to be any such
overall principle. Procedures that deal with individual employees' rights
can be appropriate; many cases illustrate the incorporation of collectively negotiated procedures for calculating individual salary or for
setting out disciplinary or grievance procedures.[128] It is noteworthy that
Parliament has directed employers to set out matters relating to discipline and grievances in the note accompanying a worker's written
particulars in a way that must envisage grievance and disciplinary
procedures being incorporated into employment contracts (EPCA s. 1
(4)). On the other hand, we saw that the CAC refused to interpret its
power to award new 'terms and conditions' in regard to obligatory
disclosure and the (now repealed) recognition procedure as including
power to insert procedural rights into the individual employment contract, despite the wide statutory words (EPA ss. 19–21, and the
repealed s. 16). But there the CAC was adopting the approach that the
judges had directed its predecessor to take under Order 1376 of 1951
(the IDT: p. 344). An award of 'recognized terms and conditions' under
that Order became individual terms of employment; but the Court of
Appeal in 1955 rejected the idea that procedural clauses in agreements
could do so; they were 'only machinery for settling a difference' between
the collective parties. A decade later this decision, Bercusson noted,

'overwhelmed the better judgment of the Industrial Court'.[129] The CAC merely followed this precedent for interpretation of the same statutory formula.

There has been more doubt about procedures that are essentially concerned with workers' collective action, either by way of the traditional formula, 'There will be no strikes or lock-out without exhausting the disputes procedure'; or, as it is put in one modern agreement: 'A fundamental understanding is that during any phase of this new procedure all normal working practices are observed and maintained.'[130] Some agreements, like the 'strike-free' agreements being negotiated in some enterprises, seem in practice to ban strikes altogether during their life. We saw, too, that in the *Partington* case the courts appeared to regard safety-men as having an individual duty, and right, to *break* a strike, based on a collective agreement between employer and union. But Kahn-Freund took the view that to incorporate a no-strike clause was a 'very artificial and strained' interpretation, that 'peace clauses' create 'collective, not individual, obligations', and that such a clause was accepted by the courts in *Rookes* v. *Barnard*[131] only by reason of an 'admission by the defendants' at trial. What the defendants admitted at trial, though, was a term of their employment contracts, which referred to the 'no-strike' clause that stated: 'The employer . . . and the employees . . . undertake that no lock-out or strike shall take place.'

Parliament certainly thinks that such clauses can be incorporated, because in 1974 it prohibited the incorporation of any term in a collective agreement that restricts 'the right of workers to engage in a strike or industrial action' unless the employment contract expressly or impliedly incorporates it and unless the term is in writing, is in an agreement made by an independent union, is accessible to the workers, *and* itself states that the term may be incorporated (TULRA s. 18 (4)). By these tests the view of Russell LJ in the *Lynott* case would prevail today. How far s. 18 (4) changed reality is another question; for, as we have seen (p. 193), industrial action will normally constitute a breach of the employment contract anyway, irrespective of any collective agreement. The collective agreement might 'restrict' these rights even further, e.g. in regard to notice of termination of employment contracts in a strike situation. It is not clear whether some modern 'strike-free' agreements mean to go that far. The effect of these agreements would be a central issue if British law ever tried to fashion a workable doctrine of 'suspension' of employment contracts as the base for a 'right' to strike. Even today, though, the issue can be important. In 1984 Hertsmere District Council wished to introduce a 'no-strike' clause directly into the employment contracts of its computer workers, fearful of 'disruption' in processing rents, rates and the like, in return for a pay premium. The union, NALGO, stated that it would disregard the provision. In 1986 the Electrical Contractors' Association said that it regarded its closed discipline agreement with the EETPU as enforceable through its workers' individual contracts.

Apart from the exact wording of such clauses, the question of the incorporation of procedural clauses generally, including no-strike clauses, involves questions of policy. It is doubtful, for example, that judges would accede to the argument, yet to be tested in the courts, that a clause that bans strikes *until* procedure is exhausted impliedly recognizes workers' rights to 'suspend' their contracts of employment by industrial action *after* going through procedure. Yet the argument is as good as many others that succeed. Take *British Leyland* v. *McQuilken*.[132] The employer had made an agreement with the union about the discontinuation of a department. All employees would be interviewed to establish a list of those who opted either for retraining *or* redundancy. Managerial policy changed. McQuilken, an employee, was told he could choose between transfer to another place or, possibly, retraining; and he was not given any interview. He claimed a redundancy payment, and the tribunal saw the refusal to implement the agreement as a constructive dismissal. The EAT rejected that conclusion:

the terms of the agreement between the [employer] and the unions did not alter the respondent's individual contract of employment. That agreement was a long-term plan, dealing with policy rather than the rights of individual employees.

Such decisions suggest that democratic union procedures might involve putting draft agreements on redundancy made at establishment level to meetings of members, perhaps with a ballot, in order that the more pertinacious among them may demand that the agreement spell out expressly such minimum procedural rights for individual workers. A clear statement in the collective agreement that its benefits are to be enjoyed by each worker could take the edge off judicial policy. But, then, if it were still possible for a court to 'separate' some obligations, it might be that certain of the collectively agreed terms – at one level or other of agreement – would be held to be 'appropriate' either to the main employment contract or to the collateral agreement. The complexities that can arise here are also an opportunity for judicial creativity. The test of policy will be whether the courts permit, as Pain J. did not in *Bond*, management discretion to prevail over the arrangements bargained at the various levels.

It is uncertain whether this will be the judges' direction. The Court of Appeal was prepared in 1985 to hold that the right of a hospital shop steward to 'facilities', and to negotiate under agreements in a Whitley staff agreement, might be incorporated into his employment contract. Indeed, it was difficult to hold otherwise where regulations declared that his 'conditions of service' should be those negotiated in the Whitley procedures and approved (as these had been) by the Secretary of State.[133] There was no hint that 'conditions of service' could not include procedural rights, though the questions were left open whether this could include his rights 'as a trade union representative' as well as his rights 'as an employee', and whether 'collective rights' could enter the contract of employment. But the employers had suspended him, after a sit-in, to try to stop the closure of the hospital, and then dismissed him. For the court this was the end of his rights. The right to enter the premises as a shop steward 'could only stem from the contract of service'. This is yet another example of the inevitable logic of the common law, which begins with the property rights of the master and individualizes the rights of workers. The worker acquired a right to enter only to the extent that the employer granted him a licence to do so, and that could be revoked – and had been, by the termination of his employment contract.

It would require great strength and perception by union negotiators to achieve a collective clause clear enough to persuade the courts that its operation through a contract of employment ousted the employer's residual rights to keep the worker off the premises. On the other hand, the House of Lords has been prepared to accept (without deciding the point) that a collective agreement, which required consultation between the union and the employer before the workers (television technicians) were asked to work on certain programmes, could give the workers a right to refuse where no consultation had taken place.[134] The consequence would have been that the union officials in threatening that the work would be 'blacked' would have committed no tort, because the workers would commit no breach of contract in refusing to work on the programme. Such a clause is surely enforceable via the workers' contracts. There is nothing inappropriate about incorporating it merely because it relates to a procedure for consultation.

Statutory props to the system

Parliament has intervened in the traditional British system to support, rather than to regulate, collective bargaining. Kahn-Freund declared in 1954, and again in 1968:

All statutory methods of fixing wages and other conditions of employment are by the law itself considered as a second best. All British labour legislation is, in a sense, a gloss or footnote to collective bargaining.[135]

Donovan added: 'Parliament has long been committed to the view that the best means of settling such questions is collective bargaining.' There have been very few attempts to make collective agreements legally binding, as in a highly exceptional Act of 1934 on the cotton industry long since repealed. Dockers' remuneration and conditions must be, by Orders of 1967 and 1976, 'in accordance with the national or local agreements for the time being in force'; but this is part of the statutory scheme that replaced casual labour by status under the Act of 1946. Other statutes may support bargaining *machinery* but do not control its outcome (as with the teachers' Burnham machinery). The 'primacy' of voluntary collective bargaining is illustrated too by the ministerial power to take certain agreements out of parts of the employment protection legislation (p. 231) or to give legal force to supplementary schemes in the area of redundancy or social security, such as the Redundant Mineworkers (Payments Scheme) Orders, which 'influenced the broad shape' of other special schemes in shipbuilding and steel.[136]

But Parliament has often sought to provide by law support or 'props' for collective bargaining. The character of these 'auxiliary laws', as Kahn-Freund called them, must never be mistaken for regulatory legislation. Here, too, wartime experience has been important.

Unilateral arbitration

Under pressure of war it was felt necessary both in 1915 and again in 1940 to introduce forms of compulsory arbitration as part of a regulation by law of the labour market. The munitions tribunals of the First World War left little overt trace;[137] wage regulation ended in 1919. But Order 1305 of 1940 continued until 1951. It rendered strikes and lock-outs illegal and imposed compulsory arbitration in trade disputes, with penal sanctions. Prosecutions were brought during the war (including that against 4,000 Kent miners: p. 29) but not subsequently in peacetime until an abortive attempt a decade later to prosecute the leaders of unofficial strikes in London's gas plants and docks. Kahn-Freund pointed out that the drastic wartime powers were tolerated in peacetime so long as they were not used. Even so, it is in retrospect remarkable that the trade unions' support for the Labour Government extended to their accepting the illegality of strikes, even if they benefited in other ways from the arbitration system. But as soon as it was used for prosecutions, the wartime Order was revoked in 1951 and replaced by Order 1376. This did not revive the illegality of industrial disputes; but it did continue certain features of compulsory arbitration, the Minister having power, after attempting a voluntary settlement, to refer an 'issue' or a 'dispute' to a tripartite tribunal. Its awards were made compulsory terms of the relevant employment contracts (the modern usage of this 'sanction' is in direct descent from that lineage: p. 290). Up to its abolition in 1958 this tribunal made nearly 1,300 awards, and its procedures were popular among those trade unionists who were, or felt, unable to use strikes or to whom recognition was refused by employers.[138]

The next Government revoked the Order in 1958 under pressure from employers (who even then had begun to complain about trade union power), putting nothing in its place for some months until it enacted the Terms and Conditions of Employment Act 1959. This Act permitted the 'Industrial Court' (forerunner of the C A C) to 'extend' terms of voluntary collective agreements to employers who were not parties to them, by enforcing 'recognized terms and conditions' (that is, employment terms that had been collectively established in a trade, industry or district by organizations of employers and of workers *representing* a substantial proportion of the employers and workers involved). Awards operated as compulsory conditions in the employment contracts of workers employed by an employer who was observing terms that were less favourable than the 'recognized terms'. By this means, a less than prodigal son could be called back into the collective fold. The days of undercutting could be numbered; for an employers' association could report a claim against the black-sheep employer, as well as a trade union. In the eight years of this jurisdiction, 106 separate awards were made; the union succeeded in 59. In many the machinery was effectively used against employers who refused to recognize a union.[139]

The E P A 1975, Schedule 11, continued this jurisdiction (now given to the C A C) but grafted on to it a jurisdiction to make an award, when there were no 'recognized' terms to enforce, terms not less favourable than the 'general level' observed for comparable workers by employers in the trade or industry whose circumstances were similar to the employer in question. By this route of unilateral arbitration the union could obtain terms of employment for workers who were engaged on terms below the generally accepted minimum level, the employment terms being looked at as a whole (Figure 5). Where a national or district

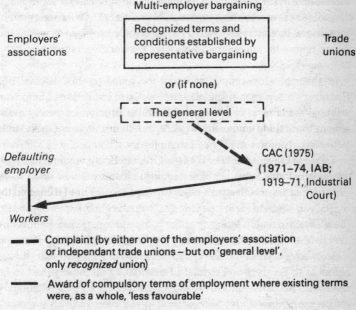

Figure 5. The machinery of E P A 1975, Schedule 11 (repealed 1980)

representative agreement set minimum terms, the general level claim was inappropriate; only if there were no such terms could the 'general level' be used, by the low paid for example, to reach at least the floor of wages in their trade.

The courts again played a restrictive role in their interpretation of this jurisdiction.[140] It is true that this machinery was also used by the unions, white-collar unions particularly, in some periods as a gateway to evade Government incomes policy, as is mentioned below. The C A C heard a modest number of cases, 1,939 references from 1975 to 1980 when the jurisdiction was repealed. It kept close contact with A C A S conciliators to pursue the primary aim, getting parties to settle cases voluntarily through their own machinery. It saw its arbitration work 'not as a panacea but [as] an important tool in the current framework of industrial relations'. It was a prop to the bargaining system.

When it operated on the sectors where 'federated' firms made multi-employer representative agreements and enforced the 'going rate', it reached workers unable to attain by bargaining even the minimum established by agreements. The addition of the 'general level' claim expanded that mechanism. Indeed, 228 awards (117,000 workers) were for 'general level' in 1979, and 47 (21,243) for 'recognized terms'. Some 90 per cent of the successful claims were for workers earning below the average wage.[141]

In 1980 the Government repealed the schedule (E A 1980 s. 19). Except for a few months in 1958, this was the first time our industrial relations system had enjoyed no unilateral arbitration machinery available to low-paid workers with weak, or no, bargaining machinery since 1940. The claim was made by perhaps the most competent of Ministers in charge of the Bill in 1980: 'We want to get back to a voluntary system, and we think that Schedule 11 is standing in the way there.' What was a prop to the eyes of collective *laissez-faire* had become, for the new policy of 1980, an obstacle to the operation of 'voluntary' market forces. As for the problem of undercutting by unfair competition, the same philosophy demanded logically that firms, and workers, should stand, or fall, on their own feet. What the C A C had described as a support that 'should continue to be given to established negotiating machinery' had to be removed. Research, however, suggested that its alleged inflationary effects were 'limited'. It was most used by the 'comparatively low paid', and it was at the time of its removal not only contributing to the solution of disputes but also achieving its principal objective, 'helping the low paid'.[142] Observers quickly suggested that the repeal of Schedule 11 began the 'impetus towards non-unionisation as a desirable state of affairs'.[143]

Fair wages

In response to the 'evils of sweating', the House of Commons in 1891 resolved that those who made contracts with Government should observe currently 'accepted' rates for their workers. The up-to-date version was adopted in the Fair Wages Resolution 1946, and local authorities followed suit with parallel clauses. Kahn-Freund regarded this as 'one of the cornerstones of British labour law'. A more sceptical assessment called it 'a last resort for workers unable to obtain fair wages through their own efforts'.[144]

The Fair Wages Resolution (FWR) was not positive 'law'. But as an instruction by the House of Commons, it ensured that the Executive obliged contractors to meet fair standards or lose their public contracts, in order to protect workers who are vulnerable through lack of trade union organization. Employment conditions should be *either* not less favourable than those established in the district by representative employers' organizations and trade unions in the trade or industry *or*, in the absence of such conditions, not less favourable than the 'general level' of conditions observed by employers whose general circumstances were similar in that trade or industry (the origin of the similar 'general level' provision in the 1975 Act). Once again collective bargaining (multi-employer bargaining) is taken for granted as the norm in the first limb of the formula; in effect, the minimum going rate was the fair rate. The second limb supports it by not allowing workers without bargaining structures to fall below a minimum. This reformulated the standard of 1891: currently accepted conditions came to be measured by a minimum 'general' or a bargained level. Disputes under the Resolution were referred by the Minister to the C A C (formerly to the 'Industrial Court') after attempts at conciliation. The High Court again interpreted its jurisdiction narrowly, insisting that the 'general level' jurisdiction could not be utilized if there were established recognized terms under the other limb, even if those were not the effective minimum rates in practice and had long been left behind by rates established on top of them by bargaining. The decision illustrated the manner in which the Fair Wages Resolution became entangled with incomes policy, since it was the 'Pay Board' that argued for the narrow construction.[145] A worker could not of course sue his employer for 'fair wages' until an award inserted a term into his employment contract.

In 1979 success was achieved by unions in 171 out of 242 awards (60,523 workers); many of the disputed cases turned on whether an employer fell into a particular 'industry' or not.[146] In 1983 only twenty-six references were received; but the Resolution was useful, the CAC had said in 1982, in getting more general industrial problems 'cured'. The pattern showed that references had been used to deal with pay 'anomalies' during incomes policy periods before 1980, but the CAC had been vigilant against 'collusive' cases. 'Incomes policy' was not the only mainspring of FWR cases. Awards continued into 1983 and 1984 on existing references such as one applying a local authority fair wages clause reducing hours and increasing pay by £4 a week for street-sweepers employed on 'privatized' work in Milton Keynes.[147]

In 1982 the Government gave one year's notice that the Fair Wages Resolution was to be rescinded. The necessary resolution took effect from September 1983. The notice was required because of ILO Convention No. 94 of 1949, which requires public sector contracts to include a clause modelled on the pattern of the British fair wages arrangements. The Convention permits states to 'denounce' the Convention periodically; the first opportunity for the British Government to denounce on notice was in 1982, when it seized the chance. The reasons given were parallel to those on Schedule 11 of the EPA, especially the stimulation of competition and the deregulation of the segmented labour market, 'to create jobs'. Awards in 1982 had largely gone to the low paid (in both absolute and relative terms), typically to workers earning £85 per week or less; and in a 1984 award the CAC decided that clauses in existing contracts continued, despite the rescission of the Resolution itself (a neat parallel to the pendant terms of employment contracts when the employer withdraws from a collective agreement).

It cannot be pretended that either Schedule 11 or the FWR presented a 'solution' to the general problems of the low paid, still less an 'adequate minimum wages policy'; that requires a broader perspective.[148] But the FWR never had such ambitions. It was, if not a corner-stone, at least a prop for the British structure of collective bargaining. Without it the structure is weaker, as workers soon discovered. In 1984 the privatization of cleaning for the NHS led to 'a cartel' of cleaning companies imposing lower conditions (especially on fringe benefits or working hours, which were alleged to amount to cuts of up to 60 per cent for some workers). The disputes arose with contractors whose workers had previously been covered by the FWR.[149]

The fair wages principle was taken further in a few exceptional statutes, which made compliance with 'fair' standards the condition of a licence, subsidy or similar privilege in, for example, the film industry, sectors of transport, broadcasting and aviation. Those that, like the Public Passenger Vehicles Act 1981 (repeating a 1960 Act), demand operators pay wages not less favourable than those that would have to be observed under a contract which complied with 'any resolution of the House of Commons for the time being in force' on fair wages, are neutered by the repeal of the FWR in 1982. In some cases, as in broadcasting in 1984, this has been supplemented by an express repeal. For drivers of companies' (own) lorries a more complex scheme has existed. An Act of 1938 required their wages to be as favourable as established bargained rates in trades that were 'comparable' or the general level of workers outside road haulage in the district or under a minimum wage Order (other lorry drivers were covered by a Wages Council). A claim could be brought by either a worker or the union to the CAC; failure to observe an award was both a breach of contract by the employer and a criminal offence. The Act was repealed in 1980 (EA 1980 s. 19 (c)). The repeal was directly blamed for outbreaks of industrial action in 1984 when dockers turned away lorries of 'cowboy' firms who allegedly undercut by paying their drivers rates below those agreed in the haulage industry's agreement, which one report ascribed to 'cut-throat competition' in the industry.

The tenor of the times now favours maxima rather than minima for workers. The Local Government Act 1985 s. 51, for example, gives an 'advisory body' the function of advising the Secretary of State about the remuneration of staff (other than teachers) transferred from councils being abolished (the GLC and the six metropolitan councils) so that he can make Orders. But the advice is on whether increases in their salaries are *greater* than the body considers 'appropriate for that class of employees', in which case he can by order direct that they be paid at a lower rate and 'deem' their salary be that amount with retroactive effect.

The general policy, too, has been applied to bodies other than central Government that insert 'fair wages' clauses in contracts, notably local authorities (many for nearly a century), nationalized industries and health authorities. The latter were circularized by the DHSS that they should discontinue specifying minimum conditions as part of the drive to privatize their services competitively. The issue has also apparently been raised how far requirements on subcontractors are invalid by reason of 'restraint of trade' – the doctrine of the common law thought to be expelled from trade union law in 1871. Most local authorities provide for reference of disputes to arbitration; but some (e.g. the GLC, Sheffield and Bristol city councils) retain the right to pay workers of the contractor the difference that makes up a 'fair wage' and recover it from him if he is found to be in default, a valuable use of 'contract compliance'. The Department of the Environment recommended in 1983 that local authorities stop these practices and followed up by proposals for legislation to render void terms in contracts for certain services (e.g. street cleaning) that do not 'directly relate' to the performance of the contract *and* any performance by other subcontractors or suppliers. Such a general prohibition would go far beyond 'fair wages'. Many local authorities require even higher standards than statute imposes in respect of discrimination, the employment of local workers, training or the non-use of such exploited groups as homeworkers.[150]

Wages Councils

Britain does not have a legal minimum wage for all workers as some countries do. Wages by themselves will not tell the whole story; they must be placed in the setting not only of fringe benefits, but of social security payments and other measures for maintaining income. The decline in the real level of some social security benefits since the 1970s has not been met by other measures on income maintenance. Rates of wages also mean little without considering taxation. Since 1978 taxation has tended to become more retrogressive. A worker, married with two children, paid as a percentage of his earnings in 1978 (and in 1985): with half-average earnings, 2.5 (5.0); on average earnings, 34.6 (37.3); on five times average earnings, 48.8 (42.6); and on twenty times average earnings, 74.3 (55.6). For millions of low-paid workers, social security benefits are as important as the wage, especially when caught in the 'poverty trap' (when benefits are lost by small increases in wages). The position of families in this position became relatively worse as against more prosperous groups in the 1980s.[151]

Even so, the wage or salary is for most workers their central sustenance. A study by Cambridge economists has presented strong social and economic reasons for an effective legal minimum wage; they concluded that 'without extensive unionization minimum wage control requires legal backing'.[152] Low-paid workers have tended to be less well unionized than others; and the Low Pay Unit calculated in 1985 that, of full-time workers, one in six men and one in two women earned less than the Council of Europe 'decency threshold'.

It was the plight of the 'sweated trades' that caused Parliament in 1909 to pass an Act to protect groups of exploited workers by a legally enforced minimum wage because they were unable to help themselves. Some experiments with minima in particular industries tended to be swallowed up by effective collective bargaining, as with the minimum wage Act for coal-miners in 1912, removed finally as irrelevant from the statute book in 1950. The 1909 measure was to have greater legal effect. Churchill introduced the Bill, speaking of such workers having 'no organisation, no parity of bargaining'; the good employer was 'undercut by the bad', and the bad 'undercut by the worst'. From this origin arose the minimum wage legislation for protected groups. By the 1980s there was an Agricultural Wages Board under Acts of 1948 and (Scotland) 1949, and the Wages Councils Act 1979 had consolidated earlier measures. Since the First World War the Minister has, after the necessary inquiries and consultations, been able to set up a tripartite Wages Council by Order for an industry.

He may act on his own initiative or on an application through ACAS of a Joint Industrial Council or of the unions and employers' organization together, so long as 'no adequate machinery exists' for voluntary collective bargaining. The Wages Council, with a tripartite structure itself, is – or should be – both a replacement and an encouragement for collective bargaining, the union and employer members being joined by independent third parties. Voting on a council is by 'sides', the independents abstaining if the union and employer sides disagree. In its modern form a council can (after publishing a draft to enable representations to be made) make Orders fixing terms and conditions of employment for the workers concerned after exhausting the careful procedures laid down for it. Such Orders automatically become terms in employment contracts of the workers in the industry (a worker can recover up to two years' back-pay); but failure to pay the minimum *wage* is also a crime for which the employer can be prosecuted (Wages Councils Act 1979 ss. 14, 15). After 1975 the Minister has been able to establish a Statutory Joint Industrial Council (SJIC), which is, in effect, a council without the independent members and with the power to go to ACAS to break any deadlock. This was intended to be a half-way house, further encouraging collective bargaining.

The character of Wages Councils also draws attention to their long having been regarded as props to the collective bargaining system. Since 1953 forty councils have been abolished. As with their creation, requests may come from a Joint Industrial Council or jointly from unions or employer; the ground must be that the council is no longer necessary to maintain a reasonable standard of pay. But here the union alone can make such a request, a change originating in various criticisms made by the Donovan Report, which saw some councils as obstructions to the growth of voluntary bargaining. In fact, trade unions have been the usual applicants when they concluded that a council was hindering collective bargaining. The Secretary of State may refer the issue to ACAS (which has many other advisory roles in the structure). In recommending an SJIC for the toy manufacturing industry in 1976, ACAS described its objective as 'fostering the conditions for a transition to voluntary collective bargaining'. In one sense, the first objective of any Wages Council should be to commit suicide.

Although criticisms have been made of Wages Councils (by the Donovan Report among others) most of those made before 1980 were within the frame of the system's own objectives: the protection of minimum conditions, the protection of employers against undercutting and the fostering of collective bargaining. One vexed problem has been enforcement. In 1985 there were twenty-six Wages Councils covering some 2.7 million workers in a wide range of industries, mainly catering, clothing manufacture, retailing and hairdressing. Agricultural workers have their separate board (with a minimum wage in 1985 of £89.90). Enforcement is mainly the responsibility of the Wages Inspectorate. It can both prosecute employers and claim arrears for underpaid workers in the 390,000 'establishments' covered outside agriculture. Some two-thirds of Wages Council workers are part-time; four-fifths are women; and about one-twentieth are under eighteen. Full-time adult rates in 1985 ranged, on Government figures, from £63 to £72 per week. In 1984 the Inspectorate found only about 6 per cent of workers inspected to be underpaid. Even so, it inspected the wages of only 184,000 workers in 27,000 establishments by visit. Underpayments were £2.4 million. The visiting Inspectorate now numbers only 120. Eight civil claims and two criminal prosecutions were launched. The inspectors naturally prefer persuasion to legal action; but this machinery for enforcement is manifestly inadequate. In 1978 there were 150 inspectors, 16 prosecutions, 16 civil actions and 32,000 establishments inspected.

In 1984, however, the Government raised different questions. The minimum rates for young workers were said to be too high. This 'may mean that there are fewer jobs available for the young'. It was claimed that the system of inspection placed undue 'burdens' on employers. We must 'free the labour market from any unnecessary and artificial restraints which may affect business performance, competitiveness and jobs'.

One difficulty facing abolition of the councils was I L O Convention No. 26, 1928, ratified by Britain with ninety-four other countries, from Uruguay to Fiji. This requires wage-fixing machinery where no other effective regulation controls 'exceptionally low wages'. Like other Conventions, however, it can be 'denounced' on giving notice. Britain's next chance was in 1985. The Government set out its proposals; either abolition or severe reform. 'Deregulation is desirable in principle. Pay is best settled between employers and employees in the light of their particular circumstances.'[153] The 'bureaucratic burdens' of Wages Councils caused 'inflexibility in the labour market'. Young workers should either be excluded altogether or allowed only a percentage of the minimum rate.

Critics saw little evidence that jobs would be created by the abolition of Wages Councils nor proof that market forces would produce a floor of wages acceptable in either economic or social terms. One said abolition would result, 'after five years, in the creation of just 8,000 jobs'.[154] The Government relied on Treasury studies that slower rises in pay would increase job opportunities and that minimum wages laws destroy jobs.[155] An official study that reported that the clothing industry council contributed to the loss of jobs over thirty years was matched in 1985 by the official study on retail sectors, which found 'no strong presumption' to that effect.[156] One study of the position, here and abroad, suggests that it provides little evidence for or against minimum wage legislation; the impact depends on 'how the labour market is believed to operate'.[157] Some employers, including the CBI, called for no more than 'reforms' (such as cutting out young workers). The Auld Committee (1984) on the Shops Act concluded that abolition would entail 'a strong likelihood of exploitation of some shopworkers'; so protection is needed more 'when jobs are hard to find'.

The Wages Bill 1986 aims to replace the 1979 Act, to exclude workers under twenty-one years of age and to restrict Wages Councils to Orders fixing minimum rates of wages. The exclusion of other terms (as to holidays, for example) is a severe limitation. The comparative evidence is that causal links between various types of minimum wage legislation and rates of unemployment are very uncertain.[158] Meanwhile, the other option chosen by many countries (a general, national minimum wage) still awaits adequate British investigation.[159] The experience of those countries with a basic minimum wage might well be studied afresh in any reshaping of labour law for the low paid. The contradictions of British policy in 1986 are illustrated by the proposed 'job-start' experiment in seven areas – 'to make lower paid jobs more attractive' – where a worker engaged after twelve months' unemployment is to be paid £20 weekly for six months, so long as the gross wage is less than £80 a week. This is a curious product of determination to keep 'wage' rates low and of desperation about the high rate of long-term unemployment. The partial deregulation of Wages Councils industries in 1986 may be a test case for these policies.

Incomes policy

There was one post-war development that might have changed the shape of labour law altogether, but did not. It can hardly be denied that

successive governments have through the post-war years been centrally concerned with the control of inflation . . . [and] until very recently been concerned to reconcile that goal with that of maintaining a high level of employment.

Davies and Freedland perceptively point out that for all the 'lip-service' paid to it by the Donovan Report (in which the problems of inflation and 'wage-push' were treated as somewhat 'marginal'), the Report's prescriptions were less significant to subsequent governments of both parties than 'anti-wage-inflation strategies'.[160] Donovan did recommend legislation imposing on *all* arbitrators a duty 'to take incomes policy into account'. None was passed. It also recognized, though, the problems involved in this formula when arbitrators gave no reasons for their awards. What Donovan faced, and rightly backed away from, was the prospect of eroding the confidence of employers and unions in voluntary arbitration.

From 1948 to 1979 recognizably similar 'incomes policies' were pursued by different governments to control growth of wages, often of prices, and sometimes of dividends, in order to resist inflation. All relied upon 'voluntary' means, such as the establishment of bodies like the National Board for Prices and Incomes. But in two periods, 1966–9 and 1972–4, first a Labour and then a Conservative Government enacted statutes to do the job by law. The precise policies were in many ways different, the Labour Government preferring the method of guidance from the NBPI, and of 'standstill' or 'pause', dams behind which the wage demands built up, whilst the Conservative Government's intervention rested more firmly on imposed norms through a Pay Board, though the results were not so different. The importance for labour law is that in both of these periods the State resorted to legal enactment of criminal offences to enforce the preferred strategy on incomes.

It is perhaps odd that in none of these developments were principles of labour law and arbitration taken over and harnessed to the Keynesian anti-inflation processes even when pay policy was statutory. Still less was the general structure of the law, with its 'voluntarist' bargaining principles, transmuted. This has been attempted in other countries – in Canada, for example, with 'compensation restraint' legislation on public employees.[161] Why did that not happen here?[162] Patterns of bargaining and of industrial action often irked the planners; but even the Industrial Relations Act 1971 did not, or could not, change them totally. Neither the pay restraint statute of 1966 nor even that of 1972 set out to restructure arbitration (the Act of 1896 and the Industrial Courts Act 1919 were not mentioned in either of them) or union or employer rights, let alone the bargaining patterns and legal structures around them. Even more significant, what labour law saw as exceptional areas of legal regulation (the 'props' to the bargaining system, like the Fair Wages Resolution) were largely accepted into and absorbed by incomes policy as justifiable norms. Almost invariably government came to accept as special cases awards under the unilateral arbitration machinery (the 1959 Act, forerunner to EPA 1975, Schedule 11), the 'fair wages' statutes like the Road Haulage Act 1938 and the Fair Wages Resolution, as exceptions to normal rules of the current incomes policy allowing lower-paid workers an exceptional rise. Later, 'orderly progress' towards equal pay for women was also accepted as a reason for an exceptional increase.[163] Indeed, the CAC itself in 1978, a later period of 'voluntary' incomes policy with many of the same exceptions, recognized that some cases were brought to it by the union and employer under the Fair Wages Resolution or Schedule 11, to avoid 'the impact of pay policy'.

To say that the arbitrators' job is to decide the parties' disputes is not to say that they do not consider, amongst other matters, the 'public interest'. On occasion this even appeared in their terms of reference ('taking account' of the White Paper *Prices and Incomes Standstill*, said the terms for a special Court of Inquiry in 1966). Arbitrators are there to solve disputes; but many, the CAC included and all those founded on 'regulated' arbitration, came to use the signposts of the labour law props like the Fair Wages Resolution to indicate what the public interest was.[164] The Orders of Wages Councils (which until 1975 were made by the Minister on the council's proposal) were not formally removed from statutory incomes policy norms; yet the transfer to them of power to make their *own* Orders without ministerial approval was enacted in 1975. The NBPI had in 1967 demanded a 'radical reform' of the Wages Council system so as to assist prices and incomes policy in monitoring protection of the low paid. Yet this did not happen. Instead, the 'gloss to collective bargaining' in labour law statutes broadly remained unchanged in shape and even took on in part a new function, a prop to exemption from incomes policy. So too, the terms of reference of ACAS between 1975 and 1979 could have subjected it to the immediate demands of pay policy in its conciliation work, but did not do so.

The statutes of 1966 and 1972 naturally invalidated employment contracts that went above the 'norm' or broke the 'standstill'. They also imposed criminal sanctions on any employer who paid above the permitted norm, and on unions or groups of workers who tried by industrial action to compel or influence him to do so.[165] But for established industrial relations and labour law policies – with their history of Master and Servant Acts, judicial creativity in conspiracy and other crimes and memories of wartime prosecutions like that of the Kent miners – such crimes were anathema. The influence of those traditional policies is easy to find even in the statutes on incomes policy. Any 'criminal or tortious liability for conspiracy or any other liability in tort' (and in 1972 liability for 'unfair industrial practices' under the 1971 Act) was expressly excluded. Indeed, in 1966 the Prices and Incomes Act genuflected to labour law by providing that any 'difference of opinion' between an employer and workers about the standstill or the obligatory pay policy restraint qualified as a trade dispute, thereby preserving freedom to lock out and strike on the issue (s. 17).

Kahn-Freund took it that his audience in 1967 would 'understand how important this was', in view of the 'checkered history of British law of trade disputes' because at the time it seemed obvious that not even anti-inflation policy should be permitted to drag labour relations back to such nineteenth-century doctrines as conspiracy. Others, like Clegg, saw great dangers to pluralist values and 'cherished principles of democratic thought' if we extended criminal sanctions.[166] What could the law do with employers who made agreements to pay the wage increase 'on the expiry of the standstill'? Or with workers who stopped work, not for wages above the norm, but to 'freeze our end of the bargain'? This is what some of them did.

The territory of labour law policy was in fact stoutly defended. Its net of relationships between unions and employers and between both and the Ministry of Labour (the role of which was then distinct from that of the Treasury) created, as it were, a magnetic field that repulsed, rather than attracted, those whose dominant aim was anti-wage-push-inflation. The Social Contract of 1975 to 1978 was a compact between these two fields of social force, expressed essentially between the unions and the Government.

By 1978 the Social Contract itself had disappointed those who wanted a more egalitarian policy, even though it too continued the customary exemptions for 'fair wages' awards, equal pay and other low-pay categories. But incomes policy did not invade collective bargaining to the extent that some expected.[167] Institutional changes in the structure of collective bargaining naturally occurred while incomes policy was in operation, especially from 1964 to 1974, but not in the direction that made the 'planning of incomes' any easier; for the spreading of work-place bargaining with the growth of shop stewards was 'given an important stimulus (if again, one which was not altogether intended) by the existence of incomes restraints'. Nor could the incomes planners ignore the alleged causative link between rises in prices and earnings and the ever more rapid union growth between 1969 and 1979.[168] Some of them saw union growth as antagonistic to their incomes policy. Never-theless, the EPA 1975 promoted the 'extension' of collective bargaining through ACAS; even the 1971 Act had stated its aim to 'promote' collective bargaining 'freely conducted', so long as it had 'due regard to the general interests of the community'.

The spirit of the Donovan Report was alive in Whitehall throughout this period, at times playing a role as central as incomes policy, if not more significant in the development of labour law. This is even more remarkable when one considers that incomes policy was itself a cause of strikes. There were some limitations on traditional conciliation machin-ery, and inhibitions were put by government pay criteria upon the settlement of disputes, so that up to 1973 'the pursuit of an incomes policy seems to have had a deleterious effect on the pursuit of industrial peace'.[169]

The easy, but perhaps facile, answer to the question why incomes policy, as a central concern of government, did not step in to sweep away the structure of the old industrial relations policy altogether, and labour law with it, is no doubt 'trade union power'. This was one of the factors shaping the Act of 1971. One of the reasons – but not the only or even the main reason – given then for 'clipping the wings of the unions' was to rescue the national interest from inflation. On their side, some trade unionists saw the Act too as imposing a 'surrogate incomes policy'. But at that level of abstraction almost any legislation touching unions, employers or the labour market can be called an 'incomes policy'. Fiscal measures in the Budget, or even announcements of labour law changes announced as part of a Budget package (including the proposal in 1969 to enact two 'penal' provisions of *In Place of Strife*, or the review of Wages Councils and the increase of the qualifying period for unfair dismissal rights to two years announced in 1985), come within this category. In the story so far, these two instances are the closest the

Treasury comes to victory over labour law; but the second was not an application of 'incomes policy' justified on grounds of 'fairness'; it was part of the dismantling of laws perceived as obstructions to the pricing of labour into jobs at lower wages. To announce such measures as part of a Budget is certainly to stress the link between labour law and overall economic policies. Yet the fact, in many ways remarkable, remains that at no time between 1945 and 1980 did any administration of government melt down the structure of labour law and reshape it in the mould of incomes policy. Indeed, some blamed the alleged failures of incomes policy on repeated Government 'concessions' to trade unions and workers (ranging from the closed shop and union 'immunities', to tighter rent control and housing subsidies), although the economic effect and importance of any such measures has been doubted.[170]

In another sense, however, trade unions *were* crucial in all incomes policies of the post-war period. The public policy that emerged in Britain from 1917 onwards in the sensitive relationship of law to industrial relations to shape our labour law did not spring fully armed from the head of Donovan. It was created out of struggles for the right to have a voice in society by workers in trade unions and the response to that challenge. Incomes policy did not face some abstract philosophy of 'voluntarism' but real people, in unions and in management. Sensible architects of incomes policy took account of this; partly they proclaimed their policies to be 'fair' to both these constituencies; partly they knew that in the last resort the legitimacy of their policy rested on consent. Labour law policy was part of a dialogue between social and economic values. Government wanted – or felt it to be in its interest – to keep order in the debate. But workers, wrote Phelps Brown, could not be made by legal sanction 'to perform work that is enjoined', or to 'do a good day's work at their present wage'.

The ultimate safeguard against cost push by groups who have it in their power to assert it is their understanding and free acceptance of the reasons for not doing so.[171]

So it was for three decades. But there had been a different school of thought awaiting its moment, one that saw the obstructions in the 'market', in particular the density of trade union membership and activity, to be the main cause of economic ills. Ostensibly it rejected any of the versions of post-war incomes policy. Instead it preached faith in

competition through market forces. If need be, the bipartisan acceptance from 1944 onwards of the priority of full employment was to be
jettisoned, at any rate for a period. The effect of this new policy upon
labour law and industrial relations is the critical element in the present
decade, one in which the most powerful influence over incomes has
become unemployment.

Much of the story of 'incomes policy' thus described leaves out of
account the specific problem of the 'public sector'. This sector includes
workers of many varieties, from employees of nationalized corporations
to Crown employees and local government. But in great measure for all
of them government is, via taxation, the paymaster in the last resort.
Few Governments, therefore, can fail to have a more explicit 'incomes
policy' in the public sector. Winchester has described the 'transformation' in public sector industrial relations in the two decades before 1983.
Public sector employment substantially increased and with it public
expenditure; trade union density, too, grew larger.[172] By the 1970s
controls over public sector pay had become a central issue, confronting
the wage militancy of workers and unions whose relative position was
being eroded. By 1976 the pay restraint policies of the Labour Government survived by isolating more obviously powerful public sector groups
(miners and electricity supply workers won high pay settlements; so did
the police, after a threat of militant action, and the firemen after a
protracted strike). Public sector strikes increased in 1978–9. Great
hopes were placed upon the Clegg Comparability Commission, and the
'review bodies' for the armed services and for top salary earners
(including judges), for doctors and for dentists. A system of 'cash limits'
was transmitted to the next Conservative Government in 1979, which
applied it most drastically.

'Comparability' with private sector pay was now viewed unfavourably
in Whitehall, and the civil service dispute of 1981 (partly the result of the
Government withdrawing support for across-the-board comparability
and long-standing arbitration arrangements) was but one of many public
sector strikes during 1980–5. The consequent Megaw Report of 1982
suggested a new system in which comparison with outside jobs would
'have a much less decisive influence than in the past'. In place of the Pay
Research Unit, which had facilitated ostensibly objective comparability, it proposed a Pay Information Board. The structure of Civil Service
pay bargaining was still in flux; and as Hepple noted in 1982:

Central to the question of public sector pay is cash limits, and significantly Megaw sidestepped the issue with an ambiguous recommendation that 'realistic' pay assumptions should be built into cash limits.[173]

The Government came forward with new proposals in 1985 for a pay structure with only limited comparability (the need to avoid that, or a form of salary indexation, was said to be the reason why it stayed its hand on plans to introduce new laws to restrict industrial action in 'essential services': p. 670). Whether a new structure could be agreed with the Civil Service unions was uncertain, and many Civil Service unions in fact rejected it early in 1986. One of the effects of the recent developments may have been to end an era in public sector industrial relations that, as Winchester put it, 'was based on an implicit understanding that government would be good employers' and unions would avoid industrial conflict. 'Different forms of incomes policy have disturbed customary pay relativities and undermined the principle of comparability.'

The tendency away from comparability as a dominant concept and from the right of unilateral arbitration may, by itself, indicate more, rather than less, bargaining in which the unions rely more on their negotiating strength. Here the public sector incomes policy is likely, whatever its form, to collide regularly with the new bargaining apparatus. In 1985 the Government's new proposals had a built-in 'override' for government to suspend any new Civil Service agreement 'to safeguard the public purse or public policy'. It seemed unlikely that such a lid could stick effectively on the public sector as a whole. Robinson has shown that by 1985 male non-manual workers in the private sector (in employment) had improved their position over 1980 by 11 per cent. Only police and firemen in the public sector had maintained similar income growth, whilst almost all other public employees suffered a cut in real income (5 per cent for Civil Service principals and university teachers).[174] The schoolteachers' strikes in 1985–6, when the lost ground sought to be recovered was more than 30 per cent, suggested that many groups might fight hard for such claims if their bargaining strength improved.

Disputes in the public sector are likely, then, increasingly to involve claims that affect the 'public purse' and overall welfare, fiscal and social policies. The labour legislation of the 1980s tempts government to label them 'political' disputes, even to use the new restrictions upon strikes and 'trade disputes' as one weapon to restrict earnings in the public sector, to use labour law directly in pursuit of *that* incomes policy. But we must note that the new policy in labour law, resting upon restriction of the rights of workers in unions, upon the removal of props to collective bargaining and upon the weakening of employment protection rights, finds a partial parallel even in some of the neo-Keynesian schools. Such writers maintain as a central objective the pursuit of full employment; nor do they share the ambition of deregulating the economic market or of rolling back the Welfare State. Nevertheless some of them make proposals that would smash the traditional mould of labour law just as union leaders feared might result from the mild proposals of *In Place of Strife* in 1969. Meade, for example, has proposed 'not-quite-compulsory arbitration' on wages; strikes against arbitral awards would be unlawful, automatically terminating employment contracts; damages would be recovered against unions and workers ('by deduction at source'); supplementary social security benefits to strikers' families could be 'loans'. So, he wrote in 1982, the 'rule of reason would replace the exercise of muscle power'.[175]

The confrontation continues, then, between traditional labour law and 'incomes policy' in the traditional sense. Both 'wage fixers' and free marketeers may wish to use the law to break up negotiated patterns of labour relations or block off what they see as pressures to inflation. That this did not happen in the incomes policies of the 1960s and 1970s by way of the reconstruction of labour law may be ascribed to both the strength of workers' unions and the respect for, or at any rate acquiescence in, the fact and the values of collective bargaining as a democratic process by Governments of both political parties in those decades. If government in the 1990s were again to essay a more immediate intervention, the positive planning of labour law, as part of the planning of incomes and of society, might come back on to the agenda.

Non-unionism and the closed shop

We have seen that since 1975 some attempt has been made by labour law to protect workers who are active in trade union matters against dismissal or other disciplinary penalties imposed for that reason and

even to ensure for them some time off for those activities (pp. 309 ff.).
Those modest individual rights were intended to assist in the protection
of freedom to associate, which is at the very root of workers' liberties
and of collective bargaining itself. As Donaldson P. himself said in a
1973 case under the Industrial Relations Act, for the union the dismissal
of an official puts the 'whole prestige and credibility of the union' at
stake so that compensation to that individual 'is an inadequate remedy'.
Special protection for the union's representatives among the work-force
is therefore a commonplace among modern systems of labour law in
Europe. But this is only part of the protection that a union will seek in
order to carry on effective collective bargaining, make collective agreements and jointly administer them and many other workplace practices
with the employer. The employer too often sees advantages in such
protection. The stability of the other bargaining party is in his interests;
and his arrangements with one union may, often will, interlock with
inter-union structures (as when, in a multi-union situation, unions form
a 'Joint Trade Union Negotiating Panel' for bargaining). In the 1970s
management involvement in the operation even of more formal 'closed
shops' spread fast for just such reasons.[176] The cost-conscious employer
recognizes that there are savings to be made by collective, rather than
fragmented, bargaining.

It is sometimes said that the 'right to belong to a union', which is part
of this structure, must be matched by a 'right not to belong' or a 'right to
dissociate'. The Industrial Relations Act 1971 gave some protection to
each right (s. 5). The Donovan Commission disagreed. At that time, in
1968, it was still lawful under common law for the worker's employment
contract to stipulate that he must *not* join a union (known as the
'yellow-dog contract' or 'the document'). Contrasting this with a
requirement to join the union, Donovan said:

the two are not truly comparable. The former condition is designed to frustrate
the development of collective bargaining, which it is public policy to promote,
whereas no such objection applies to the latter.

Kahn-Freund, too, rejected the equation between the 'freedom to
organize' and the 'freedom not to organize', a 'fallacy' resting on
'shallow legalism'.[177] British judges have nevertheless invariably supported the right to 'dissociate'. Judges still have in mind the approach of
Erle J. in 1869 that a person cannot 'alienate' his freedom 'to dispose of

his own labour or capital according to his will' either for a time or generally: 'it follows that he cannot transfer it to the governing body of a union'.

We discuss later some of the cases in which this matter has arisen, where the worker is in dispute with his union (p. 810). It was mainly in those cases that Lord Denning MR expounded his 'right to work', a notion intimately related to his approach to unions as a whole, which he has always made explicit: 'This case reminds me of the story of David and Goliath, with a difference. Goliath is winning all along the line.'[178] He employed the same phrase against an employer in *Langston's* case – 'a man has a right to work, which the courts will protect' – though the case was not decided on that ground. Taken as anything more than a purple flourish, such a 'right' is meaningless unless someone has a *duty* to provide work. As Megarry VC observed in 1978: 'Who is under a duty to provide the work? Who can be sued?' The 'right' can hardly mean that a man can demand 'any employment he chooses, however unsuitable'.[179] The 'right' is not about that, of course; it does not proclaim the illegality of unemployment. In practice it is about the right to work as a non-unionist. In less extravagant language, a (negative) right-not-to-belong is said to flow from a (positive) right to associate, even though we have seen that our law hardly protects any such 'right' to associate for workers. Yet even Lord Scarman went on record in the Grunwick inquiry as declaring that the 'right to join a union' and 'the right not to join a union' are *both* 'recognised by English law'.[180] There are few of our judges who perceive the collective realities in the way chosen by the Danish judge (dissenting) in the Court of Human Rights:

The so-called positive and negative freedom of association are not simply two sides of the same coin or . . . two aspects of the same freedom. There is no logical link between the two.[181]

The subject is usually discussed in Britain in relation to the 100 per cent union membership arrangement (UMA) or closed shop, to which we come below. But it is a much wider issue than that, one bound to be perceived differently in various industrial relations cultures. It is, for example, not the case, as is commonly believed, that other systems of law forbid all similar 'union security' arrangements that limit the ambit of non-unionism and fulfil at least some of the functions of our UMA. Where unions are ideologically divided (into Communist, Socialist and

Catholic unions, for example) pressure to join a particular union cannot be allowed. How could the law there permit a devout Catholic to be compelled to join a Communist union? Or compel an atheist to join a Catholic union? It is for this reason that French and Italian law enshrines the right of a worker to belong to a union of his choice. Yet in both France and Italy, despite the doctrine of union 'equality', the law has gradually increased the advantages and status of 'representative' unions in respect of both bargaining rights and rights of activity at the work-place. Unions are seen as 'equal in law' even though some functions can be fulfilled only by 'representative' unions, nationally or at enterprise level.[182] One aim in such arrangements is to identify the workers' bargaining bodies amidst the multitude of unions. In other systems closer 'union security' arrangements are found even with ideological unions. After 1927 in the Netherlands it became lawful to compel a worker to join *one* of the (then) three union confederations, which were divided on religious and ideological lines.

In systems where, as in Britain, *membership* is the basis of union strength, practice differs. Certain forms of 'union preference' in hiring or representational rights are permissible in Australia,[183] and to some extent in Sweden, but not in West Germany (though Kahn-Freund doubted whether it was 'advisable to look for a job in a coal mine in the Ruhr' without a union card). The 1985 Hancock Report on Australian labour law has recommended no change in 'union preference' arrange-ments (and associated exceptions for conscientious objectors), which are part of 'the maintenance of harmony of industrial relations'. In the United States a degree of 'union security' is allowed in federal law by way of 'agency shop' agreements to make compulsory, with certain exceptions, the payment of union dues (though even this is prohibited in many state 'right to work' laws – again a misnomer, Gould remarks, since 'the legislation does not provide for any rights to work').[184]

Since 1980, by contrast, and especially since the Act of 1982, British law has more and more been based upon a policy of 'individualism', which

sees unions as an illegitimate distortion of the market relations between the employer and the individual employee and as an interference with personal freedom which is threatened by the union aspiration for collective solidarity, discipline and 100 per cent organization.[185]

It would not be right to suggest, however, that the statutes of the 1980s represent a totally new strand in the thinking of some parts of the Conservative Party. When the new text of the Fair Wages Resolution in 1946 required an employer to recognize 'the freedom of his work-people to be members of trade unions', an amendment was unsuccessfully moved to stop it becoming a requirement for a closed shop by preserving a 'choice' of union. The 'individualism' of the Industrial Relations Act 1971 (s. 5) resulted in a worker having a general right *not* to join a union, whether registered or not. And although demands for the absolute right of non-unionism were significantly absent from influential policy statements of 1958 and 1968,[186] there is a line of thought reaching back to the nineteenth century that rejects unions as coercive, exemplified by a speech of Earl Wemyss in 1891, when he said:

if there is one man who objects to join the union the whole power of the State and of the Empire ought to be brought to bear for [his protection], regardless of what the majority may be on the other side.

General non-unionism

This policy, though, has expressed itself increasingly in the modern law by amendment of that part of it which controls the employer's right to discipline or to dismiss a worker who is a non-unionist. To the extent that the employer is prevented from doing this, his freedom to enforce his agreements about trade unionists' rights to organize and bargain is limited. In this respect our new system has reaffirmed its ancient individualist basis. It is useful to remind ourselves of the reason. At the turn of the century, the Law Lords held union officials liable for a 'conspiracy to injure' for having organized a strike and a boycott through the employer's customers to stop him employing non-unionists; but we saw (p. 29) that in 1924, and again in 1942, this liability gave way to a judicial recognition that workers had a legitimate interest in withdrawing labour in protest against non-unionists (though not to hound them).[187] By this time the Trade Disputes Act 1906 had also protected a simple conspiracy to injure in a trade dispute (s. 1). The general understanding in the 1960s, therefore, was that so long as the means were within the general law 'customary trade unions methods' to exclude non-unionists were lawful.[188]

The Industrial Relations Act 1971 limited not only forms of the closed shop, declaring the 'pre-entry' shop void (where workers must be union members before hiring) and trying to establish 'agency shops' and a few specially 'approved' closed shops for unions that registered (ss. 7, 17). It also established a worker's right to be a member of a (registered) union and a right to 'refuse to be a member' of a union (registered or unregistered). From this it followed that an employer could not lawfully interfere with these rights by dismissal, discipline or refusal to hire; and 'irregular industrial action' by workers inducing him to do so was unlawful (ss. 5, 33). Most unions did not register. When the 1971 Act was repealed, the earlier bipartisan policy on dismissal was continued, the closed shop returned to legality and some protection for trade unionists was enacted.

Now, however, common law had to coexist with the new statutory floor of rights. If the former saw action as not unlawful merely because it was aimed at non-unionists, when would the new statute see an employer's dismissal or action short of dismissal as 'unfair' to the non-unionist? There were three possible answers: always, never or sometimes. Not surprisingly, Parliament took the third course. The debate after 1974 was, therefore, largely taken up by disagreements about how many times 'sometimes' should be. Since 1982 the new policies have taken the answer much nearer to 'never'.

Action short of dismissal

It is useful to look at non-unionism and 'action short of dismissal'. In 1975 there was no congruence here with the rights of trade union members (p. 309). The employer was not to engage in ASD 'for the purpose of compelling' a worker to become a member of 'a trade union which is not independent' (EPA s. 53). The object was to prevent the employer from forcing him to join a 'house union' controlled by the employer, outside the definition of independence (p. 280). But five years later, by a swift stroke of the draftsman's pen, the legislature deleted the words 'which is not independent' (EA 1980 s. 15, now EPCA s. 23 (1) (c)). The employer now must not 'compel' a worker to join *any* union – independent or otherwise. Remembering the approach of *Carlson's* case (p. 317) to the rights of a worker who is a member of a non-recognized union, it seems possible that the new formula might make the employer liable for ASD, not only when he prefers unionists to the non-unionist in promotions and the like, but also if he concludes an agreement with a union conferring benefits only on members of the union. Dunn and Gennard report: 'Although in open shops unionists have sometimes pressed for member-only benefits, management agreement has almost never been secured.'[189]

Among the exceptions, Greenwich Council was reported in 1984 as having made with its recognized unions an agreement that only members would receive certain negotiated benefits, including interest-free loans for travel. In 1977 Brighton Corporation agreed with a union as part of its transport closed shop that new employees excluded from the union would retain employment but not enjoy the benefits negotiated at local level by the branch. To gain a remedy, the non-unionist would now have to prove an element of 'compulsion' rather than encouragement to join the union. This may be 'a fine distinction' but it is an important one – as where a check-off deduction made from a worker's wages after he had instructed no more deductions by way of union contributions to be made (because he had resigned) was held not to constitute ASD since the employers had no wish to 'compel' him (their administrative machine continued to deduct while a dispute leading to his dismissal went through procedure).[190] In some countries, West Germany for example, members-only agreements are banned on a different ground, namely that such a collaboration trespasses on the 'independence' of the *unions*.

The 1982 Act specified certain forms of employers' conduct as statutory ASD: namely, action to enforce any requirement that a worker must pay money in place of being a union member (such as payment to a charity, which is often employed as a compromise in disputes between non-members and workers in the union) and any deduction from pay by the employer on the same ground. This is all doubly important now for the union because the employer is not the only party who may have to pay compensation for ASD. In a special provision for non-unionists the 1982 amendments provided that where the worker complains of ASD by the employer to compel him to join, and he (or the employer) claims the employer was induced to do so by industrial pressure by a union, an official or a worker, he (or the employer) can 'join' that union or person to the proceedings. The tribunal can then award either all or some of the compensation against the 'joined' third parties, as it considers 'just and equitable' (EPCA s. 26A). It is doubly important for the tribunals in such cases to remember, as the EAT said in 1978, that compensation for the employee is the basis of the award, 'not a fine on the employer however tactfully wrapped up'. No parallel procedure exists for the union member where the employer was induced to take ASD against him by a third party. We return to 'joinder' below (p. 381).

Dismissal of non-unionists

As for dismissal, the 1974 Act had not dealt generally with this issue outside the closed shop, and strangely (in view of the expansion of liability for ASD) nor did the 1980 Act. But in 1982 a parallel change in the EPCA was wrought. Here the existing formula making unfair a dismissal by reason of refusal to be 'a member of a trade union which was not an independent union' was replaced by dismissal for the reason that the worker is not a member of a union or a particular union or has refused, or proposes to refuse, to become or remain a member (EPCA s. 58 (1) (c)). This returns the position broadly to that under the Industrial Relations Act 1971 but with important additions. First, the non-unionist can apply for 'interim relief' (p. 316) to reinstate him pending the full hearing, if he can show that he is likely to win on this ground; but he need not, as the union member must, produce any 'certificate' to this effect (EPCA s. 77).

Secondly, he is entitled, if he proves dismissal for this reason, to a compensatory award and a basic award, in 1986, of a minimum £2,200 (s. 73 (4A)). Deductions for contributory fault may be made but not in respect of any refusal to join a union, or to cease to be a member or carry on activities of a union (even if not independent), or a refusal to make payments, or objecting to deductions, in place of joining a union (s. 72A). In addition, if he asks for reinstatement, he must be awarded a 'special award' – that is, £11,000 minimum (or 104 times one week's pay, whichever is greater) up to £22,000 maximum – and if the award is made after an order of reinstatement has not been complied with, unless the employer shows it was not reasonably practicable to do so, the special award is increased to £16,500 (or 156 times one week's pay, whichever is the greater: s. 75A, as amended for 1986, reductions again being possible for contributory fault, by the same fraction as the basic award, or more if that is just and equitable, though a 'week's pay' is not here subject to the normal limit of £155).

Thirdly, as in the case of dismissal on union grounds, the non-unionist needs to prove no continuous period of employment to qualify. It was with this characteristic that the 1982 Act firmly placed the 'negative' right on a par with, in some ways even above, the positive rights of trade unionists. Lastly, as in the case of ASD, the 1982 amendments give to the non-unionist (and the employer) the right to 'join' and to exact such part of the compensation as the tribunal thinks just and equitable against a union, official or worker who induced the dismissal by actual or threatened industrial action (EPCA s. 76A). To this policy of making the union or its members pay we return in considering the closed shop (p. 381).

Union security and the closed shop

The interrelationship of the law on discipline and dismissal of non-unionists and on workers' rights as trade unionists was highlighted, but not created, by the law on the closed shop after 1974. We saw that once the tort of 'conspiracy to injure' was put aside, the common law appeared to challenge the legality neither of pressure for 100 per cent membership nor of the agreements that many employers have for decades been willing to make to that end. The legislation of the 1980s, especially the Act of 1982, made incursions into the legality of action by workers and the defence of a closed shop. Before 1982, for example, a 'trade dispute' within which industrial action might be lawful by reason of 'immunity' against certain tort liabilities included industrial disputes between 'workers and workers'. But now a trade dispute can exist only if the dispute is between workers and their own employer. Disputes between workers (or their unions) about demarcation and recruitment and 'disputes between unions and individuals over the maintenance of closed shops' are no longer included and are therefore more easily regarded as illicit in the civil law of tort.[191] The classic analysis of the closed shop in 1964 by McCarthy identified its functions as including recruiting and retaining members, maintaining 'discipline' and the observance of union rules and customs, as well as control of entry to the job (which is direct only in the relatively rare 'pre-entry' form, where jobs are available only to union members). These, however, were not the reasons for the phenomenon: the demand for it arose out of problems of 'organizing' the work-force (high turnover of workers, for example) or 'controlling the labour force' (to enforce union rates or to maintain solidarity) or controlling the 'alternative work-force' (an aim of both craft unions and unskilled workers).

McCarthy's study estimated that one worker in six was directly affected. Not all unions then (or now) actively sought 100 per cent closed-shop arrangements. The first objective is union strength. Nor are all agreements, as we shall see, the iron vice that is usually portrayed to the public. Nor are they all functionally the same; the plant closed shop may represent the independence of the stewards, while industry agreements may be part of highly centralized structures. By the 1970s the practice in its many forms had grown rapidly to include about one in four, but by the end of the decade the decline of closed-shop activity became 'dramatic', and by 1982 the figure was nearer one in five.[192] In this development, however, management seems to have played a more prominent role. In the 1970s closed shops became more formal, almost all new agreements being 'post-entry' (where new workers join after engagement); many more covered white-collar workers. Hart's survey confirmed the greater willingness by management to conclude formal agreements with unions; and indeed very often 'managers felt in control of their UMAs'.[193]

As far back as 1970 a breakaway strike at Pilkington's, when 8,000 workers defied the sole union, illustrated the dangers of cosy union–management relationships blinding it to the needs of members. Some judges recognized 'the convenience' to management, as Widgery J. put it in 1968, 'to be able to negotiate with a single union on behalf of the [workers] as a whole'. But closed shops organized at the top, rather than won spontaneously from the bottom, run the risk of becoming a system of closed industrial discipline. What Dunn has called the 'autochthonous' nature of the closed shop in Britain (springing from the very soil of the system) is indicated by the chronology both of its recent rise and of its decline. Its upsurge began in the late 1960s before the 1974 Act – and reached 5.2 million workers before the decline set in to about 4.5 million in 1982, again *before* the legislation of the 1980s took effect. The arrangements dating from earlier periods he has labelled 'robust', whereas the more 'fragile' UMAs of the 1970s have been far more susceptible to changes in management attitude and, possibly, in the law.[194]

Problems have arisen even where union membership is not compulsory, only encouraged. In arrangements with Japanese car firms in

1984–5, where one union was given the right to represent *all* workers with sole recognition rights (plus flexibility of trades, common conditions for staff and manual workers, and arbitration of disputes – in some, 'pendulum' arbitration where the arbitrator, assuming he can find the 'final' offers, must choose one side's case without compromise), some trade unionists objected to the 'beauty contest' in which the *employer* chose the union, leading to the headline 'Nissan chooses A U E W'. The decline in the old closed shop, however, to a major extent follows, in the words of A C A S in 1984, 'the changing patterns of employment away from older production industries'.

The public debate on the closed shop has been carried on largely in terms of 'individual rights'. Kahn-Freund concluded that the closed shop could be justified in terms only of 'the need for an equilibrium of power', not of 'ethical sentiments, only in terms of social expediency'; and he approved McCarthy's comment that people often derive benefit from institutions without 'feeling an obligation to contribute' (like the Marriage Guidance Council), though the latter offered his own separate and persuasive functional justifications of the practice.[195] But few need to associate maritally to earn their daily bread. Allan Flanders asked, if workers were to share in determining their working conditions, 'What is the answer if they insist that among those must be the condition of not having to work alongside the non-unionist?'[196] Against this classical 'free-rider' argument stood the individual's assertion that he wished to work without joining the association.

There is no *logical* way of demonstrating the superiority of either of the two arguments – 'I want to work in my job at the going rate but not join the union', and 'I want to work in my job but not alongside those who contribute nothing to our machinery that wins the going rate.' One objection to the 'free-rider' analysis is that 'obligations' are not created 'by conferred benefits even when involuntarily or accidentally conferred'.[197] Perhaps not; but by that token the non-unionist appears to be obliged to consider *returning* the wage-rise whence it came. Other commentators have more usefully emphasized the legitimacy of the closed shop 'as ritual . . . a *symbol* for the affirmation of what are seen as traditional trade union values'.[198] It may well be that the closed shop came to operate for workers 'as a kind of *rite de passage*, a ritual endorsement of the collective values of the trade union movement'; whilst, on the other side, writers made it – and the law about it – the object of a 'moral panic', alleging that its evils would erode democracy, as part of the wider argument that 'liberty owed more to individual freedom in the labour market than to free trade unionism'.[199] The description of 'moral panic' is apt when one reviews some of the literature of the 1970s that ascribed so many evils to the closed shop, not least unemployment, which has roughly trebled since that time.

The post-entry closed shop expanded in the early 1970s and then declined against a background of confused debate in which philosophical arguments about 'positive and negative rights to associate', 'custom and practice', 'economic power', 'free-riders' and 'human rights' were all present, no one argument being necessarily exclusive of the others.[200] The law was only one factor among many in the development. The attempt by the 1971 Act to render the closed shop inoperable by law failed partly because management 'defended it almost as tenaciously as did lawyers'.[201] After 1974 the legal provisions were a factor contributing to greater formality, but at best they were one of the 'four interlocking variables' – 'economic forces, legislation, management and trade union attitudes', in Dunn and Gennard's words. And as Clegg remarked, a closed shop is 'coercive', 'but the coercion lies in the agreement or understanding or arrangement which imposes a closed shop, and not in the law on unfair dismissal'.[202]

Non-unionists and the UMA

The collective perspective of this 'coercion' (that is, the interests of the individuals who are the majority) is usually less readily understood by lawyers than the minority dissent. Sellers LJ in 1963 did recognize the 'free-rider' argument that workers might object to non-unionists enjoying benefits won from the employer 'whilst outside the union and avoiding its obligations'. But by 1974 the frontiers of legal challenge were inevitably individualized and since then have been found along the boundaries of the new unfair dismissal law. The employer was unable to plead union pressure as a defence to unfairness (now EPCA s. 63: p. 194); but if there was a UMA the dismissal of a non-unionist was declared to be fair *so long as* the latter was not in a special category. From 1974 to 1976, the period of a minority Labour Government, this category included workers who objected to union membership altogether on grounds of religious belief or who objected to joining a particular union on 'any reasonable ground' (TULRA, Sched. 1, para. 6 (5)). The second proviso (to which a tribunal in 1976 objected as requiring a 'political decision') was in the same year deleted. In that year the law also attained the definition of a UMA that now governs: namely, an agreement or arrangement made between one or more employers and independent trade unions relating to a class of employees, having the effect in practice of 'requiring the employees' to be, or to become, members of the union, or one of the unions, party to it or of another specified independent union (TULRA s. 30 (1)).

Two initial problems appeared, concerning the UMA: the *practice*, and the *reason* for the dismissal. At first the definition required 'every employee' to be a member. This meant a watertight 'practice', which rarely exists in reality. In very many closed-shop employments, exceptions are made formally or informally: a few workers do not either wish or bother to join or are just not recruited; so long as no anti-union battle starts, no one bothers about it. In 1976 the present, more realistic wording was inserted. So too, in order to be fair, the dismissal originally had to arise from a 'practice' under the UMA 'for *all* employees' to belong to the union, again a very strict test. But from 1976 the UMA needed to have only 'the effect in practice of requiring the employees' of that class to join (now EPCA s. 58 (2)). After some erratic decisions, the Court of Appeal took note. A milkman had joined the TGWU and, contrary to his employer's UMA with USDAW and to a TUC disputes committee award in favour of USDAW (p. 824), he refused to join that union. It was alleged that ten out of about ninety milkmen refused to join USDAW. It was held that a sufficient 'practice' had been proved; the dismissal was fair.[203]

Problems still remain in this area. In a controversial tribunal decision of 1978 an employer was not himself a party to the UMA, but his employee painters were required to work at a BP refinery where all employees had to be union members under a UMA made between BP and the unions. He was allowed to rely upon the UMA when he sacked the painters for refusing to go there because they had ceased to be members of a union; the dismissals were held to be fair.[204] The Act demanded a 'practice', said the tribunal, not a UMA to which the employer is a party; but it is doubtful whether the courts today would accept that interpretation.

As to the *reason*, the Act required that the principal reason 'for the dismissal' must be the worker's not being a member. Generally in unfair dismissal cases the employer's proof of belief on reasonable grounds is adequate. He might reasonably, but mistakenly, believe a worker to be a non-unionist. Suppose, for example, he had been misled by a shop steward into thinking the worker had lapsed his membership of a union when his arrears had only put him 'out of benefit' (p. 811). In 1981 an extraordinary decision of the EAT about the dismissal of a coppersmith demanded that the employer prove both the fact of non-membership and that this was the reason for the dismissal. The fact that the employer's belief might be 'genuinely held' was inadequate.[205] What is more, if the UMA is linked to a dismissal procedure, the employer cannot be heard to say that he acted for that 'reason' unless he can prove that he followed the procedure at least in all 'essential' ways, otherwise the courts see him as not having given 'proper consideration' to it (as where an employer failed to comply with one step in an appeals procedure, even though many other procedures had been exhausted, including an appeal to the Independent Review Committee, for a worker expelled from a union).[206] These judicial additions to the Act, for such they are, contrast starkly with the interpretation of trade unionists' rights.

Part of the legal definition and the exception in cases of 'religious belief', which was provided from 1974 onwards, also caused difficulty on the industrial front. In the 1960s railway management was unfavourable to a UMA; but in 1970 one was negotiated. It came to be enforced in 1975, against a background of high union density, resentment from some workers and threats of breakaways. Management refused to exempt 'Christian convictions' which could not be proved in the texts proffered by workers, despite their honest belief. This the EAT, rightly, would not accept.[207] (By 1985 railway management had swung so far the other way that it wanted to scrap its closed shop.) The 1980 Act extended the 'religious belief' exemption to grounds of 'conscience or other deeply held personal conviction' by reason of which a worker refused to join a union or all unions (now EPCA s. 58 (4)). The definition appeared to leave it open to a union and employer to bring in a UMA and impose it on existing non-union employees. The evidence shows this has not often been done; the majority of UMAs in the 1970s exempted existing non-union employees, and the trend was increasing.[208] But the 1980 Act also exempted existing non-members in the employment before the UMA came into effect (now EPCA s. 58 (4), (5)).

Contrary to widespread belief, there is little hard evidence of unions bludgeoning members into strikes, as Dunn and Gennard show. Nevertheless, in the early 1980s the dismissal of some individuals, especially a Miss Joanna Harris and four Walsall dinner-ladies, was vigorously publicized by the Freedom Association and the Government. Whether or not such individual dismissals were unfair, the Government refused to wait for the context of the surveys then about to appear before legislating further in 1982. The Prime Minister even spoke of the closed shop, plus secondary picketing, enabling 'small groups to close down whole industries'. The resulting legislation was unusual in a number of ways. First, compensation was to be paid *retrospectively* to those workers whom the Government (aided by an 'assessor') considered to be unjustly dismissed (by 1980 standards) between 1974 and 1980 (EA 1982 s. 2, Sched. 1; the Secretary of State could set aside any tribunal findings, and £2 million was devoted to the fund). Dunn and Gennard estimated that a maximum of 490 persons (nearly 100 the result of three disputes) were dismissed for closed-shop reasons in the whole decade after 1970. The Government, estimating it might make 400 payments, advertised for claimants. By March 1984, 250 out of 547 applications had been approved, some others being 'settled', to the tune of £956,000. On constitutional grounds the scheme caused great anxiety.[209] Inevitably, in 1985 calls were made by some unions for the retrospective repayment to *them* by a Labour Government of sums paid in fines by reason of the 1980s legislation on strikes, a demand that (despite favourable resolutions at the TUC and Labour Party conferences) Labour Party leaders firmly rejected.

The railwaymen's case

The Government justified the unprecedented scheme largely by reference to the three railwaymen *Young*, *James* and *Webster*. They were dismissed as non-unionists after the commencement in 1975 of the railway UMA. None objected on religious grounds. Young objected to the two available unions largely by reason of political activities and 'intolerance', Webster on broad philosophical grounds of individual rights and the damage done by the 'union movement', James because he was dissatisfied with NUR support for his own grievances at work. After failing at a tribunal, they took their case to the European Human Rights Commission and thence to the Court of Human Rights at Strasbourg. (Its judgments bind the Government morally, but do not have the legal force of the EEC Luxembourg court's judgments.) Article 11 (1) of the Human Rights Convention declares that everyone

has the right . . . to freedom of association with others, including the right to form and to join trade unions for the protection of his interests.

But Article 11 (2) adds:

No restrictions shall be placed upon the exercise of these rights other than such as are prescribed by law and are necessary in a democratic society . . . for the protection of the rights and freedoms of others.

Arraigned before the Court, the UK Government defended the 1974 Act, which it had just amended, and vigorously argued that it did not break the Convention. By eighteen votes to three the judges from various countries rejected its plea; the UK stood in breach of Article 11.[210] Rarely, however, has such a strange judgment been so misunderstood and misrepresented. First, it did not interpret the Convention to include a 'negative' right to dissociate within the concept of 'freedom of association' (though six of the majority were prepared to go that far). Secondly, the court said it was 'not called upon to review the closed shop system as such'. Nor did the judgment rest upon 'conscientious' grounds. What it *did* decide was that 'compulsion' to join a union 'may not always be contrary to the Convention', but 'in the present instance' it was by reason of being 'directed against persons engaged before the introduction of any obligation to join a particular trade union'.

The core of decision, therefore, related to imposition of a UMA on *existing* non-union employees. The majority went on to say that 'the right to freedom of association' implies a 'choice as regards trade unions' that workers 'join of their own volition'. As to Webster and Young, the court may not fully have grasped the significance of the right to 'contract out' of political activities in Britain (p. 768). As for James, his 'freedom of choice' was limited only when he found the NUR of 'no advantage'. Whatever it thought about individual rights, the Government understood the dangers of this reasoning and at the hearing denied to the court any wish to see British unions 'developing in the direction of ideological pluralism' (the structures we noted above in France or Italy). In fact, a multi-union system based on membership produces industrial anarchy if no structural restraints can be placed on each worker's choice. The Law Lords understood this in 1983 when upholding the TUC's inter-union disputes principles that forbid the 'poaching' of members (p. 832). Lord Denning had struck them down as contrary to public policy (and to Article 11), pronouncing: 'even though it should result in industrial chaos nevertheless the freedom of each man should prevail' (p. 833). Even the Government's own Code of Practice on the Closed Shop, however, recommends the TUC principles. The Strasbourg judgment illustrates the perils of poor comparative labour law, resting on the export of abstract principle; and it is no criticism therefore to note that half of the majority judges came from countries with 'pluralist' union movements, while the three dissentients were from Scandinavia and Iceland with structures more comparable to the British. The Government accepted the judgment and ultimately paid some £125,000 to the three. In 1985 it likewise paid a further £30,000 compensation and costs to six painters who had been dismissed by Hull Council some years before.

There is another, crucial point on the railwaymen's case. The Labour Government in its pleadings to both the Human Rights Commission and the Court of Human Rights had pleaded a defence based on Article 11 (2). It argued that the 1974 limitations on freedom of association were 'prescribed by law' and 'necessary' in a democratic British society to protect the interests of those individuals who were *in* unions. In 1980 the Conservative Government withdrew that defence. Over the strong dissent of another minority judge, the court proceeded, without full agreement, to hold that the British law of 1974 was not 'necessary . . . to achieve a proper balance between the conflicting interests' within Article 11 (2). It based this conclusion upon a concept of 'proportionality' (one, Lord Diplock said in the *GCHQ* case, 'recognized in the administrative law of several' European countries, but not in Britain). Such a concept gives to judges rather than to elected governments the power to decide whether a law is 'proportional', i.e. fair. Article 11 (2) is based not on what is fair or proportional but on what is 'necessary' in a particular industrial relations system. The failure of the Government to pursue this defence leaves a question mark hanging over the entire decision.

The right to dissociate and the UMA

Predominance of individual rights to dissociate must 'weaken the power of organized labour to compete with the power of capital. Freedom of association cannot have been intended primarily to produce this effect.'[211] Yet the Government in 1981 wanted to go further. Its Green Paper of 1981 recommended a ban on 'union labour only' practices, which, as we have seen, the 1982 Act effected in extended form when it prohibited both commercial practices and industrial action to support 'union labour only' and pressure to extend collective bargaining (p. 72). Unfair dismissal law in a UMA was also tightened. The dismissal of a non-unionist was no longer to be fair, in addition to the 1980 categories of 'conscience or deeply held personal conviction' and 'existing employees', in cases where he refused to pay money or accept a wage deduction for not being a union member; or where he was a qualified member of a body with a 'written code' and was excluded from or refused to join the union because it would be a breach of that code for him to join or take part in an official strike; or where a complaint to a tribunal against exclusion from a union (p. 793) was pending or had succeeded (EPCA s. 58 (7), (8), (13)). If 'grounds of deeply held personal conviction' were widely interpreted, few of the other grounds would be necessary; but practice has differed. *Mr Shackcloth's* objection to remaining a member of the union under a UMA with his employers, who explained the position fully and for whom he had worked before, was – rather like that of *James* – based upon his decision that it had 'let him down' in various industrial grievances. His dismissal was held not to be fair; for a deeply held conviction that the union had let him down was enough; no 'moral consideration' was involved; the Act expressly contrasted such a conviction with 'conscience'.

Mr Sakals, a bus driver, also based his deep conviction 'largely upon political grounds'. Supported by the Freedom Association, which appears regularly in the modern cases, he came forward as a libertarian who relied upon Article 11 of the Convention. The EAT upheld the tribunal in rejecting his case; he had 'no objection to membership as such', only to 'compulsion to become a member'. The Convention could not be used to widen the clear meaning of a statute.[212] *Mr McGhee* fared little better. He had become dissatisfied with his union, the TGWU. He was still 'in sympathy' with trade unions, and had no 'philosophical' objections. No doubt, said the tribunal, he 'felt very strongly that he had been poorly treated by the union', but this was not a deeply held personal conviction. The EAT refused to disturb this decision; it was not manifestly perverse such as to 'offend reason'. In such an investigation into conscience and conviction, the tribunal was 'particularly, perhaps even uniquely, dependent upon the impression' made by the member when giving evidence. Here the EAT was backing off, wisely, for this is in truth a horrendous statutory formula to apply. When the same issue reaches the Court of Appeal, however, a more interventionist pose may be expected.

Because, after 1982, a dismissal by reason of non-unionism is unfair (s. 58 (1) (c)), then as soon as the employer loses the protection of 'fair' dismissal in a UMA situation under one of the new limitations, he has lost the case (the same result had in effect been enacted in 1980). But the limitations on the UMA set out so far are slender compared with what is to come. In the 1980 Act a clause had been inserted to permit fair dismissals of a non-unionist in *new* UMAs only if there had been a ballot of employees concerned. In such a case, it followed that a non-unionist who is employed at the time of the ballot must also be exempted. In 1982 this was tightened up for all UMAs. The ballot must now take place within five years before the dismissal. The majority obtained in a secret ballot must be: (1) in a first ballot in a new UMA, 80 per cent of those entitled to vote (including the sick and the absent); (2) in other cases, either 80 per cent of those entitled to vote or 85 per cent of those voting (s. 58A). The Act does not say who should hold the ballot. An unsuccessful ballot vitiates dismissals, however established the UMA may be. The constituency of employees voting must not be defined by reference to union membership or non-membership (s. 58A (6)). These provisions are supplemented by the Secretary of State's Code on Closed Shops (1983), which polishes some of the corners, solves few problems and must be taken into account by courts and tribunals.

The 1982 Act deals logically, to a great extent, with ASD in a closed shop, making the position of the non-unionist largely coterminous with his position in relation to unfair dismissal (EPCA s. 23). But there is one sting in the tail. The position of the trade union member suffers one more adjustment. The law had previously restricted the right not to be penalized for trade union activity in a UMA to members of the unions specified in the UMA. Now, however, a UMA is to be 'disregarded' if it has not been validated by a ballot (s. 23 (2B)). Despite the *de facto* closed shop, the activities of all unions then count as equal; the new law invites and protects the 'poaching' of members.

Joinder

The employer has ceased to be the only defendant in unfair dismissal cases. Since 1980 the employer has been able to 'join' the union where it has induced the dismissal or ASD by actual or threatened industrial action and make it pay some or all of any compensation. Supporters urged the Government to allow the claimant non-unionist also to have the right to 'join'; but the Government refused on the ground that, in such a delicate area, the employer should decide whether the union should be sued. Any other scheme could contribute to a 'running sore' in a plant's industrial relations. In 1982 that policy was jettisoned. The claimant now has an equal right to 'join'.

With this step 'the law crosses a legal and ideological Rubicon'.[213] It smashes the Donovan scheme for excluding strikes and industrial action from the jurisdiction of courts and tribunals (the courts, as Browne-Wilkinson J. has said, have not been entrusted with 'the allocation of blame in relation to industrial disputes'). Now the tribunal *is* asked to allocate blame: what is 'just and equitable' in regard to pressure arising out of organizing or 'financing' (e.g. by payment of strike pay) a 'strike or industrial action, or threatening to do so' because the claimant was a non-unionist (see now EPCA ss. 26A, 76A). The effect on the work of the tribunals could, in terms of workers' confidence, be severe, particularly since the third party joined can be an individual as well as the union. In 1985 three employees of Cory King, a tugboat firm, obtained 'interim relief' after being sacked. A ballot on the UMA had succeeded with more than an 85 per cent majority; but they had left the union before the ballot was held. This put them in an exempted category. Union members refused to work with them. Cory King 'joined' the union to the action; the claimants then joined some shop stewards, four other workers (one was a son of one claimant) and the union's area official. The tribunal awarded the entire compensation against the union.

In such a case, an individual could be made to pay part or even all of at least £24,200 (including a basic and a 'special' award) or even more, if there is a compensatory award (p. 369). But what of the 'union'? When will *it* be liable for the acts of officials or even members? The 1982 Act lays down a rigid code on this problem in respect of liability in 'tort' arising from industrial action (p. 530). But that code does not apply here; the 'vicarious liability' of the union is not in the legal category of 'tort'. Instead, the rules of the common law seem to apply, making the union liable for anyone who acted within his 'authority' for the union (e.g. a full-time official). As we know, it is very difficult to know when shop stewards act within their 'implied authority' as agents of the union.[214]

Ballots and the UMA

The effect of 'joinder' is only beginning to be felt by labour law. So too, the impact of the need for compulsory ballots with overwhelming majorities to validate UMAs for purposes of dismissal and discipline is still uncertain. The TUC policy of opposition to the Acts of 1980 and 1982 was rapidly put under great pressure, linked to its advocacy of abstention from *all* ballots imposed by the new laws and from receipt of Government funds available for postal ballots for certain purposes (p. 785). The TUC 'Wembley Recommendation' (No. 7, 1982) calling for trade union members of tribunals and the EAT not to serve on 'cases arising from the application' of a UMA under anti-union legislation (with which trade unionists should not be 'involved in any way') has not been uniformly observed – even, it seems, in joinder cases. On the ground, ballots have been regularly held since November 1984. ACAS knew of 94 ballots in mid-1985, of which 74 won the necessary majority. Ballots were won at Cossor Electronics but not at Reuters (where unions boycotted the ballot). A union resignation at British Gas led it to 'review' its UMA so as to observe 'the legislative framework'; the Freedom Association had British Rail in its sights as a 'target' (a breakaway union there was certified independent in 1984). Trade unionists who wanted to use the new ballot procedures pointed to favourable votes for the UMA being followed by high votes for industrial action on pay claims, e.g. by 8,000 GUS employees in USDAW. In 1985 the TUC was under pressure to reconsider its policy of unions refraining from participation in such ballots. But the ballots held represented a small proportion of enterprises covered by a UMA. By 1986 the new laws appeared to have had only a limited effect.

Controls for non-unionism

Such inconclusive developments so far suggest that Dunn and Gennard may be correct in thinking that industrial relations problems and economic factors will have 'a more significant impact on the future of the practice than the niceties of the law'. If so, this will prove to be a further example of Kahn-Freund's thesis that law is a 'secondary force' in labour relations. Such a thesis is not, though, a principle written on tablets of stone. Legal regulation has evidenced in the 1980s new capabilities to affect the vitality of trade union organization. Never since the nineteenth century has there been such a determined drive to diminish the strategic strength of unions and to do it by using 'the law'. Often it is not the substance, certainly not the 'niceties', of laws that matter on the ground so much as 'the theatre' or rhetoric of the law.[215] Four unjustly dismissed dinner-ladies portrayed on television did far more to create attitudes to the closed shop than new Acts of Parliament, and certainly more than the attenuated reports about the thousands of dinner-ladies who were contemporaneously resisting through their unions (and UMAs) reductions in pay.

Nor should it be thought that further union targets are lacking. The practice, for example, of the 'check-off', which normally accompanies a UMA, whereby the employer deducts the subscriptions and pays them over to the union, experienced a warning shot across its bows in 1984 (p. 763). It could be put at further risk from the repeal of the Truck Acts by the Wages Bill 1986 (p. 393). The check-off has spread far outside closed shops; the TUC in 1979 estimated that it covered 50 per cent of all workers; Brown in 1980 estimated coverage at 75 per cent of all trade unionists in manufacturing. Government figures for 1980 suggested the check-off applied to 65 per cent of public sector establishments employing manual workers and 35 per cent in the private sector (for non-manual the figures were 62 and 18 per cent). Given the parlous financial condition of some unions, the growing importance in industrial confrontation of the public sector and the determination, as the 1984 Act shows, of Government to intervene – or to invite the courts to intervene – in the arrangements of both unions and management that contribute to union security, it is not unlikely that more legal controls will be proposed for the check-off agreement.

Government has very clear ambitions for its policy in the 1980s. The

Secretary of State, Mr King, said in 1984: 'the new laws would virtually mark the legal extinction of the closed shop in this country'. His predecessor, Mr Tebbit, graphically explained the nature of his 1982 law: 'it will provide the most comprehensive and the most effective statutory protection for non-union employees that we have ever had in this country'. Collective bargaining no longer retains its 'primacy'. Policy has turned turtle since Donovan, indeed since Whitley. McCarthy's conclusion in his meticulous study of the closed shop in 1964 no longer commands the assent it once did in governments of various party colours – 'every worker ought to join his appropriate trade union. This I believe.' The gulf now opened up by the new policies on trade unionism and non-unionism, like those on auxiliary and supportive legislation, makes the arguments that have previously divided opinions on these matters since the First World War in Britain look like shadow-boxing. They throw into question the relationship that will emerge in the 1990s between the law and collective bargaining itself. Changes in this relationship ultimately affect every worker and every part of labour law, including the regulatory legislation, to which we now turn.

[5] Statutory Protection of Wages, Hours and Safety

Collective bargaining in Britain matured in an environment full of legislative intervention. Apart from such areas as job security, discussed in Chapter 3, and what is left of the 'prop' legislation (Chapter 4), the modern law now reflects that context in Acts of Parliament dealing especially with three matters: (1) protection of wages, (2) hours of work and (3) safety, health and welfare at work. Of these, the last provides much the greatest volume of legislation, a vast corpus leading back to the last century. We shall consider its main aspects, not least because any assessment of the fluctuating boundaries of legal enactment and autonomous bargaining must take account of it and because few things are more important to the worker than the security of his life and limb. The labour lawyer cannot overlook the Chief Inspector of Factories' judgment:

It is deplorable that, on average, every week in 1984 three people were being killed in this country on construction or demolition sites and two people were being killed in some kind of maintenance work.

In a developed system of law, the first of the three headings should, no doubt, be 'protection of *income*', bringing together the provisions of social security, wage protection legislation and collective bargaining. Although in our system those areas of law do not interlock as a unity, it has been pointed out that, in the modern law after 1975, Parliament effected a 'crucial transition from a statutory floor of rights dealing primarily with the termination of employment' to one concerned also 'with the content of the employment relationship' about security of earnings.[1] On the other hand, Government policy in the 1980s has increasingly looked to 'deregulation' in some of the areas traditionally covered by legislation.

Protection of wages

'Truck' and wages

From 1464 onwards statutes have tried to stop abuses that came to be described as 'truck' and 'Tommy shops'. 'Truck' means the practice where the worker is paid otherwise than in money (e.g. in kind), while under the second practice the worker would be given vouchers that he could exchange only in shops under the employer's control. The first modern Act to stop 'truck', in 1831, was the result partly of pressure from the newly legalized unions.[2] Related practices were manifold, such as those struck at by Bradlaugh's self-explanatory Payment of Wages in Public Houses Prohibition Act 1883. Yet, as we shall see (p. 393), these protections are today falling victim to 'deregulation' in proposals to repeal the Truck Acts.

The Truck Act 1831 demands that wages be paid in cash – 'in the current coin of this Realm only' – and any agreement to the contrary is illegal and void. Indeed, the employer otherwise commits a crime (in 1887 an exception was inserted for agricultural workers, e.g. payment of food or tied cottages, but this is now administered by the Agricultural Wages Board, the industry's Wages Council). Similarly, the employer must not set off sums said to be owing for goods supplied, nor specify how wages shall be spent. Certain deductions could exceptionally be made (e.g. for medical attendance, or provender for beasts), and later statutes added others (e.g. for income tax or social security, super-annuation deductions in docks or Wages Council industries); and attachment of wages through the employer can be achieved to secure payment of maintenance orders or judgment debts (Attachment of Earnings Act 1971). Otherwise, the employer must not deduct from the wages; the worker's consent to deductions is by itself no defence. In 1936, for example, after the depression in the trade, employees of a cotton company agreed to take shares in the enterprise with payment deducted from wages. They were successful in recovering all the sums deducted, Scott L J saying: 'The money must be paid over so completely and finally that it then and there becomes the workman's very own.'

Workmen and cash wages

But the 1831 Act did not apply to every employee. An amending statute of 1887 applied it to all 'workmen', meaning all *manual workers*, other than domestic or menial servants. Managers and foremen are also excluded. The test is whether 'manual labour' is the substantial part of the employment or merely ancillary to the job. It is noteworthy, too, that 'homeworkers', whom we met in Chapter 2, were expressly protected after 1887, even where their earnings were not strictly 'wages'. So judges held a bus driver with repairing duties to be a 'manual worker', but a tram driver was not; a hairdresser was not; a seamstress was (see also, on the definition of 'factory', p. 432). If manual labour is present, however, the contract need not be one 'of service'; the Act reaches out more widely than the ambit of 'employees' to include all workers with contracts 'personally to execute any work or labour'. As the number of white-collar workers in the work-force increased, these lines of division became less defensible. But *Brooker*, a foreman on the salaried staff, who was still paid in cash and a member of the TGWU, which made an agreement with the employer (incorporated into his employment terms) agreeing 'in principle' to payment by cheque, failed in his challenge to payment by Giro-cheque. He was not a 'workman'; his duties were mainly supervisory; he was a foreman with ancillary manual tasks; so he had no right to be paid in cash.[3] Had he been a manual worker, however, his claim would not have been defeated merely because he had cashed the cheque.

This prohibition upon 'cash-less wages' has caused the statute to be criticized. In *Brooker's* case it led the judge to be prepared to accept a Giro-cheque as 'coin of the realm', an analysis that seems incorrect. It is nevertheless hard to see why only white-collar workers can be paid partly in luncheon vouchers or, conversely, why they should be less well protected against abusive deductions by employers (until recently they were not as well organized in unions as manual workers were); whereas the manual worker can claim large sums for deductions of meal charges (as one did in a test case involving thousands like him in 1940). In fact, even the 1831 Act permitted payment by agreement by draft or order on a bank within fifteen miles that was licensed to issue notes (but this was made redundant when the Bank of England acquired its monopoly). In 1960, therefore, the Payment of Wages Act introduced wider exceptions to payment in cash to workmen. Payment by money order or cheque or direct into a bank account is permitted if the workman has made a written *request* for that method of payment. There can be no requirement to do so, e.g. in the employment terms; nor is the agreement of a union sufficient (as in *Brooker's* case); and the worker or employer can cancel the arrangement on four weeks' notice. But since 1960 few manual workers have requested payment by cheque. (When it was said in Parliament that the workers had not asked for the Act, an interjection claimed: 'It may be their wives.')

Few banks have observed opening hours that are convenient for manual workers, though some now open on Saturdays. A survey of 1985 showed that 65 per cent of British adults had current bank accounts (although these included overwhelmingly those in social 'A, B and C1' groups, most other working men and women above the age of twenty-one had one too). Employers have increasingly complained about the problems of transporting large sums of cash to pay wages and about the private armies of guards needed to protect them; but, as we shall see, their purposes are now being served in a more radical amendment than the careful 1960 Act. In 1984 most of the inquiries and complaints sent to the Wages Inspectors under the Truck Acts concerned alleged illegal deductions, including 'fines', to which we turn shortly.

The check-off

The Truck Acts appear at first to inhibit the spread of the 'check-off', the deduction of trade union subscriptions at source by the employer. Research for the Donovan Commission in 1968, which recommended the efficiency and stability of the practice, showed that some 2 million trade unionists worked under a check-off system, mainly in the public sector; but by the 1980s it has spread, independently of any closed-shop practices, to most union members in large private sector establishments and includes even white-collar staff.[4] The system can contribute greatly to union strength. On the other hand, it may decrease contact between members and stewards (as 'collectors') and leave the employer in a powerful position in the union's lines of organization. In discussions about union records of membership in 1984 (p. 781) it was often said that in some branches the only reliable record was the employer's check-off list, usually today on the computerized pay-roll. Yet all this, in law, depends upon the Law Lords' decision in *Hewlett* v. *Allen*, 1894.[5] There, a worker was required to join a social club, the employer deducting the subscription from wages and paying it to the club's treasurer. These deductions were held not to infringe the Truck Acts. The reason was not the consent of the worker (membership of the club was obligatory for that employment); it was the payment by the employer of part of the wage, at the worker's request, to a *third person*. If the employer deducts sums for himself, that is illegal (as when an employer deducted rent for houses of which he was the landlord). In *Hewlett's* case the employer made no deduction from the wage; he paid part, by consent, to another person.

The analogy with check-off is clear. If the employer fails to pay the sum to the union, the amount remains unpaid 'wages'; but the better view is probably that he holds it on trust for the union. Deductions payable to other third parties escape the Truck Acts for a similar reason, such as payments to occupational pension trustees. In *Williams*, 1975, the judges upheld the acquittal of an employer who continued to check off union dues after the worker had notified him orally that he wished them to cease; but there the worker had initially agreed that the authority to make the deductions would cease only on his leaving the employment or by 'written instruction from the union office'.[6] Subject to such self-imposed limitations, the worker is free to stop the check-off or part of it; for example, he may notify the employer that he no longer wishes to pay the amount of the union subscription that goes to the union fund. The Trade Union Act 1984 makes the employer's obligation very strict where the worker informs him in writing that he is 'exempt' from the obligation to contribute to the political fund (p. 763) and has notified the union of his objection to contributing to it.[7] The employer must ensure that the 'political' contribution is not thereafter deducted (s. 18), a provision that deprives the reasoning of the *Williams* decision of any effect on that matter. But the 1984 section applies only to the political fund contribution. The reasoning of *Williams* remained valid on the union check-off in general and was, indeed, independent of the Truck Acts, in so far as it rests upon the binding character of the worker's initial request to pay to the third party.

Fines and deductions from wages

The right of the employer at common law frequently extends to deductions, for example for careless work (we saw he has the right to sue for loss caused by the worker's negligence: p. 179). However, whereas a court will enforce a clause in the contract that stipulates for a sum to be paid in such circumstances if it is a genuine pre-estimate of loss, it will not enforce it if it is a 'penalty', merely meant to deter the breach of contract. Employers wanted a method whereby deductions from wages for negligence or inefficiency could be safely made. The Truck Act 1896 provided it, on certain conditions. It applies to 'fines', damaged goods and sums charged for materials; and it covers shop assistants in addition to manual workers; but it does not apply to cotton weaving in Lancashire and some other counties (which is relevant to *Sagar* v. *Ridehalgh*: p. 175).

Fines payable *by* the worker are specifically covered. Particulars of the specific offences and amounts of fines must be given; each must be contractual in a written contract signed by the workman or in a notice put up in the workplace; and the method of calculating the amount must be ascertainable; the fine must relate to an offence causing damage, loss or 'interruption or hindrance' to the employer; and the amount must be 'fair and reasonable' (s. 1; the conditions for deductions for damage or in respect of materials are similar: ss. 2, 3; but there the amount must, in addition, not exceed the loss to the employer). So, where workers were fined under a rule posted in a factory in 1901 demanding 'good order and decorum', the judge decided the employer was entitled to impose fines for dancing to music during meal hours; the offence was specific, and the resulting dust was likely to damage the machines.[8] Infringement by the employer is a crime; and if the employee sues within six months he can recover sums illegally deducted. The employer must keep a register of fines and have it, with the relevant contracts, available for inspection.

Difficulty has been caused here as elsewhere by the definition of 'wages' and 'fines'. As a worker in Disraeli's *Sybil* asks: 'What *is* wages? I say 'tain't sugar, 'tain't tea, 'tain't bacon. I don't think it's candles; but of this I be sure 'tain't waistcoats.' If the remuneration is made up of different packages, are they all part of the 'wage'? The wage is the sum agreed as payable for the work. A way round the Truck Act 1896 is immediately apparent, as a 1945 case illustrated. B C employed spinners on contracts providing for termination at one day's notice and a right in the employer to 'suspend' a worker for misconduct, with a proportionate stoppage in his pay. A spinner was suspended for two days for refusing to clean a machine. The Court of Appeal held that the two days' money was never payable as wages; so B C was entitled not to pay it. It was not a deduction; the right to receive it never existed; and, said one appeal judge, 'You cannot deduct something from nothing.' Similarly, in *Sagar's* case (p. 175) the 1896 Act did not apply to the industry; but had it done so, the court held the deductions for bad work would not infringe it because they were not fines deducted from wages, but only part of the method of calculating the wages.[9] This method of evasion became widespread in areas where the work-force was not well unionized.

The Act came suddenly into prominence just as proposals to repeal it appeared. In 1985 the High Court weakened the meaning of a 'fine'. *City Petroleum Ltd*, which was prosecuted, had been deducting sums averaging 17 per cent from the net pay of an employee who was a cashier at a petrol station.[10] He had been induced on recruitment to sign a declaration that he was responsible for *all* cash and stock shortages on every shift he worked and would make them good by payment or deduction; this was repeated in his 'job description'. The court reasoned that 'fine' could not cover all deductions; otherwise there was no place for the 'fine' allowed in the separate section on deductions for damaged goods (s. 2). Therefore 'fines' must be restricted to 'financial penalties'; even though such penalties might in effect compensate the employer, in this case the justices had been right to decide the deductions were not fines. This was, said Goff L J, a liability without fault (for the cashier need not be at fault about the losses) but it was not a 'penalty', only a liability to make good certain losses to the employer. The decision appeared to drive a coach and horses through the 1896 Act as far as the protection of the worker went.

By contrast, in *Sealand Petroleum* v. *Barratt* the court upheld the conviction of a company that employed B., aged eighteen, a forecourt attendant, who on applying for the job signed a form that made him responsible for 'any loss of cash, stock, tools or equipment as a result of your breach of contractual or other duty', and reserved the right to deduct an amount up to the loss from his pay, the exact sum to be determined by reference to 'all the facts of a particular case', including cash deficiencies and replacement value of missing items. He was told that if he failed to take the registration numbers of cars taking petrol without payment, the amount would be deducted from his pay. Others had access to the till; and the manageress checked it in his absence. Deductions were made, in one week the full wage of £55.90. The court noted the unfairness for this worker (young, inexperienced and not 'trained in bookkeeping') of the employer unilaterally calculating the deduction. This was a 'fine' that did not meet the demands of the 1896 Act. No notice was affixed at the workplace; nor was the 'contract' wholly in writing as it required (s. 1 (a)); nor were the amounts fair and reasonable (s. 1 (d)); nor did the contract clearly specify a means by which the amount of deductions could be 'ascertained' (s. 1 (b)).

Barratt's case is important. For we shall see that in the Wages Bill 1986 it was proposed to strip away all these protections and allow deductions wherever 'consent' had been given in writing. As the case shows, for an inexperienced, young worker desperately looking for a job this condition by itself is little protection. But first we must note the range of similar statutory protections.

Extension of protection and itemization

Many other statutes complemented the Truck Acts in an attempt to protect wages against deductions. An Act of 1874 prohibited 'frame rents' in hosiery manufacture (whereby workers were charged rent for machinery let out to them). The same industry originated a different style of protection, the 'particulars clause' that spread to all textile factories; piece-workers must be given clear written particulars (extensively detailed) of wage rates and the work to be done (Factories Act 1961 s. 135: the particulars must 'not be expressed by means of symbols'; inspectors now inspect the particulars; and the control has been extended, with modifications, to other industries, from pen-making and steel foundries to shipbuilding and rubber toy-balloon manufacture). The only remedy here is a prosecution. It was logical, therefore, in the reforms of labour law that followed the repeal of the Industrial Relations Act in 1974, to extend both the scope and the remedies of such a protection. Without repealing the older provisions and in addition to the statement of written particulars required since 1963 (which must state the rate of remuneration or the method of calculating it: now EPCA s. 1 (3)), employers generally were in 1975 required to provide an itemized pay statement on the occasion of each payment (now EPCA s. 8, with particulars of any different methods of calculating parts of it). Such a statement will also reveal deductions; and if a tribunal finds that unnotified deductions have been made from the employee's pay in the preceding thirteen weeks it can order the employer to pay a sum not exceeding them *whether or not* the deductions were made in breach of the employment contract (EPCA s. 11 (8)). However, the employer can meet his obligations by giving the worker a 'standing statement of fixed deductions' once every twelve months (s. 9). Where the worker gets tips from customers they are not 'wages'; in consequence, a proportion demanded by the employer is not a deduction that needs to be stated under the 1978 Act.[11] Conversely, however, a worker who retains an *over*payment of wages may be guilty of theft.[12]

Other statutes went further, for example in the protection of the wage calculation for miners paid by the weight of material extracted. Since 1887 the weighing of coal near the pit-mouth and deductions for alien substances have been controlled by statute; miners have had the right to appoint, at their own cost, a 'check-weigher', elected by the workers. The cost may be deducted from wages; but the employer must afford every facility to the check-weigher (including a shelter from the weather), who in turn must not interfere with ordinary working. The Webbs record the bitter resistance of many coal owners to the workers' check-weigher: 'His calculations were hotly disputed and his interference bitterly resented.' The modern statute, the Mines and Quarries Act 1954, gives miners a further right to elect one of their number as one of the people to inspect the mine and its documents to ensure compliance with safety regulations. An Act of 1919 extended similar check-weighing protections to other industries, such as iron, steel, cement manufacturing and certain quarries.

The fate of Truck Act protections

The division between manual and non-manual workers in the application of the Truck Acts became increasingly anachronistic: 'an absurd, atavistic freak', as Kahn-Freund put it.[13] Three major inquiries between 1908 and 1968 produced no radical reform, though none proposed mere

abolition. The Government set out in 1983 to replace the whole structure – that is, to repeal not only all the Truck Acts and the Payment
of Wages Act 1960, but also the hosiery statute of 1874, the public-
house statute of 1883, the Checkweighing Act of 1919, and the other
check-weighing legislation. These, said Secretary of State King, were
'nineteenth-century leftovers'. Employers pressed for abolition:
'Repeal Truck Acts Now!' declared the EEF *News* in 1985. It was to
repeal all these statutes that Part I of the Wages Bill 1986 was devised,
and for good measure the 'particulars clause' in factories was included as
well. But there are two very different issues. The first largely concerns
payment in cash; the second relates to deductions.

First, it is undoubtedly true that far more workers receive wages in
cash in Britain than in most comparable countries. But in the quarter of
a century since the 1960 Act most of them have voted with their feet to
keep it that way; and this refusal to opt for cashless wages may have
more to do with the available facilities for cashing cheques or orders
than with innate conservatism (few of the comparative statistics also
compare bank opening hours). The case for extending any legislation to
all employees was obvious; and the cost for employers involved in
transporting cash wages plainly indicated that some movement towards
payment by cheque or the equivalent, such as direct credit to bank or
other accounts, is reasonable. But in such a change – a major one – it
would be wise to require of the employer prior information to, and
consultation with, the workers' trade unions.

Secondly, the question of deductions is very different. It is true that all
workers are now entitled to an itemized wage statement, but the
protection of the Truck Act 1896 has, if anything, been reduced by
modern judicial decisions. There is a case for modernizing it and
extending it to all workers, and for ensuring that the Wages Inspectorate
enforces it. The Inspectorate to enforce the 1896 Act dropped from 60 in
1979 to 46 in 1985. Few prosecutions are ever brought. No employer has
in the last decade sought exemption, as the 1896 Act permits by order of
the Secretary of State. Yet the evidence is that deductions have been
made on an increasing scale. One standard petrol-station clause makes
the attendants responsible for all losses, including thefts caused by their
'error', enforceable by deductions; in 'a typical case' a cashier was found
at night checking seventy lines of produce.[14]

Deductions from wages have increased severely in the last decade, especially for workers who handle stock and cash and whose union protection is weak. When faced with such practices in other contexts, the EAT has been prepared to limit the interpretation of such clauses (e.g. by finding that a forecourt attendant was not to be responsible for losses caused by other people's dishonesty).[15] Nor is it unimportant that contravention of the 1896 Act is a crime; nor that repeal of the Truck Acts requires Britain to renounce yet another ILO Convention (No. 95, 1949, Protection of Wages), one ratified by eighty-two other countries. One year's notice of denunciation was given by the Government in September 1983.

These protections will go with repeal under the Wages Bill Part I. This proposes to disallow deductions from the wages of any worker unless authorized under statute, or by a term in the worker's contract, or by a written agreement made by the worker (not, it seems, necessarily an agreement with that employer). The contractual 'terms' include all express and implied terms so long as the employer has 'notified' the worker of them before the deduction. The check-off is protected by a provision for deductions paid to third parties with the written consent of the worker. Variations in the terms cannot apply to deductions on account of the worker's 'conduct' retrospectively. But the employer does not make a 'deduction' under this Bill by deficiencies caused by 'error' in computing gross wages, nor if he stops pay because of industrial action (p. 199). A worker's remedy is by complaint to an industrial tribunal, normally within three months, for repayment of the amount. All other remedies go; the Inspectorate fades away.

The recognition that there is a bigger problem appears in the Bill where it makes special provision for retail workers, i.e. workers who carry out retail transactions (including financial services) directly with the public. Here the deduction must not exceed one-tenth of the gross wages payable on one particular day. Without more, this further exposes the weakness of the general control mechanism, the need for written 'consent' from the worker, which is in any event little more than a rehearsal of common law principle. For retail workers all payments or calculations relating to cash shortages or stock deficiencies are brought within the Bill; but the employer must notify them of total liabilities before his demand. Liability for such shortage or deficiency may arise from 'dishonesty or other conduct' or 'any other event' for which there is 'contractual liability'. Thus, liability for *other* people's dishonesty is clearly envisaged. On the final payment of wages, however, the one-tenth limit is removed. On dismissal, the retail worker may find that much more has been deducted from his final pay package. If a retail employer sues his employee for amounts due for cash shortage or stock deficiency, the court must arrange for payment at a rate not exceeding the 10 per cent that could be recovered under these arrangements.

The protections afforded in retail employment where workers are less effectively organized in unions – bar staff, petrol-station attendants, many shop assistants, car-park attendants (invariably disabled workers) – are minimal. In earlier consultations the Government had considered making retail deductions unlawful. So too, it had been proposed that features of the 1896 Act should be retained for all workers, with a requirement to display notices as to penal and compensatory deductions, that the Inspectorate be retained to enforce the law, or an obligation to consult recognized trade unions be included. The drive to deregulation ousted all such proposals. The Bill confirmed in a new area the policies of the new labour law. For all the antiquated oddities of the Truck Acts and associated legislation, they were a stronger brick in the floor of rights for manual workers than the 1986 Bill provides. This characteristic is likely to emerge when tribunals deal with cases of dismissal alleged to be unfair by reason of practices that include such deductions. Employers are likely to argue that they must be taken to have acted reasonably in respect of deductions and fines if they have satisfied the paltry requirements of the 1986 statute. The tribunals and EAT should not allow this measure to affect the view they have taken in the past of unreasonable deductions, whether or not imposed under the employee's written 'consent'.[16]

Guarantee payments

We have noted (p. 230) that when the employer has insufficient work for employees, those who lose pay (e.g. because they are paid by piecework or by the hour or have contracts permitting suspension without pay) were provided with statutory protection in 1975 (now EPCA ss. 12–18). The floor of protection is very low, and, as we saw in Chapter 4, this is an area where parties to collective agreements providing better protection have taken advantage of the possibility to have 'exemption orders' exempt the bargained scheme out of the Act's provisions (s. 18).

Moreover, if the worker is paid any contractual pay, this is set off against the statutory payment. To qualify, a worker must have been continuously employed for one month, another problem for casual workers if they have no right to work for such a period.[17] Then there must be a failure by the employer to provide work on a day on which the worker would normally work caused either by a diminution in the needs of the business for work of that kind, or by any other extraneous occurrence, such as a natural disaster, affecting normal working (s. 12). No payment can be claimed for days that are not normal working days (such as annual holidays); nor where the cause is industrial action, whether strike or lock-out, involving the employer or an associated employer; nor where the employer reasonably offers work or requires attendance for part of the day. No payment is made where the worker unreasonably refuses the offer of suitable alternative work, suited to his abilities, even if outside his normal employment contract (s. 13).

If he manages to surmount all these hurdles, the worker receives no princely sum from the employer for his workless days. The maximum period for which he can claim is five days in 'rolling quarters' (three months must elapse since the last payment), and the maximum amount to which his 'guaranteed rate' can rise on each day is currently £10.70. Perhaps it was a mark, however, of the plight of many workers that ACAS received 1,092 cases concerning guarantee payments in 1984, far more than in any of the preceding four years, though only 140 went to the tribunals, which have jurisdiction over complaints.

The provisions on guarantee payments, along with payments on suspension for certain medical reasons (p. 230), were meant to be reorganized in the later 1970s, with social security provisions, into a new scheme for short-term wage protection with a new State fund to reimburse employers. Instead, the overlapping provisions of employment protection for guarantee payments and of unemployment benefit remained structurally unresolved, a problem that the Employment Subsidies Act 1978 and the Temporary Short-Time Working Compensation Scheme (p. 506) appeared to make worse, as was shown by writers at the time.[18] It was questioned whether such wage guarantees were appropriate to place on employees, transferring cost to the consumer, rather than upon the general tax system by way of social security. The system of guarantee payments produced many anomalies in regard to the adjacent law on entitlement to unemployment benefit and to guaranteed week agreements. The Social Security Commissioners had excluded a worker from being 'unemployed' when he was covered by a collectively negotiated guaranteed week (e.g. five days' employment or forty hours' rated pay) even if the union and employer later agreed it could not be effective in the emergency that arose (such as the 'three-day week' imposed by government in 1974).[19] The guarantee payments introduced in 1975 only nibbled at the edge of the problem of income maintenance in an era that requires a coherent policy blending labour law with social security and job-creation law, something no British government has yet attempted.

The employer's insolvency[20]

If the employer becomes 'insolvent', the employee has two avenues of redress. First, he may be able to claim as a preferred creditor (i.e. among those paid off with priority) in regard to four months' remuneration with a limit (in 1985 it was £800, other than for agricultural workers, whose priority may extend to a year's remuneration: Companies Act 1985, Schedule 19, paras. 9–12; replaced by Insolvency Act 1985, Schedule 3, Part I, para. 5, Part II, para. 3). In this context, remuneration includes wages or salary for services rendered, guarantee payments, payments on suspension for medical grounds, payments for time off, statutory sick-pay, protective awards in redundancies and certain accrued holiday remuneration. Priority in an insolvency is also, however, accorded to the Inland Revenue, Customs and Excise, social security authorities and the trustees of any occupational pension fund; and the procedure of 'proving' in an insolvency is a long process.

The second method is for the employee to claim directly from the Redundancy Fund. This can be done in respect of arrears of pay (including guarantee payments, medical suspension payments, payments for time off, protective award payments and statutory sick-pay), up to eight weeks, sums to compensate for inadequate notice, holiday pay over the previous year up to six weeks, basic award compensation for unfair dismissal, and a reasonable repayment of apprenticeship fees (EPCA s. 122 (1), (2)). The maximum amount obtainable here for a debt owing over a period of time, however, is fixed by Order (in 1986 it was £155 per week), so that the maximum recoverable in pay and other periodical payments is £1,240. The Redundancy Fund recovers by way of the Secretary of State standing in the shoes of the employee in the employer's insolvency (EPCA s. 125), and provision is also made for the recovery of sums due to an occupational pension scheme by the insolvent employer (s. 123). A similar system operates for the recovery of maternity pay (ss. 40–42: from the Maternity Fund) and redundancy pay (ss. 106–8), but in these cases the employee can recover if it is proved either that the employer is insolvent or that the employee 'has taken all reasonable steps (other than legal proceedings)' to recover the payment from the employer and that he has failed to pay it in full. If a scheme under a collective agreement has taken over, by exemption order, from the statutory redundancy scheme, the worker may recover from the Redundancy Fund either the statutory sum or the sum under the agreement, whichever is the less.

The worker is given the right to sue the Secretary of State in the tribunal if payment is not properly made (EPCA s. 124). When *Ms Cox* claimed from the Maternity Fund, the Minister refused payment of a sum as maternity pay during her pregnancy because her employer became insolvent the week after she left work (she gave notice she would be absent for eleven weeks before confinement); she therefore could not be 'absent from work', since there was no work. The EAT rejected the argument; her right to maternity pay accrued at the time she left, and the fund must pay her.[21] But in *Morris*, 1985,[22] the EAT decided that the maximum payable meant not 'take-home' pay but gross pay, so that the sum paid must be net after all deductions for tax and national insurance contributions.

A more difficult problem arose in *Westwood*.[23] Where the employee is entitled to a payment in lieu of minimum statutory notice under EPCA s. 49 (p. 202) he may claim it from the fund in an insolvency; and this claim, under s. 122 (3), is a claim to a statutory debt rather than for damages for wrongful dismissal. But the Department of Employment took the view that the claim was of the same nature as a breach of contract claim, and unemployment benefit received or wages in a new job immediately acquired must therefore be deducted from the amount (p. 211). The House of Lords agreed with this way of looking at the problem; benefits received in the statutory notice period had to be deducted. But the employee need account by way of mitigation only for *net* benefits; so, because Westwood was unemployed for more than a year, he became entitled to a refund from the Redundancy Fund, having run out of entitlement to unemployment benefit when he received the lower supplementary benefit. His statutory debt would be reduced only by that lower sum for the twelve weeks (the period of notice he should have had). The difficulty in this decision, which led to consequential amendment in social security regulations and absurd complexity, really arose from the Law Lords' approval of *Parsons's* case[24] and the principle of deducting social security benefit from damages – which, we have suggested, displays some hostility to the Welfare State (Chapter 3, p. 213). The employee is entitled to 'pay', e.g. unpaid wages to which he is contractually entitled before the insolvency. Similarly, he is entitled to pay in lieu of notice. It seems absurd that the unemployed worker should have to account for social security benefits as deductions from either amount, the effect of which in an insolvency is to grant the Department of Employment a rebate on what he is paid by the DHSS. The Cork Report on Insolvency (1982) understood the objectives of the scheme better when it wished to reorganize the insolvency rights of employees on the basis that this is 'a social measure' the cost of which 'ought properly to be borne by the community'.[25]

Despite the anomalies in the two systems of insolvency rights – it is inexplicable, for example, that the Insolvency Act 1985 did not even align the different monetary maxima – insolvency claims have been important to workers in the 1980s, especially with the simpler procedure under the EPCA. For 'in practice . . . claims for unpaid wages due to employees', the Cork Report noted, 'are relatively unimportant' in normal insolvency process. More usually banks that have advanced money for wages make such claims on insolvency. The payments from the Redundancy Fund grew during the recession. Payments from the fund on insolvency (s. 122) were recorded for the following years as: year ending April 1979, 40,439 (£9.9 m.); year ending April 1983, 109,317 (£46.1 m.); year ending April 1985, 86,431 (£44.1 m.). Equivalent redundancy payments (s. 106), of which 80 per cent are estimated to be insolvency cases, were: 1979, 29,247 (£14.6 m.); 1983, 74,980 (£72.3 m.); 1985, 51,706 (£57.2 m.). Maternity Fund (s. 40) payments, some 80 per cent in insolvency, were lower: 1979, 19 (£2,106); 1983, 40 (£10,120); 1985, 49 (£13,709).

Company liquidations on a compulsory or creditors' winding-up (the vast majority for insolvency) increased from 6,150 in 1978 to more than 14,000 in 1984. Bankruptcies in 1984 reached their highest level for a decade. The processes of insolvency law are likely to continue to be of some concern to workers attempting to salvage a pittance from the wreckage. Their entitlements should not be cramped by the legal technicalities of an area still not rationalized after the Insolvency Act and Companies Act of 1985. In a liberal interpretation of the law Nourse J. decided that, although a court could not wind up a company if no advantage would accrue to the petitioner (and this usually means he must show there are assets within the jurisdiction), he would make a winding-up order against an insolvent foreign company trading in Britain but without assets here, because if he did so he might give the petitioning workers thereby a right to claim from the Redundancy Fund under EPCA s. 122. It would, he thought, be 'a lamentable state of affairs' if winding-up was excluded by 'the technicality' that the workers' rights were against the fund rather than against the company's assets in Britain.[26]

When the rights of employees in insolvency are comprehensively reconstructed as part of a plan for the protection of earnings, this spirit might profitably infuse the reform. Such an inquiry should also lead us to question whether the rights of employees should not be enforced in some degree against not only the company or a guarantor fund but those human beings in control of the company who may have walked away from the insolvency made safe against claims by the doctrine of limited liability. Further, it may be asked whether the rights of workers should depend upon the one 'event' or determination (of 'insolvency', however defined) and whether in place of such concepts, developed for purposes of commercial law, the interests of employment and employees should not be inserted much more widely, as is being suggested in other countries, by way of 'provisional' or temporary decisions demanded of the enterprise before dismissals are accepted for financial reasons.[27] The redundancy provision (s. 106) already goes wider than insolvency to include other financial difficulties, and the Insolvency Act 1985 points down the same road.

Hours of work

'The maximum duration of the working day is established by law.' So states the Constitution of Italy, whose labour laws have long placed controls on working hours, at base resting on the 'three eights' (daily eight hours each of work, of repose and of 'personal activity freely chosen').[28] In France, unions wanted and won the 8-hour day by law in 1919 and the 40-hour week from the 1936 Popular Front government. The law came to control daily maximum hours (normally 10), the working week (48) and the basic week (39 hours); collective agreements in France can extend daily hours but normally not beyond 12.[29] In both countries the modern position is vastly more complex, of course, because both general and particular laws (dealing with young workers and women, for example) and collective agreements in practice provide a tapestry of norms, not least with the introduction in both countries of types of 'solidarity contract', agreements to share working hours sometimes with State subsidies, parallel to, but now far more developed than, the old British Temporary Short-Time Working Compensation Scheme (p. 506).[30] Nevertheless, such systems start out from the legal regulation of working hours, and both have a general 'labour inspectorate'.[31]

The picture in Britain has long been very different – at least for adult male workers. Yet the method of legal enactment over hours and conditions of work might have become more prominent. Reformers in the nineteenth century naturally turned to the law, and some trade unions were not averse to its use. The area that came to be regarded as proper for statutory controls is, however, largely the one they came to occupy before the modern era of collective bargaining began. Nor was the tide a simple unimpeded flow of legislative progress. No doubt, the factory legislation reflects 'English practical empiricism',[32] but the stream of statute ebbed and flowed on movements that were significantly related to the strength of groups who called for, or who resisted, reforms.

The banning of the use of young boys as chimney-sweeps, first attempted in 1788, was not achieved until Lord Shaftesbury's Bill of 1875, when magistrates were still refusing to convict because there was no strict proof of the age of unfortunate boys of 8 or 9 so abused. Indeed, there was 'a drastic increase in the intensity of exploitation of child labour between 1780 and 1840'.[33] The path of reform legislation was not smooth. Views differ on whether it came about because 'collectivism' was adopted as a social necessity or in order to 'redistribute' individual freedom.[34] More important, the victories of Tory reformers like Shaftesbury, and of the trade union movement, along with their defeats, set the frontier for factory legislation that bounded collective bargaining in the industrial relations system that later emerged. It was, and is, complex legislation; not all of the details can be described here, but certain features of its history and present state must be noticed. The new moves in 1986 to deregulate certain areas can then be seen in context.

Hours of women and young workers

The first of the Acts controlling hours and conditions for young workers was one passed 'for the health and morals of apprentices and others' in 1802. But it was little more than an extension of the Elizabethan Poor Law relating to apprentices and it was poorly enforced. The factory system introduced the more savage exploitation of an advancing Industrial Revolution, especially for child, young and women workers. In 1833 an Act resulting from reformers' pressure for the Ten-Hour Day limited the textile employment of young workers to ten hours, and also provided for the appointment of four inspectors to enforce the Act's provisions. These inspectors were not wholly dominated by the employers, as had been predicted, and the Factory Inspectorate became, as we shall see, a primary agency of enforcing the modern statutes. Whilst, no doubt, the success of the Inspectorate's enforcement methods and style must not be overrated,[35] its creation was one of the most important innovations in our labour law.

The next fifty years saw a swaying struggle between reformers, unions and inspectors, on the one hand, and many employers, magistrates and judges along with parliamentary pressure groups, on the other. In the 1844 Act, women workers were brought within the statutory protections; but children of eight might be employed, and the Inspectorate's powers were reduced. Daily hours of women and young persons were restricted to ten by an Act of 1847, but employers found ways of evading this, with the co-operation of the magistrates (p. 578), so that 'factory legislation was in complete chaos'.[36] An amending statute of 1850 provided for an increase in hours. Some opponents of controls over the appallingly long hours worked by women and children asserted that the measures had the object of restricting men's hours, since they could not work in some factories without the children's help. This was not the last time working men had to determine their attitude to the protection of children and women working beside them; moreover, attempts were repeatedly made to exclude women altogether from the legal regulation (their hours of work, it was said in 1874, could be left to their 'good sense and increasing intelligence') – including some by Liberal women as late as the 1890s, decrying the limitation on their opportunities. Women and boys under ten had been banned from underground work in the mines in 1842. In 1867 factories and workshops other than textiles were brought within the skeleton of statutory control. But a secure and enforceable ten-hour day for women and young persons appeared on the statute book only in 1874, with an enforced minimum age of ten for factory employment. Even then many areas of work remained outside the regulation; the pressure to maintain women's maximum hours in laundries at 14 was continuous, reflecting a 'middle-class dread of personal inconvenience'[37] (even today women's daily hours in laundries may be extended to 10 on two weekdays if the employer gives a week's notice to the inspector: Factories Act 1961 ss. 110, 115). But the Act of 1878 consolidated the law and may be accounted the first modern Factories Act – all little more than a century ago.

In the modern law the hours and conditions of women and young persons have been regulated by a barrage of statutory provisions, mainly those applying to 'factories' (p. 432). Under the Factories Act 1961, for example, total hours may not exceed 9 in a day (11 including breaks) or 48 in a week, commencing not earlier than 7 a.m., ending by 8 p.m. (1 p.m. on Saturdays); spells of work may not exceed 4½ hours (or 5 with a ten-minute break) followed by a half-hour rest (ss. 86, 87; on notices see s. 88). The Act follows with numerous exceptions (e.g. in sausage manufacturing and, of course, laundries; or for women who are in management; or where a five-day week is worked, when a twelve-hour day is allowed: s. 100), and the Minister can approve other particular exceptions. More important, a general exception permits women's overtime outside the hours fixed, within strict limits imposed by the Act (e.g. up to six hours in a week). The Act also protects certain holidays for women and young workers (e.g. bank holidays and Christmas Day). Two statutes passed in 1920 and 1936 gave general effect to I L O Conventions under which the employment at night of women or young workers under eighteen was banned, except in strictly defined circumstances, in any industrial undertakings. The Mines and Quarries Act 1954 controls the above-ground hours of women and continues the prohibition on their working underground (in 1842 they were 'dragging trucks of coal to which they were harnessed by a chain and girdle on all fours, in conditions of dirt, heat and indecency which are scarcely printable').[38]

Below school-leaving age (sixteen) children are normally excluded from employment. The ban is total below thirteen (though, as was shown in the case of a milkman in 1978, a crime is committed only if the lower age is known).[39] It seems unlikely that the prosecutions (a mere nineteen in 1980–4) represent the number of breaches of this law. Below sixteen, none may be employed in a mine, factory or transport; nor in industrial undertakings except where a member of the family is employed; and the entertainment industry is specially regulated. Part-time jobs below sixteen are controlled; when the Secretary of State takes up powers to make regulations under the Employment of Children Act 1973, he will exercise major control where the law has long given local authorities extensive powers to intervene.

Young workers (under eighteen) are protected by most provisions applying to women and by some more: restrictions apply to continuous employment and shift work and to work at night in certain industries. Young male workers are exempt from certain restrictions (e.g. on shifts in certain industries, such as iron and steel, or on continuous employment with men). The Shops Act 1950 regulates the conditions of shop-workers and especially young assistants, over hours, half-holidays and meal-times; and any repeal of the Act, to which we return below, would have serious implications for all shop-workers as many of its protective provisions are not (as the Auld Report, 1984, pointed out)[40] reproduced in other statutes. Restrictions on hours in certain occupations (such as cinemas, news-agency messages, hotels) were introduced in 1938 and extended in 1964.

The Secretary of State has long had considerable powers to grant exemptions, on application from an employer or even a union or JIC. The most important derive from the Factories Act 1961, under which in 1974 some functions were transferred to the Health and Safety Executive (HSE). The general power to grant exemptions under that Act and the 1920 Act on women's and young persons' hours arises where it is thought appropriate in the public interest for the efficiency of industry or transport. Most exemptions relate to extended daily hours, overtime, shift work, week-end work and, above all, night work. Women workers have 'very few rights in the whole process', and 'in practice very few applications for an exemption order are refused'.[41] The published figures are very strange. Exemption orders never seem to vary much in number. In July 1970 there were orders covering 153,000 women and 15,500 young workers; in July 1979, 230,000 and 18,500; in July 1983, 151,000 and 15,000; in July 1985, 185,000 and 18,000 (the year in which the Government decided to cease publishing detailed figures). It seems unlikely that this type of variation is a true reflection of changes in the pattern of hours, especially as this is the period of great increase in women's employment and of the lurches of the recession, especially too as the recorded exemptions nearly doubled between 1964 and 1970. Successful prosecutions of employers for excessive hours in 1984 numbered 9 for young workers and 2 for women (total fines £3,750); 5 convictions for overworking *children* produced an average fine of £160 a case (the Government announced in 1985 that the HSE was 'reviewing the position' of regulation of part-time child workers – not, one suspects, before time). It is impossible to escape the impression that the Health and Safety Commission (HSC) and the HSE – no doubt with other pressing problems, as we shall see – give this matter a low priority; and that courts regard it as scarcely criminal (rather like some motoring offences). This is a view that would be supported by those who want to 'deregulate' employment hours for women workers. Some would abolish all special regulations of women's conditions at work, allowing even underground mining work as is found now in parts of the United States.

Just as the 'women's rights' opposition to that regulation in the late nineteenth century included the Working Women's Protective and Provident League (and some other noble middle-class bodies) as well as industrialists, Liberals and some trade unionists, so the modern argument in favour of deregulating all or most restrictions at work has cut across the usual party lines. In 1968 a tripartite NJAC report was divided on the issue, but the Government tentatively advocated deregulation. Later, repeal received qualified support from the EOC;[42] TUC policy turned in the opposite direction, while some industrialists shared the view of the writer to *The Times* back in 1902 that all regulation of the labour market makes 'trade groan under the restrictions of the grandmother who is so terribly abroad in the land'.

In 1985 the Government favoured repealing 'unnecessary restrictions and out of date discrimination on women's hours of work' so as to reduce the burdens on business, though 'this will also better ensure equalities of opportunity in employment'.[43] On the other hand, the weakening of

Wages Councils (p. 354) is criticized, understandably, by women's movement writers for undermining the position of low-paid women. The EEC draft Directive on part-time workers is supported by the argument that it would not reduce employment opportunities for women merely by levelling *up* employment protection.[44] The issue is perhaps properly seen not as one of principle; for 'freedom in the labour market' has a meaning for a worker, man or woman, only as it operates on them in practice. In proposing the end of control over shift work, for example, the EOC has sensibly demanded equally that any woman losing employment thereby must be compensated; workers' views on shift work should be consulted; and workers with special domestic commitments, such as young children, should enjoy preference as to choice of shifts. These conditions would work only if women workers along with men were adequately unionized; the last demand puts in issue the whole question of 'family' rights and the private life of the worker (p. 449). Unless it was matched by an increase in parental equality, it might become merely a method of covert protection for women. In the Britain of tomorrow, however, full parental equality is unlikely to occur. The EEC member States' Recommendation (1984) for a programme of 'Positive Action for Women' requires Britain to adopt a policy 'to eliminate existing inequalities affecting women in working life'.[45] It would be useful to approach this task in terms of the practical issues (shift work, night work, child-care provisions at work and the like) and to require negotiation with women workers and their unions where social discrimination leads to inequality for women in employment. Just as useful might be better enforcement of the law that we have long had.

Into this situation the Government threw the Sex Discrimination Bill 1986, which aims to repeal most of the protective legislation affecting women's hours: the Act of 1936 on night work; the restrictions in mines and quarries (above ground) concerning working hours, rest intervals, and starting and finishing hours (6 a.m. and 10 p.m.); the factory legislation restricting hours (11 in a day, not more than 9 of them working; or 12 and 10 with overtime; 48 in a week), starting and finishing hours (normally 7 a.m. and 8 p.m.), Saturday half-days, rest intervals every 4½ hours, standard meal-intervals, restrictions on overtime, control of seasonal work, notification to the inspector and in a register and notices of overtime particulars, the provision of separate rest and meal rooms, Sunday working restrictions, the provision of public holidays, and the control of shift work. There are many flexibilities built into the statutes in addition to the Minister's power to exempt by Order; for example, special adjustments of hours for factories on a five-day week, for special trades such as bakeries and newspapers, and (inevitably) for 'pressure of work' in laundries. The Secretary of State is given power by the 1986 Bill to revoke any Orders or regulations made under this legislation. There are many such. Regulations of 1938, for example, modify provisions on hours, seasonal or other special pressure of work, and overtime (increased to an annual limit of 150 hours) in laundries. Other regulations range from hours in net-mending and bottling to confectionery work and florists. One of the more general regulations on shift system, originally made under a 1936 Act and continued under the Factories Act 1961, provides for the way in which women and young persons must be 'consulted . . . by *secret ballot*' on proposed arrangements for shift working; in the absence of a majority of the workers giving their consent the Minister cannot grant the necessary application by the employer for approval of the arrangements. It will be interesting to see whether this order is revoked along with the rest.

The Hours of Employment (Conventions) Act 1936 gives effect to an international Convention prohibiting the employment of women normally between 10 p.m. and 5 a.m. in industrial undertakings. The repeal of it and of the associated provisions for factories on night work in the 1986 Bill is likely to be one focus of attention. For the same Government that introduced this measure stresses the dangers of increasing crime rates. The provision of public transport at night has not improved in the 1980s. Some measure of special protection for women who are forced to take night-time employment, perhaps in part-time and insecure jobs in the secondary labour market, might not be thought an unreasonable accompaniment of new laws for 'equality' of treatment with men. In fact, the absence of any auxiliary measures concerned to mitigate the possible exploitation of women workers suggests that the 1986 Bill was more concerned to relieve business of its 'burdens' than to proffer real social equality to women.

Men's hours
It has become orthodoxy to think that the working hours of men belong to the domain of collective bargaining. Attempts were made to regulate

men's hours, though, in the middle of the last century. J. M. Cobbett moved Bills in 1853 and 1855 for this purpose; soon after the initial protections for women and children, he asked whether the 'adult male' should be 'worked to death or not? – fifteen hours a day! Sixteen hours a day! . . . Talk of Freedom! The man in the factory is not free.' Others promoted the same idea in the ensuing decade. The legislation protecting the hours of women and children, however, could strengthen the hand of men's unions. The Webbs made famous the remark of the Oldham Spinners' secretary that the men's industrial battle for shorter hours in early collective bargaining was 'fought from behind women's petticoats'; and the 'Short-Time Movement' of the 1870s clearly had men's interests in mind as much as women's. It was, after all, trade union experience which taught that reductions of hours won by the skilled would be shared by the unskilled 'because many tasks required skilled and unskilled men to work together'.[46] Some unions later in the century were ready, even eager, to see legislation used to put into effect general demands for shorter hours even for working men. The Miners' Federation, for example, successfully pressed such a demand; after 1908 the daily stint underground was limited, a curb now continued in the Mines and Quarries Act 1954 (seven hours, save if set aside in times of national danger).

The railway unions, too, saw their members suffer from extremely long hours demanded by the employers. Said an official to a guard who in 1871 had worked eighteen hours and asked when he might be free: 'You've got twenty-four hours in a day like any man, and they are all ours if we want them.'[47] The Railway Servants (Hours of Labour) Act 1893 actually gave the Board of Trade powers to impose reasonable hours for the men. So too shop hours were regulated in an Act of 1886, though a parliamentary report six years later said it was unenforced, 'even to a great extent unknown'. Other unions, and even the TUC, looked for a period to general 'legal enactment' on hours; but at the turn of the century 'few trade unions continued to believe that there was any reasonable prospect of getting it'.[48]

The unions did not object to such legislation ideologically, as Dicey did, as constraining 'the right of a workman of full age to labour for any number of hours agreed upon between him and his employer'.[49] They largely jettisoned the method of enactment on hours of work because collective bargaining was perceived to be a more profitable approach.

The Acts that appear in the modern law, therefore, are exceptional; they usually control hours in occupations where overwork brings special dangers to the men, the public or both. An Act of 1954 limited the hours of night work in bakeries; under an Act of 1936 the hours of sheet-glass workers on continuous shift are limited, to give effect to an ILO Convention. The Shops Act 1950 limited working hours of shop assistants; and the Transport Act 1968 (passed for 'protecting the public against risks which arise in cases where the drivers of motor vehicles are suffering from fatigue') controls the hours of drivers of public-service and certain other motor vehicles, a code of protection now extended and fused into the less stringent EEC Community law on the subject, including the requirement to operate the tachograph.[50]

The advent of collective bargaining as the main control over the working hours of men (and, despite the statutory provisions, largely for women too) meant that the campaign that has been central to most trade unions in Western Europe in the 1980s, namely the campaign for reductions in working hours without significant loss of earnings, naturally had a different emphasis in Britain from that in many other countries where regulatory legislation is a more normal context. Union pressure everywhere plays a role; even the West German engineering industry experienced its biggest strike and lock-out for three decades early in 1985 on the issue of the 35-hour week. There is strong support within the EEC for a primary role for legislation in achieving the diminution of annual working time, leaving choices open between the reduction of weekly or daily working hours, the introduction of 'flexitime' systems and the increase of annual holidays.[51] Opposition from the British Government prevented a Community 'Recommendation' on the subject being issued in 1984. The TUC in 1984 adopted guidelines for unions bargaining for reductions of working time. Such agreements have been regularly made; but those (covering 850,000) in that year recorded a deceleration in the rate of their conclusion.[52] Few British negotiations have confronted proposals as novel as those in United States agreements in 1985 (e.g. at General Motors and International Harvester), where the company guaranteed a certain amount of employment hours over a period (three years in one case) against each unit of output, 'time banks' of work on which workers threatened by technological redundancy may draw.

The TUC recorded in 1985 a significant shift towards reduction by way of basic holiday improvement, but little progress in the reduction of overtime (either as such or linked to job saving; indeed, overtime working appeared to be increasing). On pressing the Government for action on this issue, the T U C found that the Secretary of State refused to join in anything, even the E E C 'Recommendation', that would 'represent legislative interference in collective bargaining'. The T U C itself has not called for comprehensive legislation. It remains to be seen whether this deceptive unity in favour of the method of autonomous negotiation will survive into the 1990s. If reductions and reorganization of working time are to contribute to job creation in the rapidly changing labour market of the 1990s, the practical instincts of unions and management in Britain may yet come to see a place for supplemental legislation that helps to set a firmer framework for the hours of employees. Like so many other problems, the place of legislation on men's hours, and women's, is likely to be determined by the manner in which such a legislative framework contributes to policies leading back to fuller employment.

An alternative approach is to see all this legislation as yet another obstacle to the workings of the economic market and to set about deregulation. This is the main aim of two measures introduced in 1985–6. Since the restrictions upon women's working hours in bakeries in the factory legislation would be repealed by it, the Government proposed in the Sex Discrimination Bill 1986 also to repeal, almost by a side wind, the 1954 Act limiting men's hours in bakeries. That Act made it a criminal offence for the employer to employ workers in excess of the hours permitted for night work. Night baking was limited, for example, to twenty-six weeks for each worker in a year; but the Minister could grant exemption from most controls where employers' organizations and trade unions had agreed in collective agreements upon different conditions; six such orders were made between 1957 and 1974. Attempts to protect sweated workers in night bakery go back as far as 1848, when night bakers, for example, were reported to be employed for 20 hours out of 24 in Dundee (the same town that saw a strike of bakery workers nearly a century later). Gladstone (then thirty-seven, an early de-regulator anticipating modern trends) opposed legal restrictions on working hours in 1848: 'it would be so entirely abhorrent to the genius of the constitution and the people that it would not be endured'.

After reports by committees in 1919 and 1937, modest legislation was passed in 1938 controlling night baking; and after a further report in 1952, the 1954 Act was presented as a 'sincere effort' by the Conservative Government to solve deep-seated problems of the industry. It was in fact a bipartisan measure. The object, Government spokesmen said, was to use the Act as a basis on which employers and unions could build collective agreements under the exemption orders. Even so, the U K did not ratify the I L O Convention (No. 20 of 1925) on night bakery work. No further committee of inquiry was felt necessary in 1986. In the event of repeal of the 1954 Act, though, bakery workers will be protected against exploitation in night work in many other countries, but not in Britain.

The Shops Bill 1986 was the second measure to point in the same direction. It did not, as many thought, deal only with liberalization of shop hours on Sundays. It proposed that the provisions in the Shops Act 1950, which gave shop assistants a weekly half-holiday and secure meal intervals, should 'cease to apply' to shop-workers who had attained the age of 18.[53] An amendment to delete 'cease' and insert 'continue', moved by Lord Denning and supported by the Earl of Stockton (the Conservative ex-Prime Minister Macmillan) was carried in the House of Lords by a majority of one. The Government, therefore, had to decide whether it would accept the defeat of this deregulatory proposal, which appeared ill advised to many, especially as young workers would not be protected where a Wages Council existed (for example, the two retail trade councils, which covered one million workers) until they were twenty-one under proposals of the Wages Bill 1986 (p. 354).

Not all control over conditions was covered; the Shops Act requirement, for example, of seats for women shop workers was not to be repealed. Nor was the prohibition lifted on women working in mines underground. The House of Commons, however, voted against the 1986 Bill as a whole, a defeat that caused the Government to drop it. In general, the 1986 measures of deregulation did not point towards a reduction of working hours without loss of income. They deal with areas where trade union organization, and therefore collective bargaining, is relatively weak and where deregulation means a further increase in managerial power and prerogative and increased difficulty for workers to resist whatever demands are made on them.

Safety, health and welfare

The early Factory Acts included crude attempts to provide some protection on hours and welfare to children and young workers; but as the factory system developed and new machinery was introduced, new dangers to the person of the worker appeared. The concern for women workers coincided with inspectors' reports in the 1840s of terrible accidents suffered especially by girls and women, whose dress made them most vulnerable. The Act of 1844 demanded secure fencing of certain dangerous machinery and forbade the cleaning of machinery in motion. Once again there was resistance, especially from the National Association of Factory Occupiers (Dickens called them the 'Association for the Mangling of Operatives'), and Parliament relaxed the requirements in 1856. The great Inspector Horner complained that the engineers to whom 'arbitration' was assigned were more likely to be concerned with the machines than with the prevention of accidents. Although factory owners declared that 'either the Factory Acts must be modified or the industry of England would seriously decline' (an early version of the economic argument for deregulation), statutory protection was extended beyond textiles to other enterprises in which elementary standards of sanitation and conditions of work were demanded.[54]

It was not until 1878 that anything like a modern statutory control appeared; the secure fencing of machinery was made a strict duty on the employer, and a start was made in banning young workers from very dangerous factories (such as those involving white lead). At the turn of the century, pressure from Radicals and trade unions (especially the miners and cotton operatives)[55] secured an improved structure, and the Act of 1901, consolidating a jumble of earlier statutes, was the first comprehensive piece of factory legislation, which remained the basic code until the Factory Act 1937, itself overtaken later by the Factories Act 1961. Thus, by the time modern collective bargaining came largely to occupy the territory of workers' pay and related conditions, the method of legislation had been firmly established as the basic determinant of conditions affecting the safety, health and welfare of many groups of workers, and few wished it otherwise.

Many workers were left unprotected. From the 1860s, for example, Plimsoll promoted a thirty-year campaign to help the crews of 'coffin ships', but he was strongly opposed to industrial pressure or union militancy, 'preferring that all progress should come by legislation'. So too, the greatest of reformers, Lord Shaftesbury himself, objected to union 'agitators' (let alone the Chartists, even if their programmes included ten-hour Bills and factory legislation). The varied pressures of unions and reformers meant that belated extensions of safety and welfare legislation did not reach agricultural workers until an Act of 1956, or office workers generally until the Offices, Shops and Railway Premises Act 1963, a victory in a struggle starting with a Bill of 1923, not uninfluenced by the new strength of white-collar unions. As with hours of work, some protections covered only particular groups (e.g. seats for women shop assistants or bans on women or young workers in lead-compound work). Unlike legislation on hours, most applied to male workers too, not only in the various Acts, but in dozens of regulations that Ministers acquired power to make under them.

New regulations are commonly made after drafts are issued for consultation (not always with speed, as with 1985 drafts on safety in the docks, where problems arising from new technologies were identified years earlier). Even today, ninety-six sets of regulations under the safety legislation, from the Flax and Tow Regulations 1906, to the Diving Operations at Work Regulations 1981, supplement the statutes.[56] The 1961 Factories Act itself covers health (11 sections on standards of cleanliness, sanitation, etc.), safety (45 sections on guarding and fencing of various types of machinery, on safe floors and stairs, fire-security, fumes, etc.) and welfare (seating, first aid, etc.), as well as particular matters such as the protection of eyes and underground work, and the notification of accidents and industrial diseases. The object of these provisions, like those in related Acts concerning agriculture, offices and mines, is (as Lord Denning put it in 1952) 'to prevent accidents to workmen'. Moreover, in 1949 a judge remarked that the legislation is there

not merely to protect the careful, the vigilant and the conscientious workman, but, human nature being what it is, also the careless, the indolent, the in-advertent, the weary and even perhaps in some cases the disobedient.

But the courts, and indeed most lawyers, come across this legislation not in the context of accident prevention, but more and more in that of compensation in civil actions for the victims of industrial accident or (just as important) disease. The cases arise from the web of complex civil duties, which interlock with specific statutory duties applicable to particular places of work ('factories', 'offices', etc.), often applying to the 'occupier' and varying in particular situations (dangerous machinery, lifts, etc.). In what follows we can touch upon only the more salient aspects of this complex area of law.

The concentration upon compensation, rather than prevention, is itself a curious story. In 1878 the statute allowed the Secretary of State, *if* he thought fit, to divert part or all of the fine imposed upon a delinquent employer to the benefit of the injured worker or his family. In *Groves* v. *Lord Wimbourne*, 1898,[57] an employer whose unfenced machinery had mangled a workman's fingers argued that this must mean the injured worker could not sue him directly. The judge agreed; but the Court of Appeal rejected this plea, holding that the duty to fence was owed under the statute *to* the worker. He could therefore sue for a 'statutory tort', which the Act implicitly provided (we shall see in Chapter 8 that the Employment Act 1982 has made explicit use of such 'statutory torts' concerning strikes and the extension of collective bargaining). Co-incidentally, the Workman's Compensation Act 1897 had introduced a form of compensation payable by the employer in some industries (they insured against the liability) for accidents arising 'out of and in the course of employment' of a worker. This is one of the most difficult phrases known to English law,[58] and although the 1897 Act was extended, workmen making claims not only lost their common law rights to compensation in the courts but also became enmeshed in difficult litigation.

This system was replaced in 1946 by the social security 'industrial injury' benefits made available by the national insurance scheme. Moreover, the Employers' Liability (Compulsory Insurance) Act 1969 required every employer carrying on business to take out an 'approved policy' of insurance against liability to his employees for bodily injury or disease arising 'out of or in the course of their employment'.[59] (We noted earlier that insurance companies have been known to exercise their right to stand in the shoes of the employer and claim an indemnity from any other employee of his who was responsible for the negligent injury making him liable, although this is not normally done: p. 179.) The insurance factor has long been ambiguous; it ensures that the injured worker obtains compensation if the employer is liable, but there is no guarantee that insurance companies adjust the premiums, either at all or adequately, to penalize employers with bad safety records. The effect of variable premiums on accident costs is still uncertain; indeed the deterrent effect has been said to be minimal;[60] and insurers of large companies tend not to distinguish the safety premiums so much if they have all the insurance business of a company, including fire, cars and the like. The sanction with more immediately deterrent effect might be a prosecution; but what strategy should be employed in its use, if the overriding objective is accident *prevention*?

We now look, therefore, at accident prevention and the enforcement of the safety statutes generally, then at the civil liabilities of the employer (1) at common law and (2) under the safety legislation for 'statutory torts'; and finally at compensation under social security law. First, however, we must note the changes of 1974, when a new and determined effort was made to use the law flexibly and effectively in the drive for safety at work.

The reforms of 1974

A major attempt to rationalize the law and its administration followed the Robens Committee Report of 1972.[61] The Health and Safety at Work Act 1974 provided for new bodies to secure safety and to administer the law, for a set of overriding duties for employers and for the operation of trade union safety representatives and safety committees at work. The main aims of the Act are stated to be securing the health, safety and welfare of persons at work and in the workplace, and controlling explosives, other dangerous substances and the emission of 'noxious or offensive substances' (HSWA s. 1). There is extensive power for the Secretary of State to make regulations (s. 15), including power to revoke any of the earlier safety legislation (several Orders had been made by 1986; but most of the earlier legislation was still intact). The Act established a new, tripartite Health and Safety Commission (HSC) and a Health and Safety Executive (HSE). Their task is to encourage research and training about safety, disseminate advice and information and (the HSE) to administer and enforce the safety laws. The HSC may publish Codes of Practice, which do not create offences but are to be taken into account in criminal cases so as to put the burden of proof on the employer, if he is in default

(s. 17). Enforcement may also be devolved to local authorities. Inspectors now come under the HSE (or the local authority), the separate Inspectorates that had grown up before 1974 (for factories, mines, offices, etc.) now being consolidated into a Health and Safety Inspectorate, though with specialized branches, with rights to enter premises, take samples, require information, hold machinery, etc. (ss. 20, 25).

The overriding duties begin by stating the duty of the employer to ensure the health, safety and welfare of all his employees (s. 2 (1)) and extend to the employer's plant, system of work, handling and transport of substances, provision of training, workplaces and access, and the working environment (s. 2 (2)). He also owes a similar duty to others coming on to his workplace (s. 3). But there are three features of great importance. First, the employer's duty here, as elsewhere in the primary duties of the HSWA, is to comply *as far as is reasonably practicable*. This contrasts with many duties in the previous legislation (e.g. Factories Act 1961 s. 14), which are *strict* duties, making him liable even if he is not negligent. As Asquith LJ said in 1949, 'reasonably practicable' is a narrower term than 'physically possible'; it requires a balance between the size of the risk and the 'sacrifice in the measures necessary for averting the risk (whether in money, time or trouble)'. It remains open to the employer, therefore, here to argue he knew there was some risk to his workers but that the cost of providing for it would have been disproportionate. The balance of cost against sacrifice of the workers is a delicate judicial task. Secondly, breaches of their duties in the HSWA do *not* create statutory torts in civil law (s. 47), although they are criminal offences. (We shall see that, for their part, the judges have recently insisted that not all statutory crimes are statutory torts: p. 639.) Thirdly, the employer must normally be someone employing an 'employee' in the strict sense (or apprentice) with all the problems that creates (p. 110). The 'trainees' under the Youth Training Scheme do not necessarily fall within the category of 'employees', and special regulations had to be issued to protect them, deeming them to be 'employees' for this purpose (No. 1919, 1983); in 1984 the HSC asked the HSE to review the position of all trainees and students. Neither the employer nor the self-employed entrepreneur must expose other persons to risks arising from the business, and those who are occupiers of workplaces (including installations and even vehicles) are obliged to ensure they are safe for those using the premises, within, as usual, the 'reasonably practicable' limit (ss. 4, 5).

So, where a fire broke out on a destroyer under construction in a shipyard, caused by a welder's torch but exacerbated through carelessness by employees of subcontractors, *Swan Hunter* – the employers – were convicted of a breach of s. 2 (for they had not shown that it was not 'reasonably practicable' for them to have given proper information to the subcontractors' employees in caring for the safety of their own workers); they also contravened s. 3 (they had endangered other persons coming on to their workplace).[62] The avoidance of civil liabilities and restrictions of the duties to criminal offences in this part of the HSWA is illustrated also by s. 7, which imposes a duty on the employee to 'take reasonable care' at work for the safety of himself and others (though whether he has started to be 'at work' can cause problems) and to co-operate with the employer as is 'necessary' to enable his duties to be fulfilled. Moreover, he must not interfere with anything provided for health, welfare or safety under the Act (s. 8; but the employer may not charge for them, s. 9).

Accidents and the Inspectorate

In the 1960s the battle to reduce accidents at work was being lost. The total of serious injuries in workplaces reported under the 1961 Act in 1969 (322,390) was 50 per cent higher than in 1963; even fatal accidents were not declining (649 against 610). Changes such as the introduction of statutory sick-pay in 1983 have altered the basis of reporting so that it is not easy to compare figures for recent years. The HSC and HSE do not publish comparable statistics (they intended 'to restore an adequate flow of information by mid-1985'); but a broad picture may be gained. The 1982 figure for *all* serious injuries reported to the HSC enforcement authorities was 389,800 (as against 345,000 in 1978, and 325,000 in 1976); a year later there were said to be 'approximately 300,000 people injured',[63] though trade union estimates put the figure higher. The statistics published after 1983 record so far only deaths and 'major injuries'. The HSC gave as the annual total of these, including coal and agriculture, for 1981 to 1984: 12,423, 12,761, 12,890, and 12,678 (deaths reported in 1981–4 were: 447, 471, 443 and 432). Comparison with the earlier decade is, therefore, difficult; but there seems as yet to be no clear evidence that the trend of accidents at work is downwards. The cost to industry and the nation has been estimated at more than £2,000 million; the cost to the families involved is incalculable. Moreover, new forms of disease and ill-health appear. Stress has increased at all levels;[64] 'tenosynovitis' (or 'data processor's disease') appears also to have increased sharply. (The latter has been the subject of international trade union guidelines, and in Britain APEX published a special report on new VDU hazards in 1985.)

The climate of the labour market has its effect on the record, and reporting, of accidents. The Chief Factory Inspector told of a case in 1983 where the parents of a seventeen-year-old worker whose arm was trapped in a machine promised to waive all compensation claims and even pay for damage to the machine if only he could retain his job (such are the 'priorities' engendered by 'fear of the loss of one's job').[65] The world of Lord Bramwell more than a century ago seemed set to return; in 1866 he dismissed a claim for compensation for a child whose fingers were crushed, saying that if the fingers had injured the 'delicate construction' of the machine, it was the child who would be liable to pay. This was a strange moment to propose relaxation of safety requirements for small business (the sector where, the HSC reported in 1985, many small firms had standards 'well below what is acceptable' and where the HSE said that 'a disproportionately high percentage of accidents' occurred). Government proposals to do so included relaxing the threshold of the HSWA duty to prepare a written safety policy for from 5 to 20 employees, and 'specific training to safety Inspectors to increase their awareness of smaller firms' interests'.[66] The 'Plan of Work 1985–6' of the HSC indicated that 'self-regulation' of employers would be encouraged. In 1986 the Government 'looked to' the HSC to propose the repeal of 'obsolete' legislation.

The Inspectorate hardly has adequate manpower for its job. The four inspectors of 1833 grew to more than a thousand (including the specialist inspectors). But, whereas the total in 1979 was 1,424, by 1984 it was cut to 1,242. The number of inspectors 'in the field', who spend some 80 per cent of their time visiting about 600,000 workplaces, fell from 1,098 to 915; and the 1984 HSE report confirmed:

The decline in the number of visits has continued and is now almost 13 per cent below the level of 1979 and 1980. This is again, as in past years, almost exactly in line with the fall in the number of inspectors.

For all the efforts of the Inspectorate, employers, workers and unions, the confidence of the HSC that this will be 'one of the major epochs in the development of safety law' seems questionable. A grim straw in the wind was the reported threat of mass resignation in 1985 by nuclear installations inspectors (100 or so inspectors came within three votes of a strike; a third of them were over fifty-five, and salaries had fallen well below those of engineers in the nuclear plants whose work they licensed).

Enforcement (1): prosecutions

The ultimate method to enforce safety standards is to prosecute offenders against the Acts and regulations, normally the employer (or 'occupier'); it may be, though rarely, the worker himself (e.g. under HSWA s. 7). In 1969, 2,657 prosecutions were brought by factory inspectors, and 2,482 convictions were obtained. The figures for 1980 were 2,438 and 2,227; and for 1984, 1,855 and 1,649 (the average penalty was £329). The great majority were for safety offences (in 1984, 1,185, 1,075, average £331). The pattern is startling when one appreciates that the 1974 HSWA leaned away from civil actions towards criminal offences as the basic legal sanction for the new general duties. But this is to overlook the long-standing policy of the Inspectorate. From the 1840s onwards, the inspectors have tended to avoid prosecution wherever possible. It can be said that this has led to the 'conventionalization' of factory crimes, removing the social stigma, a process that may be an 'inevitable consequence of using the criminal law to regulate middle-class behaviour' and possibly also an inevitable consequence of 'constraints' upon the early inspectors, who needed the co-operation of the mill-owners.[67] Factory inspectors have long stressed that their primary aim is to secure safe conditions, not convictions. The inspector, the 1964 Report said, 'has both to enforce the law and to act as a consultant and adviser to industry'. Today the status of the Inspectorate is secure, but constraints upon its resources continue to discourage a high-profile policy on prosecutions. Moreover, prosecution is rare in the Crown court on indictment, rather than before magistrates, where penalties are low fines; of some 9,000 prosecutions begun in 1980–3, only fifteen cases were taken on indictment. Practitioners have long denounced the absence of 'a real threat of prosecution and punishment'.[68]

While the Inspectorate may be open to criticism for maintaining an unduly gentle prosecution policy, the law itself still hampers its work. The Chief Inspector's 1984 Report told the story of the firm that employed teenagers on metal fabrication; after notices requiring them to improve these conditions, the company went into liquidation. But another company (with a new name but largely the same management and work-force) then opened up in the works; after new notices, it was prosecuted and fined £1,000; but the fine was never paid because that company was also dissolved. Yet 'in an adjacent area' a business 'under yet another name' later employed some of the same workers in similar work. This interaction of limited liability and company law with safety at work indicates that the Inspectorate should step up its prosecution against the *human beings* responsible. If a director, manager or company officer has consented to, or been careless as to, a breach of the HSWA, he can be prosecuted (s. 37; so too under many other statutes). Similarly, even where the Crown is immune from prosecution, the person whose default caused what would have been a contravention of the HSWA may be guilty of an offence (s. 36 (2)). Specific provision might also be made whereby workers could pursue civil claims for damages more widely against companies that take over substantially the same business as the 'employer' whose default caused their injury. We have seen that the TUPE Regulations 1981 do not include within the rights 'in connection with' the employment contract enforceable against a transferee a protective award on redundancy (p. 299); but it is arguable that the claim for damages at common law (p. 426) *is* connected with that contract. The worker should have the right to follow with his claim both successor companies and the human beings responsible for the unsafe conditions that have impaired his life, limb or health.

Enforcement (2): administration and notices

In many cases it is the very visit of the inspector that leads to an improvement; this is what makes the decline in visits so serious and the need so urgent to increase the numbers – and pay – of the Inspectorate. The HSWA 1974, however, gave new powers to the inspectors, beyond those of inspection noted above but short of a prosecution. The most important are improvement notices and prohibition notices. The inspector may serve an *improvement notice* on a person who is contravening the statutory provisions where it is likely he will continue or repeat the offence, requiring him to remedy it within a stated period (s. 21). Failure to do so is an offence sanctioned by a fine, which can be imposed for each day of non-compliance. A *prohibition notice* may be issued where the inspector believes that an activity falling under the statutory provisions involves a risk of serious personal injury; it must specify the contravention of the law; it requires the activity to cease, either immediately or after a period, or the risk to be remedied (s. 22). Appeals lie to industrial tribunals; improvement notices are suspended during appeals but not (unless the tribunal otherwise decides) prohibition notices.

The inspectors have made extensive use of these powers: in 1982, 3,800 improvement notices were issued and 1,472 prohibition notices (173 of them 'deferred'). In 1984 improvement notices totalled 3,321; prohibition notices 1,800 (175 deferred). But against this total of some 5,100 notices must be set the 7,090 notices in 1979 and 5,970 in 1980, the vast majority of them improvement notices.[69] It is true that further notices can be served by local authorities where they act as enforcement agencies; but they do not change the general picture. The tribunal is not of course the ultimate court of appeal; the judges have shown a tendency to restrict these procedures on further appeals as to law. The Court of Appeal decided only by two to one that improvement notices can be served in respect of common parts of a block of flats as 'places of work' for people working there; but such a notice must not be used for 'a test' case, the judges restricting it to a particular contravention *prior* to the notice and insisting that the sections under HSWA s. 2 are limited by what is 'reasonably practicable'.[70]

Enforcement (3): workers' safety representatives

Before 1974 there was little place for workers in the law on safety at work. Coal-miners have had a right to appoint representatives to inspect the mines effectively since 1811 and they co-operate closely with the mines Inspectorate. In a few industries 'safety supervisors' must be appointed, as under the Construction Regulations 1961; the weakness here is to protect the independence of the person appointed.[71] But the law made no general provision for workers' representatives and joint committees in which employers and unions could play a role, of the kind that are known in many other European countries. Pressure increased, though, for workers to play a role as of right in safety prevention; indeed, as early as 1893 there was experiment in appointing workers as 'assistants' to inspectors administering the factory laws (the year that saw the first women inspectors). Voluntary action had extended joint consultative bodies at both company and industry level; but the Robens Committee in 1972 decided that the time had come for 'a statutory requirement dealing in general terms with arrangements for participation by employees'. In 1974 the HSWA provided for safety representatives and safety committees (s. 2). The law was now providing, said the chairman of the HSC in 1978, 'an additional force in the workplace at the point where accidents take place'.

Today the employer must provide workers with a written safety policy statement (except where employees number less than five). Then (as we saw in Chapter 4: p. 312), *recognized* trade unions may appoint safety representatives amongst employees (as far as reasonably practicable, with two years' employment in that or similar employment: Safety Representatives Regulations No. 500, 1977, Reg. 3 (4)). The functions and work of the representatives are elaborated in regulations, in a Code of Practice and in notes of guidance. The employer is under a duty to consult with the representatives to promote and develop safety methods and their effectiveness. If requested by the representatives, the employer must form a safety committee for which *suggested* functions are given only in the guidance notes. The pattern of workers' representation on safety is thus aligned with the patterns of union structures recognized for negotiation, and the HSC takes the view that disagreements about the operation of this machinery should be settled 'through the normal machinery for the resolution of industrial relations problems'. Voluntary arrangements are preferred for the solution of problems on the ground arising from the regulated pattern.

The regulations, filled out by the code and notes, provide that the functions of representatives are to investigate hazards, causes of accidents and employees' complaints, to raise issues with the employer, carry out inspections and consult with the inspectors, and to receive information and attend the safety committee meetings. We have seen that time off with pay is provided (p. 312). After written notice to the employer, they have power to inspect, but only where conditions of work have substantially changed, the HSE has notified of new hazards, a notifiable accident or disease is involved or the employer agrees to the inspection. Considerable importance is attached by the HSC and HSE to the request by the safety representatives that an inspector be called in; conversely, some improvement notices are issued by inspectors as part of a pattern of enforcement of which the final stage is not a prosecution but agreement between the workers' representatives and the employer. Some concern was once expressed about the legal liabilities of a safety representative. Suppose he failed to take action when he should have done so, e.g. failed to raise an issue about dangerous plant with the employer, and a workman was injured, could he be liable? The HSWA and the regulations explicitly maintain the criminal offence of failing to take care of himself and others (s. 7; so too, s. 8 on interfering with anything provided for safety). But the regulations provide that, apart from this, none of the primary functions given to a representative are to be taken 'as imposing any duty on him'. The HSWA permits regulations to exclude civil liability (s. 47 (2) and s. 15), but these regulations do not include a general exclusion. Even so, since the primary functions do not impose a duty, the effect of the Act may be to exclude such civil liability (outside their primary functions, the work of representatives is described in terms of powers rather than duties).

The annual HSC and HSE reports reveal many areas where neither joint regulation nor inspection appear to make adequate provision in advance (the introduction of robotics, a matter of concern in many countries, may be an example). In others, the nuclear industry for example, the employer is permitted to refuse information to the safety representatives that it would be 'against the interests of national security' to reveal, and necessarily has an unusually close relationship with the inspectors (nuclear inspectors spend a high proportion of time on licensing issues). The Robens Report pointed out that too much reliance on licensing tended to place primary responsibility on the licensing authority rather than on the employer.

The ability of safety representatives to influence events in time has sometimes been questioned; their equivalents in Sweden and Norway have limited powers to suspend work where there is an immediate danger to life or health and no other immediate remedy is available. Developments in other countries show parallels with the British path since 1974. An Irish committee in 1984 expressed confidence in joint bodies but a 'distrust of legalism'. French reforms of 1983 strengthened the position of the highly regulated, workers' 'health, safety and working conditions committees' (workers themselves also have the right to 'withdraw' if they have reasonable grounds to suspect serious and imminent danger to their health or lives at work, provided the withdrawal does not create even greater dangers).[72] On the other hand, the mixture of shop steward and safety representative capacities in the same worker is objectionable to many (as it was to Robens, which sharply distinguished between 'participation in' and 'bargaining about' safety); the HSC has declared in favour of this distinction. Many shop stewards, though, are also safety representatives; these now number some 200,000, and the extension of joint structures, from which 'legalism' has been excluded as far as possible by the legislation itself, has been one lasting result of the reforms initiated by enactment in the 1970s.[73]

Accident rates nevertheless remain high. The question is whether workers' representatives can help to bring them down without further legal powers.

Compensation for industrial accidents and ill-health

(1) Civil actions

It is not at all clear that we should include, within the 'enforcement' of safety, the civil action in tort for compensation that an injured workman may have against his employer. The object of the action itself is not accident prevention but compensation for the injury; and we have noted (p. 416) that the deterrent effect on the employer, either directly or through his insurance company (he must be insured after the 1969 Act), is uncertain. Such actions are, though, very common. This is hardly surprising, given the low levels of benefit in the social security system for such workers. Broadly, the worker may sue the employer for either (a) breach of duty owed to him at common law; or (b) breach of a duty owed to him, explicitly or implicitly, under one of the Acts or regulations.

Each of these headings comprises a huge mass of legalistic case law. For example, in a case of the second kind, a company hired out a crane with the services of a driver (its employee) to a builder who was erecting a prefabricated barn. The builder directed the crane to land supported by an old wall. The crane crashed and the driver was badly injured. The Construction Regulations 1961 made it the duty of every 'contractor' and 'employer of workmen who is undertaking' building work to ensure stability and secure support of the crane. The hirers claimed it was the builder who was 'undertaking' the building work, not them, but the Court of Appeal disagreed and made them liable to pay damages.[74] The company was acting through its employee, the driver; and he was 'undertaking' a building operation vicariously on its behalf (even though his services were let out). This interpretation better served 'the social purpose of these regulations'. (Such welcome attention to social purpose is not apparent in every judgment.) But the judges made it clear that the position would be different, at any rate under *these* regulations, if the crane was hired out without an operator. On the other hand, in 1985 a miner failed in his claim against the NCB because a roof-fall that injured him down the mine did not occur at a 'working place' under the Mines and Quarries Act 1954, to which the employer's duty would apply to make it secure (though a fall on the previous shift *was* at a 'working place'). Dillon LJ said he would not adopt a wide construction of the words in the Act merely because 'the section was enacted for the protection of workmen'.[75]

What follows can be only an outline of civil actions for compensation and of State social security provisions in section (2).

(a) *The duty at common law.* A worker injured by the negligence of another person who owes him a duty to use care can claim damages from that person whoever he is, whether his employer, his fellow employee, the occupier of premises to which he is sent, consultant specialists brought in to the works, or manufacturers of appliances that he uses. The critical question in law is whether a duty of care is owed to him. But we have seen (p. 179) how from 1837 onwards judges decided that an employer was not 'vicariously' liable (as the employer would be to other injured persons) if the worker was injured at work by another employee where the two workers were in 'common employment'. The preposterous reason given was that the worker was assumed to 'run this risk' of his fellow worker's carelessness. This judicial doctrine conceived in the service of the master's ideology was reversed by Parliament only in 1948, though by then many judges had grown ashamed of it and found ways round it. Today it is dead and buried, and the employer (or his insurance company: p. 415) must pay damages so long as his careless employee was acting 'in the course of his employment'. This sounds an easy test, but it is not. A worker may still be within the course of his employment even if he is acting carelessly, or dishonestly, or even contrary to express orders, so long as he is still on his employer's work or something incidental to it (albeit not authorized), and not on 'a frolic of his own'. It is a fine line. Where three apprentices were sent by the employer to a technical school and two were making a wooden arch, the third chipped at it with his chisel. The first tried to stop him in a stupid way; the third snatched the chisel away, injuring the eye of the second. The employer could be held liable for the act of the first (he was acting incidentally to his authorized work) but he was not vicariously liable for the third and therefore not liable for his acts to pay damages to the second.[76]

The judges also developed a different principle. The employer, it was decided, owed a *personal* duty to each employee not to expose him to unreasonable risk. This personal liability of the master to the worker exists separately from any vicarious liability for careless acts of fellow workers. It was refined in the 1930s and 1940s by judges more favourable to claims by injured workers, steering them round the rocks of the 'common employment' concept; they had not impliedly consented to risk the *employer's* carelessness. This duty, sometimes summed up as the master's duty to provide a reasonably 'safe system of work', is a duty imposed by law (breach of which is a tort); but it may also be seen as a duty implied in the contract of employment. The latter method of analysis may help an employee who alleges a 'constructive dismissal' (p. 177), but a breach of the employer's duty by itself is not enough; to amount to a repudiation and 'constructive dismissal' it must be of such a quality that it indicates the employer is no longer bound by the employment contract (as where a 54-year-old woman was kept working in freezing conditions).[77] A similar problem is whether a worker's right of action to claim damages against his employer could be enforceable against a transferor of the business (which on principle it should be, as it is 'connected with' his contract of employment: p. 299).

In order to succeed in a *personal* claim, the worker must show he is an 'employee' (the duty to the self-employed is not the same: p. 123) damaged by the breach. The personal duty, said Lord Wright in 1938, is 'to take reasonable care for the safety of his workmen'. The duty cannot be delegated; it is personal to the employer. The 1938 case was a strong one because there the employers were compelled by law to delegate management of their mine to a manager, but they were still liable for the unreasonably dangerous state of the mine from which a miner suffered his injury. In one of the high points of judicial creativity in favour of injured workers, Lord Wright led the Law Lords to say that the duty covered 'provision of a competent staff of men, adequate material and a proper system and effective supervision'. Some judges have exaggerated the duty (liability still requires proof of negligence), like Danckwerts LJ who said in 1967 that an employer's life was so hazardous that it was 'a good deal safer to keep lions or other wild animals in a park than to engage in business involving the employment of labour'.

The employer must take reasonable care to safeguard his employees from foreseeable risks. But if he (or his agent) has no reason to know of curious proclivities of fellow workers, he is not personally liable (nor is he vicariously liable if the act done is outside the scope of the employment). Where scrap-metal workers jokingly rolled a live shell to and fro in 1966 and the plaintiff, on being told by another employee, 'Hit it', did so with a sledge-hammer, he failed in an action against the employers. But when an employer sends his worker on to premises of another, the duty rests upon him to the extent that he can be expected to know the nature of those premises (as where a window-cleaner proved that his employers had failed to lay out a safe system of work).[78] In providing proper instruction, the employer must take account of the peculiarities of the individual workman (the need for a one-eyed man to wear goggles is clearly greater); but judges have refused to see the relationship of employer and worker as one 'equivalent to that of nurse and imbecile child'. Where in 1976 a worker was, *unknown* to the employers, unable to read, they owed no duty to him beyond the normal obligation to display notices advising workers to wear safety spats against molten metal.[79]

The personal duty, then, is one to take reasonable care for the safety of employees, not a guarantee of safety. The employee must prove negligence – that is, failure to provide against reasonably foreseeable hazards. Moreover, as an appeal court judge said in 1964: 'a workman who seeks to recover damages must prove his case'. Some injuries will speak so directly of carelessness that the employer will find he bears the burden of disproving negligence (as where a crane just collapsed; but the employers were able to prove positively it was no fault of theirs or of any workers for whom they might be vicariously liable). Where the employer is careless in respect of a foreseeable type of injury he must pay damages for all loss of that type (as when a worker's lip was burned but he eventually contracted cancer). The employer will not however be liable for unforeseeable types of damage even if directly caused by the negligence (as where a worker was exposed to an unreasonable risk of rat-bites, but he contracted a rare disease through coming into contact not with the teeth but with the urine of the rats).

Practice goes a long way to determine standards. In 1985 the appeal judges exculpated an employer who provided no gauntlets for his carpenters (one had cut his wrist); this was not usually done, and there was no 'significant practice' by the carpenters to use them.[80] But suppose the employer pleads that he has observed the 'general practice' in the industry; he has done what all the other employers do. In many cases this will be enough for the judges. Where an employer knew no more about an illness contracted by many of his workers than that it caused minor discomfort (in fact it could cause Raynaud's phenomenon, a far more serious disease, which can lead to gangrene), he was not liable to the employee who contracted the serious disease for not warning him (the employers were 'safety conscious'; they had followed 'standard practice').[81]

But in 1984 Mustill J. in a seminal judgment (a test case for some 20,000 workers) inserted a dynamic element into the 'general practice' formula.[82] The case arose from the noise in the defendants' shipyard (the problem of noise is of importance at work; great attention has been given in the E E C to a proposed Directive on the subject; but industrial deafness did not become a 'prescribed disease' as an industrial injury until 1975: p. 443). *Thompson*, aged sixty-two, had been a ship-repair worker since 1936 and had been made rather deaf by the noise at work. The employers claimed that the risk of deafness was an accepted and inescapable feature of the industry; they had provided muffs and taken other measures according to the general practice of employers, one largely accepted by the authorities and the unions. The judge held that the workers could not complain of the injuries up to 1963; but after that year, knowledge of the problem and of preventive measures had advanced, so the employers were under a duty to depart from the 'same line of inaction as other employers in the trade'. They were not obliged to 'blaze a trail'; but the duty moved with the times and they were liable for that part of the damage caused after 1963 (for Thompson £1,350). The judge said:

It may be said these are small awards . . . So they are . . . if it is felt that the existing provisions for industrial injuries benefits in the field of deafness are too ungenerous, the remedy must lie elsewhere.

Parliament was forced by less enlightened decisions to intervene in respect of defective equipment supplied to the worker. Employers supplied a drift and hammer to a worker in 1959; the drift looked all right but it was defective, and a chip flew into his eye. He could sue the manufacturers if negligence could be proved against them (the H S W A today makes it a crime for the manufacturer or supplier who supplies goods for use at work not, as far as reasonably practicable, to ensure they are safe: s. 6); but the Law Lords held that he could not sue the employer if he was not at fault personally in some way. The Employer's Liability (Defective Equipment) Act 1969 makes the employer liable for fault of a third party in respect of defective equipment used in the business. But, as with most principles in this area, the Act's liability covers only a limited area, not least because the worker is still left to prove the 'fault' of some third party that has led to a 'defect' in the equipment.[83]

If the employer is in breach of duty, the two main common law defences open to him are 'contributory negligence' and 'consent'. Until 1945 a plaintiff who could be shown to have contributed by his own carelessness to an accident was allowed to recover nothing. This harsh common law rule was displaced in 1945 by an Act that gave the courts discretion to reduce the damages in such a case of contributory negligence by the amount they considered just. But 'consent' was, and is, a complete defence where the worker freely encountered and consented to the risk. As early as 1891, however, most judges came to recognize that workers had to run risks without their free 'consent'. When a navvy took work where stones were slung across his place of work in an unsafe manner, he had not 'consented' to the risk of being hit merely because he knew the facts. Findings of consent today against workers are rare; consent, it has been said, must be 'freely given'. Some risks inherent in the employment are assumed by the worker (as where a stockman was injured by a bull, but the farmer had exercised due care). The defence operates only where the worker has accepted the risk of the employer's *negligence* (or fellow worker's negligence for whom he is liable). Where the worker willingly takes part in acts that carelessly increase risks, he may then be held to have consented to the risk (as in the case of the man who hammered a live shell, a type of case to which we return; p. 435).

(b) *Breach of statutory duty*. If an employer breaks one of his statutory duties (e.g. to fence a machine), thereby causing damage to the worker of the kind the statute aims to prevent, the worker usually has a right to sue the employer for damages. The right is based upon the duty owed to him by the employer through which the Act implicitly permits a civil action for a statutory tort. If, therefore, the Act clearly intends not to provide a civil remedy (e.g. the HSWA, which excludes civil remedies for breach of its general duties or for duties imposed by regulations made under it unless they provide otherwise: s. 47), the worker cannot sue. But since *Groves* v. *Lord Wimborne*, 1898,[57] the judges have interpreted most of the other health and safety legislation (there is some doubt as to provisions on welfare) such as the Factories Act 1961 and its regulations, and the Mines and Quarries Act 1954, as incorporating that intention. In 1970 Lord Hailsham LC commented that the way liability depended on interpretation of 'deceptively simple' sections often made 'the protection afforded to the worker . . . illusory and unreal'.

The special benefit to the worker arises when the statutory duty does not require him to prove negligence as such at all. As Rigby LJ said in 1898, 'once there has been a failure in the performance of an absolute statutory duty . . . there is no need for the plaintiff to allege or prove negligence'. Of course, the worker may allege both. He may ride both horses at once and needs to get only one past the post. But he may fail on both, as where a paint sprayer injured his back but failed to prove that in not warning him against lifting things his employers were either negligent or in breach of the Factories Act 1961 s. 72 (which strictly prohibits a person being employed to lift heavy loads 'likely' to injure him; nothing indicated that this load would be likely, or 'probable', to injure the worker).[84] But a steel worker who stumbled and damaged his ankle in a shallow pit on the factory floor succeeded, even though he could prove no negligence, for the section relevant here (s. 28) required all 'openings in floors' to be 'securely fenced' unless the work made that 'impracticable'. (The accident happened in 1978; judgment was given late in 1981.) The pit was an 'opening'; it should have had a cover; a cover would not make it impracticable to do the work (this section did not say 'so far as *reasonably* practicable'); the worker recovered £1,500 damages.[85]

A man walking backwards in a foundry who fell over scrap metal embedded in sand on the floor failed to prove that his employers were in breach of a duty to see the floor was, 'so far as reasonably practicable, kept free from any obstruction' (s. 28). The Law Lords were not sure this was an 'obstruction'; and anyway it was not reasonably practicable to keep it off the floor during such work. The same section demands that all floors be, as far as reasonably practicable, free from any substance likely to cause persons to slip. When metal plates were temporarily placed on the floor with a slippery substance on them, employers in 1964 were in breach of the section, both as to an 'obstruction' and as to a slippery substance.[86] If a person works at a place where he may fall more than six and a half feet without a secure foothold, means must be provided, so far as reasonably practicable, to ensure his safety 'by fencing or otherwise' (s. 29); but in 1985 the E E G B was not liable to a worker who fell down a hole, because it was marked off by coloured tape.

Each section of an Act or regulation has to be considered separately. But for the injured worker, three primary questions arise: namely, whether the provision covers his workplace, covers him and covers by its terms the event and damage that occurred. For example, a worker who was repairing a neon sign attached to a building was held in 1967 not to be covered by regulations dealing with work *on* a building. We have encountered the miner struck by a roof-fall in 1985 but not able to rely on a section of the 1954 Act because he was not at a 'working place'. Similarly, the Factories Act 1961 applies only to 'factories'. Essentially, the complex definition of 'factory' is a place where, for trade or gain, persons are employed in manual labour in making, altering, repairing, ornamenting, finishing, cleaning or breaking up articles or adapting them for sale, or slaughtering cattle or other animals, together with other premises specially listed (s. 175). Almost every part of the definition has been tested in the courts. 'Manual labour', for example, includes physical exertion, even if slight; but it must be a substantial element in the work (we met the same requirement in the Truck Acts: p. 387). The words include, the Law Lords held in 1968, the diagnosis and repair of faults in television and radio sets: the manual work was not 'merely ancillary or accessory' to the work.[87] Secondly, suppose the person injured is a visiting window-cleaner or a maintenance mechanic come to mend a machine. If a provision imposes duties in favour of persons 'employed' or 'working' in the factory, it covers those working 'for the purposes of the factory' – but not, judges have said, such visitors as policemen or firemen doing their own work. Some sections apply to limited groups only, such as the prohibition upon women or young workers cleaning transmission machinery or a prime mover while it is in motion (1961 Act, s. 20).

Lastly, the event and damage must fall within the duty imposed. Sections 12 and 13 of the 1961 Act, for instance, require flywheels directly connected with prime movers and all transmission machinery to be securely fenced. Section 14 demands that every other 'dangerous part of any machinery . . . shall be securely fenced', unless it is made otherwise as safe as if it were so fenced. But 'a dangerous part of any machinery' has been curiously interpreted. In 1897, when a flying shuttle flew out of the loom and hit a worker, 'dangerous' was limited to cases where 'in the ordinary course of human affairs danger may be reasonably anticipated', taking account of possible carelessness by the worker. The capricious test of 'reasonable foreseeability' was thereby imported as to the damage, even though the duty to fence applies strictly (judges have held that machines must be fenced even if they then become useless or 'a museum piece'). Some things are not 'part' of machinery. When a safety clip in a hook designed to stop loads slipping amputated a crane driver's finger, the Court of Appeal refused to see it in 1981 as 'part of the machinery' appropriate for fencing; but the Law Lords included a mobile crane in 1969, capable of moving under its own power, which squeezed a worker against its wheel.[88]

In 1946, however, the Law Lords had raised a new hurdle in a case where a woodworker was injured by ejected slivers of wood: the object of the fencing is 'to keep the worker *out*, not to keep the machine or its products *in*', said one. Where the machine threw something out at him, he could not claim damages for breach of s. 14. In 1962, when an electric drill bit shattered, and a piece pierced the worker's eye, the Law Lords held this was not a 'dangerous' part (a fragmentation of this sort was not foreseeable), and the duty did not apply because this was a case of the machine breaking *out*. A low point was reached in 1964 where, when Sparrow slipped at work, his tools were thrown against an unfenced, dangerous part of the lathe, resulting in his hand being lacerated by another part of it. The Law Lords decided that s. 14 imposed no obligation to fence, but some judges had reservations; it appears to fall within the section if the dangerous parts come in contact with the worker's clothing or glove. And in 1977 a worker succeeded even though his contact was not with the dangerous, revolving drum of a machine but with the rubber fabric covering it, Lord Edmund-Davies saying he would be 'greatly dismayed' if the section did not cover such a case.[89] Judges have refused to include the product made in the factory, e.g. engines made by the factory's machinery; so fans attached to an engine for testing purposes fell outside the section for the 'simple reason', said Lawton LJ, 'it only became a dangerous part when it was on a product of the factory'.[90] Explaining to injured workers why their right to compensation turns upon such distinctions is not an easy task for their lawyer.

There are fashions and phases in judicial thinking, as in all other areas of life. Many of these interpretations of the law, increasingly narrow in the 1960s where the statutory duty to fence was concerned, seemed to display a feeling that workers' claims for compensation had gone far enough; the decisions certainly pay scant attention to any policy of accident prevention. By the 1970s some judges tried to save what they could from the wreckage of judicial interpretation of the once 'strict' duty to fence. *Johnson* worked on a lathe in which a boring bar moved slowly, machining a rotating steel workpiece. His hand was drawn into the 'nip' between the boring bar and the rotating workpiece and crushed when using an unapproved method of cooling. The employers argued that the bar was not dangerous in itself and that therefore there was no breach of the section. But the 'nip' created by the moving and stationary parts was itself 'dangerous', said the majority of the Law Lords; the machine was 'a single complex'; it should have been fenced. The earlier cases, said Lord Hailsham LC, created distinctions 'which neither logic nor common sense' justified, but they could be rectified only by legislation (it can be done here by regulations). Even so, Viscount Dilhorne dissented; the bar was not dangerous, and no one could foresee that the worker would 'put his hand inside'.[91] Where *Uddin* had climbed on to a platform that he knew to be prohibited – chasing pigeons with designs 'not actuated by benevolence' – and reached over a dangerous machine, which wrenched off his arm, the employer's argument that he was no longer a person 'employed on the premises' within the protection of the Act was rejected by the judges. He was protected even though acting for his own ends in an 'action of extreme folly'. Once a part of a machine was dangerous, the Act protected even the 'utterly stupid' worker.[92]

The careless worker. As we have seen, however, since 1945 a worker who does not take care for his own safety can have his damages reduced for 'contributory negligence'. *Uddin's* damages were reduced by three-quarters. A worker who was injured by an unguarded machine in motion for testing, when he tried to wipe grease from the pulley with a rag, had his damages wiped out by a 100 per cent reduction in 1985, Goff L J saying: 'There comes a point in time where the degree of fault is so great that . . . the fault is entirely that of the workman'.[93] The judges have gone further. Even where an employer has failed to provide a safety device demanded by the Act, he will wholly escape liability if it can be shown that the worker would not, on the balance of probabilities, have used it even if it had been provided. The Law Lords advanced this principle in a case of 1962 where the worker had been killed; the employer's breach of the law in not providing any safety belts was not the *cause* of the accident, they said, because the worker would probably not have worn them. This argument has, time and again, released employers from liability despite their failure to fulfil such duties, as where evidence was adduced to show that an illiterate workman would not have used safety spats even if he had been told about them (because he did not inquire of his fellow workmen what the notices said or what spats were).[94] This retrograde development of hypothetical causation occurred in face of earlier decisions in the 1950s that refused to allow an employer in default to use this argument that a worker would not use the equipment. It is no contribution to accident prevention, for it allows the employer to take less care if a worker is known to be habitually careless.

In cases of breach of *statutory* duty, as opposed to the common law duty, for decades after 1887 judges held that the worker's 'consent' was not normally any defence for the employer. Common employment was still alive; and it was felt to be against public policy to allow a worker to 'waive' breach of a statutory duty that, after all, involved a criminal offence. Yet in the last two decades the judges have resiled even from this rule. We saw that in actions for common law negligence 'consent' does not arise from mere knowledge and consent must be 'freely given'. In 1965 the two *Shatwell* brothers, George and James, employed as shotfirers by ICI, engaged in an operation they knew to be very dangerous, improper and in breach of statutory regulations; these were regulations that put the duty to abstain from the operation on them, not upon the employers. Both were injured in an explosion. George sued ICI alleging it was 'vicariously' liable for the statutory default of James, their employee, acting within the course of his employment. The Law Lords decided that George had 'consented' to the risk; that would be a complete defence against James; there was, therefore, no liability for which ICI could be vicariously responsible.[95] This was a special case where the statutory duty was imposed on the *employee*. As Lord Pearce said, 'consent' could be available only where the employer was not himself in breach of statutory duty and not vicariously in breach of any such duty. Lord Reid insisted this was not mere 'contributory negligence'; it involved two fellow servants combining to disobey an order deliberately in full knowledge of the risk. Moreover, he left open the case where the employer's own breach of statutory duty arises from one servant's 'disobedience that puts the master in breach of a statutory obligation'. The House of Lords, however, by reviving the old doctrine of consent for this type of case, opened a door long believed to be locked.

Some judges have made use of *Shatwell*. In the coal-mines, for example, there is a statutory prohibition on disorderly conduct and on disobedience of rules laid down for workers' conduct. Miners jumped from a 'man-rider' while it was still moving, in contravention of the rules, and in the disorder *McMullen* was jostled and injured. Caulfield J. refused to award 'this fine young man' damages. That was not 'harsh'; it was to stimulate his sense of safety for himself and his fellows. They had all been disobedient together, so none could sue the employer. He did what 'he knew to be wrong and he was undertaking the risk which he knew to be existing'. The judge was glad to hear that the union as well as the management was urging these 'good, healthy young men, who do want to get home early' to stick to the rules; but there would be no damages. If this had been the approach in 1887, one wonders whether the judges would ever have devised the rule banning 'consent' as an answer to a breach of statutory duty. Very different were the tones of the careful judgment of Mustill J. about *Storey*,[96] who had also disobeyed warnings by riding on a conveyor and had been killed as a result. Here the statutory duty alleged against the employers was to make rules to secure safe transportation; this means that they must create a mechanism to secure compliance with orders; only if workers made this impracticable did they escape. Here the NCB had only given warnings and left the rest to its workers; its system of enforcement had little disciplinary content and was 'toothless'. So *Storey* could succeed; but although 'consent' was no bar, his damages were reduced by 75 per cent for his contributory negligence. The reasoning is a better approach than *McMullen's* case, which may rest strictly on the principle that the only duty broken was one placed on the worker.

Damages, death and undetected accidents. Where, like *Storey*, a worker dies, the 'estate' of the deceased worker has since 1934 been able to sue the employer for damages for the tort; as it were, an action brought by his ghost for such items as pain and suffering. But a different claim may be brought under the Fatal Accidents Act 1976 by a dependant (e.g. the widow, husband or child, and since 1982 a 'common law spouse'). The damages payable by the defendant whose tortious act caused the death are for the damage resulting from it to the dependants plus, in the case of a spouse or parents of an unmarried minor, a fixed sum for 'bereavement' (amendments of 1982 prevent damages being recovered twice over against the employer by the 'estate' and by the dependants). The basic test is the amount of the benefit that could reasonably have been expected by the dependants in future. The circumstances of the dependant must therefore be considered; but the distasteful process of considering a widow's prospects of remarriage was abolished by an Act of 1971 (though this factor must be considered for any other unmarried female claimant). The 1976 Act prevents account being taken of any insurance money, or pension, payable on the death; but where the widow receives from the occupational pension scheme a widow's pension on the death this has been held in *Auty's* case, 1985, to mean that she cannot claim more for the lost chance of receiving a retirement pension later.[97] Moreover, where the widow would have given up working to start a family but for the accident, she cannot increase her damages by reason of that.[98] Where the deceased was guilty of contributory negligence the damages are reduced by the proportion of his fault.

The damages awarded to the worker (or, in case of death, to his dependants) have always been a lump sum and are recoverable once only for the employer's tort. Proposals made in 1978 for periodical payments have not been adopted. But in 1985 it became possible for the judge to award to the worker 'provisional' damages, where there is a chance that he will develop a disease or deterioration of condition as a result of the employer's breach of duty, specifying the period within which the worker may return to apply for 'further damages'. The sum may include 'special' and 'general' damages (special damages mainly include loss of earnings caused by his absence from work). In *Auty's* case, 1985, the court also confirmed the rule that the likelihood of inflation cannot affect the lump sum awarded. We have seen that in actions for damages judges do not take account of sums payable to the worker from insurance policies; but they do deduct sums received as unemployment or supplementary social security benefit (p. 212). What is more, under the Administration of Justice Act 1982 s. 5, savings attributable to a stay in hospital must now be deducted.

The conflict between the argument that the plaintiff must not benefit twice and the view that a tortious employer must pay in full for his wrongdoing was solved in a 'judgment-of-Solomon' manner in respect of 'injury benefit' (to which we come below: p. 439) by an Act of 1948. This provided that 50 per cent of these national insurance benefits, paid and likely to be paid over five years, must be deducted from the damages. But in 1985 a further deduction was demanded. *Palfrey* sustained a nasal fracture at work because of his employer's negligence; but his damages (£3,300) suffered a deduction of some £300 because he had received that amount as statutory sick-pay (p. 174).[99] This, as we shall see, is an extraordinary decision, partly because the payment of 'industrial injury benefit' was merged with payment of statutory sick-pay in 1983. The judge reaffirmed 'the common law position . . . that benefits received from the state must be taken into account in the assessment of damages'. Thus the employer (or his insurer) who by his wrongdoing injures the worker is subsidized by the judges out of the Welfare State.

The worker is normally given three years in which to bring a legal action for personal injuries (it was reduced from the normal six in 1954 for no apparently good reason). The time runs from the moment the damage is first suffered or when he first knew (with such advice as he should have taken) that his injury was attributable to the negligence or breach of duty of the employer. His belief or suspicion is not the same as his knowledge; so, where a worker believes for ten years that his employers' unsafe working conditions have caused what becomes severe dermatitis, he is allowed to sue them by a writ issued within three years of the date of his actual knowledge that it is so.[100] The court has a further power to allow the worker to sue 'out of time' where it would be equitable to do so. A cotton worker had to leave the spinning mill after thirty years in 1965, and worked as a gardener, because of deteriorating bronchitis, which his doctor put down to smoking. In 1979 he was found to have byssinosis, a disease caused by dust in the mill. The judge permitted him exceptionally to bring an action against his former employers; the greater prejudice would be suffered by the worker if his case were stopped.[101]

(2) State benefits for injury at work

Far more workers in recent years have benefited from the social security 'industrial injury benefit' than from awards of damages, although the latter few have each received more money. The Workmen's Compensation Acts between 1897 and 1945 provided compensation for a growing number of workers injured in accidents due to and in the course of their employment without proof of negligence by the employer. Weekly sums were paid – an important innovation – and the employers were insured against liability. But the amounts were small (usually less than half-pay); a claim could be settled with a lump sum; the claimant worker had to waive civil claims against the employer; and bitter litigation took place between workers, backed by unions, and employers, backed by insurance companies, often up to the House of Lords. Some industrial diseases also fell within the scheme; but employers often dismissed workers who showed early symptoms of these conditions.

In 1942 the Beveridge Report recommended that this scheme should be replaced by universal insurance against injury at work. The State would now insure against disability caused by such accidents or by prescribed industrial diseases. This was accomplished by an Act of 1946, by which the principle of regular fixed 'injury' benefits was established under the national insurance scheme introduced then with the Welfare State. Benefits were paid for personal injury arising out of and in the course of a worker's employment, and lasted for six months (at a higher rate than ordinary sickness benefit) after which a 'disablement benefit' was payable for serious 'loss of faculty'. All persons in insurable employment were covered. Broadly, this scheme was continued by the Social Security Act 1975, which brought it and the Industrial Injuries Fund into the social security pool (it is not irrelevant, Ogus and Barendt remark, that this fund, unlike the non-industrial fund, was then showing a healthy surplus).[102] Other changes were also in train. The industrial injury benefit had in origin been much higher than ordinary sickness benefit, but gradually this differential declined and the validity of a separate payment was questioned. More important for government was the high cost of this separate industrial injury scheme. In consequence, the Social Security and Housing Benefit Act 1982 abolished payment of a separate industrial injury benefit, though disablement benefit remains. After 1983 this means that the worker who is entitled to benefit receives his statutory sick-pay from the employer for the initial period and sickness benefit after that (p. 174). But the claimant does not have to satisfy the normal contribution conditions for sickness benefit; incapacity attributable to industrial injury or a prescribed industrial disease is sufficient.[103]

The basic requirement, drawn from the earlier Acts, is a prescribed disease or 'personal injury caused by accident arising out of and in the course of the employment' (Social Security Act 1975 s. 50). The injury must be 'a hurt to body or mind' (including artificial attachments only where they have an 'intimate link' with the body)[104] and must arise 'by accident', i.e. an occurrence, a 'mishap', not a process. It may be caused by a third party, as where pupils killed a schoolmaster. Lord Diplock in 1972 said it must be 'external', affecting the claimant's anatomy physiologically or psychologically or his bodily activity; but a series of events may suffice (like the rubbing of tight boots issued for work which irritated an old wound, penetrated the skin and infected the foot; or repeated explosive reports from a machine that caused dermatitis and a psychoneurotic condition). This distinction can be somewhat arbitrary. A chemical worker exposed to harmful substances for eighteen years who died was affected by an 'indefinite number of so-called accidents', which became 'a process'.[105] The accident must 'cause' the injury; but it is enough if the occurrence acts upon a previous condition, as where a movement at work by a bakery worker with an unhealthy back was 'the last straw' in putting out a disc.[106]

The most difficult problem is whether the injury arose both 'in the course of' and 'out of' the employment. In 1966 the Court of Appeal decided that a fitter's mate injured while waiting his turn outside a 'smoking booth', five minutes after he should have resumed work from a tea-break, could properly be denied benefit when hit by a fork-lift truck because, having interrupted his work, he was not injured in the course of his employment. More liberal decisions have followed. A worker who acted at work as a football-pool agent and was hit by a spanner when he was picking up contributions from the floor was still in the course of his employment (he had not left his machine), so there was no 'material interruption'. But in 1981 a seaman allowed ashore to buy lemonade and injured when using a 'short cut' to board the ship, instead of the normal access, was held not to be in the course of his employment; 'he was ashore in order to visit the dock shop for his own personal purposes'.[107]

A margin will be allowed around working hours, so that injuries to a policeman coming back from a permitted lunch off the premises, and to a biscuit worker arriving early for work who slipped in the canteen, qualified; but an injury to a psychiatric nurse who arrived early only to enjoy a game of billiards did not qualify, even though this might 'refresh' him before his exacting duties on the ward.[108] Such sporting activities may qualify. An accident befalling a fireman playing volleyball in a recreational period fell within the formula, for the game improved his morale; similarly, a mental nurse joining the patients in a cricket match was still in the course of his employment. But in *Michael's* case the appeal judges held that a policeman playing football for his force team was not covered.[109] Attendances at union meetings connected with employment have been included;[110] but the formula is rather arbitrary. So too is the additional requirement that the injury must arise *out of* the employment. There must be sufficient 'causal connection' with the employment. The Act (s. 50 (3)) deems that (in the absence of evidence to the contrary) an accident arising in the course of arises also 'out of' the employment; but the judges have held that this presumption applies only if there is *no* such evidence.[111] The employment risk need not be the only cause (a worker was covered who lit a cigarette near a gas leak at work; but not one who, going to fetch materials, fell and fractured an ankle, there being no fault in the floor and no contact at all with the premises).[112]

Thus a 'common risk' – one to which the worker is not exposed more than members of the public – is not enough. The Commissioners' decisions on this have been even harder to follow. A lorry driver hit in the eye by grit was held to have run a common risk, but another, hit by an object thrown by children, qualified because it was a 'risk of the road' affecting drivers. In 1982 the Commissioner thought that 'walking, standing, sitting, etc., are all part of everyday human activity'; so accidents happening during them would not arise *out of* the employment unless there was a special danger 'because of some inherent, idiopathic characteristic' of the worker. After the judges had held in 1958 that a bus conductor attacked by youths was exposed only to a common risk, Parliament intervened with what is now s. 55 (1) of the 1975 Act. This provides that an accident is treated as arising out of the employment if it arises in the course of it, *and* if it is caused by another person's misconduct, skylarking or negligence (or steps taken in consequence), or by an animal or by the worker's being struck by an object or by lightning; *and* if the worker did not contribute to the accident by conduct outside or not incidental to the employment. So, where the worker was hit by a playful snowball in a smoking break and moved after the youth responsible in order to remonstrate, he qualified when his fingers were slammed in a door. He had not contributed to his injury since he was not chasing in order to retaliate.

The Act deals with the worker's contravention of the law or of his employer's orders in other cases. The general rule is that he still qualifies so long as the accident would have arisen anyway *and* the improper act was done for the purposes of, and in connection with, the employer's business (s. 52).[113] A dockworker's misconduct in driving a truck against orders, killing himself when he drove it into the water, was such that he was held to be totally outside his employment.[114] (Even after an award of benefit, moreover, the worker is subject to his duty not to behave in a manner likely to retard his recovery: s. 90 (1).) The Act also provides that if a worker is injured whilst travelling to work as a passenger on transport operated by or for the employer (other than public transport), the accident is deemed to arise out of and in the course of his employment if it would have been deemed to be so had he been obliged to ride in it. But this is strictly interpreted. Walking to or from the vehicle is not included, and where the driver of a vehicle provided by the employer drove four passengers on home in his own car, the Act did not apply to this unauthorized transport.[115] But travel of any kind to and from work may be within the course of employment if the facts so allow. This question of the meaning of 'arising out of and in the course of employment' is so uncertain that appeal judges in 1985 declared it was one of 'fact' for the adjudicating officer. Two police officers injured in road accidents when going to work had their claims disallowed; after three years their cases wearily came to the Court of Appeal, and the disqualifications were upheld (though a contrary decision 'might also have been upheld', said Donaldson MR).[116]

Industrial diseases. Certain industrial diseases are specified in regulations by the Secretary of State for particular occupations or kinds of work where he is satisfied that they are a risk of that employment or work. The worker can claim benefit if he shows that he suffers from a prescribed disease in relation to his occupation and the disease developed as a result of employment in that occupation. For some diseases, there is special provision, e.g. pneumoconiosis (where employment of two years is required) or occupational deafness (where the employment must be ten or twenty years, according to occupation). From time to time extensions are made in the list of prescribed diseases (Regulations No. 377, 1980); Raynaud's phenomenon was added for some jobs in 1984; but such changes take a long time (that disease had been investigated since 1954).[117] After the abolition of injury benefit in 1983, regulations define the 'date of onset' applicable to a disease for benefit purposes.

Disablement and further disability. Disablement benefit is now available when ninety days have passed after the industrial accident (or disease) when the worker, as a result of it, suffers from 'loss of physical or mental faculty' of more than one per cent (Social Security Act 1975 s. 75; Social Security and Housing Benefit Act 1982 s. 39). The loss of 'faculty' indicates, said Lord Diplock in 1972, 'impairment of the proper functioning of part of the body or mind' causing disability to act. It must be caused by the accident. One difficulty here is: who is to determine the 'causation', the doctors or the social security authorities? After a prolonged battle, the medical authorities won the right to determine that a loss of faculty did not result from an accident at work. The disablement itself is normally assessed on a statutory scale (a gruesome schedule: loss of thumb, 30 per cent; loss of hand and foot, 100 per cent; and so on). But if the condition is not in the statutory list, the scale is fixed by the medical authorities. If there is an extraneous cause that contributed to the disability, this is taken into account within the guidelines laid down in regulations.[118] Up to 20 per cent disability, the benefit has been a gratuity measured by the years likely to be affected; above 20 per cent, a pension, also graded, is payable (for 100 per cent, the 1986 maximum is £62.50). The smaller percentage disabilities (below 15 per cent) are soon to be scaled down or even phased out.

There are a certain number of additions that may be made to disablement benefit (such as unemployability supplement, special hardship allowance, hospital treatment, constant attendance and exceptionally severe disablement allowances). There are also procedures for review. Sometimes the severities even of the benefits for disability are exemplified by claims for them. A labourer, hit on the head by a chandelier, succeeded in claiming 10 per cent for life disablement allowance; he was also granted a special hardship allowance because he could not follow his regular occupation. Later reports described his disability as being psychiatric, though it was a condition to which the accident had contributed. The Commissioner decided that no special allowance was payable for a disability arising out of a 'condition' that itself resulted from the loss of faculty.[119] In 1985 injury to a gardener's hand was assessed by the medical board at 10 per cent for life, and a special hardship allowance was awarded as he was likely never to be capable of resuming his occupation. The second allowance was disallowed after a surgeon attributed the symptoms to a rheumatoid disease; but the Commissioner restored it, because the adjudicating authorities had no right to displace the medical authority's decision about the causation of his disability.

Damages and insurance for accidents at work. The Beveridge Report in 1942 justified a separate State insurance benefit for industrial injury, in place of the old, much criticized workmen's compensation scheme, on three grounds: some industries to which labour had to be recruited were of a dangerous nature; the employer should not be liable except when at fault; the injured worker was 'under orders'. Some decades later many found these reasons increasingly unconvincing (though the last ground touches a reality that the common law, in the more liberal judgments on 'consent', has itself recognized, and it is part of the wider point that injury is suffered in the course of labour for the benefit of the employer's enterprise). It was argued that compensation for the disabled should be allotted according to need, with earnings-related benefits. As Abel-Smith wrote, 'distinctions between work-generated disability and home-generated disability' are not meaningful (the interpretation of accidents arising 'out of and in the course of employment' hardly makes for rationality). Nor should compensation of the injured depend upon 'the identification of the negligent'. The critics of the tort system also doubted its contribution to accident prevention and dubbed it no more than a 'forensic lottery', a protracted, costly procedure that gave large prizes by luck to no more than a fifth at most of workers injured at work.[120] It must be admitted that a test like the judges' distinction between keeping the worker out and not the machine in is an unattractive basis on which to award or refuse compensation to a worker for a mangled arm.

Radical spirits pursued the goal of abolishing the anomalies of both tort litigation and industrial injury benefits by providing State insurance for all who lose their earning power, whether at work or not, by sickness or incapacity.[121] Similar proposals were made to replace the law of tort entirely in Australia and New Zealand, legislation in the latter country maintaining a separate scheme for earners, though not for accidents *at* work.[122] In Britain the Pearson Committee Report on liability and compensation for personal injury in 1978, to which a great quantity of evidence was given favouring the retention of separate industrial insurance benefits, recommended the continuance of the 'mixed system' (except for car accidents) but with State insurance gradually making the civil action in tort the 'junior partner'. The higher industrial 'preference' benefit should be retained in modified form and extended gradually to other injuries but deducted fully from any damages awarded. The tort action should be retained, because its abolition 'would deprive many injured people of a potential source of compensation without putting anything in its place', in the absence of a comprehensive no-fault insurance system.[123]

Although the Pearson Report evoked criticism, not least for its proposal to preserve tort actions and the 'preferential' injury benefit,[124] some critics may have overlooked the political realities in their advocacy of comprehensive insurance to abolish the law of tort. Any exclusive State insurance system is bound to be in the grip of the Treasury and provide far smaller sums to many of the injured workers now lucky enough to obtain damages. We have seen that cost pressures led government to wipe out the differential when injury benefit was merged into sickness insurance in 1983 (and that even though, as Pearson found, costs here were only 11 per cent of compensation paid, a much smaller figure than in the litigation system that provides the tort remedies). The litigation process is usually criticized for delay, cost and unpredictability; but the damages awarded for injury are not extravagant compared with other jurisdictions. One of the most important functions of trade unions, derived from the days of 'workmen's compensation', is the support of their injured members' costs in civil actions[125] (the worker who is not a member may be able, if he is poor enough, to obtain legal aid). Many argue that the trade union presence in damages claims and the publicity that the cases attract are an integral part of pressures on employers to improve dangerous working conditions, along with safety representatives and negotiating machinery (the TUC in 1985 promoted new guidelines for union negotiators on compensation schemes for occupational diseases, long-term ill-health and industrial accidents, and their relationship to individual damages claims).

Lawyers should perhaps turn their minds not so much to the abolition of workers' rights to sue in tort for damages as to the provision of cheaper and improved legal services, including such initiatives as neighbourhood law centres, so that the enforcement of rights becomes less expensive and more rapid. Moreover, the injured worker frequently becomes a disabled seeker after more limited employment, one of the disadvantaged entrants and re-entrants to the labour market to whom we turn in the next chapter. Meanwhile, there remains a paramount need to use the law to moderate what the Robens Report called the 'tragedy and suffering' as well as the 'economic cost to the nation' of injury and disease at work:

For both humanitarian and economic reasons no society can accept with complacency that such levels of death, injury, disease and waste must be regarded as the inevitable price of meeting its needs for goods and services.

[6] Social Discrimination at Work

'Discriminatory employment practices', three leading United States lawyers write, 'are a manifestation of prejudicial patterns of behaviour in society generally.'[1] Many workers bring to their subordinate status as employees additional disadvantages that derive from discrimination against them in the wider society. Pressures for fair and equal treatment cause the law to intervene (though with what effect needs careful investigation) but not always with the same intensity. In Britain some protection is offered against racial and sex discrimination; in the United States religion is added, whilst in Northern Ireland discrimination by reason of religion or political opinion is outlawed.[2] In Italy the Workers' Statute 1970 prohibits the employer from even an inquiry into a worker's 'political, religious or union opinion' or from preventing their expression at work. The ILO standards required that states take measures against distinctions that impair equality in employment 'on the basis of race, sex, religion, national extraction or social origin' (Convention 111, 1958). The abolition of discrimination on the basis of social origin implies profound social change, not least for the young. In Britain, whilst social discrimination on grounds of sex or race remains a blot on the face of our society, the law addresses other types of prejudice only to a much smaller extent. No doubt subjective prejudice is not easily susceptible of legal sanction and, as Lustgarten says, we must not build up 'an exaggerated faith in the efficacy of law'; but patterns of behaviour can be affected by the law, as experience with discrimination in the United States demonstrates. The 'fundamental right of individuals to equal treatment and equal respect' should lead, Hepple has declared, to an extension of the law against discrimination to include, in the context of poverty, 'the disabled, the older members of the working population who suffer from age discrimination, and generally discrimination on grounds of social origin'.[3]

Throughout the 1960s, signs arose that many societies wished not only to abolish such discrimination but to enforce also the worker's right to a decent and protected personal life. Writing in 1978, Giugni detected a 'general trend' in Western European labour laws towards the exclusion of personal, or private, characteristics from relevance in the employment relationship, 'granting protection to privacy, private life in a strict sense'. Such a general principle would extend freedom at work and include freedoms 'such as political and religious freedom and equality, racial equality, and sexual equality'.[4] British law has not advanced far since then in this direction; but we do have the legislation on sex discrimination (SDA 1975), equal pay (Eq. P. A. 1970, effective from 1975) and discrimination on grounds of 'colour, race, nationality or ethnic or national origins' (RRA 1976 s. 3). There are also, as we shall see, important areas of EEC law to be considered on sex discrimination and equal pay.

Foreign workers

Discrimination on grounds of nationality falls also within the provisions of EEC law, whereby the Community guarantees equality to nationals of member States in the labour markets of all such states. Aliens in Britain, as in other countries, suffer particular legal disabilities (they may not be ships' pilots, for example, and entry into the Civil Service is narrowly restricted); and, in practice, an employer may discriminate against them. More important, many Commonwealth citizens and even some citizens of the United Kingdom are 'non-patrials' – that is, they have no right of abode in Britain. Non-patrials may be subjected to restrictions in obtaining a work permit and in changing jobs; leave to enter the country can still be refused even if a work permit has been granted (though not where one grandparent was born in the United Kingdom).[5] Moreover, an employer wishing to hire an alien or non-patrial must satisfy the Department of Employment that 'no suitable resident labour is available' for the vacancy.

But the overriding EEC law (here directly applicable in British courts) establishes a right of 'free movement' for individual workers within the Community, granting nationals of member States equal rights to take employment (other than in the public service) in the other States. It therefore forbids such restrictions as quotas or similar discrimination in regard to both hiring and employment conditions as well as freedom of association in unions (though nothing is said about transnational

EEC union operations).[6] Limitation of entry is permitted where the Government finds a person unacceptable by reason of public policy, health or security grounds.[7] But once admitted, equal treatment for the worker is required, not only in labour law but also in taxation and social security rights.[8] These rights also extend in great measure to the worker's family (children, for example, must be accorded equal opportunity to suitable education).[9] Parallel provisions have led English judges to strike down discriminatory residence periods for entry to vocational education; and the ECJ has insisted upon equality for students as well as workers.[10] The movement of workers from other EEC countries into Britain has so far been relatively small; but if unemployment rates decline in the next decade the provisions under the Treaty of Rome for 'free movement' of workers and 'freedom of establishment' may grow in importance. The limitations on the power of the Westminster Parliament to insulate the British labour market in the Community are not widely appreciated. After the 'Single European Act' 1986 (of which few have heard) its powers will 'in the long term', a House of Lords committee reported, become weaker.

It is perhaps odd that such legal strides have been made to attack employment discrimination in respect of nationality and sex within the EEC when so many other areas of discrimination remain in the domestic labour market. The two groups widely recognized as bringing disabilities from society upon their entry into it are women and racial or ethnic minorities. After a brief consideration of discrimination relating to private life and personal characteristics, we deal with sex and racial discrimination, and with equal pay. Then we shall consider the discrimination that falls today upon large numbers of young workers.

Private life and social prejudice

'Does a man's private life matter? Does it make him unfit to be a head teacher? Should he be dismissed for it?' So asked Lord Denning in 1980 about a divorced master in a religious school.[11] Few specific provisions about private life appear in our law. We have seen that our social security law does not always respect the line between private and work-related activity (Chapter 3, p. 216). But there are some explicit protections. It is unlawful to treat a person on the ground of marital status less favourably than an unmarried person of the same sex would be treated (S D A s. 3 (1) (a)); or to discriminate *indirectly* by applying to the person a requirement that would be applied equally to an unmarried person but (1) is not justifiable on other grounds, (2) is detrimental and (3) is such that it can be complied with by a *considerably smaller proportion* of married than unmarried persons of that same sex (s. 3 (1) (b)). Single persons are here not protected, though they may be able to prove indirect sex discrimination (p. 463). As the protection for marital status, for men and for women, appears in the S D A 1975, no qualifying period is needed to complain to a tribunal about dismissal on this ground; and, although compensation cannot be recovered twice over for discrimination and unfair dismissal (E P C A s. 76), such dismissals followed by improper failure to comply with an order for re-employment attract the higher award of compensation of between 26 and 52 weeks' pay (E P C A s. 71 (2) (3)).

Dismissal on the ground of *pregnancy* is also specifically denoted as unfair (E P C A s. 60: unless the woman is incapable of continuing in her job) but, for reasons that have never been entirely clear, the employee must here serve for the qualifying period, now two years, before she enjoys that protection. Absence through pregnancy, however, does not affect continuity (E P C A, Sched. 13, paras. 9, 10). The courts have varied in their approach to such sections. In 1980 the E A T by majority refused to see a dismissal by reason of pregnancy as one based on *sex* discrimination ('When she is pregnant a woman is no longer just a woman. She is a woman . . . with child and there is no masculine equivalent'),[12] and comparison of like with like is the basis of the Sex Discrimination Act 1975. But five years later the E A T regarded that as a 'highly unusual case'; the bare question of dismissal by reason of pregnancy would normally 'be a half told tale' of factors relevant to discrimination; comparison might be made of a pregnant woman and a sick man about to be away for medical treatment.[13] So too, when a woman employee decided to marry a man in a rival firm of travel agents, a risk arose of inadvertent leakage of information. The employers after discussion with the rivals decided to dismiss her; and the rivals retained the husband in employment. This was held to be a discriminatory dismissal, but on grounds of sex, not 'marital status', because the employers had assumed that the man would be the family bread-winner.[14]

Personal characteristics: dress, sexuality

The worker who is picked out for inferior treatment because of personal characteristics that are unconventional or socially unacceptable receives little protection even in the general law of unfair dismissal – still less in recruitment, where the law scarcely enters the stage. Where the employee's conduct or attitude is not related to his work (as with the length of a ledger clerk's hair) a dismissal may well be held to be unfair (E P C A s. 57: p. 237). To this extent it is right to say that it is unfair to dismiss a worker on the ground that he or she is unconventional.[15] But the employer will normally argue that the ground for dismissal is work-related. Work rules may insist on conventional behaviour or dress. In 1984 Electronic Data prohibited beards, casual dress and alcohol over lunch to establish the 'corporate culture'. The dismissal of a worker in another firm some months later because he had retained his beard gave rise to spontaneous industrial action by his colleagues.

In the judgment of 'fairness' in unfair dismissal, however, social attitudes easily find a place in the tribunal's assessment of 'conduct', 'substantial reason' and reasonableness. It is not difficult to see such preconceived attitudes at work in some decisions, such as upholding the dismissal of a homosexual worker at a camp whose work did not require him to be in contact with the children and whose psychiatrist testified that he was no danger to young persons ('a considerable proportion of employers would take the view that the employment of a homosexual should be restricted', as the tribunal knew 'on the evidence *and* on their experience'). So too, with a drama teacher at a technical college who had twice been convicted, and punished, for acts of gross indecency and whose plea that his 'private and personal life' would never lead him to betray his professional trust was of no avail.[16] Indeed, in such cases the tribunal, because it asks whether the decision falls within the 'band' of decisions that *might* be regarded as reasonable by employers (p. 245), is compelled to admit into its calculations employers at the far end of the spectrum who put into practice the most retrograde social prejudices and Victorian values towards minority groups. Thus, the dismissal of a teacher of teenagers who was convicted of possessing cannabis – he never used it but allowed others to grow it in his garden – was held to be fair in 1982 (though three years earlier the dismissal of a teacher similarly convicted of possession who was rarely in contact with children was found unreasonable).[17]

A lesbian accounts clerk regularly wore badges with slogans such as 'Gays against Fascism' and 'Gay Switchboard'; when her employers objected to one saying 'Lesbians Ignite' she refused to remove it and was dismissed. The E A T insisted (rather disingenuously) that this was *not* 'because she was a lesbian or because of anything to do with her private life', but because of her 'conduct at work'. That *could* be 'offensive to the customers and to fellow employees'. The dismissal was therefore reasonable.[18] The issue here is not merely tolerance of gay or lesbian workers. Toleration has increased; but the law and its society are still a long way from insisting upon a worker's right to express whatever form of sexuality he or she embraces as a normal part of life by establishing an equal personal freedom for those who assert, and for those who deny, that 'heterosexism is an oppression',[19] and to base their norms of give and take upon the equal validity of both philosophies. It is possible, perhaps likely, that a complaint by a dismissed worker whose badge was directed at heterosexual combustion would have received rather different treatment.

One natural consequence of social prejudices (especially at a time of high unemployment) is the need for the applicant for employment to conceal his or her characteristics or history. This frequently leads him or her into what the lawyer must describe as material misrepresentation, which, as it induces the contract, gives the employer the right to rescind it. Fear of mental illness is widespread in our society. When, therefore, a worker with a history of mental illness applied to be an agent for the Prudential, he replied to questions about illness, physical or mental, without disclosing that history at all. He was 'completely satisfactory' in his work and he had not seen psychiatric doctors for four years. The employers discovered the truth only in the course of his applying for life insurance. The E A T accepted that the 'medical history *coupled* with the fact that [he] had deliberately misled the employers' was 'some other substantial reason' on which a reasonable, and therefore fair, dismissal could be built.[20] In other cases of dismissal on grounds of health, an independent report on the worker's medical condition has been required; but here it was dispensed with – 'it would not have made any difference' – nor was it unreasonable of the company not to offer alternative work. The misrepresentation (necessary to get the job) weighed against the worker, along with his private history of mental illness, though neither had ever affected his capacity to do his work. As Lord MacDonald said in 1980, in the case of a dismissed epileptic worker, a reason for dismissal, 'particularly one which most employers would be expected to adopt', can remain 'substantial' and sufficient 'even where modern sophisticated opinion can be adduced to suggest it has no scientific foundation'. Whilst such judicial attitudes abound, fairness for the unconventional will remain an illusion.

Criminal records and family life

A similar problem, especially in respect of hiring, can arise in respect of other aspects of personal life. Take persons with a criminal record. The Rehabilitation of Offenders Act 1974 made it improper to exclude a person from an office, profession, occupation or employment on the ground that he has a criminal conviction that is deemed by that Act to be 'spent'. The applicant for employment or employee is specifically entitled to reply in the negative to questions about such previous convictions. But this protection by way of affirmative action to help ex-convicts is rather limited. Regulations exclude the operation of the Act in respect of work in health, administration of justice, social work, teaching, betting, insurance, finance and explosives (SI No. 1023, 1975). Dismissal by reason of a 'spent' offence is unfair; but where the past offence does not fall within the Act, a worker who has falsely denied any previous offence will be caught in the same trap, as where a guard was dismissed 'reasonably' because his 'dishonest concealment' destroyed the confidence 'of master and servant . . . there is no rule of law that employers must follow and extend the social philosophy which found expression in the Rehabilitation of Offenders Act'.[21] The Code of Practice on Disciplinary Practice (1977), however, establishes that no criminal offence 'outside employment' should be automatic grounds for dismissal; the employer should consider whether the worker is 'unsuitable for his or her type of work or unacceptable to other employees' (the new 1985 draft is substantially similar).

For such groups, finding employment is a larger problem than avoiding dismissal. There are others to whom the law offers very little in respect of assistance in either respect. For example, by the early 1980s one in eight families were one-parent families, mainly women who found work only in low-paid 'women's work' such as distribution, food, textiles or insurance.[22] No labour law protection is offered to them. On the other hand, social policy in the EEC has led the Commission to propose a Directive for 'parental leave' from work, available, in addition to maternity leave (p. 483), to both or either of the parents. Such leave is extensive in Sweden, full-time until the child is eighteen months or part-time until the child is eight or has been at school one year; in France, after one year's service, unpaid leave of up to two years is available to either the father or mother to care for children under three; such schemes exist in many other EEC countries.

The European Parliament has proposed additional leave for parents to care for handicapped children. Such proposals would bolster the right to decent family life at least for women and men who do enjoy employment. Moreover, the introduction of some kind of paternity leave has long been recognized as a necessary part of any attempt to reduce sexism in society.[23] Though Government backing is lacking, the CBI encouraged member firms in 1985 to make arrangements for paternity leave with individual employees, not through collective agreements (its survey found only 7 per cent of employers with such arrangements). In family law, it is true, some judges have recognized a high priority for family needs, as when the Court of Appeal reversed a Dickensian decision that an unemployed father should not be allowed custody of his four-year-old son – which would stop him entering gainful employment (he must 'get back to work', the judge had said, to discharge his 'duty to society to seek remunerative employment') – because he was an excellent one-parent family, and the needs of the child must come first.[24] This philosophy of family law could profitably infuse some parts of labour law policy; the denial of parental leave, for instance, discriminates against the young children of the poor. But the British Government has rejected such proposals; they would be costly and 'a wrong signal to the labour market'.[25]

Political tests and computer data

It is startling to discover that, whilst these proposals for bolstering workers' rights to a better family life are widely supported in the

Community, less attention has been paid to discrimination (especially in hiring) by reason of political or ethical belief. Some countries, as we have seen with the Italian workers' statute of 1970,[26] protect the worker's right to have and express political opinions and religious and union beliefs. British law offers virtually no protection. We have seen (p. 313) that a militant trade unionist can be dismissed soon after engagement by reason of his union record without the employer infringing the statutory prohibition on dismissal for trade union activity.[27] Organizations conduct 'labour screening' for employers; black lists of workers said to be subversives or otherwise undesirable are common in certain industries; in 1983 the *Sunday Times* spoke of employers 'imposing more stringent political tests on the humble lathe operator than are applied to teachers or Whitehall clerks'.

Civil servants have since 1953 been subject to explicit restrictions on their political activities, but after the Armitage Report (1978) the Government relaxed them, dividing Crown servants into three groups: those (mainly industrial) free to engage in politics; senior civil servants free to engage only in local politics; and the rest, free to engage in all political activity with permission. In 1984 the Prime Minister said of this last group that they could 'do what they wish in their own time', but it must not affect the discharge of their duties.[28] Confidence in this approach was not increased by the prohibition on union membership at the GCHQ (p. 277), by evidence of a register of civil servants' beliefs (on nuclear disarmament, for example), by Government declarations that it would not accept 'subversives' in public offices or as negotiators for Civil Service unions, or by the revelations that BBC employees had been regularly 'vetted' by MI5 and that other public figures were subjected to telephone tapping.[29]

As early as 1970 one Civil Service union expressed concern at the information about workers being compiled on computers. The Data Protection Act 1984 now requires a 'data user' and computer bureaus to register and to observe certain principles designed to prevent the improper collection of information and its unnecessary disclosure, and to afford individuals a right of access to information held concerning them. There are, however, wide exemptions from these statutory duties; they cover data kept for national security, on home computers or on files for pay-roll and accounts held only for that purpose (s. 32). Nor does the Act cover manual records. (It has been said that 'by 1987 all black-lists will be in buff folders'.) Computerized personnel records are subject to registration, with rights of inspection by workers concerned. Moreover the Convention adopted by the Council of Europe in 1981 calls for special protection for data concerning 'racial origin, political opinions or religious or other beliefs, and personal data concerning health or sexual life'; the Home Secretary has power to introduce additional safeguards (s. 2 (3)), and much may depend on how that power is used. Furthermore, the definition of 'personal data' (s. 1 (3)) means that information about organizations (such as unions) is not covered; and although attributes of and opinions about a worker are covered, 'an indication' about an individual (e.g. that he will be made redundant) is not – a distinction pregnant with litigation.[30]

The disabled

One disadvantaged group protected by Parliament both in hiring and in firing is the disabled. Once again the labour law origins lie in wartime. The Disabled Persons (Employment) Acts 1944 and 1958 normally require employers with twenty employees or more to give priority in recruitment to persons registered as disabled ('green card holders') up to a quota of 3 per cent of their work-force unless the employer obtains a permit from the Department of Employment excusing him from the quota. The Minister has power to fix other percentages for specific industries (used only for shipping) or specially to designate certain employment for the disabled (e.g. attendants in car-parks). The employer must not terminate such a worker's employment without 'reasonable cause' if it means his quota will not be met. Although the employer is criminally liable for failure to observe these duties, the worker is afforded no specific civil remedy (though it seems arguable that the employer should be liable for breach of statutory duty). If he claims that his dismissal is 'unfair', the EAT appears to believe that, whilst an employer should give such a case 'special consideration', the ultimate test is still no higher than one of 'reasonableness'.[31] The scheme was begun to help those injured in the war. Now a worker can register if injury, disease or congenital deformity cause him to be substantially handicapped for work otherwise suited to him. Until 1982 payment of unemployment benefit was conditional upon registration for the disabled.

The total of voluntary registrations in 1985 was some 404,000 (in 1981, 460,000), but some could take work only in sheltered conditions. Jobcentres and local authorities found sheltered work for 1,000, and open work for 11,000, in the second quarter of 1985. The revelation that few government departments were employing the 3 per cent quota was met in 1984 by the explanation that many disabled persons do not now register, which is why only one-third of employers subject to a quota fulfil it. The MSC reviewed the quota scheme and proposed in 1981 that it should be replaced by a Code of Practice with a new statutory duty on employers to take reasonable steps to promote employment opportunities for disabled people. The Government preferred the MSC to draft a Code of Practice, and this was published in 1984, providing advice and encouragement to management – especially line management – and employees about disabled workers and the special MSC services and help available.[32]

The principle and public policy of endorsing fair employment opportunities for those who bring serious disability to their search for employment have thus been ratified; but the modernization of the legal structure within which this is done has not. A Code of Practice, valuable though it is, does not give the worker who is not hired the remedies a Disabled Workers Discrimination Act might provide. An MSC working group report of 1985 on the quota scheme revealed many other defects. Even within the present system, the granting of permits on condition that employers 'notify vacancies' to, and 'consider sympathetically' applications from, suitable disabled people should, it proposed, be changed into an obligation upon employers to 'give preference' to them. It showed that the total number of disabled persons can be put at anything from 1.2 million to five times that number, according to the definition employed. The present scheme is badly enforced and has been 'inadequately resourced over a long period of time'. In 1983 the ILO adopted a new Convention (No. 159) and Recommendation (168) on vocational rehabilitation of the disabled of which the Government ratified the latter on promoting opportunities for employment. If the former were ratified more extensive provisions than our present legislation would be required to help the disabled with training and job opportunities.

Discrimination: sex and race

Apart from the Sex Disqualification (Removal) Act 1919, a measure of narrow importance, discrimination was permitted by the law on grounds of sex or race until 1968.[33] The common law did not, as Lord Denning asserted in 1949, ensure that persons should 'not suffer any disability or prejudice by reason of their race'. Moreover, a society that was increasingly multiracial yet increasingly segregated remained blind to its racist character, and the history of sloth and resistance to legislation, depicted by Hepple and by Lester and Bindman, now screams at us accusingly from the record (fifteen Bills were promoted by back-bench MPs between 1953 and 1965; only one received second reading debates – on Fridays). A Race Relations Act of 1965 (mainly concerned with public discrimination and incitement to racial hatred) was extended, rather unsatisfactorily, to employment in 1968. But in 1975 – International Women's Year – pressures for sex equality led to the Sex Discrimination Act (which also amended the Equal Pay Act 1970).

Sex discrimination had been well documented. 'If it were not for the *normality* of this sort of prejudice these facts would surely have given rise to legal measures long before [1975].'[34] This was a period, as we saw in Chapter 2, when more women were entering the labour market, though the legislation took insufficient account of the increasingly 'atypical' forms of employment they came to enjoy. The Act covered discrimination in education, housing, provision of services and goods, as well as employment for which complaints were directed to the industrial tribunals. It established the Equal Opportunities Commission (EOC), which both advises individuals and has more general functions to implement the Acts and to promote equality between men and women and the elimination of discrimination. This was an important moment for race discrimination too. Reform of the unsatisfactory 1968 Act was not easy. It was therefore decided to twin a new racial discrimination measure with the (now acceptable) structure of the sex discrimination legislation. So, complaints to tribunals are provided by the Race Relations Act 1976, and a body, the Commission for Racial Equality (CRE), was set up, fashioned in many ways parallel to the EOC.

The similar structures of the two Acts, therefore, require that we discuss the fundamental legal issues of both together, if only to avoid duplication; but this does not imply that the problems addressed in sex and racial discrimination in employment are always parallel. Indeed, only time will tell whether the manoeuvres that produced the RRA 1976 were tactically brilliant or unhappily opportunist.[35] Nor must we forget the 'chastening lesson', as Aaron put it, 'that law is ultimately powerless to extirpate racial and other types of discrimination in employment. Law can eliminate the uglier, overt manifestations of such discrimination.'[36] We live in a society that carries structures of discrimination in its bones. Each year the reports of the EOC and CRE testify to this (the 1984 CRE report recorded black unemployment twice as high as for white people; the rate for men with O levels was: white 9, Asian 18 and black 25 per cent). Can anyone doubt that such factors, while not the only cause, contributed to the urban riots of the 1980s? To achieve the wider objective, labour law can only hope to play its part with other social and economic policies and with a determined attack upon the evils of discrimination generally. But many believe the law could contribute more to this objective than our present legislation does.

We consider the scope of the legislation, the nature of unlawful 'discrimination' and the methods of enforcement under the Acts.

Scope of the Acts

The prohibition of discrimination is wide in the employment field. It applies to partnerships as well as to trade unions, to bodies that confer qualifications for a trade or profession, to vocational training bodies, to employment agencies and to the MSC (SDA ss. 11–16, RRA ss. 10–15). However, a trade union may still reserve seats by sex on an elected body, such as the NEC, where it considers this necessary to secure a reasonable number of that sex upon it, though the electorate must not be sex-divided (SDA s. 49); also 'positive' discrimination (or better, 'affirmative action') may be taken by training bodies, employers or unions in certain circumstances to promote training for members of one sex to increase their numbers in a job (SDA ss. 47, 48), and similar provision on education, training and welfare is made about minority racial groups (RRA ss. 35–38). Primary liability for discrimination in employment lies on the employer, who may escape where it is exercised by his employees only if he has taken reasonably practicable steps to prevent it (SDA s. 41, RRA s. 32); but any person who knowingly aids discriminatory acts is liable, including a union or an employee for whom

the employer is vicariously responsible (s. 42, and s. 33). Sex discrimination did not in 1985 apply under the 1975 Act to employers of less than
five employees (s. 6 (3) (b); but this will be amended by the Sex
Discrimination Bill 1986 because the ECJ held that it contravenes the
EEC Directive (76/207) on equal treatment of the sexes. The exclusion
of occupations in private households, however, in personal jobs such as
'personal maids', is permitted by EEC law out of 'respect for private
life': p. 449.[37] Nor does the SDA apply to provisions in relation to the
'payment of money' under the contract of employment or to death or
retirement (i.e. pensions) (ss. 6 (4), (6), 11 (4), 12 (4)). Discrimination
for reasons of national security is excluded from both Acts (SDA s. 52,
RRA s. 42).

Both Acts apply to 'contract workers' – that is, persons working under
a labour supply contract (SDA s. 9, RRA s. 7) – and to those employed
'under a contract of service or of apprenticeship or a contract personally
to execute any work or labour' (SDA s. 82, RRA s. 78, also the Eq.
P. A. 1970 s. 1 (6)). It must not be thought that every 'self-employed'
person or 'independent contractor' (p. 112) is included; a sub-
postmaster whose duties were only to see that work was done but not to
perform it himself was excluded in 1981. And while the 'doing of work'
includes research, an agency agreement in *Gunning's* case, 1986, for the
distribution of newspapers, requiring supervision of the work, was held
not to include a sufficient personal obligation to fall within the execution
of '*any* work or labour'.[38] The EAT's approach was to extend the
statutory prohibition widely:

> those who engage, even cursorily, the talents, skill or labour of the self-employed
> are wise to ensure that the terms are equal as between men and women and do not
> discriminate between them.[39]

But the Court of Appeal judges rejected this liberal approach and
applied protection only to those with a contract 'the *dominant* purpose
of which was the execution of personal work or labour'. This hardly
seems to fit the social purposes of the Act. Even if they fall within this
definition, though, the sex discrimination prohibitions do not apply to
certain groups, such as ministers of religion, nor in certain respects (such
as height) to police and prison officers (SDA ss. 17, 18, 19). The race
prohibitions do not apply to rules about immigration or Civil Service
regulations restricting entry to Crown employment (RRA s. 75).

A vexed question is the relationship of the SDA 1975 with the legislation of long standing passed to protect women in employment that we met in Chapter 5. One school of thought, which has included the EOC, believes that the legislation must eventually be repealed to establish equality.[40] The EOC has a duty to keep under review discriminatory provisions in the health and safety legislation and report upon it. The Act, however, expressly validates discrimination 'necessary . . . to comply with a requirement' of an Act in force before 1975 or a regulation under it (SDA s. 51). (It may be debatable how far this provision is entirely in accordance with EEC law, such as the 1976 Directive on equal treatment.) Thus the special protections of the Factories Act 1961, such as restrictions on hours worked in a factory (ss. 86–93), continued after 1975 until the 1986 Bill (p. 411). These provisions have been widely interpreted. In *Page's* case, 1981, a woman lorry driver complained that she was not allowed to drive lorries carrying chemicals that could be harmful to women of child-bearing age. She stated that she 'did not anticipate becoming pregnant'. The employer relied upon the general duties to care for the health and welfare of employees under HSWA 1974 s. 2, and the EAT accepted this as being sufficient. It was enough for the employer to see a risk to which the woman employee was 'particularly vulnerable'. In other contexts, too, the EAT has ousted the SDA where action under an earlier statute did not seem to be strictly 'necessary' for compliance (as in the case of men-only fellowships at a college).[41]

The ECJ judgment of 1984[37] found the SDA defective in three respects: it fails to provide a method for declaring void provisions in works rules, occupational or professional codes (despite s. 77) and collective agreements (p. 323); it exempts *all* employment in private households; and it exempts employers with five employees or less. The Government, obliged to legislate, was naturally reluctant to abolish the exemption for small businesses, having itself slashed employment protection laws in such enterprises (e.g. p. 235). We saw, however, that the Sex Discrimination Bill 1986 aimed to comply in all three respects.

Discrimination

Discrimination may be direct or indirect. Direct discrimination involves treating another person less favourably on racial grounds, or on grounds of sex. Indirect discrimination arises from *a requirement or condition* that is or would be applied equally to others, or those of another sex, but (1) is such that the proportion of persons of the same racial group, or the same sex, who can comply with it is considerably *smaller* than the proportion of the other persons, or other sex, who can comply; (2) is *not justifiable* irrespective of racial grounds, or grounds of sex, for the person to whom it is applied; (3) is *detrimental* to that person because he or she cannot comply with it (R R A s. 1, S D A s. 1, applying equally to discrimination against men: s. 2). The prohibition applies in regard to both hiring and treatment during employment and dismissal, and relates to job offers or advertisements, including selection, promotion, training and other benefits such as facilities or services (S D A s. 6, R R A s. 4). The law on discrimination, therefore, here sets an important precedent in so far as it applies to selection and hiring.

The ground for the discrimination must be the prohibited ground (sex or race). Where, therefore, the employer discriminates on other grounds, his action is not unlawful under these Acts. But where the employer applies a general assumption – for example, that women cannot do the work – he may be guilty of sex discrimination. Where the employer dismissed a waitress on discovering she had four young children, the worker recovered £260 for loss of earnings and injury to her feelings because the employer had assumed it was women with young children who were less 'reliable' (a discrimination that related to both her sex and her marital status). But an employer who ran down the lighter side of his packing warehouse (in which women mainly worked) as against the heavier side (employing mainly men) was not guilty of discrimination in 1980, even though some women employees became redundant.[42] Lord Denning adopted the dubious analysis of two establishments, 'a natural division', like porters and waitresses in the Inns of Court doing heavy and light work; so too, the warehouse was 'two establishments'. Similarly, where workers were found to have sorted themselves into different racial groups, neither the union, F T A T U, nor the employer *Pel Ltd* was made liable for their failure to take positive action to combat this racial division (lack of communication by the employer went to 'efficiency', not less favourable treatment) – though it must be remembered in the case of a union that acts directly or indirectly inducing or aiding unlawful discrimination are themselves unlawful (R R A ss. 31, 33, S D A ss. 40, 42).

At first in *Peake* the Court of Appeal decided that minor discrepancies could be overlooked (*de minimis non curat lex* – 'the law is not concerned with trifles'), especially where they involved 'courtesy and chivalry' to women. There women were allowed to leave work a few minutes early to avoid the rush. This may still cover a case where requirements, on clothing for example, are minor and no more than strictly necessary, even though different for the sexes.[43] But in *Ministry of Defence* v. *Jeremiah*[44] the Court of Appeal applied a stricter standard. The dirty work on 'colour-bursting' shells was allocated only to men. A male worker's complaint was upheld, Brandon L J in particular refuting the notion that discrimination must be adverse or hostile to their interests before men could complain: 'the sole question to be answered in this case was whether the men examiners were put under a disadvantage by comparison with the women examiners'. The *Peake* doctrine appears to apply now only to trivial distinctions. In particular, *Greig's* case, 1979, makes it clear that such a test is not likely ever to apply to the selection of employees, as opposed to the treatment of existing employees.

Indirect discrimination

Indirect discrimination goes further. It was borrowed from the decisions in the United States whereby intention to discriminate is not the test of unlawfulness where, for example, a discriminatory pattern (e.g. in high-school tests) is established, 'practices that are fair in form but discriminatory in operation'[45] (though later US decisions appear to allow some discrimination in 'a compensation system that is responsive to supply and demand and other market forces').[46] For this doctrine to weigh significantly against discrimination (especially on racial grounds) it must be strictly applied.

In 1984 the branch of a union objected to a black road-sweeper being allocated to their work as refuse collectors because, the council believed, of his colour (though they gave other reasons such as his bad attendance record). To avoid industrial action the council's officer revoked the appointment, with the worthy intention of safeguarding industrial peace and a collective agreement. Whilst motive may be evidence of the ground for an action, worthy motives could not excuse action that apparently discriminated on the ground that the worker was black. The judge distinguished a case where an employer engages a worker by mistake of less than the required height and a racially prejudiced employee points this out because he is black; if the employer dismisses solely on the ground of height, this is not racial discrimination. The majority of the Court of Appeal agreed there was material on which the CRE could have concluded that the worker was treated in a way different from the way he would have been treated had he been white.[47] Nor had the officer of the council a right to be heard by the CRE personally as a matter of 'natural justice'. But a dissenting appeal judge thought the evidence did not show that the officer *must* have acted on racial grounds; he would have decided the case for the council – a line of argument that, were it accepted, would shatter the slender structures of the statutory powers of the CRE to fight racism. For, as we shall see, unless the CRE is backed by the judges wherever it has a basis for its judgment, it will be powerless. It should not be assumed that union pressure is always of this kind. Soon after that judgment in 1984, the alleged racial prejudice of a foreman led thousands of Austin Rover car workers to strike over the dismissal of a black fork-lift-truck driver.

The three parts of indirect discrimination – the 'requirement or condition', 'detriment' and 'justifiability' – have been interpreted variably by the judges, as follows.

The requirement or condition. Where a promotion procedure was alleged to disadvantage women by the very vagueness of its tests, which allowed for subjective sexism, the need to satisfy it was accepted as a condition in 1983. But in the same year the Court of Appeal appeared to demand of selection tests (when a civil servant from Sri Lanka complained of rejection for promotion by reason of tests based on language, nationality, experience and age) that they must be an 'absolute bar'; here the complainant had failed by reason of 'personal qualities' (maturity and common sense, for example).[48] This definition can clearly allow for tests that are indirectly discriminatory or at least would be better dealt with under the heading of 'justifiability', discussed below. But in *Holmes's* case, 1984,[49] the EAT rejected a further relaxation of 're-quirement or condition', where the Home Office argued for its demand that a woman civil servant must return after maternity leave to a full-time, not a part-time, post; it rejected the extraordinary argument that the demand was too 'fundamental' to be a requirement or condition. Even so, it declared, somewhat mysteriously, that in other cases the demand for full-time staff might be 'sufficiently flexible as arguably not to amount to a requirement or condition at all'.

If such a requirement is imposed, what is the right comparison to determine whether a 'considerably smaller' proportion of persons of that sex or race can comply with it? The legislation demands comparison of like with like, persons in 'not materially different' circumstances (SDA s. 5 (3), RRA s. 3 (4)). But this still allows a discretion to the tribunals. *Deirdre Kidd*, a part-time worker in a factory with an all-women work-force, found that the 'last in, first out' principle for redundancy was to be broken by the employer dismissing part-time workers first; she complained that the requirement that to enjoy seniority one must be full-time hit women more than men, and married women more than single women, because they looked after their children. But the EAT upheld the comparison made with *households* generally where home care for children was needed; and no evidence had been adduced to prove that 'within this section of society a requirement to be [full-time] . . . was one with which a considerably smaller proportion of married than of unmarried women could comply'. Child care did not now represent an obstacle to all households; married fathers (perhaps victims of redundancy) sometimes cared for the children. The tribunal was right to reject 'generalised assumptions' for, said Waite J, 'Ours are times of far-reaching changes.'[50] That may be so; but the reasoning is startling.

The EAT insisted that no different principle was being applied than in previous cases. In *Clarke* v. *Eley (IMI) Kynoch Ltd*, 1983,[51] for example, dismissals of part-time workers in redundancy, agreed with the union in breach of the LIFO principles of seniority, were held to be both sex discrimination and therefore an unfair dismissal as an improper selection in redundancy (p. 249). Whereas LIFO might have 'a limited discriminatory effect, taking part-time workers first is grossly discriminatory'. The evidence showed that 100 per cent of part-time workers in that (mixed) work-force were women, whereas 80 per cent nationally were women. 'It is still a fact', said Browne Wilkinson J., 'that the raising of children tends to place a greater burden upon them than upon men.' It is difficult to believe that in such cases the Act envisaged that women part-time workers would succeed only if they adduce statistical evidence on the number of wives and fathers who take on (or share) the child-rearing functions in British families.

In *Holmes*, Waite J. refused to be frightened by the prospect of 'a shoal of claims by women full-time workers alleging that it would be discriminatory to refuse them full-time status'. In *Kidd*, whilst repeating that each case 'will depend on its own facts', he raised the plaintiff's hurdles by narrowing the comparison. In earlier cases the more liberal spirit prevailed. In *Price*[52] a requirement that applicants for Civil Service posts should be between 17½ and 28 years old was tested by whether fewer women could comply within the 'pool' of qualified men and women (as against the total male and female population); the E A T accepted from 'knowledge and experience' that fewer women between their mid-20s and mid-30s were able to seek employment as they wished, though statistical evidence had also been adduced to this effect. The equivalent comparison in racial discrimination confirms the interpretation that the question is whether the persons involved 'can' comply *in practice*. When a school refused to accept a Sikh boy, *Mandla*, because of a rule against his wearing a turban, the Law Lords held that he could not comply with the ban 'consistently with the customs and cultural conditions of the racial group' and that discrimination was therefore established.[53] The same should apply in employment cases.

Detriment. Secondly, what is meant by the condition being to the plaintiff's 'detriment'? A transfer of a black worker, by reason of pressure from other workers, to a different job that was less attractive though equal in pay and status was held to be a detriment in 1981. A differential check upon black workers, because it was feared that a black person might enter the premises when he should not, was accepted in 1983 as a detriment. So too was the transfer of *Kirby*, an interviewing clerk (who had passed on information about racialist practices by employers) to less interesting filing work[54] – though he lost his case for the astonishing reason that he had not been treated 'less favourably' than another clerk would have been who disclosed confidential information, reasoning that, if upheld more generally to those disadvantaged by reason of their struggle against racist or sexist behaviour by the employer whereby they are led into a breach of other duties of their employment, could tear a hole in the protective legislation.

Such a result was skilfully avoided in the *Showboat* case.[55] A white manager of an amusement centre was dismissed because he refused to carry out an instruction to exclude all young blacks from it. Direct discrimination 'on racial grounds' within s. 1 (1) (a) of the Act was capable, it was held, of including a person who had been disadvantaged by reason of resistance to racial instructions, even though that matter is dealt with also elsewhere in the R R A (s. 30). Indirect discrimination (s. 1 (1) (b)), in regard to requirement, proportion and detriment, must relate to the person against whom it is exercised; but in deciding whether an employee has been treated 'less favourably on racial grounds' when he resists such a policy by his employer, his treatment must be compared to what would have been done to a man 'having all the same characteristics as the complainant except his race or his attitude to race'. This makes it all the more remarkable that the respondent in *Kirby's* case was not even liable for 'victimization' (both S D A s. 4 and R R A s. 2 make unlawful discrimination by victimization by reason of proceedings, information or allegations effected in order to enforce the Acts; once again the answer was that the M S C would have punished workers who released confidential information, Act or no Act).

In *Jeremiah's* case, Brandon L J saw 'detriment' as meaning nothing more than 'putting under a disadvantage', a question of fact to be answered by the tribunal. But more recent decisions have been more guarded. In *De Souza* the E A T insisted that it must be a disadvantage 'in relation to employment', not merely an act of prejudice. There, one manager had said to another, 'Get your typing done by the wog.'[56] Popplewell J. declared:

However deplorable it may be to describe a coloured person as a 'wog' to a third person, it is not and cannot be construed as putting her under a present or future disadvantage in relation to her employment.

Such a view seems remote from the real world. Yet the Court of Appeal agreed. Racial insults were not enough. It must be such that the 'putative reasonable employee could justifiably complain about his or her working conditions or environment'. Here the 'reasonable coloured secretary' would not have thought she was disadvantaged within the employment context. It is doubtful that many black workers would agree. One wonders whether the learned judge would feel under a 'disadvantage in his employment context' if counsel or the Law Lords deplorably but regularly told parties 'get your cases tried by that capitalist pig'. Such judgments display a disturbing absence of social experience and imagination.

The Scottish E A T took a rather more severe view of sexual harassment. It allowed an appeal from the dismissal by a tribunal of a complaint that two male school laboratory technicians had harassed a female colleague by constant suggestive remarks and conduct with sexual overtones, including physical contact. Sexual harassment by itself is not covered by the Act; nevertheless they would not have acted towards a man in the same way, and the evidence of 'detriment' lay in her having been compelled to seek a transfer to another school.[57] (Would it have been different if they had been bisexual and *would* have done the same to a man?) It is true that in *De Souza* the Court of Appeal denied that a worker had to wait until she is forced to leave her employment before she can know that she has enough evidence to prove 'detriment' in her employment. But it is an odd way for the appeal tribunals to enforce the anti-discrimination legislation to leave open even the slightest possibility that a black woman worker, harassed sexually at work whilst being called a 'wog', might still not succeed in her complaint to a tribunal. It is time the judiciary ruled that racism and sexism are in themselves detriments to their victims in their working environment.

Justifiability. Thirdly, even if the complainant has proved a requirement of the right category and a detriment in employment, the employer may escape by proving that the discrimination is 'justifiable'. Here the judges have veered first towards a strict, but later a more relaxed, test. One of the first test cases was *Steel* v. *UPW*, 1978.[58] A system for the delivery of mail, agreed between the union and management, gave the better 'walks' to senior Post Office employees. A postwoman complained that this operated unfavourably to her because seniority was measured by membership of the permanent staff, which was not available to women until 1975. The Post Office would be willing to bring in greater equality after the present agreement had worked its way to an end; as the judge put it: 'supporting sex equality – but not yet'. Phillips J. insisted that the onus of proving justification was on the employer; he must prove the case is genuine and necessary; the continuing effect of the discrimination must be weighed against the discriminatory requirement; and the discrimination must be shown to be *necessary*, as against a practice that is convenient: 'The touchstone is business necessity.' This was a test frequently applied. As Browne-Wilkinson J. said in 1983, racial and sex discrimination are 'emotive matters':

there is no generally accepted view as to the comparative importance of eliminating discriminatory practices on the one hand as against, for example, the profitability of a business on the other.

Such a recognition of the value-laden nature of the problem may be important in future EEC developments, for in 1984 the EC Commission, whilst prepared to presume indirect discrimination in a measure that 'predominantly affects workers of one sex', felt it should be justifiable on proof that it was unintended and 'objectively justified'.[59]

Soon after, however, when the need to maintain whatever constraint law could exercise against racism was certainly no less, the Scottish EAT and the Court of Appeal both relaxed the standards. Both cases concerned a works rule prohibiting beards at work, a rule clearly discriminatory indirectly against Sikhs; but in both the rule was upheld as justifiable 'irrespective of the colour, race, nationality or ethnic or national origins' (RRA s. 1 (b) (ii)) of the workers concerned. As Lord Fraser put it in a later decision, it was 'purely a matter of public health and nothing whatever to do with racial grounds'.[60] The judges treated the question as one of fact; the purpose of the employers was more prominent than any test of business necessity.

The Court of Appeal soon confirmed the relaxation. In *Ojutiku*,[61] the MSC had restricted access to certain management training opportunities to those who had specified educational qualifications and work experience because these would be required by employers, it thought, in considering the trainees for jobs. The qualifications disadvantaged black applicants; and the employers concerned may have been intending to discriminate. The 'necessity' test was displaced. The decision in *Steel*, said Kerr LJ, put a 'gloss' on the concept of justification under the SDA which 'clearly applies a lower standard than the word "necessary"'. The rule might be justified by 'good grounds'. Here 'the prospects of would-be managers would not be enhanced by such persons attaining the paper qualification of a diploma'; secondly, the rule maintained the standard of that qualification. Because of its 'limited funds' the MSC was entitled to limit places in the course to those likely to benefit in their careers. Where the need for economy leads a body to differentiate directly by race or national origin in fees charged for courses, it is unlawful, as in the *Orphanos* case; but where indirect discrimination is involved, the *Ojutiku* test opens a back door to subjective preferences.

Eveleigh L J said the test was whether the reasons for the action would be 'acceptable to right-thinking persons as sound and tolerable reasons'.

This weak interpretation of 'justifiability' was approved in 1983 by the Law Lords: it need not be a 'necessary condition' but 'in all the circumstances justifiable without regard to the ethnic origins of that person' (or, of course, sex or marital status). The relaxation, indeed, appears to have encouraged employers to present arguments that would clearly have been impossible under the 'necessity' test. It became necessary for the E A T to hold specifically that the mere fact that the bulk of industry is organized on the basis of full-time employment as the norm cannot self-evidently justify by itself a requirement that a woman must work full-time.[62] So far from the earlier cases has the law now drifted that it is proper for a tribunal in 1985 to accept a 'marginal advantage' to the employer of full-time workers over part-timers in the shift-work patterns. Waite J. upheld such reasons as 'sound and tolerable reasons', even 'realistic and sensible', for

under the competitive conditions of modern industry small advantages of that kind, though singly they may be of little account, can cumulatively make a crucial difference between success or failure in attracting or maintaining orders.[63]

This judgment confirms the influence of the recession and of changes in prevailing philosophy upon the courts. The barrier of 'business necessity' stood firm in the 1970s against indirect discrimination. In the 1980s the market-oriented demand for competitiveness sways the judges to accept in its place the judgment of 'right-thinking' people and marginal influences on the bottom line (leading one commentator to conclude that they need to be educated 'as to the basic facts of life').[64] Worse, this has given rise to a worrying position at the level of the tribunals. Where an Asian woman, one of 240 applicants responding to an advertisement of vacancies at the D H S S local offices, was met with demands for a level of English language at O-level that she could not meet (though she had similar qualifications abroad) the tribunal rejected her claim of indirect discrimination. She was otherwise well qualified. They restricted the 'pool' of comparators to all persons of Asian origin and of the indigenous population with secondary education and decided that Asians 'can comply' with such a standard as well as others. The E A T by a majority rejected such an approach. As a matter of common sense not requiring statistics (though they were in evidence) the ability to pass such examinations was bound to be affected by its being in a second language. Moreover, the requirement was a detriment (on which the tribunal had also probably erred). But the decision still went against her. The tribunal had found the requirement to be 'justifiable'. That was a decision of fact that (though no doubt other tribunals might say it could not be justified on any grounds) the E A T decided it could not set aside.[65] 'That different tribunals can legitimately come to widely differing decisions', it has been commented, 'in so emotive an area gives much cause for concern.' The tribunal should surely not be free to apply its own subjective value judgments once a prima-facie case is established without the respondent proving that there are no other reasonable ways of reaching his objective.

Both the S D A and the R R A provide for specific situations in which arrangements for selection, promotion or transfer, or refusal of employment are justified. These are the cases of 'genuine occupational qualification' (G O Q). In relation to sex discrimination, G O Q covers reasons of physiology (other than physical strength or stamina) affecting the nature of a job and its authenticity; considerations of decency and privacy involving physical contact, undress or sanitary facilities; living-in on premises affecting privacy; hospital, prison and similar requirements; personal services for welfare, education, etc. requiring one sex; restrictions imposed by law; and jobs held by a married couple (S D A s. 7). But where such a vacancy occurs and the employer already has enough employees of that sex who it is reasonable to employ on those duties, the G O Q has no application. The R R A has a narrower list of G O Qs. Subject to the same condition, it includes actors, models, personal welfare services and jobs involving work where food or drink is consumed by the public in 'a special ambience' for which a racial group is required for authenticity (the so-called Chinese-waiters provision: R R A s. 5). These provisions may assist an employer against a worker other than the one to which they are primarily directed. In the *Timex* case[66] redundancy procedures based on L I F O indicated that a woman supervisor should be made redundant, but they were waived so that the two other male supervisors were dismissed in order to retain the woman to deal with the personal problems of female employees. This was not a case of sex discrimination by reason of the G O Q; the woman was appointed to the sole remaining supervisor post for reasons connected with decency and privacy. But the E A T disagreed with the tribunal in seeing the case as one of dismissal (when the G O Q could not apply) but as one of discrimination 'against the man by selecting the woman to do the revised job' or 'in failing to transfer the man to do the revised job' (when it could).

Proof of discrimination

The reality of the law in action depends more often than not upon procedure and the burden of proof. In general this is left by both the SDA and RRA upon the complainant. It is not an easy task. The Annual Reports of the EOC and CRE regularly disclose the difficulty of assembling the evidence, especially perhaps in race cases ('In many of these cases proceedings could not be brought . . . because our inform-ants did not wish to be identified': CRE, 1984 Report, para. 30). It is true that in cases of indirect discrimination the burden of showing 'justifiability' lies on the employer, but that is after the initial case has been made out by the claimant. Where an issue of comparison arises, the claimant may be required to put forward sophisticated statistical evi-dence. As Lustgarten commented in 1977, the approach in *Price's* case,[52] whereby the restriction was to be judged against the 'pool' of 'qualified' men and women,

may be to open a Pandora's box. Where is information on the number of men and women meeting particular qualifications to be found? The more numerous and specific these are, the less likely the statistics corresponding to them will exist.[67]

Since then things have not been made much easier. The curiosities of *Kidd's* case[50] led Waite J. to note that disagreement between the parties as to the proper section of the population for the proportionate com-parator necessitated a preliminary decision by the tribunal. But he was 'confident' the tribunals could cope, by 'preliminary hearings on specific issues' or adjournment in mid-hearing. Will a complainant alleging discrimination be likely to accept as just a procedure that begins by requiring that his case be heard twice? Proposals, such as those by Lustgarten, to centre on the employer's *record* throughout his enter-prise, e.g. on promotions, or for the creation of an independent body to give evidence on other aspects of discrimination, might have offered a better way. In its 1983 report the CRE, whilst recognizing the dangers of ethnic records, repeated its call for such records to be kept: 'Equal opportunity policies, like any other policies, need to be subject to audit.' Such records could, of course, play a major role in discrimination cases, both on race and sex. What prevents obligatory records and mandatory disclosure of them is a quaint distaste for the facts.

The EAT began well by insisting that in all but frivolous cases the evidence of the employer must be heard and that tribunals should not decide there was 'no case to answer'; and that the very fact of a claimant with superior qualifications who is denied a job creates a case on which the respondent should be heard and, inferentially, should have some reasons to present. As the Northern Ireland Court of Appeal has declared, once discrimination is proved between members of different sexes, there is a case to answer. But discrimination means an unfair, or at least prima-facie unfair, preference.[68] It is also true that in the *Perera* (No. 2) case, 1982,[69] the EAT attempted to guide tribunals by indicating that indirect discrimination might be proved even by statistical evidence that was not perfect or 'elaborate'. The employer could always reply with better statistics. The attempt in *Kidd* to stress the variable nature of the exercise, dependent upon each set of facts before the tribunal, whose decisions are therefore less vulnerable to appeal, may represent an attempt to shield such cases from a more strict test that might be to the taste of the Court of Appeal if the issue came to it as a matter of legal principle. In the United States 'courts frequently have a difficult time' determining the right boundaries for comparison, and the weight of decisions and literature on statistical evidence is very great.[70] A mere glance at that example makes one ask again whether the great offensive (which will be needed) to liberate Britain from race and sex oppression at work will best be mounted through the medium of court litigation and evidence assembled for each case, or by increasing the intervention of investigatory bodies, with ultimate powers of compulsion, which can look at individual cases in the context of work groups and industries.

In a few cases the complainant may be handed his or her evidence on a plate; for example, there may be an advertisement of a job that is discriminatory (SDA s. 38, RRA s. 29). In other cases the primary evidence in the tribunal may disclose discrimination, as where the nature of the interview conducted by a butcher of a woman who answered his advertisement for an assistant, as evidenced by his manner and demeanour, indicated discrimination against women (though he had no such intention).[71] These are indeed cases where the sight of the witness in the flesh matters a lot. But more often he or she will have little concrete proof to hand of the reason why the job was refused or the promotion denied. Regulations made under SDA s. 74 (Regulations No. 2048, 1975) enable a complainant to serve a form on the employer asking certain standard and useful questions; the replies are admissible evidence; and a refusal to reply without reasonable excuse permits the tribunal to draw adverse conclusions (also RRA s. 65, and Regulations No. 842, 1977). But the employee will want more than this. Why should he or she not see the relevant books and papers of the firm at an earlier stage than any procedure now offered? The tribunal has a jurisdiction to order 'discovery' of documents by both sides, similar to that enjoyed by the High Court. The problem is, when should it make such an order? The employer may allege that the papers concerned are so confidential that disclosure would damage the business for reasons unrelated to the litigation. To compare the reasons for a woman's rejection for a job might involve looking at all the references of the other candidates; and they might object to this. Such problems are particularly acute in a system where the court or tribunal is seen to preside over 'adversarial' proceedings and the parties fight it out, rather than 'inquisitorial' procedures where the starting-point is that the court will investigate the truth for itself.

A prolonged battle about discovery took place in *Science Research Council* v. *Nassé*[72] where unsuccessful applicants for promotion or transfer sought the discovery and inspection of confidential documents about others who were considered by management for the same posts, one alleging sex, the other race, discrimination. The Court of Appeal set aside orders for discovery, Lord Denning stressing that confidential documents should rarely be subjected to such an order. The Law Lords agreed with the result but on narrower grounds; the test was whether discovery was needed in order fairly to dispose of the proceedings, and the tribunal itself should look at the documents to decide whether, as a last resort, confidential reports should be disclosed. Restrictive conditions could be placed upon discovery, such as the 'covering up' of passages or holding a hearing in camera (excluding the public). Lord Fraser, in particular, recognized that the relevant 'confidential information is almost always in the possession of the employer and . . . may be of vital importance to the complainer'; and Lord Scarman added: 'If a document is necessary for fairly disposing of the case, it must be produced, notwithstanding its confidentiality.'

The decision of the tribunal, however, is not outside the purview of review by the appellate courts. In *British Library* v. *Palyza*, 1984,[73] complaints of two library employees of racial discrimination that caused them to be passed over for promotion by an interviewing 'sift' board led the tribunal to accept their applications for disclosure of the reports on fellow employees (they had seen their own) subject to the exclusion of some passages. The E A T decided that it had power not only to set aside a tribunal's order for discovery; it could look at the documents itself, particularly when the decision had been made, and appealed, before the hearing had begun and no evidence had been heard. It recognized that, under the procedures now developed, 'the inquiry which the tribunal has to make into the relevant material is inquisitorial in nature [although] it takes place in the context of adversarial proceedings'. The principle is 'fairness, not absolute justice'. A party would not be required to adduce a document that is in his favour but which he wishes to withhold. The E A T undertook its 'invidious task' of reading the documents; it decided that they contained nothing necessary for disposing fairly of the proceedings. The judgment ends on an apologetic note, not least for disagreeing with the industrial tribunal when neither body could explain the reasons for its decision. Despite the addition of inquisitorial procedures, the legal machinery could do little more than rough justice and hope the losing side would trust it. As such, it may reveal some of the limits of what the law can do in the employment sector with deep-seated social discrimination on grounds of race.

The same lesson emerges in relation to proof of discrimination where the very institutions of employment tend to be rationalized by conventional 'objectivity'. The cases on promotion are perhaps the most difficult, though it may be that tribunals are now more ready here to infer direct discrimination from the evidence rather than enter the maze of indirect discrimination. The E O C report for 1984 records such a decision for Mrs Hay, who was passed over for a short-list after a promotion interview by the West Lothian College of Further Education where she had been teaching for eight years. Three years earlier Browne-Wilkinson J., in a case on promotion brought by an Indian-born photographer that was remitted to the tribunal, urged tribunals 'to forget about the rather nebulous concept of the "shift in the evidential burden" . . . it is more likely to obscure than to illuminate the right answer'. They should look at the evidence as a whole, understanding that proof of discrimination will normally consist of inferences to be drawn from the primary facts. If they indicate discrimination, the employer must give an explanation, and the tribunal must decide whether it is adequate. Perhaps even more important, he reminded them that 'it is highly improbable that a person who has discriminated is going to admit the fact, quite possibly even to himself'.[74] There, as so often in promotion and transfer cases, the tribunal had to make up its mind whether the evidence of the employers that they were not motivated by racial discrimination could be accepted.

Enforcement and remedies

The two main avenues of enforcement for discrimination legislation are individual claims and action by the agencies, the EOC and CRE. Action in the ordinary courts by individual workers damaged by discrimination is displaced (SDA s. 62, RRA s. 53) in favour of a claim presented to an industrial tribunal, normally within three months (SDA ss. 63, 76, RRA ss. 54, 68). This immediately highlights again the use of these tribunals as maids-of-all-work; and, although attempts are made to ensure that wing-persons sit, in the appropriate cases – women or people with experience in race relations (p. 266) – a strong case can be made for the creation of separate tribunals at least in the latter type of case.[75] The tribunals can award three remedies: a declaration of rights; compensation up to the limit applicable in compensatory awards for unfair dismissal (in 1986, £8,000: p. 254); and a recommendation for action by the employer to remove the discrimination, though unreasonable failure to observe such a recommendation is sanctioned by compensation, which is surprisingly still subject to the same limit (SDA ss. 63, 65, RRA ss. 54, 56). The 'recommendation', however, must not be couched as an order, certainly not an order to increase salary.[76] In promotion cases, perhaps the most difficult to prove, the EAT has not always been tough with employers, finding 'reasonable justification' for not responding, or not responding quickly, to the proposals.[77]

The most frequent remedy in the tribunals has been compensation. In sex (race) cases, the amount recovered in conciliated settlements or tribunal awards exceeded £749 in 1984 for only 29 (14) claimants; in 1983 for 23 (15). In 1981–4, out of 988 (1,297) tribunal applications, 261 (181) were settled by official conciliation; 157 (97) succeeded at a hearing; and 68 (62) awards of compensation and 75 (32) recommendations were made. The compensation is awarded on the same basis as damages in tort in a County court (i.e. foreseeable damage that is a direct result) and includes provision for compensation for injury to feelings (SDA s. 66 (4), RRA s. 57 (4)). In 1983 the EAT referred to the 'statutory tort of unlawful discrimination'. But the Court of Appeal has decided that such injury must be strictly proved to have flowed from the discrimination as such; in a case of dismissal, for example, it must 'result from the knowledge that it was an act of sex discrimination that brought about a dismissal'.[78] Where a tribunal awarded a derisory sum (50p) to a part-time waitress dismissed when it was discovered she had four children, and had improperly taken into account her activities after dismissal as a reason for reducing the amount, the EAT set its award aside, but only in favour of a figure of £100, which had been agreed by the parties in addition to the £160 compensatory award.[79] Waitresses are hardly well protected by such remedies against the unjust removal of the job on which the family may depend.

Moreover, if the complaint is of *indirect* discrimination, no compensation can be awarded if the employer proves that he did not apply the requirement or condition with an intention to discriminate on the prohibited ground (SDA s. 66 (3), RRA s. 57 (3)). This limitation is unlikely, however, to be the reason for the small amounts actually awarded by the tribunals. Most complainants believe they have been directly prejudiced. Of the 982 SDA applications completed in 1981–4, 678 were complaints about direct discrimination; for the 1,300 RRA applications, the figure was 1,089. In both race and sex cases the biggest single category of subject matter is dismissal (regularly about half the complaints) with refusal to hire coming next. Of the 583 race cases decided in 1981–4, 83 per cent of complaints were dismissed, an alarming figure on any basis. Leonard's survey of SDA and Eq. P. A. cases 1976–83 concluded that at 1983 prices 50 per cent of awards were for less than £300.[80] These figures disclose a sorry picture, scarcely one in which legal remedies are even denting the institutions of prejudice still strong in employment.

The agencies and discrimination

The agencies, the EOC and CRE, have primary roles in enforcing the legislation: namely, powers to assist individuals to bring complaints (SDA s. 75, RRA s. 66), to act against discriminatory advertisements (SDA s. 72, RRA s. 63), to seek an injunction to restrain persistent discrimination (SDA s. 71, RRA s. 62), to issue 'non-discrimination notices' and enforce them (SDA ss. 67–70, RRA ss. 58–61) and to issue Codes of Practice (SDA s. 56, RRA s. 47). Both in addition have functions to promote research, keep the law under review and submit proposals to the Government for its amendment. The assistance given to individuals illustrates still further the very small proportion of successes in the tribunals out of all the cases on which persons felt strongly enough to approach the agencies. In 1984 the CRE received more than 1,200 complaints of individual discrimination and 765 applications for assistance in tribunals (470 about dismissals, 179 about refusals of employment), of which it supported 108 (18 were successful, 38 settled, 52 dismissed). The EOC received 1,382 'inquiries' about sex discrimination (other than equal pay) and supported 270 cases in the tribunals or on appeal out of 390 requests (17 per cent of SDA cases succeeded in tribunals).

Tribunal work, valuable though it is, concentrates on the tip of the discrimination iceberg; the great mass is hidden below the social surface. The CRE project of 1980 is now famous in which three applications were made for jobs in Nottingham; two purported to come from persons with superior qualifications but plainly black; the third, white candidate was chosen by nearly half the 100 firms tested. In 1985 few could doubt the deep pattern of racialism in British society. The 'set-piece attacks' against Asians in London led police to say they were not random; the low achievement of black children in schools was ascribed by the Swann Report largely to the depressed socio-economic status of the families; and a 1985 CRE survey in Leicester showed that white applicants were four times more likely to be given jobs than equivalent black workers.[81] In Birmingham, where riots occurred in 1985, 20 per cent of school-leavers were black but they got only 8.7 per cent of the jobs.[82] Similarly, the segregation of jobs into 'men's' and 'women's' persisted.[83]

Both the EOC and the CRE have continually called for a change in the burden of proof to allow individuals an easier remedy for discrimination, and have called for other amendments to the two Acts. Even so, the differences in nature between the social structures embodying the two forms of discrimination – both grave, but not always parallel – began to make it doubtful whether the urgently needed measures against each of them require that the patterns of the two statutes, aligned for tactical reasons in 1975–6, should necessarily always remain identical. The wide-ranging Barber survey in 1985 showed that when unemployment for white males stood at 11.0 per cent it was 29 per cent for 'West Indians' and 34 per cent for 'Pakistanis'. For young male workers the rates were 20, 45 and 25 per cent.[84] A Government Minister reacted: 'If the best person gets the job, then that is what everyone should support.' More depth and sensitivity than this are required.

In such a social situation, the work of the agencies to promote equality assumes increasing importance. The CRE in 1983 and the EOC in 1985 issued Codes of Practice. Like the codes issued by ACAS on employment matters, these codes set up standards; they do not create offences but are to be taken into account by industrial tribunals on relevant questions (SDA s. 56A, RRA s. 47). (Now that the Secretary of State's employment codes are to be considered also by the courts (p. 308) a similar extension should be made here.) The codes spell out the character of the unlawful practices and recommend further action. For example, employers should state that they are 'equal opportunity employers'; steps should be taken by employers and agencies to prevent indirect discrimination; promotion, training and transfer should be notified to all workers, and selection tests generally should be freed from discriminatory characteristics; applicants from 'particular racial groups' at factory gates should not be treated less favourably than others (CRE code, section 1). The GOQ for a job should be regularly re-examined to see if it still applies; an equal opportunities policy must be seen to have active support from top management (EOC code, paras. 17, 35). Both recommend positive action that can be taken under the Acts to remedy disadvantage, such as in training (SDA ss. 47, 48, RRA ss. 37, 38). What effect these codes will have by themselves remains uncertain. The CRE followed up the code by approaching large employers in the private sector, and it has recorded that ethnic monitoring has begun to increase: 'we shall be increasingly emphasising the need for practical measures to deal with under-representation' (1984 Report). But the work needs more support from government, not necessarily by new laws, but by measures such as 'contract compliance' (parallel to the old FWR: p. 350), which the TUC emphasized in 1986.

The agencies and the judges

The pursuit by the agencies of their enforcement role by way of non-discrimination notices after a formal investigation has brought them into somewhat discordant contact with the courts. The formal investigation must follow terms of reference drawn up by the Secretary of State, and the agency is obliged to notify persons concerned and is given power to require information (SDA ss. 57–61, RRA ss. 48–52). An appeal against a non-discrimination notice lies to the tribunal, and the sanction for persistent contravention of a notice is a County court injunction (SDA ss. 68, 71, RRA ss. 59, 62). In *Amari Plastics*, 1982,[85] the CRE had instigated a formal investigation into a company and concluded that the company had contravened the RRA. Instructions had been given not to employ 'coloured' applicants. A notice was therefore issued, itemizing ten contraventions. The company appealed against the findings of fact by the CRE, which refused a request for detailed particulars of the notice. The Court of Appeal upheld a tribunal order that the CRE should deliver particulars of the facts found by it in the investigation relevant to the notice, not merely those relevant to the reasonableness of the requirements made in the notice. The company was allowed to appeal on issues of fact as well as issues of law: 'There must', said Lord Denning MR, 'be a proper judicial inquiry as to whether those findings of fact are right. That means evidence of witnesses, with opportunity of cross-examination, and the like.' It was Lord Denning who had said in 1978 in the *Nassé* case of the right of the agencies in the course of a formal investigation to demand information and 'compel discovery of documents on a massive scale': 'You might think that we were back in the days of the Inquisition. . . . You might think we were back in the days of General Warrants.' In the *Mandla* case, 1982, Kerr LJ had referred to the inquiries of the CRE as 'an inquisition', and Oliver LJ spoke of 'an engine of oppression', leading Lord Fraser to say such strictures were 'entirely unjustified'. The chance for the courts to interfere was unhappily enlarged by Woolf J. when he accepted in the *Westminster CC* decision that, even though the avenue of appeal provided by the RRA had not been exhausted, the High Court might in some cases intervene by way of judicial review against a notice where all that was in dispute was a question of law (though in that case, he held, the CRE had not erred, a finding upheld by the appeal judges).[86]

The House of Lords confirmed the grip of judicial control by its decision *In Re Prestige Group p.l.c.*, 1984.[87] The CRE decided to investigate the Prestige Group, though at that time it did not positively believe that unlawful discrimination had occurred. The company was kept fully informed. Later the CRE informed it that, subject to any representations it wished to make, it was minded to conclude that contraventions of the RRA had occurred in three factories, whereby applicants were given preference if they knew an existing employee and were considered suitable for hourly paid employment only if they passed certain tests in English. After considering the company's representations, written and oral, the CRE decided there had been a breach (RRA s. 28) and made a non-discrimination order. The company appealed. The Law Lords found that the 'clumsily drafted' sections 49 and 50 of the Act raised an ambiguity as to the powers of the CRE. Lord Diplock distinguished its power to conduct a 'general investigation' from its power to conduct an investigation into a 'named person'. He read the Act to mean that the latter could be *begun* only if there was already a belief that that person might be guilty:

In the absence of [such] belief . . . why should those persons alone be picked upon to have their activities investigated to the exclusion of the activities of other employers engaged in the same industries as the persons named? . . . The news that it is to be undertaken soon gets around . . . understood by many . . . as pointing the finger of suspicion of racial bias at the persons who are named in it. . . . putting the employer and those who act in a managerial capacity in his establishments to some degree of inconvenience, dislocation of the employer's business, and expense.

He refused to make a 'purposive' interpretation of the Act, which would give the CRE power to launch such an investigation at a stage anterior to suspicion of guilt; that would not serve 'any useful purpose'. The CRE was bound to hold a 'preliminary inquiry' after the belief was formed that a person could have acted unlawfully; only after that could it hold the formal investigation. Lord Diplock himself commented that an investigation could 'drag on for several years'. Under the Law Lords' interpretation of the Act, a company with expensive lawyers might make it last a decade. Lord Diplock ended by criticizing the CRE for bringing the appeal 'out of the pocket of the taxpayer'.

As so often before, the protection of the individual (here, a company) weighed heavily in the balance against the effective operation of an administrative agency given the task by Parliament of enforcing a sensitive area of public policy. The judgment is dominated by the legal perspective of the CRE 'primarily fulfilling a policing and accusatory function', rather than 'the wider statutory aims of the promotion of good relations and equality of opportunity'.[88] This customary attitude of the courts (which may 'ensure the impotence of anti-discrimination law')[89] has now been joined, as we have seen (p. 350), by reported Government pressure on local authorities not to include equal opportunities clauses in contracts that do not relate directly to performance of the work. The UK Government in 1985 also proposed that EEC laws should not extend any further regulations on equal treatment for men and women.[90] In the same month the CRE proposed to government that the RRA should be strengthened, with wider powers of investigation (to counter the *Prestige* decision), legal aid for complainants and separate divisions of tribunals for race cases; the code was being accepted by companies and unions, but employers, unions and, above all, the structures of the labour market were still found wanting.[91]

It may be that legislation, as has been said concerning sex equality, can cure only the 'blatant abuses', any more radical change being dependent upon a reappraisal of social attitudes to women's roles at home and in the labour market: 'Legal intervention in these kinds of issues is only really successful when supported by social attitudes.'[92] So too, 'the main guideline of action against racial discrimination should be to take effective measures against underlying social evils', aiming at 'Full employment and a guaranteed standard of human rights'.[93] Legislation has a role to play, but success requires a general involvement in equal opportunity policies that are not 'hived off, but seen as an integral part of employment policy and practice in general'.[94] Such policies, though, also require from courts and tribunals a sensitive understanding of their purpose and the urgent need for those seen as opinion leaders to put their full weight against discrimination. Refusals to make 'purposive' interpretations do not help.

Maternity rights

In addition to the right not to be dismissed by reason of pregnancy (EPCA s. 60: p. 450), two further rights were in 1975 enacted concerning maternity: a right to maternity pay and a right to return to work after pregnancy (now EPCA ss. 33–48 and Schedule 2). In 1982 a further right was enacted to time off for antenatal care (now EPCA s. 31A). The extent to which this employment protection has added to employers' burdens has, as with other such laws, been controversial. An estimate found that in 1980 an employer with ten women workers might expect one to stop work to have a baby every three years.[95] Of the 330,000 working women having babies in that year, fewer than 16 per cent qualified for maternity pay; part of the reason is undoubtedly the 'complexities and strict requirements' of the statutory provisions.[96] Collective agreements often add to these rights; there is extensive provision on pay and return to work in public sector agreements. The Civil Service allows forty weeks' leave and three months' full pay.[97] A worker may prefer to rely upon contractual rights. Miss *Lucas* made a 'nebulous agreement' with her employer to return to work after her baby was born. She did not follow the statutory procedures even though she was qualified to do so, but she received an amount equivalent to maternity pay. After the birth she was told on inquiring that her job no longer existed. The EAT decided this was a dismissal; she had not exercised her statutory rights; the employment contract had continued during the period she had been 'given permission' to be absent to have her baby; and the employer finally recognized this by giving two weeks' pay in lieu of notice. It was open to her to claim unfair dismissal by reason of her pregnancy. Very different are cases where a woman tries to enforce her statutory right but fails to qualify (as where she gives 5 days' notice of return to work instead of the necessary 7).[98]

Although the legislation provides that where contractual terms (e.g. from a collective agreement) are more generous than the Act, the woman can take advantage of whichever right is 'in any particular respect' the more favourable (EPCA s. 48), in *Bovey* it was held that this does not enable the employee to pick out bits of one and of the other to put together the best mixture. When a full-time Grade 1 physiotherapist said she wanted to return part-time after maternity leave, the employers agreed so long as she fell to basic grade. She later claimed the right to return part-time (under the contract) and at Grade 1 (under the statute that said her conditions were to be no less favourable). The E A T rejected this, saying the contract was here a collateral agreement to her employment, not covered by the Act, and the right to work part-time on basic grade was not 'divisible'; it was not clear what was 'more favourable' to her (despite her own clear choice); and any other result would have 'most unfortunate and inconvenient consequences'.[99] The E A T acted 'in true paternalist fashion', writes Bercusson (who also doubts 'the capacity of all-male tribunals to decide questions of maternity rights').

Qualification

The maternity rights accrue to an employee only after two years' continuous employment; additionally, her contract of employment must continue until immediately before the eleventh week before the expected week of confinement (E P C A s. 33). If she is dismissed by reason of her pregnancy, fairly or unfairly, before that time, she can still be qualified, though for return-to-work rights she must give notice before, or as soon as reasonably practicable after, the dismissal. The requirement of two years' 'continuous employment' (normally of sixteen hours weekly) restricts the benefits largely to women working full-time (p. 205). Upex and Morris noted in 1981 that only 54 per cent of women who worked satisfied the requirement, making the provisions of the collective agreements they describe even more important, especially in their provision for the increasing proportions of part-time workers.

The statutory provisions on notice are complex. The worker must give notice first that she will be absent by reason of pregnancy and, second, that she wishes to return to work. The first notice must be in writing in regard to maternity leave. For maternity pay, the employer may accept oral, but can demand written, notice. Both must be given twenty-one days before her absence begins, or if that is not reasonably practicable, as soon as is reasonably practicable. It is not enough that she could not make up her mind about returning to work, for in that case it *is* 'reasonably practicable' for her to act within the time limit.[100] Employers complained that this left employees free to give notice even when they were not sure they wanted to return in order to protect their rights. In 1980, therefore, a new requirement was inserted for a third notice. By this the worker is required to confirm her intention to return seven weeks after the birth if the employer asks her to confirm her plans (she must reply within fourteen days of his request; now EPCA s. 33 (3A)). She must also give a fourth notice at least twenty-one days before the day on which she proposes to return, to which we come below (s. 47).

Maternity pay

Maternity pay is payable whether or not a woman intends to return to work after the birth of her child; but the State maternity allowance benefit is deducted from it (s. 35). The deduction is rigorously enforced. Thus where a woman in 1980 worked for X by day and for Y in the evenings, for more than sixteen hours weekly, X paid her maternity pay at 90 per cent of earnings less maternity allowance (then £15.75 a week). She claimed maternity pay also from Y at 90 per cent of her wage, £17.20; but the EAT agreed that nothing was payable because the same deduction had to be made from that amount.[101] Maternity pay is funded by the Maternity Pay Fund from employers' contributions, which provides an employer with a rebate in full in respect of the statutory maternity payments (EPCA ss. 37, 39). If an employer makes payment to a woman not entitled to it, the Secretary of State has discretion to give a rebate if he considers it just and equitable. Where the employer is insolvent or where the worker has taken all reasonable steps to obtain her pay (other than action in the tribunal) the Secretary of State may pay her directly out of the fund (ss. 40, 41). In 1984 the Minister rejected the claim of an employee whose employer was insolvent, even though she had given a proper notice, on the extraordinary ground that she was not 'absent from work' because of pregnancy, because there was no work to do at the ruined enterprise; both the tribunal and the EAT managed to interpret the Act so as to give her the money.[102]

Maternity pay is nine-tenths of a 'week's pay' (calculated as for redundancy, p. 220, but without a maximum) less the amount of the social security maternity allowance, and lasts for six weeks after the absence begins (ss. 34, 35). The absence, we have seen, will normally begin in the eleventh week before confinement; it cannot be earlier; but she may choose to leave later, in which case the six-weeks period runs from the time she leaves. Where a teacher's contract provided that she must leave in the eleventh week before confinement and she wished to continue until a later week, her right to choose to do this under the statute was upheld (by the two lay members of the EAT, outvoting the judge), and the contractual term was held void as attempting to oust her statutory rights.[103] But if the worker receives payment under a contractual maternity pay scheme this is set off against the statutory right. Today maternity pay is taxable; but it has become more important for those who can claim it than the social security payments as 'maternity allowance' which (in 1985–6, £29.15) is now paid at a lower level than unemployment benefit.[104] The Government plans to transfer statutory maternity allowance to employers to administer in 1987 in a similar fashion to the transfer of sickness benefit (p. 114) after the enactment of the Social Security Bill 1986.

The right to return

The statutory right is a right after pregnancy to return to work in the job held before leaving 'on terms and conditions no less favourable than those which would have been applicable to her if she had not been so absent' (EPCA s. 45). The employee must return by the end of the twenty-ninth week after the date of the confinement. The qualifications must be met, especially the notices set out above, each within its own time limit (the notice of absence and intention to return; notice of confirmation, if requested; and notice of intended date of return). Subject to the new rules introduced in 1980, a refusal to take the woman back to work (either at all or to a proper 'job') counts as a dismissal (s. 56), which may give her a remedy for unfair dismissal. It is odd that the sanction is left to act in this indirect manner; there seems no reason why such a dismissal should not be treated as automatically unfair when the employer has broken his obligations and is able, so long as it is reasonable, to justify dismissal of a temporary replacement in her job (s. 61).[105] The employer may postpone her return for up to four weeks if he gives his reasons; and the employee may postpone her return to a date even beyond the twenty-ninth week in the case of (1) an interruption of work, such as industrial action, or (2) her inability to work by reason of proven illness lasting not more than four weeks (s. 47).

The right to return to her 'job' on terms and conditions 'not less favourable' is more difficult. First, although the woman's continuity of service is preserved generally throughout, the Act does not preserve it during her absence in respect of 'seniority, pension rights or similar rights' (s. 45 (2)). On her return she may therefore have lost that period, e.g. for LIFO schemes in redundancy. Secondly, a 'job' is not the same as a 'post'. It means the nature of the work she is employed to do under her employment contract and the *capacity* and *place* where she is so employed (EPCA s. 153 (1)). If she is put at the same grade in a different department with differently organized tasks, that may be enough. But where a permanent grade CG3 clerk found another clerk in her post and was placed in an unestablished, 'supernumerary' CG3 clerk's post on her return, this was not the same job; she was deemed to be dismissed, and unfairly.[106] This protection was, however, severely diminished in two ways by the Act of 1980 (EA 1980 s. 12). First, if the employer says her job is no longer available, he may offer the woman 'suitable' alternative employment; if she unreasonably refuses this, or accepts it, she cannot claim for unfair dismissal (now EPCA s. 56A). The employer must prove that it is not reasonably practicable to accept return on the normal conditions (by reason of circumstances other than redundancy), that he or an associated employer has offered alternative employment suitable to her and appropriate for her to do, and that the new terms are not 'substantially less favourable' than her normal conditions. The second change applies to small firms. If the employer and any associated employer together employed five employees or less immediately before her absence, and he can show that it is 'not reasonably practicable' to allow her to return to work on the normal terms and that it is not reasonably practicable for him or any associated employer to offer 'suitable' alternative employment, his obligation to take her back to work is extinguished altogether. This reaction to a situation that Daniel described in his survey of 1980, as one where the employer with ten women employees 'will generally receive a formal notification of return once every thirty years', seems excessive, if not irrational. Small business men seemed to 'fear the prospects and implications through lack of awareness of the qualifying requirements'.

Equal pay

The sex discrimination legislation does not apply to 'any provision for the payment of money' that would be included, directly or indirectly (e.g. through a collective agreement), in a contract of employment or be regulated by it (SDA s. 6 (5), (6)). These matters are meant to be regulated by the Equal Pay Act 1970, as amended in 1975 (Eq. P. A.). As we shall see, it was also fundamentally amended in 1983. The two Acts, said Bridge LJ in 1978, 'are closely interlocking' and should be applied 'as a harmonious whole'. The basic dividing line is that the Eq. P. A., not the SDA, applies to 'payment' to the employee. But the Eq. P. A. brings within 'pay' other conditions of employment such as hours, holidays and sick-pay, though it excludes conditions related to or connected with 'death or retirement' (except for access to occupational pension schemes: s. 6 (1A)). A qualification of six months' service is required (s. 2 (4)). Also, like the discrimination legislation, the 1970 Act applies widely to employees, to apprentices and to those under 'a contract personally to execute any work or labour' (s. 1 (6)).

The legislation resulted from a century of pressure, much of it industrial, and has, as we shall see, been greatly influenced by EEC law. From 1888 the TUC aimed at equal pay for men and women doing the 'same work'; by 1946 three Royal Commissions and three committees had sat on the issue; by 1961 it was achieved in the non-industrial Civil Service; trade union opinion accepted the need for legislation in this area in order that the UK should ratify, as it did in 1971, the ILO Convention on equal pay (No. 100, 1951).[107] The struggle for equal pay from 1967 of the sewing-machinists at Ford (which led to a strike and influenced the introduction of the 1970 law) finally succeeded in November 1984, after a claim under the Eq. P. A. had been rejected (even in its 1983 version) largely because the job evaluation of 1967 had assigned unequal value to the work of the women and the men with whom they claimed comparison.[108] Soon after, 270 of the women went on strike; a new panel evaluated the jobs afresh and awarded equal pay. The legal 'floor of rights' still needs the support of industrial action.

Much complexity and subjectivity goes into unequal pay. The discrimination against women is in great measure a social status taken into employment. Women are paid less than men, writes Rubenstein, because of 'the attributes they bring to the job', because of 'the jobs they are in' and because 'they are women'. Unequal pay is a social institution. Although it often exists, 'prejudice, in the form of discriminatory animus against women, is not an essential component of discrimination'.[109] As Davies noted in his incisive analysis of the CAC's work, the employer may claim that 'he is paying the rate for the job but his assessment . . . may be unconsciously biased by the status of the people who are performing the work'.[110] Other writers have stressed 'the institutional rather than the economic factors' determining pay and job structures: 'jobs are not feminised because they are deskilled, but deskilled because they are feminised'.[111] On the other hand, no scientific test can determine the precise relationship of different jobs.

'Job evaluation is', as Rubenstein describes, 'essentially a method for systematising subjective judgments.' Even so, by 1980 some 55 per cent of manual and 56 per cent of non-manual workers were covered by job evaluation schemes, and the Eq. P. A. was one factor that stimulated its spread (another was its popularity with US owners of enterprises). But this is an overall picture, and there is considerably less chance of women workers than men being covered by such a scheme[112] since women are still largely segregated into 'women's jobs'. Some 60 per cent of women workers are in clerical, welfare or educational jobs, and in industry women are still mainly unskilled workers. The fact that average hourly female (full-time) earnings rose from 63 per cent of men's in 1970 to 74 per cent in 1984 is not attributable merely to differences in market conditions. The rise to 76 per cent in 1977 must have been affected by the coming into force of the Eq. P. A. in 1975 (there were 2,493 applications to the tribunals in the two years 1976–7), the fall to the 1984 level reflects the different labour market in which the law is a weaker instrument.[113] In 1983–4 there were only 105 applications. The pay gap seems to be widening. Weekly earnings of full-time manual women workers averaged 62 per cent of men's in 1983, but 60.5 per cent in 1985.

Equal pay under the 1970 Act

The 1970 Act inserted into contracts of employment an implied term, the 'equality clause'. Unlike most other employment protection legislation, the right to equality is thus a *contractual* right; yet it is enforced not in the ordinary courts but in the tribunals (s. 2), where up to two years' arrears of remuneration can be recovered. Non-contractual provisions are not included, such as an informal arrangement that graded university teachers by age, an 'age wage norm' that played no part in their employment terms.[114] The equality clause introduced by the Eq. P. A. had three effects. It enforced equal terms in the contract of the woman (or man where he is treated unequally) in the same employment (which includes employment by associated employers at the same establishment or any other where common terms of employment are observed): (1) to eliminate the less favourable terms where men and women are employed on like work (s. 1 (2) (a)); and (2) where the work had been rated as equivalent by a job evaluation exercise. Also, (3) provisions in collective agreements and pay structures applying to men or to women only could be amended by the CAC (s. 3). Into this picture, however, EEC law later intervened on the entry of Britain in 1973, an intervention that in turn gave rise in 1983, as we shall see, to the *equal value* amendments of the Act. In 1986, as we shall see, further changes in the law were needed (see p. 919).

As McCrudden points out, the overriding test of 'same establishment', which has in Britain continued after 1983, excludes many women from benefit, e.g. homeworkers or those in small establishments with no comparable men.[115] One outstanding issue at the base of our equal pay law is why women should not be allowed some measure of comparability across the frontiers of the enterprise and in relation to hypothetical, as well as actual, 'comparators' among men workers.

(1) *Like work.* The first test arises only where there is 'like work', defined as work of 'the same or a broadly similar nature', and the differences are not of 'practical importance' having regard to the frequency with which they arise (s. 1 (4)). This clearly refers to the nature of the tasks in practice performed, not merely to the terms of the contract or title of the job. It is about 'things done' not contractual obligations, one judge put it. The courts encouraged a 'broad brush' approach. The addition on one side of greater responsibility has frequently led them to see jobs as not broadly similar, as with a clerk-packer and a storeman-packer whose supervisory duties differed in 1978. But men employed at the counter of a betting-shop were found to be on like work with a woman, *Ms Shields*, employed on the same tasks. The claim that men had to 'deal with trouble' was unsupported by evidence that the problem in reality occurred.[116] In that case too, the Court of Appeal endorsed the concept that a 'difference in working hours was an irrelevant factor', a problem that returns later in respect of part-time workers. Indeed, the early refusal to count differences in

working time marked a determined stand by the judges against erosion of equality by market factors. Similarly, in *Dugdale*[117] the work of women quality controllers was broadly similar to that of male quality inspectors in another department even though the women did not work the night shifts obligatory for men, nor work on Sundays as men could and did (this would have been unlawful under the Factories Act 1961 s. 93), nor lift the heavier weights or use the greater versatility required of the men. The EAT insisted that tribunals must examine the work actually done (including the work on the Sunday shift, for example); as in the redundancy cases (p. 228), 'the mere time at which work is performed' could not be a difference in the work done. The 'like work' test was, and is, therefore a major inroad on inequality; but with it Parliament did little more than put a tentative toe into the ocean of women's low pay.

(2) *Job evaluation: jobs rated as equivalent.* This applies only if either the woman's job and the man's job have been 'given an equal value' in terms of demands (e.g. effort, skill or decisions) on a study evaluating the jobs of all or any of the workers, or it would have been given such a value had not the evaluation used 'different values for men and women' under any such heading (s. 1 (5)). The subjective elements in job evaluation – it has been called 'ultimately itself a method of collective bargaining or dispute resolution'[118] – may express themselves as veiled discrimination, and the EOC has drawn up a code for allotting unbiased points to jobs (a list that has itself been criticized).[119] The scope of the right to challenge a completed job evaluation study before the tribunal is uncertain. Where the employers and employees or their union have agreed upon it, the Law Lords held in 1980 that the scheme can be relied upon even if it has not been applied in practice.[120] So too, in *Arnold*, 1982,[121] where a woman catering supervisor's job was classed as in the same grade as that of a man vending supervisor by a revised job evaluation study that the union and employer never agreed to implement, the EAT held that the woman could rely upon it, even though individual supervisory workers had the right to challenge their own gradings under it. A challenge in the tribunal might be mounted only in the case of (rather inadequately defined) 'fundamental' or 'plain' error in the study. Under this provision of the Eq. P. A. job evaluation is not compulsory; but the 1983 amendment, as we shall see, 'imposes an obligation to assess job content, i.e. a form of job evaluation'.[122] When

we come to consider that issue (p. 499) we must remember that the 'rationalities' of job evaluation cannot freeze the fluidities of real working life; and even under such schemes local management experiences pay pressures to which concessions may be made that threaten the 'integrity' of a graded scheme.[123] Job evaluation is no substitute for dynamic industrial relations.

(3) *Inequality in collective agreements and formal pay structures.* It would have been inadequate for the legislative intervention in 1970 to allow individual enforcement of equal pay for 'like work' or work rated as equivalent but to do nothing about formal pay structures imposed by the employer or agreed in collective agreements. Consequently, where a provision for either applies a provision to men or to women only, they may be referred to the CAC (s. 3; the same is true of Wages Councils' orders: s. 4). The reference may be made either by one of the parties or by the Secretary of State (s. 5). The CAC must amend the agreement (or structure) by extending the offending provision to both men and women and then eliminate the lower of the two pay rates; but no agreement can be extended to workers (men or women) not already covered by it or to create grades not envisaged (for men or for women) in it (s. 3 (4)). This provides the CAC with a powerful instrument of intervention; but references have declined. There were twenty-five awards in 1977 and 1978; only one in the years 1980–4; this work 'is virtually at an end' – CAC Report, 1981. The courts played a role in this. The CAC took jurisdiction in cases where the employer had appeared to remove discriminatory pay structures; in order to examine the reality, it looked at such questions as whether men predominated at the top of an apparently unisex structure or whether some work was historically done mainly by women. But in *R.* v. *CAC, ex parte Hy-Mac Ltd*[124] the High Court insisted that it had no jurisdiction where the agreement 'does not *on the face of it* contain any provision applying specifically either to men or to women', or – possibly – where it was a 'sham'. This 'rather brutal reminder', as Davies called it, of the judges' strict reading of the Act without consideration of the implications was joined by an equally strict refusal to countenance the trend in some CAC awards to revise pay structures by encouraging, or even itself completing, rates for new grades. The terms of the judgment left the CAC little scope; its awards had in truth, Davies showed, 'saved the section from its own inherent limitations and absurdities'. The CAC

itself has noted that attention now is upon individual tribunal cases on 'equal value'; but it wonders whether these cases will be

symptomatic of latent weaknesses within pay structures or collective agreements requiring examination in a wider context. The advantages of the broader approach, in which account can be taken of the collective repercussions of individual claims, may yet become evident [1984 Report].

This sorry story is also illustrative of the difficulty of applying 'principles of abstention and intervention' as concepts describing judicial policy in this area, especially when correcting inequality between comparable men and women tends to have 'a ripple effect on differentials in general'.[125] The classical concept of 'abstention' dealt with the exclusion of common law illegalities to allow for collective bargaining (Chapter 1), but it accommodated many legislative interventions to protect weaker groups of workers (from 1909 the Trade Boards, now Wages Councils, the great majority of whose workers have always been women (p. 350), the fair wages legislation and Fair Wages Resolution). The limited intervention of the 1970 Act raised the question of whether the policy of protecting sex equality in employment was to be pursued predominantly by individual judgments or through machinery that could take account of those ripple effects in the collective bargaining picture generally. The C A C could do that better than the courts.

But this structure was put in question by the E C J judgment of 1984[37] which, we have seen, demanded amendments to the S D A in respect of collective agreements, whether or not they were legally binding, together with works rules, union rules and rules of professional bodies (Chapter 4, p. 323). The Sex Discrimination Bill 1986 took the opportunity to propose total repeal of the C A C jurisdiction under Eq. P. A. s. 3. Instead, collective agreements were put within the ambit of S D A s. 77, the section whereby a term of a 'contract' unlawful by reason of discrimination within the S D A is 'void' unless the term is discriminatory against a 'party', in which case the term is 'unenforceable against that party'. Where a term is discriminatory against a party, any person 'interested' in the contract may ask the County court to modify or remove the term (s. 77 (2)), and a term in contravention of the S D A or Eq. P. A. is unenforceable by any party in whose favour it operates (though the 1986 Bill retains the right to enforce the rest of the agreement). Oddly, the Bill's definition of 'collective agreement' differs in two ways from TULRA (s. 30): it does not include 'arrangements' alongside agreements, and the term 'trade union' is replaced by the words 'organization of workers' (as it is in SDA s. 12 and RRA s. 11) to include all such organizations, wider than the usual term 'trade union' (p. 718) and used here so as to be doubly sure to catch all groups of workers even if not within TULRA s. 28 (would a local group of shop stewards and workers be an 'organization'?)

The difficulty with the Bill as published was that it appeared to provide no enforcement mechanism for a collective agreement that contained provisions for unequal pay or, indeed, sex discrimination generally. A term that offends the 'equality clause' without a material factor defence (p. 497) is deemed to be 'unlawful' under the SDA. So, under the 1986 Bill the SDA unlawfulness swallows up the issue of equal pay into discrimination generally (a development some writers have held is the logical consequence anyway of EEC Directive 76/207 on equal treatment). But the discrimination on pay is hardly likely to be aimed against either 'party' to the collective agreement, i.e. the union or the employer. Application to the County court would not, therefore, be available under s. 77 (2). But the jurisdiction of the CAC would now be repealed. It could be argued that a party interested might apply to the High Court for a declaration that the discriminatory term was void; but this remedy (here in 'private law') is uncertain. The lacuna as to remedy suggested that parliamentary time might be needed to insert into the Bill some machinery of enforcement if the ECJ judgment was to be fully implemented; but the Government resisted such changes. Suspicions, however, that the scheme partly originated from a dislike in Government quarters of the CAC were fuelled by the discovery that the CAC jurisdiction under Eq. P. A. s. 4 to deal with unequal pay provisions in Wages Council orders was also to be repealed by the Wages Bill published in 1986 (without, it seemed, a replacement). Just when the CAC was more urgently needed than ever, it was being put out to grass.

(4) *Equal pay and the impact of EEC law.* A decade earlier, by the time the Eq. P. A. came into effect in 1975, the writ of EEC law already ran in Britain. The foundation-stone, the Treaty of Rome, itself required that each member State should ensure the application of the principle that 'men and women should receive *equal pay for equal work*' (Art. 119). Moreover, equal pay 'without discrimination based on sex' was spelled out to mean the same unit measurement in piece-rates and

the same time rates for 'the same job'; and 'pay' included all wages, salary and 'any other consideration whether in cash or in kind'. At first sight this Article merely requires that each State should legislate; but in 1976 the ECJ decided that Article 119 was 'directly applicable' law in member States as regards discrimination, for it was 'part of the social objectives of the Community', which is intended 'by common action to ensure social progress'.[126] Thus Article 119 provides an 'enforceable community right' in British courts, which are obliged to interpret all legislation so as to be consistent with it, under the European Communities Act 1972 s. 2 (1) (4). (The EAT was able to reject 'with relief' the claim in 1982 that actions based on Article 119 should be brought in the ordinary courts and claims under Eq. P. A. in the tribunals; that would indeed create 'a chaotic result'.) Where there is a doubt about the meaning of Community law, a British court may refer the case to the ECJ (Art. 177 of the Treaty), but this practice is normally left to the Court of Appeal or House of Lords unless the EAT considers that they are likely to do so. Not only will this increase delay; the judgments of the ECJ are rather different in character and may, as Hepple politely puts it, 'be couched in the ambiguous language of compromise between the Court's members'.

In addition to Article 119, in 1975 an EEC Directive on Equal Pay, 75/117, put further flesh upon the bones of Community law, also directly enforceable and binding in Britain. This went beyond the terms of the Treaty and declared that in Article 119 the 'equal pay principle'

means, for the same work or for work to which equal value is attributed, the elimination of all discrimination on grounds of sex with regard to all aspects and conditions of remuneration.

Further, where a 'job classification system is used' it must be based upon the 'same criteria' for men and women and 'exclude any discrimination on grounds of sex'. The ECJ has declared that these provisions of the Directive are no more than a clearer rendering of Article 119 itself. To these EEC sources must be added the Directive on Equal Treatment, 76/207, requiring equal treatment of men and women in employment, the potency of which was felt in 1986 (p. 919).

The differences between this code of EEC law and the British Eq. P. A. are manifest. Just how wide is 'pay', under Article 119, for example? The ECJ has held that it includes travel facilities for male workers who have retired, thereby outlawing the discrimination against retired women, and additional payments to male employees only to compensate for their entry into an occupational pension scheme, which also determined other benefits, because the gross pay was discriminatory.[127] British law already ensures equality of access for men and women to occupational pension schemes (Social Security Pensions Act 1975 s. 53); but the ECJ decisions clearly cut across the British provisions that the 'equality clause' does not operate in relation to terms connected with retirement (Eq. P. A. s. 6 (1A)), and the sex discrimination prohibition in employment does not apply to retirement (SDA s. 6 (4)). The extent to which pensions count as deferred 'pay' under Article 119 is not entirely clear. The courts have so far understood the Article not to apply to access to such benefits. So, where an employer in a redundancy situation offered employees immediate pensions at fifty-five, which was ten years earlier than a man's but only five years earlier than a woman's normal retiring age, the EAT decided that the scheme fell outside both Article 119 and the two British Acts.[128] But in 1985 an unmarried civil servant objected to contributions required from him towards a widow's pension scheme that women were not required to pay (a scheme contracted out of the State system is obliged to have such a provision for male members). Contributions were returnable to bachelors on retirement or death; he asserted that the levies were unlawful under EEC law. The EAT requested a ruling from the ECJ whether this was correct under Article 119, Directive 75/117 or Directive 76/207, or any permutation of the three.[129] The law in this area awaited clarification from the ECJ.

The Eq. P. A. applies to men and women working contemporaneously. Where a stock-room manager resigned and a woman, with slightly different duties, replaced him at a lower salary at *Macarthys Ltd*, the English courts found no remedy in the Act; but the ECJ on reference held that Article 119 was not so limited and required that such a woman replacement be given equal pay. In the confusion of sources on the subject it was perhaps uncharacteristically harsh for Lord Denning to say that the employers 'had no right to look at our English statute alone. They should have looked at the Treaty as well.'[130] For the problem of discovering what the law is in Britain had been intensified by another crucial issue, the defence that an employer might offer. We must note, though, that some comparable man must exist for the woman to succeed; she cannot even under Article 119, it seems, claim to compare herself with a 'hypothetical' man, or one working in another establishment.[131]

The defence of genuine material difference

In cases of 'like work' or work rated as equivalent, an employer has a defence if he proves that the variation between the woman's and man's terms is due to a material factor, not the difference of sex. This factor must be a material difference (Eq. P. A. s. 1 (3) (a)). Here everything turns on the judicial understanding of 'material difference'. It must be genuine; it must explain the differential in pay;[132] and it must be 'material'. But this surely cannot be allowed to include the workings of the labour market. As Browne L J said in 1979, 'it would frustrate the purpose of the Act' if the man demanded higher pay and the employer could agree 'because of some bargaining factor'. There, in the *Clay Cross* case, a woman clerk was paid less than a male clerk whose rate in his previous job had been maintained. The fact that he was the only applicant for the post was insufficient. The economic circumstances of, or reasons 'personal' to, the employer (as against personal to the *employee*) were irrelevant.[133] But the E C J in 1980 and 1981 appeared to regard it as legitimate to consider whether economic circumstances accounted for the difference, at any rate where the employment is successive and not contemporaneous, by way of an implication in Article 119.[134] The E A T therefore permitted the employer's changed economic circumstances (reduced profitability and decreased volume of the work) as proper factors allowing the defence to be argued where a woman manager was paid less than her male predecessor.[135]

Comparisons between full-time (male) and part-time (women) workers cause similar difficulty. Such a differential in pay was accepted as justifiable under s. 1 (3) in 1979 because the machinery was left idle for longer by a part-timer. But the terms of the E C J judgment in *Jenkins* led the E A T to understand that the (overriding) implication in Article 119 permitted the employer a defence where he could point to factors 'objectively justified and . . . in no way related to any discrimination based on sex'; but in other passages the judgment appeared to require little more than no 'covert intention to discriminate'. Even so, there was no objection to the British statutes giving to employees 'greater rights than they enjoy under Article 119'; therefore the EAT held that the employer must still prove that the difference is 'in fact reasonably necessary' for reasons other than the sex of the worker, in that case a part-timer (e.g. to reduce absenteeism or obtain maximum utilization of plant). This might involve

increased labour costs at a time when they and the country can ill afford it. This may in turn lead to a decrease in the total number of women employed. But it is not our function to weigh these factors.[136]

As we shall see, this echo of the CAC's question as to the best way to handle such issues returns when the defence arises in 'equal value' cases. For these notions, in the words of Davies and Freedland, 'constitute the very pivot upon which the whole law of equal pay turns'.[137] An individual decision may affect unknown numbers of workers, as where a nursery nurse's rejected claim to equal pay with clerical workers was said to affect 19,000 other nurses.[138] Non-discriminatory reasons that prove a 'material difference' can rest on such factors as service, payments, grading, qualifications needed for the job or age and infirmity. The practice of 'red circling' has caused further problems here. It arises when responsibilities for which workers receive a higher rate are removed, but they continue to receive that rate as against others on like work. Women operators in police communications, for example, were upgraded when given the duties of training recruits; a new male operator failed in his claim to equal pay with this 'red circled' group even when two years later the duties were taken over by others.[139] But the 'red circle' must not have been drawn for reasons of sex discrimination; it must rest on the 'personal equation'; and, even if justifiable initially by reason of the employees' personal characteristics, the tribunal must decide whether with the passage of time it has ceased to be so.[140]

Mrs Rainey was an NHS prosthetist earning some £3,000 a year less than her nine male colleagues. The men had all transferred previously into the NHS from their private sector practice in a composite deal at higher pay bargained with their union, when it was found the normal rates could not staff the NHS service. This material difference was accepted by the majority of Scottish appeal judges as one not dependent on sex discrimination. It was needed to provide a prosthetic service in the NHS by an adequate method of entry. Although it was a 'grey area', the differential was necessary and sufficiently related to 'personal' characteristics of the employees. It was similar to a 'red circle' case, protecting the pay level of a group – no more transfers at the higher rates would be made – though the case was 'curious and exceptional, and unique', said Lord Emslie. Lord Cameron agreed; the pay differences reflected a 'personal equation'; the 'genuinely material differences' depended on the facts of the case; one could consider 'the personal state of matters . . . at the time that determination [of pay] was made' in considering the variation between 'her case and his' (Eq. P. A. s. 1 (3)). Lord Grieve dissented. These special circumstances were not 'personal' to the man, only to the group of male prosthetists; they were 'collateral'. Parliament intended equal pay for like work to govern such a case. The majority judgment gives 'market forces' (and among market forces, it would appear collective bargaining) a major role. The Scottish E A T had seen *Rainey* as an attempt to secure, not equal pay, but increased pay for all N H S prosthetists, which was not a 'proper use of the Equal Pay legislation'. The appeal judges did not go so far;[141] but they did allow the structures of the market credence as factors that justify the maintenance of unequal pay on the ground that they are personal to the workers (invariably men) who are more highly paid.

'Personal differences' is a weak reed on which to rely, for it can easily excuse covert inequality. This issue is bound to go to the Law Lords for their determination; and if they follow the majority judges in Scotland, the Equal Pay Act will be in shreds. But a satisfactory solution surely needs a body like the C A C to inquire into the methods by which equal pay can be introduced rather than an adjudication of phrases in the Act. The very concept of 'equal pay for women' is in conflict with that of 'the market'. Its enforcement must necessarily curtail market forces, and for this job an expert body is needed, alongside the courts.

The 1983 amendments: equal pay for equal value

In 1982 the E C J ruled that the United Kingdom was in breach of its obligations under Directive 75/117 because equal pay was available for work of equal value under the Eq. P. A. only where the employer had chosen to carry out a job evaluation study.[142] After some delay, amendments were made to the Act of 1970 in regulations of 1983 (No. 1794, 1983; together with the Procedure Regulations: No. 1807, 1983, setting out the new tribunal rules of procedure, 'I T Rules', in the schedule).[143]

Doubt still remains whether these fulfil all the requirements of Community law.[144] The amendments made two major changes. First, even where there is no 'like work' or non-discriminatory job evaluation, if the woman's work is of 'equal value' to that of a man, the equality clause entitles her to corresponding conditions to the man (new Eq. P. A. s. 1 (2) (c)). Secondly, the defence of material factor available under s. 1 (3) to the employer is varied in an 'equal value' case: he must prove here that the variation is genuinely due to a material factor that is not due to sex, but then that factor *may* (not must) be a material difference (new s. 1 (3) (b)).

But in equal value cases a new and protracted procedure was laid down (now Eq. P. A. s. 2A and 1983 Procedure Regulations). In addition to any pre-hearing assessment, the tribunal invites the parties to adjourn to seek a settlement. It then itself considers whether there are reasonable grounds to think the work is of equal value. If there are none, it rejects the claim (as it did in the case of the Ford sewing-machinists).[145] At the next stage, it hears the parties, if either so wishes, on the question of whether pay variations are genuinely due to a material factor other than sex (the employer's first chance). It then invites an expert (nominated by A C A S and paid for out of public funds) to prepare a report evaluating the work (I T Rule 7A); the expert has certain powers to require information from persons concerned. If the expert takes more than forty-two days, the tribunal must inquire into the delay; it may dismiss him and start all over again; it may also ask for explanation of items in the report. The report is admitted as evidence (unless a party convinces the tribunal that its conclusion could not reasonably have been reached or is for some reason other than its conclusion unsatisfactory, in which case the process begins again). The parties may cross-examine the expert and may also, on giving notice, each call one expert witness of their own. The hearing then – at last – takes place on the question of equal value, with the experts open to cross-examination; but parties may give evidence as to facts only if the tribunal's report is shown not to include information withheld by a person that prevented it from reaching a conclusion, or relevant to the employer's defence of 'material factor'. Otherwise no evidence on fact is permitted (I T Rule 8 (2C), (2D)). The employer's defence is also decided at this stage (his second chance).

This protracted procedure, established by regulations that Lord

Denning criticized for their 'tortuosity and complexity . . . beyond compare', has at the centre of it the report of the independent expert, a form of obligatory job evaluation required before an equal value claim can succeed; but the Government was forced to permit one expert also to each of the parties and cross-examination, which it had wished to exclude. The individual claim cannot, in practice, be pursued without a consideration of the wider work-force. The employer's defence of 'material factor' here need not be a *difference*: Eq. P. A. s. 1 (3) (b), and, as we saw, it may be argued at two separate stages. (In a case against Short Bros. in 1985 the tribunal reserved full exploration of the defence until the expert's report had been completed, which seems more logical.) It must still be proved to be the 'genuine' reason for the variation and not the difference of sex. In these cases, however, it appears to include 'commercial factors such as skill shortages and other "market forces"'.[146] But, since to admit as a conclusive defence the fact that women will take the job when men will not would 'annihilate the Act', Rubenstein concludes that 'market forces' may be allowed but only where reliance upon the defence is not discrimination (direct or indirect) under the SDA.[147] The new material factor defence, McCrudden also believed, would let in market value but only to the extent that such direct and indirect discrimination was excluded and might relate to such matters as personal qualities (e.g. seniority), profitability, wage structures in the market and collective bargaining.[148] This seems logical; but it is still uncertain how far such limitations will hold. Nor is it clear why a wider defence should apply to the equal value claim assessed by the ACAS expert (s. 1 (3) (b)) than the defence of 'material difference' open in a case based on a job-evaluation scheme (s. 1 (3) (a)).

The consideration of this wider defence illuminates anew the uncertainties inherent in the 'equal pay, equal value' formula. The definition of 'value' is a central problem in economics. Are we to adopt Ricardo's absolute value or Marx's labour theory, or perhaps accept that value has 'no operational content. It is just a word.'[149] The operation of the tribunal system depends nevertheless upon the validity of the evaluation of jobs and of their value by the experts. Management consultants involved in the work in 1985 pointed to the danger to analysts' credibility if they became 'employers' analysts' and to the 'imbalance' between advice available respectively to employers and to workers, especially those outside unions.[150] Their report testified to the increasing practice of employers in putting their own experts forward. As for the defence, the tribunals must clearly allow such factors as flexibility and experience as the basis of the employer's defence in equal value cases as in others, as where male fish packers did a wider range of jobs than a woman in colder temperatures and needed extra training. But other women fish packers won equal pay with a male labourer after the employer's expert's report had failed to dislodge the A C A S expert's judgment, which the tribunal accepted as deserving 'equal' value, even though their jobs were not given precisely the same values as his, and the tribunal overruled the expert's exclusion of five of the women.[151]

It was *Hayward's* case that hit the headlines when the equal value amendments came into effect in 1984, where a cafeteria cook (supported by the E O C and her union) established her work as of equal value to that of men working in the shipyard as painters, engineers and joiners.[152] The independent expert's report (which ignored the effect on values of the men's work of a collective agreement not yet implemented) was not there, however, met by any employer's expert's report, the employers having failed to appoint one. Nor did the employer plead the defence of 'genuine material factor' until it was too late to do so, a rather important element in the history of the case.

Even so, the judgment had to be implemented on the ground. The tribunal had left the precise figures to be agreed. This meant evaluating just what Miss Hayward's 'pay' really was. For her too – and no doubt for the expert in her case – the question arose: 'What *is* wages? . . . 'tain't waistcoats' (p. 390). Or was it? What about her staff status? The collective agreements said the men were skilled; she was unskilled. Her sick-pay and conditions were superior; the employers said she was already £550 a year better off than the comparators when one looked at the figures. Her reply was that she was entitled to compare 'pay' in the narrow sense; the tribunal need not compare the whole package of conditions in every case; the Act applied to 'any term' of the employment contract (Eq. P. A. s. 1 (2) (c)). The tribunal, second time round, noted the overriding E E C Article 119, which seemed to demand equality of conditions 'whether in cash *or* in kind', and in an appeal in 1986 the E A T agreed that one had to look at the 'overall package'. In the tribunal the employer's contentions were sternly rejected by the minority member as leading to appalling 'leap-frog' problems. (If the employers were right, all the men must have a valid claim!) A year had passed since the original award. The result needed further hearings. (The C A C would surely have done better.)

It was reported, too, that Miss Hayward's supervisor and a chef colleague were demanding equivalent rises. As in 1985, other cases emerged in the tribunals, employers expressed concern about rising wage costs (one consultant said the Government might have 'spawned a monster', a 'time-bomb ticking away in the heart of British industry'). But some division appeared in trade union circles about the way forward. Some unions encouraged a flood of claims; A P E X and the bakers' union joined forces in this, the former promoting 150 cases in Birmingham alone, some of them taking male comparators in different unions not the same union as in *Hayward*. (The inter-union complexities have not begun to be explored.) Others believed legal claims took too long and could not be relied upon to be proper test cases. An official of Miss Hayward's union declared: 'We believe we can best help women members for the time being through the negotiating machinery'; and the union negotiators for women workers in municipal authorities preferred this approach to tribunal judgments that might be 'pyrrhic victories'.[153]

It is perhaps necessary for lawyers enclosed in the verbiage of the equal pay laws to remember that it is not yet proven that the method of negotiation cannot help more women workers in the medium term than spectacular and just but individual victories. Employers' responses on tests for promotion and similar matters that indirectly discriminate against women often claim that change will cause 'conflict with the unions'.[154] Whether or not that is an excuse, collective action will be needed at least to supplement legal processes, however intensive. Not that the effectiveness of legal process should be judged merely by the number of judgments recorded. By late in 1985 it was clear that large numbers of claims had been wholly or partly successful in negotiation, where the 1983 amendments on equal value had been strong bargaining weapons. Equal pay for women, though, will be secure only when its justice is adequately understood and practised by men. The size of that task seems large enough to need the work both of enlightened collective bargaining and of an improved and clarified Act that concentrates not on the vague formulas of Community Directives but upon practical issues that obstruct further progress towards equality and the search for *procedures* whereby both the individual case and the social problem can be better negotiated.

Young workers and discrimination

When young people enter the labour market they bring with them the advantages and disadvantages of the education that society and their families have provided for them. This is the moment where the structures of the educational system and of the employment system intersect. For many, the problems produced are now reflected in the provisions of the revised Youth Training Scheme (YTS). The use of the law increasingly in the last two decades to promote industrial 'training' is another illustration of law providing 'machinery' rather than imposing regulation. It may be analysed as part of the policies for 'job creation' for all workers,[155] though the two decades of development since the Industrial Training Act 1964 hardly testify to clear, overall interventions by any administration since then in pursuit of a long-term manpower policy. Many of the training measures, especially in the 1980s, have concerned young people and their proposed training in skills needed by the economy, to help them find jobs. The meaning of those labour law measures has to be set in the context of our school and further and higher educational system, for it is there that the young are first sorted into those more, and those less, likely to be permitted to enter and to succeed in the labour market, and on what terms. Here too the role of legally established institutions has become critical, especially now the Manpower Services Commission. The MSC was established in 1974 partly 'to help people train for and obtain jobs which satisfy their aspirations and abilities and to help employers find suitable workers' (Report, 1976–7). By 1984 it recorded an objective of providing that young people below eighteen could continue 'in full-time education or . . . planned work experience combining work-related training and education' (Report, 1983–4). Any training at all that helps a school-leaver to find a job is particularly welcome when so many young workers have been unemployed for more than one year. No criticisms of the schemes provided should fail to have that in mind. But the social function of these labour law institutions may be scrutinized perhaps by asking: How many families who encourage their children to go on to a university or polytechnic have considered the alternative of YTS?

Education and industrial training

Of some 8 million pupils at school in Britain, 93.5 per cent attend State schools, the rest independent schools. The latter (in England, the 'public' schools) see many pupils staying on after the age of sixteen; in consequence they send a much higher proportion to universities, polytechnics and other full-time courses. These represent numerically an élite sector compared with equivalent post-school institutions in comparable countries. The low proportion of working-class students in such British institutions was one of the concerns that led to attempts two decades ago to expand the higher and further education sectors – in itself of great moment for the labour market. The Robbins Report (1963) advanced the objective of making university courses 'available for all those who are qualified by ability and attainment to pursue them and who wish to do so'.

Numbers of places increased, but the proportions of students in terms of social class have changed remarkably little at all degree-giving institutions. In 1974 the percentage of school-leavers from State schools who went on to such institutions was 5.6; in 1978 it was 6.6; and in 1983, 6.7. From independent schools the percentages were: 1974, 33.4; 1978, 36.2; 1983, 35.6. The openings to positions of authority in industry are more numerous for those with degrees. Maintained schools now send some 18 per cent of their pupils on to some kind of other colleges of further education; but independent schools send 30 per cent. University entry has become more difficult (by tests at A-level) just at the time State school resources have been reduced and their teachers forced into prolonged strike action over grim salary scales (p. 631). At the other end of the hierarchy, that traditional avenue of 'training' for workers' offspring, the apprenticeship (itself often in the past an avenue of entry also into the organized trade union movement), has over the past two decades fallen away. The annual entry to apprenticeships in 1962 was 142,000; by 1985 the figure was 40,000. Three out of five companies now offer no formal training at all to employees.[156] In 1985 official figures disclosed a total of 82,000 apprentices in Britain (along with 40,000 'other trainees' in industry) – a small proportion of the figure in the 1960s. In 1985 the Engineering Industry Training Board put annual apprentice entry to the industry as 15,000 a year less than in the mid-1970s; and it estimated that by 1989 entry of trained craftsmen and technicians would fall to 5,000 (the intake in 1984 was 11,000; natural wastage takes away 20,000 a year). The MSC discovered accelerating skill shortages in both old and new technologies, and a near-collapse of the apprentice system. Very few YTS entrants have the opportunity to qualify in such skills. Comparatively, Britain had the lowest percentage of pupils remaining at school after sixteen in 1985 of all the major Western European countries except Spain; at 64 per cent it is far lower than the percentage in West Germany (84), Japan (73) or the United States (79). Into this educational picture, framed darkly by the massive youth unemployment of the 1980s, the programmes for job creation and training for young workers have to be placed.

Industrial training and job creation

Schemes to improve industrial training generally have abounded since the 1960s. The object of the Industrial Training Act 1964 was to make levies upon employers (appeals on them were the first jurisdiction of the tribunals) to create Industrial Training Boards for each industry. Sixteen out of twenty-three of these were abolished after 1979; those in engineering and construction are still active. What is left of that scheme operates under the Industrial Training Act 1982, the new umbrella statute. The last decade has seen a plethora of schemes, too, for subsidizing employment, of which the two main survivors are the Job Release Scheme under an Act of 1977 (and now also the Part-Time Job Release Scheme, where older workers are paid to leave employment, in whole or in part, earlier than retirement age, creating openings for younger workers) and the Job-Splitting Scheme under which employers were paid sums for creating part-time jobs out of a full-time job. For five years after 1979, under the Employment Subsidies Act 1978, the Temporary Short-Time Working Compensation Scheme replaced earlier job-subsidy schemes (some of which were questioned by the EC Commission under Community unfair competition law). This supplemented the pay of workers on short time in nearly a million jobs before it was phased out in the 1980s. Most of its provisions were set out informally in what Freedland has neatly dubbed 'leaflet law'.[157]

In the 1980s the MSC, increasingly put in charge of developments, fostered schemes more directly aimed at young workers in the climate of growing unemployment. The Community Enterprise and Community Industry schemes support work of use to the community, largely temporary jobs to take the edge off long-term unemployment; it is planned to increase them to some 230,000 or more. A direct subsidy was offered to employers in 1982 under the Young Workers Scheme; they could claim £15 a week for each worker under eighteen in the first year of employment who earned less than £40 (even if the employer would have recruited them anyway and irrespective of the effect upon older workers). The TUC called this a plan 'to undermine union rates of pay'. It ended when a two-year YTS was introduced in 1985 (though a parallel New Workers scheme was revived in 1986). As with the other plans, these schemes provided for no trade union participation, let alone guarantees concerning the bargaining of conditions. The MSC is perhaps the supreme example of a tripartite body whose trade union members can expect to see no guaranteee of specifically trade union characteristics in the schemes that it promotes. More important was the Youth Opportunities Programme (YOP) created in 1978 out of earlier schemes. In its four years YOP included 1.8 million people; it offered 'work experience' schemes and 'work preparation' courses with a tax-free allowance. Nearly half of all school-leavers went into YOP in 1982; but increasingly they failed to find a job when they came out of it. With the new plan for 'training',[158] YOP was transmuted into the YTS.

Little attention was given to the lessons already learned about the legal complexities of what was being done. Although there was debate about the Government's (thwarted) wish to exclude school-leavers from social security supplementary benefit if they refused to join the scheme,[159] the exclusion of trainees from employee status went un-heeded; that could have, as we saw in Chapter 2, serious consequences in the loss of employment protection rights.[160] Gradually, special reg-ulations afforded some protection to trainees concerning race and sex discrimination and in health and safety.[161] Indeed, deep concern about the number of accidents suffered by YOP and YTS trainees led to a major effort by the MSC, including the recruitment of safety advisers and scrutiny of safety conditions. The fact that such protections were not provided from the outset of the YOP and YTS schemes illustrates the casual manner in which even bodies like the MSC took insufficient account of the interests of young workers. After all, the contract of apprenticeship is surrounded by legal rules dating back to the fourteenth century. It is true that many legal principles attaching to this contract 'to teach and instruct' in a trade or profession – such as the right to moderate physical correction of the apprentice – have become out of date; but those principles also provide considerable protection for the apprentice.[162] Broadly, the employment protection legislation, too, was applied to apprentices. It is remarkable, then, that we should have created a new kind of 'trainee' without having adequately stipulated for his rights in respect of the sponsoring employer. The contract between the MSC and a managing agent or sponsor is not one that can be directly relied upon by the trainee, as he is a third party to that contract (though the young workers have erroneously been referred to that contract for their employer's 'obligations' by the MSC and even by the TUC). What is more, the law has seen little difficulty in treating other 'trainees' as employees (as with the trainee social worker in Scotland in 1984: p. 214) but not young trainees on these schemes (p. 119). Those setting up and running schemes that would inevitably risk the criticism of 'cheap labour' owed it to the young unemployed recruits to accord them equivalent legal status, not least when they were integrated in a tripartite body like the MSC. They could have demanded that the law on apprenticeship be adapted to protect these young trainees. In not doing so, they failed to discharge a central responsibility.

YTS, training and education

YOP had been criticized as not providing courses or training that helped entrants to find a job and as providing employers with cheap labour out of a public subsidy. The letter to an MP became famous in which a farmer complained that other farmers had 'got a free boy. Where is my free boy?' Some unions opposed the scheme on this ground; but the pressures of unemployment and the continued presence of TUC representatives on the tripartite MSC, where they have grounds for claiming that they improved the scheme compared to Government proposals (e.g. in defeating – so far, at least – the plan to withdraw social security rights; though those who refuse a place without 'good cause' have been disqualified for six weeks: p. 215), have drawn most unions out of that posture. How far this 'new political pattern in labour law', with the re-emergence of 'some degree of consensus',[163] will preside over a scheme that militates against collectively bargained conditions whilst taking large numbers off the register of unemployment remains to be seen. Attention has focussed mainly upon the training aspect of the scheme, and that is important. But the meaning of the 'consensus' on YTS will ultimately be tested in the effects upon the social structure.

Under the scheme a young person, normally a school-leaver of sixteen, takes up a position with an employer. He does not, however, become an 'employee' unless the employer offers this status (it appears that few have). In the time that he spends in this position, he undergoes 'work experience' and, originally, a period of thirteen weeks 'off-the-job' training. Trainees are paid £27.30 a week (1985–6). Two versions of the scheme were set up. Mode A involves employers sponsoring a place with a contract with the MSC. They are paid some £2,000 a year. Under Mode B the MSC acts as managing agent and organizes places in training centres, community projects or colleges. The great majority of the places are in Mode A and increasingly so. In July 1985 the Government, which had earlier planned 300,000 Mode A and 160,000 Mode B places, announced that from 1986 the YTS scheme would be extended into a two-year scheme with twenty weeks' 'off-the-job' training and £35 a week in the second year (seventeen-year-old school-leavers would be eligible for a one-year scheme), and the total would reach 500,000. Later Government estimates for YTS in 1986–7 were 362,000. A trainee would have a formal 'training agreement': 'Every 16-year-old school-leaver will be assured of two years of good training and work experience. Every parent should know that too.'[164] A two-year period with improved training could mark a step forward. On the other hand, the scheme's relationship to employment remained ambiguous. In 1985 only 56 per cent of YTS trainees were finding jobs at the end of the one-year course, though some others returned to education. Moreover, the scheme had all the appearance of keeping young people off the job market. Abuses of the scheme had been revealed: some managing agents charged a fee for each trainee (thereby demonstrating, it has been said, 'that the young people are carrying out productive work for their sponsor, but without being paid for it').[165] Such criticisms led the Government to propose a training standards advisory service to monitor the quality of training (though how the inspection of training will take place is uncertain unless a proper inspectorate is provided or unions are given that function).

The same year also saw a more significant change in regard to the

MSC. For some years, criticism of English and Welsh schools has concentrated upon a lack of 'standards', especially in vocational subjects suited to employment needs. The introduction of the TVEI (Technical and Vocational Education Initiative) in 1982 in schools was accompanied by Government pressure to see that 'social' education should not form a part of YTS schemes. One aim of policy is that 'all young people in school should have the opportunity of following a more relevant and practical curriculum leading to the achievement of recognised standards of competence and qualification'.[166] In so far as this refers to the inadequate development of applied science and engineering in the educational system, it repeats a long-standing aim. But in so far as the policy as a whole counterposes 'training' and 'education', it pursues a different objective – one addressed to the task of helping 'young people to make themselves more suited to the likely patterns of employment'.[167] There is a risk that the YTS certificate will merely mark out a young trainee as a 'good worker'. At the other end of the spectrum, in the welter of policy statements in 1984–5, it was made clear for higher education in degree-giving institutions that whilst employers must increase their attention to science and technology, they will, 'understandably, often choose recruits in management by reference to general ability and leadership qualities'. On the other hand, *training* is to 'help young people progress from education to work as smoothly and effectively as possible'.[168] The division between the leaders and the led is inherent in the policies and the language of the various White Papers.

The movement of educational resources into the province of 'training' was sharply marked by another event, the transfer in 1984 of control over a wide area of work-related further education (and its resources) to the MSC from local authorities. The year-long resistance of the latter was fruitless. The aim was that this sector should be 'closely geared to labour market needs'. It is clear that this area of policy cannot address the problem of absence of jobs; but neither is the MSC a body of experience in education nor (like local authorities) responsible to an electorate. It is concerned with training. 'Training' is thereby divorced – for the mass of young people – from education. It was not always so. Proposals for further education for all between 16 and 18 are not new. In 1959 the Crowther Report called upon government to implement 'a provision of compulsory part-time education for all young persons of 16 and 17 who are not in full-time education'. But that education, although relevant, was not to be 'training'. Had the YTS 'trainees' been seen in that light, it is unthinkable that their legal status would have been so uncertain and so unprotected. The point was overlooked when it would not have been for either a 'Crowther student' or the traditional apprentice.

The trainee in YTS today, therefore, is typically a sixteen-year-old school-leaver to whom society offers no employment. As such he or she is, by the very pattern of our educational system, more likely to come from a household of the ruled than of the rulers. Instead of a real job, he undertakes a period of activity in which 'policies are fast blurring the distinction between training and work'.[169] He does work; but is not (except by grace of the employer) an 'employee'. He is paid; but is not paid a 'wage' in the market for his labour power, only a paltry 'allowance' fixed by government. The institutions that plan his training are gradually being removed from the sector of education. The fact is inescapable that while others prepare to study amid dreaming spires, he *is* a free boy. In addition, the young woman trainee faces the in-built bias about 'women's jobs'. The machinery thus established by the law poses fundamental questions about freedom, equality of opportunity and education in a pluralist democracy. The labour lawyer sees quickly enough the problems for collective bargaining and especially, in conditions of mass unemployment, the dilemma for trade unions in YTS. But there are wider issues, the organization (and reorganizing) of work, the reduction of working hours and work sharing, for example, and the inherent assumptions in YTS – as it is now – on such matters. To assess the social impact, we must place job creation and training for young workers in the context of our divisive educational system. For employers and trade unions these wider issues are also inescapable; for the 'training' of so many young people for whom jobs are still increasingly precarious will add a new dimension to conflict at, and about, work, just as YTS challenges the unions, in particular, to find new ways to express young workers' interests. The general relationship of the law to industrial conflict must be our next concern.

[7] Industrial Conflict and the Law

The freedom of employees to combine and to withdraw their labour is their
ultimate safeguard against the inherent imbalance of power between the employer and the individual employee. This freedom has come to be accepted as a
hallmark of a free society.

So said the Government Green Paper on *Trade Union Immunities* in
1981. To protect such a right is not to approve, or disapprove, of any
particular withdrawal of labour or of the conduct of any particular
dispute. But it does recognize the fundamental importance of that
freedom in a democratic society. In 1908 the United States union leader
Samuel Gompers (no revolutionary by any standards) said:

It is our aim to avoid strikes but I trust that the day will never come when the
workers of our country will have so far lost their manhood and independence as to
surrender their right to strike.

Today he would have recognized the equal place of women workers.

Agreement on the importance of this freedom, however, leaves open
the question of how far it is or should be protected or limited by law –
that is, not only by the general law (against violence, for example) but
also by laws that specifically apply to collective action to exert economic
pressure in industrial conflict. Such laws may apply to workers and
employers, to all workers only, to workers taking 'unofficial' action (not
approved by their unions) or 'unconstitutional' action (in breach of
procedures agreed in a collective agreement), or they may be special to
particular groups of workers (in the public sector or 'essential services'),
to workers who fail to observe procedures laid down by the law or some
other obligation, or to workers who target a forbidden employer (because the law designates him a 'neutral'), or to workers who take action
in solidarity with other, weaker groups of workers. The industrial action
may be (at first often is) partial. Management may tighten up work
discipline (e.g. by more strict enforcement of rest periods) long before
it considers a lock-out, and workers may engage in a 'go-slow', work-

to-rule, or working without enthusiasm before proceeding to a total withdrawal of labour. We have seen in Chapter 3 how those actions normally involve a breach of the contracts of employment in Britain.

Little more than 150 years ago under laws of many kinds all these forms of industrial action by workers were illegal. The employer has rarely had anything to fear from a lock-out except a claim for damages for breach of an employment contract if he failed to give proper notice to terminate contracts (notice of 'variation' will not do: p. 153); and even then damages are normally quantified at no more than the wages payable to a worker for that period of notice. On the other hand, the result of the struggle by unions of workers to emerge from the various illegalities is, as we noted in Chapter 1, in Britain the modern system of 'immunities'. In this chapter we shall look at the development of the law in relation to (1) the *early illegalities*, especially the application and development of the *criminal* law; (2) the *civil status* and vulnerability to legal process of the unions before and after the *Taff Vale* case, 1901, and in the modern, civil law after the 1982 Act; (3) the law and the conduct of industrial action, especially through *picketing*; (4) the civil law 'immunities', the concept of a *trade dispute* and acts done 'in contemplation or furtherance of a trade dispute' ('ICFTD'). After we have considered these areas of the law, without undue technicality but with sufficient attention to its twists and turns, we can address the 'right to strike' today.

Early criminal illegalities

In 1800 trade unions were illegal. In the Industrial Revolution workers employed by the entrepreneur and the factory system were replacing domestic production; but already early in the process 'the workers in every trade were becoming very much alive to the necessity for defending their standards'.[1] Four things joined, however, to make their combinations illegal, indeed criminal. They were: wage fixing; the Master and Servant Acts; the Combination Acts; and the common law of the judges. First, wages were still in theory fixed by State authorities, largely by the magistrates in quarter sessions. So, in legal theory at least, they could not be bargained or left to a 'free market'. The laws of 1349 and 1351, which imposed 'pre-Black Death wages' and required all able-bodied men to work, were re-enacted by Tudor legislation (one statute aimed 'to banish idleness'), and from this source wage-regulation Acts gave magistrates the jurisdiction that was finally abolished only by statutes of 1813 and 1824 (although in fact they had long since ceased effectively to fulfil wage-fixing functions). New relations of production and the new ideology of 'free competition' that had come with them led to the view that all such wage regulation had, in Lord Sidmouth's words, 'pernicious consequences'. Some workers did try to improve their lot by agitating for the restoration of the proper operation of wage fixing, but by the early nineteenth century 'It is not surprising that the working classes sought other means of redress.'[2]

That alternative means was combination. Between the fourteenth century and 1800, however, statutes had also made workers' combinations illegal, either generally or in particular trades ('if workmen do conspire, covenant or promise together . . . that they shall not make or do their work but at a certain price or rate' – 1548). Nor could the servant be allowed to leave his work unfinished. For this purpose there were the statutes under the second heading, the Master and Servant Acts. These, as we have seen (p. 141), made a breach of his contract of employment a criminal offence for the servant (for which he could ultimately be imprisoned with hard labour) but only a civil offence for the master. Originating also in the 1349 ordinance, these statutes were refurbished in 1766 and 1823, codified in 1867 and repealed only in 1875 (a particularly fierce and effective campaign by the Glasgow Trades Council contributed greatly to the repeal). The servant could be imprisoned over and over again for the same breach of contract. As Lord Ellenborough put it in 1817, these laws existed to sustain the master's 'superior authority'. The Benthamite reformers of 1824 took little interest in the 'intolerable oppression' these laws allowed.[3]

Third, encouraged by the French Revolution to see all organizations of workers as a potential source of Jacobin revolution, the Government passed the Combination Acts of 1799 and 1800. The 1800 Act rendered criminal all agreements or meetings for advancing wages or altering hours and many associated activities. Other laws already prohibited many such combinations, but the Combination Acts generalized the prohibition and facilitated procedures for prosecutions before magistrates. Prosecutions were numerous. But the common law added a fourth weapon. The judges saw union organization as the crime of conspiracy, irrespective of these statutes. That appears to be the case in the prosecution of the *Journeymen Tailors of Cambridge* in 1721; and Grose J. said in 1796:

each may insist on raising his wages if he can, but if several meet for the same purpose it is illegal and the parties may be indicted for a conspiracy.[4]

Conspiracy was to be a recurring theme in the criminal prosecution of workers for three-quarters of a century, and in civil cases long after that.

The unions: bare legality 1824–5

'The first twenty years of the nineteenth century', wrote the Webbs, 'witnessed a legal persecution of Trade Unionists as rebels and revolutionists.'[5] Yet such combinations grew and took on various forms, partly to avoid the wicked mien of a trade union, appearing as artisans' clubs, working men's groups and 'friendly societies'. (These last received some encouragement from authority as promoting thrift.) In the provisions for members' old age or sickness, for out-of-work and funeral benefits, the friendly society left its mark upon our modern trade unions with their 'friendly' or 'provident' benefits. Benthamite reformers, led by the Charing Cross tailor Francis Place, opposed demands for further repression with the argument that all 'artificial' restraints should now be lifted. In 1824 they skilfully engineered the repeal of the Combination Acts. Once the 'oppressive laws [are] replaced', said Place, 'combinations will lose the matter which cements them into masses'. But their hope that 'freedom of combination would soon teach the worker its futility' was dashed.[6] Despite an improved economy, a rapid increase in prices provoked a wave of violent strikes, and a less permissive statute was hastily passed in 1825.

Historians seem to agree that this episode exemplifies the importance of the economic factors in these developments just as much as, if not more than, the importance of laws against trade unions.[7] But the 1800 Act had clearly forced workers into more clandestine practices. Nor is it clear that we may speak of the 'ineffectiveness' of the Combination Acts,[8] at any rate if we include other legislation under which prosecutions were often brought.[9] In view of Kahn-Freund's reliance upon this example, the point is of more than historical importance. Under the 1825 Act combinations by masters and workmen were expressly legalized. But the equality was formal. Workers' combinations were permitted for the 'sole purpose' of agreeing on *their own* hours and wages, nothing more. A series of vaguely worded offences was set out in s. 3 of the Act: pressure in industrial disputes by violence, 'threats', 'molestation', 'intimidation' or 'obstruction'. The judges' approach to these forms of 'coercion' in the 1825 Act remained of importance well beyond the reforms of 1871–5, which are the basis of the modern law. There is even a curious echo in the laws of the 1980s of this insistence that the legality of workers' action should be confined to disputes directly about their own employment conditions (p. 556 and Chapter 8).

These were not the only legal weapons used against workers attempting to create unions in the early nineteenth century. The grandiose but precarious schemes for national organizations in earlier years, like the 'Philanthropic Hercules' of 1818 or the Owenite 'Grand National Consolidated Trades Union' in 1834 (with Benbow's projected 'Grand National Holiday of the Productive Classes') collapsed in the face of bitter opposition and of prosecutions that helped to deter recruiting. Thompson marks this period as one when 'the rulers of England', whose class interests the law had served, 'surrendered to the law' in the strategy they adopted. Even so, their acceptance of trade unions was no more than acceptance of their place in 'peaceful negotiation', not, as Fox puts it, acceptance of their 'interference in the employer's authority with respect to the deployment of resources at the workplace'.[10] Unions, especially of the unskilled, were often secret societies. Six unfortunate Dorchester labourers, the 'Tolpuddle martyrs', were prosecuted in 1834 under an Act of 1797 (passed after the Nore Mutiny) forbidding 'unlawful oaths', and were sentenced to seven years' transportation for administering a union oath, though formal trade unionism was still rare among farm labourers (the government being more concerned about the incendiary riots of the 'Captain Swing' gangs in 1830).[11]

In the decade to follow, the movement towards general unionism disintegrated, and the political programme of the Chartists dominated the working-class movement. Though they fought for the Ten Hour and other factory legislation, they play a curiously small role in the legal history. We can only speculate what the difference might have been had the more political programmes of Chartism influenced the unions in the 1860s (though unions outside the 'aristocracy' of craft workers appear to have given support to 'moral force', though not to 'physical force', Chartism).[12] The reason for their defeat. Hobsbawm says,

in Chartist Britain, as on the revolutionary continent of 1848, was that the poor were hungry, numerous and desperate enough to rise, but lacked the organisation and maturity which could have made their rebellion more than a momentary danger to the social order.[13]

There was 'little basis, at the end of the 1840s, for confident predictions of a strong future or mass growth for the unions and collective bargaining'.[14] Every union, as the Webbs said, had its 'romantic legend', the 'midnight meeting' and the 'secret oath'. The 'New Model' unions that emerged after 1850 found greater maturity and stronger organization in a period of general economic buoyancy. The flavour of revolutionary tactics gave way to the strategy of those who were fighting for a stake in society. With the Amalgamated Society of Engineers in the van, craft unions built stable funds and an organization other unions had lacked, except for the miners and cotton workers whose discipline and resourcefulness were already established.[15] The miners' union appointed a solicitor in 1844 (a remarkable event when we consider that few large unions even today have an in-house professional lawyer on headquarters staff).

These unions were the force behind the evidence given to the Royal Commission of 1867 and the pressure upon Parliament to change the law. They carried over, too, the craft exclusiveness towards other workers and tough bargaining with conciliatory attitudes to employers, whilst their political ambitions were 'largely restricted to trade union affairs'.[16] They were not 'apolitical'; but their aims were 'concrete aims, aims that could be realised within the existing society', very different from the 'political commitment of Continental trade unions during their formative stages, a commitment to working class action with the purpose of changing the very structure of society'.[17] This attitude was both confirmed and given direction by counsel from Harrison and other Positivist advisers to concentrate on the security of their funds and sufficient freedom of industrial action, not to go further into legal status and be exposed to crippling litigation in the courts.[18] Many unions had registered under the Friendly Societies Act 1855 in the hope (forlorn, as we shall see) of acquiring legality and protection with minimum risk.

The courts were unable, even if they were willing, to reinterpret the liabilities fast enough to grant these new (at heart 'respectable') trade unions legality. Except for very few, such as Rolfe B., judges did not wish to do so; many of them feared, as did Earl Wemyss later, the 'coming democracy and trades union tyranny'. The essence of the wrongs inherent in 'molestation', 'obstruction', 'threats' or 'intimidation', under the 1825 Act, s. 3, was, in the words of Sir William Erle (later Erle J.), 'the intention to coerce the will of another', in particular to coerce the free will of a man in the exercise of his 'right to dispose of his own labour or capital as he chooses'. Within this he included peaceful persuasion of a worker to leave work if done with 'some corrupt or spiteful motive'.[19] In 1832 a letter informing an employer of a forthcoming strike was held to be criminal 'molestation'. In 1851 Erle J, in a prosecution for organizing a strike by sweated tin-plate workers, told the jury it was 'molestation' when 'a manufacturer has got a manufactory and his capital embarked in it . . . if persons conspire together to take away all his workmen'.[20]

The reforms of 1871

British labour law now stood at the crossroads. The first phase, the minimum repeal of the laws that made trade union combinations totally illegal, had been accomplished in 1824–5. But many other criminal illegalities – such crimes as 'molestation', and the Master and Servant Acts – impeded effective union action. One way lay a route to a right to associate and right to strike (as in France, though there too the more radical leaders argued against a law granting a *right* to associate in 1884 for fear this 'poisoned pill' of legal status might lead to greater control and integration).[21] The other road, which was taken in Britain, led to step-by-step protection and reform in successive statutes. In the Molestation of Workmen Act 1859, Parliament gave some relief from the judicial interpretation of 'molestation' by excluding from liability peaceful persuasion to quit work, but only in strikes that concerned wages or hours and did not induce a worker to break an employment contract (a critical proviso). Thus a strike to induce a non-unionist to join a union led to a conviction in 1867, and Baron Bramwell (the authentic voice of the common law) declared in a prosecution of tailors who had peacefully picketed shops in London that they were guilty of molestation and conspiracy if their action included 'abusive language and gestures' or anything 'calculated to have a deterring effect on the minds of ordinary persons by exposing them to have their motions watched and to encounter black looks'.[22] We shall see that in the mid-1980s this formulation came to be of considerable contemporary interest (p. 547).

Extensive union agitation secured further reforms in 1871 from the Liberal majority elected on the new urban franchise. Two Acts, partly based on the minority report of a Royal Commission to which the 'junta' of new union leaders had given evidence, dealt with civil status and with criminal law. The latter was subject to serious amendment in the House of Lords, in particular by insertion of the crimes of 'persistent following' and 'watching and besetting', which are with us today. This criminal law Act did repeal the 1825 statute (but unhappily also that of 1859) and confined 'molestation', etc. to acts that could give rise to binding over to keep the peace (i.e. *violent* threats, etc.). It was also thought to have kept conspiracy liability at bay, at least where the combination had done, or had in view, no act illegal in itself. These provisions were supplemented by the Trade Union Act 1871, which excluded any criminal liability (which was uncertain) by reason of a 'restraint of trade' in respect of the 'purposes of any trade union' (s. 2). We return to that Act shortly (p. 522).

The first omens were poor. Wives of strikers were imprisoned for molestation by way of banging kettles at a strike-breaker and for saying 'Bah' to blacklegs.[23] More important, in *R.* v. *Bunn*, 1872 (p. 17), the organizers of a strike by gas workers against victimization were convicted of conspiracy. There were two strands to this judgment. One dubbed the combination illegal because it had threatened to call men out in breach of employment contracts – an act, we recall, still capable of being itself a crime. This was a conspiracy to use means unlawful in themselves, a defence to which was at the time hard to find. But Brett J. went even further, holding the combination *as such* to be illegal, even if no act to be done was itself unlawful (a 'simple' conspiracy) because it still involved molestation, i.e. 'an unjustifiable annoyance and interference with the masters in the conduct of their business'; or, as he put it to counsel, 'a conspiracy founded upon an interference with a person's free will, by threats and intimidations'.[24]

The Times commented that the court had 'to maintain the rules of fair fighting and with whatever reluctance they must be enforced'. The reaction of the unions (which had been misled, not for the last time, into the belief that liberty was already theirs) was one of intense anger, the London Trades Council meeting to discuss the 'critical legal position'. The use of conspiracy was important because for this common law offence the judge was able to give sentences many times the maximum permitted for parallel crimes under the Act of 1871 (though in *Bunn's* case they were later reduced by the Home Secretary), a phenomenon met again in the case of the Shrewsbury pickets (p. 541).

Trade disputes: the 1875 bedrock

A new campaign of agitation won, surprisingly quickly, a new Royal Commission and a new Act which delighted the unions. It was felt that working-class power had been used for the first time to extract from the political machinery successful legal protection for the industrial movement. Selective support had been given in the election of 1874 to candidates across party lines (other than the first of the 'Lib–Labs') according to their answers to questions. The new Conservative Government incurred union hostility when it appointed a Commission; but within a year Disraeli, acutely aware of the strength of a growing working-class vote, imaginatively offered a Bill that met most union demands. In 1875 it became law and established the foundation of modern labour law. The fledgling TUC was so ecstatic that a telegram of congratulation was sent to the Minister; and George Howell, retiring secretary, doubted that there was further need of the TUC or its Parliamentary Committee, which had organized the campaign. In the next five years, though, unions were more concerned with the economic depression than with the law. Legal controversy was to re-emerge later in further cases on picketing and in the cases on civil liability for strikes, when militant and more radical 'new' unions began to organize the unskilled workers in the 1880s and 1890s.[25]

The 1875 Conspiracy and Protection of Property Act repealed the Master and Servant Acts (s. 17),[26] codified yet again crimes connected with 'intimidation', 'molestation' and picketing (s. 7: p. 541) and expressly provided for criminal liability in some strikes in breach of employment contracts (s. 4, in public utilities, repealed in 1971; s. 5, endangering life or property, still law: p. 654). But its most important section invented a golden formula that became the bedrock of British workers' rights to organize and take effective industrial action. In s. 3 it reversed *Bunn's* case by providing that a combination to do or procure any act 'in contemplation or furtherance of a trade dispute' should not be a criminal conspiracy *unless* the act itself would be punishable as a crime. The common law 'simple' conspiracy, where the objection is taken to the combination as such, was excluded from trade disputes. In substance, this is still the basis of the freedom to withdraw labour in Britain. In form, it was the first of the trade dispute 'immunities'. There were many other crimes that the section did not affect: riot, unlawful assembly, breach of the peace, sedition 'or any offence against the State or the Sovereign'. Those crimes concerned public order and security. But *simple* criminal conspiracy was henceforth banished from trade disputes. A line was drawn between public order and industrial disputes. It was not thought necessary to define a 'trade dispute'; indeed, so obvious did the meaning appear to be that such a definition entered the next Act of 1906 only at a late stage in Parliament (p. 554). Only after the enactment of this protection, understandably at the time not seen as a 'privilege' or 'immunity', can we begin to speak of a 'right' or, more accurately, 'liberty' to strike in Britain.

In the modern law (the Criminal Law Act 1977) a different method of supplying the 'immunity' against simple criminal conspiracy was used in the context of a general reform of the English criminal law. The common law crime of conspiracy itself was abolished (except for two forms not relevant here, such as conspiracy to corrupt public morals), and s. 3 of the 1875 Act was repealed. A new crime of statutory conspiracy was created, committed only when a combination or agreement involves the commission of a criminal offence. The labour law formula is, in effect, generalized. Further, the penalties for statutory conspiracy are limited to either a fine or a period of imprisonment not longer than the maximum available for the offence involved. Moreover, if the acts are to be done in contemplation or furtherance of a trade dispute, the offence is disregarded if it is a summary offence not punishable by imprisonment. These provisions are of some importance in relation to picketing.

The civil status of unions

Trade unions did not shake off – and have not yet fully shaken off – the aura of illegality. In civil law, too, they had an 'unlawful' status – for example, under the doctrine of restraint of trade (discussed in Chapter 2), which could harass their day-to-day administration. In *Hornby* v. *Close*, 1867,[27] the United Order of Boilermakers, which had registered under the Friendly Societies Act 1855, wanted the help of the courts to prosecute an official who had embezzled the funds. It was refused. Blackburn J. summed up the position:

> I do not say the objects of this society are criminal. I do not say they are not. But I am clearly of opinion that the rules referred to are illegal in the sense that they cannot be enforced.

Because of that civil status, the court could not lend its aid to an association in restraint of trade. The unions found they could not protect even the money they had thought safe behind the friendly society machinery. At first Parliament reacted only with minor statutory amendments concerning such thefts. But the main reform came in the Trade Union Act 1871, which was for a century the charter of union legality. It did three things, which still underlie the modern structure of the law.

(1) Restraint of trade

The 'purposes of a trade union' were not to be unlawful by reason merely of being in restraint of trade so as to render any agreement or trust 'void or voidable' (s. 3). For nearly one hundred years this was thought to confirm the lawful civil status of union rules, the contract that established the association. Then in a case in which a worker had been wrongly excluded from his union in breach of the rules, one judge purported to invalidate a rule on the grounds that it gave the NEC power to exclude members 'for any capricious reason', that it was an invalid rule because it was 'in restraint of trade' and s. 3 of the 1871 Act did not apply because that section applied to 'purposes', and this rule was not 'proper to the "purposes" of this or indeed any trade union'.[28] This remarkable distinction between rules and purposes was a door that could let in anew the old common law doctrine. In consequence, when the modern law was enacted in 1974 it was enacted that the 'purposes' should not be unlawful *and* that the 'rules' should not be unlawful or unenforceable only by reason of restraint of trade (TULRA s. 2 (5)). Without this protection a union is even today normally an unlawful association in civil law.

(2) The rule-book and the courts

Parliament also exacted a price, which the unions were very ready to pay, in s. 4 of the 1871 Act, which declared: 'Nothing in this Act shall enable any court to enforce directly' large parts of the union's agreements with members (the right to benefit, for example, or liability to penalties or agreements on terms for accepting employment) or its agreements with other unions (p. 724). The intention of both sides, unions and Parliament, was to keep these union affairs out of the courts. That section was repealed in 1971 and not revived in TULRA 1974; there seemed no good reason then not to allow members and unions to enter normal contractual relationships. (We shall see in Chapter 9 that this decision carried hidden consequences of immense importance.) But this section has been, and is, of great interest because it illustrates the manner in which judges can manage these 'special' laws on unions. If they decide that the common law is, after all, rather different from what it is thought to be at the time the statute was passed, then in the light of their subsequent pronouncement as to the 'true' common law doctrine, the statute may come to have a different effect from what it was meant, or thought, to have.

In restraint of trade cases, for instance, some judges early in this century began to suggest that not *all* unions' rules were unlawful; some might not be in restraint of trade since they were not 'unreasonable'. But this apparent alleviation was not welcome to the unions. They preferred to be legalized by the Act, rather than by the judges, because if the union was lawful at common law then it did not *need* the 1871 Act's exclusion of the doctrine of restraint of trade; therefore s. 4 did not apply, and the rules could be 'directly enforced' in the courts – a development in which Kahn-Freund detected a judicial inclination to recapture control of internal union management.[29] Today, however, most union rules are thought to be in restraint of trade at common law; most recent judgments assume this. But because s. 4 was repealed in 1971, in recent litigation involving the miners' unions the courts have been able for the first time to apply remedies that had not been available for a century (p. 744).

(3) Unincorporated status

The third reform of the 1871 Act introduces the vexed question of the precise legal status of trade unions. As we saw in Chapter 1 (p. 56), they have always resisted corporate status. They do not see themselves as, nor are they, command structures; and they have always rejected proposals, like those of the 1894 Royal Commission and even the Donovan Commission (1968), to incorporate them. The tortuous development of the law has gone through three main phases, an understanding of which is critical to the modern law and the rights and liabilities of unions: (a) the administrative register, 1871–1971; (b) the incorporation register, 1971–4; (c) the list, 1974. In discussing them, we must also consider the impact of the issue of legal status upon union liabilities in industrial conflict. Without that context the issue becomes a sterile exercise in antiquated jurisprudence.

(a) *The 1871 Act* (s. 6) offered an administrative register on which unions could, if they wished, register with the Registrar (of Friendly Societies). Some minor tax benefits and administrative gains eventually accrued; but the section said nothing about legal status. Coming so soon after the Companies Acts 1844–62, which incorporated registered companies, the Act was believed not to have changed union status as an unincorporated association that held its property through trustees (the Act made this obligatory). Most major unions registered under the 1871 Act (the most important modern exceptions were NALGO and the Union of Post Office Workers (now UCW), which created some odd features in internal union law: p. 752). As one Law Lord said in 1956, 'the comparative ease with which the garb of registration may be donned and doffed hardly accords with the view' that on registration the union acquired 'legal personality'. The Act required the trustees to be sued in matters concerning the property. Nothing whatever suggested that 'the union' could be sued in its name; companies could, because the legislation of the same era *said* they were 'corporate' bodies. With an unincorporated association, a 'representative action' can sometimes be employed whereby some members can be sued on behalf of *all* the members; but this is allowed only within very narrow principles (all the members must, for instance, have the same common interest and no separate defences). Certainly at the end of the nineteenth century, wrote Lord Asquith (who later became a Law Lord), 'the Acts of the

'70s were conceived to have made no difference in this regard' (to unions' availability to civil action), and everyone 'must have supposed that actions against unincorporated bodies of large and fluctuating membership, such as Trade Unions, were impracticable'.[30]

Of the five relevant cases in the 1890s, liability was imposed on two unions, but they did not contest the action; in *Lyons* v. *Wilkins* (p. 542) an action against the union itself was dropped; and in two others the representative procedure was rejected because it had no application in *tort* actions (with which a judge agreed as late as 1951, though the Court of Appeal held otherwise six years later).

Taff Vale and liability of union funds. In 1901 the Law Lords explosively shattered those beliefs as to union status by their judgments in the *Taff Vale* case. The effect of the decision was to lay trade union funds wide open to attack in the courts without limit in situations of industrial conflict. The fact that employers did not immediately press home this advantage, and that the next five years saw a period of relative industrial peace compared with the years immediately before 1914, did little to moderate the alarm in trade union circles and the speed with which unions strove to reinforce the TUC and their links with the 'Labour Representation Committee'.[31] Like *Rookes* v. *Barnard* some sixty years later, *Taff Vale* was an important trigger to legal change, the more so because the law seemed 'so clearly settled to the contrary', as Asquith wrote, that 'public opinion was unprepared for any such decision'. Election posters of 1906 depicted a judge handing to an employer a scourge with which to beat workers. The same year, 1901, had also seen the Law Lords develop the doctrine of *civil* conspiracy against the unions in *Quinn* v. *Leathem* (p. 31). In the previous decade the 'new' unions had organized the unskilled, the worker who had no skill to 'buttress' by restrictions, whose

only chance therefore was to recruit into one gigantic union all those who could possibly blackleg on him – in the last analysis every 'unskilled' man, woman or juvenile in the country; and thus to create a vast closed shop.[32]

Now the onslaught against these unions and their militant, for a time socialist, leaders after the turbulent dock strike of 1889 constituted 'a developing counter-attack by the propertied classes against the industrial organisation of the working people'.[33] These industrial battles, by reason of the employers' efforts to bring in 'free labour', often from

Ireland, to break strikes, turned the lamp of the law with renewed ferocity upon the practices of picketing.

Into this hot climate was launched the *Taff Vale* judgment, progenitor of the 1906 Act's protection and its repeal in 1982. The Taff Vale Railway had allegedly victimized a signalman, John Ewington, who had led a demand for a wage increase. From this tiny spark and the ensuing strike, together with the railway manager's 'passion for litigation' and willingness to import strike-breakers and the union's perception that the company was prosperous and a good target, a huge conflagration ensued. The company sought an injunction against the union and its officials; the officials were held to be guilty of tortious conduct; and an injunction was issued.[34] But the Court of Appeal unanimously disagreed with the injunction against the *union*. A registered union could not sue or be sued; it was not an entity known to the law; if the 1871 Act implied anything it was 'the exact contrary' of the judge's decision. But the House of Lords agreed with the judge.

Two strands were interwoven in the Law Lords' judgments. Two judges (including Lord Lindley) treat an action against the union's registered name as an extended use of the 'representative action' procedure. But two others treat the registered union as a 'legal entity' (or 'quasi-corporation'), arguing that this was the implied intention of the 1871 Act. Both views incorporate the union sufficiently for the purpose: 'Though not perhaps in the strict sense a corporation', said Lord Brampton, it was 'nevertheless a newly created corporate body created by statute, distinct from the unincorporated trade union' (which it could apparently become by deregistering). Lord Halsbury L C, at the risk of assuming his conclusions, expostulated:

If the Legislature has created a thing which can own property, which can employ servants, and which can inflict injury, it must be taken, I think, to have impliedly given the power to make it suable in a Court of Law for injuries done by its authority and procurement.[35]

The unions had, of course, not been 'created' by Parliament (they were created by working people), and the very question for the Law Lords was whether 'it' existed in law at all. Here, as in other judgments, the Law Lords spoke of the legislature 'creating' unions, when what they were referring to was their legalization by Parliament, in order to treat them as quasi-corporate bodies even though Parliament had not so enacted. The immediate consequence was the threat to union funds in tort actions where liability was being widened (including the benefit funds for sickness and the like). Beyond the injunction, the union had to pay £23,000 damages (and £12,000 costs). It was inevitable that, after the landslide Liberal victory in the 1906 election, the *Taff Vale* judgment should be reversed. After some confusion – many Bills were introduced[36] – the chosen method was not one that clarified the judgments concerning the civil status of registered unions. Instead, such was the shock of *Taff Vale* that the Trade Disputes Act 1906 s. 4 declared that no action was to be allowed against a trade union (whether in its registered name or through a representative action) 'in respect of any tortious act alleged to have been committed by or on behalf of a trade union'. An exception (obscurely drafted) provided for tort actions against the trustees concerning a registered union's property outside trade disputes. Also, the union remained liable in contract; and individuals, officials and others remained liable in tort (they were defendants in many actions after 1906, backed by the union). Nevertheless, critics fastened upon this section as 'outrageous', as Professor Dicey, the jurist, put it in asking the Women's Liberal Unionist Association

to think what it would mean if the terms on which women – domestic servants, for instance – laboured were really regulated by the caprice or even the serious doctrine of a trade union.

(Domestic service was then the second largest category of employment.) Lord Halsbury declared in 1906: 'This is a Bill for the purpose of legalizing tyranny.'

Without doubt, the removal of liability in tort from unions altogether, not just in trade disputes, was a drastic remedy for *Taff Vale* that created its own problems (the Webbs disapproved of it). To anticipate a little, the 1974 legislation re-enacted the same exemption from tort liability (TULRA s. 14 (1)); unincorporated employers' associations received the same exemptions because under the 1906 Act most of them were still 'trade unions' (p. 718). But it also provided in clearer and wider terms the exception that actions in tort could be brought *outside* trade disputes for negligence, nuisance or other torts causing personal injury or connected with use of property (s. 14 (2)). Even so, since the Crown could after 1947 be made liable (to certain remedies) in tort, Dicey's question was frequently posed: why should a union be 'a privileged body exempted from the law of the land'?

Research reveals, however, that under the modern union's protection from tort liability, 'managements were confident of the effect of the threat to the union arising from its *de facto* responsibility to meet any award against its officials'.[37] Indeed, critics rarely asked for total obliteration of the protection, even in debates preceding the 1927 Act after the General Strike or in the Conservative lawyers' proposals of 1958. Donovan proposed a limitation to torts committed in trade disputes.[38] The law under which union funds had not been attacked in the nineteenth century was, as Lord Loreburn L C said in 1906, not merely procedural but 'a law of principle'. To ask whether the tort exemption put unions 'outside the law of the land' could allow for only one answer. It did; but that way of putting the point denied the problem and was therefore the wrong question. It assumed that the 'ordinary' law of the land was neutral and just. After *Taff Vale* it was not. A very different answer might be given if it were asked whether the common law of tort, by providing employers with the ability to wipe out union funds through suits for damages, permitted adequate liberty for unions to do their job in collective bargaining. As Mr Woodcock, General Secretary of the TUC, said in 1964: 'It is not a privilege to be allowed to do the job you are there to do. It is your right.'

Many solutions might have been advanced to meet this real problem. We come to the compromise enacted in 1974 shortly. What is important for the moment is that any 'half-way house' admits that the problem exists and that the simplistic formulation of Dicey is fallacious. One such answer is to make the trade union liable in tort, both to injunctions and damages, but to adjust the law of tort to take the edges off the raw common law. One might, for example, clarify the principles of vicarious liability and limit the amount that may be recovered in damages. Yet by itself this is not necessarily an answer. The risk of financial extinction of the unions is still real. The purpose of the exercise must be to amend the 'law of the land' to allow for the continued existence and functioning of the unions. Everything therefore turns upon the degree of protection afforded against both remedies, damages and injunctions.

(b) *The 1971 Act.* The 1906 Act was repealed in 1971. The Register set up under the Industrial Relations Act 1971 gave full corporate status to any trade union that registered on it. Indeed, only such bodies were allowed under that statute the title of 'trade union'; the rest were in law 'organisations of workers' (leading some to suggest that the Trades Union Congress should be renamed COW). Unions that kept off the Register were nevertheless able to be sued or to sue 'in the name of the organization' (s. 154). Actions in the NIRC, such as that in *Heatons* v. *TGWU* (p. 54),[39] were therefore brought against the union as such, as were actions in respect of other 'unfair industrial practices', which were frequently the equivalent of tort liabilities (as with s. 96 on inducing breach of contract, which applied to unions not on the Register). One of the privileges of the corporate 'trade union' was a limit on the damages that it could normally incur (s. 117; £5,000 with a membership of less than 5,000, scaled up to £100,000 if 100,000 or more). For the non-registered union there was no limit. Another advantage from which the unregistered union was excluded was the tax concessions that had been given since 1893 on the 'provident benefits' of unions on the 1871 Register. In High Court actions involving tort, immunities were granted to those acting in furtherance of an 'industrial dispute', but there was no further exemption for the union (s. 132).[40]

(c) *Modern union status and liability*. In repealing the 1971 Act, TULRA 1974 confirmed the protection against the 'restraint of trade' doctrine (s. 2 (5)) and revived the union protection from tort liability as noted above (s. 14). The latter section prevented actions in tort against trade unions, but allowed actions against the trustees, outside trade disputes, for torts connected with union property or causing personal injury. It is that section which was repealed by the Employment Act 1982. The 1982 Act, however, did not alter the way in which TULRA 1974 had settled the more general question of trade union status. Under TULRA there is no register at all. But a union may, if it satisfies the definition of 'trade union' (TULRA s. 28) and does not have a name misleadingly similar to an existing listed union, be placed upon a 'list' kept by the Certification Officer (CO). If he refuses, the organization can appeal to the EAT on both fact and law (TULRA s. 8, EPCA s. 136 (3)). The list is not relevant to legal status as such, but listing brings certain advantages, such as the tax benefits for provident funds, and is the condition needed to apply for a certificate of 'independence' (EPA s. 8: p. 280).

In 1974 unions wanted to get rid of the semi-corporate status judges had so often thrust upon them. Now, therefore, whether or not they are 'listed' – or even independent – the status of all trade unions is governed by TULRA s. 2 (1). This states that, except for the five incidents set out below, a union 'shall not be, or be treated as if it were, a body corporate'. The five special incidents in the section, though, give a union: (i) capacity to make contracts; (ii) capacity to have property belonging to it held by 'trustees in trust for the union'; (iii) capacity to sue or be sued in its name; (iv) capacity to have criminal proceedings brought against it; and (v) liability to have judgments or orders made against it enforced 'as if [it] were a body corporate'.

The strong wording of TULRA – 'shall not be treated as if' – has been held to create a situation different even from that of the union on the 1871 register. It was never formally decided before 1971 just how far one should refer to a union on the old register as 'a legal entity' or 'quasi-corporation', and little really turned on that because the judges tended to attach to such unions any corporate incident necessary to their purpose.[41] But the question arose how far unions had all become 'quasi-corporate' bodies after the 1974 Act. Because unions can now sue or be sued, conclude contracts and be beneficiaries under a trust, many have assumed that all unions after 1974 are in the same legal position as to status as a union registered under the old Act. But the courts have not taken this view. In 1946, for example, under the old 1871 Act a court decided that, since *Taff Vale* gave such a union quasi-corporate status, it must have the capacity needed to sue for defamation in defence of 'its' reputation. In 1980 this was held no longer to apply. The judge argued: the 1974 Act, s. 2(1), has prohibited the court from *treating* the union as a body corporate outside the five incidents there set out. The 1871 Act contained no such wording. There is therefore no longer any 'body' known to the law that can possess a reputation.[42] The union *shall not be treated* as a body corporate so it cannot have the 'reputation' a body corporate might have. To this legal status and its mysteries we return in Chapter 9.

The Employment Act 1982 and union liability

The 1982 Act did three things. It made unions liable in tort; it set out a code of vicarious liability (s. 15); and it limited damages against unions in certain tort actions (s. 16). By repealing s. 14 of TULRA, it removed the protection that had prevented an action in tort. Now the union can be sued (TULRA s. 2 (1) (d)) even in tort (EA 1982 s. 15 (1)). The principle behind *Taff Vale* is revived. The advantage to plaintiffs who sue in tort is obvious. Before the 1982 Act two officials of a railway union were ordered by a High Court injunction to withdraw a tortious recommendation to members to 'black' certain newspapers (which the workers claimed carried accusations that they were dishonest) and to refuse to drive trains carrying them. But after they complied, the plaintiffs were still confronted with 300 drivers who refused to drive the trains with the newspapers aboard. There had been a parallel in 1972, when some of the dockers' shop stewards had to be chased around London by those trying to serve notice of writs upon them (though later changes in procedure cured part of that difficulty).[43] It is much easier to sue the union once it is liable in tort. The object, then, in the 1980s is to attempt to coerce it into policing its members.

Tort liability now exposes the union to both injunctions and awards of damages. But awards of damages are limited by the 1982 Act *unless* the liability arises from personal injury caused by negligence, nuisance or other breach of duty, or a breach of duty has arisen in connection with ownership, occupation, control or use of property, real or personal (s. 16 (2); an ominous exception that seems to go wide enough to include use of union circulars or the like containing defamatory material). Otherwise damages are limited by ranges of membership: £10,000, for 5,000 or less up to £250,000 for 100,000 or more. (In federal unions, members of constituent unions count as members of the federation.) Such limits apply 'in any proceedings in tort' by a plaintiff. Where there is more than one plaintiff, or where one plaintiff commences more than one set of proceedings, the union may be liable up to the limit in *each* case. The Secretary of State may vary the limits by Order. The limits apply to damages but *not* to costs (the bulk of the costs of a winning party is normally paid by the loser), nor to fines imposed for contempt of court in consequence of a failure or refusal to carry out an order of the court.

This device of monetary limits, therefore, taken over from the 1971 Act's provision for its registered unions, is scant protection in the face of the wide liabilities in tort at common law that now threaten a union and can rapidly reduce its funds. As we saw in the case of British Rail's claim for £200,000 in 1985, some employers who stay their hand during a dispute threaten to enforce their legal rights against unions who allegedly acted tortiously in authorizing a strike, to the extent of claiming heavy damages after it has ended (p. 90). It has also been affirmed in the *NGA* litigation that a court will award exemplary damages, on top of the plaintiff's loss, against a union if it is 'necessary to teach [it] that tort does not pay' (the union there having acted, the judge thought, in 'jubilant defiance' of the court order).[44]

A further limitation, or perhaps clarification, is introduced by the 1982 Act in s. 17. Awards of damages or costs (but *not* fines for contempt of court) are not recoverable against certain 'protected' funds. These comprise, first, property belonging to trustees otherwise than on trust for the union, or belonging to a member or an official 'otherwise than jointly or in common with the other members' (this introduces a difficulty concerning just what is 'union property': p. 721); second, the political fund, provided that the fund is, and was at the initiation of proceedings, prevented by the rules from being used to finance industrial action; and, third, any separate fund available only for 'provident benefits' (benefits for sickness or injury, superannuation, loss of tools by fire or theft, funeral expenses and provision for deceased members' children). None of these protected funds can sustain a union's day-to-day needs, for example in payment of officials' salaries or union running expenses.

Tort and vicarious liability

The question therefore becomes critical: *for whom* is the union now liable in tort? What happens if a shop steward organizes action by members that causes losses to an employer? Is the union liable 'vicariously'? We have seen that the Act of 1971 left aside this issue of vicarious liability to common law principles and that the judges had to apply concepts of 'express and implied authority' to test the liability of a union for unofficial action by shop stewards in such cases as *Heatons* v. *TGWU*[39] (p. 55). In judging 'implied' authority, the Law Lords insisted that the court would look not only at the rules but also at the union's policy and practices, including a shop steward's handbook. If the liability of the union is perceived as part of a strategy to avoid the personal 'martyrdom' of individual defendants, the question cannot be left so uncertain. The House of Lords, after all, followed up the liability of the TGWU in *Heatons* with a decision that it was *not* liable for London Airport shop stewards in the *General Aviation Services* case,[39] where the facts would seem not dissimilar to most observers of industrial relations, Lord Wilberforce saying that industrial relations and disputes are 'so complex and sometimes so opaque that it may be the exception when the ultimate result, reached with difficulty in one case, can be applied to another'. It is notable that the Law Lords rejected the argument that to escape liability in tort (as opposed to liability for *contempt* for not seeing that the court's order is carried out: p. 707) the union must withdraw the apparent authority of stewards. The question was whether stewards had a 'general implied authority' to act for the union and all its members.

It has been suggested that, because the House of Lords was deciding the *Heatons* case in relation to the 'unfair industrial practices' in the 1971 Act, the test in the common law of tort for establishing the 'authority' of stewards may even now not be finally settled.[45] But the judges are likely to follow the *Heatons* route at common law, especially as it was made clear that 'this question of authority is the only question before the House' and that no 'new development' of the law about principal and agent was involved, and tort liability was 'closely connected' with liability under the 1971 Act. For example, Scott J. applied the *Heatons* test as the basis of 'ordinary principles of vicarious liability' in *Thomas* v. *NUM (South Wales) Area*[46] when making that union liable for a common law tort in picketing organized by its lodges.

The Act of 1982 set out to construct a firmer and arguably a tighter net to avoid personal martyrdom and induce greater union discipline over members and 'officials' (a term legally defined to include both full-time officers and lay officials such as shop stewards and branch officials: TULRA s. 30). The effect is to make the union more available to an employer or third party in respect of both damages and injunctions (without removing any personal liability of an official or other individual: s. 15 (8)). The 1982 code on vicarious liability makes the union liable for the authorization or endorsement of action given by three types of 'responsible person',[47] namely:

(1) *Top officers and the NEC.* First come the President, General Secretary or the 'principal executive committee' of the union (NEC) whatever the rules say (s. 15 (3) (a), (c)). Here liability is absolute. Authorization by any of these makes the union liable. One problem is whether the liability arises if the top officer or committee is not acting properly either under the rules or under the law. Since the section defines

each of the 'top' positions as the person who 'holds the office' of President or General Secretary (or the nearest equivalent office) and the committee as the body 'exercising executive functions', it appears that the section means to make the union liable for those exercising *de facto* power, whatever the legal validity of their status (s. 15 (7)). And a failure to comply with the 1984 Act as regards the election of the NEC does not affect the 'validity' of its actions (TUA 1984 s. 1 (6)). But there must surely be some further limit. Suppose the 'committee' purports to authorize action at a meeting with two members present when its quorum is twenty. This should not, it is suggested, create liability in its union. Nor is it clear what meaning the words 'authorization' or 'endorsement' have in regard to, say, an NEC in relation to union rules. The example has been produced of union rules that give the executive committee exclusive power to control, or to authorize, strikes or to decide upon the ending of strikes.[48] In such a case, a nod and a wink, or even a failure to act, by the NEC might be held to constitute an *implied* authorization. Yet the section also gives the General Secretary or President power to make the union responsible, whatever the NEC says.

(2) *Persons empowered by rules*. The second group that makes the union vicariously liable comprises any person 'empowered by the rules' to authorize or endorse the kind of action in question (s. 15 (3) (b)). It may be argued that this is narrower than the *Heatons* test because, although it rests upon agency and authority in the common law sense, it is confined to the rules. But the word 'rules' is extended beyond the union's rule-book to include 'any other written provisions forming part of the contract' of membership (s. 15 (7)). It is true that a shop stewards' handbook might not normally be seen as part of the membership *contract*; but if that was an incident defining the authority of shop stewards which came up 'from the bottom', from all members, in *Heatons* (as the Law Lords insisted it was) the only legal mechanism that could bind them all in law to this arrangement is a contract, and the only contract that could do this is the union membership contract. This type of case, therefore, seems to cover the *Heatons* ground.

(3) *Full-time officers and repudiation*. The third group includes any other official employed by the union, or a committee to which he regularly reports, unless he is 'prevented' by the rules from authorizing or endorsing the kind of action in question (s. 15 (3) (d), (e), (4) (a)).

This appears, though it is not certain, to include cases of 'prevention' express and implied; e.g. where the rules allot exclusive authority to a body to call strikes, the NEC for example, which cannot be delegated to the official in question, he must be understood to be 'prevented' from acquiring that authority. There is a further escape route. Even if the official is not prevented from giving union authority under the rules, the union escapes if his act is *repudiated* by someone in category (1), provided that the repudiation is made in writing to him without delay, as soon as reasonably practicable after his act has come to their knowledge. The repudiation, though, is ineffective if after it any of those same persons in category (1) behave 'in a manner which is inconsistent' with it (s. 15 (4) (b), (5), (6)).

Thus under these convoluted provisions, if such an officer approves a strike and the rules do not prevent his having authority to do so, the union is not liable if, say, the President repudiates his action. But it becomes liable again if, say, the NEC then resolves that he is to be supported. It is by no means clear whether 'inconsistent behaviour' can include omission to act. Clearly such acts as paying strike pay or lending support to 'unofficial' strikers are sufficient. But what can a union do to assist in the resolution of a strike in which it has repudiated its employed official's endorsement? Again, must the union notify *only* the official (or committee) of the repudiation, as the section demands? Or should it go further and inform its members? Or management?

Such questions of responsibility lay beneath the surface in *Austin Rover Group Ltd* v. *AUEW (TASS)*[49] (the dispute we met in Chapter 1: p. 77), though that case went on from the issue of liability to that of contempt. The strike decision was made by the union side of a Joint Negotiating Committee (after a majority vote); management was notified of it by its co-ordinator on behalf of 'the trade union side'. The unions would carry out 'their traditional methods' of implementing it, he said. Of the thirty-six members from eight unions on the NJC, TASS had two representatives (one of whom seems to have been a full-time official – though this is not clear – who 'did not disassociate TASS' from the decision). An injunction was granted ordering TASS to 'withdraw and cancel any instruction, direction or decision' that members should strike, and to inform its members of that withdrawal. But TASS (which had not appeared in court to contest liability) took the view that it had never issued any such instruction and was 'not in any way bound' by the

JNC decision, though its members did participate in the strike. Austin Rover now sought the punishment of TASS for the contempt of court. Hodgson J. decided there had been a contempt, for TASS had not taken 'sufficiently vigorous steps to distance' itself from the strike. But it was not guilty of a serious contempt, so he imposed no penalty.

The strike was over; and it was not, of course, now possible for TASS to contest the company's initial assertion that the JNC unions were all represented by 'officials who were duly authorised' to take strike action. This question becomes more than ever important after 1984, when the Trade Union Act s. 10 has made it a condition of any 'immunity' under TULRA s. 13 in a trade dispute that a ballot of members must be held. Under that Act too, authorization or enforcement of industrial action by the union is measured by the code on 'responsible persons' in EA 1982 s. 15. No strike ballot was held at *Austin Rover*. To this we return below (p. 625).

Further, the special code in s. 15 does not apply to all actions in tort against trade unions. It is confined to the 'industrial torts', i.e. those based 'on a ground specified in' TULRA s. 13 (1) (p. 579) or an alleged conspiracy to commit such a tort. (Broadly, these are inducement of breach of contract, unlawful interference with performance of a contract, threatening to do either of these or threatening to break a contract or interfere with its performance – the torts involved in normal economic pressure in a trade dispute.) If, therefore, some *other* tort is relied upon by a plaintiff, the code of vicarious liability in s. 15 is displaced in favour of the common law test, i.e. the *Heatons* test of agency and authority (p. 54). But liability in tort does not in reality run in such watertight compartments. There may be a 'mixed' case. In the *NGA* case,[44] for instance, the union was made liable for a mixture of torts: conspiracy, inducing breach of contract, 'unlawful interference', intimidation (threatening to break contracts) *and* 'nuisance'. This last, we shall see, is a relatively frequent civil liability involved in picketing. Ironically, it was one of the grounds of liability (in the form of 'watching and besetting') in *Taff Vale* itself.

In such mixed cases it is arguable that the court should test the liability for 'industrial torts' by EA 1982 s. 15, and the common law torts (e.g. nuisance) by the common law test. It might be argued that there is an analogy in some of the cases in regard to assessment of damages. In 1984, for example, the Northern Ireland Court of Appeal faced damage done by a union partly through torts protected by the equivalent of the s. 13 immunity in a trade dispute and partly through other unprotected torts (i.e. nuisance and trespass). The court decided that the plaintiff's damages should be assessed separately under each heading.[50] But it does not seem to be the intention of the 1982 Act to split up the torts in this way for the purposes of vicarious liability. The Act appears to apply the code in s. 15 to liability as a whole whenever '*a* ground' – i.e. one of the grounds – relied upon in the proceedings included an 'industrial tort'. An authorization of the relevant strike action by the President of a union would then bring liability automatically. But suppose the plaintiff in a 'mixed' case fails to establish any liability *except* for the tort of nuisance (not an 'industrial tort' within TULRA s. 13); or suppose he withdraws all the grounds of complaint *except* nuisance in the middle of the hearing. The judge must, it appears, now jettison the s. 15 code and revert to the *Heatons* test, and ask, say, whether the President had express or implied authority under the union's rules, customs and practices to authorize the acts done (in some unions he certainly would not).

The problem will arise rarely but it will be particularly significant when a plaintiff's claim turns out to be based upon diverse torts and the agents of the union other than the top officials are claimed to have acted on behalf of it. There will obviously be a great overlap between the common law test (did they have 'authority', express or implied, to act for it?) and parts of the s. 15 code (were they 'empowered by the rules' to do so; or were they not 'prevented by the rules' from doing so, and not repudiated?). Take *Thomas* v. *NUM (South Wales Area)*, 1985,[46] where the picketing was held to involve the tort of 'unreasonable harassment' of the plaintiffs in their use of the highway, a rather novel tort akin to nuisance, which is not protected by TULRA s. 13. The national NUM was not liable since it had not organized this picketing at all. But the Area union was liable. Indeed, the judge thought that this was the 'real question', rather than any liability of the Area executive officials, another indication of the significance of union liability in tort. The lodges had organized the picketing, he found, and had been supported by the Area executive council in its 'policy'. The rules said little about the power of the lodges; but they were 'constituent parts' of the union. Their powers were 'sensibly enough left to practice and custom'. From all this he concluded that the lodges possessed implied authority to act 'on behalf of the Area Union' in approving and organizing the picketing (as part of its advancing the interests of its members).

This was the common law test, another case of implied authority. Would the answer have been the same if E A s. 15 had applied – that is, if liability had been for an 'industrial tort'? Interestingly, the plaintiff had in fact pleaded such a tort (interference with, and prevention of performance of, the working miners' employment contracts); but the judge held there had been no such tort committed. If there had been, the Area union might have been liable because the lodges were impliedly 'empowered' to authorize the picketing and act on its behalf. But s. 15 (3) (b) requires that they be 'empowered by the *rules*'. The judge did stray outside the rule-book (as *Heatons* allows) into the 'customs and practice' of the union to find the necessary authority, but those factors go beyond the extended definition of 'rules' in s. 15 (7). It is not likely, however, that the courts would see any great distinction between the two cases. The implied authority might still be discovered in such a case as inherent in the 'rules' (as defined in s. 15 (7)). Indeed, the facts of the *NUM (South Wales Area)* case illustrate the rather stricter properties of E A s. 15 compared with the common law test. The judge found that the President and the General Secretary were responsible for the picketing policy put into effect by the lodges. Had it been applicable, therefore, it seems that the 1982 Act would have made the Area union strictly liable for them, whatever the 'rules' said (s. 15 (3) (a), (c)).

A refusal to allow 'repudiation' as an easy method of avoiding liability was illustrated in *Express and Star Ltd* v. *NGA*, 1986,[51] where the union was fined £15,000 for contempt. An order had been made restraining it from inducing its members to take action in breach of employment contracts in a long-standing dispute about new systems of work that would 'virtually eliminate' composing-room jobs. The union duly notified members as required of a withdrawal of blacking instructions; but the judge found that a 'task force' of a full-time official and branch officials had encouraged further blacking 'by nods, winks, the turning of blind eyes and similar clandestine methods of approval which did not appear in the records'. Was the union responsible? It failed in its argument that this was all done at branch level and that each branch was a separate unit in a federal union. Moreover, the code of vicarious liability in E A 1982 s. 15 was used in these contempt proceedings

because this was a 'step in the same proceedings' as those in which
the writ was served (an argument that would exclude it in favour
of the *Heatons* test if the original tort was not an s. 13 industrial
tort).

The Court of Appeal agreed that the purported compliance by the
union was no more than a 'pantomime' conducted by the NEC and
regional officials designed to secure the opposite result. The union was
vicariously liable for them and stood in 'flagrant' contempt. But the
appeal judges refuse to apply s. 15 to contempt proceedings. They are
not proceedings in tort, so the code in s. 15 is not relevant. To this we
return (Chapter 8, p. 707). The union had argued that the General
Secretary had repudiated the actions of this full-time official; and he
would have repudiated another if he had known of his action. The union
was not responsible. The judge and the Court of Appeal rejected this
'disavowal'. It was, said the former, 'a conditional and half-hearted
reprimand', no more. To satisfy s. 15 (5) as a repudiation there must be a
'disowning of the acts of the official to all the members concerned',
as well as to 'the victims of the tort'. This went well beyond the requirement in s. 15 (5), which is to notify only the *official*, and appears
to rest upon a wider obligation imposed by the court in a contempt
case.

There is a further question. It relates to the 'joinder' of the union in a
case of unfair dismissal in an industrial tribunal, where a non-unionist
alleges that the union had induced his dismissal by taking, financing or
threatening industrial action (p. 381; EPCA s. 76A, introduced by EA
1982 s. 7). The 1982 Act says nothing at all about the principles of
vicarious liability in this situation. If an official calls a strike in protest
against the presence of a non-unionist at work who is then dismissed, the
union's liability to 'joinder' will presumably be judged, therefore, in the
tribunal and in appellate courts by the *Heatons* test. Yet if the union is
sued (even by the same plaintiff) for the same action as an 'industrial
tort', the code of s. 15 will apply. The three situations must be considered separately, even where the plaintiff is the same: (1) a High Court
action for a 'non-industrial tort', e.g. nuisance alone (common law test
in *Heatons* applies); (2) a High Court action involving an 'industrial tort'
(the special code in EA s. 15 applies and probably applies also to liability
as a whole in a 'mixed' case); (3) a tribunal action for unfair dismissal
with 'joinder' (probably the common law *Heatons* test applies).

The new provisions in EA 1982 s. 15 do not go in the direction in which Donovan pointed:

Trade union leaders do exercise discipline from time to time, but they cannot be industry's policemen. They are democratic leaders in organizations in which the seat of power has almost always been close to the members.

The members have no say, under EA s. 15, as to the 'authority' of the NEC or top officials (once elected) to bind the union, since the rules are ousted. The element in the code that looks to actions, or repudiations, by this top echelon – seen in the reality of a General Secretary besieged by television reporters with news of a decision by a full-time officer or shop steward, asked whether he will or can 'repudiate' the former or approve the latter and told that a writ is expected summoning the union to court in two days' time – divides the membership from a leadership of whom 'policing' functions are inevitably increasingly required.[52] Most important of all, the 1980s legislation cleared the way to the enforcement of common law liability in tort against the union and against its property. This, as we shall see, was the linchpin of its strategy.

Picketing

Quite frequently there are occasions when pickets are there in large numbers and all is peaceful and no great difficulties are caused. They are sometimes there for comradeship or solidarity. You must not assume that on every occasion there is a mass picket there is going to be trouble.

So said the Chief Constable of South Wales in 1980. His colleague for West Midlands added: 'the vast majority of picketing situations, even those involving quite large numbers of people, are carried out peacefully and often without the presence of the police'.[53] This evidence rebutted the common image of picketing, especially mass picketing, which conceives of it in terms of angry and even violent confrontations with police such as had been seen exceptionally at the Saltley Coke Depot miners' picket in 1972, at the Hadfield Steel Works in 1980 and at Grunwick's in 1977, when 18,000 workers came to support the workers' demand for union recognition. Even so, this is an area where the administration of the criminal law and the police assume a more important role, one that caused controversial concern in the violent episodes accompanying the miners' strike of 1984–5.[54]

The relationship between picketing and the law is a useful introduction to various issues in industrial conflict, both in criminal and in civil law. The right to picket peacefully in order to persuade other workers not to work or enter the workplace, and to inform people about the dispute, is an essential weapon on the workers' side in trade disputes. It was not won easily, nor is it clear how far the law permits it even today. A central limitation is still found in s. 7 of the Conspiracy and Protection of Property Act 1875, which codifies the crimes that had previously gone under such names as 'threats' and 'molestation'. This provides that a person commits a crime who, with a view to compelling any other person to do or abstain from doing anything lawful, 'wrongfully and without legal authority' does any of five things: (1) uses violence to or intimidates such other person, his wife or children, or injures his property; (2) persistently follows him; (3) hides his tools or property, or hinders their use; (4) 'watches or besets' any place where he is; or (5) follows him in the street with two or more others in a disorderly manner. A proviso in 1875 permitted 'attending' at or near a place (i.e. on the highway; the law has never allowed pickets to trespass) in order to communicate or obtain *information*.

Both the English and the Scottish courts appeared to interpret 'intimidation' not in the severe sense it assumed under the 1825 Act, but more moderately, as requiring threats that would arouse in 'a person of common sense . . . a natural alarm of personal violence or of violence to his family'.[55] More recently, in upholding convictions of the Shrewsbury building-site pickets in 1974, the Court of Appeal went wider and included all threats of 'force or violence', not necessarily personal violence.[56] (The flying pickets there were also convicted of the crime of unlawful assembly, a gathering to 'endanger the public peace'.) The section is still strictly applied. When Inland Revenue union officials followed non-strikers in Scotland who drove to deliver financial mail so as to ensure the flow of government funds during selective strikes by Civil Service unions in 1982, they were convicted of persistent following.[57] The language of this judgment creates serious legal risks for pickets who follow non-strikers.

Even stricter applications of the section were made at the turn of the century in a crop of decisions that issued against the fierce picketing of 'free labour' non-unionists introduced to break strikes (some of them mere thugs, like the Deptford 'Eye-Ball Buster Gang'; others escorted to work by cavalry and 'a file of military').[58] In an action heard twice, *Lyons* v. *Wilkins*, 1896 and 1899, the Court of Appeal rocked the unions back on their heels by appearing to declare peaceful picketing unlawful as a common law 'nuisance' and, its criminal equivalent, as 'watching and besetting'.[59] The judges held that the 'compulsion' in s. 7 need not be aimed at the same person as the person beset (a strange interpretation) and, more important, that the proviso on communicating or obtaining information did not exempt a case of 'peaceful *persuasion*' (as the 1859 Act had done, short of inducing breach of contract) because that went beyond information. The pickets here had indulged in persuasion not to work. This, said Lindley LJ, was unlawful watching and besetting:

such conduct seriously interferes with the ordinary comfort of human existence and ordinary enjoyment of the house beset and such conduct would support an action . . . for a nuisance at common law.

Persons commit the tort of nuisance if they use the highway in a way that unreasonably interferes with the plaintiff in the comfortable and convenient enjoyment of his land. Picketing may escape liability for nuisance if it takes place, it was said in 1975, 'without violence, obstruction, annoyance or molestation'.[60] The *Ward Lock* decision of 1906 established that the crimes in s. 7 relate only to actions already wrongful in the *civil* law (e.g. watching and besetting is the crime coterminous with the tort of nuisance).[61] The Scottish courts applied a rather stricter principle in *Galt* v. *Philp*, 1984,[62] to a sit-in, holding that 'besetting' can be committed inside as well as outside a building and that a civil wrong protected by a trade dispute 'immunity' in tort (such as interference with contracts within TULRA s. 13) may still be the basis of a criminal prosecution under s. 7 (in England the civil wrong would be trespass, which has no trade dispute immunity). Both lines of authority agree, however, that s. 7 does not here create any *new* civil wrong. There must be a tort before there is a crime.

The statutory right to picket

The judicial decisions also have to take account of Parliament's effort to provide a positive right to picket peacefully in trade disputes. The Trade

Disputes Act 1906 s. 2, responding to the retrograde decision in *Lyons* v. *Wilkins*, replaced the proviso to s. 7 of the 1875 Act with a new formula:

It shall be lawful in contemplation or furtherance of a trade dispute to attend at or near a place 'merely for the purpose of peacefully persuading or communicating information *or of peacefully persuading any person to work or abstain from working'*.

This formula, which was thought for many years to establish a right of peaceful picketing, was repeated (with the omission of places of residence) in 1974 by TULRA s. 15. It was repeated in substance even in the 1971 Act, s. 134, where 'it shall be lawful' was redrafted into: 'it shall not constitute a crime', or 'a tort', etc. In 1906 Dilke had proposed an amendment to add the words 'and such attendance shall not be held to be a nuisance', but this was lost by five votes.[63] The wisdom of his perception was proved by subsequent judicial insistence that the tort of 'nuisance' (and therefore 'watching and besetting' under s. 7) is not protected by the formula. This history is a very serious matter for labour law generally. The judiciary has refused to bow the head of the common law even in face of Parliament's stricture that it must give way to 'lawful' picketing. Dilke's amendment was lost partly because the Attorney-General declared that the existing clause would make peaceful picketing 'lawful for all purposes'. History proved him wrong. The right to picket has never protected trespass in the civil law of tort nor associated criminal liability, such as breach of by-laws for taking part in a demonstration in an aerodrome.[64] But if judges go on to say it does not protect any 'obstruction' or 'nuisance' it is scarcely a right to picket at all.

In *Tynan* v. *Balmer*, 1967,[65] the defendant led some forty pickets in a circle outside a factory. No serious obstruction was proved, but it was found as a fact that their object was to 'seal off the highway' so as to persuade drivers not to enter. He was convicted of the crime of obstructing a constable in the execution of his duty after refusing a request to move the pickets away. In analysing the position, Widgery J. held that he must 'leave aside' the statutory protection in trade disputes, and ask

whether the conduct of the pickets would have been a nuisance at common law as an unreasonable user of the highway . . . if one imagines these pickets as carrying banners advertising some patent medicine or advocating some political reform, it seems to me that their conduct in sealing off a part of the highway would have been an unreasonable use of the highway.

Common law nuisance prevailed over the statutory right. The Law Lords confirmed that approach in *Broome* v. *D P P*[66] in 1974. There a construction union official, in his efforts to persuade a driver not to enter picketed premises, stood in front of a lorry for a few minutes – no longer, the magistrates thought, than was necessary for peaceful persuasion. The House of Lords held he was guilty of the crime of obstruction of the highway. Lord Reid likened pickets to hitch-hikers:

One is familiar with persons at the side of the road signalling to a driver requesting him to stop. It is then for the driver to decide whether he will stop or not. That, in my view, a picket is entitled to do. If the driver stops, the picket can talk to him but only for so long as the driver is willing to listen.

The fact is that the motor car and the bus carrying squads of workers past lines of pickets have overtaken the 1906 formula on lawful picketing. Efforts at the time of the E P A 1975 to permit pickets to persuade persons 'whether in a vehicle or not', or even to permit a 'reasonable obstruction' to allow them to explain their case, came to naught (there were strong Home Office and police objections). The only method left to stop vehicles passing a picket line is to bar the way by a mass picket. Although Lord Salmon in *Broome* had said that proof would be needed even here that the purpose was 'prevention of entry' rather than 'peaceful persuasion', mass picketing can readily be seen to be a civil nuisance and criminal obstruction. Indeed, *Verrinder's* case, 1982,[67] showed that something far short of mass picketing can be held to be a tortious nuisance. Lorry-driver members of the T G W U, who saw their haulage contracting work decreasing and 'cowboy' operations undercutting established employers, secured the agreement of other T G W U workers at the docks to service only approved lorries. They picketed the docks, severely affecting the business at the terminals. The judge granted an interlocutory injunction against this 'nuisance' largely because they had attempted 'to compel the company' to ban the 'cowboys' and 'scalliwags' and 'to control the container traffic'. With that as the nub of liability the judgment echoes the 'molestation' doctrines of the last century.

Further statutory changes in the 1980 Act narrowed the picketing 'immunity' in trade disputes. The 1980 Employment Act redrafted TULRA s. 15 and limited the right to attend in trade disputes 'for the purpose only of peacefully obtaining or communicating information or peacefully persuading any person to work or abstain from working', to attendance at or near *the worker's own place of work*. In the case of an official of a union, he may attend only at or near the place of work of his member 'whom he is accompanying and whom he represents'. (The worker must be one of those he is appointed or elected to represent: substituted TULRA s. 15 (4)). If a worker normally works at more than one place or at a location that it is 'impracticable' to picket (an oil-rig, perhaps, or a shop in an arcade far from the highway) he may attend at or near the employer's premises from which he works or his work is administered (substituted s. 15 (2)). An unemployed worker has the right to picket only if his dismissal was connected with the trade dispute or one of the circumstances giving rise to it. If a worker's 'attendance' is outside these limits, any act done 'in the course of picketing' is deprived of immunity in tort under TULRA s. 13 (EA 1980 s. 16). These provisions have been said to introduce an 'imbalance . . . in that employers can transfer work' to another establishment where it 'becomes unlawful to picket. Employers can transfer work but unions cannot transfer pickets.'[68]

The new formulation has many uncertainties. For example, a 'place of work' is not always obvious, as the social security decisions on unemployment benefit show (the entire Ford Dagenham estate has there been regarded as one 'place of employment').[69] But contrary to those who argued that the statutory protection could apply to minor crimes – after all, it *did* begin, 'It shall be lawful'; and s. 134 of the 1971 Act *had* specified that picketing should not be either a tort or an 'offence'[70] – the Government insisted that the statutory provisions and their amendments affected only the civil law. (The civil law changes on picketing also relate to the removal of the 'immunities' in TULRA s. 13 in regard to *secondary action*, which we discuss below: p. 605).

This is of some importance by reason also of the Secretary of State's Code of Practice of which a court must take account on any relevant questions (EA 1980 s. 3 (8)). The code contrasts with the TUC's earlier, sober guidelines (reissued in substantially the same form in 1986) by treating a band of pickets as something to control rather than something to make effective within reasonable limits of peaceful persuasion. The 'picket organizer' described in it should apply for 'directions' from the police – not what a citizen normally has to do when pursuing a 'lawful' activity. He is presented as a mixture, in McCarthy's words, of 'a scoutmaster and a friendly regimental sergeant-major'.[71] Pickets should not cause 'distress, hardship or inconvenience to members of the public who are not involved in the dispute', and should ensure that all 'essential services' are maintained. The code's most famous provision tells unions to ensure that 'in general the number of pickets does not exceed six at any entrance to a workplace; frequently a smaller number will be appropriate'. After 1980 the police who previously had been concerned mainly with the 'mechanics of the law and the peaceful nature of picketing' came inevitably to be concerned with who was picketing, where and in what numbers,[72] and possibly (though they claimed to reject the role) in identifying pickets and their 'place of work'. The identification of pickets can be a difficulty in civil suits for injunctions, although the problem is now partly solved for a plaintiff by the availability of the union as a defendant.

Picketing away from the place of work in the miners' strike, entailing loss of 'immunity' under TULRA s. 13, gave rise to a number of, though not many, legal claims by third parties for injunctions, such as those by hauliers in Scotland and Durham and a coal-extraction firm in South Wales. The most important action legally was that brought by *Read (Transport) Ltd*, which secured interim injunctions, breaches of which later led to fines and then sequestration of the South Wales Area union's funds.[73] The NCB obtained injunctions against picketing in Yorkshire within a fortnight of the commencement of the strike, but then informed the court it would not press contempt applications for breaches as that would not be 'constructive'. *The Times* complained that other possible plaintiffs, such as the CEGB and BSC, had brought no proceedings. In the *Read (Transport)* case proof that the union was responsible for the picketing appears to have been based upon the reported claim by the President of the union that he could control the level of pickets when he offered to cut their numbers. The union's subsequent contempt liability was based upon breach of the injunctions by 'union officials'. The same firm obtained injunctions against the TGWU for the picketing of its lorries in the docks.

In 1985 the code on picketing was put to use by Scott J. in *Thomas's* case.[74] As we saw, working miners in South Wales sought injunctions to restrain the Area union organizing pickets at pit-heads where they worked, and a declaration that picketing at other pits and premises was unlawful and that expenditure on it was *ultra vires* (i.e. beyond the union's lawful powers). They had gone in to work in vehicles with police protection, past some fifty to seventy striking miners (six close to the gates), who hurled abuse at them. The judge held that watching or besetting under s. 7 of the 1875 Act was proved only *after* a civil tort was shown. The picketing here was not an 'assault' (there was no ability to reach the miners in the vehicles). Nor had the contracts of employment been disrupted (they got in to work). The 1980 amendments, though, had deprived the picketing of immunity under TULRA s. 13; many miners were not attending at their *own* pits, and the South Wales Area union was vicariously liable for their actions. The organizing of picketing that carried a *risk* of criminal offences being committed was not necessarily *ultra vires* for the union (a point to which we return in Chapter 9). But he considered that 'mass picketing' must, although 'secondary picketing' did not necessarily, constitute 'a nuisance and an offence under s. 7'. The *Ward Lock* case showed that picketing 'peacefully and responsibly conducted' need not be a nuisance at common law. In any case, it did not follow that an obstruction of the highway would be a tort 'actionable at the suit of the working miners' who had not suffered 'special damage'. Each plaintiff could sue only in respect of picketing at his own pit – an important point (p. 645).

This scrupulously careful analysis pointed towards judgment for the defendants, but it was not to be. The judge went on to find a tort in the 'unreasonable harassment' of them while exercising their right to use the highway. This might be seen as 'a species of private nuisance', but the 'label for the tort' did not matter. He therefore granted injunctions against picketing at the collieries where they worked, which after consulting the code (which could be relevant both to criminal offences and torts) he formulated so as to allow lawful pickets for peaceful persuasion 'in numbers not exceeding *six*'.

This judgment sets two landmarks in civil law. First, the tort for which the defendants were made liable had scarcely any place in the plaintiff's case (which 'shifted considerably in the course of the nine-day hearing' in the interlocutory proceedings and is demolished in the judgment point by point). It is a vague tort of 'unreasonable harassment', one not hitherto known. If pickets are to be advised what they can lawfully do, the 'labels' of the law *do* matter. 'Harassment' as a tort is in direct line of descent from the 'molestation' and 'coercion' of 1825, albeit that they were also crimes. Secondly, the code's chosen 'six pickets' were thrust into injunctions, without discriminating among the five collieries, as a magic formula, 'a guide to a sensible number'. The judge agreed: 'Any number chosen is necessarily arbitrary'; but he thought 'six or thereabouts' might help with the 'intimidatory' abuse and threats.

The fact is that in discovering a lawful picket so rarely – even in the civil law – the judges are doing little more than echoing the orthodox voice of authority. This has changed little since the last century, when Lindley LJ refused to believe lawful action could make a strike 'effective' (p. 17). Lord Bramwell encapsulated received wisdom when he said in Parliament in 1891: 'there is nothing unlawful in picketing, provided that it is lawfully practised, but that is what it never is'. In the early weeks of the miners' strike in 1984 the *Guardian* reported that 'most of the picketing has been peaceful and thus entirely legal'; but the gut feeling of the system remained with *The Times*: 'The point about picketing – any and every form of picketing – is that it is a form of intimidation.'[75] By this standard the judgment in the *Thomas* decision cannot count as illiberal. But its formulation of principle has, we shall see, ironically contributed to increasingly illiberal developments in the sphere of the criminal law. The only indisputably lawful pickets are those who attend near their own workplace in small numbers and who keep out of the way.

Further crimes for pickets

The criminal law disposes of many other weapons, in addition to s. 7 of the 1875 Act, not least the crime of obstructing a constable in the execution of his duty. If a constable has 'reasonable grounds' to anticipate a *breach of the peace* by pickets, their refusal to obey his lawful orders is a crime. So, when a picket, ordered to move away by a constable who had decided two pickets (instead of three) were enough at a factory gate, responded by saying, 'I know my rights', and 'pushed gently past' the policeman, he was 'gently arrested' and later convicted of obstructing him in the execution of his duty.[76] This ability to make a pre-emptive strike was much used by the police in the 1984 miners' strike, extending the range of the 'anticipation on reasonable grounds' geographically and chronologically. The police who, on threat of arrest, turned round Kent miners driving to the Midland coalfields at the Dartford Tunnel under the Thames, despite their protests that they intended to do no more than picket peacefully, achieved considerable notoriety. Nor would the High Court grant interlocutory injunctions against the police to stop them doing so. Earlier cases had suggested that police can arrest for this offence where they anticipate 'in the immediate future' a breach of the peace as 'a real, not a remote possibility'. But in *Moss* v. *McLachlan*, 1985, a police cordon stopped a convoy of striking miners at a motorway junction heading into Nottinghamshire, who then blocked the road with their cars and tried to push past the cordon. The police were held to have good grounds to stop the convoy and to arrest them because there was evidence from the 'words and deeds of the men' that a breach of the peace was intended; the risk of a breach of the peace was sufficiently 'imminent, immediate and not remote'. The court went on to say they were entitled to take account of what they had seen in newspapers and on television in judging who should be turned back and where.[77]

The discretion that this gives to the police is very wide and somewhat alarming. Also, the police used nationally in the miners' strike were trained (for the first time on this scale) in riot equipment and methods. The figures from the Government soon after the strike showed that 11,312 charges were brought during the strike; 646 were for riot and unlawful assembly; 275 charges were brought under s. 7 of the 1875 Act (mainly 'watching or besetting'); 4,107 for conduct 'likely to cause a breach of the peace' (Public Order Act 1936 s. 5); 1,682 for obstructing a police constable and 640 for obstructing the highway. Fewer than 10 per cent of the miners prosecuted were charged with offences involving violence, however; and of the 5,653 cases tried by March 1985 some 27 per cent ended in acquittal. Many 'watching and besetting' charges failed.

Whether history will approve the administration of British justice in this testing period is still an open question. Certainly some magistrates were thought to use their power to fix conditions on bail and to 'bind over' in unaccustomed ways; one miner was compelled to move to the North of Scotland; others were prevented from visiting NCB premises even when they could not easily reach their homes without doing so. The condition of 'no picketing other than at your own place of work' was regularly used, as with Yorkshire miners after their arrest in August 1984 charged with the serious crime of unlawful assembly (in February 1985 these charges, like many others, were dropped). The even more serious charge of riot, for which life imprisonment could be imposed,

was entered against some miners, especially after fierce clashes at the
Orgreave pit in June 1984 involving 8,000 assembled police and
thousands of miners from many areas in scenes 'without parallel in an
industrial dispute this century . . . a gift to the government's campaign
against the miners' picket line violence'.[78] A year later the prosecution
evidence collapsed – 'slipshod work', the judge called the police evidence. Fifty-nine charges of unlawful assembly and more than ninety of
riot eventually collapsed either by acquittal or through withdrawal by
the prosecution. The defence claimed many charges had been devices to
assist in breaking the strike. By 1986 the evidence was strong that
Orgreave had in reality seen a fierce pre-emptive strike by the police.
The practices of the police and of the magistrates on the ground
probably had the greatest legal effect on the day-to-day conduct of the
dispute, or at any rate on its perception by the public.

The first case of this sort to reach the High Court was an illustration.
The Mansfield justices imposed a condition on miners charged with
obstruction or breach of the peace forbidding them to picket or demonstrate, other than 'peacefully' at their 'usual place of employment' (a
clear reference to the 1982 changes in TULRA s. 15, which had been
asserted to apply only to the civil law). The judges held that magistrates
could have regard to the 'matrix of events' in their local community.
Defendant miners felt that little account was taken of their individual
cases in what seemed like 'group justice' at the time. The magistrates
acceded to police submissions on bail conditions in some 90 per cent of
the cases. Indeed, the Mansfield justices' clerk – in the 'supermarket
justice', as Wallington puts it, of that court – affixed standard conditions
to bail forms even *before* individual applications for bail were heard, a
practice doing the bench no credit, said Lord Lane LCJ, though the
clerk's correct anticipation of the conditions imposed by the bench did
not vitiate its decisions.[79]

Picketing and public order

The refusal of the courts to allow the statutory 'right' to picket peacefully ('It shall be lawful . . .') to displace certain crimes (such as obstruction
of the highway) and civil liabilities (such as nuisance) has always meant
that, in reality, picketing has taken place largely at the discretion of the
police. Although both police and government reject any relationship

between the police and the enforcement of the civil law – the Green Paper of 1981 insisted that it must not 'seem that the services of the police were being enlisted on behalf of the employer. . . . Abandoning the principle of the neutrality of the police could have serious implications' – there does appear recently to have been a gradual convergence in this area of the civil and the criminal law. The use of the code's suggestion on 'limitation of numbers', including the magic formula 'no more than six', and the limitation to the workplace in bail conditions are perhaps the most obvious examples.

Experience in the miners' strike illustrates the fragile line that now divides the law of 'picketing' from 'public order' laws, if indeed it has not been erased. Police methods in that strike tended to contribute to an escalation of violence in a form not present in many earlier disputes. It has always been clear that pickets, like anyone else, are liable for crimes of violence and disorder, whether they be riot, violent disorder, assault, breach of the peace or even obstruction. It could not be otherwise. But if the law is administered so as to make criminal even the smallest obstruction and to use serious charges that are later unsubstantiated to take workers off the picket line, the reaction of workers may be to lose confidence in having any right at all to 'persuade' anyone peacefully, and the public may be led to draw the conclusion from the ensuing confrontation that picketing equals violence.

This trend was accentuated in the White Paper on *Public Order Crimes* of 1985.[80] New offences (including conduct intended or likely to cause fear of, or provoke, unlawful violence and 'disorderly conduct') were proposed to replace some existing offences (unlawful assembly, for example), with new powers to control marches, processions and 'static demonstrations'. Picketing peacefully to persuade was distinguished from picketing 'to intimidate or obstruct'; but 'intimidation' was to become an arrestable offence. The White Paper also envisaged that new police powers would apply to pickets (whether they were at their own place of work or not). The police would acquire power to impose conditions on 'static demonstrations' if they reasonably apprehend 'coercion of individuals', disorder or serious disruption; and failure to comply with such conditions was to be a crime. The (civil) *Thomas* judgment[74] was cited for the view (in the *criminal* law) that 'coercion' is a wide liability, precisely the hostage to fortune offered by the judge's doctrine of 'unreasonable harassment'. Even under the punitive Trade

Disputes and Trade Union Act 1927 it had to be shown that pickets had caused 'reasonable apprehension' of 'injury' to a person's business, occupation or employment before they were guilty of 'intimidation' (s. 3 (1), (2)): repealed in 1946). Crimes based on 'coercion', left at large and unrelated to any act threatened or done that is unlawful *in itself*, find their true pedigree in Erle's 'essence' of the 'molestation' crimes in 1825, namely 'the intention to coerce the will of another' or, as Bramwell B. put it in 1867, to 'coerce that liberty of mind and thought by compulsion and restraint'.[81] Under these recommendations public order law would reassume its place in the ordering of the labour market, with grave dangers to civil liberty.

The Public Order Bill 1986 largely followed the lines of the White Paper. Under it, conditions can be imposed by the police on processions or 'public assemblies' to prevent disorder, disruption or 'intimidation'. Crimes such as riot, violent disorder and affray are redefined, but to them are added threatening or insulting words or behaviour likely to cause fear of violence or to harass or 'distress' another person. This crime requires an 'intention' or 'awareness' of the effect; but a constable can arrest if he 'reasonably suspects' someone of committing it; and 'violence' includes 'violent conduct towards property' as well as towards persons. What is more, a constable is to have power to arrest anyone suspected of committing offences under s. 7 of the 1875 Act (such as 'watching or besetting'). Apart from their merits for public order generally, these proposals do not address the industrial relations problems as such. If the distinction between (licit) 'peaceful' picketing and (illicit) picketing 'to obstruct' or 'to coerce' is to be anything more than a genuflection to convention, licit picketing must be released from the overpowering grip of crimes of obstruction and the tort of nuisance. A concentration on 'intimidation' or 'coercion' by strikers of non-strikers, where no act in itself unlawful is done, is pregnant with dangers. In a hot-tempered dispute, it is unlikely that pickets attempting to make a case to strike-breakers in buses will avoid everything that magistrates can later see as reasonable evidence on which a constable suspected the 'scabs' might be distressed.

In real life, 'peaceful persuasion' is no longer a right but a risk. Whilst the objections to enabling pickets to stop or delay persons travelling on the highway are obvious, picketing in the age of the car and the bus must, if it is to have any reality, allow for an opportunity of some kind to put the pickets' case to those entering the premises. It would not be unreasonable to require the employer whose premises are lawfully picketed to play some role in this as his contribution to maintaining a peaceful ambience to what is his dispute as well as that of the strikers. We managed for decades on the old legal formulas largely because police discretion was used wisely in the great majority of cases by local police forces who knew their own area. That era may have passed. Violence cannot be accepted by the law; but the reintroduction of an industrial dimension to the debate refutes the proposition that the problem of picketing is only, or even primarily, one of public order.

If workers are to have a right to picket peacefully and meaningfully, a peaceful picket line must be understood to be *not* just another 'static demonstration'. It is an assembly of working people demonstrating in 'comradeship or solidarity', as the chief constable said, to put their case, often their only opportunity to engage the attention of a wider audience. Authority, however, has understood this point. Attention in the modern media is more readily gripped by a screen full of scenes of violence or disorder in which the industrial problem is often buried. The wider the ambit of criminal liability and the more vague its language on crimes of 'coercion', the easier it is to present of a picket of any size as disruptive or 'intimidatory'. In such a situation wider civil liberties are at stake – and at risk – from the clamp fixed upon the industrial right of peaceful picketing.

Trade disputes

For the protection of those acting in industrial conflict from industrial torts in civil law, the 'immunities' mainly rested, and rest, upon the golden formula: 'acts done in contemplation or furtherance of a trade dispute'. Everything turns, therefore, upon the meaning of this formula. The definition of it, however, is an expression of policy, not a philosophical exercise. For it has never been easy to divide the industrial neatly from the social, the economic from the political dispute. It was said in 1954 that this concept

rests on a theory of society and of politics which, even in 1906, was open to grave doubt and which today is plainly untenable . . . it is hardly possible to think of any major labour dispute in which the government is not somehow involved . . . it may be possible to carry on with the present law for many years to come but . . . its foundations are shaky.[82]

On the other hand, the problem is not solved by trying to define what is lawful industrial action, in Viscount Radcliffe's words, 'by its substance'.[83] This sounds sensible; but the very nature of what this 'substance' *is* often is the subject of conflict and controversy. The meanings move in response above all to the shifts of power between classes in society, both as they are and as they are perceived.

Take a recent example. Merchant seamen have for many years been treated in the Dreadnought Seamen's Hospital at Greenwich. In 1984 it was threatened with closure as the result of central government policies. Amongst other actions, some seamen withdrew labour in protest. Was this, or should it be, a 'trade dispute'? There is not much point in appealing to 'substance' in framing the answer, for this will depend on values and choices. The seamen felt deeply about it. Should the law penalize them for their stoppage? Or penalize their employer if he punishes them for it? Under the traditional British test, set out in 1906, those stoppages might possibly have been effected in furtherance of a trade dispute. In 1985 they would clearly fall on the other side of the line.

Whatever the strict logic of the matter, all systems of labour law in an industrialized democracy need some fixed point of reference by which to divide the lawful from the unlawful industrial dispute, somewhere along the spectrum that runs from the obviously 'political' (the electoral process, for example) to the obviously 'economic' (a dispute over a wage claim), as we see again in Chapter 10. The philosophical foundations of such a line may be 'shaky', but the need to draw it is inescapable. In Britain, for good or ill, this function has largely been fulfilled by the concept of acts done in contemplation or furtherance of a 'trade dispute'.[84]

The first definition of the 'trade dispute' formula in 1906 (T D A s. 5) was in essence repeated in revised form by T U L R A 1974 s. 29. It is made up of four parts: (1) the dispute; (2) the parties; (3) the content; (4) the 'furtherance or contemplation'. The second and third of these were severely amended in 1982 in a restrictive manner.[85] Let us look at the four constituent parts of this golden formula.

(1) *A dispute* between the parties is essential: an existing dispute for 'furtherance', an imminent dispute for 'contemplation' (see (4) below). The courts have found a dispute to exist when an employer and union

were 'sparring for an opening'; and a claim for union recognition that is rejected can be a dispute. But we shall see later that sometimes the judges refuse to recognize the existence of a dispute if a union refrains from going through the motions of making a demand (as in the *Stratford* case: p. 565).

(2) *The parties.* The position in 1974 was as follows: the parties to the dispute could be 'employers and workers' (or a trade union on behalf of workers: s. 29 (4)) or 'workers and workers' (s. 29 (1)). A dispute between two employers has never been sufficient. Because 'worker' meant '*any* worker', even if not employed by the employer in dispute (s. 29 (6)), a trade dispute could exist between an employer wishing to do business with someone and the union organizing the employees of that person. Thus British law recognized the legitimacy of workers taking action against an employer other than their own, either in their own interests or in solidarity with that other employer's workers. NALGO employees of a health authority engaged in a trade dispute when they objected to the authority introducing a private computer firm to do work in its management branch.[86]

Where some workers say they are 'content' with their conditions, a claim by a union on behalf of other workers in the industry that the employer should raise their rates to a reasonable minimum may appear in court as a dispute both between union and employer and between workers and workers (as in the case of apparently compliant seamen employed on bad conditions in a 'flag-of-convenience' ship).[87] A union or employers' association could be a party to a dispute on behalf of its members (s. 29 (4)). The terms 'worker' and 'employment' include a person who performs 'services' (other than for a professional client) and government employment (other than the armed forces or police): ss. 29 (6), 30.

The courts have on occasion gone behind the 'corporate veil' of a company or the other legal forms in which business is carried on to find the real 'parties' in a dispute (for example, where an enterprise is transferred to a company from a partnership with the same controllers).[88] But this is not an exercise on which a union can place reliance; for, as we shall see when we come to 'secondary action' in Chapter 8, judges normally stick to the legal forms in industrial disputes.

In 1982 three major changes were made (EA 1982 s. 18). First, s. 29 (4) was repealed; a union can no longer automatically be a party.

But it seems that it still represents its member workers if the court is persuaded that it is their agent. As Lord Wright said in 1943: 'It would be strangely out of date to hold, as was argued, that a trade union cannot act on behalf of its members in a trade dispute.' The effect of the repeal of s. 29 (4) is to require the union to prove that agency more strictly.

Secondly, disputes between workers and workers were excluded. This did far more than cut out 'demarcation disputes' (or 'who does what?') among workers, a type of dispute that is much less common now than in the 1960s. Even in such disputes the employer, as Donovan pointed out, is rarely 'neutral'. But the courts have a habit of analysing other disputes in this way, such as disputes over the presence at the workplace of non-unionists or members of splinter unions, as in *White's* case;[89] though where the employer faces such a demand from the union workers it is more logical to regard him as a party to the dispute.[90] A rather different argument was sometimes heard, namely that there is no dispute with the employer if he gives in. Buckley L J declared in 1973:

If someone threatens me with physical injury unless I hand over my wallet and I hand it over without demur, no one could . . . sensibly say that there had been any dispute about my handing over the wallet.[91]

This particular erroneous analysis is reversed by TULRA s. 29 (5), which is still law. At the time of the threat a dispute would have arisen if he had resisted. The Act makes it clear that such an act is done 'in contemplation' of a dispute. But we may expect the courts to analyse disputes 'where union men have refused to work with a non-union man', as Lord Denning put it, as not now included in the new definition because they are seen as essentially disputes between workers and workers.

The third change arises from the definition of 'worker' and the ambit of a trade dispute. The 1982 Act demands that the dispute must be between 'workers and *their* employer'. Also, a 'worker' is newly defined as 'a worker employed by *that* employer', or a person unemployed whose dismissal was connected with the dispute or one of the circumstances giving rise to it (E A 1982 s. 18 (2), (6) amending TULRA s. 29 (1), (6)). Parallel amendments to s. 29 (2) secure a similar result in government employment. The restriction of workers to disputes with *their own employer* about their *own* employment finds its direct precedent in 1825 (p. 516). This is one of the most important changes made by the 1982 Act. Under the previous definition, workers who saw their jobs threatened by the practices of another employer could take action against him and still fall within the trade dispute formula. But they would now, after the 1982 s. 18, be in dispute with an employer *not* their own and therefore have no trade dispute. The change was a body-blow to the International Transport Workers' Federation (ITWF), which tries to secure civilized conditions for crews of flag-of-convenience ships. The crew members are usually terrified of acknowledging the help of the ITWF; and, unless it can secure the authority of one of them (in many cases the authority is withdrawn after the owners come to hear of it), the ITWF is left acting on behalf of workers (other seamen) who are not employed by the owners and therefore outside the pale of the newly restricted 'trade dispute'.

Thus restricting the range of 'trade dispute' accords with the general policy, noted in Chapter 1, of restricting workers' industrial action *within their own unit of employment*. Sympathy strikes or solidarity action, whereby a strong group of workers comes to the aid of a weaker group, is struck at by this provision. It is true that, once there is a trade dispute, even under the new definition other workers employed elsewhere may act in 'furtherance' of it (EA 1982 s. 18 (7)), but then they will normally be indulging in 'secondary action' – action not against their *own* employer – and lose the immunity of TULRA s. 13 for that reason, as we see later (p. 597). In such cases identification of the 'parties' to the dispute is now doubly important, as we see when we deal with employers' associations (p. 568).

(3) *The content.* Under the Acts of 1906 and 1974 the dispute had to be *connected with* one or more of the 'employment matters' (as we shall call them) set out in TULRA s. 29 (1) (a)–(g). These may be summarized as: (a) terms and conditions of work, and physical working conditions; (b) engagement, non-engagement, dismissal or suspension; (c) allocation of work or duties; (d) matters of discipline; (e) union membership or non-membership; (f) facilities for union officials; and (g) machinery for negotiation or consultation and procedures on these matters, including recognition. Moreover, after the 1976 amendments, matters to which a dispute related could occur outside Great Britain. This general formula provided liberty of action by workers in a withdrawal of labour and militated to some extent against interventions by judges into the merits of industrial disputes – although, as we shall see, it

was not as wide as its detractors claimed in the 1970s. So long as the dispute was *connected with* the required content, even the addition of 'malice' or spite made no difference, as when an official in 1912 who hated the bandmaster brought out the band on strike for higher wages. But it was otherwise if the spite ousted the employment content, as when in 1909 a deceitful union official threatened a strike (which he had no power to call) to 'punish' a non-union worker in respect of an eight-year-old fine. That was a personal grudge, as was the hounding by union officials of a member who had refused to join a one-day strike; he stalked out of a union meeting calling the committee 'a shower', which the judge relied upon as 'a tolerably accurate' though 'no doubt much condensed' account. Thereupon officials treated him as expelled contrary to their NEC's wishes and in pursuit of 'their own ruffled dignity' stopped him finding work over a very wide area (*Huntley* v. *Thornton*, 1957).[92]

So, when the ITWF blacked a flag-of-convenience ship in which the Hong Kong crew enjoyed miserable conditions, the Law Lords in *NWL Ltd* v. *Woods*, 1979,[93] accepted that this action was *connected with* the employment conditions of the crew, even if the action was part of a general ITWF campaign against flags of convenience. Demands about conditions of employment were 'connected with' a dispute even if a wider, predominant object existed, even one 'to bring down the fabric of the present economic system by raising wages to unrealistic levels', said Lord Diplock (thereby adding fuel to the fire of the new Government's plans to revise the allegedly dangerous immunities). This example, however, was legally ambiguous. Lord Scarman put it better when he said that the connection might be broken if a personal or 'political' motive excluded the employment connection to the point of its being 'a sham' or a 'pretext'.

In *BBC* v. *Hearn*, 1977,[94] the Court of Appeal had taken that view. To support the campaign against apartheid and the union policies against racialism, union officials told the BBC that their members would take whatever industrial action was necessary to prevent the transmission of the Cup Final for television broadcasts via satellite to South Africa. Pain J. held that in effect this was a demand for new employment conditions (to work on terms that included no South African transmission) and therefore a trade dispute. But the Court of Appeal disagreed. Although 'conditions' had a very wide meaning, the dispute had not 'reached that stage'. It was a threat unconnected with their conditions of employment and not therefore a trade dispute. This left open the question: suppose it does reach a 'stage' where the union is saying, 'Unless you revise our members' employment terms to exclude that unwanted work, they will strike'? Can the union thereby draft its members back into a trade dispute? What is the difference between this and the demand, for example: 'Unless you revise the terms on wage rates (or: on Saturday working; or: on working in Wales) they will strike'? Those surely are trade disputes. In 1968 Davies L J had similarly construed a notice that workers would not work with non-unionists after a certain date as an 'offer to continue [to work] on different terms' (p. 192). This question whether the union demand or the strike notice can by its drafting determine the status of the dispute has acquired new importance in the law of industrial conflict today.

In judgments of the Law Lords, a *frisson* of concern is detectable about this logical argument. In 1983 Lord Cross said in *Universe Tankships Inc. of Monrovia* v. *I T W F*:[95]

A trade union cannot turn a dispute which in reality has no connection with terms and conditions of employment into a dispute connected with terms and conditions of employment by insisting that the employer inserts appropriate terms into the contracts of employment.

There the I T W F demanded from flag-of-convenience shipowners better conditions and back-wages for the crew and (as had become usual) a contribution to the Seafarers' International Welfare Fund, which helps seafarers throughout the world. A majority of three Law Lords decided that the demand for the contribution was not 'connected with' the employment conditions of this crew or of 'anyone at all'. It was parallel to an extraneous demand for, say, a payment to a 'political party' or a revolutionary 'guerrilla group' (an attitude that Lord Scarman, in the minority, found 'unjust to the point of cynicism'). But the majority insisted it had no connection with the listed employment matters. The fact that it was put in a collective agreement was not enough, said Lord Russell, to transmute an obligation that 'lacks the legal characteristic of a term and condition of employment'.

The *Universe* decision showed how fragile even the old test was (Lord Diplock took 'the blame' if his *N W L* judgment had misled anyone). A trade dispute has never comprised action that furthers something essentially and recognizably 'political' (although, as Roskill LJ warned in 1973, this is a dangerously ambiguous word). The 'political' element was clear in a one-day strike in 1971 against the Industrial Relations Bill and in a union stoppage in support of a TUC 'day of action' against the Employment Bill in 1980. Neither was in furtherance of a trade dispute even then. But beyond that, the occasions on which the judges might wish to find that the 'connection' with employment matters has been broken by 'non-industrial' policy objectives were always uncertain.

In the *Hadmor Productions* case, 1983,[96] a television union, the ACTT, 'blacked' films made by the plaintiff company from being transmitted on ITV because it and its members feared that redundancies would be caused by the introduction of programmes made by such 'facility companies'. This was a case of refusal to do particular work. The Law Lords held that the evidence was 'overwhelming' that the dispute was connected with employment matters, even though the ACTT had a general policy of non-co-operation with such companies. The Court of Appeal was wrong to equate this to *Hearn's* case and hold that the union's motives were not 'fear, rational or irrational, of future redundancies', but 'political only'. These were the years when the Court of Appeal began to interpret 'trade dispute' in a fashion more narrow than had ever been seen before. Just before the ban on 'secondary action' became law, it held in *Duport Steels*, 1980,[97] that the steel unions were unprotected by the golden formula. In a pay dispute with the nationalized BSC they had extended their strike action into the private sector steel companies, partly to put pressure on the Government to make more money available. The Court of Appeal said it had become a dispute (or become a second dispute) between the unions and the Government. But the House of Lords rejected this analysis (indeed, counsel for the companies conceded he could not even defend it). The dispute was still connected with, and still furthered, the wage claims, even if one of its purposes was to 'coerce the Government', said Lord Diplock. This extended action ('so injurious to the nation') was protected by the ('intrinsically repugnant') immunities, he said, though he added that the strike ('contrary to the general law') caused in his view 'untold harm to industrial enterprises unconcerned with this particular dispute and to the nation itself'. 'The general law', it will be observed once again, is the common law. Even though Lord Diplock was there forced to accept the trade dispute, the strike, though granted 'immunity', still suffered the moral indignation of the ancient common law.

The 1982 amendments on content

The British courts have not been alone in confronting the task of dividing the 'political' from the 'economic'. Australian unions, for example, raised the issue in a rather different form when they withheld members' labour from building projects on environmental grounds ('green bans'), challenging town planning decisions – 'the exercise of authority of a governmental character', as one judge put it, for 'socio-political objectives'. So too, the same legal system has experienced difficulty in defining for constitutional and for labour law purposes an 'industrial' dispute or matter.[98] Comparative inspection of this problem reveals its centrality to the development of a labour law system in a plural democracy.

This is what made the 1982 amendments in Britain so important. The 1982 Act, s. 18, struck out the words 'connected with' and required that a 'trade dispute' must now be a dispute that *relates wholly or mainly* to one or more of the listed employment matters (TULRA s. 29 (1), as amended). The policy of this change, so concise in compass yet so critical in consequence, is to confine unions to 'economic' matters in the market-place in a very strict sense, and to exclude 'socio-political objectives', except in a subsidiary role. So, in the *Mercury* decision[99] (which we met in Chapter 1, p. 73) the new statutory definition was shown to have very restrictive effects. The union campaign and its members' refusal to connect Mercury gave rise to a dispute that the Court of Appeal decided was not 'wholly or mainly about fear of job losses' (Dillon LJ). It did not have the 'predominant purpose' of preventing them (May LJ). It was mainly 'about' (as the judges saw it) the Government's liberalization and privatization programmes for British Telecommunications, a 'political and ideological campaign' in which 'jobs' was only one issue. May LJ saw the industrial action as 'the thin end of the wedge' of a broader campaign against privatization. Such an approach can now be used to exclude a range of disputes that in the past have qualified for legality. We might take, for example, the seamen's strike of 1966, which a vexed Prime Minister Wilson attacked as a 'strike against the State' organized by a 'tightly knit group of politically motivated men'; or the strikes at London Airport in 1969 against 'creeping denationalization', when a private foreign firm was awarded servicing contracts. Similarly, in 1984 widespread industrial action opposed the privatization of hospital services (at Barking Hospital picketing by NUPE workers went on for more than a year).

In 1985 further Government privatization plans, of gas for example, were threatened with strike action (by NALGO and GMBAT). The legal status of such action must be highly uncertain when judges have a free hand now to ask broadly, 'What is it *mainly* about?' Labour law changes here dovetailed into overall Government policy. Society was to be privatized and deregulated. The legitimacy of workers' opposition was to be reduced. Their protest, as the process accelerated, would increasingly be perceived in the court room as 'mainly' a protest against the whole policy within which they feared for their jobs – as, in a sense, it was bound to become. Meanwhile, the new definition affects all types of cases. Take the 1984 decision in *Crazy Prices*,[100] where the Court of Appeal in Northern Ireland decided (under the equivalent of the old 1974 law) that an imminent dispute about the price of bread that was sold in the plaintiffs' shops and that union members delivered (the union insisting upon the maintenance of bread prices as part of its policy of maintaining members' employment prospects, which were threatened by undercutting from Britain) was connected with the workers' employment. 'The relevant phrase "connected with" . . . is wider than "about" or "concerning",' said Lord Lowry CJ.

In Britain today it seems unlikely that such workers or their union could satisfy the 1982 test by reformulating their demands in terms of employment 'conditions'. Suppose they said, 'We demand that our employment terms be altered so as to exclude any obligation to deliver imported cut-price bread'? We have seen (p. 559) that there are strong indications that judges may reject this ploy, whatever its logic. In 1984, for example, journalists refused to provide copy to the employer, *Dimbleby*, because they objected to the non-union enterprise to which he began to send the newspaper for printing. They were suspended and dismissed (in itself before 1982 a likely connection; but not now). Lord Diplock, in a breathtaking passage, declared that this was not a dispute 'as to the terms and conditions of their employment':

There was . . . no vestige of any claim by the NUJ itself or by the NUJ journalists that their current contracts of employment by Dimbleby – and it is only their *current* contracts that can be relevant to this case – contained a term entitling them to refuse to comply with instructions given to them by Dimbleby to provide copy.[101]

For him it passed 'beyond the bounds of credibility' that a newspaper owner would agree to such a term. On the evidence, the journalists acknowledged they were breaking their contracts. But what if the evidence had shown that they had claimed *new* terms of employment? It cannot be right to say the court will look only at their *current* terms, for that would, as Simpson says, exclude 'a dispute over a pay claim'. Obviously the employer had not agreed to such a term; this was why there was a dispute. This is usually why disputes arise. Lord Diplock's hyperbole, though, shows the way the judicial wind blows.

The judge at first instance had found there *was* a trade dispute in *Dimbleby* concerning employment terms; but in the Court of Appeal, Donaldson M R said this was 'clearly wrong'; there was no 'suggestion that their terms and conditions of employment should be altered'. 'Had there been any such suggestion' the court would anyway apply Lord Cross's test in *Universe Tankships*: a trade union cannot turn a dispute into a trade dispute by insisting on new terms. This was a pronouncement, to which several other Law Lords have given their agreement, of profound importance to the future development of the law. It was clearly his concern about this problem that led Lord Diplock to his extravagant answer about *current* contracts. It looks as if the judges are moving towards a position where the reality of what a dispute is mainly 'about' under the 1982 law is largely in their power to determine, no matter *how* the union or the workers formulate their claim to the employer. By insisting that a union cannot 'turn a dispute into a trade dispute' by a formulation of the workers' demands as demands for new employment conditions, the Law Lords are treading a highly dangerous and illiberal path, one that goes in the same direction as, but beyond, the 1982 Act. For this approach would enable them to exclude any demands made by a union relating to workers' employment terms as not being part of the 'reality' of the dispute, merely an attempt to turn what *they* saw as the real issue into a contest that satisfied the statute. This is something more than evaluating the evidence, which any court must do. It is the creation of a device by which the court can get out of the evidence, whenever it wishes, a mechanism made more available by the strict wording of the 1982 formula.

Next, the 1982 Act's redefinition of 'workers', confining them to workers employed by the employer in dispute, applies both to the parties to the dispute and to the 'workers' mentioned in the list of employment matters. The terms or physical conditions under which 'any workers are required to work' now refer only to them. Similarly, Lord Diplock held in the *Dimbleby* case that 'the allocation of work or the duties of employment between workers or groups of workers' in s. 29 (1) (c) now means allocation among workers employed by their *own* employer who is party to the trade dispute and no one else. It could not now mean, as it might before, the allocation of the work of printing Dimbleby's newspapers to non-union printers employed by another firm. The courts are likely to attach a similar meaning throughout the list of employment matters even where the word 'worker' does not expressly appear (e.g on facilities for union officials, or 'matters of discipline': s. 29 (1) (d), (f)).

The 1982 Act also changed the ambit of matters arising abroad by reintroducing a proviso that was forced upon the minority Government in 1974 but later expunged in 1976. A trade dispute can relate to matters occurring abroad now only so long as the *persons* whose actions are said to be in contemplation or furtherance of the trade dispute are likely to be affected themselves, in respect of an employment matter within the normal list, by the outcome of that dispute (TULRA s. 29 (3)). This presumably refers to the workers in the trade dispute, although technically it refers to the organizers of their strike, since they are the persons whose actions are in furtherance of the dispute. It is not clear how directly or to what extent they must be 'affected', but the proviso is clearly another limitation upon industrial action taken in Britain in solidarity or sympathy with workers in another country, who perhaps are employed by a company there that is part of a multinational group of companies, or by a transnational enterprise that controls the workers' employer in Britain. We have seen, however (p. 103), that transnational industrial action by workers is a rarity. Moreover, action in this country by reason of an alleged injustice abroad, for example the exploitation of workers employed by a company of the same multinational group in, say, Portugal or South Africa, would appear to be a trade dispute only if it relates 'mainly' to the conditions of the workers employed by the British company. The alternative argument would be that the workers abroad were engaged in a trade dispute mainly about their employment conditions and that the British workers were 'affected', in which case it is not clear how far the British court would consider the legality of the action under the foreign civil law (the point was raised in a case concerning Olympic Airways in 1966, but not decided).[102] In any event, today the British workers would often lose immunity for indulging in 'secondary action' (p. 597).

(4) *The furtherance or contemplation* of the dispute has always been the final requirement. 'Furtherance' refers to an existing or, Lord Scarman has said, 'actual' dispute; whereas a dispute is in 'contemplation' if it is likely or 'imminent', whether it eventually occurs or not. A dispute, it was put in 1981, cannot be conjured up out of 'groundless fears'. There must be reasonable evidence of its imminence or likelihood. Similarly, where in 1945 officials induced brewery employees to disclose confidential information to strengthen their hands in preparation for bargaining with the employers, they were held to have no trade dispute in contemplation. A union official has never been permitted to prepare for and create his own dispute and then contemplate or further it. In cases of a rather different kind, defendants have been held to 'further' purposes other than employment matters, when this heading is used as an alternative to reasoning about 'content'. One may say either that the dispute has the wrong content, or that it has the right content but the defendant was really 'furthering' something different.

In *Stratford* v. *Lindley*, 1965,[103] for instance, a company in the S. group refused on many occasions to negotiate with either the T G W U or the Watermen's Union, unions that organized lightermen in its employment. It suddenly recognized the T G W U, which organized the great majority of lightermen. The Watermen at once put an embargo on barges hired out and repaired by another company in the S. group, freezing its business. The Court of Appeal thought this was a dispute over recognition and therefore a trade dispute. The Law Lords, however, disagreed. First, some of them doubted whether there was any 'dispute' at all, on the extraordinary ground that the union had not, yet again, approached the company to ask for recognition. Secondly, they all held that the union was furthering not a trade dispute, but 'inter-union rivalry' and its own 'prestige' (p. 583). Moreover, in coming to this conclusion, the Law Lords were prepared to judge industrial necessities. Lord Pearce asserted that the Watermen members employed by the company were 'adequately protected' by the agreement with another union, the TGWU (which they had chosen not to join), so there was 'no practical need for any intervention by the defendants'. Other judges have taken a similar line. Donaldson MR, in the *Mercury* case, found it 'inconceivable that if the dispute was wholly or mainly about jobs the union would not have approached BT' under the job security procedures of a collective agreement, even though the union had testified that, in its view, action within the agreement's procedures was not appropriate to protect jobs in that situation. Dillon LJ decided that 'natural wastage' and the collective agreement 'would avoid redundancies from technological advance'. But the court had no adequate evidence to make such a difficult judgment.

Nor is it possible for a defendant within the procedures of an interlocutory case to put to the court the industrial hinterland properly required for such evaluations. In any event, it is not clear why it is the job of the court to interpose its judgment on such questions, including the right moment for a union to invoke a procedure in a collective agreement or whether workers are adequately protected by one of two unions. Nor did the members of the union in the *Mercury* case share the judicial view that their jobs were safe, give or take 'natural wastage'. This was what they took action 'about'. By insisting that their action was mainly 'about' politics the judges contributed to the politicization of the union action under the new laws which they find in no way repugnant. It was no little irony that some months later British Telecom reportedly announced to the unions of its technical and engineering employees that by 1994 staff would need to be substantially reduced.

This quick route home – 'they were furthering something else, not a trade dispute' – was often taken by Lord Denning MR. In *Torquay Hotel Co.* v. *Cousins*, 1969,[104] the TGWU was organizing hotel workers in Torquay, to the alarm of hoteliers and the annoyance of another union to which an arrangement had once allocated that area (though it had recruited few workers). The Torbay Hotel refused recognition to the TGWU, whose local officials, L. and P., called a strike and organized pickets round it. There was no doubt that at the Torbay there was a trade dispute. The matter was conveyed by N., at regional level, to C., the general secretary, who authorized official strike pay. The local union members read a report that the managing director of the Imperial Hotel (owned by the *Torquay Hotel Co.*), who was a prominent member of the hoteliers' association, had declared in a speech that they would 'stamp out' the TGWU in the town. The *Imperial* had no TGWU members. Furious at this intervention, the workers moved across to picket that hotel as well, with which L. declared 'a dispute' now to exist. News of that dispute was given to Esso, which supplied oil under contract to the *Imperial*. P. declared the union would 'cut off supplies' (Esso drivers were in the TGWU). The *Imperial* sought other oil from a firm, Alternative Fuels, in Cheshire, which was warned by a local TGWU official about the dispute (Figure 6). The Court of Appeal upheld the granting of interlocutory injunctions against the union officials involved. There was a trade dispute at the Torbay Hotel, but the action taken against the *Imperial* was not in furtherance of it. That action was 'personal', taken to 'punish' the managing director; the pickets were furthering not the dispute but 'their own fury'. Their 'furtherance' had gone too far, so they had lost protection.

This is one of the few cases when an employers' association has played a role, though the judges took little account of it. In 1980 a CBI

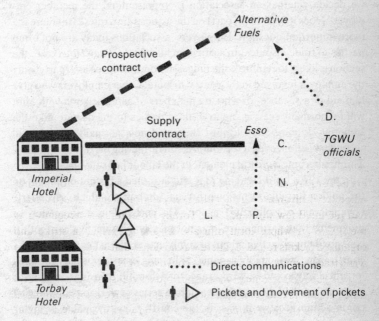

Figure 6. *Torquay Hotel* v. *Cousins*, 1969

'feud' against the plaintiffs.[106] This exuberant bout of idiopathic judicial creativity was too much even for the Law Lords and was brought to an end in a trilogy of House of Lords decisions just before the new legislation began its course with the Employment Act 1980.[107] In *Express Newspapers Ltd* v. *McShane*, all the Law Lords except Lord Wilberforce rejected the objective test of 'furtherance'. Even if the 'immunities' tended to 'stick in judicial gorges', Lord Diplock could not agree to this wholly new test. The word 'furtherance' was 'purely subjective'. The issue of 'furtherance' was that of 'honesty of purpose alone not the reasonableness of the act or its expediency'. There, in order to assist in a wage claim by journalists against provincial newspaper employers, the union called on its members at the Press Association to come out on strike in support. About half the P A workers went on strike. The union then called out its members employed by the national newspapers. These extensions of the action were still in 'furtherance' of the dispute. They were in fact a classic case of stronger groups in a union rendering assistance to a weaker group.

But Lord Denning stuck to his guns. In *Duport Steels* he disallowed union action against the private steel companies in their dispute with the B S C because, as we saw, it did not further *that* dispute and because the court had a 'residual discretion' to grant an injunction. This second point we shall meet again, and it is of importance (p. 693). On 'furtherance' and 'content', though, the Law Lords responded tartly. The words in the statute were clear. The Court of Appeal had failed to construe the Act 'in the way in which this House had plainly said it was to be construed', said Lord Scarman. Even counsel for the employers had admitted that he could not possibly rely upon the reasoning of the Court of Appeal. This, it was said, 'strayed beyond the limits set by judicial precedent and by our (largely unwritten) constitution'.

More than one Law Lord said it was only Parliament that could change the law. As they were aware, the new Government's Bill that became the 1980 Act *was* just then before Parliament and about to change it. The judgments of Lord Diplock and Lord Salmon in effect wished the new Bill Godspeed. As Griffith wrote, the 'disagreement between the Court of Appeal and the House of Lords presented a clear difference of tactics', but not of overall policy.[108] Lord Denning had gone too fast. But the venom in the words with which most Law Lords described the 'immunities', the very base of labour law (with the notable exception of a few, like Lord Scarman), was of immediate political relevance to the debate about the proposed legislation, into which the Government soon afterwards introduced the provision that was to become s. 17 of the 1980 Act on 'secondary action' and that fulfilled the same policy in a different way (p. 597).

This extraordinary episode illustrates better than any other the specific British problems that beset the attempt to devise a frontier to cut off the illegalities of the common law from legitimate liberties and functions in industrial conflict. Here, the relationship of the judiciary to the unions defies anything other than a class analysis. Indeed, in labour law 'the policy of "reform" has never found an answer to the problem of the judiciary or of the legal profession with which it is enmeshed'.[109] It is still an open question whether the 'new generation of lawyers' of whom Kahn-Freund dreamed can be part of a lasting solution. What is more, as Davies and Freedland put it, the story must cause any government wishing to restore traditional areas of liberty of action – whether by 'immunities' or 'positive rights' – 'to consider very carefully not just the appropriate substantive law to be passed but also the nature of the courts to which interpretation of the law will be entrusted'.[110] We shall find in Chapter 8 that the same question emerges with even greater force from consideration of the *procedures* of the courts through which the 'labour injunction' is granted. The history of the golden formula, especially the definition of 'trade dispute', reveals that there is not one problem, but three. To the problem of the principles of substantive legal definition are added the problems both of procedure and of the philosophy of the judiciary.

A further point about the golden formula should receive more attention. British labour law since 1875 has stood on a liberal base in one major respect. The 'immunities' have been accorded not to official as against unofficial bodies, or even (traditionally at least) to those who accept procedures laid down by the State as against those who do not. Trade unions are not divided into State-groomed sheep and outcast goats, as they sensed they might be under the Act of 1971. The law does not even mark out, as in France and Italy, some unions as more 'representative' than others, although curiously the Act of 1984 gives 'official' union action a lesser status because, as we shall see (p. 623), the obligation to hold a strike ballot applies only to it, not to unofficial action. The area of liberty protected by the 'immunities' has tradition-

committee took British employers to task for not showing 'greater employer unity and solidarity in industrial relations', urging them not to 'poach labour' or take work away from companies hit by strikes, but to curb 'competitive instincts' as is done in 'mutual financial support schemes which have operated successfully in some European countries'.[105] The Engineering Employers' Federation was reported to have an 'indemnity fund' in 1968 to help members affected by strikes; but little more seems to have been done systematically. The *Torquay* case suggests that, even if this practice became more widespread, such links between employers are unlikely to affect the judges' analysis.

The 1980 Act foresaw argument in this area in regard to 'secondary action'. Here, as we shall see in Chapter 8, it becomes essential to know which employers are 'parties' to the trade dispute. It is therefore provided that for the purpose of this issue (only), where an employers' association is a party to a dispute, an employer who is a member of it is regarded as a party also 'if he is represented in the dispute by the association' (E A 1980 s. 17 (7)). The obscurities are obvious. How do we decide whether an association *is* 'representing' the member employer? Does it depend (in part) on the association's rules? But there is a more important question. Employers' associations today are not often parties to trade disputes. In a situation like the *Torquay Hotel* case, the section is likely to reinforce the judges' tendencies to see as a 'party' only the employer involved in the central dispute. Other employers who give him aid or assistance, or who are members of an association with him, will be normally seen as 'neutral' third parties to the dispute, like the Imperial Hotel. Action against them will now normally be unlawful secondary action, even if the union is still furthering the dispute (p. 597). This has become a critical element in the labour law of 1986.

In the 1970s Lord Denning M R had launched a further onslaught on the golden formula in his own judicial attempt to attack 'secondary' (sympathetic or solidarity) action. He declared in a succession of judgments that 'furtherance' was not merely a 'subjective concept'; it contained an 'objective' element. Only acts done that could be, in the court's view, 'reasonably capable' of helping one side or the other in a 'practical way' could be 'furtherance' of a dispute. By using tests such as these he led the Court of Appeal into a series of decisions disallowing union action because it was, in the court's view, incapable of giving practical support, or was too 'remote', or in other cases was part of a

ally been the preserve of *any* person who acts 'in contemplation or furtherance of a trade dispute'. It is perhaps odd that the judiciary has never adequately appreciated this libertarian element in the structure. True, the action envisaged will normally be collective, a combination of labour in a union on one side, and the aggregation of resources or capital that is the employer or employers' association on the other. Indeed, the formula applies to the lock-out equally as to the strike (a parallel not permitted by some systems of law for the obvious reason that in social reality strike and lock-out are not on the same plane). The golden formula re-emphasized the recognition of an individual interest in, and individual right to, action in combination. It makes clear the fact that there are consequences for individuals, rather than for abstract entities, inherent in any rearrangement of the lines around the trade dispute 'immunities', the boundaries within which the collective interests of individual workers may be lawfully pursued. This fundamental characteristic of a liberty to take industrial action as an individual right to act in combination was this far at least recognized by our law after 1906 as applicable equally to all. It is this that has been misdescribed in the 1980s as a legal 'privilege'.

Industrial conflict: summary and agenda

It may be useful briefly to summarize the main points already made, in preparation for the territory ahead in Chapter 8 concerning the 'right to strike' today.

(1) The criminal illegalities of trade unions and of their activities were the subject of statutory amendment between 1824 and 1875. Only in 1875 were simple criminal conspiracy excluded from trade disputes and the Master and Servant Acts repealed. (The former is now the subject of the 1977 Criminal Law Act.)

(2) The illegality attaching to the civil status of a trade union by reason of restraint of trade was removed by the 1871 Act, and now rests on TULRA s. 2 (5). Today a union may make contracts, be a beneficiary and sue or be sued; but it is not, outside such specific provisions, ever to be treated as a body corporate (TULRA s. 2 (1)). The exemption from tort liability, devised in 1906 as an answer to the *Taff Vale* case, was removed in 1982, when a special code of vicarious liability for unions was

enacted for the 'industrial torts' (EA 1982 s. 15). Limits are placed on damages awardable in industrial tort actions against unions (ibid. s. 16).

(3) The right to picket peacefully was thought to be established by Parliament in 1906 (TDA s. 2). Picketing, however, is at risk not only of various crimes such as 'watching and besetting' or 'persistent following' (s. 7 of the 1875 Act) but also of liability in the criminal law for obstructing the highway or obstructing the police, and in the civil law the tort of nuisance, despite the statutory 'right'. The statutory 'right' to picket peacefully has been restricted to a worker's own place of work (TULRA s. 15, amended by EA 1980 s. 16). Recent developments in both the civil and the criminal law (influenced by the Code of Practice) suggest that wider liabilities than nuisance and obstruction are being applied; and proposals on reform of 'public order' offences reinforce the danger that the law may increasingly relate to peaceful picketing as a matter not of industrial conflict but of 'coercion' and public disorder.

(4) The golden formula protecting acts done 'in contemplation or furtherance of a trade dispute' (ICFTD) has been restricted in regard to both 'parties' and 'content' in the 1982 Act (TULRA s. 29, amended by EA 1982 s. 18). Although some attempts to narrow the old doctrine judicially were rejected by the House of Lords in 1980, the judicial decisions both on 'furtherance', on 'parties' and on 'content' show that a wide interpretation of the new legislation can be expected, especially where a judge decides that a union is trying to 'create' a trade dispute that 'in reality' is not there.

From this base we are ready to inquire into the 'right to strike' today. Much of this chapter will remain relevant, above all the golden formula, which is the basis of the 'immunities' in trade disputes. We shall, though, for the most part be concerned with the civil, not the criminal, law. Picketing has brought together in this chapter both civil and criminal liabilities; but the civil liabilities to which we now come turn again and again on whether there is enough evidence of a common law tort and whether the defendant acted ICFTD so as to acquire a trade dispute 'immunity' (and, if he did, whether the 1980s legislation has destroyed that immunity). In interim proceedings we shall see that those issues are approached by the judges in rather special procedures, not least when they grant an injunction 'to preserve the status quo until the rights of the parties have been determined' at the full trial.[111] The substance of this chapter is the platform from which we can launch our investigation.

[8] The Right to Strike

Where the rights of labour are concerned, the rights of the employer are conditioned by the rights of the men to give or withhold their services. The right of workmen to strike is an essential element in the principle of collective bargaining.

These are not the words of a trade union leader but of a Law Lord, Lord Wright in the *Crofter* case, 1942.[1] The judgment was a high point of judicial 'non-intervention' given at the height of the war from the lips of a pupil of Scrutton (p. 33). Lord Wright knew that the 'right' to strike that he was defending was a social right, protected in British law only by statutory protections in the form of 'immunities'. Such a 'right' can hardly exist in the normal legal sense when a call by a union for members to strike implies that each must break his employment contract. Yet, as Sir Robert Megarry V C said in the first major judgment delivered in the miners' strike in 1984, 'a trade union with no power to call a strike would be a poor thing'. This chapter asks how far the exercise of that power is lawful today.

Industrial action and the workers

The word 'strike' is used here in a broad sense to include various types of 'industrial action'. Full-scale withdrawals of labour tend to take the limelight in discussions about industrial conflict. But the strike by workers and the lock-out on the employer's side are often preceded in practice by other workplace sanctions: a go-slow or an overtime ban by workers, a decreasing 'margin of tolerance', in McCarthy's phrase, from management. This must affect our consideration of strike statistics. For instance, in the international 'league table' of working days 'lost' or 'idle' per 1,000 employees, the annual averages for 1974 to 1983 put Britain towards a middle position (Italy 1,300, Spain 1,000, U K 440, France 170, Sweden 140, West Germany 30). But both the character and the reliability of such figures need attention. Italy reported all stoppages; France, neither 'political' nor public sector strikes; West Germany, only strikes of ten workers or of one day or more; the UK, not political strikes nor those of less than ten workers or for one day.[2]

Despite their difficulties, the international statistics do at least make it clear that legal regulation of the bargaining system does not by itself correlate with either a low, or a high, pattern of strikes. Some systems (in Sweden and West Germany, for example) have for long had more regulation than there is in Britain, and their figures are lower; but others with far tighter legal regulation have normally had far more strikes (as in Australia and the United States). The legal systems are concerned largely with the symptoms rather than the causes of disputes. The writ and the injunction may help to defeat a stoppage, but the grievances behind the strike or the lock-out spring from deeper sources. Indeed, it has been remarked that in the international setting of advanced industrialized countries Britain is one of the few in which strikes per worker may be said to have decreased if one compares 1965–9 with 1975–81.[3]

There is a large literature about whether Britain is afflicted by a special 'disease' of strike-proneness. At the time of the Donovan Report (1968) the dominant element in workers' action was the short, 'unofficial' stoppage. More than 95 per cent of stoppages were then of that character, and about half of these, Donovan said, 'concerned wages'.[4] More than half the strikes beginning in 1984 were also officially reported as related to pay. Such 'causes' take us only a limited way towards an understanding of the industrial activity that, as Edwards says, 'reflects part of workers' attempts to gain control over their working lives', albeit that 'such attempts are often limited and sectional'.[5] The number of recorded stoppages maintained a yearly average in the 1970s of between 2,000 and 3,000; but the total days idle fluctuated between 6 million in 1976 and 29 million in 1979. In the 1980s average annual stoppages have fallen to around 1,400, but days lost have fluctuated between less than 4 million in 1983 to 26.6 million in 1984 (of which some 22 million arose from the miners' strike). The pattern of strikes, too, has changed since the 1960s. Since 1970 there have been more and longer 'official' union strikes, and more in the public sector and in service industries (but then the old manufacturing industries have declined). Of the various explanations for the distribution and patterns of strikes, few have escaped criticism. Large plants appear to be rather more prone to stoppages;[6] and in some of these the incidence of industrial action on the shop floor may have been greater than the figures reveal.[7] In the wave of strike activity across Western Europe in the 1970s Britain had fewer strikes about 'non-pay' issues but experienced fierce sectional battles, especially over public sector pay in 1978–9. Informed opinion now regards the picture of Britain as a 'uniquely strike-prone' country as one of the nation's 'simplistic myths', but the differences in the analyses of stoppages that do occur have grown, if anything, wider.[8]

An authoritative survey of strike activity divided activity into four phases after the war; the post-war peace, 1946–52; the return of strikes, 1953–9; the shop-floor movement, 1960–8; and the formal challenge, 1969–73.[9] These are also periods of particular significance for the lawyer, for they mark (if one allows for belated reactions by the courts to social change) remarkable parallels with changes in judicial policy and 'creativity'. The lower levels of factory-level industrial action in the early 1980s (that is, outside such battles as the health-service or coal-industry strikes) are frequently ascribed to a lasting fear of unemployment – the 'new realism' – among workers in a weak labour market. Whether it is true that strike activity usually increases in an improving economy has yet to be tested in the Britain of the 1980s. Some writers believe the 'new realism' is likely to be 'ephemeral'. At all events, 'Workers do not strike for fun.'[10]

In day-to-day work relationships partial withdrawals of labour or of co-operation are of comparable importance to full-scale strikes in terms of managerial control over the work process and the managerial interest in an uninterrupted flow of operations. This phenomenon places industrial action as part of the 'conflict in a struggle between workers and employers for control over the terms on which labour power is translated into effort'.[11] On the other hand, the complexities of any serious stoppage rarely support the view that 'there is a single reservoir of discontent permeating all forms of industrial action'.[12] Surveys have noted the difficulty of even defining a 'strike' or 'industrial action', not merely in legal or theoretical terms, but also in practice on the shop floor. The exercise involves not only a description but also 'a social process on the part of both workers and management', whose different perceptions lead even to 'differences in the strike records of unions and employers'.[13] This difference is not irrelevant to the difficulties that the law encounters in defining a strike. Indeed, the influence of these factors is felt at the juridical level even in systems that deal in over-arching concepts and rights. The French 'right to strike' does not permit predominantly political strikes, a go-slow or a work-to-rule – a point to be remembered when we discuss 'positive rights'. The very definition of 'strike' in each country depends as much on the local industrial culture as upon reason or logic.[14]

British law knows of two different legal definitions of 'strike or industrial action'. Both are enacted for specific purposes. The first is the definition for the purpose of 'freezing' weeks of employment in the calculation of continuity of employment (p. 209; essentially this is a cessation of work in combination, or a concerted refusal to continue to work, in a dispute to compel an employer – i.e. any employer – to accept employment terms: EPCA, Sched. 13, paras. 15, 24; with a parallel definition of 'lock-out'). The second definition appears in the law on compulsory ballots for union industrial action (TUA 1984 s. 11 (11); there a strike means 'any concerted stoppage of work'; there is no definition there of 'industrial action': p. 625). Elsewhere in the law there is no general definition of a strike, lock-out or industrial action, though those specific statutory definitions are sometimes used by judges as analogies or reference points. Indeed, we saw that for the purposes of excluding the jurisdiction of industrial tribunals on unfair dismissal in cases involving industrial action the courts have fastened upon concerted pressure on the employer by a total or partial withdrawal of labour from normal working as the essential element, whether or not there is any breach of the workers' contracts of employment (EPCA s. 62: p. 193).

Common law and Parliament

We have observed that there is a high likelihood that workers who take part in strikes or even in any other industrial action short of a strike, such as a go-slow or work-to-rule, will be in breach of their contracts of employment (p. 190). This is at the hard core of modern British strike law. The strike has been called 'a repudiatory breach which the employer may or may not treat as one upon which he will act' and so determine the contract. If he keeps the contract alive and takes the strikers back he can still discipline them for it and can even take account of their disloyalty in selections for redundancy or put them at a disadvantage on re-engagement in terms of their risk of being fairly dismissed.[15]

Just as combination, 'conspiracy' and 'coercion' were at the heart of many of the nineteenth-century developments, so breach of contract, and especially breach of the employment contract, is the base on which much of the civil law of this century rests. Any attempt in Britain to create a positive right to withdraw labour would need to change that and give the worker an individual right to take industrial action with others without breaking his employment contract.

The history described in Chapter 1 showed how our law did not take that path. Instead, from 1875 onwards Parliament provided for those organizing industrial action 'immunities' in trade disputes against tort liabilities. The judges then expanded tort liabilities. Parliament then, belatedly, countered the judicial expansions of liabilities by adjusting the 'immunities' (often with some gaps or uncertainties remaining). But in 1980 the process changed. Parliament began to narrow or destroy the 'immunities', joining in on the other side. Legal analysis of the legality of strikes today, therefore, involves not two but three questions:

(1) Is there liability at common law (or sufficient proof of it in 'inter-locutory' proceedings)?
(2) Is there an 'immunity' against it?
(3) Has that 'immunity' now been removed?

Let us in parenthesis note that the classical pendulum that swung to and fro between 1875 and 1980 – judge-made liability, parliamentary immunity, then more liability – did not arise merely from the peculiarities of 'creative' judges (though it is often best illustrated by them). It derived from the very nature of the common law, its attitude to property and to the social order, its ability to achieve mutations in its doctrines, and its relationship to Parliament. When, as in 1964 or 1969, the judges created a new tort (like intimidation) or, as in 1982, imported into labour law a new doctrine of 'economic duress' so that trade dispute immunities were outflanked, they repeated a process as old as the common law. This is one reason why legislation finds it hard to come to grips with this elusive creature. We find direct parallels more than a century ago. Take the 'Ten Hours Act' of 1847. It restricted (from the following year) the hours of work of women and young persons in factories to ten a day and fifty-eight a week.[16] But employers evaded the statute by the 'relay' system – that is, by carefully staggered, instead of continuous, periods of work and short rest periods; 'scattered shreds of time', 'hours of enforced idleness which drove the youths to the pot house and the girls to the brothel'.[17]

Convictions by magistrates were rare, though the English factory inspectors honourably resisted Government pressure not to prosecute. In 1850 the whole matter came before the Court of Exchequer. Parke B., who presided, had already said, according to the Attorney-General, that the intention of the Act was undoubtedly to require continuous work periods, but 'as it is a law to restrain the exercise of capital and property, it must be construed stringently'. The court did just that. Under the Act, hours should be reckoned 'from the time when any child or young person shall first begin work'. But it did not, the judges found, clearly provide for simultaneous *ending* of work. So Parliament could not be 'assumed' to have placed that 'larger sacrifice' upon factory owners. Were it otherwise, mill owners would be deprived of the 'full control of their capital' – and mill-women restricted in their employment, 'which is their capital also'.[18] *The Times* said this made the Act a 'mere nullity'. Lord Shaftesbury wrote: 'The work is to be done all over again.'[19] A compromise Act of 1850 regained some, but not all, of the ground.

The approach of the common law judges there is familiar to a student of modern 'immunities'. This is not to say that the law and the courts are the same now as they were then. Workers are no longer prosecuted for striking on 4,914 counts in an indictment measuring 57 yards.[20] Nor is it to deny that great judges on occasion do put aside part of this constraint – although sometimes this is not easily done even when a liberal occupant of the bench desires to do so. But the stringent attitude to statutes restricting rights of property and of capital is not the exclusive preserve of those earlier times. Let us now see how it has developed in ours.

Torts and immunities

The central immunities in trade disputes

The Trade Disputes Act 1906 concentrated on providing protection in trade disputes mainly against the torts of inducing breach of employment contract and 'simple' conspiracy to injure (Chapter 1, p. 18). It also protected trade unions (but not officials) in *all* tort actions, a protection removed in 1982 (Chapter 7, p. 525). When in 1974 the Labour Government repealed the Industrial Relations Act 1971, it reconstructed in modernized form the framework of law that had been the foundation of British industrial relations after 1906 for over half a century (TULRA 1974–6). As things have turned out, one section has dominated the legal scene, not least because it has been the main object of attention in the legislation of the 1980s. This is TULRA s. 13, which is still the basic law, although it has been much amended in the 1980s. An understanding of this section is the key to an appreciation of today's developments; let us, therefore, summarize its provisions.

s. 13 (1)   *An act done by a person ICFTD is not actionable in tort on the ground ONLY*

> (a) *that it*
>> – *induces a person to break a contract, or*
>> – *interferes, or induces another to interfere, with its performance,*

or (b) *that it is*
>> – *a threat to do an act falling within (a), or*
>> . – *a threat that a contract will be broken (whether he is a party to that contract or not).*

[s. 13 (2)   'For the avoidance of doubt' it was declared that an act ICFTD was not a tort on the ground only that it was an interference with the trade, business or employment of a person or his right to dispose of his capital or his labour (repealed EA 1982 s. 19 (1)).]

[s. 13 (3)   'For the avoidance of doubt' it was declared that either (a) an act within s. 13 (1) or (2), or (b) a breach of contract committed ICFTD, was not 'unlawful means' for the purpose of liability in tort (repealed EA 1980 s. 17 (8)).]

s. 13 (4)   *An agreement or combination to do an act ICFTD is not actionable in tort if the act, if done by an individual, would not be actionable in tort.*

The parts in *italics* have since been restricted; those in [brackets] repealed. It will be seen that the legislation of the 1980s repealed subsections (2) and (3) (in, respectively, E A 1982 s. 19 and E A 1980 s. 17 (8)). The *italics* indicate that the other provisions have been restricted. Subsections (1) and (4) have been narrowed in their operation by various provisions of the Acts of 1980, 1982 and 1984. The reader will find that s. 13 (1) is usually at the heart of things. It deals, as can be seen, mainly with acts done ICFTD ('in contemplation or furtherance of a trade dispute', defined in Chapter 7) that induce a breach of a contract or interfere with the performance of a contract or threaten to do so. No part of this section (the basic trade dispute 'immunity' on which the 'right to strike', as Lord Wright called it, depends) has gone unscathed in the Acts of 1980–4. Our view about the existence of an adequate 'right to strike' in our law depends largely upon how far we judge T U L R A s. 13 to be necessary and the new restrictions of it to be acceptable.

The tort liabilities: an agenda[21]

In making an informed judgment on this issue, there is no alternative to an examination of the tort liabilities relevant to the 'immunities'. Too many people – in all industrial and political camps – offer opinions on the matter without making the effort to do this. The myth has grown up that the law is here so complex and 'difficult' that only a few lawyers can understand it. Nothing is further from the truth. The issues are relatively straightforward. In the sections that follow, we shall look at the main tort liabilities, recalling what was said about *tort* in Chapter 1 (p. 3) and the relevant statutory 'immunities' in trade disputes as they stand today. Then we look at the remedies available to judges, especially injunctions. We may take, as an agenda, the main areas of tort liabilities and related matters involved in industrial action:

(1) Simple conspiracy to injure and other forms of conspiracy.
(2) Inducing breach of contract, with which we consider 'secondary action' and industrial action to extend union negotiation or union labour only, and their effect on 'immunity'.
(3) Bare interference with trade or employment.
(4) Bare interference with contract.
(5) Intimidation (the civil liability, not the crime).
(6) Strike ballots as they now relate to these torts.
(7) Damage done by unlawful means (including sit-ins).

(8) Other liabilities (such as inducing breach of equitable obligations and economic duress).

We shall consider, too, the incidence of these liabilities in emergencies and general strikes; liabilities of particular groups of workers (such as seamen or postal and telecommunications workers); some relevant social security provisions; and lastly, the critical question of remedies, especially labour injunctions in interlocutory proceedings, and contempt of court. Let us begin with conspiracy.

Conspiracy

Conspiracy as a tort has taken two forms: (1) 'simple' conspiracy to injure, where no act unlawful in itself is to be done; and (2) conspiracy to do damage by 'unlawful means'. We shall see later that 'unlawful means' is not easy to define. The statutory shield against the *crime* of 'simple' conspiracy in trade disputes was, we saw (p. 520), provided in 1875. When the courts turned to developing civil liability for conspiracy, striking down union activities as 'combinations to injure' (*Quinn* v. *Leathem*, 1901:[22] p. 30) even though no act unlawful in itself was done, Parliament enacted a parallel protection in trade disputes (TDA 1906 s. 1). The modern parallel to that section is TULRA 1974 s. 13 (4), which states that acts done ICFTD are not to be actionable in tort if the act is one that, if done without any such combination, would not be actionable in tort. Within the area of trade disputes, 'simple' conspiracy is not actionable.

Simple conspiracy to injure

Two developments must be noted, one in statute law, the other in the cases. First, the legislation of the 1980s characteristically operates by removing or restricting the 'immunities' in TULRA 1974 s. 13. Usually this is done by removing a protection against liability for an individual tort, as with 'secondary action' where a defendant is exposed to the tort of inducing breach of contract (EA 1980 s. 17, removing TULRA s. 13 (1): p. 597). But elsewhere the whole of s. 13 is removed, including s. 13

(4) on conspiracy, as in the case of 'secondary picketing' (away from the place of work: E A 1980 s. 16 (2)), action to extend negotiation or union labour only (E A 1982 s. 14) and union strikes without a ballot (T U A 1984 s. 10). In the first case, if the secondary action is tortious and not protected in trade disputes, conspiracy is also not protected, because the act 'if done without the combination' *is* actionable in tort. But where s. 13 (4) has been repealed, liability for 'simple' conspiracy to injure is also reintroduced. It is important therefore now to see what its liability involves.

The courts came to accept trade union objects as 'legitimate' in cases such as *Reynolds* v. *Shipping Federation*, 1924, and the *Crofter* case, 1942, described in Chapter 1 (p. 29). Judges even came to accept 100 per cent union membership as proper, Harman J. remarking in 1957: 'It is not for English lawyers to dislike or distrust the principle of the closed shop.' Lord Wright in 1942 saw the 'true contrast' between those combinations where the 'real object' is a 'legitimate benefit of the combiners', such as better wages or conditions, and those where 'the object is deliberate damage without any just cause'. Where objects or motives are mixed, the judge must decide what is 'the predominant object'. Most of the modern cases have followed the *Crofter* principle. When Lord Diplock thought union action 'misguided', in 1983, he would not impose liability for simple conspiracy to injure: 'the purpose was not to injure Hadmor, however inevitably injury to Hadmor might be one result of the blacking'. The same approach was maintained where the defendants were made liable for other torts, as in *Stratford* v. *Lindley*, because they acted in pursuit of what they genuinely believed to be 'fundamental trade union principles'.[23] The test to be applied is the predominant object of the defendants.

It is still up to the judges, however, to define 'legitimate' trade union principles and objects. Where officials of the Musicians' Union organized a boycott of a ballroom that ran a colour bar among dancers, their action was held in 1958 to be legitimate (musicians could not 'insulate themselves from their audience'); the welfare of their members was being advanced even if not translatable into 'detailed financial terms'. (Even though racial discrimination is today the subject of statutory prohibition, it is not clear that a combination to promote a colour bar would be tortious conspiracy, since the prohibition does not create a tort: pp. 459 and 638). But in *Huntley* v. *Thornton*, 1957, members of a union committee (other than two who had throughout genuinely pursued union interests) who aimed to injure a non-striking member by hounding him personally in pursuit of a 'grudge' were made liable in damages for conspiracy.[24] There is an immediate overlap here with the 'furtherance' of a trade dispute; for in the same case the judge said these defendants 'were not furthering a trade dispute but a grudge' or a 'personal matter'. Where the predominant purpose is regarded as 'illegitimate' by the judge, the defendants will often lose the 'immunity' under the formula I CFTD and be liable also for simple conspiracy. But not necessarily; they may still have legitimate union interests even if the court rejects their claim to have acted in furtherance of such a dispute, as in *Stratford* v. *Lindley* (their furtherance of 'inter-union rivalry' displaced the trade dispute but was not an illegitimate objective: p. 565).

Conspiracy to use unlawful means

There is another form of conspiracy, a conspiracy to do damage by 'unlawful means', or to do acts unlawful in themselves. Where the acts are tortious, s. 13 (4) will not apply. So it does not protect a union that organizes pickets who commit the tort of nuisance or 'unreasonable harassment' (p. 542). It was for some time uncertain whether the same test of 'intent to injure' as in 'simple' conspiracy should apply to such cases. In *Lonrho* v. *Shell*, 1982,[25] where oil companies had committed the criminal offence of supplying oil to the illegal Rhodesian UDI regime to the damage of Lonrho, they were not liable for conspiracy as a tort because for that liability to arise, said Lord Diplock, 'injury to the plaintiff and not the self-interest of the defendants must be the predominant purpose'. We return to 'unlawful means' below (p. 635).

The intent to injure

Suppose, however, a group of defendants include some whose object was a genuine union purpose and others who went beyond this into a vindictive or other illegitimate object. The *Huntley* case shows that the first group may be dissociated from liability as not being parties at all to that conspiracy; two union officials there confined their activity to 'genuine' union purposes. After the *Lonrho* judgment, the same logic appears to apply even if unlawful means are used. For example, pickets attending at their own place of work (protected by s. 13) should not lose their protection in a trade dispute as conspirators *merely* because they are joined by pickets from another workplace (from whom s. 13 protection is withdrawn; EA 1980 s. 16: p. 545). This could be of great practical importance for the liability of a union if officials for whom it is liable were responsible for organizing the first, but not the second, group of pickets. On the other hand, if a defendant is a party to everything to be done to further the combination's objects, he can be liable even if he is unable himself to do the tortious act. This seemed to be why the union official Silverthorne was liable as a party to the conspiracy involving 'intimidation' by threats to break employment contracts by airport draughtsmen in *Rookes* v. *Barnard*, 1964 (p. 39), even though he had no such employment contract to threaten to break. Such a threat, which he had agreed to promote, was 'in its nature' actionable, said Lord Devlin, so he could be sued for it along with 'the conspirators, if any, as well'. Section 13 (4) (then TDA 1906 s. 1) could be no defence. But in this case the Law Lords did not require that, where unlawful means are used, liability in conspiracy should turn upon the existence of 'predominant intention to injure'. And the *Lonrho* case has been understood, in the *Faccenda Chicken* case 1984, to mean that where the combination does acts that are unlawful *and* actionable by the plaintiff as civil wrongs (for example, 'breach of confidence', which is not a tort) it is an actionable conspiracy even if the defendants' purpose is not predominantly an 'intent to injure'.[26] Where the individual tort is one actionable by the plaintiff the courts may yet not require a predominant intent to injure before imposing liability on all parties to the conspiracy.

There is another principle, however, that judges might use in such cases to cut through the knots woven round conspiracy, namely the liability of persons for tort where each contributes to its commission 'in furtherance of a common design'. Each then becomes individually a 'joint tortfeasor', as part of 'concerted action to a common end'. Indeed in 1853 Erle J. spoke of a person who 'procured' a wrong as a 'joint wrongdoer'. If the judges wish to expand anew liability for 'combinations' they may turn to the principles of law concerning joint tortfeasors, to which TULRA s. 13 (4) does not as such apply. There is some uncertainty about the principles of 'joint tortfeasors', and therefore room for judicial 'creativity'. We shall meet the concept again (p. 644).

The immunity in s. 13 (4) is lost where the act to be done is a tort; the immunity is preserved if the act is actionable in some manner *other* than 'in tort'. For example, a combination of workers who break their contracts of employment in a trade dispute can be sued by their employer, as in *NCB* v. *Galley*, 1958 (p. 213); but they are not for this reason alone liable for the tort of conspiracy in a trade dispute – an important point in view of the possibility that damages for such a tort can be larger than for each such breach of contract. We return, however, to 'breach of contract' as unlawful means below (p. 635).

Inducing breach of contract

It is a tort knowingly and intentionally to induce any person to break his contract to the damage of the other contracting party without lawful justification. This is the central civil liability. It was established in *Lumley* v. *Gye*, 1853,[27] by a majority of three judges to one, reshaping the older principles of law that sprang from the master's property rights *in* his servant into principles resting on a contract *with* him. The judges made it clear that the modern tort consisted in a 'procurement of a breach of contract' or knowingly (sometimes put at the time as 'maliciously') 'inducing another to break a contract'. Historically the decision in *Lumley* v. *Gye* was an 'enormous extension' of liability.[28] Even sixty years later eminent lawyers denied the validity of any such tort. Just as the judges after 1875, on the demise of 'simple' conspiracy in trade disputes as a crime, developed simple civil conspiracy, so as the Master and Servant Act crimes for breaking employment contracts wound down to their end, the common law courts developed a generalized civil liability in tort for inducing a breach. This first occurred at the very moment when the 'New Model' unions were recreating the labour movement. In two decisions some three decades later the judges showed signs of creating an even wider liability for inducing or persuading a man not to *make* a contract with another. But that liability was ultimately rejected and is not part of the modern common law, at least so long as the means used are in themselves lawful. The tort is committed against the other party to the contract by inducing its *breach*. In 1963 a majority of the Court of Appeal held that where a person is so induced by persuasion to break an obligation, *he* cannot sue for he should have resisted the blandishments of the inducer 'by strength of will'. The other party to the contract is the proper plaintiff for this tort, an important proposition, as we see later (p. 641).

Inducing breach of employment contract and the 1906 Act

The *Lumley* v. *Gye* tort made union officials an easy target for attack. They had no right even in trade disputes (in the absence of a doctrine of 'suspension' of contracts) to induce a workman to say, as Lord Denning put it, ' "I am going to stay away one day" (just to please himself)'.[29] It was to this problem that the 1906 Act, s. 3, was directed to protect in trade disputes the bare liberty to organize a withdrawal of labour (p. 24).

The cases decided after 1853 in the courts, the Donovan Report noted, involved liability for inducement of breach of *employment* contracts, not other contracts. As late as 1952 Jenkins L J said the Court of Appeal had 'been referred to no case' in which strike organizers had been made liable for breach of 'contractual relations between the strikers' employers and the persons with whom they deal' (i.e. a commercial contract) even though 'almost every strike' must cause such breaches. This is an important historical fact. On the other hand, desperate attempts to have the judges lend assistance to strike organizers before 1906 failed. In 1905 the House of Lords rejected the argument that a defence of trade union principles or of wage standards provided any 'justification' for the tort, when miners had been called out on strike against very low wage rates in breach of their employment contracts. Lord Halsbury L C (an important character in this period) 'absolutely refused to discuss' any analogy with cases where 'justification' had been allowed as a legal defence against the *Lumley* v. *Gye* tort on 'moral or religious grounds'. Only once, it seems, has this vague defence of 'justification' been allowed in an industrial case, where chorus girls were brought out in breach of their contracts when low wages had forced them into prostitution to make a living.[30] In the common law sexual corruption may 'justify' inducing breach; starvation wages alone could not.

Even so the Bill introduced in 1906 did not originally deal with this tort. It was left to Sir Charles Dilke to introduce an amendment – 'at 5.0 p.m. on a Friday afternoon', Lord Robert Cecil later complained – which the Liberal Attorney-General accepted in a confused debate. Few such important amendments have been introduced into British law, as this was, formally and without a speech. In this way the first 'limb' of s. 3

of the 1906 Act came to provide that an act done ICFTD 'shall not be actionable on the ground only that it induces some other person to break a contract of employment'. From the very outset this 'immunity', without which strikes are illegal, was castigated as a 'privilege'. Dilke and Lord Chancellor Loreburn later defended it against the Conservative Opposition charge that it was an 'absolute disgrace . . . a new privilege'.[31]

The judicial extensions

This 'immunity' did not, and does not, protect from liability in trade disputes where some extraneous tort is committed (assault, slander or nuisance, for example). The trade dispute protections have always been confined to torts committed by economic pressure. Nor has statute ever covered the breach of employment contract itself (i.e. the worker's own liability to his employer). Only its inducement is protected. But after a long period of quiescence, in the 1960s the judges increased the width of the common law liability beyond inducing breach of employment contract. We saw in *Thomson* v. *Deakin*, 1952 (p. 36), how careful the court was, towards the end of the period of 'non-intervention', about the need for a defendant's *knowledge* of the contract. By the time of *Stratford* v. *Lindley*, 1965,[23] that approach had gone. The Law Lords said, for example, that a defendant need not know the 'precise terms' of the contract. Then in *Emerald Construction Ltd* v. *Lowthian*, 1966,[32] where construction union officials had organized action that caused the breach of 'labour-only' lump contracts, Lord Denning brushed aside the argument about knowledge:

Even if they did not know of the actual terms of the contract but had the means of knowledge – which they deliberately disregarded – that would be enough. Like the man who turns a blind eye. So here, if the officers deliberately sought to get this contract terminated, heedless of its terms, regardless whether it was terminated by breach or not, they would do wrong.

The need for an *intentional* inducement of a breach was similarly relaxed. In the same case Diplock LJ said it was enough to intend to bring the contract to an end by breach if there were no way of ending it lawfully. A defendant who does this 'runs the risk' that, if his act causes a breach, he will be liable. A tort of intention had become one in which recklessness could cause liability. It was enough, Slade J. held in 1978, 'to apply pressure or persuasion' to cricket players to withdraw from their contracts, even if the defendant believed in good faith that 'the player's contracts were not legally enforceable'. The decision was matched in the *Solihull* decision, 1985, where the judge rejected as a defence a genuine belief by teachers' leaders that they were procuring no breach of contract in the industrial action because the duties involved (attending events out of school hours, lunch duties, etc.) were believed to be voluntary: 'honest doubt as to the facts' was different from 'doubt as to the legal result of known facts'.[33] Judges have even begun to 'deem' defendants to have knowledge of contracts in their line of business and so to 'deem' them to intend to interrupt such contracts. Apart from this, plaintiffs have for many years frequently sent to the defendants the very contracts involved before or with service of writs demanding an injunction to stop them disrupting performance. (The Donovan Commission was told that employers regularly served commercial contracts upon a union 'as soon as a strike is threatened'.) Both points were illustrated, as we see shortly, in the modern law in *Merkur Island Shipping* v. *Laughton*, 1983.[34]

Once the judicial pressure was on, few of the traditional common law points available to union defendants were left to argue. There had, for example, been a distinction – a difficult one, but it was there in the judgments – between 'inducement' (or 'procurement') and 'advice' (or 'information'). The Donovan Report backed this classic approach: a union official who advised a person about a dispute did not necessarily commit a tort, even if he drew attention to 'possible dangers' of industrial action. Even as the ink was drying on the pages of the Report, the judges were proving that it could not any longer be taken at its face value. A Scottish court in 1968 held that a 'suggestion' made by someone 'desperately anxious' for a result could be an inducement, where union officials had addressed workers who then took action to support a claim for recognition. In the *Torquay Hotel* case, 1969[35] (p. 566), a broad approach to inducement was used (we see it again in the Alternative Fuels aspect of the case: p. 593). Winn LJ rejected claims that union officials had done no more than 'advise' the oil companies of the dispute at the Imperial Hotel, adding a bizarre analogy:

A man who writes to his mother-in-law telling her that the central heating in his house has broken down may thereby induce her to cancel an intended visit.

A whisper of the classic approach was heard in 1976, when the Court of Appeal reverted to the strict principles of the law by accepting that the evidence of a union official 'informing' his members in the docks about negotiations with a flag-of-convenience ship 'blacked' by the ITWF – 'It would be their decision [to take industrial action], not mine' – was not sufficient evidence of a 'procurement or persuasion'.[36] We saw in Chapter 1 how important this approach to the *evidence* can be in such interlocutory proceedings. In more recent cases trade union action has usually been assumed to involve the inducement or instruction of members to take action. Even where a judge held that workers reached a decision to take action 'independently' (the evidence, he thought, was contradictory but was enough proof of an inducement to grant interlocutory injunctions) the appellate courts found there *was* a 'serious case' on inducement.[37] In the *Austin Rover* case, 1985, an order that a union should withdraw an 'instruction, direction or decision' that it claimed it had never made was the basis of contempt proceedings.[38] In such cases the workers' industrial action involves a breach of their employment contracts. There may be cases where, if management breaks a 'status quo' agreement, industrial action can be taken without such a breach; but no court has as yet upheld such a claim. We touch on this under 'Intimidation' (p. 617).

Commercial contracts and the indirect tort

Much more serious, however, was the great leap taken by the courts in the 1960s from employment contracts into commercial contracts. The Achilles' heel of the 1906 Act's s. 3 turned out to be the fact that it protected inducement to break only *employment* contracts. Yet no judgment attacked that vulnerable point for half a century. Until 1952 the Court of Appeal had not heard of a claim based on breach of a commercial contract. Then came *Thomson* v. *Deakin*.[39] We recall (p. 36) that the TGWU officials had declared a boycott of Thomson's, a non-union firm (after 1926 all its workers had to promise not to join a union). Bowater's learned that its lorry drivers would not wish to deliver supplies to Thomson's and therefore informed the firm that it could not honour its supply contracts – that is, it would break them. The Court of Appeal rejected Thomson's application for an injunction against union officials. Let us remember the date. Only the year before, 1951, the fruitless prosecution of the dock strike leaders had led to the repeal of Order 1305, the wartime Order under which strikes were unlawful (waking and then killing off a regulation that by consent of the TUC leadership had slumbered on for a remarkable six years into the peace). In the High Court, Upjohn J. held that the union officials had induced a breach of the drivers' employment contracts; but this was protected by the trade dispute immunities in the 1906 Act; the fact that a commercial contract was also broken was not sufficient to create liability. The Court of Appeal stressed that it was not concerned with 'social conduct' but with legal principles. The defendants had not procured or induced Bowater's directly to break the commercial contract. They had caused it to be broken, if at all, *indirectly*. And an indirect inducement of breach was tortious only if some 'wrongful means' was used in the course of it. To this the plaintiffs replied that there was 'wrongful means', namely the direct procurement of breach of the lorry drivers' contracts of employment. But the court was not satisfied that the lorry drivers *had* broken their employment contracts. Bowater's had not ordered the men to load the lorries; they, said Evershed MR, 'took the line that they would not order any man either to load or to drive paper to the plaintiffs'. The indirect procurement of breach of the commercial contracts had therefore been effected without any illegal means. It was true that the union officials had let Bowater's know of the position; but this was mere 'information'.

The judgment of Jenkins LJ in this case became a classic source. He cautiously set out the four requirements by which liability for *indirect* inducement was 'strictly confined': first, knowledge of, and intention to procure breach of, the commercial contract; second, the defendant procured the workers to break their employment contracts (the unlawful means); third, the workers *did* break those contracts; fourth, the breach of the commercial contract was a 'necessary consequence' of the workers' action. The decision in *Thomson* rested mainly on the absence of the third link in the chain. Although the defendants succeeded in the case, it is clear, as O'Connor LJ said in 1983, that 'Jenkins LJ was laying down the ingredients of what he regarded as an extension of actionable interference in the context of the facts' of the *Thomson* case. It unlocked the gate for any court that wished to intervene afresh.

The new opportunities were seized in *Stratford Ltd* v. *Lindley*, 1965,[40] just one year after *Rookes* v. *Barnard* (p. 39). There, we recall (p. 565), the Watermen's Union had put an embargo on barges hired out by Stratford Ltd and instructed members employed by the hirers not to handle the barges, in order to put pressure on the Stratford group of companies (one of which had refused it recognition). The union notified the employers' association, regretting 'any inconvenience'. The Law Lords held, as we saw, that this was not a trade dispute (p. 565). They also held that the plaintiffs were entitled to an interlocutory injunction because the union officials had committed the tort of inducing breaches of the hiring contracts. The majority judges in the Court of Appeal thought there was no evidence that the officials knew enough about those contracts (one of the defendants present in the Court of Appeal was so carried away by Lord Denning's judgment that he rose and applauded until restrained). But this was now swept aside by a looser test as to 'knowledge'. Thereafter the Law Lords diverged. Lord Pearce treated this as a case of *direct* inducement. The union had informed the hirers through the employers' association, but this was an inducement, not mere 'information': 'The fact that an inducement to break a contract is couched as an irresistible embargo rather than in terms of seduction does not make it any the less an inducement.' In such a case there was no need for the breach to be a 'necessary' consequence. The majority of the Law Lords held this was the tort *indirect* inducement of breach of the commercial contract. To bring this about the officials had directly induced their members to break their employment contracts with the hirers. There was no trade dispute (so the 1906 Act s. 3 could not apply). Thus the direct inducement of the members was a tort; and this was the 'unlawful means' that made into a tort the indirect inducement of breach of the commercial contract (Figure 7, p. 592).

(Some remarks in the judgments, especially that of Lord Pearce, suggested that even if the 1906 Act s. 3 had applied by reason of a trade dispute, the direct inducement of the workers might have remained an 'unlawful' means even though it was not 'actionable' under that section. This was an error that was to haunt the law until it was corrected in 1983: p. 595.)

For a time the new judicial enthusiasm for imposing extended liabilities upon union officials led some judges and commentators to suggest even that the 'unlawful means' was not needed for the *indirect* form of the tort. A moment's reflection shows the dangers. Suppose A makes a contract to supply special goods to B; he does not have them but he

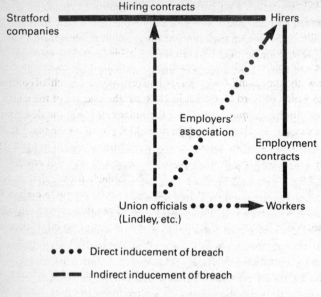

Figure 7. *Stratford* v. *Lindley*, 1965

knows where he can purchase them cheaply. C, with the intention of deliberately ruining A, secretly buys up the entire stock of the goods, thereby indirectly ensuring that A must break his contract. Lord Denning insisted in 1969 that such a man 'who corners the market' by lawful means does not commit a tort. So too, indirect interference with contract by union officials is tortious only if they use unlawful means – 'else we should take away the right to strike altogether'. This was in *Torquay Hotel Ltd* v. *Cousins*, 1969[41] (p. 566), where a further complication arose. We recall that the TGWU officials notified Esso of the dispute at the *Imperial*, with effect that oil supplies were stopped. This may have been a direct procurement; but if not, it was indirect with wrongful means (inducing the tanker drivers to break their contracts otherwise than in a trade dispute: p. 591). The court was prepared to grant an injunction to prevent further acts that would procure breach of the supply contract when oil was ordered under it. But the defendants argued that this was no tort; there was no *breach* by Esso in failure to supply. The reason was that there was in the contract a clause saying:

'neither party shall be liable for any failure to fulfil any term' of the contract if prevented by 'any circumstance whatever . . . not within their immediate control' (including specifically 'labour disputes').

This was a very important moment for the law. No previous case had made a defendant liable except where he procured a *breach*. Indeed, as we saw, the judges in *Lumley* v. *Gye* had regarded a 'breach' of contract, in the words of Lord Herschell in 1898, as 'the essence of the cause of action'. In the *Torquay Hotel* case the judges all found the defendants liable despite the clause. Lord Denning M R extended the tort liability into a new principle of 'interference' (we return to this on p. 614). The other Lords Justices, however, held that the tort was still committed even if the failure to perform by Esso was a 'breach' for which it was not 'liable' in damages. The fact that the *Imperial* could not sue Esso for damages because of the exemption clause did not prevent it from suing outsiders who procured that 'breach' for damages or an injunction. So the defendant who had been forbidden in 1966 to 'turn a blind eye' to the contract was now told that, however hard he fixed his eyes upon it, he could not take advantage of its terms, certainly not of a clause that is 'an exception from liability for non-performance'. Lawyers noted that Russell LJ agreed that it would be different if the clause was 'an exception from obligation to perform'. It must surely be right that unions, like anyone else, have the right to persuade a man not to do what he is not obliged to do. More recent cases, such as the *South Wales* miners' case, show that there is a need for the plaintiff to show that the acts of which he complains were capable of 'preventing the performance of a primary obligation' in the contract.[42] But the mere existence of an exemption clause stopping one contracting party suing for damages is not enough to exclude the tort of inducing breach.

There was a further point in the *Torquay Hotel* decision, not about the Esso contract but about Alternative Fuels. That company had no contract with the *Imperial*; but the Hotel had approached it for deliveries (one had reached it, the pickets taking the number of the tanker). A union official had approached Alternative Fuels and spoken of 'repercussions' if it supplied any more oil. The Court of Appeal granted an injunction in respect of these deliveries also, on this basis: the official had not inquired whether there was a contract. But neither had he added: 'Of course if you have contracted to deliver some more, it can't be helped.' The officials had shown an intention to stop supplies from this firm *if* any contract for delivery *were* made. The injunction was therefore granted.

By this stage it was clear that in industrial action the risk of tort liability was very high, whether or not there was a trade dispute. The 1906 Act 'immunity' was confined to inducing breach of employment contracts. A breach of commercial contract (sometimes even of a commercial contract yet to be made), of which the defendant perhaps knew little, could attract liability for direct inducement (if the union was polite and unwise enough to 'inform' the parties to it) or for indirect inducement where any 'wrongful means' could be found. The statement of Jenkins LJ in 1952 remained, and remains, true – that to say 'X is black' is not a tort. But unless the union emasculated its industrial action by adding, 'Of course we will ensure that no contracts are broken', its officials stood in peril. Even the Donovan Report's statement that it was not illegal simply to communicate information 'to persuade [someone] not to enter into or to renew contractual relations' had plainly been left behind by the breathtaking rapidity with which in practice liability had been extended by the courts before 1970.

Once again it would be insufficient to see this development in the law of tort as one exclusively aimed by a prejudiced judiciary at workers and trade unions. Life is not as simple as that. In the two decades after 1960 one can detect a gradual enlargement of liabilities for this and other types of 'economic torts', a phenomenon that appears to be related to protection of proprietary and contractual relationships in a period of economic buoyancy of which trade union growth was a part (and it may be the case that this general trend outside labour law has been put into reverse gear in the recession of the 1980s).[43] The economic and social conditions had clear effect upon the judgments. But no study of the judges' decisions can fail to conclude that the brunt of the extensions fell upon the unions more severely and more quickly than on any other recipient. With the same assertion, and no doubt the same conviction, as the judiciary of 1901 that it was merely applying the principles of tort liability to new situations equally for all, the judges developed in the decade after 1963 a new jurisprudence for the control of trade union action. Its function was to restrain the apparent rise of a power that the inner lights of the common law had identified as increasingly dangerous to the social structure. By the 1970s even the pleas by the ITWF that it was not liable to shipowners for this tort in its defence of oppressed seamen looked forlorn indeed. In the *Merkur Island* case,[44] the ITWF had asked the TGWU for help in 'blacking' a Liberian flag-of-convenience ship, as a result of which tugmen eventually acted in breach of contract against sub-charterers of the ship by refusing to service it. Arguments that the principles of Jenkins LJ did not extend to an 'indirect interference at a second or third stage', which was too remote, were firmly rejected in both the Court of Appeal and House of Lords. Unlawful means anywhere in the chain of supportive action is enough.

This case raises two other points. Where the tort appears in its 'indirect' form, the liability may be categorized as part of the wider tort of doing damage by 'unlawful means'. That is, inducing workers to break their employment contracts is a tort. So, if damage is deliberately done by that 'unlawful means' then the defendant is liable. This damage may be by way of causing a breach of the commercial contract; or it may 'prevent the performance' of that second contract. Where indirect *unlawful* means is present, a 'breach' of the commercial contract is not strictly required (this is perhaps the proper analysis of *Torquay Hotel* v. *Cousins*). The House of Lords held in *Merkur Island*,[44] applying the four requirements of Jenkins LJ of 1952, that once there was a tort present in the indirect means, the injury to the commercial contract need not be strictly a breach; it could be any 'prevention of due performance of a primary obligation under the contract'. In this case, as in the *Torquay Hotel* case, exemption clauses were present; the contract of charter for the ship released the charterers from liability to make payments for hire for periods lost through industrial action and gave them an option to cancel. Even so there was still a prevention of performance of the charter for which the ITWF was liable because it had procured the tugmen to break their employment contracts (and by 1983, as we shall see, p. 598, they were protected by no immunity). But, secondly, where there is a trade dispute the inducement of workers to break their employment contracts in furtherance of it is not normally 'actionable' under TULRA 1974 s. 13 (previously TDA 1906 s. 3). Surely then it does not remain 'unlawful means'. Some judges thought it did, especially Lord Pearce in *Stratford* v. *Lindley*, 1965 (at least when the plaintiff was not the primary employer). By 1983, however, opinion had moved against this illogical proposition, and through Lord Diplock the Law Lords declared that it was 'wrong'.[45] If the industrial action was called to further a trade dispute, and so protected, this was not an unlawful means on which a tort could be built for the interruption of the commercial contracts.

TULRA 1974–6: the basic immunities

The judicial extension of this tort, and especially its extension in regard to *commercial* contracts, led the Donovan Report to propose a parallel extension of the trade dispute 'immunity' in s. 3 of the 1906 Act (a majority of seven said for unions and their officials only; a minority of five, for all those acting ICFTD). The tort now encompassed all contracts; so should the 'immunity'. A Bill of 1970 aimed to put this into effect, but it fell on the defeat of the Labour Government. The proposal was reintroduced in 1974 and (after a period in which a minority Government submitted to a confinement of the immunity to employment contracts) it was enacted in 1976, so that the immunity in TULRA s. 13 (1) was applied to inducing breach of *any* contract ICFTD. The Opposition complained (as in 1906) of 'new privileges', and Lord Hailsham expostulated that 'any civilized man' would have decided the cases of the 1960s similarly to protect 'innocent third parties' and that 'a judge has not the right to create a tort'. But there was no other way to save the immunity on which the legality of strike action had been based since 1906. Manifestly Parliament had then meant to put trade disputes outside the grip of the *Lumley* v. *Gye* tort. As Lord Scarman put it in 1979: 'Briefly put, the law now is back to what Parliament had intended when it enacted the Act of 1906 – but stronger and clearer than it was then.'[46] The form of the 'immunity' was extended to cover commercial contracts. The substance was a consolidation of what had been provided for lawful industrial action since 1906. But no single item was more controversial in the politics of labour law in the late 1970s than the repeated assertion that the 'privileges of the unions' had been extended by the Government of the day. In fact, the form of the 'immunity' had been extended, but not the substance.

It was in its new form that the 'immunity' of TULRA s. 13 came to incur the intense displeasure of many judges and Law Lords in the decisions of 1980, even though they could not bring themselves to agree with the extravagant limitations placed by the Court of Appeal upon the trade dispute formula. Lord Diplock reached that conclusion with 'considerable reluctance', seeing this 'much extended' and 'repugnant' immunity as 'granting to trade unions a power, which has no other limits than their own self-restraint, to inflict by means which are contrary to the general law untold harm'.[47] The judgments of this period clearly illustrate the way innovations in the common law acquire automatic legitimacy, whilst the trade dispute legislation of Parliament has to prove its salt. Lord Diplock and judges who thought like him (the vast majority) did not see liability in tort as having been extended. Liability for interference with commercial contracts had been extended beyond any point that was or could have been envisaged in 1906. But since this was part of the common law, the new liability acquired a legitimacy equal to that of principles that had been there for centuries. For Lord Diplock it was the statutory 'immunity' that had been 'much extended', cutting down the 'general law' (i.e. the common law). In this way the judgments on this tort in the 1960s and 1970s constitute an important political statement by the judiciary, one with which future Parliaments will have to deal. That statement has been re-emphasized by the judicial silence concerning the legislation of 1980–4. The Acts of 1980–4 are not repugnant to judges, if only because they readmit the extended common law to control trade unions and trade disputes by destroying the immunities.

Let us now turn to two restrictions of the 'immunities' in TULRA s. 13.

(1) Restriction of secondary action

The first major amendment of strike law was the removal of 'secondary action' from the protection of TULRA s. 13 (1) (EA 1980 s. 17). Essentially, this may be thought of as removing any difficulties that might be in the path of a plaintiff in a case like *Stratford* v. *Lindley*. The term 'secondary action' in the Act means action (usually by a union) that induces another to break his contract of employment (or interferes or induces him to interfere with it; we return to this aspect on p. 614) or threatens to do so, *where his employer is not a party* to the trade dispute: s. 17 (2). Thus virtually all types of industrial action are covered where the workers are employed by a company that in law is not a 'party' to the trade dispute, no matter how direct their interest in the dispute. This provision dovetails neatly into the 1982 redefinition of trade dispute, confining it to disputes between workers and their *own* employer

(p. 556). Where secondary action is 'one of the facts' relied upon to establish liability for interference with a *commercial* contract, the 'immunity' in TULRA s. 13 (1) does not protect: EA 1980 s. 17 (1). So sympathetic or solidarity action, or what many would call assistance of the weak by the strong, is subjected to tort liability. The section makes no demand for a breach of the commercial contract; the indirect means relied upon to establish liability (the industrial action by workers employed by the 'secondary employer') has no 'immunity', and is therefore unlawful means under the common law.

In cases of this sort, then, the court must now undertake the three-stage inquiry:

(a) Is there a common law cause of action in tort?
(b) If so, is it protected by a trade dispute immunity under TULRA s. 13?
(c) If so, is that protection removed by EA 1980 s. 17?

We see the drastic effect of EA 1980 s. 17 well illustrated by *Merkur Island Shipping Corpn* v. *Laughton*[44] (Figure 8). The ITWF was responsible for procuring the boycott by tugmen, in breach of their employment contracts. This indirectly caused the prevention of performance of the charterparty (notwithstanding the exemption clauses). The ITWF had knowledge (and would have been 'deemed' to know anyway) of the charterparty contract. The tugowner employers of the tugmen were not parties to the trade dispute. That dispute was between the crew and the owners. So inducement of the tugmen to boycott the ship was 'secondary action', and interference with the charterparty contract had no 'immunity' under TULRA s. 13 (1). If the tugmen or their union had tried to 'turn their secondary action into primary action' by 'creating a trade dispute with their employers',[48] e.g. by demanding new terms excluding the 'blacked' ship from their work, the court might not have accepted this transformation (p. 559), although logically it should do so. Trade unions in a position of bargaining strength may see the new law on secondary action as increasing the need to secure from employers an agreement that members will not work on certain types of task without consultation with the union.

Gateways to legality – gateway (i): first customer or supplier. Great stress was laid in discussions on this new law in 1980 on the fact that there are certain 'gateways' to legality in the section. The main one is in

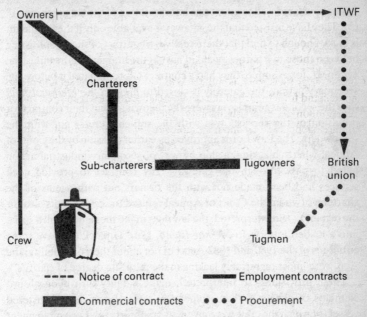

Figure 8. *Merkur Island Shipping Corpn* v. *Laughton (ITWF)*, 1983

s. 17 (3), which provides a defence where two conditions are met: (a) the principal purpose was directly to prevent or disrupt the supply of goods or services during the dispute between the primary employer, party to the trade dispute, and the 'secondary' employer; and (b) the secondary action (together with any similar action by other workers) was likely to achieve this purpose. The second test is objective; but it is linked to the first test, which requires a *subjective* purpose. The word 'directly' seems inappropriate, since the action is by definition an indirect interference. What is more, the 'supply' in (a) is defined to mean supply 'in pursuance of a contract subsisting between them' (the secondary and primary employers: s. 17 (6)). But the defendant frequently has no means of knowing whether such a contract between those precise parties exists. It has been argued that, since the definition requiring a 'subsisting contract' is inserted into (a) and not (b), all the gateway requires is that the defendant's intention or 'purpose' is to disrupt such a contract, whether or not it turns out to exist. Otherwise the section makes the gateway 'a casino' or a 'lottery' in which the union has to gamble.[49]

The courts refused to adopt this interpretation of the language of s. 17 (3). They have insisted that the gateway is available only if the defendant is lucky enough to find that there really *is* a contract of supply subsisting between those two parties, valid in law, at the moment of the industrial action. If, for example, they had a contract but terminated it before the secondary action, the gateway is closed to him. In the *Merkur Island* case the secondary employers were the tugowners; but their contract for provision of tug services was with the sub-charterers, not with the shipowners. The Law Lords approved an earlier decision by the Court of Appeal where 'blacking' a ship by way of secondary industrial action failed to pass through the gateway. The contract to provide dock services had been made not with the owners but with agents of the charterers (whom the Court of Appeal refused to see as agents also for the owners).[50] So interpreted, the law does make the right to call a strike into a loaded lottery. In *Merkur Island*, Lord Diplock did have some criticisms of the 1980 and 1982 Acts but not about their palatability; the Acts were 'most regrettably lacking in the requisite degree of clarity'.

These provisions, so interpreted, make liability turn upon absurd elements of chance. Where shipowners of a Panamanian registered vessel (of which the crew were given, as 'a subterfuge', two employment contracts: one, for public view, on ITWF standard terms, and one, the 'effective contract' agreed in Indonesia, under which they were paid) obliged their charterers to see that the port services were arranged under contracts not made on their behalf as parties to them, they were able to obtain an injunction against the ITWF. They saw to it that their contracts for the charter, and later for the sale, of the ship were made known to the ITWF, which had threatened to induce the port workers to 'black' the ship in breach of their employment contracts. (The pilots were excluded from this; they were self-employed; and 'secondary action' is defined in terms of contracts of *employment*.) The defence under s. 17 (3) was not available. The commercial contracts were made between the 'ship's agents' and the tugowners, etc. The owners here, in a belt-and-braces exercise, had by telex made it clear that the ship's agents were not in law their 'agents'. No doubt, said Staughton J., it was 'a little surprising' that the legality of industrial action should depend upon so small a point, i.e. who in law made the contract for port services, since the economic effect might be thought to be no different and it was 'not easy to tell' who was contracting for the tugs.[51] The union could not tell. He decided, however, that it might well be that the 'agents' were the owner's agents when the ship *entered* the port, but the charterer's agents when *leaving* it. Such a law on the right to take industrial action might stick in the gorge of an experienced trade unionist, or even a reasonable bystander. The emphasis in 1980 upon this 'gateway' as holding a reasonable 'balance' in trade disputes was little more than an italicized false prospectus.

Gateway (ii): associated employers. There are two other gateways in the 1980 Act. One, s. 17 (4), is a gloss on the one we have just discussed and deals with 'associated employers' (typically a group of companies: p. 98). Here the union's purpose must be directly to prevent or disrupt supply (under a subsisting contract) of goods or services between a person and an associated employer of the primary employer in the dispute; and those goods or services must be in *substitution* for those lost in the dispute by the primary employer. The 'secondary employer' can be either that person or the associated employer; and the action must be likely to achieve the purpose.

In *Dimbleby & Sons* v. *N U J*, 1984[52] (p. 562), the Law Lords used their interpretation of s. 17 (4) to narrow the ambit of the more important gateway in s. 17 (3). Journalists refused to supply copy to their employer, *Dimbleby's*, because its newspaper was being sent for printing to T. Bailey Forman's in Nottinghamshire. This was a business with which the NUJ had a long-standing trade dispute, in which twenty-eight journalists had been dismissed and not reinstated. *Dimbleby's* sought interlocutory injunctions against the NUJ. We recall that the courts refused to find a trade dispute between the journalists and *Dimbleby's*; so this was 'secondary action'. It was argued that the action disrupted commercial contracts between *Dimbleby's* and T. Bailey Forman's; these were the nub of the complaint. But 'T. Bailey Forman's' was not one company. It was a group of companies, most with identical controllers and the same office. The newspaper company in the group was *T B F Ltd*, the printing company *T B F (Printers) Ltd*, also non-union. The old trade dispute was with *T B F Ltd*. But the supply contract was between *Dimbleby's* and *T B F (Printers) Ltd* (Figure 9, p. 602). Section 17 (3), said the Law Lords, was not satisfied. The party to the trade dispute was not the party to the commercial contract. It was argued that the Lords should lift the 'corporate veils' of the T. Bailey Forman enterprise and judge the case on the economic realities (p. 100).

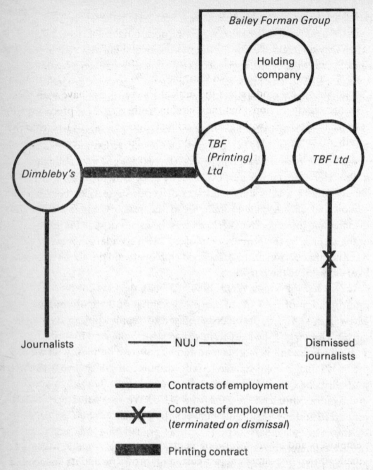

Figure 9. *Dimbleby & Sons Ltd* v. *NUJ*, 1984

But 'little time needs to be spent', said Lord Diplock, on this argument. It was a 'quite impossible construction' of s. 17 (3) because s. 17 (4) dealt with 'associated employers'. *TBF Ltd* and *TBF (Printers) Ltd* were associated employers: if the courts were to lift the corporate veil under s. 17 (3), then s. 17 (4) would 'make nonsense'.

There have nevertheless been cases where the courts have been prepared to look behind the veil of a company's 'personality' to see who the real parties are to a trade dispute. Here s. 17 (4) brings in all 'associated employers' in cases of *substituted* goods and services. It does not say that the judges can never pierce the corporate veil in cases other than substituted goods in order to avoid a result that the Court of Appeal admitted was 'curious' and 'odd'. For if T. Bailey Forman's *had* been one company the NUJ would not have been liable for the secondary action. One can understand the difficulties courts can have with these extraordinary sections; but there are, in truth, dozens of precedents in which judges have (without any specific statutory authority) 'pierced the veil' of company personality. The mere fact that one company is 'associated' with another by way of control is not enough. But where all the companies in a group are extensions of the controllers (as Lord Diplock said of a company in 1983: 'In effect, it is [the shareholders] with limited liability') judges have been known to pierce it. A precedent of 1938 showed that in a tightly knit group, a subsidiary could be treated as 'agent' of the parent. Looking at a group in 1976 Lord Denning said: 'The three companies should for present purposes be treated as one'; and the other judges agreed.[53] It is not such a radical idea; United States courts in analogous labour law situations do it regularly.[54] Yet in secondary action cases our judges say of company personality: 'The trouble with any doctrine which involves disregarding the legal form . . . is that once one starts on the process one does not know when to stop.'[55] The danger that once started judicial disregard for formality might dissolve into undisciplined licence seems a poor reason why the law should remain in this state.

When the civil prohibition upon 'secondary action' was introduced in 1980 it was claimed to be fair and just, not least by reason of the s. 17 (3), (4) gateways, and that the Bill proposed merely the protection of employers and others who were 'neutral' in a trade dispute. Much was made of the 'first-supplier, first-customer' provision and its 'associated employer' supplement, which were paraded as a protection of the right to strike, notably by Mr Prior, Secretary of State, who always took along charts to prove it. It was clear, though, that the conditions upon entry to these gateways, together with the complexity of the seemingly easy question of who is a 'party' to a trade dispute, would be likely to render the remaining 'immunity' a hit-and-miss affair at best. The law, being drafted along formal and legal, rather than economic and realistic, boundaries, permits companies linked to a firm in dispute easily to appear as 'neutrals', even if they are in the same group. It encourages employers, as shipowners were quick to spot, to organize their commercial contracts in such a way that the union cannot find the gateway at all. Back in 1958 Conservative lawyers found it 'difficult to see why it is improper' for workers to engage in 'sympathetic or secondary' strike action, at any rate 'if, without it, employees will have insufficient bargaining power'.[56] The bargaining strength of many workers today is less than it was then, yet it is into today's labour market that the new restrictions have been inserted. The 1982 amendments that redefine 'trade dispute' interlock with the secondary action provisions. We saw in Chapter 7 how narrow the path to the golden formula itself has become. Nor is it just a question of sympathy strikes. Any secondary action suffices. As soon as shop stewards seek support from workers servicing the factory where their members are in dispute, they are exposed to the risk of an injunction unless they are lucky enough to find that the relevant 'parties', 'contracts' and 'substitute goods or services' are so arranged that by chance they have in their hands permission to go through a gateway to legality. By 1984 even this would not suffice, unless they had held a ballot (p. 623); but even before that, in real life there was scarcely enough left of the 'immunity' in TULRA to constitute what is normally known as a 'right' or liberty to strike in solidarity with those whose economic interests are similar or even identical.

Any doubt that employers would when appropriate be advised to arrange their corporate structures with this in mind disappeared by 1986 after the Wapping affair. The production of *The Times* and the *Sun* was moved by News International (NI) from Fleet Street to a new site at Wapping, a veritable fortress housing new technology, despite a dispute with the print unions, NGA and SOGAT. Some 5,000 print workers were dismissed, and the print unions were excluded from Wapping. Industrial action was taken, but its legality was inhibited by 'buffer companies'. NI, itself a subsidiary of the transnational NC, published the papers through TN and NG respectively.[57] The group of companies also contained, it was found, separate companies for distribution (NID), for supplies (NIS) and for advertising (NIA). There were also six other subsidiaries of which the functions were less clear. (One of the NI advisers came from T. Bailey Forman's.) Newspaper wholesalers made their contracts with NID; outside typesetting or printing firms made contracts with NIS. The companies in dispute, the primary employers of the print workers, appeared to be TN and NG. Action to 'black' distribution or typesetting, therefore, by workers employed by wholesalers or by typesetting firms was secondary action even though many belonged to the same unions and had a direct interest in the dispute. But their employers' commercial contracts were not made with any employer party to the dispute, only with NIS or NID.

It was suggested, however, that even if s. 17 (3) could not apply, the gateway in s. 17 (4) ought to apply. All the companies in the NI group were said to be 'associated employers' under the same control. Even so, the goods or services were not supplied *in substitution* for those that would have gone to the primary employer companies but for the dispute. It appeared, for example, that NID would always have arranged distribution of the papers once this corporate empire was established (it was not the only such group to be created). There did not appear to have been any 'substitution'. Industrial action taken by the two unions led to injunctions, fines and sequestration. The liabilities rested in great measure upon restrictions introduced by the Act of 1984 as to ballots, as we shall see (p. 634); but the risk of illegality through 'secondary action' was plainly present, too, in the web of corporate veils in which the NI group could catch the unions of its sacked employees.

If the 'success' of labour legislation is tested by how far its concepts affect behaviour and become part of the industrial culture, the authors of the 1980 Act were perhaps able to claim modest progress when they saw employers arranging their affairs in this way. More interesting still, in 1985 haulage firms in Liverpool proposed to the TGWU (alongside longer driving stints, more temporary workers and amendments to the guaranteed week) a clause whereby the union would not take action against other operators by secondary action when a dispute arose with one company. They preferred to secure the result by agreement rather than go to the courts. 'Secondary action' had entered the language of bargaining.

Gateway (iii): picketing. The third gateway of escape from the secondary action liability relates to picketing. Where a worker satisfies the new requirements as to lawful 'peaceful picketing', e.g. attending at or near his *own* place of work in a trade dispute only for the purpose of peaceful persuasion (TULRA s. 15 as substituted by EA 1980 s. 16: p. 544), then an act done in the course of this attendance by such a worker is relieved from liability for secondary action provided he is employed by an employer who is party to the dispute (s. 17 (5) (a)). Employees of 'secondary employers' are thus excluded. But union officials are protected rather more widely. If an official satisfies the new TULRA s. 15 (1) (b) he is relieved from the secondary action liability and retains the protection under TULRA s. 13 (1) in respect of interference with the commercial contract (s. 17 (5) (b)). As we have seen (p. 545), under the new picketing formula such an official must be acting ICFTD and accompanying a member whom he 'represents'; and the member must be attending at *his* place of work. But the official seems to pass through this gateway if all these conditions are met, even if the member is an employee of a 'secondary employer' attending at his permitted place for picketing.

This is a suitable place to recall the more general point that where a person pickets otherwise than at the permitted place (normally at or near – not in – his own place of work, for purposes of information or peaceful persuasion and in contemplation or furtherance of a trade dispute) he loses the protection of the whole of TULRA s. 13 (EA 1980 s. 16 (2): p. 545). Sometimes, however, despite sections 16 and 17 of the 1980 Act, TULRA s. 13 (1) can still bring about protection. For example, union rules are a contract. One complaint about the NUM in *Thomas's* case, 1985,[58] by dissident miners was that it, or its national co-ordinating committee, had encouraged 'secondary picketing' in South Wales, thereby inducing breaches of contract, including breaches of the South Wales Area union's rules. The judge agreed that any such inducement had 'plainly been done in contemplation or furtherance of a trade dispute' so that the 'immunity' of s. 13 (1) applied. Nor was it ousted by EA 1980 s. 17, for there was here no 'secondary action'. No employment contract was involved. Nor was it ousted by s. 16 (2) of the 1980 Act on secondary picketing; for these defendants, the national NUM, were 'not being sued for acts they have done in the course of picketing. They are being sued for inducing breaches of the South Wales union's rules.' There was no 'arguable case' against these defendants. Draftsmen of the 1980 Act had left a tiny hole.

(2) Action to extend negotiation or union labour only

We recall that the 1982 Act set out to make unlawful as torts business practices relating to the supply of goods or services that have as one of their purposes either the requirement that work is to be done only by union members (or non-unionists) or the requirement that the contractor or customer shall negotiate or consult with or recognize a union (EA 1982 ss. 12, 13; Chapter 4, p. 286). Any person who is 'adversely affected', e.g. a customer, can bring an action for damages or an injunction or both. Terms to the same effect in contracts for the supply of goods or services are void. But these sections do not affect terms in the ordinary collective agreement, which is not legally binding since no 'contract' exists in it at all.[59] These statutory 'business torts' are aimed at removing from closed-shop practices, and from collective bargaining itself, the support an employer might otherwise give by 'leaning on' his customers or suppliers.

The Act goes on, however, in s. 14 to remove the 'immunities' of the whole of TULRA s. 13 from three types of industrial action. First, it removes the 'immunity' where the union 'attempts to induce another to incorporate in a contract' a term that would be void under ss. 12 and 13. Although action taken to persuade contracting parties to a commercial contract for goods or services that they should agree on union labour, or on recognition of unions, does not of itself attract immunity, it is conceivable that a union might take action in a trade dispute with that aim. If it does, the 'immunities' of TULRA s. 13 are lost (s. 14 (1) (a)).

Secondly, these 'immunities' are lost where the union attempts to induce anyone to contravene s. 12 (2) or s. 13 (2) by indulging in the forbidden practices, e.g. refusing to contract, terminating a contract or 'determining not to enter into a contract . . . for the supply of goods or services' if *one* of the reasons is a prohibited ground (i.e. union or non-union labour only, or union recognition): s. 14 (1) (b). This enactment is important if the business man has committed the tort under s. 12 (2) or s. 13 (2). Some might argue that a person who induced him to commit it would be liable as a joint tortfeasor (or a conspirator if the intent to injure is proved) – that is, jointly committing the new 'statutory tort' which has never attracted the 'immunity' of TULRA s. 13 anyway. It is not impossible for Parliament to grant more immunities than may be needed and, conversely, to take away even those that do not apply. But Parliament appears to have taken a stronger view here. The business man is liable because the 'statutory tort' explicitly places upon him the 'obligation' to comply with ss. 12 (2) and 13 (2). When, however, it deals with anyone who induces him to contravene that obligation, Parliament in s. 14 (1) explicitly refrains from imposing on them the same duty. The statutory tort is not applied to them. Nor is it made a tort to induce the statutory tort. Their penalty is the removal of 'immunity' in TULRA s. 13, so that they are liable if they have committed a relevant common law tort, such as inducing breach of contract, even in trade disputes.

This very important distinction between the common law tort and the 'statutory tort' in EA 1982 ss. 12 and 13 finds its most important consequence in the range of persons who can sue for damages caused. For the statutory tort, any persons 'adversely affected' can sue (ss. 12 (7), 13 (4)). But the range of possible plaintiffs for damage done by inducing breach of contract seems much narrower. We return to this on p. 641.

Thirdly, and most serious of all, the Act removes the 'immunities' of TULRA s. 13 from action that (a) induces workers to break their contracts of employment (or interferes with those contracts, or threatens so to induce or interfere, or threatens that they will be broken) and (b) interferes with the supply of goods or services, or can reasonably be expected to do so, where the action is taken for a prohibited reason, whether the supply is under a contract or not (EA 1982 s. 14 (2)). At once we see a parallel to secondary action (p. 597). Here it is no defence that the workers were induced to break employment contracts in furtherance of a trade dispute or even that they are taking action against their own employer in that dispute in order to induce him to take the prohibited action. Everything, therefore, depends upon the prohibited reasons. These are: either (a) that the work to be done is or is likely to be done by persons (other than the workers mentioned above) who are union members or are non-unionists (s. 14 (3) (a), (b)) or (b) that the supplier of the goods or services (other than the employer of the workers mentioned above) does not, or is not likely 'to recognize, negotiate or consult with a union' (s. 14 (3) (c), (4)). The section requires only that a prohibited reason be *one* of the reasons for the action. No matter how many good 'trade dispute' reasons for the action may exist, they are all vitiated if any one of these prohibited reasons makes even a subsidiary appearance. Nor is any account taken of an employer's legal duties to consult (e.g. on redundancies, or on safety: Chapter 4, p. 294). Pressure through the one employer to see that the other employer fulfils that duty to consult is still prohibited.

The extreme character of s. 14 of the 1982 Act disturbed many commentators.[60] The test of liability will be motive or 'reason'; and the court must go into what one judge in 1942 called 'the quagmire of mixed motives', looking for the prohibited reason that will vitiate the whole no matter how subsidiary. Once it is found that workers have taken or threatened industrial action even partly for the prohibited reason (say, that their employer is going 'soft' on his practice of asking subcontractors or maintenance firms to send only union men on to his site, or to consult with the unions of men they are sending) their action becomes unlawful. Both their own employer and outside parties who suffer loss will be able to sue for the interference to their business by the unlawful means (of inducing breach of the employment contracts).

The demand by workers for a UMA or for consultation at the workers' own place of work is still lawful. What is rendered unlawful is persuading their employer to use his business practices relating to the supply of goods or services to achieve the prohibited objectives in other employments. It is the first time since the Combination Acts that collective bargaining as such has been an illegal purpose by statute. Many companies do make such demands of their contractors. In 1964 McCarthy reported that craft workers employed on maintenance work were often required by 'the industry they serve' to be in union membership. An electrician who wanted to work in Fleet Street would need to join the union; but if he serviced 'a pickle factory he may well be able to lapse'; so too, managements may find it 'convenient to accept a craft union card as evidence of experience and competence'.[61] In a tribunal case in 1978 evidence was given that maintenance and other workers had been 'put off the BP refinery site on one occasion simply because one of the employees of a flooring subcontractor did not hold a current union card'. Nor is objection to 'cowboy' workers, bringing with them low standards, inadequate training, safety hazards and the undercutting of agreed rates of pay, confined by any means to craft workers or to the construction industry.[62] It is true that the 1982 Act does not prohibit the employer's saying to his contractors, 'I want you to pay union rates.' But he must not say, 'I want you to negotiate with the union.' The section is four-square in line with a policy of replacing the 'going rate' with the market rate.

When the 1982 Act is not harsh, it is haphazard. This is particularly true of these illegalities associated with collective bargaining, which were tacked on to the Bill at the last minute. Take workers in the same union employed by neighbouring companies A and B, at both of which they strike for union recognition. A is willing to grant recognition; but one of the twenty union complaints is that B will not recognize it and that

A should persuade B to do so. If B is a supplier of goods or services to A, the industrial action at A is now deprived of 'immunity' (s. 14 (2), (3) (c), (4)). But if A is supplying goods *to* B the section does not bite. The union-labour-only dimension of s. 14 was tested in *Messenger Newspapers Group* v. *NGA*, 1984.[63] A typesetting subsidiary of the group in Stockport, which published free newspapers, made recognition and union membership agreements with the NGA. A second subsidiary was set up in Bury, but negotiations with the union broke down. A third, in Warrington, began to print the papers. In the new companies, workers were given an option whether to join the union, but voted against it. The union called a strike at Stockport to support the practice of 100 per cent union membership, and picketing began at Bury and Warrington, some of which led to violence. The Stockport company dismissed the union workers on strike. The plaintiff company (the holding company in the group run by Mr Shah) obtained injunctions against the 'secondary picketing' and in respect of letters from the union to advertisers asking them not to advertise in the papers, for which liability arose under s. 14. The union broke the injunctions, was fined £675,000 and had its assets sequestrated. In the action for damages it was held liable for torts of inducing breach of contracts by the suppliers of advertisements (though it had failed in the attempt), of 'intimidation' by threats of unlawful acts and of nuisance, conspiracy and various forms of interference with business by unlawful means. It was liable because 'responsible persons' had authorized the actions (within EA 1982 s. 15 (3)).

Moreover, the action taken at some companies in the group was 'secondary action' as against the plaintiff company. Above all, the purpose of the union was 'to compel the plaintiff to accept the closed shop which in itself is unlawful because of the combined effect of s. 12 and s. 14 of the 1982 Act'. Damages, including aggravated and exemplary damages to punish the union, were awarded. It was not a tidy judgment; but it illustrated the way one company in a group can appear as a winning plaintiff when action is taken by employees of another subsidiary to maintain union membership agreements. There is no provision for 'associated companies' to be viewed together in ss. 12–14 of the 1982 Act. But there is a right of action for a very wide range of plaintiffs, to which we return (p. 641). Both in the *Dimbleby* case and in the *Messenger* dispute the union's attempts to resist the judgments ultimately failed.[64] In the first, the NUJ returned to action against

Dimbleby, against which members had continued to act even after the House of Lords judgment. Attempts to 'black' his appearing on BBC television were met with another injunction at the suit of the BBC, which members obeyed. In the NGA case the six members dismissed in the *Messenger Group* dispute were a rallying-point for a time, as was the sequestration of the union's assets. NGA members took 'spontaneous' action at national newspapers, none of which were published for two days in June 1984. Some papers dismissed their workers; all issued writs for damages against the NGA, claiming a total of £3 million. One commentator remarked that the *Messenger* dispute 'must be counted as a success for the Employment Acts' even if they allowed 'small, unrepresentative employers to push their own economic advantage at the expense of the best traditions of British industrial relations'.[65]

Bare interference with trade or employment

The word 'interference' has come to be one of the most confused terms in the English law of tort. In discussing it, an essential distinction must be kept in mind. Where it involves no act or means unlawful in itself, we are confronted with a *bare* interference, the equivalent at the individual level of the 'simple' conspiracy by a combination. Where, however, the interference is accompanied by, or affected through, some *unlawful means* (interference by 'unlawful means') it may – not necessarily will – become actionable by reason of the illegality inherent in those means. For example, 'restraint of trade' renders a contract illegal or unenforceable, but the Law Lords made it clear in 1892 that no action in tort can be mounted by someone injured – even intentionally – merely by reason of that illegality. In 1982 they refused to allow an action in tort merely because damage had been suffered by reason of contravention of a penal statute. If you do me harm by breaking a statute, I cannot always sue you even if you committed a crime. We return to this issue of unlawful means below (p. 635), though it will be necessary to point to a few cases here where judges have recently confused these two forms of 'interference'.

We saw in Chapter 1 that at the turn of the century some judges appeared to think that bare threats or 'coercive' interference with the affairs of another could be as such torts, just as Sir William Erle in 1869 asserted that a bare interference with a person's 'freedom to dispose of his labour or capital as he willed' was capable of being a tort. With this principle of law at their disposal the judges could outlaw social and industrial pressures according to their own social policy. The House of Lords rejected that doctrine in *Allen* v. *Flood*, 1898,[66] where Lord Herschel said that there was 'a chasm' between doing an act that 'violated a legal right' and an interference where 'no legal right was violated'. This liberal judgment was a reaction, it is said, to Lord Chancellor Halsbury's efforts to engineer the opposite result. (Three years later he was to pack the court when two liberal Law Lords were not invited to sit so as to make his counter-attack in *Quinn* v. *Leathem*, 1901, where the Law Lords created the tort of conspiracy to injure.)[67] Many judges – we may term them the 'Halsbury party', which has astonishingly included at times as fine a judge as Lord Devlin[68] – have been fighting back ever since in an attempt to erode or to reverse *Allen* v. *Flood*. But so far as the common law can ever be certain (and this is less than some people think) the case law establishes that the proposition of Erle that bare interference is a tort is 'the leading heresy'.[69]

In 1906, however, Parliament could not be sure it would go that way in the courts. Halsbury was eighty-three but still alive. The Royal Commission had three years earlier recommended that a statute should make things clear by declaring that a person was not liable for doing a lawful act only on the ground of 'interference with another person's trade, business or employment'. In consequence, Parliament enacted the 'second limb' of T D A 1906 s. 3, stating that an act done I C F T D was not actionable on the ground only that it was 'an interference with the trade, business or employment of some other person' or with his right 'to dispose of his capital or his labour as he wills'. In 1974 T U L R A s. 13 (2) enacted precisely the same formula (p. 579), but prefaced it with the words, 'For the avoidance of doubt'. This phrase means that Parliament was, or thought it was, declaring what the law was anyway. It was not unimportant, though, to repeat the formula in 1974. The Law Lords had decided in 1966 that they were not necessarily bound any longer by their own previous decisions, a constitutional innovation too little remarked (today they are bound by judicial decisions only of the European Court of Justice in Luxembourg). And it was but a decade since Lord Devlin's expressed misgivings about *Allen* v. *Flood*.

In *Rookes* v. *Barnard*, 1964, however, save for Lord Devlin, the Law Lords had had no doubts whatever about the status of s. 13 (2) (or limb 2 of TDA s. 3, as it then was: p. 43). As the law stood, there was no liability in tort at all for a bare interference with trade, business or employment. If this had not been so, the *Rookes* case would have been argued differently. It may be unusual for Parliament, the Law Lords agreed, to grant an 'immunity' where no tort exists, but so it was. The provision was now 'nugatory', or 'pointless'.[70] But Lord Reid understood the history of it. Parliament had, he said, 'put in a provision which would be necessary to achieve their object if the law should go one way but unnecessary if it went the other way'. The provision was, in other words, insurance against the rejuvenation of Halsbury.

More recent decisions have been replete with profound misunderstanding. It is not impossible that TULRA s. 13 (2) might one day have provided a defence to some new wrong created by the judges (perhaps 'economic duress', if this ever became – as it yet has not become – a tort: p. 650). But none has so far appeared. Even so, courts in the 1980s began to ignore the history of the law on 'interference'. In *Plessey Co.* v. *Wilson*, 1982, the Scottish courts thought that it was at least arguable that s. 13 (2) gave an 'immunity' to a 'sit-in' in a trade dispute.[71] This constitutes a trespass in English law and is similarly actionable in Scotland, at least if damage occurs.[72] The Scottish judges relied in part upon the judgment of Lord Diplock in the *Hadmor* case.[73] Unable to 'fathom' all the twists and turns of the 1974 legislation, he had said the reference to 'interference' in s. 13 (2) 'must be intended to refer to an act of "interference" that would be actionable, if it were not done in contemplation or furtherance of a trade dispute', i.e. an interference 'by unlawful means'. That was, he thought, 'too plain and unambiguous to justify resort to legislative history'. The judgments in *Rookes* v. *Barnard* that decided the opposite were probably not in his mind at this point (though he cited the case on the next page of his judgment).[74]

The *Hadmor* judgment was given in February 1982, a fortnight after the Employment Bill was published. At 2.25 on the night of 13–14 July 1982 in the (legislative) House of Lords the Lord Advocate moved a new clause to repeal TULRA s. 13 (2). He gave great prominence to both Lord Diplock's and the Scottish judgments. It seemed, he said, that s. 13 (2) might become a 'charter for sit-ins'. By 2.40 a.m. it was all over; the clause became s. 19 of the Act. There can be no doubt that Lord Reid's historical understanding of s. 13 (2) was correct, that Lord Diplock's interpretation was wrong and that the latter, coming when it did in 1982, sparked the hitherto motionless engine for its repeal. No demand for its repeal had appeared in the Government Green Paper on *Trade Union Immunities* (1981). All this was some sixteen years after the (judicial) House of Lords had taken power allowing it to overturn *Allen* v. *Flood*. The ghost of Halsbury stalked the chamber in glee that July night.

Bare interference with contract

From 1853 onwards judges affirmed that a breach of a valid contract was an essential constituent of the *Lumley* v. *Gye* tort. In interlocutory proceedings they have been prepared to accept evidence of the contractual terms that is 'scanty' or 'tenuous',[75] (*Dimbleby's* contract with TBF (Printers) Ltd, for instance, was a rather vague oral understanding). But in cases not involving trade unions the courts have not been prepared to make A liable for an act 'which he knows is likely to render less valuable certain contractual rights of B as against C without actually interfering with the performance by C of the contractual obligations'.[76] To do this would be to risk making economic competition into a tort.

Lord Denning's tort of interference with contract

The innovation that Lord Denning MR purported to make in his judgment in *Torquay Hotel Ltd* v. *Cousins*[41] is, therefore, of great importance. We recall that the defendants' argument that the exemption clause in the contract with Esso meant that there was no 'breach' was rejected by two judges within the ordinary principles of liability (p. 593). But Lord Denning created a new tort: 'The time has come when the principle [of *Lumley* v. *Gye*] should be further extended to cover deliberate and direct interference with the execution of a contract without that causing any breach.' Three things, he said, were required: (1) *interference* with performance, which included an act that 'hindered' or 'prevented' performance without causing a breach; which was (2) *deliberate* and (3) *direct* (indirect interference 'is only unlawful if unlawful means are used'). This was a new departure. The word 'interference' in earlier judgments had clearly referred to a breach of contract. Lord Denning said his tort was needed. He gave the example of a singer under contract to sing to whom 'an ill-disposed person, knowing of her contract, had given her a potion to make her sick'. She would not be in breach; but he would be liable in tort for preventing performance. No new tort was needed, however. The reason for liability there would be the use of unlawful means in administering the 'potion' without her consent. Liability has always included a case where unlawful acts directly prevent performance (as 'by removing the only available essential tools or by kidnapping a necessary or irreplaceable servant').[77] But it has not previously gone further. In 1969, however, Winn LJ, without deciding the point, also leant in favour of liability if a person prevented 'a particular mode of performance' that the contracting parties expected, perhaps 'from a normal course of dealing', even if there was no breach. But in the *Stratford* case, 1965, Lord Donovan had found the assertion that such a bare interference with contract was a tort 'as novel and surprising as I think the members of this House who decided [the *Crofter* case] would have done' in 1942.

In 1974, therefore, Parliament was in a dilemma. It faced yet another case in which the common law was unclear. If Lord Denning's tort existed, the old 1906 formula for immunities could be outflanked. In consequence, it added to the trade dispute 'immunity' for an act that induces a breach of contract, an act that 'interferes or induces any other person to interfere with its performance' (TULRA s. 13 (1), as amended in 1976). From that time on, the draftsmen of parliamentary Bills came to include the 'interference' formula as a natural part of the 'inducement' immunity. It might, in Lord Reid's words, prove 'necessary' when the common law was clarified. As Lord Devlin had said in 1964, the draftsman of a statute could not begin: 'If it be held that interference is wrongful'; he would assume it was and draft accordingly. 'If it was not, the enactment would be otiose but harmless.' But when the 'immunities' came to be *restricted*, the same formula was used. So in describing 'secondary action' that deprived a person of the s. 13 (1) immunity, the draftsman naturally defined it by reference to an act that 'induces another to break a contract of employment or interferes or induces another to interfere with its performance' (where the employer is not a party to the trade dispute: E A 1980 s. 17 (2)).

In the same way, when the 1982 Act restricted the liberty to take industrial action undertaken for an extension of negotiation or for union labour only, it adhered to the same wording (i.e. acts that have induced a breach of an employment contract or 'interfered or induced another to interfere with its performance'). As we shall see, a similar formula was used in 1984 on strike ballots (TUA 1984 s. 10 (1), (2)). Not unnaturally, therefore, judges have begun to say that the inclusion of 'interference with performance' along with 'inducement to break a contract' amounts, as Lord Diplock has said, to 'Parliamentary recognition that the tort of actionable interference with contractual rights is as broad as Lord Denning MR stated'.[78] It would be surprising if this were correct in general terms. One would, in the first instance, expect Parliament to indicate the ambit of 'interference'. One problem with Lord Denning's tort is to know what kind of 'hindrance' imports liability, a particularly important question in industrial disputes. Indeed, it is difficult to think of any industrial action that does not 'hinder' the performance both of the employer's commercial contracts and of employment contracts of any workers remaining at work. The new tort would remove any doubt as to the automatic illegality of all industrial action under the judges' common law.

Secondly, there is no case after 1969 in which the new tort has been crucial to the liability of the defendants. A few judges have referred to it with apparent favour, though not in any case where the point was fully contested.[79] In many cases 'interference' has been used to mean 'inducement of breach'. In others, judges have cited Lord Denning's words with approval, but normally only in cases where they confronted indirect interference by unlawful means. Lord Denning's new principle, however, was concerned with *direct* and deliberate interference short of causing breach without unlawful means. Thus Lord Diplock refers, in the *Merkur Island* case, to liability arising from interference causing 'non-performance of primary obligations under a contract', even though damages were not payable for breach because of exemption clauses. But he himself makes it clear that this was a case of 'interfering by *unlawful means* with the performance of a contract', and he describes the unlawful means as the tort of inducing 'the tugmen . . . to *break* their contracts of employment'.[78]

Even if the exemption clauses there meant that the charterers were exempt from the obligation to continue payment, the interference with performance was done through unlawful means, the inducement of the tugmen now constituting 'secondary action'. We shall see (p. 635) that not even every illegal act constitutes 'unlawful means' for this purpose; so it would be absurd if an otherwise lawful act that directly hindered performance, even deliberately, could be a tort. If this were so, it would not be lawful for one employer to persuade a skilled man (crucial to the business and expected by his present employer to remain) to give proper and lawful notice and transfer to him with higher pay in order that he can compete more effectively with the other employer.

In the absence of unlawful means, the statement of the law in the Donovan Report of 1968 is best: 'Mere interference by itself is not actionable anyhow.' This is consistent with the way Lord Denning himself has stated the liability in several subsequent judgments: where a person 'deliberately interferes with the trade or business of another and does so by unlawful means, that is by an act which he is not at liberty to commit'.[80] This is the more accurate principle (though, as we shall see, the Law Lords have apparently placed a rather narrow definition on 'unlawful means'). If the judges followed Lord Denning in his 1969 tort it would constitute a major and unjustified intervention against both competition in commercial law and trade unions in labour law.

We shall find that the Trade Union Act 1984 requires a trade union to hold a ballot of the members taking action where a call to strike or take industrial action involves inducing either breaches of, or 'interference' with, contracts of employment. This language has been seen by some to support Lord Denning's principle and recognize bare interference as a tort. We shall argue, however, that a close interpretation of the sections (TUA ss. 10, 11) reveals the opposite result and shows that Parliament must have been speaking of an 'interference' that also involves a breach of employment contract (p. 630). The core of the argument is that the Act demands a question in the ballot only where such a breach is involved. Because of the obscurities in the 1984 Act, however, the arguments about bare interference are likely to acquire new prominence. We return to them below in that context.

Intimidation

Between 1793 and 1964 the tort of intimidation played little, if any, role in the law. It may appear as a distinct wrong in a claim for damages; but in so far as it consists in a threat to commit a tort, it adds little to a claim for an interlocutory injunction, at least where the defendant has not yet acted. Suppose a union threatens to call a strike by way of secondary action and the employer seeks an injunction. The cause of action is based on the threat to induce breaches of employment contracts that will interfere with his commercial contracts (EA 1980 s. 17), and the injunction will rest on the so-called *quia timet* form (because the tort is feared or threatened). This is the basis on which a court, faced with the threatened tort, restrains the defendant from doing any act that procures a breach of contracts made 'now or hereafter' (as in the *Torquay Hotel* case).

We have met the tort in its 'three-party' form: A says to B, 'Unless you withdraw that benefit (lawfully) from C, I will commit this (unlawful) act against you.' There C is the plaintiff. Although some writers have thrown doubt on it, the judicial decisions also recognize the 'two-party' form: where A says to B, 'Unless you refrain from that act, from which you will (lawfully) benefit, I will commit this (unlawful) act against you.' There B is the plaintiff. In each case it is the person who suffers the damage by reason of a deliberate threat of unlawful action who can sue.

We recall that 'intimidation' was revived as a separate heading of tort, and extended from threats of violence even to a threat to break a contract, a form not hitherto known as a tort (Chapter 1, p. 41), at the instance of the (third party) plaintiff in the dramatic decision in *Rookes* v. *Barnard*, 1964.[81] Were it not for that extension of liability, the trade union defendants would have been protected by the trade dispute immunities of 1906 on conspiracy and inducing breach of employment contracts. A few judicial statements subsequently suggested that a threat to break employment contracts in a trivial way might not be actionable because that would cause the employer no real damage.[82] But normally after 1964 a threat to strike (it could be an *implied* threat, as Lord Devlin made clear) has constituted the tort of 'intimidation' at common law because of the threatened breach of those contracts. It is one strange result in the common law of the Law Lords decision in the *Rookes* case that, if workers themselves strike, the employer has an action for breach of contract (Chapter 3); but if they threaten to strike, the employer appears to have a choice. He can sue for 'anticipatory' breach of contract (the term for such an announcement that a party will break an agreement) or he can sue for the tort of intimidation. He cannot obtain an injunction to prevent a breach of the employment contracts (Chapter 2; TULRA s. 16). But on principle, he can seek an injunction against a tort (though the court should in its discretion refuse injunctions that are only a roundabout method of specifically enforcing personal contracts). These are only a few of the complexities that show how the Law Lords contravened the logic of the law in extending this tort into breaches of contract. But that is water under the bridge – unless that form of the tort is abolished by Parliament outright. English law does not, and should not, regard the very breach of contract (even an intentional breach) as a tort, as some US jurisdictions do.[83] So why should a threat to break it be a tort?

Parliament and intimidation

To restore elementary legality to industrial action in 1965 Parliament brought threats to break employment contracts within a trade dispute 'immunity'. When the modern pattern of equivalent 'immunities' was collected together in TULRA 1974–6, therefore, it was natural for the draftsman to insert in s. 13 (1) (b) equivalent protections for threats to commit acts ICFTD that are protected within s. 13 (1) (a). The equivalent was a threat to induce another person to break a contract (or, for safety's sake, to interfere with its performance). There was, however, one addition: a threat that a contract (whether one to which he is a party or not) will be broken (or its performance interfered with). Thus TULRA s. 13 (1) (b) covers both the *quia timet* forms of the substantive torts of inducing breach of contract and the tort of 'intimidation' in all those forms, plus the *Rookes* v. *Barnard* form of a threat to break a contract. But later, because the 1974–6 legislation took that form, so too did the definition of 'secondary action' (EA 1980 s. 17 (2) (b): namely, a threat to induce breach of, to interfere with, to induce interference with or to break an employment contract). So did the prohibition to take industrial action in order to extend negotiation or union labour only (EA 1982 s. 14 (2) (b)). In secondary action or the prohibited extension of negotiation or union labour only, intimidation is no longer protected since TULRA s. 13 is displaced. It is noticeable, however, that the formula on 'threats' is not repeated in the equivalent section on strike ballots, to which we turn below (TUA 1984 s. 10 (1), (2): p. 625).

The principle of the tort of intimidation

In *Rookes* v. *Barnard*,[81] though, the Law Lords did maintain one essential common law principle, based upon the decision in *Allen* v. *Flood*. Lord Reid said:

there is a chasm between doing what you have a legal right to do and doing what you have no legal right to do, and there seems to me to be the same chasm between threatening to do what you have a legal right to do and threatening to do what you have no legal right to do.

So they decided that the threat to break employment contracts (or as Lord Reid put it, rather differently, acts done 'to conspire to threaten an employer that his men will break their contracts with him unless he dismisses the plaintiff') was 'intimidation' just as much as threats of violence (an equation that not all other common law countries have accepted).[84] But the Law Lords rejected the idea that liability could extend into threats, however 'coercive', to do acts in themselves lawful.

We return later to the element of 'unlawful' acts or means: p. 635. We shall find that the Law Lords have said in 1982 that acts which are 'unlawful' by reason of a contravention of a penal statute do not constitute unlawful means for the purposes of the law of tort unless the intention of the statute on its proper construction is that the plaintiff shall be permitted a civil remedy for the breach.[85] A threat to commit an act – even a criminal act – of this kind, where the Act allows for no civil action, now appears to be outside the range of civil intimidation. Where, however, A threatens to commit a contravention of the statute against B to the damage of C, and the act would give B a civil right of action if it were committed, the logic of the judgments in *Rookes* v. *Barnard* seems to give C a right to sue for intimidation. This is yet another odd result of the *Rookes* case. In fact, there Lord Devlin assumed that a threat of any criminal act gave rise to the tort of intimidation. It is uncertain how far the 1982 judgment has finally defined liability in this area.

Intimidation as a tort has been said to need an 'or else' element: 'Change the employment conditions or else we will strike.' It is possible, however, that the courts might see as a tort open to damages and an injunction a threat to break employment contracts (or a threat that 'workers will break' them) even without an 'or else' demand (although usually the facts reveal at least an implied objective, as Templeman J. once observed, to make the employer 'come to his senses'). A threat to lock-out whatever happened would similarly be wrongful (unless adequate notice of dismissal was given). Even in 1964, however, Lord Reid distinguished between threatening the employer and 'merely informing [him] that the men would strike if their terms were not accepted'. This distinction has a long pedigree in the case law. Where there is no 'or else' element the older cases suggest that the announcement of a strike or lock-out is at most warning of an impending breach of contract. This was joined by a third possible interpretation in *Morgan* v. *Fry*, 1968,[86] where the union official's statement that workers would not work with non-unionists from a certain date was treated as 'an offer' by the workers to continue working 'on different terms', which was there accepted by the employer. We saw in Chapter 3 that this is virtually the only way a strike notice, as opposed to a notice to quit, can affect the legality of the workers' strike action.

Unhappily in most of the recent cases the area of trade dispute immunity has been reduced to such a small compass that the distinctions between the various types of tort liability have not been carefully considered by some judges. In *Hadmor Productions Ltd* v. *Hamilton*[73] one of the torts put against the union defendants, ACTT, was intimidation by the 'blacking' of the plaintiff's films, by way of a threat to break, or procure breaches of, employment contracts. In the Court of Appeal new evidence was admitted to the effect that the union and Thames TV had agreed that Thames would not require ACTT members to transmit programmes produced by facility companies (like the plaintiff) except after prior consultation with the union. The union claimed this clause was incorporated into their members' employment contracts, and therefore a threat to 'black' the programmes where no consultation had occurred was no breach of contract. We have seen the difficulties that can arise in respect of the incorporation of collectively agreed terms into employment contracts (p. 338). Here Lord Diplock refrained from answering the 'interesting and difficult questions of law into which it would be inappropriate to enter upon a motion for an interlocutory injunction' (the courts are not always so shy, as we saw in the *Mercury* case: p. 561). The Law Lords decided the case for the defendants on the easier ground that a trade dispute existed; but the definition of trade dispute has changed since the *Hadmor* decision and the incorporation question is therefore now of even greater importance. The Law Lords were clearly prepared to consider the incorporation of the consultation clause, which would give a worker the right to refuse to work on particular materials unless his union was consulted without any breach of contract. Such reasoning could be of profound importance in days when the ambit of the common law is doubly important because of the shrunken condition of the 'immunities'.

Anderman suggested in 1975, in an important analysis of 'status quo' clauses, that the common law analysis of the work contract paid inadequate attention to the clauses in collective agreements that stated, or implied, that the status quo at the workplace should not be changed until a procedure of consultation had been exhausted.[87] It is indeed arguable that, where strike action is expressed in a clause of the collective agreement to be prohibited until after the exhaustion of procedure and the clause enters the employment contracts of workers (provided that it satisfies TULRA s. 18 (4): p. 340), then by implication the employer must have agreed that strike action without breach of employment contracts is an option for workers after the procedure is completed. No court has gone – or at present is likely to go – this far (though this is no reason why a statute should not). The step in the *Hadmor* case would have been nothing like so great. All that was suggested there was that the workers should be entitled not to work on materials on which the employer had agreed they should not work until he had discussed the matter with their union. Why Lord Diplock found this interesting point to be difficult is unclear. The clause was not inappropriate for incorporation (p. 338).

Somewhat surprisingly both Lords Devlin and Denning have suggested that the tort of 'intimidation' allows for a defence of 'justification'. The difficulty lies in finding, if the defendant has threatened an unlawful act, the sort of consideration that can validate the illegality. In the only modern application, Lord Denning MR met the claim against the union official in *Morgan* v. *Fry*, 1968,[82] by saying that he 'might well be justified' in committing intimidation against the dock employers in order to get rid of the plaintiffs, who had broken away from the union and who were 'really troublemakers who fomented discord in the docks without lawful justification or excuse'.

In 1973 he went further and was prepared to judge the strength of the plaintiff's case by whether he acted out of 'conscience' or 'out of malice and with intent to injure' or even had 'brought everything upon himself by his own eccentric conduct'. Few judges would go so far. Nor is it desirable that they should, for it leaves common law liability wholly at the discretion and industrial eccentricities of the court. Lord Devlin in *Rookes* itself thought that a more limited doctrine might be admitted – namely, a defence where a party threatens to break a contract against a person who is already in breach of obligations owed to him. This is as far as most judges would be likely to go.

Summary so far

It may be useful to recapitulate the skeleton of the inquiry so far. *Bare interference with trade or employment* is no tort; and there is no better case for accepting *bare interference with contract* as a tort, though Lord Denning M R held otherwise. But *inducing breach of contract* is a tort. So too, *intimidation* as a tort is constituted by a threat to induce *breach* and a threat to *break* a contract. Industrial action by workers is normally a *breach of their employment contracts*. Where the act is done in contemplation or furtherance of a *trade dispute*, both those torts are protected by 'immunity' in TULRA 1974–6 (s. 13 (1)). Simple *conspiracy to injure* was similarly protected (s. 13 (4)). But since then protection has been stripped away in respect of all three torts in regard to '*secondary*' *picketing* (E A 1980 s. 16) and *action to extend negotiation or union labour only* (E A 1982 ss. 12–14). The protection of s. 13 (1) is also removed from '*secondary action*' (E A 1980 s. 17), subject to three rather ineffective 'gateways' to legality (E A 1980 s. 17 (3)–(5)). In other words, taken together with the narrowing of the definition of 'trade dispute' and the renewed tort liability of the union discussed in Chapter 7, the new legislation hands back to the industrial torts of the common law, in their certain and uncertain forms, a very wide area of industrial action.

Strike ballots

Parliament then introduced further restrictions. The Trade Union Act 1984 Part II is different from what has gone before. Its conception was announced on that same night of 14 July 1982 (p. 613), for it was then that the Government made what was rightly called by Lord McCarthy 'an amazing announcement at this time of night' (it was 3.20 a.m.), namely that a 'consultative document' with proposals for new legislation would soon be published. The Green Paper, *Democracy in Trade Unions*, was produced in January 1983.[88] For the first time in a Government paper the unequivocal statement was made that 'Trade union power . . . springs from legal immunities and privileges.' Since 'the law had granted these privileges' it was necessary to consider whether individual members were 'adequately protected and whether those who exercise power in the name of the membership are properly accountable to the members'. Moreover, it said, the 'unique legal status which trade unions enjoy' and their leaders' power to damage 'the economic and commercial interests of others' make it essential for union internal affairs to command 'public confidence'. The paper made proposals for new regulation of elections, industrial action and political funds.

The new law contrasts markedly with the Donovan approach to compulsory strike ballots. For one thing, the Bill in the form in which it was introduced required unions to hold a ballot, but it did not demand a favourable result from the workers voting before validating a strike. Many observers found this to be absurd; and so it was, by Donovan standards. But the 1984 Act had rather different objectives, as can be seen by the way the debate on compulsory strike ballots had developed. Donovan rejected such ballots; experience in North America suggested that they tended to produce votes in favour of striking. Moreover, settlements of disputes might be delayed. Should there not be a vote on them? And who was to set the questions? The decision when and how to hold a ballot should continue to be decided by a union's rules and practices, especially when compulsion to ballot could not be applied to the small-scale unofficial stoppage against which the law should lean. That discussion in 1968 centred upon the reform of the industrial relations systems. Subsequently compulsory ballots in emergencies were proposed (*In Place of Strife*, 1969) and, on a grander scale, enacted (Industrial Relations Act 1971 s. 141), both based on objectives that related to the reform of industrial relations, however wrong-headed.

When the issue surfaced again, the Green Paper of 1981 put forward two 'general approaches' for discussion: first, the right of a proportion of union members to 'trigger' a ballot; second, the encouragement of non-mandatory ballots by the provision of public funds. Funds had already been made available for ascertaining the views of members about industrial action in 1980 (EA 1980 s. 1). The 1983 Green Paper discussed the same two proposals, plus the idea of a ballot triggered by the employer, again speaking of reform (one difficulty with 'triggered' ballots was that militants might use them to embarrass 'more responsible leaders'). Overall the debate still seemed to allow for unions' justifiably differing in the ways in which they sought their members' views (some, like NALGO, regularly balloted members, others, like the BIFU, were bound by rule to do so).

The 1984 ballots

As against these proposals, the 1984 Act is startling in its novelty. Without the support of a favourable ballot, a union loses its s. 13 'immunity' in every official strike or industrial action in respect of liability for inducing a breach of, or interference with, an employment contract. Consequential interferences with commercial contracts are also deprived of protection. The protection of 'simple' conspiracy in s. 13 (4) remains, for what it is worth. Unofficial action is not affected and retains whatever 'immunity' is going.

The justification for such an idea was twofold. Government spokesmen said it was the 'minimum obligation' for the union's 'privilege' of immunity from civil obligations; and it was also a means of 'giving the unions back to their members'. The current of individualism was now dominant, no longer checked by considerations of collective bargaining functions. But the new proposal, by not prescribing any special circumstances ('emergencies', 'triggers' and the like) when ballots are needed and by demanding them for all 'official' action, from a small shop-floor stoppage to a national strike, is able to take its stand on the democratic 'right' of every member to vote. There was little debate about whether the law should not equally insist on a form of voting on other issues (say, settlement of disputes, or industrial policy or even decisions by employers) and whether, and why, the law should demand that unions alone should be subject to government by referendum; nor about whether members of a union should also have the right to decide democratically upon the conditions of, and the question put in, the ballot. Indeed, in its first version the Bill had not demanded a majority vote in the ballot, and the requirement of majority support was inserted because it seemed odd not to demand it.

But the point of the strike ballot is not merely to ensure that the majority of members agree; it is also to put an obstruction in the path of official strikes. The remedies for not holding a ballot do not bring direct benefit to members, unless one or more of them wished to go to the courts for an injunction in the absence of a ballot. The plaintiffs and beneficiaries are invariably employers or third parties. The effects and functions of imposed strike ballots are much wider than any that can be related to the internal legitimation of industrial action. For example, we shall see that in many negotiation situations the time required will cramp the union's options and 'reduce flexibility in collective bargaining', whilst the mandatory application of the ballot to all members likely to be involved – and no others – at one and the same time discloses to the other side the union forces to be deployed and prevents an extension to new groups of workers as a surprise tactic.[89]

The experience of the 1984 Act has confirmed the fact that many employers are now more prone to litigate, a very different social context from that of the 1970s. But the Act could not have become the intimate part of industrial tactics that it became for some unions had not the procedure of the High Court required no more of such a plaintiff than that he prove a 'serious case' to be argued before he is able to obtain an interlocutory injunction against a union going on to industrial action without a ballot. Full proof of liability is not required in such proceedings – only an arguable case for it, as we shall see when we deal with the labour injunction (p. 685). Tactically, the unions were caught flat-footed. Objecting to the charge of being 'undemocratic', they also opposed this particular form of ballot being imposed by law and in many cases the offer of State aid to implement it. It was not an easy posture to sustain; and after the failure of the London Tube strike in 1985 (p. 86) pressures grew inside the TUC to change the policy of non-co-operation, which at one point threatened to lead to a scission (p. 786).

The scope of the Act

The problems involved in implementing the 1984 Act are not to be underestimated, even though under the 1980 Act in a postal ballot State money may be available (s. 1, and Funds for Trade Union Ballots Regulation No. 1654, 1984), while for secret workplace ballots the union has legal rights to use the employer's premises (s. 2). The obligation to hold a ballot arises whenever a trade union 'authorizes or endorses' action, within the meaning of the code on vicarious liability in EA 1982 s. 15. Unless there is a ballot in which a majority votes 'yes' to an 'appropriate question', the 'immunities' of TULRA s. 13 are withdrawn. The requirement for approval by a majority (s. 10 (3) (b)) was introduced by amendment in the House of Lords. Where the ballot requirements are not satisfied, the loss of the s. 13 'immunities' makes the action actionable in tort against both the union and relevant officials where they have 'induced a person to break his contract of employment or to interfere with its performance' (T U A 1984 s. 10 (1)).

Three points arise here. This formulation, first, does not include 'interference'. It speaks of 'inducement to interfere'. The section is confined to persuasive inducement of the workers themselves. Mere interference, short of causing breach and without unlawful means, would be unaffected. Secondly, the 'interference' induced appears at first sight to mean some industrial action that is less than a breach of employment contract. Otherwise the word seems to have no function. The section therefore appears to include, say, an abstention from voluntary, non-contractual overtime in its demand for a ballot. But this would constitute a gigantic limitation on work-people's freedom. It would mean that they would act illegally because without a ballot they refused to do what they had no obligation to do. What is more, where industrial action without a ballot is relied upon in a case based upon indirect inducement of breach of, or interference with, a 'commercial contract', the 'immunity' is lost equally in respect of that cause of action (s. 10 (2)). Thirdly, the formula does not include 'threats'. This might be thought to prevent legal action arising during negotiations on the basis of the union threatening a strike without a ballot. The plaintiff cannot, it is true, rely upon 'intimidation' in the form of a threat to break a contract. But in such a case an employer can argue that he seeks a *quia timet* injunction based upon another tort. The tort threatened would normally be that of inducing breach of employment contracts without a ballot, within the 1984 Act.

In the *Austin Rover* case, 1985,[90] 'five days' notice' was given of the strike, but proceedings were not begun until two days after it started. But in *Shipping Company Uniform Inc.* v. *ITWF*, 1985,[91] the action was brought explicitly on a *quia timet* basis, before any 'blacking' took place. As well as incurring liability for secondary action, the ITWF was held liable under the 1984 Act, because no ballot was 'foreshadowed'. Indeed, no ballot was possible. The (relevant) 'members' of the ITWF were other unions; but the 1984 Act demanded a ballot of union members with 'contracts of employment'. Instead of holding that the

Act was therefore inapplicable to the ITWF, Staughton J. held astonishingly that it did apply to make the ITWF liable, because 'they cannot
and do not hold a ballot'.

It seems, therefore, that despite the omission of the usual 'threats'
formula, a plaintiff can obtain his injunction on the basis of a threat by
the union to induce breach of employment contracts by industrial action
without a ballot. This draws the High Court into the industrial process in
a new way. The judge can offer – and already some have offered – to
adjourn the case while a union holds a ballot before reconsidering its
projected strike. The judge is now involved directly in the bargaining
process, ostensibly defending union 'democracy', at the instance of the
plaintiff employer. The Act thereby encourages the sort of procedure
adopted by the Court of Appeal in the AUEW action in the *Austin
Rover* dispute: closed sessions in which the judges decide what to do by
unknown standards of discretion. The consequences for the place of
'law' may be profound.

Intimidatory questions and interference

The Act lays down strict rules for the ballot. Entitlement to vote must be
accorded equally to all members who it is reasonable for the union to
believe will be called upon 'in the strike or other industrial action in
question to act in breach of, or to interfere with the performance of their
contracts of employment'; but to no others (s. 11 (1)). The union must
disclose its hand as to the disposition of its forces. It must follow that the
mistaken admission of any 'others' to vote invalidates the ballot.
Moreover, if anyone is denied his 'entitlement' to vote and is then
induced to join the action (perhaps by a different official from one who
mistakenly rejected his vote) and to 'break his contract of employment
or to interfere with its performance' the entire ballot is invalidated, and
the whole union loses the s. 13 'immunity'. Here the Act does not
include the usual legal principle applicable to associations, that a minor
or insubstantial irregularity in procedure may be excused and cannot be
challenged by a minority of members (p. 753). The question of the ballot
arises in an action brought in respect of the tortious industrial action,
and the High Court has no discretion to excuse innocent contraventions
of the imposed procedures. Voting must be by voting papers; voters
must not be subject to interference or constraint from the union, its

members or employees (there is no such ban on the employer or third parties). So far as reasonably practicable, there must be no direct cost to voters; there must be secret voting and proper counting, and an announcement of the result to members entitled to vote. Every member entitled to vote must, so far as is reasonably practicable, be given a voting paper in, or immediately before or after, working hours and at work or a more convenient place (s. 11 (6)). Additionally, the mandate of the ballot lasts for only four weeks. The union must authorize future industrial action, and it must begin, within four weeks of the ballot, while endorsement of existing action must take place within four weeks of the ballot. So union negotiators in a difficult dispute must reach a conclusion within four weeks of a ballot; otherwise they must call industrial action, or hold another ballot. The limitations upon union tactics in bargaining are obvious.

As Donovan stressed, in a ballot the question is of great importance. The 1984 Act requires that one of two mandatory questions ('however framed') must be put, and answered 'yes' or 'no'. They are (1) in a strike, whether the voter is prepared 'to take part in a strike involving him in a breach of his contract of employment'; and (2) in other cases, whether he is prepared 'to take part in industrial action falling short of a strike but involving him in a breach of his contract of employment' (ss. 10 (4), 11 (4)). These formulations have both industrial and legal difficulties. In industrial terms, the questions are scarcely neutral. Most workers do not wish to act illegally. The mandatory questions do not include (though there is nothing to stop the union including) a full explanation of the way in which strikes are normally a breach. As they stand, the statutory questions are loaded, even intimidatory.

In legal terms, they illustrate the remarkable confusion in this part of the Act. The law purports to deprive of 'immunity' (a) inducing breach of employment contract and (b) inducing interference with it (s. 10 (1), (2)). In parallel terms, it refers to (a) strikes and (b) 'other industrial action' (s. 10 (3) (a), (4)). These are in turn linked to 'breach' and 'interference' (s. 11 (1) (a), (2) (b); so too in s. 10 (5)). Strike is defined as 'any concerted stoppage of work' (whether or not there is a trade dispute: s. 11 (11)). So too, 'strike' is contrasted with 'industrial action short of a strike' (s. 11 (4) (b)). All of this suggests that the draftsman is working to a model where (a) the strike involves a breach but (b) the other industrial action involves an 'interference' less than breach. We have argued that inducing a bare interference with performance short of breach is not as such a tort (p. 614) and that workers should not be prejudiced for acts that are not a breach of their obligations.

Do sections 10 and 11 of the 1984 Act give support to the tort of bare interference? It is submitted that on further analysis they do not. For when we come to the questions to be placed before the voter we find a critical elucidation. The worker must be asked either 'Will you strike in breach of your contract?' or 'Will you take part in industrial action short of a strike in breach of your contract?' The second question can mean only that 'interference' short of a strike also involves a breach. If 'inducing interference' were a tort without any breach, Parliament would be compelling the union either to put a mendacious question to the members or to have no way of saving its 'immunity'. (The question would be mendacious, because on this analysis the interference on which a ballot is required is *not* a breach.) The courts should not construe an Act in a manner that compels one party mendaciously to mislead another. The only interpretation that achieves a different result is to draw boundaries of 'interference' along the obligations of the employment contract. Interference then means breach in both sections 10 and 11. The question relating to industrial action short of a strike, on this view, uses the term 'breach', in s. 11 (4) (b), in order to reinforce that point, referring perhaps to breach of a 'primary' term. Despite initial appearances, it is submitted that compulsory ballots do *not* apply to the case of industrial action without breach of employment contracts (such as a mere withdrawal of goodwill or abstention from voluntary overtime).

This interpretation is supported by the parliamentary history of the clauses (which the judges, as Lord Diplock rightly insisted in the *Hadmor* case, are unhappily not permitted to consult). In the Bill, as first printed, the question relating to action short of a strike (now s. 11 (4) (b)) had a different wording; it asked the voter whether he would take part in action 'involving him in a breach of his contract of employment *or interference with its performance*' (thereby covering both action that was a breach, e.g. a go-slow, and action that was not). The Government was constantly questioned in committee in the House of Commons as to the meaning of those final words, and, save perhaps for a ban on voluntary overtime, it was never able to define them or even to give examples. In consequence, it moved an amendment at report stage (which was not debated at all) to delete those final words 'for technical reasons'. The reason must have been that its advisers had perceived the improper width of a bare 'interference short of breach'. A court would be free to hold that it included any interference that thwarted management's wishes in any way at all (without even any requirement of concerted pressure on the employer). Those 'technical reasons' went to the root of the employment relationship.

The wrong of 'interference' could be a vehicle for a massive increase of the employer's rights over the disposition of labour power in the wage–work bargain, a new statutory pronouncement that within the factory or office he is once more 'a private legislator', his command 'as indispensable as that a general should command on the field of battle'.[92] If the courts were to hold that Parliament had confirmed the existence of a tort of 'inducing interference', the Halsbury party would after all have won, by a curious side-wind, a significant battle in its war against *Allen* v. *Flood*. Once again the meaning of the legal technicalities goes to the root of the social relationship.

English judges have a nose for danger. They avoid difficult issues if their instincts tell them the moment is not ripe and they can reach their result without them. In *Solihull MBC* v. *NUT*, 1985,[93] the union had called upon teachers in certain schools to take action by refusing to supervise pupils in lunch periods, to attend meetings outside school hours and certain other tasks. At first no ballot was held. The employing council obtained an order requiring the union to rescind its communication. Warner J. held that there was a serious case that the lunchtime duties were not voluntary but contractual. There was evidence of an implied term to that effect, necessary for 'business efficiency' modified by custom and practice; and he was not going to decide the entire issue 'on motion' (in interlocutory proceedings) but only after 'hearing full oral evidence'. The plaintiffs argued that the teachers' agreement to stay over lunch breaks was a separate 'supplemental agreement', which entitled them to free lunches. The judge thought this was 'perfectly consistent' with the main contract, though whether this could then be the contract of employment under the Act was not made clear. The council got its injunction. The judgment will merit further examination on injunction procedure (p. 700). The problems of 'interference' were studiously avoided. If Lord Denning's tort of 'bare interference' really existed (p. 614), its absence from such judgments is remarkable.

The operation of the Act

The N U T organized selective action, including withdrawal of 'goodwill' from February 1985, over salaries; for example, during three days in June alone 14,000 teachers in 945 schools of forty-five local authorities were involved. Ballots were held, and objections were raised to the questions. At first the union put a question: 'Are you prepared to withdraw your services for a period of up to (three) days if called upon to do so?' When the Department of Employment reportedly objected (though what standing it could have to do so was obscure) the union put a question including the 'breach of contract' formula, but made it clear it disagreed with the interim judgment in the *Solihull* case. A ballot by A P E X of members some months later engaged as security guards by Brinks-Mat had to be repeated as the union ballot paper did not include the 'breach of contract' question by reason of a clerical error. A S T M S prepared an interesting standard question that included the words: 'Obviously the usual breach of your contract of employment is involved: the significance of this is explained in the attached circular.' The Act seems to allow for this. In the teachers' dispute, the question was raised about the school summer holidays: if the N U T continued action into the new school year, would this need a new ballot and a new call for action within four weeks of it? The N U T announced in June 1985 that the sixth ballot of members in its dispute showed a majority of 77 per cent in favour of further industrial action, and members were keenly supporting its campaign. The selective character of the N U T action, calling on teachers in different schools each week, also raised the issue of how far a new ballot might be required for each 'call' more than four weeks from the last ballot. The better view seems to be that the Act allows one ballot to validate the whole of one piece of industrial action even if carried out in stages; but of course all the members who will take part in it must be included.

By the end of 1985 A C A S knew of 94 strike ballots (68 with majorities for action with industrial action in 38). Some Civil Service unions were included. But there were 813 recorded stoppages in 1984; and it was not clear that all ballots complied with the Act. A C A S commented that 'balloting can sometimes be an over-simple way of assessing opinion in a complex situation', though union members 'were coming to regard pre-strike ballots as an essential precursor to industrial action'.

The injunction consequent upon not holding a ballot was a factor in defeating the NUR call for the London Underground drivers' strike in 1985, but NUR policy changed in the 'one-man train' dispute six months later when by a narrow margin guards voted against a strike. Some 40,000 GMBAT gas workers voted against industrial action in May; and sporadic strike action in the Post Office in the long dispute over technology and part-time workers led to an injunction and to a plan for a union ballot to back up negotiations. A ballot of bank staff members by the (non-TUC) CBU returned a 56 per cent majority for an overtime ban on a pay claim, and its rival BIFU's members voted for such a ban but against a strike. Towards the end of the miners' strike seamen in three ships had taken industrial action to support them, refusing to let the ships sail. In proceedings brought by the shipowners against the NUS the judge suggested it should hold a ballot, which it made preparations to do in the required form. The seamen, however, insisted that they would continue their action whatever the union did (i.e. as unofficial action), and its General Secretary thought the injunction had had 'the effect of hardening attitudes at grass roots level'.[94] British Telecom obtained an injunction against action by engineers in the London branch; the union, the NCU, told them to return to work and organized a ballot. By June the TGWU, a union strongly opposed to the 1980s legislation, decided to ballot its bus crews on industrial action.

From this patchwork picture it appears that, although many of these unions might have held a vote of members anyway, the 1984 Act's demand for *its* style of ballot before industrial action had a measure of success – often after injunctions or threat of proceedings. Most of them put the mandatory question. The original TUC policy that affiliated unions should ignore the Act was not everywhere effective. Some ballots had gone against, most for, union policy; some strikes without ballots (and with injunctions) had failed; other industrial action had not. The national campaign sustained by the NUT's selective action was supported by regular ballots of members; by the end of 1985 the union had held eleven. The Secretary of State, Mr King, claimed that the ballot provisions were making a 'major contribution' to reducing strikes, citing cases in which employers had obtained injunctions against twenty-one unions.[95] Such figures must be set against the unions that hold ballots or votes of one kind or another under their own rules in regard to industrial action and other issues arising in collective bargaining.[96] But the authors and supporters of the Act ascribed great importance to the type of ballot imposed, a secret ballot, as the Minister put it, 'away from the emotionally charged atmosphere' of a mass meeting.

Against this it was said that the individual member exercising a postal vote at home as he watches his television is hardly free from an emotionally charged presentation of trade union affairs. Moreover, the union is charged not to indulge in 'interference or constraint', while the employer is free to act as he pleases within the general law. Some trade union leaders who considered that some form of 'strike ballot' was desirable, coupled that proposal with a demand that employers should be obliged to maintain the industrial status quo, and not to interfere, during the ballot. The NGA complained of intimidation of members in 1986. In the period leading to the ballot of NUR guards in 1985, British Rail dismissed more than 200 who engaged in unofficial strikes against plans for 'one-man trains' and threatened to close the entire railway system if the vote approved a strike. When the proposal was lost by a few hundred out of some 9,000 votes, BR pressed home its advantage by demanding a range of concessions from the NUR before considering their reinstatement. The loss of the guards' ballot was treated by conventional wisdom as confirmation that the unions must give up resistance to management's plans for the industry.

More generally, doubts arose about the subjection of each issue to a referendum of members – usually a particular group of members – not a method of policy-making always used in representative democracy. The legal problems, meanwhile, grew ever more complex. Some (reportedly including the UCW in a dispute with the Post Office) seemed ready to claim that a positive ballot and notice to the employer cured the breach of workers' employment contracts inherent in industrial action. Such a view had profound implications, and it seemed unlikely that the courts (especially the appellate courts) would accept it. There were more immediate difficulties. Take the *News International* dispute at Wapping (p. 604). In 1986 SOGAT was fined and had its £17 million assets sequestrated for not obeying injunctions to withdraw its instructions for action without a ballot (this may also have been 'secondary action'). The NGA called for industrial action, did not obey an injunction and was fined £25,000. Shortly before another court hearing, however, the union called off the 'blacking' of NI newspapers, whereupon the judge said that if this was not genuine the union would 'get a good clout'. The company did not proceed with its action for further punishment; but shortly afterwards the NGA declared that the 'blacking' would be reimposed, apparently by way of ballots with the required questions at three printing and typesetting companies that worked for the NI Group on supplements. Workers at two companies voted narrowly to reject industrial action; but at the third a majority was for it.[97] Lawyers debated the result. Was this all a defiance of the first order, a contempt for which the new judge put in charge of all the Wapping litigation could punish the unions? (SOGAT was also in contempt of court.) Or was it a legitimate step in new industrial action? If so, must all three companies' workers be taken together, in which case the ballot was lost, or could the third company be regarded separately? Had the union made a mistake in grouping all the workers together or was it bound to do so? Could it have had separate ballots? What does '*the* strike or industrial action' in the 1984 Act mean? How far is the union free, under s. 11 (1) of the 1984 Act, to ballot different groups of members separately even though they support one another? Apart from the ballot, if these companies had contracted with NIS (p. 604) would not their workers' action lose protection anyway as 'secondary action'? Such legalistic conundrums would clearly tie down all industrial action as long as the 1984 Act survived.

We have now discussed the more important heads of tort liability and relevant immunities that arise in industrial conflict. For convenience, they are set out summarily in Table 1 (p. 636). The table also includes other liabilities, which are now considered.

Damage done by unlawful means

Contract and unlawful means

In *Stratford* v. *Lindley*,[40] Lord Reid said: 'interference with business is tortious if any unlawful means are employed'. This was an alternative and wider way of putting the liability at the core of the case, indirectly causing breach of contract (i.e. the commercial contract) by unlawful means (i.e. inducing breach of the employment contracts). Two main

TABLE 1. The 'immunities' – a skeleton: TULRA 1974–6

Common law tort (Union protection: TULRA s. 14; repealed EA 1982 ss. 15–17)	Immunity: ICFTD (trade dispute defined: TULRA s. 29; restricted EA 1982 s. 18)	New restrictions
(I) *Action* • *Inducing* another to break contract • Bare interference with performance of contract (tort?) • *Inducing* another to interfere with performance (tort?)	In *TULRA s. 13 (1) (a)*	*Restricted:* (a) EA 1980 s. 17 (secondary action) (b) EA 1980 s. 16 (secondary picketing) (c) EA 1982 ss. 12–14 (pressure to extend negotiation or union labour only) *Union action* (within EA 1982 s. 15 (3)) Obligatory ballot TUA 1984 ss. 10–11 (uncertainty on 'interference')
(II) *Threat* • as 'intimidation' or *quia timet* form of (1), to do act within (1); *or* • as 'intimidation', to break contract, or that contract will be broken (whether or not threatener a party)	In *TULRA s. 13 (1) (b)*	
(III) *Bare* interference with trade or employment (tort?)	[*TULRA s. 13 (2)*]	*Repealed:* EA 1982 s. 19
(IV) *Deliberate* interference with contract, trade or employment by *unlawful means*	[*TULRA s. 13 (3)*] Protection as *unlawful means* for: (a) (1), (2) and (3); and (b) breach of contract	*Repealed:* EA 1980 s. 17 (8) • status of (b) remains uncertain • (limits of 'unlawful means' uncertain)
(V) *Conspiracy* • 'Simple': to injure • To damage by unlawful means	*TULRA s. 13 (4)* (See (1)–(4))	*Restricted:* • EA 1980 s. 16 (in practice EA 1980 s. 17) • EA 1982 ss. 12–14 TUA 1984 ss. 10–11
(VI) *Picketing* (torts?)	*TULRA s. 15*	*Substituted and restricted:* EA 1980 s. 16
(VII) *Other torts* (nuisance, trespass, defamation, unreasonable harassment on highway, etc.)		

problems arise in connection with the law on trade disputes. First, if there was a 'trade dispute', the inducement of workers to break employment contracts was not 'actionable' even under the 1906 Act (now TULRA s. 13 (1)). But was it still 'unlawful means'? We saw that Lord Pearce believed it was, as did other judges, at any rate if the plaintiff was someone other than the workers' employer (in the *Stratford* case, Bowater's). But this attempt to create a kind of judicial secondary action, unprotected by 'immunity', was prevented by TULRA s. 13 (3) (a), which declared that actions not 'actionable' within s. 13 (1) were not 'unlawful means' on which other tort liability could be built. That subsection was repealed by the 1980 Act (s. 17 (8)). But the House of Lords disposed of this problem by sensibly deciding in the *Hadmor* case 1983 that Lord Pearce's view was 'wrong',[73] and laying down that what is not 'actionable in tort' is not 'unlawful' in tort. This seems sensible.

There is a second problem. The 'immunities' have never displaced the illegality of the breach of employment contract itself. The employer can still sue the worker for breach of his contract, even if he cannot in a trade dispute sue the union official for the tort of inducing breach. Could he, though, sue workers and official together as a combination, or a 'conspiracy', or as joint wrongdoers, who were using 'unlawful means' i.e. the very breach itself? After all, in *Rookes* v. *Barnard*, 1964, the workers and the union official were made liable as conspirators to *threaten* a breach of the workers' employment contracts. Lord Reid said: 'It would be absurd to make [a defendant] liable for threatening to do it, but not for doing it.'[98] In 1952 even Evershed M R was willing to see a workman's breach of contract, induced by union officials, as itself an 'unlawful act' in the law of tort (not itself protected by a trade dispute immunity). Any such semantic manoeuvre could obviously outflank the immunities. Even in a trade dispute a combination of workers (breaking employment contracts) and union officials to damage X might be seen as a tort against X to which the statutes provided no defence.

Donovan accepted that the possibility of such liability should be removed. This was accordingly done by TULRA s. 13 (3) (b), which 'declared' that a breach of contract committed in contemplation or furtherance of a trade dispute is not unlawful means for the purposes of tort liability. (In fact, the draftsman was in error in making s. 13 (3) (b) declaratory – 'For the avoidance of doubt'; for, unlike s. 13 (3) (a), it was not declaring the law but reforming it.) This subsection too was repealed in 1980 (EA s. 17 (8)), thereby reviving uncertainty about liability. In the *Hadmor* decision, Lord Denning's attempt to use this doctrine of 'unlawful means' was decisively rejected by the House of Lords, which concluded that s. 13 (3) had been repealed only because it was 'otiose' once the trade dispute immunity I C F T D applied to inducing breach of *all* contracts. That was correct on s. 13 (3) (a). Unfortunately, the judgment pays little attention to the second problem of unlawful means in the form of breach (as opposed to inducing breach), to which s. 13 (3) (b) applied. The danger of judges using the breach of contract, as such, as unlawful means persists.

Many such situations would today involve 'secondary action' within the 1980 Act (s. 17 (1)–(6)) in which the primary 'immunity' of T U L R A s. 13 (1) is withdrawn: p. 597. Even so, some writers are careful to preserve the unlawful means both in inducement and in the breach of contract itself in defining union liabilities.[99] The very fact that Silverthorne was held liable in *Rookes* v. *Barnard*, 1964 (p. 42), when he was treated as a conspirator (rather than as an inducer, when he would have been protected), shows clearly how great the consequences can be of apparently technical details in this area. Parliament should establish once for all that when a worker withdraws labour in a dispute the breach of his employment contract should not be allowed to operate as 'unlawful means' in any way in the law of tort.

Unlawful means and Acts of Parliament

There is, however, a wider question. Judges have for many years regarded as wrongful the doing of damage to a person by unlawful acts generally. For example, an injunction lay to stop pickets injuring 'the property' of an employer by breaches of the old 1825 Act. More recently in 1955 the Court of Appeal granted injunctions against seamen on unofficial strike occupying their ships in breach of the penal provisions of the (now repealed) Merchant Shipping Act 1894[100] – a decision where one can already sense the increasing readiness of the judges in more interventionist mood to apply legal sanctions against an 'unofficial' strike. In *Meade* v. *Haringey L B C*, 1979,[101] union officials told the council that their members (school caretakers and manual school workers) would take strike action. When the council closed the schools, parents alleged that this was a breach of duty under the Education Act,

committed to support the unions. Although the Court of Appeal thought it was not a suitable case for an injunction (the strike was now over) Lord Denning MR regarded the council's breach of duty as 'unlawful', and the union was 'inducing them to break it' or 'hindering' the performance of their duties. Alternatively, this agreement was nothing more nor less than an agreement to 'use unlawful means'. On either basis there was no 'immunity'. In another case, he stated that even an interference by a union with 'the freedom of the press' was a tort.

The Lonrho decision. But decisions of this kind must now be seen as limited by recent statements of principle by the Law Lords in *Lonrho Ltd* v. *Shell Ltd (No. 2)*, 1982.[102] In this decision the House of Lords appeared to address itself both to the issue of conspiracy to use unlawful means and to the definition of 'unlawful means' in the form of a breach of a statute. The case itself, however, appeared not to involve intentional harm, only damage that was the 'foreseeable' consequence of such a breach. There is therefore an element of uncertainty, not unusual in the common law, about the real effects of the judgment; but within the principles there stated some questions in this murky area are clearer than they were (p. 583).

First, the tort of interference by unlawful means is confined to intentional damage. It seems right to say: 'The essence of the tort is deliberate interference with the plaintiff's interests by unlawful means.'[103] Indeed, where conspiracy to use unlawful means is alleged liability arises, according to *Lonrho*, only where the 'predominant purpose' is one, not of protecting legitimate interests, but of injuring the plaintiff. Secondly, the *Lonrho* case decided that the breach of a penal statute is not necessarily 'unlawful means' in the law of tort. The plaintiff who suffers damage cannot succeed by saying only: 'That is a crime, so I can sue you.' Not every crime is a tort. In *Gouriet* v. *Union of Post Office Workers*, 1978,[104] a private citizen was denied the right to seek an injunction against the union when it had called on members not to handle mail to South Africa as part of the anti-apartheid campaign, on the ground that criminal offences under the Post Office Act had been committed. Some statutes, however, do allow a person suffering damage to sue, for an injunction and for damages, if the courts can find that this is (tacitly) permitted by it. This occurs, as Lord Diplock put it in *Lonrho*, where either the statute has created a 'private right' for the plaintiff, which is interfered with (such as where an injured worker is allowed to sue the employer for breach of the Factories Act: p. 431), or the statute creates rights for the public, and the plaintiff has suffered 'special damage peculiar to himself'. Whether such a civil action in tort is permitted rests upon the proper 'construction of the statute'. Since the Act, by hypothesis, is silent on the point, its construction is often, as Lord Denning has said, 'Guesswork. . . . You might as well toss a coin.' But such is now the law, as the Court of Appeal confirmed in 1983.[105] Unless the breach of the legislation gives a civil right of action to the person damaged as a breach of statutory duty, he cannot use that breach by itself as a platform to mount the charge of 'unlawful means' to sue in tort. In some cases, therefore, a defendant who may be open to a criminal prosecution *can* say, 'I know it is a crime, but you cannot sue me.'

These areas of the law of tort, despite their remaining uncertainties, are important for labour law. A further point remains, on conspiracy too. We recall that in trade disputes conspiracy cannot be relied upon except where the act done, or to be done, by the combination would if done without the combination, i.e. by an individual, be 'actionable' in tort (TULRA s. 13 (4)). Here, therefore, 'unlawful means' cannot be based upon either a breach of contract itself (for that is not a tort) or upon breach of an Act that does not give rise to a right to sue in tort in the plaintiff. Even outside trade disputes, the *Lonrho* and *Gouriet* decisions establish that breach of a statute is not enough; the breach must be one actionable by the plaintiff in tort. Some – but not all – of the older cases can be made to fit this pattern. The 1955 injunction against the leaders of the unofficial seamen's strike was in part based upon a construction of the Merchant Shipping Act 1894, which gave the shipowners a civil right of action in tort against those who persuaded seamen to break the Act, i.e. not 'to proceed to sea' or otherwise to be 'absent from duty'. The *Gouriet* case itself was a decision falling on the other side of the line. No civil right of action for the plaintiff, as a member of the public, could be found by the judges in the Post Office Act 1953.

It is less clear what view the courts would take of industrial action (otherwise lawful) that induces, or compels, a person or a body to act in breach of statutory duties (e.g. inducing the council to shut the schools in breach of statutory duties, as in *Meade's* case). Will a plaintiff be allowed to sue the union in such a case only if the breach of statutory duty gives him a right of civil action first against the council, e.g. as a parent to whom duty is owed? Logically, this seems to follow from the

Gouriet and *Lonrho* decisions. If a citizen (e.g. a non-parent) cannot rely on the breach as 'unlawful means' against the body breaking its statutory duties (such duties may be enforced by the Attorney-General, but that is another matter) he surely cannot plead it as 'unlawful means' to create a tort against a third party. This logical view, however, may not attract some judges if they are in an interventionist and 'creative' mood. After all, if this argument is correct, *Rookes* v. *Barnard*, 1964, was an illogical decision. For Rookes was allowed to sue for the threat to break a contractual duty owed, not to him, but to the employer. It was, of course, an illogical decision; but no British court has yet admitted so. More important, where a council or other body is exercising 'public' functions the courts may now permit 'judicial review' to persons with a 'sufficient interest' seeking a declaration or even injunction.[106] The possibility cannot be excluded that that public law jurisdiction may be used as an analogy to lever the liabilities of unions in private law open more widely than the logic of the current precedents suggests. We have seen (p. 158) that the High Court quashed the decision by Liverpool City Council in 1985 to withhold pay from teachers who could not teach when schools closed on a 'day of action' organized to support the council in its battle with the Government on the application of a teacher and an N U T official.

The range of plaintiffs who can sue

A related problem is: what is the range of plaintiffs who can sue for such torts, and especially for the use of 'unlawful means'? The plaintiff must be someone who is damaged or threatened with damage. But this is not enough. A tort may damage a wide range of people, yet only some of them may be able to sue in the courts. The problem is of growing importance when Parliament not only reintroduces the old common law torts into labour law by removing 'immunities' but creates a few more of its own. For example, we can now see the reason why the 1982 Act defines the persons who can sue business men for the statutory tort created out of attempts to extend union negotiation or union labour only (the prohibited purposes) by way of contractual and business practices. They include all persons 'who may be adversely affected' (E A 1982 ss. 12 (7) (d), 13 (4) (b)). This definition was inserted so that there should be no doubt about a civil right of action being widely available for contravention of these sections of the 1982 Act. A union that threatens to induce or induces this statutory 'business tort' is expressly deprived of the 'immunities' of TULRA s. 13 (EA 1982 s. 14 (1) (b)). The same is true where it induces a breach of employment contracts, even in a trade dispute, so as to disrupt the supply of goods or services with one of those prohibited purposes in view (s. 14 (2), (3): p. 606). For example, persons 'adversely affected' under the statutory tort may include advertisers in a newspaper whose advertising is obstructed, as in the *NGA* case. But then they would be proper plaintiffs at common law, for those whose business is struck at by the industrial torts can sue. (In the *Wade* case, 1979, the plaintiffs included nineteen newspapers and publishers, two advertisers and two local authorities.)[107]

But suppose a union succeeds, by threat of industrial action, in inducing two employers (one a company, the other a local council in breach of its statutory duty) to withdraw custom by not renewing contracts with X Ltd, a firm of suppliers, because it does not consult with its own employees' union and has dismissed the union members in its work-force. Suppose that firm goes bankrupt in consequence, thereby ruining A, an employee, B, a shareholder, and C, a client (Figure 10). All might be persons 'adversely affected', with consequential rights of action against the company and the council under ss. 13 and 14 of the 1982 Act. Both are liable for the 'statutory tort' created by EA 1982 s. 13. But the 1982 Act does not say that the union can be made jointly liable for that statutory tort along with the company or the council. Nor does it create duties for the union parallel to those of the company and council, or create any tort of 'inducing' this statutory tort. Indeed, the Act of 1982 specifically creates the 'statutory torts', actionable by anyone 'adversely affected', only on the part of a person who is under a duty 'to comply' with the sections concerned with the business behaviour (ss. 12 (7), 13 (4)), not with the industrial behaviour. The latter is left to s. 14; and this section withdraws 'immunity' in respect of the tort of inducing breach of contract and allied 'industrial torts' in trade disputes (compare telecommunications: p. 658).

But who can sue for *those* torts? The courts surely should not use the concepts of 'joint torts' or conspiracy to extend the ambit of this very special 'statutory tort' (it is one of the rare occasions when refusing to make a contract can be tortious). If the union is sued for the common law tort of interference with business by unlawful means, however (there being no trade dispute immunity, because the union is likely to disrupt supply of goods or services, and one reason for its action is a prohibited ground, non-consultation by X Ltd: s. 14 (2), (3) (c)), it is not at all certain what the range of plaintiffs is. The union may accept that in support of the workers of X Ltd and the claim by union (2) to consultation rights, it intended to procure indirectly interference with the

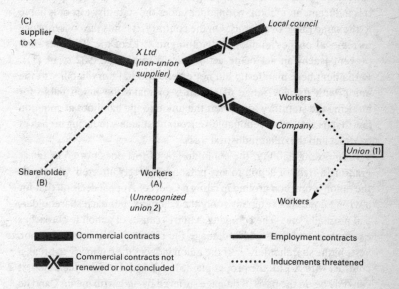

Figure 10. Employment Act 1982, sections 13, 14

business of X Ltd in what might be secondary action legitimated by the 'gateway' of E A 1980 s. 17 (3), were it not for the 1982 provisions, which have now made the means unlawful as a threat to induce breach of employment contracts. But it had no intention to damage A, B or C; nor was damage to them a *necessary* consequence under the classic test of Jenkins L J in *Thomson* v. *Deakin*, 1952 (p. 590).

This is of the utmost importance, for the 1982 Act appears to bar the attempt to extend the liabilities of the union by reliance on the 'statutory tort'. Sections 12 (7) and 13 (4) create that tort in respect of a contravention by anyone under the 'obligation to comply' with the prohibitions on certain business practices (ss. 12 (2), 13 (2)) and they thereby open up liability to the wide range of persons 'adversely affected'. The statute then deals with a union, or other person, that 'induces or attempts to induce, another . . . to contravene section 12 (2) or 13 (2)'. But it deliberately refrains from enacting that it becomes, in consequence of this inducement, a 'joint' wrongdoer under the statutory tort or is liable to the same range of persons. On the contrary, it limits the consequence to removal of the 'immunity' ('Nothing in s. 13 of the 1974 Act shall prevent [such] an act being actionable in tort': EA 1982 s. 14 (1)). Parliament here manifestly did not extend the statutory liability to the union with its new range of plaintiffs or make the union liable for inducing the statutory tort; it left the union to the liabilities at common law that its acts, now 'actionable', encounter, namely inducing breach of contract and the other industrial torts.

In imposing liability, the common law of tort does not go as far as granting a right of action to any person 'adversely affected'. As for B, the union is on good ground in citing a Court of Appeal decision that for a wrong done to a company, only the company, not each shareholder, can normally sue: 'The company acquires causes of action for breaches of contract and torts which damage the company. No cause of action vests in the shareholder.'[108] If the union induces the company to break a contract with X Ltd, the proper plaintiff is X Ltd. If C sues the union, it can only be on the basis of damage suffered by 'unlawful means', and he cannot then succeed unless he proves the union knew that his interests would be injured and intended to do him damage. If this were not the law, the liability of someone who induced a breach of contract might be limitless. To allow an action merely by proof of interference by 'unlawful means' (i.e. inducing breaches of contracts that are many removes away) would open up civil action to each of one million commuters prevented from reaching work by a rail strike from which trade dispute immunity is removed by the 1980s legislation in some manner. Indeed, *Mr Falconer*, a traveller stranded in London by an NUR stoppage during the miners' strike, was awarded damages by a County court in

1986 against the NUR. Although some judgments speak loosely of an action for anyone damaged by 'interference with trade or business by unlawful means' and although the Law Lords have been willing to allow an action for economic loss negligently caused by the supply of faulty articles,[109] C cannot succeed merely by proving that the union intentionally used tortious means against, and caused damage to, X Ltd, which then caused consequential damage in the end to him. The defendants, Jenkins LJ said in his classic judgment in 1952 on indirectly causing a breach of contract, must have 'counselled action by employees in itself necessarily unlawful . . . *designed to achieve that end*'. If there is to be liability to a wider range of persons, this must be done by statute. For example, the EEC Treaty, a majority of the Law Lords has held, creates obligations actionable as 'statutory torts', so that, when the Milk Marketing Board 'abused its dominant position' contrary to Article 86 of the Treaty, a milk producer could sue the board. But he was a person directly damaged (struck off the list of suppliers) and clearly within the purview of the Article as someone it set out to protect. And even in such cases there is not necessarily a right to damages.[110]

We find another guideline in the picketing cases. Liability imposed in the *South Wales* miners' case was wide in so far as it rested upon 'unreasonable harassment' of groups of working miners in their use of the highway in and out of work. But Scott J. did not give all the plaintiffs a global or 'class' remedy against the picketing as a whole. If the picketing was tortious,

then the rights of the plaintiffs thereby affected are being infringed. But their rights are not joint rights, they are individual rights. Picketing at Cynheidre cannot be tortious vis-à-vis a plaintiff who works at Merthyr Vale. The only persons who can be entitled to claim injunctions to restrain picketing at, for example, Cynheidre are plaintiffs who work at Cynheidre. . . . None of the plaintiffs has any cause of action in tort in respect of picketing at a pit at which he does not work.[111]

The fact that workers who picket are guilty of the tort of nuisance, or of the analogous tort of 'harassment', does not give a right of action based on that 'unlawful means' to all miners or other persons damaged in consequence at other Welsh pits, still less to persons in the coal industry generally, even if the defendants could foresee that they might be deleteriously affected. Now that the common law is ushered back into industrial relations, its principles concerning the appropriate range of plaintiffs must be strictly observed by the courts. Extensions of liability by way of loose talk about 'technicalities' will merely be a cover for further inroads against workers and unions. If Parliament wants to go further, it must say so as it appears to have done in E A 1982 ss. 12–13, in the case of business men liable for the statutory torts there created. A plaintiff can sue only for a tort that is a tort *as against him*, not because the defendant has committed an act that is a tortious breach of duty owed to others, in respect of which he suffered loss.

Sit-ins and work-ins

No 'immunity' protects workers who in a trade dispute enter the premises and occupy them. (We have seen that the erroneous idea that TULRA s. 13 (2) might do so led to its repeal anyway in 1982: p. 613.)[112] Alternatively, the workers who are in the premises lawfully with the permission, or 'licence', of the employer may refuse to leave the premises and engage in a 'sit-in'. In both cases they are guilty of the tort of trespass. Any original 'licence' terminates when the employer withdraws it or when they exceed its express or implied terms. We have seen in the case of the NUPE shop steward how quickly the courts link permission to be on the premises with the contract of employment and the employer's property rights.[113] Such an occupation is not necessarily a crime (at any rate in England and Wales). Intentional damage will give rise to criminal liability under the Criminal Damage Act 1971, but mere wrongful possession of a workplace is not a crime (though it is of residential premises and foreign missions, and the former could include some places of work). Violence, or the threat of it, to secure entry contrary to the wishes of an occupier is a specific offence (Criminal Law Act 1977 s. 6) and one that limits the means by which an employer can try to force his way in against trespassing occupiers. But where the workers *entered* as trespassers, their possession of a 'weapon of offence' is a crime, and such weapons include any article 'intended' by the person having it to cause injury or 'adapted' for that use (s. 8). There are of course certain places protected by local by-laws on or even near which a criminal offence may be committed by occupation or demonstrations, such as Heathrow Airport.[114]

There has sometimes arisen a procedural problem for employers who wish to evict those sitting in or where, as has sometimes happened, the workers try to keep production going in face of a threatened closure, 'working in'. An injunction, including a mandatory injunction ordering the defendants to leave, is effective against those named. It can also affect those who assist such persons in defiance of the order; aiding and abetting a contempt is itself a contempt of court. But the plaintiff may not know the names of all of the occupants; or those named may be replaced by others unknown. To meet this type of situation the procedure of a possession order was invented in 1970, mainly to deal with squatters (now RSC Order 113). In June 1984 the NCB made use of possession order proceedings to evict miners whose numbers and identity were uncertain from the Betteshanger Colliery in Kent where they were staging an underground sit-in. The plaintiff serves a summons on persons named by leaving a copy of the summons at the premises or by any other manner the court directs, and he deals with unnamed persons by fixing a copy of it on the door or puts one through the letterbox. A final order can be made five days later or earlier 'in cases of urgency'. In 1970 a judge made an order against a sit-in; he saw the position as 'not substantially different from students at an university'. The order may relate both to the premises occupied and to any other parts of the property threatened with wrongful occupation.[115] The sheriff acting under this order can evict all occupants found on the premises. In addition to this we must note that the courts have begun to allow an action against 'representative defendants' in an unusually wide way to order members of an organization to stay away from or out of premises.[116] Also, new procedures facilitate application for the delivery up of any goods wrongfully held, such as tools in a factory (Torts (Interference With Goods) Act 1977; RSC Order 29, R. 2A).

There have been a number of celebrated 'sit-ins' and 'work-ins' in the years of the gathering recession. The work-in at the Meriden motor-bike factory of Triumph led to the setting up of a workers' co-operative, which managed to adapt production to new markets and survive, with government assistance, for some years. The first occupation that attracted attention and support (including that of Harold Wilson, who supported the workers' 'right to work – provided they act within the law') was at Upper Clyde Shipbuilders. Although the 'work-in' there achieved an initial success in halving the redundancies required by the liquidator, it was not a tactic that could ultimately save the yard.[117] So too with Cammell Laird's Merseyside yard, which forty workers occupied (together with a warship) for more than three months in 1984, keeping in touch with pickets and union officials by CB radio. They had been dismissed by the company in their fight against redundancies and privatization. When they defied the orders of the court to leave the premises, the company applied to have them imprisoned for contempt of court. Eventually they left peacefully; but thirty-seven were sent to prison for a month for the contempt of court, since they refused to apologize. The sentence excited little public attention in the middle of the coal strike.

Other liabilities

The common law

The mandatory 'unity' of the common law presents special problems for labour law. Laski once said: 'Most lawyers have a half-conscious belief that the Common Law provides, so to say, a law behind the law which is enacted by Parliament.' Most judges, at any rate, seem to acquire such a belief. We have seen, too, how even a new principle of liability is granted, on its accession, immediate status with other common law principles as if it had always been part of the corpus (even though Lord Reid has confirmed that no one now believes the 'fairy tale' that it has). No doubt the lack of a statist tradition in Britain has contributed to this independent legitimacy of the common law but, whatever the reason, in practical terms it gives the courts a curious power over labour relations. One watches, for example, doctrines grow in areas of commercial or property law, often responding to new relationships in those areas. Once the new 'common law principle' is formulated, however, its judicial passport takes it everywhere; there is nothing to stop counsel citing it and the judge using it in an area quite unlike that in which it originated, where its impact may fulfil a totally different social function or policy. Labour law is, therefore, at risk not only, sometimes not so much, from 'creative' judges in the employment cases, but from the creations of judges and legal principles in other branches of the law. We take two illustrations.

(1) *Inducing breach of equitable obligations.* Some obligations are

imposed by the courts upon persons because of the relationship they bear to others, many of them first invented by the courts of 'equity' before 1875. A director, for instance, owes a 'fiduciary' duty to his company; he must not stand in a position where his personal interest conflicts with his duties to his company, and he must not make a 'secret' profit from his office. If a union induces a director to break that duty, the company can bring a successful action for an injunction and for compensation. In the same way, when union officials induced agents of an insurance company not to remit moneys collected as premiums to the company in the course of industrial action, they were made liable for inducing breaches of the agents' fiduciary duty.[118] We saw in Chapter 3 instances of a fiduciary duty being applied to an employee to strengthen the obligation of 'confidentiality' and 'fidelity' owed to the employer.[119] Two points are at once apparent. The duties exist independently of contract; and, because of this, no 'immunity' is available in trade disputes from TULRA s. 13 (1). In a similar manner, duties of 'confidence' or fiduciary duties may originate in a relationship sustained by a contract (a director often has a contract with his company) but survive the termination or expiry of the contract and continue to bind the person concerned.[120]

On the other hand, there is little difficulty where there is a contract in formulating these obligations as express or implied terms of that contract. A director or insurance agent may have a contract of employment (or a contract for services). To induce a breach of this in furtherance of a trade dispute will, without more, be protected by TULRA s. 13 (1). There is something slightly absurd in the prospect of lawful industrial action turning into unlawful industrial action merely because a lawyer puts a different label on the same obligation. Indeed, in some of the cases where the obligation arises independently but a contract exists, judges have been careful in commercial law to treat a breach as a breach of contract; though it is also true that injunctions have been granted against third parties who procure the abuse of confidential information even though the tort of inducing breach of contract has *not* been committed.[121] In some trade dispute cases, however, officials who procured members to impart confidential information were treated as committing the tort of inducing breach of contract.[122] But even in the law of contract we find the equitable remedy of an injunction being granted against a third party who has not induced a party to break a contract but assisted him in evading an injunction issued to prevent a breach (rather like a person who 'aids and abets' a contempt of court).[123]

Most of these decisions have been developed in property or commercial litigation. Labour law, though, is immune from none. The more 'high-tech' the work that is performed, the more likely it is that judges will come to see those performing it as subject to duties of loyalty, or of 'confidence', which do not necessarily depend upon the contract of employment. The wrong of 'interference with equitable duties' is such an obvious point of departure for further 'creativity' that it is perhaps surprising that thotection in TULRA s. 13 (1) was not extended in the 1974–6 period to procuring breach of equitable duties. One major difficulty against doing so was undoubtedly the seamless web of 'equitable' and 'fiduciary' duties that lead up to that pinnacle of equitable obligations, the duties of a trustee. The question might arise from any such extension of the immunity how far industrial action should be protected in regard to procurements of a breach of trust. But even a 'high-trust' employee is still a long way from being a trustee for his boss.

(2) *Economic duress.* Until recently the doctrine of 'duress', by reason of which a contract or transaction can be set aside, was restricted to threats to life and limb or, in some cases, to property. From 1976, however, a 'more flexible test' was adopted, first by Kerr J., who said that a plea of 'compulsion or coercion' generally was now available to a party to a contract. (We detect at once, and again, the irresistible attraction of 'coercion' for the common law.) The essence of the new doctrine, the judges decided, is 'coercion of the will'. Or, in Lord Scarman's words, it rests on 'the victim's intentional submission arising from the realisation that there is no other practical choice open to him'.[124] 'Mere commercial pressure' is not enough. In *B. & S. Contracts* v. *V G Publications*, 1984, B. & S. contracted to erect stands at Olympia for V G and planned to use the redundant workers from its insolvent Welsh factory for the job. When the workers arrived they refused to work until paid £4,500 outstanding of the sums to which they (wrongly) claimed to be entitled as redundancy pay. B. & S. threatened that if this amount was not paid (as an extra) by V G, it would cancel the contract (citing a clause in the contract on which it was not entitled to rely). V G paid up to B. & S., but then deducted £4,500 from the price. The Court of Appeal upheld its action; the extra sum had been extorted from it by 'economic duress'.

We detect immediately an overlap with tort. B. & S. had threatened to break its contract. This was capable of being the tort of 'intimidation'. But economic duress is wider than tort; the pressure, in Lord Wilberforce's words, 'must be one of a kind that the law does not regard as legitimate'. Lord Scarman is on record for the view that duress can 'exist even if the threat is one of lawful action' (and he has even said that duress is now 'a tort' in its own right, which most judges do not so far accept). Many of the relevant cases have concerned companies; and it is not obvious how 'the will' of one large corporation is, in reality, 'overborne' by that of another. The doctrine is full of uncertainty. Where does commercial pressure end and illegitimate demands begin? But for all its uncertainties it was inevitable that the courts in Britain would one day apply this new principle to labour relations.

Yet in other jurisdictions this automatic transfer was not inevitable. A Canadian judge decided in 1966 that duress could not be 'strictly applied' to collective agreements; for 'all such contracts are entered into under considerable pressure, often accompanied by strikes . . . or as a result of lockouts', and such an agreement should not be set aside for 'duress' when it was 'signed after such industrial conflicts as a result of protracted negotiations'. This seems common sense. Any large-scale industrial dispute may – usually must – end by the 'will' of one party being 'coerced'. Indeed, it may be preferable that the will of one or other side be coerced by pressure into some agreement than that the two sides should fight to the death. To apply the new illegality of economic duress to this process is an instance of the judiciary demanding the right to declare what is and what is not 'legitimate' pressure. What lock-out ever has been, or is ever likely to be, invalidated on the ground that it is vitiated by 'economic duress'? Whatever purpose the doctrine has in commercial transactions, in labour relations its social function is to limit the pressure that can be applied by workers and their unions. In doing so, its role objectively is yet another attempt to reopen *Allen* v. *Flood*. Pressure put on workers to settle or face years of unemployment is not regarded as illegal duress by our judges; and even if it were, the doctrine gives them no remedy except to renounce their contracts.

The doctrine was apparently transferred to labour law in *Universe Tankships Inc. of Monrovia* v. *ITWF*, 1983, another case of a flag-of-convenience ship 'blacked' by the ITWF to assist the crew and enforce international minimum conditions.[125] But care is needed here because of the concessions made by counsel. The ITWF lifted its boycott of the ship because the shipowners paid the crew's back-wages (more than £70,000) and the usual further sum into the international Seafarers' Fund. But the shipowners had all along intended to claim the whole of the money back. As soon as the ship had sailed, a writ was issued alleging economic duress. The owners then had the crew assign the back-wages over to them (by what arguments or pressures is not revealed). Now they claimed the other amount paid to the ITWF for the fund. Was there duress? All of the Law Lords seemed to agree that there was. Lord Diplock accepted that the shipowners' will was coerced and 'the financial consequences' of not having the ship for hire would be 'catastrophic'. Lord Scarman saw the case as 'an excellent illustration' of the 'lack of any practicable choice'. But all of these judgments were based upon the crucial fact that counsel for the ITWF *conceded* in the House of Lords that it had been guilty of economic duress. The point remains open for another case to argue, though the attitudes of the Law Lords and judges in the lower courts seem clear. Even so, the 'will' of the shipowning company was never investigated in this case. It had formed the intention from the outset of claiming back all the money that it paid to the crew and to the ITWF with apparent consent, as soon as the ship had sailed. For the present, though, it looks as if the judges agree that such industrial pressure constitutes duress.

It is still open to question why the actions of the ITWF (if lawful in other respects) should suddenly be vitiated by this imported novelty. How else were the oppressed Asian crew of this ship ever to be paid decent wages except by someone 'coercing the will' of the Liberian company that owned it by refusing to service it? No alternative 'commercial pressure' was available. Further, and worse, why should the ITWF be guilty under the semantic twists of 'economic duress', when looked at from the law of tort (and this, too, was an agreed concession between counsel) it had at that time an immunity by way of TULRA s. 13 (1), provided that it had acted in furtherance of a trade dispute? This was the second concession in the case. We have seen that by a majority the Law Lords astonishingly decided that this was not a trade dispute. As the law then stood, by three to two they decided that the demand for the sum to the fund was not adequately 'connected with' the seamen's employment even on the pre-1982 definition (Chapter 7, p. 559). This was the point that decided the case. It may be replied that at least the Law Lords thereby limited the impact of economic duress in industrial negotiations by the creative decision to render its boundaries in trade dispute cases coterminous with the immunities available to the same facts looked at as incurring liability in tort. This was judicial legislation, for there was no 'immunity' in TULRA for economic duress (for the good reason that Parliament in 1974 had no idea that any such liability could possibly arise in trade disputes). But even this is not certain. Lord Scarman appears to decide that way; but there would, on his view of duress, be many cases of 'economic duress' where the employer might win by arguing that there was no equivalent tort, or certainly no tort to which an immunity attached.

Lord Diplock saw the statutes on trade disputes as 'indications' as to 'public policy' about what demands could be accepted as 'legitimate in the field of industrial relations', even if they were otherwise economic duress. Lord Cross thought the statutes were 'guidance'. Neither puts the point in 'absolute terms'. Moreover, Lord Brandon held that he accepted this point only as a concession for 'this appeal alone'; and it should, in his view, 'be made quite clear' that the Law Lords were not 'giving the seal of approval' to it. Total confidence cannot be expressed about the common law, then, in the next case in which the point is fought. We may yet see an employer claiming back a wage increase forced out of him by the duress in what is normal industrial pressure for acts that further a trade dispute and receive 'immunity' seen as a tort.

So another common law doctrine enters the industrial-relations stage from the commercial wings. Once more, it makes the task of the parliamentary draftsman difficult. Can he write a Bill in which he has confidently inserted protection against appropriate forms of economic duress, whether he composes in terms of 'immunities' or of 'positive rights'? The new doctrine yet again speaks the language of 'coercion', but this time in terms of 'economic' compulsion, which most trade unionists and many an employer would reckon to be part of the very stuff of collective bargaining. It is a doctrine of no possible value to workers. It springs from Scrutton's 'certain class of ideas' inherent in the logic of the common law, far removed from industrial conflict. One of the tasks of the labour lawyer is to watch the judges' decisions in other areas of law for rumblings of doctrines of the common law that may later descend like thunderbolts upon industrial relations. The most difficult task for Parliament is to anticipate such developments. An attempt to provide for economic duress in TULRA in 1974 would have been thought absurd.

Special groups of workers

Among many other problems relating to strikes, there are two that require brief attention here. They are, first, the special legal position of certain groups of workers; and second the problem of 'emergencies' and 'general strikes'. Bridging the two is the proposal for laws to render strikes in 'essential services' unlawful, a matter that the Government actively considered in 1985. It is helpful first to list the specific areas in which special provisions are made.

(1) Workers on strike in breach of contract causing special danger

Any worker who breaks a 'contract of service or of hiring' having reasonable cause to believe that the probable consequence of doing so (alone or in combination with others) will be to endanger human life, cause serious bodily injury or expose any property to destruction or serious injury, commits a crime. So says the Conspiracy and Protection of Property Act 1875 s. 5, in what may be seen as the last vestige of the old master-and-servant legislation. The section already offers what some demand – criminal liability for strikes that damage property or person, so long as the employment contracts are broken. The Donovan Report confirmed, however, that up to 1968 there had not been a prosecution for this crime. Nor has this section been used since, when more strikes have taken the form of longer, damaging strikes in the public sector. Donovan recommended that the section be 'left undisturbed', largely because to repeal it might give the wrong impression. This is what has happened.

Another section of the 1875 Act, s. 4, made it a crime for workers to strike wilfully in breach of contract in the gas, water and (as extended in 1919) electricity industries if they had reasonable cause to believe that the consequence would be a substantial deprivation of supply. One result was that unions in these industries sometimes gave strike notice to terminate contracts, so as to avoid the possibility of breach. Donovan found that this section, too, had scarcely ever been used. When an electricity strike was threatened in 1948 at London power-stations, notices were posted drawing workers' attention to the liability (by the General Secretary of the T U C);[126] but this was still a time when strikes were in theory illegal generally, two years before the wartime Order 1305 was rescinded. The section was repealed by the Industrial Relations Act 1971, and little has been heard of it since.

(2) Police and armed forces

In some comparable countries, members of the armed forces may be members of a trade union (in West Germany, for example), and in a number police may organize in unions (France and West Germany); strikes by police are known but are rarely lawful. In Britain members of the armed forces are in practice excluded from union membership (though on occasion unions have demanded the right to organize them), and the organization of a strike would be the crime of incitement to disaffection. After the trauma of the police strike of 1918, statute (now the Police Act 1964 s. 53) made criminal any actions likely to cause disaffection and a breach of discipline by members of the police force. The police are forbidden by the same statute to join a trade union, though permission can be given to a recruit to maintain his existing membership. The Police Act establishes an association for the police to join, the Police Federation. This organization has a curious status. Nothing appears to prevent it from engaging in public controversy; indeed, its members have debated on several occasions whether they should demand a right to strike, and resolved in favour in 1976 when discontent over pay became severe. The consequent Davies Report on the police recommended a large increase plus regular increments linked to average earnings. On that basis its rejection of freedom to strike was accepted by the Federation.[127] If a government failed to maintain the wage indexation arrangements, the demand for a right to strike for the police might be revived. Since it is not in law a trade union, the Police Federation is not obliged to establish a 'political fund' before it engages upon anything within the broad area of 'political activity' now defined by the Act of 1984 (p. 761). There has, however, been an increasing tendency for the Federation to intervene in matters of social and political controversy.

A further problem arose from the Government's policy to 'civilianize', and save on, certain 'support' or ancillary jobs. Workers numbering about 45,000 in these areas found that their salaries were falling far behind the large increases given to the police. By 1985 civilian fingerprinting specialists, members of NALGO, in pursuit of a three-year-old claim for higher pay and a new career structure, took part in a two-week strike, including picketing, in West Yorkshire, which resulted in most of their demands being granted. The Police Federation called for a review of 'civilianization' and for consideration of no-strike regulations for workers out of uniform. The further question arises whether, if it claimed that 'national security' was involved, the Government could exclude such staff from various forms of employment protection and from the right to various membership, as it did for workers at *GCHQ* (p. 136).

(3) Aliens

Also in 1919 the Aliens Restriction (Amendment) Act provided that if any alien 'promotes or attempts to promote industrial unrest in any industry in which he has not been bona fide engaged for at least two years' he commits a crime. Not only does this xenophobic guard against foreign agitators, posted in fear of the Russian Revolution, still slumber on the statute book; the Act is rejuvenated by the Transfer of Undertakings (Protection of Employment) Regulations 1981, Reg. 8 (4), which permits certain of its provisions to override an otherwise unfair dismissal.

(4) Merchant seamen

Merchant seamen in British ships have long been placed under special legal restrictions in order to protect the safety of vessels as well as the interests of the owners. The Merchant Shipping Acts 1970 and 1974 maintain certain crimes whilst the ship is at sea, such as disobedience that impedes the progress of the voyage (seamen are not, however, subject to s. 5 of the 1875 Act: p. 654). The 1970 Act, though, enabled a seaman to give forty-eight hours' notice to terminate his employment, whether or not permitted under his contract, in contemplation or furtherance of a trade dispute, provided notice is given after the ship is safely berthed in the UK (s. 42 (2)). Giving notice to terminate in this exceptional way was not, however, uncommon among seamen under the older laws, in order, like the workers in gas or water undertakings in earlier eras, to escape the criminal liabilities attaching to those in the industry. In the big seamen's strike of 1966, which ended with 26,000 on strike from 800 ships in its sixth week, seamen terminated their contracts by the appropriate contractual notice as ships docked.[128] What is new about the 1970 Act is the period of forty-eight hours, which cannot be contractually increased.

(5) Post and telecommunications

From the time of Queen Anne the Post Office, which became a semi-autonomous public corporation in 1969, has operated under a special legal regime. Even so, it is surprising to find that its workers have never escaped from criminal liabilities affecting strike action, especially having regard to the relative absence of special laws restricting the rest of the public sector. The most important crimes are wilfully detaining, endangering or retarding any postal packet or soliciting any of these acts (Post Office Act 1953 ss. 58, 59, 68). In the *Gouriet* case[129] the selective 'blacking' of mail to South Africa was held to be a crime (though not one, as we have seen, for which a member of the public like Gouriet, to whom the statute gave no private right and who suffered no special damage, could sue). Despite assurances from the Attorney-General that general, rather than selective, strike action stands outside these crimes, it is not easy to see how Post Office workers would escape them; the Attorney-General's reasoning has been gently described as 'not unassailable'.[130] Sorters who refused to handle mail addressed to Grunwick's during the recognition dispute there in 1977, and who were disciplined by the Post Office, were seen by the courts as guilty of crimes, though an injunction was refused to local customers deprived of mail who asked the court to force the Post Office to come to terms with them whilst permitting them to continue their criminal acts.[131] On the other hand, Post Office workers have taken general industrial action on a number of occasions within the last twenty years, none of which have given rise to prosecutions. This has led some observers to the conclusion that the official explanation offered by the Attorney-General may be right, perhaps because in general rather than selective action workers do not 'wilfully' retard the mail.

Some incidents, however, raise the question whether some plaintiff or other will try to add alleged crimes under the Post Office Act (as unlawful means) to the other available wrongs. For example, 800 staff walked out of Mount Pleasant sorting office in 1985 over the introduction of a new coding machine and the suspension of two colleagues who refused to use it, despite an injunction (issued just before the walk-out; there had been a meeting but no ballot). Earlier in the year the Freedom Association threatened to sue both the union and the Post Office when the former threatened industrial action if 900 post offices were closed, citing the Act as a main weapon.

After British Telecom was 'privatized', the Government insisted that a right to strike survived its new legal deal for telecommunications in the Telecommunications Act 1984. The statute does indeed repeal the criminal provisions of the Wireless Telegraphy Act 1863 and Telegraph Act 1868 that stood parallel to those in the Post Office legislation, confining criminal liability now to the intentional interception of messages and the like. But a new civil liability is created. The telecommunications system is to operate by way of orders made by the Director-General. The licensed operator owes a statutory duty to 'any person who may be affected' not to contravene such an order. Civil liability arises for loss or damage both in respect of a breach of duty by the operator (unless he took all reasonable steps and exercised due diligence) and of any act inducing the breach or interfering with performance 'which is done wholly or partly for the purpose of achieving that result' (s. 18 (5)–(7)). It is clear, therefore, that industrial action by telecommunications workers might easily amount to a contravention of statutory duty (either by an interference or by inducing a breach by the operator), a tort actionable by a wide range of persons. The Government, however, insisted that strikes would not necessarily import such liability. This arises, said Lord Mackay, 'where employees take action not for the purpose of improving their terms and conditions of employment but for the purpose of bringing about a breach of the licence conditions'. It therefore rejected an amendment that would have provided an 'immunity' in trade disputes, to the extent that other workers still enjoy any.

In reality, however, telecommunications workers who take action for higher pay will know that the telecommunications system they have left unattended is one that the licensed operator may well be unable to make effective. This, at any rate, is what their employer is likely to tell them. The 1984 Act does not fix liability only on those who act 'wholly' for the purpose of disrupting the system; it includes those who act 'partly' for that purpose. It need not be the predominant purpose. One recalls the judges' interpretations of 'knowledge and intention' in the tort of inducing a breach of contract ('like the man who turns a blind eye': p. 587). It is unlikely to profit a union that its affidavits aver a 'purpose' of calling out workers for a trade dispute objective, whilst claiming that disruption of the system had never crossed its mind. A glance at the judgments in the *Mercury* case (p. 561) provides guidance as to the way the judges are likely to respond. Nor is it likely that this sector will find industrial relations easy in coming years, not least through redundancies and the adjustment of a public service structure to a more commercial ethos. In 1983 a work-to-rule by telephone engineers was smashed by a lock-out; and in 1985 various overtime bans have been imposed against demanning in an enterprise making unprecedented profits. Such action of course might well lose the normal 'immunity' today for other reasons, for example as 'secondary action' or for lack of a ballot. But the insistence that there must be a further civil liability by way of breach of statutory duty here must rest upon a judgment that telecommunications require unusual treatment. It prompts the question too whether this

is the start of a long line of statutory torts (in which trade dispute immunities will have no part to play) providing civil redress for industrial action which affects or threatens 'essential' supplies or services.[132]

(6) Other public sector employees

There are few special legal restrictions applying to such workers. Sometimes it has been said that 'firemen cannot strike'; but their prolonged stoppage in 1977, and their victory in it, proved that they can. Nor is such a stoppage unlawful by virtue of special legislation. Firemen may risk contravention of the ordinary law, including s. 5 of the 1875 Act ((2) above), if property or life were foreseeably put in jeopardy by a strike in wilful breach of contract. On the other hand, disciplinary regulations made under the Fire Services Act 1947 do control their conditions of service, and industrial action might readily amount to a breach of this 'statutory code of discipline', where the standard of proof is not that of criminal law (beyond reasonable doubt) but of civil law (the balance of probabilities).[133] We may note too that a 'retained' fireman's obligation to remain on call does not as such constitute 'employment'.[134] To procure him to break that duty would not therefore constitute inducing breach of an employment contract (e.g. for the purposes of secondary action).

In the National Health Service new problems were raised by the industrial action of ambulance men and ancillary workers in 1978–9 and the eight-month national dispute in 1982 involving all types of health workers except doctors and some craftsmen.[135] (There is a growing sector of private medicine, but few proposals are heard for special legal control of its workers.) A DHSS circular of 1979 encouraged local health authorities to take a firm stand: to introduce volunteers in place of striking workers and not to pay any wages where workers reduced services substantially. In fact, on both occasions management usually reached arrangements with the unions at local level, a process facilitated by the voluntary codes adopted by health service unions themselves (apart from the Royal College of Nursing, which is not affiliated to the TUC and does not organize industrial action of any kind) and by a TUC guide on the conduct of disputes where emergency services must be maintained. Volunteers to do work of striking staff were used in 1982, in the main from internal staff in order to avoid undue friction with unions. A Government plan existed for the use of troops but they were not used, nor were there any prosecutions under the 1875 Act, s. 5. Among manual workers, the policy of 'privatizing' cleaning services has given rise to sporadic local action, such as that in Newcastle in 1985 when porters and technical staff refused to cross the picket lines of 300 domestic staff; or the strikes in a Cambridge hospital for nine months (where nurses and sisters held meetings to condemn the private firm) and a stoppage where neighbouring hospitals experienced sympathetic action to support domestic staff at Scarsdale. Perhaps the most important consequence of the industrial action was the proviso that the Government put upon the new Review Body of 1983 to consider the pay and conditions of nurses and allied workers – namely, the right of the Government to exclude from its recommendations any group or union that takes industrial action.

Such bodies are of increasing importance to public sector pay. Judges have shown that they are ready, via 'judicial review', to control radical elements on them. One held in 1985 that the NUT was unreasonably 'frustrating the intention of Parliament' on the teachers' panel of the Burnham Committee by refusing to co-operate with a representative from a non-TUC union, PAT, who was nominated by the Government contrary to all precedent.[136] The court's process of judicial review was thus harnessed to attempts to splinter the union negotiating side. The NHS is perhaps the outstanding example of the Whitley Council structures, with complex disciplinary and negotiating procedures. It has also provided little publicized evidence of union members operating the codes of conduct to maintain accident and emergency cover during disputes. But unions cannot maintain such codes unilaterally. Without management understanding and co-operation such codes can boomerang on the union and appear to members as the cord that ties a hand behind their backs. This was illustrated in May 1985 when NUPE felt compelled to withdraw from the 1979 TUC code drawn up after the 'dirty jobs' strike and largely maintained in the 1982 health service dispute, in favour of local discretion for union branches. There had been complaints that the codes had been used to justify strike-breakers; and one official complained that now in disputes 'The first thing management does is slap the TUC guidelines down in front of you.'

(7) Civil servants and local government

Both central and local government share the characteristic that they depend ultimately for their finance upon public funds, mainly through forms of taxation; so 'the centre of decision-making is in the political sphere'.[137] In the latter case, decisions to pay employees higher wages may be challenged by judicial review or by the district auditor, though the council must be shown to have acted in a way no reasonable council could have done. The Law Lords in 1925 struck down equal pay as dependent on 'some eccentric principles of socialistic philanthropy [and] . . . a feminist ambition to secure the equality of the sexes'. In 1983, however, management's acceptance of the claims of striking staff who had brought services near to collapse was not in law objectionable to the judges (though it would be if the object was 'to undermine the incomes policy or to sabotage for political purposes the national negotiations').[138]

Central government civil servants are Crown employees open to dismissal at pleasure, as the *GCHQ* case confirmed (p. 135), but also covered by either the employment protection laws or negotiated schemes of at least equivalent value (e.g. on redundancy). It is still uncertain whether they have 'contracts' of employment. But in respect of industrial action they, and their unions, are normally said to stand in the same position as other workers. In the Act of 1927 civil servants were compulsorily segregated into separate trade unions, and all public authorities were forbidden to demand union membership, but that Act was repealed in 1946. The definition of a 'trade dispute' specifically provides that a dispute between 'a Minister of the Crown and any workers' may be a trade dispute between them and their employer even if he is not their employer if it relates to matters referred to a statutory joint body on which he is represented or to matters that statute requires to be settled under the Minister's statutory powers; and civil servants are 'workers' (TULRA ss. 29 (2), 30 (1), as amended 1982).

The state of the 'immunities' is now such that any large-scale industrial action by public employees is bound to risk the label 'political'. The new definition of 'trade dispute' (EA 1982 s. 18, amending TULRA s. 29: p. 557) as applied in the *Mercury* decision (p. 561) allows judges easily to conclude that the 'main' substance of a dispute with government (the workers' employer or the paymaster of their employer) is about the Government's policy rather than the immediate wage claim. Ironically, the more such a dispute pursued by public employees relates to the central issue of pay, the more likely it is now to risk being in law a 'political' dispute with government about overall economic and fiscal policy. These were the realities of the teachers' pay claim in 1958–6. Such action is inevitably both 'industrial' and 'political'. The selective strike action in schools was for a salary increase. The 'employers' (largely local authorities) claimed they had insufficient money from government. 'We are not willing to make additional resource available for 1985–6,' said the Secretary of State six months into the action; 'The Government would want a clearer statement of teachers' duties.' The Government argued the case in public and took the political consequences when it then ratified the proposals of the Top Salary Review Board for huge pay increases for generals, judges and top civil servants. Under the old test of 'connection', the teachers' action was clearly a trade dispute. Under the 1982 Act it might have been questioned.

Recent cases have illustrated parallel problems. Many of the modern statutes concerning loss of 'immunity' are couched in terms of inducing breach of a contract of employment, e.g. secondary action (EA 1980 s. 17), or the need for a ballot (TUA 1984 s. 10). In *Benwell's* case, 1985 (p. 159), the court distinguished nurses from prison officers because the former 'enter into a contract of employment', but prison officers are 'appointed by the Home Secretary' under statutory powers and could therefore claim 'judicial review'. So too, a registrar of marriages has, in *Miles's* case (p. 198), been held to be a 'holder of an office', not employed by the local authority. The division made in the *Walsh* case by Donaldson MR and May LJ (p. 159) between 'ordinary' cases of employment contracts, where unfair dismissals claims go to the tribunals, and office-holders or statutory appointees, for whom judicial review is available, suggests that the latter do not always serve under the normal contract of employment. If so, this would be another case where procuring a breach of duty would not fall within 'secondary action' or the need to hold a ballot (EA 1980 s. 17, TUA 1980 s. 18). Prison officers took industrial action in 1980 and 1986; and in 1985 the Government sought an injunction against Civil Service unions threatening to strike without a ballot (a rare instance of the Government appearing as plaintiff under its own 1980s legislation). Such developments are bound ultimately to revive the question whether civil servants or other Crown servants do not have 'contracts of employment'[139] (Chapter 2).

In many comparable countries State officials of varying range scarcely fall within normal labour law jurisprudence at all, but fall within 'public law'. West German *Beamte* (who include nearly half the railway staff) and French *fonctionnaires* are examples. In such countries these workers have had to struggle for rights not merely to strike (which some still do not have) but even to organize in trade unions.[140] Even in Sweden this was not accomplished until 1966. In the United States federal employees have a right to join unions, but their strikes can be visited with dismissal. President Reagan in 1981 sacked thousands of air controllers and broke their union, PATCO. Four-fifths of the states provide for some kind of collective negotiation with public employees. This backward condition still relates to the strange claim that collective bargaining somehow infringes a state's 'sovereignty'.[141] A prevailing right to strike has intersected with the special status of public sector workers in some countries to prompt the formulation of 'self-governing' codes by unions involved. In Italy, for example, *autoregolamentazione* by public service unions (beginning on the railways, and now supported by a law of 1983 and protocol of 1984) contrasts markedly with the much more strike-prone air controllers organized in breakaway unions whose strikes are illegal under a law of 1980. The 1984 protocol provides a code for transport as a whole: 'its only sanction is merely political: an appeal to public opinion'.[142] These State supports for self-discipline in a conflict-prone system merit closer examination in Britain in the light of the customary practice of unions ensuring safety in Britain, e.g. in the NHS, steel and other industries. Self-regulation by unions can work only with direct or indirect support from government and with the understanding of the immediate employer.

The contrast generally with Britain is interesting. The State here did not adopt the position that its sovereignty or dignity was infringed by collective bargaining. Nor were its employees governed by a separate *droit public* (public law) applicable to those who maintain *le fonctionnement du service public* (the State Civil Service), for the very good reason that there was no such separate law. The advent of Whitleyism secured that not only collective bargaining but, for the most part, ordinary private law too came to govern public industrial relations. It is, indeed, one of the dangers of the new rigid judicial division between 'public' and 'private' law in Britain (associated with judicial review: p. 157) that the judges might come to recognize special legal *rights*, as well as duties, for the State in its collective relations with its workers. Some see the ready displacement by the judges of all trade union rights at $GCHQ$ by virtue of the prerogatives of the Crown as soon as the words 'national security' are heard as a dangerous precedent in this direction.[143] The use of the Royal Prerogative in this case to forbid union membership, and the removal, by certificate, of rights in the employment protection legislation from workers at the sensitive communications headquarters on grounds of 'national security', led many to ask which other civil servants might fall under similar prohibitions. Although the ILO Freedom of Association Committee had regarded the action as a breach of the ILO Conventions regarding trade union rights, the House of Lords refused to go behind the Government's claim of 'national security', making the slow progress of the issue to the European Human Rights Commission and Court a process of more than usual interest. Even if there is no such ban, however, it would be in logical conformity with its policies if the

Government were to lean, contrary to tradition, increasingly against union membership in sensitive jobs in the Civil Service.

Certainly, many established practices in the Civil Service are in a state of flux, threatening collective bargaining and long-standing Whitley machinery for dispute resolution. In this condition, civil servants may have few legal defences, as when 'normal' retirement ages are changed, affecting dismissal compensation[144] or (as with *Dudfield*: p. 332) when negotiated terms are excluded by government from employment conditions. Such problems have been largely avoided by non-legal methods, above all by the use of arbitration in disputes over pay and conditions that began with the agreement of 1925, a separate Civil Service Arbitration Tribunal being established in 1936. Even industrial action has tended to be dealt with by way of the domestic 'disciplinary code'. Two changes of policy are critical here. In 1981 the Government refused at first to go to arbitration, then agreed subject only to a right of veto via Parliament. By 1984 it refused once again to activate the arbitration machinery. Secondly, the principle of 'fair comparison' with other earnings (elaborated through a Pay Research Unit) was steadily eroded in place of a greater element of market bargaining. This trend accelerated after the Megaw Report of a committee of inquiry, following a severe strike in 1981. The committee recommended against both special legal liabilities restricting the freedom of civil servants to strike, as in West Germany or the United States, and the imposition of 'no industrial action agreements'. Instead it proposed that no industrial action should occur until a long period elapsed following any breakdown in negotiations, and made recommendations for new bargaining structures ending in arbitration but closer to 'market forces'.[145] Soon innovations like 'clerical work measurement' and bonuses for 'good performance' by senior civil servants were brought in. By 1985, when the Government imposed a general 4.9 per cent 'settlement' in the annual wage round, unrest in the Civil Service over its relative and absolute salary position was intense. In 1986 a weak comparability formula was offered.

The likelihood of continuing industrial action among civil servants remains high. How far legal regulation can change the patterns remains uncertain. It would be ironic if Britain, which led the field from the Whitley Committee onwards in assuring industrial rights to State and public employees, should now try to copy the ways of countries in which those rights are still restricted. It was perhaps a fear that this wedge was being inserted by a thin end that caused the uproar with which the *GCHQ* case was greeted and the industrial demonstrations against the Government's threats to dismiss the employees there who refused to resign from their unions.

General strikes, emergencies and the State

On 11 May 1926, in the middle of the General Strike, Astbury J. declared:

The so-called general strike called by the Trades Union Congress Council is illegal. . . . no trade dispute does or can exist between the Trades Union Congress on the one hand and the Government on the other.[146]

The same day Sir John Simon, a former Home Secretary, declared that a general strike had 'a wholly unconstitutional and unlawful character'. The TUC, which had called out 2 million workers in support of the miners in their bitter struggle against wage cuts enforced by the coal owners after government subsidies were removed, denied that there was a challenge to the constitution: 'The sole aim of the Council is to secure for the miners a decent standard of life. The Council is engaged in an industrial dispute.'

Under the law as it then stood, Astbury J. was probably wrong. The strike action was in furtherance of the miners' trade dispute; and in any event no crime or other wrong against the State (such as sedition) had been committed. 'What distinguishes a General Strike', wrote one lawyer, 'is that it is more likely to succeed.'[147] This was the general response, too, to the vague, unconvincing assertions by the Attorney-General in 1951 when prosecuting dockworkers (under the marcescent Order 1305), who said that strikes causing breach of contract or interference with 'the policy of the State' could be criminal offences and who (by now Lord Shawcross) wrote in 1970 that those who incited 'industrial action for political purposes' committed the crime of conspiracy. None of that had any secure base in legal principle. How far the courts would be prepared to apply the crime established by s. 5 of the 1875 Act ((2), p. 655) is uncertain since it has scarcely, if ever, been used. This is not unrelated to the fact that safety cover has normally been provided in strikes by unions in dangerous trades voluntarily (e.g. in steel, coal and gas), there being a strong tradition in Britain, as the Government Green Paper of 1981 accepted, for strikers to 'ensure that essential services are maintained'.

A closer look at the General Strike of 1926 and its legal consequences is still useful. The Act of 1927 that followed it was much more restricted than the employers' lobby demanded. They wanted a Royal Commission with the objectives of removing 'the immunities of the 1906 Act' and ending the 'privileged legal position of the trade unions'.[148] Baldwin and the majority of the Cabinet refused to change sections 3 and 4 of the 1906 Act (trade dispute immunity for inducing breach of employment contract and the protection of unions in tort). The Government's 1927 Act contented itself with imposing 'contracting-in' to the unions' political levy (Chapter 9); making new forms of 'intimidation' on picket lines illegal; banning sympathetic action that coerced the Government; preventing closed shops in part of the public sector; and stopping Civil Service unions affiliating to the TUC. The Act was deeply resented by the labour movement, and its repeal was the first priority of the Labour Government in 1946. But the more interesting question today is whether the employers' lobby of 1926 would have been satisfied by the surgery carried out on the 'immunities' between 1980 and 1984.

Emergencies today

As for emergencies created by a general strike generally, the Criminal Law Act 1977 leaves the crime of conspiracy restricted to combinations to commit acts in themselves criminal. On the other hand, the redefinition of 'trade dispute' and the restriction of the 'immunities' make it almost inconceivable that a court would refuse an injunction against sympathetic, or 'secondary', action that takes the form of a general strike. Moreover, if the unions who are parties to the primary dispute have broken the orders of the courts against them so as to stand in contempt of court, other workers and unions who assist them – or 'aid and abet' them – in their defiance may themselves be in contempt and vulnerable to fines, imprisonment or sequestration of property. Just how far the third party can lawfully go is open to doubt, as we shall see.

In this situation, various proposals have been heard in the 1980s about special legal measures that might be desirable either in 'emergencies' or in respect of 'essential services'. After the 1984 Act little has been said about holding special ballots in 'cooling-off' periods (the use of which under the 1971 Act proved valueless), since the need of a ballot is universal in 'official' action. Widespread industrial action may give rise to civil remedies of injunctions and damages on the principles already discussed in this chapter. Nevertheless, we must make further examination under each heading. As to 'emergencies', the Emergency Powers Act 1920 (amended mildly in 1964) gives the Government the right to make a proclamation if essential supplies for the community are threatened and thereafter govern with special powers by regulation. The Act is cautious in that, although the powers can be extensive, they cannot include any form of compulsory military service or industrial 'conscription', nor may they make it an offence to 'take part in a strike' or peacefully to persuade anyone to do so (a limitation that the 1981 Green Paper ominously questioned). The proclamation must be renewed within one month. The regulations must be approved forthwith and regularly renewed by Parliament. There were three proclamations in the 1920s (one covering the General Strike), and nine more have been made since 1945 (four dock strikes; the seamen's strike of 1966; railways, 1955; electricity, 1970; coal, 1972; and coal and electricity, 1973). None was issued in the miners' strike of 1984–5.

The State, the military and emergencies

This overt power is really only the tip of the iceberg. First, the 1964 amendment to the Act of 1920 made the Defence Regulations 1939 permanent, thereby allowing the armed services to be used without any proclamation or consultation with Parliament on 'urgent work of national importance'. The Government and Defence Council have relied upon these powers sometimes when they have moved in troops to offset the early effects of large strikes. Between 1947 and 1981 troops were used in at least twenty-four disputes, ranging from strikes by air controllers and dustmen to the national firemen's stoppage.[149] Troops laid netting for car-parks in the rail strikes of 1982, and drove in the ambulance strike of 1981. A wide power to use troops by virtue of the Royal Prerogative is suggested by the Queen's Regulations for the Army, which permit the use of troops 'in aid of the civil authorities' generally. The law here does not confine use of troops to an 'emergency'. Whelan cites at least eleven further trade disputes since 1945 in which the military was 'ready to intervene', a condition where civil control becomes far more problematical than where Parliament has been informed via a proclamation. Another review of thirty-six occasions when troops were deployed in post-war industrial disputes questions the legitimacy of using Royal Prerogative powers (a claim not likely to be upheld in the courts) and proposes clarification of the law (which is highly desirable).[150] It seems clear that Governments – of all parties – have relied upon these general powers, instead of indulging in the more democratic and humbling procedure of a proclamation, though Wiles points out that the 'technological sophistication' of many essential services today makes the use of the military increasingly difficult.[151]

This serves to remind us that the disposition of military personnel, not as substitute labour, but as part of the forces of social order, must now be seen also in the context of the national planning of the police – especially riot police – forces. Troops were used to break strikes on numerous occasions before 1914, but at Tonypandy in 1910 the Home Secretary preferred to send 270 London police officers. From the first day of the 1984 miners' strike a sophisticated National Reporting Centre operated at Scotland Yard. The important distinction between sending troops and using police in Britain has usually been that the latter were local, the former 'foreigners'. The dangers of organizing police squads that can be operationally used in a national strategy are obvious; they will not share with local police forces the inhibition born of the need to live with the community after the strike is over.[152] Indeed, the traditional distinction between the use of troops and the use of police to contain industrial disputes that are perceived as involving social disorder may not now be so clear cut. With the emergence of specialist units and common training with special army units, by the 1980s 'the divide between the police and the military', Wiles has shown, 'has shifted considerably'. The police concept of a 'normal' industrial dispute was linked *inter alia* to their command structures, and today's increased 'professionalism' could lead police to lose 'patience with the politicians and try to define the operational law of industrial disputes for themselves'.[153] Police discretion has, in operational terms, long defined the law locally on picketing. But the definition of what is lawful by police organized nationally in the face of industrial action categorized as 'disorder' is a very different matter.

In planning for emergencies, government has acquired new legal strength from the *GCHQ* decision. The Law Lords confirmed that decisions taken under the Royal Prerogative will not be open to judicial review by the courts if taken by reason of 'national security'. In that case it involved a ban on trade union membership among civil servants at a secret communications centre; they also appeared to include within the same rule 'the defence of the realm' or decisions relating to the armed services. There is here a further layer to the inquiry. Since 1919 there has existed in government the STO (Supply and Transport Organization) with its own committee of senior Ministers (the story is legend of its preservation on ice by the Labour Government of 1929, to be handed over intact to its successor in 1931). This was a rather more important product of the period than the Act of 1927. Its development into the modern CCU (Civil Contingencies Unit) has been revealed in great detail by Jeffery and Hennessy,[154] showing that for more than sixty years all Governments – and in particular the top officials of the Civil Service – have maintained continuous vigilance over industrial contingencies, ready to act in any emergency, and in an atmosphere of secrecy little short of conspiratorial. Removing extreme disruption may, they say, be sensible or even desirable: 'In exploring this avenue, the government, however, ought not to take material advantage from the unions' self-restraint.' One aspect of interest and concern is the apparent involvement of employers in preliminary planning at this level, something that must inevitably be taken into account in considering any collaboration by trade unions in patterns of self-regulation for the purposes of the safety and maintenance of community services before and during any widespread industrial action.

Essential services

This, then, is the framework in which the problem of disruption of 'essential services' must be seen, one of continuous and deep government involvement in advance, not a sudden union incursion on to some neutral battleground. The preparations, of which something is now known, made by the Government between 1981 and 1984 for what was seen as an inevitable and bloody battle with the NUM are a recent illustration of such long-term planning. As yet the exact place of the CCU in that is uncertain. There are further layers to penetrate.

Government has been ready to legislate *ad hoc* to deal with particular problems; it did so in 1980 to offset the consequences of the prison officers' action, and in 1979 to lessen the impact of a three-year dispute about new computers in which civil servants withdrew their support for the Scottish court system. We have seen, too, that in more general legislation the Telecommunications Act 1984 specifies that field as one in need of special treatment.

There are other standing laws that affect certain industries, for example nuclear power. As Lewis has shown, ordinary restrictions together with statutes on nuclear safety and official secrets make lawful industrial action improbable in the nuclear industry and the use of troops highly likely in a dispute.[155] The Atomic Energy Authority's special constabulary has special powers and is armed; 'national security pervades and limits the collective relationship' of unions and management. The sensitivity of some other areas of employment has received attention. A sit-in by British Aerospace workers in 1984 (which ended peacefully after skilled negotiation by the local police) was of great concern to the company and to government because of projects that included 'highly sensitive military orders'. In a different way, industrial action by DHSS computer staff, which lasted many months in protest against new shifts introduced unilaterally, threatened to wreck the payment of housing and social security benefits to millions of claimants. In October 1984 the entire DHSS statistics for the year were reported to be locked in a strike-bound computer. It is as yet uncertain how far action of this sort might incur liability, apart from ordinary torts, for inducing a breach of statutory duties (p. 640) and, indeed, what remedies would be effective if torts were committed. But the Government no doubt had this kind of problem in mind in setting out to consider 'essential services' in 1985. There have also been moves for the replacement of key civilians in critical posts with military personnel, a tendency curiously contrary to the 'civilianization' of the police.[156]

In 1984–5 many proposals were aired to make further provision for restricting strikes in 'essential services'. Zealots, such as Neal and Bloch, have pressed for the introduction of criminal liability for strikes in services that are, or are deemed by a Minister in his discretion to be, 'essential'.[157] The discretion is important because a definition of 'essential' is almost impossible. As the Green Paper of 1981 pointed out: 'so interdependent and interconnected are firms and industries that there is almost no major strike which will not ultimately affect the interests of the economy or community as a whole'. Definition of an 'emergency' is therefore difficult, and 'great difficulty' would be encountered in defining what services are 'essential'. The Institute of Directors had a try in 1984: they included gas, water, sewage, electricity, ambulance, fire brigade, burial and certain health services, plus perhaps oil transport in the private sector.[158] One might add telecommunications, broadcasting, railways, airports, docks, data processing, road transport, food processing and numerous others. Instead of criminal penalties, this proposal chooses compulsory procedure agreements and binding 'pendulum arbitration' (or 'final offer', where the arbitrator must choose either the union's or the employer's last offer, where he can identify it, without amendment). Both ideas reflect in part new-style agreements made between certain unions (the EETPU, for example) and Japanese car firms, which contain, in effect if not in form, 'no-strike' clauses. But a *compulsory* procedure 'agreement' is a contradiction in terms. It is legal regulation in drag. In reality such proposals edge closer to the illegality of all strike action (for it would presumably have to be illegal for workers in the other industries to combine in industrial action with, or in support of, the essential groups forbidden to withdraw labour). Nor would it seem logical, if 'essential services' demand such Draconian measures, to leave enforcement to the choice of employers; government would be compelled to intervene.

At this point the distinction between penal civil law and criminal law is wafer thin. Moreover, the importance of the availability of unions as defendants, rather than individuals who might introduce the 'martyrdom' factor, is once more apparent. We recall the desire of members of the judiciary to end 'self-help' in industrial conflict. The authoritarian element in such a policy is a paradoxical result, 'advanced by its own logic as pursuit of the ethic of freedom through competition'.[159] The hard-headed thinkers in this school of thought drew their conclusions on this point a decade ago, spelling out the way 'the union organisation would be affected if the right to coerce were ruled out'. They put the point without beating about the bush: 'Ideally, what is needed for the emancipation of labour is the enactment of the principle underlying the British Combination Acts 1799 and 1800 . . . adapted to the 1970s.'[160]

If we experience laws of this kind in the final years of the 1980s it is to be hoped that they will be discussed for what they are – an assertion that modern society, its structures and its markets are too fragile, too complex, too conflictual, too full of 'problems' to allow any longer a general freedom of withdrawal of labour, and that penal law must be used to suppress contravention of its regulations. The interdependence of services and industries in an industrialized community today cannot be denied, though it is sometimes forgotten that this is not wholly a modern phenomenon. Those who wish for such freedoms to be preserved will be obliged to produce practical proposals to that end about maintaining the community in the midst of conflict if they are to inspire confidence in others. For this they need to develop an equally clear view about the place of the State – troops and all – and the possibilities of self-regulation by trade unions that can be attained by compromise in the context of pluralist policies that face the realities of power, inequality and the legal system.

Realistic discussion on these matters is hardly within earshot of conventional condemnation of 'political' strikes against the 'Government' or the 'State'. We have noted in this and the preceding chapter the dangers of the concept 'political strike' – which, Lord Roskill pointed out in 1973, can so easily be used to condemn action of which one 'subjectively disapproves'. Such simplistic analyses are supported even by writers on political theory who treat the issues in abstract categories, such as 'When is coercive political strike action valid?' MacFarlane, for example, replies to such a question that in 'a modern democratic State based on universal suffrage' the 'political' strike may be justifiable to preserve the State against 'internal subversion or government subversion' or for 'saving the community from the catastrophic effects of a morally indefensible government policy'. This begs questions at every step (by now we surely know that one man's 'indefensible policy' is another woman's 'policy without any alternative'). The central problem with such writing as far as law is concerned is its assumption that it is a neutral force. A general strike, he writes, is justifiable only if there is 'a direct political threat' to democratic practices or 'to the rights of trade unions to exist and operate'.[161] What rights? Such nostrums assume that in 1926, 1984 or whenever it may be trade unions have a bundle of 'rights' and have enough 'rights' to 'operate'. Operate to what effect? Since in reality they have few, scarcely any, 'rights' in our law, there can hardly ever be a threat to them sufficient to justify a general strike in defence of them.

We need a starting-point that is more real and more stimulating, for example Miliband's provocative conclusion that 'British unions are not strong enough by themselves to dictate terms to employers and the state; but they are too strong to be forced into co-operation.'[162] New measures on 'essential services', on top of the experience of 1980–4, may put this optimism to the test.

Social neutrality and State intervention

In 1954 Kahn-Freund declared that 'neutrality of the state towards trade disputes has found expression in social welfare legislation'.[163] At that time of non-interventionist consensus, orthodoxy regarded the spheres both of social security and of conciliation and arbitration as parallel in that respect. We discussed the latter in Chapter 4 (p. 307). There is a case to be made for the view that from the Act of 1896 to the work of ACAS today the machinery supported by the State to assist in the conciliation and arbitration of disputes is in Britain less interventionist than in most other comparable systems. It is easier to address the problem in that way rather than use the absolute category of 'neutrality'. Arbitration might have become compulsory; but, except in time of war or in exceptional cases of props to collective bargaining (see Chapter 4), it did not. Courts of Inquiry still have the function, not of making legally binding pronouncements, but (as the Ministry of Labour put it in 1965) 'of informing Parliament and the public of the facts and underlying causes of dispute'. They can be a form, as McCarthy and Clifford put it, of 'public conciliation'.[164] ACAS maintains this tradition as best it can, still advancing the merits of the conciliator whose skill 'can help the parties to weave into the fabric of a settlement acceptable to both sides' the thread of compromise, thereby speeding 'the process of necessary industrial reform' (1984 Report). But in so far as public policy moves towards *compulsory* arbitration or 'agreements', its function will change; the State will value compromise less than it did.

A valuable survey has shown that the use of arbitration, conciliation and similar machinery provided by the State was most prominent in the period following the war; it then declined rapidly until the 1960s and rose to new peaks in the 1970s. But, most important, such phenomena 'can all be regarded as part of the search for a viable incomes policy' (Chapter 4); and 'the evidence indicates that on balance incomes policy has both provoked particular strikes and done a great deal to raise the general level of strike activity'.[165] Perhaps this echoes the unfortunate manner in which 'incomes policy' has become, unnecessarily, the equivalent in the ears of many people of 'wage restraint'. On the other hand, the 1980s have shown that the absence of a formal incomes policy (or, as some would put it, the introduction of unemployment as an incomes policy) does not put an end to strike activity. The question in 1986 was whether the bodies that, like ACAS, still favour a less interventionist approach would be able to survive many further rounds of legal regulation.

Social security

Secondly, there is social security. For the worker who engages in industrial action or who is locked out, one of the first questions is whether he has any entitlement to social security payment. In 1900 the courts had already established the general principle that strikers should have no benefits by way of Poor Law relief if they were able to obtain and perform work at wages that would support themselves and their families, though some relief might be given to the families themselves.[166] This principle, which links with the general theme that social security should not support 'voluntary' unemployment, was taken over into national insurance in 1911, and in a sense it is still the basis of our system today. It is not a satisfactory explanation, though, of parts of it; for example, the concept that unemployment insurance should not assist 'voluntary' unemployment has never justified in full the disqualification of workers who suffer a lock-out equally with those who go on strike. Moreover, there is no exception for those who leave work for 'good cause' in a dispute (the law was said not to wish to judge the merits of strikes and lock-outs).

Some now wish to abolish the right of such families to draw supplementary benefit; for this might be said to assist strikers against the employer. Others see the disqualification of workers from unemployment benefit thoughout the length of disputes as far from 'neutral' if strikers have a legitimate grievance.[167] What is more, workers on strike for long periods may cease to be qualified with adequate contributions, and this may prejudice their rights both for unemployment benefit and benefits under bargained redundancy schemes, as with some miners in 1985. Clearly this is an 'indirect compulsion to return to work', as Kahn-Freund himself said in 1972. English law has never achieved 'neutrality' – if indeed it is possible to achieve it. For in a dispute social security benefit is either paid (when the workers are stronger) or not paid (when they are weaker). State policy is better seen in the context of the labour market as a whole. In truth, what was approved by a wide band of opinion in the 1950s and 1960s, including the Donovan Report, was not the 'neutrality' of, but a balance of interventions by, the State. Indirect pressure to take work, even on strikers, was accepted as part of a package in which the State maintained its commitment to full employment, to the availability of work at conditions above a minimum floor, to traditional freedoms to withdraw labour and to social welfare to assist the poorest, including strikers' families.

In this context Parliament's attempt to insulate the Welfare State from industrial conflict was taken as a guide to policy. So, the right to a redundancy payment in case of lay-off or short time is excluded where it is caused by a strike or lay-off even in foreign lands (EPCA s. 89 (3)). And where employment is lost by reason of a stoppage due to a 'trade dispute' at his place of employment the worker is disqualified from unemployment benefit throughout the stoppage (except where he has become bona fide employed elsewhere) unless he proves he is 'not participating in or directly interested in' the dispute (Social Security Act 1975 s. 19 (1), as amended by EPA s. 111). (The Social Security Bill 1986 aims to replace 'participation' by 'withdrawal of labour in furtherance of the dispute'.) Here 'trade dispute' has broadly its old meaning (i.e. before the 1982 amendments noted in Chapter 7), namely a dispute between employers or employees, or employees and employees, connected with employment, non-employment or employment terms or conditions of any person (whoever is his employer). Until 1975 there were further disqualifications for workers helping to 'finance' the stoppage (e.g. through their union) or workers in the same 'grade or class' as those interested in the dispute; but on Donovan's proposal these were deleted in 1975.

The disqualifications that remain have caused great difficulty. 'Participation' has included taking part at any time, even for a day. Cases where pickets came to persuade a worker to join in a dispute have been held to entail a 'trade dispute' between the pickets and their employer or between him and the pickets (though not necessarily where workers are only forcibly prevented by pickets from entering the works). Disputes are also included arising from the employer's alleged failure to observe health and safety legislation.[168] But in 1985 a more liberal view of 'participating' was taken by the Commissioners; a participant may now withdraw and cease to be disqualified, though he may be disqualified on other grounds, such as (in that case) his 'direct interest'.[169] It will be seen that here the ambition of the claimant will not be to seek a wide definition of 'trade dispute', as it would be if he were trying to rely on an 'immunity' ICFTD, but in a narrow construction that might allow him to escape the net of disqualification. The 'place of employment' has been held to include the whole of the docks in which a dockworker worked; and the statutory definitions mean that places that comprise any 'step in an integrated process of production' on a site are included (leading to the whole of the Ford Dagenham estate being held to be one 'place'). The fact that the employer has not done all that might have been expected of him does not prevent the stoppage being 'due' to the dispute.[170]

The most difficult problems have arisen in connection with the disqualification of workers 'participating in or being directly interested in' the trade dispute, a proviso introduced in 1924. We have noted the similar problems about dismissals of workers who 'take part' in industrial action (p. 195). Here the 'participation' includes a subjective element, knowingly doing or refraining from something concerning the dispute; but attending a meeting called to find a settlement has been held to be enough, as has a refusal to blackleg by doing the work of strikers. Recent decisions seem to be even more strict. Where a dispute arose over compulsory redundancies instituted by a multinational corporation, mass meetings issued an ultimatum to it to withdraw its proposals. The claimant, X, a work study engineer, attended the meetings and supported the opposition. During a holiday period, which ended on 18 April 1983, workers led by shop stewards occupied the factory. The employers advised the rest of the work-force not to report for work. On the evening of 18 April, X notified his head of department that he opposed the sit-in and was available for work in any other factory of the corporation. But the Commissioner held that he was disqualified; the latest date by which he could dissociate himself from participating was the morning of 18 April, and since he was participating in the dispute then it was too late for him to withdraw.[171]

'Direct interest' is more difficult. Where employees' pay and conditions are bargained with relation to the rates of other workers there is always an 'interest'; but it would be unduly wide to hold, as some decisions did, that a strike by the latter disqualified the former if they happened to be thrown out of work in the dispute. Recent decisions have therefore stressed the 'directness' that is required of the interest. But this still allows for wide disqualifications, for, as Lord Brandon has put it, a narrow and legalistic interpretation might allow for 'deliberate and calculated evasions' of the statutory scheme. In *Presho's* case, 1984,[172] the claimant was a unionized production worker in a factory where maintenance engineers in a different union went on strike for a pay claim. Without the maintenance of machines, all production workers were laid off for five days. The employer's practice was to apply alterations in structure of pay to all workers. The Law Lords held there is a 'direct' interest in cases where (1) an employer will apply the outcome of a dispute to both strikers and another group of workers, including the claimant, and (2) this 'across-the-board' result happens automatically by reason of either a collective agreement or 'established industrial custom and practice at the place of work concerned'. Here, therefore, the worker was rightly disqualified by the Commissioner. A worker's interest in the *outcome* of the dispute (which is not what the Acts says) was 'very much the same thing' as his being interested in the *dispute* (which is). Although the relationship of the outcome to the neighbouring group must be 'automatic', the process can still be uncertain if there is argument about just what the employer's 'practice' is and when there will be a break in 'the chain of causation'. Such matters under the *Presho* test appear to be largely in the hands of the employer. If he decides to apply the outcome of disputes, whatever they may be, to workers other than the strikers, he appears to have the power to exclude them from unemployment benefit if they are thrown out of work by the stoppage, even if they have no knowledge of, or are even opposed to, the purposes of the strike.[173] The Court of Appeal had taken a narrower approach to avoid unreasonable hardship for such claimants; not so the Law Lords.

Since the disqualification of such workers lasts for the whole period of the stoppage, the question of whether they or their dependants can obtain supplementary benefit assumes great importance. Broadly, they cannot; but their families can (Supplementary Benefits Act 1976 s. 8), though regulations of 1983 restricted the payments available for the family's 'additional requirements'. Supplementary benefit, which unlike unemployment benefit has no contribution qualification, is meant to be the safety-net below which no family should fall, taking account of a (rigorous) assessment of its 'resources'. But in 1980 the Government introduced a new deduction to be applied to such benefit. In 1984–5 it was reduced by £16 per week (originally it was £12; for 1985–6 it is £17). This is an amount that strikers are 'deemed' to receive from a trade union (whether they are in fact members or not and whether a union does or can pay strike benefit or not): Social Security (No. 2) Act 1980 s. 6. In 1984 Government estimates put the savings arising from the 'deemed' deduction of £15 (as it was then) at £19.8 million. Attempts to challenge the application of this deduction in the miners' strike of 1984 failed (the mining unions pay no strike pay);[174] and, as Mesher comments, this deduction may have increased bitterness in the dispute. In addition, the same Act abolished any 'disregard' of income in assessing resources, except for strike pay up to the statutory figure. Where, therefore, a husband was on strike in 1985, the basic normal supplementary benefit for the wife (other than payments for housing and for children) was reduced from £22.45 to £6.45. (The effect of raising the 'deemed' strike pay in 1984 by £1 was to cancel the £1 general increase in benefit, in effect reducing it 5 per cent in real terms.) If both spouses are on strike, no normal benefit is payable. No deduction will be made if any part of £17 is paid by the union as strike pay to the worker, but if it comes to him as a 'hardship' payment 'by reason of being without employment', account is taken in full. Moreover, the rules about previous earnings mean that when the last week's earnings before the strike are more than two and a half times basic scale rates for the family unit as a whole, the excess is counted as income for the following week.[175]

If a striker (or, we must remember, a worker thrown out of work by the dispute at his workplace, even by a lock-out) is single he cannot claim benefit; but he could before 1980 seek some assistance for 'urgent need'. 'However "undeserving", a striker was not allowed to starve. This protection', writes Lynes, 'no longer exists.' Fewer emergency payments can now be made. The miners' strike was held not to be a 'disaster' that allowed urgent payments (R(SB) 24/85). The regime is less harsh when the dispute is over; payments can continue for fifteen days (as they can for unemployment benefit). But this benefit is ultimately recoverable from the worker's wages, normally through the employer. Any loan, advance or *ex gratia* payment made or offered by the employer in this fortnight is taken into account in full. Employers have complained about the rules concerning supplementary benefit on return to work because they can endanger a harmonious settlement after a severe dispute.[176]

Gennard has shown that supplementary benefit has played much less of a role in financing strikers than legend asserts. There is evidence to suggest that in the miners' strike of 1984–5, as might have been expected in such a protracted dispute, the take-up by miners' families was much higher than in the strikes of 1972 and 1974.[177] That these are not the only relevant areas of social welfare law was illustrated in the same strike. A claim by a striking miner that he was entitled to family income supplement was rejected by the Court of Appeal.[178] Under the Family Income Supplements Act 1970 and Regulations No. 1437, 1980, this benefit is payable only when a family's 'normal gross income' from either or both spouses' employment falls below certain limits. The claimant earned much more than the limit in his employment when at work (especially when not 'subject to an overtime ban imposed by his union'). Now in the strike he earned nothing; his wife earned £51 a week; their only other income was £13 a week in child benefit for the two children. The judges said 'normal' income meant income when he was at work. They justified this interpretation largely by the fact that, if the wife had not been earning at all, the family could not have claimed FIS benefit because it is available only to supplement low-income families. The court insisted upon equal misery for all. (FIS is perhaps one of the most quirkish of the welfare benefits. A mother in full-time work, but absent because of sickness, lost her benefit because though she was 'in' work she was not 'at' work.)[179]

A source of support that was once important to strikers – tax rebates – was dealt with in the Finance Act of 1981. This permits the Government to withhold repayments when unemployment benefit is being paid or when the worker is involved in a trade dispute (the Inland Revenue Staff Federation estimated in July 1984 that the Government was retaining £6.8 million, and that was less than half-way through the miners' strike).

There has been a detectable drift in recent years in these areas of social security law towards a stricter regime of discipline for workers who take any industrial action (or who are locked out), a tendency that matches the movements in labour law and general government policy. Older elements survive; for example, we recall the provision preventing the refusal of work of a suitable kind being a disqualification from unemployment benefit where the vacancy is a consequence of a stoppage in a trade dispute (Social Security Act 1975 s. 20 (4): p. 108). But the balance of the system between the prevention or punishment of industrial conflict and the provision for human need is, overall, very different from what it was three decades ago. The notion that the State should be industrially 'neutral' in social security – never more than a myth, but once a useful one – has been jettisoned.

Remedies: damages and the labour injunction

Damages

Remedies in tort actions are awards of damages and injunctions. Some of the cases we have discussed ended with an award of damages, such as *Rookes* v. *Barnard*, 1964 (p. 39), and the *Messenger Newspapers* case, 1984 (p. 610). In the latter, the court awarded not only the damages that normally accompany a finding of liability, namely the loss intended or directly flowing from a tort, but also sums representing 'aggravated' and 'exemplary' damages. Both of these are ways of marking the court's displeasure at the defendant over and above the loss he has caused to the plaintiff. The former are related more to injury to the plaintiff's dignity or feelings, while exemplary damages are punitive. The NGA had to pay both aggravated and exemplary damages by reason of what the judge saw as its 'jubilant' defiance of the law and its malicious treatment of the plaintiff. The amounts awarded were: for loss by expenditure, including sums spent before the torts to safeguard the enterprise, £70,051; for loss of revenue, £20,000; as aggravated damages £10,000; and exemplary damages, £25,000. But here no loss of profit was claimed, as it normally would be (compare the £3 million claim: p. 611).

A plaintiff must take reasonable steps to mitigate loss caused to him; and it is arguable (though the cases are not clear) that the defendant cannot be made liable to pay compensation for losses that are neither intended nor foreseeable. A more difficult problem can arise when the defendant has committed various torts, all contributing to the plaintiff's loss but some of them protected by a trade dispute 'immunity'. Suppose some workers go on strike against their own employer for a wage claim. They persuade other workers to break their employment contracts and strike with them, but in the course of picketing they commit the torts of nuisance and of trespass on the employer's property. The Northern Ireland Court of Appeal faced such a problem in *Norbrook Laboratories Ltd* v. *King*, 1984.[180] It held that the 'immunity' is not lost merely by reason of the other torts (so long as they are not the means of the very inducement, when the 'unlawful means' would deprive the defendant of the 'immunity'); and, therefore, that the damages payable to the plaintiff must be limited to the loss caused by the nuisance and trespass, and exclude that attributable to acts 'within the golden formula'.

We have seen that a claim for damages brought against a trade union is often subject to a statutory limit according to the number of members it has (p. 531; EA 1982 s. 16). We do not repeat those details here, but note three points. First, the limit is applicable 'if the union has' so many members. There might be a dispute about how many members it 'has', or had at a particular time. Indeed the section is not itself very clear about what *is* the relevant time (the time of the judgment; or the writ; or the tort – all are possible). A court might look at the central register that a union must maintain (TUA 1984 s. 4); but this might be out of date compared with the relevant time. There are no 'independent' records, except those of the CO, and they are usually published more than a year out of date. Secondly, the limit applies 'in any proceedings' in tort. Ways of evading the limit may be found. It only applies to each plaintiff; so the number of plaintiffs might be increased where, say, numerous companies have suffered loss. Even one plaintiff may bring more than one set of 'proceedings'. Indeed, it is not entirely clear what a set of 'proceedings' is; if a company issues six different writs against a union for different torts, or in respect of different acts, during the course of a strike, it does not necessarily follow that they all must be consolidated into the one action, although no doubt the union would ask for the consolidation of all claims arising from one strike into one set of 'proceedings'. Thirdly, the limits do not apply to torts causing personal injury, nor to torts where the breach of duty is 'in connection with ownership, occupation, possession, control or use of property' (of any kind: s. 16 (2). It is arguable that the limits do not apply, therefore, to defamation in a union journal. Clearly much wig-scratching will accompany the search for breaches of duty that arise 'in connection with union property', for more than one set of 'proceedings', and for ways of assessing the number of union members. There may likewise be argument about the precise funds maintained in the 'protected property' (p. 532; s. 17) when it comes to enforcing the award of damages.

The problem of damages is also likely, however, to arise in a rather different connection, now that the 'immunities' are so restricted. The difficulties present themselves in the form not so much of how much a plaintiff can recover, but of how many plaintiffs can recover loss directly caused to them. Take the abolition of 'immunities' where one of the grounds for action is pressure to extend or maintain consultation with a union. We have considered a similar problem in connection with loss caused by unlawful means (p. 643). We posed the problem of a company that, induced by its workers' union, withdrew custom from a supplier because it had ceased to consult with its employees' union and had dismissed its union members. This is a statutory tort under E A 1982 s. 13, and all persons 'adversely affected' can sue. But does this mean that every client and customer of the supplier can sue the company for loss directly caused, and so on down the long line? It seems so. What then of the union that induced the first company to act on this ground? It has no 'immunity' by reason of s. 14. But this is to say only that it is liable to persons who can sue it for threatening to induce breaches of employment contract and of commercial contract. This may extend to the supplier; but it would be a great extension of the law to say that, generally, its customers, and their customers, can sue for that tort to the end of all 'adverse effect'.

The case might be put differently against the union, i.e. that it is a 'joint tortfeasor' or 'conspirator' with the company to commit the statutory tort under s. 13. But we saw that the 1982 Act in s. 14 (1) specifically refrains from imposing on the union the 'statutory tort' and its wider range of plaintiffs. For 'inducing' the company to contravene s. 12 or s. 13, the union is to lose its 'immunity' in trade disputes. Parliament sometimes imposes liability for inducing new statutory torts (as with telecommunications: p. 658). But here Parliament appears to have put a wider liability upon the company (s. 13) than upon the union (s. 14).

The regulation of industrial relations by way of the law of tort, which is the policy of the Acts of 1980–4, is likely, then, to make actions for damages important in two different ways: first, where a plaintiff company claims huge damages against a union and attempts to find ways to attenuate the protection of the limit on damages (EA 1982 s. 16); secondly, where a large number of different plaintiffs claim sums that in total are very large, but each individual claim is one set of proceedings. In the second type of case the result may turn less upon the law about remoteness of damage than upon the range of proper plaintiffs. We took the example of ss. 13 and 14 of the 1982 Act. But the problem might arise where a union endorses a strike by members in a public service without a ballot (TUA 1984 s. 10) and thousands of customers bring actions for loss suffered. In the summer of 1985 lawyers spoke softly about 'those commuters' who might consult them about claims if a rail strike occurred in which the union lost 'immunity'; (claims that we have argued should not succeed: p. 644). One cannot be confident that the judges, in 'creative' mood, would not extend the range of plaintiffs as we have so far known it in the law of tort, or that the Government will not legislate to do so. Also, whether or not the union is liable, the persons who have done the tortious acts, union officials for example, are fully liable personally in the absence of immunity for loss to plaintiffs who have standing to sue. Damages are important to them, especially if every disappointed customer can sue from Wick to Wyoming.

Injunctions

Even so, the injunction is a more important remedy here than damages, even though the plaintiff has a right to his damages but the injunction lies within the discretion of the court. A court may grant the plaintiff a final injunction at the trial ordering the defendant not to commit, or not to repeat, the tortious acts. But long before the final trial, the plaintiff in this sort of case wants to stop the action at once. He can make use of the so-called 'interlocutory' procedure of the High Court. Moving quickly after the issue of his writ, he can go to the court to stop the defendant doing him some allegedly irreparable damage, asking the judge to grant him an 'interlocutory injunction' (in Scotland 'interim interdict', where the principles are similar though not identical). For example, if a defendant is about to knock down his house a plaintiff may ask the court·

to stop him, at least until the question whether he has a right to do so can be properly tried. An interlocutory injunction may also be granted to prevent an alleged breach of contract, such as a breach of rule by, say, a wrongful expulsion from a union (though normally not where it would amount to the enforcement of a contract not specifically enforceable, such as a contract of employment). At this 'interlocutory' stage, both the facts and the legal issues may still be uncertain. Indeed, one object, said Lord Diplock in 1975,

> is to protect the plaintiff against injury by violation of his right for which he could not be adequately compensated in damages recoverable in the action if the uncertainty were resolved in his favour at the trial.

All injunctions, whether in prohibitory or mandatory form, are discretionary. Both the High Court and the County court have power to grant a final or interlocutory injunction or to appoint a receiver. Where 'the case is one of urgency' an application may be made to a judge *ex parte* (that is, in the absence of the defendant) rather than *inter partes* (that is, after due notice so that the defendant can defend the application). A plaintiff cannot apply to the court before he issues his writ or originating summons *except* 'where the case is one of urgency' (Rules of Supreme Court, Order 29, R. 1 (2), (3)). Clearly, a legal system that had no 'interlocutory' remedies at all would be defective, exposing the plaintiff to whatever irreparable damage a defendant might choose to commit before the law's delays ushered the litigation through trial to final judgment. On the other hand, interlocutory adjudications, especially those resting on *ex parte* motions, must be very closely scrutinized, and 'urgency' narrowly interpreted, to avoid the risk of prejudicing the defendant. To grant any injunction against a defendant who, it turns out, has done no wrong is an injustice.

The labour injunction

Transfer this pattern of procedure to labour law and a very different picture emerges. The principles remain (roughly) the same. The 'basic purpose of the grant of an interlocutory injunction is to preserve the status quo until the rights of the parties have been determined in the action' (RSC, note, O. 29/1/2). But what status quo? The union is of course faced – and has been faced long before the legislation of 1982–4 restricted the 'immunities' – by the (legal) fact that even in trade disputes it does not have any rights, only torts-that-are-not-actionable. The employer is faced with what he alleges is unlawful industrial action. He says that if it is not stopped, it will cause him very great damage. But if it is stopped, the workers will lose the advantage of 'striking while the iron is hot'. It is little use to them for a court to discover, months later at 'full trial', that their action was not actionable after all, when the industrial dispute has been lost with the help of the court's injunction.

The tendency is, therefore, for the interlocutory battle over the 'labour injunction' in most cases to be the real fight. Most cases of this kind do not go on to full trial; but the court, of course, speaks of the case as if it will. 'More may come out at the trial' is a common theme in interlocutory judgments. 'The union may succeed at the trial, but if it does it will have been a close run thing,' said Dillon L J in 1984, agreeing to grant an injunction *against* the union. Union officials are sometimes understandably mystified to hear that they 'may win' at trial (i.e. their action may well be lawful) but they must suffer this 'interim' order not to continue the strike, even though the order may last for years. After the interim proceedings the employer may delay bringing the case on to trial and so give the union no chance to prove its full case. Indeed, he may never do so. Even when the court orders 'a speedy trial' this usually means, at best, a delay of many months. An effective interlocutory injunction during this period benefits the employer in the most simple way: he has stopped the strike. The only alternative for the union is defiance of the order. Some 'interim' orders obtained by employers have lain on the file for years, while the 'status quo' (a ban on the strike) is preserved.[181]

Without scrupulous care by the judiciary – and sometimes even with it – the interlocutory labour injunction can become a great engine of oppression against workers and their unions. This was the case in the United States where they were banned from the federal courts by statute in 1932 (though their siblings have reappeared since). As was said in the classic U S study of labour injunctions:

The injunction cannot preserve the so-called status quo. . . . The suspension of activities affects only the strikers; the employer resumes his effort to defeat the strike. . . . Moreover, the suspension of strike activities, even temporarily, may defeat the strike for practical purposes and foredoom its resumption, even if the injunction is later lifted.[182]

We have seen the value placed by employers today upon easy access within days, even hours, to such injunctions when the industrial action threatened is deprived of 'immunity', as with the London Underground train strike (Chapter 1, p. 86) or the *Austin Rover* case (where punishment for breach of an order was exacted upon one union weeks after the strike had failed: p. 77). The question here is how much further the law will go; whether it will provide the employer with his remedy when the illegality is not so clear. The Law Lords even felt compelled to point out to the Court of Appeal in 1980:

If judges were to grant injunctions notwithstanding that they know that it is highly probable that the acts that they are enjoining are perfectly lawful, it is unlikely that voluntary respect for the law would continue.[183]

Injunctions: *ex parte* and *inter partes*

One difficulty is that we are here concerned not so much with legal principle as with legal practice. The statement of legal principle in this area invariably gives even more scope than usual to the judge to interpret the rule, or to make exceptions to it, and vary the result in his discretion; and while lawyers may be interested in the formulations of principle in the judgment, the employer and the workers are interested in the result. For example, the application for interlocutory relief is supposed to come after the writ has been issued and the statement of claim filed (the document from which the defendant can best understand the nature of the case put against him); yet in many cases the 'notice of motion' is issued with or even before the writ, and a statement of claim may not be issued at all or issued much later. In *Thomas* v. *N U M (South Wales Area)*[184] the writ was issued on 7 January 1985, but the notice of motion was dated 3 January and it was brought into court on 22 January (a fairly leisurely progress for such a case not unrelated to the dates of the legal vacation). This must have been accepted as a matter of 'urgency'. Yet the matters of which complaint was made (in affidavits dated between 21 and 26 January) came to a head in November 1984 (though in part they were continuing in 1985). In *Mercury Communications*[185] the plaintiff's writ, notice of motion and main affidavit with thirteen exhibits all had the same date; two later affidavits were available to the defendants as the hearing began. Moreover, critical new evidence was permitted from the plaintiffs in the Court of

Appeal. In such cases the lawyers for the plaintiff often give the defendants sight of draft affidavits in advance, but this may be only days or hours before the hearing.

There is little point in the defendant objecting to such procedural defects. For one thing, his lawyers will be busy trying to reply to the affidavits received before or sometimes even during the hearing. The normal minimum period of notice required to start such proceedings is two clear days, but leave can be obtained for shorter notice, and in some cases notice is simply shorter in fact. Indeed, many actions are begun by a unilateral application by the plaintiff, *ex parte*, where the judge hears only the plaintiff in a case of 'urgency'. When tort liabilities expanded in the 1960s, plaintiffs began to put this procedure to more effective use. Davies and Anderman wrote in 1973:

the High Court has not found the requirement of urgency a difficult one for the plaintiff to meet, and many of the injunctions granted by the High Court in labour disputes have been granted, initially, *ex parte*.[186]

So, in the *Ford Motor Co.* decision on collective agreements, 1969 (p. 319), an injunction was granted *ex parte* by the judge, and that order stood against the defendants for a week until he was convinced that the plaintiff's case was quite hopeless. In the *Hull Trawlers* litigation of 1970[187] mandatory injunctions were issued on an *ex parte* motion and were not discharged by the Court of Appeal, even though it found their mandatory form in *ex parte* proceedings 'most unusual' and 'very odd'. At a later hearing the employer claimed the strike had been 'effectively broken' – as indeed it had. Even if the defendant union's lawyers hear about the *ex parte* motion and arrive panting at the door of the court, the judge still has a discretion as to whether they be heard; although present, they were not heard at the first hearing in the *Torquay Hotel* case 1969 (p. 566). To deal with such glaring injustice, Parliament provided in 1974 that, where a defendant is likely to claim that he acted in contemplation or furtherance of a trade dispute (that he did so; not that he has a defence), the court shall require that notice be given by the applicant to him, and that he must have an opportunity to be heard (TULRA s. 17 (1)). The section made little difference in practice. The Law Lords have set a low standard for deciding when the defendant is 'likely' to make this claim of 'trade dispute'.[188] The judge may decide about this issue on the information before him (from the plaintiff) and is not obliged to make his own inquiries. There is a very strong case for prohibiting *ex parte* injunctions in any case against a union or in an apparent trade dispute either altogether or at least before information is obtained from ACAS about it.

One of the picketing cases arising out of attempts by drivers in 1981 to stop 'cowboy' firms undercutting on wage rates illustrates the place of the *ex parte* injunction. Drivers picketed the docks at Liverpool; but they had acted unofficially. The employers obtained *ex parte* injunctions against four members of an *ad hoc* committee and a TGWU official prohibiting all of them from organizing picketing. This seems to have come at a critical moment for the strikers, especially in their relationship with the union, the TGWU. A week later the case was argued *inter partes* but the injunctions against the drivers, though not the official, were continued. The picketing, the judge held, constituted a 'nuisance'. The injunctions undoubtedly played some part in defeating the industrial action by drivers in dock areas.[189] We have seen that although pickets may be guilty of 'nuisance', the mere fact of picketing is, as Scott J. said in the *South Wales* miners' case, 1985, 'not *per se* a common law nuisance'. Whatever the merits of the dispute, the *ex parte* orders in many of the picketing cases were therefore issued on the basis of a highly uncertain liability.

The *ex parte* application has a wider range than this suggests, however. Not only have a considerable number of labour injunctions since 1974 begun with *ex parte* applications and many others made notice to the unions little more than a formality (the *Austin Rover* proceedings were in court with great rapidity), but even when the matter is being fought *inter partes*, with the defendants doing the best they can to put their case together, the plaintiff can still make an application *ex parte*. This is, as it were, a motion within the existing proceedings.

One can understand the origins of such a procedure. Suppose during a recess in the court hearings a defendant makes a new attempt to knock a house down; the plaintiff must be able to reach the court quickly to stop it. But in the industrial sphere this opportunity gives the plaintiff yet another tactical advantage, which he is fully entitled to use. In *Clarke* v. *Heathfield*, 1985,[190] discussed fully in Chapter 9, dissident miners had successfully challenged the NUM for calling a strike in breach of union rules. In this action the plaintiffs sued the trustees of the NUM in respect of their disposition abroad of union funds over preceding months, claiming that they should be removed and a receiver put in their places. The matter was heard *inter partes* by Vinelott J. on 29 November 1984, when by agreement it was adjourned for a week. In other proceedings six days before, Nicholls J. had ordered the union to authorize sequestrators (who had taken over the union's funds in other proceedings) to be paid the funds in a Luxembourg bank. On the 29th the plaintiffs were told that the union was applying to a court in Luxembourg for release of part of the money which had been frozen there. On 30 November, therefore, on the first day of the adjournment period, they applied *ex parte* to the court (as they were entitled to do) for the installation of a receiver for a week. Mervyn Davies J. granted the application, and the Court of Appeal, which had exercised its discretion in favour of hearing the defendants (who were not only defendants in the *ex parte* motion, but also officers of the union already in contempt of court), upheld this 'unusual' order.

We are not concerned with the merits of that litigation, only with the graphic illustration it represented of the procedural possibilities. Many of the other miners' cases saw the use of more conventional interlocutory motions, legitimate uses of existing procedures, but of great significance to labour relations. Proceedings of this kind, however justifiable the claim, frequently belong as much to the theatre of industrial conflict as to the application of the law. The likelihood of 'full trial' is in most cases small. Moreover, the plaintiff who is allowed to have his *ex parte* orders for one or two weeks is naturally encouraged to plead his case on the basis of the widest possible assertions of liability ('interference with business' and the like); so that by the time the union comes into court, its protestations of innocence or assertions that no such torts exist ring against the background of orders already made from which it now must struggle to free itself. This difficulty was compounded by another judicial creation, which we must now examine.

The Ethicon test

The tactical advantages in this procedure lie with the plaintiff. This has always been important. But now, when the substantive law and its uncertainties have moved fundamentally against the prospective union defendant, it is doubly important. So too, this is an area where the control of developments by judges is at its strongest. In most legal systems it is naturally over the procedures of their own courts that judges have their tightest grip. This was remarkably illustrated by a decision in 1975 – as Kahn-Freund said, 'a piece of judicial legislation of quite exceptional importance', *American Cyanamid Co.* v. *Ethicon*.[191]

Before this time, there were two conditions to be met before a plaintiff could obtain his interlocutory injunction. First, he had to show that he had a prima-facie case against the defendant (i.e. he had a case that, as the evidence stood, looked as if it would win at the full trial). Secondly, on the 'balance of convenience' he ought to be granted the interim remedy (i.e. he would suffer more harm if the interim remedy were not granted than the defendant would suffer if it was). It is obvious that the employer's hand was the stronger under this second test. Moreover, one price always demanded of a plaintiff to whom an interlocutory injunction is given is his 'cross-undertaking in damages'; in other words, if the full trial discloses that he ought *not* to have had this interim injunction, he must compensate the defendant. The defendant can then recover full compensation for loss but he must prove that it was caused to him by the injunction,[192] not an easy matter for a trade union when the 'damage' will have been to its industrial bargaining position and its members' conditions. As Lord Denning MR said in 1975, even the undertaking in damages in such a case would be 'no use to the defendants, seeing that they will not suffer any pecuniary damages'.

There had long been some uncertainty about how precisely to formulate the first criterion. In *Stratford* v. *Lindley*[193] in 1965 it was put by Lord Upjohn (a great authority on such procedures) in terms of whether the plaintiff could 'establish a prima-facie case that the respondents have committed the tort'. This much at least the plaintiff had to prove. But ten years later, in the *Ethicon* case (not a labour law, but a patent law decision) this test was rejected. The proper test, Lord Diplock and the Law Lords held, is whether the plaintiff can convince the court that 'the claim is not frivolous or vexatious; in other words, that there is a *serious question to be tried*'. This was a very important change in the law. It was at once evident, and judges commented upon it, that under this '*Ethicon* test' the plaintiff seeking a labour injunction was now in an even better position. Proving a serious case to be tried, or a point that is 'arguably triable', is easier than proving a prima-facie case. He still had to persuade the judges that he could prevail on the second test, the 'balance of convenience'. But an employer alleging that the strike will, if not prohibited, cause him gigantic financial loss is always a target of sympathy more easily identifiable for judges than a union whose prospective loss may be great but is far more intangible. It is difficult to match the employer's evidence of loss of profit by evidence showing the 'damage' that will occur to workers by not being permitted to strike at the right moment. *Ethicon*, a decision on patent law, also illustrates once again the nature of the insistence upon across-the-board common law tests. The 'serious question' test may well be a sensible one for cases on 'confidential information' or on patents; but when applied to labour law, by making so much turn on balance of convenience and lowering the first hurdle to be cleared by the plaintiff to the level of a mere arguable point, it deals most of the cards to the plaintiff before the game begins.

Parliament and the Ethicon test

Parliament, seeing *Ethicon* as just such a danger in the field of labour injunctions, used the EPA 1975 as a vehicle to introduce an extra provision on the matter (it became TULRA s. 17 (2)). The object of the amendment was to restore Lord Upjohn's test in labour injunction cases and to add a test that would modify the outcome of the *Ethicon* principles. The legislation, beset with problems that are relevant to any future change of the law on procedure, ended up in an unhappy state. First, it did not apply to Scotland (s. 17 (3)). This allowed some judges to argue that it could not have changed the law in England since the two must not get out of step. Secondly, some support was given for a limited interpretation by the fact that the draftsman had been allowed to insert the opening words: 'It is hereby declared for the avoidance of doubt' – a formula Parliament is supposed to use only when it is declaring, not changing, the law. (When the draftsman and the Lord Chancellor's Department, speaking as the legal experts, insist that these words must go in, it is no easy task for Cabinet Ministers to keep them out, let alone for back-benchers or advisers.) The new provision (s. 17 (2)), which is still law, like s. 17 (1), requires that where in an interlocutory injunction application the defendant claims that he acted ICFTD the court must 'have regard to the likelihood' of his establishing a trade dispute *defence* in exercising its discretion whether or not to grant the injunction. The provision is clearly less relevant today than in 1975 by reason of the recent restriction of these defences. But even before this restriction, Lord Diplock, in *NWL* v. *Woods*, 1979,[194] said that the section appeared to him to be merely 'a reminder addressed by Parliament to English judges' to take these things into account. It did not 'expressly enjoin the judge to have regard' to other defences, only to the 'practical realities' in this type of case. It was not out of accord with the *Ethicon* test.

Public interest injunctions

By this time, the Court of Appeal, led by Lord Denning MR, had gone further, almost ignoring s. 17 (2) in granting labour injunctions on the basis of a 'balance of convenience' test, even though there seemed to be arguable points of law in favour of a trade dispute defence. By 1978 the Court of Appeal alarmed the Law Lords by granting interim injunctions, almost exclusively on its own appreciation of 'the public interest'.[195] Commentators saw this use of the labour injunction, even as the immunities stood then, as 'a device for effectively settling industrial conflict in favour of capital and at the expense of labour'.[196] The House of Lords saw the danger of this approach and called the Court of Appeal back within the customary conventions of legal argument. But when it did so, it introduced yet another test itself. There were cases where, instead of merely balancing convenience between the parties once there is a serious question to be tried, even if there was a likelihood of success for the defendant in proving a defence, the court should nevertheless grant an injunction, because, it said:

the consequences to the employer or to third parties or the public and perhaps the nation itself may be so disastrous . . . unless there is a high degree of probability that the defence will succeed.[197]

The plaintiff must prove just an arguable point. The defendants have to show their defence is 'highly arguable'. Why should this be do? If there is an arguable defence, it is arguable that – on the evidence so far – the defendant is acting lawfully, whatever 'disasters' ensue. In this assertion of jurisdiction to issue 'public interest' injunctions, Lord Diplock was joined even by others who, like Lord Scarman, had been prepared to give some separate meaning to TULRA s. 17 (2), independent of the balance of convenience test. Here, in the new test, is a back door through which a court can pass in any major conflict, a new gateway to the granting of labour injunctions. Although presented as a mere procedural appendix, this was a significant development effected at the time of the public service strikes of 1978–9. It was proof again of the effect of social events even upon more liberal judges, and further proof of the importance of this procedure. Certainly a power to issue injunctions whenever the judge thinks there are disastrous consequences to 'the nation' renders the argument about substantive principles of liability of less significance.

It was clear that both the Court of Appeal and the Law Lords were responding to the clamour raised against strikers who at that time included some grave-diggers and many hospital workers. Lord Salmon in the *Express Newspapers* case, 1980, used the occasion of a case about journalists to stray into an attack on workers at 'the Charing Cross Hospital' whose action preventing oil deliveries, he said, had brought cancer patients 'near to death'. (This charge they denied; but they had no opportunity of answering in his court.) It was partly on this that his Lordship based a call for the law 'to be altered'. Whatever the merits or demerits of the industrial action at that hospital, we cannot expect trade unions to forget this kind of judgment when we discuss the discretionary powers of the judges.

Balance of convenience and the practical realities

Lord Diplock in the *NWL* case had ventured down a rather different road, one of great importance in the 1980s. Speaking in 1979 he stressed that the judge in exercising his discretion on balance of convenience under *Ethicon* must take account of all the 'practical realities'. In a labour injunction case he should recognize that the real dispute is between employer and union (not the official who at that time was always named as defendant); that the union's action is all part of the bargaining; that this can be promoted effectively only if the union can 'strike while the iron is hot'; and that these 'exceptional' types of case 'seldom if ever come to actual trial'. The union's need to act (the 'now-or-never' imperative) is correctly diagnosed in this passage. Lord Diplock went on to say that where the grant or refusal of an injunction would have the 'practical effect' of putting an end to the action, then the 'likelihood' of a trade dispute defence at trial must be seriously considered, though it was not 'paramount'. These statements, which seemed to be an advance into the reality of the matter, made many believe that hope for such defendants survived. But in practice few union defendants in labour law have been helped. Nor have many decisions since 1980 given effect to TULRA s. 17 (2), although its applicability has been eroded by the shrinking girth of the trade dispute defences. Lord Diplock had more to say on the 'realities' in *Dimbleby & Sons* v. *NUJ*.[198] After 1982 a trade union can be a defendant in a tort action. So a plaintiff may now be more likely to go on to trial for recovery of damages than in the days when only a union official was defendant. The judge need not, therefore, exercise his discretion 'on the assumption that the case will never proceed to trial'. By this Lord Diplock has generally been thought to mean that the judge should be *more*, not less, ready to grant the interim injunction.

Even before the 1982 Act was effective, Lord Diplock was leaning in this direction. In *Hadmor Productions*, 1983 (one of the last cases where the defendants managed to prove a 'trade dispute' under the old definition), the defendants had arguments on which to rely in addition to those that arose in the interim proceedings. So the court should not, he said in his decision, act on the assumption 'that this action will never come to trial but will in effect be finally disposed of by these inter-locutory proceedings'. Lord Diplock is here keeping his options open and the judicial discretion as wide as possible. The question was, first, whether the plaintiffs had proved an issue to be tried (he thought they had, though with 'considerable misgivings') and, secondly, where the balance of convenience lay, including TULRA s. 17 (2), i.e. whether it was 'more likely than not' that a trial on this evidence would bring success for the defendant by reason of a trade dispute 'immunity':

This is a factor in favour of refusing to grant an interlocutory injunction . . . not necessarily conclusive . . . a weighty factor; and the greater the likelihood the greater is the weight to be attached to it.

It is instructive to contrast the reasoning in other areas of the law. In *Cayne* v. *Global Natural Resources*, 1984,[199] for example, the Court of Appeal refused an interlocutory injunction to a shareholder who alleged that shares were being issued to maintain the directors in office as part of a merger deal. The dispute revolved upon the question of whether the merger was for the benefit of the existing board of directors (when it would be invalid) or of Global as a company. The court agreed with the judge below that no injunction should be granted before the company general meeting was held. If it were, 'that would be an end to the substance of the matter'. This was not a case 'which lends itself to the convenience test'; the court must approach it on the broader principle of doing its best 'to avoid injustice'. Kerr L J said that here 'the realities' were these: if an injunction were granted, the plaintiffs might get control of the board, and they would then stop the proceedings against the company to avoid 'self-inflicted blood-letting in public'. If an injunction were refused, the plaintiffs might or might not continue the case. Global had pleaded a defence, with evidence in support, so it would be wrong 'to decide the entire contest' summarily on untested material now before the court. May L J agreed; this was no 'holding operation', as in *Ethicon*. It would effectively preclude the defendant 'from having his rights determined in a full trial'. Indeed, he added, where a plaintiff sought an interlocutory injunction, justice required that that defendant should be entitled to dispute the plaintiff's claim at a trial and if the grant of the injunction would preclude this then it should not be granted on an interlocutory basis.

These judgments reinterpret the *NWL* speech of Lord Diplock, but one may doubt whether they will find any reflection in labour law. For they are based on the *legal* 'realities'. Once the plaintiffs got their way at the meeting, they could control the company board and the corporate litigation. The injunction, in other words, would bring about an end of the matter by a change in legal control. In a labour injunction case the judges are likely to 'distinguish' *Cayne* as different, because the trade union suffers no *legal* disability under the interlocutory injunction in regard to disputing the claim and putting its case at trial. Yet in reality it may have lost the dispute in *fact* long before that – with the help of an interlocutory injunction.

Injunctions and the adequacy of damages

A similar point arises in respect of damages. If damages are an adequate remedy, the normal rule is that an injunction will not be granted. In the *Garden Cottage Foods* case, 1984,[200] the Law Lords held that the company of Mr and Mrs Bunch could be adequately compensated in damages for the wrongs done to it by the Milk Marketing Board through its breaches of the EEC Treaty. It was not too difficult to calculate what that loss would be. 'There could hardly be a clearer case of damages being an adequate remedy,' said Lord Diplock. There is scarcely a reported labour injunction case where that argument has prevailed. Partly this is because the employer's evidence usually points to inestimable further disasters if the remedy is refused. Also until 1982 the union could not be defendant. But unions had met damages awarded against their officials arising from union action. Some losses could be enormous; in claims brought by national newspapers the evidence filed suggested that loss from a strike would reach millions of pounds a week. But it is open to the judge to say that 'there is no reason to suppose that the defendant union will not be fully able to meet any damages that may be awarded'.[201] After 1982 the union can be defendant but with limits on the damages awardable (p. 531). In *Mercury Communications*,[185] May LJ held that the loss would exceed the £250,000 limit in EA 1982 s. 16 (3), and therefore damages could not be 'adequate'. The financial limits on damages payable by unions thus become an ambivalent protection. In this context they can *increase* the likelihood of a labour injunction because the limited damages available may be said not to be an adequate remedy for the plaintiff.

In *Shipping Company Uniform Inc.* v. *ITWF*, 1985[202] (p. 627), the judge did the sums in a novel way. If no injunction were granted, the owners could let the ship lie 'blacked' with substantial losses, or pay the ITWF the £225,000 demanded (mainly wages for the crew). The maximum damages recoverable from the ITWF would be a little above that sum plus interest (£250,000; EA 1982 s. 16 (3)). If an injunction were granted but the ITWF were to succeed at the trial, it would have wrongly lost the chance to obtain that sum; but the plaintiff's undertaking in damages apparently could not cover the crew of the ship, unless the owners agreed to extend it. He concluded that if the owners were prepared to extend that undertaking to cover the loss to the crew, 'the balance of convenience favours the grant of an injunction: otherwise it does not'.

Sometimes a trade union finds, however, that the damages principle just is not applied because of an overriding discretion in the court. Where the TUC General Council called for a 'day of action' in protest against the 1980 Act, the General Secretaries of some unions were sued to stop them inducing members to break employment contracts in a 'political strike'. They argued that the plaintiffs (national newspapers) had a full remedy by way of damages, a very arguable proposition; but Griffiths J. rejected it. The *Ethicon* case did not compel a judge to refuse an injunction because damages might be adequate; to do so would be to give the defendant 'a licence wrongfully to infringe the plaintiff's right merely because he was rich enough to pay'.[203] Yet this is what seems to have happened to Mr and Mrs Bunch. We shall find decisions in Chapter 9 where, in actions brought by members against their union, judges pushed aside the 'adequacy of damages' principles as not applicable. It is not clear why they should do so.

The judge's discretion and the evidence

In *Garden Cottage Foods*, as in countless earlier cases, the Law Lords insisted: 'The function of an appellate court is initially that of review only.' The discretion belongs to the judge who hears the case. Appellate courts can change his decision only if it is based on a misunderstanding of the law or of the evidence (or an inference from it), or if it can be shown to be wrong by reason of fresh evidence on appeal or a 'change of circumstances', or occasionally, Lord Diplock added, when the judge's decision is 'so aberrant that it must be set aside on the ground that no reasonable judge regardful of his duty to act judicially could have reached it'. This pliable test rarely favours the union. In *Mercury Communications* v. *Scott-Garner*,[185] for example, where the judge below had refused the injunction, the plaintiffs were allowed to put in fresh evidence about a formal job security agreement (p. 73). Donaldson M R found it 'a little surprising' that no one had mentioned it before. Moreover, the judge had misdirected himself on the law. Two Lords Justices agreed: the judge had 'erred in his approach'; 'We have had the benefit of . . . important additional evidence.' In such cases the new evidence sometimes gives to the appeal the flavour of a new hearing of what by then looks like a new case.

This brings us to two other factors: the nature of the 'evidence' and, with it, the benefit of difficulties. Even under the old prima-facie case test, plaintiffs often succeeded in proving on very thin evidence torts like inducement of breach of contract. Evidence of the very contract itself has been accepted even when it was, in the judge's words, 'sketchy', or 'tenuous', or 'meagre'. But a defendant's 'knowledge' of or 'intention' to interfere with the contract is readily inferred.[204] All this evidence is given on affidavit. This means that it is not subjected to cross-examination. The normal principles of evidence are relaxed. In interlocutory proceedings an affidavit 'may contain statements of information or belief with the sources and grounds thereof' (RSC, O. 41, R. 5); it is not confined to the normal limits of information put forward by a witness of his own knowledge. Indeed, the practice has arisen whereby a plaintiff will support his affidavits by exhibiting great bundles of press cuttings, which may include both reports of facts on which he relies and large quantities of extraneous and prejudicial material. Every lawyer knows that judges vary on how much of such 'evidence' they will 'let in'.

Theoretically, a party may ask for a witness to be cross-examined (RSC, O. 38, R. 3). But there appears to be no recorded labour injunction case in modern times when that has been done (the Supreme Court Practice says it is 'very rare' in any type of interlocutory proceedings). Counsel for the union, whose first job is after all to win if he can, realizes that it will be regarded as rather 'bad form' if he makes the unusual demand for cross-examination, especially if he fails to shake the witness to the core. The drawing up of affidavits for these interlocutory proceedings (they start with a 'statement' taken by the solicitor from the witness and are then passed to counsel for drafting before being sworn by the witness) has consequently become a very fine art by a veritably pointillist school of lawyers. Only in this context can one understand at all what it means for a trade union's solicitors to receive notice of a writ, a notice of motion and (perhaps) one or more draft affidavits, for an action that is to come on in a few days, with more affidavits undoubtedly in the pipeline (the plaintiff has had weeks if not months to prepare them to prove his 'serious question' fit for trial). The general secretary of the union is probably at a conference in Scotland, and the other officials who are needed immediately for statements are busy at work for union members around the country. From the outset many such cases are a tactical battle about procedure rather than a test of rights.

Secondly, there is the balance of difficulty. One of the reasons for the House of Lords reasoning in *Ethicon* was its disapproval of the lower courts' indulging in a 'trial of the action' on inadequate evidence 'without the benefit of oral testimony or cross-examination'. Obviously, rights should not be decided on inadequate evidence or on obscure legal premises; but by definition in interlocutory proceedings the evidence will not be complete, and this penumbra of doubt will make it difficult too to characterize the legal principles. In labour injunction cases the benefit of factual doubt invariably falls in favour of the plaintiff, and the *Ethicon* test makes matters worse for defendants even on the legal issues.

Take *Solihull MB* v. *NUT*, 1985.[205] The critical issue was whether a ballot under the TUA 1984 should be held before the union induced teachers to withdraw co-operation. This turned on whether that action was in breach of their contracts. The plaintiffs alleged there were 'supplemental contracts' as well as the main employment contracts. The defendants denied this, particularly if they were said to be oral. Warner J. thought the extra agreements were 'consistent' with the contractual documents. So it was 'improbable' that there was 'no serious issue to be tried'. (A further advantage accrues to the plaintiff when the test is turned into this negative form.) But the teachers further said there was a 'custom and practice' that limited their duties of attendance. The plaintiffs countered with the allegation that there was an 'implied term' in the contracts to the contrary. So there was 'a direct conflict of evidence'. How should this be resolved? The judge concluded that this was 'not the sort of conflict one can resolve on motion, on affidavit evidence, without cross-examination and before discovery' (i.e. the disclosure of documents that takes place before a full trial). Proof of custom and practice needed 'full oral evidence'. Not to grant the injunction, though, would do harm to the children in schools; whereas if it were granted the union would have the choice of holding a ballot or going to arbitration (and the cost of a ballot could be recovered under the cross-undertaking if the union won). An injunction was granted.

At every stage of that argument the difficulties are likely to be resolved against the union. The practice has a long pedigree. In the 1960s judges in interlocutory proceedings, even in the days of the prima-facie case test, 'were prepared to find that plaintiffs had established prima-facie cases on the basis of novel points of law and dubious interpretations of the facts'.[206]

It would be wrong to say that all difficulties always benefit the plaintiff. But the width of the discretion creates maximum uncertainty. The judge may as easily say, 'This is all too difficult for interlocutory motion. It must go to trial, so I will *not* grant an injunction', as he may conclude, 'so I *will* grant an injunction'. On some occasions the court has said, as Upjohn J. did in 1953, that the case involved 'startling but admitted' facts (a custom and practice) that needed to be explored at trial, and therefore an interlocutory injunction would *not* be granted. And in the *Meade* case (p. 638) there was so much dispute about both facts and law (especially about liability for procuring a breach of statutory duty) that two members of the Court of Appeal shrank from granting a mandatory injunction, especially as the industrial dispute was almost over (though Lord Denning would not have been deterred). In the same year the court refused to determine in an interlocutory case the hitherto uncertain question whether hindering a public body in the performance of its public duties was a tort; but injunctions granted *ex parte* were continued on other grounds against the union ('there will be much to be said on both sides at the trial', said Lawton LJ, but as usual there seems to have been no trial).[207]

In other cases defendants have lost interlocutory actions that have involved points of law, often taken to the Court of Appeal or even the House of Lords. The *Stratford* case, 1965, took six months to reach the Law Lords, and touched the innermost recesses of the law of tort, as did the Court of Appeal in *Torquay Hotel*, 1969, all in 'interlocutory' proceedings. Nor have judges in recent cases, such as *Mercury Communications*, 1984, or *Dimbleby*, 1984, been deflected by any 'conflict of evidence' or by the difficulty of the legal issues. Lord Donovan said in the *Stratford* case:

the present proceedings are interlocutory proceedings in a case in which the facts may well not have been fully and accurately ascertained. It is not, therefore, an occasion for deciding disputed propositions of law based on alternative hypotheses as to what the crucial facts may hereafter turn out to be. It is desirable, I venture to think, that the minimum necessary to refuse or restore the injunction should alone be decided.

But a lot of new law was made in the case, and the defendants lost anyway. That is the way the 'minimum necessary' usually goes.

Unusual remedies and the status quo

Mandatory injunctions are on principle more difficult to obtain than prohibitory orders. At this interim stage the court will think very carefully about ordering the defendant to do, rather than refrain from doing, something. Lane LJ said in 1977, when the Court of Appeal refused a mandatory injunction claimed against the Post Office, that only 'in the most extreme circumstances' should it 'interfere by way of mandatory injunction in the delicate mechanism of industrial disputes and industrial negotiations'.[208] Yet orders telling the union to act are regularly made in industrial conflict cases. The union is frequently ordered to withdraw instructions or revoke decisions or take other steps to end the industrial action. The Court of Appeal expressed the view in a labour injunction case of 1949 that this is an 'exceptional' form of relief; but that was in the days of non-intervention.

In one of the miners' cases, after counsel for the plaintiffs had rightly drawn the Post Office case to the judge's attention (that was his duty, as the defendants were not present or represented), Nicholls J. granted a mandatory injunction against the *N U M (Yorkshire Area)* (based upon breach of the contract in the Area rules) ordering it to hold elections, saying it was 'a very exceptional form of relief . . . to be exercised with great caution'.[209] (This part of the order was later discharged by consent because of misunderstandings in it about facts not then before the judge.) Other cases of that period saw more exceptional remedies granted. The receiver appointed in *ex parte* proceedings in place of the trustees of the national N U M was 'very unusual', said O'Connor LJ. Five months earlier, in the first major civil case of the strike, *Clarke* v. *Chadburn*[210] (where the defendants were not in court), Megarry V C invalidated N U M conference resolutions altering the union rules on the ground that they ignored earlier orders of the court in two *ex parte* applications – a point of law 'devoid of any direct authority' – and then engaged in a further novelty by granting a declaration. There is no such remedy as an 'interim declaration of rights', only a final declaration. In interlocutory proceedings, an injunction is available; but its enforcement needs a further application to the court, and this the plaintiffs wished to avoid. After 'some hesitation' on this 'matter of such public concern', the Vice-Chancellor granted an interlocutory injunction *and* a final declaration of rights in *interim* proceedings.

The tendency to extend the scope of the remedy of declaration into interlocutory proceedings is doubly disturbing when it is recalled that in other areas of the law judges have begun to introduce the startling concept that failure to abide by its terms can lead to punishment by the court (even though this remedy is not a 'coercive order': Chapter 2,

p. 151). Such remedies seemed in 1984 to be less willingly dispensed in the Scottish courts, where the principles applied appeared to resemble the older English approach; for on appeal in a claim that the Scottish Area Mineworkers' Union had acted in breach of union rules, Lord Jauncey said in the Court of Session: 'I am not persuaded that the pursuers [plaintiffs] have a prima-facie argument . . . it follows that interim interdict will be refused.'[211] In England, when it comes to granting discretionary remedies against unions, judicial discretion has been less unbending.

Because the remedy of injunction (and of receivership) is discretionary, it is impossible to list all the factors that a court may take into account. But problems in other areas do not appear to have barred plaintiffs seeking a labour injunction. The object of the injunction is to restore the status quo. But, as Lord Diplock said in the *Garden Cottage Foods* case, 'The status quo is the existing state of affairs: but . . . existing when?' His answer was, existing

during the period immediately preceding the issue of the writ claiming the permanent injunction, or if there be unreasonable delay between the issue of the writ and the motion . . . the period immediately preceding the motion.'

If this was applied to labour injunctions, it would mean that the plaintiff might have a right only to the status quo immediately before the writs, i.e. possibly after the strike had started. Clearly the courts will not apply Lord Diplock's rule to mean that. Indeed, when the point arose in the *Mercury* case, the Court of Appeal appears to have accepted counsel's argument that 'the relevant status quo ante, prior to the union's action complained of, was Mercury's entitlement to be interconnected to BT installations'.

Where a plaintiff has delayed unreasonably or comes to the court in breach of some obligation of his own (without 'clean hands', the old cases have it) the court is entitled to exercise its discretion against him. We saw something analogous in *Chappell's* case, where all the workers were individually tainted by their union's threats of industrial action (p. 166). It is hard to find union defendants who have won a labour injunction case on similar grounds, though Lord Denning's attempt to stop 'trouble-makers' obtaining relief might come into this category.[212] Indeed, the policy of encouraging the court to assess the cleanliness of employers' hands may encounter other objections; the result of courts entering more often upon this kind of reasoning would inevitably be their entry into the merits of industrial disputes, which it once was Parliament's wish they should avoid. The unions, at any rate, would not be likely to profit from a judicial power to weigh the 'merits' of industrial disputes. On the other hand, it may be questioned whether the court should see a shipowner who prepares two different sets of contracts for his crew (p. 600) as a plaintiff whose hands are clean in the eye of equity.

Parliament and court procedures

The procedures and practice of the labour injunction to a great extent eluded Parliament's attention under its previous policy of maintaining a broad area of trade dispute liberty through the 'immunities'. In part this was because the prima-facie case test was maintained in principle at least until the 1960s saw its relaxation alongside the rapid extension of the substantive principles of the law of tort. Content to intervene only against the abuses of *ex parte* injunctions in 1974 (TULRA s. 17 (1)), Parliament was stung by the *Ethicon* decision into further – if curiously 'declaratory' – action, which became TULRA s. 17 (2). But today the 'immunities' are tattered waifs in the land of trade disputes, and the courts operate mainly within their own concept of the 'balance of convenience'.

The two go hand in hand, substance and procedure. No serious consideration of the freedom to withdraw labour can be undertaken without examination of the procedural rules that determine the outcome of litigation. In this territory judges largely make their own operational rules, and Parliament is still something of a trespasser except when it rubber-stamps changes to the Rules of Court. But Parliament is in a difficulty in that the *principles* applied by the judges are those applied generally to all cases, even though the reality of labour injunctions is special. Intervention is easily portrayed as introduction of special 'privilege' for unions. But now that there has been a significant increase in 'the seeking of an injunction or the threat to seek an injunction', perhaps because employers have, as Evans suggests, a new 'sense that the arsenal contains live ammunition',[213] the disadvantages suffered by unions in labour injunction procedure become a matter of even greater importance. With the new legislative policy on labour law in the 1980s the injunction gradually has become the weapon more readily used in industrial disputes. Sometimes it is used more quickly by 'secondary' than by 'primary' firms, often highlighting the differences between the hawks in management with legal and commercial backgrounds and their traditionally more dovelike personnel counterparts, or between large and small firms in their readiness to go to law (and to press home the remedies) in the context of their own patterns of industrial relations.[214] By the time a small newspaper and printing firm showed it was possible to cripple a major union by injunctions, fine, sequestration and damages in the *NGA* case, 1983, the idea that 'the law should be kept out of industrial relations' (whatever it meant) could no longer be said to be a tenet so widely shared among managers. The labour injunction seemed to have entered upon its inheritance.

Contempt of court

It would be wrong to leave matters there without a brief mention of the consequences that follow from the wilful breach of an injunction. The power of the High Court here is formidable. A person's refusal or failure to obey an order of the High Court in a civil case, sometimes called 'civil contempt', is punishable in the discretion of the judge by way of a fine or imprisonment or 'a writ of sequestration against the property of that person' (RSC, O. 45, R. 5). It was once thought that a fine was inappropriate in civil cases because it is a punishment and the process of enforcing the court's orders should be primarily coercive rather than punitive. But in the modern cases judges have taken the power to fine in place of committal to prison or 'sequestration' (i.e. seizure) of property. Indeed, in 1966 it was laid down that in imposing a financial penalty the court could 'take into account, in addition to other factors, the injury to the public interest which must be deemed to be involved in the breach'. A fine, of course, is lost to the 'contemnor' for ever, whereas the property sequestrated is returned to him if and when he is released from the contempt (normally through his 'purging' it by an apology) less any fines and costs incurred. Costs can be extensive since sequestrators are normally highly priced accountants.

A further modification was introduced in 1981 whereby the court can secure that an unpaid fine is levied against a contemnor who fails to pay, by the normal process for enforcing a civil debt (against his property in an action brought by the Queen's Remembrancer: Contempt of Court Act 1981 s. 16). This provides an alternative to imprisonment of the contemnor. But because the liberty of the subject may be at stake in contempt proceedings, proof of service (unless the court dispenses with it) and proper notice of the terms of the order to the defendant must be strictly proved. So too, the breach of the injunction must be proved beyond all reasonable doubt. This was the ground on which the first group of dockers' shop stewards was released in 1972 at the instance of the Official Solicitor. Similarly, because he was not wholly convinced that the NUM and its President, Mr Scargill, had full knowledge of the relevant order, the judge in 1984 adjourned for a week the hearing at which he was eventually to fine them in their absence £200,000 and £1,000 respectively for 'wilful and repeated disobedience of an order of the court'.[215] The union President had said (and the NEC later approved): 'There is no High Court judge going to take away the democratic right of our union to deal with internal affairs.' This defiance was given 'maximum publicity', the judge said, 'by a powerful body'. This led to a writ of sequestration against *all* the NUM's assets a fortnight later. The series of contempt judgments played a considerable role in the industrial and psychological battle of the miners' strike, one that left some laymen surprised when they discovered that it arose originally out of a breach of contract (p. 730). Most cases illustrate the need to prove a clear breach of the injunctions, though a few slip rather below that level (as where the leader of unofficial strikes by electricians in Fleet Street once claimed that he could do nothing to 'withdraw any order, instruction, direction or advice', because he had given none; and the judge held he could 'have done something to reverse the situation. . . . Everybody knew what it [the order] was intended to operate against'; he was fined £350).[216]

Since organizations cannot be imprisoned, remedies against them are a fine and sequestration. In the NUM case, as in most cases, the sequestration was applied for in the first application, and the fine imposed was payable within fourteen days. The sequestration, ordered when the money was still unpaid, related to the initial and continuing contempt, not merely to the non-payment. Under the 1971 Act, Donaldson P. had in the *Con-Mech* case initiated a procedure of 'sequestrate first, fine later'. He ordered sequestration of a given amount of the union's property (£100,000) and decided later what the fine should be to be taken out of the funds (£75,000).[217] In the case of 'a body corporate' sequestration can also be levied against the property of 'any director or any officer' (RSC, O. 45, R. 5 (1) (ii)), and a director can be made personally liable for the company's default even if he has taken a purely passive role (though penal proceedings are unlikely if he did). Although trade unions are not incorporated bodies, nevertheless for the purposes of enforcement by way of 'punishment for contempt . . . against any property held in trust' for the union, execution proceeds 'as if the union were a body corporate' (TULRA s. 2 (1) (e)). It is therefore arguable that the courts can here apply the rules on companies to unions.[218]

Contempt and vicarious liability

Another problem arises when we ask whether a union is liable to contempt proceedings for acts of officials or members. A body corporate, e.g. a company, has its liability tested by the normal principles of 'vicarious liability' applicable to organizations that embody a command structure. But to assess the liability of trade unions, the courts have had to adapt the normal principles of vicarious liability. We saw (p. 55) that in the *Heatons* case the union was initially liable for 'unofficial' 'blacking' organized by shop stewards because this was within the courts' idea of their implied authority to act for the union.[219] The union rules alone are not definitive; the courts can look at the union's customs, practices and policies. But in the context of contempt, a parallel problem arose. Once made liable, was the TGWU in contempt of court in *Heatons* because it had done nothing to stop the 'blacking' after the orders of the NIRC made some four months earlier and now upheld by the Law Lords? The Law Lords decided that the union had disobeyed the orders 'wilfully' because it had done nothing to withdraw the authority of those stewards who had in law 'authority' to act for it. 'Advice' to the stewards to act lawfully was insufficient. There must be a curtailment of the stewards' authority by way of 'an order' to stop the 'blacking'; if necessary the union must discipline them.

This additional element is also reflected in the rules established by the 1982 Act in its code on the vicarious liability of unions for industrial torts (p. 533). We recall that this makes their initial liability arise from either the acts of the NEC or two top officials, or those of officials (e.g.

stewards) empowered with authority under the rules, or those of certain other full-time officials, unless they are repudiated (E A 1982 s. 15 (3)). In Chapter 7 we saw that this third group can be 'repudiated' by the first group so long as it is an unequivocal repudiation (p. 535). Does this statutory code on liability oust the *Heatons* test when it comes to contempt of court? Judges have taken that view. In *Read (Transport) Ltd* v. *N U M (South Wales Area)*, 1985,[220] the union was liable for torts that included procuring breaches of contracts of employment by reason of picketing, i.e. 'industrial torts' to which a s. 13 defence might, once, have applied. Interim injunctions ordered the union 'by its agents or servants or otherwise' (the usual format) not to continue to encourage members to do this. The initial liability in tort was based upon the acts of officials, mainly those of the president (E A 1982 s. 15 (3) (c)). Three months later an application was made for punishment of the union and its officials for contempt. The union put no evidence before the court. The judge concluded that he ought to fine the union £50,000, to be paid within forty-eight hours. It was not paid. He ordered sequestration of the entire assets. The officials were not punished. The judge appeared to use the same principles of vicarious liability on contempt by the union as for the initial liability, namely s. 15 of the 1982 Act. Another attempt by a judge to use s. 15 in contempt proceedings, and even to extend its scope (the *Express and Star* case: p. 538), was rejected by the Court of Appeal in 1986.[221] The section was held not to be relevant in contempt proceedings; it was concerned with proceedings 'in tort'. The issue in contempt is whether the union has broken the terms of the injunction through its servants or agents, on the common law basis.

This is the correct approach. It does not settle all the problems in contempt proceedings, as the *Heatons* case itself shows; but it avoids difficulties inherent in applying s. 15. We note two of them. For example, in a 'mixed' case (involving both an 'industrial tort' within T U L R A s. 13 and other torts, e.g. nuisance) it may be that s. 15 demands the application of its code in determining liability. But the section does not purport to change the principles of the law concerning contempt. If, therefore, a union was allegedly in breach of an order to discontinue picketing by reason of the tort of nuisance, it ought to be permitted to argue its case on contempt by reference to the principles in *Heatons*, not s. 15 of the 1982 Act. Where there is no 'industrial tort' this must be the case. Further problems arise where the breach is of an order not to commit or continue a breach of a contract constituted in the union rules (a problem, we shall see, that could not easily arise before 1971: p. 725). Vicarious liability is not an issue that arises frequently in relation to breaches of contract; but its equivalent, the responsibility of a contracting party for agents' acts or statements, raises analogous questions.[222] Under the Act of 1971 Donaldson P. showed a propensity to make unions liable even for the acts of members; but this approach would be seen by most judges as erroneous then and now.[223]

There is nevertheless another argument against applying E A 1982 s. 15 at all in judging responsibility for contempt even in tort cases. It is this: section 15 sets out rules, in proceedings based on the industrial torts, 'for the purpose of determining in those proceedings whether the union is liable in respect of the act in question' (i.e. the tort). Suppose the union is made liable to an injunction for such a tort. Then a local official or shop steward acts in a manner contrary to the injunction. To argue that the tests in s. 15 apply to the contempt proceedings does not fit well with T U L R A 1974. This states, in s. 2 (1) (e), that judgments and orders 'in proceedings of any description' against a union 'shall be enforceable by way of . . . punishment for contempt or otherwise against any property held in trust for the union . . . to the like extent and in like manner as if the union were a body corporate'. It would be very odd if in contempt proceedings the company and union were, in face of that language, treated similarly for the formalities of execution, but differently for purposes of vicarious liability. This is a rare case where the union *is* treated 'as if' it were a body corporate. It would seem appropriate that the normal common law doctrine of vicarious liability should limit the extent of punishment of its property. As we saw (p. 708), the Court of Appeal decided that s. 15 was inappropriate in contempt proceedings in the *Express and Star* case (though it upheld the fine on the union for its officials' acts which it had encouraged with 'humbugging pretence').

Enforcing contempt orders

None of the special statutory protections for union funds apply to fines and sequestrations for contempt. The statutory limits on damages are not relevant (EA 1982 s. 16), nor is the section making the provident benefits fund and political fund 'protected property' (s. 17: p. 531). Part of a political fund was once seized, in 1973, by sequestrators of the AUEW's assets in the *Con-Mech* litigation, though whether through bad luck or bad judgment was never made clear. But only the property held on trust for 'the union' can be seized. In the *NGA* sequestration, when the union refused to pay fines of £150,000 in 1983, Donaldson MR said the court might have allowed the union, by varying the order of sequestration, to retain sufficient moneys 'to carry on its *lawful* trade union activities' if it had appealed to the Court of Appeal. In the same case, and that of a SOGAT branch in 1986, sequestrators had to return funds that turned out to belong not to the union as a whole but only to one branch. In 1984, the NUM (South Wales Area) reportedly raised the point that the sequestrators in the *Read (Transport)* action had taken some £200,000 held on separate trusts in a hardship fund for miners' families, though whether this was correct was never clear. Sequestrators today operate by way of telephones and keyboards. While thousands of miners in South Wales were barricading their headquarters, the sequestrating accountants were quietly tracing funds by telephone through the union's bank accounts (they found £707,000). Here is another mark of the shift of enforcement proceedings away from people, towards property. The last thing the sequestrators were likely to do, mindful of the mistakes of 1972, was to send officers of the court marching up the road towards the 5,000 miners surrounding their head office. They asked other unions and banks for details of funds held for, and donations made to, the South Wales union. For a third party is obliged to conform to the sequestrators' demands in regard to union property without consulting his union client; for they are agents of the court. Even third parties, such as auditors, who hold no property but possess information needed by the sequestrators, must divulge it to them.[224] In carrying out their task sequestrators return to the court for instructions, often in private hearings.

The contempt cases involved applications by the plaintiffs. This is the normal way in which disobedience by the defendant is punished. If the plaintiff chooses to let his injunction lie upon the record despite the defiance of the defendant (as the NCB did in March 1984) that is his affair. This is a point of fundamental importance to 'civil contempt', and is quite different from a 'criminal' contempt (interference with a witness at a trial, for example). The initial duty broken (i.e. the tort committed) is one owed in civil law to the plaintiff; it is not a criminal offence, and not a duty to the court. It is open to the plaintiff and defendant to settle their differences at any time – indeed, in industrial conflict this may be a most desirable result – and the decision by the plaintiff not to press the charge of disobedience may well be a part of that. The order is made 'for the sole benefit of the other party to the civil action', Lord Diplock said in 1974, and there is no point in punishing the offender if he 'chooses not to insist on its enforcement'.[225] In certain rare cases the Attorney-General may move the court to enforce the orders in the public interest; and if there is a matter that is 'urgent' the court itself may take steps to do so, though 'only in exceptional cases'.[226] In this respect, civil contempt is still different from criminal contempt, where no such waiver by the victim can operate and where the contempt is from the outset a blow aimed at the administration of justice.

Some judges, however, have rejected or disliked this distinction, at any rate if the contempt is 'contumacious'. Donaldson P. in *Con-Mech* and other cases in the NIRC attacked it ('it is not open to the parties to settle the matter of the contempt'). Others have given added weight to the rule of the court ('The plaintiff cannot waive the order, but as a rule the court will pay attention to his wishes').[227] Megarry VC recently thought there might be a more sweeping change:

there should be some relaxation by the courts of their present restraint upon themselves in enforcing their orders in cases where these are being openly flouted and the administration of justice brought into disrespect.

This last phrase edges closer to the field of criminal contempt. This is a route by which the courts in some other common law countries (e.g. Canada) have increased the initiatives taken in civil cases by the judges themselves to punish defendants. It would be a dangerous road for the courts to take on labour injunctions in Britain. Such injunctions arise from the dispute between the plaintiff and the defendant union. If the plaintiff settles the dispute, judicial intervention to punish the union is hardly likely to benefit either industrial relations or the legal system.

A defendant union is usually in contempt because of decisions taken by its democratic processes that have led its members to be unable to accept an injunction. Some judges have shown an understanding of this. The style and character of the South Wales miners' defiance allowed

Scott J. in 1985 to release them from their contempt even without apology. Other judgments during the miners' strike show rather different emphases. To encourage courts to launch forth unilaterally on the enforcement of their own orders could sink the judiciary deeper in the slough of conflict. What is more, it would improperly inhibit the civil rights of the industrial parties to compromise a dispute, for which they would come to need the court's permission. No court in England has the right to stop a plaintiff freely waiving an ordinary civil claim.

Aiding and abetting a contempt

Two further questions are of profound importance, namely the range of persons bound by the injunction, and the position of third parties who assist them. On the first, the rule is that the persons bound by the injunction are those named in it. Where they are named in a 'representative capacity', the class of persons represented is bound, a dangerous form of relief if applied without discrimination, as we noted in the Animal Aid case.[228] Indeed, it was because the courts in the United States began earlier this century to use wide, unspecific orders that the 1932 Norris–La Guardia Act was passed to ban the labour injunction in the federal courts. The injunction had been used to include within its sweep 'all persons whomsoever' might think to do the acts forbidden. In this way, 'The imminent threat of irreparable harm to property . . . does service against all persons, indefinable and undefined . . . a code of conduct governing the whole community.'[229] English courts have never used the injunction in this way. But even the narrower injunction that binds defined persons must be carefully scrutinized. As Canadian writers have noted: 'Beginning as a device for the protection of private property rights, it ends by shading over into delicate public policy judgments about the proper conduct of labour controversy.'[230] This social function finds expression in the obligation on the part of third parties not to 'aid or abet' a defendant to break the court's injunction. A third party who knowingly assists in a breach (and wilfulness is required)

is liable for a contempt of court by himself. It is true that his conduct may very often be seen as possessing a dual character of contempt of court by himself and aiding and abetting the contempt by another, but the conduct will always amount to contempt of court by himself.[231]

It was said in 1897 that the third party is guilty of a criminal contempt, since he is not a party to the original action but is really impeding the course of justice. On the other hand, such an aiding and abetting has been treated as 'unlawful means' for the purposes of the civil law, and as civil contempt in itself.[232] Since the plaintiff would be unlikely to agree to 'waive' the breach by a third party, the distinction is here less important.

Suppose an employer obtains an interlocutory injunction (1) prohibiting named pickets from picketing at a place and (2) prohibiting the union 'by itself, or by its servants or agents' from organizing the picketing instructing members to strike. It is a contempt for the pickets to continue to attend at that place and for the union, or anyone else, knowingly to encourage or assist them so to break the order. This includes any corporation whose 'servant acting in the course of his employment knowingly assists in the breach', as Eveleigh LJ has said, 'on grounds of vicarious liability'. So too, any union is liable whose official, as its agent, acts in that way (the Court of Appeal appears to have settled that this is tested not by EA 1982 s. 15, but by ordinary principles of vicarious liability, as we saw: p. 708). But other members of the union may replace the pickets so long as they are not a covert conspiracy to assist in a breach of the order. Acting only on their own behalf they are not bound by the order, even if they subvert its purpose. The employer must seek a further injunction against them. It is here that we see the advantage of being able to obtain an order against the union, which was not possible when the immunity in tort existed. In our example, the union and its officials must refrain from organizing pickets and must not instruct members to strike. But, again, the members not named in the order do not commit a contempt merely by striking, unless they do so as a way of knowingly aiding or abetting a breach of the order. Just where that line is to be drawn is sometimes difficult to establish. But it cannot be too often stated that when an injunction bans a union and its officials from organizing or encouraging a strike, workers commit no wrong in respect of the injunction merely by withdrawing, or continuing to withdraw, their labour.

More difficult cases arise. In September 1984, for example, the national NUM stood in contempt of court primarily by reason of its failure to accept the judges' interpretation of its rules as to whether the strike was 'official'. Thereafter it engaged in a succession of refusals to obey orders of the court, ultimately leading to sequestration of assets and the appointment of a receiver. Stress was put by the judges on the fact that the union would not undertake to abide by all orders of the courts, past and future. Indeed, this contempt by disobedience of 'interim' orders went on to survive even the discontinuance of the whole action by the plaintiffs eight months later. But other unions, it was found later, had loaned or given money to it. One General Secretary said: 'The miners have been sustained by my union.' Did this aid and abet the contempt? Some, including the sequestrators, argued that even the separate Area miners' unions acted improperly if they had given money to the national NUM. The TUC refused assistance for fear of aiding and abetting contempt, even after the strike was long over (p. 741). When he lifted the sequestration, late in 1985, Nicholls J. said that those who had given money to the NUM would not be punished – 'but they would not be treated so leniently in any future sequestration'. Professional advisers must not 'assist' a breach of an order; and solicitors could be liable if they assisted conduct 'which they knew was *or might constitute* a contempt'.[233]

This last formulation, wider than earlier precedent, could be highly restrictive in practice, not least because the boundary lines of permissible conduct are not entirely clear. Some indirect benefits to the contemnor seem to be allowed. When the seamen's union (NUS) wished to pay donations to the NUM, Scott J. disallowed it because of the sequestration (it could serve no purpose of the NUS to pay money to the sequestrators). But he distinguished donations for

more limited and specific purposes, such as alleviating hardship and distress among the families of striking miners. I imagine . . . that a payment impressed with a trust for such a purpose would not be liable to be seized by the sequestrators.[234]

If its NEC took the view that such alleviation of hardship of the miners' families was in the NUS members' interests, 'enhancing the possibility that more collieries will stay open . . . thereby there will be more coal for transport round the coast and the enhancement of employment prospects for [the seamen]', tending to promote 'trades union principles of solidarity', this would not be beyond their lawful powers. Together with benefits to families, this reasoning allows for indirect benefit to the contemnor from conduct that does not directly 'assist' it in the contempt as such.

We know that doctrines from other areas have a habit of descending on sensitive points of labour law. We should therefore note the 'Mareva' injunction, an order developed in commercial law since 1970. It was first used in interlocutory proceedings to stop a party from removing assets from Britain so as to bind banks and other third parties, in whose hands the property must be 'frozen' as soon as they have notice of the order. Now its ambit is even wider, and in family and wardship actions, orders have been made 'binding upon the world at large'.[235] We encounter the 'Mareva' injunction again on p. 746.

Purging and release

Release of the contemnor from the orders of the court normally requires some 'purging' of the contempt, including the doing of any act ordered to be done and frequently the giving of an apology. Until this is done no application by the contemnor will be heard except at the discretion of the court, though he may defend new actions or applications against him.[236] Discharge may, however, be obtained in the case of a fine if it is paid by a third party, even if that is done without, or even against, the consent of the contemnor. This has happened in many countries, especially where union leaders are imprisoned or threatened. An anonymous business man paid the fine to release O'Shea, a union leader in Australia in 1969. In Britain donors contributed money in the *Con-Mech* case, 1974; and Mr Scargill's fine of £1,000 was paid in 1984 even though, said the judge, 'it has been widely reported that the payment was not by him or anyone acting on his behalf or with his approval'. But it was enough that it was paid.

This illustrates the fact that the fine is a punishment for the contempt, whereas other sanctions may or may not be. For example, a writ of sequestration may be used as punishment, as the machinery for the payment of a fine. Such a writ was issued in the interim stages of the *Heatons* case, for example, and in the *Con-Mech* case, as a vehicle for the collection of fines.[237] But sequestration may also, or instead, be a means of coercing the defendant to obey the court's orders. If the fine were merely coercive it would be illogical to allow a third party to pay it off; but most sanctions have retained the original purpose of the jurisdiction, to compel the contemnor to obey. This purpose of coercion is distinct from punishment, which is why a contemnor committed to prison who refuses to repent may be set free after a period in gaol. Watkins L J said in such a case in 1983: 'It is pointless to keep him where he is.' The release of the imprisoned shop stewards by reason of the union's being found liable by the Law Lords in the *Heatons* case, 1972, stretched this principle to breaking-point.

When, a fortnight after the end of the miners' strike, the NUM (South Wales) went back to the court in 1985 to request discharge from the sequestration of its funds (less the fine of £50,000 and costs of nearly £100,000), the plea was resisted by the sequestrators, who argued that conditions should be imposed (including the disclosure of moneys received from other unions). Scott J. rejected any such conditions in an enlightened judgment. He decided that the contempt had been adequately punished and, as to coercion, no further breaches of the orders had been reported, and the strike was over anyway. 'The court is not troubled by the absence of a formal apology,' he said; the union had 'recognized the authority of the court'. The important thing was that 'the rule of law has been seen to prevail'.[238] But similar attempts by the national NUM failed even months later. In giving the receiver permission to pay the Area unions money that was their property but became entangled with the national union funds (partly by reason of union members' subscriptions being deducted in a check-off by the NCB and then paid over nationally), the judge imposed conditions to prevent any 'covert support' for the national NUM, which he still saw as defying the law. It was reported that Area unions had paid for national officials' salaries and that this had been questioned sequestrators.[239] Whether the courts would insist upon an apology in such a case remained uncertain. The appointment of a receiver complicated matters still further (we return to this in Chapter 9, p. 734).

In all this, the exact role of the sequestrators is unclear. Where a party returns to the court to ask for a release, it may be questioned whether the rule of law requires that these agents of the court must resist such an application, as opposed to giving the court any information it requires. In some of the miners' cases, sequestrators seem to have cast themselves almost in the role of mini-Attorneys-General. Since they are the agents of the court, however, the judges have control of, and responsibility for, them.

The centrality of procedure

By 1985, then, the law on injunctions and contempt of court had entered the innermost processes of industrial conflict and trade union administration, and not only in the miners' cases. It appeared in the *Austin Rover* cases. TASS was found to be in contempt but was not penalized; the TGWU was fined weeks after the collapse of the strike called with a ballot (p. 77). In 1983–4 industrial action by the NGA had been defeated by strategies including actions for injunctions, damages, punishment for contempt by fines and, then, sequestration.[240] In 1986 the NGA and SOGAT were fined, and the latter's assets were sequestrated. The procedural aspects of the law relating to strikes, which have too often been ignored in discussions about labour law, now occupy the centre of the stage. This is why they have received attention here. Labour law must now take account of the court procedures that breathe life into the skeleton of substantive legal principle.

One feature, however, of the miners' litigation was different: the appearance as plaintiffs not only of employers or customers suing in tort, but of members of the union itself suing not in tort but for alleged breach of the contract in the rule-book. This is not as unprecedented in strikes as some observers appeared to think. The litigation that followed the *Taff Vale* case, 1901, featured similar actions, as when one member sued his union, the *Yorkshire Miners' Association*, over strike pay in 1905.[241] The Law Lords approved an injunction to stop the strike pay. That was a time, one year before the Trade Disputes Act, when, Phelps Brown wrote, 'the impression was strong and the threat real that any strike would result in the union's funds being mulcted, and there were few strikes.'[242] In one respect, however, the law then presented obstacles to such actions that do not exist today. These arose out of the impact of the law on the relationships between members of unions amongst themselves, and between the members and their union. To those relationships we now turn.

[9] Trade Unions and Members

For many years the legal definition of a trade union provided by the Trade Union Acts of 1871 and 1876 was a long way from the social reality captured by the Webbs when, some seven decades ago, they defined it as 'a continuous association of wage earners for the purpose of maintaining or improving the conditions of their working lives'. The old legal test, repealed in 1971, referred to the objects of 'imposing of restrictive conditions on the conduct of any trade or business' as well as 'the regulation of relations between workmen and workmen [or] masters and workmen'. But it also brought within its compass even combinations with those objects for the regulation of relations between 'masters and masters'; so the odd inclusion of some employers' associations within the old legal meaning of 'trade union' must be borne in mind whenever cases in that century after 1871 are considered.

Today things are different. TULRA 1974 defines separately 'trade union' (s. 28 (1)) and 'employers' association' (s. 28 (2)). There are two parts to the modern definition of 'trade union'. First, it must be an organization (permanent or temporary) that consists wholly or mainly of workers of one or more descriptions. Secondly, its 'principal purposes' must include 'the regulation of relations between workers of that description or those descriptions and employers or employers' associations'. A federation or similar organization may also be a 'trade union' if (1) it consists of constituent or affiliated organizations that are themselves trade unions (or of their representatives) and (2) its principal purposes include the regulation of relations between workers and employers or employers' associations, or the regulation of relations between its constituent or affiliated organizations (a phrase that appears to bring the TUC within the definition). Such bodies as the International Transport Workers' Federation (ITWF) are clearly within the definition. We must remember, too, that 'worker' is defined so as to include not only those employed under contracts of 'service' but also those self-employed under contracts for 'services' (other than those who work for a professional client, a proviso that has been held to apply to solicitors, so that the Law Society is not a trade union). Included also are those employed in the National Health Service and in government employment (other than the armed services); but the police are excluded (TULRA s. 30 (1)). Many actors and musicians are union members employed under contracts for services.

The definition of 'employers' association' is nearly a mirror image of that of 'trade union', substituting 'employers or individual proprietors' for workers. Such organizations, however, do not fall under the requirement, as trade unions do, that they must be unincorporated bodies (noted in Chapter 7, p. 530). They have the option of being incorporated, e.g. as companies, or unincorporated. In 1978 the Test and County Cricket Board was able to show that it was an organization of employers but failed to qualify as an 'employers' association' because its principal purposes were not the regulation of relations between employers and workers, largely because on such matters it was 'responsible not to the members' but to a superior body, the Cricket Council.[1] This decision is of some importance, we see later, in regard to the status of some union branches.

The Trade Union Acts that lasted for a century commencing in 1871 offered a trade union the advantage of placing its name on a register maintained by the Registrar of Friendly Societies. We saw in Chapter 7 how this registration, which for decades appeared to have no effect on the unincorporated status of unions (then, as now, they had to have their property held by trustees), was seized upon in the *Taff Vale* case to make them 'quasi-corporations' open to legal suit in their registered names. We saw, too, that today a union is not, 'and shall not be treated as if it were, a body corporate'; yet it has the capacity to make contracts, to be the beneficiary for property held on trust for it, to sue and be sued, to be prosecuted and to have judgments enforced against it (TULRA s. 2 (1): p. 530). On the repeal of the Industrial Relations Act 1971, all registers were abolished, and the Certification Officer (CO) was empowered to establish a 'list' of trade unions on which an organization may be entered if it satisfies the definition. If the CO refuses listing, the organization may appeal to the EAT on any question of law or fact (TULRA s. 8, EPCA s. 136 (3)). Inclusion on the list is evidence that the organization is a trade union. Unions on the list receive the traditional tax relief in respect of sums paid as 'provident benefits', and listing is a requirement for a certificate from the CO that the union is 'independent', which we have seen in Chapter 4 to be an important attribute in regard to the rights of unions and of officials and members (EPA s. 8: p. 280).

The rules and the union

The union rules are a contract, first between the union and each member, and secondly 'the mutual contract', as Lord Diplock recently put it, 'between its members'. Before the *Taff Vale* case it was natural to regard the contract as one simply between members (there was no legal entity in 'the union' to be a party). Today the union also has the capacity to make a contract with each member (TULRA s. 2 (1)). Lord Denning has more than once complained that this contract is 'a fiction', saying the rules are 'more like by-laws'; but this view, he later accepted, 'went too far'. The contract in the rules is no more fictitious than many contracts of adhesion that an individual enters into today on terms already fixed (contracts to travel on trains, for instance, or contracts of insurance). Indeed, union rules will normally contain a democratic procedure for altering the terms, usually by a special majority of members or special conference. Great difficulties can arise here. One rule of the AUEW(E) gave benefits to its members – in unemployment or sickness or on disablement, for example – but provided that this rule could not be amended in the normal way but only after approval by 40 per cent of the members 'affected'. An AUEW(E) member successfully challenged the union's attempt in 1985 to amend the rule in a normal rules revision conference by deleting the special proviso. Young workers under eighteen are bound by a contract of membership when it is as a whole for their benefit. (TULRA, Schedule 1, para. 31 (1), impliedly recognizes the validity of membership for persons over 16.) The ILO Conventions ratified by the United Kingdom recognize the right of trade unions to draw up their rules 'without previous authorization' and to be free from interference impeding the 'right to draw up their constitutions and rules, to elect their representatives in full freedom, to organize their administration and activities and to formalise their programmes', freedoms that the 'law of the land' must not impair (Freedom of Association Convention No. 87, 1948, Arts. 2, 3, 8). But no law in Britain sets out these rights in positive terms.

Trustees

Under TULRA 1974 all trade unions must have trustees; but only listed unions receive the benefit of 'automatic vesting'. This is the automatic transfer of property to the names of new trustees on their death or removal, provided certain formalities are met (TULRA s. 4). Without such an arrangement, an unincorporated association needs to have all its title deeds, etc. altered every time a trustee retires or dies and is replaced. Under TULRA, and unlike the Act of 1871, it seems possible for a union to appoint a corporate trustee (a company limited by guarantee, for example), which dispenses with any such difficulties; but few appear to have done so. Most unions do not expect their trustees to be active managers of the funds. Under most rules, three or four trustees commonly elected at the union's conference from members not holding office are required to act in accordance with the directions of the NEC (national executive committee), and their position is often an honour rather than a burden. They are, however, liable for any breach of trust, for example investments not permitted either by the general law or by the rules of the union.[2] The rule-book, as well as being the basic membership contract between the union and its members, is the document that sets out the terms of the trust, so that dispositions of property outside the terms of the rules make the trustees liable to the union.

The primary beneficiary under the trust is, as TULRA s. 2 (1) (b) states, 'the union'. Indeed, this was the interpretation most judges put upon the previous statutes (even though they spoke of trustees holding assets on trust for 'the union and the members thereof'). This does not prevent a member from having an 'indirect beneficial interest' in the fund constituted by the union's assets, which he is entitled to protect if it is misused,[3] though we shall see that there are limits upon his ability to do so (p. 752).

There are as yet uncharted seas of difficulty surrounding the concept of property held on 'trust for the union'. First, although all property that 'belongs' to the union must be 'vested' in the trustees, few unions take formal steps to put property other than land, offices, investments, bank accounts and the like into their names. Frequently, for purposes of administration, certain top officials and executive employees have mandates to operate bank accounts in accordance with the rules. There is nothing necessarily wrong in this so long as the trustees know what is being done. More important, the union's trustees may hold property distinct from the general property of the union. A members' super-annuation scheme, for example, is subject to special rules for actuarial examination and must be a separate fund (TULRA, Schedule 2). In 1985 nineteen unions maintained twenty-six such schemes. Similarly, the trustees may hold other property on special trusts that are different from those constituted by the rules as a whole; for example, a 'hardship fund' to support members' children or relatives, or funds donated to charitable purposes. Such a fund would appear not to be the property of 'the union'. On the other hand, a fund raised by working members' voluntary donations to help members on strike (for which there was no provision in the rules themselves) was held to be a 'fund of the union'.[4] The moneys were paid to the union 'for the benefit of their members who were out on strike', said the judge; this made them 'funds of the union', even though 'the trusts are not those on which their other funds are held'. An even more difficult problem may attach to branch funds. These will frequently be held by branch trustees or by branch officials. In some cases, despite the existence of separate trustees, the union rules mean that the branch members have no 'right to its funds in the branch as distinguished from a right to them in the society'; thus everything is the property of the one union.[5] But some branches, and even more some sections, of modern unions clearly do have their own separate property. Indeed, some may be in law separate trade unions (a point that arises, we shall see, under the 1984 Act: p. 776).

These are issues of the utmost importance in time of trouble. For example, in 1983, when the total assets of the NGA were sequestrated, the sequestrators took over not only the funds of the national union, but also those of chapels, branches and regions.[6] Each of these retained its own share of contributions collected from members and each had autonomy in the application of such funds within the national rules and policy. Not only did Scottish banks object to satisfying an English court's orders in this case (they did so in the end), the union lost its ability to pay any wages or benefits. (The TUC agreed to make a grant of £420,000 to the NGA, most of which was apparently paid to its members, 'in lieu of the union's contractual obligations to them which sequestration made it unable to fulfil', payment for its 'lawful functions' that was apparently not inhibited by the fears of contempt which were to arise in the case of the NUM a year later: p. 742.) But the Manchester branch of the NGA objected. It claimed it was an autonomous society, founded in 1797; and it succeeded in recovering its separate property from the sequestrators, though on conditions that stopped it feeding the national union. Where a union is a federation, as with the NUM, each Area union is a separate trade union; but there may still be separate branch or other funds within the Areas. Complaints were made in 1984 that sequestrators of the NUM (South Wales Area) funds had seized a separate hardship fund. Gennard has suggested that, in a union not centrally funded, like the NGA, if all branches 'declared UDI and regained their funds' sequestration might be nullified. But it is unlikely that such a declaration could by itself alter the trusts on which property was held, whatever they were (although Scott J. in 1985 envisaged that money given on special trusts to the South Wales Area NUM, for relief of family hardship, for example, would not become union property available for sequestration: p. 714). In the case of a sequestration (p. 705), however, the question what is 'union property' can be a matter of difficulty and may well have been somewhat overlooked in some recent sequestrations. When SOGAT suffered sequestration in 1986 it was reported that 63 per cent of 'its' property was 'owned' by branches; some of it was saved from seizure.

The 1982 Act provided that 'damages, costs or expenses' awarded against a union or trustees in whom 'property is vested in trust for [the] trade union' are not recoverable from property 'belonging to the trustees' in some *other* 'capacity' (EA 1982 s. 17). This manifestly recognizes that such trustees may be holding certain funds otherwise than as trustees for 'the union'. (The section makes the same point about members or officials; i.e. they may hold property that does, or does not, belong to them 'jointly or in common with the other members'.) Property that is not 'union property' is protected from the award of damages. Two other funds may, we saw, also be protected against such an award (political fund and provident benefits fund: p. 532), but these funds clearly *are* union property. In 1985 there was doubt about sums that were in the hands of NUM (South Wales) officials after a sequestration order against all its assets for disobeying an order of the court. The union argued that these were 'donations earmarked for specific union purposes . . . in effect, trust moneys for which the union was not accountable to the sequestrator'. But the court was not called on to decide the point. Few of these different problems, as we shall see, were illuminated in the proceedings, which gave a new prominence to union trustees in 1984–5 and put them at the centre of the legal stage (p. 734).

Control of the rules

The Trade Union Act 1871 contained a short list of subjects on which a registered union was required to have some rules (objects, trustees, and inspection of books, for example). Otherwise like other unincorporated societies the union was free to adopt whatever rules it chose as the contractual base of the members' association. The doctrine of restraint of trade was prohibited from rendering the union's 'purposes' unlawful, and since 1974 this has been clarified by specifically excluding that doctrine from application also to union rules (s. 3 of the 1871 Act; now TULRA s. 2 (5); an 'immunity' that also applies to unincorporated employers' associations: s. 3 (5); p. 719). But in 1871 the object of the legislature was at once to legalize and to distance the unions. In consequence Parliament enacted that 'nothing in this Act' was to enable a court to enforce *directly* any agreement (1) between union members as to the terms on which they would be employed or do business, (2) for payment of union subscriptions or penalties, (3) to apply union funds for benefits to members, and (4) that was an agreement between one union and another (TUA 1871 s. 4). This section was a price readily paid by the unions for the removal from their shoulders of the burden of 'restraint of trade'.

Although now repealed, this section is important to an understanding of the modern law. From Parliament's point of view the aim was to keep agreements of domestic concern to trade unions out of the ordinary courts. In practice, although certain remedies were unavailable, courts began to enforce the rules as a contract in two ways. First, at the turn of the century, judges held some unions to be lawful at common law, i.e. not in restraint of trade, and therefore took jurisdiction over the rules.[7] But today most unions appear to have rules that are in restraint of trade at common law and therefore in need of the statutory protection. Secondly, however, courts began to grant remedies to members who were expelled or disciplined or who complained of improprieties in ballots or improper disposition of union funds *ultra vires* the rules. They evaded s. 4 by deciding that these remedies involved only the 'indirect' enforcement of the agreements set out in the section.[8] But where s. 4 of the 1871 Act did apply, the prohibition was strict; for example, members of the TGWU who sued for strike pay in 1963 were met by the barrier of s. 4 (3).

Today there is no such barrier. The Industrial Relations Act 1971 repealed s. 4 of the 1871 Act, and it has never been revived. Parliament no longer wished to distance the unions in 1974; so it seemed natural that all agreements between members and unions in the rule-book should be fully enforceable in the courts as contractual obligations on both sides. Few understood at the time what a great leap this step was in 1974. The 1971 Act required all union rules to conform to certain 'guiding principles' (s. 65) and imposed further requirements on the rules of unions on its register (Schedule 4). These two were repealed by TULRA 1974–6,[9] so that the main requirements made by statute today may be listed as: (1) a compulsory term implied in the rules that members have a right to resign on 'reasonable notice' and complying with 'reasonable conditions' (TULRA s. 7; this operates as a compulsory implied term in the rule-book contract); (2) the need for rules providing for the appointment and removal of auditors who audit the annual return (TULRA, Sched. 2, Part 1, para. 11); we may add too (3) the prohibitions against racial or sex discrimination in regard to the admission or treatment of members (RRA 1976 s. 11, SDA 1975 s. 12 – although provisions are allowed reserving positions for members of one sex on elected bodies where a minimum number of that sex is thought to be necessary, i.e. women's seats, so long as arrangements for voting or membership are not discriminatory: SDA s. 49; or discriminating in facilities for training for posts or encouragement of one sex to hold posts where the numbers of that sex in the previous year were comparatively small: s. 48 (2); see the similar provisions in RRA s. 38 (3) (4)); (4) the requirement of equality in membership, treatment and availability of posts demanded for EEC nationals (EEC Regulation 1612/68, Art. 8); (5) protection against discrimination for members and for applicants who wish not to contribute to the political fund under the Trade Union Act 1913 (discussed on p. 761).

In addition the rules are now overridden by legislative regulation concerning the election of the NEC (TUA 1984 Part I: p. 771). Further, where the employment involved is subject to a UMA, or 'closed shop', industrial tribunals have jurisdiction to declare expulsion from, or a refusal to admit to, membership unreasonable and to award compensation (EA 1980 ss. 4, 5: dealt with on p. 793). We may note, however, that from the time of the Donovan Report the TUC has made proposals to affiliated unions concerning the rules, especially in regard to admission, discipline and expulsion (an expelled member, for example, should remain a member until a proper appeals procedure had been exhausted). The TUC, moreover, set up its own Independent Review Committee to review certain types of exclusion in 1976 (p. 793). An authoritative survey in 1980 concluded: 'There are probably few instances of injustice to individual members' in the application of union rules.[10]

The rules and industrial action

Since s. 4 of the 1871 Act was not revived by TULRA 1974, union rules are in general now enforceable like any other contract of association. In practice some rules of trade unions reflect the old law, e.g. in providing for a right of inspection of books by members and others who have an interest in the funds, which the 1871 Act demanded of registered unions.[11] But the contractual 'rights' of the union against its members (more accurately, of the majority against the minority) are restricted by a number of factors, not least the attitude of the judges, which leans in favour of the individual member and against the union and the majority. This approach finds expression in the policy of construing the rules strictly against the union when a dispute arises with a member, and implying the requirements of 'natural justice' in procedures of discipline and expulsion. Where the expulsion of a member is concerned, one can readily understand that the union should be put to the test of proving the right of the majority to expel, even where there is no closed shop and a job is not necessarily immediately at risk. We may ask whether the fears of those judges who saw the need for Trade Union Act 1871 s. 4 have been justified, whether the courts, as Lord Robson put it in 1912, are

compelled to give full effect by decree or injunction to contracts whereby workmen had bound themselves . . . to refrain . . . from working at their trade at all, except by leave of their union.

Lord Robson was speaking of a refusal to *take* a job, which would not normally involve, as a strike would, the breach of a contract. The right of the union to enforce the rules is not likely to be one that the union seeks to enforce in court, but its existence may be important in terms of the internal discipline and solidarity of the union in the work that it has to do in collective bargaining for its members as a whole. For the union loses its *raison d'être* if it cannot continue the struggle of negotiation for its members.

The right to call members out to take industrial action may not include a situation where the action would break another agreement. Lord Denning in 1979 thought that was the case where the union stood in breach of a (legally enforceable) collective agreement. *Partington's* case, 1981,[12] is another odd example, which we met in Chapter 4. The union had made an agreement with employers that certain gas workers would fulfil safety tasks by staying at work in a strike. The member, who appeared (though not very clearly) to be one of these workers, had this agreement incorporated in his contract of employment (so the judges held, without consideration of T U L R A s. 18 (4): p. 340). He went into work on safety tasks in the middle of a strike. Read literally, the rules allowed for his expulsion in these circumstances; but the Court of Session refused to give them this meaning. The agreement with the employers meant that the union had limited its power to expel where the members involved fell within the safety agreement, even though it was a separate transaction entered into subsequent to the contract of membership. The agreement – apparently *not* legally enforceable; a normal collective agreement – between union and employer was made enforceable on the union by reason of its incorporation into the member's employment contract. One may ask, in the light of this decision, whether the rule-book is ever enforceable when the strike called is 'unlawful', today for example through lack of an 'immunity' in a trade dispute.

Shaw L J said in 1979 that to limit the power of a union body to a power to require members to terminate rather than break their employment contracts 'would, in practice, be futile and inexpedient'. In 1985 Scott J.[13] took an equally careful course in respect of picketing. It must, he held, be *ultra vires* for a union 'deliberately to embark on a series of criminal acts'. It would not, however, necessarily be *ultra vires* the rules (i.e. beyond their lawful ambit) to embark on a series of acts that 'carried the risk' that crimes or torts might be, but would not necessarily be, committed: 'in the ordinary conduct of business a large number of companies take this sort of risk open-eyed and frequently'. He left open the position where the union's action in picketing is bound to involve torts; it 'might depend on the nature of the tort'. We recall that particular plaintiffs may not have the right to sue for certain torts even if damaged (p. 642). There are good reasons to suggest that the approach of Scott J. is correct and that the union can rely upon powers in the rules except where its action must necessarily lead to a crime or possibly a tort in respect of which the plaintiff can sue, having regard to any consent that he has given by way of the rules or otherwise. There is, however, authority (far removed from the field of labour law) for the proposition that a contract to commit a tort is unenforceable, even illegal. The problem has arisen today by reason of the severe restrictions on the liberties of trade unionists to take lawful industrial action. Organizing strike action frequently amounts to an actionable tort today. It would be ironic if Parliament, which in 1974 made union rules enforceable as a contract to reinforce the bonds of the union, had by 1984 so far diminished the legality of strike action that the union cannot enforce that contract in respect of this critical area against members, while minority members can enforce it against the majority members or the union (except in respect of strike or other benefits that stem from illegal industrial action).

Interlocutory remedies

This description of the issues leaves out of account the important effects of interlocutory remedies, especially the 'labour injunction', which we noted in Chapter 8, in disputes between member and unions. The courts have been prepared to prohibit union disciplinary measures on the most narrow, sometimes even hypothetical, interpretations of the rule-book where objection is taken by a member to industrial action. The procedural elbow-room enjoyed by the court is such that the difficulties in the principles of substantive law do not always need to be probed. In *Shotton* v. *Hammond*, 1976,[14] the plaintiff member had refused to take part in a strike approved by the district committee, though it was arguably contrary to union rules and policy and certainly contrary to the wishes of the general secretary. The district committee, which was in conflict with the national bodies of the union over some matters of policy, subsequently refused to endorse his election as a shop steward (its approval being necessary if he was to act as such) unless he agreed to abide by whatever decisions the committee took. The union argued that there was adequate appeal machinery inside the union; this was where the final decision should democratically be made. Oliver J. decided that the committee was obliged to apply its discretion fairly; this 'was part of the contract between the member and the union'. This it could not have done when it insisted that the plaintiff must abide by its instructions even if they were unlawful, i.e. contrary to the rules. Indeed, although the court was 'reluctant to interfere in a union's domestic affairs', on the basis of the *Ethicon* principles and the balance of convenience (p. 690) he granted a mandatory order that the committee should convene a meeting within fourteen days to approve the election and ratify it at its next normal meeting. It was 'not the function of the court, nor was it equipped to attempt, to conduct the affairs of a trade union'; there was 'no precedent' for granting of a mandatory order upon a domestic tribunal by the court exercising its discretion. But in this 'unusual' case he would grant one: 'the balance of convenience is all one way'.

The House of Lords illustrated a similar approach in *Porter's* case, 1980,[15] a dispute about the meaning of the rules of the NUJ. This was a sequel to the *Express Newspapers* case, 1980 (p. 569). The union NEC had called for an all-out strike by provincial journalists and for sympathetic action by national and broadcasting members by 'blacking' material to the Newspaper Society. Dissident members had refused to comply, and after the strike was over several hundred members were expelled under a rule that permitted expulsion for conduct detrimental to union interests, including a failure to comply with such an instruction to strike. The plaintiffs complained that the strike order was unlawful because it infringed other rules, especially a rule that the NEC should hold a ballot for types of widespread action of this kind. The union contested this interpretation of the rules. The plaintiffs sought, and obtained, an interlocutory injunction to stop any disciplinary action against them until trial of their action challenging the expulsions. There were serious questions raised of disputed fact and law (i.e. interpretation of the rules). Therefore, 'the balance of convenience, save in exceptional circumstances . . . requires the status quo to be maintained until the trial of the action' (Lord Salmon). The issues could not be determined on affidavit evidence. But the Law Lords did interpret the rules, and in the plaintiffs' favour. They then granted them the (theoretically) interim remedy that was critical. It is true that in *Porter* any improper expulsion would have had serious effects for the plaintiffs. The strike was over, but non-members would find difficulty in obtaining work in certain closed-shop employments at that time. It is, however, by no means clear that the Law Lords would have decided differently during, or even before, the strike. There may have been reasons to restrain the majority NUJ members from expelling the minority. But the fact that the parties were in dispute about an arguable point of law on the facts available on affidavit is surely not adequate. If it is, the judge can find against the union whenever he wishes. The labour injunction may then be even more unjust in the area of contract than it was in the land of tort.

In *Esterman* v. *NALGO*, 1974,[16] Templeman J. went even further. In pursuit of a dispute, the NALGO NEC held a ballot of members, which was needed before a strike could be called, except for action taken in 'emergencies'. Only 49 per cent of members voted for strike action. The dispute developed, and the NEC later ordered selected branches to withdraw assistance from running local elections. The plaintiff refused to do so and was called before her branch on disciplinary charges, including one of being 'unfit for membership'. Her main case was that she found the NEC order objectionable and dishonourable. The judge granted her an interlocutory injunction, banning the very hearing of the disciplinary charges by the union 'until the trial of the action', because a reasonable member 'might' have doubted – as he did himself with some force – whether the order given was within the powers of the NALGO NEC. The court is here granting a notionally 'interim' injunction, preventing disciplinary action in accordance with the rules, on the basis that a member 'was entitled to doubt' the validity of the NEC decision. Indeed, the judge concluded that 'no reasonable tribunal could bona fide come to the conclusion that disobedience of this order demonstrated any unfitness to be a member'. This was of course the very issue to be decided by the union branch and appellate bodies. The order was 'pending trial'. It is difficult to believe it was not the end of the matter. The branch was not even allowed to discuss the issue. This interlocutory procedure gives judges the chance to insist that certain issues are too difficult to try 'on affidavit evidence and on motion'; but they then proceed to interpret the union's rules on the spot and to give the plaintiff the injunction needed to stop either the disciplinary proceedings or the industrial action or both.

The miners' case

The fundamental contract in any union is the rule-book. Upholding the rules is a central article of faith in a trade union, quite apart from the law.

But the obligations in the rules are various, owed by the majority and minority, the union itself and the individual member. There is often disagreement about what is meant by the rules, a dispute that may not be fully explored in interim proceedings for an interlocutory injunction.

In addition to the cases on tort that we met in Chapter 8, the use of such injunctions to inhibit industrial action was evidenced in the many civil actions brought by dissident miners during the long miners' strike of 1984–5 (early in 1985 it was estimated that there were some twenty separate actions on foot, although most were dropped after the strike ended). The history of these actions is of importance to an understanding of the contract in the union rule-book, of the approach of the courts to its enforcement and of the new significance of both to the place of civil law in union affairs and strikes. A caveat, however, must at once be interposed. In some of the crucial legal actions, either the national union (NUM) or the relevant Area union being sued (or both) did not appear in court to contest the initial liability. In many cases, therefore, the court did not always have the advantage of full arguments for the defence in the interlocutory proceedings (e.g. that there had been no breach of the rules). This was so for most of the judgments before November 1984. Neither the legal nor the industrial merits of the miners' unions' actions are our concern here – for example, whether ballots should or should not have been held, what justifications there were for the strike or for closures, and so on. What matters here is the relationship of the law to the member, the union and the strike. Nor is this simply an academic or theoretical exercise; the social background must be kept continuously in mind for the very understanding of its nature.

In 1984 a miner was a member of two unions, his Area union and the NUM. In March 1984, faced with the announcement of pit closures, the NUM decided not to hold a national ballot on a strike (as required by its Rule 43 for 'national' action) – a decision that caused great controversy – but instead to sanction 'Area strikes', as it could do under another rule, Rule 41. Under this procedure, in each of the Areas the different Area union rules had to be satisfied for a strike called at that level.

When, therefore, the court was presented with evidence that the *Derbyshire Area* rules required a 55 per cent majority for a strike and that in an Area ballot in March only 49.9 per cent of members had voted in favour, it was presented with a strike in that Area manifestly called in breach of contract. Eventually in September 1984 Nicholls J. granted an injunction and a declaration against this Area union and the NUM. The orders made the strike and union instructions not to work 'unlawful' in the sense of being a prohibited breach of contract; and they also stopped any disciplinary actions against dissident members. Earlier interlocutory proceedings before Megarry VC concerning the Derbyshire Area had extracted undertakings not to discipline the dissident miners.[17] Nicholls J. further held that a 'national call, coupled with threats and the need to cross a so-called "official" picket line to get to work, in my judgment is entering upon a national strike'. Lack of a ballot under Rule 43 therefore constituted a breach of the national NUM rule-book contract and so rendered the strike 'unlawful' under that contract too. This was an unusual action in one respect. The course that the rapid interim proceedings had taken allowed it to proceed as a 'final trial' from September onwards.

Actions brought in the other Areas on strike (most miners in Nottinghamshire refused to strike, but elsewhere the great majority had come out) succeeded in similar fashion, except one. In *Scotland*, no breach of the Area rules was shown in interim proceedings.[18] There Rule 41 appeared to be satisfied: and the court was 'not prepared to conclude that an Area and a national stoppage could not run in parallel', so that no prima-facie case existed to show that the picketing was related to an unlawful national strike, rather than to the lawful Area strike. However, in the second half of 1984 dissident members obtained interlocutory injunctions against the unions in other Areas, for example in the *North Wales Area, North Western Area, Midlands Area, Durham Area* and the separate *Durham Mechanics (Group No. 1) Area*.[19] Interlocutory injunctions were obtained by dissident miners in these cases, usually banning disciplinary action against them 'pending trial or further order', mostly on the basis of a 'serious case to be tried' in respect of failure to observe Area rules for a 'Rule 41' strike. In the *Midlands Area* litigation Mervyn-Davies J. relied heavily on the *Ethicon* principle. There were serious issues to be tried on the legality of the strike; balance of convenience favoured the plaintiffs; the adequacy of damages was not a test that could be applied. Strategies as to defendants differed: the Area union or its executive committee was made a defendant in all those cases; in one, the 'Point of Ayr Lodge Committee' was sued; in three the national NUM was joined, and in two the National Executive Committee of the national union. The addition of the national NUM and various other personal defendants in some of the actions was an important straw in the wind. It was to bring the judges closer to the persons involved, within touching distance of the personal relationships inside the unions.

The Vice-Chancellor, Sir Robert Megarry, had also discounted the 'adequacy of damages' guideline in *Clarke* v. *Chadburn*[20] when granting interlocutory injunctions in the first case in the sensitive *Nottinghamshire Area* (deeply divided but with a majority at work throughout the dispute). The plaintiffs needed 'an injunction to protect them, not damages for loss', he said – though if this is the guiding principle, damages would seem to be an adequate remedy in very few cases. The plaintiffs sought injunctions to prevent disciplinary action, instructions not to work and representations by the union that it was a breach of union rules to continue to work. The interim orders included orders to stop any such representations or instructions. On the 'balance of injustice', said Megarry V C, these interlocutory injunctions should stand. There was an arguable case that this *was* a national strike under Rule 43 (even though the NUM executive committee and conference had decided it was not) and therefore had been improperly called without a national ballot. Also, there did not appear to be 'fair treatment' of the members by their union; this was 'relevant in deciding whether to grant or withhold the remedy' (a formula that adds further to the court's discretion). Later the plaintiffs made further applications. A national conference of the NUM was about to consider putting a new disciplinary clause into the rules. Although this became known as the 'Star Chamber' clause (Rule 51), it was a 'blanket' clause penalizing action by members contrary to the 'interests of the union' of a kind that a majority of unions (including some NUM Area Unions) have for many years included in their rule-books, as a recent survey confirmed (p. 799).

Introduced at this time, the new NUM rule was bound to be provocative to those not on strike; but this by itself was not enough to make it illegal. Megarry V C granted orders on two *ex parte* applications requiring the conference to be postponed and later ordering the union not to discuss the new rule. The argument was mainly about mandating the Nottinghamshire Area delegates; but this part of the case was rendered less relevant when the Nottinghamshire delegates voted with the minority against the new rule anyway. This left the order not to discuss it. But the conference *had* discussed it and adopted it by a large majority.

This, however, was by then a contempt of court. What was the effect on the new rule, which had been duly passed according to the rules? In the absence of precedent – and on interlocutory motion – Megarry V C made a *final* declaration that the rule itself was void; he said of the defendants: 'those who defy a prohibition ought not to be able to claim that the fruits of their defiance are good and not tainted by the illegality'. (It is not clear what would happen if eventually at a 'full trial' such a defendant won his case. Presumably the 'final' declaration would be retroactively quashed, and the rule would be resurrected by some judicial magic retrospectively. This makes the novel remedy very odd and highly prejudicial.)

There can be no doubt that this was a decision of a difficult and somewhat novel point of law in interlocutory proceedings of a kind that courts in other circumstances might have found unsuitable for decision on motion. An injunction was then also granted, quite logically, to restrain the NUM from acting on the rule. We have seen (p. 711) that the Vice-Chancellor went on to speculate whether the courts should not have further powers to initiate enforcement of their own orders – an idea that many saw as another warning shot across the unions' bows. The dispute in Nottinghamshire survived the strike, with the union in 1985 deeply divided, some of the new officers aiming to make it independent of the national NUM. The President of the (old) Area union was locked out of his office but obtained an order that a ballot should be held before independence was declared, as eventually it was (p. 743).

Contempt of court and receivership

Meanwhile, litigation originating in the Yorkshire Area sparked developments that led to another contempt of court. We must take up the story of 'contempt', therefore, on which we set out the principles in Chapter 8 (p. 705). In *Taylor and Foulstone* v. *NUM (Yorkshire Area)*, 1984,[21] dissident miners sought interlocutory orders against both the Area and the national union. They complained of a breach of the NUM Rule 43 (the absence of a national ballot) and of a breach of the Yorkshire Area rules (these required an Area ballot; but the union, which did not at this stage appear, claimed throughout that a majority in a previous Area ballot was sufficient, a point that was never fought out in the proceedings). On the same day of September on which he gave his main *Derbyshire Area* judgment, Nicholls J. also granted interlocutory injunctions restraining both the Yorkshire Area union and the NUM from urging members not to work or cross picket lines, and in particular not to do so by describing the strike as 'official'. He also granted mandatory orders compelling the Yorkshire Area to hold new elections according to its rules as amended by a timetable, to stop members being 'deprived until trial of the right . . . to elect representatives'. (It was later discovered, however, that there had been no substantial breach of the election rules, and those mandatory orders were discharged by consent.)

It was this September order making the strike call invalid (technically only in the Yorkshire Area) and prohibiting the unions (by their servants and agents) from describing it as 'official' that rightly attracted greatest attention. It was an interlocutory order against the NUM; but the news media were not likely to report the judgment as an interim one that established 'a highly arguable case'. The nation was caught up in heady, industrial warfare. The headlines were unqualified: 'Pit Strike Unlawful'. Miners in some Areas knew, or thought they knew, that the strike was 'official' and apparently lawful. Indeed, it was so in Scotland; and later it was accepted for the purposes of other litigation about South Wales that it was 'called in accordance with the rules of the South Wales union and is therefore an "official strike"'.[22] Within a fast-moving week, the NUM President, Mr Scargill, declared with the support of his NEC that the NUM in its fight against pit closures would not accept the court ruling, and in a private hearing Vinelott J. granted leave for contempt proceedings. Service of papers was effected on Mr Scargill in the middle of a Labour Party conference. In this, the seventh month of the strike, violent confrontations on the picket lines continued; the Prime Minister called on the nation to face 'the most testing crisis of our time'; some Labour MPs said the judgment should be 'resisted'; the Bishop of Durham said the Government should work for peace between 'local police and local miners'; severe bail conditions were upheld in the Divisional Court; two policemen being stoned saved the life of a picket; a senior police officer apologized to a village after two days of police 'raids' to arrest villagers stealing buckets of coal; the Chancellor of the Exchequer called the cost of the strike 'a worthwhile investment for the nation'; and a Police Federation spokesman was 'fearful' whether the police would be able to serve a Labour Government. The NUM President 'fully expected' to be put in prison when he refused to pay his fine of £1,000. But not only did an anonymous donor pay it, Nicholls J. had ordered that, if unpaid, it should be enforced through the new procedures by the Queen's Remembrancer (p. 705). Martyrdom was being firmly ruled out. Before October was over, however, the judge had ordered the sequestration of all the property of the NUM, after its failure to pay a £200,000 fine.

This was a period that illustrated very well the way 'legal frameworks have ideological, as well as deterrent and punitive effects', and the more immediate fact that 'the neat lawyer's distinction between civil law and criminal law is not part of everyday consciousness'.[23] The NUM judgment entered the mind of the nation as a pronouncement of 'the law', in black and white, not tones of interlocutory grey. No doubt many arguments might have been added had the NUM been represented in court from the outset. But the nature of the interlocutory procedures and the very character of the *Ethicon* test make it unlikely that no injunctions at all would have been granted, whatever arguments the union had advanced, especially having regard to what experienced barristers call – and take very seriously in predicting judgments – 'the climate of opinion at the time'. The plaintiffs in all these actions seem to have had 'arguable' points, serious questions to send to trial, something less than frivolous or vexatious points. This is all they needed. Once an *arguable* breach of contract was put to a court, some injunction or other ('pending trial') was all too likely to challenge the 'official' nature of the strike and be given publicity accordingly. Even the most cautious leader of the unions would be placed in a dilemma by such an action (only one member of the NUM executive committee resigned at this juncture). The ballot rule was not the only rule relied on by plaintiffs in some of the legal actions. More than 150,000 members of the union were still on strike; many had seen their wives and children experience months of great hardship; families were divided, sons and fathers vowing never to exchange words again. A demand that the union leadership should renounce the 'official' character of the strike at that point, however justified in legal procedure, was a demand for its industrial crucifixion.

No doubt it was its legal duty to obey. No doubt 'the law' was properly administered, albeit with a few judicial innovations on the way that should be noted. But there were few laymen who understood that the strike was 'unlawful' in the sense that it was a breach of an interim order to remedy a possible breach of contract. As a defiance of the court, the union's stance was a defiance of the law. Some commentators did explain that the judgments were concerned with the 'common law of contract', and therefore not with the Government's laws that amended the 'immunities' and liability in tort; but the nature of the liability and, more important, the interim procedures and remedies did not feature prominently in the excitement of events. Indeed, scarcely was there time for anyone except the lawyers to comprehend these before issues of 'contempt of court', with its semi-criminal connotations, took over the stage.

Further proceedings by other dissident miners were launched in November 1984, this time against the trustees of the NUM and trustees of the Yorkshire Area union individually (in the latter case, though, the interlocutory proceedings were stood over until the 'trial' – which never took place). The main defendants were the three trustees of the NUM, in whom all the union property was vested and who were obliged by the rules to carry out the orders of the NEC. These trustees, appointed in the first week of the strike, were the President, Vice-President and Secretary of the union. It had come to light that virtually all the union's funds had been moved abroad to Zurich, Dublin and Luxembourg. The sequestrators were unable to lay hold of the money partly because they were not recognized by the courts abroad and partly because of steps taken by the trustees. The plaintiffs now alleged that the trustees had put the funds 'in jeopardy'; and that they were not 'fit and proper persons' to be trustees, particularly because of their defiance of the courts and obstruction of the sequestrators. They should be replaced by a receiver. The trustees argued that the funds were safe (and earning good interest) and that they had throughout carried out the instructions of the NEC (and indeed the union's conference). Mervyn-Davies J. decided that they were entitled to obey only lawful instructions from the NEC; moreover, they had obstructed the sequestrators by refusing to repatriate the funds, and they had refused to obey the orders of the courts generally. They were not fit to be trustees and should be replaced by a receiver (the order on this *ex parte* motion was to run for seven days for the reasons already explained: p. 690).

The High Court can appoint a receiver in any case where it is just and convenient (RSC, O. 30, R. 1); but this had never been done before in a trade union case. The Irish judge dealing with the funds in Dublin said later that the idea of a receiver came from 'continental lawyers' trying to trace the funds. The decision, we saw in Chapter 8, was approved next day by the Court of Appeal in *Clarke* v. *Heathfield*.[24] The court stressed the fact that the defendants, being already in contempt (after the *Taylor and Foulstone* proceedings), could be heard by the judges only in their discretion. The decision to appoint a receiver rested in part on the refusal of the defendants to obey the mandatory order granted by Nicholls J. the week before to the effect that they must write to the Luxembourg bank authorizing payment in full to the sequestrators. They had failed to do this or to purge their contempt generally. It was a 'drastic remedy' to extend the receivership to all the union property, said Stephenson LJ, but the Luxembourg bank had to be 'convinced of the receiver's title'. An undertaking had been offered by the defendants that they would not move the money. (In so far as the allegation was that the funds were 'in jeopardy', it was a long way from the company law usage where the 'jeopardy' is usually the danger of the assets charged being taken in execution by unsecured creditors.)[25] If the judge had had an undertaking 'on which he could have relied, he would not . . . have been justified in making the order'. But counsel for 'the sequestrators convinced the judge that the undertaking offered was, in view of the record of continuous contempt . . . an undertaking on which he could not rely'. Thus the sequestrators played a central role in securing this interlocutory receivership.

The receivership was therefore in one sense caused initially by the union's disobedience and was, that far, in aid of the sequestrators. A week later, in renewing the order for a receiver (an accountant took over from the provincial solicitor appointed at the first hearing) Mervyn-Davies J. – the judge who was to manage the receivership long into 1986 – laid greater stress on the trustees' record, which showed 'their conduct in future may bring about further depletions of the Union funds' (further fines for contempt might be imposed); and they had made the funds 'unavailable for the purposes for which they were contributed by the general membership'. The nature of the receivership was much debated in the subsequent Irish litigation in Dublin. It is a widespread principle that a court will not enforce the *penal* orders of a foreign State, and the Irish judge, giving judgment four months after argument, decided that the sequestration was essentially a foreign penal order and therefore not enforceable in an Irish court. He was, however, 'not satisfied that the receivership [was] simply an indirect method of enforcing the sequestration' and thereby also penal. But the receiver was temporary; the English order appointed the receiver 'for the time being, until new trustees are appointed or, on a change of heart, the removed trustees are restored'. The Irish court therefore preferred to keep the funds (£2.5 million) frozen in Ireland 'until permanent trustees of the union's property are identified or appointed'.[26] Two weeks later everyone – the union, sequestrators and the receiver – consented to the release of this Dublin fund (less costs outstanding). It was paid to the receiver, who now also had most of the money repatriated from Luxembourg and Zurich (less servicing and court costs, and less a large sum retained by the Luxembourg bank in case it needed an indemnity).

Receivers and sequestrators

By 1985 there therefore existed a situation without precedent in British trade union law. The sequestrators had been ordered by Nicholls J. in September 1984 to take possession of all the NUM assets. But they had been able to find only a few thousand pounds. Most of the money had gone abroad, and, when foreign courts and banks were shy of recognizing the sequestrators, the union trustees did not bring it back when ordered to do so by the court in November. This refusal was a major factor, as the Court of Appeal made clear, in their being seen as not 'fit and proper persons' to be trustees in the receivership action. From December 1984 there were, therefore, *two* agents, or 'officers', of the court entitled to acquire the assets of the NUM. The trustees were ordered to transfer all such assets into the control of the receiver 'save in so far as the same are transferred to any sequestrators'. An accountant was ultimately appointed as the 'Receiver of the income, assets, property and effects' of the NUM ('save in so far as the same may from time to time be in the possession or control' of the four other accountants appointed as sequestrators by the court) with power 'to carry on legal proceedings in the name of the [union] in any jurisdiction' so that he could recover union property. (At one hearing in Britain it was questioned whether the barrister acting for 'the union' at the insistence of its NEC had the *right* to do so without the agreement of the receiver, a point not fully resolved.)

The receiver was an agent or officer of the *court*, not of the union; the distinction is of great importance. In company law, for instance, the receiver of a company appointed as agent of the court operates 'adversely to the company', whereas a receiver appointed out of court by creditors carries on the business as the agent of the company.[27] This receiver does not appear to have been appointed to carry on 'the business' of the union. The idea was inapt. He was to collect and manage the assets; but his exact status was open to argument. Tension was reported between him and the sequestrators, each going privately back to the High Court for instructions from time to time (apparently to the different judges who appointed them, though whether this was more than convention is not clear).

Although the receivership may not have been a penal measure in itself, the use of this remedy was novel: 'a sort of legal *deus ex machina* brought in . . . in reality to pull the sequestrators' – and the court's – chestnuts out of the fire'.[28] It was widely seen as a step in aid of the purposes of the sequestration. In February 1985 the receiver attempted to have the sequestration terminated or at least 'put on the back burner', having reportedly put aside £400,000 to cover the sequestrators' costs. The sequestrators, however, successfully opposed this bid. The union had not purged its contempt. They still had much to do. For example, they had begun upon an investigation of third parties who might have assisted the old trustees or the NUM. They had made inquiries of other unions and of the TUC, to see whether by helping the miners any of them had been 'aiding and abetting the contempt'. Sequestrators cannot, however, be indemnified by the court, and these accountants needed reassurance about their costs. So the Government, in an extraordinary move in a civil action, gave them a Treasury guarantee. A receiver is entitled to such 'proper remuneration' as the court allows (RSC, O. 30, R. 3); and once he had acquired the union funds from abroad, everyone's costs could come out of that money.

Various questions arise. One is whether this is a rational way of conducting trade union law. The union had clearly defied the court order not to call the strike 'official'; but was it sensible that its members should still be deprived of its assets many months after the end of the strike? The introduction of a receivership, complementary to sequestration, meant that now the union had to make two different applications to the court before regaining use of the depleted funds. The NUM elected three new trustees preparatory to an application in July 1985 to have the title to the union assets returned. The receiver objected, and the court adjourned the matter until October, then November. But in August the plaintiffs in the Yorkshire Area action, *Taylor and Foulstone*, with the approval of Scott J., abandoned their entire action against both the N U M and the Yorkshire Area union after a union undertaking not to take disciplinary action against them for their conduct during the strike.[29] From the point of view of all the parties, abandonment was sensible; but it left the union, and the law, in a bizarre situation. The assets of the union were still sequestrated because of the contempt; title to its assets was in a receiver; but the court action itself was now dead. The discontinuance of the action by the plaintiffs, which was reported to include an agreement to co-operate in seeking an end to the sequestration, seemed to be in the nature of a 'waiver'. If so, there was no one left to enforce the contempt, unless the court decided to do so unilaterally – a course that would be highly exceptional (p. 709). But it seemed to be the accepted wisdom that, although the legal action was dead, the sequestrators could continue without further legal steps as to their position. Certainly some unions came rightly or wrongly to feel that sequestration of funds was an inevitable part of the new laws. In 1986 S O G A T suffered sequestration immediately when it disobeyed injunctions against industrial action at Wapping (p. 634).

Aiding and abetting contempt

By early in 1985 the N U M appeared to be in dire financial straits. Donors at home and abroad had given assistance; but was this aid improper by reason of 'aiding and abetting' the contempt? Indirect aid that benefits a contemnor is not always illicit, such as the payments for 'limited and specific purposes', e.g. to alleviate hardship among miners' families, to which Scott J. referred in *Hopkins* v. *N U S*, 1985.[30] The T U C had set up a Miners' Solidarity Fund and a Hardship Fund 'to relieve the hardship of miners and their families'.[31] Those funds were not sequestrated and continued to operate. But after the strike ended, the N U M asked the T U C for help by way of a trust fund to pay staff and outside creditors. It was reported to need more than £25,000 a week. This request was rejected in circumstances of some importance. Sequestration may contain, we have seen, a penal and a coercive element.

Third parties are allowed to assist in regard to penalties; they may pay a
contemnor's fine. But an attempt to provide aid to the contemnor that
reduces the coercive effect of the sanction runs the risk of 'aiding and
abetting' the contempt, though it is not clear where the line is precisely
to be drawn. Helping miners' families was lawful even though, in one
sense, it indirectly relieved the presssure on the NUM. The TUC
Report (1985) reveals that it was advised to obtain 'legal clearance' for
the requested trust deed – a step to which, after initial 'reluctance', the
NUM agreed. The TUC decided that the project should be 'checked
legally with the solicitors for the receiver and the sequestrators'. The
receiver replied that he would regard 'the payment by any party of any
outstanding liability' of the NUM, and 'any device' like a trust deed, as
a 'contempt of court' for which he would feel 'obliged to apply to the
court'. This reply could hardly have been unexpected.

To leave the law as stated by a receiver seemed to rule out testing a
carefully structured scheme in the court (however hostile). To regard
any settlement of, or assistance with, a contemnor's liabilities to *any*
third party as necessarily a contempt is a view open to challenge. In the
NGA case the TUC had paid some £400,000 from a 'defence fund' for
union members deprived of benefit by sequestration. But the opinion of
the receiver in the NUM case may have reflected his special claim to
deal with the union's property rather than his relationship with the
sequestrators. The receiver, however, clearly did not regard it as his
function to 'manage the business' of the union. He refused to release
funds, for example, to pay the union's affiliation fees to the 1985 TUC
(at which a motion was passed demanding that a Labour Government
compensate the union for all fines levied upon it). Nothing was more
clearly in the interests and well-being of the union than its attendance at
that Congress; and the TUC General Council even used its powers to
amend the rules to 'defer payment' by the NUM for that year to
facilitate it. Against this deferment of an NUM liability – a plain and
direct benefit – the receiver took no action. Logic might demand that
deferment, or even the guarantee, of debts to some at least of the other
outstanding creditors of the union might be equally lawful. Practice in
the miners' strike did little to clarify the dark corners of past judicial
decisions on aiding and abetting contempt (p. 712); but it showed how
uncertain principles of law can be applied at their widest against those
who feel unable to challenge them.

The effect and function of contract remedies

The accelerating financial difficulties of the NUM and Area Unions coincided with other developments. Some Areas were reported to be selling investments to keep going. The national NUM had no assets and now needed £30,000 a week for basic requirements. When this situation extended well into 1985, it would be naïve to believe that someone somewhere was not supporting it a little. The miners now in control of the Nottinghamshire Area were intent upon seceding from the national federation by forming a 'Union of Democratic Mineworkers' (a local secession in Nottinghamshire under George Spencer lasted for eleven years after 1926; but this time a national union was planned). They planned an amalgamation with another Area union and one smaller group.[32] Such a merger under an Act of 1964 requires only an ordinary majority in a ballot (p. 842), avoiding any need for a higher majority if required in the Areas' rule-books. It was successfully achieved in 1985. Before the ballot, they began work on the breakaway, for example withholding members' contributions allegedly due under existing arrangements to the national NUM. The court rejected a claim by 'loyalist' miners that this might involve breaches of contract meriting an interlocutory injunction. Even though no 'firm decision' had then been taken by the Area miners, the judge allowed the process to continue because the dissidents agreed to abide by a decision 'at an eventual full trial' on whether this money should be refunded to the NUM. It is not clear how 'serious' was the question raised, but the denial of an interim remedy, based on the same contractual principles as earlier actions, here assisted the breakaway. Moreover, this took place at a time when the NCB accorded recognition, in practice, to the incipient breakaway organization.

It is noticeable that the function of the law of contract, as it emerged in this long line of miners' cases, was less to strengthen the bonds of the overall association than to fragment it. In these cases the plaintiffs, of course, took their stand on the common law right to enforce a contract, a democratic right to have the contract observed. Although we shall see later that there are considerable legal limits on a minority member's right to do this (which were not tested in the miners' cases: p. 752) the moral force of such a stance is powerful. On the other hand, in the great majority of the cases the rights of minority and majority in the various unions were never finally established; the remedies were in most of them discretionary, interim remedies in interlocutory proceedings, decided without a full trial, injunctions that, once issued, could not in the short term easily be challenged. Defendants like the NUM, especially after it was in contempt of court, could not escape from 'interim' orders even when the plaintiffs, as occurred in the *Taylor and Foulstone* case, discontinued and abandoned their action. The court orders and punishment for breach of them remained in place even though the 'case' was dead. They were still hanging over the NUM by a kind of juridical levitation. The union saw applications to appoint the new trustees (apparently 'fit and proper persons') in the receiver's place drag on from hearing to hearing in the 1985 winter. The judge demanded assurances from the old trustees to co-operate with the receiver. The sequestration finally ended (with a 'perfunctory' apology) on 14 November 1985. But the receivership was still in place in May 1986. Indeed, the receiver was then still actively pursuing proceedings for contempt against certain banks and other defendants (including officers of the NUM) for what they had done to help move the funds abroad in 1984. One bank paid £600,000 in settlement. Reportedly some of this help was given *before* the Yorkshire Area writ was issued; the case seemed likely therefore to test how far contempt can be committed or 'aided' even before a case has begun in court at all.

It is hard not to believe that the historian will detect an element of rubbing the NUM's nose in its plight in some of this. But it was all within the judges' discretion; and until the hearing lifting the sequestration the NUM had not apologized to the court. It was perhaps one of those occasions when it was not good, in Churchill's words, for a union to be brought in contact with the courts – and especially not good for the courts. Some of the remedies granted were highly unusual (like a final declaration in interim proceedings). They included one that could not have been granted in the first century of modern trade union laws – the receivership. In 1928 the court in *Samson's* case[4] rejected an application for a receivership of union funds allegedly misapplied. At that time, we recall, Trade Union Act 1871 s. 4 prohibited a court from directly enforcing agreements for the application of union funds for benefits, and as between the union members the court decided that the rules were thereby unenforceable. A receivership could not be imposed on an association with unenforceable rules. That section was repealed in 1971 and was not resurrected by TULRA 1974. Ironically, by a quirk of legal history the jurisdiction to appoint such a receiver arose, therefore, almost accidentally because of the repeal of s. 4. No one discussed receiverships at the time of either the 1971 or 1974 Act. Nor was anyone heard to complain in the century after 1871 that members of unions were deprived of basic democratic rights because they could not apply to the court for a receivership. Indeed, we shall see that after *Cotter's* case, 1929 (p. 754), the right of a member to do so where all the legal points are contested is problematical. His right to complain even of a breach of trust is limited (another point not litigated fully in the miners' cases). So novel was this remedy that the 1985 edition of the Supreme Court Practice still carried the old rule (wrongly) that receiverships were not an available remedy against funds of trade unions.[33]

The revival of the receivership was not entirely, however, a matter of chance. It was all part of the general movement away from enforcement against the person, with the attendant risk of 'martyrs', noted in Chapter 1, towards sanctions levied against the property of unions. To some extent some of the remedies fell upon the miners' unions as they did in these cases by reason of their own tactics (some of the non-appearances in court, for example). But, appearance or not, the novel uses of old and new remedies by the courts in the interlocutory proceedings were just as important, especially in respect of union funds. For if the judges had imprisoned union officers in 1984, it is inconceivable that they would still have been in gaol so many months after the end of the strike, when the union funds were still both sequestrated in 1985 and in receivership in 1986. More generally, the opinion was widely held that all would have been different in this strike if there had been a national miners' ballot at the outset. This may be so; but with hindsight, certainly as far as the law and the courts go, especially in interlocutory proceedings, it seems a questionable view.

An additional point must be mentioned. The receiver was appointed in the *Clarke* proceedings against the trustees, a civil action, closely connected with the sequestration order for contempt arising from the *Taylor and Foulstone* case on the union's breach of contract. It has been suggested – not least in some trade union circles – that a receivership will be relevant only to that kind of case but not to tort actions in which the trade dispute 'immunities' (and the 1980s legislation) might be pleaded. This is not the case. If the court is convinced that the trustees have ceased to be 'fit and proper persons' to continue in office it may, in its discretion, appoint a receiver. So if a union broke court orders made in a tort case arising from an industrial dispute, sequestration might follow (as in the *NGA* case); but so too might receivership. A plaintiff might, for example, allege that the very funds 'put in jeopardy' by the trustees' improper payments were those from which he would seek payment of his damages. The real reason, however, why a receivership might not expand into such a case is not that the court could never see it as a 'just and convenient' remedy, but that there is another remedy lurking in the wings that may one day be adapted for use against trade unions in such circumstances. This is the 'Mareva' injunction, mentioned in Chapter 8 (p. 715). After 1975 the judges extended the use of injunctions in commercial cases so as to seize a defendant's assets *before* judgment, initially to stop him spiriting funds abroad, then to prevent him 'dissipating or concealing his assets so as to make judgment against him worthless or difficult to enforce'.[34] A significant body of precedent now supports this flexible and discretionary remedy of the 'Mareva' injunction. After we have seen 'economic duress' transplanted into labour law, it would be rash to think that the courts might not develop, as their next 'interim' sanction, a 'labour Mareva'.

The flexibility of receivership

The flexibility of the remedy of receivership has, however, been illustrated in other developments concerning unions and their members. The character of union rules as a contract and of the interventionist temper of the courts was evidenced further by a very different use of the remedy in *Bourne* v. *Colodense Ltd*.[35] Here the receivership was imposed on the *member* in order to compel the union to act. B. had claimed damages for injury caused by his employers but lost his case along with other workers, all members of SOGAT. The employers were awarded costs against the plaintiffs of some £50,000. But they were not paid. SOGAT, as is usual in such cases, had assisted the members in the litigation. The employers now sought an order for a receiver (under RSC, O. 30) against B. and the other workers. If appointed the receiver would then enforce the 'contract' between B. and SOGAT to indemnify B. as to his liability in costs (the receiver would then pay the employers). But no one had said the union would indemnify B. as to all his costs. The union rules said that members should 'apply' for legal benefit, but B. had not done and apparently would not do so. The Court of Appeal was not deterred. Lawton LJ had 'no hesitation' in finding an 'understanding of both parties that the union would keep [B.] free from personal liability if his claim was dismissed'. As for the rules (which demanded a member's application), the court should construe them as they would be understood by a member. Not all

the terms of the agreement between the members and the union are to be found in the rulebook, particularly as respects the discretion conferred by the members on committees or officials.

This astonishing statement (relying on the *Heatons* case: p. 54) was used to support the conclusion that SOGAT was bound by *implied* contract with the member to indemnify him (without application) for legal costs, a contract that both parties denied but the employers were happy to enforce by way of a receiver. This decision too could not have been reached in the days of s. 4 of the 1871 Act. It is an approach that could have serious implications, complementing as it does a new statutory tendency to put into the contract of membership unspecified 'written provisions' *outside* the rule-book: EA 1982 s. 15 (7) (though that speaks of the contract between 'a member and the other members', apparently omitting the contract between members and union made by virtue of TULRA s. 2 (1) (a)). Significantly, Lawton LJ emphasized the area of discretion of officials or committees 'as to the way in which they may act on the members' behalf'. It is in just this area where, under the *Heatons* test of 'implied authority' (or now EA 1982 s. 15 (3) (b)), the court's creativity could expand a union's liability in tort, just as it was expanded in contract in *Bourne's* case. So the policies of the courts and of the legislature move in the same direction. What the court did here was construct a new contract between the member and his union, and compel him to enforce it at the behest of the employers in their favour. The policy was to ensure payment to the employers, and their lawyers, of the costs in the action they had won. Questions must remain about the legal reasoning – and use of the receivership – by which this policy was fulfilled.

The Court of Appeal also took comfort from the fact that the *objects* in the union's rules included one 'To provide legal advice to members for themselves, their wives and children'. This showed, it said, that the promise of indemnity that – to its surprise – the union was held to have given the member was not therefore *ultra vires*. This raises a different and important question: the doctrine of *ultra vires*. The words mean acts that are 'beyond the powers' of an organization. We now consider the relationship of this doctrine to the democratic concept (which the law in principle supports) that decisions in any association are normally to be taken by the majority of its members.

Ultra vires and majority rule under the contract

Where a body is set up by or under a statute, its legal powers and capacities (its *vires*) are determined by reference to the relevant legislation. If it does acts that fall outside those legal capacities (*ultra vires*) they are in law void. Where a body is allowed to register for *any* lawful purposes, like a registered company under the Companies Acts, it has the capacity to do any acts within 'the purposes of its incorporation as defined in the objects clause, which have to be set out in its memorandum of association'.[36] If such a company engages in a business outside its registered objects, the transactions are a nullity, for it has no legal capacity to enter into them. This doctrine applies to all corporate bodies (with the odd exception for historical reasons of a corporation formed by Royal Charter). But where an organization is only an unincorporated association 'the doctrine of *ultra vires*', as Lord Denning has said, 'has no place'. There is no separate corporate body; so an act outside the purposes in the rules is just a breach of contract with the other members. 'Breach of contract is one thing,' an Australian judge once put it, 'but *ultra vires* or incapacity is another and quite different thing.'[37]

Where then do trade unions stand? After the *Taff Vale* case in 1901, courts applied the *ultra vires* doctrine to what they had come to see as 'quasi-corporate' registered trade unions. In *Yorkshire Miners' Association* v. *Howden*, 1905,[38] miners who had gone on unofficial strike in a dispute about payments for 'bag-dirt' were subsequently granted strike pay by the union. A member challenged the legitimacy of these payments because the rules allowed for strike benefit only where the union had previously sanctioned the strike or when members were thrown out of employment. The union believed the members now to be locked out. But the judges treated these payments as 'beyond the powers of the association' and therefore void and invalid. The case illustrates the way that any member (or in the case of a company, any shareholder) can challenge an *ultra vires* transaction. Similarly, in *Martin* v. *Scottish*

TGWU, 1952,[39] a worker wanted to join the union during the war; he was accepted as a temporary member 'for the duration of the war'. But the union had no rules providing for the admission of members on a temporary basis. The transaction was *ultra vires* and void. Nor could it be ratified by a vote of the membership; for it is a mark of this doctrine that, since the body has no legal *capacity* to do the act in question, that capacity cannot be made valid by ratification on the part of the members. It must change its objects to gain legal capacity to do the act in the future. In 1951 the electricians' union gave funds to members on unofficial strike, which was not allowed by the rules; it was held that dissentient members

were entitled to a declaration that it was *ultra vires* the union for any payment to be made out of their funds in furtherance of a strike not authorised under . . . the rules of the Union.

We must here make a cautious distinction. Sometimes the phrase *ultra vires* is used in a rather different sense to mean acts that the law *forbids* the association in question to do. Companies, for example, are sometimes said to act *ultra vires* if they pay dividends outside those which company law allows. But there the point is that the act is something the association can never lawfully do, whereas in a case of 'true' *ultra vires* it may be able to alter its objects so as to acquire capacity to do such an act in the future. Thus when in *Thomas* v. *NUM (South Wales Area)*[40] Scott J. spoke of its being '*ultra vires* for a union, or indeed any company, deliberately to embark on a series of criminal acts' (p. 727) he was using the words in this second sense – a rather confusing sense, but one often employed. No objects clauses in the rules could ever give an association legal authority to do criminal acts. But that is why he was cautious about extending this version of the principle to a series of tortious acts, and also refused to extend it to conduct that merely carries a 'risk that criminal offences might be committed'. Still less would he regard a series of acts by a union or a company 'which carried the risk that torts might be committed' as *ultra vires*. This was a risk that 'a large number of companies' regularly take 'open-eyed and frequently'.

An example of *illegality* of this kind arose in *Byrne* v. *Foulkes*[41] where the losing candidate in the election for Secretary of the electricians' union proved a conspiracy by defendants, members of the Communist Party who controlled the union, to rig the elections. It was, as counsel called it, 'the biggest fraud in the history of British trade unionism', the only one in modern times (others have been alleged but none so far proved). An important illustration of the application of *ultra vires* in this sense of illegality concerns payment by a union of the fines of members who have been convicted of offences, e.g. on a picket line. Whether the union has capacity to pay such moneys to members, i.e. *ultra vires* in the true sense, is determined by the objects found in the rules. But it is unlawful (or *ultra vires* in the other, confusing sense) for a union, whatever its objects clauses may say, to promise to indemnify members' crimes *in advance*. Payments as specific reimbursements made in respect of past offences may be lawful. This was applied in 1985 to invalidate a resolution stating that 'subsequent fines will be paid by the NUM (South Wales)'; but the judge accepted that the union had power within its objects to take the lawful course of paying members' fines after the event, so long at any rate as this did not crystallize into a promise to go on doing so and indemnify crimes in the future.[42]

There is, though, one further problem. A registered company sets out its 'objects', usually at great length, in its 'objects clause' in its registered memorandum of association. But the rule-books of trade unions, although they do normally have a rule headed 'objects', are not required to set the objects out in one part of the rules (or, indeed, at all now; the 1871 Act required it of registered unions). In consequence, courts can look at the statement of objects and the other rules to see, as one judge said in 1900, 'what the real object and scope of the association is'. Even so, not every breach of rules is *ultra vires*, nor is every 'object' a rule enforceable by members. The union may have the power to enter a transaction but break one of its rules, as it were, incidentally. Where the TSSA had a rule requiring the union 'to improve the conditions and protect the interests of its members', a member was not allowed to sue the union in reliance upon it where he alleged that the union's officials had not properly pursued his interests in a dispute with the employers. The court will not hear every dispute or squabble internal to the union; what was relied on here belonged to the objects, in the sense of the 'overall aims', not to the obligatory 'rules' of the union, which created rights for its members.[43] In *Bourne* v. *Colodense Ltd* a further defect in the court's judgment was its reliance upon the 'objects' rule of SOGAT. This was a failure to make the basic distinction.

A union can change its rules, including its objects rules, so long as this is allowed by the rules themselves. The 'alteration-of-rules rule' invariably requires a special majority or a resolution at a special conference. The court will view such rules strictly and invalidate a new rule if its adoption has not followed the precise procedure required. Where union rules for the alteration of rules required a two-thirds majority 'at a general meeting', but the rules permitted the council to conduct a vote of all members 'on any question' *and* gave 100 members the right on petition to have all members vote on any resolution at a general meeting (setting up a seemingly endless circle of repetitive procedures), the House of Lords leaned in favour of regarding a vote of the entire membership called by the council as the definitive procedure. The Law Lords did not go outside the rules for their interpretation, stating that the same 'canons of construction' should be applied to the rules as are 'applied to any written documents'.[44]

A discriminating interpretation of the rules of the seamen's union was made by Scott J. during the miners' strike. One union object was the promotion of the adoption of trade union principles. A special meeting could raise funds by levy for any lawful object up to certain limits. The NEC had power to make all necessary by-laws that were binding until the next general meeting, where power lay to alter the rules. A general meeting in 1984 expressed support for the NUM in its dispute. The NEC approved payments to the NUM in September and passed a by-law to impose a levy on members for six months for further funds to support the miners. A member sought a declaration and injunctions to stop the levies and the payments. The judge held that the power to make by-laws did not include a power to make levies; they were therefore *ultra vires*. The payments, however, were different. The strike called by the NUM had not been shown to be unlawful or illegal in any sense other than that it was in breach of the NUM rules. The NUS could support it out of *its* general fund so long as payment was within *its* objects, as this was. But the NUM's funds were now sequestrated, so that it was 'difficult to see how in those circumstances a payment out of' NUS funds to the NUM 'could be said to be a payment in pursuit of the objects' of the NUS.[45]

The rules of the union, then, are a contract, setting out the capacities of the union, its government and constitutional procedures, and the rights and obligations of members. Today, after the extinction of s. 4 of the 1871 Act, the member can sue for a breach of the rules as a breach of contract. He can, in a case where the breach has caused him loss, claim damages (for example for wrongful expulsion) to put him in as good a position, so far as money can do it, as if he had never been excluded from the union, taking into account, of course, all the contingencies . . . and remembering, too, that it was his duty to do what was reasonable to mitigate the damage.[46]

We saw in the miners' cases that a member can obtain an injunction to prevent a breach of rule, sometimes even a mandatory injunction ordering the union to take action to cure a breach, and may obtain in interlocutory proceedings both those remedies and, now, even a receivership and exceptionally a final declaration of rights. There is more to be said, though, about all this – and about *ultra vires*. For this we must look at a further legal principle.

Majority rule and minority complaints

Because of the ever spreading scope of the formidable remedies that may be granted by the court, especially those granted on the basis of an 'arguable case' and 'balance of convenience' on interlocutory motion, it is of some importance to clarify the occasions on which a member is *not* permitted to bring a legal action for a breach of the rules. Here many of the recent miners' cases are no safe guide because the defendant unions or officials did not present any argument to the court, either at all or at a sufficiently early stage, so that the points of law often went by default (in our system of adversary justice the judge cannot be expected to decide every point in the absence of one party). This was the case, for example, in *Taylor and Foulstone* v. *NUM (Yorkshire Area)*,[21] in *Clarke* v. *Heathfield*[24] and in some of the actions in other Areas.[19] (This is no criticism, simply a fact; no doubt the points will be argued if any of these cases go to 'full trial'.) Where then does the limitation lie? The boundary of the member's standing to sue is set by a principle carrying the Dickensian title 'the rule in *Foss* v. *Harbottle*', a judgment of 1843. Once again it is in large measure a company law principle, but one applied by the judges to any association with power to sue in its own name. It was therefore applied to registered (though not unregistered)[47] unions after the *Taff Vale* case, 1901, and applies today to all unions (TULRA s. 2 (1) (a): p. 530).

The courts in the nineteenth century realized that if every member could sue for every wrong done in, or to, an association, litigation would be endless. In any event, the minority must accept that the majority ultimately governs the association, not the court. They therefore brought together two earlier principles. First, the 'procedural irregularity' principle: where there is a mere internal, procedural 'irregularity' it is for the majority to set it right. Secondly, the 'proper plaintiff' principle: where a wrong has been done to the association it is for the association to sue, not the minority member, and for the majority to decide when it will sue and when not. These made up the two prongs of the 'rule in *Foss* v. *Harbottle*'. It is 'founded on principle but it also operates fairly by preserving the rights of the majority'.[48] As Russell L J said in 1929, the rule in its two prongs

really works by means of something in the nature of a dilemma. The only possible plaintiff to stop an *intra vires* act is the corporation itself. If an individual is in a position to be able to use the name of the corporation then the majority are in agreement with him. If he is not in a position to use that name, then the majority are in disagreement with him and he is not entitled to bring an action in his own name.

There are three situations where the rule plainly cannot apply or must be ousted. They concern (1) acts that are *ultra vires* (for here the majority cannot 'ratify' or approve what has been done); or (2) other cases where a simple majority cannot confirm the transaction, as where it invades the individual and personal rights of a member; or (3) where there is 'fraud' by those in control of the association (when the rule is 'relaxed in favour of the aggrieved minority', who may bring 'a derivative action on behalf of themselves and all others'). Because in these three situations the majority cannot ratify, the minority member can sue.

These principles were set out in the classic judgment of Jenkins L J in *Edwards* v. *Halliwell*, 1950.[49] There two union members challenged an alteration in contribution rates, which had been changed at a delegate conference when the rule-book stated that such changes needed a two-thirds majority on a ballot of members. Such a step, said Jenkins L J,

invaded the individual rights of the complainant members, who are entitled to maintain themselves in full membership . . . until the scale of contributions is validly altered by the prescribed majority obtained on a ballot vote.

The rule in *Foss* v. *Harbottle* had 'no application at all' to their personal rights, which the court would support by a declaration. But a breach of the rules will not give a minority member such a 'personal right' to sue if the court regards the error as a mere procedural irregularity. Even if, for example, there have been breaches of the rules through mistakes made in union elections, as in *Brown* v. *AUEW*, 1976,[50] when 600 out of 29,000 members were disfranchised through postal ballot errors, the court will not entertain an action by a minority if the irregularity is such that the election was 'conducted substantially in accordance with the . . . rules'. (We may contrast the lack of any such rule in the Act of 1984: p. 628.) Members in 1919 were not allowed to pursue complaints of breaches of rules in convening delegates to a union meeting that decided by a large majority not to join the 'London Whitley scheme'. Petersen J. said: 'This was not *ultra vires* . . . if it was passed irregularly it might be ratified by a subsequent resolution . . . simply a question of the internal management of the union.'[51] In a strong application of the principle, Goff J. in 1966 refused a member an injunction where a union council proposed to cast its votes at a TUC Congress contrary to the union's conference resolutions, which were binding under the rules. On the other hand, as we shall see, a failure to follow proper procedures when the member's personal membership is at stake (as in expulsion) is not 'a mere irregularity in procedure' but naturally a breach on which he can sue.[52]

Most of those decisions concerned the 'irregularity' principle. In *Cotter* v. *National Union of Seamen*, 1929,[53] they joined with the other prong, the 'proper plaintiff' principle. The Court of Appeal faced a member's complaints about a union loan of £10,000 to the 'miners' non-Political Movement'. The court found this was not *ultra vires*; one object in the rules allowed funds to be used to extend the adoption of trade union principles. But the plaintiff had a string of other complaints: delegates to the special meeting had been elected not by districts, as the rules demanded, but by branches; inadequate notice had been given; the meetings of the executive council had been irregularly called. The President, it was said, had a personal interest in the loan; and the breaches of rules and defects in procedure would make it a 'breach of trust' for the officers to pay out the money. The Court of Appeal rejected the motion for an injunction, on the basis of the rule in *Foss* v. *Harbottle*. The 'irregularities' affected 'internal management of the union, which could be regularised by the majority of members'. The plaintiff claimed that more was at stake, saying he had a personal right to stop this money being improperly expended in a breach of trust. But the judges held that this supposed 'individual right' of a member to sue for breach of fiduciary duty in disposing of union money (even if all the allegations were true) went too far. The loan was an *intra vires* act, 'which could be sanctioned by the majority'. Any such wrong was done to the *association*, for which action must be brought by *it*, with the support of the majority, not by a minority.

This aspect of the principle is well known in company law. If a director breaks the 'fiduciary duty' that he owed to the company (the duty of loyalty, or duty not to make a 'secret profit' from his office, for example), the right of action is in the *company*, not each and every shareholder. This is why the company, acting through the ordinary majority of shareholders' votes in general meeting, can grant him what Harman LJ called in 1970 'absolution of his sins'. The right to sue, Upjohn LJ said in 1963, is a sword in the company's hands; but 'it may sheathe the weapon'. Where the wrongdoing is so bad that it amounts to a fraudulent misappropriation of the company's assets by those in control of it, the courts will exceptionally allow the minority to sue in an action on behalf of all the shareholders (a 'derivative action') to enforce what are, in effect, the company's rights against the wrongdoers (it should be done normally by a 'representative writ', and the exception is strictly limited).[48] All this applies to trade unions.

In the miners' cases, minority members did not encounter many of these difficulties, especially if the court held the breach of union rule to be *ultra vires*, either in the true sense or in the sense of general 'illegality'. Each member then had a personal right to sue. In the circumstances of the *Thomas* case Scott J. pointed out that there was no need of a 'derivative action'; the plaintiffs were not seeking to enforce the union's rights and recover money or damages 'for a wrong done to the South Wales Union'. Each member had a right to sue 'on his own behalf to restrain *ultra vires* activity'. Other actions were started, however, alleging breach of fiduciary duty against *individual* members of the Executive Committee of the NUM and of certain Area unions. The fate of such actions is uncertain; but if they alleged ratifiable breaches of fiduciary duty, they appeared to be doomed to failure under the rule in *Foss* v. *Harbottle*. If this were not so, each member might be entitled to sue all the members of the NUM Executive Committee personally, and some 5 million writs might be unleashed on the same matter. This obviously could not be allowed. In one such action the plaintiff was reported to have argued that the action was brought *both* in a personal capacity *and* in a representative capacity as a 'derivative action'. Had these cases gone to trial they would have involved much greater procedural complexity than the interim, reported decisions of 1984–5.

For it was not clear which of the miners' legal actions, where liability was established for breach of contract in the absence of appearance by the defendant unions, would have been affected by the *Foss* v. *Harbottle* argument. Some or all the plaintiffs in, say, the *Yorkshire* or *Midlands Area* cases might have encountered difficulty because some of the breaches of union rules alleged by them might have been shown by the defendants to be arguably either an 'internal irregularity' or a 'wrong done to the union', and therefore within the rule in *Foss* v. *Harbottle*. Many judgments, however, have held that expenditure of union assets upon strikes otherwise than in accordance with the union rules is *ultra vires* (in the true sense). The *Yorkshire Miners* case in 1905 held just that. When, therefore, in *Taylor* v. *N U M (Derbyshire Area)*, 1985,[54] it was shown that £1.7 million had been paid out of the Area union's funds on the strike, that the rules provided for the payment of money to members on an authorized strike, but that this strike (as an earlier interlocutory order of Nicholls J. had established) had not been properly authorized under the union rules, Vinelott J. held that the payments were *ultra vires*. But officers of a union, like directors of a company, are strictly liable to restore any funds misapplied *ultra vires*; and the rule in *Foss* v. *Harbottle* does not prohibit a suit by an individual member to enforce that liability.

This action was brought against three officers (President, Treasurer and Secretary) and the *Derbyshire Area* union. The plaintiffs added the union as a nominal defendant, as is usual in a 'derivative' action when the action is to recover money for the benefit of the union. (Counsel for the defence, though, claimed *he* was acting for the union as well as for the officers; but in view of the 'urgency' the judge let that pass.) Moreover, this was an action for 'summary judgment', a claim that there was no possible defence and therefore the defendants should be found liable at once (i.e. the three officers should pay £1.7 million of union funds expended). The judge could see no defence. The misapplication of funds was *ultra vires*; and this 'cannot be ratified by any majority of members however large'. Yet in his discretion he refused summary judgment. There was perhaps a way out. There was evidence that the 'majority of members approves the expenditure' (for despite the loss of the early ballot the great majority of miners in the Area were still out on strike). A majority might in the future take the view that it was not in the interests of the union to make these officers 'personally liable'. There was no immediate advantage in bankrupting them; some 'machinery' might be found whereby the members would prevent them being made personally liable.

The common sense of this decision of the judge in December 1984 was manifest. No judge could have thought, nine months into the strike, that much good would come of the bailiffs or the Queen's Remembrancer trying to seize £1 million from the homes of three Derbyshire union officials. But the reasoning behind it did leave the law in a very odd state. The decision meant (1) that where officials misapply funds *ultra vires* they are liable to restore them, and a majority of members cannot absolve them by ratifying their acts, and therefore a single member can sue; but (2) that the majority may decide not to make them personally liable – in effect, decide not to sue them. Then the single member cannot get his judgment; or at any rate not summary judgment. The incongruity of those propositions suggested that something had gone wrong.

One factor had, indeed, been overlooked in all the cases since 1974: the *principle* of 'Taff Vale' had been repealed in 1974. The *Taff Vale* case, 1901, had caused the judges to treat a union registered under the 1871 Act as a 'quasi-corporation'. It was therefore natural and logical to treat it as a body to which the *ultra vires* principle applied. So it was in the *Yorkshire Miners* case, 1905, and in *Edwards* v. *Halliwell*, 1950. Upjohn LJ spelt out the position under the old register in 1963: 'Trade unions share one attribute with true corporations; they are subject to the rule of *ultra vires*.' As Vinelott J. significantly said in 1985, the registered union was 'treated as analogous to a company' in this regard.

But in 1974 the legal status of a union was not restored to precisely the same status as the registered union under the 1871 Act. All registers were abolished, leaving only the 'list'. And in TULRA, except for the five specific corporate incidents (including the capacity to sue or to be sued, which is enough to bring the association generally within the rule in *Foss* v. *Harbottle*), it was enacted that a union 'shall not be, *or be treated as if it were*, a body corporate' (TULRA 1974 s. 2 (1)). We have seen how because of this a judge in 1980 rejected the plea that a union had, like a company, its own reputation, sufficient to sue in defamation (as the old registered union had). After 1974 this would be to treat it as a 'body corporate' and could not be allowed.[55] So the 'analogy with a company' cannot any longer be permissible. The doctrine of *ultra vires* – which is the characteristic mark of a body corporate or 'quasi-corporate' – does not and cannot on this reasoning apply to modern trade unions at all.[56] A member is still able to sue on his personal rights for a breach of contract constituted by a breach of the rules. But this is a very different thing from breaches that go on to be *ultra vires*. There is normally no difficulty about the majority of members 'ratifying' what has been done by way of breach of contract and absolving those who have broken the contract of association from their sins. The body corporate cannot do this when it falls within the *ultra vires* rule. An unincorporated association can, because the rule does not apply to it. After 1974 a trade union must be treated as an unincorporated association (save only for the five exceptions: capacity to sue, be a beneficiary, contract, suffer prosecution and suffer execution or punishment). So T U L R A seems to rule out *ultra vires* as far as trade unions are concerned. On reflection, this appeared to be the true principle that ought to lie behind the difficulties in the *Taylor* judgment. But the judicial habit of applying the doctrine to unions is likely to die hard. It is done frequently. Even so, the proper logic of T U L R A seems to be the exclusion of *ultra vires* from trade union law.

Like other judges, Vinelott J. in *Taylor's* case, 1985, saw the union officials as owing 'their fiduciary duty *to the union*'. Indeed, it was the nub of the plaintiff's claim that they were relying 'on an alleged breach of fiduciary duty by the officers of the union to *it*'. This is the usual analysis, parallel to the position of the trustees who hold the property for and owe their duties to 'the union' according to the majority of judgments. In *Clarke* v. *Heathfield*, 1985, the action against the N U M trustees themselves, Stephenson LJ spoke of 'all the members of the union as beneficiaries'. But T U L R A 1974 makes it clear that 'the union' is the primary beneficiary, to which the trustees must therefore owe their primary duties (s. 2 (1) (b)). This does not prevent the union members having an enforceable interest in the funds, an 'indirect beneficial' interest, as Vinelott put it in *Taylor's* case. This analysis makes sense of the cases on majority rule, and was the view of the Court of Appeal in *Cotter* v. *N U S*, 1929.[57] The suggestion by Lord Denning, therefore, in 1963 that the officials of a union are in a direct 'fiduciary position towards the *members'* cannot now be accurate. They owe their duties to and through the union (which has the capacity to be the beneficiary of such proprietary rights, and to sue, from TULRA 1974 s. 2 (1)). The position is different where trustees hold for members (and ex-members) of the union who are direct or ultimate beneficiaries of a fund. In *Cowan* v. *Scargill*, 1984,[58] the trustees of the miners' pension fund may have been in that position. The five NUM nominees resigned after Megarry J. stopped them insisting upon an investment policy for the fund aimed at British industry and the benefit of the coal industry, rather than accept conventional financial advice for maximizing returns. In 1985 their places were filled by the court by five persons who were to be 'deemed to be the nominees of the union'.

Trade unions and political activities

In 1910 the House of Lords applied yet another form of *ultra vires* to trade unions. This – quite different – doctrine is sometimes known as '*ultra vires* the statute'. It came about because the support for parliamentary candidates that unions gave in the nineteenth century to Liberals or Independents moved decisively in the first decade of this century to support for, and active participation within, the new Labour Party. It was generally believed to be lawful for unions to give such support and spend funds upon it; and a judge declared it to be so in 1907. But in the *Osborne* case, 1910,[59] when a member of the railwaymen's union challenged his union's compulsory levy to be used in support of the Labour Party, the Law Lords pronounced it invalid and *ultra vires*. They did not however apply the 'true' *ultra vires* doctrine applied in the *Yorkshire Miners* case, 1905 (p. 748), testing the political activity against the objects in the union's rules. All the Law Lords except one tested it against the definition of a 'trade union' in the Trade Union Acts 1871–6. The unions, said Lord Atkinson, were 'quasi-corporations' defined by statute: 'A definition which permitted all things not in themselves illegal would be no definition at all and would serve no purpose at all.' The Act's objects did not include expenditure 'to subsidise . . . a scheme of parliamentary representation' within its definition.

There are occasions when a test similar to this can be used, for instance when a statute sets up a body and defines its powers, such as the legislation creating the National Coal Board. The Trade Union Acts were not of this kind; they provided, like the Companies Acts, for bodies that would (as the 1871 Act said registered unions must) define their *own* lawful 'objects' in the rules. The judgments showed not only that the Law Lords wished to treat the unions as quasi-corporate, but also that they were determined to confine these dangerous and only recently illegal associations. The aged Earl of Halsbury declared of the 1871 Act: 'it can hardly be suggested that it legalises a combination for anything'. The Scottish courts then applied the same reasoning to political activity for municipal representation.

No more explosive decision could have been delivered in 1910 at a time when the pressure for 'direct' militant action was beginning to grow stronger inside some trade unions. An MP did not then receive a salary, and sixteen Labour Members lost their only income as a result of the *Osborne* judgment. Kahn-Freund believed that the reasons for the decision are 'today of purely historical interest' and that, while the decision was 'incompatible with democratic principles', the 'restoration of an unqualified power' in trade union rules to demand contributions for political activity would also be objectionable.[60] Yet the trade union is the *only* association or body to which this principle on political expenditure has been applied in Britain. Its special position in the legal system rests still upon the fallacious reasoning in this judgment, which, the Webbs wrote, resting on the current 'animus and prejudice' against trade unions, was greeted with 'undisguised glee' by the 'governing class' and lawyers who still resented the passing of the Act of 1906. As to trade unions and 'politics', they wrote: 'There is not a day passes but something in Parliament demands its attention. On this point Trade Union opinion is unanimous.'[61]

The effect was to debilitate the new Labour Party in the elections of 1910; for all political levies, whether or not a union's rules made them compulsory (as in the *Osborne* case), were made illicit by the judgment. Many other union activities not explicitly mentioned in the 1871–6 definition also seemed to be rendered of doubtful legality, such as educational work or mutual insurance of members. The result of the outcry that followed the House of Lords decision was eventually the Trade Union Act 1913, 'a fragile settlement' of the issue, as Ewing has rightly called it.[62] The Act restored to the unions the normal ('true') doctrine of *ultra vires*, subject to new rules about political expenditure. The true doctrine of legal capacity and *ultra vires* now applies to unions by virtue of TULRA s. 28 (1). Since 1913 trade unions have been allowed lawfully to pursue any activity within their stated objects except for the application of funds directly or indirectly 'in the furtherance of political objects' within the statutory definition. If it applies funds for 'political' purposes, the 1913 Act provides that the union must (1) adopt by ballot political rules approved (now) by the CO (originally the Registrar) to establish a political fund, and (2) provide for the exemption from any obligation to contribute to that fund of any member who gives notice that he wishes to 'contract out' of it. The rules for the fund must also be approved by the CO.

The Act of 1913

This close network of control maintained the gap between the liberty of unions and of other associations; and so it has remained. It is widely assumed that the sums given by public companies to the Conservative Party (which must normally be disclosed but which the law does not regulate by enforcing rights for shareholders or customers to contract out) is expenditure within their express or implied powers and objects (though this view has been challenged, and a judgment of 1983 making gifts from the League Against Cruel Sports to the Labour Party *ultra vires* that body, a company limited by guarantee, created renewed interest in the point).[63] In the 1983 election year it has been estimated that some £2.7 millions went as gifts from companies to the Conservative Party, £0.5 million to bodies politically sympathetic with it, and £32,000 to the Liberal–SDP Alliance. The *total* funds of the fifty-eight unions then having political funds were £6.6 millions. Since the Companies Act 1967 s. 19 (Companies Act 1985, Sched. 7), companies have been obliged to disclose their political donations in an annual period, but that is all. The Hansard Society, whilst recognizing that this creates inequality in the electoral system, has failed to find evidence that company donations necessarily influence Government policy. Others have proposed a code of conduct whereby companies would inform shareholders in advance about political donations (some, though few, do so).[64] The issue here leaves the realm of labour law. The debate, one of great difficulty, is about the right way to finance political parties in a democracy. But within labour law trade unions today are the only bodies regulated as to political activity. The matter might be thought, therefore, to require special sensitivity on the part of any administration in government formed by a party to which trade unions do not normally give material support, to avoid any impression that it is trying to starve out its Opposition.

A further point concerns 'contracting out'. The 1913 Act demanded that the member be given the right, of which he must be given notice, to contract out of the levy to the political fund and that by contracting out a member shall not be excluded from any benefits, or otherwise put under any disability or disadvantage, 'except in relation to the control or management of the political fund'. Nor may contribution to the fund be made a condition of membership (TUA 1913 s. 3). A drastic change was made in this compromise structure in 1927, when 'contracting in' was substituted for contracting out (that is, only members who *gave* notice paid the political contribution), but contracting out was restored in 1946. The latter arrangement gives the political fund the advantage of human apathy (the contributions to political funds rose from 38 per cent of members in TUC unions in 1945 to 60 per cent in 1948); but the Donovan Report, after close consideration of the arguments, strongly rejected proposals that the contracting-in system should be reintroduced. As Ewing shows, no studies have disclosed evidence of a significant scale that members fail to contract out 'through force or fear'. Indeed, the courts are vigilant to protect exemption for them.

In *Reeves's* case, 1980,[65] a problem had arisen from the employer's computerized pay-roll and the check-off of union subscriptions. Reeves complained to the CO (who hears complaints under the 1913 Act). He had contracted out, but the union contribution was still deducted, which included 8p in the first week of each quarter as a political contribution. The employers said they could not adjust the computer programme to deduct 32/52nds of a penny less each week from his wage than from other workers. The union had tried to refund Reeves in advance, not always successfully; and he objected, anyway, because to have any of his money deducted at all was a 'disadvantage' to him. The CO substantially accepted the argument; but on appeal (permitted on points of law after 1975; now EPCA s. 136 (2)) the EAT accepted that the wording of the 1913 Act allowed a refund, even a refund in arrears, but only where it was not possible to pay it in advance and as soon as possible afterwards. Although a liberal interpretation in some respects (the court said 'disadvantage' meant one of substance) the litigation proved how careful union administrators must be in dealing with exempt members, even where it is the employer's computer that is really in control. The Act of 1984 introduced a new procedure whereby a contracted-out member can certify the fact to his employer, who thereupon must not deduct any political contribution under a check-off of union dues, but must not otherwise deny the check-off to that employee if it is used for the other union members (TUA 1984 s. 18).

In its Green Paper of 1983 the Government had also raised the issue of 'contracting in' once more ('those who wish to make a political contribution should be required to take a positive decision to do so'). In the passage of the Trade Union Act 1984, to which we return below, an amendment to restore contracting in was heavily defeated in the House of Commons, and the Government held discussions on the matter with the TUC. These resulted in the Government agreeing not to take this step and the TUC issuing a 'Statement of Guidance' re-emphasizing to unions the importance of members' rights to contract out, the importance of full information for members and of clear and detailed annual returns to the CO.[66] This guide to 'good trade union practice' was accepted 'as an alternative to legislation'. But the Government later made it clear that it still had the matter in mind; Ministers spoke of reconsidering 'contracting in'; and in 1986 Mr Bottomley, a junior Employment Minister, said he was 'not satisfied that all trade union members are being made aware of their rights to contract out'. The Government's reaction was not entirely unconnected with the results of 1985 ballots, to which we come shortly.

Statutory 'political objects'

The third issue arising from the 1913 Act concerns the definition of statutory 'political' objects. The 1913 definition was a limited one: broadly, the expenditure of money on expenses or maintenance of candidates for, and Members of, Parliament (and the equivalent in local government), in connection with the selection of such candidates or the registration of voters, or on holding 'political meetings' or distribution of 'political literature' unless the main purpose was furtherance of the 'statutory' (roughly meaning *industrial*) objects of a union (TUA 1913 s. 3 (3)). Thus trade unions could adopt wider political objects (several rule-books include an object for 'the furtherance of political objects of *any* kind'), in which case the 'political' expenditure on activities of a kind not within s. 3 (3) can be financed from the union's general fund. So, in *Coleman's* case, a contribution to a district trades council 'campaign against the cuts' (by 'any Government of whatever party', leading to inadequate public services) was placed by the CO in the area outside the statutory definition. It may have been political; but it was not within the *statutory* meaning of 'political'. There the word 'political' meant 'party political', as the Registrar had held in 1925, the adjectival form of 'party politics', not of 'polity'.[67] So too, a lobby of Parliament by miners against pit closures has a 'political objective, at the same time it is clearly an industrial objective', said a Scottish judge in 1965:

In one sense any dispute between employer and employee in a nationalised industry takes on the complexion of a political dispute, since the employer is in some sense the State, which is a political body. . . . [but] This, in my view, is a fundamentally industrial demonstration.[68]

In general, moneys in the general fund cannot be transferred to the political fund (nor after the 1984 Act can it be used to discharge any liability for that fund – a loan or overdraft, for example: TUA 1984 s. 14 (3)). Expenditure to help in the building of a new headquarters for the Labour (or any other) Party must come from the political fund, even though the investment was made at market rates on independent advice.[69]

It is here that the 1984 Act has drawn the net even more tightly by amending the statutory definition of 'political'. Parts of the amendments merely update the old s. 3 (3): candidates for, and Members of, the European Assembly are included, for example, alongside MPs. Certain areas are clarified, bringing in contributions to or for any service, or property for use by, or 'on behalf of', a political party. Contributions include 'loans'. But elsewhere the concept is clearly extended. Expenditure 'connected with' elections to 'political office' (including registration of voters, selection of candidates or candidatures) or maintenance of a holder of 'political office' is covered, and that now means not only MPs, MEPs or local councils, but also 'any position *within* a political party'. Thus any expenditure by a branch connected with a local Labour Party ward's elections (even *indirectly*) is included in TUA 1984 s. 17, substituting a new TUA 1913 s. 3 (3), although this will not include the 'ordinary administrative expenses' of a branch meeting discussing normal union business: new s. 3 (3B). Nor did the old definition appear to include groups *within* political parties discussing, say, the elections to the party leadership; but the new one seems to do so. More important, the definition now includes holding any meeting the 'main purpose' of which is transaction of business in connection with a political party. The insertion of the 'main purpose' test was a concession made by the Government in passing the TUA 1984. It may be said to bring this part of the new definition closer to that of the old, though there is no express exception, as in the old definition, for industrial 'statutory' objects. A meeting called to pursue a campaign against closure of a local plant jointly with local trades councils and local political parties might obviously be held to have a 'main purpose' of transacting business *in connection with* those parties. Finally, there is included the production or distribution of literature, films, recordings or advertisements the 'main purpose' of which is 'to persuade people to vote for a political party or candidate or to persuade them not to vote for a political party or candidate' (new s. 3 (3) (f), inserted by TUA 1984 s. 17).

In debates on this clause, the 1983 campaign by NALGO (which had no political fund) against public expenditure cuts was often mentioned. Such a campaign would appear to be included in the new definition, which includes persuasion to vote or not to vote for any candidate, or any of the candidates of the political parties (for example, the Green Party). Although the 'main purpose' test was eventually inserted here too, *Cleminson's* case might well be differently decided now, putting unions at a disadvantage compared with campaigns mounted by 'organizations which have complete freedom to promote cuts and privatization'.[70] One reaction to the developments was for more unions to adopt a political fund, like the hosiery workers in 1986. Even Civil Service unions moved in this direction (an overwhelming majority voted for a fund in the Inland Revenue staff union). The Government criticized these unions for compromising their 'neutrality'. In one sense it was of course true that the adoption of political funds by Civil Service unions would testify to the crisis of concepts and frailty of the conventional line between the 'political' and the 'social'.

In general, the new definition strengthens the demand for expenditure concerning most types of controversy on public or social issues to be financed out of a union's political fund. If, therefore, the union has a tradition of not having such a fund, as with NALGO and Civil Service unions, its ability to engage in such public debate must be somewhat weakened after the 1984 Act not only in contrast to companies and such organizations as the Freedom Association, but even compared with, say, the Police Federation, which does not happen to be categorized as a 'trade union'. The view of the Conservative Government when the Act came into force was different. Ministers insisted that the ballots were about whether unions would engage in 'party politics'. Secretary of State King said that

campaigns on matters like jobs, health and safety and other issues affecting the members' interests may certainly be financed from unions' general funds provided that their main purpose is not to persuade people to vote in a particular way.

Most unions put the matter rather differently to their members, stressing that the issue was not merely direct affiliation to the Labour Party (much of the political fund is always spent on other activities) but whether the union was to have the *right* to engage in campaigns on all social issues, including anything defined as 'political' merely because it entailed criticism of a party whether it was in government or not.

Political fund ballots

This made even more important the second major innovation in the 1984 Act. Under the 1913 Act a union was obliged to adopt political objects by a fair ballot. But the 1984 Act requires that the political fund be validated by regular ballots with at most ten-year intervals. But where a political fund resolution had been approved more than nine years before this part of the Act came into effect (March 1985) it was deemed to have been passed nine years before that date (TUA 1984 s. 12 (3)). Most unions with political funds adopted them more than nine years before 1985. The same rule was applied to unions that had amalgamated within the nine-year period; their political fund resolution was the date of the earliest adoption by any of them (s. 12 (5)). This made 1985–6 a critical twelve months for union political funds.

These ballots are supervised by the CO, as under the 1913 Act, but more closely than the 1913 law, which demanded a fair ballot and largely left it to the Registrar to ensure that this happened. For example, all members must be given an equal entitlement to vote, whether employed or not (only 'overseas' members can be excluded, but here that includes Northern Ireland: s. 13 (2), (7)). The Furniture Trades union in 1985 issued ballot papers to non-paying retired members in order to be safe under the Act, a step that caused questions as to whether these persons really were still 'members'. There must be no constraint or interference by the union or its officials (once again, constraint by employers is remarkably left out); and so far as reasonably practicable, the member must be enabled to vote in secret, without direct cost to himself, have a ballot paper supplied or available at a time and place proximate to his work, and be given a convenient opportunity to vote either by post or at his workplace or a choice of either: s. 13 (2). Recognized unions can require an employer to provide facilities for a ballot on the work premises (EA 1980 s. 2), and regulations of 1984 (No. 1654) permit a union that has a political fund to apply to the CO for State funds in regard to expenditure on such a ballot. But a union is not entitled to State finance if it is balloting members for the first time on a political fund, or in any other case where no resolution for one is in force (Reg. 6). This distinction belies the argument that the 1984 Act and the regulations are merely intended to ensure decadal democratic approval of such funds. For this purpose it would be equally important for government to offer funds to all unions, whether or not they have existing political fund rules. Before the money is paid, the CO must be satisfied about a long list of conditions, in particular that voting must be by post (payment is essentially for postal expenses, which limits the apparent options in the 1984 Act), and may pay only part of certain items (e.g. for first-class posting or costs of 'heavier quality' paper than is reasonable).

If a resolution is passed, the Act confirms that the only property that can go into the political fund is restricted to political contributions and assets from the fund's administration (dividends, etc.): s. 14. Borrowing from other funds appears to be prohibited; as we have seen, no other fund may be used to discharge the political fund's liability (s. 14 (3)). If a resolution is defeated in one of the ten-yearly ballots, no new property may be added (other than contributions already collected or income from administration). The defeat may lead to the retention of a fund in the hope of a favourable ballot later; or in limited circumstances some political expenditure may be continued for six months (s. 15 (1)). Alternatively, the fund may be wound up and transferred to other funds of the union (s. 14 (2)). On the loss of a ballot and consequent cessation of a resolution, it may be difficult to wind up some check-off arrangements quickly; if political contributions continue to be collected for such reasons, the members concerned may apply for payment of them; if they do not, the fund may pass to the general fund (s. 15 (3), (4)). The union must ensure that collection of such contributions ceases as soon as reasonably practicable, and any member (contracted out or not) may apply to the court for orders on that matter (s. 16). The contracted-out members are, however, protected in other ways. Nor does the cessation of the political fund and its rules destroy their right, under the 1913 Act, s. 3 (2), not to be excluded from benefit or subjected to a disability or disadvantage by reason of their exemption (other than in the management of the political fund); the CO retains jurisdiction while the rules exist.

Contracted-out members

The jurisdiction of the CO (and before him of the Registrar since 1913) may be reckoned one of the more successful informal jurisdictions in British labour law. Until 1971 the decision of the Registrar was final, with no appeal to the judges. Few complaints were ever made; and very few appeals have been taken to the EAT from the CO since 1975. The CO hears the member who is 'aggrieved' (he must be a member or the jurisdiction of the CO is lost) on account of an alleged 'disability' or 'disadvantage'. He has a discretion to make such order as he thinks just (TUA 1913 s. 3 (2)). For example, where he finds an unintentional breach but one that is being cured by an amendment to union rules, as with SOGAT in 1982, he may decide not to make any order. *Mr Double* complained in 1982 that as a contracted-out member of the EETPU he was not allowed to vote at his branch on a motion concerning the nomination of a candidate to a local Labour Party to which the branch was affiliated; but the CO held that this affected only his position in regard to management of the political fund, from which the affiliation fees and the right to nominate arose. But in *Birch's* case, 1950,[71] a member succeeded despite the Registrar's rejection of his case. As a contracted-out member, he was ineligible under the NUR rules for any office involving management of the political fund. He was removed from office as branch chairman when it was pointed out that branch officers controlled the fund. The Registrar held this was permissible. At that time Birch could not appeal to the EAT (it did not exist). Instead,

he sought a declaration from the High Court that the NUR political
fund rules themselves offended against the 1913 Act (even though
they had been approved by the Registrar when the fund was set
up). The judge agreed that they did offend, largely on the ground
that discrimination was allowed under the Act only in regard to
offices 'solely or mainly' concerned with the management of the
fund.

No doubt Birch would today appeal to the EAT from the CO's
decision that he was not 'aggrieved' in respect of an improper disadvantage. But this jurisdiction of the CO is based on a *breach* of the political
fund role (TUA 1913 s. 3 (2)). The member appears still to be able to
challenge the approval of those rules themselves by the CO himself
(under s. 3 (1)), by way of judicial review in the courts. The CO cannot
deal with alleged breaches of the general law. In *Reeves's* case, for
example, complaints could not be entertained about alleged breaches of
the Truck Act 1831. Nor has he powers over the disposition of the
political fund chosen by the union; a member who claims that his branch
may use the political funds of his branch to support the Conservative
Party will be heard in the High Court.[72] The issue is there the proper
interpretation of union rules. The 1913 Act does not prevent all forms of
political discrimination in a union. It could not help the baker who in
1935 was alleged to be a 'disruptive element' because of his connection
with the 'Bakers' Rank and File Movement'. The EETPU maintains a
ban on the eligibility of Communists and Fascists for office. But we shall
see that the 1984 Act makes some odd distinctions in this area in its new
regulation of elections to the NEC (p. 775).

Despite the occasional allegations of improper discrimination against
contracted-out members and other breaches of the 1913 Act, as Ewing
emphasizes, the number of complaints has never been large. This was
true at the outset (68 in 1913–21, 26 of which fell outside the jurisdiction) and later. More important, the number of 'formal hearings', the
best indicator of serious cases, is small. Between 1969 and 1984 there
were 232 complaints (76 from one workplace about one union in 1979),
but only 17 formal hearings were held by the Registrar or CO. Although
his procedures unfortunately do not include any great space for conciliation, reliance upon his discretion not to make an order has preserved
for the CO the benefits of informality constructed by his predecessor,
the Registrar.

Unions and political funds

Since the 1984 Act trade unions have treated the first ballots for decadal renewal of the political fund resolution as an issue for all members, not just those contracting in. The issue in both legal and social terms is whether a union shall have the right to engage, if it chooses, in the areas of social controversy now falling within the rather wider definition of 'political objects' under the 1984 Act. This, too, appeared to be the way in which many members perceived the question in 1985. By early 1986 members had voted to retain political funds in 38 unions, often by majorities larger than the percentage of contracted-out members; the hosiery workers and the Inland Revenue staff adopted a fund for the first time. Other unions in the Civil Service, including the CPSA, IPCS and CSU, were considering the same step.

Such developments raise the question anew, however, whether it is right that the law should require these special and (whoever pays) expensive measures of trade unions alone. Writers predicted that either by the operation of its 'agreement' with the TUC 'or by further legislation' the Government would ensure that a significantly smaller number of trade union members ended up paying the levy.[73] Companies are not regulated in this way. No other body of persons, associations or institutions in British life is so regulated, and in the absence of a sensible debate about the financing of the political processes of our democracy, none is likely to be. In any union it has always been open to members to pass a motion to terminate a fund as well as to establish one. Scandals and improprieties in unions proven by evidence rather than legend are few; machinery is more than adequate to meet them, including an appellate court that will (quite properly) spend two days of argument on whether a contracted-out member was justly dealt with concerning 32/52nds of a penny a week. One may ask why it is that the screw should be turned here on trade unions when it takes so many years to establish even 'self-regulatory' agencies in the City of London against the warnings of a respected adviser that action is urgently needed to prevent 'further serious scandals undermining public and international confidence',[74] for which the evidence is abundant. There is a more fundamental point. The ILO Committee of Experts noted in 1983:

It is increasingly apparent . . . that a trade union's activities cannot be restricted solely to occupational questions, since the choice of a general policy – in economic affairs for example – is bound to have consequences on the situation of workers . . . trade unions must be able to devote attention to matters of general interest – i.e. 'political' in the broadest sense of the word – and . . . they must be able to express their views publicly on government economic and social policy.

Political links should not 'compromise the continuance of the trade union movement'; but lawful political activity has long been part of ensuring the 'social and economic well-being' of workers.[75] Seen in this context, the British legislation of the 1980s erodes this liberty on two sides. On one side is the constriction by the State of the lawful 'trade dispute' and, as the *Mercury* case illustrated (p. 561), translation by drafting of industrial conflicts into illicit 'political' disputes. On the other, the 1984 Act restricts the very area in which, without meeting special conditions, a union may engage in that political activity through which alone voters may be persuaded and laws may be changed. But in 1984 the tendency of policy was for more, not less, State intervention in the internal affairs of trade union members.

Control of elections and union democracy

Union elections

The same ILO Committee of Experts' report confirmed that the Convention (No. 87) on Freedom of Association, which provides for the right of organizations 'to select their representatives in full freedom', means that 'legislation which regulates in detail the internal election procedures of trade unions is incompatible with the rights of trade unions recognized by Convention No. 87'. This does not prevent legislation intended 'to promote democratic principles' or to regulate elections in the interests of the rights of individual members. Only in Australia and the United States do comparable legal systems closely control the electoral processes, but in both countries the most radical measures followed the revelation of scandalous practices in parts of the trade union movement. Such legislation has given rise to discussion that contrasts different attitudes to 'democracy' in unions. The legislation in Australia, for example, tends to ensure that control is established by members through their 'voting in elections'. On the other hand, if democracy is measured by the *level* of active participation by members in the day-to-day affairs of the organization, an entirely different conclusion is likely to be reached.

Some unions there experience a 'low level in participation by the rank and file', resulting in the dominance of small groups.[76]

Davies and Freedland, noting the different meanings and tests used for the concept of 'trade union democracy', found that most schools of thought agreed that in Britain

democracy exists within trade unions to a sufficient degree and that for those who have doubts these do not particularly focus upon the issue of secret ballots for trade union ballots.[77]

Indeed, even after the ETU ballot-rigging scandal a quarter of a century ago, few proposals were heard in the 1960s for new regulations on this matter. The Donovan Report (1968) proposed new machineries for complaints about alleged election malpractices, but it proposed to leave election rules for the union to determine. The Industrial Relations Act 1971 provided 'guiding principles' for internal trade union affairs, some of which concerned elections (such as no 'arbitrary or unreasonable' rejection of candidates, and secret voting in a ballot).

The idea of imposing rigid structures was not attractive to these different schools of thought, both because no malpractices were proved to justify it, and also because the structures and practices of British trade unions are so diverse that no one type of legislative model would be appropriate for the government of all. Some unions elect a national or principal executive committee (NEC) by direct, others by indirect, elections, some by a mixture. The GMBAT has on its NEC a directly elected General Secretary, indirectly elected lay members (through regional councils) and appointed regional officials. The TGWU has a lay NEC elected partly geographically by constituency of branches, partly through the trade groups. The AUEW(E) elects its NEC, 'appeal court' and full-time officials by postal ballot, but its national committee (its conference) by indirect branch ballot. The CPSA (Civil Service) uses workplace branch ballots to elect the NEC, but some members are entitled to use a postal ballot; NALGO has sixty NEC members directly elected, but nine more from sections and committees to ensure representation of smaller groups. Some unions use the 'branch block vote' (where the majority carries the whole branch); more use the votes cast for candidates in branches. Some branches are geographical, others are workplace branches. Some 59 TUC unions in 1983 provided for the whole membership to elect the NEC, while in 22 it was elected at a delegate conference, 3 by a national committee and 12 by local committees. Others used mixed methods.[78] Donovan concluded that one set of 'model election rules' for all these bodies would not be practicable.

The authoritative survey of Undy and Martin in 1984 illustrated how dangerous generalizations can be about this varied pattern of developing institutions. Each in its own way is touched by the tradition of 'direct' democracy, which was brought into the modern movement; few of them even remotely resemble the oligarchic machines that modern mythology describes. Indeed, with a low density of full-time officials to members compared with comparable foreign unions, the surprising feature is that the reliance upon lay officials (i.e. upon hard-pressed branch secretaries in many unions) has not produced a much higher tally of malpractices. Publicity concentrates upon charges of impropriety, as in the case of the election for the TGWU General Secretary in 1985 where the headlines were full of such charges for many months, but the proof of proper conduct of a new election tended to disappear to the back page. More important, the Undy and Martin survey convincingly showed that 'no single system of voting maximizes turn-out and secrecy and minimizes the opportunity for malpractice'. Further, no particular system of elections gave rise necessarily to any particular result in terms of 'political' make-up of the NEC or senior officials: 'Postal ballots and high turn-outs do not therefore result in right or moderate candidates winning elections.'[79]

There have been occasions on which the legislature has required mandatory ballots in trade unions and controlled their operation. The Act of 1913, as we saw, required a fair ballot for the adoption of political fund rules; and the Trade Union (Amalgamations, etc.) Act 1964 requires ballots to approve a merger in each of the amalgamating unions. In each case the requirement was part of a scheme to facilitate moves towards a condition of the law that trade unions desired; and it is too often overlooked that the 1964 Act was part of a long process to liberate trade unions from the regulation before 1917 under which, in Citrine's words, 'it was difficult, if not impossible, for many unions to merge' (p. 820). For the 1983 Government Green Paper to point to these Acts as legislation 'already recognised and accepted by trade unions' was hardly a useful way, therefore, to outline the case for new regulation over internal elections to the 'principal executive committee (NEC)'.[80] Indeed, the election of officials was as much a target as election of the NEC; but the proposal was to make a start at the top 'with the governing body'.

The 1984 Act and NEC elections

This is what Part I of the Act of 1984 has done. The reasons given for it were twofold. First, regulation over internal elections was a necessary 'price' for the 'legal immunities' (Chapters 7 and 8). Second, the unions should be 'handed back to their members'; or as the Green Paper had put it, leaders are often 'out of touch with their rank and file', appearing to be 'neither representative of the majority of their members nor directly responsible to them'. The first point leads back to the debate about 'immunities' and 'privileges'. The second no doubt describes a condition that on occasion arises, but stands in need of evidence if it is meant as anything like a generalization about British unions. But by 1984 reform of labour law did not accord to empirical evidence the priority that it acquired in the pragmatic days of Donovan. Kahn-Freund had found the essential mark of our unions to be 'direct democracy'; the very

potentiality if not the actuality of – more or less spontaneous, more or less organized – action by the rank and file . . . explains, amongst other things, why the law plays so much smaller a role in our labour relations than in those of otherwise comparable countries.[81]

Yet in 1984 the Government introduced legislation apparently to re-create 'democracy'. The difference was, as so often, one of meaning. Kahn-Freund was speaking about democracy in action, the individual member as part of a collective organization. Some complain that Britain has had too much of that, on the shop floor. The Government concentrated upon the forms of representative democracy, insisting that for trade unions (though, once more, not it seemed for any other association) only one form could be democratic, direct election of the whole NEC.

The Act of 1984 enacts that every trade union must elect voting members of its 'principal executive committee' (NEC) in direct elections by its members (TUA 1984 ss. 1, 2). No indirect elections are permitted. The law does not demand that a union should change its rules; but the provisions of Part I of the Act override the rules in so far as they contradict them. The election must take place at least every five years for every person who is a voting member. Any person who is a voting member of the NEC by virtue of holding 'another position', e.g. an office such as General Secretary or President, must be similarly elected (directly and every five years), and any term in an employment contract with the union to the contrary is disregarded. (A small exemption lets out some officers, once elected under the Act, as they near retirement: s. 8). A 'voting member' includes a member who may vote in any circumstances and thus includes a casting vote. Amendments made by the NUM in 1985 abolished the casting vote of its President, who is elected under its rules to retiring age.

The Act sets out the permissible arrangements concerning constituencies and candidatures (s. 2). On the first, all members must be accorded 'entitlement to vote . . . equally' except where the Act permits. The Act permits members to be excluded by the union's rules from voting if they are in one of the specified classes, *all* of whom are excluded by the rules, namely (1) unemployed members, (2) all members in arrears with contributions (apparently to any specified extent) and (3) 'apprentices, trainees or students or new members' (words not otherwise explained). Constituencies may be devised by the rules restricting the entitlement to vote of members falling within a class determined (1) by trade or occupation, (2) by any geographical area, (3) as a separate 'section' of the union or (4) by reference to any combination of (1), (2) and (3). But no member must be 'denied entitlement to vote' at all elections otherwise than by virtue of belonging to an excluded class.

As to candidates, no member is to be 'unreasonably excluded' from standing; but to this there are three additions. First, no candidate can ever be required, directly or indirectly, to be 'a member of a political party'. Second, a member is not taken to be 'unreasonably excluded' if the ground of exclusion is that he belongs to a class all the members of which are excluded by the rules. Third, in interpreting the second provision, no rule may provide for 'a class to be determined by reference to those members which the union chooses to exclude' (s. 2 (9)–(12)). The third provision is obscure; it appears to mean that the union (e.g. the NEC) cannot specify particular members as disqualified. But the second provision makes it clear that the *rules* can exclude a class. Since the first provision bans only the requirement to be a member of a party, it appears that the Act permits rules that exclude members of a political party as candidates – and also Roman Catholics or other groups, so long as the law on sex or racial discrimination is not infringed. This is an odd structure for a law designed to promote democracy.

The construction of the Act is slipshod. One example arises from the question: to which bodies does Part I apply? It applies to every 'trade union' (as defined in TULRA s. 28 (1): p. 718; except that a federation with no individual members is exempted, as in effect is the ITWF, and a new amalgamation is given a year's grace before Part I applies: s. 7). But two sections reveal a hidden minefield of difficulty in this notion of a 'trade union'. The definition of a 'section' of a union 'includes any part of the union which is itself a trade union' (s. 9 (1)). Similarly, a duty is imposed on 'every trade union' to compile a register of names and addresses of members, which may be kept by means of a computer (s. 4). This duty is particularly difficult for large unions with mobile or short-term workers in membership, where not even the local branch secretary may know who has ceased to be a member (by lapsing with contributions, for example). Perhaps with this in mind, the section continues by providing that any duty to keep a register 'falling upon a branch under this section by reason of its being a trade union' shall be treated as discharged if the national union is keeping a register properly (s. 4 (3)). Here then are two sections (ss. 9 (1) and 4 (3)) that recognize that a 'branch' or 'a section' *inside* the trade union can itself be a (separate) 'trade union'.

This curiosity has long been with us. Certain other legal obligations of a 'branch or section' as to records, audits or annual returns to the CO falling upon it 'by reason of its being a trade union' under TULRA ss. 10 (4) and 11 (8) can be discharged by the national union discharging the duties for the union as a whole. In the Acts of 1871, 1876 and 1906 there were provisions to deal with union branches that were themselves 'trade unions'; and the matter has been discussed in the courts, e.g. in relation to the secession of a branch.[82] We have noted that a branch or section may have separate branch property and trustees; but this is not enough. To be a separate trade union the branch or section must have its own 'principal purposes', which include the regulation of relations between workers and employers and bring it within the definition of TULRA s. 28. We saw that the court applied a parallel condition strictly to the

Cricket Board's claim to be an employers' association (p. 719). But there are indeed sections and branches that have this purpose and prove it by engaging in negotiation with employers. They may well be trade unions in their own right. The Government doubted that there were many; but there were enough to insert s. 4 (3). The importance of the point is this: where branches *are* separate 'trade unions' in law, the 1984 Act appears to demand that direct elections using its procedures must take place not only to the NEC but also to the 'principal executive committee' of each of those *branches*. This was not the intention perhaps; but the Bill was enacted with little attention to such matters.

The point is likely to arise in other contexts, however, because, when attacked, a union may want to present the appearance of an association of autonomous units. In *Express and Star Ltd* v. *NGA*[83] on a hearing about contempt, the NGA argued that it was 'a federation of independent units', each branch acting separately. The judge found the rules to be 'monolithic not federal' and to constitute one undivided union. On the other hand, the problem of the 'branch as a separate union' must be distinguished from the question of how far a particular statute accepts acts done in relation to a branch or section as acts done in relation to the union. This second issue turns on the wording of the statute. For example, the definition of a UMA whereby employees are required to be or become members of a union party to the agreement, states that 'references in this definition to a trade union include reference to a branch or section of a trade union' (TULRA s. 30 (1)). Otherwise a closed shop made with a branch would fall outside, but an agreement with a union would be inside, the definition. The 1980 Act, however, gives a person unreasonably excluded from a trade union in a UMA a special remedy, as we shall see, but states that a reference to a trade union 'includes a reference to a branch or section or a trade union' (EA 1980 s. 4 (10)). Here, however, the words mean an 'organizational unit' of the union; there is no need for it to be a separate trade union (p. 793).

Great attention was given to mandatory election procedures in the 1984 Act. Here the Government originally intended to provide for two options: postal ballots and workplace ballots (not branch ballots, of any kind; they are banned). But the progress of the Bill was impeded at a late stage by a revolt of peers in the House of Lords, not the quarter from which wisdom might expectantly be awaited on either trade unions or democracy. The Government felt compelled to accept their demand, however, to give priority to *postal* ballots, of which many peers had obvious hopes not justified by the findings of Undy and Martin. The basic conditions in s. 2 remained: the vote must be in secret, without interference or constraint from the union or its officials, members or employees; as far as is reasonably practicable the member must be able to vote without direct cost. Every member entitled to vote must, so far as is reasonably practicable, be sent by post to 'his proper address' a voting paper and be given a convenient opportunity to vote by post (s. 2 (7)). Where, however, the *union* considers that there are reasonable grounds for believing that a workplace ballot would satisfy 'the requirements of s. 2' instead of a postal ballot, it may make the voting paper available before, after or during working hours and give the members a convenient opportunity to vote either by post, or at the workplace in the same period, or either of these (but no other alternative) (s. 3). There is no machinery for the union to seek clearance in advance about the workplace ballot – as even the Australian legislation allows, where the Registrar has power to permit an election under the rules otherwise than by postal ballot if this is likely to lead to 'fuller participation' by members (Conciliation and Arbitration Act 1904 s. 133AA (3), as amended 1983). Here the union must take a chance. The reason for this rather unattractive structure in the Act was the Government's determination not to give an administrative body any functions and repeat what they felt was the mistake of the State Registrar under the Act of 1971.

Remedies

The union, then, must carefully consider the enforcement procedures of the Act in case there is any slip. At first, the Government gave only the High Court power to declare a contravention of Part I and make enforcement orders on an application made before or within one year after the election. An enforcement order by the court may order any step needed to remedy the defects in the election and may order a fresh election; in this case, unless it considers it 'inappropriate', the court *shall* require the election to be conducted by postal ballot. Any member who was a member at the time of the order may bring 'obedience' proceedings in case of default; and at the end of this road stands contempt of court. But the same lordly rebellion that promoted postal ballots caused another remedy for default to be inserted. The members may apply also to the CO, but for a declaration only (s. 5). He may specify steps taken by the union to remedy the fault, or give his reasons for a declaration. But he may also add 'written observations on any matter arising from, or connected with, the proceedings', all of which may eventually be 'brought to the notice of the court' (s. 6 (2), (4)). The peculiarity of the procedure before the CO is that there is no appeal, even on a point of law (as there is in every other judicial or quasi-judicial jurisdiction that he enjoys: EPCA s. 136). This means that if he decides against the union, adding whatever 'observations' he sees fit about the union's affairs, the union has no appeal under the 1984 Act. If the member then chooses not to proceed in the High Court to obtain an enforcement order, this is the end of the case, no matter how wrong the decision of the CO may be. It is a matter for speculation how far the High Court would consider an application by the union for judicial review. Kidner concluded: 'the refusal of the government to grant a right of appeal is inexplicable'; but 'it is arguable that a court would allow judicial review of a declaration of the Certification Officer'.[84] However, when the case goes the other way, if the individual loses his application to the CO, he has another bite at the cherry; for he can still apply to the High Court to see if it will take a different view. And if there is an enforcement order, any other member can bring 'obedience' proceedings if he alleges default, even if the first complainant does not wish to pursue the matter. Law is often tested by its procedure for enforcement, as we found with the labour injunction in Chapter 8. By this test, the Act does not 'hand the union back to its members'; it hands it over to any individual who wishes to pursue and harass it about accidental contraventions.

For the obligations of a union under Part I of the 1984 Act are very strict. The primary obligation is that every member must be 'accorded entitlement to vote' (s. 2 (1), (4)). The Government, in refusing to accept amendments aiming to give a union a defence in cases of unintentional and excusable mistake, asserted that a refusal of an 'entitlement' to vote was different from an 'accidental' refusal of an 'opportunity' to vote. In practice, this seems an unlikely distinction of any value in interpreting the Act as it stands. If the branch secretary of the Bradford branch of the AB union mistakenly confuses membership lists and tells X, a fully qualified member, that there is no vote for him because, on the records available, he is marked as a member in arrears and therefore disqualified under the union rules (a ground permitted by s. 2 (2)), from the point of view of X he has been denied his 'entitlement' to register a vote. There is nothing in the Act to suggest that the CO or the court can accept the perspective of the branch secretary and call it a mistake. No doubt both would exercise their discretion in regard to the declaration or, in the case of the court, any enforcement order that was given. But they do not appear to have the flexibility that even the common law gives judges in the law of associations, permitting them to reject a complaint of irregularity in an election if the rules have been 'substantially' observed (*Brown* v. *AUEW*: p. 754) or if there is a mere 'irregularity' in procedure (p. 753). Nor is there anything in the Act – as again there is in the common law – to prevent multiplicity of actions, that is dozens of complaints concerning the same incident, which ought to be dealt with in one action. No doubt, once more, the court will adjust its procedure to this problem as far as it can. But it hardly seems right tacitly to leave such a problem, and the trade union, in the hands of the judges and the CO. In any statute devised in 1984 to hand the association 'over to its members', Parliament ought to have offered some solution to the procedural difficulties that arise between the individual member, or minority, on the one hand, and the majority on the other. This is, after all, a problem that has been around, as the 'rule in *Foss* v. *Harbottle*' testifies, since 1843.

Nevertheless, if a union elects an NEC or members of it, or an officer who has a vote on it, otherwise than in conformity with Part I of the Act, this does not affect 'the validity of anything done' by the NEC. Thus transactions and decisions of the NEC are still valid acts binding the union. For example, an instruction to members to strike without a strike ballot would bind the union and render it vulnerable to action for an injunction. But Part I of the Act does not require that unions should alter their rules, though they are under an obligation to obey the Act in their method of elections. The rules are still a contract, but the Act supplants them in the areas it touches. This set a problem for unions opposed to the Act in principle but who wanted to have a lawful NEC. If they altered the rules, members could say they had voluntarily chosen to comply; if they did not, they would have to explain to members why, in this one case, they were to ignore the rules in so far as they deal with NEC elections, a recipe for little less than administrative chaos. McCarthy has predicted that union rule-books will be redrafted;[85] but he also saw the 1984 Act as promoting an increase in 'factionalism' and in the efforts of outside groups who provide assistance to members in elections or in litigation against the union. By early 1986 the Government knew of nineteen unions changing their rules (some were doing so 'provisionally', during the life of the Act). Othcrs, including N A L G O, were reported to be refusing to observe the Act as to elections to the NEC.

The register of members

At the same time that the new clauses insisting upon the priority of postal ballots were inserted into the 1984 Bill, a clause was inserted requiring every trade union to maintain a register of the names and proper addresses of its members and to secure that it is 'kept up to date'. A register can be kept 'by means of a computer'; as we have seen, a branch that is a separate trade union is excused if the trade union itself is maintaining the register (now T U A 1984 s. 4). The 'proper address' of a member is his home address or any other address 'which he has requested the union in writing to treat' as his address. Most trade unions have not kept a computerized central register. Indeed, large unions with mobile membership find their most accurate membership records at branch level, and even there the branch secretary (a lay official doing the job in his spare time) may well not know which of his members has 'lapsed' from membership through non-payment of contributions or who has been recruited by shop stewards in the last week. This is so even in unions with regular postal ballots. In a well known speech, a General Secretary of the A U E W(E), Sir John Boyd, once said: 'We rely on 2,558 branch secretaries. . . . To have a register of 805,350 voters out of a membership of 1 million is a wonderful achievement.' But the 1984 Act, which on this matter was brought into effect immediately it received Royal Assent, demands, so far as is reasonably practicable, accuracy in accordance with each member's written request (which he can make at any time). The person who often has the most accurate list of members is the employer, at least where a check-off system is in operation; but the section imposes no obligation upon him to co-operate with the union in fulfilling its duties. By 1986 some large unions were co-operating in computerizing membership lists. We shall see whether this can solve the problems.

Union government and democracy

In the light of the new Act let us return to the issue of the government of, and 'democracy' in, trade unions. It is fashionable to say that the concept of a union as a 'voluntary association' is out of date, that trade unions are not social clubs, but that they are, in Kidner's phrase,

trade representation organisations which a person should be entitled to join for the protection of his interests and whose internal conduct must be regulated to ensure that they function 'properly'.

For unions are 'no longer *perceived* as purely voluntary'. Such arguments used to be deployed in regard to the closed-shop agreements made by employers and unions because then union membership is connected with the job. Even there, however, many U M A agreements have always been 'more liberal than the law demanded', and the '"conscript army" jibe' is largely unjustified; the evidence on admissions and exclusions is that 'the actual operation of [union] rules does not generally carry potential abuses into practice'.[86] United States analyses that make the analogy between trade union government and government of the State, and demand party oppositions and factional politics as the necessary condition of union democracy, overlook the fact that party oppositions cannot, as a faction in a union can, secede from the body politic. The organization of a group with a separate programme, therefore, may pose a 'mortal threat' to any union, the threat of a breakaway; and this, Kahn-Freund concluded, is why

there is a formidable case against an overdose of elective democracy in a voluntary body, and especially in a body always and inevitably threatened by disruption, because it is a fighting body which may be attacked by outside hostile interests working from inside.[87]

This does not mean that a union may not be judged by the extent to which its leaders are accountable to its members or its policies are representative of their expressed interests. But that is a more complex test than periodical elections of the N E C and officials, and certainly different from government by perpetual referendum, which is not (despite the modern omnipresence of opinion polls) a form of democracy adopted in other bodies. Many writers have examined the levels and channels of union membership participation as a whole and the checks and balances of power found in different unions.[88] Some place emphasis upon the capability of the union as a voluntary organization to fulfil the interests of the workers in it;[89] others upon the degrees of 'dispersion' of decision-taking in the governmental structure and the differences between decision mechanisms for collective bargaining and for other matters, as they operate in fact rather than in theory.[90] The government of a union depends, Turner suggested, on the relationship of three groups: the full-time officials, the lay members who take an active role in its management and the majority of the rank and file.[91] Clearly a trade union is not a self-contained 'system'; unions are associations of workers 'who are already organised by those to whom they sell their labour power and whose actions they are designed to influence'.[92] Trade union 'democracy' must be placed within that social reality. A meticulous system of voting that left a union inoperative as an engine of collective bargaining and of wider social influence in society might accurately register the representation of factions but would weaken it as a trade union.

As Allen puts it:

trade union organization is not based on theoretical concepts prior to it, that is on some concept of democracy, but on the end it serves. In other words, the end of trade union activity is to protect and improve the general living standards of its members and not to provide workers with an exercise in self-government.[93]

Martin has argued that

in practice government concern with ensuring that trade unions operate according to a particular conception of democratic procedures becomes indissolubly linked with government desire to achieve specific outcomes: the desire to promote democracy becomes linked to the desire to produce a specific outcome.[94]

This has a much wider importance than the election of the NEC or officials. The Webbs, writing about the nature of trade unionism, concluded: 'the very fact that, in modern society, the individual . . . necessarily loses control over his own life, makes him desire to regain collectively what has become individually impossible'.[95] In Australia, the Industrial Court acknowledged the difficulties for unions whose elections are determined by individuals 'who take no interest in union affairs', though this is no reason for not aiming at a high level of voting and, as Rawson puts it, seeking 'to involve the voters in other union activities too'.[96]

It is useful to look at the 1984 Act in this light. Some of the controls over election procedures are open to criticism on the ground that by disallowing greater variety than the one method of *direct* election they prevent unions from adopting machinery better suited to their needs, not for the satisfaction of an internal democratic imperative, but for the purpose of the external, effective representation of members' needs. Because of such dangers the Donovan Report presented its proposals for – and even the Industrial Relations Act 1971 enacted – only model standards to which union rules should attain, permitting each union to adopt its own suitable methods. Even the *registered* union under the 1971 Act was merely required to have rules making 'provision for the election of a governing body and for its re-election at reasonable intervals', which every British rule-book does.

Martin considered three possible justifications of the 1984 Act: union 'privileges'; protection of individual members; elimination of corruption. He demonstrated convincingly that none supports these particular regulatory provisions. Indeed, such provisions themselves become 'undemocratic' when in the name of defending the members they reduce the union's 'ability to improve – or defend – union members' economic conditions'.[97] There is a further feature of the legislation to which the Webbs' remarks are relevant. Here and on other matters (strikes, UMAs, political fund resolutions) the 1984 Act imposes a ballot that, as far as it can, *individuates* the members of the union. None of these ballots may take place at the branch of the union itself. The Act establishes a hierarchy of balloting methods: branch or other union-related ballots are prohibited; ballots at the workplace are usually permitted (but only grudgingly for NEC elections); postal ballots are encouraged (especially for NEC elections or when, as we shall see, State funds are available) and may be demanded (as when a court imposes this requirement in an enforcement order under TUA 1984 s. 5).

What is the reason for this hierarchy? The evidence is that postal ballots do not necessarily raise turn-out by a significant degree. Nor, despite the innuendo of some participants in the debates, has there been any substantial evidence of 'ballot-rigging' in any British union since the ETU scandal of the 1950s, against which, as Donovan reported, 'No rules, however elaborate, would be proof.' (The ETU used postal ballots.) Accepting the will of the peers-in-revolt, who had carried their demand by 85 votes to 65 against Government and Opposition and thereby imposed postal ballots as the primary norm for NEC elections, the Minister, Earl Gowrie, spoke of some unions currently electing their leaders at branch meetings: 'Theirs is the democracy of the activist.' The price of a vote 'is to give up a whole evening. . . . The Bill gets rid of all that.' Trade union 'activism' is indeed a target of the Act. One of its functions is the promotion of an individualized perception by the union member, which may be expressed at home and by post without the inconvenience of collective trade union experience or discussion of policy or candidates at the branch meeting. The structure favours passive, rather than active, trade unionism. In this it is said by many to cut with the grain of events. In the modern labour market the tendency is said to encourage the worker to regard himself as less of a person collectively involved with others, more as a 'free' individual who controls his own life in the multinational market. The insistence upon individualized ballots is part of an attempt to prove that 'democracy' consists only in the individual franchise rather than in a wider and collective participation in union affairs.

Funds for ballots

The statutory demand for secret ballots raises the question of their cost. After 1980 public funds could be made available by the Secretary of State in a scheme (EA 1980 s. 1) for unions that met the regulations on ballots, an offer that was at first taken up only by unions not affiliated to the TUC. The scheme, made by regulation, now allows payment for ballots, for five purposes: (1) taking views of members on strikes or industrial action under the 1984 Act; (2) election to the NEC under the rules and under the 1984 Act or elections of senior officers who will hold office as employees; (3) ballots on amalgamations under the Act of 1964; (4) ballots to approve a resolution for a political fund (so long as the union has a political fund already; not for adopting such a fund for the first time); (5) obtaining a decision of members on a 'proposal of an employer' relating to pay, hours, performance, holidays or pensions (Regulations No. 1654, 1984). The Act of 1980 permitted a scheme to include the election of workplace representatives, such as shop stewards, but the regulations have not done so. Each of the headings carries special conditions; for example, voting must normally be by postal ballot, but strike ballots on industrial action are permitted to be workplace ballots to the extent that the 1984 Act allows (p. 626), and that Act's provisions about constituencies and candidates are applied to elections to the NEC. All ballots must be secret and, so far as reasonably practicable, without direct cost to the member. The union must apply to the CO for payment within six months; no payment may be made until any legal proceedings relating to a ballot have been 'finally determined' (with appeals to the House of Lords, this could take a very long time). The CO may pay such sum as he considers reasonable for printing voting papers and a limited amount of other literature, plus postal costs (second-class mail or a reasonable sum if a more expensive method is necessary).

By the middle of 1985 applications under the scheme by 28 non-TUC unions had resulted in awards of £197,000 for 79 ballots. The largest payments were made to the Royal College of Nursing for ballots on election of officers and the NEC, and on an employer's offer. More than fifty ballots related to elections; only four to industrial action. But in the same year the AUEW was awarded £1.2 million for 154 ballots for elections of its officials. This was not only expenditure of a different order; it was the first occasion when a TUC union had accepted money under the scheme, though the EETPU had also made applications, and a group of smaller white-collar unions, some of them TUC unions, resolved to do the same. The special TUC meeting of 'executives of affiliated unions' in 1982 had adopted the eight 'Wembley Resolutions' in opposition to the new legislation. One of these stated: 'Affiliated unions shall . . . not seek or accept public funds for union ballots under the Employment Act 1980 ballot funds scheme.' In consequence, it was proposed in 1985 that the AUEW, the second largest union, should be suspended or even expelled from the TUC.

One feature of union disagreements on this matter is their illustration of the diversity of British unions and, therefore, the different ways in which particular parts of the legislation have an impact upon them. Unions such as the AUEW or the EETPU have used postal ballots for many years. Most unions in this category are of craft origin, in some others a mobile and dispersed membership has made postal voting essential (as with merchant seamen and actors); so too, postal methods are used in small white-collar unions with little history of industrial action. In some, postal voting has favoured the political 'right', in others the 'left'; and while the turn-out in postal ballots is often high, that achieved by workplace procedures does not always compare badly.[98] For the unions accustomed to using postal ballots, the acceptance of State money was bound to appear less of a compromise with principle than for unions that used other methods judged for many decades to be suited to their union needs to secure representative democracy. The latter perceived the finance in the State scheme as part of the legislative compulsion to change the electoral methods chosen through their own democratic machinery. After fierce disagreements during the TUC Congress of 1985, the AUEW was persuaded to consult its members afresh about accepting funds; but not surprisingly they voted to use State rather than union money. The prospect, however, of another clash with the TUC 'Wembley Resolutions' remained high unless, as seemed likely, TUC policy changed in 1986.

The powers of the CO, Lewis and Simpson have noted, allow him to object to 'interference' by the union in the elections but not by press influence; nor can he ensure 'that there is any balance by, for example, ensuring that subject to the union's rules all candidates are entitled to have an election address distributed together with the voting paper'. The regulations give the CO power to finance material 'which explains' the question to be voted on, or 'the procedure for voting', but no more. The supervision of the CO, they suggest, would become 'an even greater threat to trade union autonomy' if workplace ballots were more extensively included in the scheme.[99] We may also note that the absence of any express prohibition of 'interference' by the employer is pointed up by EA 1980 s. 2, under which an independent recognized union has the right to use of the employer's premises (so long as he and any associated employer employ more than twenty workers) for the purpose of a secret ballot falling within the scheme for payments. The employer must permit the use of the workplace, so far as reasonably practicable, to give his workers who are members of the union 'a convenient opportunity of voting'. The remedy, in case of unjustified refusal, is for the trade union to make a complaint to an industrial tribunal, which can make a declaration and an award of such compensation as is just and reasonable, having regard to the employer's default and the union's expenses. This is the only case where the tribunal can award compensation to the union as such; but such awards, if they exist, are rare. There is a further feature of importance. The remedy for the employer's breach of duty is expressly confined to this type of complaint and these specified remedies (s. 2 (8)). This provision is inserted to ensure that the breach of duty cannot be relied upon in any action brought in tort as 'unlawful means'. There is no equivalent subsection in some of the legislation that imposes obligations upon trade unions (e.g. the duty to keep a register: TUA 1984 s. 4), though a parallel provision is inserted to confine the remedies for failure to elect the NEC according to the 1984 rules to those provided under the Act (TUA 1984 s. 5 (10)).

Exclusion and discipline of members

The administration of a trade union, like any other association, and especially a large union, is bound to lead to conflicts between the majority and individual members in which each side has its arguments and its merits. The common lawyer tends to respond more quickly to the argument advanced by the individual member, for his training and experience have attuned his ears to the cry of individual oppression. The same cry, however, for many trade unionists may echo the note of a 'blackleg' or a 'scab', someone who has let them down in crisis of battle and with whom they wish to have no more to do. Few lawyers have the same instinctive understanding of the union that sees itself as defending its security against an errant member. The Donovan Report avoided the quick assumption that (here) the minority is always right, concluding that 'trade unions in the main respect genuine conscientious objections', for example on grounds of religious belief; but it recommended that if a union rejected a reasonable compromise (such as conscientious objectors paying sums to a charity in lieu of contributions in a closed shop, a solution favoured by the 1971 Act for registered unions), redress should be available to the individual before an independent review tribunal. A solution along these lines was sought, as we shall see, in closed shops by unions affiliated to the TUC; but in 1980 legislation intervened in regard to admission and expulsion of members also in closed-shop situations. Outside UMA employment there is no special legislative control.

Admission

Since the rules are a contract, the primary test for the legitimacy of admission of a worker to a union is whether it is done in accordance with the rules. We saw in *Martin's* case, 1952, that a union is unable to admit a person to a type of membership for which the rules make no provision (p. 748). On the other hand, where the union has failed to observe some procedural steps necessary for admission, where the worker is fully qualified for ordinary membership and where the union has for a period treated him as a member, the union will not be allowed to dispute his membership: 'a person can become a member of a trade union by conduct'.[100] Moreover, where a union has represented to persons that they enjoy a particular status of membership, it will be 'estopped', i.e. prevented, from going back on that representation if they have relied and acted upon it (e.g. where the Nottingham NUM had in 1984 represented that members would remain 'financial members' and not be in arrears if they failed to pay their contributions during a strike, even though the rules provided that members could not stand for office if they were three months in arrears).[101] What is more, and this is fundamental, the courts do not have the power to strike down the rules of the union merely because the judge finds them 'unreasonable', nor to imply terms into the rules, as the judge said in that 1984 case, on the ground only that the rules as they stand produce 'absurd results'. If the rules are illegal, then they cannot stand (except for the doctrine of restraint of trade: TULRA s. 2 (5)); but 'unreasonableness' alone is not a ground on which the court can invalidate the contract.

'I know of no principle of public policy', said Diplock LJ in 1963, 'which entitles the court to treat as void a term of a contract because it is unreasonable.' That case, *Faramus* v. *Film Artistes' Association*, 1964,[102] went to the House of Lords. F. had joined the union in 1950, stating that he had never been convicted of a criminal offence. The union organized film 'extras', an occupation in which unemployment rates were high, and would have been higher had not admission been restricted to about a quarter of the applicants. There were 1,700 members; 5,000 more wanted to be admitted; in the Court of Appeal it was noted that if membership increased much more, the 'members would hardly earn a living wage'. The union had a closed-shop agreement, and the rules aimed to exclude, amongst others, dishonest persons, going so far as to declare that no person convicted of any criminal offence (except minor motoring offences) was eligible to enter or retain membership of the union. The union discovered that F. had been convicted of offences when he was seventeen, in 1940 in Jersey under Nazi occupation. It is not clear what brought this to light or why the union took the course it did, especially why it did not seek to cancel F.'s membership because of his misrepresentation, since a contract induced by such a misstatement is voidable. Instead, it relied on the rules. The House of Lords upheld its stance, Lord Pearce saying:

if all who wished were admitted, there would not be an adequate living for any. This rule is partly directed to that purpose and it is no more unfair to keep out one man because he has been convicted albeit trivially, and so put another in his place, than to keep persons out simply because there is no room for them.

The judgments in this case are a rare example of the court's taking into consideration the collective problems of the union and the industry. It has been said to be a 'non-interventionist' decision; but the word might also be used of cases where the judge has abstained from paying regard to the collective, rather than the individual, interests involved. There could hardly be a 'fair' method by which to decide who should be among the 5,000, and who among the 1,700. Selection was bound to be largely arbitrary. The rule in *Faramus* was certainly harsh; but it was not illegal. Moreover, since it dealt with the 'eligibility' of persons to become or remain members, F.'s admission, having always been in breach of it, was a breach of the rules and void from the beginning; therefore he had in law never been a member at all. No question of expulsion arose. Since the doctrine of *ultra vires* was thought to apply, no ratification of his void membership was possible, even though he had served on the union's committee. On the same principle a rule might have the same effect with members who had been properly admitted; that is, a rule might refer to an event on which their eligibility or membership automatically came to an end (for example, upon arrears in subscriptions for a certain number of weeks; most union rule-books contain such a provision). We shall return to this issue.

A large number of trade union rule-books include provision for the applicant for membership to be given reasons if his application is rejected. Furthermore, the survey in 1980 disclosed that fifty-five unions with 5 million members provided machinery for an appeal against such rejection, the most common being a right of appeal from the branch to the NEC.[103] But an applicant whose request for admission is rejected cannot sue for breach of contract even if there has been a breach of rule. He is not a member and therefore not a party who is able to sue on the contract. In *Faramus*, Lord Pearce said: 'cases of expulsion without a fair hearing come in a different category from cases of refusal of an applicant for membership'. Some have challenged this view of the common law. In *Nagle* v. *Feilden*, 1966, the Court of Appeal faced a case where the Jockey Club was alleged to have refused a trainer's licence to someone because she was a woman (this was before the Sex Discrimination Act 1975).[104] When she sued, the club asked the court to strike out the claim as disclosing no possible cause of action in law. The judges refused (and this was all that was decided). But Lord Denning MR went on to say that an association 'who have the governance of a trade' must not refuse an application without a fair hearing; if they reject an applicant 'arbitrarily or capriciously' the courts could intervene (he disagreed with one of his own earlier judgments: 'that was seventeen years ago. . . . The right to work has become far better recognised since that time').

Few judges have since supported this broad doctrine of the 'right to work'. One judge did so in 1978, distinguishing it from 'restraint of trade', which is excluded from application to unions by TULRA 1974 s. 2 (5). We saw in Chapter 4 how the language of the 'right to work' doctrine is false. The judge does not offer the plaintiff the right to a job, only the right to sweep away rules of a union or trade association. What Hepple has described as 'the loaded "right to work" idea in the context of the closed shop'[105] is a way of pre-empting issues in a delicate policy debate in order more easily to advocate control of trade union rules. The Law Lords took a more balanced view in *Faramus* of the function of the law. In 1971 Lord Denning came back to the charge; a judge more than 300 years before had said that 'public policy is an unruly horse' and might run away with a judge who mounted it:

I disagree. With a good man in the saddle, the unruly horse can be kept in control. It can jump over obstacles . . . and come down on the side of justice as was done in *Nagle* v. *Feilden*.

But Megarry V C in 1978 rejected the simplistic 'right to work' doctrine when dismissing a claim by an applicant for a licence as a boxing manager from the British Boxing Board of Control, which in practice controls the occupation. He drew an analogy with a closed shop; but treated this as a case where the highest duty of the board was to act fairly. This was not a body dealing with the plaintiff under contract or statutory obligations, when a duty to observe 'natural justice' would normally arise (that is, a duty to hold a hearing and give reasons). There might be cases where the plaintiff had a 'legitimate expectation' (of the renewal of a licence, for example); then some higher duty might be owed, but that was not so here. Here the board was under no obligation to give its reasons. As to the 'right to work', if someone has a right,

then some other person or persons must be subject to a duty. . . . Yet who is under the duty to provide the work? Who can be sued? The 'right to work' can hardly mean that a man has a 'right' to work at whatever employment he chooses however unsuitable he is for it.[106]

As an Irish judge said about an applicant refused membership of a union in 1959: 'He is certainly not deprived of any right of property . . . he is, at most, only deprived of acquiring a right.' These judgments erect obstacles of logic and common sense that are more difficult to surmount even for a well mounted steed. The truth is, as Elias has said (albeit with apparent approval), the doctrine of a 'right to work' is here an attempt to strike out union rules according to judicial concepts of 'reasonableness', by a doctrine that evades the *Faramus* decision 'disguised in a new form'. The Irish judges took the lead in semantics and sense when one said in 1978 of 'the undoubted human right to work' that it

places upon the State the obligation to so order the economic resources of the country and the organization of industry and labour that persons will not find themselves denied the opportunity to work . . .

– at, he added, 'a just wage'.[107]

Exclusion from union membership

The 1980 Act brought in new legal regulation. Indeed, in its original form T U L R A 1974 had included regulatory clauses, insisted upon by an Opposition majority in the House of Commons, that gave the tribunals and the courts certain powers over 'arbitrary' exclusions or expulsions by a union. These were removed by the Amendment Act 1976. But in the discussions leading up to that measure, the T U C agreed in 1976 to set up, in consultation with the Secretary of State and A C A S, an Independent Review Committee (I R C), which all affiliated unions agreed to treat as a final committee of appeal on the exclusion of members in closed-shop situations where they have been dismissed from their jobs. (Since the present writer is Chairman of this body, the account of it below is drawn from the published sources indicated.) Davies and Freedland see the I R C as an attempt at

reconciling the general insistence that individuals aggrieved by the conduct of trade unions have some recourse to an independent body outside the union, particularly where there [is] a closed shop, with the reluctance of trade unions [to be subject to a] body remotely resembling the courts.[108]

Although the I R C deals with refusals to admit as well as with expulsions from a union, its terms of reference have necessarily meant that few of the thirty-six claims that fell within its competence up to 1985 were concerned with admission. In some cases the I R C, not being bound to the formalities of judgment alone, upheld an exclusion but recommended that the union should 'sympathetically consider' an application from the complainants; in others the union has been required to confirm the complainant's acceptance into membership.[109] Since most of the cases before the I R C, however, have been concerned with expulsions, it is convenient to return to it below under that heading (p. 813). Another reason for doing so is the introduction in 1980 of a new jurisdiction for the industrial tribunals to review exclusions and expulsions from unions in closed-shop situations, to which we now turn. Whether the new opportunity to go to a tribunal is a major reason for the decline in the case-load before the I R C (it received a total of 49 complaints in the five years up to 1981; and in the following three years only 5), or whether this is part of a general decline in disputes between members or applicants and trade unions, remains uncertain (especially when we note that the I R C itself has been stipulated as 'the final level of appeal' in a significant number of new or redrafted U M As).[110] By comparison, in 1984 A C A S received notice of 18 new cases under this heading of tribunal jurisdiction under the 1980 Act (compared with 76 and 16 in the two previous years); 76 per cent of such cases before it were settled by conciliation, only 9 cases (14 per cent) went to the tribunals.

The 1980 Act s. 4 gives to a worker covered by it in a closed-shop situation the right to complain to an industrial tribunal that an application for membership has been unreasonably refused by, or that he has been unreasonably expelled from, the union (including any branch or section of it). Since the cases that arise frequently involve refusals to readmit, both aspects are considered here, though it is necessary to add at once that the rights in regard to expulsion are specifically given in addition to the extensive rights enjoyed under the common law, discussed below (p. 797). Rights against sex or racial discrimination in the SDA 1975 or RRA 1976 (Chapter 6) and the prohibition against making contribution to the political fund a condition of membership (TUA 1913 s. 3) are also unaffected. The worker is covered by the section only if he is 'in, or is seeking to be in' employment to which a UMA applies. The precise extent to which a worker must have a particular job opportunity in view is uncertain; but the EAT has held that he need not have a particular job in mind, it is enough if he is actively seeking work in the relevant area of employment.[111] The union made respondent to his claim must be a union specified in that agreement. The complaint should normally be presented within six months of the refusal or expulsion (EA 1980 s. 4).

The Act then makes two important definitions. First, if the union delays unreasonably in replying to an application, this amounts to a refusal on the last day on which it might reasonably have been accepted. Secondly, if the rules provide that a member 'ceases to be a member on the happening of an event specified in the rules', he is treated as if he has been expelled (s. 4 (9)). This means that all the members who 'lapse' through non-payment of contributions counts under this Act as having been 'expelled', apparently in order to close up an obvious loophole of possible evasion by automatic termination. However, few of such members would be able to prove much loss, or be able to prove they had been treated unreasonably. An attempt was made in *McGhee* v. *TGWU*, 1985,[112] to stretch the concept of expulsion still further. The member refused to pay a fine of £5 imposed by the branch in the course of a dispute that originated out of his not wishing to be a member of the union in a UMA employment. The union told him six months later that, as the rules allowed, he now counted as standing in arrears. He responded by resigning, despite attempts to get him to change his mind. He claimed that this was a 'constructive expulsion' (rather like a 'constructive dismissal': p. 236), but the EAT was unable to find any such concept in s. 4 of the 1980 Act. If Parliament had wanted such a doctrine, it would have said so. If there is an exclusion or expulsion, the tribunal (from which an appeal lies to the EAT in this type of case on law and on fact; in a 1985 case it exceptionally allowed the Bakers' Union to put in new evidence on appeal) must determine the reasonableness of it 'in accordance with equity and the substantial merits of the case' (s. 4 (5)). The novelty for the union is that compliance with its rules is not enough. In UMA employment the *Faramus* principle is here reversed. Indeed, industrial tribunal decisions show that they are prepared to conclude that not only the union's actions but the rules themselves are unreasonable and to invalidate the refusal to admit or the expulsion on this ground.[113]

The EAT, though, in the very few cases that have reached it has shown an inclination not to extend the jurisdiction beyond the strict terms of the Act. In *Goodfellow's* case, 1985,[114] members of a London branch of NATSOPA were 'regular casuals' for a newspaper, not on the staff but available for shift work regularly for different employers. The complainants had worked regularly for a magazine, but it closed down. Under the UMA they became members of the relevant 'chapel' of the union wherever they worked. On the closure they 'surrendered' their shifts and, in accordance with an arrangement in the industry to deal with unemployment, signed an undertaking not to seek other shifts in the industry to make up this loss. Later the branch refused their application to seek other shifts. Their complaint failed primarily because they had not been refused membership of the branch; they were still members of the London branch and, what is more, were trying to go back on their undertaking. Section 4 was there, the EAT thought, to stop a union 'arbitrarily' banning an 'outsider' who wants a job in the closed shop. A similar result was reached in *Kirkham's* case, 1983.[115] An employee on a newspaper chose voluntary redundancy but later wished to return to the industry. The union, which was party to the UMA, decided he must be a member in category 3, 'casuals', because of the redundancy arrangements, rather than category 1, 'regulars'. This meant he could not obtain regular employment in the industry. The tribunal found that he had been unreasonably excluded from a 'section' of the union; but the EAT disagreed. Although it thought the union had acted unreasonably, to come within s. 4 a branch or section must be one that is specified by the UMA. Here only the union was specified by the UMA, and he had not been excluded from that. The words 'branch' and 'section' meant at most 'organizational units' of the union, of which a person could have membership; here this was the union, not a particular category of union membership.

The Code of Practice on closed shops issued by the Secretary of State in revised form in 1983 puts strong pressure upon tribunals where expulsions from the union relate to members who failed to join in official industrial action. The code is to be 'taken into account' by tribunals and courts. Members should not be disciplined for refusing to take part, it says, where it is reasonable to believe the action is unlawful, a breach of the criminal law or a risk to public safety, where the member's code of professional ethics would be infringed (see the provisions on dismissal: p. 379), and where a procedure agreement is broken or where no secret ballot has been held (para. 61). The last two items went far beyond the legal inhibitions upon strikes at the time the code was issued (now the TUA 1984 requires secret ballots for official action) and were widely criticized for that reason as making new law by a code. The further provision in para. 56, that in rejecting applications the union may consider whether the number of potential applicants 'has long been and is likely to continue to be' so great as to pose a 'serious threat of undermining' collective bargaining, requires something more than proof that wage levels will not be maintained.

Under the 1980 Act the remedy for unreasonable exclusions or expulsions is compensation; but via a very strange procedure (s. 5). If the tribunal upholds a complaint and the union admits, or readmits, the complainant, his compensation is assessed on a second application to the tribunal. Here his maximum is parallel to unfair dismissal compensation (£12,650 in 1986, i.e. the basic and compensatory awards together: p. 253 – though the complainant will not obtain more than his loss). If the union does not admit or readmit him, his second complaint goes (strangely) direct to the EAT, which can award whatever is just and equitable, not merely his loss, but with a limit tied to unfair dismissal compensation including the maximum possible additional award (p. 250; currently £20,710). There is no jurisdiction to enforce membership as such (in contrast to the High Court, discussed below), but the usual unfair dismissal principles apply requiring the complainant to mitigate his loss and diminishing his compensation for 'contributory fault'. A printer who applied to a closed-shop employer whilst his application for union membership was still under consideration was found by the EAT to be guilty of such 'fault'. He 'knew he was running a risk', because the union might regard his taking the job as 'queue-jumping'. So his compensation for an unreasonable refusal to admit (£2,000, representing loss of earnings and employment opportunity, and 'injury to feelings' and to his personal life) was reduced by 15 per cent.

Discipline, expulsion and the courts

The High Court has a general jurisdiction over discipline and expulsion. It applies two major principles in respect of all unions, whether there is a closed shop or not. First, the union must act strictly in conformity with its rules. Secondly, it must observe the principles of 'natural justice'. If either of these principles is contravened the member may obtain damages, a declaration and an injunction. As we have seen in the miners' cases, he may seek an interlocutory injunction in order to prevent the union from acting. In some cases, as in *Esterman's* case (p. 730), this may occur even before the relevant meeting of the committee or other body in the union.

In the last century, the jurisdiction of the court over associations, especially in cases concerning clubs, was said to rest on the injured member's 'property rights'. But later it came to be seen as dependent on the contract, express or implied, made between the members, or between members and union; and this is still the modern basis of it. Like other contracts, the rule-book cannot exclude the court's jurisdiction on questions of law (as opposed to fact); for, as Scrutton LJ put it in 1922, 'there must be no Alsatia in England where the King's writ does not run'. Lord Denning remarked in *Lee's* case, 1952, that the parties could make a domestic tribunal 'the final arbiter on questions of fact, but they cannot make it the final arbiter on questions of law'.[116] (Attempts to oust the jurisdiction of the court over a binding contract are different from a clause stating that the agreement is 'not legally enforceable', for then there is no binding contract at all; but there is no known union rule-book that purports to be legally unenforceable.)

We saw in Chapter 3 that defining a 'question of law' is not always easy. For example, *Lee* had been fined and ultimately expelled for infringing his guild's rules on 'unfair competition'. The court, however, decided that the guild had misunderstood the meaning of those words, and the proper interpretation of the contract was a question of law for it to decide. This does not mean the court can always impose whatever meaning it sees fit; if the rules define 'competition' clearly, that meaning must prevail. It is the jurisdiction of the court to find the meaning of the rules that cannot be ousted. *Mr Leigh*, a railway guard, wanted to accept nomination for President of the N U R in 1969. But the secretary said the rules stated he must be a member of the Labour Party. He had applied to join the Labour Party after resigning from the Communist Party, but had not yet been accepted. The judge held that the rules did not mean that candidates for President had to be members of the Labour Party at the time of nomination; so Leigh could obtain his qualification in time to become President, if he was elected.[117]

So it is not 'reasonableness' but a breach of the contract in the rules (however technical the breach) that puts a member's case on its feet. Where the rule in question states an offence or procedure, the court will seize on any failure to observe the rule strictly. In 1923 an aged member of a union was expelled – put under 'sentence of industrial death', the judge called it – for being twenty weeks in arrears with subscriptions; but the judge discovered that the executive had acted two days too early under the rule and stopped the expulsion on that ground. In *Bonsor* v. *Musicians' Union*, 1956,[118] the member, a musician who died before the case reached the House of Lords, who had been forced to take other jobs after his expulsion (such as removing rust from Brighton Pier), had been fifty-two weeks in arrears, twice as long as was needed under the rules for a valid expulsion. But his expulsion was wrongful because the rules said it could be effected only by the branch committee. He had been expelled by the branch secretary. The individual member is here entitled to pursue the letter of his bond with the union, and there is no 'Daniel come to judgment' in the court to deprive him of his remedy if it is infringed by one jot or tittle.

Bonsor's case went to the House of Lords by reason of obscurities at that time in the law about the union's status (especially about the extent to which a union registered under the 1871 Act was 'quasi-corporate') and consequent doubts about liability to pay damages for the breach of contract with the member. These are now clarified by the capacity to be sued and to conclude a contract in TULRA s. 2 (1). After the Law Lords' decision, damages became an established remedy, alongside declarations and injunctions, the right to which survives the member's death (a widow recovered damages for her husband's expulsion in 1968). In *Edwards* v. *SOGAT*, 1971,[119] a skilled fitter in a closed-shop firm had become a 'temporary' member instead of a full member after a dispute. He had authorized the necessary check-off from his wages, but the union failed to arrange matters properly due to a muddle. He fell into arrears and ceased (it was thought) to be a member. In consequence the employer dismissed him with notice. He then refused to take labouring jobs, obtained a job in a non-union firm, but lost it without fault on his part. The union, which acted as an employment agency for members, refused to readmit him; then it belatedly admitted the mistake; but it still offered him only inferior jobs. The Court of Appeal decided he had acted reasonably in not taking all the jobs offered, for the purpose of mitigating his damage. Apart from the duty to mitigate, Lord Denning said such a plaintiff must be put

in as good a position, so far as money can do it, as if he had never been excluded from the union, taking into account, of course, all the contingencies which might have led to his leaving his employment anyway.

The loss up to the date of trial can be calculated; but the assessment of future loss – what Sachs LJ called 'a quantification of the difference to his future earning capacity likely thereafter to result from the union's wrongful act' – involves the court in something like guesswork. Damages for mental distress on principle ought not to be included; we have seen that they are not awarded in respect of breach of contract in a wrongful dismissal (p. 213). The *Edwards* case went to the Court of Appeal on the question of damages; the three judges, by different routes of calculation, awarded £3,500; and one appeal judge kept carefully to that issue. But greater interest centred upon the dicta of the other two judges, to which we return (p. 810).

Many disciplinary rules are concerned with specific contraventions by members, from arrears in contributions to misapplication of funds. But others will be more general, e.g. expulsion by reason of conduct that in the opinion of a union committee is detrimental to the interests, welfare or reputation of the union. The 1980 survey found 'a very general or "blanket" clause' under which the union can discipline a member for 'a wide range of unspecified offences' in the rules of sixty-nine unions with 11.2 million members.[120] The most common involve action 'contrary or detrimental' to union aims or interests, or action 'likely to bring the union into disrepute'. Some are even wider (one allows the union conference to expel anyone whose expulsion 'appears to be expedient'). Many unions allow for expulsion of a member who disregards a lawful instruction of an official or authorized body; some retain a rule protecting members from those whose conduct is likely to lead to the break-up of the union. To these must be added specific offences especially, but not only, in the craft, or what were the craft, unions. The language tends to become different as the social place of the union changes. The teachers' unions speak of 'unprofessional' conduct; many white-collar unions have disciplinary codes just as strict as those of the manual unions but expressed in more genteel terms. For it does not take a union long to discover that without some code of discipline the minority can render the union ineffective as a 'fighting unit'. What the T U C has attempted to do since its report on rule-books in 1969, with some success, is encourage affiliated unions to rearrange the rules so that they are clearer and are brought more closely to the attention of members.

The legal approach to the rules nevertheless frequently conflicts with that of the trade unionist. If there is no power to expel set out in the rules, there can be no lawful expulsion. And where there is a specific enumeration in the rules of the cases in which a member can be deprived of membership, 'there is no scope or necessity', said Plowman J. in 1972, 'for the implication of any additional obligation', i.e. any implied term for breach of which he can be expelled. Moreover, a rule specifying the offence of acting in a manner 'detrimental to the interests of the union' cannot always justify the penalties imposed. In *Silvester* v. *NPBPW*, 1966,[121] a night driver for the *Daily Mail* worked various kinds of overtime. He gave up all overtime for domestic reasons; but the branch, to whom it was a disadvantage if a member gave up all overtime, censured him and ordered him to resume. He applied to the union's appeal court, but the branch meanwhile fined him £10 for failing to carry out its order, acting under a rule banning acts 'to the detriment of the interests of the union'. The only rule on overtime as such was one that restricted it to eight hours; and the driver was not obliged to work overtime under his employment contract (the union disapproved of members being so bound). The branch withdrew his membership card; and the 'appeal court' in the end varied the penalty to a fine of £20. But Goff J. ruled that these actions were all invalid. In particular, he would not accept that overtime was optional as between the employer and the member but compulsory as between him and his union. There was no basis for the finding that he had acted detrimentally to the union's interests. There was another point: the General Secretary had stopped his appeal until he 'carried out the provisions of the general rules'; but this he had no power to do.

In all these cases, particularly ones like *Bonsor*, the initial mistake is made by a lay official or officials, say a branch committee, in effect running the union in their spare time. This does not excuse the breach of the rules, nor diminish the member's rights. But it is useful to have in mind in considering the 'merits' of the case that what from one perspective is a 'David and Goliath' struggle (an image cherished by Lord Denning) is from another a mistake made by a tired individual trying to deal with branch affairs. It is an extraordinary fact about the British trade union movement that it runs on hundreds of thousands of lay officials. Shop stewards in many unions tend to meet full-time officials when there are 'problems'.[122] Some shop stewards or 'conveners' are in effect full-time; but it is significant that their 'numbers are far higher than the size of the full-time union bureaucracy'.[123] Another factor is important. In many unions customs and practices grow up and crystal-lize that, while they may be sensible, may not in the legal sense be in pre-cise accordance with the rules. Most of the time this does not matter, but if a dispute touching those very rules comes into court it matters a great deal. Perhaps it is here that the trade unions have paid the biggest price for the distance that history placed between their offices and the lawyers.

Exhausting internal remedies

Although a contract cannot oust the jurisdiction of the court, it can require that the parties should submit to arbitration or to some other procedure before they resort to action in the courts. Indeed, since 1979 commercial contracts can oust the control by the courts to an increased extent where arbitrations are involved.[124] A union rule-book may there-fore demand that a member must 'exhaust internal remedies' before resorting to the courts – that is, use all the internal union appeals machinery before he brings a legal action. Unions vary in their structure on this matter. The 1980 survey found 75 unions out of 79 with a membership of 11.6 million with some right of appeal; large unions tended to have several stages of appeal, often from branch to regional or district level and then to N E C or special appeals tribunal. Many required appeals to be heard quickly, sometimes within twenty-eight days; but in others there were long delays because the appeal body met occasionally or was the delegates' conference itself. The TUC recommendation is that penalties should not be enforced while an appeal is being pursued; and all TUC unions now inform members of their right (when they are in a closed shop and otherwise within the terms of reference) to appeal to the IRC. Some rule-books state positively that members should not go to the courts before the appeal procedure has been exhausted.

In 1951 Viscount Simonds stated the classic English legal principle in such a case: 'this [the union appeal machinery] is the appeal the respondent was bound by his contract to pursue before he could issue his writ'. He should do what the contract required before launching a legal action. Where there is an express rule requiring the member to exhaust internal remedies, this would still seem to be the correct principle to be applied. But the judges have moved away from it. They have in recent decades restricted this principle, at least in respect of rule-books that do not manifestly demand exhaustion as a pre-condition of legal action but merely provide the member with the opportunity of an appeal within the union. Where there is no such pre-condition, the member can now take his case to court. In 1965 Ungoed-Thomas J. said that there might be no barrier if a member was actually expelled during the course of domestic appeal procedures. In *Leigh's* case Goff J. went further. Where, he said, there was even an express provision in the rules that a member should exhaust domestic remedies, the court was not absolutely bound by this, but the plaintiff must show cause why the court should interfere with the contract; but where there were internal appeal remedies without obligation to use them, the court would normally hear the case, though it could require the plaintiff to resort to them. By 1972 Plowman J. in *Radford's* case[125] decided that, since there was no requirement in the rules to have recourse to the appeals machinery, he had 'jurisdiction to deal with the matter, subject to a discretion to withhold it until domestic remedies have been exhausted'. Questions have been raised about this discretion, which enables the courts to push aside the domestic procedures in an approach that has been said to 'leave out of account a legitimate trade-union interest in autonomy of decision'.[126] Few judges today are likely to refuse to hear a case because a member has not exhausted internal remedies.

In a considerable jurisprudence the courts have also discussed the issue whether an illegitimate decision to discipline a member by, say, a branch of the union – one that breaks the rules or fails to accord with natural justice – is 'void' or 'voidable' (i.e. whether it is a complete nullity, or a defect that can be cured by some later and proper procedure). In *Lawlor* v. *Union of Post Office Workers*, 1965,[127] members organizing unofficial action in London were ultimately expelled from the union, but without giving them the chance to answer the charges, a breach of natural justice. The union claimed that they should have processed their appeal first to the next annual conference, and that any defect of procedure could be cured there. Ungoed-Thomas J. noted that it was 'debatable' whether such an improper procedure made the initial decision 'void or voidable', but

If it is void, it has been said to be not subject to appeal at all. But only the courts can decide whether it is void or voidable, and whether, in this case, the executive council decision is a complete nullity.

So the case had to come to the court to decide whether the case could go to the conference (and not to the court). These legal Chinese boxes have also been paraded where the internal appeal machinery has already been used. *Leary*, a long-standing member of a union, was elected as an area official. At a meeting of a branch of which he had no notice it was decided he was in arrears and he was expelled; and the branch committee ratified the decision with a far from perfect procedure. At later meetings of the NEC and the appeals council Leary presented his case, but eventually it was rejected. He was expelled and excluded from office. Megarry J. decided that under the rules the only body that could expel Leary was the branch committee. But its decision was void. An appeal body could not cure this initial defect: 'Why should he be told that he ought to be satisfied with an unjust trial and a fair appeal?'[128]

On this basis, internal appeals procedures are legally of little value (and Viscount Simonds can hardly have been talking sense in 1951). But worse was to follow in later cases. The Law Lords (sitting as the Judicial Committee of the Privy Council on an appeal from New Zealand) in 1979 had to decide whether a stewards' inquiry held in breach of the procedures required by natural justice, which disqualified a racehorse owner, had been legitimated by a later hearing by the committee of the Jockey Club to which appeals went but which had confirmed the verdict.[129] The initial decision, said Lord Wilberforce, was 'void' but not legally non-existent until a court said it was. Moreover, the judgment of Megarry J. was 'too broadly stated', correct in only some cases:

these may very well include trade union cases where movement solidarity and dislike of the rebel, or renegade, may make it difficult for appeals to be conducted in an atmosphere of detailed impartiality and so make a fair trial at the first (probably branch) level an essential condition of justice.

But in other bodies it was – or might be – different. Here those who accepted the 'Rules of Racing', like the owner, must have accepted that fair treatment at the later hearing of the committee could settle the matter; the court, therefore, should not interfere. So there is no 'automatic rule' about appellate bodies. They can be used to cure an invalid first stage hearing when in the end 'justice can be done' or the complainant has had 'a fair deal'. Except, it appears, in trade unions. Where the Law Lords obtained their evidence about union branch meetings in this case about a Jockey Club in the Antipodes, or what survey they had made into renegades or the fevered solidarity of trade unionism and its effects, one cannot know. In *Leary's* case, faulty though the first branch proceedings had undoubtedly been, the case went through five stages, culminating in a two-day hearing by the appeals council which heard the witnesses, all cross-examined, of which a transcript '147 foolscap pages long' was put before the judge ('in single spacing', he remarked). We cannot know what might emerge if the Law Lords' test was applied to that. What does emerge is that a different standard is suggested by them for appellate procedures in trade unions.

Natural justice

The phrase 'natural justice', said Maugham J. in 1929,

is of course used only in a popular sense and must not be taken to mean that there is any justice natural among men. . . . The truth is that justice is a very elaborate conception, the growth of many centuries of civilization, and even now the conception differs widely in countries usually described as civilized.

The principles of natural justice are, then, a man-made product, and there may be disagreement about their precise nature in any situation. There is often argument about what is 'fair'. The conception may differ widely in diverse groups or classes in the same country. It is, for instance, not clear on which occasions it will be regarded as necessary for justice to be done in England to allow in legal representatives (nor when to keep them out).[130] Three features, however, were stated by Lord

Hodson in 1964, and have often been accepted by the courts as the basis of natural justice:

(1) The right to be heard by an unbiased tribunal.
(2) The right to have notice of charges of misconduct.
(3) The right to be heard in answer to those charges.

As to the *tribunal*, the nature of the organization must be kept in mind. The problem may be one to which no member can bring an 'open' mind in the sense that all have heard about it in the union. What the officials or body adjudicating a case must do, said Viscount Simonds in 1951, is act in good faith and not make up their minds before the hearing but show

a will to reach an honest conclusion after hearing what was urged on either side and a resolve not to make up their minds beforehand . . . however strongly they had shared in previous adverse criticism of the [member's] conduct.[131]

The tribunal must, however, be properly constituted to that end. Where members of a union had given evidence against the President in a libel action and were reported by him for various offences against the rules, it was not proper for the President to chair the area council that referred the members' actions to another committee, which then met under the President's chairmanship to charge and then convict them (the area council met to confirm the decision, under the President's chairmanship).[132] No person should act as both prosecutor and judge. It was no defence to show that the President had not influenced the proceedings and that justice had in fact been done. To this extent, natural justice is a matter of procedure. All reasonable steps must be taken to avoid the appearance of bias. Various societies become restive when people give evidence in ways they do not like; a well known national society was fined £10,000 in 1985 for punishing an officer for what he had done as a witness.

The very nature of a union may nevertheless make this difficult for one side or the other in a serious dispute among the members. Take the case where the delegate conference is the final appeal body for disciplinary offences. L., who was President of her union, published an attack on a section of the membership, saying they were 'militants' and 'dedicated to the total breakdown of the welfare state'. The NEC regarded this as improper use of her office; this resolution was overtaken by one deploring the views expressed by her. L. obtained numerous interlocutory injunctions against the NEC and had obtained one stopping the NEC from circulating an agenda for the coming conference containing any of the motions to censure her. The difficulty was that the NEC wished to move resolutions condemning L. before she was heard; and conference might discuss them as a policy body but might then have to deal with the same matter as a final appeal body if the disciplinary proceedings that were threatened actually came about. The Court of Appeal therefore continued injunctions (on the *Ethicon* principle) preventing the NEC from condemning L. before a 'fair inquiry', and stopping the conference from resolving on motions condemning L. in regard to matters that could lead to disciplinary proceedings.[133]

Secondly, the need for adequate *notice of the charges* goes closely, in practice, with the third element, the right to a proper *opportunity to be heard* in answer to them. In *Radford's* case, 1972, the judge answered the union's case by saying that the member

was held to have voided his membership without having been given any advance notice that his membership was at stake. What he was told was that the committee proposed to investigate his action of seeking legal advice. He was never charged with anything at all. That, in my judgment, is sufficient to render the branch committee's determination void.

The Law Lords adopted a similar, strict application of the principle in a Privy Council case brought by an expelled member of a Trinidad oilfield union in 1961. He did have notice of the charges and denied them; but the meeting was adjourned to a later date, when he could not attend because of a prior engagement at a 'mock trial'. At the second meeting the charges were differently framed, sufficiently to allow for his expulsion. This was enough to vitiate the proceedings.[134] So too the woodworkers' union's failure to give *Mr Hiles* a chance to answer a charge at an appeal committee that he had broken the rules when he sent out a circular opposing the Government's wages 'freeze' in 1967 was enough to cause an injunction to be issued stopping disciplinary penalties.[135]

But the flexible character of the court's concepts of fairness emerges when other aspects of union government come before the judges. If, for example, there is not a charge of breach of the rules, something that needs a hearing and argument on both sides, but only a decision to be made by a committee whether or not to confirm the appointment of a member to a position in the union, do the principles of natural justice apply, and if so what are they? In *Breen's* case, 1971,[136] where a committee had to decide whether or not to approve the election of the plaintiff as a shop steward, Lord Denning was in favour of applying the principles as they might apply to charges (one issue was how far the committee had improperly taken into account charges of dishonesty against the member, which he had had no chance of answering). Having been 'elected to this office by a democratic process he had . . . a legitimate expectation that he would be approved by the district committee unless there were good reasons against him'. They ought, moreover, to *tell* him the reasons; it was 'intolerable that they should be able to veto his appointment in their unfettered discretion'. But the other two appeal judges would not go so far. The committee was under a duty to act fairly; if charges were made against him he should be asked to answer them, though in their absence he need not be invited to attend. Here, so long as it acted in good faith, the committee was under no obligation to give him the reasons for its decision (the judge having found as a fact that the improper considerations did not influence the members). Many lawyers have predicted that we can expect 'creative' judges in the future to lean towards Lord Denning's view.

Protection of officials

In this area of union internal government, it would be absurd to place the full weight of the natural justice doctrine on every committee that has to exercise a discretion affecting the members. On the other hand, the courts have made it clear, as in *Breen's* case, that they will intervene in such cases if there appears to be a failure to act 'fairly'. No harm can come of this, so long as the judges take account of the interests of the union's members as a whole and of the realities of administering these organizations. But where the judges perceive a member and lay official to be oppressed by an unfair exercise of discretion on the part of the union's machinery of government, they will protect him even to the extent of mandatory orders that tell the committee involved what its decision must be. This we discovered in *Shotton* v. *Hammond*, 1976 (p. 728). It is no accident that both *Breen* and *Shotton* involved a union structure where the election of the shop stewards represented the direct democracy of the plant. We may contrast the full-time official (who may be either appointed or elected) and may remain (or be obliged to become) a member of the union as well. In this event, if his office is terminated in a manner alleged to be improper, he will appear in court in two distinct capacities. The judge distinguished the two in *Taylor* v. *NUS*, 1967,[137] in granting an injunction to an appointed official (having employment 'during the will and pleasure' of the NEC) who had been rendered ineligible to stand for certain other union offices by a disciplinary procedure that infringed natural justice (the general secretary acted as prosecutor and judge, and raised his 'Communist associations' in private after the hearing was over). An injunction was issued to prevent this wrongful infringement of his rights as a member under the contract in the rules; but a declaration for breach of the employment contract was rejected, except in so far as his eligibility to union office was concerned. He also recovered damages.

This attempt to unravel the two strands of the employment contract and the union membership contract is important if the judges are to observe the principle that the remedies of injunction and declaration do not normally lie for breach of a personal contract of employment. In Chapter 2, however, we saw that in *Stevenson* v. *URTU*, 1977,[138] the Court of Appeal appeared to depart from this principle. The full-time officer and member, whose employment lasted while he gave 'satisfaction to the NEC', was dismissed without a proper chance to answer charges against him; and the court granted a declaration that the decision to dismiss was 'in breach of the [union] rules, in breach of natural justice, *ultra vires* and null and void'. In the case of officials who are full-time employees and also members of the union, it appears that the judges are prepared to spill over into the contract of employment remedies that are more appropriate to the membership contract in the rules.

This is no doubt easier to do where the official is elected and action is taken against him *qua* member. In *Leary* v. *NUVB*, 1970,[139] a rule provided that members who were six months in arrears 'shall be excluded at the discretion of the branch *committee*'. Leary, an elected area official responsible to the NEC, was expelled by a resolution of his branch but without notice to him. The branch committee endorsed the action, but again without notice and at an improperly constituted meeting with active participation by members who should not have been there. He appeared later before the NEC and appeals council on appeal

(p. 803). Megarry J. decided that the lack of natural justice and breaches of rule at branch level were fatal to the expulsion, against which an injunction was issued. But the judge noted the distinction between officials who were elected (as here) and those who are appointed. The latter normally become employees of the union, responsible only to the NEC; the former may be responsible to their electorate. Megarry J. refrained from granting Leary an injunction to stop his removal from office, mainly on the 'balance of convenience' but partly, too, because he doubted whether the relationship between the union and the official permitted it.

In an earlier case in 1967 Buckley J. decided that in the case of 'an elected officer', when someone 'other than those who elected him' tried improperly to remove him from office, the law relating to employer and employee should not prevent the granting of an injunction. There appears to be good sense in this approach. More union officials than one might suspect turn out to be in law the employees or 'servants' of the union; for instance, in 1963 a worker acting as 'sick-steward' for the union was held to be a servant of the union when he was injured while pursuing his duties for the union.[140] Wherever an *elected* official is prejudiced by action in breach of the rules or in contravention of natural justice an injunction appears to lie on the basis of the union contract. Where the appointed official is similarly treated, if the union rules are inextricably bound up with his employment, as in *Stevenson's* case, there may be no objection to permitting similar remedies; but if he relies upon his employment contract alone, the decisions before that case suggest that an injunction and declaration will not normally lie. If the union officer is not a member and not elected, there does not seem to be any good reason why the union should be placed under obligations greater than those of any other employer in private law.

Natural justice: contract or public policy?

The general approach of the courts in these cases is to favour the individual. But it is not the approach found in every case where an individual is disciplined by a body that he has joined, as Griffith has shown in his penetrating comparison of the cases concerning union members and those involving students.[141] We must now ask what the juridical basis is for this intervention by the judges. In 1952 Lord

Denning said that a stipulation in the rules to oust natural justice would be void. One rarely finds a rule of anything like that nature and, despite the cases which the lawyer meets in court, trade unions do, as the Donovan Report agreed, operate within just procedures in a vast majority of cases. There have been remarkably few court cases since 1975; but infrequency of injustice is no reason for denying a remedy, though it is a good reason for fitting the remedy to the needs of overall union security. There were reasons for believing, however, that the rule-book could substantially control its own procedures, i.e. that the rules of natural justice could, as implied terms, be modified by that contract. In 1949 Tucker L J said that the application of the principles of natural justice depends on 'the circumstances of the case, the nature of the inquiry, the rules under which the tribunal is acting . . . and so forth'. The Court of Appeal found that the Jockey Club's rules did not demand any hearing at all by the stewards when they withdrew a licence; so they could not be challenged in such a case for holding a 'defective' hearing. So too, in 1929 a judge appeared to believe that a union could modify the need for a hearing in a disciplinary case. As a United States judge said in 1945: 'The ideas of natural justice are regulated by no fixed standard: the ablest and the purest men have differed on the subject.'

The modern cases seem to establish that the principles of natural justice are imposed by the judge as a matter of public policy and cannot be waived by the union rules or any other agreement between the parties. In *Hiles's* case the earlier judicial statements were doubted; and in *Edwards* v. *SOGAT*, 1971,[142] Lord Denning M R said that no trade union 'can give itself by its rules an unfettered discretion to expel a man or to withdraw his membership'. Although he said this in the context of propounding a 'man's right to work' and asserting that the rules were 'more like by-laws' than a contract (both propositions that later developments have proved to be misguided), other judges have joined in asserting the illegitimacy of rules that offend against natural justice. In *Radford's* case Plowman J. declared that, if the union rule before him 'were one for automatic forfeiture of membership without the necessity for any charge or hearing by the union, it would in my judgment be *ultra vires* and void'.[143] But that very case poses one of the many problems inherent in this approach and not yet solved by the courts. The rule in question read:

Any action taken against the [union] by individual members or members acting collectively . . . shall be declared a wilful breach of rules and shall void the membership of the member or members so acting.

Because of the wording, the judge thought the rule required a hearing; since there had not been a proper hearing with notice of the charges, the expulsion was void. But what if the action of the member had been said *automatically* to terminate his membership? Plowman J. would have struck the rule down as contrary to public policy. Megarry J. took the same approach in the case involving disputes in a constituency Labour Party in 1969, when he said:

I cannot believe that the principles of natural justice can be ousted by the simple process of describing expulsion by another name, or resting it on an alternative theoretical basis.[144]

In this case it was argued that the members had ceased to be members on doing the acts that broke the rules; but the judge refused to accept this interpretation. Nor would he see this breach as a 'repudiation' or resignation.

Yet there are some instances in which acts will bring about automatic cessation of membership. Megarry J. himself[145] accepted in 1973 that if 'a member of a society' disregarded his obligations under the rules for several years, he could not thereafter claim to be a member, even if the correct procedure 'has not been followed'; this would amount to an implied resignation; it happened in 'many thousands of clubs and societies'. In trade unions, not only is there a statutory right to resign on reasonable notice and conditions (TULRA s. 7), virtually all rule-books include a rule under which membership terminates automatically after a certain period of arrears of subscription (usually after a twilight, shorter period in which the worker remains a member but, being 'out of compliance', is not entitled to benefit). Some rules are absolute; some not. For example, in the TGWU after 6 weeks' arrears (13 for seafarers) the member cannot claim benefit, but after 13 (26 for seafarers) he 'shall be deemed to be no longer a member of the Union unless the branch and/or the branch committee . . . decides by resolution' otherwise. So common are these rules that Parliament, as we saw, included such an automatic termination within the statutory concept of 'expulsion' in closed-shop situations (EA 1980 s. 4 (9): p. 794). But it would seem absurd to do so in all cases. The most common termination of trade union membership, as with clubs and societies, is 'lapse' through non-payment of subscriptions. Nor would it be reasonable to imply the obligation to have a full 'hearing' merely because the branch, or an official, is obliged to consider whether there is anything that makes this a special case (as in the T G W U rule). There is nothing here speaking, as in *Radford*, of a 'wilful' breach. Membership just ends at the stated period of arrears.

We have seen that some judges speak of rendering 'void' *any* rule that provides for 'automatic forfeiture'. Taken literally, this would render void hundreds of union rules about 'lapse'. It is suggested that such judgments go further than the true principle of law. They stem from statements by Lord Denning in the period (now past) when he was attempting to acquire judicial power to invalidate rules that were, as he put it in 1954, 'contrary to natural justice, or what comes to the same thing, contrary to what is fair and reasonable'. But we saw that the Law Lords held a decade later in the *Faramus* case[102] that it is not the same thing at all. The court does *not* have competence to invalidate rules merely on the ground that the judges consider them to be unfair or unreasonable. Indeed, the House of Lords recognized in this case that a worker might be ineligible for membership by reason of certain facts or be discovered to have been ineligible. What is more, we shall find in *Cheall's* case (p. 832) that the House of Lords accepted that the N E C can bring a person's membership to an end without any hearing, where a union rule gives it power to do so, e.g. in order to put into effect an award of a T U C Disputes Committee in a dispute between competing unions. Once judges begin to control the substance of the union rules generally, rather than the *procedural* provisions that relate to disciplinary situations, they resume the drive to control union rule-books that their forbears expressed through such doctrines as 'restraint of trade' and against which Parliament had to provide in 1871 and again in 1974 (T U L R A s. 2 (5)). The cases in which judges have claimed a general jurisdiction over the substance and 'reasonableness' of union rules, and the right to invalidate all automatic forfeiture provisions, are in fact relatively few, cases like *Radford*, *Edwards* and some other judgments by Lord Denning. None are at House of Lords level, where the reasoning in *Faramus* stands opposed to them. Offences of a disciplinary character demand the application by way of public policy of the principles of natural justice. Beyond that, on any further extensions of the jurisdiction of the courts Parliament must be the arbiter. This is indicated by the very existence of s. 4 of the 1980 Act (p. 793).

The closed shop and the IRC

When Parliament created a new jurisdiction for UMAs in 1980 it gave it not to the High Court but to the industrial tribunals. It is convenient to remind ourselves of the differences in the closed-shop situation. Today the non-unionist is most unlikely to be subject to a 'fair' dismissal by the employer, either because there has been no ballot with the required majority, or because he objects to joining on grounds of conscience or deeply held personal conviction, or because one of the other exempting categories applies to him (EPCA ss. 58, 58A: Chapter 4, pp. 373–80). If he is unreasonably refused admission or unreasonably 'expelled', as defined in the 1980 Act, he can, if employed or 'seeking' employment within the area of the closed shop, obtain compensation from the union (EA 1980 ss. 4, 5). Moreover, in reaching decisions in regard to the closed shop, the tribunals and their appellate courts, and indeed all courts, must take into account the Code of Practice on the Closed Shop, which extends the means by which a case may be decided in his favour, especially in disciplinary proceedings associated with industrial action. The code demands that 'procedures on exclusion or expulsions' comply with the 'rules on natural justice' and that TUC Disputes Procedures should be heeded and decisions of the Independent Review Committee 'fully taken into account' (p. 184).

It cannot be doubted that if a closed shop is operated by management and the union with rigour and to the letter (which few are) a new situation can arise for the worker. He may face a 'closed discipline' situation, where to lose union membership is to lose the job, or vice versa, or where the union may collaborate with the employer in enforcing disciplinary penalties against workers, e.g. the withdrawal of fringe benefits or even imposing fines. The latter was possible in an agreement made by the electricians' union (now EETPU) in the electrical contracting industry in 1967 where a National Joint Industry Board could impose a wide spectrum of penalties on workers, including fines up to £1,000. In such cases the worker may look elsewhere for his defence, and the same might be true where an employer signs up one union for his work-force, as in agreements made by the AUEW and the EETPU. By 1985 the latter claimed to have agreements with ten electronics companies whereby it represents all staff except top management, after the first with Toshiba in 1981.[146] Some unions have been favourable to a more open structure among unions at the place of work and, traditionally at least, less favourable to 100 per cent agreements with employers where they can involve penalties for workers. Certainly, in a 'closed discipline' situation, where the member may be scarcely aware of paying his subscriptions because they are deducted by check-off, his trade union experience may not reach a high level. History records large groups of the work-force rebelling against such a situation, as when some 8,000 members of the GMBAT, before its reforms in the years that followed, threatened to break away from the union at Pilkington's, one manager complaining: 'We would never have had this trouble if the union had been more militant.' On the other hand, unions that make single-union agreements claim this enables them more easily to provide services to members.

In 1976, as we saw (p. 792), the TUC, in consultation with the Government and ACAS, appointed the Independent Review Committee (IRC) to which its unions agreed cases could be brought by members for final review.[147] Its terms of reference are limited to hearing cases from persons who have been dismissed or given notice by the employer as a result of being expelled from, or refused admission to, a union in a UMA. It is required to be satisfied that internal procedures have been exhausted and to attempt to resolve the matter 'by agreement' (a feature that some have criticized on grounds of delay). It must then decide whether to make a 'recommendation' that the union should accept the person into or back into membership. Of the 23 cases going to a hearing between 1976 and 1985, recommendations were made in 14 (involving 19 complainants), and in each, the affiliated union in question complied. A number of the other cases among the 36 within its terms of reference involved the IRC in conciliation. No recommendation was made to admit or readmit in 6 cases (22 complainants). Since the IRC does not have the advantage of the presence of the employer before it, recommendations aimed at the re-employment of the successful complainant can take effect only through the efforts of the union, a limitation of great importance for the worker involved. At the first hearing, the present writer, as Chairman, stated that the IRC would render to the best of their ability independent recommendations based upon common sense and fairness. . . . We have no illusions about the difficulty of our delicate task. But we shall endeavour to reach conclusions which strike a just balance between the interests of individual complainants and the interests of trade unions seen in the context of the whole trade union movement.

The IRC normally requires the union to show that it has acted in accordance with its rules, acted fairly in conformity with natural justice and acted reasonably in the circumstances. Where in *Dennis and EETPU*, 1976, the union had no rule permitting it to expel (lacking the normal 'model rule' in a case where a TUC Disputes Committee had awarded against it: p. 824) the IRC ruled against it; and where in *Thompson and NUDBTW*, 1979, the union had expelled a member in conformity with its rules who had worked in an anti-union firm that had been 'black' since ejecting the union in 1963, the IRC decided he was unreasonably expelled, largely because he did this thirteen years before becoming a member.[148] But in many such cases the IRC made further suggestions aimed at improving the job prospects of the complainant and relationships with the unions concerned. In some of its decisions, such as *Buxton's* case, the IRC has appeared to some observers to favour the union rather than the individual; in others it has been said the individual was favoured, as in *Walmsley and SOGAT*, 1977, where an expulsion (fairly effected within the rules) was disallowed by reason of factors that included his support from other workers in the same chapel and the different treatment accorded to other members.[149] The terms of reference bind the IRC to ensure that all internal procedures have been exhausted. Government spokesmen in 1980, when discussing the provisions that became s. 4 of the 1980 Act, stated, with some justification, that the IRC procedures take 'a good deal of time'. On the other hand, some unions, as Ewing and Rees report, adopted the practice of not carrying out an expulsion until the case has been dealt with by the IRC.

The IRC has from the outset given a high priority to its conciliation work. Even where no agreement proves possible in the early stages, it has frequently engaged in what it came to describe as 'post-hearing conciliation'. That is, it hears the arguments of both sides in the normal way and deliberates upon a decision. Having reached a decision, it does not announce it but asks both sides whether they will agree to a further attempt to conciliate, if necessary by the IRC seeing each party separately. If the conciliation fails, the decision reached earlier is announced to the parties in the usual way. This can sometimes assist in finding a way for the union and the complainant to resolve their differences by a solution that offers a more hopeful route back to employment for the worker. Two cases of 1981 illustrated the process. In one, a disagreement about observance of TGWU rules in a strike, the parties agreed upon a way back into the union for the complainant; in the other, NATSOPA representatives agreed to recommend renewed membership for the complainant upon his giving satisfactory assurances.[150] In one of those cases a barrister represented the complainant; in others there were solicitors, and in one an MP. In some cases the IRC met to 'clarify the facts'; when that was done in *Clark's* case, 1983, the complainant and the union were able to tell it that agreement had been reached about union membership following discussions with the IRC's secretariat (which is provided by the TUC).[151] Of the 23 hearings, post-hearing conciliation was conducted in 13; but this figure does little to indicate the increase in the use of the procedure between 1976 and 1985. Ewing and Rees rightly note that success is more difficult to achieve in cases involving disputed disciplinary measures against a member. The evidence of conflict at rank-and-file level between the complainant and a body of workers at his old workplace sometimes led the IRC to recommend that a job be sought for him in another department or plant or that he be readmitted to a different union branch.

In a number of cases unions have not taken objection to the IRC hearing cases before the worker involved was 'dismissed' in the normal legal sense; and critics have proposed that the need for a dismissal, or notice of it, be withdrawn from the terms of reference. There are two points of interface with other procedures. The first is with the TUC Disputes Principles and Procedures, to which we come below, where a worker has got into the 'wrong' union from the point of view of these Principles.[152] As to the other, the IRC has felt obliged to adopt the position that it cannot continue to hear a case if action in the courts has begun or is about to begin. The addition of the jurisdiction for industrial tribunals by s. 4 of the EA 1980 has increased the likelihood of this arising; but relatively few (of the few) complainants after 1980 seemed to take this course. An action in the High Court is almost as likely. Three meetings were held for 'clarification' in a dispute between six members who had been 'suspended' from the Film Artistes' Association. Although it saw evidence of a 'dismissal', the IRC decided initially that the suspensions were not expulsions but 'of a finite or temporary character'; but further evidence of 'prolonged suspension' could well become 'evidence of expulsions'. By the third hearing, when there was still disagreement about the competence of the IRC to hear the case, it transpired that legal proceedings involving two complainants were about to come into court ten days later. The IRC felt, therefore, that it should proceed no further with the cases.[153] In three cases it recommended that unions give sympathetic consideration to readmitting or admitting the members, and it had reason to believe that this was done. It cannot, of course, award compensation, although in some cases arrears were waived or paid. The informal character of the IRC enabled it to assist, with the agreement of the parties, in matters that did not fall within its remit; and in 1982 its members conducted, on the request of the TUC and the union involved, a protracted inquiry into internal disagreements within a union.

The number of complaints reaching the IRC has further declined over the years, as we saw (p. 793). Until further statistics are available for cases in the tribunals under s. 4 of the 1980 Act it will not be possible fully to test the hypothesis that there are few instances of unfair treatment by unions in expulsion and exclusion among the many millions of union members in Britain. But the absence of 'a rush of applicants' to either the IRC or to the tribunals under s. 4 of the 1980 Act has suggested to commentators of very different inclinations that closed shops have not given rise to massive disciplinary injustices.[154]

The TUC, mergers and members

Perhaps the most startling fact about trade union membership in Britain in the 1980s is the rate of its decline. Trade unionism fell considerably faster than employment. In 1979 the total UK trade union membership of 13.3 million represented more than 55 per cent of the potential work-force (in 1960 it had been 9.8 million, or 44 per cent). By the end of 1984 it had fallen to 11.1 million, a decrease of 17 per cent. In the same period total employment in the UK fell by some 8 per cent. This is partly explained, no doubt, by the changes in the labour market and by the rapid deindustrialization of Britain since 1979; the older industries made high proportions of manual workers redundant, most of them trade unionists; 'new' jobs have been created in large measure for part-time married women, service workers and the self-employed (all difficult for unions to recruit). Some, though inadequate, comfort could be drawn by trade unions from the fact that this trend is an international one. ILO figures show that in all industrialized 'market countries' trade unions have lost members in the recession. In Sweden the decline for 1981 was 4 per cent, in West Germany 2.5 per cent; in France and Spain there was a fall; only Denmark and Norway showed a rise in 1980–2. In the United States trade union density has been falling for years and by 1984 declined to some 19 per cent of the work-force. Bain and Price predicted that union density in Britain was likely to fall after 1983, but later

stabilize when unemployment stops increasing and then, assuming inflation continues at a moderate rate, to fluctuate slightly around a declining trend. . . . How steeply declining this trend will be, however, will largely depend upon how employers behave.[155]

To this we shall return in the next chapter.

The most important unions are affiliated to the Trades Union Congress. In 1980 there were 109 affiliated unions with a total membership of 12.2 million. By 1983 they had fallen to 102 unions with 10.5 million and by 1985 stood at 91 unions with 9.9 million members. Of the major unions (the top ten now account for 6.4 million members) only two grew significantly over the previous year without the aid of a merger, namely the two main teachers' unions (the NUT and the NAS/UWT).

Since 1868 an important feature of membership of a major British union has been representation in the affairs of the movement as a whole through the TUC. In the post-war period, and even before that, the TUC has been composed of unions that were growing larger. Membership did not increase every year; there were losses and fluctuations in the 1920s; but from 1938 when they organized 30 per cent of potential members, unions, as Price and Bain show,[156] enjoyed a gradual and steady expansion until 1980. The next five years were the first modern period of serious and steady loss of membership to challenge the movement. The link with unemployment and with the closures in the heartland of trade unionism, manufacturing industry, is clear; but the need to find explanations for the gap between the decrease in employment and the decrease in union membership has highlighted research on other factors, such as the correlation between union density and the size of establishment. Other studies suggest that union membership is influenced in important measure by the jobs and industries in which people work, together with their region, but that other personal characteristics do not appear to affect it significantly (such as marital status, as opposed to sex).[157] Nor are the gains and losses that occur to be explained convincingly as losses by 'militant' and gains by 'moderate' unions; the two unions of schoolteachers registered their increase in membership during a period of sustained and militant policy in the selective action of 1984 (though membership trends seem uncertain in 1986). Never has the need been stronger for British trade unions to discover exactly what is happening to the membership. The developments led the *Financial Times* to note that 'the greater stress on the merits of free markets has raised new doubts about the economic utility of unions'.

The new pressure of decreasing membership has fallen upon a movement that is in many ways unprepared for it. The small proportion of full-time officials and the low level of subscriptions, compared to other movements that organize on a basis of membership density, is matched by a weak organizational 'centre' and sometimes, it must be said, a lack of vision. But it is part of the purpose and the democratic function of the TUC *not* to take to itself the work of its constituent unions. In consequence, as membership drops and the financial problems of each union increase, the need for more money per head at the centre grows; the TUC annual affiliation fee per member was raised from 60p to 70p for 1986. In 1984 the NUR owned assets of £191 per head of each of its 136,000 members. Even the largest of British unions is hardly opulent; the TGWU was 'worth' some £60 million, but its expenditure totalled £41 million (some £28 million on administration); it had 1,640 employees, 1.47 million members and a surplus on the year of £4 million. In the previous year NUPE had an income of £15 million, an expenditure of £14 million and administrative costs per member rising at 14.4 per cent; ASTMS was recorded as having £4.2 million funds, £9.6 million income and £8.9 million expenditure. There was not a lot of 'fat' to be taken out of such organizations. Certainly they could not withstand too many actions for large damages. One of the ways in which most of the larger unions have increased, or lately maintained, their size of membership is by mergers. It is in this area, as in inter-union relationships generally, that each union comes into contact with the law on one side and the machinery operated by and through the TUC on the other. We look first therefore at mergers and then, secondly, at the TUC's Disputes Principles and Procedures.

Mergers and the TUC

George Woodcock, the General Secretary, said to the TUC in 1963: 'We have to face as a fact that diversity is with us and will be with us.' So far he has been proved right. The 'multi-unionism' of the British movement is as marked now as a century ago, if not more so. It has every type of union. Some are 'industrial', the NUM for miners and the NUR for railwaymen (though the TSSA organizes white-collar grades and ASLEF, a craft union, most drivers). Others are 'craft' unions (the NGA in printing). But although most large unions have their roots either in craft (the AUEW) or in general workers' unions (the TGWU), in the 1960s the tendency of all major unions was, as Hughes put it, to become 'large "open" unions which take a broad definition of their sector of operation'.[158] The union merger has long been an important mechanism in such developments.

Union mergers were particularly prominent between 1911 and 1922, prompting the Government in the middle of the First World War to facilitate amalgamations by the Act of 1917. The nineteenth-century statutes had required a majority vote of two-thirds of the members in order to merge (unions sometimes disbanded to get round this and urged members to join the new one). But the more relaxed 1917 Act permitted mergers after a ballot in each union with 50 per cent of members voting, and votes in favour exceeding votes against by 20 per cent. A great wave of mergers began in the decade after 1963 when again, as unions and others desired, Parliament facilitated the process in the Trade Union (Amalgamations, etc.) Act 1964. Among the main reasons for union mergers have been technological change, reorganization of capital and competitive recruitment (the boilermakers absorbed the blacksmiths and shipwrights in 1962–3), or increase in size and scope to improve bargaining strength (as in the absorption of staff associations by white-collar unions, such as ASTMS), or just the need for a place to go to remain effective and solvent (as with the Agricultural Workers' entry into the TGWU, which in 1984 also took in the 148 members of the Sheffield Sawmakers' Protection Society, founded in 1797).[159] A steady stream of mergers continued into the 1980s; the office of the CO at the end of 1984 was 'concerned with 40 proposed mergers of trade unions'. The expanding range of union activities has put intense pressure on the resources of smaller unions with few resources. Moreover, some larger unions have a structure well adapted to mergers; the distinctive trade group structure of the TGWU, in particular, allowed it more easily also to accommodate the Plasterers (1968), Chemical Workers (1972), Vehicle Builders (1973), Stevedores (1982), and Dyers and Bleachers (1982); but its membership declared for affiliation to the TUC in 1985 was approximately back to the figure for 1969. In the last two decades

the fortunes of major unions have become increasingly dependent . . . on their success, relative to rivals, in grasping new opportunities. Policy and strategy have become salient factors in structural development.[160]

Policy in the narrow sense has been one factor in the development of the engineering union. The attempt to transform the loose federation of four unions in the AUEW (the engineers, construction workers, foundry workers and white-collar TASS) foundered in the face of the implied incorporation of the federal rules, which did not allow it without unanimous consent, into each union's rule-book.[161] Some of the difficulties were related to the fact that officials in the 'right-wing' engineering union are elected, but in the 'left-wing' TASS are appointed. This led to the full merger of the first three unions in 1984 (the AUEW also absorbing the Gold and Silver Trades and the Toll Turners, to maintain its membership at one million). TASS (expanding to nearly a quarter of a million in 1985) had to go its own way, merging with the Sheet Metal Workers, Patternmakers and Metal Mechanics, with the politically sympathetic Tobacco Workers, and keeping an eye on the electronics sector in competition with the EETPU. Not every proposal, though, came to fruition: the journalists (NUJ) and printers (NGA) failed to agree amidst redundancies caused by new technology; the BIFU took in some building society associations but failed to convince other non-affiliated banking unions; political problems stopped the Civil Service CPSA and SCPS from merging. More important, most large unions have not only allowed some newly absorbed unions to retain their own identity, e.g. as separate sections, but have also developed their own white-collar sections in positive competition with the 'white-collar' unions. So white-collar workers in the TGWU join the ACTSS. The EETPU, formed when the electricians merged with the plumbers in

1968, absorbed various small white-collar groups (including some, like UKAPE, that had vigorously opposed TUC unions under the 1971 Act) and in 1984 supported an umbrella organization, the Council of Managerial and Professional Staffs, with fifteen affiliated staff associations, to provide 'an alternative to TASS or ASTMS'. But it lost the Boilermakers, who preferred to amalgamate with the General and Municipal Workers to form GMBAT. Unions of all kinds merged, craft with general, white-collar with manual.

Small bodies, rivals to TUC unions, have also been established regularly over recent years, 'a network of breakaway unions' receiving organizational and legal aid from such bodies as Industrial Relations and Personnel Consultants. Here we find the Association of Professional Ambulance Personnel, the Professional Association of Teachers and the Nationally Integrated Caring Employees (or NICE).[162] Though small, these unions are not likely to merge with TUC organizations, not least because of their opposition to industrial action.

Although the total number of unions fell to 371 in 1984 compared with 519 ten years before and more than 1,000 in 1939, there was little evidence of the 'rationalization' of union structures to which both Donovan and the TUC had looked forward in the 1960s. Instead, in the 1980s unions were compelled to spend increasing amounts of precious resources upon competition with other unions in which the prize of a successful merger might sometimes restore the treasury. Union structures and practices in 1986 were as competitive as ever. The potential inter-union difficulties make more important than ever the success of the TUC machinery that we discuss below. Competitive unionism can keep a union on its toes in responding to the needs of members; and in an age when 'competitiveness' has the seal of official approval, the higgledy-piggledy character of amalgamations may appear less important than it did a decade ago.

Despite these developments, paradoxically unions and union members have also often worked increasingly together. The widespread impact of multi-unionism is offset by joint bargaining structures and joint shop stewards' committees and meetings, though the latter occur less frequently among white-collar groups and there appears to have been a decline in the 1980s in 'combine' committees of shop stewards.[163] The practice of and structures for working together arise for trade unionists in the day-to-day struggle at the workplace. These are sometimes reflected by formal structures at a different level through joint operation of the representatives of various unions, e.g. in the Post Office, universities, television and the Civil Service, where there has long been the Council of Civil Service Unions. At a different level again, to co-ordinate collective bargaining unions established in 1973 a series of Industry Committees through the TUC (eleven in number in 1984). Each deals with an industry or sector (from Construction and Health Services to Financial Services and Fuel and Power). Sub-groups in that year pursued issues as disparate as radioactive waste, race relations in the NHS and the privatization of steel. On occasion unions in dispute have requested a panel of such a committee to adjudicate on disputes between them; and through such committees TUC intervention has been facilitated in certain disputes.

The 1964 Amalgamations Act

Perhaps because it marked a liberation of unions from previous legal restrictions, there has been little criticism of the Trade Union (Amalgamations, etc.) Act 1964 (TU(A)A). The Act facilitates mergers by amalgamations and by 'transfer of engagement' (a form introduced in 1940 where one union transfers members and property to another). The fundamental requirement is that the merger must be approved by a simple majority of the votes recorded in a ballot. This applies whatever the rules of the union say, except for rules adopted after the 1964 Act, which may impose a requirement for a higher majority. In an amalgamation both unions must hold a ballot; in 'transfers' only the transferor union. In the ballot 'every member' of the union is entitled to vote 'without interference or constraint' (not limited, as in the 1984 Act, to interference by the union) and with a 'fair opportunity' to vote. The notice to members and the proposed 'instrument of amalgamation' (or 'transfer') must be approved by the CO. Arrangements are made for the disposal of property and changes of name. Further, any member may complain to the CO if he alleges within six weeks that the voting arrangements did not satisfy the Act. Until 1975 the jurisdiction of the old Registrar (predecessor of the CO) was exclusive. He could, if he saw fit, at the request of a union or complainant, transfer a case to the High Court; but otherwise the validity of the resolution approving a merger could 'not be questioned in any legal proceedings whatsoever'. This exclusion of the courts was changed (for what reason, other than tidiness, was never very clear) in the EPA 1975, after which an appeal from the CO has lain to the EAT on questions of law (now TU(A)A 1964 s. 4 (8)).

The 1964 Act overrides the union rules in so far as it demands that every member is entitled to vote and must receive the approved notice within certain time limits. But its simple code requiring a 'fair opportunity' for members to vote, which the CO is able to interpret to meet particular needs, contrasts with the more cumbersome regulation of the 1984 Act, and especially with the extraordinary remedial procedures of its Part I on elections (p. 738). Very few complaints have been made to the CO or the Registrar before him. In 1983 he received fifty letters of complaint about three mergers; none was pursued to a hearing. In 1981 the CO refused to interpret 'interference' to include a union campaign for a 'yes' vote, or 'constraint' to include misleading statements (though a 'blatant untruth' might be); nor in the circumstances was an employer's refusal to provide facilities for a 'no' vote a 'constraint' (such a point would be unarguable, as we saw, p. 778, under the 1984 Act); nor was a member's inability to vote through sickness in the 1985 UDM merger (p. 828). Members who have complained that union rules were broken because all members voted (including apprentices, to whom the rules gave no vote, as in a case of 1967 before Pennycuick J.) or because procedures in the rules had been ignored (as in Mr Gormley's complaint of 1982) have lost because of the overriding provisions of the Act. The CO has a discretion to overlook breaches of the timetable; but if ballot arrangements have not satisfied procedures agreed by the union and required by the Act, especially if the defect has affected the outcome of the ballot, he will require a new ballot to be held.[164]

TUC Disputes Principles and Procedures ('Bridlington')

There is, however, another legal dimension that can arise where two TUC unions are competing for membership. Certain principles were laid down at the 1939 Bridlington Congress for TUC machinery relating to disputes between affiliated unions (they clarified the proposals of the 1924 Hull Congress; but they are often still referred to as the 'Bridlington Principles'). In a modified form these have today become the TUC Disputes Principles and Procedures. The Principles (and the Notes to them) are stated to be 'a code of conduct accepted as morally binding', not intended to be 'a legally enforceable contract'. Neverthe-less, the rules of the TUC are a contract; and they impose obligations upon affiliated unions (including the duty to notify the General Secret-ary of certain stoppages of work, mainly those arising from disputes between unions, or involving 'directly or indirectly large bodies of workers'). A dispute between affiliated unions can be referred by the General Secretary to a Disputes Committee. Affiliated unions are under the rules 'bound by any award of the Disputes Committee and shall comply forthwith with such award'. The sanctions include, ultimately, suspension or expulsion from the Congress. The same sanctions can arise where an affiliated union is found by the General Council, after proper hearings, to have acted in a manner detrimental to the interests of the union movement. This was at the centre of the charge brought against the EETPU in 1985–6, some of whose members were found to be working in the Wapping works of News International. The union gave undertakings demanded by the TUC in the interests of the printing unions and their 5,000 dismissed members. But a resolution instructing the EETPU to tell its members to refrain from work normally done by print workers – which could be understood to mean not crossing the picket lines – was lost by 15 votes to 14, apparently on the ground that this might involve the TUC in an unlawful instruction and bring it into court.

Under the TUC Disputes Procedures, complaints come before a Disputes Committee, which is made up of senior trade unionists not concerned in the dispute. These are required to be resolved 'in accord-ance with the Regulations governing procedure in regard to disputes between affiliated organisations'; the procedural 'regulations' are thus incorporated into the contract under the TUC rules (Rule 12 (e)). A Disputes Committee is charged by those regulations to 'have general regard' to the interests of the trade union movement and declared principles and policy of the TUC, but must 'in particular be guided' by the Principles as amended from time to time. The Principles thus escape the net of direct contractual obligations, but they must be the 'particular' guide of a committee in its work.

The Principles address two problems, both of which can be relevant to mergers and to inter-union competition. By way of preface, they encourage 'joint working agreements' between unions, such as agreed spheres of influence or 'recognition' of another union's cards; and in this context the Notes also encourage mergers and consultation with other interested unions before a merger is considered, especially with non-affiliated organizations. The first major problem addressed is 'poaching' from other TUC unions. A union must require an applicant who has been a member of another union to complete the form asking for details of his membership of that union, dealing especially with resignation, discipline, penalties, arrears, etc. Inquiry must be made of the other union, and, if it objects, his application should be rejected until consultation or TUC adjudication has solved the problem. He must not be admitted if he is under discipline, engaged in a trade dispute or in arrears (Principles 2, 4, 6). The most common reason for a union to refuse an applicant is his failure to clear arrears with another affiliated union. The more general problem is dealt with by Principle 5, which forbids a union to 'commence organizing activities' among grades of workers at an establishment or undertaking in which 'another union has the majority of workers employed and negotiates wages and conditions'. The Notes (which have 'equal status and validity' with the Principles) state, however, that even where a union does not have a majority, another incoming union should consult with the established union; in such a case a Disputes Committee will have regard to that union's having once had, or its efforts to gain, a majority membership; the likely prospect of its acquiring recognition; and any other collective bargaining or 'representation arrangements'. This Principle and Note aim at stability of bargaining structures and the avoidance of 'raiding' which may not involve direct poaching. But, as we shall see, its enforcement has special problems in the case both of a merger and of 'single union' collective agreements.

The enforcement at the workplace level of the 'Bridlington Principles' seemed to cause little legal difficulty until 1956, when the common law control over expulsions intervened. In *Spring* v. *NASD*[165] a Disputes Committee decided that the plaintiff should, according to the Principles, be in a different union. Obedient to its obligations, the NASD expelled him. But it had no rule in its rule book that permitted his expulsion. In consequence the court held it to be invalid. The court would not imply a term giving the union that power. The TUC in consequence recommended that affiliated unions should adopt a 'model rule'. In its revised form, this gives the NEC (or other appropriate body) of a union power to terminate, by six weeks' notice in writing, 'the membership of any member if necessary in order to comply with a decision of a Disputes

Committee of the Trades Union Congress'. In order to rely on this rule the union must observe it meticulously. Thus when the AUEW expelled a member in 1977 before a Disputes Committee had made any award, it could not rely upon it (nor upon another rule giving the council power to do whatever was necessary for the welfare of the union). There were threats in the 1970s, though they came to nothing, to test the validity of the Principles in the courts, in particular when the EMA appeared likely to take TASS and the TUC into the High Court to prevent application of TUC procedures in a dispute, one of the rare occasions on which an affiliated union has issued a writ against the TUC. But in 1976 the 'model rule' and the Principles were tested in a different type of case, and found wanting.

In *Rothwell* v. *APEX*, 1976,[166] ASTMS organized about a quarter of the staff at General Accident Insurance; but for years its efforts to recruit more had been frustrated by the staff association (SAGA), which was not affiliated to the TUC. Another TUC union, APEX, successfully negotiated a merger by transfer of engagements with SAGA. ASTMS complained to a Disputes Committee alleging breach of Principle 5 (which at that time had rather different Notes). The award stated that APEX was in breach of Principle 5, that ASTMS was the 'appropriate union' at General Accident and that APEX should not proceed with the merger. The instrument of transfer was however registered to complete the merger. The award was adopted in the proceedings of that year's Congress, whereupon the TUC told APEX to implement it. When APEX sought to expel the ex-SAGA members under its own Rule 14 (identical with the 'model rule'), the latter sought a declaration that this was wrongful. Foster J. decided in their favour. There were two main grounds. First, Rule 14 applied to awards only if they were within the terms of reference of the Disputes Committee. Principle 5 could not apply because ASTMS did not have in membership a majority of the employees involved (the Notes at that time did not help ASTMS); and anyway the Committee had not been asked in its terms of reference to decide which was the 'appropriate' union in general terms. More important, 'organizing activity' did not include mergers, so Principle 5 could not apply. Secondly, by the time the award was made APEX was 'legally bound' (presumably by contract) to merge with SAGA. Moreover, when the TUC demanded that APEX comply, the instrument of merger was registered and the TUC could not lawfully demand that it be undone. Thus we see that at two points the unions (and their members, if threatened with expulsion) involved in a merger could raise legal objections to implementation of the Disputes Committee award, first when the contract to merge is made (seemingly a contract conditional upon successful ballots), and secondly when the instrument is registered with the CO. The judgment was unclear, but this part of it appeared to rest upon a liability for threatening to induce a breach of the contract to merge in the first place and, in the second, on a liability for interfering with the statutory right to merge.

The latter could be of great importance to the impact of the law. In the dispute between the NUM Nottinghamshire Area and the national NUM, it transpired in 1985 that the former was considering, as a method of breaking away from the latter and of avoiding the need – if there were one – of any special majority that might be required by its *own* rules, a merger under the 1964 Act with another friendly union, which might be accomplished by a simple majority vote, to form the 'Union of Democratic Mineworkers'. The partners in the exercise proved to be the South Derbyshire Area Mineworkers' Union and an organization formed by coal workers in Durham. This seemed to involve a new use of the 1964 Act. The overriding power of an ordinary majority for a merger was part, as we have seen, of a historical process of loosening the bonds restraining union mergers. At the time it was not devised as a way for a union to break its bonds with other organizations to which it is linked or federated. The difficulty of breaking up some federations was illustrated in the *AUEW* case.[161] The approval of the CO to the merger sought by the Nottinghamshire Area NUM in 1985 was likely to be an important precedent. A trade union need not be 'listed' to make use of the 1964 Act. A breakaway group from a non-federal union might do so.

Foster J. in *Rothwell* did not raise objection to the 'model rule' on the ground that it did not provide for a hearing for the ex-SAGA members; but it was inevitable that one day a plaintiff would raise issues of this kind, possibly attractive to the individualist tendencies of the courts. The Principles do involve a procedure

in which the interests of the individual are disposed of by reference to collective interests; and this will always arouse the sensibilities of the courts, however fair the adjudication between the unions can be made.[167]

The TUC Disputes Principles and Procedures have been redrafted twice since that time; but remarkably no action was taken to remove the coach and horses driven through Principle 5 in *Rothwell* by the assertion that 'organizing activities' did not include 'mergers'. TUC history in the 1980s might have been very different had that been done. In itself it was a startling interpretation. What better way of 'organizing' a work-force than to take it over, not individually, but *en bloc*? Yet this was the one element in the judgment accepted by the TUC unions – perhaps because competition was so strong. What is more, Ball saw in the TUC awards up to 1980 'a clear policy' to observe the 'line of legal demarcation between organizing activities and mergers resulting, in some cases, in weird and contradictory decisions'.[168]

The problem, as a TUC report in 1979 revealed, was that a significant number of unions wished to retain the freedom to merge, at any rate with unaffiliated organizations. This has happened frequently since and is, for some unions, a major weapon in the competition for members. But there are further legal difficulties, such as the right of resignation (TULRA s. 7). An award of 1985 confirmed the marginal effectiveness of the Principles in this area. A member of the TSSA joined a staff association that later merged with the EETPU. At some point, which was not clear, he had resigned from the TSSA, which alleged that the EETPU should not have taken him into membership via the merger. The Disputes Committee's award favoured the EETPU. Whenever the worker resigned from the TSSA, the decision confirms the problems inherent in this area of inter-union relations for the TUC Principles.

In other ways, however, the efforts of the Disputes Committees, by patient work which receives little public recognition, promote joint understandings between unions and better industrial relations thereby, with no loss of trade union strength. In recent years Committees have, amongst other things, arranged for ballots of workers to decide between the AUEW(E) and ASTMS to see which union had the 'required percentage' or 'necessary support' to negotiate for them; arranged for a joint approach to an employer by the NGA and the GMBAT; made complex proposals to the EETPU and NALGO for a working settlement rather than go to a formal award; and made an award building on existing agreements between the ISTC and the TGWU, whose members worked cheek by jowl and both of which had some recognition rights.

Cases of 'poaching' still occur, some innocently. The AUEW was found to have accepted forty-six TGWU members into membership; it was required to exclude them from membership, even though the TGWU had no recognition rights at the firm; Principle 2 had been infringed. Similarly USDAW proved that ASTMS had contravened Principle 5 by 'commencing organizing activities' in Woolworth without consulting USDAW as 'the appropriate union' for its staff. From 1981 to 1984 there were 55 Disputes Committee adjudications, which is about the same yearly average as in the 1960s. In the same period, of the 128 disputes dealt with by conciliation 83 concerned organization or negotiating rights, 36 'poaching' and similar claims, and 9 disputes about demarcation arising from new technology.

By 1985 some of the Principles bore the signs of strain. Various complaints were brought by unions, such as APEX and the NGA, which had been squeezed out of representation by companies that had signed agreements with one union only, to act exclusively for the workers, such as the EETPU at Hitachi (where other unions lost existing rights) and the AUEW at Nissan. Disputes Committees decided in favour of most of the unions that made such agreements. The unions squeezed out took the matter to the 1985 Congress, where a motion was passed demanding that the negotiation of 'one-union' agreements should respect the bargaining rights of existing recognized unions. There was a distinct danger of the Committees falling into disrepute in such cases, despite their efforts to find practical arrangements. In the Hitachi dispute, for example, the award went to the EETPU, but the Committee criticized that union for failing to consult the other unions, which already had members and rights in the plant, and for not resolving the inter-union dispute before signing the agreement giving it sole recognition. (Had the EETPU 'poached' a single member of another established union it would have broken the Principles.) Further, the Committee tried to draw up a code under which new recruits would be informed of their rights to join other unions, officials of other unions would be involved in representing the members in grievance procedures and the EETPU would consult the other unions on matters affecting its members. But full implementation of such a plan would appear to be difficult when the company is determined to deal with one union only as the heart of its industrial relations policy. These parts of the Committee's conclusions had the appearance of beating the air.

Some unions called for a more general revision of the TUC Principles. Some of the new agreements appeared to allow the employing company to choose which union would represent all the workers, a procedure productive of neither democracy nor healthy competition and one that put the TUC Procedures into baulk. Delay in hearing increasingly difficult Disputes Committee cases, moreover, was alleged to result in individual workers, whose ultimate status depended on the outcome, being fed up and lapsing from union membership altogether. A review of the Procedures and Principles had occurred from time to time; by now it had become urgent. The TUC General Council faced up to implementation of the 1985 Congress resolution as the year came to a close. New wording for a Note to the Principles was adopted to be recommended to all affiliated unions in the Congress whereby affiliated unions should not enter into sole negotiating agreements, or a variety of other recognition agreements, where an existing union would be deprived of existing recognition or negotiating rights. The interests of all unions affected should be taken into account. The redrafting, however, was rather behind events. These were the days of the Wapping dispute in which the dispossessed print unions called for stronger TUC action against the EETPU (p. 604). The pressure of events brought change, but slowly.

Textual revision of the Principles and Procedures, however, could not be expected to solve all the problems. Some unions, such as the EETPU, openly avowed a new, 'realist' style – some said a new species – of trade unionism. The difficulties behind the operation of the TUC Principles and rules were differences in strategy and perception between unions as to workers' best interests, divergencies that could do little either to moderate the pressures of competition or to increase the effectiveness of the TUC, which in the last resort rests upon a broad consensus in the movement as a whole. Even in less difficult times, inter-union disputes had been of some complexity and delicacy. Without the patient work of these TUC Disputes Committees, industry and the public services would be immeasurably poorer, and individual workers generally would suffer along with employers and the public from the inevitably more arbitrary consequences of multi-unionism. If the Principles cannot be adequately revised with imagination to make them as effective and relevant as the 'Bridlington Principles' were for decades after 1939, the greatest losers are likely to be a divided trade union movement and the workers who are its members.

TUC machinery and public policy in the courts

In 1983 the Court of Appeal pierced the whole structure of the Principles with a shattering blast of 'public policy'.[169] Very serious problems would have arisen had not the Law Lords reversed its judgment. The case was almost a re-run of *Rothwell* – but with a difference. There was no merger to complicate the issues. *Cheall*, a security officer at Vauxhall Cars, was a member of the ACTSS (TGWU), but disenchantment led him to resign and join APEX. The APEX officials knew he had been in the ACTSS but failed to inquire about him. A Disputes Committee decided that clearly Principle 2 had been broken and it required APEX to expel him. APEX had the power to do this under Rule 14 (the 'model rule'). But Cheall claimed the expulsion was unlawful on three grounds.

First, he complained that he had not been heard and had therefore not been accorded the fairness that 'natural justice' demanded. The courts rejected this approach, on the ground that, although in a dispute natural justice requires that the parties be heard, before a Disputes Committee the only parties are the two unions in dispute. It would be impossible for it to hear all the persons, perhaps many thousands, who might be affected by the outcome of such an adjudication; nor were they entitled to make such a demand. Secondly, in the Court of Appeal, Slade LJ and Lord Denning MR, against the dissent of Donaldson LJ, held that APEX could not rely upon Rule 14 because it had brought about the circumstances to which that rule applied by its own wrongful recruitment of Cheall. But on final appeal the Law Lords demonstrated the error that this reasoning disclosed as a matter of contract law. The true principle is that a party to a contract is not permitted to rely upon a clause in the contract where he is taking advantage of his own breach of duty owed to the other party. APEX denied any breach of duty owed to Cheall. But Cheall complained that APEX had broken its duty in not giving him a hearing before its own executive council. In a decision of great importance to expulsion and 'automatic cessation' clauses in rule-books, the Law Lords agreed with the trial judge that there was 'no legal obligation on APEX to . . . grant him an opportunity to be heard'. APEX had to fulfil its duty to act within its rules and in the best interests of its members by complying with the award. Rule 14 allowed it to terminate his membership without a hearing, merely by giving notice.

This left the third argument, that the TUC Principles, Procedures and Notes, and awards under them, were all void as being contrary to public policy, in particular in restricting the right of an individual to 'join and remain a member of the trade union of his choice'. In *Rothwell* the judge had refused to decide the case on this ground, saying, 'Public policy is always a dangerous ground for a court to use to decide a case.' But now it was the centre-piece of Lord Denning's judgment, for which he relied upon Article 11 of the European Convention on Human Rights, which we met in Chapter 4 (p. 377). Freedom of association, he declared, was part of the common law for associations, 'whether it be a social club, a football club or a cricket club'. The Convention recognized the same basic principle, and the railwaymen's case (p. 376) showed that a worker must be allowed to join the 'union of his choice'. Rule 14 could not stand. It was argued, he said, that the rule and the TUC procedures were necessary 'so as to keep order in industrial relations. If it were not for the Bridlington Principles there would be chaos. Trade union would fight against trade union.' But to this Lord Denning had an answer (just after the Falklands war):

Even though it should result in industrial chaos, nevertheless the freedom of each man should prevail over it. There comes a time in peace as in war – as recent events show – when a stand must be made on principle, whatever the consequences.

It hardly needs to be stated that such an absolute principle of membership 'choice' would wreak havoc in any system of multi-unionism. The Law Lords rejected it. Freedom of association, they said, had to be 'mutual'; the 'body of the membership' of APEX represented by the APEX Council was not willing to accept Cheall in the light of the TUC Disputes Committee award. No rule of public policy prevented unions from entering into this kind of arrangement when they considered it to be in their members' interests, thereby 'promoting order in industrial relations and enhancing their members' bargaining power with their employers'. The judges could not intervene. Lord Diplock added: 'If this is to be done at all, it must be done by Parliament.'

The Law Lords in this judgment saved the TUC Disputes Principles and Procedures from illegality and must be given credit for so doing. Yet it is an extraordinary proof of the attachment of the common law to its individualistic precepts that two judges of the Court of Appeal felt bound in 1983 to strike them down as void, one by an odd application of contract law that would have emasculated them, the other with the club of public policy that would have killed them off unless Parliament had come to their rescue (the last thing voluntary procedures of this kind would wish to seek). In rejecting those judgments, the Law Lords went in a direction in which other sources have pointed, namely the desirability of supporting the valuable TUC machinery. ACAS has regularly promoted the TUC Procedures to solve inter-union difficulties; and even the Secretary of State's 1983 Code of Practice on Closed Shops urges unions to have regard to the TUC Principles and Procedures and relevant findings of a Disputes Committee. They are critical to the maintenance of stability in British collective bargaining. Even so, there was a 'sting in the tail of Lord Diplock's judgment'.[170] His 'human sympathies' were with Mr Cheall, he said, but he was 'not in a position to indulge them' in this case. He added:

Different considerations might apply if the effect of Cheall's expulsion from APEX were to have put his job in jeopardy, either because of the existence of a closed shop or for some other reason.

Those untutored in the ways of the common law might ask why, when the interests of the 'body of union membership' and of the TUC unions would remain the same, the fortuitous addition to the facts of a closed shop at Vauxhall's for security officers might afford to Lord Diplock or to any other judges a new opportunity to indulge their sympathies by adding a 'different consideration' to the law. But the principles of the common law do not so easily doff completely their preference for individuals nor shift so readily into a collectivist gear.

The *Cheall* judgment was an important advance in the application of judge-made law to trade union problems. History may nevertheless suggest that the judgment was not unrelated to the social context in which trade unions had by 1983 become patently weaker, society more fragile and the need for 'order' more pressing. The attitude of the common law remains unpredictable and its approach to trade unions fickle. Its first love remains the individual in this area of the law.[171] Protection for the individual must have some priority in any civilized system of law. But it is precisely the definition of this 'individual' – how far he is perceived as an individuated trader of his labour power in the market or as a worker whose very employment demands collective organization to promote his individual freedom – that will determine the future policies of the judiciary and the legislature in the law governing relationships of workers with their unions and unions one with another.

[10] Changing Laws and Workers' Rights

It would not be in the spirit of this book to conclude it with a project of specific reforms for British labour law. Rather, it is hoped that its chapters have stressed the interrelationship of the various parts and the need to consider contiguous legal and social problems, from the definition of 'employee' to the 'right' to organize, from job creation to the poverty trap. The pursuit of a policy in one part of labour law must take account of its effects upon the others and of the effect upon society generally. It is not, therefore, an area of law that we can, or ought to, discuss without making apparent our attitudes. It is a place where law, politics and social assumptions meet in a person; those who believe that they are so 'impartial' as to be above policies or prejudices are either arrogantly naïve or dishonest with themselves and others. The preceding chapters evince an open positive preference for collective bargaining, both as a realistic recognition of conflicts of interest and as machinery for the peaceful mediation of social change – for which individual workers have a need, to which they have a right and through which they can influence their working conditions and the joint administration of life at work. In this chapter we consider some underlying problems and issues in Britain and in other countries that may influence discussion about labour law in the next decade. Let us begin with some that found little place in Donovan.

Industrial democracy

For three decades after the Second World War, in many countries of Western Europe this seemed to be the era of industrial democracy, an idea whose time had come.[1] The systems in experiment differed sharply. In Sweden a strongly pluralist base was maintained; between 1973 and 1976 trade unionists took seats as minority members on company boards, unions were afforded extended rights to bargain over strategic decisions of management, even to veto aspects of manpower policies such as subcontracting. By the 1980s the much modified 'Meidner plan' for economic democracy through wage-earner funds was introduced, whereby a slice of profits buys shares for collective ownership through trustees (thereby, it was found in 1985, providing industry with a useful source of new capital). Equally collective, but more unitary, was the West German development of 'co-determination', supplementing enterprise Works Councils with employee representation upon the Supervisory Councils of large companies, participation to the extent of one-half in coal and steel, and by 1976 generally just less than one-half in other large enterprises. Although this is not always formally representation through trade unions, most representatives have come to be trade unionists. Those more unitary structures coexist with collective bargaining, giving West German labour law 'various, concurrently existing and uncoordinated models of co-determination on the enterprise level'.[2] This was the form that most influenced early thinking in the EEC, especially on the draft (as it still is) Fifth Directive on 'Harmonization of Company Law'.

There was little at the time of Donovan to suggest that Britain would take seriously the idea of introducing legal structures to facilitate the extension by law of participation by workers either through their unions or in other ways in decision-taking in industry. Collective bargaining was the approved road, as it had become in the United States and later in France and in Italy. As we saw in Chapter 1, authorities like Kahn-Freund insisted that the 'land of collective bargaining' was distinct from, and inescapably alternative to, the 'land of company law' as a base for industrial democracy – even though he knew well the limits of collective bargaining, how nationally it could rarely reach the big, strategic corporate decisions and how transnationally it barely registered:

at the international level we have management but neither government nor effective union power. The entire basis of our thinking on collective labour relations and collective labour law is destroyed by this development.[3]

It is difficult to overestimate the shock caused by the conclusions reached by majority opinion inside the TUC in 1973–4 that collective bargaining must be 'broadened' and that this should include both extending the existing field of negotiation, with new statutory rights to support consultation and information, and joint control by way of workers' representatives through unions as half of the members on large companies' boards of directors and boards of nationalized industries (where workers voted for it – enterprise ballots are not a new idea). The proposals of the majority Bullock Report contained not only the more detailed elaboration in labour law and company law of a similar plan, but also important consequential proposals for trade unions themselves. Not the least important was the requirement in industrial democracy structures of a 'Joint Representation Committee' of unions, white- and blue-collar together, at enterprise and group level.[4] We have seen in Chapter 9 that, with some notable exceptions (e.g. the print unions), mergers have not stemmed advancing competition among hard-pressed British unions; and it must be for speculation how far the formation of such Joint Committees in the 1970s, building on existing organization, from shop stewards at enterprise level to TUC industry committees at the other, might have given the trade union movement a relatively stronger base on which to face the economic and legal blows of the next decade.

The experiment, however, came to naught. Trade unions did not identify legislation on industrial democracy, especially in the face of fierce management hostility, as 'so central and important . . . that it was worth jeopardising the range of other policy initiatives which the trade union movement could expect from a Labour government in power' (especially, of course, the employment protection statutes of 1974–8).[5] We saw in Chapter 4 that the attempt was there made to extend the scope and depth of collective bargaining by provision of individual rights (shop stewards' time off, rights to union membership and activity) and union rights (on disclosure, consultation on redundancy, pensions and safety, as well as the recognition experiment), a path down which such initiatives as the EEC draft 'Vredeling' Directive still point. Britain did not in the end adopt its own form of participative structures by law; and the joint 'consultation' that has since continued, even increased, in industry is qualitatively different from joint decision-making.[6] Sweden and West Germany, however, had their different, participative structures in place before the worst of the economic crisis arrived; and both had by 1985 survived it better than average in Europe. It is hard to believe that in each its own form of worker participation has not made a positive contribution.

The debate on this specific area of 'industrial democracy' fell silent in Britain not for legal reasons or through defects in the Bullock proposals (though no doubt they were many) but because of the recession and spiralling unemployment, a context in which neither trade unions nor management saw much point in it as an immediate issue, especially after the sharp change of direction in labour law policy in 1980. Oddly enough, whereas experts believed in the 1960s that 'the prospects for worker participation seem even more remote in America than in Europe',[7] it is in the United States that interest in it has most sharply increased in the 1980s. Unions have made agreements, providing for board-level representation, 'lifetime' employment and expanded consultation, in ways that may even change, Craver suggests, the conventional labour–management relationship.[8] But the existing US labour legislation insists on a classic adversarial posture for bargaining purposes, fearing the risk of constraint or interference by the employer over any 'labor organisation'.[9] The relatively more general economic buoyancy has been an important factor in this period, together with the need for US unions to find new avenues out of the decline that beset them for more than a decade – although some of the plans, e.g. for employees on corporation boards, were no more than an attempt by management to negotiate reorganizations that involved extensive redundancies.

Collectivism and individualism in the crisis

There is, however, a very different philosophy little noticed at the time of Donovan, now prominent in Britain two decades later, a form of individualism that aims to break the mould of earlier policy. The pace of change both in technology as such and in the relations of production has posed new challenges to established patterns and institutions in economic and industrial relations (as many British advocates of experiment in industrial democracy had predicted). In Britain the challenges were the more sharp by reason of patterns of inadequate investment, international competition and, some held, low productivity.[10] Analyses that centred on market competitiveness and monetarist economics have put in issue not only such institutions as employment protection legislation but, much more profoundly, the collective base of labour relations. Two very different reactions may here be usefully contrasted to this crisis in the labour market, in Italy and in Britain, both of them highly 'conflictual' industrial cultures, the former having added in the last three decades robust and fluid collective bargaining to its legally regulated base with extensive employment protection measures, not least in the Workers Statute 1970, and the Redundancy Fund (CIG) from which 80 per cent of wages may be provided for many workers when 'suspended' – not dismissed – by reason of redundancy.[11]

Faced with the need for increased efficiency, influential voices in Italy promoted the reform of employment protection 'guarantees'; efficiency, once thought of as the prerogative of the employer, they wrote, now 'constitutes a principle of action valid for everyone'. Workers' guarantees must be extended to 'submerged' workers; but they must be made more 'flexible', allowing for rapid adaptations 'according to the needs of the economy which is already on the threshold of a post-industrial age'.[12] The 'new information technology' favoured 'decentralisation of responsibilities' among workers; new groups of workers in the 'post-industrial enterprise' must be accommodated with whom management may feel able to deal 'on an *individual* basis'. There is 'change and *discontinuity*' at all levels; but

Collective action and representation seem to be preferable in terms of industrial democracy as opposed to a return to individual bargaining . . . particularly . . . if the dramatic implications of technological change are to be socially controlled.[13]

Such an approach, an insistence upon new flexibility in the labour market coupled with maintenance of 'social control' through the adapted institutions of collective bargaining and of law together, has nurtured remarkable changes. At first, the 'crisis laws' of the later 1970s seemed uncertain temporary measures, but developments in the 1980s displayed a more permanent character. Part-time employment, traditionally an outcast in Italian labour law, was legitimized, for example, in a law of 1984 that protects conditions and ensures a role for collective bargaining (an employer who infringes the law or an agreement on hours, numbers, etc. can be prosecuted). This

introduces a normative framework for part-time work . . . and leaving room for collective bargaining, acts as an instrument of job creation, reabsorbing the secondary labour market, with a better opportunity to work for those who . . . have a particular need and interest to find a job with hours shorter than normal, not to speak of restoring elasticity to the productive system.[14]

The opportunity was taken through the introduction of a more 'flexible' employment relationship to proceed by consent by introducing a code that did not overlook the protection of workers and provision for their unions. The same Act makes provision for new 'training-work' contracts for those aged between 15 and 29, relaxation of strict rules on hiring and fresh support for 'solidarity agreements' reducing hours and even wages (both 'internal' agreements saving jobs and 'external' ones allowing new recruitment, building on the experience of the French *contrats de solidarité*). Earlier measures on workers' 'guarantees' were sustained in the tripartite 'Accords' of 1983 and 1984, making collective bargaining more flexible, loosening the *scala mobile* (wage indexation) and achieving progress on union 'self-regulation' in public service industrial action. In 1985 this attempt to increase efficiency by consent and social control had the remarkable effect of prompting Italy's most radical trade unions (the CGIL) actually to propose the termination of the CIG, long the citadel of labour's strongest defences, in return for a three-year maximum period of redundancy payments and stronger State labour market policies for training and job creation.[15]

The problems confronting Britain in the 1980s bore some similarities, and many of the objectives were the same: increased competitiveness, efficiency and 'flexibility'. The industrial context was different, but in some respects only in style. As for the law, there was no need to legislate to make such institutions as part-time work respectable; but the same case could be made for legislation aiming at efficient use and 'social control' in its adaptation. In an old economy, already sharply de-industrialized, workers and management faced harsh choices:

In the real world workers have to determine their interests according to circum-stances . . . above all according to the distribution of power as entrenched in the prevailing political and economic relations of capitalist society.

Both 'efficiency' and 'mobility', it was said, were values that had a place in 'working class interests'.[16] But for this to be so, labour market policy would need at least to reflect those interests. Having rejected Bullock, would management come up with an alternative whereby a negotiated social transition by consent could be achieved? Were other avenues to be explored through which workers' choices might be registered as part of a process of change with consent and social control? We shall never know. Instead management was offered a work-force made relatively more docile by high and rising unemployment and the opportunity of taking industrial problems back into the High Court – an offer that could not be refused, as we saw in Chapter 8, by a surprisingly large number of employers.

From 1980 overall policy was straightforward. Reliance upon the 'economic market' was more and more resolute. Influential voices offered econometric proof that

union power, even if only a modest nuisance in the 1960s, has become a major obstruction by the early 1980s. . . . To my untutored legal mind it seems a simple and attractive course to abolish the 1906 [Immunities Act], except for the peaceful picketing clause . . . to abolish the closed shop, and to institute a Labour Monopolies Commission.[17]

One million jobs, it was claimed, had been taken from the poorest 'in the course of five economic cycles' by trade unions – though nowhere else in Europe was this simplistic analysis made, where often unions had comparable social rights in different legal form. When, therefore, employment protections were weakened, as with unfair dismissal (Chapter 3), when Truck Acts were repealed or maternity rights restricted in small businesses (Chapters 5 and 6) or the props to collective bargaining removed (Chapter 4), they were accompanied by no compensating measures of 'social control' through law or collective bargaining. Others of this school had concluded: 'The rate of wages which is best for the workers as a whole is that which is determined in the free market.' The useful function for collective bargaining was said to be 'negotiating about those things which, unlike prices or rates of wages, are *not* adequately determined by the market process'.[18] Minds, tutored and untutored, deduced that the statutory 'props' to the going rate had to be removed, like unilateral arbitration, the Fair Wages Resolution and Wages Councils for the young (Chapter 4). The prime culprits, trade unions, must have their 'power' curtailed both by the workings of the labour market when the unemployed lapsed from membership, by changes in social security law and by legal curbs upon workers' industrial action and forms of organization especially where they dared to cross the boundaries of employment units (Chapters 7 and 8). Illegality was attached to industrial pressure to extend collective bargaining; increasing State control over internal union affairs and upon methods of consulting members in industrial action was justified by the thesis that the law was both restricting union power to improve the working of the labour market and 'handing them back to the members'.

Such measures have not, of course, changed the industrial relations scene totally, especially in larger enterprises.[19] As part-time work and subcontracting increased, however, no tripartite or bargaining machinery mediated the changes; no neo-corporatist offer even like that of 1971 was made; the programmes allocated to the MSC were justifiably seen to aim as much at depressing unemployment statistics as at policies for education and employment of a new generation of young citizens. Theory had it that, as 'union power' was curbed by new laws, unemployment would fall – but it increased. If the Italian style looked like a call to man the pumps while a grand old ship afloat in new currents was repaired and modernized, the British scene resembled an older, if stately, engine careering towards the water as the driver lectured the boilermen to work harder. More important, a democratic collective tradition began to be jettisoned.

Individualizing labour relations

British labour law policy in the 1980s might no doubt be satisfied with decentralized, 'business' or enterprise unionism. On the other hand, certainly in the new high-technology industries, in private services and in the secondary labour market, there is nothing to suggest that its preference would not be for an even more individuated labour market. The tendency of the policy at every point is hostility to collectivism. We have detected this inclination in each preceding chapter. Why should it not be so? If trade unions are perceived as no more than obstructive monopolies whose undue 'power' has 'destroyed jobs', the individuation of labour relations should be, wherever possible, a target at which State intervention should aim. In this philosophy effective trade unionism, as we have known it, must be a surplus value. Trade unions in a democracy are destined to live in tension with the State; but a policy of individuating the work-force demands that they pass into a condition of hostility to government, or give up their functions. The restoration of common law rule over collective industrial relations is a central part of this individuating process. We have seen how common law individualism in general, and its distaste for workers' combinations in particular, survived from the last century into this, not merely in its substantive principles but also in its professional relationship to society and, above all, in the procedures and remedies that come naturally to it (Chapters 8 and 9). Furthermore, we know that the special status of common law regulation by judges frequently makes the task of Parliament difficult when it wishes to pass a statute to change 'the law' that is to be interpreted in those very courts. In labour relations, the 'general law' is for judges common law; statutory protections are normally, at best, exceptions. We should do those who have promoted the hegemonic role of the common law in industrial relations the courtesy of believing that they knew what they were doing. What is less clear is how far they wish to go, or will be driven to go by the dynamics of the forces that propel them.

One system that has gone further is that of the United States. US trade union membership is now small; it fell from nearly 35 per cent of the work-force in 1954 to around 19 per cent in 1985. The union decline in a growing work-force in the 1970s was measured in percentages; since then there has been a decline in absolute numbers. The growth of the tertiary sector (by 1990, service industries will employ 75 per cent of the work-force) is one reason; the fragmentation of the labour market another (20 per cent of workers hold a part-time job; more are self-employed or short-term employees); the geography of the new industries and technology (decided by capital) concentrated in non-union areas yet another. Weak at the outset of the economic upturn in the 1980s, the labour unions face 'exportation of production jobs from United States factories to "low cost" underdeveloped nations', and have failed to connect with the needs of female and minority-group workers; by 1979 they were winning less than half the representation elections in 'bargaining units'.[20] British unions have done better on some points; but these are all problems on which they cannot be complacent. An important additional factor, however, has been the diverse practices of 'union avoidance' or 'union-free environments' adopted by many US employers, plain 'union-busting' on the part of some. The 'avoidance' of the union may for some be a result of personnel policies; in others it is a central policy objective; for all, there is at hand an army of management consultants to advise about the matter (they should register under the Act of 1959, a precedent to which British attention should be paid).[21] In its review of the position in 1985 the AFL–CIO declared:

Nor are anti-union actions confined to not-yet-organized or just organized employers. Employers with long-standing collective bargaining relationships are closing unionized plants and diverting work to their established non-union plants or to new plants established in non-union areas in the United States and elsewhere.[22]

The legal irony is that, whilst U S labour relations have thus become less collectivized, this is the one 'common law' jurisdiction that long ago gave up the individual *contract* of employment as its primary base.

The extent to which management has to a serious degree begun to adopt any such 'union avoidance' policies in Britain is unclear. Some instances of refusal to recognize unions, to extend recognition to new branches of work or to continue existing negotiating patterns have arisen in the 1980s. Some employers have made life more difficult for shop stewards, bypassing them in dealing with the work-force; more have been content with the shift in bargaining power.[23] For many with a large work-force 'individualizing' labour relations would be very costly; and public policy now concentrates on the small firm. Some prominent U S consultants have begun work in Britain, and British firms have entered the field. Small firms increasingly prefer non-unionism (as in the *NGA* and *Dimbleby* cases: pp. 610 and 601); some managements have shown little reluctance to profit from 'splits' in the trade union movement (whether breakaways from the NUM or divisions in the TUC); firms that actively discourage unions include large corporations such as IBM and Citibank ('the best interests of all Citibankers are served without the presence of a union').[24] Moderate white-collar and steel-workers' leaders joined at the TUC in 1983 in condemning the 'climate of anti-unionism and fear of unemployment', the 'screening out' of employees favourable to unions, the 'framing of activists' and attempts to end the check-off.[25] The *GCHQ* affair (p. 277) struck at the moral base of collective labour relations not least because public service trade unionism has such long roots in Britain. The legislative elevation of the status of non-unionism in the 1980s – promoted to equal, if not superior, status to trade unionism, as we saw in Chapters 4 and 8 – encouraged those who believed that the tide of technology was running counter to the grain of 'old-fashioned' trade unionism. Individualism was the fashion, management prerogative the result, not least over 'atypical' employment.

The direction of recent British policy is therefore a major reason why more cannot be currently attempted by law to repair the disabilities of the disadvantaged in the labour market (Chapter 6). A strategy for equality in sex and race would require the co-ordination of agencies with greater legal powers and the participation of stronger trade unions – in short, a programme with in-built social control. As it is, even the enactment of EEC standards on sex discrimination (difficult enough against the uncertainty of such concepts as 'equal value') is met by British policy in the 1980s in a state of defensive schizophrenia, fearful that further regulation will contradict its precepts on the need to deregulate the employer's environment and reduce his – immediate – costs. Nor should it be assumed that the discrimination legislation in general, even at its present low levels (the one area of social control that has been relatively safe from dismantlement since 1975), will always be immune from the arguments that concentrate on the 'burdens on business'. As we saw in Chapter 5, policy in 1985 seeks to reduce regulation even in health and safety (it is claimed, without reducing standards). Every opportunity is taken to stress to the EEC that 'priority should be given to action to reduce the administrative and legislative burdens on business, particularly on small and medium-sized enterprises' (some forty existing or projected Directives and regulations are condemned as 'excessively burdensome').[26] The protections that set out to safeguard the weakest and the poorest can never be secure against such arguments.

Other features have lent further velocity to the flight from collectivism. One is the dominant concept of 'democracy' that underlies the 1984 legislation on trade union 'ballots'. The individualist but autocratic assumptions of the new regulation are apparent in allowing for only one permissible form of 'democracy' in unions, organizations that are at once representative and organizational, that exist not to hold proper elections but to hold proper elections *and* serve the interests of their members in the struggles of the workplace and of society (Chapter 9). Of all the legal mystifications that have fuelled the drive against trade union 'power' so as more easily to enact the recent legislation, however, none has been more extensively deployed than the complaints about the 'immunities', about which debate revived in 1985. As we saw in Chapters 1 and 8, the social function of the 'immunities' in British labour law has been to provide elementary collective rights – to organize, to bargain and to withhold labour – which the common law was unable to grant whether judges wished to do so or not (though what would have happened had they so wished cannot be with certainty assessed). The 'immunities' are often mystified into extravagant 'privileges'. By others they are sometimes presented as a colossal mistake, an albatross hung round the neck of the labour movement in 1906. They are neither. They are a form of drafting.

Non-intervention and rights

It is no way surprising that as, on the one side, the labour market fragmented in an economic and social crisis far more profound than was foreseen in the 1960s and, on the other, the argument for legislation to make unions ineffective was supplemented by semantics that turned legal 'immunities' into social privilege, a new debate should have broken out especially among those who sought possible alternatives to, or even modifications of, the labour law patterns of the early 1980s. It was not a new debate, for the suggestion to replace 'immunities' by 'positive rights' had been canvassed by different groups at the time of Donovan and even before. Since the analysis of 'non-intervention' or 'collective *laissez-faire*' rested upon a system founded on trade union liberties in the form of legal 'immunities' and upon a society enjoying at the time comparative equilibrium and consensus, it is natural – perhaps unavoidable – that this analysis should also now be called into question. Indeed it would be strange if what was acceptable in 1960 needed no amendment in 1990.

From his first exposition of 1954 onwards, the 'non-intervention' of Kahn-Freund (Chapter 1) deployed a description of an industrial relations system in its relationship to law. Beyond this, however, it became an enlightened strategy, though rarely the religion some critics detected. At times it was a language, at others a code, for the defence of autonomous trade unionism; in part it was a brilliant rationalization of history advanced as a reason for pluralist practices and values. The historical analysis has not been replaced; but the prognosis that was built upon it expected society and the balance of its classes to remain more static than proved to be the case.

As we approach the 1990s an abstract debate about 'voluntarism', 'legalism' or 'non-intervention' is increasingly irrelevant. Not only has it been said that such concepts suffer an inherent 'weakness as a tool of social policy', not least when government is bound to intervene in economic and industrial management, but also that 'the tradition of legal

abstention has arguably made it easier' to introduce restrictive legislation and a 'retreat from social progress' in industrial relations.[27] But it
does underestimate the resolution of the Government of 1980 to think
that it would have been greatly deterred from legislating if British trade
unions had enjoyed 'positive rights'. The Fair Wages Resolution did not
last long. Nevertheless, modern government, even a 'market' government, is obliged to engage in attempted economic management to a
much greater extent than the Cabinet of 1906. This is why it is so remarkable that labour law structures were not swallowed up by incomes
policy (Chapter 4; a 'positive rights' structure might perhaps have
been affected more). More important, 'voluntarism' is as weak or as
strong as the *social*, not the *legal*, conditions allow; for it rests to a
significant extent upon autonomous union bargaining strength. When
unions have little option but to acquiesce, their consent, like that given
out of Hobson's choice after the General Strike of 1926, may still be
given to a system that at least does not deny them a place, however
lowly. Unless the realities of power behind the social equilibrium are
kept in view, 'non-intervention' may appear to be content with the
existing balance; this is what gave legitimacy to the 'radical critique' of
the analysis.[28] Now, however, when full employment is no longer the
central focus of public policy, when deregulation and market forces
assume the profitable places of the Welfare State, the social power of
trade unions is marginalized in legal and economic steps that reduce or
eliminate social control over national resources. As Crouch suggests:
'Economic liberalism does not imply a weak state; it is merely opposed
to detailed government interference with the rights of property
owners.'[29] In face of such developments, bare 'non-intervention' would
indeed be a weak policy. Nor could it remain a central tenet if we
believed that, socially, the employer had become 'the agent of the
consumer, the instrument of the public', an idea with which Kahn-
Freund flirted at the end, and which opens the way to the State control of
trade unions that he still resisted.[30]

Problems of rights and immunities

In such a situation it would be absurd not to consider seriously the
prospect of an alternative type of labour law based on 'positive legal
rights'. After all, if we started with a blank sheet of paper to devise a

structure of labour law, we would be more likely to speak in terms of 'rights' – rights to organize, to bargain, to withdraw labour – than of 'acts that are immune from liability in trade disputes'. The objectives are social, not legal. Each of us would then add a list of our favourite rights, and duties. The confusing semantics of 'immunities' could be put aside in the design of objectives, and the 'power' of the industrial parties analysed in concrete terms of property, poverty and equality. Such a debate might also focus more clearly the rights of workers in the public sector (those who ultimately may be most at risk in policies of union restriction). It would permit direct discussion of the purposes of trade unions and their rights, the place of management, the role of non-unionists, and the relationship of each to industrial democracy and economic management in as straightforward a manner as is left to us for debates about political economy.

But the legal debate is not the social debate. Nor can we begin with blank paper. We inherit the State structure – or perhaps, in certain constitutional respects, 'compared with the rest of Europe, a state-less structure'[31] – and a specific legal system to which the very free trade unions themselves relate historically by way of 'immunities'. The special problems for new positive rights in Britain derive partly from this history, from the institutionalized power of the common law, and from the lack of a method of giving parliamentary legislation a 'constitutional' status beyond the reach of the common law perspective of judges.[32] It is therefore important that the debate on 'positive rights' be carefully conducted.

First, no system of labour law is either all 'immunities' or all 'rights'. Even in Britain certain 'positive rights' have been won, for example on peaceful picketing in trade disputes: 'it shall be lawful to attend', say the statutes from 1906 onwards. But in the face of such general liabilities as obstruction and nuisance, the interpretation of that right was compressed by judges even before 1980 to the level of a narrow trade dispute 'immunity'.[33] Nor do 'positive rights' by themselves guarantee results. West German workers have a positive right to strike; but its judicial limitation by doctrines first of 'social adequacy' and then of 'proportionality' restricted it to a narrower area than the freedom enjoyed by British workers for nearly a century before 1980. French workers in the public sector find that they are the subjects of exceptions from the constitutional right to strike. Because they see legalized picketing as an exception for workers from the 'general law' – whatever the wording of the statute – English judges are prone to accept its equation with civil disorder despite the historical evidence, and therefore ready to turn the flanks of the statutory 'rights' in order to equate the liberties of peaceful pickets with those of hitch-hikers (Chapter 7). The experiment between 1975 and 1980 with a positive duty on employers to recognize unions on the recommendation of ACAS (Chapter 4) also reminds us of the similar use of 'judicial review' when statutory agencies are used in support of workers' industrial and social rights.

To the problem of interpretation is then added the structural issue of substantive principle. Positive rights in labour law could not be left at the mercy of antagonistic common law doctrines, as developed from time to time. At present, for example, the worker has no 'right' to strike because his individual employment is normally not suspended but broken in industrial action – a feature that surprises the European civil lawyer. It is often argued that, before one can speak of a *right* to strike, the law must go further, banning all prejudice at the hands of the employer against employees who strike. This is a viewpoint of unimpeachable logic, though it would require great changes in the rule that strikers cannot, except within narrow limits, avail themselves of our unfair dismissal law (Chapter 3).[34] The Donovan Report illustrated the awkward questions posed even by the primary problem of suspending employment contracts (e.g. can the employer ever dismiss the worker during a strike? What happens if the strike never ends? Is a strike notice of fixed length a requirement? May the striking worker moonlight?). In Ireland proposals for such suspension have come to demand as preconditions a strike ballot and one week's notice. Strikes and 'industrial action' would need to be defined. Would we include a work-to-rule, for example? This type of action is within the right to strike in Italy and West Germany, but not in France; while in Sweden even one worker has a right to 'strike' so long as it is official union action. Again, in what way could the judges' 'creative' innovations in the common law be prevented from nibbling away at the new rights? We recall the advent of 'economic duress' in 1982, the uncertain principles of actionable damage by 'unlawful means', the historical lessons of conspiracy in 1901 and of 'intimidation' in 1964 (Chapter 8). The advocates of positive rights are understandably impatient at what Bercusson calls 'legislative pirouettes attempting to circumvent the legal perspective by stipulating immunity'.

At times it looks like a game. But it may be unduly optimistic to believe that

The advantage of a rights-based system is that the right could exist regardless of common law developments. So even if the judges developed new causes of action, this would be largely irrelevant in the labour field because they would always be secondary to the primary statutory right.[35]

There is no such guarantee that the common law would 'come to a virtual standstill'. Even the White Paper of 1981 saw the need (but proposed no method) for a system of positive rights to 'insulate any legal right to strike from the common law'.

In different forms various comparable systems of labour law encounter analogous problems. In every industrialized democracy the law has to provide a limiting factor for industrial rights. In Italy, where the constitutional freedom to strike is perhaps at its most broad, neither the 'right' nor the (wider) 'liberty' to strike extends to strikes that subvert the constitutional order or the exercise of rights and powers expressing popular sovereignty.[36] The French constitutional right to strike is interpreted as accepting 'mixed', politico-economic strikes, but not 'political' strikes narrowly defined (unless, possibly, strikes in defence of institutions of the Republic). In Britain the limiting factor has since 1906 been the golden formula based upon the 'trade dispute', now restricted by the new legal policy after 1982, which gave to many industrial disputes the character of a 'political' and unprotected status, as we saw in Chapter 7.[37] These lines between the industrial and the non-industrial are a reflection of policy, not of philosophical categories. As Fox says, their categorization is 'shifting and conventional'. The problem is not confined to a system of 'immunities', and a system of British positive rights would be obliged to draw its own line. Otherwise it would have no chance at all of rendering any part of the common law 'irrelevant in the labour field'. Judges could mould the boundaries of the statute, just as they have moulded the meaning of the golden formula. If 'rights' were to overtake the common law in this labour field, the definition of a 'trade dispute' would need to be replaced by a definition of the 'labour field'. Certainly, the introduction of positive rights changes the manner of the discussion; it does not change – nor by itself solve – the problem. Indeed, there are those who say that the judiciary of the High Court will never accept that Parliament has forbidden them to be, in Lord Scarman's phrase, 'some sort of back seat driver in trade disputes'. More of them seem to share the wish of Sir John Donaldson MR to be in poll position.

The extreme character of this problem in the real situation in Britain is a reflection of the place of the common law and therefore of the judges, on the one hand, and of the acuity of social conflict, on the other. Yet it is not, as is often thought, uniquely a British problem. In Australia submerged beneath Commonwealth and State compulsory arbitration machinery lies the largely unreconstructed common law, operating especially in the State courts. When a Labour Government proposed to repeal Commonwealth statutory liabilities for 'secondary boycotts' in 1984 it was necessarily led to propose that, where a dispute went into the conciliation and arbitration machinery, no tort actions should interfere with this process. It did so by proposing not that tort liabilities be excluded but that 'an application for an injunction shall not be heard or granted by any court' in relevant actions in tort.[38]

Civil law systems also have recent experience. Starting with the unprecedented *Corfu* case in 1972, French judges began to make unions and trade unionists liable in damages for loss caused by 'fault' (analogous to tort) in industrial action, sometimes by reason of an occupation of premises or blockades, sometimes by reason of breach of collective agreements and the motives of the defendants. So concerned did French lawyers become that this trend in the judgments might 'neutralize the constitutional right to strike' that in 1982 the Government introduced a measure to grant a 'relative civil immunity' for collective industrial action, retaining nevertheless liability in damages for criminal acts and acts 'manifestly not connected with the exercise of the right to strike or trade union rights'. This immunity Bill was not destined, however, to join the reforms of 1982; the Constitutional Council annulled it as unconstitutional on grounds of infringing constitutional 'equality before the law', a decision much questioned by French labour lawyers.[39] Whether these continuing judgments signal a French *Quinn* v. *Leathem*, or whether that judiciary will avoid such a contest with its labour movement, we cannot know. But when a labour law system like the French – containing trade union rights, including a right to strike, of constitutional status that judges respect – begins to experience such novel civil liabilities (workers have had to pay non-strikers massive losses; workers' representatives were made liable to pay for the damage to an employer's deteriorating goods) and stumbles into a debate about 'immunities' at a time when its Government is introducing new rights for unions and workers (the *lois Auroux*, with their right to bargain, rights of 'expression' for workers in the enterprise, new limits on the disciplinary powers of management), it is permissible to speculate about the effect of economic and social change upon courts other than our own. Further, it poses ever more sharply the question of how laws introducing basic, positive rights into British labour law could be guaranteed an understanding reception from a judiciary most of whom, like Lord Diplock, have found even the frail, native immunities to be 'intrinsically repugnant'.

This is not to say that some of our 'immunities' could not, or should not, be replaced by 'rights'. It is to recognize the difficulty of the task, and the need for concrete, rather than theological, debate. An agile CBI committee in 1980 favoured the consideration of 'a better legal framework', and in it 'even perhaps . . . a positive right to strike, *subject to reasonable limitations*'. It is idle to declare for or against 'rights' as such. We need to know *which* rights, and with *what* limitations. More generally, there is a natural fear, as Simpson put it about recognition rights in 1979, that the legal framework 'can easily be amended in pursuit of policies contrary to those for which it was envisaged'.[40] Rights are not immune from judicial restriction. Moreover, the limitations in any such enactment will necessarily reflect the interest of management in continuous production and control of work. Indeed, any labour law provisions that are part of a package of measures aiming at social reconstruction by agreement must necessarily convince management that they will, in the traditional Donovan sense, contribute to improved industrial relations. Workers in unions would need to be similarly convinced of the utility of a rights-based approach.

'Limitations' set in a statute might prove to be less flexible than a non-interventionist pattern, within which changes in bargaining strength are accommodated by social rather than legal amendment. This leads us to the most difficult issue of all. If anything emerges from the recent cases, it is that, here as elsewhere, the life of the common law is procedure. The miners' cases and others of 1984–5, irrespective of the merits of particular litigation, re-emphasized this central point. The land of the interlocutory injunctions was little more disturbed by TULRA 1974 s. 17 (2) (p. 692) than a pond by a pebble. A central issue of British labour law reform is whether Parliament can assert control over the civil remedies and court procedures. In labour relations a positive right is of limited value to a defendant if the plaintiff can obtain an injunction.

Even if workers in Britain regained liberties to organize and to act in combination, in substance and in form, if all the problems of common law principle were solved, if legislative ways were found to suspend employment contracts and to block off the judicial 'creativity' that every decade or so invades labour law with the class partiality of a new tort, the enterprise might come to naught if a union or its officials were still subject at a few hours' notice to an interim injunction to 'preserve the status quo until full trial'. The limitations of the positive rights (and there would be some), just like the limits on the golden formula and 'immunities', would provide even the average employer's lawyer with enough stuff to fill a 'serious case to argue'. The judge would, as today, no doubt assure trade union defendants that their rights would be fully explored and enforced at the full trial. Meanwhile, on the 'balance of convenience' he would normally grant the interim injunction banning workers' industrial action, leaving over the difficult questions – 'things that can only be ascertained by the court after hearing full oral evidence' – to the full trial, months or years away, or never.[41] If need arises, as we learned in 1984–5 (Chapter 9), the plaintiff now may obtain even a declaration or a receivership, all in 'interlocutory' proceedings. If the defendants disobey the interim order, contempt of court is inevitable; and the consequences of this may endure long after the industrial action and even after the legal action has been abandoned. The relative absence of this practical issue from the debate on 'positive rights' reflects its absence from much other labour law discussion. Its importance was the reason for the extended treatment in Chapters 8 and 9. To alter the balance in the court room we need to find ways to change the unjust procedure of the labour injunction and to stop pretending that it is merely a problem of judicial 'discretion' in each case. This task is not impossible, but it is crucial.

Such considerations do not foreclose the issue. They do not detract from the assertion that a worker should, in an industrial democracy, enjoy social rights to organize widely with other workers, to withdraw labour and to have negotiations conducted with his employer by freely chosen representatives. They do attempt to recognize the character of the legal problems, both for 'positive rights' and for 'immunities', problems increasingly profound after the judicial pronouncements of the last decade. A 'framework of law' is tested in courts; unless both substantive and procedural dimensions are addressed, reform will founder. There is no reason to continue with procedures that can be shown to be unjust to trade unions. The judiciary must eventually understand that the failure of a modern Lord Wright to speak out on this matter could put in issue the legal system as a whole. If the relationships between organized workers and the courts remain so primitive that Parliament cannot rely upon the judiciary to understand the nature of laws that take their ground not in individualism but in collective autonomy, then certain decisions may have to be put elsewhere to other bodies for decision. We saw that a parallel problem has arisen in regard to the industrial tribunals and employment protection law. Indeed, in asking more directly what is the job that has to be done, proposals for reform now extend even to the replacement of the tribunals by arbitral machinery (Chapter 3).

The labour law discussion illustrates how far from radical are the discussions about courts generally in Britain. We have accepted the need for specialized tribunals in labour law. There is no reason to exclude from our minds the appointment of labour law judges in the Continental manner, selected from among young lawyers who choose to be such judges early in their career, and who then acquire experience in the field. Nor would it follow that the normal appellate courts should necessarily review all their decisions. A self-contained industrial magistracy must be an item on the agenda. The option might be considered, too, whether a suitable body should certify that a matter falls within the 'labour field' or is a 'trade dispute' (whichever limiting factor is used), just as the High Court is now prevented from passing upon the 'independence' of a trade union if it arises in litigation, since the question must be handed over to the Certification Officer (EPA 1975 s. 8). It will be said that such decisions will immediately be made subject to 'judicial review' or that in this or similar ways there is no escape from such limitation by the judges. As Griffith made clear, dealing with the CRE and the *Prestige* case, 1984 (Chapter 6, p. 481):

The idea of a public authority invested with the power to investigate, to adjudicate and to decide, while providing persons affected with opportunities to make representations, was too much for the senior judiciary, reared in the tradition of private rights, to accept.[42]

This is an issue, a general political issue, that must be confronted by any administration in government intending to use such bodies, as it must, in the urgent struggle against discrimination. So too, for legislation that means business in labour law if it heads in a direction different from that of the 1980s.

Such an approach also will involve consideration of the abrogation of certain torts altogether, reviving such parts as are necessary by careful statutory provision. The approach by way of 'immunity' for nominate torts has been rendered doubtful by reason of the judges' record. Such parts of the tort of inducing breach of contract, for example, as are needed by commercial law could be resurrected after a general legislative execution. The common law crime of conspiracy was dealt with in this way in 1977. The whole field of tort liability for intentional acts must be similarly scrutinized. If 'immunities' have been shown to be unavailing for the implementation of Parliament's purpose by way of protection against specified torts, its legitimate authority is entitled to displace that of the common law more fundamentally. As Humpty Dumpty said, the question is which is to be master – that's all. Similarly, in the fashion of the Australian Bill, interim injunctions could be prohibited in cases where the court was informed by an appropriate body that a dispute fell within alternative procedures. Whatever legislative form they take, the social rights will be effective only if served, not dominated, by legal procedures.

By this point in the legal debate, it is a matter of little more than drafting whether particular clauses of a labour law code are constructed in the language of 'rights' or of 'immunities'. 'Rights' may be preferable because they say what they mean; 'immunities' will be unavoidable if only to protect their flanks. Concentration should be focussed upon the content of the social rights as they operate in practice. Nor should we despair of there being no judges who can appreciate the political and legal point. Those who urge that the tripartite E A T has expressed a sufficiently liberal and different approach to have its jurisdiction expanded – and secluded from the superior appellate courts – lead us to examine anew how independent of the old traditions and of management ideology this court really is in employment protection law. What would it make of the labour injunction? In 1982 Lord Scarman spoke calmly of areas of executive discretion and decision where 'co-operation calls for a high degree of judicial restraint. The ambit of executive decision and executive discretion must be defined in statute: and judges must respect it.' Similarly, in the litigation on the recognition procedures of 1975 and even the injunction cases of 1980, he showed a wish to plumb the industrial relations realities and an inclination to break (as Parliament manifestly intended in 1906 and 1974) with the judicial traditions of the past as 'back seat driver' in industrial conflict.[43] Nor should it be assumed that there are not younger members of the bench who would not necessarily relish another round of sterile conflict with both workers, unions and a Government determined to construct a modern system based upon the rights of individual workers to combine in autonomous collective bargaining, with effective rights to organize, to bargain and to strike. But if Parliament lacks the determination to insist upon new forms of judicial procedures, such voices will be lost in the robed crowd.

Theory and practice

Among other questions of importance to the future of labour law in the 1990s are some relating to theory, to practice and to research. In the Donovan era a tradition had grown up that labour legislation should be based upon knowledge and therefore upon research. Subjective social policy choices are inevitable; but they can – and should – be based upon scrupulous objectivity about the social facts. Brown and Hepple have documented the way in which this tradition was ruptured in the events involving political interference with research, which led to the dissolution of the Panel for Monitoring of Labour Legislation in 1983.[44] The legislation in 1980–5, restricting employment protection, union activities, defences against low pay and the closed shop, frequently rested on arguments not easily sustained by reference to current research (Chapters 3, 4, 8 and 9). The research base of policy needs urgently to be restored. For the effects of legislation in practice upon different areas of industrial relations *behaviour* is still uncertain; this is true, for example, even for the legal innovations of the Social Contract period.[45] The legal provisions upon unfair dismissal appear to have contributed to the growing formality of procedures; and the place of the industrial tribunals generally may have introduced a more 'lawyer-like' climate at the level of personnel managers and even of shop stewards. This the judge who was president of the E A T in 1982 called the law that now 'both employer and employees voluntarily accept', based upon 'principles of fair industrial behaviour', of which the 'Industrial Tribunals should have a uniform view'; a precedent pointing the way to a role for legal regulation in 'other sectors of labour relations'.

Changes in industrial relations practice there have been; but how deep and how centrally instigated by the new laws – how far behaviour on the shop floor determined by reference to agreed principles or to 'custom and practice' has been replaced by that based on accepted legal (or what are believed to be legal) principles – is more uncertain. The Warwick team found evidence that the legislation has had effects of this kind, an increase in individual as opposed to collective approaches, contributing, for example, to an increased importance of the personnel function or a shift in authority away from lower level supervision, though the impact was smaller, perhaps necessarily, on small firms.[46] What is less well established is the precise manner in which such laws complement or obstruct the growth and activities of trade unions or collective bargaining, or even the initiatives of managers whose aim is to introduce more participative, along with more efficient, work practices. For the initiative lies normally with management, and through management will law most often be mediated to the worker.

This process of invasion of industrial relations by State norms is sometimes described as 'a process of juridification'. Kahn-Freund described the West German labour law system – especially at Works Council level – as having, in contrast to the British, all the advantages and disadvantages of 'bureaucratization and "juridification"'. Recent analyses, especially by Simitis, however, have questioned the validity of this distinction, advancing the view, as Clark puts it, that the trend towards juridification is 'a universal feature of all democratic industrial societies, including Britain'.[47] Industrialization, the thesis runs, 'excludes alternatives'; and 'the long road from the Factories Act (1833) to the Employment Act 1982 is a single confirmation of progressive juridification'. Some British writers have suggested that there had been a deep, even irreversible, trend towards legal regulation, especially between 1963 and 1978. Simitis argues that juridification 'significantly increased' in the Social Contract period, as well as in the 1980s. State control of internal trade union affairs in the 1984 Act and 'legal scrutiny' by ballots for closed-shop agreements in 1982 are examples. No doubt the degree to which employers have used new opportunities in the court room to settle industrial conflict, or unions have accepted forms of association or procedure prescribed by the State, may now afford fresh material for the thesis.

Yet neither in Britain nor in other countries does this apparently uncompromising historical process appear to be an unbroken line of advance. In Italy the trend of the 1980s was still 'to intervene in order to support, not to replace . . . [even] to promote forms of self-regulation'.[48] Similar objectives underlay the British laws of 1975, in the main tradition of the 'props' to collective bargaining (Chapter 4). Nor is it clear that the new laws have fundamentally 'juridified' British industrial relations in practice and in fact at the workplace. Simitis regards many such laws as forms of 'indirect steering' by which the State 'instrumentalises' collective bargaining, tying the self-regulation of the parties (workers and employers) to labour market rules set by it. There are many problems here. One might doubt whether the modern European 'State', for example, is capable of all the 'steering' that the theory attributes to it. Direction of the social facts may be more often in the hands of international corporations. (We saw that Kahn-Freund recognized in 1972 that the first force to colonize labour relations was the international enterprise.) Apart from such problems of the 'State', however, the British case seems far more complex than the theory allows. True, the direct, legal regulation of conflict has now made greater use of civil and criminal sanctions in Britain and, more important, has confused the civil and the criminal law (Chapters 7 and 8). But the legislation of the 1970s aimed to encourage collective bargaining, while the restrictive legislation of the 1980s has reintroduced control of unions not by statutory regulation (except perhaps in respect of electoral and strike ballots in the 1984 Act) but by enthroning the common law once more as mistress of the rules of the game. If the word 'juridification' is applied to this process too, so that more common law regulation equals more 'juridification', the value of the concept is diminished, for this process began not with industrialization but with Henry II.

Throughout Western Europe schools of thought have made demands for 'deregulation' of the labour market, most vociferously in Britain; similar voices resist the 'oppressive' character of State intervention, which in improving workers' conditions begins, Simitis says, upon a 'colonization' or 'occupation of their life-world'. This complaint comes more often from the employer when his rule-making powers at work are confined. Then regulation becomes 'authoritarian' (as in nuclear industry or in US safety regulation). Simitis finds one answer in a gradual 're-individualization' of a (still protected) employment relationship. Moreover, in the 'electronic cottages' of the future, with homeworking and 'telecommuting', collective bargaining will not be adequate, and greater legal regulation will become inevitable. State intervention, representing the community as a whole, will be increasingly needed to restructure the labour market in 'high-risk' technologies.

Despite the recognizable points of contact with British experience, this persuasive thesis seems not entirely to fit. It may not take full account of the ambition of democratic social control in a period of change found, for example, in the Italian and the French legislation. With such legislation autonomous social forces, unions and management, find space for flexible, joint regulation within a developing legal framework. As Clark says: 'All juridification involves state intervention, but not all state intervention necessarily involves juridification.' We are back to the distinctions met in Chapter 1 between different kinds of 'law' and the need to assess the impact of each upon the realities of work. The index of how much 'more law' there is may tell us little. In fact, we can be surprised at how much law there was in 1900. Nor was the emergence of trade unions from illegality indicative merely of 'State recognition'. The primary forces at work were social not legal. Few people believe, with Lord Halsbury in 1901, that the legislature 'created' trade unions. Nor is there an unbroken line of British development towards statutory juridification. Collective agreements that the 1971 Act attempted to 'juridify' were (relatively) 'dejuridified' by TULRA 1974; and in that process the causative social forces included management as much as trade unions. Indeed, as the contrast in Britain between 1972 and 1984 suggests, the relative effect of laws upon unions and workers is to a great extent dictated by the economic and social environment:

things which may have a disastrous effect in a declining labour market can be absorbed by a buoyant economy and . . . a healthy union movement can 'take' a great deal of legal intervention, whilst weak unions may be its victim.[49]

Labour law tomorrow

Such theses as juridification, just like comparative studies of other countries' systems, are valuable because they demand from us answers to uncomfortable questions and inquiry at the level both of theory and of practice. It was the same with collective *laissez-faire*. They remind us that the interventions of the State in the life of the worker need to be studied and assessed at all levels, in terms of economic result, of social class, of democratic principles and of human rights, in social security law as much as in employment and discrimination protection, in trade union law along with health and safety. We are unlikely to understand the drift without a secure understanding of our own history. Many in 1986 predict an increase in overall governmental action in the labour market; it may be that new technologies and new industrial relationships will accentuate this need. In 1979 Crouch presented stark alternatives: *neo-laissez-faire* or 'bargained corporatism', the first pursuing the logic of the economic market, the second promoting State action in tripartite deals with employers and unions.[50] Both, though, risk new interventions with an autocratic tendency: the first because market individualism, despite support from finance capital, implies periods of high unemployment and social instability, which reinforce its dependence upon a strong, central State, even upon 'the police and the armed forces', to sustain it; the second because, despite its likely adherence to radical social transformation, even 'industrial democracy', it may be seen as a threat by autonomous groups, in particular trade unions and shop-floor workers, with constrained containment within settled policies such as incomes policies (quite apart, we might add, from the risk it may run of resistance from capital or, not quite the same, from management).

In whichever direction Britain moves in the 1990s, projects for new labour laws must be tested in concrete terms by their effect upon real people, the condition and quality of their lives, their prosperity and their – real, not theoretical – liberty. Research must test realities and curb policies which, like the mistakes on 'trainees', compound the errors of the past; and theory must draw its strength from experience. Even the magic of 'juridification' must cast no false spells. For, as Klare observes, 'the political tendency of regulation as such cannot be determined *a priori*'.[51] It depends on who is to be regulated, and for what. Regulation of work on asbestos benefits workers; deregulation of combinations did, but of pensions may not. The lessons from our laws on dismissal or equal pay may be uncertain or ambivalent. But in the future regulation is inescapable, just as it was in the past. The crucial question is not 'how much' but: of what sort and to what end?

The context for tomorrow's labour law may be more desperate than that of previous years. The hard economics of the market, not least the international market and the transnational forces within it, will test the capacity of domestic policies in Britain to provide for the needs of workers and their families and, above all, for the weakest in our society. The power of law as the instrument for achieving the aims of such policies must constantly be in question. As in race relations, so in industrial relations: 'to use the legal approach as the primary weapon is to begin with second best'.[52] Even as a secondary force, the powers of law in its many forms are qualified. But it has a necessary place in the ambition to regain social *consensus*, to recapture full employment, to regenerate economic advance and to confront the disfigurements of disability and inhumanity suffered by those disadvantaged by race, sex, age or poverty.[53] Because we live in a society whose inequalities are strongly related to social class, it should be no embarrassment to discuss the class character of the legal product. Lawyers, whether in offices, chambers, courts or colleges, have an obligation in these choices to the citizens in whose service we teach or practice the law; and we do now stand before the immediate and unavoidable choice between a more civilized democracy and a tortured disintegration of social structures. The paradoxical need is for radical change but also change negotiated by social consent.

Still subordinate in the employment relationship and in the market where labour power is sold, most workers will judge the lawyer's work by its contribution to the struggle against twin evils, unemployment and social deprivation. The British labour lawyer, however, can, if he chooses, share in one special, hard-won bequest, the values and the traditions of free trade unionism and of autonomous collective bargaining of which it is an integral part. These are freedoms in which management has a stake as well as workers, values to be cherished if we are to negotiate a difficult journey of social transition as a democratic, efficient yet decent society. Workers will continue to need and to practise the protection and the fraternity that come from autonomous association at work one with another. Labour law may be judged by them also by its role in the defence and promotion of these human rights for tomorrow's workers and their children. From this liberty shared in industrial democracy we may yet hope to repair the conflicts and oppressions that have all too often marked so far the relations between the worker and the law.

Notes and References

1 Foundations of Labour Law

1 H. Phelps Brown, *The Growth of British Industrial Relations* (1959), p. 355. The modern textbook is G. Bain (ed.), *British Industrial Relations* (1983).

2 O. Kahn-Freund, in A. Flanders and H. Clegg (eds.), *The System of Industrial Relations in Great Britain* (1954), p. 45.

3 O. Kahn-Freund, respectively, *Labour and The Law* (3rd ed. 1984; P. Davies and M. Freedland, eds.), p. 18; K. Renner, *The Institutions of Private Law and Their Social Functions* (1949), Introduction, p. 28.

4 See Wedderburn and W. T. Murphy (eds.), *Labour Law and the Community* (1982).

5 See on union density: G. Bain and R. Price, Chap. 1, in Bain (ed.), *Industrial Relations in Britain* (1983); and on trade unions, R. Hyman.

6 A. Flanders, *Management and Unions* (1970), p. 99.

7 W. McCarthy and S. Parker, 'Shop Stewards and Workshop Relations' (1968, Donovan Commission, Research Paper 10), pp. 54, 56; see too M. Terry, in G. Bain (ed.), *Industrial Relations in Britain* (1983), and the survey in (1985) 345 I R R R 2.

8 A. Marsh, *Employee Relations Policy and Decision Making* (1982, CBI), p. 187; W. Brown (ed.), *The Changing Contours of British Industrial Relations* (1981), Chap. 7.

9 W. Daniel and N. Millward, *Workplace Industrial Relations in Britain* (1983), p. 291.

10 See C. Craig, J. Rubery, R. Tarling and F. Wilkinson, *Labour Market Structure, Industrial Organization and Low Pay* (1982), Chap. 6; C. Pond, in G. Bain (ed.), *Industrial Relations in Great Britain* (1983), pp. 193–4; P. Townsend, *Poverty in the UK* (1979), pp. 645–9.

11 See R. Edwards, *Contested Terrain: The Transformation of the Workplace in the 20th Century* (1979), pp. 11–12, 166–74; J. Atkinson, 'Flexibility, Uncertainty and Manpower Planning' (1984) I MS Report No. 89; and, with D. Gregory (1986) *Marxism Today*, April, 123; (1984) 325 I R R R 15; but see K. Mayhew and B. Rosewall (1979) 41 *Oxford Bull. of Economics and Statistics* 81.

12 H. Braverman, *Labour and Monopoly Capital* (1974), p. 65.

13 Clark and Wedderburn, in Wedderburn, R. Lewis and J. Clark (eds.), *Labour Law and Industrial Relations* (1983), p. 145.

14 O. Kahn-Freund, 'Labour Law', in *Law and Opinion in England in the 20th Century* (1959; Ginsberg, ed.), p. 241.

15 H. Clegg, A. Fox and A. Thompson, *A History of British Trade Unions* (1964), pp. 215–39.

16 *Springhead Spinning Co.* v. *Riley* (1868) LR 6 Eq. 551.

17 O. Kahn-Freund and B. Hepple, *Laws Against Strikes* (1972), p. 4.

18 Wedderburn, 'Industrial Relations and the Courts' (1980) 9 ILJ 65.

19 *Trade Union Immunities* (Cmnd 8128, 1981), para. 384.

20 *NWL* v. *Woods* [1979] ICR 867, 886 (HL).

21 R. Simpson (1980) 43 MLR 327, 336.

22 *Express Newspapers Ltd* v. *McShane* [1979] ICR 210, 218; rev'sd by HL [1980] AC 672; see the comments of Lord Diplock, p. 687; Lord Salmon, p. 690; and in *Duport Steels Ltd* v. *Sirs* [1980] 1 All E. R. 529, 541, 548 *per* Lord Edmund Davies; 550 *per* Lord Keith.

23 P. Elias and K. Ewing [1982] CLJ 321, 344.

24 J. A. G. Griffith, *The Politics of the Judiciary* (3rd ed. 1985), pp. 185, 234.

25 O. Kahn-Freund (1944) 6 MLR 112, 143 (the legislation in the USA 1935, Germany 1918, France 1936); and see Wedderburn, Chap. 3, in Wedderburn, Lewis and Clark, *Labour Law and Industrial Relations* (1983).

26 E. Hobsbawm, *Worlds of Labour* (1984), pp. 152–3; and on 'human rights' pp. 309–11; compare D. Kennedy (1981) Ind. Rel. L. J. 503, 506.

27 O. Kahn-Freund, *Labour Relations Heritage and Adjustment* (1979), p. 47.

28 A. Fox, *History and Heritage* (1985), pp. 162, 435.

29 See Val Lorwin, *The French Labour Movement* (1954); H. Grebing, *History of the German Labour Movement* (1969); D. Horowitz, *The Italian Labour Movement* (1963) and Wedderburn (1980) 9 ILJ pp. 66–79.

30 G. Stedman-Jones, *Languages of Class* (1983), p. 178.

31 See R. Kidner (1982) 2 *Legal Studies* 34, 46–52; and see M. Beer, *History of British Socialism*, Vol. II (1929), pp. 237–45.

32 H. Phelps Brown, *The Growth of British Industrial Relations* (1959), p. 215, and Chap. IV *passim*.

33 B. Napier (1977) 6 ILJ 1, 9; and on 'unitary' approaches, A. Fox, *Beyond Contract; Work, Power and Trust Relations* (1974), pp. 248–54.

34 Browne-Wilkinson J., *Midland Plastics* v. *Till* [1983] ICR 118, 123–4.

35 In M. Ginsberg (ed.), *Law and Opinion in England in the 20th Century* (1959), pp. 224, 244; on law as a secondary force, *Labour and the Law* (3rd ed. 1984), pp. 18–28. On conventional 'pluralism' in the USA: K. Stone (1981) 90 Yale L. J. 1059.

36 Respectively A. Wilson (1984) 13 ILJ 1, 24; R. Lewis (1979) 8 ILJ 202, 228.

37 See 'Lessons from the Industrial Court' (1975) 91 L Q R 181, 191–2; *Guardian*, 30 November 1983; *Time Out*, 1 December 1983.

38 C. Crouch, *Class Conflict and the Industrial Relations Crisis* (1977), pp. 255–72; R. Hyman, *Strikes* (3rd ed. 1984), Chap. 3; P. Davies and Wedderburn (1977) 6 I L J 197; Fox, op. cit. (notes 28, 38), on unitary and pluralist frames of reference.

39 E. Batstone, *Working Order* (1984), pp. 340–2.

40 See L. Panitch, *Social Democracy and Industrial Militancy* (1976); J. Goldthorpe, Chap. 12, in T. Clarke and L. Clements (eds.), *Trade Unions Under Capitalism* (1978); Wedderburn, R. Lewis and J. Clark, *Labour Law and Industrial Relations* (1983). See too Chapter 10.

41 See H. Collins, *Marxism and Law* (1982), p. 25.

42 J. Griffith, *The Politics of the Judiciary* (3rd ed. 1985), pp. 227–30; R. Miliband, *Capitalist Democracy in Britain* (1982), pp. 116–21.

43 [1898] A C 1 (HL).

44 [1901] A C 495; see on the judges involved, J. A. G. Griffith, *The Politics of the Judiciary* (3rd ed. 1985), pp. 54–8.

45 [1901] A C 426.

46 166 *Parl. Deb.*, 4 Dec. 1906, HL, col. 693–4.

47 *Short History of English Law* (1928), p. 337.

48 *Samples of Lawmaking* (1962), p. 11.

49 *White* v. *Riley* [1921] 1 Ch. 1; *Reynolds* v. *Shipping Fedn* [1924] 1 Ch. 28.

50 See P. Renshaw, in B. Pimlott and C. Cook (eds.), *Trade Unions in British Politics* (1982), pp. 98–104; A. Fox, *History and Heritage* (1985), pp. 306–16.

51 [1923] C L J 8.

52 [1942] A C 435.

53 *Lonrho Ltd* v. *Shell Petroleum* (No. 2) [1982] A C 173, 189.

54 A. Fox, *History and Heritage* (1985), p. 335; M. Morris, *The General Strike* (1976), pp. 289–91.

55 K. W. Wedderburn (1972) 10 B J I R 270, 275, and, on the 1950s, pp. 277–8.

56 R. Miliband, *Parliamentary Socialism* (1973), p. 206.

57 C. Grunfeld (1971) 9 B J I R 330, n. (1).

58 *Thomson & Co. Ltd* v. *Deakin* [1952] Ch. 646 (C A).

59 Lord Denning M R, *Emerald Construction Ltd* v. *Lowthian* [1966] 1 W L R 691, 700–1; see Chapter 8, p. 587.

60 Warner J., *Solihull M B* v. *N U T* [1985] I R L R 211; see Chapter 8, p. 631.

61 *A Giant's Strength* (1958, Conservative Inns of Court Association), p. 11; see too J. Lincoln, *Journey to Coercion* (1964).

62 See C. H. Rolph, *All Those in Favour: The E T U Trial* (1962).

63 D. Lloyd, 10 *Current Legal Problems* (1957), p. 41; Denning L J, *Lee* v.

Showmen's Guild [1952] 2 QB 329; R. Graveson (1963) 7 Jo. of Soc. Public Teachers of Law 121, 126; and see W. E. J. McCarthy, *The Closed Shop* (1964), Chap. 10.

64 See Lord Devlin, *Samples of Law Making* (1962), pp. 11–14.

65 O. Aitkin, in B. Roberts (ed.), *Industrial Relations* (1962), p. 226: 'no longer are [unions] fighting to protect and establish themselves . . . they are established and in possession of considerable power'.

66 See e.g. B. C. Roberts, *Trade Unions in a Free Society* (1959), p. 25, and *Evidence* to Donovan Commission (Day 33, 1966), pp. 1406, 1433–4.

67 See P. Townsend, *Poverty in the UK* (1979), Chaps. 4–7.

68 [1964] AC 1129 (HL), reversing [1963] 1 QB 623 (CA).

69 14 *Federation News* (GFTU) (1964), p. 30, and see p. 41 on 'repressive tendencies'; on differing views about the new tort: Wedderburn (1964) 27 MLR 257; Hoffman (1965) 81 LQR 116.

70 Russell LJ and Lord Denning MR, *Morgan* v. *Fry* [1968] 2 QB 710; see Chapter 3, p. 192.

71 See R. Hyman, *Strikes* (3rd ed. 1983), pp. 197–9, and sources cited.

72 H. Phelps Brown, *The Origins of Trade Union Power* (1983), p. 173.

73 J. A. G. Griffith, *The Politics of the Judiciary* (3rd ed. 1985), pp. 185–90.

74 Kerr LJ, *B. & S. Contracts* v. *VG Publications* [1984] ICR 419, 428; see Chapter 8, page 650.

75 See *Parl. Deb.*, 16 Feb. 1965, HC, col. 1017 (Gunter, Minister of Labour); 24 June 1965, HL, col. 456 (Dilhorne sat judicially 26 times as an ex-Lord Chancellor 1964–9); 25 March, HC Committee A, col. 115 (Heald).

76 Such correlations are not always valid: see P. Edwards, Chap. 9, in G. Bain (ed.), *Industrial Relations in Britain* (1983).

77 H. Clegg, *The Changing System of Industrial Relations in Great Britain* (1979), pp. 315–16.

78 *Report of the Royal Commission* (Cmnd 3623, 1968); and see the Research Papers Nos. 1–12 (1966 to 1968). Criticism arose from this limitation: K. Hawkins, *British Industrial Relations* (1976).

79 P. Jenkins, *The Battle of Downing Street* (1970).

80 H. Clegg, *The Changing System of Industrial Relations in Great Britain* (1979), p. 311.

81 D. Barnes and E. Reid, *Governments and Trade Unions* (1980).

82 K. W. Wedderburn (1972) 10 BJIR 270, 282.

83 See B. Simpson and J. Wood, *Industrial Relations* (1973), p. 179; also B. Weekes, M. Mellish, L. Dickens and J. Lloyd, *Industrial Relations and the Limits of Law* (1975); A. Thomson and S. Engleman, *The Industrial Relations Act* (1975); M. Moran, *The Politics of Industrial Relations* (1977).

84 W. Simkin, *Mediation and the Dynamics of Collective Bargaining* (1971),

p. 205; B. Aaron and K. W. Wedderburn, *Industrial Conflict – A Comparative Legal Survey* (1972), pp. 352–64.

85 H. Clegg, *The Changing System of Industrial Relations in Great Britain* (1979), p. 323.

86 B. Weekes *et al.*, *Industrial Relations and the Limits of Law* (1975), p. 42; S. Dunn and J. Gennard, *The Closed Shop in British Industry* (1984), p. 48.

87 *Trade Union Immunities* (Cmnd 8128, 1981), para. 243.

88 N. Lewis, 'Con-Mech: Showdown for NIRC' (1974) 3 ILJ 201, 212–13; Wedderburn (1974) 37 MLR 187.

89 See *Heatons Transport (St Helens) Ltd* v. *TGWU* [1972] ICR 285 (NIRC); 308 (CA); and [1973] AC 15 (HL). See the useful accounts by P. Davies (1973) 36 MLR 78, and J. Griffith, *The Politics of the Judiciary* (3rd ed. 1985), pp. 64–70, 195–8. See too D. Wilson, *Dockers* (1974), Chaps. 6, and 13 on containerization.

90 *Trade Union Immunities* (Cmnd 8128, 1981), para. 329; Lord Denning, *The Due Process of Law* (1980), p. 39.

91 *Democracy in Trade Unions* (Cmnd 8778, 1983), pp. 14–15, para. 52(a); on the 1984 cases, see Chapter 9, pp. 730–46.

92 K. Jeffery and P. Hennessy, *States of Emergency* (1983), p. 237.

93 Weekes *et al.*, *Industrial Relations and the Limits of Law* (1975), p. 223.

94 Sir John Donaldson, 'The Role of Labour Courts' (1975) 4 ILJ 63, 68.

95 P. Kahn, N. Lewis, R. Livock and P. Wiles, *Picketing, Industrial Tactics and the Law* (1983), p. 193, and generally.

96 E. Batstone, *Working Order* (1984), pp. 70–3.

97 See R. Taylor, in B. Pimlott and C. Cook (eds.), *Trade Unions in British Politics* (1982), pp. 206–8.

98 See Clark and Wedderburn, in Wedderburn, R. Lewis and J. Clark (eds.), *Labour Law and Industrial Relations* (1983), pp. 184–98; J. Clark, H. Hartman, C. Lau and D. Winchester, *Trade Unions, National Politics and Economic Management* (1980): and see Chapter 10 below.

99 S. Dunn and J. Gennard, *The Closed Shop in British Industry* (1984), p. 125; K. Ewing and W. Rees (1983) 12 ILJ 148.

100 Clark and Wedderburn, in Wedderburn, R. Lewis and J. Clark (eds.), *Labour Law and Industrial Relations* (1983), p. 188; see too J. Clark on 'juridification' (1985) 14 ILJ 69; and Chapter 10, pp. 856–60.

101 L. Dickens *et al.*, *Dismissed* (1985), pp. 252–5. See too J. Clark and Wedderburn, 'Juridification: A Universal Trend? British Experience in Labour Law', a response to S. Simitis, 'Juridification of Labour Relations', in G. Treubner (ed.), *Juridification of Social Spheres: a Comparative Analysis* (forthcoming, 1986).

102 O. Kahn-Freund (1977) 6 ILJ 65, 75–6; see the reply by P. Davies and Wedderburn (1977) 6 ILJ 197.

103 Bullock, *Report on Industrial Democracy* (Cmnd 6706, 1977); see Chapter 10, page 836.

104 See R. Nobles, 'Conflicts of Interests in Pension Funds' (1985) 14 ILJ 1.

105 J. Elliott, *Conflict or Co-operation? The Growth of Industrial Democracy* (1978), p. 290.

106 *Parl. Deb.*, 25 July 1979, HL, col. 1942; and see *Building Business, Not Barriers* (1986, Cmnd 9794), Chap. 7.

107 See Davies and Freedland, *Labour Law: Text and Materials* (2nd ed. 1984), p. 140; see too Wedderburn, Chap. 2, in P. Fosh and C. Littler (eds.), *Industrial Relations and the Law in the 1980s* (1985).

108 *The Times*, 18 April 1985; *Financial Times*, 24 April 1985.

109 See *The Relationship Between Employment and Wages* (1985, HM Treasury); *Employment, Real Wages and Unemployment* (1985, Bank of England, Panel Paper No. 24); R. Layard and P. Minford, in C. Greenhalgh, P. R. Layard and A. Oswald (eds.), *The Causes of Unemployment* (1984); *We Can Cut Unemployment* (1985, Charter for Jobs).

110 C. Craig, J. Rubery, R. Tarling and F. Wilkinson, *Labour Market Structure, Industrial Organization and Low Pay* (1982), p. 139; Chapter 4, pp. 353–4.

111 *Labour Research*, February 1985, p. 42.

112 W. Daniel and N. Millward, *Workplace Industrial Relations in Britain* (1983), p. 289.

113 [1984] Ch. 37, 81, 89, 92, 99; Ewing and Rees (1984) 13 ILJ 60.

114 *Trade Union Immunities* (Cmnd 8128, 1981), paras. 200, 324.

115 Wedderburn (1984) 13 ILJ 73, 80–1.

116 Engineering Employers' Federation, *Response to Green Paper* (1981), p. 2; *Financial Times* (leader), 30 November 1981.

117 R. Taylor, *Workers in the New Depression* (1982), p. 184.

118 P. Kahn, N. Lewis, R. Livock and P. Wiles, *Picketing* (1983), p. 166.

119 See the analysis by E. Hobsbawm, 'Inside Every Worker There Is a Syndicalist Trying to Get out', *New Society*, 5 April 1979.

120 Clark and Wedderburn, in Wedderburn, Lewis and Clark (eds.), *Labour Law and Industrial Relations* (1983), p. 206.

121 Either as aiding and abetting the contempt, or through the combination of TULRA 1974 s. 2 (1) (e), and RSC, O. 45, R. 5; see Chapter 8 below.

122 See R. Undy and R. Martin, *Ballots and Trade Union Democracy* (1984), p. 110.

123 Report III (4B), *Freedom of Association and Collective Bargaining: General Survey* (1983, ILO 69th Session), para. 172.

124 *1980s Unemployment and the Unions* (1980), pp. 58, 64.

125 F. A. Hayek, *Law, Legislation and Liberty* Vol. 1 (1973), p. 142, Vol. III (1979), pp. 82, 89–90; and *The Times*, 7 August 1984.

126 A. Fox, *History and Heritage* (1985), pp. 187–9; H. Clegg, A. Fox and A. Thompson, *The History of British Trade Unions* (1964), Chaps. 2 and 4.

127 John Lloyd, *Financial Times*, 17 October 1984, p. 40.

128 See John Lloyd, *Understanding the Miners' Strike* (1985, Fabian Soc. No. 504); B. Towers (1985) Vol. 16 Ind. Rel. Jo. No. 2. p. 8; M. Crick, *Scargill and the Miners* (1985); *Strike* (1985, Sunday Times Insight Team).

129 *Taylor* v. *NUM (Derbyshire Area)* [1984] IRLR 440; [1985] IRLR 99; but see Chapter 9, p. 731; also K. Ewing (1985) 14 ILJ 160.

130 *Clarke* v. *Heathfield* [1985] ICR 203 (CA); and (No. 2) [1985] ICR 606.

131 See *Daily Telegraph*, 4 December 1984; but compare *Sunday Telegraph*, 12 December 1984 (where the links were denied).

132 *Thomas* v. *NUM (South Wales Area)* [1985] IRLR 136; and see R. Benedictus (1985) 14 ILJ 176; and *Read (Transport)* v. *NUM (South Wales)* [1985] IRLR 67.

133 See P. Kahn, N. Lewis, R. Livock and P. Wiles, *Picketing, Industrial Disputes Tactics and the Law* (1983); see too, on policing the strike, P. Wallington [1985] 14 ILJ 145.

134 [1965] AC 269 (HL); (No. 2) [1969] 1 WLR 1547 (CA).

135 See P. Wintour, *Guardian*, 12 February 1986.

136 R. Tur, in Wedderburn and Murphy (eds.), *Labour Law and the Community* (1982), Chap. XVI, now in W. E. J. McCarthy (ed.), *Trade Unions* (1985), pp. 294–6; and now A. Shenfield, *What Right to Strike?* (1986, IEA); C. Hanson, *Trade Union Reform, the Next Step* (1986, Inst. of Dirs.).

137 See Lord Kaldor, *The Economic Consequences of Mrs Thatcher* (1983), p. 54.

138 *The Times*, 9 July 1984.

139 *Parl. Deb.*, 8 Feb. 1982, HC, col. 744.

140 See too the analysis in Clark and Wedderburn, Chap. 6, Wedderburn, Lewis and Clark (eds.), *Labour Law and Industrial Relations* (1983). On tendencies within trade union structure towards 'business' or 'enterprise' unionism, see W. Brown in *Personnel Management* (1983), p. 48.

141 *Multinational Gas and Petrochemical Co.* v. *Multinational Gas and Petrochemical Services Ltd* [1983] Ch. 258; see (1984) 47 MLR 87; see on the law, the Cork Committee Report on *Insolvency Law and Practice* (Cmnd 8558, 1982), Chap. 51.

142 *Regent International Hotels (UK) Ltd* v. *Pageguide Ltd, The Times*, 13 May 1985.

143 See now *Cox* v. *ELG Metals* [1985] ICR 310 (CA); and see *South West Launderettes* v. *Laidler* [1986] IRLR 68.

144 See Hadden, *The Control of Corporate Groups* (1983); K. Hopt (ed.), *Groups of Companies in European Laws* (1982).

145 *Poparm Ltd* v. *Weekes* [1984] IRLR 388; see Chapter 3, p. 209;

Washington Arts Assoc. v. *Forster* [1983] ICR 346 (company limited by guarantee).

146 *Gorictree Ltd* v. *Jenkinson* [1985] ICR 51, 53.

147 *Green & Son Ltd* v. *ASTMS* [1984] ICR 352; *UCATT* v. *Burrage and Lytton* [1978] ICR 314.

148 See Gower, *Modern Company Law* (4th ed. 1979), p. 133; cf. Whincup (1981) 2 Co. Law. 158.

149 *Dimbleby & Sons Ltd* v. *NUJ* [1984] 1 WLR 427, 435; *Examite* v. *Whittaker* [1977] IRLR 312; Simpson (1984) 47 MLR 577.

150 *Parke* v. *Daily News* [1962] Ch. 927; on *ultra vires* today, see *Rolled Steel Products* v. *BSC* [1985] 2 WLR 908, 938–49, 955–7 (CA); cf. Gregory (1985) 48 MLR 109.

151 D. Prentice, *Companies Act 1980* (1981), Chap. 17; and (1981) 10 ILJ 1.

152 See Wedderburn, in K. Hopt and G. Teubner (eds.), *Corporate Governance and Directors' Liabilities* (1985), Chap. 1. (Milton Friedman calls any such diversion from profit maximization 'sheer unadulterated Socialism'.)

153 E. Herman, *Corporate Control, Corporate Power* (1981), p. 235. And see Wedderburn, 'Social Responsibility of Companies' (1985) 15 Melb. U. L. R. 4; R. Wallace, *Legal Control of the Multinational Enterprise* (1982).

154 P. Davies, in Hopt (ed.), *Groups of Companies in European Law* (1982), p. 228; and see R. Bean, *Comparative Industrial Relations* (1985), Chap. 8; Hadden, op. cit., pp. 2–6; Wedderburn (1972) 1 ILJ 12.

155 *Financial Times*, 'Multinationals Turn the Tables', 12 and 23 March 1985; Ford had just launched an 'employee involvement' programme for white-collar staff: ibid., 12 and 23 Feb. 1985. International councils also exist in Britain for over sixty other TNEs: *Labour Research*, July 1984, 178.

156 See on the *Akzo* affair, H. Northrup and R. Rowan (1978) 9 Ind. Rel. Jo., No. 1, p. 27.

157 X. Blanc-Jouvan, in F. Schmidt (ed.), *Discrimination in Employment* (1978), p. 344. On the prospect of 'harmonization' of labour law in EEC: B. Hepple, Chap. II, in J. Adams (ed.), *Essays for Clive Schmitthoff* (1983).

158 R. Blanpain (ed.), *Comparative Labour Law and Industrial Relations* (1982), p. 93; P. Davies, in Hopt (ed.), op. cit., p. 227; T. Kennedy, *European Labor Relations* (1980), Chap. 8; R. Blanpain, *The Badger Case and OECD Guidelines* (1977). On the 1984 revision of the OECD guidelines, see J. Rojot (1985) 23 BJIR 379. On the UN Code, P. Maynard (1983) 4 Co. Law. 3.

159 See G. Aubert (1984) 3 Bulletin de droit comparé du travail (Bordeaux) 5, 10.

160 Herman, op. cit., p. 301. Not everyone favours transnational bargaining: H. Northrup and R. Rowan, *Multinational Bargaining Attempts* (1979). See too J. Stopford and L. Turner, *British and the Multinationals* (1985), Chaps. 6, 9.

2 The Employment Relationship

1 I. Smith and J. Wood, *Industrial Law* (2nd ed. 1983), p. 97.

2 A. Ogus and E. Barendt, *The Law of Social Security* (1982), p. 77; see generally Chaps. 3 and 12.

3 Social Security Act 1975 s. 17 (1) (a); Social Security Regulations No. 564, 1975, Reg. 7 (reasonable restrictions).

4 R(U) 9/83, and R(U) 1/185 respectively.

5 Social Security Act 1975 s. 20.

6 R(U) 10/61; R(U) 28/55; and see R(U) 2/77.

7 Supplementary Benefits Act 1976 s. 5; Supplementary Benefit Regulations No. 1299, 1980, Reg. 8; see T. Lynes, *The Penguin Guide to Supplementary Benefits* (1985), Chap. 12. On men over sixty: Regulations No. 463, 1983.

8 Health and Social Services and Social Security Adjudications Act 1983 s. 25, Sched. 8; and Social Security Regulations Nos. 451 and 613, 1984. For earlier problems see R(SB) 3/84 and 36/84. See J. Mesher [1983] Jo. Law and Society 135.

9 See Ogus and Barendt, op. cit., Chap. 16 and Supp.; H. Knorpel (1984) 21 CMLR 241. A worker who is available for work in one country and receiving benefit there is not eligible to claim benefit in another: *Aubin's* case [1982] ECR 1991.

10 R(SB) 2/85; cf. *Scrivner* v. *Centre d'Aide Social de Chastre*, ECJ, 122/1984; see the useful review by P. Watson (1985), European L. R. 335.

11 Supplementary Benefit (Conditions) Regulations No. 1526, 1981, Reg. 8; No. 907, 1982.

12 Supplementary Benefits Act 1976 ss. 10 (centres for re-establishment training) and 25 (crime).

13 *R. v. Sec. of State for Social Services, ex parte Cotton*, *The Times*, 5 August 1985, 14 December 1985 (CA).

14 See Clark and Wedderburn, in Wedderburn, R. Lewis and J. Clark (eds.), *Labour Law and Industrial Relations* (1983), pp. 146–53.

15 A. Fox, *Beyond Contract: Trust, Power and Work Relations* (1976), pp. 183–4.

16 P. Davies and M. Freedland, *Labour Law: Text and Materials* (2nd ed. 1984), p. 83.

17 *WHPT Association* v. *Secretary of State for Social Services* [1981] ICR 737, 748, 751.

18 From the fourteenth century, then Tudor and later legislation, including the Poor Laws: see Holdsworth, *History of English Law*, Vol IV (1945 ed.), pp. 380–402; Clark and Wedderburn, op. cit., pp. 146–9.

19 *Narich Ltd* v. *Commr. of Payroll Tax* [1984] ICR 286 (PC); *Morren* v. *Swinton and Pendlebury BC* [1965] 1 WLR 576.

20 *Withers* v. *Flackwood* [1981] IRLR 307; *Market Investigations* v. *Minister of Social Security* [1969] 2 QB 173.

21 *Ready Mixed Concrete Ltd* v. *Minister of Pensions* [1968] 2 QB 497.

22 [1980] IRLR 201 (CA).

23 *Newland* v. *Simons & Willer* [1981] IRLR 359; *Coral Leisure Group Ltd* v. *Barnett* [1981] ICR 503; C. Mogridge (1981), 10 ILJ 23.

24 *Hyland* v. *Barker (NW) Ltd* [1985] IRLR 403.

25 See Upex (1981), 10 ILJ 124 and (1979), 8 ILJ 102, for these and other cases; *Whittaker* v. *MoP* [1966] 3 All E. R. 531; and see P. Leighton (1983) *Employment Gazette* 197.

26 *Methodist Conference (President)* v. *Parfitt* [1984] ICR 176 (CA) (not employee); *Davies* v. *Presbyterian Church of Wales* [1986] 1 All E. R. 705 (HL: servant of God, not of church).

27 See *Labour Market Quarterly Report* (March 1985, MSC); *Employment* (Cmnd 9474, 1985); *Sunday Times*, 31 March 1985.

28 See I. T. Smith (1985) 14 ILJ 18, and for number of workers p. 31.

29 P. Leighton (1983) 91 *Employment Gazette* 197 (self-employment); on part-time work (1984) 320 IRRR 2.

30 C. Hakim (1984) 92 *Employment Gazette* 144, 145 (homework, outwork and freelances); and (1984) 92 ibid. 7, 11 (homework estimates).

31 Quoted by B. Hepple and B. Napier (1978) 7 ILJ at p. 97.

32 'Nabisco's Strategy for Change' (1985) 351 IRRR 7.

33 J. Atkinson, op. cit., Chapter 1, note 11; *Financial Times*, 21 August 1985; and (1984), 325 IRRR 13. On Engineering Employers' Federation proposals, see *Financial Times*, 18 October 1985; on 'temps' and subcontracting (1986) 365 IRRR 2. See too, J. Robertson, *Future Work* (1985).

34 M. Syrett, *Temporary Work Today* (1985, Fedn of Recruitment and Employment Services).

35 B. Hutchins and A. Harrison, *A History of Factory Legislation* (1903), p. 171; on outworkers and homeworkers today: Factories Act 1961 s. 133; Homeworker Order No. 394, 1911 (as amended).

36 *Wiltshire Police Authority* v. *Wynn* [1980] ICR 649, 656.

37 *Hawley* v. *Fieldcastle* [1982] IRLR 223; *Daley* v. *Allied Suppliers* [1983] IRLR 14; but a 'supervisor' of a YOP scheme became an employee: *Glasgow City DC* v. *McNulty* (1984) 251 IRLIB p. 11. See Health and Safety (YTS) Regulations No. 1919, 1983; and Chapter 6.

38 *Carmichael* v. *Rosehall Eng. Works* [1983] IRLR 480, 482.

39 Davies and Freedland, *Labour Law: Text and Materials* (2nd ed. 1984), p. 37; see too B. Hepple, (1986) *King's Counsel* (forthcoming).

40 P. Leighton (1984) 13 ILJ 86; R. Rideout (1966) 19 Current Leg. Problems 11.

41 'Temporary Workers and the Law' (1978) 7 ILJ 84.

42 *Wickens* v. *Champion Employment* [1984] ICR 365.

43 P. Leighton (1985) 14 ILJ 54, 56; and *Contractual Arrangements in Selected Industries* (1983, DE Research Paper No. 39), p. 23; on continuity, *Ford* v. *Warwickshire CC* [1983] ICR 273 (HL): fixed, short-term engagements of teacher for specific courses; annual holidays between contracts do count for continuity as 'temporary cessations of work' (EPCA 1978, Sched. 13, para. 9 (b); see Chapter 3, p. 205). But cf. *Surrey CC* v. *Lewis* [1986] IRLR 11 (three separate contracts; normal hours of work inadequate for continuity).

44 *Construction Industry Training Board* v. *Labour Force Ltd* [1970] 3 All E. R. 220. See, on 'the lump', B. Mordsley (1975) 38 MLR 504; C. Drake (1968) 31 MLR 408.

45 [1976] IRLR 346; cf. *Donaghey* v. *Boulton & Paul* [1968] AC 1; *Inglefield* v. *Macey* [1967] 2 KIR 146 (timberman); and now *McDermid* v. *Nash Dredging*, *The Times*, 17 April 1986.

46 *Rice* v. *Fon-A-Car* [1980] ICR 133.

47 T. Austin, 'The Lump in UK Construction', in T. Nichols (ed.), *Capital and Labour* (1980), pp. 302–13. For the 1985 'Right to be Self-Employed Bill', see *Parl. Deb.*, 4 Feb. 1986, HC, col. 147.

48 P. Leighton (1983) 91 *Employment Gazette* 197, 202; A. Cragg and T. Dawson (1981, DE Research Paper No. 21), p. 31.

49 *Gorictree Ltd* v. *Jenkinson* [1985] ICR 51.

50 Social Security Regulations No. 564, 1975, and No. 1105, 1982; see Ogus and Barendt, op. cit., pp. 131–5.

51 [1983] ICR 728; P. Leighton (1984) 13 ILJ 62. See too note 67 below.

52 *Surrey CC* v. *Lewis* [1986] IRLR 11; but see *Ford* v. *Warwickshire CC* [1983] ICR 273; note 43 above.

53 On that draft Directive (1984) 130 EIRR 27; Part-Time Work draft Directive (as amended) ibid. 31; and on both IDS *Employment Law Handbook*, 31 'Part Timers, Temps and Job Sharers' (1985), Appendix 1.

54 For a legal and economic analysis, R. Disney and E. Szyszczak (1984) 22 BJIR 78.

55 *Foreningen af Arbedejdsledere* v. *A/S Danmols Mikkelsen*, *The Times*, 29 July 1985 (ECJ).

56 See O. Robinson (1984) 15 I. R. Jo., No. 1, p. 58 (part-time in the EEC countries); on EEC social security and self-employed, M. Forde (1979) 8 ILJ 1.

57 J.-P. Jallade, *Towards a Policy of Part-Time Employment* (1984). A report by J. Atkinson to the NEDC showed that most large companies had by 1985

increased use of part-time, temporary and shift work; *Financial Times*, 3 December 1985.

58 See C. Hakim (1984) 92 *Employment Gazette* 144, 149 (homework, outwork and freelances).

59 *Burdens on Business* (1985, DTI) p. 4; also A. Smith, 'The Informal Economy', *Lloyds Bank Review*, July 1981, 45; cf. R. de Grazie, *Clandestine Employment* (1984, ILO).

60 E. Hobsbawm, *Labouring Men* (1964), p. 116.

61 P. Townsend, *Poverty in the United Kingdom* (1979), p. 465. On the objections to the 'curse' of home work a century ago, see the graphic picture in S. and B. Webb, *Industrial Democracy* (1914 ed.), pp. 539–45.

62 U. Huws, 'The New Technology Homeworkers' (1984) 92 *Employment Gazette* 13; *The New Homeworkers* (1985, Low Pay Unit); *Homeworking* (1985, TUC); above, note 35.

63 C. Hakim, 'Homework and Outwork' (1984) 92 *Employment Gazette* 7; cf. C. Hakim and R. Dennis, *Homeworking in Wages Councils Industries* (1982, DE Research Paper No. 37).

64 Compare the Italian debate: G. Ghezzi and U. Romagnoli, *Il rapporto di lavoro* (1984), para. 127; G. Mariucci, *Il lavoro decentrato* (1979), pp. 140–45; A. Grieco, *Lavoro parasubordinato e diritto del lavoro* (1983).

65 See the valuable critique, K. Ewing (1982) 11 ILJ 94; HC Select Committee Report, *Homeworking* (1981, HC 39).

66 *Wiltshire CC* v. *NATFHE* [1980] ICR 455; *Brown* v. *Knowsley BC* [1986] IRLR 102; see too *Ryan* v. *Shipboard Maintenance* [1980] IRLR 16.

67 [1984] ICR 612 (CA); J. Warburton (1984) 13 ILJ 251. See the failure to prove an 'overriding' contract from a series of short-term engagements in *Boyd-Line* v. *Pitts* [1986] ICR 244.

68 G. Pitt (1985) 101 LQR 217, 241.

69 *Financial Techniques Ltd* v. *Hughes* [1981] IRLR 32; contrast *Marley* v. *Forward Trust* [1986] IRLR 43 (see Chapter 4, p. 335; a manifestly inferior decision).

70 *NCB* v. *Galley* [1958] 1 All E. R. 91.

71 See *IRS Guide to Youth Training Scheme* (1983); *Employment* (Cmnd 9474, 1985), pp. 15–17; *Education and Training for Young People* (Cmnd 9482, 1985); and *Parl. Deb.*, 1 July 1985, HC, col. 24.

72 See *Kodeeswaran* v. *Att.-G. of Ceylon* [1970] AC 1111 (PC); *Council of Civil Service Unions* v. *Minister for Civil Service* [1985] ICR 14, 39 (GCHQ).

73 *Gascol Conversion Ltd* v. *Mercer* [1974] ICR 420; Hepple (1974) 3 ILJ 164; see Chapter 4, p. 335.

74 [1982] ICR 54, 58.

75 See P. Leighton and S. Dumville (1977) 6 ILJ 133.

76 *Hawker Siddeley Power Eng. Ltd* v. *Rump* [1979] IRLR 425; *Simmonds* v. *Dowty Seals Ltd* [1978] IRLR 211; P. Leighton and J. Doyle (1980) 9 ILJ 116.

77 *Jones* v. *Associated Tunnelling Co. Ltd* [1981] IRLR 477; see p. 177.

78 *Mears* v. *Safecar Security Ltd* [1982] ICR 626.

79 P. Davies and M. Freedland, *Labour Law: Text and Materials* (2nd ed. 1984), p. 279, approving *Howman & Son* v. *Blyth* [1983] ICR 416.

80 A. Marsh, *Employee Relations Policy and Decision Making* (1982, CBI), p. 185.

81 S. and B. Webb, *History of Trade Unionism* (1920), p. 249.

82 D. Simon, Chap. 6, in J. Saville, *Democracy and the Labour Movement* (1954).

83 *Universe Tankships of Monrovia Inc.* v. *ITWF* [1983] 1 AC 366; *Pao On* v. *Lau Yiu Long* [1980] AC 614, 636. *B and S Contracts* v. *VG Publications* [1984] ICR 419: Chapter 8, p. 650.

84 *Hennessy* v. *Craigmyle Ltd* [1985] IRLR 446, 448; and *The Times*, 24 May 1986 (CA).

85 See A. Siopis (1984) 100 LQR 523, on *Commercial Bank of Australia* v. *Amadio* (1983) 46 ALR 402.

86 *Schroeder Music Publishing Co.* v. *Macaulay* [1974] 3 All E. R. 616, 623.

87 *Greig* v. *Insole* [1978] 1 WLR 302, 326; G. Treitel, *Law of Contract* (6th ed. 1983), pp. 317–18.

88 *National Westminster Bank* v. *Morgan* [1985] 2 WLR 588, 600; but see D. Tiplady (1985) 48 MLR 579; and see note 84.

89 *Alec Lobb Ltd* v. *Total Oil* [1985] 1 All E. R. 303, 313; Dillon LJ.

90 *Peterborough Labour Social Club* v. *Monoghan*, *The Times*, 6 December 1984; *Kelman* v. *Oram* [1983] IRLR 432; *Barry* v. *British Railways Staff Assoc.*, COIT 570/170, IDS *Employment Law Handbook*, 31, p. 89.

91 *Condor* v. *The Barron Knights* [1967] 1 WLR 87.

92 [1981] IRLR 195.

93 *Hare* v. *Murphy Bros. Ltd* [1974] ICR 603.

94 *Chakki* v. *United Yeast Ltd* [1982] ICR 140; contrast *Notcutt* v. *Universal Equipment Ltd* [1986] 1 WLR 641 (CA).

95 *Shepherd & Co.* v. *Jerrom* [1985] IRLR 275.

96 G. Treitel, *The Law of Contract* (6th ed. 1983), p. 772; G. de N. Clarke (1969) 32 MLR 532.

97 *Lumley* v. *Wagner* (1852) 1 De G. M. & G. 604 (the other side of the coin to *Lumley* v. *Gye*; see Chapter 8, p. 585); *Warner Bros.* v. *Nelson* [1937] 1 KB 209; *Page One Records Ltd* v. *Britton* [1968] 1 WLR 157.

98 *Esso Petroleum Ltd* v. *Harper's Garage* [1968] AC 269, 300; [1967] 1 All E. R. 699, 721; approving *Kores Mfg* v. *Kolok Mfg* [1959] Ch. 108.

99 *Eastham* v. *Newcastle FC* [1964] Ch. 413; *Greig* v. *Insole* [1978] 1 WLR 302.

100 *Webster* v. *Southwark LBC* [1983] QB 698; on 'martyrs', see Chapter 1, p. 56.

101 *Strange* v. *Mann* [1965] 1 WLR 629; *Spafax* v. *Harrison* [1980] IRLR 442; *Home Counties Dairies Ltd* v. *Skilton* [1970] 1 WLR 526.

102 Denning LJ, *M & S Drapers Ltd* v. *Reynolds* [1956] 3 All ER 814, 820.

103 See *Alec Lobb Ltd* v. *Total Oil* [1985] 1 All E. R. 303, 313; note 88 above.

104 *Bull* v. *Pitney-Bowes* [1966] 3 All E. R. 384; *Bridge* v. *Deacons* [1984] AC 705 (PC).

105 *Garden Cottage Foods Ltd* v. *Milk Marketing Board* [1984] AC 130; *Lonrho* v. *Shell* (No. 2) [1982] AC 173; see Chapter 8, p. 638. But see as to remedies under the Treaty: *Bourgoin SA* v. *Ministry of Agriculture* [1985] 3 All E. R. 585 (CA).

106 [1964] AC 40, 65; see on public law dismissals: G. Ganz (1967) 30 MLR 288; H. Collins (1984) 13 ILJ 174.

107 *Burdett-Coutts* v. *Herts CC* [1984] IRLR 91. The view of Asquith LJ that a declaration for an unaccepted repudiation is a 'thing writ in water' and 'of no value to anyone' was approved in *Gunton* v. *Richmond on Thames LBC* [1980] IRLR 321, 327.

108 See *Shook* v. *Ealing LB* [1986] IRLR 46; see Chapter 3, p. 188.

109 *Miles* v. *Wakefield MDC* [1985] IRLR 108 (CA).

110 *Vine* v. *National Dock Labour Board* [1957] AC 488; see too *Taylor* v. *Furness Withy Ltd* [1969] 6 KIR 488 (contract with dock employer one of employment within the scheme).

111 See further O. Kahn-Freund on 'Status and Contract' (1967) 30 MLR 635.

112 W. Holdsworth, *History of English Law*, Vol. 1 (revised ed. 1956), pp. 246–64.

113 *Hayes* v. *Bristol Plant Hire Ltd* [1957] 1 All E. R. 685; *Parsons* v. *Albert Parsons Ltd* [1979] ICR 271.

114 *Hannan* v. *Bradford CC* [1970] 2 All E. R. 690; *Sec. of State for Trade* v. *Douglas* [1983] IRLR 63, 65 (coastguard). But see *Jones* v. *Lee* [1980] ICR 310; see Chapter 6, p. 449.

115 *Council of Civil Service Unions* v. *Minister Civil Service* [1985] ICR 14, Lord Diplock pp. 35–9; Lord Scarman p. 34; Lord Roskill pp. 42–5.

116 *McClelland* v. *N. Ireland General Health Services Board* [1957] 2 All E. R. 129 (HL); *Vidyodaya University of Ceylon* v. *Silva* [1964] 3 All E. R. 865 (PC); *Birch* v. *University of Liverpool* [1985] IRLR 165 (CA).

117 *Gunton* v. *Richmond-upon-Thames LBC* [1980] ICR 755, 764, 777; on the effect of breach of the employment contract, see *London Transport Exec.* v. *Clarke* [1981] ICR 355; see Chapter 3, p. 188.

118 *Malloch* v. *Aberdeen Corporation* [1971] 1 WLR 1578; on the Act of 1973,

see C. Harlow and R. Rawlings, *Law and Administration* (1984), pp. 277–83.

119 *Scott* v. *Aberdeen Corporation*, 1976, SLT 141.

120 See the valuable Chap. 5 in J. Griffith, *The Politics of the Judiciary* (3rd ed. 1975).

121 *R.* v. *Liverpool CC, ex parte Ferguson* [1985] IRLR 501.

122 *R.* v. *Secretary of State for Home Dept, ex parte Benwell* [1985] IRLR 6; *R.* v. *East Berkshire Health Authority, ex parte Walsh* [1984] IRLR 278 (CA).

123 W. Robson, *Justice and Administrative Law* (1951), p. 32; S. De Smith, *Judicial Review of Administrative Action* (4th ed. 1980; J. Evans, ed.), p. 3.

124 S. De Smith, op. cit., pp. 227–33.

125 *R.* v. *Herts CC, ex parte NUPE* [1985] IRLR 258; see Mary Stokes (1985) 14 ILJ 118. On unfair dismissal: *Kent CC* v. *Gilham* [1985] IRLR 18; see Chapter 3, p. 245.

126 H. Collins (1984) 13 ILJ 174; see his discussion of *Davy* v. *Spelthorne BC* [1984] 1 AC 262.

127 See *Vine* v. *National Dock Labour Board* [1957] AC 488; *R.* v. *Hampshire CC, ex parte Ellerton* [1985] 1 All E. R. 599 (discipline regulations of firemen).

128 *R.* v. *BBC, ex parte Lavelle* [1983] ICR 99; J. Beatson and M. Freedland (1983) 12 ILJ 43.

129 *Stevenson* v. *URTU* [1977] ICR 893; cf. *Taylor* v. *NUS* [1967] 1 All E. R. 767. But the Supreme Court of Ireland has held a union officer is an 'office-holder', not a servant: *Connolly* v. *McConnell* [1983] Ir. R. 172.

130 See S. De Smith, op. cit., p. 230.

131 *Francis* v. *Kuala Lumpur Councillors* [1962] 3 All E. R. 633 (PC); Chitty on *Contracts*, Vol. 1 (25th ed. 1983), p. 984.

132 *West Midlands Co-op Soc. Ltd* v. *Tipton* [1985] IRLR 116 (CA); [1986] 2 WLR 306 (HL). And see *National Heart and Chest Hospital* v. *Nambiar* [1981] ICR 441; *Greenall Whitley* v. *Carr* [1985] IRLR 289.

133 *Hill* v. *C. A. Parsons Ltd* [1972] Ch. 305; Hepple [1972A] CLJ 47.

134 *Chappell* v. *Times Newspapers Ltd* [1975] ICR 145; see Chapter 4, p. 328.

135 *Jones* v. *Lee* [1980] ICR 310, 320–1; on private life aspects, see Chapter 6, below.

136 *Irani* v. *Southampton and SE Hampshire HA* [1985] IRLR 203, 209, doubting whether *Barber* v. *Manchester RHB* [1958] 1 WLR 181 was correctly decided.

137 [1985] IRLR 252 (CA).

138 *Secretary of State for Education* v. *Thameside MBC* [1977] AC 1014; *R.* v. *GLC, ex parte Bromley LBC* [1983] 1 AC 768 (HL). See J. Griffith, *The Politics of the Judiciary* (3rd ed. 1985), Chap.5; C. Harlow and R. Rawlings, *Law and Administration* (1984), Chap. 11.

3 Job Security and Dismissal

1 Lord Wright, *Luxor Ltd* v. *Cooper* [1941] A C 108, 137.

2 Viscount Simonds, *Lister* v. *Romford Ice Co. Ltd* [1957] A C 555, 576.

3 Stephenson L J, *Mears* v. *Safecar Security Ltd* [1982] I C R 626, 649–51.

4 *Howman & Sons* v. *Blyth* [1983] I C R 416, 421. On these developments see Richard Lewis, 'Privatization of Sickness Benefits' (1982) 11 I L J 245, on the Social Security and Housing Benefit Act 1982; see too (1983) 292 I R R R 2 on statutory sick-pay; Social Security Act 1985 ss. 18–21; Sick Pay Order 1985, No. 67; and Statutory Sick Pay Regs. 1986 Nos. 318, 477.

5 [1931] 1 Ch. 310, 312–14; see *Marshall* v. *English Electric Ltd* [1945] 1 All E. R. 653. See also the discussion of *Sagar* by H. Collins in *Marxism and Law* (1982), pp. 59–60, 71, 86, 99; but the employer's appeal to custom succeeded; and the reduction was possible because Lancashire weaving had been long exempted from the Truck Act 1896 (S I 1897 No. 299); see Chapter 5.

6 See the Donovan Commission's *Report* (Cmnd 3623, 1968), para. 35; O. Kahn-Freund, *Labour Relations, Heritage and Adjustment* (1979), p. 67.

7 *Bond and Neads* v. *C A V Ltd* [1983] I R L R 360, 366–7. See too *Edwards Ltd* v. *Evans* (1985) 315 I D S Brief 11 (no implied right to lay off drivers during miners' strike; constructive dismissal).

8 *Duke* v. *Reliance Systems* [1982] I R L R 347, 349.

9 H. Collins, 'Capitalist Discipline and Corporatist Law' (1982) 11 I L J 78, 170, 176. Cf. P. Elias (1981) 10 I L J 201; H. Glasbeek (1984) 13 I L J 133.

10 *Jones* v. *Associated Tunnelling Co. Ltd* [1981] I R L R 477.

11 See the interesting material in P. Davies and M. Freedland, *Labour Law: Text and Materials* (2nd ed. 1984), pp. 318–47.

12 *Breach* v. *Epsylon Industries Ltd* [1976] I C R 316; on the main principle, *Turner* v. *Sawdon* [1901] 2 K B 653.

13 See *Greig* v. *Insole* [1978] 1 W L R 302, 326.

14 *Langston* v. *A U E W* [1974] I C R 180, 190; ibid. (No. 2) [1974] I C R 510; B. Hepple (1974) 37 M L R 681, 684.

15 *Pepper and Hope* v. *Daish* [1980] I R L R 13.

16 *White* v. *London Transport Exec.* [1981] I R L R 261; *Post Office* v. *Roberts* [1980] I R L R 347, 350 (no duty to be reasonable). There is an obligation to instruct and train an *apprentice*; see too p. 184.

17 *Lister* v. *Romford Ice and Cold Storage Co.* [1957] A C 555 (HL).

18 *Morris* v. *Ford Motor Co.* [1973] 1 Q B 792; but *Lister* was reaffirmed in *Janata Bank* v. *Ahmed* [1981] I C R 791 (C A). On the 1977 Act, G. Treitel, *Law of Contract* (6th ed. 1983), pp. 200–6.

19 [1982] I C R 693, 695, 698, 702–3 (implied terms treated as a question of fact, when the orthodox rule makes them a matter of law).

20 See A. Döse-Digenopoulos and A. Höland (1985) 48 MLR 539, 544, on West Germany.

21 On high-trust and low-trust relations, see A. Fox, *Beyond Contract: Trust, Power and Work Relations* (1974): in the former, parties have 'a diffuse sense of long-term obligations; offer each other spontaneous support . . . communicate freely . . . [and] are ready to repose their fortunes in each other's hands' (p. 362).

22 *Courtaulds Northern Textiles* v. *Andrew* [1979] IRLR 84; *Wetherall (Bond St) Ltd* v. *Lynn* [1978] ICR 205.

23 *Lewis* v. *Motorworld Garages Ltd* [1985] IRLR 465 (CA).

24 *Faccenda Chicken Ltd* v. *Fowler* [1986] IRLR 69 (CA).

25 Ungoed-Thomas J., *Beloff* v. *Pressdram Ltd* [1973] 1 All E. R. 241, 259–60. On the complexities of 'confidence' see W. R. Cornish, *Intellectual Property* (1981), Chap. 8; Jefferson (1984) 13 ILJ 115.

26 *General Nutrition Ltd* v. *Yates*, *The Times*, 6 June 1981; (1981) 2 Co. Law. 227.

27 See *Thos. Marshall* v. *Guinle* [1978] ICR 905, 922–6, Megarry VC; *Horcal* v. *Gatland* [1984] IRLR 288 (CA); *Maintenance Co. Ltd* v. *Dormer* [1982] IRLR 491 (fiduciary duty of managing director not to allow duty and interest to conflict; good grounds for fair dismissal); *Prudential Assurance Co.* v. *Lorenz* (1971) 11 KIR 78 (fiduciary duty of insurance agent: see Chapter 8, p. 649).

28 *Sybron Corpn* v. *Rochem Ltd* [1983] ICR 801, 815, Stephenson LJ.

29 'High Trust, Pensions and the Contract of Employment' (1984) 13 ILJ 25, 32.

30 *Nova Plastics Ltd* v. *Froggett* [1982] IRLR 146.

31 *Cresswell* v. *Board of Inland Revenue* [1984] ICR 508; see *Financial Times*, 18 February 1984; and 24 May 1986 (wide professional duties implied into teachers' contracts).

32 E. Batstone, I. Boraston and S. Frenkel, *Shop Stewards in Action* (1977), pp. 155–8, 176.

33 *Sec. of State for Employment* v. *ASLEF* (No. 2) [1972] ICR 19, 30, 54–6, 62, 72.

34 B. Napier (1977) 6 ILJ 1, 7–11; and O. Kahn-Freund in *Labour and the Law* (3rd ed. 1983), p. 28, the 'unitary approach to labour relations . . . should be firmly rejected'; conflicts of interest are 'inevitable in all societies'.

35 P. Davies and M. Freedland, op. cit., pp. 316–17.

36 *Payne* v. *Spook Erection Ltd* [1984] IRLR 219 (system unfair to both workers and foreman); *Palmanor Ltd* v. *Cedron* [1978] ICR 1008 (language); see too *Isle of Wight Tourist Board* v. *Coombs* [1976] IRLR 413 ('she's an intolerable bitch on a Monday morning'); see the treatment in S. Anderman, *Unfair Dismissals* (2nd ed. 1985), pp. 82–8.

37 *Solihull MB* v. *NUT* [1985] IRLR 211.

38 *London Transport Executive* v. *Clarke* [1981] ICR 355 (Lord Denning retaining the exception in part); see *Gunton* v. *Richmond-upon-Thames LBC* [1980] ICR 755 (Shaw LJ diss.).

39 *Harrison* v. *Norwest Holst Group* [1985] IRLR 240 (CA); see on the earlier cases, P. Kerr (1984) 47 MLR 30; P. Elias (1978) 7 ILJ 16. See too *Shook* v. *Ealing LB* [1986] IRLR 46; and *Peyman* v. *Linjani* [1985] Ch. 457 (CA) on the general law of contract and election.

40 *Bliss* v. *SE Thames RHA* [1985] IRLR 308 (CA). See on this 'knotty problem' H. Carty (1986), 49 MLR 240, 243.

41 *Hunt* v. *British Rail Board* [1979] IRLR 379, 381; *Cox Toner* v. *Crook* [1981] ICR 823.

42 *Walker* v. *Josiah Wedgwood* [1978] ICR 744.

43 *Blyth* v. *Scottish Liberal Club* [1983] IRLR 245 (Scot.).

44 *Wilson* v. *Racher* [1974] ICR 428; cf. *Pepper* v. *Webb* [1969] 1 WLR 514 (the earlier gardener's case).

45 *Ogden* v. *Ardphalt Asphalt* [1977] ICR 604; *Devis* v. *Atkins* [1977] AC 931 (HL); but see too *Greenall Whitley Ltd* v. *Carr* [1985] IRLR 289, and *West Midlands Co-op. Soc.* v. *Tipton* [1986] 2 WLR 306.

46 *Rasool* v. *Hepworth Pipe Ltd* [1980] ICR 494.

47 X. Blanc-Jouvan, Chap. 4, in B. Aaron and K. Wedderburn (eds.), *Industrial Conflict, A Comparative Legal Survey* (1972), pp. 184–5; see too B. Aaron, Chap. 2 on strikes and lock-outs. The 'right' to strike causes no breach of contract, by being exercised, in many other systems of law: G. Giungi, *Diritto Sindacale* (1984); *qui iure suo utitur, neminem laedit*, p. 217 ('you do no legal wrong when you exercise your rights').

48 *Puttick* v. *Wright & Sons* [1972] ICR 457.

49 *Stratford* v. *Lindley* [1965] AC 269, 315 (and see (1965) 28 MLR 206); *Cummings* v. *Chas. Connell*, 1969, SLT 25 (where the guarantee of eighteen months' employment was not decisive in holding the nature of lock-out to be a breach). On 'status quo' clauses see S. Anderman (1975) 4 ILJ 131.

50 *Chappell* v. *Times Newspapers* [1975] ICR 145; *Fisher* v. *York Trailer Co. Ltd* [1979] ICR 834 (lock-out when workers refuse to sign); see Chapter 2, p. 166.

51 See P. O'Higgins [1968] CLJ 223, (1973) 2 ILJ 152; but it does not seem that the mere existence of an agreement to exhaust collectively agreed procedures is enough, cf. M. Freedland, *The Contract of Employment* (1976), pp. 102 ff; and K. Foster (1971) 34 MLR 275.

52 [1964] AC 1129, 1204; *Stratford* v. *Lindley* [1965] AC 269, 285.

53 [1968] 2 QB 710, 724–8, 731; on the lightermen, see *Stratford* v. *Lindley*, above, note 49.

54 [1977] QB 284; which also discussed EPCA s. 92; this applies where an

employer ends the contract during a notice period, when a redundancy payment is payable. See too s. 110, whereby an employer may demand that a redundant employee on strike may make up the time lost.

55 See *Dimbleby & Sons Ltd* v. *NUJ* [1984] ICR 386, 408–9; *Haddow* v. *ILEA* [1979] ICR 202 (delay did not prevent employers from 'accepting' breaches of striking teachers by dismissals); *Rasool* v. *Hepworth Pipe* [1980] ICR 494 (attendance at mass meeting in working time a breach); *Express Newspapers* v. *McShane* [1980] AC 672; and see Chapter 8, below.

56 'Lessons from the Industrial Court' (1975) 91 LQR 181, 192.

57 P. Wallington (1983) 46 MLR 310, 317.

58 The definitions for the purpose of 'continuity of employment' are sometimes consulted as an analogy (EPCA, Sched. 13, para. 24: Chapter 3, p. 205, below). A different definition of 'strike' appears in the TUA 1984 (Chapter 8, p. 623). 'Irregular industrial action' in the 1971 Act, s. 33 (now repealed), required a breach of contract.

59 *Power Packing Casemakers Ltd* v. *Faust* [1983] ICR 292.

60 *Naylor* v. *Orton Smith* [1983] IRLR 233; *Midland Plastics Ltd* v. *Till* [1983] ICR 118.

61 *Coates* v. *Modern Methods, etc. Ltd* [1982] ICR 763 (Eveleigh LJ dissenting: the worker's 'reason for not going in to work . . . was her unwillingness to expose herself to abuse'; she did not 'act in concert with the other strikers'); cf. *McCormick* v. *Horsepower Ltd* [1981] ICR 535.

62 *Hindle Gears Ltd* v. *McGinty* [1985] ICR 111. On difficulties of 'taking part' see *Jang Publications* v. *Munir* (1986) 297 IRLIB 11.

63 P. Edwards and H. Scullion, *The Social Organization of Industrial Conflict* (1982), pp. 256–7; the adoption by the law of perspectives of other social sciences does not always make parallel the legal and the sociological consequences. Dismissed workers can now be found arguing that managers were 'in reality' taking part even though they continued to carry out certain duties (e.g. where all the employees were NGA members at the *Kent Messenger*: *The Times*, 11 February 1986).

64 *Courtaulds Northern Spinning Ltd* v. *Moosa* [1984] IRLR 43, 46.

65 *Williams* v. *National Theatre Board* [1982] ICR 715, 720.

66 See B. Aaron and K. Wedderburn (eds.), *Industrial Conflict, A Comparative Legal Survey* (1972), p. 65; and B. Hepple, 'Lock-Outs in Britain', *Recht der Arbeit* 33 (1980), 25 (English).

67 *Labour and the Law* (2nd ed. 1977), p. 138; see now 3rd ed. 1983; P. Davies and M. Freedland, eds., p. 173, where older cases are mentioned.

68 *Henthorne* v. *CEGB* [1980] IRLR 361, CA.

69 A collective agreement on 'lay-off' applied only where there was no work; *Bond and Neads* v. *CAV* [1983] IRLR p. 366. But see the criticisms of B. Napier [1984] CLJ 337.

70 *Royle* v. *Trafford B C* [1984] I R L R 184.

71 *Miles* v. *Wakefield M D C* [1985] I R L R 108; but see Eveleigh L J, dissenting.

72 A. Herman, *Financial Times*, 28 February 1985, citing C. Dickens, *Little Dorrit*, attacking the *Miles* judgment in the C A.

73 *Gibbons* v. *Associated British Ports* [1985] I R L R 376. On *Crothall Ltd* see *Financial Times*, 9 January 1986.

74 *Rowan* v. *Machinery Installations Ltd* [1981] I R L R 122.

75 See respectively R(U) 2/77; R(U) 2/74; D. Lewis (1975) 4 I L J 110; A. Ogus and E. Barendt, *The Law of Social Security* (2nd ed. 1982), pp. 109–10.

76 On the historical puzzle of this divorce from the common law, S. Jacoby (1982) Comp. Lab. Law 84, 102–20; and see P. Fenn and C. Whelan (1985) 20 Stanford J. Int. Law 353.

77 See *Dalgleish* v. *Kew House Farm Ltd* [1982] I R L R 251.

78 *McClelland* v. *N. Ireland General Health Services Board* [1957] 1 W L R 594.

79 *Morris* v. *Bailey Ltd* [1969] 2 Lloyds' Rep. 215 (C A); see note 73, above.

80 *Marriott* v. *Oxford and District Co-op. Soc.* (No. 2) [1970] 1 Q B 186; see above, p. 139; cf. *Miller* v. *Hamworthy*, *The Times*, 14 May 1986 (C A).

81 *Lipton Ltd* v. *Marlborough* [1979] I R L R 179, 181,

82 *Tracy* v. *Zest Equipment* [1982] I C R 481.

83 *Igbo* v. *Johnson Matthey Ltd*, *The Times*, 3 May 1986 (C A); but it is unclear just how far s. 140 affects termination by 'consent'. *Birch* v. *University of Liverpool* [1985] I R L R 165 (university lecturer in premature retirement); see too *Morley* v. *Morley* (*C T*) [1985] I C R 499 (volunteer for redundancy can be 'dismissed').

84 See R(U) 1/83; *Crewe* v. *Social Security Commsr* [1982] 2 All E. R. 745, 750; cf. R(U) 4/85; and Social Security Act 1985 s. 10 (requires 'dismissal').

85 *Finnie* v. *Top Hat Frozen Foods Ltd* [1985] I R L R 365 (Scot. E A T).

86 See E P C A, Sched. 14, Parts I (normal working hours) and II (week's pay), for details; see *Lotus Cars Ltd* v. *Sutcliffe* [1982] I R L R 381 for a strict interpretation on overtime.

87 *Westwood* v. *Secretary of State for Employment* [1985] A C 20 (H L); but on exhaustion of entitlements see Regulations No. 1259, 1984.

88 *R.* v. *National Insurance Commsr, ex parte Stratton* [1979] I C R 290; *Chief Supp. Benefit Officer* v. *Cunningham* [1985] I C R 660 (C A); R(U) 7/80; R(U) 3/83; see A. Ogus and E. Barendt, *The Law of Social Security* (2nd ed. 1982), pp. 84–101.

89 Employment Protection (Recoupment, etc.) Regulations No. 674, 1977; on reduction of the 'prescribed element', *Mason* v. *Wimpey Waste Management Ltd* [1982] I R L R 454. See too on 'recoupment' Chapter 3, p. 254; and R. Upex, *Termination of Employment* (1983), pp. 160–3.

90 *Lake* v. *Essex C C* [1979] I C R 577 (C A) (but see note 31 above); but weeks of absence envisaged by the contract 'count': *Secretary of State for Employ-*

ment v. *Deary* [1984] ICR 413; *Flack* v. *Kodak* [1985] ICR 820; *The Times*,
31 May 1986 (CA) (intermittent periods).

91 *Ford* v. *Warwickshire CC* [1983] ICR 273; cf. *Lord Advocate* v. *De Rosa*
[1974] ICR 480 (continuity and redundancy). On increased use of short-
term and temporary contracts, see *Labour Research*, November 1985, 277;
and N. Meager (1986) *Employment Gazette* 7; and Chapter 2, note 33.

92 Compare *Corton House Ltd* v. *Skipper* [1981] ICR 307; and hours 'on call'
may not count: *Suffolk CC* v. *Secretary of State for Environment* [1984] ICR
882 (HL), a very restrictive decision. See further on continuity, J. Harvey on
Industrial Relations and Employment Law (1986) Div. 1 (B).

93 *Surrey CC* v. *Lewis* [1986] IRLR 11; *Hellyer Bros.* v. *McLeod* [1986] ICR
122; but see *Boyd Line* v. *Pitts* [1986] ICR 244 (continuous contract made
out of series of voyage contracts).

94 *Jeetle* v. *Elster* [1985] ICR 389.

95 *Melon* v. *Hector Powe* [1981] ICR 43 (leaving the workers with redundancy
claims against the transferor); *Lloyd* v. *Brassey* [1969] 2 QB 98.

96 *SI (Systems and Instruments) Ltd* v. *Grist* [1983] IRLR 391; but see a
contrary EAT tendency in *Kennedy Brookes Hotel* v. *Reilly* (1983) 242
IRLIB 8.

97 *Apex Leisure Hire Ltd* v. *Barratt* [1984] ICR 452 ('immediately before' a
question of fact); *Delabole Slate Ltd* v. *Berriman* [1985] IRLR 305 (CA);
Sec. of State for Employment v. *Spence* [1986] ICR 181.

98 Transfer of Undertakings (Protection of Employment) Regulations No.
1794, 1981, Regs. 5, 7. On the relationship with the Directive on Acquired
Rights of Workers on Transfers of Undertakings, EEC 77/187, see B.
Hepple (1982) 11 ILJ 29; (1976), 5 ILJ 197. See too on the TUPE Regs.,
Chapter 4, p. 298. There may be little 'net gain' on continuity compared with
EPCA, Sched. 13: I. Smith and J. Wood, *Industrial Law* (2nd ed. 1983),
p. 154.

99 *Hadden* v. *Univ. Dundee Students' Assoc.* [1985] IRLR 449.

100 On 'hiving down' see the invaluable studies of P. Davies and M. Freedland
(1980) 9 ILJ 95 (especially on *Pambakian* v. *Brentford Nylons Ltd* [1978]
ICR 665), and *Labour Law: Text and Materials* (2nd ed. 1984), pp. 580–7.

101 *McGrath* v. *Rank Leisure Ltd* [1985] IRLR 323; the employee dismissed by
the transferee is automatically unfairly dismissed unless the latter proves
dismissal was for an 'economic, technical or organization reason entailing
changes in the workforce' and was reasonable (Reg. 8); see p. 243. Both
transferor and transferee can be liable: *Fenton* v. *Stablegold Ltd* [1986]
IRLR 64; but see *Bullard* v. *Marchant*, *The Times*, 26 February 1986.

102 *Hair Colour Consultants* v. *Mena* [1984] ICR 671, 673–4; cf. *Charnock* v.
Barrie Muirhead [1984] ICR 641. For an odd result: *Poparm Ltd* v. *Weekes*
[1984] IRLR 388 (Chapter 1, p. 98); so too *South West Launderettes* v.

Laidler [1986] IRLR 68 (50 per cent shares in husband and in wife not sufficient).

103 *McGorry* v. *Earls Court Stand Fitting* [1973] ICR 100; on the limits of continuity: *Bloomfield* v. *Springfield Hosiery Finishing Co.* [1972] ICR 91.

104 W. Gould, *A Primer of American Labor Law* (1982), p. 108; H. Sinay and J.-C. Javillier, *Droit du Travail* (1984), pp. 311.

105 *Dunk* v. *Waller and Son Ltd* [1970] 2 QB 163 (apprenticeship, however, has a special, protected character not necessarily transferred to all employment); contrast trainees: Chapter 2, p. 119.

106 [1964] 1 QB 95; reluctantly applied, *Nabi* v. *British Leyland Ltd* [1980] 1 All E. R. 667.

107 *Shove* v. *Downs* [1984] ICR 532 (not discussing *Parsons*; damages included sums in respect of life insurance, private health insurance and company car).

108 Law Reform (Personal Injuries) Act 1948 s. 2 (1); *Denman* v. *Essex AHA* [1984] QB 735, *Haste* v. *Sandell Perkins Ltd* ibid.; see Chapter 5, p. 438.

109 *Basnett* v. *Jackson* [1976] ICR 63; *Millington* v. *Goodwin Ltd* [1975] ICR 104.

110 *Plummer* v. *Wilkins* [1981] 1 All E. R. 91, 94; *Lincoln* v. *Hayman* [1982] 2 All E. R. 819 (CA); *Palfrey* v. *GLC* [1985] ICR 437 (statutory sick-pay deductible).

111 *Westwood* v. *Secretary of State for Employment* [1985] ICR 209, 220; see Chapter 5, p. 399.

112 *Bliss* v. *SE Thames RHA* [1985] IRLR 308.

113 *NCB* v. *Galley* [1958] 1 WLR 16.

114 *Strathclyde Reg. C.* v. *Neil* [1984] IRLR, 11, 14 (Scot.).

115 See A. Ogus and E. Barendt, *The Law of Social Security* (2nd ed. 1982 and Supp.), Chaps. 3, 12; Tony Lynes, *Penguin Guide to Supplementary Benefits* (5th ed. 1985); B. Hepple, T. M. Partington and B. Simpson (1977) 6 ILJ 54.

116 See *R.* v. *Social Security Commissioners, ex parte Sewell, The Times,* 2 January 1985 (appeal to Commissioner needs his leave); ibid., 2 February 1985 (leave to appeal granted by court where Commissioner gave no reasons for refusing). See too on SSAT, J. Mesher (1983) 10 Jo. of Law and Soc. 135.

117 A. Ogus and E. Barendt, op. cit., p. 448; R. Walker, R. Lawson and P. Townsend, *Responses to Poverty* (1985).

118 Social Security Advisory Committee, *First Report* (1981), p. 25; R. Pauley, *Financial Times,* 18 October 1984.

119 Social Security Act 1975 s. 20; see the valuable note by J. Mesher (1978) 7 ILJ 56.

120 R(U) 16/52; Social Security Act 1985 s. 10 (new s. 20 (3A) in Social Security Act 1975); for definition of 'redundancy' see p. 225.

121 Respectively R(U) 16/52; R(U) 15/53; R(U) 33/51; R(U) 18/52.

122 Convictions: R(U) 24/55; R(U) 1/71 (and see R(U) 1/71; R(U) 25/56); trade union: R(U) 2/77; drinking: R(U) 14/57 (the employer had 'additional reasons for wanting to get rid' of the fitter).

123 A. Ogus and E. Barendt, op. cit., pp. 499–501, on the regulations. The Government plans to raise the limit to 13 weeks in October 1986.

124 R(SB) 57/83; R(SB) 4/85.

125 R(SB) 2/82; on clothes ragged through 'normal wear and tear', *Supplementary Benefit Officer* v. *Howell*, *The Times*, 11 April 1984; I. McKenna (1985) 14 ILJ 138, 141.

126 *Lowe* v. *Rigby* [1985] 2 All E. R. 903 (CA); see Chapter 8.

127 R(SB) 18/81.

128 See, respectively, Supplementary Benefits Act 1976 s. 10; Social Security and Housing Benefit Act 1982 s. 38; T. Lynes, *Penguin Guide to Supplementary Benefits* (1985), pp. 194, 231–2; Supplementary Benefits Act 1976 s. 25.

129 J. Mack and S. Lansley, *Poor Britain* (1985); S. Bazen, *Low Wages, Family Circumstances and Minimum Wage Legislation* (1985, PSI No. 643). The Low Pay Unit calculated the New Earnings Survey meant that 8 million *full*-time workers earned 'poverty wages'.

130 See generally C. Bourn, *Redundancy Law and Practice* (1983).

131 See *McKindley* v. *William Hill* [1985] IRLR 492 (worker unsuitable).

132 *Spencer* v. *Gloucester CC* [1985] IRLR 393 (CA); *Paton Calvert* v. *Westerside* [1979] IRLR 108.

133 *Standard Telephones Ltd* v. *Yates* [1981] IRLR 21. *Hindes* v. *Supersine Ltd* [1979] ICR 517; *Taylor* v. *Kent CC* [1969] 2 QB 560.

134 F. Meyers, *Ownership of Jobs* (1964), p. 112.

135 P. Davies and M. Freedland, *Labour Law: Text and Materials* (2nd ed. 1984), p. 438.

136 EPCA s. 64; *Waite* v. *GCHQ* [1983] ICR 653: 'normal' is presumed to mean contractual retiring age, unless a different 'practice' is proved; if neither is proved, it is 60 for women, 65 for men; but from 1986 it will be 65 for both (p. 919, note 167); cf. *Hughes* v. *DHSS* [1985] ICR 419 (HL).

137 P. Townsend, *Poverty in the United Kingdom* (1979), p. 646.

138 See on the 1970s, J. Gennard, in *Workforce Reductions in Undertakings* (1982, ILO, studies in seven countries), pp. 107–40.

139 C. Grunfeld, *The Law of Redundancy* (2nd ed. 1980), p. 5; part of the 'larger changes rolling relentlessly forward' (p. 2).

140 S. Parker, C. Thomas, N. Ellis and W. McCarthy, *Effects of the Redundancy Payments Act* (1971), p. 3.

141 See R. Fryer's indictment of the idea that compensation was adequate 'for the great majority of workers who lose their job' (1973) 2 ILJ 1, 11; and his

'Redundancy Values and Public Policy' (1973) 4 Ind. Rel. Jo., No. 2, p. 2; and M. Bulmer, 'Mining Redundancy' (1971) 2 Ind. Rel. Jo. No. 4, p. 3. See too P. Lewis, *Twenty Years of Statutory Redundancy Payments in Britain* (1985), especially pp. 28–41.

142 C. Bourn, *Redundancy Law and Practice* (1983), pp. 73–4: it aimed to make 'a great change in attitudes of workers towards redundancy'.

143 See the valuable studies on the schemes by W. Rees (1982) 11 ILJ 178; and on redundancy pay and the miners' strike 1984–5, (1985) 14 ILJ 203.

144 *Sunday Times*, 4 April 1984.

145 H. Levie, D. Gregory and N. Lorentzen, *Fighting Closures* (1984), pp. 195–9, on the effects of reports of high redundancy payments.

146 As with Swan Hunter, *Guardian*, 8 January 1985; on directors' payments, *Financial Times*, 14 February 1985 and 12 July 1984; *Labour Research*, January 1984 and October 1985.

147 *Turvey* v. *Cheyney* [1979] ICR 341; see the summary by R. Upex, *Termination of Employment* (1983).

148 *CPS Recruitment Ltd* v. *Bowen* [1982] IRLR 54.

149 *Newham LB* v. *Ward* [1985] IRLR 509 (CA). See too *Stapp* v. *Shaftesbury Society* [1982] IRLR 326 (CA); *West Midlands Co-op. Soc.* v. *Tipton* [1986] 2 WLR 306 (HL).

150 *Dixon* v. *BBC* [1979] ICR 281; see too *Lee* v. *Nottinghamshire CC* [1980] IRLR 284.

151 *Brown* v. *Knowsley BC* [1986] IRLR 102. *Wiltshire CC* v. *NATFHE* [1980] ICR 455.

152 See Kerr on *Receivers* (16th ed. 1983; R. Walton, ed.), pp. 313 and 154–7; *Nicoll* v. *Cutts*, *The Times*, 20 May 1985.

153 *Anderson* v. *Dalkeith Engineering Ltd* [1984] IRLR 429; cf. *McGrath* v. *Rank Leisure Ltd* [1985] IRLR 323; *Secretary of State for Employment* v. *Anchor Hotel* [1985] IRLR 452.

154 *Vaux and Associated Breweries Ltd* v. *Ward* (1968) 3 ITR 385; (No. 2) (1970) 5 ITR 62.

155 *Chapman* v. *Goonvean and Rostowrack China Clay Co.* [1973] ICR 310, 321; overruling *Dutton* v. *Bailey Ltd* (1968) 3 ITR 335.

156 *Johnson* v. *Nottinghamshire Police Authority* [1974] ICR 170, 176; *Lesney Products Ltd* v. *Nolan* [1977] ICR 235, 238.

157 C. Bourn, *Redundancy, Law and Practice* (1983), p. 132.

158 *Jones* v. *Associated Tunnelling Ltd* [1981] IRLR 477; cf. *Little* v. *Charterhouse Magna Assurance Ltd* [1980] IRLR 19 (total mobility of general manager).

159 *Hindle* v. *Percival Boats* [1969] 1 All E.R. 836 (CA).

160 *O'Hare* v. *Rotaprint Ltd* [1980] ICR 94, 98; for the assistant manager, *Ranson* v. *Collins Ltd* [1978] ICR 765.

161 P. Davies and M. Freedland, op. cit., pp. 530–52; and H. Collins (1982) 11 ILJ 255, on the problems of both approaches.

162 [1983]·ICR 1; *Nelson* v. *BBC* [1977] ICR 649; and *Broomby & Hoare* v. *Evans* [1972] ICR 113 (painters replaced by self-employed).

163 *Pink* v. *White* [1985] IRLR 489.

164 *MacFisheries* v. *Findlay* [1985] ICR 160, 162.

165 *Murphy* v. *Epsom College* [1985] ICR 80, 90, 92–3, 96; on the changed function of redundancy, *Elliott Turbomachinery Ltd* v. *Bates* [1981] ICR 218, 220.

166 *K. MacRae Ltd* v. *Dawson* [1984] IRLR 5 (EAT Scot.).

167 See A. Ogus and E. Barendt, op. cit., pp. 91–101; and on the relationship to EPCA, B. Hepple, M. Partington and B. Simpson (1977) 6 ILJ 54.

168 On Temporary Short-Time Working Compensation Scheme payments, see the pioneering article by M. Freedland (1980) 9 ILJ 254; on power to make employment subsidies, Order No. 830, 1984; and see pp. 396, 506.

169 *Devonald* v. *Rosser* [1906] 2 KB 728 (piece-worker's right to payment); *Browning* v. *Crumlin Valley Collieries* [1926] 1 KB 522 (mine), see Pain J.'s treatment in *Bond* v. *CAV* [1983] IRLR 360, 366–7.

170 *Tocher* v. *General Motors Ltd* [1981] IRLR 55; on s. 140, P. Schofield (1981) 10 ILJ 176; *ILEA* v. *Nash* [1979] ICR 229; on 'common law' trial periods see note 147, above; and now *Igbo's* case, p. 202, note 83, above.

171 Restrictively construed in *Cartwright* v. *Clancey Ltd* [1983] ICR 552. On the exemption in electrical contracting, see (1976) 131 IRRR 2; L. Dickens *et al.*, *Dismissed* (1985), p. 238.

172 See A. Sisson and W. Brown, in G. Bain (ed.), *Industrial Relations in Britain* (1983), p. 151; R. Taylor, *Workers in the New Depression* (1982), p. 141; W. Brown (ed.), *The Changing Contours of British Industrial Relations* (1981), p. 117; W. Daniel and N. Millward, *Workplace Industrial Relations in Britain* (1983), p. 279.

173 *Simmons* v. *Hoover* [1977] QB 284.

174 See on periodical payments, the ILO study, *Into the 21st Century: The Development of Social Security* (1985); P. Ashby, *Social Security after Beveridge* (1984); for reform proposals, B. Marsh (1985), Law Soc. Gaz. 1557. See too P. Lewis, *Twenty Years of Statutory Redundancy Payments in Great Britain* (1985).

175 B. Hepple, 'A Right to Work?' (1981) 10 ILJ 65, 82.

176 See B. Napier (1983) 12 ILJ 17, on the new ILO standards, which also deal in a wide sense with redundancies; pp. 24–7.

177 S. Anderman, *Unfair Dismissal* (2nd ed. 1985), p. 1, the best account of the current law in detail.

178 See s. 141 (2); *Janata Bank* v. *Ahmed* [1981] ICR 791.

179 EPCA, Sched. 9, para. 2 and s. 138 (4); EPA 1975 s. 121; and Chapter 2, p. 136, on the *GCHQ* case.

180 See Chapter 2, pp. 115–16; C. Mogridge (1981) 9 ILJ 23; *Hyland* v. *Barker Ltd* [1985] IRLR 403 (period of illegality of contract not included for continuity).

181 *Wickens* v. *Champion Employment* [1984] ICR 365; but see *Cox* v. *ELG Metals* [1985] ICR 310 (CA; associated employer's employees working abroad counted); *Keabeech Ltd* v. *Mulcahy* [1985] ICR 791 (see p. 121).

182 See *Employment* (Cmnd 9474, 1985); Wedderburn, in P. Fosh and C. Littler (eds.), *Industrial Relations and the Law in the 1980s* (1985), p. 97; R. Lewis and B. Simpson, *Striking A Balance?* (1981), pp. 23–9. See now S. Evans, J. Goodman and L. Hargreaves, *Unfair Dismissal Law and Employment Practice* (1985, DE Research No. 53), Chap. 6 (little evidence of 'employment deterrence').

183 [1985] IRLR 89.

184 *McNeill* v. *Chas. Crimin* [1984] IRLR 179 (Scot.) (temporary change in duties not a repudiation); *Millbrook Furnishing Industries* v. *McIntosh* [1981] IRLR 309 (change in status and work, without loss of pay, of uncertain duration a constructive dismissal).

185 *Wadham Stringer Commercials Ltd* v. *Brown* [1983] IRLR 46 (demotion); but a breach does not always flow from a mistaken, if insistent, interpretation of the contract: *Financial Techniques Ltd* v. *Hughes* [1981] IRLR 32 (CA; unless there is a 'threat to the current contractual rights' of the employee, Templeman LJ, p. 37).

186 *Genower* v. *Ealing, Hammersmith and Hounslow AHA* [1980] IRLR 297; *Hollister* v. *NFU* [1979] ICR 542.

187 *Trusthouses Forte* v. *Aquilar* [1976] IRLR 251, 253.

188 *Devis & Sons Ltd* v. *Atkins* [1977] AC 931; *Monie* v. *Coral Racing* [1980] IRLR 464.

189 See *Greenall Whitley* v. *Carr* [1985] IRLR 289; *National Heart and Chest Hospitals Board* v. *Nambiar* [1981] IRLR 196 and *West Midlands Co-op. Soc.* v. *Tipton*, [1986] 2 WLR 306 (HL). See too *Stacey* v. *Babcock Power Ltd* [1986] IRLR 3 (EAT, pick-up of business after dismissal notice for redundancy; failure to offer alternative job unfair).

190 *McCrory* v. *Magee* [1983] IRLR 414 (CA NI); *Hotson* v. *Wisbech Conservative Club* [1984] IRLR 422.

191 *Smith* v. *City of Glasgow DC* [1985] IRLR 79 (Ct S.); *Henderson* v. *Granville Tours* [1982] IRLR 494 (but this issue might be dealt with under reasonableness); cf. *Grootcon (UK) Ltd* v. *Keld* [1984] IRLR 302.

192 *Sutton and Gates Ltd* v. *Boxall* [1979] ICR 67; on conduct, see *Thomson* v. *Alloa Motor C.* [1983] IRLR 403 (Scot. EAT).

193 *James* v. *Waltham Holy Cross UDC* [1973] ICR 398, 404.

194 See *Wass* v. *Binns* [1982] ICR 486; *British Labour Pump Ltd* v. *Byrne* [1979] ICR 347; *Murray MacKinnon* v. *Forno* [1983] IRLR 7, 8. On the 1985 draft ACAS code, *Disciplinary and Other Procedures in Employment*, see (1985) 294 IRLIB 7.

195 *Dobie* v. *Burns International Security Services* [1984] IRLR 329 (but injustice made dismissal unreasonable).

196 *Hollister* v. *NFU* [1979] ICR 542, 552–3.

197 Respectively, *Holden* v. *Bradville* [1986] IRLR 483; *Howarth Timber Ltd* v. *Biscomb* [1986] IRLR 52, 56. See too *Graham* v. *ABF* (1986) 297 IRLIB 9 (no consultation; selections for redundancy unfair).

198 *Yusuf* v. *Aberplace Ltd* [1984] ICR 850, 858.

199 *Chubb Fire Security Ltd* v. *Harper* [1983] IRLR 311, 313.

200 *Richmond Precision Ltd* v. *Pearce* [1985] IRLR 179.

201 J. Bowers and A. Clarke (1981) 10 ILJ 34, 43.

202 An IDS survey, cited by E. Armstrong, *Straitjacket or Framework?* (1973), p. 74.

203 H. Collins (1985) 14 ILJ 61, 62.

204 *Berriman* v. *Delabole Slate Ltd* [1985] ICR 546 (CA) (change in pay of workers not enough); *McGrath* v. *Rank Leisure Ltd* [1985] IRLR 323.

205 *Gorictree* v. *Jenkinson* [1985] ICR 51; *Anderson* v. *Dalkeith Engineering* [1985] ICR 66.

206 *Premier Motors Ltd* v. *Total Oil Ltd* [1984] ICR 58; but not a 'protective award': Chapter 4, p. 299; *A. Jowett Ltd* v. *NUTGW* [1985] IRLR 326.

207 *Forth Estuary Eng. Ltd* v. *Litster* [1986] IRLR 59 (but compensation was remitted to another tribunal).

208 *Barratt Construction Ltd* v. *Dalrymple* [1984] IRLR 385; cf. *Maund* v. *Penwith DC* [1984] ICR 143 (competing reasons); *Howarth Timber Ltd* v. *Biscomb* [1986] IRLR 52.

209 *Iceland Frozen Foods Ltd* v. *Jones* [1983] ICR 17.

210 *Thompson* v. *Smiths Shiprepairers Ltd* [1984] ICR 236, 247 (noise at work); *Stacey* v. *Babcock Power* [1986] IRLR 3.

211 *Kent CC* v. *Gilham* [1985] IRLR 18, 22 (CA); see too Chapter 2, p. 162; on compensation: *Gilham* v. *Kent CC* [1986] IRLR 56.

212 *Royal Society for Protection of Birds* v. *Croucher* [1984] ICR 604; *Kingston* v. *British Rail* [1984] ICR 781 (prison sentence SOSR; worker alleged racial harassment); *Anandarajah* v. *Lord Chancellor's Dept.* [1984] IRLR 131 (ejection of union representatives).

213 *Siggs & Chapman* v. *Knight* [1984] IRLR 83, 85.

214 *Bailey* v. *BP Oil* [1980] ICR 642.

215 *Monie* v. *Coral Racing Ltd* [1980] IRLR 464 (CA).

216 See *Greenall Whitley p.l.c.* v. *Carr* [1985] IRLR 289, 297.

217 *Rasool* v. *Hepworth Pipe* [1980] ICR 494; on discipline after acquittal, see *Saeed* v. *GLC* [1986] IRLR 23.

218 *Williams* v. *Compair Maxim* [1982] ICR 156 (guidelines); *Gray* v. *Shetland Norse Preserving* [1985] IRLR 53 (absenteeism; no trade union in a 'small enterprise'); *Wass* v. *Binns* [1982] ICR 486 (no warnings on earlier, or chance to explain later, misconduct).

219 *Rolls-Royce Ltd* v. *Dewhurst* [1985] IRLR 184, 186.

220 *North Yorkshire CC* v. *Fay* [1985] IRLR 247 (CA); no 'bumping' redundancy.

221 *Holden* v. *Bradville Ltd* [1985] IRLR 483 (selection unreasonable for lack of consultation; worker might have 'sporting chance' to persuade employer to replace her on redundancy list by a colleague).

222 *GEC* v. *Gilford* [1982] ICR 725; *Thos. Scott* v. *Allen* [1983] IRLR 329.

223 *Clarke* v. *Eley (IMI) Kynoch* [1982] IRLR 482 (and see Chapter 6, p. 465). See too *BL Cars Ltd* v. *Lewis* [1983] IRLR 58; the overriding test is still: was the selection one which a reasonable employer could have made? The worker may attack the criteria used for selection in a redundancy under s. 57 (3), but in effect this requires him to prove that 'the employer's decision has fallen below the lowest acceptable standard of management practice', S. Anderman, *Unfair Dismissal* (2nd ed. 1985), p. 206.

224 *McDowell* v. *E. British Road Services* [1981] IRLR 482; on unfair selection for redundancy and LIFO, *Morris* v. *Acco Co. Ltd* [1985] ICR 306.

225 *Cross International Ltd* v. *Reid* [1985] IRLR 387 (Watkins LJ dissenting, putting the employer's needs to keep his business in being and skilled workers in employment as sufficient to justify his choosing the rest contrary to agreement).

226 *Henry* v. *Ellerman Lines* [1985] ICR 57.

227 L. Dickens, M. Jones, B. Weekes and M. Hart, *Dismissed* (1985), Chap. 4, pp. 105–6.

228 See Clark and Wedderburn, in Wedderburn, R. Lewis and J. Clark (eds.) *Labour Law and Industrial Relations* (1983), p. 208. For an economic analysis see P. Fenn and C. Whelan (1982) 2 Int. Rev. of Law and Economics 206.

229 *Coleman* v. *Magnet Joinery Ltd* [1975] ICR 46; but see *Hill* v. *Parsons* [1972] Ch. 305; Chapter 2, p. 166.

230 See L. Dickens, M. Hart, M. Jones and B. Weekes (1981) 10 ILJ 160, and (1982) 20 BJIR 257; P. Lewis (1981) 19 BJIR 316 and (1983) 21 BJIR 232; and L. Dickens *et al.*, *Dismissed* (1985), Chap. 5.

231 K. Williams and D. Lewis (1981) 89 *Employment Gazette* 357; P. Lewis (1982) 45 MLR 384; and see K. Williams (1983) 12 ILJ 157.

232 L. Dickens *et al.*, *Dismissed* (1985), p. 111. See too on unfair dismissal and 'job property': P. White (1985) 16 Ind. Rel. Jo. No. 4, 98.

233 S. Estreicher (1985) 16 Ind. Rel. Jo. No. 1, 84, 88; on Germany, A. Döse-Digenopoulos and A. Höland (1985) 48 MLR 539; on Quebec and France, B. Napier, J.-C. Javillier and P. Verge, *Comparative Dismissal Law* (1982), p. 145; G. Camerlynck, G. Lyon-Caen and J. Pelissier, *Droit du Travail* (12th ed. 1984), p. 334 (reinstatement in France to be 'proposed' by the court under the 1973 law), pp. 723–7 (representatives); (1985) 141 EIRR 10, and 137 ibid. 17; and generally, P. Sherman (1981) 29 Am. Jo. Comp. Law 467. On 'constructive discharge' in the USA: R. Lieb (1985) 7 Ind. Rel. L. J. 143.

234 M. Grandi and G. Pera, *Commentario breve allo Statuto dei lavoratori* (1985), pp. 69–91; G. Ghezzi and U. Romagnoli, *Il rapporto di lavoro* (1984), pp. 336–9, 424–6; T. Treu, in (1984) 23 Giornale di Diritto del Lavoro e Relazioni Industriali 497, 517.

235 *Amalgamated Metals Foundry, etc. Union* v. *Broken Hill Proprietary Co.*, Case No. 3690/81, 2 August 1984 (the 'Job Protection' case).

236 See S. Evans, J. Goodman and L. Hargreaves (1985), 14 ILJ 91.

237 L. Dickens *et al.*, *Dismissed* (1985), p. 232.

238 [1972] ICR 501; cf. *Morris* v. *Acco Ltd* [1985] ICR 306 (unfair selection in redundancy; employer's intentions not a relevant factor). The maximum ceiling is applied only after *ex gratia* payments from the employer are taken into account: *McCarthy* v. *British Insulated Callender Cables* [1985] IRLR 94. The failure to increase it in 1986 may not affect many tribunal awards (below, p. 259), but it could affect negotiations in many settlements. The Government gave no explanation for the special treatment to this maximum.

239 See *Manpower Ltd* v. *Hearne* [1983] IRLR 281, 283; and the valuable exposition in S. Anderman, *Unfair Dismissal* (2nd ed. 1985), pp. 303–8, and 414–23; and R. Upex, *Termination of Employment* (1983), Appendix C.

240 *Daley* v. *Dorsett Ltd* [1982] ICR 1.

241 *Courtaulds Northern Spinning* v. *Moosa* [1984] ICR 218. The Secretary of State has power under the EA 1982, Sched. 3, para. 7, to make an Order allowing interest on compensation; cf. *Morris* v. *Acco Ltd* [1985] ICR 306; R. Upex, *Termination of Employment* (1983), Chap. 4. *Moosa* was approved in *Gilham* v. *Kent CC* (No. 3) [1986] ICR 52, as the correct approach.

242 *Wm. Muir* v. *Lamb* [1985] IRLR 95; *Gardner-Hill* v. *Roland Berger Technics Ltd* [1982] IRLR 498.

243 *Lee* v. *IPC Business Press* [1984] ICR 306.

244 *Warrilow* v. *Robert Walker* [1984] IRLR 304.

245 *Iggesund Converters* v. *Lewis* [1984] IRLR 431.

246 *Finnie* v. *Top Hat Frozen Foods* [1985] IRLR 365 (Scot. EAT).

247 *Holroyd* v. *Gravure Cylinders* [1984] IRLR 259.

248 *Sutton and Gates Ltd* v. *Boxall* [1978] IRLR 486; *Nelson* v. *BBC* (No. 2) [1980] ICR 110.

249 *Moncur* v. *International Paint Ltd* [1978] IRLR 223.

250 *Ladup Ltd* v. *Barnes* [1982] ICR 107.

251 P. Davies and M. Freedland, *Labour Law: Text and Materials* (2nd ed. 1984), p. 503; (1982) 227 IRLIB p. 14. On effects of pre-hearing assessments: P. Wallace and R. Clifton (1985) 93 *Employment Gazette* 65 (and G. Smith ibid. 182); also J. Angel, *Industrial Tribunals* (1984).

252 A. Döse-Digenopoulos and A. Höland (1985) 48 MLR 539, 557.

253 W. Daniel and E. Stilgoe, *The Impact of Employment Protection Laws* (1978, PSI); R. Clifton and C. Tatton-Brown, *Impact on Small Firms* (1979, DE Research Paper No. 6); *Financial Times*, 21 March 1985 (UMIST survey for DE). The 1985 survey for government: *Burdens on Business* (1985, DTI). See too now the official study of 1985, above, note 182.

254 L. Dickens, *et al.*, *Dismissed* (1985), pp. 255–60; P. Lewis (1981) Ind. Rel. Jo. No. 2 19, 26. On the irrationality of different legal exceptions for small firms: I. Smith (1985) 14 ILJ 18; cf. *Building Businesses, Not Barriers* (1986), Cmnd 9794).

255 B. Hepple in G. Bain (ed.), *Industrial Relations in Britain* (1983), pp. 409–12; and Chap. 22, R. Blanpain (ed.), *Comparative Labour Law and Industrial Relations* (1985).

256 L. Dickens *et al.*, *Dismissed* (1985), Chap. 8; L. Dickens (1978) 9 Ind. Rel. Jo. No. 4 p. 18.

257 H. Collins, 'Capitalist Discipline and Corporatist Law' (1982) 11 ILJ 78, 92; and ibid. 170, 177; contrast P. Elias (1981) 10 ILJ 201; (1978) 7 ILJ 16, 100.

258 See H. Forrest (1980) 43 MLR 361; F. Bootham and D. Denham (1981) 12 Ind. Rel. Jo. No, 3, 6 (dismissals of trade unionists: Chapter 4, p. 312).

259 S. Evans, J. Goodman and L. Hargreaves (1985) 14 ILJ 91, 104–5.

260 R. Munday (1981) 10 ILJ 146, 158–9; compare L. Dickens, M. Hart, M. Jones and B. Weekes, (1984) 37 Ind. Lab. Rel. Rev. 497.

261 L. Dickens *et al.*, *Dismissed* (1985), pp. 73–84; K. Wedderburn and P. Davies, *Employment Grievances and Disputes Procedures in Britain* (1969), Chap. 12; W. Hawes and G. Smith, 'Patterns of Representation' (1981, DE Research Paper No. 22). For a tribunal chairman's defence, see W. Leslie, 'Legalism in Industrial Tribunals?' (1985) *Employment Gazette* 357; on lay members, (1986) *Employment Gazette* 117.

262 L. Dickens *et al.*, op. cit., p. 46 and Chap. 7 on tribunals' 'efficiency', Chap. 2 on representation. On employers' associations, K. Sisson, in G. Bain (ed.), *Industrial Relations in Britain* (1983), p. 130.

263 Wedderburn and Davies, op. cit., p. 245; see too Clark and Wedderburn, in Wedderburn, Lewis and Clark (eds.), *Labour Law and Industrial Relations* (1983), pp. 173–84.

264 Cf. M. Mellish and N. Collis-Squires (1976) 5 ILJ 164; R. Martin and R. Fryer, *Redundancy and Paternalist Capitalism* (1973).

265 See (1974) 37 MLR 1, 23.

266 B. Napier, 'French Labour Courts, Institution in Transition' (1979) 42 MLR 270, 284; J.-C. Javillier, *Droit du Travail* (2nd ed 1982), p. 586; cf. S. Van Noorden (1980) *Employment Gazette* 1098, 1102.

267 See L. Dickens *et al.*, *Dismissed* (1985), pp. 278–84; see too K. Wedderburn, 'Conflicts of Rights and Conflicts of Interests in Labor Disputes', in B. Aaron (ed.), *Dispute Settlement Procedures in Five Western European Countries* (1969). On tribunal flexibility and the 'adversarial' nature of procedure: *Neale* v. *Hereford and Worcester CC* [1985] IRLR 281, 287; but compare the CA [1986] IRLR 168.

268 See A. Fox, *History and Heritage Social Origins of the British Industrial Relations System* (1985), esp. Chap. 4; and now *Man Mismanagement* (2nd ed. 1985), esp. Chaps. 7 and 8.

269 See the judicial preference for individual consultation over collective action: *Holden* v. *Bradville Ltd* [1985] IRLR 483; *Lafferty Construction* v. *Duthie* (1985) 295 IRLIB 14 (consultation on redundancies of non-unionists as well as union); and Kilner Brown J. in the *Crothall Ltd* decision (note 73, above).

270 L. Dickens *et al.*, op. cit., Chap. 9 'An Arbitral Alternative'; but see H. Glasbeek (1984) 13 ILJ 133, 150–2 (North American arbitration may be only marginally different from the tribunals given the similarity in the concrete nature of the relations of production); see too K. Stone (1981) 90 Yale L. J. 1509, and Chapter 10.

4 Collective Bargaining and the Law

1 O. Kahn-Freund, *Labour and the Law* (3rd ed. 1983; Davies and Freedland, eds.) p. 154; Allan Flanders, *Management and Unions* (1970), p. 222.

2 See H. Clegg, *The Changing System of Industrial Relations in Great Britain* (1979), pp. 115–23; A. Flanders, op. cit., p. 99.

3 E. Hobsbawm, *World of Labour* (1984), pp. 254–6; cf. E. P. Thompson, *The Making of the English Working Class* (1963), Chap. VIII.

4 A. Fox, *History and Heritage* (1985), p. 174; cf. Clegg, op. cit., Chap. 3.

5 See the classic studies by E. Batstone, I. Boraston and S. Frenkel, *Shop Stewards in Action* (1977); and W. McCarthy, *Shop Stewards* (1966, Donovan Commission Research Paper No. 1).

6 See W. Brown (ed.), *The Changing Contours of British Industrial Relations* (1980); K. Sisson and W. Brown, in G. Bain (ed.), *Industrial Relations in Britain* (1983), pp. 137 ff.; W. Daniel and N. Millward, *Workplace Industrial Relations in Britain* (1983), Chaps. V–VIII.

7 See note 5, above; M. Poole, W. Brown, J. Rubery, K. Sisson, R. Tarling and F. Wilkinson, *Industrial Relations in the Future* (1984), pp. 31–3; and E. Batstone, *Working Order: Workplace Industrial Relations over Two Decades* (1984). (It is doubtful how far decentralization has gone; cf. the IDS Study, reported in *Financial Times*, 7 January 1985.)

8 See D. Winchester, in G. Bain (ed.), *Industrial Relations in Britain* (1983), pp. 163–76; B. Hepple, in Wedderburn and Murphy (eds.), *Labour Law and the Community* (1982), Chap. VII.

9 Wedderburn, in Fosh and Littler (eds.), *Industrial Relations and the Law in the 1980s* (1985), Chap. 2, n. 128; L. Neal and L. Bloch, *The Right to Strike in a Free Society* (1983, Centre for Policy Studies).

10 See Chapters 1, p. 11, and 2, pp. 117–18.

11 ILO, 234th Report, Case No. 1261, 226 Session, 31 May–2 June 1984, p. 87; *Council of Civil Service Unions* v. *Minister for the Civil Service* [1985] ICR 14 (HL).

12 G. Bain and R. Price, in G. Bain (ed.), *Industrial Relations in Britain* (1983), p. 19; G. Bain, *The Growth of White Collar Unionism* (1970).

13 O. Kahn-Freund, *Labour and the Law* (3rd ed. 1983), p. 88.

14 As in *R.* v. *PO, ex parte ASTMS* [1981] ICR 76.

15 *Financial Times*, 8 February and 9 March 1985; see too Chapter 9, p. 781.

16 E. Rose and C. Selby, 'Some Reflections upon Recognition' (1985) 16 Ind. Rel. Jo. No. 1, 70.

17 *Squibb UK Staff Assoc.* v. *Certification Officer* [1979] ICR 235; and see *Annual Report*, Certification Officer (1976), Chap. 2; (1979), supplement on 'Staff Associations'.

18 'The New Structure of Labour Law in Britain' (1978) 13 Israel Law Jo. 435, 456.

19 On Sweden, Folke Schmidt, *Law and Industrial Relations in Sweden* (1977); H. Gospel (1983) 21 BJIR 343 (and USA). On France see (1982), 11 *Droit Social*, November, 'La Négociation dans L'Entreprise' (G. Lyon-Caen, ed.); and *les lois Auroux* (1983), 1 *Droit Social*, January; 'Les Réformes IV – Un Nouveau droit du Travail?' (J. Laroque, ed.).

20 On the USA: M. Hart (1979) 8 ILJ 201; W. Gould, *A Primer on American Labor Law* (1982), pp. 109–22. See now on Britain, W. McCarthy, *Freedom at Work* (1986, Fabian Society).

21 See R. Simpson and J. Wood, *Industrial Relations and the 1971 Act* (1973), pp. 106–18.

22 *Commodore Business Machines* v. *EETPU*, 78/339, para. 21; see also below, note 129.

23 Notably Lord Scarman, *UKAPE* v. *ACAS* [1981] AC 424; B. Simpson (1980) 9 ILJ 125; R. Lewis and B. Simpson, *Striking a Balance?* (1981), Chap. VII. Repeal was effected by Employment Act 1980 s. 19.

24 *Powley* v. *ACAS* [1978] ICR 123, 135 Browne-Wilkinson J.

25 *Grunwick Processing Laboratories Ltd* v. *ACAS* [1978] AC 655 (HL). See the excellent case study of all aspects in P. Elias, B. Napier and P. Wallington, *Labour Law Cases and Materials* (1980), Chap. 1, Part 4; and see B. Simpson (1979) 8 ILJ 69; R. Beaumont (1981) 19 BJIR 238; J. Rogaly, *Grunwicks* (1977); and ACAS, *Annual Report* (1980), Part II. Obligatory recognition persists in N. Ireland: SI 528/1982, art. 22.

26 *NUGSAT* v. *Albury Bros.* [1979] ICR 84.

27 *R.* v. *CAC, ex parte BTP Tioxide* [1981] ICR 843; J. Bowers (1983) 4 Co. Law. 35; *USDAW* v. *Sketchley* [1981] ICR 644 (representation in grievance procedure not recognition; no negotiation). The CAC was prepared to see 'representations' as a 'limited scope of recognition': *Babtie Shaw & Morton* v. *UKAPE*, 82/4.

28 I. Smith and J. Wood, *Industrial Law* (2nd ed. 1984), p. 40.

29 *Cleveland CC* v. *Springett* [1985] IRLR 131.

30 *Messenger Newspapers Group Ltd* v. *NGA* [1984] IRLR 397, 399; see too Chapter 8, p. 610.

31 On subcontracting and draughtsmen, see R. Lewis and B. Simpson, 'Disorganizing Industrial Relations' (1982) 11 ILJ 227, 233; see on the loss of trade dispute 'immunities', Chapter 8.

32 See too Wedderburn, in P. Fosh and C. Littler (eds.), *Industrial Relations and the Law in the 1980s* (1985); P. Davies and M. Freedland, in O. Kahn-Freund, *Labour and the Law* (3rd ed. 1983), p. 269.

33 H. Phelps Brown, *The Origins of Trade Union Power* (1983), p. 215.

34 CAC, *BL Cars* v. *GMWU* 80/65 ('moral' duty), *Rolls-Royce* v. *ASTMS* 80/30 (preparation); *BP Chemicals* v. *TGWU* 86/1 (impediment); see on CAC decisions: 215 IRRR (Jan. 1980) 8, and 290 ibid. (Feb. 1983) 2.

35 *Kodak* v. *ASTMS* 82/16; 288 IRRR (Jan. 1983) 14; and the CAC record generally see: H. Gospel and P. Willman (1981) 10 ILJ 10.

36 *Civil Service Union* v. *CAC* [1980] IRLR 274 (also, no impediment).

37 *British Timken* v. *AUEW and EETPU* 85/3 (disclosure of pay bill and pension fund details; profits, order book, etc. left to consultation in agreed machinery).

38 F. Mitchell, I. Sams, D. Tweedie and P. White (1980) 11 Ind. Rel. Jo. No. 5, 53, 61 (case studies); A. Marsh and R. Rosewall (1976) 7 Ind. Rel. Jo. No. 2, 4.

39 See *Redgrave's Health and Safety in Factories* (2nd ed. 1982; Fife and Machin, eds.), Part 2.

40 See HSWA s. 79; and (1985) 110 H. and S. Info. Bull. p. 2.

41 For the 'state of play' see 97 H. and S. Info. Bull. (Jan. 1984) p. 7; and on Britain and for interesting comparisons in Australia, W. Creighton (1982), Jo. Ind. Rel. 337 (Aus.).

42 See (1984) 104 H. and S. Info. Bull. p. 6.

43 W. E. J. McCarthy, *The Role of Shop Stewards in British Industrial Relations* (1966, Donovan Commission Research Paper 1), p. 734.

44 See *Lifting the Burden* (Cmnd 9571, 1985), p. 23.

45 It may be necessary one day to reconsider the relationship of the EPA and the Directive; cf. M. Freedland (1976) 5 ILJ 24.

46 [1984] ICR 352, considering *NUT* v. *Avon CC* [1978] ICR 626 (notice issued immediately after consultation begins; breach of the section).

47 *TGWU* v. *Ledbury Preserves Ltd* [1985] IRLR 412.

48 *Spillers-French (Holdings)* v. *USDAW* [1980] ICR 31.

49 *Hamish Armour* v. *ASTMS* [1979] IRLR 24; *USDAW* v. *Leancut Bacon Ltd* [1981] IRLR 295.

50 See 'Job Security Procedures' (1983) 305 IRRR 2.

51 W. Daniel and N. Millward, *Workplace Industrial Relations in Britain* (1983), p. 198.

52 S. Wood and I. Dey, *Redundancy* (1983), pp. 12–16.

53 See on the TUPE Regs., B. Hepple (1982) 11 ILJ 29; P. Davies and M. Freedland, *Transfer of Employment* (1982); and R. Elkund (1985) Comp. Lab. Law 71 (comparative).

54 *R. Seligman Corpn* v. *Baker* [1983] ICR 770; *SI (Systems & Instruments) Ltd* v. *Grist* [1983] ICR 788; Chapter 3, p. 207. On restriction of 'commercial venture': *Hadden* v. *Univ. of Dundee Students' Union* [1985] IRLR 449.

55 *Apex Leisure Hire* v. *Barratt* [1984] ICR 452; *Premier Motors* v. *Total Oil (GB)* [1984] ICR 58. But see *Bullard* v. *Marchant*, *The Times*, 26 February 1986 (dismissal before transfer, transferee liable).

56 [1985] IRLR 326; and on the protected period *Green & Son Ltd* v. *ASTMS* [1984] IRLR 135; P. Robertshaw (1985) 14 ILJ 130.

57 *Consultative Document on Draft EC Directive* ('Vredeling' and draft Fifth Directive), DE and DTI (1983), pp. 1, 38, with the texts as at that time; see now C. Docksey (1986) 49 MLR 281.

58 See (1985) 133 EIRR p. 10; (1985) 134 EIRR p. 2.

59 A. Ogus and E. Barendt, *The Law of Social Security* (1982), p. 187. For the statistics: (1985) *Employment Gazette* 494.

60 See P. Davies and M. Freedland, *Labour Law: Text and Materials* (2nd ed. 1984), pp. 362 ff. Also on pension funds, H. McRae and F. Cairncross, *Capital City* (1984), pp. 102–8: and R. Nobles (1986) 49 MLR 42.

61 See H. Wellington, *Labor and the Legal Process* (1968), p. 84.

62 M. Freedland (1977) 6 ILJ 188 on the two White Papers (Cmnd 5904 and 6514).

63 See R. Minns, *Pension Funds and British Capitalism* (1980); *Cowan* v. *Scargill* [1984] ICR 646; *Financial Times*, 2 February 1985.

64 See R. Nobles, 'Conflicts of Interest in Trustees' Management of Pension

Funds' (1985) 14 ILJ 1: J. Hyman and T. Schuller, 'Occupational Pension Schemes and Collective Bargaining' (1984) 22 BJIR 289.

65 Social Security Pensions Act 1975 s. 31; Occupational Pensions Regulations No. 1927, 1975.

66 E.g. Health and Social Security Act 1984 ss. 19, 20; Social Security Act 1985 ss. 1–4; see 'Personal Pensions' (1984, DHSS Consultative Document); and the valuable note by G. Moffat (1985) 14 ILJ 134. The reform proposals may not help those most in need: *Selective Social Security* (1986, PSI).

67 S. and B. Webb, *History of Trade Unionism* (1920), p. 337.

68 See Wedderburn and P. Davies, *Employment Grievances and Disputes Procedures in Britain* (1969), Chap. 4, and McCarthy, Research Paper No. 1 and Marsh, Research Paper No. 10 for the Donovan Commission.

69 Lord Amulree, *Industrial Arbitration in Great Britain* (1929), pp. 46–9; W. Houldsworth, *History of English Law*, Vol. XIII (1952), pp. 336–9.

70 A. Fox, *History and Heritage* (1985), p. 251; Lord Askwith, *Industrial Problems and Disputes* (1920), pp. 77–8, 80–3.

71 W. Brown (ed.), *The Changing Contours of British Industrial Relations* (1980), pp. 49–50.

72 L. Dickens, M. Jones, B. Weekes and M. Hart, *Dismissed* (1985), Chap. 8.

73 C. Camerlynck and G. Lyon-Caen, *Droit du Travail* (12th ed. 1984), p. 993: 'en veilleuse'. See too the cautious appraisal of 'last offer' arbitration by CAC Chairman, Sir John Wood (1985) 23 BJIR 415.

74 Wedderburn (1976) 39 MLR 169. Time off work is also afforded for discharge of some public duties (EPCA s. 29), antenatal care (s. 31A; Chapter 6, p. 483) and for seeking a new job or training in a redundancy (s. 31). For safety representatives' time off, see p. 312.

75 W. Brown (ed.), *The Changing Contours of British Industrial Relations* (1980), pp. 62–9 (the numbers of stewards may have fallen in the 1980s); and on stewards' activities, W. Daniel and N. Millward, *Workplace Industrial Relations in Britain* (1983), pp. 88–104; P. Willman (1981) 19 BJIR 1 (combine committees).

76 *Menzies* v. *Smith & McLaurin Ltd* [1980] IRLR 180 (Scot.).

77 *Beal* v. *Beecham Group Ltd* [1982] ICR 460 (CA); (No. 2) [1983] IRLR 317 (EAT); Fitzpatrick (1983) 12 ILJ 258.

78 *Thos. Scott Ltd* v. *Allen* [1983] IRLR 329 (CA); *Ashley* v. *Ministry of Defence* [1984] ICR 298 (EAT). On plans to curtail time-off rights: *Building Businesses, Not Barriers* (1986, Cmnd 9794), Chap. 7.

79 *White* v. *Pressed Steel Fisher* [1980] IRLR 176; J. McIlroy (1981) 10 ILJ 58.

80 *Maund* v. *Penwith DC* [1982] ICR 732 (see Chapter 3, p. 244); and ibid. [1984] ICR 143 (CA).

81 *Marley Tile Co.* v. *Shaw* [1980] ICR 72.

82 *City of Birmingham DC* v. *Beyer* [1977] IRLR 211.

83 *Dixon* v. *West Ella Developments* [1978] ICR 856, 860.

84 *Chant* v. *Aquaboats Ltd* [1978] ICR 643; *Drew* v. *St Edmundsbury BC* [1980] ICR 513.

85 *Cruickshank* v. *Hobbs* [1977] ICR 725.

86 [1983] ICR 208. Cf. *O'Connell* v. *Tetrosyl* (1986) 125 H. S. Info. Bull. 12 (sacked safety respresentative; not trade union dismissal).

87 *British Airways Engine Overhaul Ltd* v. *Francis* [1981] ICR 278.

88 See 263 IDS Brief (Oct. 1983) pp. i–iv; *Brassington* v. *Cauldon Wholesale Ltd* [1977] IRLR 479; for tribunal cases on refusal to recognize and ASD, see (1986) 318 IDS Brief 4.

89 *Carlson* v. *Post Office* [1981] ICR 343.

90 *Carter* v. *Wiltshire CC* [1979] IRLR 331 (IT) (fireman); *British Airways* v. *Clark* [1982] IRLR 238 (EAT). See on the 1971 Act, *PO* v. *Crouch* [1974] ICR 378 (HL).

91 See *Langston* v. *AUEW* [1973] ICR 211; [1974] ICR 180 (CA); (No. 2) [1974] ICR 510; Chapter 3, p. 178.

92 *UKAPE* v. *ACAS* [1980] ICR 201, 214 (HL); [1979] ICR 303, 316 (CA). But the Convention is not part of English law. *R.* v. *GLC, ex parte Burgess* [1978] IRLR 261.

93 See O. Kahn-Freund, *Labour and the Law* (3rd ed. 1983), pp. 154–5, Chap. 6 'Collective Agreements and the Law'.

94 *Ford Motor Co.* v. *AUEF and TGWU* [1969] 2 QB 303.

95 O. Kahn-Freund, *The System of Industrial Relations in Great Britain* (1954), pp. 55–8. On the Kahn-Freund 'legacy', R. Lewis (1979) 42 MLR 613; Wedderburn, Chap. 3, in Wedderburn, R. Lewis and J. Clark (eds.), *Labour Law and Industrial Relations* (1983), pp. 40–7.

96 B. Weekes, *et al.*, *Industrial Relations and the Limits of Law* (1975), Chap. 6 on various wordings of the TINALEA clause proposed by the TUC in 1971: J. Hughes and H. Collins, *Trade Unions in Great Britain* (1973), p. 145.

97 *Monterosso Shipping Co.* v. *ITWF* [1982] ICR 675, 685.

98 *Trade Union Immunities* (Cmnd 8128, 1981), paras. 241–3; Donovan Report (Cmnd 3623, 1968), para. 505 and Chap. VIII.

99 *Universe Tankships of Monrovia Inc.* v. *ITWF* [1980] IRLR 239, 246; on appeal [1983] 1 AC 366 (HL).

100 See EPCA s. 18 (guarantee payments; see Chapter 5, p. 396); s. 65 (dismissal agreements); s. 96 (redundancy); s. 140.

101 *EC Commission* v. *UK* [1984] ICR 192 (ECJ); S. Fredman (1984), 13 ILJ 119.

102 *R.* v. *Hertfordshire CC, ex parte NUPE* [1985] IRLR 258; see Chapter 2, p. 160; *Kent CC* v. *Gilham* [1985] IRLR 18 (unfair dismissal claims).

103 *R.* v. *Liverpool CC ex parte Ferguson* [1985] IRLR 501.

104 *Ellis* v. *Brighton Co-op. Soc.* [1976] I R L R 419; *Burton Group Ltd* v. *Smith*
[1977] I R L R 351.

105 *Edwards* v. *Skyways Ltd* [1964] 1 All E. R. 494.

106 See *Joel* v. *Cammell Laird* (1969) 4 I T R 206 (I T) (a clear case of incorporation: see below): so too *Singh* v. *B S C* [1974] I R L R 131 (I T) (where workers
resigned from union; the reasoning cannot be accepted unless the workers'
employment terms, which are not fully reported, meant that they were not
bound by new agreements thereafter).

107 [1975] I C R 145.

108 *Heatons Transport (St Helens) Ltd* v. *T G W U* [1973] A C 15; and see *General
Aviation Services* v. *T G W U* [1976] I R L R 224; [1985] I C R 615 (HL).

109 *Rookes* v. *Barnard* [1963] 1 Q B 623, 675 (later Lord Donovan); the decision
reversed on other grounds [1964] A C 1129 (HL).

110 [1958] 1 W L R 16 (C A); see too Chapter 3, p. 213.

111 *Sutcliffe* v. *Hawker Siddeley* [1973] I C R 560 (points of guidance); *Lister* v.
Fran Gerrard Ltd [1973] I R L R 302; *Murray* v. *Robert Rome Ltd* (1969) 4
I T R 20 (plumbing industry); *Pearson* v. *Wm. Jones* [1967] 2 All E. R. 1062.

112 *Stevenson* v. *Tees-Side Engineering Ltd* [1971] 1 All E. R. 296; compare
Jones v. *Assoc. Tunnelling* [1981] I R L R 477 (Chapter 3, p. 177).

113 See P. Leighton and Dunville (1977) 6 I L J 133.

114 *Abernethy* v. *Mott Hay and Anderson* [1974] I C R 323.

115 *Dudfield* v. *Ministry of Works, The Times*, 24 Jan. 1964; O. Kahn-Freund,
The System of Industrial Relations in Great Britain (1954; A. Flanders and H.
Clegg, eds.), p. 58. Compare *Brand* v. *L C C, The Times*, 28 Oct. 1967 (J N C
award binding on true construction of contract).

116 *Assoc. Newspaper Group* v. *Wade* [1979] I C R 664; *Partington* v. *N A L G O*
[1981] I R L R 537 (gas safety workers).

117 [1983] I R L R 139; cf. *Mears* v. *Safecar Security Ltd* [1982] I C R 626; p. 173.

118 *Morris* v. *Bailey* [1969] 2 Lloyd's Rep. 215; *Gibbons* v. *Associated British
Ports* [1985] I R L R 376; Chapter 2, p. 199.

119 *Robertson* v. *British Gas Corpn* [1983] I C R 351; Leighton (1983) 12 I L J
115.

120 *Burroughs Machines Ltd* v. *Timmoney* [1977] I R L R 404.

121 *Loman and Henderson* v. *Merseyside Transport Services Ltd* (1968) 3 I T R
108; Wedderburn (1969) 32 MLR 99; *Gascol Conversions Ltd* v. *Mercer*
[1974] I C R 420; Chapter 2, p. 136.

122 *Barrett* v. *N C B* [1978] I C R 1101; *Donelan* v. *Kerrby Construction* [1983]
I R L R 191; M. Freedland (1983) 12 I L J 256.

123 *Marley* v. *Forward Trust Group* [1986] I R L R 43.

124 *Cadoux* v. *Central Regional Council*, 12 July 1985, Ct S.; and see B. Napier
[1986] 15 I L J 53; cf. *Financial Techniques* v. *Hughes* [1981] I R L R 32.

125 *Land* v. *West Yorkshire MCC* [1981] ICR 334 (CA); *Kenny* v. *Vauxhall Motors Ltd* [1983] ICR 560, 566, affd [1985] ICR 535 (CA).

126 *Bond* v. *CAV Ltd* [1983] IRLR 360; see Chapter 3, p. 197; on collateral contracts, G. Treitel, *Law of Contract* (6th ed. 1983), p. 271; Wedderburn, [1959] CLJ 58 (the consideration in the employment cases seems to be an agreement to vary the normal arrangements).

127 [1966] 1 QB 555 (the defendant stewards were protected then by the Trade Disputes Act 1906 in any event: Chapter 8, p. 586).

128 See *West Midlands Co-op. Soc.* v. *Tipton*, [1986] 2 WLR 306 (HL); *Greenall Whitley p.l.c.* v. *Carr* [1985] IRLR 289.

129 *R.* v. *IDT, ex parte Portland UDC* [1955] 3 All E. R. 18, 25; B. Bercusson, *Fair Wages Resolution* (1978), p. 350; see above, note 22.

130 EETPU and Control Data Agreement, (1984) 327 IRRR 11. See on Toshiba and Sanyo agreements with EETPU, (1981) 253 IRRR 2; (1985) 337 IRRR 9.

131 *Rookes* v. *Barnard* [1964] AC 1129; see O. Kahn-Freund, *Labour and the Law* (2nd ed. 1977), pp. 58, 140; he regarded this part of the case as 'quite exceptional', *Labour Relations and the Law* (1965), p. 27, but that judgment seems incorrect.

132 *British Leyland UK Ltd* v. *McQuilken* [1978] IRLR 245.

133 *City and Hackney Health Authority* v. *Craig* [1985] IRLR 252.

134 *Hadmor Productions Ltd* v. *Hamilton* [1983] 1 AC 191 (HL). See on status quo agreements, S. Anderman (1975) 4 ILJ 131.

135 *The System of Industrial Relations in Great Britain* (1954, Flanders and Clegg, eds.), p. 66; *Labour Law, Old Traditions and New Developments* (1968), p. 32.

136 See W. Rees (1982) 11 ILJ 178, 180.

137 But see G. Rubin (1977) 6 ILJ 149, and (1985), 14 ILJ 33. Note the Restoration of Pre-War Trade Practices Act 1919, and its equivalent in 1944; and now Reserve Forces Act 1985.

138 See W. E. J. McCarthy, Research Paper No. 8 for the Donovan Commission (1968), pp. 31–44.

139 K. Wedderburn and P. Davies, *Employment Grievances and Disputes Procedures in Britain* (1969), Chap. 9.

140 See *R.* v. *CAC, ex parte Deltaflow* [1978] ICR 534.

141 L. Dickens, J. Hart, M. Jones and B. Weekes, *A Response to Government Working Paper* (on EP Legislation 1980: IRRU, Warwick Univ.).

142 M. Jones (1980) 9 ILJ 28, 44; on the legal issues, P. Wood (1978) 7 ILJ 65; on repeal, R. Lewis and B. Simpson, *Striking a Balance?* (1981), Chap. 7; B. Bercusson (1976) 5 ILJ 129.

143 P. Kahn, N. Lewis, R. Livock and P. Wiles, *Picketing* (1983), p. 214.

144　O. Kahn-Freund (1948) 11 MLR Pt I, 269, 274; Pt II, 429; B. Bercusson, *Fair Wages Resolutions* (1978), pp. xxv, 496.

145　*Racal Communications Ltd* v. *Pay Board* [1974] ICR 590; see p. 356.

146　See P. Wood (1978) 7 ILJ 65.

147　*Exclusive Cleaning Services* v. *NUPE* 84/13; see too *GEC Turbine* v. *AUEW (TASS)* 84/1 (company in engineering not 'turbine' industry); *Leyland Vehicles* v. *ASTMS* 83/13 (wage levels not below general level).

148　B. Bercusson (1982) 11 ILJ 271.

149　D. Brindle, *Financial Times*, 12 Nov. 1984.

150　See (1985) 342 IRRR 2. One contractor complained of 'non-commercial' questions (117 from the GLC) and exclusion of those who built Molesworth or had business links with South Africa: *The Times*, 18 December 1985.

151　S. Bazen, *Low Wages, Family Circumstances and Minimum Wage Legislation* (1985), p. 81; J. Mack and S. Lansley, *Poor Britain* (1985).

152　C. Craig, J. Rubery, R. Tarling and F. Wilkinson, *Labour Market Structure, Industrial Organization and Low Pay* (1982). See F. Bayliss, *British Wages Councils* (1962); on the historical development, P. Davies and M. Freedland, *Labour Law: Text and Materials* (2nd ed. 1984), pp. 144–54. But for 'misconceptions' on Wages Councils, see S. Keevash (1985) 14 ILJ 217.

153　*Consultative Paper on Wages Councils*, Department of Employment, February 1985, para. 15.

154　Respectively, Craig *et al.*, op. cit. (1982); H. Neuberger, *From the Dole Queue to the Sweatshop* (1984, Low Pay Unit); *Who Needs Wages Councils?* (1983, Low Pay Unit); cf. W. Wells, *Relative Pay and Employment of Young People* (1982, DE Research Paper 34).

155　HM Treasury, *Relationship between Employment and Wages* (1985); see W. Brown (1985), 14 ILJ 141; and D. Marsland, *Wages Councils Destroy Jobs* (January 1984); D. Forrest and S. Dennison, *Low Pay or No Pay* (1984, Instit. Econ. Affairs); Nat. Fedn of Self-Employed and Small Businesses, *Still Priced Out* (1985); P. Hart, *Youth Unemployment and Relative Wages* (1983, NIESR Paper No. 70); cf. *Report* of Select Committee HL on 'Unemployment' (1982, Paper 142).

156　P. Morgan, D. Patterson and R. Barnes, *Wage Floors in the Clothing Industry 1950–81* (1985, DE Research Paper 52); C. Craig and F. Wilkinson, *Pay and Employment in Four Retail Trades* (1985, DE Research Paper 51). See the review by John Lloyd, *Financial Times*, 3 March 1985.

157　S. Bazen, *Low Wages, Family Circumstances and Minimum Wage Legislation* (1985, PSI No. 643), p. 65.

158　G. Starr, *Minimum Wage Fixing* (1981, ILO), Chap. 8.

159　C. Pond and S. Winyard, *The Case for a National Minimum Wage* (1982, Low Pay Unit); F. Field, *The Minimum Wage – Its Potential and Dangers* (1984, PSI).

160 P. Davies and M. Freedland (eds.), Introduction to Kahn-Freund, *Labour and the Law* (3rd ed. 1983), pp. 4, 5–10; also *Labour Law: Text and Materials* (2nd ed. 1984), pp. 137–43.

161 L. Panitch and D. Schwartz, *From Consent to Coercion* (1985), pp. 39–57, for an interesting review.

162 See further: Wedderburn (1984) 13 ILJ 73; R. Davies, 'Incomes Policy and Anti-Inflation Policy', Chap. 17, in G. Bain (ed.), *Industrial Relations in Britain* (1983); H. Clegg, *The Changing System of Industrial Relations* (1979), Chaps 8–10 (the best brief account of the nature of various policies).

163 See the various White Papers, e.g. Cmnd 2634, 1965; Cmnd 5267, 1973.

164 R. Rideout, Chap. V 'Regulated Arbitration', in Wedderburn and W. T. Murphy (eds.), *Labour Law and the Community* (1982).

165 Prices and Incomes Act 1966 s. 16; Counter Inflation Acts: 1972 s. 5; 1973 s. 17 (8).

166 Respectively, O. Kahn-Freund, *Labour Law, Old Traditions and New Developments* (1968), p. 21; H. Clegg, *How to Run an Incomes Policy* (1971), p. 57.

167 H. Turner (1970) 8 BJIR 197, 203. On later periods of incomes policy: R. Chater, A. Dean and R. Elliott, *Incomes Policy* (1981).

168 G. Bain and R. Price, Chap. 1, in G. Bain (ed.), *Industrial Relations in Britain* (1983); see R. Undy, V. Ellis, W. E. J. McCarthy and A. Halmos, *Change in Trade Unions* (1981), pp. 314–34.

169 J. Durcan, W. McCarthy and G. Redman, *Strikes in Post-War Britain* (1983), p. 395, and Chap. 11 *passim*.

170 See R. Davies, in G. Bain (ed.), op. cit., p. 446 on S. Brittan; see too R. Layard, D. Metcalf and S. Nickell (1978) 16 BJIR 287–302.

171 H. Phelps Brown, *The Origins of Trade Union Power* (1983), p. 166.

172 D. Winchester, Chap. 7, in G. Bain (ed.), *Industrial Relations in Britain* (1983).

173 B. Hepple, in Wedderburn and W. T. Murphy (eds.), *Labour Law and the Community* (1982), p. 77.

174 Derek Robinson, *Guardian*, 19 July 1985.

175 J. Meade, *Wage Fixing: Stagflation Vol. 1* (1982), p. 118, Chap. VIII.

176 W. Brown (ed.), *The Changing Contours of British Industrial Relations* (1980), pp. 55–9.

177 *Labour and the Law* (3rd ed. 1983), pp. 24, 240.

178 *PO* v. *Crouch* [1973] ICR 366, 374 (rights of member of splinter union); [1974] ICR 378 (HL).

179 *Langston* v. *AUEW* [1974] ICR 180, 190; *McInnes* v. *Onslow-Fane* [1978] 3 All E. R. 211, 217; B. Hepple (1981) 10 ILJ 65.

180 *Report of Court of Inquiry* (Cmnd 6922, 1977), paras. 56–7.

181 Judge Sørensen, *Young, James & Webster* v. *UK* [1981] IRLR 408, 420
    (Eur. Ct Human Rights); see too below, p. 376.
182 See e.g. G. Camerlynck, G. Lyon-Caen, J. Pélissier, *Droit du Travail* (12th
    ed. 1984), pp. 645–58; and M. Forde (1984) 33 Int. and Comp. L. Q. 134.
183 See the excellent account in W. Creighton, W. Ford and R. Mitchell, *Labour
    Law Materials and Commentary* (1983), Chap. 28; on the Hancock Report
    (1985), see D. Rawson, 'A First Look at the Hancock Report' (1985,
    ANU).
184 W. Gould, *A Primer of American Labor Law* (1982), p. 54; see generally
    Wedderburn, Chap. 6 'The Right to Associate and Dissociate', in F. Schmidt
    (ed.), *Discrimination in Employment* (1978).
185 R. Lewis and B. Simpson, 'Disorganizing Industrial Relations' (1982) 11
    ILJ 227, 244.
186 See Wedderburn (1972) 10 BJIR 270, 283–8 on s. 5; *Fair Deal at Work*
    (1968, Conservative Political Centre); *A Giant's Strength* (1958, Inns of
    Court Conservative Society).
187 *Quinn* v. *Leathem* [1901] AC 495; and the *Crofter Hand Woven Harris
    Tweed* v. *Veitch* [1942] AC 435; *Huntley* v. *Thornton* [1957] 1 All E. R. 234;
    pp. 558, 852.
188 W. E. J. McCarthy, *The Closed Shop in Britain* (1964), p. 214.
189 *The Closed Shop in British Industry* (1983), p. 99, writing about 'open
    shops'. For agreements for members only, *Financial Times*, 20 August 1984;
    (1977) 163 IRRR p. 12.
190 P. Elias (1980) 9 ILJ 201, 206; *Sakals* v. *Utd Counties Omnibus Co.* [1984]
    IRLR 474. On West Germany, see Wedderburn, Chap. 6, in F. Schmidt
    (ed.), *Discrimination in Employment* (1978). In 1986 the NUM alleged
    ASD where the NCB paid a rise to UDM members only.
191 R. Lewis, in G. Bain (ed.), *Industrial Relations in Britain* (1983), p. 338; see
    Chapter 7, p. 553.
192 W. McCarthy, op. cit., p. 37 and Chaps. 3–5; S. Dunn and J. Gennard, *The
    Closed Shop in British Industry* (1984), pp. 145–9; see too (1980) *Employ-
    ment Gazette* 16.
193 S. Dunn and J. Gennard, op. cit., p. 113, and Chaps. 2 and 5; M. Hart, 'Why
    Bosses Love the Closed Shop', *New Society*, 15 Feb. 1979, p. 354; W. Brown
    (ed.), *The Changing Contours of British Industrial Relations* (1980), Chap. 4.
194 S. Dunn, in P. Fosh and C. Littler (eds.), *Industrial Relations and the Law in
    the 1980s* (1985), pp. 85–98.
195 O. Kahn-Freund, *Labour and the Law* (3rd ed. 1983), p. 244; W. McCarthy,
    op. cit., pp. 180–1 and Chap. 11; cf. Dunn and Gennard's 'explanations',
    op. cit. (note 189), Chap. 5.
196 A. Flanders and H. Clegg, *The System* (1954), p. 173.
197 L. MacFarlane, *The Right to Strike* (1981), p. 51.

198 B. Napier (1983) 46 MLR 453, 457; S. Dunn (1981) 19 BJIR 275; S. Dunn and J. Gennard, op. cit., p. 88 (the 'ritual' of engineering shop stewards).

199 See S. Dunn and J. Gennard, *The Closed Shop in British Industry* (1984), p. 52; S. Dunn, in P. Fosh and C. Littler (eds.), *Industrial Relations and the Law in the 1980s* (1985), pp. 83–6.

200 C. Hanson, S. Jackson and D. Miller, *The Closed Shop* (1982), pp. 14–15.

201 B. Weekes, M. Mellish, L. Dickens and J. Lloyd, *Industrial Relations and the Limits of Law* (1975), p. 62.

202 Respectively Dunn and Gennard, op. cit. (note 189), Chap. 8; H. Clegg, *The Changing System of Industrial Relations* (1979), p. 396.

203 *Taylor* v. *Co-op. Retail Ltd* [1982] ICR 600.

204 *Ashby & Bridges* v. *Coleman* [1978] IRLR 51 (IT).

205 *Leyland Vehicles Ltd* v. *Jones* [1981] IRLR 269.

206 *Curry* v. *Harlow DC* [1979] ICR 769; Chapter 9, p. 814 on the IRC.

207 *Saggers* v. *British Railways Board* [1978] ICR 1111.

208 R. Benedictus (1977) 8 ILJ 160; see S. Dunn and J. Gennard, op. cit., Chap. 7 (pp. 120–9 on the *Harris* and *Walsall* cases).

209 K. Ewing and W. Rees (1983) 12 ILJ 148; see too C. Harlow and R. Rawlings, *Law and Administration* (1984), pp. 406–9.

210 *Young, James and Webster* v. *UK* [1981] IRLR 408; M. Forde (1983) 31 Am. Jo. Comp. Law 301; on compensation see [1983] IRLR 35; also *Official Note of Hearing*, 4 March 1981, p. 41 (transcript).

211 F. von Prondzynski [1982] CLJ 256, 272.

212 *Home Delivery Services* v. *Shackcloth* [1984] IRLR 470; *Sakals* v. *Utd Counties Omnibus Co.* [1984] IRLR 474; *The Times*, 17 April 1985 (CA); and *McGhee* v. *Midlands British Road Services and TGWU* [1985] IRLR 198.

213 Clark and Wedderburn, in Wedderburn, R. Lewis and J. Clark (eds.), *Labour Law and Industrial Relations* (1983), p. 207; *Ottway, Hood, McNeill* v. *Cory King*, *Financial Times* 26 Oct. and 7 Dec. 1984, 19 Jan. 1985 (tugboat men).

214 See on *Heatons Transport* v. *TGWU* [1973] AC 15; Chapter 1, p. 55.

215 See P. Kahn *et al.*, *Picketing*, op. cit. (note 143, above), Chap. 10.

5 Statutory Protection of Wages, Hours and Safety

1 P. Davies and M. Freedland, *Labour Law: Text and Materials* (2nd ed. 1984), p. 347.

2 G. W. Hilton, *The Truck System* (1960), pp. 101–14.

3 *Brooker* v. *Charrington Fuel Oils Ltd* [1981] IRLR 147 (Cty Ct).

4 A. I. Marsh and J. Staples, in *Three Studies in Collective Bargaining* (1968, Donovan Research Paper No. 8); see S. Dunn and J. Gennard, *The Closed Shop in British Industry* (1984), pp. 78–9; W. Daniel and N. Millward, *Workplace Industrial Relations in Britain* (1983), pp. 74–7; but strong union organization may lean against the check-off: E. Batstone, *Working Order* (1984), pp. 213–14.

5 [1894] AC 383 (HL).

6 *Williams* v. *Butlers Ltd* [1975] ICR 208; cf. *Morris* v. *Secretary of State for Employment* [1985] IRLR 297 (EAT); below, note 22.

7 The decision in *Reeves* v. *TGWU* [1980] ICR 728 would not, on its facts, necessarily be affected by TUA 1984 s. 18; see Chapter 9, pp. 762–3.

8 *Squire* v. *Bayer & Co.* [1901] 2 KB 299.

9 *Bird* v. *British Celanese Ltd* [1945] 1 All E. R. 488, 491; *Sagar* v. *Ridehalgh* [1931] 1 Ch. 310. (An Order of 1897, No. 299, excluded from the 1896 Act the cotton industry in Lancashire and some other counties.)

10 *Bristow* v. *City Petroleum Ltd* [1985] IRLR 459; T. Goriely reports that Comyn J. took a different view in *Moore* v. *Morrison Road Garages*, unreported, 9 July 1980; (1983) 12 ILJ 236, 243; *Sealand Petroleum* v. *Barratt*, *The Times*, 12 February 1986.

11 *Cofone* v. *Spaghetti House Ltd* [1980] ICR 155.

12 *Attorney-General's Reference* (No. 1, 1983) [1984] 3 All E. R. 369 (CA); S. Hedley (1985) 14 ILJ 122.

13 *Labour and the Law* (3rd ed. 1983; P. Davies and M. Freedland, eds.), p. 50; on the 1961 Karmel Report, see O. Aitkin (1962) 25 MLR 220; M. Hickling ibid., 512.

14 See the valuable account by T. Goriely, 'Arbitrary Deductions from Pay' (1983) 12 ILJ 236; it seems doubtful whether any protection normally arises from the Unfair Contract Terms Act 1977 s. 3.

15 *Bristol Garage Ltd* v. *Lowen* [1979] IRLR 86, 88.

16 See *Riley* v. *Joseph Frisby* [1982] IRLR 479 (IT) (manageress unfairly dismissed when made to account for loss suffered when she was on holiday; weekly stoppages of £20 out of £67 pay).

17 See *Mailway (Southern) Ltd* v. *Willsher* [1978] ICR 511.

18 See the analyses by T. M. Partington (1978) 7 ILJ 187; M. Freedland (1980) 9 ILJ 254; B. Hepple, T. M. Partington and R. Simpson (1977) 6 ILJ 54; A. Ogus (1975) 4 ILJ 12.

19 R(U) 1/75; R(U) 1/76; Regulations No. 564, 1975 (day of guarantee pay entitlement not a day 'unemployed'); see A. Ogus and E. Barendt, *Law of Social Security* (2nd ed. 1982 and Supp.), pp. 90–2, 100–1.

20 This includes cases of bankruptcy, compositions with creditors, receiving orders and, for a company, winding-up or receivership for debenture holders

or pursuant to a charge on property; EPCA s. 127 (1); see C. Bourn, *Redundancy Law and Practice* (1983), Chap. 10.

21 *Secretary of State for Employment* v. *Cox* [1984] ICR 867.

22 *Morris* v. *Secretary of State for Employment* [1985] IRLR 297.

23 *Westwood* v. *Secretary of State for Employment* [1985] ICR 209; on the retrospective payments made to those who lost jobs since 1976 as a result of what proved to be erroneous government practice, see (1984) 258 IRLIB 12; and for new methods of adjusting social security benefits and s. 122 claims, see Regulations No. 1259, 1984.

24 *Parsons* v. *BNM Laboratories Ltd* [1964] 1 QB 95; see *Westwood's* case [1985] ICR pp. 220–1, Lord Bridge.

25 Cork, *Report on Insolvency Law and Practice* (Cmnd 8558, 1982), paras. 1434–6, recommending that the Secretary of State should not be a *preferential* creditor when standing in the employee's shoes; R. Upex (1982) 11 ILJ 268.

26 *In Re Eloc Electro-Optieck BV* [1981] ICR 732.

27 See on proposals in France, B. Bezian and E. Teynier, 'Le Droit de la Faillite à l'Heure de la Réforme' (1984), *Travail et Emploi*, September, 67, 77.

28 G. Pera, *Diritto del lavoro* (1984), p. 606 and Chap. XXVIII; G. Ghezzi and U. Romagnoli, *Il Rapporto di lavoro* (1984), pp. 185–203; L. Mariucci, *La Contrattazione Collettiva* (1985).

29 G. Camerlynck, G. Lyon-Caen and J. Pélissier, *Droit du Travail* (12th ed. 1984), p. 455. On 'solidarity contracts', ibid., pp. 139–42; O. Galland, J. Gaudin and P. Vrain (1984), *Travail et Emploi*, December, 7 (distinguishing four types); on collective agreements, *Code du Travail* (1985), Art. D.212–17; (1984) 129 EIRR 29; and *Financial Times*, 21 November 1985; (1986) 148 EIRR 3, 8 (new laws on flexible hours at risk with new government).

30 See P. Curzio, in *Crisi, Occupazione, Legge* (1985; M. Garofalo, ed.), pp. 19–53; G. Pera, 'I Contratti di Solidarietà' (1984) 24 Giornale di Dir. del Lav. e di Rel. Ind. 699–713 (on the two types in Italy).

31 The French labour inspector may grant authorization extending daily working hours in certain cases: *Code du Travail* (1985), Art. D.212–13; on Italy, M. Biagi, 'The Labour Administration in Italy', Report to XIth International Congress of Comparative Law (1982) 341.

32 S. Webb, Introduction, B. Hutchins and A. Harrison, *A History of Factory Legislation* (1903), p. vii, still the leading work.

33 E. P. Thompson, *The Making of the English Working Class* (1963), p. 331.

34 See P. Bartrip and S. Burman's summary, *The Wounded Soldiers of Industry* (1983), pp. 214–21; cf. T. Ward, *The Factory Movement* (1962): 'factory legislation was the mortal blow' to *laissez-faire* attitudes, p. 483.

35 See P. Bartrip and P. Fenn, 'The Evolution of Regulatory Style in the 19th Century: British Factory Inspectorate' (1983) 10 Jo. Law and Soc. 201,

rejecting the thesis that the inspectors 'conventionalized' white-collar factory crime to avoid criminalizing owners; *cf.* W. Carson (1979) 7 Int. Jo. Sociology of Law 37; and on prosecutions and 'moral fault', (1970) 33 M L R 396.

36 Hutchins and Harrison, op. cit., pp. 102–4.

37 Hutchins and Harrison, op. cit., p. 194.

38 Hutchins and Harrison, op. cit., p. 82.

39 Children and Young Persons Act 1933; Children Act 1972 s. 1.

40 Auld, *Report on Shops Act: Late-Night and Sunday Opening* (Cmnd 9376, 1984), pp. 65, 88, 99–100; 'shops' has a very wide meaning: Shops Act 1950 s. 74.

41 T. Gill and L. Whitty, *Women's Rights in the Workplace* (1983), p. 259; and see the practical summary of 'deregulation' issues, pp. 260–3.

42 E O C, *Health and Safety Legislation: Should We Distinguish Between Men and Women?* (1979).

43 *Lifting the Burden* (Cmnd 9571, 1985), p. 23.

44 R. Disney and E. Szyszczak, 'Protective Legislation and Part-Time Employment' (1984) 22 B J I R 78.

45 See (1985) 133 E I R R p. 27.

46 E. Hunt, *British Labour History 1815–1914* (1981), p. 243.

47 Quoted by C. Babbett-Vincent, *An Authentic History of British Trade Unions* (1902), p. 38; *Daily Telegraph*, 19 December 1871.

48 H. Clegg, A. Fox and A. Thompson, *A History of British Trade Unions Since 1889* (1964), p. 294.

49 *Law and Public Opinion in England* (1914), p. li.

50 See Transport Act 1968 ss. 96–8; Road Traffic (Drivers' Ages and Hours of Work) Act 1976; E E C Directive 543/1969, and Regs. 3820 and 3821/85 (drivers' hours from Sept. 1986). The 'statutory breaks' may not break continuity of 'working' hours; *Carter* v. *Walton*, *The Times*, 28 May 1984.

51 See R. Gulliver, *The Reduction of Working Time* (1984, I L O), especially Chap. 8; and I L O General Survey, 'Working Time' (1984, Committee of Experts, Report III (Part 4B)); and on 'flexibility' of hours, E T U C, *Flexibility and Jobs, Myths and Realities* (1985), Chap. VI.

52 See (1985) 336 I R R R 2; on the agreement at *International Harvester* in the United States, (1985) 341 I R R R 9.

53 See S. Hewitt (1986) 136 N. L. Jo. 38.

54 Hutchins and Harrison, op. cit., p. 119.

55 E. Turner, *Roads to Ruin* (1960), p. 200; J. and B. Hammond, *Lord Shaftesbury* (1923), pp. 153–5, 186.

56 See Redgrave's *Health and Safety in Factories* (2nd ed. 1982; I. Fife and E. Machin, eds.), pp. 703–1580.

57 [1898] 2 Q B 402.

58 See on this formula in the law of tort P. Winfield and A. Jolowicz on *Tort* (12th ed. 1984; W. Rogers, ed.), pp. 579–90; on social security law, see below, p. 440; and in the context of the HSWA, *Coult* v. *Szuba* [1982] ICR 380.

59 On the many defects in this statute see the trenchant comments of R. Hasson (1974) 3 ILJ 79.

60 See on the problem P. Atiyah (1975) 4 ILJ 1 and 89; and the discussion in F. Trindale and P. Cane, *The Law of Torts in Australia* (1985), Chap. 18.

61 *Safety and Health at Work* (Cmnd 5034, 1972). On the detail of the law see J. Munkman, *Employer's Liability* (10th ed. 1985). See generally R. Rideout and Janet Dyson, *Principles of Labour Law* (4th ed. 1983), Chaps. 11–13; I. Smith and J. Wood, *Industrial Law* (2nd ed. 1982), Chaps. 10, 11.

62 *R. v. Swan Hunter Shipbuilders Ltd* [1981] ICR 831; B. Barrett (1982) 45 MLR 338. The 'reasonably practicable' formula of the HSWA has arisen in argument about 'constructive dismissal' by failure to arrange proper safety precautions: *Dutton & Clark* v. *Daly* [1985] ICR 780, 784 (but is the contractual implied term still only the common law of 'reasonable care'?).

63 See P. Tydeman (on 159 years of the Factory Inspectorate) (1983) 91 *Employment Gazette* 400, 405.

64 See R. Taylor, *Workers and the New Depression* (1982), pp. 134–6; the evidence seems to show manual workers are more endangered by stress than executives. On VDU hazards, see J. Brown, *Taxes*, November 1985, 153.

65 (1984) 92 *Employment Gazette* 506; Manufacturing and Services, *Report* (1983), p. 1.

66 *Lifting the Burden* (Cmnd 9571, 1985), p. 23; and further, *Building Businesses, Not Barriers* (1986, Cmnd 9794) para. 7.14.

67 P. Bartrip and P. Fenn, 'Regulation and the Factory Inspectorate' (1983) 10 Jo. Law and Soc. 201, 218, a valuable discussion.

68 R. and B. Thompson, *Accidents at Work* (3rd ed. 1968), p. 52.

69 See HSE, *Report* (1984), p. 89; HSE, *Health and Safety Statistics 1980*, pp. 23, 24, n. (b).

70 *Select Managements Ltd* v. *Westminster CC* [1985] IRLR 344 (CA); *West Bromwich Building Soc.* v. *Townsend* [1983] ICR 257. See R. Howells (1983) 12 ILJ 182; B. Barrett (1985) 48 MLR 589, and (1984) 46 MLR 785.

71 J. Williams, *Accidents and Ill-Health at Work* (1960), p. 167.

72 See (1984) 123 EIRR 18; (1983) 109 EIRR 8; for other European countries (1980) 80 EIRR 18; on Australia, W. Creighton (1983) 9 Monash L. R. 192.

73 W. Brown (ed.), *The Changing Contours of British Industrial Relations* (1980), p. 75; W. Daniel and N. Milward, *Workplace Industrial Relations in Britain* (1983), pp. 142–4.

74 *Williams* v. *West Wales Plant Hire Co.* [1985] ICR 6 (CA); on the employer's liabilities, see J. Munkman, *Employer's Liability* (10th ed. 1985);

and for a useful survey of liability for ill-health, B. Barrett (1981) 10 ILJ 101.

75 *Hammond* v. *NCB* [1984] 3 All E. R. 321 (CA).

76 *Duffy* v. *Thanet DC* (1984) 134 New L. J. 680; cf. *Harrison* v. *Michelin Tyre Co.* [1985] 1 All E. R. 918 (employer liable where joke committed in course of employment).

77 *Graham Oxley Tool Steels Ltd* v. *Firth* [1980] IRLR 135; *Dutton & Clark Ltd* v. *Daly* [1985] ICR 780; *British Aircraft Corpn* v. *Austin* [1978] IRLR 332. But reductions in damages for contributory negligence (p. 430) do not, it seems, apply to breach of contract actions for damages; *A B Marintrans* v. *Comet Shipping Ltd* [1985] 3 All E. R. 442.

78 *General Cleaning Contractors* v. *Christmas* [1953] AC 180; *Smith* v. *Austin Lifts Ltd* [1959] 1 All E. R. 81; *Wilsons and Clyde Coal Ltd* v. *English* [1938] AC 57 (Lord Wright); *McDermid* v. *Nash Dredging*, *The Times*, 17 April 1986.

79 See *James* v. *Hepworth and Grandage Ltd* [1968] 1 QB 94; *Paris* v. *Stepney BC* [1951] AC 367.

80 *Grioli* v. *Allied Building Ltd*, *The Times*, 10 April 1985 (CA).

81 *White* v. *Holbrook Precision Castings Ltd* [1985] IRLR 215 (CA).

82 *Thompson* v. *Smiths Shiprepairers Ltd* [1984] ICR 236; cf. *McCafferty* v. *Metropolitan Police Receiver* [1977] 2 All E. R. 756.

83 See the persuasive account by Beverly Lang (1984) 47 MLR 48.

84 *Bailey* v. *Rolls-Royce Ltd* [1984] ICR 688.

85 *Sanders* v. *Lloyd Ltd* [1982] ICR 360.

86 *Jenkins* v. *Allied Ironfounders Ltd* [1969] 3 All E. R. 1609 (HL); *Dorman Long Ltd* v. *Bell* [1964] 1 WLR 333 (HL).

87 *Stone Lighting & Radio Ltd* v. *Haygarth* [1968] AC 157 (HL).

88 *Mirza* v. *Ford Motor Co.* [1981] ICR 757 (CA); *British Railways Bd* v. *Liptrot* [1969] 1 AC 136 (HL).

89 See *Close* v. *Steel Co. of Wales Ltd* [1962] AC 367; *Sparrow* v. *Fairey Aviation Co.* [1964] AC 1019; *Wearing* v. *Pirelli Ltd* [1977] ICR 90, 98.

90 *Ballard* v. *MoD* [1977] ICR 513 (CA).

91 *Callow (Engineers) Ltd* v. *Johnson* [1971] AC 335 (HL); cf. *Millard* v. *Serck Tubes Ltd* [1969] 1 All E. R. 598; J. Hendy (1969) 32 MLR 438.

92 *Uddin* v. *Associated Portland Cement Co.* [1965] 2 QB 582 (CA); see too *Westwood* v. *PO* [1974] AC 1.

93 *Jayes* v. *IMI (Kynoch) Ltd* [1985] ICR 155.

94 *James* v. *Hepworth and Grandage Ltd* [1968] 1 QB 94, 104.

95 *ICI Ltd* v. *Shatwell* [1965] AC 656 (HL).

96 *McMullen* v. *NCB* [1982] ICR 148; *Storey* v. *NCB* [1983] ICR 156; G. Holgate (1983) 12 ILJ 185.

97 *Auty* v. *NCB* [1985] 1 WLR 784.

98 *Malone* v. *Rowan* [1984] 3 All E. R. 402.

99 *Palfrey* v. *GLC* [1985] ICR 437; after five years the 50 per cent deduction of industrial injury benefit eases; *Denman* v. *Essex Area HA* [1984] QB 735. The Pearson Report (Cmnd 7054, 1978) proposed that all social security benefits payable to an injured person or dependants of a deceased person should be deducted, a recommendation accepted by the Government in 1981. See too *Westwood* v. *Sec. of State for Employment* [1984] 1 All E. R. 874 (HL); p. 399.

100 *Davis* v. *MoD*, *The Times*, 7 August 1985.

101 *Brooks* v. *J. & P. Coates Ltd* [1984] ICR 158.

102 A. Ogus and E. Barendt, *The Law of Social Security* (2nd ed. 1982, and Supp.), p. 261, n. 11; and their invaluable Chap. 8 on 'Industrial Injuries'.

103 By Social Security Act 1975 s. 50A, inserted in 1982, a worker incapable of work by reason of an industrial injury within s. 50 is 'taken' to have satisfied the contribution conditions for sickness benefit. This distinction may make questionable the equation in *Palfrey's* case (above) of injury benefit and sick-pay sickness benefits, especially when s. 2 of the 1948 Act is regularly amended to apply to other injury benefits (e.g. Health and Social Security Act 1984, Sched. 4, severe disablement allowance).

104 *Jones* v. *Secretary of State for Social Services* [1972] AC 944, 1020; R(I) 8/81.

105 R(I) 43/55; R(I) 12/68 (accidents); R(I) 7/66 (process).

106 R(I) 19/63.

107 Respectively: *R.* v. *Industrial Injuries Commsr, ex parte AEU* (No. 2) [1966] 2 QB 31 (CA); R(I) 4/73; R(I) 10/81.

108 *R.* v. *National Insurance Commsr, ex parte Reed* Annex to R(I) 7/80; *R.* v. *National Insurance Commsr, ex parte East* [1976] ICR 206; R(I) 1/59; and see R(I) 1/83.

109 R(I) 13/66; R(I) 3/57; *R.* v. *National Insurance Commsr, ex parte Michael* [1977] 2 All E. R. 420; and see R(I) 7/69.

110 See M. Turner (1977) 6 ILJ 123, reporting CI 526/75.

111 *R.* v. *National Insurance Commsr, ex parte Richardson* [1958] 2 All E. R. 689.

112 R(I) 2/63; R(I) 6/82.

113 R(I) 3/67.

114 *R.* v. *D'Albuquerque, ex parte Bresnahan* [1966] 1 Lloyd's Rep. 69 (a much criticized decision).

115 R(I) 5/80. On travelling to and from work generally see *Vandyke* v. *Fender* [1970] 2 QB 292; R(I) 14/81; and A. Ogus and E. Barendt, *The Law of Social Security* (1982), pp. 276–9.

116 *Nancollas* v. *Insurance Officer* [1985] 1 All E. R. 833 (CA).

117 See R. K. Lewis, 'Benefit for Industrial Disease' (1984) 13 ILJ 128 and (1983) Jo. Soc. Welfare Law 10; and on what follows A. Ogus and E. Barendt, op. cit., pp. 288–336.

118 See Richard Lewis (1980) 43 MLR 514. The smaller disablement sums were to be abolished under proposals made by the Government in 1986.

119 R(I) 5/84; the gardener's case, R(I) 4/85.

120 T. Ison, *The Forensic Lottery* (1967); B. Abel Smith, in P. Hall (ed.), *Labour's New Frontiers* (1964), pp. 126–7.

121 P. Atiyah, *Accidents, Compensation and the Law* (2nd ed. 1975); but see G. Calabresi, *The Costs of Accidents* (1970).

122 Woodhouse, *Reports* (Australia: Parl. Paper 100, 1974; and NZ: 1967), which led to the Accident Compensation Act 1972; see F. Tindale and P. Cane, *The Law of Torts in Australia* (1985), pp. 722–9; see on re-emergence of common law principles in the New Zealand 'no fault' system, A. Szakats (1978) 7 ILJ 216.

123 Pearson Report (Cmnd 7054, 1978), paras 273–91; J. Fleming (1979) 42 MLR 249; D. Allen, C. Bourn and J. Holyoak (eds.), *Accident Compensation After Pearson* (1979). In 1986 the Lord Chancellor announced new plans to mitigate delay and cost in civil actions for personal injuries: *The Times*, 20 February 1986.

124 See the trenchant critique by A. Ogus, P. Corfield and D. Harris (1978) 7 ILJ 143; a useful review of the position is in P. Winfield and A. Jolowicz on *Torts* (12th ed. 1984; W. Rogers, ed.), pp. 15–41.

125 See for a remarkable application *Bourne* v. *Colodense Ltd* [1985] ICR 291; Chapter 9, p. 746.

6 Social Discrimination at Work

1 A. Smith, C. Craver and L. Clark, *Employment Discrimination Law* (2nd ed. 1982), p. 1; cf. T. Ramm, Chaps. 1 and 7, in Folke Schmidt (ed.), *Discrimination in Employment* (1978), on discrimination as 'the symptom of a disease' in society.

2 See C. McCrudden, 'Law Enforcement by Regulatory Agency: Employment Discrimination in Northern Ireland' (1982) 45 MLR 617.

3 L. Lustgarten, 'Racial Inequality and the Limits of Law' (1986) 49 MLR (68, 84); B. Hepple, 'A Right to Work?' (1981) 10 ILJ 65, 82.

4 G. Giugni, 'Political, Religious and Private-Life Discrimination', in Folke Schmidt (ed.), *Discrimination in Employment* (1978), p. 192.

5 Immigration Act 1971, and Immigration Rules. See I. Macdonald, *Immigration Law and Practice* (1983); and on lack of parliamentary control, P. Davies and M. Freedland, *Labour Law: Text and Materials* (2nd ed. 1984), pp. 13–21; and D. Duysens (1977) 6 ILJ 85.

6 See Treaty of Rome Articles 48, 49, also Art. 52 (self-employed); Regulations 1612/68 and 312/76; see X. Blanc-Jouvan, Chap. 5, in Folke Schmidt

(ed.), *Discrimination in Employment* (1978); and B. Hepple, Chap. II 'Harmonization of Labour Law' in EEC, in J. Adams (ed.), *Essays for Clive Schmitthoff* (1983).

7 *Van Duyn* v. *Home Office* [1975] Ch. 358 (ECJ: scientologist excluded).

8 See A. Ogus and E. Barendt, *Law of Social Security* (1982), pp. 627–42 on Treaty Art. 51 and Reg. 1408/71; cf. Reg. 1612/68, Art. 7; M. Forde (1979) 8 ILJ 1; and P. Watson (1985) European L. R. 335 for a valuable review of ECJ judgments on free movement and social security.

9 But the family cannot remain after the worker has left; *In Re Sandhu, The Times*, 10 May 1985 (HL).

10 *R.* v. *ILEA, ex parte Hinde* [1985] 1 CMLR 716; see the critique by A. De Moor (1985) 48 MLR 482 of Art. 7 of the Treaty, and *Forcheri* v. *Belgium*, 152/82 [1984] CMLR 334; *Gravier* v. *Ville de Liège*, 293/83 [1985] 3 CMLR 20 (ECJ). And see *Single European Act* (1986, Cmnd 9758); *Report* of Select Committee HL (1986, Paper 149), p. 6.

11 *Jones* v. *Lee* [1980] ICR 310, 312; see Chapter 2, p. 167.

12 *Turley* v. *Allders Stores Ltd* [1980] ICR 66, 70.

13 *Hayes* v. *Malleable Working Men's Club* [1985] IRLR 367.

14 *Skyrail Oceanic Ltd* v. *Coleman* [1981] ICR 864 (CA, by majority; 'marital status' arguments had failed in the EAT).

15 *Greenslade* v. *Hoveringham Gravels Ltd* [1975] IRLR 114; and J. McMullen, *Rights at Work* (1983), p. 241.

16 *Saunders* v. *Scottish National Camps Assoc.* [1980] IRLR 174, 175 (EAT), [1981] IRLR 277 (Ct S.); *Wiseman* v. *Salford CC* [1981] IRLR 202.

17 *Tabor* v. *Mid-Glamorgan CC* (1982) COIT 1165/7, see (1982) IDS Brief Supp. 36 p. 21; *Norfolk CC* v. *Bernard* [1979] IRLR 220 (EAT).

18 *Boychuk* v. *Symons Holdings Ltd* [1977] IRLR 395, 396.

19 H. Kanter, S. Lefanu, S. Shah and C. Spedding (eds.), *Sweeping Statements* (1984), p. 57, on the dismissal of two lesbian child-workers.

20 *O'Brien* v. *Prudential Assurance Co. Ltd* [1979] IRLR 140.

21 *Torr* v. *British Railways Board* [1977] IRLR 184, 186; *Property Guards Ltd* v. *Taylor* [1982] IRLR 175 (spent conviction; dismissal unfair).

22 See J. Popay, L. Rimmer and C. Rossiter, 'One-Parent Families and Employment' (1982) 90 *Employment Gazette* 531.

23 W. B. Creighton, *Working Women and the Law* (1979), p. 240.

24 *B.* v. *B., The Times*, 3 August 1984 (CA).

25 Lord Belstead, *Parl. Deb.*, 25 March 1985, HL, col. 858; on the proposal, Select Committee on EEC (HL), *Parental Leave and Leave for Family Reasons* (1985; Paper 84); (1985) 141 EIRR 17 (comparative survey).

26 Articles 1, 8, 15; *Lo Statuto dei lavoratori* (1979; G. Giugni, ed.), p. 1 and p.

88 (S. Sciarra); Article 4 forbids concealed observation of workers by television aparatus.

27 *City of Birmingham* v. *Beyer* [1977] IRLR 211; but *quaere* whether his *proposed* activities do not afford grounds of action: EPCA s. 58 (1) (b); see too *Sunday Times*, 14 August 1983; *Labour Research*, February 1985, 34.

28 See C. Turpin, *British Government and the Constitution* (1985), pp. 159–63; Armitage, *Report on Political Activities of Civil Servants* (Cmnd 7057, 1978); *Financial Times*, 7 March 1984.

29 *The Times*, 4 April 1985; *Guardian*, 2 February 1985; *Financial Times*, 8 February 1985; *Sunday Times*, 8 August 1985. In 1977 employees in a BSC subsidiary were found to be politically vetted both by the Special Branch and by the Economic League: R. Lewis (1978) 7 ILJ 1, 15.

30 See (1985) 292 IRLIB 2; (1984) 42 IDS Brief Employment Law Supp. 19–25.

31 *Seymour* v. *British Airways Board* [1983] IRLR 55; *Forman Construction Ltd* v. *Kelly* [1977] IRLR 468; *Hobson* v. *GEC* [1985] ICR 777.

32 See (1984) *Employment Gazette* 71; (1985) ibid. 233.

33 See W. Creighton (1975) 4 ILJ 155 (on the 1919 Act); and on common law and history of race discrimination Bills, A. Lester and G. Bindman, *Race and Law* (1972), pp. 23–72, 107–49; B. Hepple, *Race, Jobs and the Law in Britain* (2nd ed. 1970), pp. 143–74.

34 J. Reid, 'Women in Employment – the New Legislation' (1976) 39 MLR 432; on the history, M. Snell, P. Glucklich and M. Poval, *Equal Pay and Opportunities* (1981, DE Paper No. 20), pp. 1–12; G. Schmid and R. Weitzel, *Sex Discrimination and Equal Opportunity* (1984).

35 See L. Lustgarten [1978] Public Law 178, 182–205; and his valuable survey in (1984) 49 MLR 68.

36 B. Aaron, in Folke Schmidt (ed.), *Discrimination in Employment* (1978), pp. 113–14, and Chap. 2 generally for a comparison of US and British experience; see on the background to the RRA, C. McCrudden, 'Institutionalized Discrimination' (1982) 2 Ox. J. L. S. 303, 330–7; and his 'Anti-Discrimination Goals in the Legal Process', in N. Glazer and K. Young (eds.), *Ethnic Pluralism and Public Policy* (1983); but see L. Lustgarten, 'Racial Inequality and the Limits of Law' (1986) 49 MLR 68; D. Smith (1980) *Employment Gazette* 604 (unemployment and racial-minority groups). For a striking survey of racial discrimination, legal processes and collective workers' action, see S. Feuchtwang, *Politics and Power* (1981), pp. 99–127. On the USA, see too W. Gould, *Black Workers in White Unions* (1977).

37 *EC Commission* v. *United Kingdom*, Case 165/82 [1984] ICR 192 (ECJ); S. Fredman (1984) 13 ILJ 119. (See on the 1986 judgment of the ECJ, *additional note* 170, below; and Sex Discrimination Bill 1986.)

38 *Tanna* v. *PO* [1981] ICR 374; *Mirror Group Newspapers* v. *Gunning* [1986] IRLR 27 (CA).

39 *Quinnen* v. *Hovells* [1984] IRLR 227, 229.

40 *Health and Safety Legislation* (EOC 1979).

41 *Page* v. *Freight Hire (Tank Haulage) Ltd* [1981] ICR 299; *Hugh-Jones* v. *St John's College, Cambridge* [1979] ICR 848.

42 Respectively *Hurley* v. *Mustoe* [1981] ICR 490 and [1983] ICR 422; *Noble* v. *David Gold Ltd* [1980] ICR 543; *FTATU and Pel Ltd* v. *Modgill* [1980] IRLR 142.

43 *Peake* v. *Automotive Products Ltd* [1977] ICR 968 (CA).

44 [1980] ICR 13; see too *Greig* v. *Community Industry* [1979] ICR 356.

45 *Griggs* v. *Duke Power Co.* 401 US 424, 431 (1971); *County of Washington* v. *Gunther* 101 S Ct. 2242 (1981).

46 *American Fedn of State, County and Municipal Employees* v. *State of Washington* 707 F. 2d. 1401 (1985, 9th Cir.).

47 *R.* v. *CRE, ex parte Westminster Council* [1985] IRLR 426 (CA).

48 *Watches of Switzerland* v. *Savell* [1983] IRLR 141; *Perera* v. *Civil Service Commission* [No. 2] [1983] ICR 428 (CA).

49 *Home Office* v. *Holmes* [1984] ICR 678; R. White (1985) 14 ILJ 132.

50 *Kidd* v. *DRG (UK) Ltd* [1985] ICR 405; see too *Fulton* v. *Strathclyde RC* (1985) 276 IRLIB 10 (pool of comparison for internal vacancy qualified men and women already employed; no discrimination.)

51 [1983] ICR 165.

52 *Price* v. *Civil Service Commission* [1978] ICR 27.

53 *Mandla* v. *Dowell Lee* [1983] ICR 385, 394.

54 *Kirby* v. *MSC* [1980] ICR 420. See on 'victimization' RRA s. 2; SDA s. 4.

55 *Showboat Entertainments Centre Ltd* v. *Owens* [1984] IRLR 7.

56 *De Souza* v. *The Automobile Association* [1985] IRLR 87; [1986] IRLR 103 (CA).

57 *Porcelli* v. *Strathclyde Council* [1985] ICR 177; [1986] IRLR 134, 138, Lord Brand; 'a form of unfavourable treatment . . . to which a man would not be vulnerable'.

58 [1978] ICR 181; and for the success of the claimant [1978] IRLR 198.

59 *Interim Report on Equality and Social Security* (1984), para. II (1); (1984) 122 EIRR 25.

60 *Singh* v. *Rowntree Mackintosh Ltd* [1979] ICR 544; *Singh* v. *British Rail Engineering* [1986] ICR 22 (EAT); *Panesar* v. *Nestlé Ltd* [1980] ICR 144 (CA); *Orphanos* v. *Queen Mary College* [1985] IRLR 349 (HL), Lord Fraser p. 353. But a prohibition of turbans under a 'no hats' rule can be indirect discrimination: *Kambo* v. *Vaulkhard* (1985) 275 IRLIB 12 (CA).

61 *Ojutiku* v. *MSC* [1982] ICR 661; see Lord Fraser, *Mandla* v. *Dowell Lee* [1983] ICR 385, 394–5; accepted by the EAT in *Clarke* v. *Eley (IMI)*

Kynoch [1983] I C R 165, 174. Cf. *Orphanos* v. *QMC* [1985] I R L R 349.

62 *Home Office* v. *Holmes* [1984] I C R 678.

63 *Kidd* v. *D R G (U K) Ltd* [1985] I C R 405, 416.

64 M. Rubenstein (1985) 1 Eq. Opp. Rev. 48.

65 *Raval* v. *D H S S* [1985] I C R 685; and comment (1985) 285 I R L I B 14.

66 *Timex Corpn* v. *Hodgson* [1982] I C R 63.

67 L. Lustgarten, 'Problems of Proof in Employment Discrimination Cases' (1977) 6 ILJ 212, 225, an invaluable survey; also D. Pannick, 'Burden of Proof in Discrimination Cases' (1981) New L. J. 895.

68 Lord Lowry LCJ, *Conway* v. *Queen's University of Belfast* [1981] I R L R 137, 142.

69 *Perera* v. *Civil Service Commission* (No. 2) [1982] I C R 350; affd [1983] C R 428 (C A).

70 A. Smith, C. Craver and L. Clark, *Employment Discrimination Law* (2nd ed. 1982), p. 451; see too D. Baldus and J. Cole, *Statistical Proof of Discrimination* (1980).

71 *Brennan* v. *Dewhurst Ltd* [1984] I C R 52.

72 [1978] I C R 1124 (C A); [1979] I C R 921 (HL), consolidated with *B L Cars Ltd* v. *Vyas,* ibid. (race discrimination).

73 [1984] I C R 504.

74 *Khanna* v. *Ministry of Defence* [1981] I C R 653, 658–9.

75 See L. Lustgarten, *Legal Control of Racial Discrimination* (1980).

76 *Ministry of Defence* v. *Jeremiah* [1978] I C R 984; affd [1980] I C R 13 (C A); *Irvine* v. *Prestcold Ltd* [1981] I R L R 281 (C A).

77 See for example *Nelson* v. *Tyne and Wear Transport* [1978] I C R 1183.

78 *Skyrail Oceanic Ltd* v. *Coleman* [1981] I C R 864, 871, Lawton LJ.

79 *Hurley* v. *Mustoe* (No. 2) [1983] I C R 422.

80 See the analysis of S D A and Eq. P. A. complaints by A. Leonard (1986) 86 N L J 99 and 123.

81 C R E, *Report* (1980), para. 2; *The Times,* 9 February 1985; *Education for All* (Cmnd 9453, 1985); C R E, *Beaumont Leys Shopping Centre Report* (1985).

82 *Unequal Opportunity* (1985, W. Midlands YTS Research Project); on amendments to the law see *The Race Relations Act 1976: Time for a Change?* (1983, C R E).

83 See the comparative date in C. Hakim, *Occupational Segregation* (1979, D E Research Paper No. 9); cf. E O C, *Stereotypes and Selection* (1986).

84 A. Barber (1985) *Employment Gazette* 467; *Financial Times,* 2 January 1986.

85 *C R E* v. *Amari Plastics Ltd* [1982] I C R 304 (C A).

86 *R.* v. *C R E, ex parte Westminster C C* [1984] I C R 770; affd [1985] I R L R 426 (C A).

87 [1984] ICR 473 (HL); see too *R.* v. *CRE, ex parte Hillingdon LBC* [1982] AC 779 (HL).

88 N. Lacey (1985) 14 ILJ 64, 66; and see J. A. G. Griffith, *The Politics of the Judiciary* (3rd ed. 1985), pp. 215–16.

89 V. Sacks and J. Maxwell (1984) 47 MLR 334, 341.

90 On councils that use this route to prevent discrimination: (1985) 342 IRRR 2, 5; on the EEC, *Financial Times*, 22 July 1985.

91 *Financial Times*, 5 May and 1 and 22 August 1985; A. Haynes, Report on the Code of Practice (1985, CRE); *Trade Union Structures and Black Workers' Participation* (1985, CRE).

92 B. Chaplin and P. Sloane, *Tackling Discrimination in the Workplace* (1982), p. 132; M. Snell, P. Glucklich and M. Poval, *Equal Pay and Opportunities* (1981), p. 97.

93 B. Hepple, *Race, Jobs and the Law in Britain* (1970), p. 297.

94 T. Hitner, D. Knights, E. Green and D. Torrington, *Racial Minority Employment* (1982, DE Research Paper No. 35), p. 2.

95 W. Daniel, *Maternity Rights: The Experience of Women* (1980, PSI 588), p. 114; and (1981) 88 *Employment Gazette* 296 (employers' experience).

96 R. Upex and A. Morris, 'Maternity Rights – Illusion or Reality?' (1981) 10 ILJ 218, 220–1, 237.

97 See T. Gill and L. Whitty, *Women's Rights in the Workplace* (1983), p. 210.

98 *Lucas* v. *Norton of London Ltd* [1984] IRLR 86; *Lavery* v. *Plessey Telecommunications Ltd* [1983] ICR 534 (inadequate notice; no deemed dismissal under EPCA s. 56).

99 *Bovey* v. *Governors Board of the Hospital for Sick Children* [1978] IRLR 241; B. Bercusson, in C. Drake and B. Bercusson (eds.), *The Employment Acts 1974–1980* (1981), commentary to EPCA s. 48.

100 *Nu Swift International Ltd* v. *Mallinson* [1979] ICR 157.

101 *Cullen* v. *Creasey Hotels* [1980] ICR 236.

102 *Secretary of State for Employment* v. *Cox* [1984] ICR 867.

103 *ILEA* v. *Nash* [1979] ICR 229 (now EPCA ss. 34, 140; see p. 202).

104 A. Ogus and E. Barendt, *The Law of Social Security* (1982), pp. 246–9.

105 The employer may escape unfair dismissal of the replacement even if he did not inform that worker of the risk on hiring as s. 61 requires: *Hayes* v. *S. Glamorgan CC* (1985) 293 IRLIB 12.

106 *McFadden* v. *Greater Glasgow PTE* [1977] IRLR 327.

107 See W. Creighton, *Working Women and the Law* (1979); W. Snell, P. Glucklich and M. Poval, *Equal Pay and Opportunities* (1981, DE Research Paper 20); B. Hepple, *Equal Pay and the Tribunals* (1984).

108 *Neil* v. *Ford Motor Co.* [1984] IRLR 339 (IT; but see the dissent pp. 349–50); *Labour Research*, February 1985, 48; (1985) 344 IRRR 18.

109 M. Rubenstein, *Equal Pay for Work of Equal Value* (1984), pp. 1, 27; see his

valuable Chap. 2 'Why Women Are Paid Less'; and on job evaluation pp. 86–103.

110 P. Davies, 'The CAC and Equal Pay' (1980) Current Legal Problems p. 175; see H. Phelps Brown, *The Inequality of Pay* (1977), p. 147.

111 C. Craig, J. Rubery, R. Tarling and C. Wilkinson, *Labour Market Structure*: *Industrial Organization and Low Pay* (1982), p. 84.

112 W. Brown (ed.), *The Changing Contours of British Industrial Relations* (1980), pp. 111–13; and, on women, W. Daniel and N. Milward, *Workplace Industrial Relations In Britain* (1983), p. 205.

113 (1986) *Employment Gazette* 52.

114 *Pointon* v. *University of Sussex* [1979] IRLR 119 (CA).

115 In his valuable analysis of the Equal Value Regulations 1983 (1983) 12 ILJ 197, 210.

116 *Shields* v. *Coomes (Holdings) Ltd* [1978] ICR 1159 (CA).

117 *Dugdale* v. *Kraft Foods Ltd* [1977] ICR 48.

118 P. Davies and M. Freedland, *Labour Law: Text and Materials* (2nd ed. 1984), p. 377.

119 EOC, *Job Evaluation Schemes Free of Sex Bias*; M. Rubenstein, op. cit. (note 109, above), pp. 98–101.

120 See *O'Brien* v. *Sim-Chem Ltd* [1980] ICR 573 (HL; scheme sufficiently complete and agreed even though not implemented for fear of infringing incomes policy).

121 *Arnold* v. *Beecham Group* [1982] ICR 744, 753; *England* v. *Bromley LBC* [1978] ICR 1.

122 C. McCrudden (1983) 12 ILJ 197, 202; the commonest method is a 'points system', allotting points to the factors in each job; ACAS, *Job Evaluation*.

123 See E. Batstone, *Working Order* (1984), pp. 165–8.

124 [1979] IRLR 461, 463; P. Davies, 'The CAC and Equal Pay' (1980), *Current Legal Problems* 165, 176, 177–88.

125 S. Fredman, 'Market Forces and Equal Pay' (1984) 13 ILJ 122, 124.

126 *Defrenne* v. *Sabena SA* [1976] ICR 547; see the useful summary by B. Hepple, *Equal Pay and the Industrial Tribunals* (1984), pp. 9–12.

127 *Garland* v. *British Rail Engineering Ltd* [1982] ICR 420 (ECJ); *Worringham* v. *Lloyds Bank Ltd* [1981] ICR 558 (ECJ); see now note 170 below.

128 *Roberts* v. *Tate & Lyle Food, etc. Ltd* [1983] ICR 521; the EC Commission proposes a Directive to cover this area (1983) EIRR 31. The ECJ also had before it in 1985 the issue in *Southampton and SW Hampshire AHA* v. *Marshall* [1983] IRLR 237, whether differential retiring ages were permissible under Directive 76/207; Advocate-General Slynn averred that they are not: *Financial Times,* 19 September 1985. For a valuable survey see V. Shrubsall (1985) 48 MLR 373. For State social security, see Directive 79/7,

and Commission Report of January 1984: (1984) 122 EIRR 23. The EOC backed the *Marshall* and *Roberts* cases before the ECJ. The majority of EEC States have the same retirement age for both sexes. For the ensuing judgment of the ECJ in 1986, see *additional note* 170, below.

129 *Newstead* v. *Department of Transport* [1985] IRLR 299.

130 *Macarthys Ltd* v. *Smith* [1980] ICR 672, 693.

131 On 'hypothetical' male and 'different industries' claims, see E. Szyszczak (1985) 48 MLR 139, 150–5; and McCrudden (1983) 12 ILJ 197, 209–10.

132 Probably the whole variation: *NCB* v. *Sherwin* [1978] IRLR 122; Rubenstein, op. cit., p. 130; but see *Methven* v. *Cow Industrial Polymers* [1980] IRLR 289 (CA).

133 *Clay Cross Ltd* v. *Fletcher* [1979] ICR 1 (CA).

134 *Jenkins* v. *Kingsgate Ltd* [1981] ICR 592; *Macarthys Ltd* v. *Smith* [1980] ICR 672.

135 *Albion Shipping Agency* v. *Arnold* [1982] ICR 22. But in *Jenkins* [1981] ICR 592, 613, the ECJ appears to let in economic factors in both types of case.

136 *Jenkins* v. *Kingsgate Ltd* [1981] ICR 715, 726.

137 Davies and Freedland, op. cit., p. 388, citing H. Phelps Brown, *The Inequality of Pay* (1978), pp. 155–8. But contrast Rubenstein, op. cit., pp. 130–3.

138 *Leverton* v. *Clwyd CC* (1985) 289 IRLIB 14, 15 (not in same employment; genuine material 'factor' under 1983 amendments); see too [1985] IRLR 197.

139 *Avon and Somerset Police Authority* v. *Emery* [1981] ICR 229.

140 *Ministry of Defence* v. *Farthing* [1980] ICR 705; *National Vulcan Engineering Ltd* v. *Wade* [1978] ICR 800 (CA).

141 *Rainey* v. *Greater Glasgow HB* [1985] IRLR 414 distinguishing *Clay Cross* v. *Fletcher*, note 133, above; on EAT, S. Fredman (1984) 13 ILJ 122. On the need for clear evidence as to the terms of a 'red circle' agreement incorporated into employment contracts, *Kenny* v. *Vauxhall Motors Ltd* [1985] ICR 535 (CA); Chapter 4, note 125.

142 *EC Commission* v. *UK*, Case 61/81 [1982] ICR 578.

143 See the detailed discussions by C. McCrudden, 'Equal Pay for Work of Equal Value' (1983) 12 ILJ 197; M. Rubenstein, *Equal Pay for Work of Equal Value* (1984); E. Szyszczak (1985) 48 MLR 139; R. Townshend-Smith (1984) 47 MLR 201.

144 The House of Lords registered that opinion: *Parl. Deb.* 445, 5 December 1983, HL, col. 882; see B. Hepple, *Equal Pay and the Industrial Tribunals* (1984), pp. 2–12.

145 *Neil* v. *Ford Motor Co. Ltd* [1984] IRLR 339 (IT).

146 B. Hepple, *Equal Pay and the Industrial Tribunals* (1984), p. 21.

147 M. Rubenstein, *Equal Pay for Equal Value* (1984), pp. 141–7; see *Jenkins* v. *Kingsgate Ltd* [1981] ICR 592 (ECJ) and 715 (EAT) (full-time and part-time rates allowed only if no intended discrimination and commercially necessary).

148 C. McCrudden (1983) 12 ILJ 197, 210–19.

149 Joan Robinson, *Economic Philosophy* (1962), p. 46.

150 Working Time Analysts, *Management Consultants and Equal Value Cases* (1985).

151 *Kirby* v. *Cawoods Ltd* (1985) 1 Eq. Opp. Rev. 6; *Wells* v. *Smales & Son Ltd* (1985) 281 IRLIB 11; *Brown* v. *Cearns Brown* (1986) 304 IRLIB 10 (IT).

152 *Hayward* v. *Cammell Laird Shipbuilders Ltd* [1984] IRLR 463; see too *Financial Times*, 3 January 1985; and 20 May 1986 (EAT); (1985) 311 IDS Brief 2. See a useful review of early tribunal cases (1985) 356 IRRR 2–8.

153 *Financial Times*, 30 July and 13 and 16 August 1985; *The Times*, 2 September 1985; *Sunday Times*, 16 June 1985. But on equal treatment generally see *additional note* 170, below.

154 See the IDS Study 340, *Equal Opportunities* (1985).

155 See the valuable treatment by P. Davies and M. Freedland, *Labour Law: Text and Materials* (2nd ed. 1984), pp. 27–37, and D. Metcalf, *Alternatives to Unemployment* (1982, PSI No. 610).

156 *Education and Training for New Technologies* (1984, Report of HL Select Committee, December 19), p. 35; on school-leavers and comparisons see written answers: *Parl. Deb.*, 26 March 1985, HC, col. 49, and ibid., 10 June 1985, HC, col. 332; on university entrance requirements, *Social Trends 16* (1986); on skill shortages, *Financial Times*, 8 January 1986, 27 November 1985 and 13 May 1986.

157 See M. Freedland, 'Leaflet Law: The Temporary Short-Time Working Compensation Scheme' (1980) 9 ILJ 254.

158 *A New Training Initiative: A Programme for Action* (Cmnd 8455, 1982); see IRS, *Guide to the Youth Training Scheme* (1983).

159 See in M. Freedland's valuable 'Labour Law and Leaflet Law: The YTS 1983' (1983) 12 ILJ 220–5.

160 See Chapter 1, p. 119; *Hawley* v. *Fieldcastle* [1982] IRLR 223; *Daley* v. *Allied Supplies Ltd* [1983] IRLR 14; cf. *Greig* v. *Community Industry* [1978] ICR 356; and compare the solicitor's articled clerk in *Oliver* v. *Malnick* [1984] ICR 458; [1983] ICR 708.

161 Orders under RRA and SDA, made 21 July 1983; and Health and Safety (YTS) Regulations No. 1919, 1983; see *Health and Safety on YTS* (1985, MSC); (1985) 352 IRRR 15; see Chapter 2, note 37.

162 See R. Rideout, *Principles of Labour Law* (4th ed. 1983), p. 20; G. Fridman, *Modern Law of Employment* (1962), p. 973.

163 M. Freedland (1983) 12 ILJ pp. 234–5.

164 T. King, Secretary of State for Employment, *Parl. Deb.*, 1 July 1985, HC, col. 24.

165 C. St John-Brooks, *Who Controls Training? The Rise of the MSC* (1985, Fabian Soc. No. 506), p. 9.

166 *Education and Training for Young People* (Cmnd 9482, 1985), para. 27.

167 *Better Schools* (Cmnd 9469, 1985), para. 49.

168 Respectively, *The Development of Higher Education into the 1990s* (Cmnd 9524, 1985), para. 2.6; *Training for Jobs* (Cmnd 9135, 1984), para. 31; see, too, J. Rae, 'Blame Bosses, Not the Schools', *The Times*, 18 November 1985.

169 C. St John-Brooks, op. cit., p. 5; cf. C. Benn and J. Fairley (eds.), *Challenging the MSC* (1986).

170 *Additional note*: Later in 1986 the ECJ delivered its bombshell decision in *Marshall* v. *Southampton and SW Hampshire AHA* [1986] IRLR 140 (above, note 128), in favour of the appellant dietician who had been compelled to retire at 62, when men retired at 65, from the National Health Service. (A parallel appeal in the *Roberts* case [1986] IRLR 150, above, note 128, failed.) The ECJ held in *Marshall*: (1) that the Equal Treatment Directive, 76/207, forbids a general policy of retiring women at an age different from that for men, even though the ages are linked to national laws establishing different qualifying ages for state retirement pensions (permissible under the social security Directive 79/7). (2) Such discrimination in compulsory retirement falls within the 'dismissals' disallowed by Directive 76/207 (*Burton* v. *British Railways Board* [1982] ECR 555), which prohibits any discrimination on the ground of sex with regard to working conditions. (3) As the Directive is in precise terms, its provisions can be relied upon as such by an individual against the State but not against another 'individual'. (4) Where, as here, the State was acting as employer by way of a public authority, the individual could enforce the provisions directly; the State as employer must not be allowed to take advantage of its own failure to comply with Community law. Private sector employers were not, therefore, directly affected by this judgment. But the State could remedy that distinction by implementing the Directive in national law.

The Government set out to do that by way of amendments to the Sex Discrimination Bill then passing through Parliament though one peer complained that such ECJ judgments 'interfere with the basic principles of democracy'. The insistence of the ECJ upon precisely equal treatment, i.e. men and women 'shall be guaranteed the same conditions without discrimination', direct or indirect (Arts. 2 and 5, Directive 76/207), is bound to affect many areas of discrimination discussed in this chapter. To allow direct enforcement in the 'State' or public sector whilst leaving enforcement in the private sector to national legislation was an unsatisfactory way of making law (where, for example, did it leave local authority employees?). But the judgment constituted a major impetus towards full, formal equality in employment. How far this would increase real equality in the labour market of the later 1980s remained to be tested.

7 Industrial Conflict and the Law

1 W. Milne Bailey, *Trade Union Documents* (1929), p. 4.

2 R. Hedges and A. Winterbottom, *The Legal History of Trade Unionism* (1930), p. 8; cf. J. Riddall, *The Law of Industrial Relations* (1981), Chap. 2.

3 S. and B. Webb, *History of Trade Unionism* (1920), p. 251; cf. D. Simon, in J. Saville (ed.), *Democracy and the Labour Movement* (1954), pp. 173–200; T. Tholfsen, *Working Class Radicalism in Mid-Victorian England* (1976), pp. 179–89.

4 *R.* v. *Mawbey* (1796) 6 T R 619, 636.

5 S. and B. Webb, op. cit., p. 63; but compare E. Hunt, *British Labour History 1815–1914* (1981), pp. 197–9, for a different emphasis.

6 G. D. H. Cole, *Short History of the English Working Class Movement* (1947), p. 62; E. P. Thompson, *The Making of the English Working Class* (1963 ed.), pp. 516–21.

7 E. Hunt, op. cit., pp. 198–9; A. Musson, *British Trade Unions* (1972), Chap. 5.

8 O. Kahn-Freund and B. Hepple, *Laws Against Strikes* (1972) p. 5.

9 E. P. Thompson, *The Making of the English Working Class* (1968 ed.), pp. 500–21.

10 E. P. Thompson, *Whigs and Hunters* (1975), p. 269; A. Fox, *History and Heritage* (1985), pp. 88–96.

11 E. P. Thompson and G. Rudé, *Captain Swing* (1973), Chaps. 14, 15.

12 See E. Hunt, *British Labour History 1815–1914* (1981), pp. 228–32; Wedderburn (1980) 9 ILJ 65, 74–5; A. Jenkin in L. Munby (ed.), *The Luddites and Other Essays* (1971), pp. 75–91.

13 E. Hobsbawm, *Labouring Men* (1964), p. 319, and *The Age of Revolution* (1962), p. 41.

14 A. Fox, *History and Heritage* (1985), p. 118.

15 H. Turner, *Trade Union Growth, Structure and Policy* (1962); H. Pelling, *A History of British Trade Unionism* (1963), pp. 34–41.

16 E. Hunt, *British Labour History 1815–1914* (1981), p. 260.

17 O. Kahn-Freund, *Labour Relations, Heritage and Adjustment* (1979), p. 44.

18 R. Harrison, *Before the Socialists* (1967), p. 287; S. and B. Webb, *History of Trade Unionism* (1920), p. 271.

19 See R. Hedges and A. Winterbottom, *The Legal History of Trade Unionism* (1930), pp. 43–9; N. Citrine, *Trade Union Law* (3rd ed. 1967; M. Hickling, ed.), pp. 4–8.

20 See *R*. v. *Duffield*, *R*. v. *Rowlands* (1851) 5 Cox 404, 432, 436, 463, 466, 493.

21 See J. D. Reynaud, *Les Syndicats en France* (1975), Vol. 1, pp. 6–12, 149–52; J. M. Verdier, *Syndicats* (1966), pp. 15–19; see Chapter 10, p. 851.

22 *R*. v. *Druitt* (1867) 10 Cox 592, 601–2.

23 K. Brown, in C. Wrigley (ed.), *A History of British Industrial Relations 1875–1914* (1982), p. 118.

24 (1872) 12 Cox 316, 333, 339–40, 348–9; *The Times*, 20 October 1872.

25 See H. Clegg, A. Fox and A. Thompson, *A History of British Trade Unions Since 1889*, Vol. 1 (1964).

26 This was not, as is commonly believed, initially accomplished by the Employers and Workmen Act 1875.

27 (1867) L R 2 Q B 153, 159.

28 *Edwards* v. *S O G A T* [1971] Ch. 354, 381–2, Sachs L J.

29 O. Kahn-Freund (1943) 7 M L R 192, 201–2.

30 C. Asquith, *Trade Union Law for Laymen* (1927), pp. 53, 56; Chapter 1, page 31. The Webbs report the Court of Appeal refusing to allow a union to be sued, *Warnham* v. *Stone* (1896): *Industrial Democracy* (1914 ed.), p. 858.

31 See H. Clegg, A. Fox and A. Thompson, op. cit. (1964), Chaps. 8 and 9; K. Brown, in C. Wrigley (ed.), *History of British Industrial Relations 1875–1914* (1982), Chap. 6.

32 E. Hobsbawm, *Labouring Men* (1964), p. 181.

33 J. Saville, in A. Briggs and J. Saville (eds.), *Essays in Labour History* (1960), p. 317.

34 See *The Times*, 31 August 1900; cf. F. Bealey and H. Pelling, *Labour and Politics 1900–1906* (1958), Chap. 3.

35 *Taff Vale Rlwy Co.* v. *Amal. Soc. of Rlwy Servants* [1901] A C 426, 436.

36 See R. Kidner (1982) 2 Legal Studies 34; see too p. 586.

37 S. Evans, in P. Fosh and C. Littler (eds.), *Industrial Relations and the Law in the 1980s* (1985), p. 13.

38 See *A Giant's Strength* (1958, Inns of Court Conservative Society), p. 54; Donovan Report (Cmnd 3623, 1968), paras. 906–9.

39 [1973] A C 15; and see *Howitt* v. *T G W U* [1973] I C R 1; (1973) 36 M L R 226; *General Aviation Services Ltd* v. *T G W U* [1976] I R L R 224; and [1985] I C R 615 (H L).

40 See the discussion in R. Simpson and J. Wood, *Industrial Relations* (1973), Chaps. 10 and 11.

41 *Bonsor* v. *Musicians' Union* [1956] A C 104; K. W. Wedderburn (1957) 20 M L R 105, (1965) 28 M L R 62.

42 *E E T P U* v. *Times Newspapers Ltd* [1980] Q B 585.

43 See *The Times*, 26 January 1982; *Midland Cold Storage Ltd* v. *Steer* [1972] ICR 435; P. Davies (1973) 36 MLR 78; J. Griffith, *New Statesman*, 24 November 1972.

44 *Messenger Newspapers Group Ltd* v. *NGA* [1984] IRLR 397 (the union was also fined for contempt and suffered sequestration of funds).

45 P. Davies and M. Freedland, *Labour Law: Text and Materials* (2nd ed. 1984), p. 829.

46 [1985] 2 WLR 1081, 1109, 1111; R. Benedictus on 'Tort and the Miners' Strike' (1985) 14 ILJ 176; and see note 51, below.

47 R. Benedictus (1985) 14 ILJ 176, 187, believes that s. 15 imposes an *alter ego* doctrine; but the section as a whole seems to determine vicarious liability.

48 K. Ewing (1982) 11 ILJ 209, 220–1.

49 [1985] IRLR 162.

50 *Norbrook Laboratories Ltd* v. *King* [1984] IRLR 200 (NICA).

51 [1985] IRLR 455, Skinner J.; and (1986) 322 IDS Brief 12 (CA).

52 Clark and Wedderburn, in Wedderburn, R. Lewis, and J. Clark (eds.), *Labour Law and Industrial Relations* (1983), pp. 200–6.

53 Evidence to House of Commons Employment Committee, 27 February 1980 (HC 462–i), pp. 39–40; and see evidence on 29 October 1980 (HC 462–viii); also P. Kahn, N. Lewis, R. Livock and P. Wiles, *Picketing* (1983); R. Lewis and B. Simpson, *Striking a Balance?* (1981), Chap. 8; S. Evans (1983) 12 ILJ 129.

54 See National Council for Civil Liberties, *Civil Liberties and the Miners' Dispute* (1984, First Report of Independent Inquiry); J. Lloyd, *Understanding the Miners' Strike* (1985, Fabian Soc. No. 504); R. East, H. Power and P. Thomas, 'The Death of Mass Picketing' (1985) 12 Jo. Law Soc. 305; T. Bunyan, 'From Saltley to Orgreave', ibid. 293.

55 *Agnew* v. *Munro* (1891) 2 White 611, 615; *Gibson* v. *Lawson* [1891] 2 QB 545.

56 *R.* v. *Jones* [1974] ICR 310 (the last major case before the 1977 Act where imprisonment for conspiracy exceeded the maximum available for the substantive offence); see J. Arnison, *The Shrewsbury Three* (1974).

57 *Elsey* v. *Smith* [1983] IRLR 292.

58 H. Clegg, A. Fox and A. Thompson, *A History of British Trade Unions* (1964), Vol. 1, p. 69.

59 *Lyons* v. *Wilkins* [1896] 1 Ch. 811; [1899] 1 Ch. 255.

60 See respectively *Thompson-Schwab* v. *Costaki* [1956] 1 All E. R. 652, 654 (patrolling prostitutes a nuisance); *Hubbard* v. *Pitt* [1976] QB 142 (CA); [1975] 3 All E. R. 1, 19 (demonstrating tenants); Wallington [1976] CLJ 86.

61 *Ward Lock & Co. Ltd* v. *OPAS* (1906) 22 TLR 327; so too *Fowler* v. *Kibble* [1922] 1 Ch. 487; B. Bercusson (1977) 40 MLR 268, 272–6.

62 [1984] IRLR 156; Miller (1984) 13 ILJ 111.

63 R. Kidner (1982) 2 Legal Studies 34, 50, who says this amendment would have clarified the 'positive rights' of pickets; but it was another 'immunity'; and it is difficult to think of a more 'positive' phrase than 'It shall be lawful', with which the clause began: see Wedderburn, Chap. 37, in W. McCarthy (ed.), *Trade Unions* (1985), p. 521; see also below, p. 847.

64 *British Airports Authority* v. *Ashton* [1983] I C R 696.

65 [1967] 1 Q B 91.

66 [1974] I C R 84; cf. *Kavanagh* v. *Hiscock* [1974] I C R 282.

67 *Mersey Docks and Harbour Co.* v. *Verrinder* [1982] I R L R 152; P. Kahn *et al.*, *Picketing* (1983), pp. 177–9.

68 J. Gennard (1984) 15 I. R. Jo., No. 3, 7, 19 (on the N G A affair).

69 R(U) 1/70; A. Ogus and E. Barendt, *The Law of Social Security* (2nd ed. 1982), p. 122; but see *Verrinder's* case [1982] I R L R 152, 155.

70 See R. Lewis and B. Simpson, *Striking a Balance?* (1981), pp. 171–2; *Galt* v. *Philp*, above, seems to lean heavily against this view.

71 *New Society*, 4 September 1980, p. 452.

72 See I. Smith and J. Wood, *Industrial Law* (2nd ed. 1983), p. 387.

73 *Read (Transport) Ltd* v. *N U M (S. Wales Area)* [1985] I R L R 67 (on the sequestration see *Financial Times*, 16 March 1985); *Wight Contractors* v. *N U M (S. Wales Area)*, unreported, 19 June 1984; *Banks Ltd* v. *N U M (Durham Area)*, unreported, 12 November 1984; *N C B* v. *N U M (Yorkshire Area)*, see *The Times*, 14, 17 and 23 March 1984, and 27 March, 27 May and 9 June 1984; on the T G W U, *Financial Times*, 6 November 1984.

74 *Thomas* v. *N U M (S. Wales Area)* [1985] I R L R 136; and note 46, above.

75 See *Parl. Deb.*, 6 March 1891 H L (on the 'Scotch' railway strike); *Guardian*, 3 April 1984; *The Times*, 16 March 1984.

76 *Piddington* v. *Bates* [1960] 3 All E. R. 660; *Kavanagh* v. *Hiscock* [1974] I C R 282.

77 [1985] I R L R 76; Gillian Morris (1985) 14 I L J 109. On the statistics see J. Percy-Smith and P. Hillyard (1985) 12 Jo. Law Soc. 345.

78 G. Goodman, *The Miners' Strike* (1985), pp. 108–9; see the forthcoming account by J. Lloyd and M. Adeney (1986).

79 *R.* v. *Mansfield JJ, ex parte Sharkey* [1984] I R L R 496, 502; see the useful review of policing the miners' strike, P. Wallington (1985) 14 I L J 145, 156; B. Fine and R. Millar (eds.), *Policing the Miners' Strike* (1985); and the special number on the coal dispute, (1985) 12 Jo. Law. Soc. No. 3 (P. Scraton and P. Thomas, eds.).

80 *Review of Public Order Law* (Cmnd 9510, 1985), Chap. 5.

81 Bramwell B., *R.* v. *Druitt* (1867) 10 Cox C. C. 592, 601 (intimidation of blacklegs by 'black looks').

82 O. Kahn-Freund, in Flanders and Clegg (eds.), *The System of Industrial Relations in Great Britain* (1954), p. 127.

83 Viscount Radcliffe, *Stratford* v. *Lindley* [1965] AC 269, 330; see generally Clark and Wedderburn, in Wedderburn, R. Lewis and J. Clark (eds.), *Labour Law and Industrial Relations* (1983), pp. 155–65.

84 See Clark and Wedderburn, pp. 158 ff., in Wedderburn, R. Lewis and J. Clark (eds.), op. cit.

85 See R. Simpson, 'A Not So Golden Formula' (1983) 46 MLR 463; K. Ewing (1982) 11 ILJ 209, 215; and Chapter 10.

86 *Health Computing Ltd* v. *Meek* [1981] ICR 24, 32.

87 *NWL* v. *Woods* [1979] ICR 867, 875.

88 *Examite Ltd* v. *Whittaker* [1977] IRLR 312 (CA); *Porr* v. *Shaw, Johnson and Holden* [1979] 2 Lloyd's L. R. 331 (CA).

89 *White* v. *Riley* [1921] 1 Ch. 1; Chapter 1, p. 31.

90 *Langston* v. *AUEW* [1974] ICR 180.

91 Buckley LJ, *Cory Lighterage Ltd* v. *TGWU* [1973] ICR 339, 362; Lord Denning MR at p. 353; *Quinn* v. *Leathem* [1901] AC 495; see, on intimidation, p. 617.

92 [1957] 1 All E. R. 234; *Conway* v. *Wade* [1909] AC 506; see below, p. 583.

93 [1979] ICR 867, 878, 888; B. Simpson (1980) 43 MLR 327.

94 [1977] ICR 685; H. Collins (1978) 7 ILJ 126; Wedderburn (1978) 41 MLR 80.

95 [1983] 1 AC 366; Wedderburn (1982) 45 MLR 556.

96 [1983] 1 AC 191.

97 *Duport Steels Ltd* v. *Sirs* [1980] ICR 161.

98 *Master Builders' Assoc. NSW* v. *Australian Building Construction, etc. Fedn* (1974) 3 ALR 305, 320, 325 (Aus.); see W. Creighton, W. Ford and R. Mitchell, *Labour Law* (1983), pp. 490 ff. On Italy see Wedderburn (1983) 12 ILJ 253; and Chapter 10, p. 850.

99 *Mercury Communications Ltd* v. *Scott-Garner* [1984] Ch. 27 (CA): Chapter 1, p. 73; K. Ewing and W. Rees (1984) 13 ILJ 60.

100 *Crazy Prices (NI) Ltd* v. *Hewitt* [1980] IRLR 396, 400 (labour law in N. Ireland is significantly different from that in Britain).

101 *Dimbleby & Sons Ltd* v. *NUJ* [1984] 1 WLR 427, 433 (emphasis in original); R. Simpson (1984) 47 MLR 577, 582; R. Benedictus (1984) 13 ILJ 107.

102 See K. W. Wedderburn (1972) 1 ILJ 12; and F. Morgenstern, *International Conflicts of Labour Law* (1984), pp. 112–15.

103 [1965] AC 269; (1965) 28 MLR 205.

104 [1969] 2 Ch. 106; A. Grabiner (1969) 32 MLR 435.

105 *Trade Unions in a Changing World: The Challenge for Management* (1980, CBI Steering Group) pp. 22–3.

106 See R. Benedictus (1979) 8 ILJ 100 for some of the cases.

107 *Express Newspapers Ltd* v. *McShane* [1980] AC 672; *NWL* v. *Woods* [1979] ICR 867; *Duport Steels Ltd* v. *Sirs* [1980] ICR 161; see Wedderburn (1980) 9

ILJ 65; and on Lord Denning, P. Davies and M. Freedland, in P. McAuslan and J. Jowell (eds.), *Lord Denning the Judge and the Law* (1985).

108 J. Griffith, *The Politics of the Judiciary* (3rd ed. 1985), p. 206.

109 See Clark and Wedderburn, in Wedderburn, R. Lewis and J. Clark (eds.), *Labour Law and Industrial Relations* (1983), pp. 166–73.

110 P. Davies and M. Freedland, *Labour Law: Text and Materials* (2nd ed. 1982), p. 817; see Chapter 10, p. 854.

111 *Supreme Court Practice* (1985), Vol. 1, O. 29, R. 1 (29/1/2).

8 The Right to Strike

1 [1942] A C 435, 463.

2 See (1985) 93 *Employment Gazette* 149; K. Walsh, *Strikes in Europe and the United States* (1983); R. Bean, *Comparative Industrial Relations* (1985), pp. 148–56.

3 R. Hyman, *Strikes* (1984), Chap. 7. They have fallen further in 1981–6.

4 See W. McCarthy (1970) 8 BJIR 224; H. Turner, *Is Britain Really Strike Prone?* (1968).

5 See P. Edwards, in G. Bain (ed.), *Industrial Relations in Britain* (1983), p. 233.

6 C. Smith, R. Clifton, P. Mackelam, S. Creigh and R. Burns, *Strikes in Britain* (1978, DE Manpower Paper No. 15); P. Edwards (1981) 19 BJIR 135.

7 W. Brown (ed.), *The Changing Contours of British Industrial Relations* (1981), pp. 80–100.

8 P. Edwards, in G. Bain (ed.), op. cit., Chap. 9; S. Creigh, N. Donaldson and E. Hawthorn (1980) 87 *Employment Gazette* 1174.

9 J. Durcan, W. McCarthy and G. Redman, *Strikes in Post-War Britain* (1983), pp. 398–402, 432.

10 R. Taylor, *Workers and the New Depression* (1982), p. 164. On the finances of strikers, see J. Gennard, *Financing Strikers* (1977); M. Partington (1980) 9 ILJ 243; see p. 680, below.

11 See P. Edwards and H. Scullion, *The Social Organization of Industrial Conflict* (1982), p. 257; cf. E. Batstone, *Working Order* (1984), pp. 304–34.

12 J. Kelly and N. Nicholson (1980) 11 Ind. Rels. Jo. No. 5, 20, 30; cf. J. Cronin, *Industrial Conflict in Modern Britain* (1979), p. 195.

13 E. Batstone, I. Boraston and S. Frenkel, *The Social Organization of Strikes* (1978), p. 20; cf. W. Daniel and N. Millward, *Workplace Industrial Relations in Britain* (1983), Chap. IX.

14 See B. Aaron and K. Wedderburn, *Industrial Conflict – a Comparative Legal Survey* (1972).

15 *Haddow* v. *ILEA* [1979] ICR 202, 207; *Cruickshank* v. *Hobbs* [1977] ICR 725; *Williams* v. *National Theatre Bd* [1982] IRLR 377; Chapter 3, p. 195. On election by the worker in face of an employer's breach, see *Shook* v. *Ealing LB* [1986] IRLR 46.

16 See B. Hutchins and A. Harrison, *A History of Factory Legislation* (1903), Chaps. IV, V, VI; J. T. Ward, *The Factory Movement* (1962), Chap. 14; Chapter 5, p. 373.

17 K. Marx, *Capital*, Vol. 1 (1946 ed.; D. Torr, ed.), p. 277.

18 *Ryder* v. *Mills* (1850) Parl. Papers 67 Sess. 3; xlii p. 479; *The Times*, 9 February 1850; Ward, op. cit., pp. 360–88; Marx, op. cit., pp. 278–81.

19 J. Wesley Bready, *Lord Shaftesbury and Social–Industrial Progress* (1926), pp. 228–30 and Chap. XVI generally; J. and B. Hammond, *Lord Shaftesbury* (1923), pp. 135–6.

20 *R.* v. *Selsby* (1847) 5 Cox 495n., described by S. and B. Webb, *History of Trade Unionism* (1920 ed.), pp. 209–10.

21 For details of the tort liabilities, see Clerk and Lindsell on *Torts* (15th ed. 1982 and 4th Supp. 1986), Chap. 15.

22 [1901] AC 495.

23 *Hadmor Productions Ltd* v. *Hamilton* [1983] 1 AC 191, 228; *Stratford* v. *Lindley* [1965] AC 269.

24 *Scala Ballroom (Wolverhampton) Ltd* v. *Ratcliffe* [1958] 3 All E. R. 220; *Huntley* v. *Thornton* [1957] 1 WLR 321. On combinations where some parties only are 'malicious', see *McKernan* v. *Fraser* (1931) 46 CLR 343, 401, 407.

25 (No. 2) [1982] AC 173, 189, Lord Diplock; but see Wedderburn (1983) 46 MLR 224; the case before the Law Lords did not allege any intention to injure, only the unlawful means.

26 *Faccenda Chicken Ltd* v. *Fowler* [1984] ICR 589, 602; see now [1986] IRLR 69 (CA) (conspiracy not considered).

27 (1853) 2 El. & Bl. 216, 229 (Crompton J.), 232 (Erle J.).

28 W. Holdsworth, *History of English Law* (1945), Vol. IV, p. 384.

29 Lord Denning MR, *Daily Mirror Newspapers* v. *Gardner* [1968] 2 QB 762.

30 *Glamorgan Coal Co.* v. *South Wales Miners Fedn* [1905] AC 239; *Brimelow* v. *Casson* [1924] 1 Ch. 302 (chorus girls).

31 See *Parl. Deb.*, 3 Aug. 1906, HC Vol. 162, cols. 1677–705; 5 Nov. 1906, cols. 145–58; HL, Vol. 166, 4 Dec., cols. 686–735.

32 [1966] 1 WLR 691, 700–1, 703–4.

33 *Solihull MB* v. *NUT* [1985] IRLR 211, 213.

34 [1983] 2 AC 570, 608–9 (Lord Diplock agreeing with Donaldson MR); (1983) 46 MLR 632; see, too, *Shipping Co. Uniform Inc.* v. *ITWF* [1985] IRLR 71, 73.

35 *Torquay Hotel Ltd* v. *Cousins* [1969] 2 Ch. 106; Grabiner (1969) 32 MLR

435; *Square Grip Reinforcement Ltd* v. *MacDonald* (No. 2), 1968, SLT 65; (1968) 31 MLR 550.

36 *Camellia Tanker Ltd* v. *ITWF* [1976] ICR 274; (1976) 39 MLR 715.

37 *Dimbleby & Sons Ltd* v. *NUJ*, [1984] ICR 386, 395 (CA and HL); Simpson (1984) 47 MLR 577, 580.

38 *Austin Rover Group Ltd* v. *AUEW (TASS)* [1985] IRLR 162.

39 [1952] Ch. 646; p. 36, above.

40 [1965] AC 269; (1965) 28 MLR 205.

41 [1969] 2 Ch. 106, 138. *Falconer's* case, 1986 (p. 644), seemed to involve an exemption clause in his contract with BR, excusing it from performance.

42 *Thomas* v. *NUM (South Wales Area)* [1985] IRLR 136, 148.

43 See e.g. the decisions of 1960–80 in Clerk and Lindsell on *Torts* (15th ed. 1982), pp. 700–23; and now *RCA Corpn* v. *Pollard* [1983] Ch. 135; (1983) 46 MLR 224.

44 *Merkur Island Shipping Corpn* v. *Laughton* [1983] ICR 178 (CA); [1983] 2 AC 570, 607–9 (HL).

45 *Hadmor Productions Ltd* v. *Hamilton* [1983] 1 AC 191, 231; Simpson (1982) 45 MLR 447, 452.

46 *NWL Ltd* v. *Woods* [1979] ICR 867, 886.

47 *Duport Steels Ltd* v. *Sirs* [1980] ICR 161, 177.

48 B. Bercusson (1980) 9 ILJ 215, 219.

49 Wedderburn (1981) 10 ILJ 113; and on the eight hurdles in s. 17 (3) Clerk and Lindsell, *Torts* (15th ed. 1982 and 4th Supp.), para. 15–30.

50 *Marina Shipping Ltd* v. *Laughton* [1982] 2 QB 1127.

51 *Shipping Company Uniform Inc.* v. *ITWF* [1985] IRLR 71, 74–5.

52 [1984] ICR 386 (CA and HL); *Examite Ltd* v. *Whittaker* [1977] IRLR 312; (1978) 41 MLR 80; Chapter 7, p. 555; Simpson (1984) 47 MLR 577, 587–8.

53 *DHN Ltd* v. *Tower Hamlets LBC* [1976] 1 WLR 852, 860, 861, 867 (CA).

54 See C. Morris, *The Developing Labor Law* (2nd ed. 1983), Vol. 1, pp. 725–30; cf. R. Bernstein and R. Cooper (1985) Lab. Law. Jo. 327.

55 *Shipping Co. Uniform Inc.* v. *ITWF* [1985] IRLR 71, 75.

56 *A Giant's Strength* (1958, Inns of Court Conservative Society), p. 26.

57 On the *News International* structure in 1986, see *Financial Times*, 20 February 1986; *Guardian*, 12 February 1986.

58 *Thomas* v. *NUM (South Wales Area)* [1985] 2 WLR 1081, 1121–3.

59 *Monterosso Shipping Ltd* v. *ITWF* [1982] ICR 675.

60 See R. Lewis and B. Simpson (1982) 11 ILJ 227; P. Davies and M. Freedland, *Labour Law: Text and Materials* (2nd ed. 1984), pp. 862–8 (also on the now repealed EA 1980 s. 18); cf. M. Short (1983) 12 ILJ 99.

61 W. McCarthy, *The Closed Shop in Britain* (1964), p. 68; S. Dunn and J. Gennard, *The Closed Shop in British Industry* (1984), p. 35.

62 See e.g. *Mersey Dock and Harbour Board* v. *Verrinder* [1982] IRLR 152; 'cowboy' lorries were much in evidence in the miners' strike 1984–5.

63 [1984] IRLR 397.

64 See V. Shrubshall (1984) 15 Ind. Rel. Jo. No. 2 p. 91; P. Fosh, Chap. 1, in P. Fosh and C. Littler (eds.), *Industrial Relations and the Law in the 1980s* (1985).

65 J. Gennard, 'The Implications of the Messenger Dispute' (1984) 15 Ind. Rel. Jo. No. 3, 7, 19, a valuable account.

66 [1898] AC 1, 121, 138–40; see Chapter 1, p. 30. R. Heuston, *The Lives of the Lord Chancellors 1855–1940* (1964), pp. 118–22.

67 [1901] AC 495; R. Stevens, *Law and Politics* (1979), p. 93.

68 See *Samples of Lawmaking* (1962), pp. 11–13; *Rookes* v. *Barnard* [1964] AC 1129, 1215–16.

69 Lord Dunedin, *Sorrell* v. *Smith* [1925] AC 700, 719.

70 *Rookes* v. *Barnard* [1964] AC 1129, 1192 (Lord Evershed); 1236 (Lord Pearce); p. 117 (Lord Reid); see too Templeman J., *Camellia Tanker Ltd* v. *ITWF* [1976] ICR 274, 289; Wedderburn (1974) 37 MLR 525, 539.

71 [1982] IRLR 198; but see *Phestos Shipping Co.* v. *Kurmiawan* 1983, SLT 389 (ship sit-in); Brodie (1983) 12 ILJ 170 on interim interdict (interlocutory injunction).

72 Miller (1982) 11 ILJ 115, 117.

73 *Hadmor Productions Ltd* v. *Hamilton* [1983] 1 AC 191, 229, 230 (where the minority character of the 1974 Government explains the problem about the first form of TULRA s. 13 (1); compare the *Merkur Island* case [1983] 2 AC 570, pp. 609–10).

74 See too Gibson LJ, *Norbrook Laboratories* v. *King* [1984] IRLR 200, 209 (the *Hadmor* judgment is 'not easy altogether to reconcile' with the *Rookes* reasoning); and K. Ewing (1982) 11 ILJ 213–15. The present writer had argued that s. 13 (2) (in its 1906 Act form) could protect interference by economic pressure, namely threats to break a contract, (1964) 27 MLR 257; (1961) 24 MLR 572; but no more; see p. 618.

75 *Dimbleby & Sons Ltd* v. *NUJ* [1984] 1 WLR 427, 434; *Daily Mirror Ltd* v. *Gardner* [1968] 2 QB 762, 779.

76 Slade LJ, *RCA Corpn* v. *Pollard* [1983] Ch. 135, 156.

77 Morris LJ, *Thomson* v. *Deakin* [1952] Ch. 646, 702.

78 *Merkur Island Shipping Corpn* v. *Laughton* [1983] 2 AC 570, 608; and on the tort involved, pp. 606–7, 609; Dillon LJ at p. 588 (unlawful means).

79 See Clerk and Lindsell on *Torts* (15th ed. 1982 and Supp.), p. 709; and see H. Carty (1984) 100 LQR 342; J. Tiley, ibid. 347; B. Simpson (1984) 47 MLR 577, 580; P. Elias and K. Ewing [1982] CLJ 321, 328–9; Wedderburn (1983) 46 MLR 632–4.

80 *Acrow (Automation) Ltd* v. *Rex Chainbelt* [1971] 3 All E. R. 1175, 1181.

81 [1964] AC 1129; Chapter 1, pp. 40.

82 *Morgan* v. *Fry* [1968] 2 QB 710.

83 See for an example *Seamen's Direct Buying Co.* v. *Standard Oil California* 686 P. (2d) 1158 (1984); and Wedderburn (1983) 46 MLR 224; (1964) 27 MLR 257; compare Elias and Ewing [1982] CLJ 321.

84 *Central Canada Potash Co.* v. *Govt of Saskatchewan* (1979) 88 DLR (3d.) 609, 636 (Sup. Ct Canada).

85 There was a threat to continue the wrongdoing in *RCA Corpn* v. *Pollard* [1983] Ch. 135; (1983) 46 MLR 224; see p. 640, below.

86 [1968] 2 QB 710, 731–2, Davies LJ; see Chapter 3, p. 192.

87 S. Anderman (1975) 4 ILJ 131; see too R. Hyman, *Disputes Procedures in Action* (1972), pp. 80–5; and R. Simpson (1982) 45 MLR 447, 449–50.

88 Cmnd 8778, 1983.

89 R. Martin, in P. Fosh and C. Littler (eds.), *Industrial Relations and the Law in the 1980s* (1985), p. 72.

90 *Austin Rover Group Ltd* v. *AUEW (TASS)* [1985] IRLR 162.

91 [1985] IRLR 71.

92 See K. Renner's discussion of Marx's phrase, and editorial notes, *The Institutions of Private Law and Their Social Functions* (1949; O. Kahn-Freund, ed.), pp. 104–15; compare H. Collins, *Marxism and Law* (1982), pp. 86–7.

93 [1985] IRLR 211.

94 See *Financial Times*, 18–20, 23, 26 and 27 February, 23 and 28 March, 3, 17, 20 and 25 April, 13, 21 and 23 May and 4, 6 and 15 June 1985. An agreement at *Nabisco* went beyond the Act: *Financial Times*, 9 September 1985 (ballot at all plants before any plant goes on strike).

95 *Financial Times*, 31 May 1985.

96 See R. Undy and R. Martin, *Ballots and Trade Union Democracy* (1984), pp. 32–43 and Chap. 3 *passim*.

97 See *The Times* and *Financial Times*, 11–22 February 1986.

98 [1964] AC 1129, 1168; Lord Devlin expressly left the conspiracy point open, p. 1210. See on the legal detail Clerk and Lindsell on *Torts* (15th ed. 1982 and Supp.), pp. 759–61, 772–3.

99 J. Thompson (1982) 98 LQR 342, 345; but contrast R. Simpson (1982) 45 MLR p. 452; P. Elias [1981] CLJ p. 237.

100 *Springhead Spinning Ltd* v. *Riley* (1868) LR 6 Eq. 551; *Cunard SS* v. *Stacey* [1955] 2 Lloyd's R. 247.

101 [1979] ICR 494; see *Assoc. Newspapers Group* v. *Wade* [1979] ICR 664 (press freedom).

102 [1982] AC 173 (HL); see p. 583, above.

103 Cooke J., *Van Camp Chocolates Ltd* v. *Aulsebrooks Ltd* [1984] 1 NZLR 354 (NZCA, reviewing the cases).

104 [1978] AC 435: the Attorney-General could facilitate an action if he consented to a 'relator' action in the public interest: p. 481.

105 *RCA Corpn* v. *Pollard* [1983] Ch. 135; Wedderburn (1983) 46 MLR 224 (the *Lonrho* case did not involve an allegation of intentional damage by the oil companies against *Lonrho* when they committed crimes in supplying Rhodesia: p. 228); and see Clerk and Lindsell on *Torts* (15th ed. 1982 and Supp.), pp. 731–40; 750–9.

106 See the discussion of *Gouriet* v. *Union of Post Office Workers* [1978] AC 435 and *R.* v. *IRC, ex parte National Fedn of Self-Employed* [1982] AC 617, by C. Harlow and R. Rawlings, *Law and Administration* (1984), Chap. 10. And see the action brought against Liverpool City Council by the NUT and NAHT, redundancy notices growing out of the 'unlawful rate': *Guardian*, 18 October 1985; and now *R.* v. *Liverpool CC, ex parte Ferguson* [1985] IRLR 501.

107 See *Messenger Newspapers Group* v. *NGA* [1984] IRLR 397; above, note 65; *Assoc. Newspapers Group* v. *Wade* [1979] ICR 664.

108 *Prudential Assurance Ltd* v. *Newman Industries Ltd* (No. 2) [1982] Ch. 204, 224.

109 *Hadmor Productions Ltd* v. *Hamilton* [1983] 1 AC 191, 228–9; and on the scope of economic loss caused by negligence: *Junior Books Ltd* v. *Veitchi Ltd* [1983] 1 AC 520 (HL).

110 *Garden Cottage Foods Ltd* v. *Milk Marketing Board* [1984] AC 130 (injunction not granted as damages an adequate remedy); *Bourgoin SA* v. *Ministry of Agriculture* [1985] 3 All E. R. 585 (CA) (no damages; judicial review an adequate remedy: CA).

111 *Thomas* v. *NUM (South Wales Area)* [1985] 2 WLR 1081, 1098.

112 On Scotland see J. Miller (1982) 11 ILJ 115; and D. Brodie (1983) 12 ILJ 170.

113 *City and Hackney Health Authority* v. *NUPE* [1985] IRLR 252.

114 *British Airports Authority* v. *Ashton* [1983] ICR 696.

115 *University of Essex* v. *Djemal* [1980] 2 All E. R. 742.

116 *Michaels (Furriers)* v. *Askew, The Times*, 25 June 1983 (CA; order against officer of Animal Aid binding all members to stop picketing of furriers: RSC, O. 15, R. 12).

117 See on Upper Clyde, A. Buchan, *The Right to Work* (1972).

118 See *Boulting* v. *ACTT* [1963] 2 QB 606; and *Prudential Assurance Co.* v. *Lorenz* (1971) 11 KIR 78 (insurance agents).

119 *General Nutrition Ltd* v. *Yates, The Times*, 6 June 1981; Chapter 3, p. 182; see now *Faccenda Chicken Ltd* v. *Fowler* [1986] IRLR 69 (CA).

120 See *Industrial Developments Consultants Ltd* v. *Cooley* [1972] 1 WLR 443; *Binions* v. *Evans* [1972] Ch. 359; *Malone* v. *Metropolitan Police Comr* [1979] Ch. 344; and see W. Cornish, *Intellectual Property* (1981), Chap. 8.

121 See *Cranleigh Precision Engineering Ltd* v. *Bryant* [1965] 1 WLR 1293; *Schering Chemicals Ltd* v. *Falkman Ltd* [1982] QB 1 (CA).

122 *Bent's Brewery Ltd* v. *Hogan* [1945] 2 All E. R. 570.

123 *Manchester Ship Canal Co.* v. *Manchester Racecourse Co.* [1901] 2 Ch. 37; *Pritchard* v. *Briggs* [1980] Ch. 338, 392; and Clerk and Lindsell on *Torts* (15th ed. 1982), p. 712.

124 See G. Treitel, *Law of Contract* (6th ed. 1983), pp. 310–12; *Pao On* v. *Lau Yiu* [1980] AC 614; *Barton* v. *Armstrong* [1976] AC 104, 120–1; *B and S Contracts* v. *VG Publications* [1984] ICR 419 (CA).

125 [1983] 1 AC 366 (HL); Wedderburn (1982) 45 MLR 556; M. Tiplady (1983) 99 LQR 188; M. Sterling (1982) 11 ILJ 156.

126 K. Jeffery and P. Hennessy, *States of Emergency* (1983), pp. 209–10.

127 G. Morris, Chap. III, in Wedderburn and W. T. Murphy (eds.), *Labour Law and the Community* (1982), p. 23–4.

128 P. Foot, in R. Blackburn (ed.), *The Incompatibles* (1967), pp. 169–209; also generally, J. Kitchen, *The Employment of Merchant Seamen* (1980).

129 *Gouriet* v. *UPW* [1978] AC 435, above, note 104.

130 Gillian Morris, in Wedderburn and W. T. Murphy (eds.), *Labour Law and the Community* (1982) p. 25; and her *Strikes in Essential Services* (forthcoming, 1986).

131 *Harold Stephen Ltd* v. *PO* [1978] 1 All E. R. 939 (CA).

132 H. Carty (1984) 13 ILJ 165, 167.

133 *R.* v. *Hampshire CC, ex parte Ellerton* [1985] 1 All E. R. 599.

134 *Suffolk CC* v. *Secretary of State for Environment* [1985] IRLR 24.

135 See the valuable discussion by Gillian Morris and S. Rydzkowski (1984) 13 ILJ 153; and G. Morris (1983) 12 ILJ 69, 80–2; NHS employees are generally Crown servants: *Wood* v. *Leeds AHA* [1974] ICR 535, but employment protection legislation makes special provision for them.

136 *R.* v. *Burnham Primary and Secondary Committee, ex parte Professional Association of Teachers*, *The Times*, 30 March 1985. The Government ensured that the NUT lost its majority on the teachers' panel.

137 B. Hepple, in Wedderburn and Murphy (eds.), *Labour Law and the Community* (1982), p. 68, in a valuable review; also A. Thomson and P. Beaumont, *Public Sector Bargaining* (1978); B. Hepple and P. O'Higgins, *Public Employee Trade Unionism in the UK: Legal Framework* (1971).

138 *Pickwell* v. *Camden LBC* [1983] 1 All E. R. 602; *Roberts* v. *Hopwood* [1925] AC 578 (HL), see too Chapter 2, p. 157.

139 See *Kodeeswaran* v. *Att.-Gen. Ceylon* [1970] AC 1111 (PC).

140 See Wedderburn, Chap. 6, in B. Aaron and K. Wedderburn (eds.), *Industrial Conflict – a Comparative Survey* (1972), pp. 364–77; cf. C. Rehmus (ed.), *Public Employment Labor Relations (Eleven Countries)* (1975).

141 W. Gould, *A Primer on American Labor Law* (1982), Chap. 10; H. Edwards, C. Craver and R. Clark, *Labor Relations Law in the Public Sector* (1979), Chap. 1.

142 G. Giugni, *Diritto Sindacale* (7th ed. 1984), p. 242; on political strikes in Italy, Wedderburn (1983) 12 ILJ 253.

143 *Council of Civil Service Unions* v. *Minister for Civil Service* [1985] ICR 14 (HL); see Chapter 4, p. 277.

144 On retiring age: *DHSS* v. *Hughes* [1985] IRLR 263 (HL).

145 See Hepple, op. cit. (note 137, above), pp. 76–80, on the Megaw Report (Cmnd 8590, 1982); see too the valuable Chap. 7 by D. Winchester, in G. Bain (ed.), *Industrial Relations in Britain* (1983).

146 *National Sailors' and Firemen's Union* v. *Reed* [1926] Ch. 536, 539–40; cf. J. Griffith, *The Politics of the Judiciary* (3rd ed. 1985), pp. 58–60.

147 A. Goodhart (1926) 36 Yale Law Jo. 464.

148 See G. McDonald, 'British Industry in 1926', in M. Morris (ed.), *The General Strike* (1976), pp. 307–10.

149 See C. Whelan (1979) 8 ILJ 222, and (on troops and contingency planning from 1869 onwards) Chap. IV in Wedderburn and W. T. Murphy (eds.), *Labour Law and the Community* (1982).

150 S. Peake, *Troops in Strikes* (1985, Cobden Trust).

151 P. Wiles, in P. Fosh and C. Littler (eds.), *Industrial Relations and the Law in the 1980s* (1985), p. 161.

152 See NCCL, *Civil Liberties and the Miners' Dispute* (1984, First Report of Inquiry), pp. 32 ff.; see too P. Scraton and P. Thomas (eds.) (1985) 12 Jo. Law Soc. 251–414.

153 See the valuable paper by P. Wiles, in P. Fosh and C. Littler (eds.), *Industrial Relations and the Law in the 1980s* (1985), pp. 159, 172; and P. Kahn, N. Lewis, R. Livock and P. Wiles, *Picketing* (1983).

154 K. Jeffery and P. Hennessy, *States of Emergency* (1983).

155 R. Lewis (1978) 7 ILJ 1.

156 Gillian Morris (1983) 12 ILJ 69, 83; *Strikes in Essential Services* (1986, forthcoming); on the police (1980) 9 ILJ 1; and *Financial Times*, 15 July 1985.

157 L. Neal and L. Bloch, *The Right to Strike in a Free Society* (1983, Centre for Policy Studies).

158 Institute of Directors, *Settling Disputes Peacefully* (1984).

159 Wedderburn (1984) 13 ILJ 73, 84.

160 W. H. Hutt, *The Theory of Collective Bargaining* (1975, IEA), p. 119; compare A. Shenfield, *What Right to Strike?* (1986, IEA).

161 L. MacFarlane, *The Right to Strike* (1981), p. 155 and Chap. 6 *passim*; now in W. E. J. McCarthy (ed.), *Trade Unions* (1985), Chap. 33.

162 R. Miliband, *Capitalist Democracy in Britain* (1982), p. 152; and see Chapter 4.

163 *System of Industrial Relations in Great Britain* (1954, A. Flanders and H. Clegg, eds.), p. 123.

164 W. McCarthy and B. Clifford (1966) 4 B J I R 39; see too K. W. Wedderburn and P. Davies, *Employment Grievances and Disputes Procedures in Britain* (1969), Chap. 11.

165 J. Durcan, W. McCarthy and G. Redman, *Strikes in Post-War Britain* (1983), p. 394 and Chap. 11 generally.

166 *Att.-Gen.* v. *Guardians of the Poor, Merthyr Tydfil* [1900] 1 Ch. 516; J. Fulbrook, *Administrative Justice and the Unemployed* (1978), pp. 23–8; see the invaluable review of 'Social Security in the Coal Dispute' by J. Mesher (1985) 14 I L J 191.

167 See on the policy issues: A. Ogus and E. Barendt, *Law of Social Security* (2nd ed. 1982), pp. 119 ff.; J. Gennard, *Financing Strikers* (1977); on Ireland: R. Clark, 'Towards the "Just" Strike?' (1985) 48 M L R 659; on miners who might lose two benefits: W. Rees (1985) 14 I L J 203.

168 Respectively, R(U) 4/79; R(U) 1/74; R(U) 3/69; R(U) 5/77.

169 C U 39/1985, discussed by Mesher (1985) 14 I L J 191, 194. See too his argument on when a person is 'out of employment' under s. 8 of the 1976 Act, ibid. p. 196.

170 R(U) 14/58; R(U) 4/62; R(U) 1/70; R(U) 8/80. On the 'place of work' see J. Davies on the Cementation decision (1986) 136 N L J 54.

171 R(U) 2/85. The Social Security Bill 1986 proposes to replace 'participation' by 'withdrawal of labour in furtherance of the trade dispute'.

172 *Presho* v. *D H S S* [1984] I C R 463 (H L); cf. *Watt* v. *Lord Advocate* 1979, S C 120.

173 See C. Troup (1985) 14 I L J 112; and R(U) 8/80; R(U) 13/71; for a hard case arising from the miners' strike: *Cartlidge* v. *Chief Adjudication Officer* [1986] 2 W L R 558 (C A).

174 *R.* v. *Chief Adjudication Officer, ex parte Bland, The Times*, 6 February 1985 (judicial review rejected); R(S B) 17/85; J. Mesher (1985) 14 I L J 191, 202.

175 See the helpful account in T. Lynes, *Penguin Guide to Supplementary Benefits* (1985), Chap. 13; J. Mesher, *Supplementary Benefit Legislation – Annotated* (1983, C P A G); F. Sutcliffe and J. Mesher, 'Industrial Action and the Individual', in R. Lewis (ed.), *Labour Law in Britain* (forthcoming); and J. Mesher, 'The 1980 Social Security Legislation: Great Welfare State Chainsaw Massacre' (1981) 8 B. Jo. Law Soc. 119.

176 A. Ogus and E. Barendt, *The Law of Social Security* (1982), pp. 501–7. J. Gennard and R. Lasko (1974) 12 B J I R 9; R (S B) 29/85 (loans).

177 J. Gennard, *Financing Strikers* (1977); and P. Bassett, *Financial Times* 2 January 1985. On the mobilization of resources for miners' families: A. Booth and R. Smith (1985) 12 Jo. Law Soc. 365.

178 *Lowe* v. *Rigby* [1985] 2 All E. R. 903 (C A).

179 R(FIS) 1/85 and see 2/85.

180 [1984] IRLR 200; see Simpson (1984) 6 Dublin Univ. LJ (NS) 192.

181 See *Stratford* v. *Lindley* [1965] AC 269 (HL); (No. 2) [1969] 1 WLR 1547 (CA).

182 F. Frankfurter and N. Greene, *The Labor Injunction* (1932; 1963 ed.), p. 201.

183 Lord Diplock, *Duport Steels Ltd* v. *Sirs* [1980] ICR 161, 185.

184 [1985] 2 WLR 1081, 1085–1100.

185 *Mercury Communications Ltd* v. *Scott-Garner* [1984] Ch. 37, 93.

186 P. Davies and S. Anderman (1973) 2 ILJ 213, p. 225.

187 *Boston Deep Sea Fisheries Ltd* v. *TGWU, The Times*, 13–21 March and 9 April 1970; see the 2nd ed. of this work, pp. 381–3.

188 *Gouriet* v. *UPW* [1978] AC 435 (Lord Wilberforce, Viscount Dilhorne and Lord Fraser).

189 *Mersey Docks & Harbour Company* v. *Verrinder* [1982] IRLR 152; see P. Kahn, N. Lewis, R. Livock, P. Wiles, *Picketing* (1983), pp. 177–9.

190 [1985] ICR 203 (CA); the receivership was confirmed: [1985] ICR 606. In 1986 the receiver still had control; he sued many persons for causing the union loss by aiding the contempt; see p. 739.

191 [1975] AC 396; O. Kahn-Freund, *Labour and the Law* (3rd ed. 1983; Davies and Freedland, eds.), p. 362.

192 See *Digital Corpn* v. *Darkcrest Ltd* [1984] 3 WLR 617, 621–9.

193 [1965] AC 269, 338; the older test was applied in *Camellia Tanker SA* v. *ITWF* [1976] ICR 274, because the plaintiff conceded the point; see on the developments, C. Gray [1981] CLJ 307; R. Simpson (1982) 45 MLR 448–9; (1984) 47 MLR 578–80. On earlier uncertainties, see P. Davies and S. Anderman, op. cit. (note 186, above). See too P. Wallington [1976] CLJ 86.

194 *NWL* v. *Woods* [1979] ICR 867, 879.

195 See especially *Beaverbrook Newspapers Ltd* v. *Keys* [1978] ICR 582, 585; *Star Sea Transport Corpn of Monrovia* v. *Slater* [1978] IRLR 507; R. Benedictus (1979) 8 ILJ 100.

196 B. Doyle (1979) 42 MLR 458, 462; cf. R. Simpson (1978) 41 MLR 470.

197 *Express Newspapers Ltd* v. *McShane* [1980] AC 672, 695; *Duport Steels Ltd* v. *Sirs* [1980] 1 All E. R. 529; Wedderburn (1980) 9 ILJ 65, 86–94; (1980) 43 MLR 319; R. Simpson (1980) 43 MLR 327.

198 *Dimbleby & Sons Ltd* v. *NUJ* [1984] 1 WLR 427, 431–2; R. Simpson (1984) 47 MLR 577, 578–9; *Hadmor Productions Ltd* v. *Hamilton* [1983] 1 AC 191.

199 [1984] 1 All E. R. 225; distinguished by Scott J. in *Thomas* v. *NUM (South Wales Area)* [1985] 2 WLR 1081.

200 *Garden Cottage Foods Ltd* v. *Milk Marketing Board* [1984] AC 130 (HL); and on 'discretion', *Hadmor Productions Ltd* v. *Hamilton* [1983] 1 AC 191.

201 Cf. *Cory Lighterage Ltd* v. *TGWU* [1973] ICR 339. Connoisseurs noted a

year after the strike that a judge refused to continue an interim injunction against the NCB, obtained three days earlier by the NUM for alleged failure to observe the agreed 'review procedure' before closing a pit, on the ground that the NUM would not give an undertaking to meet any losses the NCB might suffer as a result of the injunction: *The Times*, 1 March 1986.

202 [1985] IRLR 71, 76.

203 *Express Newspapers Ltd* v. *Keys* [1980] IRLR 247, 250.

204 See p. 587, above; and the cases in Clerk and Lindsell on *Torts* (15th ed. 1982), pp. 701–7.

205 [1985] IRLR 211.

206 P. Davies and S. Anderman [1973] 2 ILJ p. 222.

207 *Associated Newspapers Group* v. *Wade* [1979] ICR 664.

208 *Harold Stephen* v. *PO* [1977] 1 WLR 1172, 1180.

209 *R. Taylor and Foulstone* v. *NUM (Yorkshire Area)* [1984] IRLR 445, 451.

210 [1984] IRLR 350.

211 *Fettes* v. *NUM*, unreported, 9 November 1984; cf. *Guardian*, 7 November 1984. See generally K. Ewing (1985) 14 ILJ 160.

212 *Morgan* v. *Fry* [1968] 2 QB 710, 729; and *Cory Lighterage* v. *TGWU* [1973] ICR 339, 357.

213 S. Evans (1983) 12 ILJ 129, 146.

214 See S. Evans, in P. Fosh and C. Littler (eds.), *Industrial Relations and the Law in the 1980s* (1985), Chap. 5; and (1985) 24 BJIR 133.

215 *Churchman* v. *Joint Shop Stewards Committee* [1972] 3 All E. R. 603; *Taylor and Foulstone* v. *NUM (Yorkshire Area) and NUM*, unreported, see *Financial Times*, 5, 11 and 26 October and 24, 28 and 29 November 1984. See generally G. Borrie and N. Lowe, *Law of Contempt* (2nd ed. 1983), Chap. 13; R. Kidner (1986) 6 Legal Studies 18.

216 *Express Newspapers p.l.c.* v. *Mitchell* [1982] IRLR 465.

217 *Con-Mech Engineers Ltd* v. *AUEW* [1973] ICR 620; [1974] ICR 332, 464; and on the saga of this case, N. Lewis [1974] 3 ILJ 201; K. W. Wedderburn (1974) 37 MLR 187.

218 *Biba Ltd* v. *Stratford Investments* [1973] Ch. 281; and see *Thomas* v. *NUM (South Wales Area)* [1985] 2 WLR 1081 (Scott J. not deciding the point).

219 *Heatons Transport Ltd* v. *TGWU* [1973] AC 15. (HL).

220 [1985] IRLR 67; and see *The Times* and *Financial Times*, 31 July and 1 August 1985.

221 See *Express and Star Ltd* v. *NGA* [1985] IRLR 455; and (1986) 322 IDS Brief 12 (CA).

222 See e.g. *Dumenil Ltd* v. *Ruddin* [1953] 2 All E. R. 294.

223 *Howitt Transport Ltd* v. *TGWU* [1972] IRLR 93; see (1973) 36 MLR 226.

224 *Eckman* v. *Midland Bank* [1973] QB 519; *Messenger Newspapers Group* v. *NGA* [1984] ICR 345; *Guardian*, 25 April 1986 (SOGAT; CA).

225 *Att.-Gen.* v. *Times Newspapers Ltd* [1974] AC 273, 307–8; *Seaward* v. *Patterson* [1897] 1 Ch. 545, 555. As to the minority judgments, in which a 'contumacious' civil contempt is said not to be open to waiver: see A. Arlidge and D. Eady, *Law of Contempt* (1982), pp. 33–53; but compare G. Borrie and N. Lowe, *Law of Contempt* (1983), pp. 403–6, 462–9.

226 Megarry VC, *Clarke* v. *Chadburn* [1984] IRLR, 350, 353.

227 Salmon LJ, *Jennison* v. *Baker* [1972] 2 QB 52, 64.

228 *Michaels (Furriers) Ltd* v. *Askew*, *The Times*, 25 June 1983 (CA); see p. 647, above.

229 Frankfurter and Greene, *The Labor Injunction* (1913), p. 123.

230 'Canadian Casebook Group', B. Adell *et al.*, *Labour Relations Law* (1970), p. 479.

231 *Z Ltd* v. *A-Z and AA-LL* [1982] QB 558, 578, 581, Eveleigh LJ.

232 *Seaward* v. *Patterson* [1897] 1 Ch. 545, 554; *Acrow (Automation) Ltd* v. *Rex Chainbelt Ltd* [1971] 3 All E. R. 1175 (but *quaere* now *Lonrho Ltd* v. *Shell Ltd* (No. 2) [1982] AC 173; p. 639, above; and see *Scott* v. *Scott* [1913] AC 417.

233 TUC General Council, *Annual Report* (1985), para. 32 *et seq.*; *Taylor* v. *NUM*, *The Times*, 20 November 1985, Nicholls J.; see p. 744.

234 *Hopkins* v. *NUS* [1985] ICR 268, 276–7.

235 See *Z Ltd* v. *A-Z and AA-LL* [1982] QB 558; *SCF Finance Ltd* v. *Masri* [1985] 1 WLR 876. See M. Hoyle, *The Mareva Injunction and Related Orders* (1985).

236 *Clarke* v. *Heathfield* [1985] ICR 203 (CA); *Clarke* v. *Heathfield* (No. 2) [1985] ICR 606.

237 *Heatons Transport* v. *TGWU* [1972] ICR 285, 301; *Con-Mech Ltd* v. *AUEW* [1973] ICR 620, [1974] ICR 332, 464; *Goad* v. *AUEW* [1973] ICR 42, 108. See now *Express and Star Ltd* v. *NGA* (1986) 322 IDS Brief 12 (CA: fines may be coercive, but also penal where 'contumacy' is evident).

238 *Read (Transport) Ltd* v. *NUM (South Wales Area)*, *Financial Times*, 15 March 1985.

239 *Financial Times*, 7 June and 5 July 1985; *Daily Telegraph*, 7 June 1985.

240 See pp. 77, 535, 610; *Austin Rover Group Ltd* v. *AUEW* [1985] IRLR 162; *Messenger Newspapers Group* v. *NGA* [1984] IRLR 397; J. Gennard (1984) 15 Ind. Rel. Jo. No. 3, 7.

241 *Yorkshire Miners' Association* v. *Howden* [1905] AC 256.

242 H. Phelps-Brown, *The Growth of British Industrial Relations* (1959), p. 195; *Yorkshire Miners' Assn* v. *Howden* [1905] AC 256; F. Bealey and H. Pelling, *Labour and Politics 1901–1906* (1968), p. 224.

9 Trade Unions and Members

1 *Greig* v. *Insole* [1978] 1 W L R 302, 360–2.

2 *Bennett* v. *N A S O H S P* (1915) 113 L T 808.

3 *Taylor* v. *N U M (Derbyshire Area)* [1985] I R L R 99, 103.

4 *Sansom* v. *London and Provincial Union of Licensed Vehicle Workers* (1920) 36 T L R 666; see too p. 744, below.

5 *Cope* v. *Crossingham* [1909] 2 Ch. 148, 163 (secession of branch).

6 See J. Gennard (1984) Vol. 15 Ind. Rel. Jo. No. 3, 7, 16–17; *Financial Times*, 23 November–10 December 1983.

7 See O. Kahn-Freund (1943) 7 M L R 625; Wedderburn (1957) 20 M L R 105, 120–1; *Faramus* v. *Film Artistes' Assn* [1964] A C 925.

8 See *Amal. Soc. of Carpenters* v. *Braithwaite* [1922] 2 A C 440.

9 Control of the rules, inserted by the Opposition into T U L R A 1974 by ss. 5, 6, was removed by T U L R Amendment Act 1976 s. 1.

10 J. Gennard, M. Gregory and S. Dunn (1980) 86 *Employment Gazette* 591, 600. See too S. Dunn, Chap. 3, in P. Fosh and C. Littler (eds.), *Industrial Relations and the Law in the 1980s* (1985).

11 See *Taylor* v. *N U M (Derbyshire Area)* [1985] I R L R 65 (a member litigating against his union has a right to inspect in any event: R S C, O. 24, R. 9; O. 29, R.7A); *Hughes* v. *T G W U* [1985] I R L R 382.

12 *Partington* v. *N A L G O* [1981] I R L R 537 (Scot.); p. 333, above.

13 *Thomas* v. *N U M (South Wales Area)* [1985] 2 W L R 1081, 1117.

14 *The Times*, 26 October 1976.

15 *Porter* v. *N U J* [1980] I R L R 404.

16 [1974] I C R 620; see E. McKendrick (1986) 6 Legal Studies 35.

17 *Taylor* v. *N U M (Derbyshire Area)*, 4 and 28 June 1984; [1984] I R L R 440 (Nicholls J.).

18 *Fettes* v. *N U M (Scottish Area), per* Lord Jauncey, 9 November 1984 (Ct S.: affirming Lord Hunter, 25 September).

19 *McKay* v. *Executive Committee of North Wales Area N U M*, 13 June 1984, McCowan J. (*ex parte*); 3 September 1984, Glidewell J.; *Lord* v. *Executive Committee of North Western Area N U M*, 14 June 1984, McCowan J. (*ex parte*); 26 June 1984, Caulfield J.; *Morris* v. *N U M (Midlands Area)*, 22 August 1984, Mervyn-Davies J.; *Wilkinson* v. *Executive Committee Durham Area Union N U M*, 3 September (*ex parte*), 14 September, 12 October 1984, Glidewell J. (and see *Financial Times*, 3 March 1985, on consent to final injunctions); *Bellenie* v. *N U M (Durham Mechanics Group No. 1 Area)*, 12 October 1984 (*ex parte*), Glidewell J.; 12 November 1984, Jones J. Most of the unreported proceedings are reported as news in the subsequent day's *Financial Times*. Some are discussed in the helpful articles by K. Ewing, 'The

Strike, the Courts and the Rule-Books' (1985) 14 ILJ 160; and R. Benedictus, ibid. 176 (tort cases).

20 25 May 1984; and [1984] IRLR 350; see K. Ewing (1985) 14 ILJ 160, especially 161–8.

21 [1984] IRLR 445.

22 *Thomas* v. *NUM (South Wales Area)* [1985] 2 WLR 1081, 1120.

23 P. Kahn, N. Lewis, R. Livock and P. Wiles, *Picketing, Industrial Disputes, Tactics and the Law* (1983), pp. 70, 195.

24 [1985] ICR 203 (CA) (see Chapter 8, p. 690); and subsequently Mervyn Davies J., *Clarke* v. *Heathfield* (No. 2) [1985] ICR 606.

25 A. Boyle and J. Birds, *Company Law* (1983), p. 391.

26 *Irish Times* and *Financial Times*, 19 June 1985, *Larkins* v. *NUM*, Donal Barrington J.; and *Financial Times*, 2 and 5 July 1985.

27 *Nicoll* v. *Cutts*, *The Times*, 20 May 1985 (CA); contracts of employment terminated by receivership appointed by the court.

28 R. Hughes, *Financial Times*, 3 March 1985.

29 *The Times* and *Financial Times*, 28 August 1985.

30 [1984] ICR 268, 277. Contrast the injunction granted against North London Polytechnic, Wallington (1985) 14 ILJ p. 172; and see p. 712, above.

31 See TUC General Council, *Annual Report* (1985), pp. 40–62, from which quotations are taken. On the receiver's action against banks and other third parties: *Financial Times*, 30 January 1986; and 21 May 1986.

32 *Financial Times*, 8, 15 and 17 August 1985; *Sunday Times*, 20 October 1985. (Nottinghamshire Area voted by a 72 per cent majority, South Derbyshire Area voted by 51 per cent to join an amalgamated UDM; the next day the NCB recognized formally the UDM in Nottinghamshire.)

33 Supreme Court Practice (1985), note RSC 30/1/16; Kerr on *Receivers* (1983), p. 77, said it 'appears . . . a receiver could now be appointed'.

34 Rules of Supreme Court 1985, O. 29, R. 1/5; Supreme Court Act 1981 s. 37 (3); *CBS (UK) Ltd* v. *Lambert* [1983] Ch. 37; *PCW Ltd* v. *Dixon* [1983] 2 All E. R. 158, and 697 (CA varying the order). See too Chapter 8, note 235.

35 [1985] ICR 291 (CA); R. Kidner (1985) 14 ILJ 124. The receivership was by way of equitable execution, which is also within RSC O. 51.

36 Slade LJ, *Rolled Steel Products (Holdings) Ltd* v. *British Steel Corpn* [1985] 2 WLR 908, 939.

37 *Institution of Mechanical Engineers* v. *Cane* [1961] AC 696, 724; *Williams* v. *Hursey* (1959) 103 CLR 30, 66, Fullagar J.

38 [1905] AC 256 (HL).

39 [1952] 1 All E. R. 691 (HL); *Astley* v. *ETU* (1951) 95 Sol. Jo. 744.

40 *Thomas* v. *NUM (South Wales Area)* [1985] 2 WLR 1081, 1117.

41 *The Times*, 4 July 1961 and 1 February 1962 (CA); see C. H. Rolph, *All Those in Favour: The ETU Trial* (1962).

42 *Drake* v. *Morgan* [1978] ICR 56; *Thomas* v. *NUM (South Wales Area)* [1985] 2 WLR 1081, 1120–1.

43 *Oddy* v. *TSSA* [1973] ICR 524, 529.

44 *British Actors' Equity* v. *Goring* [1978] ICR 791, 794–5, and *Porter* v. *NUJ* [1980] IRLR 404, 410.

45 *Hopkins* v. *NUS* [1985] ICR 268; see above, p. 714.

46 Lord Denning MR, *Edwards* v. *SOGAT* [1971] Ch. 354, 377.

47 *Hodgson* v. *NALGO* [1972] 1 All E. R. 15 (the exception for relaxations where 'justice' demands them is not now good law: note 48).

48 *Prudential Assurance Ltd* v. *Newman Industries Ltd* (No. 2) [1982] Ch. 204, 224 (CA). On the rule see: Wedderburn [1957] CLJ 194; [1958] CLJ 93; C. Baxter [1983] CLJ 96; R. Gregory (1982) 45 MLR 584.

49 [1950] 2 All E. R. 1064, as interpreted in the *Prudential Assurance* case, op. cit. (note 48, above) pp. 210–25.

50 [1976] ICR 147; see too *Chapple* v. *ETU, The Times*, 22 November 1961 (four of fifty delegates improperly elected; motion dismissed; no bad faith).

51 *Goodfellow* v. *London and Prov. Union of Licensed Trade Workers, The Times*, 5 June 1919; *McNamee* v. *Cooper, The Times*, 8 September 1966.

52 *Radford* v. *NATSOPA* [1972] ICR 484, 500; see below, p. 802.

53 [1929] 2 Ch. 58 (CA).

54 [1985] IRLR 99 (and earlier [1984] IRLR 440). Vinelott J. allowed a 'derivative action' even though the writ was not 'representative' for all the members; but see Wedderburn (1976) 39 MLR 327, 329; (1978) 41 MLR 569. In such an action a member may be allowed to charge the costs to the union on company law principles, whatever the result: see *Thomas's* case, *Financial Times*, 16 Nov. 1985.

55 *EETPU* v. *Times Newspapers Ltd* [1980] QB 585; see Chapter 7, p. 530.

56 See Wedderburn (1985) 14 ILJ 127, 129; cf. R. Clayton and H. Tomlinson (1985) 135 New L. J. 419.

57 See p. 752; *Cotter* v. *NUS* [1929] 2 Ch. 58; *Clarke* v. *Heathfield* [1985] ICR 203, 205.

58 [1984] IRLR 260 and *Financial Times*, 8 February 1985; see the valuable discussions by R. Nobles (1984) 13 ILJ 167, and (1985) 14 ILJ 1.

59 *Amalgamated Soc. of Railway Servants* v. *Osborne* [1910] AC 87.

60 O. Kahn-Freund, *Labour and the Law* (3rd ed. 1983; P. Davies and M. Freedland, eds.), p. 247; on the origins of the dispute within the railway unions, H. Clegg, A. Fox and A. Thompson, *A History of British Trade Unions Since 1889* (1964), pp. 413–17.

61 S. and B. Webb, *History of Trade Unionism* (1920), p. 628.

62 See K. Ewing, *Trade Unions, the Labour Party and the Law* (1982), and the fascinating account of 1910 to 1926, pp. 38–56; K. Coates and T. Topham, *Trade Unions and Politics* (1986), Chaps. 4 and 5.

63 See K. Ewing (1984) 47 MLR 57; and P. Davies [1983] JBL 485, noting *Simmonds* v. *Heffer*, Mervyn Davies J., 24 May 1983. On company donations, Companies Act 1985 s. 235 (3), *Labour Research* (1984), August, 204, and K. Ewing, *The Conservatives, Trade Unions and Political Funding* (1983, Fabian Soc. No. 492). See too *Financial Aid to Political Parties* (Cmnd 6601, 1976).

64 Constitutional Reform Centre, *Company Political Donations* (1985); Hansard Society Commission, *Paying for Politics* (1980).

65 *Reeves* v. *TGWU* [1980] ICR 728.

66 See (1984) 252 IRLIB p. 3 for the TUC statement; and K. Ewing (1984) 13 ILJ 125.

67 *Coleman* v. *POEU* [1981] IRLR 427 (CO); *Forster's* case, Chief Registrar's Report, 1925, Part 4, p. 4 (in P. Elias, B. Napier and P. Wallington, *Labour Law Cases and Materials* (1980), p. 302).

68 Lord Kilbrandon, *McCarroll* v. *NUM (Scottish Area)*, 26 March 1965, quoted by Ewing, op. cit. (note 62, above), p. 89.

69 *ASTMS* v. *Parkin* [1984] ICR 127; *Richards* v. *NUM* [1981] IRLR 247 (Labour Party building).

70 See K. Ewing on the 1984 Act (1984) 13 ILJ 227, 239.

71 *Birch* v. *NUR* [1950] Ch. 602; *Double* v. *EETPU*, Certification Officer's Annual Report (1982), p. 27.

72 See *Parkin* v. *ASTMS* [1980] ICR 662 (but a purpose of ensuring cooperation of Conservative union MPs who allegedly were not allowed to sit on the union's parliamentary committee was outside TUA 1913 s. 3 (3) and the political rules).

73 K. Ewing (1984) 13 ILJ 227, 243; on Northern Ireland, see B. Black (1984) 13 ILJ 243. Of the 7 million union members involved, 52 per cent voted, of whom 83 per cent were in favour. One employers' association ratified a fund: (1986) 367 IRRR 12.

74 L. C. B. Gower, *Review of Investor Protection* (Cmnd 9125, 1984), para. 12.02; and *Review of Investor Protection: A Discussion Document* (1982).

75 *Freedom of Association and Collective Bargaining: General Survey* (1983, Committee of Experts, Report III Part 4B), para. 195.

76 B. Creighton, W. Ford and R. Mitchell, *Labour Law, Materials and Commentary* (1983, Aus.), p. 583.

77 *Labour Law: Text and Materials* (1984), p. 673.

78 R. Undy and R. Martin, *Ballots and Trade Union Democracy* (1984), pp. 58–60. On Europe, see A. Carew, *Democracy and Government in European Trade Unions* (1976).

79 R. Undy and R. Martin, op. cit. (1984), pp. 110, 115; and Chapter 5.

80 *Democracy in Trade Unions* (Cmnd 8778, 1983), para. 13 *et seq*.

81 O. Kahn-Freund, *Labour Relations, Heritage and Adjustment* (1979), p. 17.

82 *Cope* v. *Crossingham* [1909] 2 Ch. 148, 163; above, p. 722.

83 [1985] I R L R 455; (1986) 322 I D S Brief 12 (C A).

84 (1984) 13 I L J 193, 209.

85 Lecture to the Industrial Law Society, quoted by R. Kidner (1984) 13 I L J p. 211, and see pp. 193–6.

86 See S. Dunn and J. Gennard, *The Closed Shop in British Industry* (1984), pp. 133, 149–55 and Chap. 7 *passim* (see now in W. E. J. McCarthy (ed.), *Trade Unions* (1985), Chap. 14).

87 *Labour and the Law* (3rd ed. 1983; P. Davies and M. Freedland, eds.) pp. 273–4.

88 See A. Fox, *Sociology of Work in Industry* (1971); H. Clegg, *The Changing System of Industrial Relations in Great Britain* (1979), pp. 200–13.

89 V. Allen, *Power in Trade Unions* (1954).

90 R. Undy, V. Ellis, W. McCarthy and A. Halmos, *Change in Trade Unions* (1981), Chaps. 1, 8, 9.

91 H. Turner, *Trade Union Growth, Structure and Policy* (1962).

92 R. Hyman, in G. Bain (ed.), *Industrial Relations in Britain* (1983), pp. 61, 62–5.

93 V. Allen, *Power in Trade Unions* (1954), p. 122; but see the criticisms of R. Martin (1968) 2 *Sociology* 205 (now in W. E. J. McCarthy (ed.), *Trade Unions* (1985)).

94 R. Martin, in P. Fosh and C. Littler (eds.), *Industrial Relations and the Law in the 1980s* (1985), pp. 79–80.

95 S. and B. Webb, *Industrial Democracy* (1902 ed.), p. 850.

96 *Shearer* v. *A U E W* (1960) 1 F L R 436; see D. Rawson, 'Union Ballots and Australian Electoral Offices' (1983, A N U Ind. Rel. Papers), pp. 20–2.

97 R. Martin, in P. Fosh and C. Littler (eds.), op. cit. (note 94, above), pp. 77–80.

98 R. Undy and R. Martin, op. cit. (note 78, above), pp. 63–84, 108–9.

99 *Striking A Balance?* (1981), pp. 130, 132.

100 *Rothwell* v. *A P E X* [1976] I C R 211, 221.

101 *Liptrott* v. *N U M* (1985) 285 I R L I B 14.

102 [1964] A C 925 (H L).

103 J. Gennard, M. Gregory and S. Dunn, 'Throwing the Book' (1980) 88 *Employment Gazette* 591, 594.

104 *Nagle* v. *Feilden* [1966] 2 Q B 633.

105 B. Hepple (1981) 10 I L J, 65, 75; and Wedderburn, Chap. 6, in F. Schmidt (ed.), *Discrimination in Employment* (1978).

106 *McInnes* v. *Onslow Fane* [1978] 3 All E. R. 211, 217; see P. Elias (1979) 8 I L J 111, 113. See too R. Rideout (1967) 30 M L R 389.

107 Walsh J., quoted by M. Redmond, *Dismissal Law in the Republic of Ireland* (1982), p. 37.

108 *Labour Law: Text and Materials* (2nd ed. 1984), pp. 630–1; see too K. Ewing and W. Rees (1981) 10 ILJ 84 on the IRC, which J. Wood and I. Smith, *Industrial Law* (2nd ed. 1984), p. 358, dub 'a rather rosy view'.

109 *Mayhew-Smith and ACTT,* TUC *Report* (1978), p. 401 (admission); *Ward and TGWU*, TUC *Report* (1980), p. 345 (union to consider sympathetically).

110 S. Dunn and J. Gennard, *The Closed Shop in British Industry* (1984), pp. 140–2; R. Lewis and B. Simpson, *Striking a Balance?* (1981), pp. 117.

111 *Clark* v. *NATSOPA (SOGAT '82)* [1985] IRLR 494.

112 [1985] IRLR 198.

113 See *Day* v. *SOGAT '82* (1985) 305 IDS Brief 13.

114 *NATSOPA* v. *Goodfellow* [1985] ICR 187.

115 *NATSOPA* v. *Kirkham* [1983] ICR 241. On compensation, see *Howard* v. *NGA* [1985] ICR 101; and procedure, *Howard* v. *NGA* [1983] ICR 574; [1985] ICR 97 (CA). On contributory fault reducing compensation, see *Saunders* v. *Bakers', etc. Union* [1986] IRLR 16.

116 *Lee* v. *Showmen's Guild of Great Britain* [1952] 2 QB 329.

117 *Leigh* v. *NUR* [1970] Ch. 326.

118 [1956] AC 104; Lloyd (1956) 19 MLR 121; compare (1957) 20 MLR 105.

119 [1971] Ch. 354.

120 J. Gennard, M. Gregory and S. Dunn, op. cit. (note 103, above), pp. 594–6.

121 (1966) 1 KIR 679, Goff J.

122 W. Daniels and N. Millward, *Workplace Industrial Relations in Britain* (1983), pp. 96–104.

123 R. Taylor, *Workers and the New Depression* (1983), p. 187.

124 Arbitration Act 1979 ss. 1–2; G. Treitel, *Law of Contract* (6th ed. 1983), pp. 337–9.

125 *Radford* v. *NATSOPA* [1972] ICR 484, 499.

126 P. Davies and M. Freedland, *Labour Law: Text and Materials* (2nd ed. 1982), p. 603.

127 [1965] Ch. 712.

128 *Leary* v. *NUVB* [1971] Ch. 34; M. Kay (1971) 34 MLR 86.

129 *Calvin* v. *Carr* [1980] AC 574; but see the preference for the *Leary* approach of Hodgson J., *R.* v. *Brent LBC, ex parte Gunning, The Times*, 30 April 1985.

130 On legal representation in a different context, *R.* v. *Secretary of State Home Dept, ex parte Tarrant* [1984] 2 WLR 613.

131 *White* v. *Kyzych* [1951] AC 585, 596 (PC).

132 *Roebuck* v. *NUM (Yorkshire Area)* (No. 2) [1978] ICR 676 (the action was also improper by reason of punishing a witness).

133 *Losinska* v. *CPSA* [1976] ICR 473.

134 *Annamunthodo* v. *Oilfield Workers* [1961] AC 945.

135 *Hiles* v. *ASW* [1968] Ch. 440.

136 *Breen* v. *AEU* [1971] 2 QB 175.

137 [1967] 1 All E. R. 767.

138 [1977] ICR 893; see Chapter 2, p. 164.

139 [1971] Ch. 34; discussing Buckley J. in *Shanks* v. *PTU*, unreported, 15 November 1967; M. Kay (1971) 34 MLR 86.

140 *AEU* v. *Ministry of Pensions* [1963] 1 WLR 441; see too N. Citrine, *Trade Union Law* (3rd ed. 1967; M. Hickling, ed.), p. 296.

141 J. A. G. Griffith, *The Politics of the Judiciary* (3rd ed. 1985), Chap. 7.

142 [1971] Ch. 354 (but on Sachs LJ see the protection now of the *rules* against restraint of trade: TULRA 1974 s. 2 (5)).

143 *Radford* v. *NATSOPA* [1972] ICR 484, 496.

144 *John* v. *Rees* [1970] Ch. 345.

145 *Re The Sick and Funeral Society, St John's School* [1973] Ch. 51.

146 See (1985) 337 IRRR 9; recording the first use of 'pendulum arbitration' under an agreement, and the way in which procedural disagreements between the parties led to something more like a mediated settlement. On electrical contracting, see L. Dickens *et al.*, *Dismissed* (1985), pp. 238–40.

147 On the IRC and its work, see K. Ewing and W. Rees (1981) 10 ILJ 84–100; S. Dunn and J. Gennard, *The Closed Shop in British Industry* (1984), pp. 138–43; P. Davies and M. Freedland, *Labour Law: Text and Materials* (2nd ed. 1984), pp. 630–3; and ibid. (1st ed. 1979), pp. 548–57; (1979) 208 IRRR 2; and TUC, *Annual Reports* (1976–85). The other members are Mr G. Doughty (an ex-General Secretary and elder statesman of the movement) and Lord McCarthy, to both of whom the Chairman would ascribe such success as the Committee has enjoyed.

148 Respectively, TUC *Report* (1976), p. 396, (1979), pp. 370–84.

149 TUC *Report* (1977), p. 340; *Buxton and TGWU*, TUC *Report* (1977), p. 341.

150 *Hunter-Gray and TGWU*, TUC *Report* (1981), p. 370; *Nicholls and NATSOPA*, ibid., p. 376.

151 *Clark and ACTT*, TUC *Report* (1983), p. 345; but no such outcome was possible through post-hearing conciliation in the previous case, *Howes and TGWU*, ibid., p. 340, where the complainant was unable to accept the union's compromise offer.

152 See *Curry and NUPE*, TUC *Report* (1978), p. 406; *Docherty and APEX*, ibid., p. 392; and *Jones and NUSMW*, TUC *Report* (1980), p. 353.

153 *Doye and Film Artistes' Association,* TUC *Report* (1984), pp. 359–61.

154 See S. Dunn, in P. Fosh and C. Littler (eds.), *Industrial Relations and the Law in the 1980s* (1985), pp. 108–9; C. Hanson, S. Jackson and D. Miller, *The Closed Shop* (1982), p. 88.

155 See G. Bain and R. Price, in G. Bain (ed.), *Industrial Relations in Britain*

(1983), p. 33; Chapter 1 *passim*; and (1986) *Employment Gazette* 16, for the 1984 statistics.

156 R. Price and G. Bain (1983) 21 B J I R 46; see too the different approach (difficult but valuable for the lawyer) of A. Booth (1983) 21 B J I R 377; cf. G. Bain and F. Elsheikh (1982) 20 B J I R 34.

157 G. Bain and P. Elias (1985) 23 B J I R 71, 86; and see B. Hirsch (1982) 36 Ind. and Lab. Rel. Rev. 22; G. Bain and F. Elsheikh (1979) 17 B J I R 137.

158 John Hughes, *Trade Union Structure and Government* (1967, Donovan Research Paper No. 5), Part (i), pp. 23–5; see also Part (ii) for an important discussion of members' participation and democracy in unions.

159 See R. Buchanan (1981) 12 Ind. Rel. Jo. No. 3, 40, who suggests that company mergers are a further factor, p. 49; and see (1981) 19 B J I R 232.

160 R. Hyman, Chap. 2, in G. Bain (ed.), *Industrial Relations in Britain* (1983), p. 36, and on the A U E W pp. 46–8.

161 See *R. v C O, ex parte A U E W(E)* [1983] I C R 125 (C A).

162 *Financial Times*, 5 August 1985.

163 See W. Brown (ed.), *The Changing Contours of British Industrial Relations* (1983), pp. 59–69; W. Daniel and N. Millward, *Workplace Industrial Relations in Britain* (1983), pp. 97–100; E. Batstone, *Working Order* (1984), pp. 227–30, and on 'combines' pp. 219–21, 310–11.

164 See *McLaren and Latimer and A C T A T, Annual Report of C O* (1979), p. 18; R. Kidner (1979) 8 I L J 244; *Richards and N U M (South Derbyshire)*, *Annual Report of C O* (1985), p. 61.

165 [1956] 1 W L R 585; a similar case had arisen in *Andrews* v. *N U P E, The Times*, 9 July 1955.

166 [1976] I C R 211; P. Kalis (1977) 6 I L J 19; on the earlier period, S. Lerner, *Breakaway Unions and the Small Trade Union* (1961).

167 P. Davies and M. Freedland, *Labour Law: Text and Materials* (2nd ed. 1984), p. 617.

168 C. Ball (1980) 9 I L J 13, 16; and see the valuable discussion of the Principles in the context of the E M A case and the 1975 right to be recognized, pp. 19–26.

169 *Cheall* v. *A P E X* [1983] 2 A C 180; [1983] I C R 398 (H L), reversing [1982] I C R 543 (C A).

170 See B. Simpson (1983) 46 M L R 635, 642, who finds it 'strikingly reminiscent of similar, strictly unnecessary comments' in *N W L* v. *Woods* [1979] I C R 867 and *Express Newspapers Ltd* v. *McShane* [1980] A C 672, which were 'swiftly followed by legislation'; see above, p. 20.

171 Not in all areas, as J. A. G. Griffith shows in *The Politics of the Judiciary* (3rd ed. 1985), Chaps. 4 and 7.

10 Changing Laws and Workers' Rights

1 See Wedderburn, 'The New Legal Framework in Europe', in *International Issues in Industrial Relations* (1983, Industrial Relations Soc. Australia), 35, 49–57; generally J. Elliott, *Conflict or Co-operation?* (1978); M. Carnoy and D. Shearer, *Economic Democracy* (1980). See the useful review: E. Batstone and P. Davies, *Industrial Democracy, European Experience* (1976); C. Docksey (1986) 49 MLR 281 (Vredeling); and Chapter 1, p. 66.

2 R. Birk, in *Comparative Law Yearbook*, Vol. 4 (1980, Center for International Legal Studies), 69, 84. On the EEC draft Fifth Directive: *European Communities Directive, etc.: A Consultative Document* (1983, DE and DTI); (1983) 117 EIRR 25 (revised proposals).

3 O. Kahn-Freund, 'A Lawyer's Reflections on Multinational Corporations' (1972) Jo. Ind. Rel. Soc. (Aus.) 351, 356; see Chapter 1, p. 103.

4 *Industrial Democracy* (Cmnd 6706, 1977); Chapter 1, p. 67 (R. Lewis and J. Clark (1977) 40 MLR 323); Government proposals: *Industrial Democracy* (Cmnd 7231, 1978); *The Nationalized Industries* (Cmnd 7131, 1978), p. 13; O. Kahn-Freund (1977) 6 ILJ 65; P. Davies and Wedderburn (1977) 6 ILJ 197; R. Benedictus, C. Bourn and A. Neal (eds.), *Industrial Democracy: The Implications of the Bullock Report* (1977).

5 J. Clark, H. Hartmann, C. Lau and D. Winchester, *Trade Unions, National Politics and Economic Management* (1980; Britain and West Germany), p. 125.

6 P. Cressey, J. Eldridge, J. MacInnes and G. Norris, *Industrial Democracy and Participation: Scottish Survey* (1981, DE Research No. 28), pp. 56–7; P. Brannen, *Authority and Participation in Industry* (1983), Chaps. 2, 3, 6.

7 D. Bok and J. Dunlop, *Labor and the American Community* (1970), p. 345.

8 See the valuable review in C. Craver, 'The Vitality of the American Labor Movement in the 21st Century' (1983) Univ. Illinois L. R. 633, 672–95; W. Woodworth, 'Promethean Industrial Relations' (1985) Lab. L. J. 618; cf. the advice to ATT, A. Toffler, *The Adaptive Corporation* (1985).

9 J. Schmidman and K. Keller, 'Employee Participation Plans as s. 8 (a) (2) Violations' (1984) Lab. L. J. 772; K. Alexander (1985) Lab. L. J. 428.

10 See the useful Report of Select Committee on Unemployment, Vol. 1 (1982, Paper 142), Chap. 14; but on productivity contrast K. Williams, J. Williams and D. Thomas, *Why Are the British Bad at Manufacturing?* (1983), p. 34 (in W. McCarthy (ed.), *Trade Unions* (1985), pp. 389, 396).

11 See F. Carinci, R. de Luca Tamajo, P. Tosi and T. Treu, *Diritto del lavoro 2* (1985), Chap. XIII (La Cassa integrazione guadagni); see the helpful account of the development in (1974) 11 EIRR 15; (1977) 48 EIRR 22;

(1979) 62 EIRR 18, and 65 ibid. 12; (1980) 75 EIRR 12; (1982) 102 EIRR 12, and 104 ibid. 19.

12 G. Giugni, in an influential paper, 'Il diritto del lavoro negli anni '80' (1982) 15 Giornale di Diritto del Lavoro e di Relazioni Industriali 373, 406–8. See too the valuable review by A. Lyon-Caen and L. Marriucci, 'The State, Legislative Intervention and Collective Bargaining' (1985) 1 Int. Jo. Comparative Labour Law and Industrial Relations 87.

13 T. Treu, 'The Technology Debate' (1984) 9 Labour and Society (2) 109, 125. See too, O. Jacobi, B. Jessop, H. Kastendiek and M. Regini (eds.), *Technological Change, Rationalization and Industrial Relations* (1985).

14 M. De Cristofaro, in M. Garofalo (ed.), *Crisi, Occupazione, Legge* (1985), p. 61; on solidarity contracts, P. Curzio, p. 19; relaxation of hiring rules, M. Garofalo, p. 5; training-work contracts, C. Lagala, p. 93; early retirement, T. Germano, p. 141; see summary of the 1984 Act (1985) 139 EIRR 17. On France, see Chapter 4, note 29, and G. Camerlynck, G. Lyon-Caen, J. Pélissier, *Droit du Travail* (12th ed. 1984), p. 139.

15 'Cassa Integrazione: la CGIL per una radicale reforma' (1985), *Lavoro Informazione* 266.

16 S. Wood and I. Dey, *Redundancy* (1983), p. 15, criticizing R. Martin and R. Fryer, *Redundancy and Paternalist Capitalism* (1973), pp. 216–60; and R. Hyman, *Industrial Relations: A Marxist Introduction* (1975).

17 P. Minford, 'Trade Unions Destroy a Million Jobs' (1982) Jo. Econ. Affairs No, 2, 73; in W. McCarthy (ed.), *Trade Unions* (1985), 365, 368–9; also F. Hayek, ibid., p. 357. See the remarks of McCarthy, ibid., pp. 17–18; and H. Phelps Brown, p. 322; C. Mulvey, p. 338; B. Burkitt, p. 376.

18 W. Hutt, *The Theory of Collective Bargaining 1930–1975* (1975), p. 74.

19 See E. Batstone and S. Gourlay, *Union Structure and Strategy in the Face of Technical Change* (forthcoming); *Financial Times*, 28 October 1985.

20 C. Craver, op. cit. (note 8, above), pp. 634, 643, 648–9, 695.

21 D. Mills, *Labor–Management Relations* (1978); F. Foulkes, *Personnel Policies in Large Non-Union Companies* (1980); C. Craver (1978) 73 NW Univ. L. R. 605 (consultants).

22 *The Changing Situation of Workers and their Unions* (1985, AFL–CIO), p. 11; and see R. Freeman and J. Medoff, *What Do Unions Do?* (1984), especially Chap. 15; the AFL–CIO publishes *Report on Union Busters* monthly.

23 R. Hyman, in G. Bain (ed.), *Industrial Relations in Britain* (1983), pp. 90–1; E. Batstone, *Working Order* (1984), pp. 257–60.

24 See Chapter 4, p. 280; *Labour Research*, February 1984, p. 47; ibid., October 1985, p. 247 (on IBM).

25 W. Sirs (ISTC) and L. Mills (BIFU), TUC *Report* (1983), pp. 394–7.

26 *Lifting the Burden* (Cmnd 9571, 1985), p. 29.

27 F. von Prondzynski, in P. Fosh and C. Littler (eds.), *Industrial Relations and the Law in the 1980s* (1985), p. 56.

28 See A. Fox, *Beyond Contract: Work Power and Trust Relations* (1974); R. Hyman (1978) 16 B J I R 16; Chapter 1, p. 26.

29 C. Crouch, *The Politics of Industrial Relations* (1979), p. 186; see on trade union 'power': B. Burkitt, 'Excessive Trade Union Power: Existing Reality or Contemporary Myth?' (1981) 12 Ind. Rel. J. No. 3, 65. (Both in W. McCarthy (ed.), *Trade Unions* (1985), pp. 376, 433; see too on alternative policies, J. England and B. Weekes, ibid., p. 406.)

30 O. Kahn-Freund, *Labour Relations, Heritage and Adjustment* (1979), p. 76.

31 P. Wiles, in P. Fosh and C. Littler (eds.), *Industrial Relations and the Law in the 1980s* (1985), p. 154.

32 See generally Wedderburn, in W. McCarthy (ed.), *Trade Unions* (1985), pp. 497, 507–28; *Trade Union Immunities* (Cmnd 8128, 1981), Chap. 4.

33 The dilemma is brought out well by B. Bercusson (1977) 40 M L R 268; cf. R. Lewis and B. Simpson, *Striking a Balance?* (1981), Chaps. 8 and 10.

34 P. O'Higgins, in J. Carby-Hall, *Studies in Labour Law* (1976), Chap. 3; Donovan Report (Cmnd 3623, 1968), para. 943; see the useful discussions by X. Blanc-Jouvan, in B. Aaron and K. W. Wedderburn (eds.), *Industrial Conflict: A Comparative Survey* (1972), Chap. 4; and W. E. J. McCarthy, *Freedom at Work* (1985, Fabian Soc. 508).

35 P. Elias and K. Ewing, 'Economic Torts and Labour Law' [1982] CLJ 321, 358.

36 See Wedderburn (1983) 12 ILJ 253, on *Public Prosecutor* v. *Ardizzone*, 1983; and *Public Prosecutor* v. *Antenaci*, 1974, in (1978) 1 Int. Lab. L. R. 51 (Cort. Cost.).

37 See on this problem Clark and Wedderburn, in Wedderburn, R. Lewis and J. Clark (eds.), *Labour Law and Industrial Relations* (1983), pp. 155–72; A. Fox, *Man Mismanagement* (2nd ed. 1985), p. 162.

38 Conciliation and Arbitration Amendment (No. 2) Bill 1984 s. 3 (new s. 88 DJ (1)); W. Creighton, on Australian secondary boycotts (1981) 44 M L R 489; W. Creighton, W. Ford, R. Mitchell, *Labour Law* (1983), Chaps. 33–7.

39 See H. Sinay and J.-C. Javillier, *La Grève* (1984), pp. 364–86; J. Rojot (1984) 41 Action Juridique pp. 15–18; *Fontaine* c. *Dame Damery*, Cour. Cass., 8 déc. 1983; D. 1984, p. 90; *Gaillais* c. *Ste Tanneriès de Sireuil*, Cour. Cass., 8 déc. 1983; Bull. p. 428; and M. Forde (1984) 13 I L J 40. For an early warning: G. Lyon-Caen, D. 1979, Chr. 255. Damages of £97,000 have now been awarded to an employer against strikers for violence against non-strikers that led to closure: (1986) E I R R 6. The Auroux reforms were designed to make workers 'citizens of the enterprise': G. Camerlynck, G. Lyon-Caen, J. Pélissier, *Droit du Travail* (12th ed. 1984), p. 19.

40 R. Simpson, 'Judicial Control of A C A S' (1979) 8 I L J 69, 83.

41 Warner J., *Solihull M B C* v. *N U T* [1985] I R L R 211, 214; see Chapter 8, pp. 684–717; Chapter 9, pp. 728–46. Some of the problems are addressed in *Industrial Relations Legislation* (1986, T U C).

42 J. A. G. Griffith, *The Politics of the Judiciary* (3rd ed. 1985), p. 215; and the quotation of Lord Scarman's speech at p. 222. Compare with the analysis there, and above, of the English judiciary, the American 'critical legal studies' school, e.g. K. Klare (1978) 62 Minn. L. Rev. 265 (judicial 'deradicalization' of Wagner Act); and see K. Stone (1981) 90 Yale L. J. 23.

43 See *E M A* v. *A C A S* [1980] I C R 215, 226–36; *Express Newspapers Ltd* v. *McShane* [1980] A C 672, 692–4 (a policy unhappily not maintained at p. 695).

44 W. Brown and B. Hepple, in P. Fosh and C. Littler (eds.), *Industrial Relations and the Law in the 1980s* (1985), pp. ix–xv.

45 See Clark and Wedderburn, in Wedderburn, R. Lewis and J. Clark (eds.), *Labour Law and Industrial Relations* (1983), pp. 173–96.

46 See L. Dickens *et al.*, *Dismissed* (1985) Chap. 8, on 'juridification' pp. 252–5.

47 See the invaluable article, J. Clark, 'The Juridification of Industrial Relations' (1985) 14 I L J 69, reviewing S. Simitis, 'Zur Verrechtlichung der Arbeitsbeziehungen', in R. Zacher, S. Simitis, F. Kübler, K. Hopt, G. Teubner, *Verrechtlichung von Wirtschaft, Arbeit und Sözialer Solidarität* (1984), now in English as 'The Juridification of Labour Relations', in G. Teubner (ed.), *Juridification of Social Spheres, A Comparative Analysis* (1986). Simitis's view of Britain is questioned by Clark and Wedderburn, 'Juridification – A Universal Trend? British Experience in Labour Law', ibid., where the 'levels' of juridification are examined.

48 See G. Giugni, in G. Teubner (ed.), op. cit. (note 47, above). On increasing legalisation in Britain, see R. Lewis (1976) 14 B J I R 1, 15; (1979) 8 I L J, 202, 218–20; compare O. Kahn-Freund, *Labour and the Law* (3rd ed. 1983; P. Davies and M. Freedland, eds.), p. 60; P. Davies and M. Freedland, *Labour Law: Text and Materials* (2nd ed. 1984), pp. 258 ff., 785 ff.

49 O. Kahn-Freund, *Labour and the Law* (3rd ed. 1983), p. 153.

50 C. Crouch, *The Politics of Industrial Relations* (1979), pp. 184–95.

51 K. Klare, 'Labor Law as Ideology' (1981) Ind. Rel. L. J. 450, 481.

52 L. Lustgarten, *Legal Control of Racial Discrimination* (1980), p. 254.

53 For some well directed proposals, see W. McCarthy, *Freedom at Work* (1985, Fabian Soc. 508). See, too, now the perspectives indicated by the penetrating Chap. 8 'Participation, Bargaining and the Wider Society', in A. Fox, *Man Mismanagement* (2nd ed. 1985).

Table of Statutes

Relevant Bills likely to become law in 1986 are included.

Table of Cases

Page numbers refer to text; citation of cases is normally found in the relevant endnote (number in brackets).

Index